NEW AND GREATLY EXPANDED
THIRD · EDITION

300 YEARS OF
KITCHEN
COLLECTIBLES

by
LINDA CAMPBELL FRANKLIN

7,000+ Fully-described Price Listings
1,800+ Pictures Illustrating over 5,000 Items
111 Recipes for Old-fashioned Cooking

Together with Invaluable Advice for Collectors and hundreds of interesting
quotes from antique cookbooks, trade catalogs, encyclopedias & advertisements
and special article on "Cast Iron Molds" by David G. Smith

Author's photo on back cover
Courtesy Daniel Grogan

BOOKS AMERICANA
INC

ISBN 0-89689-077-5

TABLE OF CONTENTS

DEDICATION & ACKNOWLEDGEMENTS

This heavy tome is dedicated to my parents, Mary Mac and Robert Franklin, in whose basement I have been writing for three and a half years, and to my Grand Mamma, Willie Lee Burton, and to my brother, Robbie. The lighter parts are courtesy of the pleasure brought me by my beagle Darwin, the best flea market find I ever made. Special thanks also goes to my publisher, Dan Alexander.

I am lucky to have had the assistance, encouragement, cooperation and patience of many collectors, dealers, auctioneers, librarians and curators. Many of them first agreed to help in 1987, when I thought the book was but one year away! Many thanks to Pat Guthman, David G. Smith, Joel Schiff, Georgiana Sanders, Don Thornton, all the Holyroyds of Oregon, the Moffets, Joe Young, the Dziaduls, Carol Bohn, Sheri Ficken, Steve Stephens, Oveda Maurer, Ron Barlow, Clifford Boram, Meryle Evans, John Lambert, Anne Serio, Rodris Roth, Ann Golovin, Vern Ward, Ray Townsend, Bunny Upchurch & Kyle Goad, Kate Urquhart, Evelyn Welch, Tom Wiggins, Peggy Wainscott, Pat Gross, Dolores Thomas, Robert Carr, Karol Atkinson, Marion Levy, James Trice, Bob Cahn, Georgia Levett, Litchfield Auction Gallery, Clayton Bailey, James D. Julia, Jeannine Dobbs, A.H.T. Robb-Smith, Gail Lettick, Barbara Bowditch, Betty Landis and many many others.

Photographs include those taken by Paul Persoff of the Keillor Collection and other collections, those by David Arky, who did most of the photographs in the second edition, those bought from various sources or lent for free by others, and those taken by the author.

Cover photograph by Bill LaFevor, Nashville, TN. Large horned figural iron piece is one of a pair. Possibly a creeper, to hold small logs between the andirons; or they might be utensil rests. 19th C. Wooden piece behind is an unusually carved potato masher. Other pieces include a Dover eggbeater, stamped tin fish mold, cast iron alligator nutcracker (p.59), cast pewter hinged ice cream mold (p. 245), and skeletal mixing spoon (pp. 78, 84).

INTRODUCTION

Introductions are supposed to lay out the subject, give direction to the reader, and reveal the author's thought processes. I have but one page, but here goes! Seven years have passed since the last edition. There have been many changes in this field.

Enlightenment & Generosity. There are many more collectors (and dealers). They seek more detailed manufacturing and historical information; they form newsletters and clubs for discrete subject areas (such as apple parers, cast iron cookware, pie birds, etc.) They are, for the most part, users not hoarders, and sharers not paranoids. Collectors enjoy a lively exchange of information, and many hundreds of new friendships have resulted. More objects are being saved from being thrown out because even non-collectors are aware that old kitchen items are highly collectible. Prices have risen considerably — for good reasons (see above) and bad (see below).

Ignorance & Greed. Sellers of all kinds misrepresent origins, rarity and condition, commit unacknowledged repairs and parts replacements, refinish unwisely, and overprice objects accordingly. The worst offense is the rampant manufacture of reproductions, lookalikes and outright fakes — often advertised wholesale as distressed and in "old-looking" finishes. There's absolutely no excuse for this except Greed — the maker's, who refuses to indelibly mark his productions, and the dealer's, who hawks the stuff knowingly. I blame "Hollywall" — a show-biz/corporate profit mindset which rewarded societal cupidity in the 1980s, and foolishly and persistently admires and awards outward appearance over inner substance. The antiques and collectibles market is a clear proof of this selfish, dead-end attitude. Ten years from now collectors will all be very sorry if we don't demand that all reproductions be permanently marked with a statement such as "This is a replica - reproduction made in 199-"

***

Price Guides — What Good Are They? When using this book, remember that it is meant to inform you about all the factors influencing collectability; you should use the actual retail value ranges with healthy scepticism. The pictures were captioned after the price entries and values are sometimes lower, sometimes higher. The book was written during an awful upheaval in the economy; if some prices seem high, they should catch up about 1994. If low, be grateful.

What is the purpose of a price guide? To be a constantly-expanding, evermore detailed field map. It can be used to develop heretofore unexplored areas and markets, and to expand frontiers (of age, price and form) forward, backward and off to the sides. Sure, the immediate effect on prices is they go up, but they tend to find a more natural market level with time. Many things are actually rescued because of the revelatory light of price guides because they can also afford a lens enabling people to notice things they've overlooked. If there were a price guide to the treasures of Nature, perhaps more people would be actively involved in preservation of natural resources and endangered species.

***

Practical Usage Notes. Sources of pictures and quotes cited in captions & price listings are more fully described in the Bibliography. In price listings, you will often see "TOC", which means turn-of-century (ie. c.1890-1910).

For an **8-page Introduction** send a SASE (Self-Addressed double-Stamped #10 long Envelope) to L.C. Franklin, 2716 Northfield Rd., Charlottesville, VA 22901. You will also receive information about the proposed revival of the **kitchen collector newsletter** (first published from 1984 through 1986).

Sincerely,

Linda Campbell Franklin

A. PREPARING
I. CORE, CUT, CHOP, PARE & PIT

The two fundamental processes that underlie the selection of most of the implements and gadgets in this chapter are: (1) Removal of inedible or undesirable portions of the food (viz. pits,, and skins in the case of fruit and vegetables; bones, gristle, skin, and offal, in the case of animals, fish or fowl), and (2) Division of the edible portions into smaller pieces for various purposes. Some of the most popular and varied kitchen collectibles fall into this preparation category — including apple parers, cherry pitters, chopping knives and nutmeg graters. The most ancient of cooking tools (as separate from utensils or vessels) would be put here — anything with a cutting edge or a smashing surface. In fact, you will find a surprise three quarters of the way through: a "kitchen collectible" that is ten million years old!

The apple parer is the device with the greatest number of organized collectors. Any one of the members of International Society for Apple Parer Enthusiasts knows a great deal more than I do about apple parers, and I urge you to join them, share their camaraderie (they had their first successful conference in 1988), and learn from the newsletter. Send an SASE for information to John Lambert, 3911 Morgan Center Rd., Utica, OH 43080.

The fastest growing field of those covered in this chapter is mechanical nutmeg graters. But while there are several hundreds of apple parers, including improved versions, there are probably under two hundred mechanical nutmeg graters, very few of which (if any, besides the popular Edgar) have gone through different versions. In fact, while mechanical parers are still being made, mechanical nutmeg graters enjoyed a very short period of production, mainly in the 1860s and 1870s. Almost everyone today has one of the "coffin" types, with the little hinged compartment and a curved grating surface, and they are still being made. I know of no mechanical one. At the time of this writing, there is still no book on mechanical nutmeg graters, though perhaps one will be done in this decade.

Implements for grinding, crushing and mashing are among the most basic and ancient. They're a crude form of a knife, in a way; it takes a delicate, fine-edged "micro-knife" to cut seeds and grains for eating; a mortar and pestle are macro-mashers. Somehow "Lucy", or another very ancient ancestor had to reduce cereals (or extremely tough roots or animal parts) into something which could be eaten. So two rocks, or a rock and a hard piece of wood, were the first mortars and pestles. Cooking wasn't even necessary – at least not at first. But when it was discovered that by mashing grains and mixing the resulting meal with liquid (water, milk and blood being the choices) before cooking, the food became something a bit more durable, and also portable, a giant step forward was taken. Viewed from the end of the 20th century, surrounded by toaster waffles, hotdog buns, and evocative "hunters' grain" sliced breads, it seems an amazing feat of imagination for homo sapiens (perhaps even homo erectus) to have thought up the mortar and pestle.

For many collectors, nutcrackers are the most appealing subgroup of kitchen collectibles in the hit or mash category. They can be viewed as refined mortars, or at least miniature precision clubs. A rock and a hard place is obviously the first or earliest nutcracking contrivance, and we find many variations on the anvil and hammer theme. But the nutcrackers we are most familiar with are mechanical – based on one of two systems: the screwed press, or the levered jaw. The latter is particularly well-suited to wild and whimsical designs on the theme of animal or human mouths.

Apple corer, hand held, tin, with T handle, marked "H" on each end of handle, American, 19th C. **$15.00-$20.00**

Apple corer, tin tubular corer, wooden knob handle; piece inside keeps corer from going all the way through the pple – for making baked apples, "The Gem Apple Corer," pat'd by James Fallows, Philadelphia, pat'd Jan. 2, 1877 & sold for many years. **$7.00-$15.00**

Apple corer, tin, wood handle, "Boye Needle Co.," pat'd 1916. **$10.00-$16.00**

Apple corer & parer combined, heavy sheet steel, nickel or tin plated. "Real-A-Peel," mfd. by Tarrson Co., (another marked "Grayline Housewares, Inc."), Chicago, IL, (Grayline in Elgin, IL), 5"L, pat'd 1937 **$7.00-$12.00**

Apple corer & parer combined, tin & wood, hand held, non-mechanical, 2 parts – the corer fits into handle of a broad blade parer, "Dandy," American, pat'd 1913 **$10.00-$17.00**

Apple corer & quarterer, best to use with already sliced apples as it is rather flimsy, very narrow outer ring of tin to hold 4 tin segmenting blades which spoke out from a circular corer, 2 vertical shanks for crosswise turned-wood handle, American, 5¾"H x 4½" diameter, last quarter 19th C. **$15.00-$25.00**

Apple corer & segmenter, tin, with 2 handles, smallest of this class of tools, used by pressing firmly down on handle, S. Joseph Co., probably the importer, marked "Made in Germany", late 19th C. • We can never estimate the vast quantities of kitchen & housewares imported from Germany at the end of the 19th C. One wholesaler in NYC, G. M. Thurnauer, made regular buying trips for about 20 years to Germany & Austria, buying wood, aluminum, tin & china wares. • **German vocabulary** — blechen Geschirr: tinware. • See entry under "Berlin kettles" in Pots & Pans chapter. **$25.00-$35.00**

Apple corer & slicer, referred to as apple segmenter, cast iron frame, screw clamps to table, plunger action from top, sharp tinned steel blades form 8-spoke 'wheel' segmenter, "Climax," mfd. by D. H. Goodell, Antrim, NH, 10"H x 7"W, pat'd Feb. 16, 1869. **$135.00-$155.00**

Apple parer, all wood except for forged iron fork & handle, pale bird's eye maple, clamps to table with its own clamp, 19th C. **$175.00-$250.00**

Apple parer, also potato & turnip parer, cast iron mounted to wood, rather skeletal with several gears, simple rod crank with dogleg bend, Sargent & Foster's Patent,"Shelburne Falls, MA, pat'd Oct. 4, 1853, • According to Thomas Wiggins, this was the first mass-produced iron parer "readily available" to people at mid century who wanted to buy a mechanical parer, with replaceable parts. • The **first** widely-known apple parer, wood with a small blade and prong of iron or steel, was patented by Moses Coates, Chester County, PA, Feb. 14,

1803, and presented in a drawing in Anthony Willich's *Domestic Encyclopedia*, (1803-04 Philadelphia). Willich's purpose was to present the latest knowledge about raw materials, methods, machinery, and inventions that might be applicable to "rural and domestic economy." People have reported finding obviously one-of-a-kind, handmade parers very like Coates', so it is obvious that the rural readers of Willich built their own from the drawing and specifications. Dr. Willich himself wrote about the parer that "on account of its simplicity, and the expedition with which it works, will no doubt come into general use.... The Editor has tried the experiment with the machine, and found it to pare apples with great rapidity." • The **second** parer patented was Bostonian W. Badger's "Machine for paring, quartering, and coring apples", on Feb. 10, 1809. • *The Journal of the Franklin Institute*, for April 1838, noticed Robert W. Mitchell's "Machine for Paring, Coring, & Dividing Apples," patented April 13. Mitchell lived in Martin's Mill (Springfield), Richland County, OH. The editor wrote "This, we believe, is the **fourth** [patent #686] obtained for the purpose; ... the apple is to be placed on a fork at the end of a shaft, or mandrel, turned by a crank, whilst the paring knife, furnished with a guard, is held in the right hand, and passed from end to end over the apple; this is then pushed towards the shaft which is furnished with knives that cut it into quarters; a centre, tubular knife removing the core." • Obtained earlier, & unnumbered, but counted by the same editor as the **sixth** was a "Machine for Peeling apples and Peaches" patented Feb. 3, 1836 by J. W. Hatcher [Hatch in Gazette Index] of Bedford County, VA. The editor said "This ... is the sixth peeling machine that has been patented, and we do not think it any improvement upon the first, which was that of Moses Coates, obtained in 1803. The [Hatcher] has a spindle, with a fork to receive the apple, a second spindle with an endless screw, a cog wheel, pinion, whirl & band, & other appendages for moving the knife; the apparatus for moving the knife the only part claimed." (*Ibid.*).
$120.00-$150.00

Apple parer, bench type, all wood with forged iron fork, no attached parer on this type, American, bench: 17"H x 25"L, c.1830s-40s. • One of the oldest apple parers in the country is a <u>bench type</u> — the bench being a rather elegant plank with 3 legs, and a large 11"D wooden belt-drive wheel built into the bench. It belongs to The Bennington Museum, VT. Their records say it was made in West Woodstock, VT, in 1785 by Daniel Cox and his sons. • "Apple Butter. — Being at the house of a good old German friend in Pennsylvania, in September last, we noticed upon the table what was called apple butter; and finding it an agreeable article, we inquired into the modus operandi in making it.

"To make the article according to German law, the host should in the autumn invite his neighbors, particularly the young men and maidens, to make up an apple butter party. Being assembled, let three bushels of fair sweet apples be pared, quartered, and the cores removed. Meanwhile let two barrels of new cider be boiled down to one-half. When this is done, commit the prepared apples to the cider, and henceforth let the boiling go on briskly and systematically. But to accomplish the main design, the party must take turns at stirring the contents without cessation, that they do not become attached to the side of

the kettle and be burned. Let this stirring go on till the liquid becomes concrete — in other words, till the amalgamated cider and apples become as thick as hasty pudding — then throw in seasoning of pulverized alspice, when it may be considered as finished, and committed to pots for future use. This is apple butter — and it will keep sweet for very many years. And depend upon it, it is a capital article for the table — very much superior to any thing that comes under the name of apple sauce." Reprinted from *Gospel Banner*, in *The Farmers' Cabinet; Devoted to Agriculture, Horticulture and Rural Economy*. Phil.: Vol. III, Aug.1838 - July 1839. $300.00-$400.00

Apple parer, cast iron, "Turntable," mfd. by Lockey & Howland, after Keyes himself mfd. it, Leominster, MA, pat'd by Horatio Keyes, June 17 & Dec. 16, 1856.
$65.00-$75.00

Apple parer, cast iron, Goodell Co., Antrim, NH, 1893.
$50.00-$60.00

Apple parer, cast iron, Sinclair Scott "Top Gear", Baltimore, MD, late 19th C. $45.00-$65.00

Apple parer, cast iron, Reading Hardware Co., Reading, PA, pat'd May 5, 1868; May 3, 1875; Oct. 19, 1875; Nov. 14, 1875; May 22,1877. $75.00-$85.00

Apple parer, cast iron, "Triumph," mfd by Boutell, American, pat'd 1899. $225.00-$275.00

Apple parer, cast iron, 4 gear, C. E. Hudson Parer Co., Leominster, MA, Jan. 24, 1882. $65.00-$75.00

Apple parer, cast iron, clamps to table, "Keyes' Patent", pat'd by Horatio Keyes, Leominster, MA, marked June 17, 1856 & Dec. 16, 1856. • An earlier version, showing only June date, was mounted to wooden board. The patent for it states that "as the prominences and cavities of the apple pass [a part that Keyes called "the lip"], ... the cutter will be moved in a corresponding inverse manner ... and consequently the apple will be pared in a perfect manner. $50.00-$65.00

Apple parer, cast iron, commercial size, "Rival #296," American, pat'd 1889. $140.00-$195.00

Apple parer, cast iron, cutout on gear slightly different from other Turntable, screw clamp nut also slightly different, "Goodell Turntable '98, No. 41", Goodell Co., pat'd May 24, 1898. $80.00-$90.00

Apple parer, cast iron, has big ax head or keystone-like logo on gear wheel, "Keen Kutter," mfd. by E. C. Simmons Hardware Co., St. Louis, MO, pat'd May 24, 1898.
$80.00-$95.00

Apple parer, cast iron, heart design gear wheel, 8 gears, Sinclair Scott Co., Baltimore, MD, late 19th C.
$45.00-$65.00

Apple parer, cast iron, heart motif wheel, very like 1858 Monroe Brothers' parer, "The Waverly," mfd by L. A. Sayre, Newark, NJ, frame is 5½"H, gear wheel is 4¾" diameter, pat'd Jan. 29, 1884. $65.00-$75.00

Apple parer, cast iron, heavy multiple gears, screw clamps to table, "The Union," mfd. by O. R. White, Wooster, MA, 8"H, pat'd Nov. 11, 1866 (date incorrect.) But sold since 1864. • I can't find O. R. White in the *Subject Index to Patents*, and Nov. 11, 1866 wasn't a Tuesday. There was a parer patented Nov. 11, 1856, by E. L. Pratt of Philadelphia. But then why would it take so many years to be sold? My ads & files show this to have gone on sale in 1864, though not yet patented. Could the two Nov. 11s be a coincidence? Perhaps Nov. 11, 1866 was date the patentee sent off his application, and he used that date on

This practice was common to inventors. • 1868 ad in *American Agriculturist* stated "The knife pares going both ways, thus saving time without increasing the speed of the apple. It throws the parings from the machine. It contains a less number of parts than any other machine in the market." • This is the same as the "Union Apple Paring Machine" manufactured by the Whittemore Brothers, Worcester, MA, advertised in Aug. 1865 as "patent pending". It has several large gears, the most interesting one with cutouts in curved "rays" from center of gear. **$65.00-$90.00**

Apple parer, cast iron lathe type, angled screw clamp, large gear wheel has teeth on inside which move a small gear which turns the apple, almost round wooden knob to crank. Very clean & modern looking. "Family Bay State", D. H. Goodell Co., based on Whittemore's patent, Antrim, NH, (Whittemore's patent Aug. 10, 1869) this one late 19th & early 20th C. • An Improved Bay State was made in late 1890s & early 1900s by Goodell. It has 2 of the angled screw clamps to hold the apple out over space instead of the working parts. The "Family" one was supposed to have been a "remodeled, strengthened and otherwise improved" version of the Whittemore Bay State, suitable for "hotels, restaurants and boarding houses or any place where any considerable quantity of apples are to be prepared." The "Improved Bay State" was "adapted for packers and evaporators of fruit or in families where an extra strong parer is needed. It is practically the same as the Family ..., except in the matter of durability. The machine is larger and stronger in every way. It has a steel screw and is fastened to the table at both ends, making it very firm. ... This machine has an automatic push off for removing the cores." (Joseph Breck & Sons 1902 catalog copy.) The gear wheel is also proportionally much larger to the small gear, and the crank is more curved, and the handle is longer. • Price range for "Family" version. **$55.00-$65.00**

Apple parer, cast iron, mechanical type mounted to board, gear wheel cast with heart design used by the Monroes, in fact almost duplicates the Monroe Brothers' apple parer, only it's slightly larger, marked "Gold Medal", American, dates on parer from 1850s, but not actually made until late 1870s. • "The pies made of the **Tomatus** are excellent. As this is a new desert [sic], those who wish to make them will slice the fruit, and pursue the same process as with a common pie made of apples." *Lancaster Journal*, PA, Set. 6, 1822. **$85.00-$100.00**

Apple parer, cast iron mounted on wood, "Sargent & Foster," Shelburne Falls, MA, pat'd 1856. **$85.00-$95.00**

Apple parer, cast iron, mounted to wood, skeletal simple frame, crank mounted at right angles; one set of gears turns skinny, surgical tool-looking parer, another gear directly turns the apple stuck on the prongs, simple bent rod crank, no knob, pat'd by J. D. Seagrave, mfd by Larned & Seagrave, Worcester, MA (?), base is 10"L x 4"W (at its longest, parer is about 8"L), pat'd June 17, 1856. • Seagrave received another patent for a "Machine for paring apples" on April 18, 1854. **$80.00-$100.00**

Apple parer, cast iron, openwork wheel has heart motif, apparently a real favorite of the Monroe Brothers, (James & Edwin), Fitchburg, MA. Frame is 5¾"H, wheel is 3¾" diameter, frame pat'd May 6,1856, Sept 9, 1858, Aug. 21, 1866; wheel: Sept. 9, 1858. **$75.00-$90.00**

Apple parer, cast iron, quarter circle gear rack, pares, cores & segments, "The Thompson," mfd. by New England Butt Co., pat'd Aug. 14, 1877, by G. Thompson. **$125.00-$150.00**

Apple parer, cast iron, red wooden plank base is original, paper label on plank, "Automatic Apple Parer", mfd by Foster (is this C. A. Foster?), Shelburne Falls, MA, says pat'd 1852, but in *Patent Index* there were no 1852 parer patents. **$65.00-$90.00**

Apple parer, cast iron, "S" curve heavy wire or thin rod crank with wooden handle, lathe type parer, screw-clamps to table, bar below threaded shaft is straight — almost resembles a plumber's wrench, "Little Star," mfd by C. E. Hudson Co., Leominster, MA, pat'd June 9, 1885. • A slightly later model of "Little Star" — #125 — has a completely differently-shaped bar beneath screw that curves & dips down near apple's end. About this "Little Star" was written: "The only parer in which the paring knife always faces the fruit when brought against it." Joseph Breck & Sons catalog, 1902. **$35.00-$50.00**

Apple parer, cast iron, screw clamps to table, "White Mountain Turntable '98," mfd. by Goodell Co., Antrim, NH, pat'd May 24, 1898. • Another Goodell parer from 1898 was the "Winesap," for which I have no information at this time. **$45.00-$65.00**

Apple parer, cast iron, screw clamps to table, "Reading '78," mfd by Reading Hardware Co., PA, 11" x 6"W, pat'd 1878. **$45.00-$60.00**

Apple parer, cast iron, screw clamps to table, Landers, Frary & Clark, New Britain, CT, pat'd 1873. **$45.00-$60.00**

Apple parer, cast iron, screw clamps, spiral eccentric cam gear underneath, 2 cutters (this is 2nd model, according to an expert), S. N. Maxam, Shelburne Falls, MA, pat'd April 10, 1855. • Bob Cahn, The Primitive Man, showed this to me at Renninger's Extravaganza, June 1989. It was earmarked for an advanced collector. I didn't ask the price, nor would he have told me, because it was sold. I'm guessing price range from the rarity. If I'm way off, I know I'll hear from you. If I'm low, it'll be "Where can I get one for that?" **$400.00-$600.00**

Apple parer, cast iron, screw clamps to table, unusual starfish-like spokes to gear wheel, "Hudson's Improved," mfd by F. W. Hudson Parer Co., Leominster, MA, 7" to bottom of clamp frame, pat'd Dec. 2, 1862. • Yet another "Improved" was granted a patent on March 5, 1872, to F. W. Hudson. **$115.00-$140.00**

Apple parer, cast iron, screw clamps to table, very large toothed gear with six 3-lobe heart cutouts, 2 small gears, claimed to pare the whole apple with one & a half turns of the crank, at which point you took one apple off & put another on, then turned again one & a half times, pat'd by S. S. Hersey, (his name should be cast on frame below date), Farmington, ME, pat'd June 18, 1861. (Another patent, maybe same parer?, Aug. 30, 1864.) • This was sold by Dover Stamping Co., Boston, MA, in their 1869 catalog. **$125.00-$165.00**

Apple parer, cast iron, turntable, screw clamps, "The Centennial", Reading Hardware Co., pat'd by W. A. C. Oakes, Reading, PA, pat'd Dec. 10, 1872, July 22, 1873. **$75.00-$90.00**

Apple parer, cast iron, turntable type, nice round knob to crank, gear wheel very open casting with 4 contiguous cirles, screw clamps to table, "The Domestic", Landers, Frary & Clark, pat'd by A. Turnbull & R. L. Webb, New Britain, CT, pat'd June 10, 1873. **$80.00-$110.00**

Apple parer, cast iron, vertical turntable, screw clamps, round wood crank knob, "Transit," Hunt Mfg. Co., Antrim, NH, 19th C. $60.00-$70.00

Apple parer, cast iron, very high legs, Tippecanoe Apple Paring Machine Co., NYC, NY, c.1870s. $145.00-$165.00

Apple parer, cast iron, with 4 spoke gear wheel, one of which is elongated past rim to form handle, screw clamps to table — fancy thumbscrew, intriguing spring steel wire that curls around & has knife on end, "Non Pareil," mfd by J. L. Haven & Co., Cincinnati, OH, pat'd May 6, 1856.
• In Loris Russell's *Handy Things To Have About the House*, he said that this parer was patented by J. D. Browne, of Cincinnati, OH, on Sept. 9, 1856, and mfd. by Scott Mfg. Co. of Baltimore. $120.00-$150.00

Apple parer, cast iron, concave gear wheel with very abstract casting pattern, screw clamps to table, activated by the small gear, has push off, "Rocking Table," C. E. Hudson Parer Co., Leominster, MA, c. 7½"H x 8"W, pat'd Jan. 24, 1882, & Feb. 9, 1892. $40.00-$65.00

Apple parer, cast iron with wooden handle, fixed arc, semicircular gear rack, "The New Lightning," mfd by D. H. Goodell Co., Antrim, 7"D of half-circle gear, pat'd Oct. 6, 1863 & Aug. 23, 1864 by E. L. Pratt of Boston.
• Great looking but not all that uncommon once you start focusing on the gear. An *American Agriculturalist* ad, Aug. 1875, states: "This machine drops parings clear of machinery, does better work than any other machine, does double the amount ..., loosens the apple on the fork by the neatest arrangement ever yet invented." One dealer had it for $115.00. $75.00-$100.00

Apple parer, iron, lathe type, the same "machine for paring apples" on which he received a patent a little over a month after this, pat'd by David H. Whittemore, Whittemore Works, Chicopee Falls, MA, Worcester, MA, original patent granted Jan. 13, 1857, extension Jan. 12, 1871. • Excerpts from the "Decisions of the Commissioner of Patent" in 1871: "The invention of applicant was novel when the patent was issued and seems to be really valuable. In his sworn statement applicant [David H. Whittemore] makes no attempt to fix the ascertained value of the invention, but witnesses say it is worth $20,000 or $25,000. No reliable data for this estimate are given except in one instance. Bancroft, a farmer, who has used the machine ten or twelve years, says it is worth $10 a year to any person using it to any great extent.

"As several thousand dozen of the machines have been manufactured and sold, the estimate alluded to above does not appear to be extravagant.

From the statement of accounts it appears that applicant's receipts exceed his expenditures by only $7. There is one item of expense, however, which is not properly chargeable to the patent, viz: the sum of $250 for obtaining foreign patents. But striking out this item the balance of receipts affords no adequate remuneration for the time, labor, and expense bestowed upon the invention by the patentee, and this without neglect on his part to make diligent effort to secure such remuneration from the introduction of his invention into public use." The Examiners and Mr. Duncan, Acting Commissioner, granted the extension. [SEE also other Whittemore apple parer.] • **Other parers granted in 1857,** which may or may not represent actual production parers, are: • Machine for paring apples, J. O. M. Ingersoll, Ithaca, NY, Jan. 20,

1857; • Apple paring & slicing machine, G. H. Hubbard, Shelburne Falls, MA, Jan. 27, 1857; • Machine for paring apples, D. H. Whittemore, Worcester, MA, Feb. 17, 1857; • Machine for paring apples, B. F. Joslyn, Worcester, MA, Mar. 17, 1857; Machine for paring, coring & quartering apples, C. F. Bosworth, Petersham, MA, June 9, 1857; • Machine for paring apples, J. J. Parker, Marietta, OH, Apr. 7, 1857; • Apple paring & slicing machine, R. W. Thickins, Brasher Iron Works, NY, July 28, 1857. $65.00-$100.00

Apple parer, mostly wood, painted red, oblong wood base meant to be clamped (with a separate clamp) to a table edge, simple cast iron wheel, steel prong fork, steel cutting blade on parer. Looks homemade, but mass-produced in Maine, 7"H x 13"L x 6¾"W, mid 19th C, maybe a bit earlier. • I've been told they came with three sizes of wheels: 6"D, 7"D and 8"D. This one has a 6"D wheel. Perhaps the firm who made them had a pile of assorted wheels they'd needed before to make something else, so they just fit whatever one came to hand. $75.00-$95.00

Apple parer, strap-to-leg type, hand carved wood, forged iron fork, remnants of leather strap, American, 1820s-40s. $85.00-$120.00

Apple parer, straddle type (put it on a bench, then sit on its long board base while operating it), mostly wood, painted black, white & old red in geometric design, 2 thick chunky iron gears, wood crank, American, prob. PA-European heritage, 29"L, 19th C. • This was my treasure bought at the Keillor Family Collection auction in the mid-70s. Much, but not all, of that fabulous collection formed the nucleus of my first book, the name of which I rarely mention since it was been stolen from me, and had my name removed as author, and the son of the publisher's name put in, and that publisher is doing Bibles now. Can you see the steam from where you sit? $175.00-$250.00

Apple parer & corer, cast iron, looks like an oil drilling rig, for bakeries, hotels & dried apple industry. Can be made to pare only, without coring. "Bonanza," mfd. by Goodell Co., Antrim, NH, 15"H x 16"L, pat'd March 13, 1888, but introduced June 1890. • A Bonanza owned by my father, also one I saw in ad, have old weld-repairs to the top "beam" of the frame — perhaps a weak spot, or metal fatigue? Is everyone finding the "Bonanza" in repaired condition? One of my Illinois connections, collector Ted Phillips, reported Oct. 1988 that these Bonanzas go for $200.00 and up. • **Regional Price Variations.** — I'm in a quandary about reporting prices; I can't do a regional price guide, but some pieces, particularly patented iron gadgets, go much higher in certain areas than in others. I suspect the upward $$ trend will spread throughout the country. Over-inflated prices will tend, however, to crash the whole kitchen antiques market. $120.00-$150.00

Apple parer, corer & slicer, cast iron frame, screw clamps to table, lathe action, rather like the "Little Star," except that instead of having separate short foot above the screw clamp, this one uses cross bar of main frame, "Daisy," mfd by Hudson Parer Co., Leominster, MA, prob. based on July 11, 1882 patent for a lathe-type parer. • This was made & sold well into the 20th C. Advertisements I have for the Daisy, from various 1931 *American Cookery* magazines, state: "Cores and Slices at the same time.

Three cuts and it's ready for pies, apple sauce or canning.'' The 3 cuts are a separate step done with a paring knife. Other ad says ''...will pare, core and slice an apple in one operation — quickly.'' **$25.00-$35.00**

Apple parer, corer & slicer, extremely simple cast & malleable iron lathe type, screw clamps to table, single gear without teeth that follows (?) horizontal toothed ratchet along bottom of frame, advertising probably exaggerates utility, ''Oriole'', Scott Mfg. Co., Baltimore, MD, c.1883 **$35.00-$45.00**

Apple parer, corer & slicer, skeletal cast iron, meant to be hooked up to power source, but could be cranked by hand, 3 spindles with prongs, 4 stanchions to be bolted to surface, between them & beyond is elaborate system of gears & snapping flipping levers & push offs. ''Every part of the 'Eureka' is made with an eye to simplicity, durability and strength. All its parts are adjustable, and in case of breakage can be easily and cheaply duplicated. It has a record of 80 bushels a day by hand, and 100 bushels by power. All the operator has to do is to put the apples on the fork and the machine does the rest.'' (Joseph Breck & Sons catalog, 1902.) You could load 3 apples at a time, but was there ever one made that would pare 3 at a time? ''88 Eureka'', Goodell Co., Antrim, NH, 18½''H, pat'd Aug. 4, 1874 , April 27 & Nov. 6, 1886. • I don't know how this differs from the ''86 Eureka'', touted as an improvement on the ''85 Eureka''. I don't know why it's the ''88'', if the last patent was 1886. **$135.00-$175.00**

Apple parer, corer, & slicer, skeletal cast iron & steel commercial model, to be bolted to tabletop, 4 high oil rig stanchions or legs at one end, large toothed gear & 5 other small gears (within the legs) turned by crank, horizontal intricate spindle works unsupported at other end, ''Dandy'', mfd. by Goodell Co., Antrim, NH, 18¼'' x 19½'' x 9⅝'', pat'd Nov. 16, 1886, Mar. 13 & May 8, 1888. • It seems almost identical to the ''Eureka'', mfd. by Goodell Co., Antrim, NH, although that was sold prior to the patent on the Dandy. **$135.00-$175.00**

Apple parer, corer & spiral slicer, cast iron, nice wooden knobby handle on crank, lathe type, originally D. H. Whittemore patent, the ''White Mountain,'' mfd. by Goodell Co., Antrim, 6½''H x 11''L, pat'd April 6, 1880, May 3, 1881. • According to Tom Wiggins, one of the country's preeminent apple parer collectors, this one is an ''improvement to the David H. Whittemore parer (patent extension Jan 11, 1871)'' which didn't have a threaded shaft, and which in fact used one rod, bent to create the crank at the end of the shaft. • This parer, green enameled cast iron with steel shaft & wood handle, continues to be made. It is sold by Cumberland General Store, Crossville, TN. **$35.00-$50.00**

Apple & peach parer, cast iron, screw clamps to table, Sinclair Scott Co., Baltimore, MD, 10''L, c.1880. **$60.00-$75.00**

Apple scoop or corer, carved sheep bone, prob. English; poss. American examples around somewhere, 5'' to 6½''L, 19th C. **$28.00-$45.00**

Apple scoops or corers, carved sheep bone, with knuckle as handle grip, mostly plain but for one carved with hearts & initials ''M. C.'', English or American, about 5''L, early 19th C. **$28.00-$45.00**

Apple segmenter, tin with wooden handles, hand held, quarters & cores apple with one push, American, c.1880s. **$22.00-$30.00**

Apple segmenter & corer, cast iron frame, screw clamps, plunger presses apple down on sharp tin wheel-like plate with 8 ''spokes'' radiating from a small round hole, to make 8 segments and core in one step. The frame of this looks almost identical to a Goodell gadget for making Saratoga potato chips, patented just a few months later. No maker's mark, but probably the one pat'd by C. D. Read, Lowell, MA, 10''H x 7''W, pat'd Feb. 16, 1869. **$70.00-$90.00**

Apple segmenter & corer, cast iron round frame with 2 rectangular Mt. Joy, PA, 5½'' diameter exclusive of frame, c.1880. **$22.00-$30.00**

Apple slicer, 9 steel blades, black painted cast iron frame, apple pulled across the blades, looks like a strange xylophone & probably could be played, for those of you with a kitchenware orchestra, ''Sun,'' C. M. Heffron, Rochester, NY, pat'd June 10, 1890. **$150.00-$175.00**

Apple slicer, wood & iron, 6 slicing blades. Apple is fitted onto prong mounted to a sliding piece of wood, & is pushed through the gauntlet of slicing blades. ''Primitive'' style, but mass-produced. American, 42''L, 19th C. **$130.00-$165.00**

Bean cutter, cast iron, screw clamps to table, for making French style green beans, feed one bean at a time into a sort of diagonal chute & turn crank, has 3 steel blades, removable so you can sharpen, turned wood handle, cast design of hand at bottom, ''Harras No. 37'', ''Germany 374'', 10½''H, early 20th C. **$45.00-$55.00**

Bean slicer, 2 beans at a time, cast iron painted pale avocado green, ''Rose'', Belgian, 8⅝''L, 20th C. **$50.00-$60.00**

Bean slicer, cast iron, very ornate, japanned dark brown & bronze, beans fed into hopper & pass between 2 rollers to be sliced. Screw clamps to table, American, 6½''H, late 19th C (?). **$40.00-$50.00**

Bean slicer, cast iron painted blue, leaf design cast in it, screw clamp, 2 skinny bean-insertion places in back, turn crank & it turns 2 beans against cutting blade, tin cover holds beans in place & keeps them from flying out, no mark, 9''H, early 20th or late 19th C. **$60.00-$70.00**

Bean slicer, oak case, iron and tin, tin slots where you feed beans in, 4 cutting blades on cutting disc, which is removable for sharpening, lid of case slides off, flywheel is perfectly balanced & it almost hums as you turn crank, no mark, 14¼''W, 19th C. **$90.00-$120.00**

Bean slicer & pea sheller, cast iron, screw clamps to table, green wood handle (sometimes seen in black), ''Vaughn's,'' Chicago, IL, 12''H, early 20th C. **$35.00-$40.00**

Bean slicer & pea sheller combo, cast iron, interchangeable rollers of iron & rubber, screw clamp, American, 12''H, early 20th C. **$28.00-$40.00**

Bean stringer & slicer, little blued steel blade, springs, ''Bean-X'', Orange, NJ, 6½''L, pat. pend., TOC (?). **$10.00-$13.00**

Beetle, also called a <u>meat fret</u> or <u>steak pounder</u>, turned wood, all one piece, this one dual purpose, having a small mushroom-shaped pestle at handle's end, American, 10''L, late 19th C. **$15.00-$22.00**

Beetle, or potato masher, handmade, one piece of maple, very dried out so it feels lighter than it should, 10½''H, late 19th C. • **German vocabulary** — <u>Kartoffelkafer</u>: potato beetle. **$25.00-$30.00**

Beetle, turned wood, 2 piece, with handle that screws into large head with large age or dryness check, American, 9''L, TOC. **$10.00-$12.00**

Beetle, turned wood, handle has nice patina, head has a few chips on business end, probably for a hotel, American, unusually long: 23'', TOC. **$35.00-$45.00**

Beetle, walnut, turned of one piece of wood, nice patina, American, 12''L, late 19th C. • Added value. — As a rule, the beetles turned of one piece of wood bring more money than the two piece, as they are usually somewhat older. An exceptionally nice turning or paint on handle of a 2 piece one, however, would add $$ too. **$15.00-$22.00**

Beetle or cracker roller, turned wood, 2 pieces (head & screw in handle), narrow rows of ridges on head. Perhaps meat tenderer too? German (?), head is 8''L, handle another 5½''L, TOC. **$25.00-$30.00**

Beetle: SEE also Potato masher for wood & wire types.

Berry or fruit press, wood platform like for an oil drilling rig, tinned iron saucepan-shape berry holder is perforated on bottom, short handle. Levered presser pivots in 2 places, no mark, American, 11¾''H x 26½''L, pan about 7¼''D, mid 19th C. • Possibly patented? I've seen the Smithsonian Institution's, which I can't place a monetary value on, but I venture a price range in case *you* find one. **$175.00-$225.00**

Betel nut cutter, scissor action, iron blade & silver handle, in form of rooster, engraved steel around eyes & design is chiseled in, the betel nut was cut in half then the meat picked out with end of handle, made in India, 7⅝''L, 19th C. • Most betel nut cutters are cast brass. They look Indian, most of them, but you can be thrown off guard by some simpler ones. Betel nuts are the seeds of a form of pepper plant, and the leaves, nut "and a little lime from burnt sea shells" is chewed by "East Indian natives" from India & Malay. **$100.00-$150.00**

Boat mill — SEE Herb crusher, also Spice grinder.

Bread board, carved wood, motto "Speed the Plough" around border, American or English, about 9½'' diameter, early 20th C. • Other mottoes include "Give Us This Day Our Daily Bread", "Waste Not Want Not" and "Staff of Life." There are also 19th & early 20th C bread boards from Germany, with similar mottoes in German; I've not seen these yet at American shows. **$45.00-$55.00**

Bread board, carved wood, motto "Welcome" around border, American or English, 20th C. • Reproduction alerts. — These have turned up in such great quantities, all worn as if they'd been run through a belt sander, bleached out too (wouldn't surprise me if a police pathologist wouldn't find household bleach in the woodgrain), that I personally wouldn't advise making a big collection of these. • A company called Bread Boards, in Landisville, PA, has advertised "hand carved" and "beautifully crafted" 12'' diameter bread boards for sale to dealers. • The Country Cottage Collection, in Elkins Park, PA, sells 12'' diameter "handcrafted Breadboards from Sheffield, England. These hand-carved and turned Breadboards are part of an English country tradition dating back to 1840. Carved from durable sycamore wood, known for its rich grain and hue which mellows with age. Because each is hand-carved, no two are exactly alike." (Brochure, 1987.) Some of theirs are carved on the outer rim, one has word "Bread", and the 5th is carved on the center of the board. **$45.00-$55.00**

Bread board & matching knife, carved wood, carbon steel blade for knife, both say "Bread" —- around border & on handle, English (?), early 20th C. • Reproduction alert. — I thought the knives were not being reproduced, but saw a few obviously reproduced at a flea in 1988. Also smaller sets for "Butter." **$60.00-$80.00**

Bread grater, heavy tinned sheet iron, slightly curved grating surface with coarse punctured holes fairly close set, wood handle, American, 12''L, early 19th C. • These are still useful, and you can really work up an appetite for scraped toast. A hundred years ago, invalids were treated to toast water, which was a burnt piece of toast soaked in water, and the colored water poured off and served up. **$75.00-$100.00**

Bread grater, punctured tin cylinder, fixed & braced handle, coarse grating surface, American, 10''L, late 19th C. • Look for thickness of tin (thicker is older) & irregular, rather than absolutely regular machine punctures. By the mid 1800s punctured tin blanks were available in tinsmiths' supply catalogs, for use in making graters & probably for pie safe door panels. • Dover Stamping Co., for example, in their 1869 catalog, offered what they called "grater blanks", rather coarse, with the puncture holes exactly ¼'' apart, center to center in either direction. These could be ordered in full sheets (not given, but I believe probably 16'' x 16''), half sheets and quarter sheets. A quarter sheet, presuming the above measurement, would thus be big enough to make a grater, though square, and thus unusual. **$25.00-$35.00**

Bread grater, punctured tin cylinder, the proportions of large tomato juice can, with 2 appended cylindrical graters, much smaller, fixed midway up on 2 sides, bracket strap handle across top. The large grater has coarsest holes; the other 2 provide medium & fine grating surfaces. Called a "bread grater" in the 1891 *Scammell's Treasure House*, but probably useful for grating other things too. American, 10''H, late 19th C. • "Spinach Fritters. — Boil the spinach until quite tender; drain, press and mince it fine; add half the quantity of grated stale bread, one grate of nutmeg, and a small teaspoon of sugar; add a gill of cream and as many eggs as will make a thick batter, beating the whites separately; pepper and salt to taste. Drop a little at a time in boiling lard. If it does not form fritters, add a little more bread crumbs. Drain and serve immediately or they will fall." *Ladies Home Journal*, April 1890. • A gill in the U.S. is equal to ¼ liquid pint; in Britain it's a ¼ Imperial pint (based on metric system), but in British dialect, a half-pint. It is possible that in early 19th C American recipes a half pint was meant. Later recipes which call for a gill require a half cup or 4 ounces. **$45.00-$65.00**

Bread knife, black wooden handle, carbon steel blade, "Ontario Knife Co.," 13''L, TOC. **$8.00-$12.00**

Bread knife, "Bread" carved on wooden handle, steel blade, marked "Sheffield", English, 19th C. **$25.00-$40.00**

Bread knife, carbon steel, iron loop handle, "Comet," mfd by Christy, Fremont, OH, 12''L, pat'd Nov. 12, 1890. • Other brand names of the period include "Universal" and "Aetna" made by Landers, Frary & Clark, also "Always Sharp", the Samson "Never Crumb", and the Clyde. What intrigues me is that there are no bread knife (or cake knife) patents at all in the *Subject Index to Patents, 1790 to 1873*, and just 10 or 15 years after that they seemed to be a hot item. **$15.00-$18.00**

Bread knife, carved wooden handle, says "Bread," carbon steel blade, American, 12½"L, 19th C. • **Caution:** For some few years the carved words or mottoes, on these as well as the carved rim bread plates, have been faked on old uncarved knives, or on newly made but distressed turned wood plates. **$25.00-$35.00**

Bread knife, plain wooden handle, carbon steel blade with truncated tip, "Climax," American, 13¼"L, late 19th C. **$15.00-$20.00**

Bread knife, primitive leaf carved on handle, 19th C. **$35.00-$40.00**

Bread knife, steel blade, carved wood handle, blade marked "G. Gill & Sons", Sheffield, England, 11"L, 19th C. **$30.00-$40.00**

Bread knife, steel blade, carved wood handle says "Bread", blade has trademark silhouetted twins & "J. A. Henckels Twin Works," Solingen, Germany, sold by importers in NYC, c.1910. **$12.00-$18.00**

Bread knife, steel blade, well-carved handle in old style, dealer's label reads "Old knife, new carving"; you know what happened to that delineation of age as soon as it was sold. Blade marked "Sheffield", English, 19th C knife, 1980s carving. • **Fake alert.** — This kind of irresponsible thing drives me crazy. What right did the carver have to take an old knife & do new old-style carving on it? The intention is only to fool everyone. **"Oh, what a tangled web we weave, When first we practise to deceive !"** — Sir Walter Scott. • Value now is same as for an all new, now secondhand bread knife. **$9.00-$13.00**

Bread knife, "Want Not" on wood handle, 12"L, 19th C. **$35.00-$50.00**

Bread knife, wheat sheaf carved on handle, blade marked "Alexander E. Foulis," English, 19th C (?). **$45.00-$65.00**

Bread knife, wheat sheaf carved on handle, carbon steel blade, all very worn, unusually short, only 8"L, 19th C. **$35.00-$40.00**

Bread knife, wooden handle, pointed carbon steel blade, "Tip-Top Boy," trademark of boy's head, American, 15"L, late 19th C. **$15.00-$22.00**

Bread knife, wood handle, truncated tip to carbon steel blade, "Victoria," American Cutlery Co., 14¾"L, late 19th C. **$15.00-$22.00**

Bread knife & matching board, wheat carved on knife handle & around board, with words "Bread Knife" engraved on steel blade, English or American, 9½"D board or plate, 19th C. • One dealer I talked to said that knife and board blanks were sold for people to carve themselves. This seems a reasonable assumption, when you see the variations in the carving. The carving technique for the raised block letters is basic, but results are often strikingly different, especially in spacing & size. Mottoes relating to bread abound the world over — ranging from jokes to blessings — so it is possible that this kind of carving is a tradition, at least in some countries. I have never found a document to back up this dealer's assertion, but would appreciate hearing from anyone who knows of a catalog or such, or who knows firsthand, perhaps through a family member, of this practice. **$85.00-$110.00**

Bread knives — SEE also Cake knife. Some can be used for both, but the basic rule is that the more widely spaced serrations or scallops are on cake knives, the more narrowly spaced ones are on bread knives.

Bread or cake knife, long scalloped carbon tool steel blade, metal handle cast with encircling bands like screw threads, marked "Lightning" & "Prussia", American, 15"L, early 20th C. **$18.00-$23.00**

Bread rasp, heavy forged iron, rough chiseled teeth, wood handle. Shaped like mason's concrete trowel; standard bakery equipment, used like bread grater, American, 9"L, late 18th early 19th C. **$85.00-$125.00**

Bread slicing box, heavily varnished wood, the 2 sides have 12 slots & are attached to cutting board base. Works sort of like a mitre box — the slots guide the bread knife. Simple but efficient. American or English, 5¾"H x 13½"L, 19th C. **$75.00-$100.00**

Butter cutter, painted & nickeled cast iron, screw clamps to table edge, horizontal platform for large 1 lb block of butter, which moves at preset calibrations through the levered wire cutter. It comes through 2 crossed wires which quarters it just a millisecond before it is cut into 4 pats of any thickness. Early ad shows pats falling into basin of ice water, sold by V. Clad & Sons, Phila., early 20th C. **$45.00-$55.00**

Cabbage cutter, a box grater, worn & silky wood frame with steel blade, prob. American, 26"L, 19th C. • Added value. — Homemade ones cost more than commercial ones. Look for interesting cutouts for hanging, or interesting treatment of wood, or nice joining of sides of box, or old wrought wingnuts for adjusting blade, etc. If it has too much going for it, caveat emptor. Homemade, & big, it might be $125.00-$225.00, but 19th C commercial one is worth less. **$25.00-$50.00**

Cabbage cutter, a wood box grater, with steel blade, box well-made, probably by hand, American, 22"L, 19th C. • "**Bubble and Squeak.**" — Take from a round of beef, which has been well boiled and cold, two or three slices, amounting to about one pound to one and a half in weight, two carrots which have been boiled with the joint, in a cold state, as also the hearts of two boiled greens that are cold. Cut the meat into small, dice-formed pieces, and chop up the vegetables together; pepper and salt the latter, and fry them with the meat in a pan in a quarter-pound of sweet butter; when fully done, add to the pan in which the ingredients are fried, half a gill of fresh catsup, and serve your dish up to the dinner table with mashed potatoes." From *Godey's Lady's Book*, as reprinted in Gertrude Strohm's *Universal Cookery*, 1888. • "**Bubble and Squeak.**" — Slice of cold boiled beef; chopped potatoes; chopped up cabbage; both previously boiled; pepper, sald and a little butter; set it aside to keep hot; lightly fry some slices of cold boiled beef; put them in a hot dish with alternate layers of the vegetables, piling high in the middle." *Scammel's Treasure House*, 1891. **$75.00-$100.00**

Cabbage cutter, also called a kraut or slaw cutter, wood with 2 steel blades, "The Indianapolis Kraut Kutter", Tucker & Dorsey Mfg. Co., Indianapolis, IN, made in different sizes, pat'd 1905. **$45.00-$55.00**

Cabbage cutter, also slaw board, walnut with large heart cutout hanging hole at one end, steel blades, one replaced side molding, all the wood unfortunately refinished at some point, with dull, dead no color under surface finish typical of poorly applied Minwax® combo stains & waxes. If you can't imagine the color, think of thickly spreading brown makeup all over your face, then heavily powdering it with gray or white powder. Pennsylvania German, 20⅝''L x 7¼''W, 19th C. • **Earl F. & Ada F. Robacker Collection.** As in all the Robacker pieces described in this book, the measurements & sometimes other attributed information are adapted from author's notes & Clarence Spohn's catalog for T. Glenn Horst Auctions. <u>In this case, the Minwax® description is the author's, and has nothing to do with Mr. Spohn, Mr. Horst or the Robackers.</u> • ''If you can't see the bright side of life, polish the dull side.'' — A quote seen in passing on a PA church notice board. • Price at May 1989 auction would have been up with original finish. **$140.00**

Cabbage cutter, gray graniteware, steel blade, ''Ideal'', TOC. **$185.00-$210.00**

Cabbage cutter, or <u>cabbage plane</u>, handmade box style, wood with peg construction, one very worn (much sharpened) carbon steel blade, American, 30''L, 19th C. • **German vocabulary** — <u>Krauthobel</u>: cabbage plane, or <u>Krautschneider</u>: cabbage cutter. **Pennsylvania German** — <u>Grout-Huvvel</u>: cabbage plane. **$40.00-$55.00**

Cabbage cutter, simple wood board with steel blade, very worn, but nice patina, American (?), 34½''L x 12¼''W, to fit over large kraut barrel, 19th C. • ''Sour-Krout.— Take a large, strong wooden vessel, or cask resembling a salt beef cask, and capable of holding as much as is sufficient for the winter's consumption of a family; gradually break down or chop the cabbages in very small pieces; begin with one or two cabbages at the bottom of the cask; add others at intervals; press them by means of a wooden spade against the side of the cask, until it is full; then place a heavy weight upon the top of it, and allow it to stand near a warm place for from 4 to 5 days; then place the cask in a cool situation; keep it always covered up; strew anise seeds among the layers of the cabbages during its preparation.'' Henry Scammel, compiler, *Treasure House*, 1891. **$25.00-$50.00**

Cabbage cutter, thick carved wood, heart shaped at top, bench end or straddle type used by putting on a bench or chair & sat upon, all wood with wooden screws to adjust steel blade, cabbage pusher missing. Stood on end it resembles a simple bust sculpture, American, prob. PA, 46⅜''L, mid 19th C. **$200.00-$250.00**

Cabbage cutter, interesting swinging box that passes over blade, describing about 15 degrees of a full circle, wood, cast iron hinge, steel cutting blade, porcelain handle on heavily sprung lid to box, which acts to hold cabbage firmly, like a foller in a press, American or German, 13''H w/ 17''sweep to box, 19th C. **$150.00-$175.00**

Cabbage cutter, walnut, 1 adjustable steel blade, cast iron handle, ''Brady,'' Lancaster, PA, 25''L x 7¾''W, pat'd March 9, 1880. **$75.00-$100.00**

Cabbage cutter, walnut, 3 steel blades, ''Disston & Morss'' (or Morse? or Morris?), Philadelphia, PA, 24''L x 9''W, 19th C. • This must have a connection with saw makers, Henry Disston & Son, but at this time I can't find anything about Morss, Morse, Morris. **$45.00-$60.00**

Cabbage cutters, walnut, iron & steel, with cutout hanging holes at ends of boards (one a sort of bird's head heart, the other a tulip), one with a cutout for fitting against hip or waist while using, American, most likely Pennsylvania German, one 18½''L, one 19''L, heart one dated 1883, other about same age. • These are in the collection of the National Museum of American History, Smithsonian In-

stitution. If I had to give a value to them, I'd say the amounts below. **$250.00-$500.00**

Cake knife, cast iron handle, carbon steel blade, ''Christy,'' Fremont, OH, 14¼''L, pat'd 1889, 1891. **$12.00-$15.00**

Cake knife, clear glass, rather chunky handle, slightly serrated cutting edge, ''Cryst-O-Lite,'' 8½''L, 1930s-40s. • Clear glass is not as desirable, by a long shot, as colored. And blue would be the most valuable of all. **$10.00-$12.00**

Cake knife, corrugated cast iron handle, carbon steel blade, ''Comet'' mfd. by Christy, Fremont, OH, 14¼''L, 1890s to TOC. **$12.00-$15.00**

Cake knife, glass, beautiful cobalt color, c.1930s. **$20.00-$35.00**

Cake knife, glass, in original box, ''Vitex,'' American, c.1940s. • Glass cake & fruit knives were made in cooperation with the war effort metal drives and war materials conservation efforts. **$12.00-$15.00**

Cake knife, green glass, with flower & leaf design on handle, in its original box, ''DUR-X'', 9''L, 1938 (design patent #112059). • Also used for fruit, as it could not be stained by acids. **$20.00-$25.00**

Carving fork, for meat, steel with bone handle, 2 tined, American (?), mid to late 19th C. • Low value for lone pieces, without matching carving knife & steel. If handle is well-worked, carved as a one of a kind piece, it has definite value on its own. This one does not. **$3.00-$6.00**

Carving set, carbon steel, knife, fork & sharpening steel, ''Keen Kutter,'' by Simmons Hardware. **$50.00-$75.00**

Cheese grater, 2 turned wood parts, with punctured tin grating surface in between. The shorter knobby part has short prongs on which to fix the piece of hard cheese (this wouldn't work for soft cheese). After putting the 2 parts together you grate by working your wrists back & forth, like wringing out clothes. Very attractive pale wood. American or European, 6½''L, 19th C, or early 20th. **$30.00-$45.00**

Cheese scoop, hand machined & cut steel, ivory handle, steel shaft decorated with 4 facets surrounded by zigzags & a sort of rope or scallop design, spade-shaped concave spoon-blade has very sharp cutting edge, thumb screw holds the pusher or follower on its track inside the scoop, can be turned to lift up pusher for cleaning, English, 10¹⁄₁₆'' L, scoop is 1⅝''L x 1¼''W, c.1840s. • Not all that rare, I've seen several of them, but the work is individually done. Cast iron, necessarily thicker & less refined looking, obviated all the handwork needed to make such tools as this scoop. **$75.00-$90.00**

Cheese slicer, aluminum, very musical if you pluck the wires, ''Cut-Rite, No. 300'' mfd by Wagner Ware, Sidney, OH, 7''L x 3⅛''W, ''patent pending'', 20th C. **$30.00-$38.00**

Cheese slicer, plated wire bent in sort of hacksaw shape, including loop handle, thin steel wire stretched between frame is what slices the cheese, American, 6⅝''L, c.1920-1949. **$3.00-$6.00**

Cherry pitter, almost all wood, iron hinges. Stones 20 cherries at a time. After you load the separate hinged cherry carrier tray, you insert it into the box, fit the foller or levered press, which has 20 longish pegs, into the top so the holes line up & push out 20 pits. Pits fall out underneath, & the pitted cherries are dumped from the carrier into a bowl. Most ingenious. American, box part is 6¼''H x 6¼''L x 5¾''W, 19th C. • This stoner, owned by Meryle Evans, was described in my 2nd edition as "homemade." Instead, I think it was a handmade production piece, made in small quantities. • A picture of a similar one, possibly the original from which the 20-stone one was copied, was recently found by me in a B.K. Bliss & Son's Seed Catalog, dated 1876. It is for "Fisher's Cherry Stoner", which will with "five strokes stone one hundred Cherries. The rapidity and certainty with which it performs its work will make this machine a necessity in every household. Under or overripe fruit equally well stoned, and can be done five times as rapdily as by tghe old way by hand, and much neater, as it leaves the fruit round and in perfect shape." The Fisher, a wooden box-like hinged device with a levered top "press" with 100 pegs, and a bottom part with 100 small holes (on which to place the cherries like Chinese Checkers), was pat'd "1870". The only 2 cherry stoners pat'd that year were one by J. Marchant, Farmington, IL April 19; and one by J. N. Webster, Peoria, IL, on May 31.   **$150.00-$225.00**

Cherry pitter, cast iron, 3 legs, mounted to board, hopper & crank, lightweight casting, sort of cabriole legs nicely shaped with "spurs" like a dog's dew claws, Scott Mfg. Co., Baltimore, MD, 6¾"H x 12"L, TOC.   **$45.00-$60.00**

Cherry pitter, cast iron, brightly nickel plated, screw clamps to table, has interesting works — a platform with 4 little holed cups holds 4 cherries at a time; when the pitter is cranked, the plunger goes up & down & punches pits out, one by one, New Standard Corp., Mount Joy, PA, 10¼"H, "patents pending," prob. TOC.   **$20.00-$35.00**

Cherry pitter, cast iron, even the crank knob is cast iron, 4 legs, mounted to board that has a rectangular cutout for cherries (or their stones?) to fall through, Scott Manufacturing Co., Baltimore, MD, stem to stern 7"H x 10⅞"L, "patent pending" 19th C. • I bought one specifically because one leg was replaced with a wooden leg. What I didn't realize, blush, until I actually took its picture and studied that, was that the little mouth or spout-trough was missing. It pays to look at everything and do a run-through in your mind, especially if you are highly attracted to one element to the exclusion of others. Hope this helps you someday ... remember: "<u>Learn from other people's mistakes. You won't have time to make them all yourself</u>."   **$45.00-$60.00**

Cherry pitter, cast iron finished in blue enamel, screw clamps to table edge, punches out 2 at a time, "Home Cherry Stoner," mfd. by Schroeter Bros. Hardware Co., St. Louis MO, 10½"H x 9½"L x 3"W, pat'd Aug. 17, 1917. • According to *House Furnishing Review* in 1918, "It is fast and very convenient; is self-feeding, due to the rocking hopper which agitates the cherries, causing them to roll into pitting sockets. Hopper large enough to hold 12 or more cherries at a time.   **$35.00-$45.00**

Cherry pitter, cast iron, hopper has cranked rub plate, clamps on, deep spout, handle is missing turned wood knob, replacement is old wooden spool, "The New Brighton," Logan & Strobridge, TOC.   **$18.00-$25.00**

Cherry pitter, cast iron, long hopper, swiveling hinge above the clamp that fastens it to the table, is a sort of shock absorber while plunger-punch is in action. Hopper can be filled with about 8 cherries, which roll down one at a time for pitting, "Duke," mfd. by Reading Hardware Co., Reading, PA, 11"L, not including wooden handle on crank, "patent pending," 19th C. • **German vocabulary** — <u>Mechanischer Kirschenentkerner</u>: mechanical cherry pitter.   **$65.00-$80.00**

Cherry pitter, cast iron painted turquoise, 2 plungers, screw clamp, Rollman Mfg. Co., Mt. Joy, PA, 14"H, TOC or later.   **$30.00-$40.00**

Cherry pitter, cast iron, pits 2 at a time with 2 curved rods that have ragged sharp ends. Punches pits through holes in double trough, & when pair of pitters is pulled back through a pry-off sheet of metal, the pitted cherries are knocked into a slanted wooden trough & roll into a bowl, "The Family Cherry Stoner," mfd. by Goodell Co., Antrim, NH, 8"H, pat'd 1886. • According to Loris Russell, this was based on the patent of George Geer, Galesburg, IL, of April 9, 1867.   **$35.00-$45.00**

Cherry pitter, cast iron, screw clamp, "Cherry Stoner No. 17", & on bottom of clamp "2884", "Enterprise" not cast on piece, 12"H exclusive of screw, pat'd Mar. 31 1903.   **$30.00-$45.00**

Cherry pitter, cast iron, screw clamps to table, simple figure 8 heavy wire thumbscrew, the #17 (japanned) & #18 (tinned) can be regulated or adjusted for different size cherries, which are fed into hopper, whereupon a crank rubs them against a ridge plate which splits them & removes pits, "Enterprise #17," Enterprise Mfg. Co., Philadelphia, PA, pat'd March 31, 1903.   **$30.00-$45.00**

Cherry pitter, cast iron, square-cut letters & numbers, square hopper, comes apart for cleaning, mounted to board, name not marked, but pat'd by H. Buckwalter as a "cherry-stoner", Kimberton, PA, 5"H exclusive of board, pat'd Nov. 17, 1863.   **$125.00-$165.00**

Cherry pitter, cast iron, tinned finish, hopper & crank, adjusted by thumb screws to adapt to different size cherries, Enterprise #2, mfd. by Enterprise Mfg. Co., Philadelphia, PA, 12"H x 9"W, pat'd March 31, 1903. • The #1 was japanned, and sold for half to three quarters the price of the tinned one originally. • **Lookalike alarm**. — A brand new cherry pitter, styled exactly like the old Enterprise, is being manufactured (not to fool collectors). Cast into the body is "CHOP-RITE Pottstown U.S.A." Approximate new price: **$30.00-$45.00**

Cherry pitter, cast iron, tinned (later, c.1913, offered also in bronze japan finish), screw clamped to table, ridged wheel in center of hopper is cranked to rub stones out of the cherries, this one in its original cardboard box, "Brighton #2", mfd by Logan & Strobridge Iron Co., sold by future mfrs, Wrightsville Hardware Co., L&S from New Brighton, PA; WHCo. in Wrightsville, PA, pat'd May 15, 1866, by William Weaver, Phoenixville, PA. • Made for many years after 1866, and advertised as being made by Wrightsville Hardware in 1913. In an ad from *House Furnishing Review*, March 1913, this cherry seeder is described as being "adjustable" — like the Enterprise ones, finished in "Bronze Japan or Tinned," & "furnished either with clamp for attaching to table or with four legs." Old ones get the most money: **$65.00-$100.00**

Cherry pitter, hand held, nickeled spring steel wire, loop-de-looped so that it fits over thumb & middle finger, fed cherries one by one with other hand, & squeezed to make sharp-ended plunger push pit out, John Houck, Chicago, IL, 7¼"L, pat'd Dec. 28, 1909.   **$18.00-$22.00**

Cherry pitter, hand held, small metal device with finger holes at each side, & a plunger worked with the thumb in center, has to be hand-fed, "Perfection" is name given it by a distributer, F.W. Seastrand, American, about 4"L, marked only "PAT." Seastrand catalog is c.1910, so earlier than that.   **$10.00-$15.00**

Cherry pitter, or cherry stoner, cast iron, mounted to wood board cut out to match footprint of pitter; has tin-lined hole so whole thing could be set up over large receptacle; hopper has fabulous, almost Art Nouveau, sorrel leaf, with waving tip, cast in it, turned wheel inside hopper, which rubs cherries off their stones, ribbed on both sides; this is the improvement on the original patent, improvement pat'd by William Weaver on H. Buckwalter's patent, Weaver from Phoenixville, PA, Buckwalter from Kimberton, PA, 6''H, board 8⅞'' x 4½'', pat'd Nov. 17, 1863 & May 15, 1866. • **"Cherry Bounce.** — Take a peck of morella cherries, and a peck of black hearts. Stone the morellas and crack the stones. Put all the cherries and the cracked stones into a demi-john, with three pounds of loaf-sugar slightly pounded or beaten. Pour in two gallons of double-rectified whisky. Cork the demi-john, and in six months the cherry-bounce will be fit to pour off and bottle for use; but the older it is, the better.'' Miss Leslie, of Philadelphia, *Seventy-Five Receipts for Pastry, Cakes, and Sweetmeats. Appended to The Cook's Own Book and Housekeeper's Register ....,* by a Boston Housekeeper. Boston: Munroe & Francis, 1833. **$140.00-$160.00**

Cherry pitter, skeletal cast iron frame, with 3 spraddly but insectually grasshopper graceful heavy gauge rod legs. Hopper feeds cherries against one side of the spirally-ridged wheel that is turned with a crank that has (or is supposed to have) a slim wooden handle, marked only with patent date, but pat'd by Henry Buckwalter, Kimberton, PA, pat'd Nov. 17, 1863. • The William Weaver patent of 3 years later (May 15, 1866) is an improvement, in that both sides of the wheel are ridged, doing twice as many cherries. **$125.00-$165.00**

Cherry pitter, tinned cast iron, cranked action that pulls down vertical pit puncher, leather insert at point of impact on hopper, screw clamps to table, wooden handle (older ones natural or varnished), ''New Standard #50,'' New Standard Hardware Works, Mt. Joy, PA, 10''H x 5½''W, pat'd in the 1870s. • Also came in a 12''H size, the ''New Standard #75.'' • **Lookalike alarm.** — A similar one-cherry pitter, also of tinned cast iron, is now being made by the White Mountain Freezer Inc., Winchendon, MA 01475. It seems to be a variation of the John H. Webster May 31, 1870 patent for a straight-plunger style pitter. These were made over a very very long time; I believe the ones seen with red wooden handles are as late as the 1940s. • Another 1940s variation, the ''50A Dandy'', is made of cast iron and heavy stamped sheet metal, heavily tinned (or nickeled?), with a piston that drives pitter up and down when you turn crank. The pitter is marked New Standard Corp., Mt. Joy, but sold by White Mountain Freezer Co., Nashua, NH. (Value of 1940's one under $25.00). **$25.00-$40.00**

Cherry pitter, tinned cast iron, screw clamps, crank is not on a wheel, but at right angles & behind hopper. This one ''is intended to stone cherries with the least possible cutting or disfiguring. Every good housewife will appreciate this for preserving purposes. The most satisfactory results are obtained by dropping the cherries one at a time into the Hopper immediately after Sweeper has passed the hole. With practice one can become very expert.'' ''The New Cherry Stoner,'' Enterprise #12, c.1890s to c.1905 at least. **$40.00-$60.00**

Cherry pitter, tinned metal & wire, hand held, ''The 'HAND'-Y'', American, 3''H, c.1920s (?). **$10.00-$18.00**

Cherry pitter, worked with 2 hands, metal, put cherries on platform below, pitted by one part, split by other, no mark, 8''H, TOC. **$75.00-$90.00**

Cherry stoner, red painted cast iron screw clamp frame, tall vertical shaft has large knob at top, to be pushed down for spring action, one cherry at a time, oval concave white porcelainized cast iron receiver, ''Excelsior 85'', pat'd 1885 (?). **$75.00-$100.00**

Chocolate grater, tin & cast iron, a mechanical gadget with a rectangular spring-loaded holder for a chunk or block of chocolate, has 3 rods going length of cylindrical punctured tin grating surface, 2 of which are the track for the chocolate holder, rubbed back & forth across grater, in same way as Edgar nutmeg grater, ''The Edgar,'' mfd. by William J. Bride Co., Reading, MA, cylinder 7¼''L x 2⅛'' diameter, with handle 8½''L, chocolate holder is 2⅞''H x 2'' x 1⅞'', pat'd 1891, and again Nov. 10, 1896. • ''Caramel Potato Cake. — ½ cup butter, 1 cup sugar, 2 eggs, ½ cup milk, ½ cup hot riced potatoes, 1 cup flour, 2 teaspoons baking powder, ½ teaspoon cinnamon, ½ teaspoon [ground] clove, ½ teaspoon [grated] nutmeg, ½ cup grated chocolate, ½ cup chopped nut meats. — Cream butter and add gradually, while beating constantly, sugar; then add eggs, well beaten, milk and potatoes. Beat thoroughly and add flour, mixed and sifted with baking powder, and spices, chocolate and nut meats. Turn into a buttered and floured cake pan and bake in a moderate oven fifty-five minutes. Remove from pan and cover with Fudge Frosting. • **Fudge Frosting.** — 2 tablespoons butter, 1 cup sugar, ¼ cup milk, 1 square unsweetened sugar, ½ teaspoon vanilla. — Put butter in saucepan and when melted, add sugar and milk. Bring to the boiling point and let boil ten minutes. Add chocolate and let boil five minutes, taking care that chocolate does not adhere to bottom or sides of pan. Remove from range, add vanilla and beat until the right consistency to spread.'' Fannie Merritt Farmer, *A New Book of Cookery.* Boston: Little, Brown, 1915 edition of 1912 book. • Rare: except in ads, I've never seen one for sale. **$250.00-$350.00**

Chopping bowl, carved wood, a few minor age checks, 16⅝''L x 9½''W, mid 19th C. **$225.00-$300.00**

Chopping bowl, crudely-hewn thick wood, American, rectangle 5'' x 11'' x 4''D, very early 19th C, poss. 18th C. **$135.00-$175.00**

Chopping bowl, hand carved wood, nice patina, American, 25''L x 10½''W x 4''D, early to mid 19th C. • This proportion is most common — over twice as long as wide & not very deep. Old chopping bowls should show signs of vigorous cutting. The wonder is that they look so good on the inside; maybe really badly scarred ones were burned in the fireplace generations ago. I've seen many repaired ones, where bottom has been chopped through, bad section cut out & hole fitted with another piece of wood, flush as possible, or metal patch has been added. • Added value.— Often repaired ones bring more than those with good condition but less personality. **$75.00-$125.00**

Chopping bowl, hand carved wood, oblong, old red paint on outside, American, 22½''L x 8½''W, 19th C. • **Paint & Patina:** Old paint, red, ochre, blue, green or even gray, adds to collector appeal. But if not painted, a good scrubbed, old patina is what you should look for. These were cut from split logs, then hollowed out with a special curved cutting scraping tool called a scorp; somewhere twin bowls, made from the two halves of a log may exist. **$200.00-$250.00**

Chopping bowl, wood with old red paint on outside, oblong, American, quite extraordinarily large at 25"L x 17"W, early or mid 19th C. • Sold at a 1982 auction for $300.00. Now would depend on where it was sold if it would go much higher. **$275.00-$500.00**

Chopping knife, 2 nickeled steel rocker blades set at right angles & forming almost round shape, big wooden ball knob handle, "Androck," Rockford, IL, 1930s-40s. **$8.00-$12.00**

Chopping knife, 2 plated steel sausage shape blades, 2 tangs welded at one end, fit over a rod going through turned wooden handle at other end. By use of wingnut to loosen tangs, the distance between blades can be adjusted. "James F. Foster", Buffalo, NY, 6"H x 5¾"W, pat'd Dec. 27, 1887. **$18.00-$25.00**

Chopping knife, 2 tang straight bottom steel blade, turned wooden handle, "Brades Co.," American or English, 6"W, 19th C. **$40.00-$50.00**

Chopping knife, 3 slightly bowed, hotdog shaped steel blades, iron frame & wooden handle, called a tension chopper. "In this knife the blades are ... kept firm by the tension of the frame in which they are set. It does very rapid work, and is an excellent knife for family use. Most people consider hash a very delicious breakfast dish, in spite of all the hits newspaper paragraphers have made on it, and a good implement for making it is indispensable." *Practical Housekeeper*, 1884. American, about 6"W, pat'd 1867. **$18.00-$25.00**

Chopping knife, 4 stainless steel blades set at right angles to form bell-like shape, painted wooden handle, "A & J," Binghamton, NY, 6"H x 3"W, c.1925. • Knobs were painted green, yellow or red. Blue is not mentioned in the catalog. **$10.00-$15.00**

Chopping knife, also called a chopper, or mincer, fancily shaped cast steel blade, brass inset decoration, smooth mahogany colored handle, 2 tangs, English, c.1820s or 30s. • **Think English** as soon as you see **fancy cutouts** on the blade, or very deep blades with profiles of roosters or animals along top non-cutting edge, or combinations of brass & iron; most such pieces are not American. **$75.00-$150.00**

Chopping knife, brass & steel, handmade (at least it looks one of a kind & not commercial), tubular brass handle with long slit into which was slid, then soldered, the well-shaped steel blade with fancy shoulder, American (?), 4½"H x 6½"W, 19th C. **$120.00-$150.00**

Chopping knife, cast iron handle with cutout in top, usually painted, stainless steel rocker blade with distinct swellings at each end. This looks exactly like the "Double Action" knife, except for cutout in horizontal part of handle. I don't know if they were made by same company, 20 years apart, or if Voos got license to make them & altered handle for some purpose. marked "Voos," American, 5"H x 6⅛"W, c.1920s. • **"The Knife-Life of the Kitchen. — [A]** late product of steel ... is ... fast coming to the markets of the world. It is stainless steel. A steel (with an admixture of chromium) which resists rust, does not corrode or scale, and is impervious to food acids (with the exception of mustard, plus vinegar and salt which equal muriatic acid). ... The steel we now use is carbon steel. ... Think of

not having to scour or polish your knives. Think of the knife having an indefinite life and always looking highly polished. Soon, too, even the handle will be made of this steel and the knife will be made of this steel and the knife will look like a highly polished silver utensil. No cleaning powders must be used to clean this steel; only warm water and soap. Its advent reminds one of the early days of aluminum utensils, doesn't it? Manufacturers are planning to make kettles, pots and pans of it, as they will wear well, and will not scale and wear as do iron ones." *House & Garden*, March 1921. **$12.00-$18.00**

Chopping knife, cast iron handle with no cutout, cast steel blade shaped like baby's bottom, hence its name "Double Action." American, pat'd Oct. 20, 1892. **$12.00-$18.00**

Chopping knife, cast iron stirrup-shaped handle, 2 bell-shaped steel blades, rocker action, "N. R. S. & Co. No. 20," (Nelson R. Streeter & Co.), Groton, NY, 5½"H, pat'd May 2, 1893. **$20.00-$30.00**

Chopping knife, cast steel blade, 2 tangs, forged iron handle, marked only "Cast Steel," American, 5½"L blade, c.1870s. **$35.00-$45.00**

Chopping knife, cast steel blade, cast iron shank & turned wood T-handle, blade is lightly rocked & has very high rounded shoulders, "S. H. F.," "Bingham" (may be last name of maker or town), American (?), 7"H x 5½"W, 19th C. • There were a number of Binghams in America, including three Michigan towns named that. **$35.00-$45.00**

Chopping knife, cast steel blade, wooden handle, "Universal," mfd by Landers, Frary & Clark, 19th C. **$15.00-$20.00**

Chopping knife, cast steel, quadrant handle screws to 6 "flying buttress" blades that form bell shape, taken apart for sharpening or cleaning, J. B. Foote Foundry, pat'd 1906. **$10.00-$15.00**

Chopping knife, cast steel, wood, L. D. Wheeler, n.p. (American ?), 19th C. **$35.00-$50.00**

Chopping knife, curved steel blade, wood handle, "Henry Disston & Sons," the famous saw makers, Phila., 6½"L, 19th C. • I've never seen one, but Henry Disston did get a patent for a potato parer on Nov. 29, 1859. **$18.00-$25.00**

Chopping knife, cutlery steel blade, long tang, turned wood handle, "Mason & Parker", English, 13½"L, late 19th C. **$40.00-$55.00**

Chopping knife, deep half-ovoid blade, one tang, wood handle, marked "PERK" on blade, American, 5"W, mid to late 19th C. **$50.00-$60.00**

Chopping knife, double blade, steel with wood handle, heart shaped rivet head, American, 7"L, c.1870s. **$165.00-$180.00**

Chopping knife, double bladed rocker type, black turned wood handle, loosen wing nut to take blade off for sharpening or cleaning, distance between 2 parallel blades is NOT adjustable — it locks in only one position. Ad from Dec. 27, 1890 *Metal Worker* has imaginary dialogue between housewife & hardware clerk: "'I do not want one of those double bladed chopping knives. You cannot wash, scour or sharpen them without cutting the fingers.' 'But,' said the clerk, 'This is one of the new Buffalo ... mincing knives which opens for cleaning and sharpening.' 'Why, that's splendid. I'll take that!' said she." Called a "Buffalo Adjustable", mfd by Sidney Shepard & Co., Buffalo, NY, 6"H x 5⅞"W blade, pat'd Dec. 27, 1887. • Carpet Cutters. — A type of rocking chair in the

19th C, with relatively thin wooden rocker blades rounded on the ends, were called by some wags "carpet cutters". **$30.00-$40.00**

Chopping knife, forged crescent blade, bentwood handle, American (?), 6"W, early 19th C. **$65.00-$75.00**

Chopping knife, forged iron blade 2 long tangs, thick, slightly carved wood handle, American, 6½"H x 5"W, early 19th C. **$55.00-$70.00**

Chopping knife, forged iron, curved blade with unusually shaped shoulders leading to single shank & turned wooden T handle, American, mid 19th C. **$35.00-$45.00**

Chopping knife, forged steel, likened to an anchor, wooden handle, thin crescent moon blade, prob. American, 6"W, mid 19th C. **$50.00-$60.00**

Chopping knife, forged steel straight-bottom blade, with turned wood handle, nicely shaped cutout for hand is almost like the top of a Valentine, American (?), 19th C. **$35.00-$50.00**

Chopping knife, iron blade curves like sleeping dog, 3 tangs become one shank T handle, American (?), 6¼"H, 19th C. **$45.00-$60.00**

Chopping knife, iron blade, very fat & curved, unusual brass tang, fat cigar shaped T handle grip, American, 19th C. **$50.00-$65.00**

Chopping knife, iron & tin, pat'd May 2, 1893. **$15.00-$20.00**

Chopping knife, iron with wood tiller handle off one end (just imagine the tiller of a small sailboat to get idea of shape & angle), blade's other end is fat & rounded, American, 3"H x 10"L, 19th C. **$25.00-$35.00**

Chopping knife, ornate steel & wood, 4 brass rivets fasten handle to blade, cutout & scrolly carved wooden handle (with "horns" to cradle hand), almost a mirror image of fat scrolls of rocker blade, which also has a heart near the haft, birds perched on scrolled tips, European, poss. English, although some hints at German origin, 12½"H, 18th or 19th C (?). I think 1830s. Somehow the handle does not look as old as I think it should for blade. • This chopper has been for sale at least twice: it was shown by dealer Paul Decoste (Newburyport, ME) at a Portland, ME, show, in summer 1987. & marked $2800.00. Next (?) it was shown in the late 1980s, possibly in 1987 (I forgot to date my source), by dealer Corey Daniels, of Wells, ME. • It was in the late 1980s that very ornate choppers began to appear regularly on the market. The blades look old; sometimes you look for more wear on the handles than is there. They are so "Good" you have to wonder where did they come from. I've heard from some dealers that this ornate type is being skillfully reproduced in England for export to America. • The low in the price range is no typo. **$300.00-$2800.00**

Chopping knife, stainless steel, triple blades have spring action to make center blade look (& sound) like it's doing extra work. "Foley Chopper," 7½"H x 33¾"W, pat'd 1938. **$10.00-$15.00**

Chopping knife, steel blade, 2 tangs, turned wooden handle, "Henry Disston," Philadelphia, PA. 19th C. **$15.00-$20.00**

Chopping knife, steel blade has nicely shaped shoulder & truncated ends, 1 tang, wood handle, American, 5⅞"W, 19th C. **$50.00-$60.00**

Chopping knife, steel blade with tang split at top so the **Y** gives extra strength to handle, like an inverted wishbone tang, prob. American, 5"W blade, mid 19th C. **$50.00-$60.00**

Chopping knife, steel crescent blade, single tang with wooden handle set crooked on it, angle makes it more comfortable to use, prob. American, 5¾"W, mid 19th C. **$50.00-$60.00**

Chopping knife, steel, ovoid blade pivots for dual purpose: one edge makes scalloped cuts, other minces; wood handle, filed or chiseled tooling on shaft, American, 6½"H x 6¼"W, 19th C. **$25.00-$35.00**

Chopping knife, steel rocker blade, 2 hander has fat wooden knob at each end, marked "9," American, 9½"W, 19th C. • Still made, but with stainless steel blades since -?-. **$30.00-$40.00**

Chopping knife, steel rocker blade in fat sausage or pickle shape, top side has small section of saw teeth, rosette rivet points on blade, basketwork-looking cast iron handle, like a heat-dissipating stove lid lifter handle, American, 6½"W, 19th C. **$20.00-$25.00**

Chopping knife, steel rocker blade with truncated ends, single tang, bullet-ended turned cylindrical handle assembled from discs of varying widths & different materials — including ivory, ebony & other wood, English (?), 7"H, prob. craftsman made mid 20th C. **$145.00-$160.00**

Chopping knife, steel sausage-shape blade riveted to wooden handle 3 times the height of the blade, cutout hand hold in wood, American, 7"H x 8"W overall, early 19th C. **$60.00-$85.00**

Chopping knife, steel with upside down **Y** or <u>wishbone</u> tang, wooden handle, deep double rocker blades have truncated ends, American, 6"H x 5¾"W, early 20th C. **$18.00-$22.00**

Chopping knife, steel & wood, 2 blades, "Hercules", early 20th C. **$20.00-$25.00**

Chopping knife, turned wood T handle, single wide tang, deep nearly rectangular blade with rounded corners, marked "W. Butcher", well known plane iron maker, mid to 3rd quarter 19th C. **$50.00-$65.00**

Chopping knife, 2 steel blades, curved "hotdog" shape, high arching bentwood handle, not marked, but probably a mfd piece, American (?), 6"L blades, c.1880. • "A chopping knife with only one blade is much better than one with two blades. The blade should be almost straight across. When it is rounded a good deal, much time and strength are wasted in chopping." Maria Parloa, *Kitchen Companion*, Boston: Estes & Lauriat, 1887. It is instructive to read period literature about utensils and gadgets. While "artistically" we may admire the curved double blades, Parloa, who came with the highest credentials, founder of the original Boston Cooking School, and author of several cookbooks, obviously didn't like them. **$50.00-$65.00**

Chopping knife, cast steel & wood, rocker blade, large fat handle fits comfortably in hand, American, late 19th C. **$12.00-$15.00**

Chopping knife, forged blade, beautiful arrow-tipped tang, turned wooden handle, American (?), 19th C. **$45.00-$60.00**

Chopping knife, wrought iron in elongated bell shape, wood crosswise handle crammed down on short tang, American (?), 5¼"L, 18th C. • The iron is badly pitted, the form is beautiful. I bought it at auction of Keillor

Family Collection, once probably the largest, finest collection (now dispersed) ever assembled in the U.S.
$25.00-$50.00

Chopping knife, wrought iron, crescent blade has 2 wide tangs riveted to wooden handle, pat'd by "B. Denton," Auburn, NY, about 6"W blade, 1850s-60s (?).
$55.00-$80.00

Chopping knife, wrought iron, half moon blade with longish tang, wooden T-handle, "T. Collins," about 5½"W blade x 5½"H, 19th C. • **"To Make a Cold Hash, or Salmagundy.** — Take a turkey, and two chickens that have been roasted; cut the flesh from their breasts into thin slices, and mince the legs of the chickens; then wash and bone 10 large anchovies, add eight large pickled oysters, 10 or 12 fine green pickled cucumbers, and one whole lemon. Chop all these very small, and mix it with the minced-meat; lay it in the middle of a dish and the slices of the white part around it, with halved anchovies, whole pickled oysters, quartered cucumbers, sliced lemon, whole pickled mushrooms, capers or any pickle you like; cut also some fine lettuce, and lay round among the garnish; but put not oil and vinegar to the minced-meat till it comes to table." Eliza F. Haywood, *A New Present for a Servant-Maid; Necessary Cautions and Precepts to Servant-Maids for Gaining Good-Will and Esteem*, Dublin, Ireland: 1771. • Pickles of nuts, fruits, vegetables and meats were given a lot of space in 18th C cookbooks. The corresponding ingredients in the late 20th C would be conveniently canned (therefore preserved) pineapple or peaches, peas or corn, ham or chicken. You would find canned nuts, in liquid, in Oriental groceries, but most Western recipes requiring nuts could be made with freshly shelled, dry roasted, or packaged nutmeats. **$55.00-$65.00**

Chopping knife, wrought iron, oak handle which is ovoid in section, tang inserted through simple handle then hammered over, neat little prickery shoulder point spurs just above half-moon blade, American (?), 3¾"W blade, late 18th C. **$125.00-$135.00**

Chopping knife, wrought iron or tool steel half moon blade, single tang, simple turned wood cigar-shaped handle, "Isaac Greaves", Basking Ridge, NY, 6⅛"L x 5¾"W, mid 19th C. **$65.00-$75.00**

Chopping knife, wrought iron, proportionately small blade, 2 projections at top of each end of blade bent around & forged together to form handle loop, almost look as if they were originally intended to be tangs for a wooden handle before maker changed his mind, American, 5¹¹⁄₁₆"W, early 19th C. **$28.00-$40.00**

Chopping knife, wrought steel with wooden T-handle, half moon shaped blade, marked "Coldwell," American or English, blade is 6" W, heighth including blade, tang & handle is 7¾", 19th C. **$50.00-$65.00**

Chopping knife & chopping board, forged iron & wood, the very thick wood cutting board cut in fancy outline, blade cut at top in shape of a trotting horse, with fat turned wooden handle "tail", prob. English, 7"H x 14¼"L, 19th C. • **Figural knives,** pinned to & pivoting around a chopping board, are often described as tobacco leaf cutters, although none of the ones I've smelled have any odor of tars or nicotine. Some have been remounted to the reverse side of the board, after enough chopping has made the first surface concave. I saw a horse one at a Connecticut show in about 1984 for only $95.00. I don't know what kept me from buying it, but I guess the price

was *too* low; it was very appealing, but somehow it didn't grab me. At the prices today, I guess I've lived to regret it ... a little. If it had been a serpent or a different animal, I might have leapt at the chance to buy it. • This listing sold for $500.00 at a 1982 auction. **$500.00-$650.00**

Chopping knife & cutting board, knife hinged & mounted to simple wooden board, knife is not figural, American or English, about 16"L x 11"W, 19th C. • Price depends on details, anything unusual or special about hinge or pivot part; gracefulness or length or interesting angle of handle; thickness of cutting board (a full inch or inch and a quarter plank is older than the ¾" or ⅞" thickness of today's so-called one inch board); shape of board. Most desirable are figural knifes (often in the shape of a horse, the tail being the handle), or at least ones with little extra forged details or decoration. **$150.00-$750.00**

Chopping knife & cutting board, type that looks like food chopper but is often called a tobacco cutter, pivoting steel blade, remounted to thick chestnut block, other side of block deeply hollowed, showing where blade was mounted before, English, block 2" thick, 10⅝"L x 6⅛"W, 19th C. **$40.00-$50.00**

Chopping tool, iron fingers ride in a long slot & function, possibly, as a blade cleaner (?) or push-offs, turned wooden handles, American (?), 14¾"L, there is a patent #1666. I don't know what kind of patent so can't date. • If it's a design patent it is 1862, if a reissue patent 1864, and if a regular patent is the more doubtful 1840. And as I can't find this tool under Beef-steak chopper, Food chopper, Meat chopper or Vegetable chopper, it's possible it isn't a kitchen tool. **$75.00-$90.00**

Cleaver, figural blade of carbon steel, bird head forms hook at top front of blade, flat lead handle is a replacement, probably old, of missing wooden handle. The figure probably denoted kind of meat, by kosher dietary law, to be chopped with it. Russian or Polish kosher butcher's cleaver, 4⅛"H x 13½"L, TOC. • This one, and its mate, have a known family history, shared with me by owner Marvin Tanner. I'm sure there are non-Jewish figural cleavers. **$300.00-$400.00**

Cleaver, magnetic tool steel, turned wood handle, "I. F. W. & S. Co.," American, 3⅞"H x 12"L, blade c.6"L, late 19th C. **$15.00-$20.00**

Cleaver, steel blade, wood handle, marked with a steer and "Wm. Beatty & Sons," Chester, PA, only 6"L, 19th C. $15.00-$20.00

Cleaver, tool steel blade with big hanging hole in top front, wooden handle, "Samuel Lee, L. F. & C." (Landers, Frary & Clark), 4"W x 13"L, pat'd May 1886. **$20.00-$30.00**

Cleaver, carbon steel blade, iron handle has cutout for fingers, simple, even crude in design, American, 13"L, late 19th C. **$15.00-$20.00**

Cleaver, forged iron blade ending in upturned "genie shoe" curl, wooden handle, American or English, prob. late 18th C. **$45.00-$60.00**

Cleaver & can opener combined, also meat tenderizer, bottle opener, bone saw, hammer. Steel cleaver blade, shaped wooden handle, other tools screwed to large front end of blade, adding desirable weight. American, 14¼"L, 19th C. **$45.00-$65.00**

Cleaver & tenderizer combined, steel, cast iron handle, "Tenda-Cleve," American, early 20th C. **$10.00-$12.00**

Coconut grater, handcrafted from variety of parts made of cast iron, brass, steel, sheet metal. Upright shaft is turned iron, serrated blades act like reamer when you push half a coconut against the turning blades. Brass & wood handle. English (?), for colonial use in Jamaica or the West Indies, 7"H, mid 19th C. **$85.00-$100.00**

Coffee mills — SEE Coffee, Tea & Chocolate chapter.

Cook's knife, elongated carbon steel triangular blade, wooden handle, "Guelon", with trademark on blade of boy with ladder, French, 12"L, c.1920s. • Worth more to a person needing a really good kitchen knife than to a collector. **$5.00-$10.00**

Cookie cutters — SEE the Mold chapter.

Corer, nickeled steel tube, half of which is perforated "to reduce resistance", has effect of toothed edge around top, fitted with stop inside so core could be pushed out, turned wood knob handle, sold by Spengler Specialties, NYC, NY, early 20th C. **$10.00-$15.00**

Corer & doughnut cutter combined, tin, doughnut cutter has strap handle, corer attachment fits into "hole-making" inner ring, American, 3" diameter x 3⅞"H when corer in place, TOC. **$12.00-$18.00**

Corer & slicer combined, metal, wood handled corer fits in-to handle of slicer, American, 8⅜"L, pat'd Oct. 12, 1915. **$15.00-$22.00**

Corer, slicer, scraper combo, metal, 9¾"L, 20th C. **$15.00-$22.00**

Corn cutter, a half cylinder of heavy tin about hand sized, strap handle from top to bottom, across inside at heel end is narrow row of sharp teeth, the same distance apart as most full grown corn; above is a heavy wire which braces the cylinder & "presses out" the contents of each kernel after it is slit by cutter. As to why this would be desirable for fresh corn, the *American Agriculturist* says that the un-digested whole kernel is "just as much a foreign body as a gravel-stone", therefore "careful parents and those not blessed with teeth that can crush and grind every grain, slit the kernels by drawing a sharp knife along each row, so the digestible and nutritious contents slip out." "Yankee Corn-Cutter", maker unknown, possibly patent of V. Baker for "Green corn cutter", poss., then, Otisfield, ME, maybe the one pat'd May 31, 1870, adver-tised c.1872. **$16.00-$20.00**

Corn grater, a little wooden bench-like contrivance on 4 turned wood legs, iron grater teeth & blade, American, 4½"H x 11¾"L, c.1870s-80s. **$125.00-$175.00**

Corn grater, arched steel blade with prickers, mounted over an oval hole in board, American, 12"L, late 19th C. **$10.00-$15.00**

Corn grater, crude, homemade, half cylinder of punctured tin stuck on a wooden board, dealer's tag said "Corn Gritter", which may be local usage or phonetic spelling, anyway it makes sense if you think of grits; maybe this was used for dry corn, not fresh? American, 18"L x 7"W, late 19th C. • **"A Grater For Potatoes, Etc.** — A reader has written in to show how a grater to prepare the potatoes for yeast may be made very easily. Place an oyster or fruit can upon the stove or near a fire, until the solder is melted; this will allow the top and bottom to be removed, and the seam to be opened. Open the large piece of tin, and with a nail punch numerous holes from the inside. A nail, which will make a ragged hole, is better than a regular punch; after punching lay the tin upon a block of rather hard wood; turn the edges, to give a place for tacks, and fasten to a board. A hole may be made in the board to hang it by. We have used

such a grater for horse-radish and other purposes, and it works admirably." "Household Notes & Queries", *American Agriculturist*, NYC, April 1879. **$55.00-$75.00**

Corn grater, wood & metal, signed "C. Frankenfield", Pennsylvania German (?), 12⅞"L x 3⅞"W, 19th C. • Price estimated from May 1989 Robacker auction; this was in lot with 2 wood & tin clothespins, (which have a market value of about $8.00 at most). **$55.00-$60.00**

Crooked knife, chip carved wood, heart & diamonds on handle, blade has string-wrapped "bolster", American, prob. not Amerindian, 9"L, 19th C. **$95.00-$110.00**

Crooked knife, tool steel blade, crooked wooden handle carved with hound dog's head, much carved detail, small roundhead brass pin or tack eyes, New England, in style borrowed from Indians in lower Canada or Maine, 10⅜"L, dog's head only about 2"L, 19th C. **$175.00-$225.00**

Cucumber slicer, cast iron, screw clamps to table, complete-ly vertical round hopper or chute is cuke-sized, blades cranked, "The Patent Slicer," mfd by Spong, London, England, 9⅝"H, c.1920s or 1930s (?) poss. earlier. • Another type is very like a cabbage plane, made of wood with a steel blade, but much smaller. **$65.00-$75.00**

Cucumber slicer, silver & ivory, oblong, like tiny kraut cutter, silversmith was Hester Bateman, English, 1775. **$1500.00-$1800.00**

Cutting board, elephant form, wood, 14¾"L, TOC. **$70.00-$90.00**

Cutting board, fish shape, wood with burn rings like many cutting boards have (from being used as hot pads), American, 12"L x 7¼"W, prob. early 20th C. • Robacker May 1989 price: **$45.00**

Cutting board, pig shape, burl figured wood with very nice patina, pig has rather more detail around face than usual, PA German (?), 13⅛"L x 7⅝"W, late 19th C. • Robacker May 1989 price is a bit over the money. **$300.00**

Dough scraper — SEE in Mold & Shape chapter.

Egg opener, scissors style, nickeled steel (also available in silver plated steel), 2 round loop handles for thumb & little finger, curved "blades" with a number of longish sharp teeth on inside to pierce shell of cooked egg. According to 1890's ads, this was an "improvement" on their earlier model which had straight handles without finger loops, 1st made by Champion Egg Opener Co., by 1909 made by W. R. Hartigan, Hartford, CT, then Collinsville, CT, approx. 3½"L, pat'd Jan. 4, 1887 & Dec. 22, 1903, sold at least to 1910s. **$6.00-$10.00**

Egg slicer, nickeled metal, wires, marked in shield outline "D. R. P.", German, 8¾", early 20th C. **$35.00-$45.00**

Egg slicer, plated cast iron, wire, lever action, mounted on a round pedestal base screwed to a countertop, sold by V. Clad & Sons, Philadelphia, early 20th C. **$45.00-$55.00**

Egg slicer, sheet aluminum, hinged top with 10 wires, very cheap construction, but nifty, American, 5"L x 2¾"W, 1930s. • Extremely similar to this was one marked along the edge "D.R.G.M. Aust. Pat." and imported from Austria c.1910. I wouldn't be surprised if after the war an American manufacturer simply started making them. **$8.00-$10.00**

Egg slicer, well-made cast aluminum, cupped base holds egg, hinged slicer top is strung with 10 wires; by rotating sliced egg 90 degrees you can dice it, "Bloomfield Industries," Chicago, 4" x 4", c.1935. • **German vocabulary** — Eierteiler: egg slicer. **$12.00-$15.00**

14

Egg slicer, wood & wire, heavy green painted frame, 10 slicing wires, no maker's name, but ink stamped on bottom gives original price, 15 cents, 4⅛''L x 2¾''W, 20th C.   **$18.00-$25.00**

Egg wedge cutter, cast aluminum, put egg in cup, bring wire blades down to cut 6 wedges, German, 5¾''L, early 20th C.   **$18.00-$25.00**

Egg wedge cutter, japanned & decorated cast iron, heavy stepped plinth base, cylindrical egg holder, the blades are set in a frame that slides down 2 ''columns'' on either side of the egg to cut it into 6 wedges. Sold to restauranteurs, but useful for families too, sold by V. Clad & Sons, Philadelphia, about 8''H, early 20th C.
                                                                        $40.00-$50.00

Fish cleaner, carved wood with small steel or iron blade, handle is carved & colored portrait of woman with garters, from Belle Isle, ME, 6⅝''L, c.1880s to 1890s.
                                                                        $250.00-$300.00

Fish scaler, cast iron, ''Champion,'' American, 20th C.
                                                                        $10.00-$15.00

Fish scaler, cast iron, ''C. D. Kenny,'' American (?), 9''L, 19th C.   **$20.00-$30.00**

Fish scaler, homemade using narrow paddle carved from a piece of wood, 5 bottle caps nailed rough edge up, one cap reads ''Reading Brewery Co.'', others from Shenandoah Beer, Old Reading, etc., Pennsylvania, 8¾''L, early (?) 20th C.   **$12.00-$18.00**

Food chopper, meat or root vegetable chopper or hasher, but called a meat cutter by the inventor, painted cast iron, tin canister hopper with wooden bottom, mounted to green painted wooden base with a cast iron ratchet gear. Crank and the hopper revolves, while the chopping blade goes up and down like a pile driver or oil rig, Athol Machine Co., Leroy Starrett, Athol Depot, MA, various sizes, between about 11''H to 14''H, pat'd May 23, 1865 by Starrett. • **Recycled.** — A most amusing example of ingenious adaptation appeared in an ad in 1989. Long ago someone converted a Starrett chopper into a churn, by removing the round pan part, building a wooden framework 18''H mounted to the 18''L base, with a plunger attached to the iron where the chopping blade was once attached. A small churn replaced the tin hopper, with each crank, plunger moved up and down. Who knows now if it really worked all that well? For sale in April 1989 for $195.00. • **Previously invented.** — Mr. V. Price, of Wardour Street, Soho, London, exhibited, at the Great Exhibition, London, 1851, ''a chopping-knife for the reduction of suet, &c., into small particles. It consists of three blades fixed side by side, to the lower surface of a flat metal frame, which is hinged at one end to a fixed metal pillar or support, and at the other is provided with a handle, whereby the blades are alternately lifted and brought down upon the suet or other substance to be chopped, which is laid upon a circular wooden dish or chopping-block. Each time that the knife-frame is raised, a hooked rod, suspended therefrom, catches into the teeth of a ratchet wheel, and turns it partly round; on the axis of this ratchet wheel is a small cog-wheel, which takes in-to the teeth of a circular rack or wheel, fixed to the under-side of the chopping-block; and thus, at each ascent of the knife-frame, the block will be moved partly round, and made to present fresh portions of suet to the action of the

descending knives.'' Quoted from *Newton's Journal*, XXXIX. 132. in Andrew Ure's *A Dictionary of Arts, Manufactures, and Mines*, 2nd Vol., American ed., 1854. Mr. Price also showed a clothes washer. • **German vocabulary** — Hackmaschine: hash machine.
                                                                        $125.00-$175.00

Food chopper, mostly wood, probably homemade copy or repair (less likely to be a prototype) of Starrett or Athol chopper, made up with decorative cast iron apple parer gear, also heavy simple cast 4 spoked wheel with very thick & rounded rim, that looks like a sewing machine wheel, but is the same as the Starrett wheel; the frame is cut out of quarter-inch wood, handpainted rather crudely in brown & gold (like Starrett meat & cheese press); tin tub nailed to wooden bottom, but no gear to turn the tub, you have to turn it by hand as you crank, gear reads ''Reading Hardware Works,'' ''Reading, PA'', 19th C (the Athol chopper was pat'd 1865).   **$200.00-$250.00**

Food chopper, plated metal, screw clamps to table, works with crank, 3 discs for grating, slicing, shredding, ''Kitchmaster'', mfd by Chicago Flexible Shaft Co. (which Sunbeam was part of), Chicago, IL, c. 1934. Chicago Flexible Shaft started out in 1890 as a manufacturer of sheep shearing machines!   **$20.00-$30.00**

Food chopper, tinned cast iron, screw clamps, available with 5 cutting or grinding blades & a wooden pestle, ''The American'', mfd by American Cutlery Co., Chicago, IL, came in four sizes, viz. #10, 8½''H; #20, 9¼''H; #30, 10''H; and #40, 12''H, c.1920.   **$18.00-$25.00**

Food chopper or grinder, tinned cast iron, screw clamps, short shaft, rather large hopper, 4 ''knife'' discs (fine has 15 teeth, medium has 9, coarse has 3, and the nut butter cutter has close-set sharp diagonal grooves instead of teeth). ''Enterprise No. 501'', TOC.   **$20.00-$30.00**

Food grinder, cast iron plated with brass, unusual sheet iron trough or chute, screw clamps, large hopper, side crank, retains its fine perforated metal tapered cutter insert (probably came with several, for fine, medium & coarse), No. 1 Fruit Strainer, Vitantonio Co., (an old ad tells me this ends in o, but looks like Vitantonic Co. in casting), Cleveland, OH, 9¼''H, pat'd Feb. 15, 1888 (?).
                                                                        $75.00-$90.00

Food grinder, cast iron, strong & handsome, wedges to table edge or shelf, no screw clamp. Top plate that rests on top of table is 2 lobed like baby bottom or heart top, central PA, 9½''H, mid 19th C. • This is truly the first food grinder I've ever coveted. Dealer Darryl Dudash exhibited it at Hillsville, VA, late 1988.   **$150.00-$200.00**

Food grinder, cast metal, ''Classic #1'', 20th C.
                                                                        $15.00-$20.00

Food grinder, plated iron, hopper hinged to remove cutters for cleaning, ''Russwin #2'', Russell & Erwin Mfg. Co., New Britain, CT, 1902 patent.   **$22.00-$30.00**

Food grinder, tinned cast iron, Keen Kutter #K110, Simmons Hardware, 20th C.   **$20.00-$30.00**

Food grinders, enameled cast iron, screw clamps to table, wooden crank handles, some mottled emerald green like malachite, others slightly lighter plain green enameling, one plain green one has red painted wooden handle, the other plain varnished wood, part of paper label on one reads ''-ARPER No. 40'' (''Harper''); one of plain ones is still in original cardboard box, ''National Mincer, V. Enameled, Spong & Co., Ltd.,'' Harper; Spong, London, England, 9''L and 6⅞''L mottled ones; 7½''L plain green ones, c. 1920s or 1930s. • First I've ever seen. Collected by Wanda Hegedus, whose daughter, dealer Nancy Conklin, Silver Creek, NY, had them wholesale priced at $35.00 and $45.00, which is way under the money. **$75.00-$115.00**

Food mill, and meat grinder, tabletop, zinc plated cast iron frame, hopper & crank, a piece at bottom of shaft slides into cutout in base — a shaped & "molded" cast iron platform. Painted white, with white rubber feet, complete with various cutters & blades, in original cotton bags, "Rayflex Foodmaster", Rayflex Mfg. Co., Bridgeport, CT, about 7"H, c.1930s, but "patent pending". **$25.00-$35.00**

Food mill, cast iron, "Dana Mfg. Co.," (their ice cream freezers were more famous), Cincinnati, OH, TOC. **$15.00-$20.00**

Food mill, cast iron, graniteware hopper, wooden pusher, American or German, c.1880s. • **German vocabulary** — Passiermaschine: food mill (indirect translation … the kind of German word that makes mastery of the language so difficult). **$50.00-$65.00**

Food mill, cast iron, screw clamps, "Keen Kutter #11," mfd by E. C. Simmons, 9½"H, pat'd May 29, 1906. • Size #10 seems to go for half this, according to seller ads. **$25.00-$40.00**

Food mill, cast iron, screw clamps, "Keen Kutter #10," Simmons Hardware, pat'd May 15, 1904. **$20.00-$28.00**

Food mill, cast iron, screw clamps, "Eveready #55," 8"H, 20th C. **$18.00-$25.00**

Food mill, cast iron, screw clamps, "Rollman Food Chopper #12," Rollman Mfg. Co., TOC. **$12.00-$18.00**

Food mill, cast iron, screw clamps, "Winchester," TOC. **$30.00-$40.00**

Food mill, cast iron, screw clamps, "Chipaway Food Grinder," 20th C. **$8.00-$12.00**

Food mill, cast iron, screw clamps, "#7, O. V. B." (Our Very Best), Hibbard, Spencer, Bartlett & Co., 8"H, pat'd May 17, 1904. **$18.00-$22.00**

Food mill, cast iron, screw clamps, should have several blades, "Universal #2," Landers, Frary & Clark, pat'd Oct. 12, 1897, April 18, 1899 & in 1900. **$18.00-$25.00**

Food mill, cast & plated iron, red Bakelite® or other molded phenolic resin handle, original box, "Acme Rotary Mincer," American, 1935. **$18.00-$22.00**

Food mill, cream painted cast iron, varnished round wood pusher, marked "P. C.," 9¾"H, early 20th C. **$15.00-$18.00**

Food mill, metal, saucepan-shaped, hook opposite handle, mark is old good luck symbol (backwards swastika) & "DILVER", Dilver Mfg. Co., -?-burger, PA, 8" diameter, pat'd Nov. 3, 1903 & Mar. 17, 1906. **$30.00-$40.00**

Food mill, saucepan body of plated metal, graduated or stepped ridges down into bottom, which comes off with bayonet fastening, cranked blades, choice of grating or straining surfaces, this one has only the insert for fine grating, looks like a Mouli, but isn't marked, French (?) or American, early 20th C. **$20.00-$30.00**

Food mill, sheet iron & wood, handmade, with wrought iron handle, mounted to wooden board, with varous adjustments, no mark, American, hopper 4"D, board 16½"L, early 19th C. **$250.00-$300.00**

Food mill, tin, 2 front teeth, green stained wooden handle, wire forms feet & handle, only 1 blade, "Moulinette", "Made in Engdand", but a French device originally, "pat'd in all countries", 20th C. **$30.00-$35.00**

Food mill, tin with wood pusher, screw clamp, "Edith," German, small, early 20th C. **$20.00-$25.00**

Food mill, cast iron, 2 cutters (one of which reverses coarse to fine, other is marked "Universal Bread Crumber"), "Universal," Landers, Frary & Clark, pat'd 1897 & 1899. **$25.00-$30.00**

Food or meat grinder, cast metal, steel, Winchester #W33, 20th C. • Winchester made several sizes, including #W11 ($40.00-$50.00), #W12 (about $60.00-$70.00), #W13, a very large one ($75.00-$90.00), #W32 ($50.00-$65.00). The #W33 is valued between… **$50.00-$60.00**

Food or meat grinder, plated cast iron, screw clamps, opens to clean, Rollman Mfg Co., Mt. Joy, PA, advertised in 1902. **$20.00-$25.00**

Food or meat grinder, tinned cast iron, screw clamps, in original box with different blades, "Universal #1", Landers, Frary & Clark, New Britain, CT, TOC. • Early Hamburgers. — We tend to think of hamburgers as 20th C fastfood, but as far back as 1853 the term "dodger", meaning a soft, flat, pancake sort of patty (usually made with cornmeal), was applied to a minced beef patty called a beef-dodger. **$30.00-$40.00**

Food press, cast iron frame & sheet iron rectangular press box, decoratively painted & japanned in dark red & gold, vertical screw press action with heavy iron presser foot, perforated insert for bottom, "Starrett's Patent Food Press #1", mfd by Athol Machine Co., Athol, MA, 9½"L x 6¼"W, pat'd Apr. 15, 1873. **$65.00-$95.00**

Food press, potato ricer, etc., heavy tin, 4 parts, viz. straight-sided kettle with side handles, bottom & first inch up side of seeding pan is perforated; it sets down into top of kettle; another insert pan has fine wire mesh in bottom; the "plunger", as it was called by the manufacturer, is a thick wooden disc with a sadiron-type wood handle, that was 'skated' around to mash food through the insert pan into the kettle. Ads state that this would "revitalize cold potatoes" as well as seed strawberries, raspberries, etc., and could be used to strain soup or gravy, etc., "Stocking's Simplex Straining and Seeding-Press", mfd by The 4-S-Food-Press Co., NYC, NY, pat'd Feb. 10, 1903. **$20.00-$25.00**

Food press, white porcelainized iron & tin, iron juice catcher, lion's paw feet, lion's head design, marked only "No. 00", French, 8¾"H, 19th C. **$120.00-$150.00**

Fruit baller, 2 red wooden turned handles, nickeled steel lever handles terminate in hinged perforated cutting ring, used by pulling handles apart to cause hinged blade to scoop out ball of melon, American, 5¼"L, with open ring blade 1½" diameter, pat'd Mar. 29, 192-? [would be 1921 or 1927]. **$4.00-$8.00**

Fruit baller, cigar shaped red wooden handle with a stainless steel shaft out each end, one with a small bowled scoop, other with an even smaller scoop; both bowls have a small air release hole, probably Androck or A & J or the like, American, 7¾"L, 1940s. **$3.00-$5.00**

Fruit & vegetable press, also called a potato ricer, japanned iron, cast iron levered handles, hopper looks like steam shovel, "Henis," mfd by Charles F. Henis Co., Philadelphia, PA, pat'd Nov. 1, 1881. • The patent design for this, which Henis called a "Disintegrator and Strainer", had a perforated tin hopper like the steam shovel mentioned above, but the opposing presser handles were wooden paddles. We don't know if Henis maybe manufactured them at first with wood. **$12.00-$18.00**

Fruit, wine & jelly press, plated cast iron, cranked auger-like bit fits into openwork tapered part connected to large bowl-shaped hopper, 2 legged screw clamp frame. **Ad copy from 1889** reads: "For seeding and extracting Juice from all Fruits & Berries. Every housekeeper should have one. With this press, can be extracted the juices from Strawberries, Raspberries, Cranberries, Huckleberries, Gooseberries, Elderberries, Black-berries, Cherries, Currants, Peaches, Plums, Tomatoes, Pineapples, Pears, Quinces, Grapes, Apples, etc. The seeds and skins are discharged perfectly dry. Nothing is wasted." Enterprise Mfg. Co., Phila., 12"H x 11"L, (The #46 is 19"H x 18"L has added value.) pat'd Sept. 30, 1879, still for sale early 20th C. **$50.00-$65.00**

Garlic press, wood, 2 hinged parts like a lemon squeezer, American (?), 19th C. **$75.00-$90.00**

Grape press, tinned sheet iron reservoir in black painted cast iron frame; downcurved tapered lever; lift lever to push wood pusher or foller down; 4 wide spraddled leg rests so press fits on various sized bowls or pots; includes 3 perforated tin inserts with fine to coarse openings, "Littlefield's," (or Little Field's), English (?), 7" diameter, 7½"H, with 14"L lever handle, pat'd June 16, 1868. **$75.00-$100.00**

Grape scissors, tool steel & black painted iron, longish handles with same size loop ends, stubby blades with broad flat jaws, one edge of one has cutting blade, flat spring steel insert holds stem until it can be dropped into basket, pat'd & mfd by S. W. Valentine, Bristol, CT, 8"L, early 1870s. **$10.00-$15.00**

Grapefruit corer, nickel plated steel, sharp edged cylinder with moving cutter blades inside, worked by 2 handles that stick up. Turner & Seymour Mfg. Co., Torrington, CT, 7"L, coring part 1¾" diameter, pat'd May 28, 1923, & Aug. 18, 1925 (?). • Overkill for grapefruit, no? Collector Robert Rollman wrote "Have you ever heard of a grapefruit corer? What core? The size itself would preclude such activity for it would destroy half the fruit. The most common designation given in antique shops where I have seen these is a 'fruit baller.' Yet, when I tried ours on melon it did not make a very nice ball." Hear hear. In my first book, I identified this as a baller; but I have seen actual ads for this from the 1920s, calling it a grapefruit corer. **$6.00-$8.00**

Grater, 2 parts, cylindrical tin hopper for food, steel cutting blade is marked, turned wooden pusher, "Spong & Co.", London, 3"H cylinder, tin part 8"L, wooden pusher 9¾"L, 1920s or 1930s. **$50.00-$65.00**

Grater, blue enamelware, demi-round with hoop handle opposite end with 2 steadying feet, 9"L, late 19th C. **$65.00-$100.00**

Grater, blue painted cast iron & blue enameled sheet metal, clamps to table edge, Art Deco-ish geometric pattern cast into iron, wood pusher, "Helvetia," 20th C. **$55.00-$100.00**

Grater, cast iron frame, screw clamp, cranked tin cylindrical grater for carrots, etc., pat'd & mfd in Montpelier, VT, by Enos Stimson, c. 10½"H x 11½"L, pat'd Aug. 14, 1866. **$60.00-$85.00**

Grater, enamelware, wide rectangle cut out at one end for handgrip, circular rayed pattern of punctured holes, bottom embossed "IDEAL," Czechoslovakian import to U.S.A., late 19th C. **$45.00-$55.00**

Grater, fairly thin sheet brass, punctured grating holes, plain steel handle & frame, marked "DRGM & DRP" in a diamond lozenge, the DRP possibly ORP or GRP, as it was poorly struck, German, 14¼"L, 19th C. • DRGM stands for <u>Deutsches Reichs-Gebrauchsmuster</u>, the pre-1918 mark meaning registered trademark of Germany; DRP stands for <u>Deutsches Reichspatent</u>, which I thought dated to modern times, after the division of Germany. This grater is much older than that. (If the initials are ORP or GRP, I don't know what's what). **$185.00-$200.00**

Grater, fixed handle is not reversible for left & right handed users, wooden handle, box says "For Nuts, Cheese, Farfal & Nutmeg", Farfal is small formed bits of pasta. "Mouli", mfd by Moulinex, French, 8"L, "patent applied for", c.1945. **$18.00-$22.00**

Grater, half cylinder of pierced copper mounted to board, unusual in copper, American (?), 22"L x 5" x 3½."19th C. **$135.00-$150.00**

Grater, handmade, half cylinder of punctured tin tacked to long narrow wooden paddle with lollipop handle, prob. American, 15½"L x 3¾"W, mid 19th C. **$160.00-$180.00**

Grater, homemade mechanical grater in wooden frame, crank turns 2 flat cutout cast iron gears, which cause cone shaped punctured tin drum to revolve, sheet metal trough under grater was put on with brads, American, frame 7"H x 11" square, early 20th C. **$25.00-$35.00**

Grater, pierced tin cylinder with wide strap handle bridging the top, this one has only 2 grating surfaces, fine & medium, but others have 3, including coarse, American (?), 7½"H, pat'd 1901. • This type comes in many sizes, from just a few inches high to 16"H, maybe even bigger. Sometimes the handles are of heavy wire. **$15.00-$20.00**

Grater, pierced tin half-cylinder on wooden paddle back, American (?), 10"H x 3½"W, late 19th C. • Age can generally be determined by thickness of wooden back, the craft or shaping of it, patina on the tin, and hand- or machine-punctured grating teeth. **$28.00-$45.00**

Grater, punctured brass with twisted wrought iron handle & frame, marked "L. K. 7" (or possibly 9), English or German, 16"L, mid 19th C. • In this instance I am not giving a value that I think is appropriate (which would be about one fourth market prices), but am reporting prices asked at antique shows, at least in the North- and Southeast, since the mid 1980s. • The combination of decorator dealer is so widespread now that it is difficult to peel off that part of price which attaches to the decorating potential. Look at stripped down ice cream dishers — brass is considered a useful decorator metal & nickel isn't, so it gets stripped. **$275.00-$285.00**

Grater, punctured sheet brass, strap brass frame, a pronounced trapezoidal shape, reeded border (narrow ridge, size of slender reed or stalk) to grating surface done with a punch & mallet, moving it along bit by bit so rather uneven, American (?), 11"L, early 19th C. **$185.00-$200.00**

Grater, punctured tin, "Gilmore," pat'd 1897. **$5.00-$7.00**

Grater, punctured tin, rounded rectangle, wide tin strap, held like a curry comb, American (?), 4¼"L, prob. early 20th C. **$7.00-$12.00**

Grater, punctured tin with heart motif, carved wood hoop, American, 7⅞"L x 4"W, c.1870s. **$200.00-$225.00**

Grater, punctured tin with wide tin strap handle, oval grating surface, held like a curry comb, paper label says "Easy to use. Grates rapidly. Safe and Sanitary for all grating purposes," "Bromwell's Greater-Grater,"

Saranac, MI, 20th C. • Hard to find with original paper label. Such documentation is worth $$ to collectors. **$8.00-$12.00**

Grater, rectangular, aluminum (?), large center field is fine punctured surface, top has a few rows of large pierced holes for coarse grating, bottom has pivoting potato peeler of tinned steel, going width of grater, "Triple Helper", with profile Indian head, mfd by Chief Products, Los Angeles, CA, pat'd but no date. c.1940s (?). **$12.00-$18.00**

Grater, revolving, cast iron screw clamp frame, double gears, punctured tin rotating grater drum, very similar, except for shorter drum, to Enos Stimson's "Grater for carrots, etc.," American, poss. mfd 15+ years before appearance in 1881 cookbook. **$60.00-$80.00**

Grater, revolving, rectangular wooden box with lid, tin grating drum inside, 2 drawers below, American, 9½"H x 9¼"L, poss. late 18th C, more likely early 19th C. • Sold at 1982 auction; estimated between $150.00 & $175.00. Rare & interesting, especially with the two drawers, it made only $50.00. I vote it back up. **$125.00-$150.00**

Grater, revolving, tin, cast iron screw clamp frame, wood foller or pusher, "B M E No. 620," 13"H, c.1930s. **$15.00-$20.00**

Grater, revolving, tin & cast iron, very heavy duty large size, clamps to table, American (?), c.1880s. **$18.00-$25.00**

Grater, revolving, tin, wood & nickeled metal, 3 grating drums, screw clamps to table, American (?), c. 1925. **$10.00-$15.00**

Grater, revolving, tin & wood with very simple stamped sheet metal frame, knobless crank & 3 grating drums, prob. American, poss. German though not marked, 6½"H, early 20th C. • **German vocabulary** — Reib-maschine: grating machine. **$12.00-$18.00**

Grater, semi-cylindrical brass, with iron handle, English, 14"L, early 19th C. • These have become a popular "smalls" item brought in by container loads. They are usually highly polished, and quite handsome (and expensive). There is no evidence that they were ever plated. Decorative value accounts for high prices. **$85.00-$125.00**

Grater, stamped & punctured tin, slightly curved, nice oval opening for hand, no mark, American (?), 9 ½"L, c.1910. **$8.00-$12.00**

Grater, tin, mechanical, with 3 grating discs that insert in frame & slide back & forth to fine or coarse grate or to slice, "Safety Veg-E-Grater," Knapp-Monarch Mfg. Co., Webster City, IA or St. Louis, MO, 12½"L, 20th C. **$18.00-$25.00**

Grater, tin & wire, 2 grating surfaces, a slicer & a Saratoga (French fry) slicer, "Ekco," American, 10½"L, 20th C. **$8.00-$12.00**

Grater, tin & wire, 3 grating surfaces plus a slicer, "All-In-One," American, 10⅝"L x 4¼"W, c. 1940. **$5.00-$8.00**

Grater, tin & wire, half is a woven wire mesh, other half is machine-punched tin, "Kitchen Novelty Co." (Atlantic City, NJ), mfd in Germany, 12½"L, c.1890s to 1910. • **German vocabulary** — Reibe: grater, Reibeisen: tinned iron grater. **$10.00-$15.00**

Grater, tin with wire handle, "A Gadget Master Product #8," "Made in U.S.A.", 10"L x 7"W, 20th C. **$8.00-$12.00**

Grater, box style, wood frame fitted with drawer with porcelain knob, hand-punched tin grating surface set into frame, American, 15"L, prob.1830s-50s. • I don't know where else to put this, but it's funny. From *Journal of the Franklin Institute*, Philadelphia, 1836, comes this description of Ebenezer B. Story's, Buffalo, NY, **grater patent:** "This grater consists of a sheet of tin perforated with holes, and placed in a box in a sloping direction, so as to make an angle of fourteen degrees with the horizon. 'The length of the box on the top is to be two feet one and one fourth inch. The length of the bottom ... is one foot eight and one fourth inch; the width ten inches, the height thereof nine inches. The size of the grater may be varied to suit the wishes of the person for whose use it is made. I claim therefore the invention of such grater, and such improvements as herein set forth and described.'" To which the editor adds "A more trifling patent than this does not often find its way to the office." Yet it did happen. Amazingly uninventive inventions were granted patents in the early days. **$160.00-$200.00**

Grater, revolving, green painted cast iron, screw clamps, wooden handle, "Lorraine Metal Mfg.," 8½"H, 20th C. **$18.00-$25.00**

Grater, white enamel, countertop, American, 19th C. **$35.00-$40.00**

Grater, wood & tin, "Favorite," 12½"L x 3"W, TOC. **$18.00-$25.00**

Grater & slicer, double action, wood, steel, one blade makes thin julienne strips, other makes ¼" thick slices, American, 16"L, late 19th C. **$25.00-$40.00**

Grating machine, all wood bench-style frame & hopper, levered pusher, punctured tin drum, "H.P. Arthur's Vegetable Grater," Martinsburgh, NY, 13¾"H x 13"L x 6"W, pat'd Oct. 8, 1867. **$150.00-$185.00**

Grist mill, cast iron, clamps to work surface, great big wheel with curved spokes, mill & hopper are small & behind wheel, chute below, "Apache," mfd by A. H. Patch, Clarksville, TN, wheel is approx. 16" diameter, late 19th or early 20th C. **$65.00-$75.00**

Grist mill, for corn, cast iron, screw clamps, Arcade, TOC. • **Reproduction alert** — A new tinned screw clamp cast iron mill for cereal of flour is sold by White Mountain Freezer Co. Large hopper, natural pale wood handle; it could be mistaken for an old one, although it doesn't look as old-fashioned as other White Mountain mills. Price for a new one is half again as much as for the antique. **$35.00-$45.00**

Hasher—See Food chopper, Athol.

Herb boat or grinder, also called a herb crusher, cast iron boat, bootjack legs, interesting because wheel is wooden & its narrow edge is ribbed, & had straight wooden handles; wheel possibly replaced original iron one. Prob. Oriental, early 19th or late 18th C. • This one is credited to the kitchen of the Whim Greathouse in Time-Life's *Cooking of the Caribbean Islands,* and is probably an import-from the Orient. • The value below is not for this par-ticular one, but for one with an iron boat & handmade wooden wheel. **$135.00-$185.00**

Herb boat or grinder, cast iron boat on bootjack legs at each end, rolling wheel like mill or pestle, with long wooden handles stained black, sometimes called a go-devil, American, European, Chinese, one is 17"L with 7"D wheel, early 19th C. • Philadelphia collector Ellen Blaw wrote me in 1986 saying 'I have a friend who recently moved here from China ... who showed me her 'crusher' that had been her mother's, and her mother's grandmother. It is one of the 'old things' they brought with them from China; they use it for rice not spices. The feet on my friends' mill are shorter, the cut out arch is not so deep. I hope this can shed some light on this somewhat mysterious item!'' • The Keillor Family Collection had one about which Archibald Keillor said only that he thought it was American. He had traveled in China in the 1920s and 30s, I believe.. • Carl W. Drepperd, in his *Primer of American Antiques,* says that these are ''Chinese in origin but much used in America in the early 19th century.'' He goes on to say that the ''operator (of the mill), barefooted, sat on a chair and rolled the wheel with (his/her) feet.'' Other names, according to Dreppard, are sow & pig mill, and ship mill. • Another that does not have same bootjacket legs, measures 18''L x 4½''W with 7''D wheel; a third, without bootjack legs, is 13¼''L with 7'' wheel. **$165.00-$200.00**

Herb boat or grinder, cast iron footed boat-shaped mortar, rolling pestle wheel has 2 long wooden handles, wheel was operated by the feet in Asian countries, primarily China, where they originated (?). Another name for it is ship grinder. No marks, prob. Asian, 26''L boat, excep tionally large, was in a Nov. 1989 Garth auction. Smallest I ever heard of.) • **Ballast?**— You rarely see these; when you do they are always given an American provenance, c.1800. But clues pointing to a Chinese origin are impossible to ignore, and it is possible to suppose them ballast on early China Trade ships to America, beginning in 1784 with the ''Empress of China'' and continuing into the 1840s. Canton blue & white china was packed into the holds as ballast on tea, spices, lacquers, and silk & cotton cloth. So why not the heavier herb boat. **$170.00-$250.00**

Herb boat or grinder, wooden brick shape mortar has boat shape depression cut in it, rolling hardwood crushing wheel with long side handles, like the all cast iron mill above, the Keillors believed this was either European or Asian in origin, box 5''H x 12½''L with approx. 7''D wheel, early 19th C. The late Archie & Myra Keillor, Early American Industries Association and discerning as well as omniverous collectors of kitchen wares, tools, dairy implements, etc., died in the 1970s. Their family kitchen collection appeared first in my first book. It was great privilege to know them, and to meet their children, and grandchildren, who have collections of their own. **$225.00-$280.00**

Herb masher or beetle, turned maple with small head carved with concentric circles, American (?), 7''H, 19th C. **$45.00-$60.00**

Herb mill, japanned tin, sheet iron hopper, wood drawer below, small wooden handle on crank, American (?), 7''H, 19th C. **$75.00-$100.00**

Horseradish grater, homemade, wooden box, punctured tin drum, sheet iron cover with simple latches (probably appropriated from something else), American, 14⅛ x 7⅞''W, 19th C. • ''**Melon Mangoes**'' — Cut a small square out of each melon; take out the seed; shred some garlic small, and mix it with mustard seed; fill the melon full; then replace the square piece; bind it up with small twine; boil a quantity of vinegar; in which, put white and long pepper, salt, ginger, and mustard seed; pour it boiling hot on the mangoes every day for four days; put a little horse

radish, and flour of mustard, in the vinegar the last day; when the vinegar boils, take great care that the mangoes are well covered; you may pickle large cucumbers in the same way, they are much esteemed as a pickle.'' Joseph Bell, *A Treatise on Confectionary.* Newcastle, England, 1817. **$125.00-$145.00**

Horse radish grater, mechanical, screw clamp cast iron skeletal frame, cranked large tinned sheet steel disc with sharp projections, small iron shelf on left side supports radish or potato or root vegetable against vertical revolving blade. A 'bike fender' shield covers half of disc nearest to user. Replaceable blade. ''Distelhorst's'', Chicago Nickel Works, Chicago, IL, c.1890. **$35.00-$45.00**

Huller or pin feather picker—See Strawberry huller.

Juice extractor, yellow china pitcher, modernistic sharp-edged molded diagonal swags across old-fashioned round bellied pitcher shape body; reamer sets into top & is activated to turn by pressure of your pushing half a grapefruit (orange, lemon) down on it. Also came in blue or green. Ade-O-Matic Co., Los Angeles, CA, 1930. **$9.00-$15.00**

Juicer, bright tin, bright green painted cast iron, mixer & juicer part lift off, ''Made for the Deluxe Sales Co., Inc.'', NYC, NY, 9¾''H, 20th C. **$85.00-$100.00**

Juicer, cast aluminum, chromed & red painted cast iron, rack & pinion lever action type in stand, reamer cone has fine concentric ridges & small holes around base for juice, the Tilt-Top® presser has teeth all around edge, ''Juice-O-Mat,'' Rival Mfg. Co., Kansas City, MO, 7⅞''H x 6½'' x 5¾'', pat'd 1937. Improved models with colored bases, etc., selling in 1948. • **Classic.** — Orange juice lovers' all-time favorites, & people buy old ones to use, or now can buy new ones almost identical to the old. • An ad placed by Bloomingdale's in 1938 calls this the ''Streamline Juice King''. It was available in ivory with red, blue, green or chrome; also red & chrome. Was Bloomingdale's licensed to use a name they made up? **$12.00-$20.00**

Juicer, cast aluminum, screw clamps, crank turns one of 3 different-sized bladed reamers around in horizontal position over large funnel, below which is put a tumbler or bowl, ''California Fruit Juice Extractor, Sr.'', Strite-Anderson Mfg. Co., Minneapolis, MN, c.1929-30. • They also made a smaller Junior model in bright colors. **$40.00-$50.00**

Juicer, cast aluminum, simple lever action, mounted to board, cup & reamer set at angle, Rival Mfg. Co., Kansas City, MO, c.1935. • **Lookalike alarm.** — A 1976 Hammacher Schlemmer ad had a cast aluminum juice extractor very like the Rival, with pedestal base. It could be used, like the earlier one, for citrus fruits, berries, pineapple, grapes, etc. **$35.00-$45.00**

Juicer, cast iron screw clamp frame, cranked ball-bearing gear under reamer turns the clear glass bowl & its reamer cone. Bowl has side opening to funnel juice into waiting tumbler; bowl & reamer lift off for cleaning, American, c.1929-30. **$40.00-$50.00**

Juicer, cast metal frame & base, rack & pinion lever action raises ridged conical reamer up to squush half a citrus fruit against conical upper cup, ''National Juice King'', National Die Casting Co., Chicago, IL, late 1930s. **$35.00-$45.00**

Juicer, electric, footed metal cylinder, pump-like spout near top, white glass (maker called ''alabaster'') bowl & reamer. 1929 ad copy makes us giggle now: ''To meet

Fresh Fruit Juice speed requirements comes along the perfected and proved Orange and Lemon go-getter known far & near as Sunkist Junior Electric Extractor. ... Not only a handsome donation [?], but much wanted because it snaps out a glass or a gallon of juice for breakfast — or other purposes — with alacrity equaled by no other method. ... [The] whizzing cone gets all the Orange or Lemon Juice without the usual work — and mess. Two instantly removable parts to wash under faucet." "Sunkist Jr", mfd by California Fruit Growers' Exchange, Chicago, 10"H, late 1920s. **$20.00-$35.00**

Juicer, for fruit, meat & onions, a horizontal press like small bench lathe, cast aluminum frame, the retainer cup & convex plunger or press, should have shallow aluminum holder underneath to catch juice. First the retainer pivots upright to place half lemon or piece of raw meat, then put back down into horizontal position to face plunger, which is moved toward the cup by turning the wheel. "20th Century Power Juice Extractor", mfd by the Album Mfg. Co., Freeport, IL, late 1890s, though it looks much more recent. **$50.00-$75.00**

Juicer, for lemons or limes, cast aluminum-like alloy, plier action, "Ebaloy Inc., 12-1-4," Rockford, IL, 8"L, c.1930s. **$15.00-$18.00**

Juicer, for oranges, aluminum with reamer inside, crank at top, hand held, Knapps, 1930 patent #1743661. **$9.00-$12.00**

Juicer, green painted heavy stamped iron & aluminum, 4 widely splayed legs, hopper & reamer at top, side crank turns small geared wheel, very unusual & handsome, "Universal," Landers, Frary & Clark, 10"H x 5¾", TOC. **$15.00-$20.00**

Juicer, painted red cast iron, black handle, chrome top, aluminum reamer & cup, "The Juice-King", National Diecasting Co., Inc., Chicago, IL, 9"H, 1938 patent #2131440 & 1944 design patent #138983. **$7.00-$12.00**

Juicer, reamer in sort of space station stand, cranked to work, stamped aluminum & painted tin, flimsy but as cute as R2-D2, came with red or green painted base, "Handy Andy," mfd by H. A. Specialty Co., Inc., American, 10½"H x 6⅞" diameter, pat'd July 23, 1935, although on the market since about 1930. **$15.00-$35.00**

Juicer, red painted cast iron horseshoe base fits around tumbler, upright part has cast aluminum cup fixed at top, rack & pinion lever raises ridged reamer, with half an orange on it, up into cup to express juice, American, 8"H, c.1940s. • A company advertised the "Mighty OJ" squeezer in 1982, a new version of old one. **$35.00-$45.00**

Juicer, sheet metal with green finished wooden knob, screw clamps, a triple extractor, with 3 reamers, for grapefruit, oranges, lemons, even tomatoes! American, c.1931 **$10.00-$15.00**

Juicer, steel & aluminum, hand held, cup has simple wire reamer, domed lid with crank, hinged handles to be clasped firmly to increase pressure on orange inside, very small lip on side of cup for pouring juice without opening, Kwikway Products, Inc. St. Louis, MO, 6½" x 4" diameter cup, 1929 patent. **$15.00-$20.00**

Juicer, wall bracket type, heavy cast aluminum with thinner spun aluminum reamer insert, crank with wooden knob, "The Speedo Super Juicer," mfd by Central States Mfg. Co., 5 x 4¾", c. 1930. • The wall bracket is almost always missing, alas, but sometimes you can find the whole thing at a yard sale. The value is somewhat higher than the price usually asked. Value is: **$8.00-$20.00**

Juicer or reamer, aluminum, brass gears inside with stainless steel pin for reamer, wooden knob, 3 rubber feet, lift-off reamer with gear in it, "The Gem Squeezer", mfd by Quam-Nichols Co., Chicago, IL, 6"H, 1½ cup capacity, "patents pending", c.1930s. • See also Lemon squeezers; and Reamers, this chapter. **$15.00-$20.00**

Juicer & reamer, mottled garnet color Catalin® plastic (like the more familiar Bakelite® or other molded phenolic resin), reamer part screws on & holds in place a heavy duty screen seed-catcher, marked on handle "Ex-Squeeze-It" BCM, and stamped under handle "Catalan Company", Made in England, various patent numbers for different countries, c. 1930s or 1940s. **$22.00-$30.00**

Juicer — See also Reamer, & Lemon squeezer, this chapter.

Julien cutter, or julienne cutter, for cutting sliced vegetables into decorative little flowerettes or snowflake like patterns, to float prettily in clear soups, cast iron with 20 different cutting dies to be inserted. 4 legs (including 2 long hind legs) all with holes to screw securely to work surface, lever action with turned wooden handle on lever, imported by F. A. Walker, French (?), prob. about 7"L x 4"H, with 1" cutting discs or dies, late 19th C. • An American raisin seeder, pat'd 1895, is very similar to this, with long "hind" legs & lever action, so this cutter could have been made in the U.S.A. **$50.00-$65.00**

Kitchen saw, adjustable carbon steel saw blade in cast aluminum frame, very attractive modernistic form, in general outline obviously a kitchen knife; in concept like a hacksaw, "Always Sharp," mfd. by Charles Wohr, Lancaster, PA, 15¾"L, early 20th C. **$12.00-$18.00**

Kitchen saw, carbon steel, turned wooden handle, "Keen Kutter," Simmons Hardware, 13½"L, 20th C. **$10.00-$15.00**

Kitchen saw & cake knife combined, carbon steel with wooden handle, top edge is saw, the along bottom edge is scalloped cake knife, "Victor," mfd by American Cutlery Co., 14¾"L, TOC. **$8.00-$15.00**

Knife, wide steel blade, rounded end, cut out & painted wood handle is Black Americana figural black chef, American (?), 12½"L, c.1930s-40s. **$8.00-$12.00**

Knife & fork combined, tool steel, cut & filed, brass snake winds around blade & fork, hand made from crosscut saw, artisan Jim Webb, Hillsville, VA, 8¼"L, 1980s.

• **Fork Feeding.** – *The Young Lady's Friend* (Boston, 1836) advised: "If you wish to imitate the French or English, you will put every mouthful into your mouth with your fork; but if you think as I do that Americans have as good a right to their fashions as the inhabitants of any other country, you may choose the convenience of feeding yourself with your right hand armed with a steel blade; and providing you do it neatly and do not put in large mouthfuls, or close your lips tight over the blade, you ought not to be considered as eating ungenteely."

• **Naughty Forks.** — "Forks were not generally used at table until the reign of James I, in England (r.1567-1625). They were, however, known in Europe long before this. The first fork mentioned in history belonged to a Byzantine lady, who, on coming to Venice as a bride in the middle of the 11th century, brought with her a golden 'prong' as it is called in the pamphlet describing it. This fork, which probably had only two prongs, evidently caused a great sensation, for St. Peter Damian, afterwards Bishop of Ostia, mentioned it in a sermon, wherein he severely rebuked the lady for her luxury and extravagence in actually taking up her food with a golden prong, when God had given her fingers for that very purpose. "The preponderance of patties in these (Medieval) menus is probably due to the fact that fingers then supplied, to a great extent, the place of knives and forks. Spoons were used, but knives were not general till about 1563, and forks were not commonly used in England until 1611." Excerpt of "Medieval Cookery", reprinted from *Gentleman's Magazine*, in *House & Garden*, Oct. 1906. **$15.00-$22.00**

Knife, parer & corer combined, tinned steel, in original box, "Castello's Sixteen Tools in One," American, 8⅞"L, 1913. • **"Green Tomato Pickle. —** One peck of green tomatoes sliced; one dozen onions sliced; sprinkle with salt, and let them stand until the next day; then drain them. Use the following as spices: one box of mustard (ground), half an ounce of black pepper (ground?), one ounce of whole cloves, and one ounce of white mustard seed. Alternate layers of tomatoes, onions, and spices. Cover with vinegar. Wet the mustard before putting it in. Boil the whole twenty minutes." Mrs. A. P. Hill, *Mrs. Hill's New Family Receipt Book*, NY: 1870. **$10.00-$15.00**

Kraut cutters — See Cabbage cutters.

Lard & fruit press, cast iron, Griswold #2, early 20th C. **$40.00-$65.00**

Lard press, heavy varnished wood, nickeled iron hinge, corrugated inside 2 long paddle handles, American, 12"L, late 19th C. **$35.00-$50.00**

Lemon & lime squeezer, cast metal, hand held, "Quick & Easy," Erie Specialty Co., Erie, PA, 6"L, 20th C. **$5.00-$8.00**

Lemon & lime squeezer, zinc-coated cast iron, scissor action, compartment with holes to capture seeds, "Vaughn Co.,"Chicago, IL, 6"L, 20th C. • For fuller explanation of zinc and galvanizing, see an entry under Washboards in the Laundry chapter. **$10.00-$12.00**

Lemon or lime squeezer, heavy cast aluminum, works like pliers, marked "Acid & Rust Free," American, 6-7¼"L, TOC. **$20.00-$30.00**

Lemon reamer, turned hard wood, grooved end, nice patina, American, 9"L, TOC. • **Reproduction alert. —** A very well-carved wooden hand held reamer, deeply grooved, with a small, delicately rounded point & well-shaped handle, 7"L, was mfd. during the 1970s and probably still is, to sell for about $7.00. It was so well made and attractive that it could easily be mistaken for an earlier reamer. Advice on buying antique treen (turned wooden wares, etymologically related to a tree) is very difficult, especially for simple pieces that are essentially variations on the theme of a stick! Hollowed out pieces are more likely to show signs of true age, with checks, warping, more variation in patina. • Lehman's Hardware & Appliances, 4779 Kidron Rd., OH 44636 offer a similar a very inexpensive one with a hole through the end of the handle in their 1989 "Non-Electric Good Neighbor Amish Country" catalog. **$18.00-$30.00**

Lemon sqeezer, japanned cast iron, with separate, heavily-tinned cup which can be used separately as a reamer, "American Queen," c.1906. **$20.00-$30.00**

Lemon squeezer, 4 legged wooden bench, hinged top with pressing cup, long turned wooden lever, 2 inserts of heavily tinned sheet iron, possibly Shaker, 19th C. **$150.00-$200.00**

Lemon squeezer, all maple, 2 hinged arms, with holes in the concave "bowl" or cup of one part, American, 10¾"L, late 19th C. • "An old-time Philadelphia Housewife said yesterday: "None of your new-fangled lemon squeezers for me. Anything, especially acid — squeezed through metal, such as many of the improved ones are, is very bad. The wooden ones do not have this fault; neither do those made of glass or porcelain. But they all have one fault that there is no getting rid of, and that is that the skin of the lemon is squeezed so that its flavor mixes with that of the juice. This is all wrong. There is but one way to squeeze a lemon, and that is the simple, old-fashioned way, between your fingers. Plenty of power can be brought to bear, particularly if the lemon is well-rolled first." *Ladies Home Journal"*, Sept. 1889. **$45.00-$75.00**

Lemon squeezer, all wood on wooden base, hinged press,marked "The F. F. Adams Co., Erie, PA, for the Atlantic Wringer Co.," Erie, PA, 9"H x 14"L x 4"W, late 19th C. **$125.00-$150.00**

Lemon squeezer, black painted cast iron, hinged, 2 glazed white china or ironstone reamer inserts, a loose cup with 4 holes, presser is screwed to the iron, not so marked, but pat'd by T. C. Smith, NYC, NY, 8¹⁵⁄₁₆"L, marked "pat'd Apr. 7, 1868." **$65.00-$75.00**

Lemon squeezer, black porcelainized cast iron, aluminum cup, levered hinged device, marked "LIDON", mfd by Gilchrist Co., Newark, NJ, c.1906. **$10.00-$15.00**

Lemon squeezer, cast iron, "X-Ray", mfr unknown, perhaps same (also unknown) company who made the X-Ray Raisin Seeder, American, late 19th or early 20th C. **$25.00-$35.00**

Lemon squeezer, cast iron, 2 parts hinged, one corrugated "male," one fluted "female," not marked but from Matthai-Ingram Co., American, two sizes: 8½"L & 10½"L, c.1890s. **$25.00-$35.00**

Lemon squeezer, cast iron frame with fancy little legs, stands on counter top, slotted concave cup, long lever handle with enameled convex presser, sold also as a nutcracker & food press, ad claimed it was useful for 12 different kitchen processes, "All-In-One", Ford Mfg. Co., Inc., Newark, NJ, about 11"L, late 19th C. **$100.00-$125.00**

Lemon squeezer, cast iron, hinged, 8½"L with 2½"D bowl, late 19th C. **$15.00-$20.00**

Lemon squeezer, cast iron with glass insert, "King's", English, 1882. **$25.00-$35.00**

Lemon squeezer, cast iron with porcelain liner, hinged, American, patent applied for in 1888. **$30.00-$45.00**

Lemon squeezer, cast iron with pottery reamer insert, hand held, "The Arcade," Freeport, IL, late 19th C. **$35.00-$45.00**

Lemon squeezer, cast iron with unusual glass cup insert, "Williams," late 19th C. **$30.00-$45.00**

Lemon squeezer, dense, well patinated hardwood, oblong board base with decorative notches at both ends, 3 fat dowel rod legs holding 2 part squeezer above base. Lower part holds perforated female cup, upper hinged part has handle at one end with same notched decoration & male presser, PA (?), mid 19th C. • Offered for sale in 1985 by Chalfant & Chalfant of West Chester, PA. Price range mine. **$275.00-$350.00**

Lemon squeezer, hinged 2 part cast iron with milk glass reamer insert, instead of more commonly found pottery or ironstone insert, American (?), late 19th C. **$50.00-$60.00**

Lemon squeezer, hinged, 2 part broad maple paddles, 2 pottery inserts, hanging holes in both handles, German (?), TOC. **$45.00-$50.00**

Lemon squeezer, hinged, cast iron, "Pearl," American, 19th C. **$18.00-$25.00**

Lemon squeezer, iron, hinged 2 part, "Diamond Point," American, pat'd July 10, 1888. **$25.00-$35.00**

Lemon squeezer, levered hand held type, turned wood "drum" set in nickel plated iron frame & handles (also came japanned for less), white glazed porcelain inset, small pouring channel in rim of wood, "Drum", Manning - Bowman, Meriden, CT, 10"L, late 19th C. **$45.00-$55.00**

Lemon squeezer, maple, hinged male & female halves, American (?), 10¾"L, c.1870s to 1880s. **$30.00-$40.00**

Lemon squeezer, maple, hinged, with porcelain insert, 8½"L, late 19th C. **$30.00-$40.00**

Lemon squeezer, nickeled cast iron, tin plunger & cup, horizontal reamer action activated by long lever (what maker called a "positive spiral pressure"), screw clamp, small adjustable-height platform for tumbler is attached to a thin rod , "The Leader", mfd by Rocky Hill Hardware Co., Rocky Hill, CT, about 10"L, c.1908. **$65.00-$80.00**

Lemon squeezer, plated cast iron, hinged hand held press, half is reamer, half is cup with holes, no mark, American, 7¼"L, 19th C. **$30.00-$45.00**

Lemon squeezer, sheet metal frame clamps to table, iron lever, cast aluminum perforated cup, with concave glass "receiver", lever rotated to press juice, arm with ring holds glass tumbler, "Walker's Quick & Easy No. 42", Erie Specialty Co., Erie, PA, c.1906. **$45.00-$65.00**

Lemon squeezer, tinned malleable cast iron frame clamps to underside of shelf or bar, with lever in upright position so the lemon half can be put in place against reamer which is also upright. When lever is depressed to right, both cup & lever move into horizontal position, cone & cup remove for cleaning, adjustable holder for tumbler, "Perfect", Arcade Mfg Co., Freeport, IL, c.1903. **$65.00-$80.00**

Lemon squeezer, white enameled cast iron, hinged 2 part, both cups have ribbed rims. Female cup has small ring base & its handle has a projecting foot, so it can be set down on work surface & hold the juice until needed, German, about 8¼"L, 4th quarter 19th C. • **Lookalike alarm.** — In 1982, a kitchen supply shop in NYC advertised a hand held cast iron lemon or lime squeezer, with lustrous black enameled finish inside & out, hinged two-part. It does not seem to have the little foot for steadying on counter. Visible in the photograph of it is a mark inside one handle, but I cannot read it. The mark almost looks like July and June patent dates, and this could be an exactly cast copy of one pat'd in the 1880s. **$55.00-$75.00**

Lemon squeezer, wood with white porcelain insert, mark is eagle with "S" in beak, "UPW" underneath, for Union Porcelain Works, American, 19th C. **$125.00-$150.00**

Lemon squeezer or press, cast iron, a press with a screw to be tightened from above, juice collects in reservoir underneath, handle at side to resist torque of turning screw — for doing those really old, petrified lemons from the back of the fridge, marked Landers, Frary & Clark, New Britain, CT, 7" x 8" x 4", late 19th C. **$70.00-$90.00**

Lemon squeezer & slicer, hinged 2 part wooden squeezer, iron stand with 2 cutting blades, American, 15" x 7", TOC. **$160.00-$180.00**

Lemon squeezer & slicer combined, cast iron mounted to wooden board with "bite" taken out of edge at halfway point, long legged body with high tail lever, rack & pinion mechanism, had glass or china cup insert, now missing, probably for restaurant or bar or soda fountain use, no marks on squeezer itself, mark is stamped into wood board: "Acme, The F. F. Adams Co.," Erie, PA, 12"H, pat'd Dec. 20, 1887. **$85.00-$100.00**

Lemon squeezer — See also Juicer, & Reamer.

Lemon wedge squeezer, silver plated springy metal, in shape of abstract bird; lemon wedge fits between the 'wings' which were then pressed together. Not marked. 4½"L, 20th C. **$30.00-$40.00**

Marmalade cutter, cast iron, steel, wood, nice big one, probably for hotel or restaurant kitchen, "New Universal," Follows & Bates Ltd., Manchester, England, about 16"H, TOC. **$125.00-$170.00**

Marmalade cutter, cast iron with japanning & gold striping, raised letters picked out in gold, a sort of cone with a wood pusher to move orange peel across blade, mfd by Follows & Bate Ltd., Manchester, England, late 19th C. **$125.00-$170.00**

Marmalade cutter, japanned cast iron, crank handle, clamps to table, "Magic," English, about 11"H, late 19th C. **$120.00-$145.00**

Marmalade cutter, cast iron & steel, screw clamp, cheap but serviceable, "The Rapid," Follows & Bates Ltd., Manchester, England, c.12-13"H, provisional patent #25866/32, TOC(?). **$95.00-$135.00**

Meat & cheese press, brown painted cast iron in rectangular shape, yellow stenciling, tin hopper, Starrett's, (Leroy Starrett), prob. pat'd by J. I. Danforth, but mfd by Starrett, Newburyport, MA (?), 7½"H x 9"L, poss. another size too, pat'd 1873, prob. Nov. 4, 1873. **$75.00-$125.00**

Meat chopper, cast iron frame, turned wood crank handle, wooden tub, cranked gear wheels move blade & scraper inside tub, pat'd by A. F. Spaulding & S. M. Scott, MA, (Addresses in 2 *Patent Index* listings are: Winchester MA & Winchendon MA.) 8"H x 10"L, pat'd June 5, 1865 (not in *Index*), July 11, 1865, & Jan. 31, 1865. **$125.00-$160.00**

Meat chopper, galvanized metal, screw clamp, "The Home #1," 1890s. **$15.00-$25.00**

Meat chopper or grinder, tinned cast iron, height of hopper & grinder adjust with side screw & telescoping vertical frame, screw clamps to table, very similar choppers had feet for tabletop use, "The Little Giant #205", mfd by The Peck, Stow & Wilcox Co., Southington, CT, brought out in 1890, • Old P,S & W brochures I own have several choppers like this, but no 205, only a 305, as well as a 310 and a 320. • An ad in a Dec. 1890 *Metal Worker* shows the No. 222. Then, a June 25, 1892, notice (op. cit) shows the Little Giant No. 410, tinned cast iron, with sausage stuffer attachment. We learn that: "The patterns have been changed this season so as to permit the application of a meat stuffer attachment, which can be quickly adjusted to the machine. The shape of the knife has been altered somewhat, and is referred to as stronger and less liable to break. The regular series will be known as Nos. 305, 310, 312, 320 and 322, and will be prepared for the attachments, which are not furnished with them, but which can be ordered and put on at any time. The meat cutters when furnished with attachments will be designated as Nos. 405, 410, 412, 420 and 422. Another feature of the Little Giant is that two perforated plates, with holes of different diameters, are packed with each machine. All cutters made this season will be tinned instead of galvanized, which (adds) materially to their appearance. The company claim that the smallest cutter, No. 305, will easily cut 3 pounds of meat a minute.'' **$50.00-$65.00**

Meat cutter, japanned cast iron, tabletop style with horizontal cylinder, hinged top lifts off to remove harrow blade drum & crank, bolts to table, one of O. D. Woodruff's two patents, mfd by Peck, Stow & Wilcox, came in ''family'' or relatively small size, & ''medium'' size, Woodruff's patents date to Jan. 10, 1860 and Mar. 9, 1869. • Still being sold in 1890s, possibly into 20th C. **$100.00-$135.00**

Meat cutter's glove, brass wire woven mesh glove, wrist strap, protection for left hand while cutting with right, American, early 20th C. **$12.00-$15.00**

Meat & food chopper or grinder, galvanized cast iron, screw clamp, ''Saxon,'' Steinfeld Brothers, NYC, NY, pat'd 1904. **$15.00-$20.00**

Meat & food grinder, tinned cast iron, little hopper, screw clamps to table, relatively long crank behind, small family size, ''Enterprise #5,'' Enterprise Mfg. Co., TOC. **$18.00-$25.00**

Meat & food slicer, cast iron with painted frame & decals, handsome & good sized, for stores, ''Enterprise,'' Enterprise Mfg. Co., dated 1881. **$65.00-$85.00**

Meat & food slicer, cast metal, cranks, ''General,'' 20th C. **$25.00-$30.00**

Meat & food slicer, screw clamp, ''Eagle,'' 20th C. **$15.00-$20.00**

Meat & food slicer, tin, wooden handle, ''Dandy,'' 20th C. **$10.00-$15.00**

Meat & fruit juice press, plated malleable cast iron, frame has side handle for grasping with one hand, fitted into this is cup with handle, presser fits into cup & is screwed up & down with a sort of cotter pin handle above, ''Walker's Quick & Easy'', mfd by Erie Specialty Co., Erie, PA, c.1905. **$35.00-$65.00**

Meat & fruit press, nickeled brass with wood foller, ''Wilder's,'' pat'd 1906. (In 1984 I predicted some brass & flash dealer would take this piece down to the brass & buff it near to death, & price it at $100.00, and it happened. **$25.00-$35.00**

Meat grinder, cast iron, double barrel horizontal body hinged so top half lifts up, short crank, flared hopper, not marked except date, but this is an original J. G. Perry ''meat-cutter'', Kingston, RI, body 7''L, pat'd March 15, 1859. **$110.00-$150.00**

Meat grinder, cast iron painted red, white enameled hopper interior, wooden crank handle, only one blade (for medium - coarse), ''Aalwerke #5, R AALEN,'' German or Dutch, 9''H, late 19th C. **$20.00-$30.00**

Meat grinder, cast iron, screw clamps to table, ''Gem Chopper,'' Sargent & Co., NYC, NY, large size, pat'd March 8, 1892. **$30.00-$42.00**

Meat grinder, cast iron, to be mounted to table, horizontal body, 4 feet, large mouth flared hopper, large S crank with long turned wood grip, ''Perry's Patent No. 3'', Ames Plow Co., 9 ½''L, patent ext. Feb. 28, 1864, poss. made much later. **$125.00-$165.00**

Meat grinder, cast metal, white porcelainized hopper, ''Harras #52,'' German, TOC or early 20th C. **$35.00-$45.00**

Meat grinder, cast & sheet iron, cranked, screw clamp, oblong hopper, short tapered perforated tubular blade, worm screw action pushes meat against & through holes, ''Perfection'' American Machine Co., Philadelphia, 3 sizes: #1, 2 & 3, pat'd May 7, 1889. **$25.00-$40.00**

Meat grinder, homemade, oblong wooden box with lift-off top, forged iron cutting blades on long wooden axle inside, forged iron crank, described by dealer Ron Motter, Erma's Attic, Athens, OH, as having a ''bone bushing.'' Marked ''A. F.'', American (?), about 16''L, dated 1842.
• **''Bermuda Onions, Stuffed.''**— Make a round hole in the upper end of each, dig out at least half of the contents; set in a dish covered with warm, slightly salted water, and bring to a simmer. Throw away the water; carefully fill the onions with minced poultry or veal, put a bit of butter in the dish to prevent burning, scatter fine crumbs thickly over the onions, and bake, covered, a half hour.'' Marion Harland, *House & Home, a Complete Housewife's Guide*, Phila., 1889. **$200.00-$250.00**

Meat grinder, japanned cast iron, mounts to tabletop, long 2 part horizontal cylinder, hinged top half opens to lift out cutter drum with crank handle, ''Perry's Patent No. 1'', Peck, Stow & Wilcox Co., small, for families, 1890s. • J. G. Perry, of Kingston, then South Kingston, RI, had 12 ''meat-cutter'' patents between 1859 & 1869, as well as a ''meat-cutting machine'' patented Feb. 26, 1850. It would be possible, probably, to find one made in the 1860s or 1870s by Perry himself, if indeed he manufactured them before selling rights to P.S. & W. as well as Ames Plow Co. **$100.00-$135.00**

Meat grinder, large size for butchers, cast iron horizontal cylinder, flared hopper opening in top, 4 bolting legs, flywheel at end has turned wood knob, ''New Triumph #634'', Peck, Stow & Wilcox, Southington, CT, pat'd Apr. 19, 1892 & Sept. 3, 1895. **$100.00-$135.00**

Meat grinder, nickeled cast iron, screw clamps to table, thumb screw is heavy wire or small rod bent in rounded triangle — a sign of late date, different face plates for fine to coarse grinding, Chop-Rite #0, Choprite Mfg. Co., Pottstown, PA, this one late 20th C, but in production since 1870 (as ''Enterprise''). • The plating, the material of the knob on the crank, & the material and form of the thumb screw are all clues to age. Oldest would be marked ''Enterprise'', and would have by now dull plating, worn in many places, turned wood knob, and probably a cast iron rather openwork fancy screw. Latest have shiny plating, plastic knob, and the above-described simple screw. • **Lookalike alarm.**— A sausage stuffer & lard & fruit press marked ''CHOPRITE'' (CHOP-RITE?) is still being sold. It bolts to a table top or board. Lehman's Hardware & Appliances, 4779 Kidron Rd., Kidron, OH 44636 offer one in their 1989 ''Non-Electric Good Neighbor Amish Country'' catalog, which costs about $3.00. Lehman's say ''The original all-cast iron press —you've seen in antique stores — built to last for generations.'' Lehman's also has the ''Chop-Rite'' small grinders, one screw clamped, one with horizontal barrel and 4 legs to be bolted down, in No.s 5, 10, 12, 22, and 32. They also sell parts and say that ''All Chop-Rite parts will interchange with Enterprise parts IF you have the same model number.'' **$10.00-$20.00**

Meat grinder, plated cast iron, very simple long barrel, widely flared hopper, spraddled 2 leg screw clamp, worm screw cutter with crank, 2 interchangeable plates with fine or medium perforations to clamp on front, barrel & hopper pull up out of clamp base when thumbscrew loosened, "Family No. 1", Ellrich Hardware Mfg. Co., Plantsville, CT, pat'd May 15, 1888.   **$30.00-$45.00**

Meat juice extractor, also for fruit, tinned cast iron, large hopper, frame & hopper one piece, long tapered cylinder into which the grinding or pressing part inserts & turns; holes in bottom only to allow juice to drip into waiting bowl. Pulp or fibrin exits front into waiting receptacle, "Enterprise #21," Enterprise Mfg. Co., 12"H x 9"L, c.1880s, still selling early 20th C. • Catalog of c.1905 states "The use of meat juice for medicinal purposes is a growing one, and is recommended for the aged, delicate infants and invalids, in all cases where complete nourishment is required in a concentrated form."   **$20.00-$30.00**

Meat mincer, cast iron, double barrel body with large mouth, widely flared hopper at crank end, tube out other end fits onto sausage skin, or feeds ground meat to platter, latched hinged top, "Hale", pat'd by A. W. Hale, New Britain, CT, pat'd Mar. 15, 1859. • In the early 20th C this same meat cutter was sold (and the rights probably owned) by V. Clad & Sons of Philadelphia.**$185.00-$235.00**

Meat press, cast iron, 3 parts: cup, reamer & screw-action press, "Columbia #2," Landers, Frary & Clark, 19th C.   **$85.00-$115.00**

Meat press, cast iron frame screw clamps to table, T bar screw at top attached to press plate, removable cup is shaped like spade & set at 45 degree angle within frame, it has pointed front end with long slot to let out juice, "cannot clog up as in perforated pans, or soak back as is often the case. As a result more juice is obtained." "Quick & Easy", Erie Specialty Co., Erie, PA, c.1905.   **$65.00-$80.00**

Meat press, enameled cast iron, cobalt outside, white inside, 2 hinged parts, corrugated inside, hollow cast longish handles, hand held plier action, no marks, 8"L, TOC.   **$85.00-$125.00**

Meat slicer, cast iron, painted & decorated with gilt scrolls, mounted on small piece of wood, adjustable steel blades, cast iron handle looks like turned wood — the foundry casting pattern for it undoubtedly was. American (?), 17½"L, pat'd May 15, 1894.   **$85.00-$125.00**

Meat slicer, white enameled metal, wood handle, "General #208," American , 20th C.   **$35.00-$45.00**

Meat tenderer or bovinizer, hand held tool with round head fitted with 52 steel knife points; upright handle, spring-activated plate with holes through which the points pass with each downward jabbing pound, the spring pushes the plate back down, clearing the meat from the points, "Henis Bovinizer" mfd by William G. Henis' Sons & Co., Philadelphia, PA, pat'd Aug. 20, 1907. • They also made a restaurant version with a long levered action, a stationary holey plate, and below it on a platform of the frame a wooden cutting board. • Another device that looks something like a chopping knife with a double row of 9 very sharp steel blades, set in cast iron, with turned wood handle, was offered as a subscription premium in the May 1883 *American Agriculturist*. The maker isn't given, but it is called the "new and novel" Steakgreith in the ad. "Greith" is an ancient Anglo-Saxon word mean-

ing "to make ready", a word that might have survived in some isolated American community. Perhaps the inventor used the word all his life.   **$25.00-$35.00**

Meat tenderizer, all wood with 6 sharp points carved on business end, American (?), 9"L, late 19th or early 20th C.   **$15.00-$20.00**

Meat tenderizer, cast iron head with 4 concentric rings of ripples, turned wood handle, hard to read name, possibly "Jachutti Co., No. 2", Philadelphia, PA, 8½"L, 19th C.   **$30.00-$42.00**

Meat tenderizer, cast iron round cornered oblong frame, wooden axle rod stuck with many sharp steel blades, "Yale Meat Scorer," 8¼"L, patent applied for 1892.   **$45.00-$60.00**

Meat tenderizer, galvanized tin with wooden handle, 4 rows of deep teeth zigzags, no mark, American, 4½"L, 19th C.   **$25.00-$30.00**

Meat tenderizer, or meat fret, turned wooden handle, white glazed stoneware pottery with delicate blue floral decoration, round head has a waffled pattern of little pointed pyramids, European, 12"L x 3⅓" diameter, c.1890s.   **$75.00-$100.00**

Meat tenderizer, rolling type, cast iron drum with sharp prickers or spikes, turned wood handles at both ends, with brass ferrules, stamped "Charles E. Miller," also some illegible numbers, probably the patent date, 12"L, TOC. • See the Bun divider in Mold chapter; probably made by same company as idea is similar.   **$45.00-$55.00**

Meat tenderizer, rolling type, wood roller deeply carved with pyramidal points, heavy wire handle, American, roller 9½"W, whole thing 12"L including handle, 19th C.   **$20.00-$35.00**

Meat tenderizer, saltglazed stoneware head, replaced hammer (?) handle, American, 6"L, head: 3" diameter, pat'd Dec. 25, 1877.   **$75.00-$85.00**

Meat tenderizer, stoneware drum has sharp modeled points in waffled pattern, thick turned wood handle painted black, American, pat'd Dec. 25, 1877.   **$65.00-$85.00**

Meat tenderizer, stoneware head with waffled pattern, saltglazed with brown Albany slip underneath salt glaze, prob. NY state, 9"L, pat'd Dec. 25, 1877.   **$75.00-$100.00**

Meat tenderizer, vertical turned wooden handle, head set with 14 steel chisel point blades, used in same position as hand stamp, "Pettes' Beefsteak Tenderer", pat'd by M. M. Pettes, Worcester, MA, pat'd March 5, 1872.   **$35.00-$45.00**

Meat tenderizer, rolling type, small roller has steel blades set in it, long turned wood handle, American, 9"L, 19th C.   **$20.00-$35.00**

Meat tenderizer, white glazed ironstone with a waffled surface, turned wooden handle, 1890.   **$50.00-$70.00**

Meat tenderizer & ax, cast iron or steel(?), meant for a wooden handle, head has waffled meat pounder on one end, sharp ax on other, American, head only: 5¾"L, 19thC. • I hate stuff like this, being a vegetarian, so may be pricing low.   **$10.00-$15.00**

Meat tenderizer & ax, nickeled steel ax or hatchet head with curved blade, opposite a tenderizing device with 3 rows of 5 thick teeth, wooden handle, comes apart for cleaning — wingnut holds head to handle, Tyler Mfg. Co., Muncie, IN, 10" x 4¼" pat'd Dec. 5, 1922.

     $13.00-$22.00

Meat tenderizer, cap lifter, ice shaver & mincer combined, cast steel (?), heavy wooden handle, ice shaver part can bebe locked in at least 2 positions, very well-made but odd combination of functions. Bridge Cutlery Co., St. Louis, MO, 11''L, pat'd Aug. 15, 1916. **$25.00-$35.00**

Meat tenderizer & chopper, iron, homemade from old rasp, coarse rasp teeth on one side, finer on the other, has head & handle, late 19th C or early 20th. **$15.00-$20.00**

Meat tenderizer or pounder, cast iron hammer-like instrument with grid of tiny pyramids, American, 7½''L, late 19th C. **$18.00-$30.00**

Meat tenderizer or pounder, head is thick cast iron 'hockey puck', one side has wide-spaced blunt projections, other has many sharper, closer-set ridges, wood handle, American, head 3½'' diameter, late 19th C. **$40.00-$50.00**

Meat tenderizer or pounder, ironstone head with turned wooden handle, 14''L, mid to late 19th C. • **German vocabulary** — Fleisch-klopfer: meat pounder. **$135.00-$160.00**

Meat tenderizer or tenderer, cast iron, rocker action, has 20 pointed lethal teeth set 5 x 4, arched iron rod forms handle, American, 4'' x 2¾'', pat'd Sept. 20, 1892. **$18.00-$35.00**

Mincing knives—See Chopping knife this chapter.

Mortar, ash burl, nicely shaped with small pedestal base, American, 7''H x 6''D, early 19th or late 18th C. **$200.00-$250.00**

Mortar, hollowed log, bottom repaired with iron bands to hold age checks together, some kind of whitish composition (probably a clay cement) in crack on inside, rather thick walls & very beat up around edges, many insect holes & some dry rot, thoroughly ''picturesque'' & ''country''. American, 22''H, 19th C. • **''Beating Hominy.**— Soak the hominy corn ten minutes in boiling water; then take the corn up and put it into the hominy mortar, and beat it until the husks are all separated from the corn. Once or twice while beating it, take it out of the mortar and fan it; that is, throw up on a tray or bowl so as to allow the husks to fly off. When sufficiently beaten, fan it until all the husks are out.'' *The Farmers' Cabinet, Devoted to Agriculture, Horticulture and Rural Economy.* Phila.: Vol. II, No. 1, Aug. 1, 1837. **$95.00-$150.00**

Mortar & pestle, carved gray marble, simple thick walled bowl mortar with hexagonal sides, fat simple pestle, American (?), mortar 5''H, pestle 7½''L, 19th C. **$50.00-$75.00**

Mortar & pestle, cast bell metal or bronze, nearly straight sided mortar, with widely flared lip, bold square ear handles, turned with bands, long-handled pestle, mortar engraved ''N.A.D.S. + K.B.D.'' with date, European, 3¾''H, dated 1770. • This sold, with a ''small filled hole in bottom'' at Garth's, Delaware, OH, July 28, 1989. **$185.00**

Mortar & pestle, cast bell metal or bronze. There were a number of founders who cast bells & mortars. In fact, the type of flared rim this one has is called a <u>bell mouth.</u> English or American (?), 4¾''H x 3''D, 19th C. • **German vocabulary** — <u>Morser mit Pistill:</u>mortar with pestle, this one <u>Bronzeguss.</u> Often the German word for mortar is a compound of the material from which is is made (or its style or purpose) plus <u>Morser,</u> viz. <u>Messingmer</u> (brass mortar) <u>Barockmorser</u> (baroque mortar), <u>Holzmorser</u> wooden mortar), etc. Another word for pestle is <u>Stossel</u> (looks like StoBel). **$80.00-$100.00**

Mortar & pestle, cast brass, straight sides with flared rim, probably for pharmacist, no mark, 6''H, 19th C. **$50.00-$75.00**

Mortar & pestle, cast iron, 7''H x 6¾''D, prob. 1840s to 1860s. **$50.00-$65.00**

Mortar & pestle, cast iron, nice size: wider than high, 8''H x 9''D, 19th C. **$65.00-$80.00**

Mortar & pestle, cast iron, mortar has flared sides & rim, American (?), 6¾''H x 6¾''D, 19th C. **$45.00-$65.00**

Mortar & pestle, cut marble, with 4 ears or nubs around flat top, for lifting, poss. English, or a French import, different sizes, 1860s-70s. • Harrod's Stores, Ltd., of London, England, advertised these, in several sizes, in their 1895 retail catalog. They came in eight diameters: 8'', 9'', 10'', 11'', 12'', 13'', 14'' and 16''. With them you could order a simple turned lignum vitae pestle with cylindrical handle part ending in larger head, which came in five sizes to suit the mortar. **$85.00-$125.00**

Mortar & pestle, heavy turned tiger maple, both pieces attractively figured, small or large end of pestle can be used, American, mortar: 7''H x 6'' diameter, pestle: 9''L, early to mid 19th C. **$165.00-$200.00**

Mortar & pestle, heavy white earthenware, bowl-like with small pouring lip, glazed outside, inside unglazed, pestle with wild onion shaped earthenware head, with turned wooden handle screwed to it, sometimes marked on bottom, made by several potteries, notably Wedgwood. English, various sizes, 19th C. • **''Wedgwood mortar** — Mortars of Wedgwood earthenware will answer all household needs.'' Todd S. Goodholme, *Domestic Cyclopedia of Practical Information*, NY: Henry Holt, 1877. • Harrod's Stores, Ltd., of London, showed a similar mortar & pestle in their 1895 retail catalog. They called its material ''composition''. The mortar appears to be slightly off round, but perhaps that is just the drawing, which shows a rather big pouring lip. The bowl has very small ring foot, and the pestle is the wood and ironstone (''composition''?) common to the type. This was offered in several diameters: 7'', 8'', 9'', 10'', 11'' and 12''. The bigger they are the thicker. (I saw one about 14'' diameter that was well over an inch thick. Heavy as an anvil almost, and $350.00 in 1989.) **$25.00-$250.00**

Mortar & pestle, heavy white ironstone, with wood handled ironstone pestle, English (?), 6'' diameter, 19th C. • <u>Added value</u> — Really big ones bring most. Brand new white ceramic mortar & pestle sets are being made now. If you can put an old & new one side by side, you'll see differences. Generally, new ones aren't quite as heavy, often they are highly glazed on the outside of the mortar, and the wooden pestle handles aren't as nicely turned, have little patina, but lotsa varnish, and don't fit as neatly and snuggly to the ceramic business end of the pestle. **$45.00-$60.00**

Mortar & pestle, lignum vitae, the hardest densest wood available, beautiful <u>graining</u> — or <u>figure</u>, as it's called — & patina, American, 7''H, early 19th C. **$135.00-$160.00**

Mortar & pestle, lignum vitae, with slightly checked pestle, American, 7''H x 5⅜''D, 19th C. • ''A lignum-vitae mortar and pestle will last for generations, and there should be one in every kitchen.'' Maria Parloa, *Kitchen Companion*, Boston: Estes & Lauriat, 1887. **$125.00-$150.00**

Mortar & pestle, polished cast iron, flared sides with big foot, decorative swag design around side, long handled pestle, for candy makers, mfd. by Thomas Burkhard, ½ pound capacity (came in 1 pt., 1, 2, 4 & 8 qt. sizes too), c.1870s. **$35.00-$45.00**

Mortar & pestle, tiger maple with a nice figure, American, early 19th C. **$225.00-$250.00**

Mortar & pestle, turned painted wood, with pedestal base, well worn pestle with idiosyncratic worn places on handle, American, 7''H x 4½''D, early to mid 19th C. **$65.00-$85.00**

Mortar & pestle, turned wood, dark patina, chunky, footed mortar probably turned from a burl, worn on one edge from long rugged use, mortar is fitted with a ½ inch thick dowel ''leg'', splayed downward from near the top, actually a handle to be grasped with one hand while pounding. The worn area on rim is to left of this handle, so tool probably used by left-handed person. Pestle has thick handle with beetle-like heavy duty head & small rounded mushroom cap on other end, American, 7''H x 6'' diameter, pestle 7''L. Ex-Keillor Collection. **$175.00-$250.00**

Mortar & pestle, turned wood, with base, notable for height, American (?), 13½''H, 19th C. **$65.00-$85.00**

Mortar & pestle, very large hollowed out log with tall wooden pestle, top of log is waist high, hands must be raised above shoulders to use pestle or pounder, American, 19th C. • In October 1850, the *American Agriculturist* published a letter from *M* on how ''**To Make Hommony**'' (sic). The *M* stood for Maryland, where the correspondent was from. ''I have so often been asked for our Maryland receipt for making hommony, that I send it to your journal, as the surest method of making it public. Some gristmills have a way of preparing it beautifully, by making a trifling addition to the machinery of the mill, which beats the hommony while the meal is being ground; but many people still prefer the ole Negro way, and many mills have not the new machinery. I wish I could tell the quantity of water it takes for any given quantity...but the negroes do everything by guess; and when I asked the man who makes it best for me, the only answer I could get was, 'jest 'xactly 'nuff...oney don't let 'em make de corn too wet, dat spiles all.'

''Take a gum-tree or oak block, and burn or dig it out to the depth of twenty inches or two feet; rub the hollow clean and smooth, and you have the mortar. A wooden pestle, equally rude, is formed into the flat end of which drive gently, (for fear of splitting it,) the sharp end of a large-sized wood cutter's wedge; the broad end being thus ready for breaking and hulling the corn. The best corn must be carefully selected and shelled; moisten with boiling water, and put in again; this fanning and moistening...and beating to be continued until it is free from husks. Spread it out to dry, and then sift it, first through a coarse seive, which will retain only the hommony, then through a fine one, which will retain the grits. The coarse meal that remains is excellent for cakes and puddings.'' (NOTE: the husks of the corn kernels used now are removed with lye.) **$350.00-$500.00**

Mortar & pestle, white stoneware mortar with slightly flared sides, rounded rim & pouring lip, wood handled stoneware pestle, Maddock's Sons, with anchor trademark, Trenton, NJ, mortar 2¾''H x 4½'' diameter, pestle 6¾''L, late 19th C or early 20th. **$35.00-$50.00**

Noodle cutter—See Mold chapter.

Nutcracker, alligator, cast brass in 2 parts, mounted to base, American, 7½''L, 19th C. **$90.00-$125.00**

Nutcracker, alligator, cast iron, detailed casting, American, late 19th C. **$95.00-$125.00**

Nutcracker, alligator, cast iron with old silver radiator paint, cast in 2 parts: (1) upper jaw and ''naked underbody'' with legs & lower part of curving tail, (2) lower jaw & scaled top of body & tail, pretty good detail, no marks, 13¾''L, poss. early 20th C. • **Reproduction alert** — John Wright, Inc., made a black painted cast aluminum alligator, only 1¾''W x 6¼''L, in the 1960s. **$65.00-$80.00**

Nutcracker, alligator, rather delicate & small, lever action dark satiny cast iron, 2 parts: slender upper jaw, patterned back, slightly wavery tail, separate lower body unusual because it has shortish pointed ''tail'', marked ''Nestor'', 9''L, 19th C. **$125.00-$150.00**

Nutcracker, antelope head, lever type, carved wood with set in glass eyes, long horns, very detailed carving, Tyrolean (?), 8⅞''H x 3½''W nose to ear tips, 19th C. • Try to get a look at the dozens of fabulous carved wood lever crackers in Pinto's book on *Treen* (see Bibliography). Most in his collection are human — grotesque or comic characters with gaping jaws, some dating to 16th C. Very elaborate carving of all parts. Many others are dogs, or other animals. **$125.00-$145.00**

Nutcracker, bawdy legs, cast iron shapely woman's legs, large concavity in inner thighs, very unusual because painted flesh color, original because decal put on over paint: ''Souvenir of New York City'', 6''L, c.1940s-50s. **$20.00-$30.00**

Nutcracker, bawdy woman's legs with high heels, cast aluminum, no mark, 6⅞''L, c.1940s (?). **$80.00-$100.00**

Nutcracker, bawdy woman's legs, cast brass, 5½''L, TOC. **$85.00-$120.00**

Nutcracker, bawdy woman's legs, carved wood, 19th C. **$45.00-$55.00**

Nutcracker, bawdy woman's legs, cast brass, 4''L, TOC. **$55.00-$75.00**

Nutcracker, bawdy women's legs, feet well-defined, pale-colored cast brass, two almost alike — one 4½''L, other 4⅜''L, late 19th C. **$65.00-$80.00**

Nutcracker, bearded man with skull cap, lever type, carved wood, Tyrolean or Swiss (?), 19th C. **$120.00-$150.00**

Nutcracker, Black Americana man in overcoat, hands in pockets over knees, painted cast iron, modeled with ring of white hair & white eyebrows like popular illustrations of Uncle Tom, lever works lower jaw or chin , American, 19th C, prob. 3rd quarter. **$650.00-$750.00**

Nutcracker, Black Americana head of man, cast iron, more portrait than caricature, hair, brow, eyes, nose & upper lip have good detail, lower jaw worked by slightly curved short lever in back, head mounted to widely flared footed base, American, about 6''H, mid 19th C. **$400.00-$500.00**

Nutcracker, black man's head, caricatured Black Americana, painted cast iron in 4 parts: 2 flat halves of the head, riveted together, a lever (which comes out back of head) that works the jaw, & a diamond shape base to which all is screwed, very exaggerated eyes, lips & ears, partly painted red & white, no mark at all, American, 6⅛''H, looks maybe c.1880s, poss. much earlier. **$600.00-$800.00**

Nutcracker, black painted cast iron, small anvil & blacksmith's hammer, probably not a repro. of an old one, but a ''new'' idea, John Wright, Inc., Wrightsville, PA, hammer 4''L, 1960s. **$15.00-$20.00**

Nutcracker, blue-decorated Meissen porcelain frame fitted with iron screw mechanism with big porcelain knobs at each end, Meissen, German, about 6"H, 19th C.
$150.00-$200.00

Nutcracker, brass, "Big Ben," English (?), 20th C (?).
$55.00-$65.00

Nutcracker, carved boxwood lever type, one tapered handle is L shaped, the other has pivot part fitting through bottom of L, rounded on outside with small carved double - crossed squares as decoration, ball finials, carved on one lever or handle is the name, on other is a very very early date — surprising because the name sounds like a patent or trade name, on flat surface inside L lever is "Broughtons Cracknut", the inscribed date is "October 5, 1667", English, 5⅜"L, 1667 (?). • Dealers Michael & Jane Dunn, Claverack, NY, had this at a show in 1984. I did not get to examine it, and am taking description from picture appearing in *Maine Antique Digest*, April 1984. Price range mine. • **Futile Research on the Name.** — I spent several hours trying to do intuitive research on the date or the name. Leads investigated included a British regiment, originally "The Third Foot", later the "Buffs", which had the nickname the "Nutcrackers." This regiment was definitely in existence in 1667. And it fought in the Second Dutch War — one of several Restoration wars between England and Holland — which ended in 1667. With my resources, the name Broughton led nowhere, nor did I have time to really delve into the date. I did look at a very early 19th C "every day" almanach, which details events important to England on every day of the year, but found nothing significant for October 5. One of that set of books, William Hone's *The Every-Day Book*, (the one I quote here, London: 1826), yields several squibs on nuts or nut-cracking. Sept. 14, or Holy Rood, was for nutting, signifying the "fruitfulness of autumn, and the deadly cold of the coming winter." On October 31, Hallowe'en, the Vigil night for November 1, All Saints Day, it was traditional "in many parts of England" to bob for apples and crack nuts. It is possible that the elusive "Nutcrack Night" of which I have seen only passing mention, refers to the e'en of October 31.
$750.00-$950.00

Nutcracker, carved & painted wood, wrinkled man with red & green cap, like a liberty cap, Tyrolean, either Swiss or German, 6¼"L, New, but in style of 19th C ones.
$95.-00-$125.00

Nutcracker, carved & turned oak, doughnut shape pierced on one side by wooden screw used to press nut you've placed within "hole" of doughnut against opposite side, English, only 2" diameter, late 19th C. • I've also seen modern ones, especially in woods & finishes favored by Danish furniture makers.
$35.00-$40.00

Nutcracker, cast iron, 2 part, walled oblong green painted base with sort of mortar with long handled flattish plate that fits inside base, Paper label reads: "DIRECTIONS: Place cracker on a solid foundation. Place all nuts on end and hit blow with hammer or mallet. Empty the base after cracking each nut. Use 36 ounce mallet if possible until after the war." "Potter Walnut Cracker Co.", pat'd by C. E. Potter, Sapulpa, OK, pestle about 3"L, 1945 patent #2377369.
$35.00-$50.00

Nutcracker, cast iron exactly like screw-clamp model, but this one screwed to a "countersunk plate" in bottom of a shallow turned wood bowl with very rounded sides & narrow foot, "all the shells & other litter fall into the bowl & are not scattered about", The Perfection Nut Cracker Co., Waco, TX, pat'd Nov. 17, 1914, advertised in early 1917 as a new item. • This is the scarcest of the Perfection crackers.
$50.00-$65.00

Nutcracker, cast iron, lever action, Arcade Mfg. Co., Freeport, IL, early 20th C.
$50.00-$65.00

Nutcracker, cast iron, levered jaws stick out slightly over end, mounted to oblong wooden board, lower corrugated jaw stationary, upper one opens & depresses when curved lever is raised, pat'd by Rupert Frisbie, Middletown, CT, pat'd May 17, 1859.
$65.00-$80.00

Nutcracker, cast iron, mounted to oblong wooden board, long corrugated jaws stick out over side near one end, lever moves endmost jaw while other remains stationary. Similar to Frisbie patent; a letter by Ernest J. Rolland to *Spinning Wheel* in 1977 reported that both these nut-crackers are "often mistaken for a cork press," pat'd by P. E. W. & J. A. Blake, New Haven, CT, base 10½"L x 3"W, pat'd Sept. 6, 1853. (See more on the Blake Brothers under a Corkscrew entry in the Open & Close chapter.) • **Later edition.**— One of these was reported as having black painted finish, & marked "P. & S. & W. Co.", which I believe must be Peck, Stow & Wilcox, Southington, CT. • **Reproduction alert.**— An extremely similar nutcracker, with slight differences, including a board with a turned molded edge & a spring between lever & lower part. Called the "Herkimer Jr., No. 602", & being made by White Mountain Freezer Co. of Winchendon, MA. They make one mounted to larger board with a nut "firkin" attached at one end, and this one which is supposed to be "modeled after the original Herkimer cracker." I couldn't find any patent by a Herkimer.
$65.00-$80.00

Nutcracker, cast iron, nickel plated, held cupped in hand, T handle to screw, advertising "Cook Muffler Co.," American, approx. 4½"L when screwed fully in, c. 1910-1930s.
$8.00-$15.00

Nutcracker, cast iron, nickeled or tinned, clamps to table, looks like small bench vise, horizontal screw that pushes nut against end plate, big cast T handle has swelled knobs on ends like leg bone, "Perfection," Malleable Iron Fittings Co., Branford, CT, pat'd 1889.
$40.00-$60.00

Nutcracker, cast iron, nickeled, screw clamps to table top & looks like small bench vise, vertical "lathe" type action, large T handle, slightly finer casting than earlier one, ornate letters in curve to fit frame, The Perfection Nut Cracker Co., Waco, TX, 4½"H x 3¾"W, pat'd Nov. 17, 1914. • Another one, a little leaner, and made of nickeled cast steel, is very plain. It is marked "Perfection Nut Cracker Pat." Pecans, which are supposed to be hard to crack (perhaps to crack & get perfect nutmeats out), were Texas' biggest cash crop at the time the "Perfection" was patented.
$40.00-$60.00

Nutcracker, cast iron, screw clamps to table, lever action, long slightly arched lever pulled down over small nut-holding jaw, "Enterprise", Enterprise Mfg. Co., Phila., c.1914.
$30.00-$45.00

Nutcracker, cast iron, screw clamps to table, long lever, "Home," American, 19th C.
$28.00-$40.00

Nutcracker, cast iron, small square anvil-like contrivance, curved shape to fit a seated person's knee, small short column in center has concavity for nut, used with mallet or small hammer, "Lawrence," American, about 4" square, 19th C.
$75.00-$90.00

Nutcracker, cast iron, tabletop vise type, "The Hamilton," early 20th C. $30.00-$45.00

Nutcracker, cast & turned brass, with engraved decoration, sort of whoop-tee-do dancing master's leg shaped handles, squared cracking face plate tooled with little teeth for grabbing the nut, English, range from about 3½"L to 4¼"L, late 18th or very very early 19th C. • The same people who made fire tools, andirons, bells, etc., made these heavy little crackers, which are all variations on a theme. Some have more exaggerated "legs" or handles than others. $75.00-$125.00

Nutcracker, concave part of cast iron fits in palm, T handle with slightly knobby ends, screw action, this one is chrome with enameled green body, others are nickeled or even just highly polished iron, some have narrower bodies & T bar has no knobbed ends, or have a simple looped handle, mfr Frank B. Cook advertised "The Ideal"; later, without knobbed ends, "Ideal" was mfd by Cook Electric Co., Chicago, IL, 3¼"W x about 5"L, 1917 ad, then 1923 ad. $3.50-$5.00

Nutcracker, dog, bronzed cast iron, on oblong stepped base, L.A. Althoff & Co., Chicago, IL, early 20th C. $85.00-$120.00

Nutcracker, dog, cast brass, on brass base, lots of hair detail, no marks, 4¾"H without base, 5⅜"H with it, x 11¼"L, c.1870s to 1890s? $70.00-$85.00

Nutcracker, dog cast in 2 halves, plus tail lever, cast brass, rather crude & lumpy, filed roughly & bolted. Looks like St. Bernard (according to contemporaneous reports, they & Newfoundlands were most popular breeds at the end of the 19th C), no marks, 4¾"H x 11½"L, c.1870s or 1880s? $85.00-$100.00

Nutcracker, dog, cast iron with copper finish, smaller than most you see, Made in England, 8¼"L, marked on inside of tail Patent No. 273480, which is 1863. $55.00-$70.00

Nutcracker, dog, nickel plated iron, English, 8¾"L, 1863 patent #273480. • I think I'd like a kennel full of these dogs — so many variations. John Wright, Inc., in PA, made (at least in the 1960s) a very small black-painted cast iron dog, levered tail, only 5½"L. Cast in two parts, bolted through middle of body. $75.00-$90.00

Nutcracker, dog on base, cast iron, well defined hair, advertising "L. A. Althoff," Makers of Headlights, Stoves & Ranges, Laporte, IN, (or La Port?),approx. 11"L, 19th C. • This nutcracker might appeal to some stove collectors, although, for most of them, home is nowhere but on the range. It also came in nickeled finish. It is not uncommon, but prices (like with anything else), really depend on who's buying & who's selling. One with "worn nickel finish with light rust" brought only $40.00 at the Garth Auction, May 26-27, 1989, Delaware, OH. $85.00-$215.00

Nutcracker, dog, on flat base with openwork that makes it look like sidewalk grating, marvelous jowls, cast iron, "Dog Tray Nut Cracker" (for Stephen C. Foster's song, "Old Dog Tray" ?), mfd by Harper Supply Co., North Chicago , IL, 13"L, "patent applied for", 19th C. • **Reproduction alert.** — Emig Products, Inc., of Reading, PA, reproduced (at least in the 1960s) a dog on platform cracker; the platform on theirs has much more openwork & simpler pattern than old one. (Emig's was 5"H x 10"L, sold for about $5.00. $95.00-$120.00

Nutcracker, dog with belled collar, cast brass, European, 5½"L, early 19th C. $90.00-$125.00

Nutcracker, dog with levered tail, cast iron porcelainized in black & white, American, late 19th C. $250.00-$350.00

Nutcracker, dog with levered tail, crudely formed cast iron, English, 11½"L, patent No. 273480 marked on tail. $55.00-$70.00

Nutcracker, dog's head, cast iron, levered jaw, English or German, dated (? - or may be pattern number?) "1820". • **German vocabulary** — Tannenhher or Nussknacker (looks like NuBknacker): nutcracker. $75.00-$95.00

Nutcracker, dragon, griffin or even possibly dinosaur, unusual, gold painted cast iron, body's 2 parts bolt together, sawtooth ridges on back & tail, American, 13"L, 1878 patent #206454. (?). $165.00-$185.00

Nutcracker, eagle head, cast iron, on primitive 4 legged base, which is quite different from flat base of new lookalike nutcracker, American, 7"L,19th C. $75.00-$85.00

Nutcracker, eagle head, cast iron, upraised head on flat iron base, lever moves lower beak up and down, American? 6"H, 1980s. • **Lookalike alarm.** — Cumberland General Store, Crossville TN, is selling this one, and write that it is "just like those available in the 19th century;" old ones go for $250.00-$350.00 $12.00-$18.00

Nutcracker, elephant, cast iron, painted red & black, with a little white, the red has aged to a salmon color, trunk is lever, American,10" x 5", early 20th C. $125.00-$165.00

Nutcracker, elephant form, modernistic cast iron painted orange, high arched back, lever action, 20th C. $95.00-$125.00

Nutcracker, gold fish or koi with teeth in mouth, gold painted cast iron, glued-on glass eyes (poss. not original), upper fin is spring-loaded lever, English, 8"L, Regist'd #751619. Prob. c.1920s. $90.00-$125.00

Nutcracker, grotesque man's head on small round collar-base, wearing liberty cap, extremely long sausage nose curves down, forked beard, carved walnut, American (?), 6½"L from nose tip to back of head, 3rd quarter 19th C. • Offered for sale in 1987 by Paul Madden Antiques, Sandwich Village, MA. Price range mine. $350.00-$450.00

Nutcracker, hand held crossover plier type, handles flip around axis to accommodate another size nut, cast iron, English, European or American, about 6"L, 19th C. • There's quite a variety available. I like the cast iron ones best; others have nickeled or silverplated finishes. $15.00-$20.00

Nutcracker, hand held crossover plier type, handmade (?) cast iron, maybe cast in multiples then finished by hand?, hinged levers, inside face of one are tiny V gouges, the other has O gouges, English (?), 6½"L, c.1850s to 1900. $20.00-$25.00

Nutcracker, hand held crossover pliers, pointy handles, engraved steel, English, 5½"L, 19th C. $12.00-$18.00

Nutcracker, hand held crossover pliers, silver plated iron, bulbous knobs on handles, English (?), 5¼"L, TOC. • **It's In the Picture.** — One very similar to this, a crossover type with little rough projections on jaw parts, tapered turned handles, silverplated, appears in "Still Life with Apples, Walnuts and Holly", painted by American artist Eloise H. Stannard in 1899. You should always examine still life and genre scene pictures for objects in our collecting fields. At least you get an "as early as..." date. • **It's In the Catalog.** — Harrod's Stores, Ltd., London, England, carried 10 different styles of this type. The turnings of the handles (or lack thereof) as well as overall decoration, and style of jaw, vary considerably. The cheapest has nicely shaped handles narrow near the jaws, swelling out, then coming to a dull pointed end. The jaws, on both sides, have flat faces with a pattern of small nicks or gouges. The piece between the hinged jaws that determines the minimum space between the jaws while in use, is crown shaped rather than teardrop or ovoid. Slightly more expensive is one with pointed handles, two sets of turned bands, ovoid spacer, and oval grooved or fluted concavities for nuts. Another has decorated hinge pins, but wide spoon-handle levers. Another, again with oval concavity, has bamboo-like cast iron handles; another has baluster turnings with round knobs at ends; another has the crown spacer, very decorative 'rattlesnake rattle' turnings, and a zigzag line of small gouges or nicks on all faces of jaws; another is not the 2-hinge flip over type, can be used only one way (though, like the rest, as pliers are used), but the longish jaws are corrugated inside, with area for larger nuts near the handles. This "nut crack" came with allover fancy Renaissance chased decoration, or with chased head and plain handles. The handles of this one are the shapely ones of first type listed above. Harrod's nutcrackers came plated and plain, and were ordered through the jewellery, watch, electro plate & cutlery department of the huge store. **$12.00-$18.00**

Nutcracker, hand held plier type, cast iron, knobbed ends to handles, corrugated parts for 2 sizes of nuts — small (like almonds) & large (like walnuts), American? 5⅛''L, 19th C. **$12.00-$18.00**

Nutcracker, horse, modern stylized form, 2 halves screwed together, tail lever, bronzed or coppered cast iron, English, 4¼''H x 7¼''L, marked with same pat. as dog crackers, #273480. **$250.00-$300.00**

Nutcracker, jester & knight, cast brass, plier type, English or poss. American, late 19th or early 20th C. **$25.00-$35.00**

Nutcracker, lions' heads, one to each jaw, cast iron, plier type, pronounced concavity inside mouths, no marks, English (?), 6½''L, 19th C. **$60.00-$100.00**

Nutcracker, man in moon in crescent shape, mouth is pivot point, carved wood, very smooth patination, lots of expression in face, European, prob. Swiss or German, about 5'' to 7''L, early to mid 19th C. • **Reproduction alert.**— One of these in the collection of the Boston Museum of Art has been reproduced by them and mounted to small rectangular bases. A late 1980's Museum Shop catalog shows one of cast polymer resin that is 5½''H including base, and one of cast brass, which is 6''H with base. **$175.00-$225.00**

Nutcracker, man in moon, with neat little teeth, levered mechanical, carved hardwood, crescent moon, iron hinge, English or poss. American, moon if full would form 5'' circle, mid 19th C. **$325.00-$365.00**

Nutcracker, man who looks like Mr. Magoo, cast iron & wood, lever action, homemade wooden box painted yellow, 3-D cast iron front of man stands squint-eyed with hands in overcoat pockets, his feet inside box, mounted to a wooden back cut to fit his outline, lever works lower jaw, not marked, American, man is 7½''H, 19th C. **$300.00-$350.00**

Nutcracker, man's head, perhaps a comic caricature of a peasant, wearing a Phrygian liberty cap of the type worn in France before & during their revolution, large jaw with

indication of teeth, forged iron, very long lever handles, French, dated 1761. • This piece was for sale in early 1989 by Pat Guthman Antiques, Southport, CT. It is an example of the very best kind of iron work that you could hope to find. It is so extraordinary that it matters little if it be an example of the very best kind of iron work that you could hope to find. It is so extraordinary that it matters little if it be American, French, German or whatever, because it is art. • Price range mine. **$650.00-$800.00**

Nutcracker, nickel plated metal rachet mechanism & lever, black enameled metal tray, in original orange & black cardboard box, "Krag's Whole Kernel Nut Cracker," American, 7''L, c.1930s. **$40.00-$55.00**

Nutcracker, nickeled malleable cast iron, screw clamps to table, pushing down lever operates worm causing longish cupped jaws to close in, jaws stepped & with opposing concavities for small, medium & large nuts, device especially meant for pecans, "Home", Schroeter Brothers Hardware Co., St. Louis, MO, 6''H x 4''W with 7½''L lever, "patent pending" in 1915; poss. never pat'd. **$40.00-$60.00**

Nutcracker, platform lever type, cast iron, "Blake" (probably Blake Brothers & Co.), prob. New Haven, CT, TOC. **$25.00-$35.00**

Nutcracker, rocket shaped, cast iron on wooden base, adjusts for different nuts, "Reed's Rocket," American, 20th C (?). **$25.00-$30.00**

Nutcracker, rooster, cast iron, TOC. **$65.00-$80.00**

Nutcracker, sailor & girlfriend, they kiss (the nut) when handles squeezed, cast brass, 6¼''L, 20th C. **$30.00-$40.00**

Nutcracker, sailor's head with liberty cap, concave roof of mouth accommodates nut, 4 part carved base, carved wood, European, prob. Tyrolean, 7''H, c.1860s. **$140.00-$170.00**

Nutcracker, skull & bones, nut goes between face & back of skull, bones are levered handles, cast iron with some remaining copper plating, very lean & hungry, English, 6''L, register #740410, prob. c.1920s. **$95.00-$125.00**

Nutcracker, squirrel, carved wood, probably walnut, threaded screw action presses against nut, Tyrolean or English ?, 19th C. • Not as large a variety of the screw-type wooden nutcrackers as the levered ones, but others to look for include various barrels or cylinders with simple or fancy knobs to the screws — from a simple bird to a knob faceted like a golfball to a standing woman. The most commonly found wood is boxwood. **$150.00-$200.00**

Nutcracker, squirrel, cast brass of very reddish hue, 2 parts with riveted pivot in jaw, no marks, lots of detail, 7⅞''L, late 19th C or early 20th. **$90.00-$125.00**

Nutcracker, squirrel, cast iron, "Squirrel Cracker," Tyler, TX, pat'd 1913. • **Nuts & Nutcrackers.**— The Nut Museum, 303 Ferry Road, Old Lyme, CT, which is open by appointment only, has quite a collection of world nuts, art made from nuts, and a large collection of nutcrackers. Call ahead for further information. **$75.00-$120.00**

Nutcracker, squirrel on leaf, cast iron, American, 19th C. • I've seen only three in all my wanderings. A picture of five squirrel nutcrackers, from the booth of dealer Clifton Anderson, Lexington, KY, who was set up at "Atlantique City" in March 1989, makes it clear that the variations are not subtle. One squirrel, in the foreground, has the most Alert Squirrel head ... wary, tail tucked along curved back, holding a leaf on his paws, which is where the nut to crack went. Another I recognize as the reproduction I bought through the mail from someone else, smallish and very poorly cast, very furry tail, with gap between front paws. Looking at these, and at the racing, chasing busybodies in our yard, I find it impossible to call them Rodents. Anderson wanted $1500.00 for the five, which seems high. **$95.00-$125.00**

Nutcracker, squirrel on rustic branch, cast bronze or bell metal, extremely finely detailed, squirrel has funny long skinny arms & very pointed nose, lever is uplifted plumy tail widely separated from curve of back, English? or poss. American, 6''L, 19th C. • This is one of the best-looking squirrels. The abstracting is very refined; the angular slender legs, the funny little ears. It sometimes seems to be a bronzed cast iron; possibly different periods? I have also seen this one with no leaf, but mounted to a turned wooden tray or plate. **$175.00-$225.00**

Nutcracker, squirrel sitting on hind legs on huge grape leaf, cast aluminum painted black, rather crudely cast but nice idea. The tail lifts up to lever the jaw, no mark, American?, 7½''H overall, leaf 11½''L, 20th C. • Flat or dull black painted aluminum is almost a sure sign of rather recent origin (or recent painting). I think it's intended to fool the unknowing into thinking they've found a cast iron piece. There are c.1900 cast aluminum pieces of many kinds, however, but the novel metal, considered an attractive silvery pewter lookalike, was rarely painted, and usually in gold. **$30.00-$45.00**

Nutcracker, squirrel, standing high, tail curled, cast iron, good detail, American, only 5''H, late 19th or early 20th C. **$75.00-$125.00**

Nutcracker, squirrel with paws held palms up, on log, levered tail, silver gray painted light weight cast aluminum, brown log, green eyes, the squirrel & base case in 2 pieces down through center of squirrel & length of log, bolted together, dealer's tag says ''signed H. E. Cox, Norfolk, VA'', but I couldn't find any mark at all, 5½''H, log 5¾''L, looks 1980s, and pretty awful. **$15.00-$20.00**

Nutcracker, tabletop screw type, cast brass machined to look like ship's wheel, on wooden base, American, 4½''H, 20th C. **$40.00-$55.00**

Nutcracker, with its own bowl, simple footed, rimmed bowl of ''imitation rosewood, zebra ash or genuine mahogany'', with nickeled metal high rise frame like a guillotine screwed to bottom, adjustable for 4 different size nuts, lever used to move top part down to pop nut open, ''New Champion'', c.1915. **$20.00-$28.00**

Nutcracker bowl, turned wood, with cast iron round central ''anvil'' & iron hammer, American, 7''L hammer & 10'' diameter bowl, 20th C. **$25.00-$35.00**

Nutcracker & picks, nickel plated, heavily knurled, 6 picks in original box, American, c.1910. **$12.00-$15.00**

Nutcracking block, kneecap 'anvil' style, cast iron, shield shaped with raised nut holder, fits over knee & used sitting down with small mallet or hammer, American, 3½''L, 1840s-60s. **$85.00-$100.00**

Nutcracking maul or mallet, for walnuts, probably made of chestnut, but very stained, American, 11¾''L, block is 3⅞'' x 4¾'' x 2⅜'' thick, TOC. **$25.00-$30.00**

Nutgrinder, cast iron & tin, ''Climax.'' Nutgrinder, glass jar, screw-on tin hopper filled with 'fingers' that rotate when cranked, American, 1940s. **$12.00-$15.00**

Nutgrinder, green painted metal, ''Lorraine Metal Mfg. Co.,'' NY, TOC. **$22.00-$30.00**

Nutmeg & ginger mill, tin with little crank, looks like music box, brown asphaltum japanning, marked ''Portable Ginger & Nutmeg Mill'', English, 3³⁄₁₆'' x 2⁷⁄₁₆'', reg'd Nov. 11, 1857. **$130.00-$150.00**

Nutmeg grater, asphaltum japanned tin, looks like miniature bug bomb gun, label reads ''simple, economical, rapid and durable. Every particle of the nut used. Satisfaction Guaranteed. None wasted, easy to handle, a pleasure to use,' 'The Rapid Nutmeg Grater', 5¼''L, late 19th C. **$120.00-$130.00**

Nutmeg grater, big, round robust black-glazed ceramic knob (instead of the usual wood), triangular tin chute where grated meg comes out, storage in back, ''British made'', disk is 3¾'' diameter, British patent applied for, #32492/32. **$160.00-$180.00**

Nutmeg grater, cast iron crank, wire handle, ingeniously bent so as to hold nutmeg against small grating disc, handle looks like a spark striker handle, American, 7''L, 1880s. **$75.00-$120.00**

Nutmeg grater, cast iron housing for nutmeg & other cast iron parts, wire handle, tin grating disc, no marks, 7''L, c.1870s. **$90.00-$100.00**

Nutmeg grater, cast iron with tin grater, shaped like small bellows, crank handle, unpin & unhinge it & it reveals brass spring-loaded catch for cartridge holder of single nutmeg, directional arrow cast in side to show which way to turn handle, 2 holes for screwing to shelf edge or cupboard side (another model marked the same way had a screw clamp frame), not marked with name, but invented by J. M. Smith, Seymour, CT, 3⅞''L, pat'd June 7, 1870. **$275.00-$350.00**

Nutmeg grater, 'coffin style', non-mechanical, brightly tinned, with lidded storage for 1 to 2 megs at top,1980s.• **Lookalike alarm.**— This is still being made, and it's sold by Cumberland General Store , Crossland, TN, and other stores. **$2.00-$4.00**

Nutmeg grater, coffin style, tin, has lidded storage at top near hanging hole or loop, biggest variety seen in the back of these — the ingenious ways tin was poked out to create the platform inside to hold the nutmeg, mostly American, 5⅛''L to 5¾''L, 19th to 20th C. • Slightly fancier ones (usually with embossed designs on little lidded compartment, or with sliding lids) are English. **$10.00-$17.00**

Nutmeg grater, coffin type but very big, tin, with compartment, 2 grating surfaces on the curved front & flat back, ''Acme Nut Grater'', English, Register # 11467. **$35.00-$45.00**

Nutmeg grater, coffin type modified, stamped tin, has sliding lid to nutmeg compartment, back unusual in that it's stamped with an 8 rayed star, English, 6⅜''L x 2⁹⁄₁₆''W, TOC. **$30.00-$40.00**

Nutmeg grater, coffin type, very large, stamped & punctured tin, with storage box with sliding lid with embossed design, no marks, English, 6½''L x 2½''W, 19th C. **$25.00-$32.00**

Nutmeg grater, ebonized wood, or bog oak, carved to look like small champagne bottle, no marks, remnants of paper label that is illegible, European, 3¾''H, 19th C. **$70.00-$85.00**

Nutmeg grater, fancy little box grater, japanned or lacquered tin, 4''L, late 19th C. **$50.00-$60.00**

Nutmeg grater, fancy turned wood body & handle, cube of wood has working part inside, plus barrel for storing the megs, tin grater, brass side plates & cap, Champion Grater Co., invented by C. L. Gilpatric, of South Dedham, MA, but mfd in Boston, MA, 7½″L, pat'd Oct. 9, 1866; brass cap at end of handle marked April 2, 1867. **$250.00-$350.00**

Nutmeg grater, funnel-like tin cylinder joined to crosswise tin barrel, & comes out other side, wire crank has turned wood handle, spring-loaded plunger holds nutmeg, 3½″L, 19th C. **$70.00-$95.00**

Nutmeg grater, funny looking wood, wire & tin mechanical, pressure lever makes it resemble large safety pin, grating disc prob. hand-punctured, has many tiny holes, no mark, 5″L, late 19th C. **$95.00-$125.00**

Nutmeg grater, heavy cast iron with brass & wood, pinned hinges or hooks hold back on, pat'd Jan. 30, 1877. **$110.00-$130.00**

Nutmeg grater, interesting long skinny tin mechanical grater, flat piece pulls down to protect grating surface, nutmeg holder is small cylinder mounted to track along folded edges, "William Bradley", Lynn, MA, 6″L in closed-up position, "patent applied for" on one; pat'd July 26, 1854 on another. • Very similar to this one are the "Monitor", which does resemble an ironclad submarine, from 1873, and an ingenious one pat'd Aug. 17, 1897. The latter has a "smokestack" cylinder for the nutmeg, and tracks the long skinny grating surface that's like an angular tunnel. A hole in the top at one end permits insertion of nutmeg into the cylinder when it's positioned over the hole. **$120.00-$150.00**

Nutmeg grater, long tin barrel, hinged lid at end for inserting nutmeg, hinge wire is also hanging ring, grating drum made up of assembled battery of 12 toothed rings with deep & jagged teeth like harrow discs, slightly jaywhoppered, seems like overkill, stamped "The —s Davidson Automatic Nutmeg Grater", Boston, MA, 6¾″W, pat'd June 2, 1908. (I've seen this given as June 9, also a Tuesday). **$115.00-$135.00**

Nutmeg grater, long tin tube, screw caps at each end plus one ⅓ way up, like odd pocket periscope crossed with a cigar tube. Crank comes out one end, 'meg goes in hole in side, other end stores more. See also the "Standard". American, 6½″L, late 19th C. **$100.00-$135.00**

Nutmeg grater, long wooden rectangle, round turret on top with grater & crank, wire gripper holds nutmeg in place, American, 19th C. **$165.00-$180.00**

Nutmeg grater, nickel plated cast iron, hinged nutmeg holder, punctured tin disc, small crank with wooden knob, black holding handle in center of disc, American, 3¾″L x 2¾″D, c.1870s to 1880s. • **German vocabulary —** Muskatreibe: nutmeg grater. **$95.00-$125.00**

Nutmeg grater, nickel plated metal, horizontal cylinder with squared funnel below & cylindrical "chimney" or hopper above, crank in end of grater barrel, marked inside a diamond "MTE & Co.," American, 3½″L, 19th C. **$65.00-$85.00**

Nutmeg grater, nickeled cast iron, big wooden knob on crank, disk is 2½″ diameter, early 20th C. **$80.00-$90.00**

Nutmeg grater, non-mechanical, homemade, tin & wood, paddle shape with semi-cylindrical punctured tin arched grating surface, American, 4″L, 19th C. **$25.00-$35.00**

Nutmeg grater, oddly modern & efficiently mechanical, screwed pressure foot, pierced drum with grater punch holes at slight angle, no nonsense action, 7½″L, late 19th or early 20th C. **$90.00-$100.00**

Nutmeg grater, plated metal, in cylinder shape with lift-out grater that forms top, nutmegs are stored inside cylinder, no marks, American (?), 4½″L, 19th C. **$100.00-$120.00**

Nutmeg grater, pocket, carved coquilla nut with ivory trim, shaped like a barrel. Unscrew bottom for tin grater & nutmeg storage, prob. English, though poss. American scrimshander work, only 2½″L, very early 19th C.
• Coquilla nuts, from piassaba palm of Brazil, washed up on beaches, were found by sailors, who used the richly colored, hard dense material to make intricate small carvings. These carvings and turnings, snuff boxes, patch boxes, nutmeg graters, "pretties" & tokens of love, were often trimmed with carved ivory. **$200.00-$235.00**

Nutmeg grater, pocket style, ivory with tin grater inside, caps unscrew for grater at one end, nutmeg at other, English (?), 3½″L, early 19th C, or poss. late 18th. **$175.00-$225.00**

Nutmeg grater, pocket type, carved wood & ivory, nutmeg-holding lid screws onto grater part, English (?), early 19th C. **$75.00-$95.00**

Nutmeg grater, pocket type, silver, heart-like overall shape, impressed flower designs, opens at both sides, like a 2 sided compact or something, English, only 1⅞″W x 1″H, 19th C. **$140.00-$160.00**

Nutmeg grater, rotary action, large turned handle to hold in one hand, round tin grating surface screwed through center & screw also secures nutmeg holder. Metal crank, screwed to edge of disc, has a wooden knob & a small round presser foot to hold nutmeg while the crank is turned, "Gem", Caldwell Mfg. Co., Rochester, NY, c.1907. **$65.00-$85.00**

Nutmeg grater, silver, fancy cast handle like flatware knife handle, marked with 2 eagle wings with an "S" in middle, also #69, 7″L, pat'd June 29, 1897. **$110.00-$130.00**

Nutmeg grater, simple mechanical type, rigid wood frame with nearly square tin piece, the top part of which is the grating surface, across which swings the nutmeg holder, back & forth, American, 4¾″ x 4⅛″, 19th C. **$100.00-$125.00**

Nutmeg grater, slide & pivot action, wire frame, punctured tin, works like trombone, wooden holding handle & small wooden knob on foller that holds nutmeg against grating surface; made over a long time period with various knobs & handles, some stained green. Nutmeg could be moved "forward and back, and from side to side, preventing the grated Nutmeg adhering to the surface of the Grater and bringing every part of its surface into use", said 1892 ad. "The Edgar," mfd. by Edgar Mfg. Co., Reading, MA, 5⅞″L, pat'd Aug. 18, 1891. • These were pat'd (as a variation of 1891 nutmeg grater of George H. Thomas, Chicopee Falls, MA) by Charles E. Damon, of Edgar & Damon. • Classic.— As I reported last time, these have reached their limit I think, & price seems to have stabilized. Most are at lower level of this range. **$65.00-$85.00**

Nutmeg grater, spring-loaded tin cylinder for nutmeg set at right angles to cranked grating disc, skinny tin tubular handle, attached with even narrower tubes, "The H. Carsley", pat'd by H. Carsley, Lynn, MA, 3½″L, disk nearly 3″ diameter, (one without date is 4″L), pat'd Nov. 20, 1855, but made while "patent applied for". • An

anonymous **tip on grating nutmegs** appears in Aug. 1851 *American Agriculturist* , viz. "If a person began to grate a nutmeg at the stalk end, it will prove hollow throughout; whereas the same nutmeg, grated on the other end, would have proved sound and solid to the last. This circumstance may thus be accounted for: The centre of a nutmeg consists of a number of fibres issuing from the stalk and its continuation through the centre of the fruit, the other ends of which fibres, though closely surrounded and pressed by the fruit, do not adhere to it. When the stalk is grated away, those fibres, having lost their hold, gradually drop out, and the nutmeg appears hollow; as more of the stalk is grated away, others drop out in succession, and the hollow continues through the whole nut by beginning at the contrary end, the fibres above mentioned are grated off at their core end, with the surround fruit, and do not drop out and cause a hole."
$160.00-$180.00

Nutmeg grater, squeeze action, 2 halves consisting of tube with spring-held presser for nutmeg, & a curved backplate that has a curved rasping surface fixed at the bottom at right angles. This back plate is held against the palm, the fingers squeeze the cylinder with the 'meg — causing it to move back & forth along rasp. A spring is also in the pivot & assists "the grasping and relaxation of the fingers." German (?), about 5½"L, pat'd c.1902.
$40.00-$50.00

Nutmeg grater, tall tin pocket grater, side unfolds & reveals grating surface, American (?), 2¾"H, 3rd quarter 19th C.
$90.00-$120.00

Nutmeg grater, tin, a nail, spring & wood, oil can shape, 3¼"H, late 19th or early 20th C.
$90.00-$100.00

Nutmeg grater, tin body, round grating disc, wood handle & presser that holds 'meg against grater, black paper label with gold lettering, "Brown & Hasler", Lynn, MA, 7"L, "patent applied for", c.1870s to 1890s. • Several companies made nutmeg graters in Lynn, MA, but Lynn's largest industry by far were the 150 ladies' shoe factories, which in 1870 employed 20,000 people.
$120.00-$150.00

Nutmeg grater, tin, cigar cylinder with "chimney" nutmeg holder, wood knob, American, 4¾"L, late 19th or early 20th C.
$110.00-$130.00

Nutmeg grater, tin, cigar cylinder with "chimney" nutmeg holder, wood knob slightly fancier than other shorter one, grating surface differs too, American, 5⅜"L, late 19th or early 20th C.
$110.00-$130.00

Nutmeg grater, tin, combination grater, pie crimper & can opener, American, 19th C. • "**General Directions for Making Cake.**— When cake or pastry is to be made, take care not to make trouble for others by scattering materials, and soiling the table or floor, or by needless use of many dishes. Put on a large and clean apron, roll your sleeves above the elbows, tie something over your head lest hair may fall, take care that your hands are clean, and have a basin of water and a clean towel on hand. Place everything you will need on the table, butter your pans, grate your nutmegs and squeeze your lemons. Then break your eggs, each in a cup by itself, lest adding a bad one should spoil the whole. Make your cake in wood or earthen, and not in tin." Mrs. Mary Hooker Cornelius, *The Young Housekeeper's Friend*, Boston, 1846.• Twenty years after this, even longer, people were dying after being operated on by medical doctors who didn't know enough about the causes of sepsis and infection to wear clean

coveralls, cover their hair, or wash their hands or instruments. It's too bad doctors didn't learn from cookbooks.
$65.00-$75.00

Nutmeg grater, tin, looks like Mississippi steam boat, round tin bottom, sliding, spring-loaded hopper for nutmeg, little hanging wire loop, no mark, 6¼"L, late 19th C.
$95.00-$125.00

Nutmeg grater, tin, loopy wire handle, cast iron with cast iron crank, big grating disc, American, 7"L, pat'd March 9, 1886.
$75.00-$100.00

Nutmeg grater, tin, mechanical type like small Boye, but has wood knob on nutmeg housing, marked "The Del," American, 19th C.
$90.00-$120.00

Nutmeg grater, tin & nickel plated spring metal holds nutmeg in place, swings back & forth, mark stamped on back in the tin, "M. H. Sexton", Utica, NY, 4¾"L x 3"W, pat'd May 1896.
$100.00-$125.00

Nutmeg grater, tin, oblong shallow piece with diagonal grating surface and with turned wooden end. Turned wooden nutmeg 'barrel' has small wooden presser tamp that must be held against the nutmeg. The 'barrel' slides on diagonal or transverse tracks (actually kittycorner) over grater, gratings fall out front. See also the "Monitor" grater. "Unique", Steel Edge Stamping & Retinning Co., Boston, MA, advertised in 1892 (maybe. before); poss. rip-off of 1889 "Monitor".
$125.00-$140.00

Nutmeg grater, tin, simple crank mechanism, "H. Carsley", Lynn, MA, 3⅞"L, late 19th C "patent applied for". • It is always possible with "**pat apple**" (as Bob Cahn says), pieces, that a patent was never granted. Examiners in the patent office were always complaining how silly some submitted ideas were, and how they exhibited no new (and therefore patentable) mechanisms or design, and in fact, how many of them didn't work. By putting "patent applied for" on your goods, however, you put a mantle of respectability on your item, and perhaps a tiny measure of protection, though the notion that someone else might copy your unpatentable invention is wishful thinking. • Mystery writer Margery Allingham had her detective Albert Campion muse in *Flowers For the Judge* (a highly recommended mystery), while looking at a strange old key, that it "was squat and heavy and had that curious unsatisfactory appearance which is peculiar to old-fashioned patent devices which have never been really successful."
$160.00-$180.00

Nutmeg grater, tin, small box grater, oblong shape with flat side almost completely covered with grating surface, large hanging hole, pat'd by W. Bradley, Lynn, MA, pat'd Jan. 29, 1867. • **1867, a Grate Year** — The Bradley almost starts the year off for nutmeg graters. But **(1)** patent was granted Jan. 8, 1867, to L. V. Badger, Chicago, IL.; **(2)** granted Bradley; **(3)** granted March 5, to J. A. Hooper, South Berwick, ME; **(4) & (5)** granted July 16, to R. H. Chinn, Washington, DC, and to C. A. Durgin, NYC, NY; **(6)** granted July 23, to R. W. Whitney & J. P. Davis, South Berwick, ME; **(7)** granted Aug. 6, to L. Von Froben, Washington, DC; **(8)** granted Sept. 3, to A. S. Skillin and G. W. Reed, Portland, ME; **(9)** granted Sept. 24, to C. Worden, Binghamton, NY; and **(10)** Dec. 17, to W. W. Owen and D. Kelly. I have not been able to find out what was the impetus in that year. Of 27 nutmeg patents granted up through 1873, 10 were 1867 (plus the cap on

another), 2 were 1866, and 4 were 1868, leaving only 11 from 1854 (the earliest specific nutmeg grater) through 1873. I tried to check tariffs, cookbooks, periodicals, but nothing popped out as significant. Any ideas?
$110.00-$125.00

Nutmeg grater, tin, spring-loaded boxed housing for nutmeg tracks along edges of oblong grating surface, "The Boye," Boye Needle Co., American, about 6"L, pat'd Sept. 22, 1914.
$75.00-$90.00

Nutmeg grater, tin & varnished turned wood (also found with wood part stained a sort of pinky-red color), rectangular grating plate, set in braced tin frame with turned wooden end. A little straight-sided nutmeg holder with wooden screw-top, is slid back & forth over grater along diagonal edge track. Printed with direction "Press Down Lightly". See also the "Unique" grater. identified in old ads as "The Monitor", Boston, MA, 4½"L x 1¹⁵⁄₁₆"W, pat'd March 18, 1889 in circle on lid of 'meg holder. • The name 'Monitor' may appear on paper label, if any such remain, distributed or possibly even mfd. by New England Novelty Manufacturing Co., which in 1890 was apparently the only manufacturer of nutmeg graters. I suppose by that time, powdered nutmeg in tins had pretty much obviated the need for the graters. $165.00-$200.00

Nutmeg grater, tin & wire, "New Rapid", mfd by Hamlin & Russell Mfg. Co., Worcester, MA, came in 2 sizes, small and large, pat'd Dec. 26, 1877.
$45.00-$55.00

Nutmeg grater, tin & wire, curved quadrant grating surface, spring-loaded nutmeg holder with blue painted wooden foller or plunger moves in arc over grater, looks like rocket launcher, American, about 5" (hard to measure this shape), 19th C.
$120.00-$150.00

Nutmeg grater, tin & wire, strap handle, launching cylinder with spring-loaded wooden foller, wire crank with small wood knob, about 6¼"L diagonally.
$120.00-$150.00

Nutmeg grater, tin & wire, "Will grate four times faster than any other yet made", "Yankee No. 1", mfd by Hamlin & Russell Mfg. Co., Worcester, MA, c.1884.
$45.00-$55.00

Nutmeg grater, tin, with musical note-shaped hollow tin handle with ovoid hinged lid covering nutmeg storage & grating chamber. Only marking: "Press lightly". 7½"L, late 19th C.
$95.00-$125.00

Nutmeg grater, tin & wood, long square body with works at one end, nutmeg storage at other end has tin cap & little wooden knob on top to pull back spring-loaded pressure foot, wire crank on side turns grating cylinder against nutmeg, "Standard", Standard Co, Boston, 6⅛"L, marked pat'd Dec. 25, 1877; (re-?) introduced to trade in July 1890. • Although a date is stamped on this grater, a patent search fails to turn this one up. The so-called patent date sometimes turns out to be the date the application was filed for consideration, but no nutmeg grater was patented in 1878 (or 1877 either). The 25th was on a Tuesday in 1877. •This was identified as the "Rajah" grater when advertised in Simmons Hardware Co.'s 1885 catalog.
$110.00-$125.00

Nutmeg grater, turned wood, 3 part, little cup with knobbed lid which is fitted with punctured tin grating surface; lower part is fitted with the same (the nutmeg is rubbed between the 2 graters by twisting the top back & forth), & the grated nutmeg goes into bottom, poss. American, prob. English, 6"H, mid 19th C. $175.00-$200.00

Nutmeg grater, turned wood, bottle shape, meg container has screwed-on lid, rasp on end, English (?), 2½"L, 19th C.
$225.00-$260.00

Nutmeg grater, turned wood with punctured tin disc, very nice screwed-on springy wood pressure foot, pat'd by A. S. Skillin and G. W. Reed, Portland, ME, 6⅞"L, pat'd Sept. 3, 1867.
$110.00-$125.00

Nutmeg grater, wood knob & tin body, black & red paper label still attached, "The Little Rhody," American, late 19th C.
$75.00-$85.00

Nutmeg grater, wood, tin, spring-loaded, 6¼"L, late 19th C
$75.00-$90.00

Nutmeg grater, wood, tin & wire, long wooden piece with wire & wood piece to hold nutmeg against rather big grating disc, crank comes out of center of disc, paper label on long wood piece, "Common Sense" grater, invented by R. W. Whitney & J. P. Davis, not necessarily made by the inventors, who lived in South Berwick, ME, 5¼"L, pat'd July 23, 1867.
$150.00-$170.00

Nutmeg grater, wooden rectangular block with turned wood handle at one end, crank in one side, wooden pusher knob in top, revolving punctured tin grater drum at end away from handle, no mark, 6½"L, late 19th C.
$135.00-$155.00

Nutmeg grater & cookie cutter combined—See Mold chapter.

Orange juicer, mechanical, cast iron, oak base painted a dark brown, lever action, definitely for oranges not lemons, no maker, 9½"H, pat'd Jan. 31, 1886.
$200.00-$225.00

Orange peeler, small, curved steel blade with painted turned wooden handle. Held in the right hand, the blade is slipped under the peel & is drawn toward the thumb while the orange is turned with the other hand. (Works same way as successful 1980's orange peeler made by a man in the Midwest, featured on '60 Minutes' & sold through mail.) Mfd by Robert S. West, Cleveland, OH, c.1890.
$5.00-$8.00

Oyster knife, fish shaped metal, poss. CT, 19th C.
$20.00-$25.00

Oyster knife, one piece of cast tool steel, square handle so it wouldn't slip easily, sword-like blade, prying edges thin but not sharp, 'Stortz & Son,' Philadelphia, PA, early 20th C.
$25.00-$30.00

Paring knife, steel blade, wooden handle & brass bolster (a bolster on a knife is like a ferrule on a tool), handle marked 'POTATO,' American (?), 6"L, 20th C. • **German vocabulary** — Schalen-messer: paring knife (for vegetables & fruit).
$45.00-$65.00

Pastry knife, a form of dough scraper & cutter, sometimes called a chopping knife & probably used as such, this type for dividing dough for loaves of bread, for example, or for scraping pastry board. This one is made of a single wide piece of steel, top edge rolled to form a cylindrical handle, no finger cutout, American, 4½"H x 5"W, TOC. • **German vocabulary** — Teigmesser: pastry knife.
$12.00-$18.00

Pea sheller, cast iron, screw clamps, 2 sided to split the pod, goes through rollers to pop peas out, marked only with date, but pat'd by S. Ustick, Philadelphia, PA, May 5, 1868. • See a Knife sharpener entry in Dishwashing & Care chapter.
$55.00-$85.00

Pea sheller, galvanized cast iron, screw clamp, downturned spout releases shelled peas, angled hopper on top, hook at bottom of frame holds small pail to catch (we wonder how well) the shells as they were expelled from rear of cranked machine, "Acme," Acme Pea Sheller Co., NYC, 7"H, patent applied for c.1880s-1890s. • **"Puree of Peas.**— Wash a pint of green peas in cold water; then put them in a saucepan with boiling water and cook 20 minutes. Have them dry when done. Press through a colander. Boil one half pint milk, add a small onion, three or four cloves and a small sprig of parsley. Rub a tablespoon each of flour and butter together. Strain the milk over the peas, put back in saucepan, stir in the flour and butter, and let boil, stirring to prevent sticking. Season with salt and pepper and serve." *Ladies Home Journal*, April 1890. • **"Pea Fritters.**— Boil a pint of green peas until tender. Mash them while hot and rub through a colander. Season with pepper, salt and a tablespoon of butter. Let cool, add the yolks of two well-beaten eggs, a cup of cream, one teacupful and a half of flour, and a half teaspoon of soda and one of cream of tartar, sifted several times with the flour. Stir and beat well. When ready to use, beat in the white of the eggs and fry, a spoonful at a time, in boiling lard." (Ibid .) **$65.00-$80.00**

Pea sheller, sheet metal painted green, rubber feet, crank with yellow wooden knob, you roll pea pods between 2 black hard rubber rollers; presumably pods pop & peas patooie out the chute, decal label, "Holmes Pea-Sheller", Holmes Mfg. Co., Los Angeles, CA, 5¼"L, patent pending, c.1910s to 1930s. **$40.00-$50.00**

Peach parer, cast iron on long wooden board base, has 2 forks, opposing each other; the "large fork turns the peach, the small one turns upon the rod like a swivel when the peach is turned, and serves to hold up the outer end of the peach. The stone in each peach prevents the peach from being pushed on to one fork and held by that alone." mfd. by David H. Whittemore, successor to Whittemore Brothers, Worcester, MA, 1860s. • "The above machine," continues an 1868 ad, "is also superior for paring potatoes, and even when the potato is long and wilted, it works complete, the small or outer fork serving to hold up the outer end of the potato while it is being pared. It is also a good apple paring machine — the use of the small or sliding fork being dispensed with." Whittemore, earlier of Chicopee Falls, MA, also was issued apple parer & slicer patents. • **Peter Piper Peeled a Peck of Peaches.**— I have at hand the Sept. 15, 1866 issue of the weekly "*Alexandria Price Current Letter-Sheet*", a flimsy-paper report on market prices of goods from Agricultural Implements to Wamsutta cotton prints, from Ale to Shingles, published by Knox & Wattles, Forwarding & Commission Merchants, of Alexandria, VA. A run of them for a year would be more interesting, but still, there are some tidbits. For example, "DRIED FRUIT — Demand dull. Tendency downwards. We quote: PEACHES peeled ....17 at 20¢ per lb. (17 lbs at 20¢ each) PEACHES not peeled ....11 at 12 APPLES ....10 at 11." It was worth peeling peaches, in other words. As a comparative, 50 lbs of new potatoes cost 60¢ whereas sweet potatoes were $8 a bushel, and New Orleans molasses was $1.30 a gallon! **$85.00-$100.00**

Peach parer, cast iron, screw clamps, "Lightning," D. H. Goodell Co., Antrim, NH, a county fair winner in the fall of 1869, but pat'd May 10, 1870. • **Finding patent dates** is sometimes hard, but it's fun. This one eluded me at first,

but then I found, under "Parer, Fork for peach", in the Subject Index to Patents, two patents with the right dates, which were for the 4 pronged fork that slips into end of peach and sort of cradles the pit or stone. They were awarded to C. D. House, Lake Village, NH, on Aug. 17, 1869, and to D. H. Goodell, Antrim, NH, May 10, 1870. Otherwise, the machine itself is like the Lightning apple parer. • In the *American Agriculturist*, June 1872, there is this about a peach parer: "A continuous and urgent inquiry for a machine for Paring Peaches, has been <u>ringing in our ears from all Peach-growing sections, for the past five years</u>, and in response to this universal appeal, the manufacturers of the Lightning & Turn-Table Apple Parers have at last succeeded in obtaining and securing a device for Holding and Paring Peaches, which is as practical and economical as the Apple Parer, and cannot fail to come into immediate and general use." • An ad in the same magazine, a year earlier, shows a detailed linecut of the Lightning Peach Parer, with the half round horizontal gear, clearly shown with patent date of Aug. 17, 1869. • I reread a letter from collector Evelyn Welch, from Sept. 1983, exactly six years later, and found something I must have missed before. She writes, about a non-mechanical handheld peach pitter "Sometime take a peach pitter, cut a ring around a clingstone peach with a knife, beginning at the stem hole, following the line across the peach. Take the proper sized pitter for that sized peach, slip it into the peach around the pit with the line on the peach on your left, turn pitter to side, then back around under pit, and the top will slip off. Then scoop the pit out of other half. Seems the pit has a ledge on the side and this is the professional way I was taught to cut clings at the Pacific Peach Co. Cannery (now Hunt Wesson) in Oakdale, California, when I was 16 years old (1930) and proudly earned $6.00 per day. We wore white cotton gloves in case the pitter slipped. We would 'ring' a lugbox of clings with the knife, then pit them by the box. What I'm getting at is the story behind the need for a tool to remove pits. Pear pitting is different altogether." **$75.00-$90.00**

Peach parer—See Apple parer & peach parer.

Peanut shucker, wood, 2 part mill, turned on an axle by means of fancy turned handlebar-like handle. American, 19"D grinding surfaces, mid 19th C. **$250.00-$325.00**

Pepper mill, turned maple, in shape of wine bottle, with "laser engraved" label depicting a vineyard, works in guise of corkscrew with T handle, grounds come out bottom, sold through Bloomingdales in 1983 catalog, 1980s. **$35.00-$45.00**

Pineapple eye snips, cast iron painted black, scissor action with attached steel blades, one a sort of scoop beak with sharp tapered end, other an open oval, with sharp top edge nearest scoop part, W. H. Collins, NYC, 5⅝"L,1930 ad, prob. made before that. **$8.00-$12.00**

Pineapple eye snips, looks like small pair of scissors; one hardened steel blade terminates in small spoon, other has a hollow cutter that fits into spoon bowl — as the inventor put it — "adapted to engagement with each other accurately, somewhat like the beak of parrot or an eagle", pat'd by John F. Pack, on Aug. 27, 1901. **$12.00-$18.00**

Pineapple eye snips, or eye clips, nickeled steel curved cylinder, sort of with a pistol grip, with trigger near front that you pull to make top part of little cutter clip out the eye, "Patterson's", mfd by M. E. Mosher, Rochester, NY, c.1905. **$8.00-$12.00**

Pineapple eye snips, or pineapple eyer, simple turned wood handle, triggered snip with spring to return to starting position, one fixed piece like tiny cone, open along top side, which would be stabbed under the pineapple eye, before pulling trigger to cause cutter blade to come forward & slip into top of eye, completing the small conical excision, "Dixie", mfd by W. H. Glenny & Co., Rochester, NY, 5½"L, patent applied for c.1904. **$12.00-$18.00**

Poppyseed mill, green painted iron, screw clamps, "Kosmos," 20th C. • Cumberland General Store offers a new $35.00 poppyseed mill with white enameled screw clamp frame, "hand ground steel milling cone." **$30.00-$40.00**

Poppyseed mill, turquoise green painted cast iron, spun brass hopper, screw clamps to table, "Standard," prob. PA, by the cherry pitter company, in Mt. Joy, 9¼"H, c.1890s. **$28.00-$40.00**

Potato chip machine, "machined steel with spring steel knife and lasts indefinitely" ... "unexcelled for slicing potatoes, carrots, beets, onions or any vegetable or fruit...", black enameled handle, mfd by Mebhut & Platts, Ilion, NY, 8⅜"L, "patent pending" c. 1920s (?). • $2.00 was original cost. **$12.00-$15.00**

Potato cutter, stamped tin, counter top, for making french fries, "Maid of Honor", American, 1930s (?). • See also the whatzit cutter at end of Mold & Shape chapter. **$5.00-$7.00**

Potato french fry cutter or Saratoga chipper, tin cylinder with a cutting frame (like a tic tac toe game) to do 25 french fries or Saratogas at a time, "Silver's Sure-Cut," 4"H, TOC. **$20.00-$30.00**

Potato & fruit press, what other makers called a ricer, japanned malleable cast iron frame, handle & lever handle, heavily tinned plunger & perforated cup removable for cleaning, marked on top handle or lever is "Silver & Co., NY"; "Genuine Silver Press" on lower handle, Brooklyn, NY, one size only, claimed to be "the largest and most powerful", c.1880-1910. • Silver & Co. claimed in early 20th C catalog, to be "originators of the hand press and have for 30 years maintained its quality and steadily decreased its price." **$18.00-$25.00**

Potato masher, heavy twisted wire, wooden handle, American, 22½"L, large hotel or restaurant size, 20th C. **$22.00-$30.00**

Potato masher, long turned handle with little round mushroom or button end, heavy round steel head, flat disc with perforated holes in small & medium size, "Hercules", mfd by Handy Things Co., Ludington, MI, c.1904. **$12.00-$18.00**

Potato masher, turned upright wooden handle, flat mashing head of nickeled iron wire woven into intricate openwork 'snowflake', 'web', or 'gear wheel' head of heavy wire, It is particularly referred to by Parloa, as follows: "Many housekeepers prefer the kind of potato masher shown below to the wooden one. In unskilled hands it gives a lighter dish of potatoes than the wooden masher, but the wooden one will be needed for other things which the wire one would not answer." Maria Parloa, *Kitchen Companion*, Boston, 1887. American, 9"L, c.1880s to 1900. **$10.00-$20.00**

Potato masher, turned wooden handle, heavy wire, double action: push on handle & upper set of wires goes down, A & J, Binghamton, NY, 11¼"H down to 9½"H, pat'd 1912. • In 1984 there was a UPI story about an artist named Byron Randall who ran a bed & breakfast in Tomales, CA, & decorated the B&B with his collection of 384 potato mashers. Now there's a goal for you collectors! **$30.00-$40.00**

Potato masher, turned wooden handle, mashing head is 2 heavy wire flat spirals, American, 10"L, c.1920s-30s. • *Americana magazine* in Sept./Oct. 1984, & the Washington Post in 1986 did articles on a **Potato Museum** opened by schoolteacher Tom Hughes, first with about 100 mashers, 50 peelers, 40 potato cookbooks, 2000 potato recipes, jewelry & art made from potatoes, etc. In 1984, Hughes was searching for a complete original "Mr. Potato Head" game; by 1986 he had one. He also started publishing "Peelings", a monthly newsletter. The museum was in Washington through 1989, but in Nov. 1989 I saw on TV that Hughes was planning to move to "a new community". Watch collector papers for announcements.. **$15.00-$18.00**

Potato masher, turned wooden handle, twisted wire arch with 2 rows of 4 curvy zigzags, Kilbourne Mfg. Co., Troy, NY, c.1908. **$22.00-$30.00**

Potato masher, turned wooden handle with round palm-fitting knob at end, with nickeled iron L shape masher blade with 2 rows of long slots cut lengthwise, bent at right angles to the handle, Androck "potato ricer", mfd by Washburn Co., Worcester, MA, 9½"L, c.1936. • **Reproduction alert.** — That was an updated version of a somewhat older one. But another story concerns Virginia Nicoll of Meridith, NH, and her MMPM Company (My Mother's Potato Masher). She started in 1984 making a "reproduction" of the tool, which she says her grandmother "purchased from an itinerant peddler in rural Pennsylvania back in the 1800s." In my opinion, this masher dates back to the 1890s at the earliest, although MMPM ads say "patent circa 1882". Anyway, the Nicolls had a tool and die company make the mashing plate of carbon steel, with turned birch wood handle, and they have received a lot of publicity and enjoyed great sales. I have no idea how many of the original 10,000 ordered from the die-maker have been sold, or if they are now into the hundreds of thousands. **$10.00-$14.00**

Potato masher, wires bent in shape of fingers, looks like glove dryer, 2 tiers of fingers set 20 degrees or so on horizontal plane, white wood turned handle, A & J, Binghamton, NY, 11"L, 20th C. **$15.00-$18.00**

Potato masher, zigzag wire with long turned wooden handle, commercial size one, 22"L, 20th C. **$25.00-$30.00**

Potato masher—See Eggbeater & potato masher.

Potato mashers, wire & wood, various designs from a flat spiraled head, or a wire grid, to a slightly rocking set of 8 fingers stamped of steel or a criss-cross of loosely strung wires, most with wooden handles, some few have nickeled iron loop handles, American or German, most about 8" to 10"H, late 19th or early 20th C. • "**Imitation Spaghetti.**— Boil and mash potatoes, adding salt and butter, but only a tablespoonful of milk, as you want a stiff paste. Rub this through a colander into a buttered pie or pudding dish. It will fall in small, pipe-like shapes. Leave them as they lie, and, when all the potato has

passed through, set the dish on the upper grating of the oven to brown delicately." Marion Harland, *House & Home, a Complete Housewife's Guide*, Philadelphia, 1889.
$10.00-$20.00

Potato peeler, looks like lathe-style apple parer, tiny paring blade, cast iron frame, turn the handle, stick potato on spade like prong that rotates, "Nu-Way Automatic", mfd by Guaranty Products Co., St. Louis, MO, early 20th C.
$65.00-$80.00

Potato peeler, tin with gritty composition that literally sands off the peeling. Looks like a shallow oval tart pan with crimped edges, filled with the grit compo cement, with a bracket strap handle across back, "Hamlinite Peeler," maker not known, 4½"L x 2¼"W, pat'd July 20, 1920; prob. made for fewer than 10 years. •"**Silver Pie.**— Peel and grate one large white potato into a deep plate; add the juice and grated rind of one lemon, the beaten white of one egg, one teacup of white sugar, and one teacup of cold water. Pour this into a nice undercrust and bake. When done, have ready the whites of three eggs well beaten, half a cup of powdered sugar, a few drops of rose-water, all thoroughly beaten. Put this mixture on the top of the pie evenly and return to the oven, to stiffen a few moments. When sent to the table just cold lay a spoonful of currant jelly on the center of each piece to ornament if you wish." Mrs. M. L. Scott, *Home Cook Book*, 1876.
$10.00-$15.00

Potato peeler, tin with wooden handle, "Morton Salt Potato Peeler," 20th C. • **Onion peelers** are valuable but not collectible. "The earliest onion peeler I know about wore a gingham apron and sat on a chair while she peeled the onions and cried." Henry Landis, Landis Valley (PA) Museum, in response to a query in the Early American Industries "*Chronicle*", April 1951.
$10.00-$15.00

Potato ricer, red paint enameled malleable iron lever handles, tinned perforated cup, tinned metal presser, mfd by Handy Things, Ludington, MI, about 12"L, c.1940s.
$8.00-$12.00

Potato slicer, cast iron, clamps to table, potatoes fed horizontally into cranked blade disc, c.1870s.
$100.00-$125.00

Potato slicer, cast iron, tabletop, 3 knee-bent legs attached to large round slicer housing, with potato size hopper & tall vertical shaft with crank to turn blade inside, a plate could be set underneath to catch the slices of potato (or other raw root vegetables), mfd by W. L. & T. M'Clinton (?) or W. L. & T. M. Clinton, (sold in early 20th C by V. Clad & Sons), Ithaca, NY, about 15" diameter, pat'd Oct. 1-?, 187-?. (Looks like Oct. 10, 1876.
$95.00-$125.00

Potato slicer, clamp on, high cast iron frame with diamond cutouts, stanchion divides into 2 arms to take shaft for crank, the other end of which is stuck into the potato, the blade is fixed at table level, supposed to slice a potato into one long continuous spiral (although it would fall apart before it could ever get as long as the old advertising picture), advertised for making Saratoga chips or cucumber garnishes, "Saratoga Potato Peeler & Slicer", Goodell Co., Antrim, NH, pat'd 1870, 1871.
$85.00-$100.00

Potato slicer, iron mounted on wood, potato stuck on 'piston' is drawn toward revolving cranked slicing blade by long spring, sold by F. A. Walker, Boston, pat'd by S. Walker, NYC, June 6, 1865.
$40.00-$65.00

Quern, primitive grinding mill for seeds, grains, etc., used for the same purposes as a mortar & pestle. Small section of half a log, fitted with wooden peg feet, round hollowed out "mortar" portion with a millstone to fit, high bracket or "goalpost" frame above has rod or handle to turn the upper small millstone against the lower one, prob. Scottish, though found in 18th C American kitchens, about 12" to 14"L x 15" to 18"H overall, 18th or very early 19th C. •Dr. Samuel Johnson defined it thus: "The quern consists of two stones, about a foot and a half in diameter; the lower is a little convex, to which the concavity of the upper must be fitted. In the middle of the upper stone is a round hole, and on one side is a long handle. The grinder (person operating the quern) sheds the corn gradually into the hole with one hand, and works the handle round with the other. The corn slides down the convexity of the lower stone, and, by the motion of the upper, is ground in its passage." As quoted in Webster & Parkes, *An Encyclopedia of Domestic Economy*, 1848 NY edition of English book of 1845. **$175.00-$225.00**

Raisin seeder, 7 wires set into wood block, upright mushroom knob handle, "The Everett," Boston, 3⅛"H x 2"W, 1880s to 1890s.
$30.00-$40.00

Raisin seeder, also for grapes, tinned cast iron, screw clamps to table, giraffe neck arched frame, side crank moved a "saw disc" inside that rubbed against the raisins, small hopper with regulating device in side, rubber rollers, "will seed a pound in 5 minutes", embossed "Wet the raisins" cast in side. "Enterprise #36" family size, Enterprise Mfg. Co., 11"H, hopper 2½" x 2⅛", pat'd April 2 & Aug. 20, 1895; still being sold into 20th C. The No. 38, twice as expensive and somewhat larger, was for hotels, bakeries, restaurants, etc. **$25.00-$40.00**

Raisin seeder, black knobby turned wood handle, tinned ferrule, 7 closeset tinned wire needles enclosed in a ring with wire, American, 3½"L, business part is 1¼"L, late 19th C. • Date stamped on end of handle is clearly May 2. Then a date which appears either to be 1888 or 1883 (perhaps it is 1893?) A raisin seeder was pat'd May 2, 1871, by W. Curtiss, Jr., of Wolcottville, CT...this may be his. Perhaps an extension or an improvement (such as the adding of 5 more wires) of the patent was granted, and a new name "Columbian" given as a deliberate tie-in with the World's Columbian Exposition, of 1893. (May 2 came on a Tuesday in 1882 and 1893, but no raisin seeders were patented then.) • Very similar is the "Columbian Raisin Seeder", with knobbed & turned wooden handle, tin ferrule and 12 wires, and it was made in the 1890s.
$30.00-$40.00

Raisin seeder, cast iron, 4 legs, levered press has 8 wires, no maker mark, American, approx. 6"L, pat'd May 7, 1895.
$45.00-$60.00

Raisin seeder, cast iron, clamps to table, "EZY Raisin Seeder," with message to "Scald the Raisins," cast into frame, 5"H exclusive of wingnut, pat'd May 21, 1899.
• All I can say is, thank heaven for seedless grapes.
$35.00-$50.00

Raisin seeder, cast iron, ornate, 3 legs, beautifully cast with grapes & leaves, cranked wheel, sits on table. (What is probably a later casting of this seeder was nickel plated. Price now about the same.) This was in F. A. Walker dealer catalog, American (?) or maybe French — see quote below. Only 6½"H x 4"W, c.1870. • "A few days ago," wrote an editor in *American Agriculturist*, Nov. 1871, "we saw in a store a little machine which looks like a bit of European workmanship. It had a crank, and when that was turned there were all sorts of motions, evidently intended to accomplish something, but what that was we could not guess. Here was a pretty position for an editor of a household department, not to know at sight what a household implement was for. But we had our compensation. We took possession of the little machine and submitted it to one after another at the offices. At last came Mr. Judd (publisher), who has the quickest eye for 'crinkums' and the sharpest mechanical talent of any one within our knowledge. He turned the machine, looked at it in all ways, then gave up. This ingenious machine is for removing the seeds from raisins, and we have had it figured as an illustration of the wonderful mechanical ingenuity that is at work to facilitate the simple operations of the household. Every housekeeper knows that raisins are all the better for being stoned, and she also knows how tedious is the operation when performed in the ordinary manner. With this machine, the stoning is performed with comparative rapidity. It has so many parts and so many movements, that it is not easy to represent it in a drawing. The machine being fastened to the table by a clamp, the raisins are pushed one by one upon the grating. The crank being turned, the plate above comes down and holds it in place; then another plate, which contains numerous blunt needles which pass through holes in the second plate is pressed down. These needles punch out the seeds of the raisins through the grating, and to make sure that they will be removed, there works underneath this grating a blunt knife, moved by a notch on the moving wheel as it is cranked. As the driving wheel revolves, an arm comes over and pushes the seeded raisin away to make room for another. We are aware that this may seem to be complicated when shown in an engraving, but if one sees the machine in operation it appears simple enough." Thanks, I think I'll pit prunes instead. **$100.00-$160.00**

Raisin seeder, cast iron, painted black, screw clamps to table, spring tension lever action, levered part has 5 rows of prickers, then then there's a moving plate with 5 slots through which prickers fit, then a plate with oval opening with one divider across short axis, finally a fixed flat plate against which prickers hit, no mark, American, about 5"H x 6¾"L handle, "patent applied for" late 19th C.

• **"Indian Chutney.**— For this boil 1½ dozen sour apples, peeled, cored and chopped, in 3 pints of cider vinegar, adding a pound of stoned and chopped raisins, 1 pound light brown sugar, 1 tablespoon salt, ¼ pound finely chopped ginger root, ¼ pound chopped onions, chopped garlic clove, ½ pound mustard seed that has been heated in oven, and either a small fiery pepper chopped, or a shake or two of cayenne. Cook until apple is soft, stirring constantly." *The Housewife*, Nov. 1909. **$75.00-$90.00**

Raisin seeder, cast iron, wire & rubber, screw clamps to table, not so elegant as the Enterprise, "Lightning," American, 7¼"H, pat'd 1895 & March 28, 1898.
$20.00-$30.00

Raisin seeder, cast iron with "38 different parts", screw clamps to & arches over table, for a tray & a tumbler to fit underneath, long crank handle, X-Ray Raisin Seeder Co., American, 1880s. • A flyer states "The Seeder That Seeds! Finds Every Seed and Removes It! This is a model machine, composed of 38 different parts put together as

true and perfect as a watch, not a single part can possibly get out of order. It will seed raisins as fast as you can drop them into the hopper and turn the crank. When we say seed, we mean it will remove every single seed! It will simply perforate the raisin and not cut it into shreds or mutilate it, every seed will come out dry and without the slightest waste. Talk about perfection — this machine is the very acme of it. ... We will replace any defective part free of charge any time within five years!" The original price was a dollar. **$45.00-$60.00**

Raisin seeder, iron, "The Gem," Auburn, ME, 1895 patent. (Another one, slightly lower in value, is marked "Improved Gem.") **$50.00-$60.00**

Reamer, cast aluminum, pours out either side, "Wearever E-12-1", mfd by Ebaloy Inc., Rockford, IL, 6"H, 20th C. **$5.00-$8.00**

Reamer, for citrus fruit, clear molded glass, saucer bowl & ribbed reamer cone, "Ideal", American, pat'd Jan. 31, 1888. **$20.00-$30.00**

Reamer, for oranges, lemons, limes, heavy molded glass, wide lipped saucer with flat tab handle, very pointed conical reamer in center with 3 edges or "blades" full length, & 3 short ones, Easley No. 4, William F. Easley Mfg. Co., NYC, NY, 1909. **$30.00-$40.00**

Reamer, for oranges, lemons, limes, 1-piece molded glass saucer & rounded conical reamer with 4 long "blades" or sharp edges from top to bottom, plus 7 little pyramidal points in each of 4 sections, no handle, basket pattern & rope border, Easley Mfg. Co., c.1902. **$30.00-$40.00**

Reamer, green plastic, "Ex-Squeeze-It", mfd by B C M, marked "D. R. G. M.", German, 5¼" diameter, patent #362187, c.1930s. **$7.00-$12.00**

Reamer, & lipped pouring bowl which it fits into, clear glass, painted flowers, "Baby's Orange" on bowl, American, TOC. **$25.00-$35.00**

Reamer, molded glass, conical reamer has blades or sharp edges & pointed projections in waffled pattern, base has holes, edge fits over tumbler, juice goes through holes, "Easley No. 2A", Easley Mfg. Co., early 20th C, they discontinued this non-saucer style by 1910. **$35.00-$45.00**

Reamer, wall mounted, cast aluminum, usually missing wall bracket, "Mason's Sealed Sweet Juicer", c.1930s. **$8.00-$12.00**

Reamer & lemon slicer, die molded red plastic, figural little chef, c.1940s to 1950s. **$5.00-$7.00**

Reamer or orange juicer, stamped aluminum, little pan with reamer cone inside, worked by rotating handle back & forth, "rotates on pivot base. Hold orange still ... swing handle!", doesn't work very well, "Kwicky", Quam-Nichols Co., Chicago, late 1940s. **$5.00-$9.00**

Reamer—See also Juicer & Lemon squeezer.

Rutabaga slicer, or root vegetable & potato slicer, iron & brass on round wooden base, a sort of brace bit tool, blade makes "French fry" slices, or Saratoga slices, no mark, American (?), 18½"H, base is 9" diameter and ⅝" thick, c.1870s (?). **$250.00-$275.00**

Sausage filler, japanned cast iron, like a curved elbow pipe with hopper & very long down-curved lever & presser at top, has long leg in back to bolt to table, short crosspiece for bolting in front, filling funnel fitted on lower end, one of three 1st pat'd by J. G. Perry, Kingston, RI, in 1859, 1860 and 1863, mfd by Peck, Stow & Wilcox, Southington, CT, 1890s. See Meat grinders too. **$100.00-$135.00**

Sausage grinder, homemade & primitive, very powerful looking, wooden box with hand forged hook latch, hinges unfortunately replaced by someone (who may have been using it right up into the 1980s) with cheapo 1950s kitchen cabinet hinges in "Colonial" hammered surface. Lift-out wooden drum inside has iron pins set in it sort of spiralling around it, on pencil marked intersections carefully drawn by maker, American, 16½"L x 8" diameter, early 19th C. **$135.00-$175.00**

Sausage grinder, iron, hangs on wall, 27"L, pat'd 1885. **$25.00-$35.00**

Sausage grinder, all wood, except for iron nails or spikes on revolving cranked drum inside, American, mid 19th C. **$120.00-$165.00**

Sausage grinder & stuffer, cast iron, 2 hinged parts, catch on side holds top on, 2 cutting blades & crank handle, bolts to table surface, needs funnel or gun fitted to end, no mark except "12", American, 7⅝"L exclusive of crank handle, about 3rd quarter 19th C. **$75.00-$90.00**

Sausage grinder & stuffer, screw clamp, tinned iron, Enterprise #38, pat'd 1888. **$40.00-$50.00**

Sausage grinder & stuffer, wood & wrought iron, tin gun, on platform meant to bridge 2 chairs, saw horses or tables; water pump-like lever works up & down to stuff casings fitted onto gun, American, 19th C. **$100.00-$135.00**

Sausage gun, mostly wood with tin gun & iron bolts holding gun together, wooden frame pegged, on bench frame, long lever makes it look like a sculpture of an elephant, according to dealer Lenny Kislin it was made on the Yantz Farm, Red Hook, NY, 26½"H x 37½"L, 19th C. • With this one you pay for sculpture. **$350.00-$400.00**

Sausage gun, tin cylinder with strap handle & small strap loop near gun end, long snout, perforations in flat end around where snout or spout is soldered, turned wooden foller or pusher, American, about 15"L exclusive of foller, c.1850s to 1860s. • A Jan. 1850 article in *American Agriculturist* told how to make an almost identical "sausage cutter", and said the meat "is made finer or coarser according to the rapidity with which it is fed" meat into the hopper. **$65.00-$80.00**

Sausage stuffer, "Hubbard," 6 qt. capacity. **$35.00-$50.00**

Sausage stuffer, cast iron, mounted to plank, cranked, "Wagner Stuffer No. 3," Salem Tool Co., Salem, OH, c.1900 from 1859 patent. • Salem also mfd meat presses, ham pumps & brine guns. **$35.00-$45.00**

Sausage stuffer, commercial size, cast iron, hand cranked, hinged top, "Wagner Stuffer" cast in body, brass plate reads "Silver Mfg. Co.", "Salem, ORE", 36"L, prob. the J. Wagner (Pittsburgh, PA) patent of March 29, 1859. **$275.00-$360.00**

Sausage stuffer, handmade, all wood, including long box & turned screw which is cranked & slowly pushes ground sausage out end, sliding lid entire length of box for cleaning, prob. PA, 25"L x 5¾" square, c.1840s to 50s. **$125.00-$160.00**

Sausage stuffer, tin & cast iron, spring loaded lever action, mounts to tabletop, shaped sort of like an urn, "Angers Perfect No. 1 Filler," Sargent & Co., late 19th C. **$40.00-$70.00**

Sausage stuffer, tin, hard maple plunger. Different size casing funnels attached by bayonet mount at end, needed 2 people or worked plunger against belly, American, each part 18"L, 19th C. **$65.00-$80.00**

Sausage stuffer, tin & wood, hand cranked, screw clamps to table, "P. S. & W. Co., No. 112," mfd by Peck, Stow & Wilcox Co., Southington, CT, 19th C. • An 1890s brochure from P, S & W gives only one No. 112 "meat cutter and stuffer", that pat'd by A. W. Hale, New Britain, CT, on March 15, 1859. It's japanned cast iron, works horizontally, has detachable tin stuffing tube, feeds into top & has lift-out cast iron grinding drum with swirled "blades". Dover Stamping Co. offered Hale's machine in a 1869 catalog. • Maybe tin version is a bit later. **$45.00-$55.00**

Sausage stuffer, pieced tin cylinder with wood foller, casings fit over "gun" end, American, 21"L, late 19th C. **$40.00-$70.00**

Sausage stuffer, fruit & lard press, japanned & decoratively stenciled heavy tin (one design being a basket of flowers), with lid, cast iron legs and vertical center threaded rod — with beveled gears & screw, came with removable corrugated "spout" or nozzle, perforated disc, interior perforated canister, #25, Enterprise Mfg. Co., Phila., canisters depicted as 4 qt. capacity, c. 16" to 18"H, pat'd July 11, 1876, still selling early 20th C. • Sizes of japanned presses.— #5 - 2 qt. rack; #15 - 2 qt. screw; #25 - 4 qt. screw; #31 - 6 qt. screw; #35 - 8 qt. screw. • Sizes of tinned presses.— #10 - 2 qt. rack; #20 - 2 qt. screw; #30 - 4 qt. screw; #40 - 8 qt. screw. "Rack" refers to cranked rack mechanism, also on central threaded shaft. **$75.00-$100.00**

Shark's tooth, petrified, dark slatey brown, roughly triangular in shape, with tiny sawtooth ridge of teeth, works perfectly to cut things up, quite easily recognizable as a naturally occuring, ad hoc saw, which works on root vegetables (and probably meat, but I don't eat it, so don't know). about 3" to 5"L, 14,000,000 years old. **$7.00-$15.00**

Shredder, metal with green wooden handle, "Lightning 3-in-1", 8"L, c.1930s or 1940s. **$9.00-$12.00**

Slaw cutters—See Cabbage cutters.

Spice boat—See Herb boat grinder.

Spice mill, cast iron, like rowboat with troughed opening at bow & wider at stern, with the effect of a seat & raised gunwhale (sides), high bootjack legs, large wheel pestle with rough wooden handles. (See also Herb boat.) prob. American, poss. PA, early 19th C. • "**To make Tomato Ketchup.** — For half a gallon take a gallon of skinned tomatoes, four table spoonfuls of salt, four of black pepper, half a spoonful of alspice, eight pods of red pepper, three table spoonfuls of mustard; grind them finely, and simmer them slowly in sharp vinegar, in a pewter basin, three or four hours, strain through a wire sieve, and bottle it closely. Those who like the article may add, after the ingredients are somewhat cool, two table spoonfuls of the juice of garlic." *The Farmers' Cabinet*, Phila., Oct. 15, 1836. **$250.00-$300.00**

Strawberry huller, like tweezers, made from a fold of spring steel, narrows toward tips then opens into concave round discs with centers cut out, mfd. by A. S. Bunker, Lawrence, MA, c.1877. • **In the Good Old Summertime.**— "A housekeeper's work lies in the house. If she has a large family, the customary three meals take about all of her time, and her daily and weekly round of work takes her full time and strength, so that she has as little inclination as opportunity to go roaming abroad for exercise.

Last summer, for the second time in eight years, I had my cook-stove in a shanty, or rought 'lean-to' shed, adjoining the house. How can I ever again be contented to spend a summer with the family cook-stove in a walled-up kitchen, being myself the family cook? No house is worth the name of home which has nowhere about it a shady porch or airy shed where a housekeeper or a hired girl can sit down in cool comfort, to shell the peas, hull the strawberries, or peel the potatoe, where she can set her ironing table, and wash her dishes without foregoing fresh breezes, and near neighborhood to grass and vines. Thoreau, who had a contempt for such treasures as most mortals love to lay up here below, observed that when a man had compassed his desire and got him a house, it seemed after all to be the house that had got him. So it is with many women — their houses keep them quite as much as they keep the houses.'' Faith Rochester, ''Home Topics'', *American Agriculturist*, June 1876. **$3.00-$5.00**

Strawberry huller, or pin feather picker, tinned spring steel pincher, ''Nip-It,'' American, 1¼''L x ⅞''W, pat'd Dec. 18, 1906. **$2.00-$3.00**

Strawberry huller, & pin feather puller, inch wide flat piece of nickel plated spring steel, bent to ''hairpin'' curve, uses pinching action, mounted on color printed cardboard with strawberry design, ''Spee-dee,'' mfd by Kenberry, American, TOC. **$3.00-$5.00**

Strawberry huller, spring steel, stamped with strawberry design, marked ''Berry Huller,'' American, about 2''L, TOC. **$3.00-$5.00**

Sugar cutter, cast iron, clamps to table edge, has 2 legs, levered action, marked ''Bartlett & Son'', Bristol, England, about 9''L, late 19th C. **$55.00-$85.00**

Sugar nippers, beautifully tooled steel, floriate design, turned knuckle guard, 9¾''L, early 19th or poss. late 18th C. **$225.00-$250.00**

Sugar nippers, cast steel, concentric rings around pin, leaf spring good, ball ends on handles, English, early 19th C. **$150.00-$170.00**

Sugar nippers, or cutters, for store counter, grain painted wood box base, double arched iron frame or blade guard & wrought steel blade with decorative finial, turned knob for drawer underneath, turned handle for cutter's lever. Punctured tin plate to ''sift'' sugar before it fell into drawer, no mark, American, 4½''H x 11⅛''L x 11⅛''W, mid 19th C. • **Loaf or Broken Sugar.**— A bill of sale from Daniel E. Bailey, a grocer of Lynchburg, VA, dated 1839, lists two types of sugar sold to John G. Merme (?). ''Loaf sugar'' and ''Broken sugar'', the latter cost half as much. (The units of each are illegible, but probably pounds)— Loaf was 20¢ a pound, and broken it was only 11¢ a pound. For cooking, the broken would have been more convenient by far; in fact, you wonder why anyone bought a whole loaf if it weren't necessary and was so much harder to use. Perhaps the fear of adulteration (intentional or insect-ional) made people want the Loaf. Other things on that interesting Bill included 20 yards of ''counterpane checks'' for $5.00, 7 yards of ''Blue Jeans'' for $1.40, a pair of ''Side Combs'' for 6¢, and 6 pounds of coffee for 90¢. **$325.00-$400.00**

Sugar nippers, steel, not finely polished, very stylized cut design at pivot, not the usual flat leaf spring but instead a pronounced S curved spring inside, American (?), 8¹³⁄₁₆''L, early 19th C. • ''Tomato Jam.''— Remove all the seeds, pull off the skins, and boil the fruit with a pound of sugar for every pound. To every pound of tomato allow two lemons, rind and pulp, well boiled.'' • ''**Apple Jam.**— Weigh equal quantities of brown sugar and good sour apples. Pare and core them, and chop them fine. Make a syrup of the sugar, and clarify it very thoroughly; then add the apples, the grated peel of two or three lemons, and a few pieces of white ginger. Boil it until the apple looks clear and yellow. This resembles foreign sweetmeats. The ginger is essential to its peculiar excellence.'' Mrs. Cornelius, *The Young Housekeepers Friend, or, A Guide to Domestic Economy & Comfort*, Boston & NY: 1846. **$175.00-$200.00**

Sugar nippers, steel, very nice lathe turning around pin pivot & handles, finger guard pin stuck at right angles to one handle, catch or keeper as well as leaf spring intact, English (?), 8½''L, late 18th C. • **Reduced value.**— The leaf spring is sometimes broken off, and often the keeper is missing. (The keeper is a catch like those found on small pruning clippers we use in the garden) **$120.00-$150.00**

Sugar nippers, heavy wrought iron, mounted on wood, brass ferrule and unusual wooden handle, English (?), early 19th C. • **Cutting Up Sugar.**— Sugar nippers were necessary because sugar came in hard molded cones, with a heavy string or cord up through the long axis like a wick, but there so that the sugar could be conveniently hung up, always wrapped in blue paper. The cones were hard and after chunks were cut or hacked off for the table, the nippers were needed to reduce the size of the pieces. I've never understood why they didn't just grate the sugar. Conical sugar molds of pottery or wood were used by pouring hot sugar syrup into them and cooling until solid. They range from about 8''H to 16''H. These molds are very rare, especially those with some intaglio decoration inside to make a pattern on the cone. • The blue paper, by the way, was recycled by soaking to get the indigo color as a dye for cloth. And for laundry blueing? ''**Soda for Washing.** — We have been requested by a correspondent, to publish the recipe for washing with Sub-carbonate of Soda. To five gallons of water add a pint and a half of soft soap and two ounces soda. Put the clothes (after soaking over night) into the mixture when at boiling heat, rubbing the parts most soiled with soap. Boil them one hour — drain — rub, and rinse them in warm water, after being put into indigo water, they are fit for drying. Half the soap and more than half the labor is saved by washing in this manner.'' *Silk Culturist*, as quoted in *The Farmers' Cabinet*, Philadelphia, Oct. 15, 1836. **$125.00-$160.00**

Sugar nippers, wrought iron, finely finished, steel leaf spring, finger guard peg, catch intact, nice curve to little gingko leaf-shaped blades, American (?), 8¾''L, late 18th or early 19th C. **$100.00-$135.00**

Sugar nippers, wrought iron, hand held, extremely simple, leaf spring still seems fine, but I wouldn't try it out, American, 9½''L, 19th C. • **German vocabulary** — Zange zum Zerkleinern von Hutzucker: Pliers for cutting sugar loaf. Zounds! Also used are Zucherzange and Zuckerknieper — sugar nipper. **$65.00-$90.00**

Sugar nippers, wrought iron, not steel, very slender & sculptural, almost insect-like in appearance, American, 11"L, 18th C. • This has the leaf spring between the handles, but I'd never dare to try it. PLEASE PLEASE PLEASE when you examine old wrought iron pieces, don't "try them out" because all tensile strength and springiness may have been lost. And while you're at it, be very careful of cast iron, as it is easily broken under certain conditions. **$150.00-$175.00**

Toffee ax or hatchet & hammer, cast iron, "For Toffee" cast into surface, English, 7⅜"L, 19th C. **$25.00-$40.00**

Tomato knife, for slicing, steel blade rather like most vegetable knives, but with tip round & wider than blade, turned wood handle, small brass bolster, marked "I*X*L Geo. Wolstenholm & Son" on blade, & chef's cap trademark containing words "Firth Stainless", "Sheffield, England", 7½"L, Reg. #747488, July 18, 1929. **$8.00-$10.00**

Tomato knife, or tomato slicer, sort of a small cleaver like tool, with turned wooden handle, stainless steel blade much shorter than other one but with even bigger round end, marked "E-B Stainless", Sheffield, England, Reg. # 809290. **$8.00-$10.00**

Tomato peeler, wood handle, scoop-like steel blade, "Ontario" stamped on handle, 20th C. • "**Tomato Figs.**— Use thoroughly ripe tomatoes; pour boiling water over them to remove the skin; weigh them; place them in a stone jar, with an equal quantity of good sugar. Let them stand two days; then pour off the syrup; boil and skim it until no scum rises. Pour it over the tomatoes; let it stand two days; boil, and skim again. After repeating this process for the third time, they are fit to dry, if the weather suits; if not, keep them in the syrup. They will dry in a week. Pack in boxes lined with white paper, putting powdered sugar between the layers of fruit. Should any syrup remain, it may be used for making common marmalade, or for sweetening pies." Mrs. A. P. Hill, *Mrs. Hill's New Family Receipt Book*, NY: 1870. **$7.00-$10.00**

Tomato slicer, cast iron, round base screws to tabletop, vertical shaft with crank on top. Tomato is put into cylindrical holder with ⅜" horizontal slots, into which fit the 6 steel blades that you crank through the holder. Cuts 7 slices. "Rapid", sold by V. Clad & Sons, Philadelphia, about 9"H, early 20th C. **$45.00-$55.00**

Vegetable chopper, long ¼" plywood box base, midway is bent basswood arch with slot the full length of it into which fits a carbon steel knife, looks very European, marked only "MARTA" which sounds Scandinavian, but Pinto's *Treen* claims this is English, 12¾"L, 20th C. **$55.00-$75.00**

Vegetable cutter, hammered sheet iron, fish-shaped footed base with hinged iron cutter blade in abstract form of animal's head, from India, 10¾"L, poss. 19th C, more prob. 20th C. • I bought this, hesitant a bit because of feeling it wasn't "right", as a 19th C. homemade American cutting tool. Found picture of one in Pease Binder's *Magic Symbols of the World* on page 97, enabling identification. **$20.00-$35.00**

Vegetable cutters, graduated set of tapered cylindrical conical cutters, in hinged tin box with conical lid, used for making decorative shapes of sliced root vegetables, there should be about 15 cutters in the box, the smallest possibly small enough to stone olives (as an early ad stated), though I'd hate to try. Seen in F. A. Walker catalog, Boston, also Harrod's Stores catalog, London — they're either American, or European, imports from 1870s. About 8"H, last quarter 19th C, poss. more recently than that. • "A set of vegetable cutters will add much to the beauty of many a dish. Should be made of best tin. Boxes of graded cutters may be had. Use for stamping out vegetables, forced meat, jellies and also are valuable for coring apples and other fruit and stoning olives." Maria Parloa, *Kitchen Companion*, Boston: Estes & Lauriat, 1887. • 1895 Harrod's catalog shows set with fancy cutters, tin crimped to form crested medallions or heraldic scrolly shapes. They could be ordered plain or fancy; the plain coming 9, 12 & 15 cutters to the case; the fancy, 4, 6 or 9 to the case. **$30.00-$45.00**

"**Garnishing.**— The art of garnishing dishes is the art of ornamenting them, and making them look elegant, and thus satisfying the eye as well as the palate. Various materials are used for this purpose. Among the most popular are cocks' combs, plovers, and hens' eggs boiled hard, prawns and small crayfish, button mushrooms glazed, stamped pieces of vegetables such as carrot, turnip, parsnip, beet root, and truffles, stoned olives, gherkins, fried croutons of bread, aspic jelly, horse radish, cut lemon and parsley. Everything depends on the artistic arrangement of the ornamentation, determined by the taste of the garnisher. Where the taste has been cultivated, or where there is a natural faculty for decoration, the task of garnishing effectively is an easy one." Henry Scammel, *Treasure House*, 1891.

Vegetable & fruit parer, smooth cast iron, horizontal lathe type, with wheel with interior gear teeth at one end, longish sharp knitting needle-like adjustable "spear" held & pushed fruit or veggie against revolving paring fork, (Tom Wiggins says that when doing potatoes, it's just the opposite). According to contempory ads does apples, pears, quinces, potatoes, even carrots, "The Victor," mfd by Goodell Co., Antrim, NH, pat'd Jan. 5, 1885. **$75.00-$90.00**

Vegetable & fruit press, also colander, tinned steel 'saucepan' with round bottom, perforated ¾ of way up, to be set into heavy bent rod screw clamp frame, blade inside turned by center crank, mashing food against holes, "McCoy's Improved", mfd by Dilver Mfg. Co., St. Paul, MN, c.1911. • A very similar one made by Utility Sales Co., Davenport, IA, was advertised in 1911; it differed because only the bottom of the pan is perforated, and the bottom is flatter. **$18.00-$22.00**

Vegetable grater & slicer, oblong tin grating surface with alternating perforations & sharp slits, wire frame with large handle hoop at top, curled to 2 feet at bottom, stamped with mark of 2 fish, European (?), 11"H x 4¼"W, early 20th C. **$7.00-$12.00**

Vegetable knife, almost like regular carbon steel knife with turned wooden handle, except blade not pointed but has an attached very small concave round blade to scoop out potato eyes & "defective places from all vegetables designed for the table" (as opposed to livestock), Gilbert & Durand's Patent, F. Durand, Derby, CT, pat'd Aug. 16, 1870 by F. Durand & W. E. Gilbert. **$8.00-$12.00**

Vegetable & nut chopper, glass jar with paneled sides, tin lid fitted with spring action plunger above, which gave the 4 blades an extra bounce, inch thick wooden disc inside jar, marked The Ernestreich Co. (possibly meant to be Ernest Reich), Chicago, IL, 10½"H x 4¼" diameter, c.1910 to 1920. • "**Walnut Ketchup.**— Boil or simmer a gallon of the expressed juice of walnuts when they are tender, and skim it well; add 2 pounds of anchovies, 2 pounds shalots, 1 ounce cloves, 1 ounce mace, 1 ounce pepper, 1 clove garlic. Let all simmer until the shalots sink. Put the liquor in a pan till cold, bottle and divide the spices to each." Anthony Florian Willich, *The Domestic Encyclopedia*, Philadelphia: A. Small, 1821. **$12.00-$20.00**

Vegetable or slaw slicer, white porcelain (china) table that slides in wooden frame, 2 steel blades, beautiful handle tips protrude from side, gorgeous elegant piece, prob. European, 14½"L x 5¼"W, early 20th C, poss. late 19th C. **$55.00-$65.00**

Vegetable parer, aluminum frame with steel blade, "De Vault Peeler", mfd by W. R. Feemster Co., Inc., Los Angeles - Chicago, 3"W, 1935 patent #1990127. **$5.00-$7.00**

Vegetable scraper, corn grater & fish scaler combined, nickel plated iron, turned wood handle, looks like small gardening or mason's tool, with 4 different edges: sharp beveled blade, sharp corrugated edge, comb-like edge with 6 long fork tine teeth, & curved sharp edge, sold by Montgomery Ward, pat'd 1906, c.1910 catalog. **$10.00-$18.00**

Vegetable slicer, japanned cast iron & tin, freestanding tabletop, with encased horizontal revolving cylinder, side crank, does all kinds of vegetables, "Enterprise #49," Enterprise Mfg. Co., 16"H, cylinder is 11" diameter, late 19th C. **$70.00-$110.00**

Vegetable slicer, turned wood handle, twisted wire, works like kraut slicer, "A & J Pat'd", Binghamton, NY, 16"L, c.1930s. **$15.00-$20.00**

Vegetable slicer, deep fluted tinned blade with wire handle, hand operated, not mechanical, American, c. 1900. **$5.00-$10.00**

Vegetable slicer, long wooden slide frame, steel blades, feed block of wood, hanging hole at end, "The Home Vegetable Slicer," Catawissa Specialty Mfg. Co., pat'd 1898. • Collector Dorcas Luecke copied out <u>original paper label</u>, reading in part: "For slicing potatoes and similar vegetables place same in front of feed block, grip handle firmly and shove through without stopping. For cabbage head pieces place the slicer over a receptacle with the end abutting against the wall or other support and (hold) cabbage in place with the hand. Avoid hot water, rinse thoroughly and wipe knives dry. In case of accident to knives we furnish new ones at 5 cents. ... The slices being corrugated cook more evenly and in less time than if they were plain. Also slices apples for canning. Is indispensible for slicing onions, cucumbers, radishes and the toothsome raw fry and Saratoga chips. A great many dishes can be prepared with it. We claim that this is the most efficient and satisfactory vegetable slicer on the market. It is neat and convenient to handle, it is easily and quickly cleaned and ... always ready for use." **$35.00-$65.00**

Vegetable slicer, zinc plated iron with wooden handle, screw clamps to table, comes apart by unscrewing halves, "Universal Vegetable Slicer", mfd by Landers, Frary & Clark, New Britain, CT, approx. 12"H exclusive of screw, TOC. **$40.00-$50.00**

Watermelon plugger, iron gouging tool, 19th C (?). • Used to cut out a sample plug to see if the inside was red and sweet. If not, you just stuck the plug back in. My father used one when we lived on a farm in Toledo; along the same line was our practice of testing corn for ripeness by pulling down a bit of husk. If it needed more time, you crumbled some silk from a nearby stalk and dusted it over the silk of the husk you opened and closed it back up. **$12.00-$15.00**

Whatzit cutting wheel, interesting handforged iron piece like a pizza cutter, which it may be; rattail handle attaches to wheel at right angle, point of axle has star shape outlined in dots punched into iron, around rim are what may be maker's name or name of place (pizza parlor?), looks like "ALBERTOS A CASIANO" or "CASIMO" or "CASA DO CASIMO", American, wheel 4⅜" diameter, dated 1975. **$15.00-$25.00**

Whatzit grater, or ... we first thought they were graters, the ones we saw at a PA & a VA flea market. Rough punctured tin. The third one solved the mystery. It too was a cylinder with torpedo-pointed ends, rectangular strap or bracket handle in middle, punched from inside before soldering to create pattern of closely-spaced bumps on outside, no holes. Dealer Ed Wilson, at Brimfield flea market, fall '87, had 3rd one plus a little wire & tin Y shaped tool. Theirs was partly made of a Diet Pepsi can. They found out what the 'grater' was at a Boston Pops concert when they saw it being played, during a reggae piece, like a washboard; It's a musical instrument! Jamaican or Bermudan or West Indian, 18½"L x 2½" diameter, mid 20th C. **$12.00-$15.00**

Wheat berry mill, green enameled steel box with drawer, partly nickel plated, wheat berries fed into hopper, fine to coarse settings, crank has black wood knob, bracket on back, but wall half of bracket usually missing.. "Wheat Krinkler", mfd by The Wheat Krinkler Corp., Columbus, OH, 8¼"H x 6¼"W x 2¾" D, c.1930s. **$40.00-$50.00**

I-A.
Vegetable & fruit slicer,
for creating "various beautiful and attractive designs ... to make them tempting and attractive. Lattice Potatoes are exquisite garnishes; bananas sliced in these charming patterns make a most excellent dessert." Grasgreen & Ritzinger, c.1906-07.

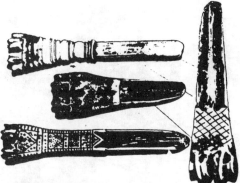

I-1.
Apple scoops or corers.
Carved sheep metacarpal bones. Decoration style dates back at least to 1200s; these are prob. 18th-19th C. Fancy one with hearts & "M.C." is 5"L. Courtesy Bob Cahn. **$35.00-$100.00**

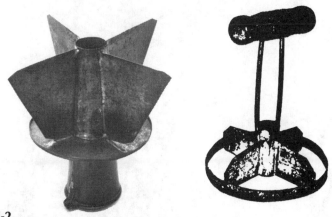

I-2.
Apple corers & dividers,
or **quarterers.** *Pieced tin, 19th C. (L) 4 3/4"H, for up to 5" apple. Collection of Meryle Evans. (R) Wood handle. 5 1/2"H x 4" diam. Ex-Keillor Collection.* **$30.00-$60.00**

I-3.
Apple corer & slicer.
Cast iron, steel, wood. Marked only "PATENTED" on quadrant wheel. 7" x 13", 19th C. Ex-Keillor Collection. **$150.00-$300.00**

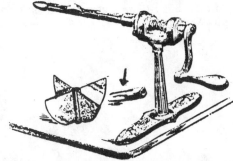

I-4.
Apple corer.
"Alcott's," pat'd by A.N. Alcott, Gowanda, NY, 2/22/1859. Converts to parer by slipping prongs (arrow) over coring shaft. Note quartering accessory. **$200.00 and up.**

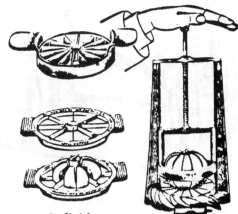

I-5.
Apple corers & dividers.
Top (L) Steel, 1 1/2"H x 4 1/2" diam. 14 or 18 segments. For potatoes too. c.1905. (L) Rollman Mfg. Co., Mt. Joy, PA, for 8ths or 12ths. Tinned cast iron. c.1901. (R) "Westerman's," with coring attachment. c.1908. **$10.00-$50.00**

I-6.
Apple corer & slicer — or segmenter.
"Climax," D.H. Goodell Mfr. 10"H x 7". Pat'd 2/16/1869, by C.D. Read, Lowell, MA. 1873 ad. **$135.00-$175.00**

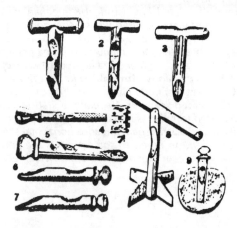

I-7.
Apple corers, *pieced tin.*
"T" handles or wood knobs. (1) c.1906. (2) 7", Geuder, Paeschke & Frey, 1925. (3) c.1904. (4) "Spengler Corer," German silver or heavy tin, perforated "saw-edged" blade, 1910. (5) 1905 Breck catalog. (6) (7) 1920 Central Stamping, 6 1/2"L, one had parer. (8) Pat'd by S. Jennie Renner, Petersburg, PA, 3/27/1877. (9) "Gem", Matthai-Ingram, c.1890. **$6.00-$20.00**

I-8.
Apple parers from Marion Levy Collection.

The late great Marion Levy let me reprint his lengthy 1979 article, "There's Fascination in Apple Parers" (The Antique Trader), in the 2nd edition. With so little room here, I can only hint at why all apple parer collectors pay him tribute. These 7 pictures (and more) illustrated his historical & mechanical overview of homemade and manufactured types. Most homemade were simple lathe types with a horizontal shaft, and frequently no gear or pulley. Levy sorted most manufactured parers into turntable, quick return, geared segment and lathe classes (each with many versions & sub-divisions). **Turntables:** *knife arm travels 360° per cycle.* **Quick return:** *knife pares 180°, lifts off & returns to starting point.* **Geared segment**: *Generally a stationary curved gear rack & a geared fork that is moved in semi-circle by a handle (supplanting a crank).* **Lathe:** *spiral-threaded horizontal shaft with crank at one end, fork on other. In some models the apple stays stationary & parer/slicer move toward apple; vice versa for others.*

Levy said "Because of their simplicity & low cost, they ultimately outsold all" other types of parers. (A) First pat'd parer, simple lathe with paring blade attached to a "sweep". Moses Coates, Downings Field, PA, 2/14/1803. (B) Homemade iron & wood parer of the Coates type. c.1810. (C) Gears or pulleys speeded up rotation. This pulley type, nearly all wood, cored & quartered. Early 1820s, type seen in Indiana & Ohio. (D) Sargent & Foster, pat'd 10/4/1853, by E.L. Pratt, Worcester, MA. Prob. first "practical parer with blade mechanically guided over the apple." Apple turned once per crank cycle. (E) Fork is geared for faster action per cycle; blade arm swivels. Pat'd 1856 by J.D. Seagraves; mfd. Larned & Seagraves, Worcester, MA. (F) First of a Lockey & Howland turntable series, pat'd 6/17 & 12/16/1856 by J. Keyes, Leominster, MA. (G) Quick return type of turntable, with the gears covered, Harbster Bros. Co. Foundry, Reading Hardware or Penn Hardware, pat'd 1868. See I-15 for a geared segment type. All photos this page by Marion Levy.

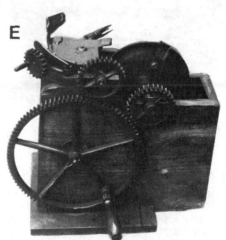

I-9.

SOME RARE APPLE PARERS, by John Lambert.

Perhaps no other kitchen collectible has such a wide and fascinating application of mechanical prinicples as does the apple parer. With the advent of cast iron gears c.1850, inventors waged a furious battle to perfect the paring machine. By 1890, after well over 100 patents, home-use parers faded in popularity; most new designs were for larger commercial models. What had occupied talented inventors for over 40 years died a quiet death. The parers — arranged by age to show evolution — on these three pages are rare; most are patented. (A) Others of this gallows-like parer exist, suggesting commercial production. The 12"H post is threaded into base; cross-piece holding blade arm lifts off easily for cleaning. "J. S." stamped on base front. c.1830. Pieces at left are the screw clamp. (B) A steel spiral track activates a sliding bar under 13 1/2" wood wheel. As it turns, bar slides 2" & pulls blade across apple. At end of 1 turn, crank handle contacts lever that transfers movement through 3 different rods to push off apple. Blade snaps back as roller falls off end of track. Very early (1840s) try for full automatism. (C) Early cast iron parer — blade still hand-held, 9"H, gear teeth are round pegs. "J.L. Havens Cin. OH." c.1850. (D) "E.L. Pratt Patent" stamped in base. First mass-produced metal parer, Sargent & Foster. Commoner model has 4 round openings in gear instead of 5 spokes. 10" x 4 1/2" base. Pat'd 10/4/1853. (E) "Yankee Apple Paring & Slicing Machine," D.F. Randall, Chicopee, MA. Pat'd 12/1855. Some (without decoratively stenciled box) marked "M.S. Ault New Haven, Conn." Pared with hand-guided knife. When a latch is flipped, apple pivots 90° for slicing by whirling blades, as user turned apple with crank on small gear. Slivers drop through box into pail. (F) "Maxam's Patent Automatic Scroll Wheel Apple Parer. Maxam & Smith Shelburne Falls, Mass. Apr. 10, 1855." Blade is advanced across apple as

follower runs on inclined spiral ridge. Blade snaps back after 3 full cranks. Intact paper label with directions. Base 4 1/2" x 9". (G-1 & 2) Pat'd by Charles P. Carter, Ware, MA, 8/26/1856. Some have paper labels. Circular corer/slicer design eliminates need for threading on shaft to advance apple forward. Use of flat spring for tension & curved blade unique. Carter held other parer patents.

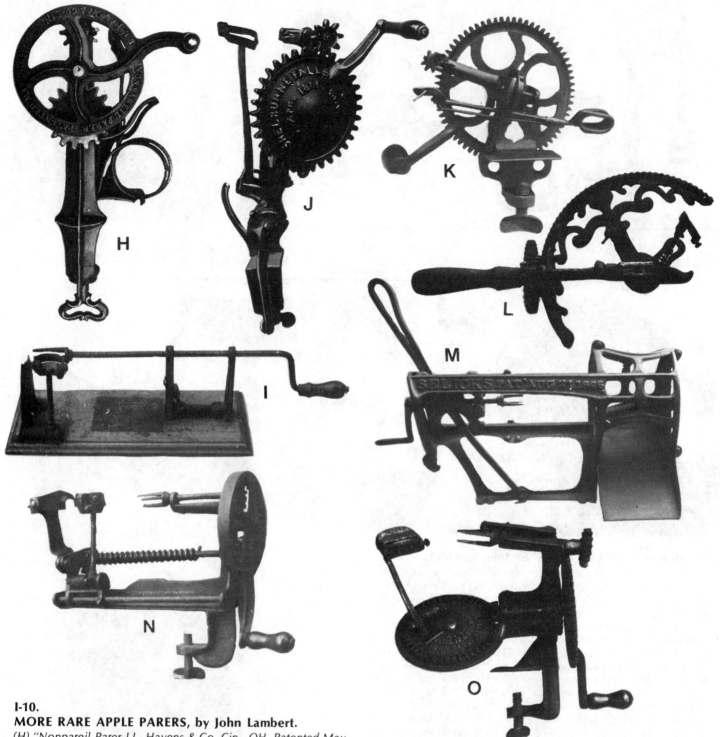

I-10.
MORE RARE APPLE PARERS, by John Lambert.

(H) "Nonpareil Parer J.L. Havens & Co. Cin., OH. Patented May 6, 1856." 1st all-metal clamp-on parer. Paring head on end of large coiled spring. 4 crank turns, then blade snaps back to starting position. Only 8 1/4"H, this small parer with clockwise movement pares flawlessly & is favorite of collectors. (I) "Whittemore, Harrington & Co's Patent. Pat. Nov. 11, 1856 and Jan. 13, 1857." Worcester, MA. 1st with threaded shaft to advance apple. Coring ring atop blade missing here. (J) Marked "S.N. Maxam Shelburne Falls, MA, Pat. Apr. 1855," but really pat'd 1/27/1857, by Clarissa Hubbard for her husband, who was killed by fall from his horse before he could submit design. 11 1/2"H parer hinged at base. Leaning right, it's cranked to right to pare. Leaning left, crank is reversed while hinged slicing knife is hand-guided toward user to slice thin rings for drying, leaving core on fork. (K) "J.J. Parker Patent Apr. 7, 1857." 5 1/2" gear. Unique in that it pares apple with 1 turn of crank which hits frame & must be cranked in reverse to start over. Parker from Marietta, OH. (L) Pat'd 6/3/1862, by Jonathan White, Antrim, NH. 9"W. Move handle

across ornate crescent arc to pare apple in 1 second. Forerunner of the "Lightning", also a half-moon type but smaller. (M) "Selick's Pat. Aug. 21, 1866." Cast iron frame, poss. early commercial model. Other Selick's are wood. After paring with hand-guided blade, user shoves lever handle forward to core & segment. 8 3/4"H x 15". (N) 8 3/4"L. Not uncommon parer, but rare breaker attachment. During paring, spiral slices kept from rotating, causing them to break off in 1/4" thick semicircles. "D.H. Whittemore." Pat'd 8/10/1869; ext'd 1/13 & 2/17/1871. (O) "Turntable," mfd. by Lockey & Howland, Leominster, MA. Pat'd 6/17 and 12/16/1856 & 11/22/1870. 6 1/2"H. Unique push-off: has split frame, so after apple pared, 1/2 frame tilts back (as shown here) to bump apple against other half, loosening it. Before crank reaches 12 o'clock position, small gear moves back in line to avoid crank. Rarest version, with turntables slanted 45° to keep juice & paring off gears.

P-1

P-2

S-2

S-1

Q

R

T

I-11.
MORE RARE APPLE PARERS, by John Lambert.

(P-1 & P-2) Top: "Missouri Apple Parer & Cutter. Mfd. by G. Bergner. Washington, Mo. Pat. Jan. 9, 1872." 18"L in position shown. After paring, the long shaft was pushed forward with palm of user's hand to core & segment apple. George Bergner was a gunmaker & as far as we know, his parer was the only model made west of the Mississippi. Truly unusual, and prized by collectors. Bottom: The shorter 12"L version is marked "Missouri Peach and Apple Parer. Mfd. by G. Bergner. Wachington, MO. Pat. Jan. 9, 1872." On most of these "Washington" is clearly misspelled with a "c". It had the added feature that pushes fruit from forks, but doesn't have a corer/segmenter. (Q) What collectors call "the Ultimate Union" parer. Marked "Pat. Nov. 11, 1866 Pat. Apr. 6, '80," but it's really a Whittemore, pat'd 11/20/1866. Highly refined device pares apple on forward movement of blade; then on reverse movement, 2nd blade (far right) slices, cores, & breaks apple into pieces for pies or drying. (R) Marked "R. & McC Speed," & known to collectors as "Speedboy." 10 3/4"H. Poss. Canadian, it closely resembles common Reading '78 model (see I-14). Real rarity is gear

lid, cast with figural resembling Gothic man with crossed arms. (S-1). "Oriole," pat'd by Robt. P. Scott, Cadiz, OH, 5/16/1871. "Scott Mfg. Co. Balt. Pat. Pnd." is mark. 12"L. Instead of rack that leans over, spiral lip has permanent gap allowing crank to be pulled back when alligned with teeth. 2-pronged fork splits old core as new apple forced on. (S-2). Quite rare "Oriole" pat'd 8/14/1883. Gate has been added to open & close gap in lip. 3-prong fork. (T) Some models marked "Jersey", prob. because they were sold by L.A. Sayre, Newark, NJ. 12"L. Pat'd 6/2/1885. Spiral lip around main gear 'worms' through teeth in rack to advance apple. Rack falls to side, so crank can be pulled back to start position. Longer-lasting than similar lathe types with threaded shafts. **All photos these 3 pages are courtesy of John Lambert.**

● *COLLECTOR'S CLUB:* **INTERNATIONAL SOCIETY OF APPLE PARER ENTHUSIASTS,** *John Lambert, Pres., 3911 Morgan Center Rd., Utica, OH 43080. Send SASE for information on newsletter & meetings.*

I-12.
Apple parers.

(L) Handmade, wood, iron crank, 2-prong fork. Clamps like bench-vise to table; pulley fitted with leather or cording belt. 18"H x 3 1/2" x 10" early 19th C. Ex-Keillor Collection. Top (R) Handmade, light-colored wood, perhaps maple, possibly made by experienced cabinet-maker. 2-prong iron fork. 6"H x 9 1/4"L. Meryle Evans Collection. (Bottom) Straddle type, meant to be sat upon. Pennsylvania German, wood painted pumpkin & dark green, cast iron gears. Needs hand-held blade. 29 1/2"L x 8"W, mid 19th C. **$250.00 and up.**

I-15.
Apple parer.

Cast iron, geared or ribbed quadrant with lever action. 23 3/4"L. Pat'd 11/2/1880 by George R. Thompson, Quincy, IL, as improvement on his 8/14/1877 patent. Pares, cores, divides & discharges core in a "single sweep of lever." Mfd. by New England Butt Co., Providence, RI, known mostly for making butt hinges. Rare & desirable.

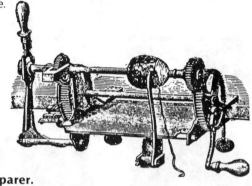

I-16.
Apple parer.

"Machine 'a peler les fruits," by French inventor Faucherre. He also invented an almond-grating machine. Screw clamps to table. Illustration from Urbain Dubois' La Patisserie d'Aujourd'hui, c.1860s. Dubois said of the picture that it was drawn too large; "in fact, it is a tiny apparatus, occupying little space."

I-13.
Apple parer.

Seems homemade, but many examples are known, with some variations in the knife arm. Three sizes, with 6" (like this one), 7" or 8" large gear wheel, red painted wood base — some have "breadboard ends". Maine, mid 19th C. **$75.00-$125.00**

I-17.
Apple parer, corer, quarterer or slicer.

"Tippecanoe," mfd. by Tippecanoe Apple Paring Machine Co., NYC. Operator stood to use it; apple held upright on 3-prong fork. Looks as if it combines treadle & cranked action. Ad from the Hearth & Home, *10/28/1871.*

I-14.
Apple parer.

"Turntable '78", Reading Hardware Co., Reading, PA, pat'd 1878. Marion Levy said "The gears are protected by an artistically-decorated bronzed cover. Mechanism canted at angle to improve visibility and insure that parings fall into a bucket. Besides a 'push-off' and 'blossom cutter,' it features an anti-reverse pawl to keep it from being cranked backwards."

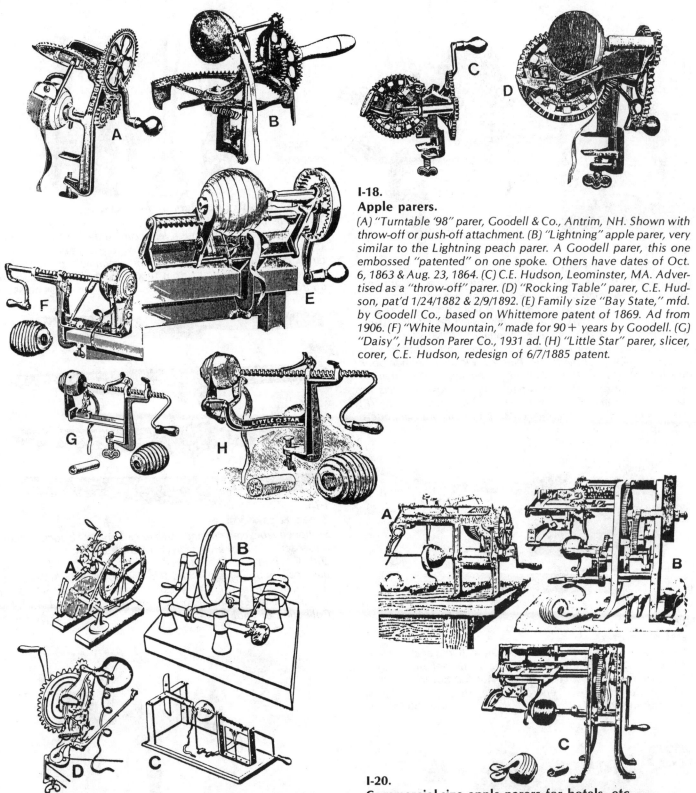

I-18.
Apple parers.
(A) "Turntable '98" parer, Goodell & Co., Antrim, NH. Shown with throw-off or push-off attachment. (B) "Lightning" apple parer, very similar to the Lightning peach parer. A Goodell parer, this one embossed "patented" on one spoke. Others have dates of Oct. 6, 1863 & Aug. 23, 1864. (C) C.E. Hudson, Leominster, MA. Advertised as a "throw-off" parer. (D) "Rocking Table" parer, C.E. Hudson, pat'd 1/24/1882 & 2/9/1892. (E) Family size "Bay State," mfd. by Goodell Co., based on Whittemore patent of 1869. Ad from 1906. (F) "White Mountain," made for 90 + years by Goodell. (G) "Daisy", Hudson Parer Co., 1931 ad. (H) "Little Star" parer, slicer, corer, C.E. Hudson, redesign of 6/7/1885 patent.

I-19.
Apple parer patents.
(A) Pat'd 8/26/1856, by Marvin Smith, New Haven, CT. Oscillating fork. (B) Pat'd 7/24/1847, by Jesse Bullock, Jr., & Sewall Benson, NYC. Looks like I-8-C, on Marion Levy's page. (C) Parer, corer & quarterer, pat'd 6/9/1857, by C.F. Bosworth, Petersham, MA. (D) Parer & slicer, pat'd 1/27/1857, by G.H. Hubbard, Shelburne Falls, MA.

I-20.
Commercial-size apple parers for hotels, etc.
All Goodell Co., Antrim, NH. (A) "Bonanza Parer & Corer." Called a "successful three-turn machine" by maker. Cast iron, mounted to board or worktable. 15"H x 17 1/2"L. Pat'd 11/16/1886 & 3/13/1888 but not, I believe, introduced until 1890. A drawing used for the "Improved '98" in c.1906-1930s catalogs shows dates 11/24/1886 & March 1881, but these are engraving mistakes. The '98 is described as being 21"H x 17"L. (B) "Eureka," hand or power. Pat'd 8/4/1874 & 4/27 & 11/16/1886, sharing a patent with "Bonanza". "It has a record of 80 bushels a day by hand." Has 3 forks, so user can continuously load. (C) "Dandy," pat'd 11/16/1886 & 3/13 & 5/8/1888. Crank 3 times to pare, core & slice one apple.
$95.00-$175.00

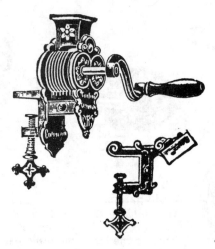

I-24.

Beetles, potato pounders or mashers.

Two at right common forms, turned wood, late 19th or early 20th C. Double headed one much less commonly found. It is found as large as 24"L, and was used mostly in restaurants. Same date range. Fancy turned handle has a white ceramic "porcelain" (probably ironstone) head. It's from 1860s, and looks like a pestle for an ironstone mortar. **$8.00-$50.00**

I-21.

Bean slicers or stringers.

Photo at (L) is a "Harras No.37" bean cutter, made in Germany, cast iron, screw-clamps to table. Feed one bean at a time into chute, turn crank, and make French-style string beans. Removable steel blades. Trademark of a hand embossed on lower casting. 10 1/2"H. Courtesy Dennis Robida, Scotland, CT. (M) 6 1/2"H "German bean cutter," yet prob. mfd. by Spong, an English firm. Exact same "slicer" in Brigette ten Kate-von Eicken's German book on kitchenwares (see Bibliography); she remarks that it's marked "gesetzltoh geschutzt" means patented, or registered, has no maker's mark, but looks just like one in a Spong trade catalog. (R) "German Bean Stringer." Both in c.1906 NYC houseware importers' catalog. **$35.00-$75.00**

I-25.

Bread & cake knives.

Scalloped & beveled cutting edges to carbon steel blades. Scallops closer-set for bread knives. Wood handles. All c.1890s to early 20th C. From top: (1) "Climax", 13 1/4"L. (2) "Tip-Top," with trademark of boy's head — the "Tip-Top Boy." 15"L. (3) "Victoria", American Cutlery Co., 14 3/4"L. (4) "Aetna" tradename, "Universal" trademark, Landers, Frary & Clark, New Britain, CT. 14 1/4"L. Collection of Paul Persoff. **$7.00-$18.00**

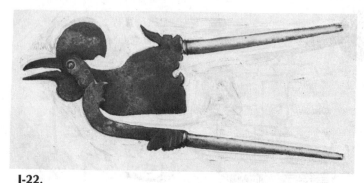

I-22.

Betel nut cutter,

often mistaken for a kitchen tool. Rooster, with iron or steel blade & silver handle, 7 5/8"L, from India. Engraved steel around eyes & chiseled design. Most are brass. The nut was but in half, then the meat picked out with end of handle. From stock of Mona Sawyer, Stamford, CT. **$100.00-$150.00**

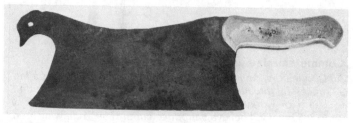

I-23.

Cleaver.

Steel blade with zoomorphic bird head. Flat lead handle replaces original wood handle. 13 1/2" x 4 1/8", Russian or Polish, 19th C. This cleaver, one of a pair used in preparing kosher food, was brought to this country in 1903; the handle was repaired about that time. Collection of Marvin Tanner. Priceless as family heirloom; very valuable for form of blade.

I-26.

Coconut grater.

Apparently hand-crafted from variety of parts, although manufactured ones exist. Cast iron bolt went through hole in table top. Brass crank with steel handle; heavy sheet metal serrated or sawtooth blades to shred an opened coconut from the inside. Quite possibly English for colonial use, perhaps in Jamaica. 7"H, mid 19th C. Located by the Primitive Man, Bob Cahn, Carmel, NY. **$85.00-$125.00**

I-27.
Cherry pitter or stoner.
Skeletal wire & stamped sheet metal, spring-activated plungers. 8"H, no mark. Seems to pit cherry on one side, and split it on other. Courtesy Arden L. Fisher. **$55.00-$85.00**

I-30.
Cherry stoner.
Cast iron, 3 wrought iron legs. Henry Buckwalter's patent, 11/17/1863. Missing wooden handle to crank. Picture courtesy of The Smithsonian Institution, Museum of History and Technology.

I-28.
Cherry stoner.
In last edition I called this "homemade." But it's a "Fisher's Patent Cherry Stoner," pat'd by C.A. Fisher, Philadelphia, 5/24/1870. "Five strokes stone 100 cherries" claims early catalog. Wood box with cherry-holder of wood, iron hinges, lever action. Does 20 at a time. Fit holder with cherries (like Chinese Checkers), insert into box, fit the levered follower into box, push out pits, which fall below. 6 1/4"H x 6 1/4"L x 5 3/4"W. Collection of Meryle Evans. **$150.00-$250.00**

I-31.
Cherry stoner.
Lightweight cast iron, 3 legs attached with wingnut bolts, mounted on plank through holes in feet. Marked "Scott Mfg. Co., Baltimore." 6 3/4"H x 12"L.

I-29.
Cherry stoners.
Two versions of cast iron 4-legged pitter, based on original patent (See I-30) of H. Buckwater, Kimberton, PA 11/17/1863, as improved by William Weaver, Phoenixville, PA, 5/15/1866. Handle on crank is also cast iron. Note one at top has wingnuts holding legs on; it's newer than other. Some marked "Scott Man'fg Co. Pat. Pending, Baltimore, MD." 7"H x 10 7/8"L.

I-32.
Cherry stoner "make-do"
or repaired piece. The Weaver patent, showing both dates, with sorrel-leaf decoration cast into hopper. Legs missing or removed purposely; body mounted to shaped wood base, 8 7/8" x 4 1/2", carved to match sinuous curves of cast iron. Iron part only 2 7/8"H; overall 6"H. Note piece at one end for mounting to tabletop. **$75.00-$125.00**

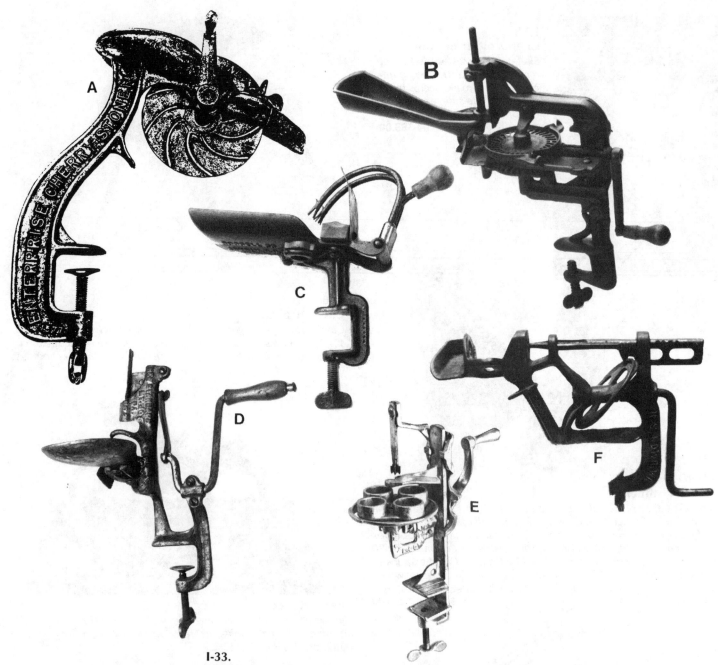

I-33.
Cherry stoners.
All cast iron; all screw clamp to table edge. (A) "Enterprise No. 2," pat'd 1903. No.'s 1 & 2 not adjustable for different cherry sizes, as were Enterprise 17 & 18. 12"L. (B) "Duke," Reading Hardware Co., "pat. pend." Very unusual. Swiveling hinge just above clamp functions as a shock absorber while pitter in operation. 11"L, exclusive of handle. Late 19th C. (C) "The Family Cherry Stoner," Goodell Co., c.1895. 8"H. Wonderful lever action plunges double pitters through cherries. (D) "New Standard No. 50," Mt. Joy, PA, 10"H, c.1900. (E) Another by New Standard Corporation, Mt. Joy. "patents pending." Nickeled iron. All parts numbered, therefore replaceable with stock parts — the touted advantage of all uniformly cast iron appliances. Feed cherries with left hand, and as you crank, platform holding 4 cherries revolves to lie briefly under punch. 10 1/4"H. (F) Another New Standard pitter, with eccentric wheel, horizontal action. Courtesy Bob Cahn. (A), (C) & (D) Collection of Robert D. Franklin. (B) & (E) Collection of Meryle Evans.

I-34.
Chopping knives with crescent blades.
Big beauty at (L) hand-forged iron, single tang branched to 2 before inserting in wood handle. 8"H x 9 1/4"L blade, early 19th C. Top (R) Commercially made, 6 3/8"H x 7 1/2"W, probably last third 19th C. Lower (R) Hand-forged, unusual curved wood handle fits hand comfortably. Collection of Meryle Evans.
$100.00-$200.00; $25.00 or so; $55.00-$70.00

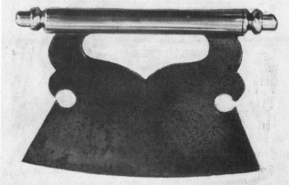

I-35.
Chopping knife,
with fancy cutout blade of wrought steel, and machined cast brass handle typical of English choppers of 19th C. 5"H x 7"W. I think these are usually overpriced, and should be worth half or less than great indigenous iron choppers as in I-34. Value range what's being asked: **$150.00-$185.00**

I-36.
Chopping knives, double-bladed rockers.
(L) Two heavy steel blades, ground & polished, riveted to steel shanks that encircle handle. Green enameled handle or plain wood. Kidney-bean shaped blades 6"W, late 19th or early 20th C. (R) Cast steel blades, truncated ends, wishbone shank. Probably c.1870s. **$20.00-$45.00**

I-37.
Chopping knives.
(L) Steel rocker blade, riveted cast iron handle with cutout, 5 1/2"H x 5 3/4"W, c.1890s. Top: Carved wooden handle, crescent carbon steel blade, 5 5/8"H x 8"W. Probably mass-produced, but on small scale, and individually finished. (R) A "Hachinette," from France. Carbon steel, wood, 6 3/4" x 5 1/4". Angel mark. Used by centering grip over blade's center, chopping down into smallish wooden bowl, which you continuously turned with your other hand. Think of this turning/chopping motion when you see I-58. Bottom: Solid steel, with all-in-one tubular steel handle, c.1890s-1920s. May be dough batch divider. **$20.00-$50.00**

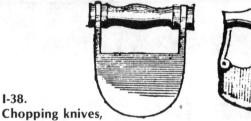

I-38.
Chopping knives,
as depicted in two early cookbooks. (L) Very substantially made "meat chopper, for chopping and disjointing bones," in Warne's Model Cookery, London: 1868. (R) "Chop knife. Iron handle, steel blade." American Home Cook Book, 1854. **$45.00-$65.00**

I-39.
Chopping knife & board.
Forged iron & wood. Blade topped by cutout trotting horse, turned wood handle. 7"H x 14 1/4"L overall. Often referred to as tobacco cutters, I believe the boards would smell if this were true of all. Ex-Seymour Collection; sold in 1982 at Christie's. Picture courtesy of Christie, Manson & Woods International, Inc. **$500.00-$650.00**

I-40.
Corn graters,
or **corn gritters** in the vernacular. (L) Called a "vegetable scorer" in last edition. Meant to slit kernels and release innards. Pieced, soldered tin, 3"H, strap handle, marked "F.A. Walker, Boston," so either mfd. or imported by them. Rare to find Walker mark on anything. Picture courtesy National Museum of American History, Smithsonian Institution. (R) Nicely made, wood, iron slitting teeth & scraping blade. 4 1/2"H x 11 3/4"L, 3rd to 4th quarter 19th C. Collection of Meryle Evans. **$35.00-$60.00; $125.00-$175.00**

I-43.
Fish scalers & combo tool.
(T) Nickeled steel, turned wood handle. A "unique culinary device... patent 1906. ...Practically the best corn grater ever invented. For taking scales off of fish or scraping vegetables it can not be excelled. It is the first and only pineapple shredder ever." Montgomery Ward catalog, c.1910. (B) Japanned cast iron fish scaler. S.B. Sexton, 1930s. **$5.00-$20.00**

I-41.
Cucumber slicer.
Ivory with silver blade. 8 1/4"L x 2 1/2"W. Beautiful tiny thumb screws adjust blade. Supposedly Asian ivory stays very white; African ivory ages to mellow golden tones. **$250.00-$325.00**

I-44.
Fruit, wine & jelly press.
Enterprise Mfg. Co., Philadelphia. Cast iron, double screw clamp. Fruit put into hopper; when cranked through, the skins & seeds came out tip; the juice poured out of the long slots the whole length of the horizontal nozzle-like barrel. 12"H overall x 11"L. Pat'd 9/30/1879; sold for years. Collection of Meryle Evans. **$50.00-$65.00**

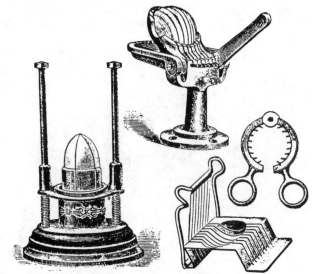

I-42.
Egg slicers & opener.
(L) Japanned & decorated cast iron, sliding cutter with 5 blades, to use in salad-making. c.1870s-80s, V. Clad, Philadelphia. Top: Slicer, for sandwiches. Lever pulls wires through. Also V. Clad. (R) Scissor-action device "to remove a portion of the shell without crushing either the removed or remaining portion of shell. Imported by G.M. Thurnauer, NYC, 1904. Last, an imported aluminum & wire slicer, of type frequently seen, made in metal or wood. c.1927 catalog. **$5.00-$50.00**

I-45.
Grapefruit corer.
It is, it is! For all you doubters — see c.1927 catalog drawings at right. Works like post-hole digger. Turner & Seymour, Torrington, CT, pat'd 5/26/1923, & poss. again in 1925. 7"H with 1 3/4" diameter corer. This one, with wire handles, the "hotel size." One shown in use (R) The household size, sheet metal. **$4.00-$7.00**

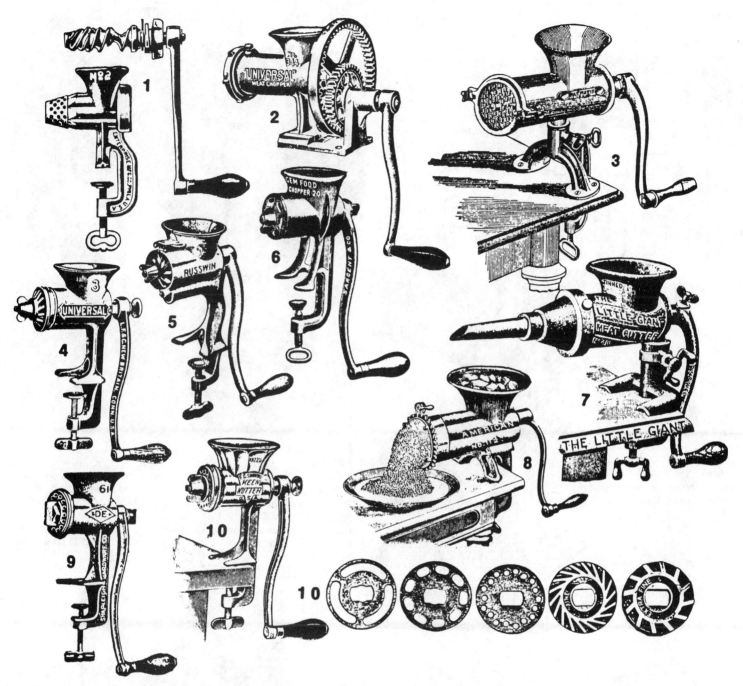

I-46.

Food grinders & meat cutters.

(1) "Enterprise No. 2" meat chopper for 1 lb. a minute. Not the most collectible Enterprise, but it shows the interior part which grinds & moves meat from hopper forward. 1905 catalog shows sizes 2, 4, 6, 8, 5, 10, 12, 20, 22, 32 & 42. (2) Tinned cast iron "Universal No. 344," Landers, Frary & Clark. Hopper 5" x 6" diameter, 9 3/4"H, "geared down to get greater ease in operation," does 4 lbs. meat a minute. (3) "Ellrich" meat cutter, Ellrich Hardware Mfg. Co., Plantsville, CT, drawing marked pat'd 5/15/189- (has to be 1888 for "patent Tuesday"). 1892 The Metal Worker ad. (4) "Universal No. 3", 4" x 5" hopper, 3 lbs. per minute. (5) "Russwin," originally Russell & Erwin. Pat'd 8/27/1901. (6) Small

"Gem No. 20" food chopper, Sargent & Co. 2 lbs. pm. For meat, vegetables, fruit, crackers, bread, boiled eggs, cheese, nuts, raisins, figs, etc. (7) "The Little Giant No. 410" cutter. Peck, Stow & Wilcox Co., Southington, CT. Stuffer attachment. 1892 ad. (8) "Great American Meat Cutter No. 112", Hibbard, Spencer, Bartlett & Co., 1870s catalog. Case/barrel 5 1/8"L x 2 1/4" diameter plate. 2 lbs, pm. (9) "Diamond Edge No. 61," with DE pierced by arrow mark. Shapleigh Hardware Co., St. Louis. 7 1/2"H, hopper is 3 3/8" x 2 5/8", 2 lbs. pm. c.1914. (10) "Keen Kutter No. 22 1/2", E.C. Simmons. 10"H, hopper 3 1/2" x 4 1/2", 3 lbs. pm. Four cutter plates; holed ones for chopping from coarse to fine. Reversible one does fine one side, extra fine other. c.1920 catalog. The more attachments, the more value. **$20.00 and up.**

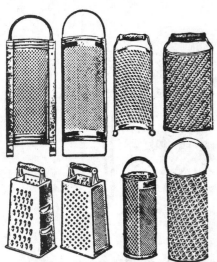

I-47.
Tin hand graters c.1905-1920.

Most in time-honored styles dating back 200 years. Top row: all curved, almost half-rounds, with metal or wood handles, different feet, some reinforced. Bottom row: two 4-sided combination graters with strap handles, 7 1/2"H. Next a cylindrical one, the "Midget", with coarse & fine perforations. 6 1/4"H. Last a 10" x 5" & (also 13" x 6") half-round. **$5.00-$20.00**

I-48.
Box graters.

(T) Most likely homemade. Wood & punctured tin, porcelain knob on drawer. Could be hung from wall. 15"L, mid 19th C. Picture courtesy of the National Museum of American History, Smithsonian Institution. (M) All tin, with white porcelain knob on drawer. Mid to late 19th C. Picture & collection of Phyllis & Jim Moffet. (B) All tin, 13"L x 7", from c.1904-1910. Duparquet, Huot & Moneuse restauranteur catalog.

$100.00 and up.

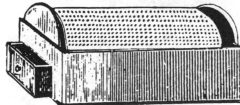

I-50.
Food mills.

Two small cast iron mills. (L) An "Improved Schroeter" almond & vegetable grater. I think a No. 10. Painted & decorated. (R) A "Schroeter's Improved Grater No. 100", Schroeter Bros. Hardware, St. Louis. Pat'd 11/1903. Colorful, decorative cast iron German-made mills bearing women's names — Anna, Inge, Victoria, Carmen, Amanda & Kitty — make a great collection. **$25.00-$55.00**

I-49.
Mechanical graters.

Wood & punctured tin. (L) Said to be a **carrot grater.** *Cast iron ribbed gears, counterweighted cast iron balance wheel. Revolving wooden drum has square nails driven into it. Only place to feed in food is a little 'mouse-hole' in front. No signs of use, no marks. 8"H x 7 1/2"L x 5 1/2"W. Looks mid-19th C. (R) "H.P. Arthur's Vegetable Grater," pat'd 10/8/1867, Martinsburgh, NY. Stenciled on top. Wood frame, metal grater drum, wood hoop & foller & crank. 13 3/4"H to top of hopper; 19"H to fulcrum of lever. Frame 13"L x 6"W. Both Collection of Meryle Evans.*
$150.00-$250.00

I-51.
Herb boats, or herb crushers.

Cast iron with wood handles, c.1800-1820s. (T) 18"L. Photo courtesy Litchfield Auction Gallery, Litchfield, CT. Ex-Harold Corbin Collection, auctioned 1/1/1989 for $750.00. (B) Wood handles stained or stove-blacked. 17"L; 7" diameter wheel. Collection of Meryle Evans. Prob. neither is American. **$200.00-$750.00**

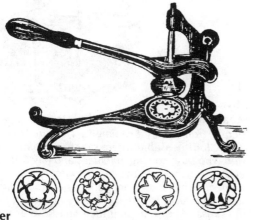

I-52.

Julienne cutter

& four steel dies for it, of 16 offered. Note eagle pattern of one. To use: cut raw vegetable in thin slices; lay a slice on the disc and press handle down. Then lay a 2nd slice on disc & press, which forces 1st slice through. Meant for cutting carrots & turnips, etc., in shapes for soups, garnishing, etc. Probably French. See more in Chapter IV. **$50.00-$150.00**

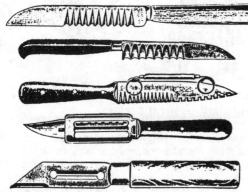

I-53.

Decorating & paring knives.

A very small selection. Scalloped ones, some German, some French, for slicing Saratoga potatoes, and raw veggies & fruits into fancy garnishes or for preserving. Also for butter — even "pudding" says one ad. Middle ones have guards. Bottom one is a "razor edge paring knife." All early 20th C. **$5.00-$18.00**

I-54.

Lemon squeezer.

Wood with heavily tinned male & female inserts. Lever action. Closely resembles early 20th C hotel lemon squeezer; this one probably mass-produced on small scale, mid 19th C. Picture courtesy of the National Museum of American History, Smithsonian Institution. **$150.00-$250.00**

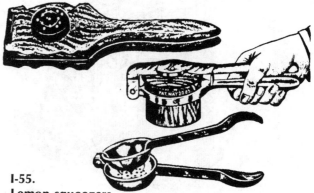

I-55.

Lemon squeezers.

Just 3 of many varieties. (T) Lignum vitae cup and bowl, 10 1/2 x 3" (also came 13"L x 3 1/2" for lemons & 15 1/2" x 4 1/2" for oranges). Late 19th C. (M) A so-called "drum" squeezer. This is the "Janes", nickeled malleable iron frame, wooden presser, zinc-lined maple bowl. Pat'd 5/20/1885 & sold for decades. (B) Cast iron with porcelain-lined cup. Berger Bros., Philadelphia. 1895 ad. **$20.00-$40.00**

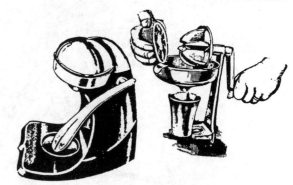

I-56.

Juicer & reamers.

All aluminum. Big one is the funny "Handy Andy", this one with red painted base. Others found green. 10 1/2"H x 6 7/8" diameter. Two-part one is accessory for another juicer. **$15.00-$25.00; small ones $2.00-$5.00**

I-57.

Juicers.

(L) "Streamline Juice King," rack & pinion action with lever. Red baked enamel with chrome. 9"H x 8" x 5 3/4". 1942 catalog. (R) "California/Florida" fruit juice extractor, for all citrus fruit. Entirely of aluminum — stamped or cast — the funnel bowl, removable aluminum strainer, reamer & frame. 13"H x 6" diameter. c.1909. **$20.00-$40.00**

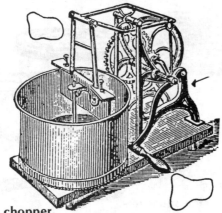

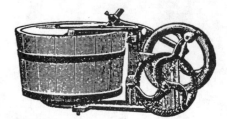

I-58.
Meat & vegetable chopper.
Also called a "steamboat meat chopper." Referred to as the "American," the "Starrett", or the "Athol" chopper. Cast iron, tin, painted wood. Pat'd 5/23/1865, by Leroy Starrett, mfd. by Athol Machine Co., Athol Depot, MA. Two outlined shapes represent cutouts in frame of choppers. Upper one on post-1877 "improved" ones. 3 sizes — 8", 10" & 12" diameter cylinder, which rotated on ratchet underneath as chopping blade rose & fell. Three larger ones, 15", 18" & 20" have intermittent gears instead of ratchet & pawl. **$125.00-$200.00**

I-61.
Meat chopper similar to the Starrett.
Picture from Henry Scammell's Treasure-House of Knowledge, 1890. "Indispensable where sausage & mince pies are favorites. Men who buy mowing machines and hay forks cannot afford to let their wives work away in the kitchen with old-fashioned implements when better ones are to be had for little money. If any husband refuses to buy it, let the wife cut off his supply of hash and sausages on trial, and then take severer means afterward if necessary." Patent dates given I-59. **$150.00-$200.00**

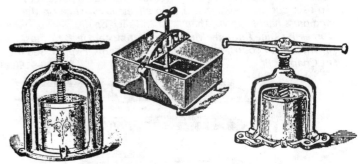

I-59.
Cast iron working parts of chopper I-61.
Has 3 patent dates: "6/5/1865" (probably mistake for 1866, the date for C.A. Foster's patent, Winchendon, MA); 7/11/1865; and "Jan. 31" with no year, but is 1865. Last 2 dates for A.F. Spaulding & S.M. Scott's patents, also Winchendon, MA). 8"H x 10"L. Cast iron but for steel blade & bucket scraper. From stock of David Antinore, at Brimfield, MA.

I-62.
Fruit, lard or meat presses.
(T) "Starrett's Domestic Press," for corned beef, boiled mutton, tongue, boned turkey, head cheese ... and for extracting juice from fruit & berries; also for pressing lard, cottage cheese, squash, turnip, &c.," Cast & sheet iron, japanned & decorated. 3 sizes: 4" deep x 6" x 9"; 5" deep x 8" x 12"; and 6" x 10" x 14". 1870s. Lower (L) "Enterprise," 2, 4, or 8 qts. Turn of century. (R) English "enameled iron fruit presser." 1895 catalog. **$100.00-$200.00**

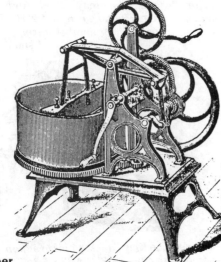

I-60.
Meat chopper,
butcher's size No. 5, Starrett patent, elevated on cast iron frame. 20" diameter chopping block inside the cylindrical can. From 1906 catalog. **$125.00-$250.00**

I-63.
Meat tenderizers, also called tenderers.
Clockwise from top: (1) Cast iron, rolling, marked only "pat appl for." (2) "Varty Mfg. Co., Chicago, pat'd 1/27/1885. Has 2 leaf springs to push meat off prongs. From the John Lambert Collection. (3) Galvanized tin, wood handle, 4 1/2"L, 19th C. Collection of Meryle Evans. (4) "Yale Meat Scorer," patent applied for 1892. Cast iron frame, wooden rod axle, set with very sharp steel blades. 8 1/4"L. Located by the Primitive Man, Bob Cahn, Carmel, NY. (5) Small rolling one has iron blades, wood handle. (6) Lawn roller type with toothed wood roller, wire handle, 12"L x 9 1/2"W. 19th C. Both collection of Meryle Evans. **$20.00-$75.00**

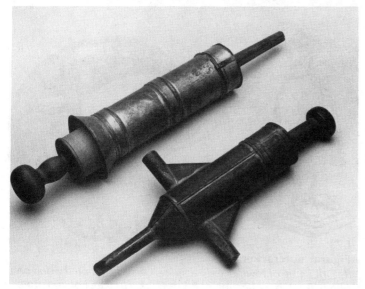

I-64.
Sausage guns or stuffers.
Pieced tin, wood plungers. Sausage casings (scraped intestines, yuck) fit over nozzle ends. Above (L) 29 1/2"L; takes different casing-funnel sizes. Other is 19 1/2"L. 1870s-80s. Collection of Meryle Evans. **$50.00-$125.00**

I-67-A & B.
Mortar with oyster attached!
Rev. Larry Pearson of Snellville, GA, found this marble mortar about 30 miles south of New Orleans, on the Mississippi's east bank "lying in the mud off shore near an old fort below Shell Beach. This area was settled in early days by the Spanish." In the water or mud for maybe 150 years or more, it's surprising only one oyster attached itself (atop projection on rim's far side). 4 1/2" x 8 1/2" across at widest points. Info & photo courtesy Larry Pearson, & Cheryl & David Hitchcock. (R) Lathe-turned mortar, with interestingly-shaped carved pestle. Red buttermilk paint. 7"H x 4 1/2" diam; pestle 9"L. Early 19th C. Collection of Meryle Evans.

I-65.
Mechanical sausage stuffers.
Top: "Stow's Patent," Russell & Erwin Mfg. Lever action in 2 sizes, for butchers or families. Pat'd 7/6/1858 by O.W. Stow, Plantsville, CT. Lower (L) "Hale Meat Cutter" and stuffer, also R & E and in their 1865 catalog, and later in a c.1900 catalog! Grinding drums lift out. Three sizes: 5", 6" 7 1/2" cylinders. Couldn't find Hale in Patent Index. (R) "Sausage meat cutter," from American Home Cook Book, 1854. There were several patents previous to 1854. **$75.00-$250.00**

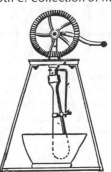

I-68.
Mortar & pestle patent.
Called a "grinding & triturating apparatus" by inventor. Pat'd 3/20/1877, by Joseph J. Lancaster, London, Ontario, Canada. Pestle has rotary motion.

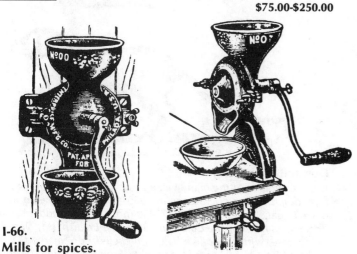

I-66.
Mills for spices.
"Enterprise," No. 00 (at left) & No. O. Decoratively painted cast iron; one for wall, one screw clamps. c.1898. **$30.00-$60.00**

I-69.
Mortars & pestles of various classic types.
Most of upper ones are cast — bell metal, bronze, brass or iron (footed one at (R) is cast iron & called "goblet shaped" by seller). Stoneware & marble ones often have a small depression or pouring lip. Knobby projections aid steadying. Sizes from 4" to 15". 18th to late 19th C classic forms. **$30.00-$500.00**

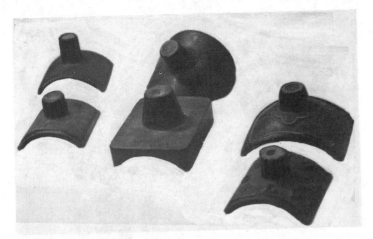

I-70.
Kneewarmer nutcrackers —
cast iron anvil part only. To be put over thigh near knee and used to break nuts with a small hammer. Size approx. 3 1/2" x 6". 2nd and 3rd quarter 19th C. Collection of Phyllis & Jim Moffet.
$50.00-$125.00

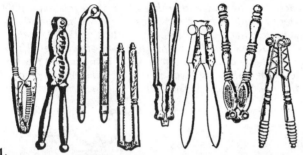

I-71.
Nutcrackers of pliers type. Also called **nutcracks.**
A confusable, because it could be used with large nuts, is the lobster cracker at far left. Next are two cast iron late 19th C. nutcracks, one made for 2 sizes; one for big nuts only. Then 5 of the "cross over" types, which reversed for small or large nuts. All but one shown in small nut position. Nickeled or plain cast iron or steel, more or less decorative. Many are English, c.1880-1930s.
$12.00-$28.00

I-72.
Zoomorphic nutcrackers.
(T) Dinosaur/dragon or griffin. Cast iron painted gold, 2-part body bolted together, sawtooth spine ridges & tail, 13"L. Pat #206454 (?). Stock of Richard Ferry, Mystic Fine Arts, Mystic, CT. (B) Alligators (not crocodiles) with blunt tips. Author's large one silver-painted cast iron, 2 parts come apart. Scaled back, tail & lower jaw lift out revealing naked underbody & legs. 13 3/4"L. Small one cast brass in reddish hue, 2 part, riveted pivot, no marks, 7 7/8"L. Collection of Peg & Ralph Latham. All turn of century.
$175.00-$250.00; $35.00-$50.00

I-73.
Figural nutcrackers.
(L) Full figure of town-crier-like figure, carved & painted wood on plinth. 8 1/2"H, collection of Priors Bank, Fulham, London, from early 19th C. book. (M) Jockey's head, in Thornhill's ad in the _Illustrated Sporting & Dramatic News_, 12/1882. English. (R) Carved hardwood toothy man in moon, iron hinge in back. 5"H. Mid 19th C. Has been reproduced by Boston Museum of Art in cast polymer resin & in brass, about 6"H with small base. This one courtesy Robert & Mary Lou Sutter, East Chatham, NY.
$225.00-$350.00 (L & R); $150.00-$225.00 (M)

I-74.
Dog nutcrackers.
Just 3 examples of the many versions of a St. Bernard or Mastiff type dog, popular dog breeds in 1860s-80s. Top Nickeled iron, 8 3/4"L, pat. # appears to be 375460 (not same as modern-style horse #273480; nor the dinosaur). This one English. (M) Dog on fancy base, with sheep-like hair, is nickeled iron, marked "L.A. Althoff Mfg. Co. Makers of Headlights, Stoves & Ranges, La Port, IN." (B) Cast brass, 5 3/8"H with base x 11 1/4"L. Probably English.
$85.00-$150.00

I-75.

Nutmeg graters.

(A) Coffin-box type, backs show 2 of many ways platform created for lidded nutmeg receptacle atop grating surface. 5 1/4"L. Early 20th C, type still sold. Judy Bancroft Collection. (B) M.H. Sexton, Utica, NY, pat'd 5/1896. Tin, nickeled spring metal holds meg. 4 3/4"L x 3"W. (Larger size known). (C) Called by 2 names: "Unique" & "Monitor", pat'd 3/19/1889 by T.L. Holt. "Unique" mfd. by Steel Edge Stamping & Retinning Co., Boston; "Monitor" made by New England Novelty Mfg. Co., Boston — possibly same co. Marked "Press down lightly." 4 3/8"L x 2"W; pinkish-stained wood frame with diagonal tracking over tin grater. Photo'd as sled. (D) 2 versions "Edgar". Older one at left. Edgar Mfg. Co., Reading, MA, pat'd 8/18/1891. 5 7/8"L. Green-painted wood; varnished wood. (E) Richard H. Chinn, Washington, DC, pat'd 7/16/1867. No marks. All tin, sliding, spring-loaded hopper, 6 1/4"L. (F) Nathan Ames, Saugus, MA, assignor 1/2 to Edmund Brown, Lynn, MA,

pat'd 10/13/1857. Tin with orig. blue paint; wood spring-activated pusher inside cylindrical holder. About 5 3/8"L diagonally. Patent drawing shows small loop handle; 1871 picture shows large "cup handle" of strap tin. (G) "H. Carsley, Lynn, MA. Patent applied for" stamped on cylindrical holder. Patent granted 11/20/1855. 3 7/8"L. Bob Cahn. (H) Skeletal form, no mark, 7 1/2"L. Screwed pressure foot; pierced drum with holes at slight angle. (I) & (J) Two versions of same grater. Cast iron, tin, wire. 5 1/4"L (Another is 7"L). Pat'd 3/9/1886. Ex-Keillor Collection. (K) "Gem", rotary motion, nickeled cast iron. Caldwell Mfg. Co., Rochester, NY. 4" x 2 3/4". 1908 ad. All not attributed are courtesy Joe & Teri Dziadul. **A 40 + PAGE BOOKLET WITH MORE ON NUTMEG GRATERS, EMPHASIZING PATENT DRAWINGS & SPECIFICATIONS, WILL BE AVAILABLE By December 1991 FROM AUTHOR FOR $12.00 ppd.**

   (A) $7.00-$12.00. Edgar: $65.00-$85.00. Others $100.00 plus.

I-76.
Nutmeg graters.

Tin & wood. Small knob in slot pulls back spring-load pressure foot to hold against grating drum. 6 1/8"L, pat'd 12/25/1877. In 1890, this design was changed so tin box part elongated to form handle & nutmeg storage, with lid on end. Spring, knob, wire crank & grating drum remained same. Mfd. under old patent by The Standard Co., Boston, and called "new" by them. (M) "Champion Grater Co., Boston, Mass." Two patent dates: 10/9/1866, and on end of brass cap "April 2, 1867." 7 1/2"L. (N) Tin, spring-loaded, rather crude wheel. No mark. 4 1/4"L. (O) Long tin 4-sided barrel holder with hinged lid at end. Grating drum encircled by battery of discs with deep & jagged teeth, like meat tenderizer or harrow discs. Stamped "The — S (?) Davidson Automatic Nutmeg Grater. Boston, Mass. Pat'd June 2, 1908." 6 3/4"L. (P) Two slightly different versions of "The Handy," with screw-cap ends to nutmeg storage chamber & spring-loaded hatch for meg being grated. Wood knobs, threads on caps, and lengths differ. 4 3/4"L x 5 3/8"L. A later one 6 1/2"L. Late 19th C. (Q) "Rapid", japanned tin cylinder with tapered nozzle. 5 1/4"L. Another measures 6 1/4"L. And by

1906, one almost identical, much stubbier, called "Ever-Ready", of nickeled brass, was only 4 1/4"L. (R) Tin, with hollow shaped tin storage handle having its own tiny ovoid hinged lid at end, underside, for putting megs in. 7 1/2"L, marked only "press lightly." (S) Skillin & Reed grater, Portland, ME, pat'd 9/3/1867. Albion S. Skillin & George W. Reed; assignors of 1/2 to Henry Hanson & J. Butler. Turned wood, tin disc, springy wood pressure foot along underneath to hold nutmeg in. 6 7/8"L. (T) "Brown & Hasler, Lynn, Mass. Pat. applied for." Wood handle & presser, tin body, black paper label with gold lettering. 7"L. (U) Stamped "Portable Ginger & Nutmeg Mill. Reg. Nov. 11, 1857." English. Japanned tin, 3 3/16" x 2 7/16". (V) Wood & tin "Commonsense," pat'd 7/23/1867, by R.W. Whitney & Joseph P. Davis, South Berwick, ME. 5 1/8"L. (W) Pat'd 6/7/1870, by J.M. Smith, Seymour, CT. Cast iron, hinged bellow-shaped body, spring-loaded cartridge for 1 meg. Directional arrow cast in for crank. Could be screwed to cupboard. 3 7/8"L. (X) Tin, wood, spring. About 6 1/4" diag. 1870s. All nutmeg graters courtesy Joe & Teri Dziadul, dealers in Enfield, CT. **$100.00 and up.**

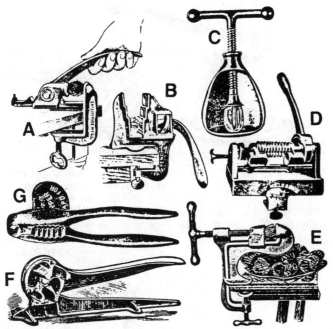

I-77.
Mechanical nutcrackers.
(Crowded in here for space reasons). (A) "Enterprise," Philadelphia. c.1910. (B) "Home", mfd. by Schroeter Bros. Hardware Co., St. Louis, MO. Nickeled cast malleable iron, 6"H x 4"W with 7 1/2" lever. Pat'd c.1915. (C) Handheld "Ideal" with old-style knobbed handle. Nickeled cast iron, c.1915. (D) "Perfect" pecan cracker, Thomas Mills & Bros., Philadelphia, c.1930. (E) "Perfection", Waco, TX. Screw clamps to table. 1917 ad. (F) Levered cracker, cast iron, from F.A. Walker catalog, 1870s (G) "Harper", nickeled cast steel, c.1910. **$20.00-$75.00**

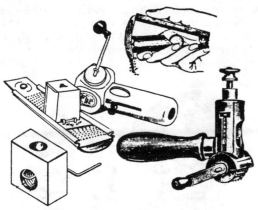

I-78.
Nutmeg graters.
Clockwise from one with hand: (1) "Automatic" squeeze-action, grating on inside of curved surface. 4 1/4" x 2 1/2", nickeled steel, c.1903. "Nutmeg is placed in the hollow tube, the tube is grasped by the hand, and 'there you are.' " A bar-suppliers' catalog said "It is the only automatic nutmeg grater where you can hold the glass in one hand and manipulate the grater with the other." (2) 1924 subscription premium from American Cookery magazine. Maker not identified, but style is 19th C. (3) Patent drawing Albert L. Platt, 10/3/1893. (4) "Boye Sanitary" grater, Boye Needle Co., pat'd 9/29/1914. Box holding nutmegs is opened by sliding it out of side tracking. (5) "Little Rhody", wood & tin, red & black paper label, 1880s. **$100.00 and up.**

I-79.
Pea sheller.
"Acme," Acme Pea Sheller Co., NYC. Galvanized cast iron, screw clamps. Pods fell out back into pail hung on frame's hook; peas fell into dish.

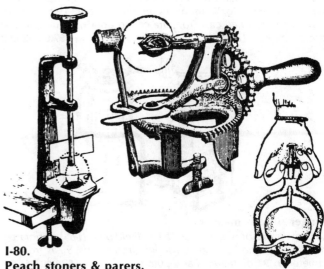

I-80.
Peach stoners & parers.
(L) Cast iron stoner, screw clamps, plunges and apparently cuts peach in half with blade. From F.A. Walker catalog, Boston, 1870s. (M) "Lightning" parer, mfd. by Goodell Co., Antrim, NH. Sargent & Co., agents (their name may appear on some gadgets like this, I don't know). Exhibited at 1869 NY, St. Louis and other agricultural fairs & won prizes. Pat'd 8/17/1869. (R) "Rollman No. 6", Rollman Mfg. Co., Mt. Joy, PA. "Patent applied for" in c.1901-05 catalog. **$35.00-$150.00**

I-81.
Pineapple Eye Clip.
"Patterson's." M.E. Mosher, Mfr., Rochester, NY. Trigger action, nickeled steel. Introduced in 1905. **$5.00-$10.00**

I-82.
Metal potato mashers.
Along back row are 4 of the scores of cleverly bent, woven, twisted, coiled & braided wire mashers, with vertical turned wood handles. Made by many makers. About 7"H to 14"H for household ones; even longer for hotel or restaurant versions. Two in front, galvanized or tinned cast iron, are called **potato muddlers**, and date at least to 1870. **$7.00-$25.00**

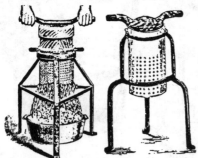

I-83.
Plunger potato mashers,
like big versions of potato ricers, a handheld press (I-85). Perforated tin cylinders, wood plungers, wrought iron stands. Sizes from 6" diameter to 9" diameter. Early 20th C. **$20.00-$45.00**

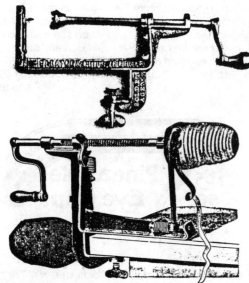

I-84.
Potato parers.
(T) "Saratoga Chips. 75 Cents" embossed on horizontal framework. "Sold by Agents" on screw clamp. Taylor Mfg. Co., New Britain, CT. Pat'd 6/18/1878. Photo courtesy John Lambert. (B) "White Mountain" parer, Goodell Co. "This machine will also pare Quinces and Pears" say ads. Late 19th C on — sold for many years. **$75.00 and up**

I-85.
Potato ricers,
or hand presses. Showing 2 basic styles — the round cylinder "drum" style, and the "V"-shaped one like the famous Henis press. (L) "Genuine Silver Press," Silver & Co., Brooklyn, removable cups. Strong & durable, "the castings are made of a peculiar composition of iron which absolutely guarantees their unbreakability." c.1910. (R) 4 1/4 x 4 1/4" cup. Tinned malleable cast iron. c.1905. **$10.00-$25.00**

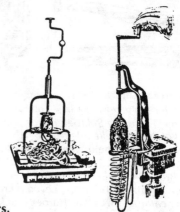

I-86.
Potato slicers.
(L) "Marguerita Macaroni" — the "only practical machine for preparing the potatoes in continuous curling strips, for boiling, stewing, or potato ribbon." Nickeled iron. Could also be used for cutting "beets, carrots, turnips, &c." for garnishing. 1914 catalog. (R) Potato slicer, pat'd 1870 and 1871 (?) or 1877 (?). A witch in a diamond-patterned dress, stirring her brew. F.A. Walker catalog, 1870s. **$45.00-$75.00**

I-87.
Potato & vegetable slicers.
(1) Also called a "citron slicer" in confectioners' catalogs. "Lightning," japanned cast iron, screw clamps. 4 cutting blades to disc. 10 1/2"L, late 19th C & sold for decades. (2) "Clinton Patent," M.L. & C.M. Clinton, Ithaca NY, Pat'd Oct. 10, 1874. Japanned cast iron. For making Saratoga potato chips up to 1/4" thick, & for apples, cucumbers & cabbage. (3) "Rapid Tomato Slicer." In Valentine Clad, Philadelphia, catalog, c.1870s-1890s. (4) "Enterprise No. 49" vegetable slicer. 16"H x 11" diameter cylinder, which revolves. Sometimes called the "Boss." Late 19th to early 20th C. **$65.00-$200.00**

I-88.
Querne.

A fairly primitive grinding mill for seeds, spices & grains. 2 round mill stones, from 6" to 10" diameter (these are 6"), the upper one turned by a handle or knob. Wood frame, 17 1/2"H x 13"L x 7"W. Swedish or Danish, 18th or early 19th C. Ex-Keillor Collection.
$200.00-$300.00

I-89.
Raisin seeders.

Clockwise from top: (1) Nickeled cast iron, very decorative casting. (Not always plated). 6 1/2"H x 4"W, 1870s. (2) "EZY" seeder, pat'd 5/21/1899. "Scald the raisins" cast into other side. 5"H, clamps to table edge. (3) "Everett," from 1890s, marked "patent applied for." Wire & wood, 3 1/8"L. (4) Cast iron with 8-wire seeder attached to lever. 4 legs. Pat'd 5/7/1895. (2) & (4) Located by the Primitive Man, Bob Cahn, Carmel, NY. (1) & (3) Collection of Meryle Evans.
$22.00-$175.00

I-90.
Raisin seeders.

Cast iron, nickeled or galvanized, screw clamps. (L) "Enterprise No. 36," Philadelphia. Embossed "Wet the raisins" along upright frame. Rubber roller inside. Pat'd 4/2/1895. A later patent seen on them is 8/20/1895. 11"H. The No. 38 was for bakers & hotels; this for family use. (R) "X-Ray" seeder, "composed of 38 different parts put together as true and perfect as a watch." 1890s.
$30.00-$60.00

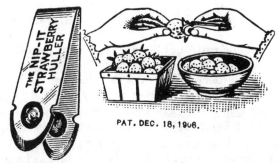

I-91.
Strawberry huller & pinfeather picker.

"Nip-It," Windsor Stephens & Co., Waltham, MA, pat'd 12/18/1906. Nickeled spring steel. "By its use one avoids stained fingers, seeds under fingernails, crushed fruit." Also for plucking chickens.
$3.00-$8.00

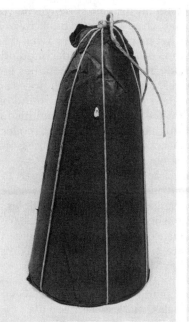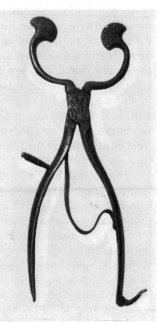

I-92.
Sugar cone & sugar nippers.

(L) Conical molded cake of granulated sugar, wrapped in blue paper & tied, as customary for maybe centuries in Europe, & in US in 18th & early 19th C. This one is from Belgium, but form is the same. About 10"H x 4 3/4" diameter. Photo courtesy National Museum of American History, Smithsonian Institution. (R) Prettiest nippers I ever saw. Steel, cut design at pivot, very stylized. 8 13/16"L. Stock of Lauri & Bill Sweetman, Laubill Antiques, Golfstown, NH.
$125.00-$175.00

I-93.
Sugar cone cutter.

For country store. Grain-painted wood box, iron arched frame or blade guard and blade. Turned wood knob and handle. Punctured tin plate for sifting sugar before going in drawer. Identified & located by The Primitive Man, Bob Cahn, Carmel, NY. Courtesy Mike & Sunny Kolba Collection.

A. PREPARING:
II. MIX, BEAT, STIR, CHURN & BLEND

"Eat and run" and "grab a bite" were the only ways to eat in mankind's earliest days. The concept of fixing a meal, let alone having a meal, had to wait for tools and techniques of preparation. The most basic of those techniques involve cutting or mashing (dealt with in the first chapter).

Implements and gadgets in this chapter accomplish the next level of preparation: they <u>change texture, taste or other attributes, mainly by creating mixtures.</u> You might argue that eggbeaters belong in the first chapter, because the "blades" cut the yolks and whites, or beat them like a mortar and pestle. But eggbeaters are here because their purpose and their effect is to <u>blend two separate or disparate parts into one.</u>

Eggbeaters are by far the most popular mechanical device in this chapter; we are beguiled by the poetry of their motion. They look like ballet dancers, twirling and spinning, (well, some of them are more like four year olds at a recital — not so graceful as primas, but just as spirited). Even when at rest their curved blades, small waists and waiting arms promise the dance to come. Those with "aprons" are wearing big tutus.

What happens when a lot of collectors pursue one category of collectible is that unknown examples surface. In addition, when a single-focus book is written, the role model collection on display in the book invites emulation. The demand part of the equation grows and the supply increases briefly when publicity brings the stuff out, then drops because desirable beaters are socked away in collections. Each new surge of publicity brings out a few more (for a first or serial appearance on the market). Patent records convince me that many eggbeaters await discovery. Although a large percentage of patented gadgets were never manufactured, numerous patented, manufactured oddities have been found in the last seven or eight years, and the possibility that they were made in commercial quantities gives hope. Prices for basic, common varieties (the foundation of any collection) are still relatively low, under $20.00; prices at the top are into the hundreds now. Don Thornton's book (See Bibliography) is out of print; let's hope that a new round of interest in beaters will elicit another book from him, one that will include many rarities that the publisher cut from his first book.

Some collectors have enough energy and room to collect churns, even floor-standing models, but most people have to treat large churns more like pieces of furniture than accessories, and consider them adjuncts to other collections. It's too bad, because so much variety exists in their form and finish.

The mixing bowls in this chapter were originally part of a larger group of bowls in the Storage and Container chapter. I moved them here because mixing bowls and beater jars are half of the whole, just as a churn body forms a whole tool with a dasher. I find it difficult to evaluate clay kitchen collectibles, because ceramics have been collected for so long, and standards, rules and lingo are well-established. When I commandeer ceramics to put into a book on kitchen collectibles, to a certain extent I have to reevaluate bowls, cookie jars, salt boxes, etc., that have already been categorized, classified, rated, and priced within another collecting context. But if we are going to compete with ceramics' collectors at flea markets and antique shows, we're the newcomers who have to abide by their rules.

Batter bowl, yellowware, big pouring lip, acanthus leaves decoration, badly cracked, alas, mark is big deep diamond, can't read name, 13⅝" diameter, 19th C. **$12.00-$18.00**

Batter jug, also called a <u>batter pot,</u> brown glaze, with tin lid and wire bail handle, from Havana, NY, 19th C. **$75.00-$85.00**

Batter jug, bulbous saltglazed stoneware, with funny stick-out ear handles, wire bail with wooden grip, tin cap on spout, tin lid (probably replacement, as it fits inside the opening, rather than capping the entire top opening) with strap handle, "Evan B. Jones," Pittston, PA, about 12"H, c.1870s to 1890s. • <u>Added value.</u> — For nice, but fairly common decoration, values up to $2500.00 or more. For terrific human or animal subjects, with excellent drawing, good detail, verve, spontanaety, over $15,000.00. It pays to study **$700.00-$900.00**

Batter jug, dark brown saltglazed stoneware, with odd clay clam shells applied on sides, as "ears" for square wire bail handle, knotty carved wood grip, tin covers on spout and top, no mark, from Bryant Pond, ME (last place in America with crank telephones), 8½"H, 19th C. **$150.00-$200.00**

Batter jug, dark brown stoneware, with what's called "Albany" slip glaze, tin cover on top, missing spout cover, wire bail, Bennington, VT, 19th C. **$175.00-$225.00**

Batter jug, saltglazed stoneware, ovoid shape, rather wide applied tilting handle at base opposite the side of the pouring spout, pretty lugs on either side with wire handle with wooden grip, a very desirable form, with unusual cobalt decoration of a leafy wreath encircling a humorous big-nosed man's profile, called by the collectors "Man in the Moon" (called by Donald Blake Webster "Punch"), has stoneware lid rather than fitted tin one, spout lid missing, also stamped with a desirable maker's mark, "Cowden & Wilcox", Harrisburg, PA, made c.1850s or early 60s. • The Robacker May 1989 auction price for this entry is a record for batter jugs, but the price breaks down to more for decoration than form. **$10,000.00**

Batter jug, squat saltglazed stoneware, ear handles, wire bail, blue decoration, viz. a sort of wreath surrounding folky man's profile with big nose & ear way up the side of the head, instead of halfway like most ears, tin lid, wire bail handle with wooden grip, Cowden & Wilcox, c.1850s to early 60s. • In Donald Blake Webster's book on decorated stoneware, is a picture of a somewhat ovoid crock owned by him with another version of the decoration. Webster's man has a huge chin. • The batter jug in this entry is similar to the Robacker one in previous entry, but surfaced on the market in the early 1980s. Price range brackets what would be expected prior to the $10,000 Robacker sale. When an auction price jolts the market, it's impossible right away to predict long term effect on the market. **$4500.00-$6500.00**

Batter pitcher, bulbous shape, 2 spouts, spongeware with brown, green & yellow glaze, American, 19th C. **$120.00-$140.00**

Batter pitcher, Rockingham flintware, yellow & brown glaze, American, 19th C. **$135.00-$150.00**

Batter pitcher, stoneware with yellow glaze, wire bail with wooden grip, American, 19th C. **$100.00-$135.00**

Beaten biscuit machine, also called biscuit brake, cast iron frame screw clamps to table, with 2 nickel plated rollers with iron crank, cast iron base rather like a sewing machine base, with marble top, the dough is fed through the rollers, which are reset closer & closer, to really work dough until it starts to form bubbles (''blisters'') that make cracking snapping sounds when they break. (For the sound, think of a mouthful of really old bubble gum.) ''The DeMuth Improved Dough Kneader & Beaten Biscuit Machine'', mfd by J. A. DeMuth, St. Joseph, MO, approx. 36''H overall, table is 30½''H x 36''L x 16''W; rollers are 2¼'' diameter x 14''L, c.1890. • I've seen one belonging to a Virginia friend, who makes beaten biscuits for her famous parties; one was bought by a Texas friend from an ad in *Antique Trader*, and had it shipped (in 3 cartons) U.P.S. I have also seen just the rollers, no base. Not a common contrivance. • These machines took some of the work out of making this Southern treat ... once made by beating the dough with a cook's axe, wooden mallet, or heavy rolling pin until it made cracking sounds. The biscuits keep very well, even frozen, aren't tough or crusty, but are dense & chewy. They are baked to the faintest tinge of tan. • **''Miss Fort's Beaten Biscuit.** — 1½ lb. flour, 5 oz. lard, 1½ tsp. salt, 2 tsp. sugar , dissolved in 1 cup water. Blend flour, lard and salt. Mix into a stiff dough with water in which sugar has been dissolved. Work well. Beat or roll until dough blisters. Bake in moderate oven until light brown. • **Beaten Biscuit No. 2.** — 1 qt. flour, ½ tsp. baking powder, 1 level tsp. salt, lard size of goose egg, ⅔ cup of milk and water, half of each with 1 tsp. of sugar dissolved in milk; have dough very stiff. Beat or roll until it blisters.'' Mrs. W. H. Wilson, *Mrs. Wilson's Cook Book*, 1914. • **''To Make Little Cracknels.** — Take three pounds of flour finely dried, three ounces of lemon and orange-peel dried, and beaten to a powder, an ounce of coriander-seeds beaten and searced [sieved], and three pounds of double refined sugar beaten fine and searced; mix these together with fifteen eggs, half of the whites taken out, a quarter of a pint of rose-water, as much orange-flower water; beat the eggs and water well together, then put in your orange peel & coriander-seeds, and beat it again very well with two spoons, one in each hand; then beat your sugar in by little and little, then your flour by a little at a time, so beat with both spoons an hour longer; then strew sugar on papers, and drop then the bigness of a walnut, and set them in the oven; the oven must be hotter than when pies are drawn; do not touch them with your finger before they are bak'd; let the oven be ready for them against [before] they are done [and] be careful the oven does not colour them.'' Elizabeth Smith, *The Compleat Housewife*, 1753. **$250.00-$500.00**

Beaten biscuit machine, tabletop model, mainly wood, cranked rollers, American, c.1860s. **$150.00-$175.00**

Beater jar, green glazed crockery, ''D. B. Wich Beater,'' American, 20th C. **$25.00-$35.00**

Beater jar, saltglazed stoneware, ''Red Wing Beater Jar, Eggs, Cream Salad Dressing,'' 20th C. **$60.00-$75.00**

Beater jar, saltglazed stoneware, blue stripe, for eggs, cream, salad dressings, made by Red Wing, advertising ''You Beat Eggs, We Beat Prices, Star Grocery, Parkersburg, Iowa,'' 20th C. • **Red Wing** is one of the most sought-after ceramic lines in this field. There are hundreds, perhaps thousands, of pieces — from flowerpots to milkjugs — available from this Minnesota city's potteries. There are a couple of books by Gary & Bonnie Tefft (see Bibliography). Organized in 1977, the Red Wing Collectors Society's 1989 address is Helen Bell, 1718 W. 6th St., Red Wing, MN 55066. • Some other potteries who made beater jars are A. S. Lauritson, Tyler, MN; Gross Mercantile Co., Bridgewater, SD; Frank J. Martin, Ackley, IA. All within same range. **$65.00-$100.00**

Beater jar, saltglazed stoneware, blue striped, advertising ''Wesson Oil For Making Good Things to Eat,'' 20th C. **$35.00-$55.00**

Beater jar, saltglazed stoneware, blue stripes, with advertising motto, ''Mix with Us, Save Dough, Rockwell City, IA'', 20th C. **$65.00-$80.00**

Beater jar, saltglazed stoneware, marked ''Holiday Greeting,'' Red Wing, dated 1924. **$60.00-$85.00**

Beater jar, yellowware, marked ''Foremost Dairies,''American, 20th C. **$45.00-$55.00**

Beater jars have grown in popularity in last 10 years or so. They are mainly 20th C saltglazed stoneware, or earthenware, usually in blue or brown, sometimes with stripes, straight sides like crocks, approx. 6''H x 4½''D. Taller than wide, they're ideal for inserting an eggbeater. Most popular ones were made by various Red Wing (MN) potteries, starting c. 1900. Red Wing's jars have various finishes: ''blue band'', ''gray line'' (grayish white with blue & red bands), ''saffron'' yellowware, etc. • Many jars were printed with a legend, message or motto on side, advertising a variety of retail or service businesses, mostly in the Midwest; examples include: Cairo Mercantile Co., Cairo, NE; E. C. Reed, North English, IA; Swanson's, West Union, IA; Semons, Athens, WI; Stewart Olson & Sons; Farmer's Elevator, Peterson, IA; Babers Mercantile, Hansel, IA; and Ardmore Lumber, Ardmore, SD. (See Rolling pins, Chapter IV, and ''Mixing Bowls,'' for other advertising stoneware.) **$50.00-$85.00**

Bowl, Saffron spatterware, with shoulder, Red Wing, with ''Christmas Greetings, 1938, Protovin, Iowa,'' 20th C. **$50.00-$65.00**

Bread machine, frame of cast iron, 4 arched legs, tinned horizontal body, various gears, side crank, horizontal bar to hang on to with user's non-cranking hand, top lifts off the ''basin'', the lower part is where the kneaded dough rested or rose. Cyrus Chambers, Jr., Scientific Bread Machine Co., Phila., about 16''H, TOC to 1910s. **$65.00-$110.00**

Bread maker, screw clamps to table, tin with cast iron gears, ''White House Bread Maker,'' American, 1902. **$100.00-$125.00**

Bread maker, tin & iron, ''Awarded Gold Medal St. Louis Exposition,'' ''Universal,'' Landers, Frary, Clark, 1904-?. **$50.00-$65.00**

Bread maker, tin pail & lid, screw clamp iron frame, iron crank. Heavy gauge wire snaky kneader fitted to lid. Stamped on lid are the directions: ''Put in all liquids first — then flour — turn 3 minute — raise in pail — after raising turn until dough forms a ball — take off cross piece — lift out dough with kneader." "Universal No. 8," mfd by Landers, Frary & Clark, New Britain, CT, 11⅞"H. (Other numbers — such as No. 4, No. 44 — are different heights.) 1904. (These were made for quite a long time.) Add $6.00-$8.00 for original paper label on pail. **75.00-$95.00**

Bread maker, tin pail, never had a lid, screw clamp, "Universal No. 2," Landers, Frary & Clark, 1904 on. **$20.00-$35.00**

Bread mixer, heavy tin pail, side handles, side crank turns "U" shaped wire blade inside, domed crimped tin lid with wooden knob, screw clamp, labeled "Chauvauquat Bread Mixer," Polar Star, mfd by Smith & Hemenway Co. (S. & H. Co.), NYC, NY, four sizes from two to 16 loaf capacity, c.1909. • A joke from the period, reported as appearing in a North Dakota newspaper: "It is reported that one of our fastidious, newly married ladies kneads bread with her gloves on. The incident may be somewhat peculiar, but there are others. For instance, the editor of this paper needs bread with his shoes on; he needs bread with his shirt on; he needs bread with his pants on, and unless some delinquent subscribers pay up, he will need bread without anything on — and North Dakota is no Garden of Eden in the winter time." *House Furnishing Review*, June 1905. **$25.00-$40.00**

Bread mixer & kneader, also called a <u>dough mixer,</u> heavy charcoal tin plate, steel & cast iron, slope sided shallow tin pan, above which is mounted frame, paddles & crank, "Universal," Landers, Frary & Clark, 1890s to early 20th C. • **Do You Need One of These?** "The process of kneading with this machine is thoroughly scientific and sanitary. It makes no difference what kind of bread flour is used. Results are always the same — better bread. Directly opposite to hand kneading is the work of the Universal. ... In hand kneading the particles of flour are necessarily pressed together, and the liquid does not thoroughly moisten each particle of the starch granules, while with the bread maker these particles are lightly held apart until thoroughly wetted ... and kneaded."
• **Reproduction alert.** — In a 1973 *House Beautiful*, a "Home Accessories" company in Massachusetts advertised an $18.00 "Old Fashioned Bread Mixer" that consists of a wooden bucket, with a cranked apparatus fitted to its rim. The ad reads "Remember the unforgettable aroma of good old yeast breads while they're baking. And, that wonderful taste sensation of a loaf still warm from the oven. Here is an 8 quart walnut finished wooden bucket with inside surfaces clear sealed. A stainless steel mixing rod & hammered aluminum diecast hardware. Free 'Old Time' bread recipes included." • **German vocabulary** — <u>Knetmaschine:</u> **kneading machine.**
$55.00-$70.00

Bread or dough mixer, sometimes called a <u>dough brake,</u> double layer of bent wood for body, nailed construction, cast iron crank, wooden knob, iron mixing blade, iron handle. Fits in crook of arm, held against body, may be American, but crank looks European, 5"H x 10"D, 19th C. • **"Bread: What Ought It to Be?** It should be light, sweet, tender. This matter of lightness is the distinctive line between civilized and savage bread. The savage mixes simple flour and water into balls of paste, which he throws into boiling water, and which come out, solid, glutinous masses, of which his common saying is, 'Man

eat dis, he no die,' which a facetious traveller interpreted to mean, 'Dis no kill you, nothing will.'" Catherine Beecher & Harriet Beecher Stowe, *American Woman's Home*, 1869. Hmmm, they sound like bagels.
$175.00-$225.00

Bread rising tray, for bakers, wood, for 6 loaves, American, about 39"L x 6⅝"W, late 19th C. **$185.00-$220.00**

Butter fork, painted wood, 5 thick tines, looks like an Afro comb, handle is like a paintbrush's, "Mrs. Bragg's Butter Fork," not marked, American, about 6"L, late 19th C.
$12.00-$18.00

Butter paddle, also <u>butter spade</u> or <u>butter ladle,</u> carved wood with very shallow bowl & short crook-necked or hooked handle, beautiful mellow patina, 8"L, 19th C.
• **What's It For?** — "For working butter, keep a wooden bowl and ladle. This last article is seldom found in New England, but always in the state of New York." Mrs. Mary Hooker Cornelius, *The Young Housekeeper's Friend*, 1859. All of the familiar types (the nearly round slightly bowled one with short crook-necked handle; the flat, straight sided, slightly rounded front edge one with angled rounded handles; and the one most resembling a spade, flat longish blade with straight edges, handle raised slightly) were shown in Montgomery Ward's 1895 catalog. I'm sure they were sold well into 20th C, (& perhaps today through dairy suppliers). • <u>Added value.</u> — Really good patina, signs of hand carving, exceptional figure in the grain, even knots, all add value, because they are signs of age or uniqueness. **$35.00-$45.00**

Butter paddle, carved tiger maple, all one piece of wood, standard shape, hooked handle has wonderful small man wearing top hat seated atop handle, incised heart midway down flat shank of handle, age crack in bowl, from PA & NY border, 10½"L, prob. early to mid 19th C. • More evidence of the folk art tradition in kitchenwares. This marvelous piece was discovered, & for sale by Doris Axtell, Deposit, NY, in 1985. Price range is mine.
$500.00-$800.00

Butter paddle, carved wood, shaped like a thick, slightly scooped ping pong paddle, 9"L x 5¼"W, late 19th C.
$20.00-$25.00

Butter paddle, carved wood with shallow convex bowl, hooked handle in exaggerated angle where it joins bowl, American (?), 4¼"D with 5"L handle, 19th C. • I never even used to look at these, but have noticed lately how much variation there is in this form, particularly in handle detail & imaginative use of grain and knots. That's one of the secrets of collecting, as you know, looking for & finding variations on a theme. Bach & Bartok did it for music! **$40.00-$60.00**

Butter paddle, maple handle, wire blade, 8¾"L, TOC.
$15.00-$18.00

Butter paddle, maple, with hanging hole in handle, rather long at 14"L, late 19th C. **$18.00-$22.00**

Butter scoop or paddle, carved lightweight pale wood, curved, slightly irregular neck, American, 8½"L, late 19th C.
$18.00-$25.00

Butter worker, for use in dairy barn or buttery, wood with remains of old blue paint on outside, a trough & 2 corrugated rollers, on skeletal frame, American, trough is 30"L, late 19th C. **$135.00-$165.00**

Butter worker, tabletop for home use, wood with corrugated swinging arm, very worn, with nice patina, American, TOC. **$65.00-$100.00**

Butter worker, tabletop, stool-like wooden frame, bentwood holder for butter & mechanism, wooden gears, iron crank handle, American, 13½''H x 9'' x 8'', 19th C.
$250.00-$350.00

Cake mixer, tin & cast iron, screw clamps to table like bread mixer, ''Universal,'' Landers, Frary & Clark, TOC.
$45.00-$55.00

Cake mixer, tin dough pail, with cast iron gears, crank & frame, screw clamps to table, ''American Machine Co.,'' pat'd 1873. **$45.00-$65.00**

Cake mixer & cream whip, tin, ''Rumford,'' pat'd 1908.
$15.00-$18.00

Cake spoon — See Mixing spoon, this chapter.

Cheese curd knife, wood, long blade to break up the curd in the process of cheese-making, American, 22''L, late 19th C. • For similar purpose, but looking quite different, is the curd knife. Two types were advertised in the turn-of-the-century Montgomery Ward catalogs: an oblong metal frame, open at one end, with a short, turned wood handle at other, many blades set across the short axis. For cutting the curds up into fine pieces. Came in one length, 20'', but five widths: 4'', 6'', 8'', 10'' and 12''. The other style had 20''L blades, set 6'', 8'', 10'', 12'', 14'', 15'' and 20''W. These thin narrow blades, set about 3 or 4 to the inch, would swish through the curds. This latter kind is, in turn, a version of a curd whip — a long implement with four or five inch-wide spring steel blades, 18''L, set into a turned wooden handle. It dates to the 1870s-90s. The value of the first two types would be under $20.00; the curd whip or whipper might bring up to $30.00. In contrast, the market value of all wood wares, especially with the kind of satiny patina that so enhances dairy implements, is much higher: **$75.00-$95.00**

Cheese curd whipper, spring steel blades, wooden grip, American, 24½''L, 1880s. **$65.00-$85.00**

Churn, all wood barrel on A frame stand, side crank, top loading, O. R. Flyers, Grafton, VT, about 46''H, 19th C. • This was advertised as being from 1826 (possibly typo for 1876?). I read listings for every Churn, every Washing Machine, & every combination patent listing in *Subject Index to Patents, 1790-1873*, also an unnumbered patents index from 1790 to 1836. No ''Flyers'', and no Grafton, VT. But two churns were patented from towns called Grafton: H.D. Smith's, Grafton, OH, May 5, 1868, and T. Conely's, Grafton, IL, June 25, 1872. • Probably thie Flyers' churn was never actually patented. **$150.00-$200.00**

Churn, cast iron wheel & handle, nickeled blades, speckled blue saltglazed stoneware body, thin wooden lid with knob, no maker's name, American, 14¾'' overall height, crock 8''H, pat'd May 15, 1906 & Feb. 26, 1907.
$160.00-$190.00

Churn, crank type with wooden paddles, glass jar with metal gears & screw-on lid, no mark, American, 4 qt. size, TOC. **$45.00-$65.00**

Churn, cranked, cream colored painted wood, has large crank wheel & smaller iron gear wheel above, natural finish lid, ''Dazey,'' 18''H body , plus 12''H wheel & frame, pat'd Dec. 18, 1877. **$85.00-$120.00**

Churn, cylinder type on 4 shoe feet, wood with iron side crank, ''R.W.,'' label shows initials over an anchor, sold through Montgomery Ward, American, various sizes, 1890s-1910. • Unless stenciled or burned-in branded names remain, few wooden churns can be identified by maker. Around 1900, many U.S. companies were making them, including Moseley & Pritchard Mfg. in Clinton, IA; Aspinwall Mfg. Co. in Jackson, MI; Frank L. Jones in Utica, NY; Anderson & Carothers of Sidney, OH; Standard Churn Co., Wapakonetta, OH; A.H. Reid, Philadelphia, PA; Stoddard Mfg. Co., Rutland, VT; Cornish, Curtis & Greene Mfg. Co. of Fort Atkinson, WI; and Menasha Woodenware Co., Menasha, WI.
$45.00-$75.00

Churn, cylinder type, on rather delicate shoe footed stand, wood painted yellow, 15¾'' x 18'' x 21'', 19th C.
$175.00-$225.00

Churn, cylinder type, sometimes called a bowler churn, tin in cast iron frame, square body, flywheel, mechanical movement, dated 1907. **$50.00-$65.00**

Churn, cylinder type, Tennessee white wood (as it was described in early catalog) box with iron hoops, iron crank, ''Diamond Balance Churn Co.,'' named for shape of its box body, various sizes from 1 to 60 gal. (the biggest were dog-, sheep- or horse-powered), pat'd May 28, 1889, Oct. 27, 1891 & Nov. 17, 1891. • Just for a price perspective, this is for the 10 gal. size: **$65.00-$95.00**

Churn, cylinder type with side crank, ochre painted wood, rectangular hopper & wooden lid, 4 sturdy shoe feet, American? 21''H x 15½'' x 19'', TOC.
$225.00-$300.00

Churn, cylinder type, wood barrel & wood frame, crank on side, lock-on lid, ''Fairy Churn,'' mfd by N. H. (or H. H. ?) Palmer Co., Rockford, IL, TOC. • **Churning.** — ''The process of churning is necessary to force out the serous fluid from the cream in order to produce butter. This is done by agitation and in a churn. There are various kinds of churns, but the best churn is the one that will preserve the proper temperature, or the same temperature that is in the churn and cream when put into it. In warm weather cold water for some time is to be put into the churn, and in cold weather scalding water, and also putting hot or cold water in the cream according to the season. As it is important to preserve the same temperature while churning — the best churns are those which are used in an horizontal position — such as the stationary barrel with dashers to move in the inside. A small churn is in use on this principle, and answers a good purpose, as a hole of sufficient size from one half an inch to an inch, may be made on the top, to let out the warm air produced by the agitation of the cream, and to admit the cool air. A barrel churn of this kind has been used, when 36 to 38 lb. of butter was made twice a week.'' *The Farmers' Cabinet*, Philadelphia, July 1, 1836, some 60 years before the Fairy Churn was advertised, though it would answer the purpose very well.
$75.00-$100.00

Churn, cylinder type, wood painted with (original?) greenish gray paint, supposedly Shaker, 19th C. • If it were absolute that this was (1) Shaker, and (2) had the old, original paint, the churn might go for upwards of $1000.00. 'Paint is all' say all the Shaker experts .
$250.00-$450.00

Churn, cylinder type, wood with beautiful patina, Canterbury community of Shakers, Londonderry, NH, 19th C. **$500.00-$650.00**

Churn, cylinder type, wooden drum with red stenciling & cow design, American, 13"H, early 20th C. **$85.00-$100.00**

Churn, cylinder type, wooden, on frame, "White Cedar, No. 1," possibly by Richmond Cedar Works, American, 8 gal. size, TOC. **$60.00-$85.00**

Churn, dasher type, barrel construction with tapered sides, one stave elongated to become handle, original old red paint, has lid & dasher, New England, 18½"H, early to mid 19th C. **$350.00-$450.00**

Churn, dasher type, barrel with old blue buttermilk paint, wide lapped band at top, 4 iron bands, has lid & dasher. American (?), 25"H x 11"D at top, 1870s-80s. **$275.00-$350.00**

Churn, dasher type, bentwood, decoration in Norwegian rosemaling paint, from "Wapa Koneta" (also Wapakoneta), OH, 4 gal. size, dated 1882. **$225.00-$275.00**

Churn, dasher type, brown stoneware, lacks wooden lid & dasher, American, 6 gal. capacity. **$55.00-$75.00**

Churn, dasher type, cooper's product, wooden staves heavy tin bands, hand forged nails, has lid & dasher, American (?), 1850s. • **No butter, thanks.** — "My greatest objection, after all, to the use of butter and cheese both, grows out of the consideration that their manufacture involves a great amount of female labor, while no permanent or substantial benefit is obtained." William A. Alcott, *The Young Housekeeper, or Thoughts on Food and Cookery*, Boston, 1838, 1842. **$250.00-$350.00**

Churn, dasher type, one elongated stave for handle, has 4 fingered wooden hoops, American (?), 12"H, early 19th C. • "**Cream.** — The peculiarly rich cream of Devonshire, England, called clouted cream, is obtained by using zinc pans of a peculiar construction, consisting of an upper and lower apartment. The milk is put into the upper apartment; and after it has stood 12 hours, an equal quantity of boiling water is introduced into the lower one. At the end of another 12 hours, the cream is taken off much more easily and perfectly than in the common way, and is also more abundant and richer. ... The same principles may be applied in the use of common pans. It would be very easy, for instance, to prepare some kind of trough, of tin, perhaps, or even wood, into which the pans could be set, and hot water afterwards introduced. As a close trough would be much better than an open one, you may have a cover with holes in which to set the pans. An ingenious yankee tinman would soon make a range in this way, sufficient for a common dairy, at no very great expense. It would last indefinitely. If it is true, that you would thus get some two pounds more butter a week from each cow, the apparatus and the trouble would soon be paid for, — to say nothing of the time saved in churning. We do not see why zinc pans — which are said to be decidely preferable to any other for the dairy — with the tin range as above, would not be quite as good as the complicated and expensive Devonshire pans. And it would be easy for a dairy woman to satisfy herself respecting the principle , without either. By using cold water instead of hot, the range would serve to keep milk sweet in warm weather." *Vermont Farmer*, as quoted in *The Farmers' Cabinet*, Phila., July 1, 1836. **$400.00-$475.00**

Churn, dasher type, pieced tin, flared sides, 2 strap handles, lid with funnel, American? 18¼"H, 19th C. **$225.00-$275.00**

Churn, dasher type, pottery, lacking lid & dasher, Catawba, NC, 19th C. **$250.00-$300.00**

Churn, dasher type, pottery, no lid or dasher, possibly "Hewell," Gillesville, GA, 19th C. • Added value. — Southern origin is the big plus. Partly this is fashion; other origins are pluses too: Texas, California, the Southwest, for example. **$250.00-$300.00**

Churn, dasher type, red cedar staves with white oak bands, has lid & cover, 19"H with 33"L dasher, 1980s. • **Reproduction alert I.** — This old-fashioned churn is being produced today and is sold through the Cumberland General Store, Rte 3, Crossville TN 38555. Their catalogue, which costs, I think, about $5.00, is a must for reference on variety of "country" kitchen items, still being made exactly like long ago. Dashers sold separately, and they have other churns. • Lehman's Hardware & Appliances, 4779 Kidron Rd., Kidron, OH 44636 offer this churn in their 1989 "Non-Electric Good Neighbor" catalog, which costs about $2.00. • **Alert II.** — "An authentic reproduction from America's past. This beautiful churn is handcrafted completely of rich, fragrant cedar with brass-colored metal bands. It makes a handsome decorative item in the kitchen or by the hearth, calling to mind the simpler life of days gone by." A little olfactory nostalgia, but actually, only the most desperate butter-maker would have used a churn "fragrant" with the smell of cedar. Ever heard of cedar butter? (Keeps moths out). This 34"H churn, with slightly tapered staves, round wooden top, and "brass-colored metal bands", probably that thin metal you find hanging treacherously off old packing crates at the dump, was advertised by Abbey Gifts of Meinrad, IN, in the Oct. 1975 *Early American Life*. **$40.00-$50.00**

Churn, dasher type, redware with dark olive-green glaze, turned wood dasher, simply beautiful, NC, 19th C. **$400.00-$600.00**

Churn, dasher type, saltglazed stoneware, bail handle, Red Wing #5. **$165.00-$200.00**

Churn, dasher type, saltglazed stoneware crock with ear handles, wooden lid & dasher, American, 4 gal. size, 19th C. **$75.00-$125.00**

Churn, dasher type, saltglazed stoneware, white & blue, 2 ear handles, wood lid, American, 3 gal. size, 19th C. **$75.00-$200.00**

Churn, dasher type, saltglazed stoneware, with target decoration, Red Wing, 4 gal. size. **$85.00-$100.00**

Churn, dasher type, saltglazed stoneware, wood lid & dasher, "Love & Fields Pottery," Dallas, TX, 20th C. **$120.00-$150.00**

Churn, dasher type, stoneware, Red Wing, 2 gal. size, dated 1915, wooden lid. **$135.00-$175.00**

Churn, dasher type, stoneware, no lid or dasher, Red Wing, 5 gal., 20th C. • Added value. — Original lid (usually wood, whether a stoneware or wooden churn) & dasher add half again as much. But it is next to impossible to know with little doubt if they are really original. Look for warping & patina that seem to match age. Lid should fit, after taking warpage into account. **$85.00-$150.00**

Churn, dasher type, stoneware with brown glaze, NY state, 3 gal. size, 19th or early 20th C. • The Milk-House of Col. M'Allister, Fort Hunter, on the Susquehanna, in 1828. "A household convenience worthy of imitation," reported visitor Judge Buel. "The Milk-house was built in the north-east side of a slope near the well, and not far from the mansion. It was composed of stout stone walls, and the roof, which rose six or eight feet above the surface of the ground, appeared to be covered with earth or tile, and was deeply shrouded with the scarlet trumpet creeper (Bignonia radicans), then in splendid bloom. The interior of the house, principally under ground, was fitted up with cisterns, in which water stood nearly to the tops of the pans of milk, which were arranged in them. The house was entered by a flight of steps on the south, and there was a window on the north, which could be opened or darkened at pleasure, to give ventilation. For want of a natural spring, which many Pennsylvanians consider almost indispensable in a milk-house, the water was conducted in a pipe from the well-pump, and after filling the cisterns to a certain height, passed off at the opposite side. The object was to obtain a cool temperature, in the heat of summer, which greatly facilitates the separation of the cream from the milk; this object was amply effected, with the labor of working occasionally at the well-pump." *The Farmers' Cabinet*, Vol. I, No. 1, Philadelphia, July 1, 1836.   **$75.00-$85.00**

Churn, dasher type, stripped cedar with 4 brass hoops, wooden lid, dasher, sold by Montgomery Ward, American, 3, 4, 5 & 6 gal. capacity, 1890s. • Very much like new Cumberland or Lehman's churns (see earlier entry), except for the brass hoops instead of white oak bands. Dasher is virtually identical.   **$55.00-$85.00**

Churn, dasher type, tin body, tin lid, wooden dasher. These & other dasher churns are sometimes called broomstick churns because of the dasher handle, which I assume was replaceable with a screw-on type broomstick handle, American, 19th C.   **$125.00-$200.00**

Churn, dasher type, tin with flared out lip, slightly conical body, 2 handles, all with original mustard paint, American, 25"H, 3rd or 4th quarter 19th C. • **Matching Toy.** — This is exactly the type of churn, color and flared lip, found on Ives "Churning Woman" (or "Lady Churner") clockwork mechanical toy pat'd 1874, right down to the mustard color. If you had that rare toy, you might want to pay two times as much for this churn to use it as a pedestal base for the toy.   **$250.00-$325.00**

Churn, dasher type, white saltglazed stoneware with blue bands, wood lid & dasher, capacity mark "No. 3," early 20th C.   **$95.00-$120.00**

Churn, dasher type, with original (or at least old) wood lid with turned knob, staved straight-sided wooden body painted light ochre, bentwood hoop at top, also iron bands, good patina & color, American (?), or poss. Canadian, 19¾"H x 9"D, c. 1830s-50s. • **"Good" or "Nice".** — I've tried to remove most instances of these two adjectives, because they are basically meaningless, being relative to physical & cultural contexts & viewpoint of the observer. Many catalog writers wear out the adjectives "very fine", "important", "exceedingly good", "good" and "nice". When you are selling something, those words add nothing to the description, and are self-serving. When you're a writer, you need a new vocabulary. I have tried to use both sparingly, to imply some degree of added desirability, without being able to go into all nuances of what makes a patina good or a shape nice. Israel Sack rates furniture with "good" being the lowest level acceptable to him. He has a mental checklist of attributes against which everything is measured; you have to develop one too. • **Biology for Sharpening Collecting Skills.** — You can practice by lining up 4 or 5 different examples of a type of collectible, similar enough to be the same species, different enough to allow (or invite) comparison. Look at each thing, make a gut or snap judgment about which you like best, which least. Turn away. Look again, and see if your eye is drawn to the same one. Now try to figure out why. (You may have to start by figuring out why you don't like the others.) The more alike the examples are, the closer they become to being a subspecies, the harder this exercise is. The less alike they are, the easier. For example: choosing between various types of churns is easier than choosing the best dasher churn, which in turn is easier than selecting the best painted wood dasher churn. To use the whole biology classification system: <u>Kingdom</u>— Material Object; <u>Phylum</u> — Collectible; <u>Subphylum</u> — Household Implement; <u>Class</u> — Dairy Implement; <u>Order</u> — Butter Making Implement; <u>Family</u> — Hollow Container; <u>Genus</u> — Churn; <u>Species</u> — Dasher Churn; and <u>Subspecies</u> — Painted Wood Dasher Churn. (P.S. Prejudice can be better understood, though not excused, if you see it as being one form of discrimination that originates in the strong, natural biological imperative to select & classify, a force also behind collecting.)   **$275.00-$320.00**

Churn, dasher type, wood with brass bands, wood lid & dasher, American or English, 28"H, 19th C.
                                            $165.00-$175.00

Churn, dasher type, wooden staves in old faded red paint, American (?), 18½"H, 19th C.   **$175.00-$200.00**

Churn, dog-powered, 2 part, wood, with painted churn body, requires treadmill & big, strong dog, maybe the Newfoundland. (I'm sure the family pet, in the sense we think of it today, was much different a century ago. Sentiment was OK for lap dogs, but a bigger dog had to work for its keep.) American, late 19th C. **$250.00-$400.00**

Churn, electric, glass barrel has embossed cow on front & back, wire bail handle, screw-on lid, long aluminum shaft & simple triangular cutout dasher blade adjustable on shaft to suit height of vessel used, embossed "Duraglas" & "Use with Gem Dandy Electric Churn" embossed on barrel, mfd by Alabama Mfg. Co., Birmingham, AL, 21¾"H with cover & motor, 2 gal. capacity, c.1947.• A 1947 ad says "Can be used with crock or jar, but we recommend Gem Dandy Duraglas jar — sold separately. 3 gal. and 5 gal. about $1.95 and $2.45." They also advertised, without delineating differences, a "Deluxe Model" motor without jar, and a "Standard Model" motor also without jar. These were $19.95 and $16.95 forty-five years ago.   **$55.00-$75.00**

Churn, electric, jar & screw-on metal lid to be mounted with motor (none here), glass barrel has embossed cows, wire bail, "Gem Dandy Deluxe Electric Churn," mfd by Alabama Mfg. Co., Birmingham, 18"H jar , mid 20th C.
                                            $20.00-$35.00

Churn, floor model, painted cast iron frame, 4 short splayed feet support 2 wheels & crank, vertical shaft with 4 large wooden paddles, heavily tinned square based sheet metal receptacle or body, Dazey Churn, St. Louis, MO, 2 sizes: a 2-wheel 6 gal. with 3 bars on sides of frame ; or 1-wheel 3 gal. with 1 bar on each side, on sale by 1910; the date Dec. 18, 1917 is prob. an improvement or extension. **$75.00-$125.00**

Churn, floor model, rectangular wooden box, side crank at one end, fancy parlor furniture-like turned & carved legs set slightly splayed, inside is oddly shaped container with foldout lids, Julien Churn Co., Dubuque, IA (?), 1870s. **$125.00-$160.00**

Churn, glass, aluminum lid with dome, "Hazel Atlas, 10K 4249" mark on jar, 13"H, 20th C. **$35.00-$45.00**

Churn, glass, cast iron gears, wooden blades, Hazel Atlas, 20th C. **$40.00-$55.00**

Churn, glass jar, egg shaped gear housing, wood blades, "Dazey Churn #80", Dazey Churn Mfg. Co., St. Louis, MO, about 17"H, glass jar c.8" square, pat'd Feb. 14, 1922. • **German vocabulary** — Buttermaschine: butter machine (this particular one: mit Glaskorper). **$50.00-$60.00**

Churn, gray stoneware with blue bands, wooden lid & dasher, "Davis Brothers" stamped into clay, 14"H, 20th C. **$35.00-$45.00**

Churn, old gray paint on wood, 4 legs, Shaker type, 19th C. **$200.00-$250.00**

Churn, on stand, heavy tin with wooden top, on iron stand, painted old blue, marked "Dazey," 20th C. **$75.00-$120.00**

Churn, "piggy" type, suspended & worked like a rocker churn, without the cradle. Pieced tin with torpedo ends, 4 little legs, rectangular built-up lid in top, with handle, American, 19th C. **$300.00-$400.00**

Churn, powered by washing machine, aluminum, Maytag, 15"H x 13½"D, early 20th C. **$75.00-$90.00**

Churn, rocker style, all wood including crank & paddles, on 4 legs, with original blue milk paint, American, 30"H, 19th C. **$185.00-$225.00**

Churn, rocker type, in wooden cradle, old red milk paint, supposedly Shaker, 19th C. • Shaker is "hot" in the same way "early American" used to be, and the attribution is often given when unwarranted and unsupported by documents or documented examples. It is hard to say if the Shakers' works will ever be sufficiently documented. Furthermore, pieces made for sale to the world at large were mass-produced, and have much less value than pieces made for community use. Study books, and visit Shaker museums. **$225.00-$300.00**

Churn, saltglazed stoneware, applied ear handles, overheated (or underheated?) & sagged in kiln, rugged but tired (or dashed-but-no-dasher), marked only with capacity "No. 6", American, 18"H, approx. diameter 7½", 19th C. • Carl W. Drepperd wrote in *A Dictionary of American Antiques* that reject ceramic wares like this were called reffus wares, and were sold cheap from what was called the reffus box. Modern collectors, always on the outlook for personality and distinctiveness (as separate from, even sometimes opposite to distinguished) often rummage figuratively through that box of refuse with great success. The pieces have tales to tell in their sagged lips, misshapen bellies, discolored glazes. • It is very hard to price things like this. I like the crazy look of it, the personality, but the maker must have been disappointed. (You may ask, if the artist didn't like it, is it art?) I was at a country auction late 1988 where a much smaller saggy churn sold for $100.00, so I assume there's a growing market for such things. **$200.00-$300.00**

Churn, square cylinder type, on stand, tin painted blue, American, TOC. **$75.00-$100.00**

Churn, tabletop, blue painted tin body, wooden top, iron stand (or frame) & gears, 4 legs, wooden dashers inside, looks like a Dazey churn, but not marked, about 18"H, early 20th C. **$50.00-$65.00**

Churn, tabletop, glass 4 sided jar, wooden beaters, screw-on tin lid, gear housed in red metal cone with handle grip on one side, & nice arching crank (with red wood knob) on other side. Embossed on jar is circle with smiling lion's head. "Monarch Finer Foods Churn," American (?), 9¾"H, c.1940s. **$40.00-$50.00**

Churn, tabletop, glass body, iron crank & screw-on lid, & wood beater blades, embossed "Dazey Churn & Manufacturing Co.", (sometimes people advertise these as "Daisy" churns — same thing, wrong spelling) St. Louis, MO, various sizes found: 1, 2, 4, 6 & 8 qts, numbered by adding "0" to quart size, pat'd Feb. 14, 1922. • **Dazey Prices Are a Doozie.** — I have not yet been able to sort out all sizes & numbers, having not found a catalog. The price range has been pretty stable for years, inching up just a bit all the time, until recently. In Oct. 1988, Collector Ted Phillips of Illinois called me about the crazily rising prices there. A #10 goes for $750.00 to $1000.00; a #20 is zooming up, now about $85.00 to $135.00. Surprising numbers of these have survived, possibly because people still enjoy using them. (Cumberland General Store sells what they call "a copy of the old Dazey," that is "imported from Far East.") • **Sizes:** the one quart is #10, the two quart is #20, etc. Often paper label is incomplete. An ad from January 1911 gives the sizes as 3, 5, 7½ and 9 pints, and — due out by March — 2 and 3 gallon sizes. Whooo boy. I hesitate printing the new prices, as everybody will think they're sitting on a gold mine, and then the bubble will burst. Believe me, it surely will, perhaps by the time this is published. $50.00-$100.00 is still the range where some can be found, but looks like the sky is the limit, up over $1000.00. An auctioneer in Springfield, MO, in March 1989, headlined the fact that he had two one-quart Dazey churns coming up. A person at a greater remove than I from the subject should write a long thoughtful essay on values vs. prices. I can't imagine paying that kind of money for something produced in quantity, hardly 60 years ago. **$50.00-$1000.00**

Churn, tabletop, glass jar with cast iron frame & gears, metal blades. "Mak-Mor Butter Machine," NYC, NY, "Makes two pounds from one pound of butter." Pat'd May 30, 1911. • This isn't really a churn, but a way of stretching butter — add one pint of milk to one pound of butter & end up with two pounds of butter! **$55.00-$70.00**

Churn, tabletop, glass, metal & wood, gear housing is domed metal top painted white, red wood crank handle, much simpler than earlier Dazeys, "Dandy Deluxe Churn," designed by J. P. Dazey, Jr., mfd. by Taylor Brothers Churn & Mfg. Co., St. Louis, MO, 1 qt. size, 1940s? **$40.00-$70.00**

Churn, tabletop, glass square jar, iron gears & lid, wood dasher-beaters, The ''Premier'' Two Minute Butter Machine, Culinary Mfg. Co., Orange, NJ, 13''H x 4¾'' square, c. 1910. • The ''Premier's'' paper labels are usually intact & mostly readable. Amazing in something washed so often. **$50.00-$65.00**

Churn, tabletop style, glass with metal lid with bulbous crank housing painted red, wood paddles, ''Dazey #4,'' 20th C. **$45.00-$70.00**

Churn, tabletop style, glass with wooden paddles, ''Elgin,'' original paper label, 2 qt. size, 20th C. **75.00-$90.00**

Churn, tabletop, tin container with wooden top, 4 short legs, ''Dazey Churn Co.,'' St. Louis, MO, 14''H x 12'' square, 20th C. **$75.00-$95.00**

Churn, tabletop, turned wood, beautiful patina, American, 13⅛''H, 19th C. Sold for $308.00 at Linden auction, 1983. **$350.00-$400.00**

Churn, tabletop type, glass jar, iron gears, wood paddles, ''Perfection MixMaster,'' American, 1 gal. size. **$45.00-$65.00**

Churn, tabletop type, top cranked, japanned tin cylinder, American, 19th C. **$125.00-$175.00**

Churn, tabletop, vivid grain painted wood, brown & ochre, American, 19th C. **$225.00-$275.00**

Churn, tabletop, wood barrel, wood blades, cranked handle, red stenciled cow decoration, J. B. Varick Co., 14¼''H x 13'' diameter, early 20th C. **$135.00-$175.00**

Churn, tin with wood paddle, ''Connfaut Can Co.,'' American, 21½''H, 40 qt. capacity, 20th C. **$135.00-$155.00**

Churn, wood, tin, iron, 2 handles, ''Buffums Little Wonder,'' American, 34''H. **$115.00-$130.00**

Churn, wooden tub on high turned legs, cranked paddles, American, 19th C. **$225.00-$250.00**

Churn & butter maker, tabletop, glass with wood, has original instructions. ''Home Butter Maker,'' American, 1 gal. size. **$35.00-$45.00**

Churn & butter worker, wooden frame, triangular A shape supports like a swing set, and indeed, the churn can swing ''when desired, but while being worked it is retained in an upright position by a board and catch'', which are midway up the frame. Over the churn body, which is octagonal with slightly flared out sides, is an arched cast iron frame with a beveled gear in the center worked by a small crank. The short, slightly curved dashers are stuck at angles up and down and around the central fat wooden dasher shaft, working like a turbine. Has 2 part wooden cover. In an 1858 Scientific American write-up, it is claimed ''This churn renders the operation of churning and preparing butter for the market very simple and easy.''pat'd by & for sale by Justin M. Smith, Lyme, CT, pat'd Jan. 12, 1858. **$200.00-$300.00**

Churn or butter maker, hexagonal glass vessel used in horizontal position, screw-on zinc caps at each end, ''Churn your butter while riding across country'', 7½''L, ''pat. appl. for'', but early 20th C. **$30.00-$45.00**

Churn or butter separator, cranked, wood body with iron hoops, spout on side has wood plug, wood handle, ''Fayway,'' American, 16''H, 19th C. • How does King Kong make butter? With a Fayway. Hee hee. **$200.00-$225.00**

Cocktail shaker, bowling pin shape, top of turned maple, unscrews from lower chromed part, American, 56 oz. capacity, same size as regulation bowling pin, late 1930s. **$35.00-$55.00**

Cocktail shaker, chrome coffee boiler shape with odd phallic spout, yellow Catalin® (or other molded phenolic resin) plastic handle & knobs, black incised bands on handle, ''Krome Kraft'', mfd by Farber Brothers, NYC, NY, 12''H, c.1930s, after 1933 (when Prohibition ended). **$30.00-$40.00**

Cocktail shaker, schoolmarm's bell shape, stainless steel, turned wooden handle screws off bell body to add ingredients; small shaker spout on side with screw cap, American, 11''H, 20th C. **$35.00-$55.00**

Cocktail shaker, World's Fair souvenir, aluminum with black letters & depiction of buildings around top border. American, 1933 — same year Prohibition ended. • Crossover competition here from Expo & World's Fairs collectors might add to price. **$80.00-$95.00**

Cocktail shaker set, rocket ship, chromed brass, the shaker body stores 4 cups, 1 small footed jigger cup, a lemon reamer, 4 spoons. Rocket has 4 fins at small bottom end. Top is larger diameter dome. only mark is ''Made in Germany,'' 12''H, prob. 1930s, after 1933 (?). • A bit scary this — what does it really represent? Not only does it look like a space rocket, it could also be a torpedo, and given the time, who knows? However, the fact that it's marked ''Made in Germany'' means it was intended for export — or at least import to the U.S.A., which required such identification after March 1, 1891. It is fabulous looking. • Estimated to sell at 1983 auction for between $300.00-$400.00, but $500.00 was realized price. **$750.00-$1000.00**

Cream separator, cast iron base, parts bolted on, heavy gauge tin top, crank, all painted in farm machinery orange, with yellow & black pinstriping, adjustable belt drive, bent wire lever regulates hole in top hopper, ''Egret'' in gold script, and shield shaped brass ID plate reading ''Entrahmen Reinigen ZU,'' which is prob. Zurich, Switzerland, 15''H x 12½''L, late 19th C. **$165.00-$185.00**

Cream separator, sheep-powered, wood & iron treadmill on wooden frame; iron base for cream separator tank, Vermont Farm Machine Co., Bellows Falls, VT, sold by Montgomery Ward, late 19th C.• Could be powered by other animals such as dogs, if they were large enough to move the treadmill by walking. **$250.00-$300.00**

Cream separator, table top, ''Royal Blue Jr.,'' American, TOC. **$50.00-$65.00**

Cream separator, tin with wooden legs, uses gravity, ''Marvel,'' 20th C. **$25.00-$35.00**

Cream whip, footed tin container, ''Hodges,'' TOC. **$50.00-$65.00**

Cream whip, glass jar with a whipper, tin, tinned cast metal gear, marked ''WHIPPO Super-Whip,'' glass jar marked on bottom with an ''I'' in an elongated diamond, about 10''H, early 20th C; there is a date but it is illegible. **$40.00-$50.00**

Cream whip, metal & stained wooden handle, Archimedean drill action, advertising legend on handle reads ''We have competition beaten to a froth and whipped to a cream paste. Henry Brooks, General Merchandise. James Store,

Virginia," mfd by A & J, mfd in Binghamton, NY, 12½"L, pat'd Oct. 15, 1907. **$30.00-$40.00**

Cream whip, nickeled sheet metal, long vertical shaft with wooden knob, rectangular perforated blade curves up to fit into sides of its glass mixing bowl, "New Dream Cream Whip," Kohler Die & Specialty, De Kalb, IL, about 12"L, c.1926. • Added value. — Costs the most with original shouldered glass "Utility" mixing bowl.
$18.00-$30.00

Cream whip, stainless steel & wood, Androck's "Turbine," Rockford, IL, c.1936. **$20.00-$30.00**

Cream whip, tin body, 4 little strap tin legs, cast iron crank & beaters inside, "Fries," American, 8"H x 6"L x 4½"W, c.1890s. • Don't Get Discouraged: **The Census & Collecting.** — If you think all the good stuff is probably gone, think again. Just look at the population figures for any given decade, and think how many probable owners of a corkscrew, frying pan, nutcracker, grater or cream whip those numbers imply. The rounded-off population of the U.S. in 1890 was 65,000,000 people. Even if we divide that by 6, to represent households of two adults and four children, that leaves almost 11 million homes. Of those, maybe one in 50 or 100 had a cream whip, but that's still encouraging — say 110,000 cream whips in use during the last decades of the 19th C. Even if only one in 10 survived rust, moving, war drives, and the unblushing blandishments of advertisers of "newer" things, there may be 11,000 of them still around. Even if there's but one in every village in the U.S., there is probably one for you. I've never bought one — one of you can have the one I didn't buy! And this hypothesis is only for something that was probably uncommonly owned to begin with. There were millions of Dover and A&J eggbeaters sold over the years; millions of frying pans; hundreds of millions of forks and spoons. Keep looking.

• Still not convinced? **Advertising Claims & Collecting.** — In many old ads you will see manufacturers' claims about the quantity sold to date. For example, in an 1890 ad for the "Morgan Broiler", made by The Sun Stamping Co., it was said that "fifty thousand Housewives bear out the claim that the broiler is a demonstrated success". Even if they stopped making them that day, that still means an awful lot of those collectible broilers are possible finds. **65.00-$75.00**

Cream whip, turbine type, steel with nickel silver curved rectangular blade. Looks like NASA skywatch dish, with cutout gear wheel & angled wood handle. Small depression or dimple in bottom of bowl fits pivot on bottom of beater so it won't slip during use, "Dunlap's Sanitary Silver Blade Cream & Egg Whip, No Splash or Waste", J. S. Dunlap; dist. by Casey-Hudson Co, Chicago, 11"L, pat'd 1906-1916. **$25.00-$35.00**

Cream whip & eggbeater, glass & stainless steel, lid, beaters & crank all in one, Androck, Rockford, IL, 1930s.
$22.00-$30.00

Cream whip & eggbeater, tin cylinder with wire dasher handle, "Lightning," pat'd 1868. **$35.00-$45.00**

Cream whips — See also Eggbeaters, Syllabub churns.

Crock, for mixing bread, saltglazed stoneware, "White Hall," 18" diameter, early 20th or late 19th C.
$85.00-$100.00

Dough bowl, trough-shaped, carved wood, very smooth patina, indicating long use, American? 24"L x 10"W,

19th C. • In Sept. 1988, at the big flea market in Hillsville, VA, I saw a large number of skillfully but primitive-looking carved dough troughs priced $35.00, which wouldn't take long to age. (I didn't see them in 1989.) **$100.00-$200.00**

Dough bowl, trough-shaped, primitively-carved oak, American, 18"L x 9½"W, early 19th C. • Value depends on patina, size, wood, & supposed age. "American" amounts to a lot of moolah. **$100.00-$200.00**

Dough box, also bread or dough brake, oblong pine box with slanting sides, cover has 'inchworm' carved handles, American, 8½"H x 23"L, 19th C. **$300.00-$400.00**

Dough box, nice slanted sides, 4 simply turned legs, on outside wood has original dark brown paint under flaking white, American, 26½"H x 41⅝"L x 22½"W, c.1870s.
$225.00-$400.00

Drink mixer, Archimedean drill action, domed snap-on metal lid with simple twisted or spiraled flat strip of metal, 4 upturned turbine blades at bottom, wooden knob at top, tall glass tumbler, "Roberts Lightning," mfd by Dorsey Mfg. Co., Boston, MA, c.1910s well into 1920s, perhaps later. **$18.00-$28.00**

Drink mixer, Archimedean drill action, glass jar with tin lid, spiral tin whipper, 16"H, pat'd Mar. 30, 1915. • Another one, same patent date, has wire finger-like beater, like a glove-drying form, worked by the Archimedean drill. This one is marked simply with a monogram of an A & D, or possibly A & P (not Atlantic & Pacific Tea), but not A & J. Maker not yet identified. The finger version is valued approximately the same as the spiral, perhaps a bit more. **$25.00-$35.00**

Drink mixer, Archimedean drill, wire with turned wooden handle, steel blades in small balloon, small pivoting "foot" on bottom seats it steady in bowl or jar, A & J, 12½"L, Oct. 16, 1907. **$22.00-$35.00**

Drink mixer, from a drugstore or soda fountain, nickeled cast metal, complete protective gear housing, golden oak base, "Quik Mix, A-1", base 8¼"H, mixing mechanism 9"H, c.1920s. **$150.00-$170.00**

Drink mixer, metal shaker & lid, "Ovaltine," early 1900s.
$18.00-$22.50

Drink mixer & measure, aluminum, graduated cup shows ⅓, ⅔, and "1 cup to top"; other side marked ¼, ½ and ¾ cup, screw-on lid, marked "Smoothie Mixer & Measure" on top, 3⅞"H x 2¾" diameter, 20th C. **$7.00-$10.00**

Drink mixer or stirrer, battery-powered, chrome, in original box, 1940s. **$10.00-$15.00**

Drink mixer or stirrer, cast metal golf club, from a club car on the "B & O" railroad, 20th C. **$15.00-$30.00**

Drink mixer or stirrer, silver plated coil with handle, "Holmes, Edwards," dated 1889. **$12.00-$15.00**

Drink mixer or stirrer, stainless steel, telescoping, "Spoonomat," 11¾"L, 20th C. **$10.00-$15.00**

Drink mixer — See also Syllabub churn.

Drink or malted milk mixer, aluminum container with lid, "Thompson's Double Malted," 7"H, 20th C. **$8.00-$15.00**

Drink shaker, for children, plastic with decals, Captain Midnight character, "Ovaltine" mixer, 20th C. **$30.00-$40.00**

Egg whip, sheet metal, on wire frame, with large flat spoon with 4 large cutouts, also used as a pastry blender, stamped at end of handle "The Vandeusen Egg Whip, C. A. Chapman, Geneva, NY, 11"L, pat'd Mar.13, 1894.
$20.00-$30.00

Egg whips or whisks, sauce whips, etc., tinned wire, usually bound-wire handles, sometimes turned wooden handles with ferrules, some have wire slip ring to adjust "ballooning" of the wire loops for beating in different size bowls, or for different needs. A sauce whip, for example, has wires bound in a longer, tighter conformation, while the egg whip has a rounder ballooning shape, American, French, etc., various lengths — about 5½"L to 12"L, 1890s to the present. • Some have been made almost identically for a century or more. Unless really unusual, the price is quite low. **$6.00-$15.00**

Eggbeater, all metal, a thin tin tube is handle grip that you move up & down the twisted wire shaft to activate Archimedean drill, no maker's name, French (?), 12¾"L, late 19th or early 20th C. **$135.00-$150.00**

Eggbeater, all metal, including heavy gauge wire handle, sheet metal gear wheel, coiled wire knob, small diameter blade "balloon," "Big Bingo #7," A & J, Binghamton, NY, pat'd 1923, made into 1940s? **$20.00-$30.00**

Eggbeater, black-finished cast iron gear & crank with black wooden knob; very unusual because gear wheel doesn't stick up vertically, but is built horizontally into black screw-on lid, long, thin wire beaters that reach almost to bottom of straight-sided embossed glass jar, "Jewel 'Beater Mixer Whipper Freezer'," mfd by Juergens Brothers, Minneapolis, MN, about 7"H, TOC. • It's not spectacular like some, but it's a very desirable addition to a beater/mixer collection. **$55.00-$70.00**

Eggbeater or liquid mixer, green glass jar, with tin screw-on lid, to which is attached the cast iron handle, gears & the wire beater blades, "Root Mason" jar, Standard Specialty Co. works, Milwaukee, WI, 12"H x 3⅞"D, pat'd June 11, 1907. • The beater itself looks like a 1873 Dover. I've never seen another one like this. In early sixties, I found this in a central Ohio antique shop, and felt sinful spending $16.00 on it … about the priciest thing I'd ever bought for my collection! **$65.00-$85.00**

Eggbeater or liquid mixer, tall Archimedean drill action, long shaft with only about 9 twists, wooden spool to run up and down the drill, large loop of wire for other hand, 2 small ballooned blades, with 2 little curved reinforcements that, by adding more cutting edges, make blades more effective. This same kind of blade is part of much older rotary "Earle's Patent." "Clipper", 13"H, pat'd Aug. 1930. **$55.00-$85.00**

Eggbeater or mixer, cast iron gear wheel with iron crank & wooden knob, set onto cast iron 'mansard' roof-like lid with scalloped edge, over tall square-sided glass container, marked on all 4 sides with various measures, ballooning whisking wires inside flare out more in later versions, "New Keystone Beater", Silver & Co., but also called the "Silver Egg Beater", Silver was in Brooklyn, NY ; Culinary Utilities in NYC (or Bloomfield, NJ?). Old model: 12"H; new: 11¼"H; container is 3¾" x 3¾"square, first pat'd Apr. 30, 1878. • Classic Keystone. — I found a Keystone (see 3 below) in Gene Florence's book *Kitchen Glassware of the Depression Era*, 3rd ed., with what appears to be a nickel-plated lid, patent date given as Dec. 1885, and the mfr as North Brothers. The date has not been confirmed. • Silver & Co., etc., had various marks depending on date. (1) "Silver Egg Beater," by Silver & Co. of Brooklyn; (2) "Silver New Egg Beater," with the Brooklyn Bridge and words "Silvers Brooklyn"

around the bridge, possibly contemporary with Bridge's opening in 1883; (3) "The New Keystone Beater," probably by Culinary Utilities Co.; (4), with modernized top — sheet metal wheel, straight edges not scalloped — but same glass container, "New Keystone Beater, Even Full," by Culinary Utilities Co.; and (5) came another "New Keystone Beater", supposedly an "improvement on Keystone Beater as hitherto known." This was made by North Brothers Mfg., and they claimed they had "secured control of the machine manufactured by Keystone Beater Co. and are now (1892) the only makers of it." Ad in The Metal Worker, late 1892. This one had simplified edge to iron lid, with deep brackets at corners, no scallops. • I believe version (2) above, dates to 1883, as patents were "pending" on earlier one. The first time I saw one depicted, it was in the of United Profit Sharing Co.'s 1914 premium catalog. The linecut shows the old iron gear, with "Silver & Co.'s New Beater" on lid. • Bulletin: Intrepid Bob Cahn found one, with more info. It's molded glass, cast iron lid has scalloped edge, but this one has its original, small chromolithographic label on the side, showing a little girl looking at a mixing bowl and the beater, and the words "The New Keystone Beater. Reduces the Work. Improves the Food. Detachable Whip. Easy to Clean. Culinary Utilities Dept., Bloomfield, NJ." Complicating the chronology now is the fact that the label's graphics look 1920s. • First price range for (1), (3) & (4); second for (2) **$65.00-$90.00; $75.00-$100.00**

Eggbeater & potato masher, 2 interchangeable cylindrical perforated steel receptacles (called a "hopper" by the manufacturer) — medium & fine holes, for cooked potato or stewed apples or eggs, nickeled cast iron vertical shaft, round topped turned wood handle; the spring steel wire that connects ferrule of shaft & top of the "hopper" provides the tension & return power as handle is pumped up & down, "Lebanon Beater," mfd by Seltzer Specialty Co., Lebanon, PA, 13"L x 2¾" diameter hopper, introduced c. 1892. • Added value for both hoppers. **$50.00-$75.00**

Electric eggbeaters and electric mixers — See Electric chapter.

Food preparer, electric, enameled metal base and bowl, lid has large central opening, blades inside, "mixes batter, juices fruits, whips, shreds, slices, chops, grinds. Eliminates the uncertainty & fatigue of food preparation." "Culinaire", mfd by P. A. Geier Co. & affiliate Continental Electric Co., Ltd., Cleveland, OH, and Toronto, Canada, c.1934. Two years later Geier had a new "Royal Culinaire", with chromium plated bowl, and a juicer attachment. **$25.00-$35.00**

Jigger & swizzle sticks, chromium top hat & 4 golf clubs, very jazzee, Chase Brass & Copper, Waterbury, CT, 1½ oz. capacity jigger, mid 1930s. $1.00 was the original price. **$20.00-$40.00**

Larding needles in case, steel in brass cylinder (or steel in japanned tin); a set of long needles in cylindrical case, used to lard in, or in effect insert or mix fat (especially strips of bacon) into lean cuts of meat before roasting, available through F.A. Walker wholesale catalog, French (?), c.1870s. **$20.00-$30.00**

Malted milk mixer, all wire frame, small sheet metal thumb piece to work Archimedean drill, for making the drink, not much to it, but it sure is fun, "Horlick's," English, 9½"H, TOC. **$25.00-$35.00**

Mayonnaise mixer, blue painted cast iron, openwork heart gear, glass jar, hole for funnel, original blue paper label on jar, "FUPA" is maker, (although it sounds like an acronym for 4 words beginning in F U P A, or P A F U) "Made in France," TOC. **$65.00-$80.00**

Mayonnaise mixer, cast iron, clamps to table, frame supports oil drip funnel behind vertical gear wheel, lower part is a hinged cast iron basket frame to hold a bowl (glass? ceramic? metal?), wire balloon whip blades, with 2 X shaped supports to hold wires, no mark, "PAT APLD. FOR" but c.1890s (?). • This belongs to Phyllis & Jim Moffet in IL, and they want to know what sort of bowl it had, who made it. Any information would be appreciated. **$135.00-$175.00**

Mayonnaise mixer, footed glass bowl, glass lid has built-in oil "funnel" with large well & small drip hole, iron frame fastened to lid, fancy iron gear wheel & short crank knob fixed on wheel, tin blades, "S & S, Hutchinson," sometimes "J. Hutchinson," Long Island, NY, 9¾"H x c.7" diameter bowl, "patent appl for" late 19th C. **$100.00-$125.00**

Mayonnaise mixer, footed glass bowl, with close-fitting lid, eggbeater can be disengaged from lid, "Ladd Beater #1," "United Royalties Corp.," American, 13"H, pat'd July 7, 1908, Feb. 2, 1915. **$45.00-$55.00**

Mayonnaise mixer, metal with original heavy glass jar that has 6 little feet & is embossed "The Holt-Lyon Jar Cream Whip and Mayonnaise Maker", cast iron "Dover" beater has elongated blades with slight crimping at curves, and 48 rather than 60 or 63 cogs in the large gear, long conical oil dripper funnel with little rod to regulate drip, Holt - Lyon Co., Tarrytown, NY, 15"H, 1910s to 1920. • A somewhat older one is 5/8" shorter & has 63 cogs to the gear; the conical oil dripper has a snap-strap that slips over grip of beater part. **$60.00-$75.00**

Mayonnaise mixer, nickeled iron top, straight-sided glass handleless cup, iron gear wheel & long crank handle, wooden knob, nickeled dasher has long horizontal fingers & a set of odd vertical fingers at bottom. Lid has oil hole with its own tiny swivel cover. "Universal Mayonnaise Mixer & Cream Whip Whipper," Landers, Frary & Clark, New Britain, CT, 9⅜"H, 2½ to 3 cup capacity, 19th C.
• **German vocabulary** — Mayonnaise schlager: mayonnaise beater. **$55.00-$70.00**

Mayonnaise mixer, tall marked glass tumbler, metal screw-on lid has mixer blade shaft, convex perforated metal dasher is horizontal, small convexity in jar's bottom fits dimple on dasher blade bottom. "Wesson Oil Mayonnaise Maker", 11"H jar, 20th C. **$25.00-$28.00**

Mayonnaise mixer & cream whip, white porcelain footed bowl, tin lid (edge or rim only) with interior crosspiece that supports cranked beater blade of tin, funnel hole in wide rim of lid for adding oil, American? 4"H bowl, 19th C. **$50.00-$65.00**

Mixer, cast iron, screw clamps to shelf, green wood handle, reamer clips onto the top, "Cake Drink Mixer, Egg Cream Mixer", mfd by New Standard Corp., Mt. Joy, PA, patent pending, c.1900. • Dealer Elissa Weitz of Lahaska, PA, said that there "supposedly is a Mount Joy bowl to use with this," and that the bowls came in a lot of sizes. **$65.00-$80.00**

Mixer, chromed white metal gears, red plastic, "Maynard Mixer," Los Angeles, CA, 11⅛"L, 1933 patent #1,910,303. **$15.00-$18.00**

Mixer, for eggs or mayonaise, footed glass "egg shaped bottom" vessel with flat metal lid fitted with upright iron beater frame, gear, side crank & 2 sets of wire blades inside bent to form 6 rectangular side wings that fit within slope of vessel, "E-Z Mixer", National Mfg. & Supply Co., Pittsburg, PA, pat'd June 30, 1903. **$75.00-$90.00**

Mixer, glass jar. short wire dasher moved up & down as Archimedean drill with white china knob, "Roberts' Lightning Mixer," 8"H, early 20th C. **$28.00-$35.00**

Mixer, nickeled metal device mounted to board, with vertical cranked wheel, metal band holds container, "Kwikmix", Schenker Mfg. Co., NYC, NY, about 8"H, pat'd 1922. **$50.00-$65.00**

Mixer, tall glass container, tin lid with snap fitting, iron shaft & nickel plated perforated dasher, there's a spring in lid so when you pump the handle up & down it really goes to town. "Jones Wonder Mixer", American, c.1910. **$18.00-$25.00**

Mixer, wind-up, clear glass container, metal top, on-off switch, American. • I wish I knew more about this. It was in *Antique Trader*, & I am including to elicit more information from readers. **$25.00-$35.00**

Mixer or eggbeater, glass vessel with slightly flared sides, fitted tin lid with attached mixer which has tall wire handle with small wood knob at top, spiraled coil "blades" inside motivated by up & down action, marked Lorraine Metal Mfg., Inc., NYC, 11"H, c. 1930s. **$24.00-$30.00**

Mixer & sifter, tightly coiled springy wire, 2 handles, squeeze action makes wires go in & out, rather like a cross between a Slinky toy & an accordion. "_____sse Carlson Co.," "Nifty Sifter," Rockford, IL (Andrews Wire Goods Co. was here about the same time), 8½"L, pat'd Feb. 1930. • Thanks readers! Vivian Robertson sent photocopy of battered advertising card — in part reading: "A 100 uses in cooking; prevents lumping of flour, sugar and ... similar ingredients... Hotel chefs have found it indispensible in preparing gravies, sauces, cake batters. ... dip into flour, sugar or other ingredients; release spring and sift into gravy skillet, stew pan, or batter bowl. ... The Nifty Sifter ... used in preparing scores of dishes where lumping will spoil the efforts of the chef." • Tiffin, OH dealer Ralph Frankart wrote me in 1984, about a woman who purchased one in 1929 in Detroit and called it a "Sprinkler." "She uses it in her baking, opens it and dips it into the sugar bowl, lets it close and by slightly opening it, sprinkles sugar on her cookies, pies, etc. Also dips it into her flour and fills it then sprinkles it on her rolling pin, rolling board, pie pans, etc. She loves it and was quite disturbed that I would not sell her mine as she wanted it as a gift for her sister." Frankart said one customer told him he paid $35.00 in about 1984 at a flea in Hershey, PA. Whew! **$8.00-$14.00**

Mixing bowl, blue & gray saltglazed stoneware, advertising message for "Dentel's, Ackley Iowa," 20th C. **$60.00-$65.00**

Mixing bowl, blue & gray saltglazed stoneware, with cherry motif, 9½" diameter, 20th C. **$35.00-$45.00**

Mixing bowl, blue & red sponged "Saffron" yellowware, wide shoulder band, narrow panelling below band, Red Wing pottery, Red Wing, MN, 7" diameter (these bowls were made in 1" increments from 5" to 10" diameter, 1930s. • Value varies widely with size, presence of advertising or name, and condition, (apt to be poor for relatively porous Saffron pieces.) **$50.00-$75.00**

Mixing bowl, blue & red stripes, Red Wing, advertising "Rock Dell," 8½" diameter, 20th C. $30.00-$45.00

Mixing bowl, blue, rust & gray spongeware, shouldered, with 6 panels, American, 8" diameter, 20th C. $50.00-$60.00

Mixing bowl, blue & rust spatter decoration, "Boyne's Grocery", West Union, IA, 8"diameter, 20th C. $55.00-$65.00

Mixing bowl, blue & rust sponged stoneware, for "Waddington's", Geneva, IA, by Red Wing, early 20th C. $110.00-$130.00

Mixing bowl, ceramic, green with pink & blue stripes, "Watt's Oven Ware," 14" diameter, early 20th C. $50.00-$65.00

Mixing bowl, creamware, white inside, English, 9"diameter, TOC. $20.00-$25.00

Mixing bowl, dark brown saltglazed stoneware, shouldered, marked "Weller", Fultonham, OH, 8"D, late 19th C. Small dimple indent inside bottom, perfect for use with some egg beaters. $25.00-$35.00

Mixing bowl, decorated china, cottage scene, girl & flowers, 9"diameter, 20th C. $25.00-$35.00

Mixing bowl, graniteware, yellow & white marbleized, American, 9½" diameter, early 20th C. $28.00-$40.00

Mixing bowl, green glaze, ribbed, square base goes up into round bowl, mark is shield with "9" inside circle, American, 9½" diameter, early 20th C. $20.00-$28.00

Mixing bowl, green glazed pottery, "Kitchen Kraft," Homer Laughlin China Co., 8" diameter, c.1940s. $25.00-$30.00

Mixing bowl, green-glazed yellowware, square base goes up to circle, molded geometric designs, no mark, American, 10" diameter, early 20th C. • If I had the '80s to do over again, I'd buy a few green-glazed yellowware bowls . What gorgeous lively color. $40.00-$50.00

Mixing bowl, large & relatively low, yellow glaze with green sponge decoration, gold rim, tiny crack not affecting use, American, 3½"H x 10¾" diameter, 19th C. $95.00-$125.00

Mixing bowl, pumpkin colored ceramic, "Watt's Oven Ware," 7" diameter, 20th C. $12.00-$15.00

Mixing bowl, red & cream spongeware, American, 8" diameter. TOC. $45.00-$55.00

Mixing bowl, redware with cream colored glaze inside, American, 16" diameter, 19th C. $65.00-$85.00

• "Caution to the Public. — Mr. Editor — Sir: Will you permit me to acquaint the public...that there is a kind of Crockery Ware, manufactured in almost every city in the Union, which is dangerous to use — and which the public will understand by the term Common Red Pottery. This ware is made of common clays from the brick yards, and when formed, is coated with a liquid called Glaze, which is nothing less than a coat of lead. The clays being of the commonest kind, cannot be subjected to any heat in the burning that will make them safe for family use — being porous — and it is very unsafe to deposit any articles of family use in them, such as milk, butter, or in fact water, as a portion of the Lead Glazing will be extracted, and the article will, in consequence, become dangerous to use. I have noticed no fewer than ten instances within the last twelve months, of families sustaining injury by the use of such ware.

"In selecting the article of crockery that is suitable for family use, it is only necessary to ascertain that the body of the ware — the clay — has been hard burnt, which any person can understand by the sound of it — if well burnt, it will have a clear sound. The poorest kind will not ring at all, and therefore can be easily detected. An article of this kind will, in the course of a month's use, become very foul. Let any one who doubts this break the vessel, and they will ascertain the fact. There is a kind of ware, however, that is manufactured in almost every city in the Union, called stone ware, which is perfectly good for family use. This ware is formed of strong and superior clays, and undergoes a great heat in the burning, — and moreover, the glazing is not a thick coat of lead, but is accomplished by throwing salt into the kiln. All kinds of Liverpool (Ohio?) ware are adapted to all purposes of family use, being made of sound clays and well burnt. As a preventive is better than a cure, if I should be the means of preventing any person suffering from the use of the poisonous article — lead — this advertisement will answer the ends I design. (signed) C. S." (Who adds) "Glass may be used in all cases, and is the most beautiful and safe article extant in manufactures." *The Farmers' Cabinet* (reprinted from *The Pittsburger*), Philadelphia, Vol I, No. 7, Oct. 15, 1836.

Mixing bowl, ribbed spongeware, mottled brown & green glaze over yellow background glaze, 8½" diameter, 20th C. $160.00-$175.00

Mixing bowl, saltglazed stoneware, adv'g "It pays to mix with Thoren Brothers, Rock City & Rock Grove, Illinois" on the inside, American, 6"H x 8" diameter, early 20th C. • Punning advertising messages are the most fun, on mixing bowls, beater jars & rolling pins. $65.00-$80.00

Mixing bowl, saltglazed stoneware, Western Stoneware Co., Monmouth, IL, 10"diameter, late 19th C to early 20th. $50.00-$65.00

Mixing bowl, saltglazed stoneware with adv'g message: "Farmer's Complete Department Store", late 19th or early 20th C. $45.00-$55.00

Mixing bowl, saltglazed stoneware, apple motif, "Watt's Oven Ware #8," "Farmer's Co-Op Elevator Co.," 8" diameter, 20th C. $50.00-$65.00

Mixing bowl, saltglazed stoneware, apple motif, Watt's "Oven Ware #7," advertises "Leistikow's," 7" diameter, 20th C. $50.00-$60.00

Mixing bowl, saltglazed stoneware with white & brown glaze, 10" diameter, early 20th C. $20.00-$30.00

Mixing bowl, sponged blue, rust & cream stoneware, Red Wing, 6" diameter, 20th C. $50.00-$60.00

Mixing bowl, sponged, Red Wing, 11"diameter, 20th C. $135.00-$150.00

Mixing bowl, sponged, no marks, 5½" diameter, nice small size, 20th C. $40.00-$50.00

Mixing bowl, spongeware, slight hairline crack, advertising message: "It pays to mix with Andrew Westin, Newberry, Michigan," 5"H x 8½" diameter, early 20th C. $50.00-$75.00

Mixing bowl, very worn inside bottom down to the clay body, yellowware, brown mocha decoration on cream band, cream slip banded decoration, small foot, NJ, 11⅜" diameter, 19th C. $175.00-$200.00

Mixing bowl, white glazed earthenware, thick sloping walls, removable & set into much deeper heavily tinned vessel with inward slanting sides, 2 strap handles with handgrip braces, little filling spout poking out on side under handle, with cap, English, 19th C. • **"Biscuit Pan.** — Hitherto consisted only of a single vessel. ... Used for beating up or whisking batters. The improved pan is formed either of metal or earthenware, inclosed within an exterior vessel, furnished with a plugged aperture, for the introduction of hot water." Thomas Masters, *A Short Treatise Concerning Some Patent Inventions ... Also the Newly Improved Culinary Utensils*, London, 1850. ("Biscuit" here is in the English sense, of crackers.) Price for 2 parts:. **$110.00-$140.00**

Mixing bowl, yellow glazed ceramic, "Kitchen Kraft," Homer Laughlin China Co., Newell, WVa, 10" diameter, c.1940s. **$30.00-$35.00**

Mixing bowl, yellow Fiesta Ware #7, 20th C. **$100.00-$115.00**

Mixing bowl, yellow Fiesta Ware #1, 20th C. **$35.00-$40.00**

Mixing bowl, yellow & green spongeware, gilt scalloped edge, 8¾" diameter, American, 19th C. **$120.00-$140.00**

Mixing bowl, yellowish green glaze, molded pattern of little "pillows" rather than concentric bands, mark is a shield with 8 in a circle inside it, also #4 (or possibly #14), American, 8½" diameter, early 20th C. **$20.00-$28.00**

Mixing bowl, yellowware, all over foliated swag design, 12" diameter, late 19th C. **$125.00-$145.00**

Mixing bowl, yellowware, deep cobalt mocha decoration on band, rolled rim, very small foot, 13¼" diameter, mid 19th C. • **Rolled rims.** — A rim or edge that is described as "rolled" may actually be rolled, such as a piece of tinware, or steel — even that which has later been enameled. The term is also used to describe the look of a rounded rim, that couldn't possibly have been actually rolled — such as a turned wooden bowl or a ceramic piece. **$350.00-$400.00**

Mixing bowl, yellowware, deep lip, scalloped rim, melon "rib" sides, American, late 19th C. • "Mixing bowls come in deep yellow and light buff earthenware. Also in white stone china. Deep yellow is made of a rather soft material and breaks easily." Maria Parloa, *Kitchen Companion*, Boston: Estes & Lauriat, 1887. **$75.00-$90.00**

Mixing bowl, yellowware, simple zigzag design around side, American or English, 5⅜" diameter, late 19th or early 20th C. **$30.00-$40.00**

Mixing bowl, yellowware, tallish with green & white bands, "Watt's Oven Ware," 20th C. **$25.00-$30.00**

Mixing bowl, yellowware, triple brown band, one wide, 2 narrow, marked "20" and "Made in U. S. A.", 8" diameter, early 20th C. **$25.00-$30.00**

Mixing bowl, yellowware, brown bands, 9" diameter, 20th C. **$30.00-$40.00**

Mixing bowl, yellowware with green sponged glaze, 5¼" diameter, 1890s. **$45.00-$55.00**

Mixing bowl, yellowware with white glaze, stepped bands, American, 8" diameter, 20th C. • **German vocabulary** — Ruhr schussel: mixing bowl. Also called a Teig schussel. **$18.00-$22.00**

Mixing bowl set, 3 nested bowls, yellowware, yellow with cream bands, turned setback bases, Watt, 6½"H x 10" diameter, and 5"H x 8" diameter, and 4"H x 6" diameter, 20th C. **$125.00-$140.00**

Mixing bowl set, Delphite glass, 3 nesting bowls in "Teardrop" pattern, Fire King, 20th C. **$28.00-$35.00**

Mixing bowls, nesting set of 3, sponged red & blue on stoneware, a Red Wing pottery, 5", 6", and 7" diameter (not complete "set" as they were made on up to 10" diameter), 20th C. **$225.00-$250.00**

Mixing bowls, opaque green — "Jadite," Depression glass, nesting set of 4, actually "Skokie Green" in catalog of manufacturer, McKee Glass Co., Jeannette, PA, 6", 7", 8" & 9" diameter, all relatively tall bowls, 1930s. • "Jadite" is the trade name for an opaque green that Jeannette Glass Co. (also Jeannette, PA) made; "Jad-ite" was used by Hocking, but it's such a perfect descriptive name — anyone familiar with green jade thinks translucent — collectors use it for wide range of very pale to rather richly green opaque glass. Price is for the set. **$40.00-$52.00**

Mixing bowls, yellow earthenware with green sponge design, some have gold-glazed rim, American, range from quite small to 14" diameter & larger. The bowls tend to be relatively shallow in relation to their diameter. TOC. **$45.00-$200.00**

Mixing machine, relatively shallow, broad tin bowl, with slanted sides, fitted with cast iron 3 legged frame that arches up to support the handle, gear & crank, & suspend the 2 kneading blades. American, probably about 11" to 13"H, c. 1860s to 1880s. • Illustrated in 1881 cookbook (but style is at least 20 years earlier). **$75.00-$95.00**

Mixing spoon, commercial or manufactured wooden spoon, of common type, but with head carved on end of handle, very African in style, high forehead, pronounced eyes & hair, American, 13"L, prob. 20th C carving, but it looks awfully good, and not "fakey folk". • I paid $3.50, surprise surprise, but believe more realistic price range: **$25.00-$35.00**

Mixing spoon, or cake spoon, tin & wire, with long slots in bowl of spoon, "Saltmans Improved Royal Rumford Cake Mixer & Cream Whip," pat'd 1908. • **"Another Way to mix Cakes.** — Take six pieces of cane about 18 inches long; tie them fast together at one end; but, to make them open, put in the middle where you tie them one or two pieces half the length: this is called a mixing rod. Provide a tall water pot as upright as can be procured, which make hot; work your butter on a marble slab, then put it in the pan, and work it well round with the rod until it is nicely creamed; put in the sugar, and incorporate both together; add one or two eggs at a time, and go on in this progressive way until they are all used; work away with the rod with all speed; and as soon as it is properly light, (which you may know by its smoothness, and rising in the pan) take it out, and mix in the flour, spices, currants, &c. &c. with a spatter [spurtle]. This is esteemed the very best mode of mixing cakes." Joseph Bell, *A Treatise on Confectionary*. Newcastle, England, 1817. Spare the rod and spoil the cake, eh? **$12.00-$18.00**

Mixing spoon, stamped & slotted metal, nickeled, green wood handle, stamped "Rumford Baking Powder," 10¾"L, 20th C. **$15.00-$20.00**

Mixing spoon, stamped tin & iron, "Rumford Cake Mixer & Cream Whip," Saltmans, 10¼"L, 20th C., unclear patent date on it looks like Oct. 9, 1928, a Tuesday. • Another "Rumford" mixing spoon has sheet metal bowl, with slots, and wire handle, stamped in one place to read "Rumford Baking Powder." **$10.00-$18.00**

Mixing spoon, tinned steel, deep bowl with 16 paired slots, deep division down center, looks like abstract skeletal rib cage, turned wooden handle with blunt end, "Ideal," manufacturer only partly legible on mine: "Mfd by ____ater." American, 10"L x 3"W, says "pat'd March 30, 1908" (a Monday. March 3, or 31 were Patent Tuesdays.) • Classic. — I still give this pride of place in my Pantheon of kitchen collectibles — for sheer design and looks and heft. Plus, I happen to love 1908 — my folks were born that year! SEE "Eclipse" mixing spoon & beater. **$18.00-$28.00**

Mixing spoon beater, tinned stamped iron with black painted turned wood handle, smallish spoon bowl is cut out leaving narrow crosspiece to which a 4 blade propeller is riveted, no mark but date, American, 10"L, pat'd Aug. 3, 1909. • From the Collection of Carol Bohn. Price range mine. **$50.00-$70.00**

Mixing spoon & fork combined, tinned iron with black painted turned wood handle, strange mechanical combination of fairly normal mixing spoon with small bowl & sliding fork mounted to shank, marked L & J Novelty Co., with trademark of L & J inside hexagon, Brooklyn, NY, 12^{15}/$_{16}$"L, pat'd 1925. **$28.00-$38.00**

Mixing spoon or beater, stamped tinned sheet metal, ridged handle shank, large bowl slotted like skeleton rib cage, small diamond cutout at top of bowl. Although handle is different, bowl is like the beautiful "Ideal". "The Eclipse Beater", mfd by Stuber & Kuck, Peoria, IL, 11"L, stamped "Pat. Mar. 30, 1903". • Again, the wrong date. The 30th was a Monday, not a Tuesday. Oddly, the "Ideal", which is so close to this in appearance, is marked with the wrong date too, it says "Mar. 30, 1908", and that was a Monday also. The year numerals are clear — we are not mistaking 1903 for 1908. **$18.00-$25.00**

Mixing spoons, slotted, tinned metal, look exactly like catbox litter scoops, in fact, such are sold for that purpose now at my local pet store, some with stamped advertising. One I have is marked "CHIEF. Lifts, whips, mixes, mashes, crushes, strains", between 10¼" and 11"L x 3½" to 3¾"W, TOC to 1970s. Most may be 1930s or 40s. Good variety in slot patterns, just as in cake turners. **$2.50-$6.00**

Mixing spoons, tinned sheet iron, or nickeled iron, with various wood handles, differences in turning, finish (natural, varnished, painted, stained), & in pattern of holes & slots in the spoon bowls, various makers, including A&J, Androck, Ecko, Samson, PM, etc., American & European, all about 10"L, 1890s to 1940s. • Cast & stamped aluminum ones (mainly German) are a sub-specialty. Advertising ones with wire handles, and those with plastic handles add even more variety to the field. **$5.00-$20.00**

Nesting bowls, spongeware, Red Wing, 6½", 7½" and 8½", 20th C. **$250.00-$275.00**

Paddle, for butter or curds, carved from burl, beautiful patina, old iron repair to handle, NJ (?), 13"L, prob. 18th C. **$900.00-$1200.00**

Pastry blender, 6 springy wire half-circles, crimped into stainless steel tips mounted to wooden handle. Several styles of wooden handle — a simple rod with turned grooves, or a thicker, tapered one — the rest is basically the same. The grooved rod is probably newer one. Androck, Rockford, IL (but poss. Worcester, MA), 5¾"L x 4"W, pat'd Jan. 12, 1929. • Androck is a combination of Andrews Wire Mfg. Co., and the location; it's unclear how and when Washburn of Worcester, MA, took on or absorbed or merged with Andrews. **$7.00-$12.00**

Pastry blender, also pie crust mixer & flaker, wire chopper (as described in the *Official Gazette* of the Patent Office), 6 wires in perfectly round hoop, threaded through 2 slots in the top (1 in each side) of sheet metal handle, "Lambert," pat'd by Clara Burchard Lambert, Pasadena, CA, 4¼"W, #1,486,255, pat'd March 11, 1924. **$12.00-$16.00**

Pastry blender, like a fork, heavy nickeled iron, wooden handle, American, 9¼"L, 20th C. **$8.00-$12.00**

Slotted spoon, yellow enameled iron, slotted, 20th C. **$18.00-$22.00**

Spurtle, oddly-shaped wooden stirring or scraping tool with hole in blade part, worn, some staining to end of blade, looks old but may not be, unknown origin, 13"L, looks like 19th C. • The word spurtle is Scottish, and refers to a cooking implement primarily used for stirring, with an edge to fit different kinds of pots, pans and kettles. They have been a longtime favorite shop project, and are so useful that one made in the 1930s of good hardwood might look about the same as one made in the 1850s. In the early 1970s, Time-Life Books, in their *Family Creative Workshop* series, had a chapter on making your own spurtle. • In 1973, Graham Kerr, the "Galloping Gourmet", introduced a set of five spurtles with their own hanging rack, made of hardwood. They ranged in length from about 8" to 13", and one flat spoon-shaped on had a pair of holes, and a shorter "butter knife" shaped one had one large hole near end of the blade, and the others were without holes in the blade, but all five had hanging holes. • An 1817 English confectionery cookbook, by Joseph Bell, calls frequently for a spatte, the same tool. **$3.00-$10.00**

Stirrer, carved wood, turned handle with small ball knob at end, wide blade is 1/3 of full length, overall it looks like a finely made canoe paddle, American, 13½"L, poss. 2nd to 3rd quarter 19th C. • $50.00 at the Garth Auction, May 5-6, 1989, Delaware, OH. **$40.00-$60.00**

Syllabub churn, small, for tabletop use, pieced tin, tapered cylindrical body, turbine blades, tin lid fits snugly, American, 9½"H x 2½" diameter at top, 1865. **$55.00-$75.00**

Syllabub churn, tin, with a tin rack (shaped like a doll stand) that adjusts in height, simple wooden handle, deeply conical bottom to churn, inside has a dasher, English or American, 9"H, inaccurately marked pat'd Apr. 14, 1875. • April 14 fell on Tuesday in 1868, 1874 and 1885, not 1875. I checked through the hundreds of churn patents in the *Subject Index of Patents 1790-1873*, which is all I have, and found several on April 14, 1868. I suspect this patent was 1874. **$60.00-$75.00**

Syllabub churn or cream whip, tin cylinder with cone shaped bottom, conical metal beater or dasher inside, wire shaft ending in wooden T handle, American, 12"L x 4"D, another recorded 11"L x 3½"D, so possibly there were 2 sizes of this patent item, (or one was mismeasured), pat'd Sept. 14, 1875. **$45.00-$60.00**

Syllabub churn or cream whipper, tin, used by shaking up & down to made the blades spin inside, sort of like a one-underpants clothes washer, only it's for one syllabub at a time, Tilden's Patent, American, 8"L x 1¾" diameter.

pat'd Aug. 1, 1865. • The only churn patent I could find for this date was granted to A. Newbrough of Madisonville, KY. No Tilden churn to be found. (Strangely, three different Newbroughs, in three different states, patented churns in the 1860s.) **$160.00-$180.00**

Toddy mixer, glass & metal, "Toddy Man," 20th C. **$10.00-$12.00**

Whip or whisk, wire, "Omar Wonder Flour," 20th C. **$6.00-$10.00**

Whisk, large flat metal with stenciled wooden handle, not for food probably, but for mixing wallpaper paste, "TIK Wheat Paste, Clark Stek-O Corp.", Rochester, NY, 14⅝"L, 20th C. **$5.00-$8.00**

Whisk, wire in flat "snowshoe" shape, wire-wrapped handle, 9"L, 20th C. **$8.00-$10.00**

Whisk, wood, tin & string, long handle you rub between palms to make it turn back & forth, small balloon blades, probably a drink mixer, American, 16"L, mid 19th C. • **German vocabulary** — <u>Schneebese</u> or <u>Schlager</u>: whisk or eggbeater. **$20.00-$35.00**

Whisks, types include: tinned steel wire with wire wrapped handles for sauces, & a more ballooning stainless steel whisk with wooden handle, adjusting ring on wires to regulate size of balloon, American? first type: 6", 8" & 10"L; second type: 12"L, new, & sold in all kinds of kitchen specialty shops & departments. Approx. new value: **$4.00-$12.00**

Whisks or egg whips, twisted wire, spoonlike in outline, with criss-cross wires, springs & wires wrapped around "bowl," or a sort of chicken wire effect of wire stretched across "bowl", various, some found in catalogs, like that of Androck, mostly American, about 12" to 13"L, mainly 20th C. **$8.00-$18.00**

II-2.
Beaten biscuit machine,
or dough kneader. Cast iron base, marble table surface, adjustable nickeled iron rollers are moved closer together so dough gets harder and harder to roll through (due to build up of gluten) & "cracks". 30 1/2"H x 36"L x 16"W; rollers 2 1/4" diameter x 14"L. Cast iron medallion on base reads: "The DeMuth Improved Dough Kneader & Beaten Biscuit Machine, Manf'd by J.A. DeMuth, St. Joseph, MO." Courtesy Margaret Minich. **$250.00-$600.00**

II-3.
Dough mixer.
Double bentwood, nailed construction. Cast iron crank with large wood knob, iron blade, iron side handle. This fits in crook of arm, held against body, and you apply plenty of body English to make it do its thing. 5"H x 10" diameter. Mid 19th C. Collection of Meryle Evans. **$175.00-$250.00**

II-1.
Batter jugs & pail.
Various stoneware batter jugs. Far (L) decorated in cobalt; next one has original fitted tin spout cap and lid. American, 19th C. Generally speaking, for non-remarkable ones, the value range of plain as well as simply decorated gray stoneware is high (as shown). Brown Albany-glazed batter jugs probably a quarter to a half the range. At far right is tin one — came in 3 sizes: 4, 6 and 8 qts. Late 19th C form, but in c.1904-1910 catalog. **$300.00-$900.00; $125.00-$300.00**

II-4.
Bread maker.
Heavy tin, cast iron crank & gears. "Sifts the flour and mixes 10 lbs. of best bread in 3 minutes." Scientific Bread Machine Co., Philadelphia. Ad in Table Talk, *4/1903.* **$85.00-$135.00**

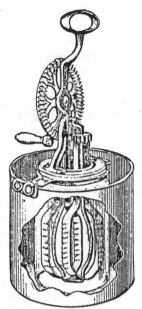

II-5.
Batter or dough-mixing machines.
Top (L) "Centrifugal Mixer," mfd. by The Sparrow Kneader & Mixer Co., Boston, MA. Tin & Cast iron; "stirrers" have horizontal cross pieces. Four sizes; 2 pans (5 or 10 qts.), 2 tanks (10 or 75 gallons). Flyer on flimsy paper, from c.1860: "Although but a few months old, hundreds of them are in use by druggists all over, who find them invaluable for compounding emulsions and ointments heretofore made with a mortar; also, for blending powders mixed by the slow, dusty and wasteful use of the sieve. ...Each stirrer in its revolution sweeps entirely outside of its centre, and the other follows in." Top (R) "Mixing machine" from 1881 cookbook, copied from c.1860s or even earlier cookbook. Lower (L) "Universal" mixer for beating eggs, whipping cream or mixing soft batters ... also for cake." A curved rod was used for kneading heavy batter or bread dough. Center (R) c.1881 "Stantan" bread mixer, heavy tin. As liquid gets mixed into flour, cranking motion causes pan to turn by itself. Lower (R) "Universal No. 4", for 4 loaves. (#8 made 8). Landers, Frary & Clark, New Britain, CT. Tinned pieced metal, with kneading rod, lid, crank, & clamp put on under the lid to provide holder for rod. Stamped on lid is: "Put in all liquids first - then flour - turn 3 minutes - raise in pail - after raising turn until dough forms a ball - take off cross-piece — lift out dough with kneader." 11 7/8"H, 1904, but sold for many years.
$75.00-$200.00

II-7.
Butter merger.
"Holt's Jar Cream Whip" being used for adding milk to butter. "Put 1 pint unskimmed sweet milk in the 1 quart jar; add 1 lb. of butter. Pour luke warm water between jar and can. Let it stand between 5 and 7 minutes. Turn crank two minutes and you will have 2 lbs. of sweet butter." Holt-Lyon Co., Tarrytown, NY. House Furnishing Review ad, 3/1911.
$60.00-$100.00

II-8.
Butter worker.
Table top model, bentwood, in simple wood frame (note well-finished post finials), wood gears, iron handle. 13 1/2"H x 9" x 8", 2nd to 3rd quarter 19th C. Note similarity to less substantial Lilly's Patent in II-6. Collection of Meryle Evans.
$250.00-$400.00

II-6.
Butter workers.
(L) "California," used in a large dairy at Point Reyes' Ranch, CA. Three-legged base screwed to floor, top revolves. Wooden "knife" fits into socket. Butter is put on top, cut and squeezed or squashed against table to remove all liquid, over & over, then patted into molds. American Agriculturist, 3/1870. (R) "Lilly's Patent," for working butter, and for adding optional salt. C.H.R. Triebels, Philadelphia, 1879 American Agriculturist ad. **$125.00-$200.00**

II-9.
Dasher, dash or broomstick churns,
(L) Gray stoneware, wood lid & dasher; 7 sizes (2-10 gals.). Old style, in 1909 catalog, costing from 40¢ to $1.50; lids extra. (R) Oak staved churn, with metal rim. Painted blue. Sizes holding 7, 9, 11, 13 1/2, 16, 20, 24 and 28 gallons, from $6.00 to $14.40, in catalog of D.J. Barry, 1924. A lot later than you'd think, and the blue paint must fool a lot of people. Similar churns were also made in cedar.
$50.00-$200.00

II-10.

Three Dutch churn mechanisms.

Article describes large horse-power churns, then large fly-wheel churns (1). (2) "At Almenaar, a churn made to go by the feet, the weight of the body being moved alternately from one side to the other, on a platform" attached by series of pivots to dasher. (3) a Gouda, Holland churn made "to work from the ceiling in a very easy way; a piece of wood, in the shape of an obtuse angle, was attached at the elbow to a pivot in one of the beams of the ceiling; the churn-stick attached to the one end" and worked by moving lever at left up & down. Article adds "in North Holland they churn using dogs in wheels, in a similar way to the turn-spits." Mechanic's Magazine, and Register of Inventions and Improvements, NYC, 3/1834.

II-11.

Dasher churn.

Gray stoneware with cobalt partridge decoration. Note beautiful spotted chest, and number "5". Impressed with mark: "T. Harrington." 18"H. Photo courtesy Litchfield Auction Gallery, Litchfield, CT. Ex-Harold Corbin Collection, auctioned 1/1/1990. Price realized: **$4200.00**

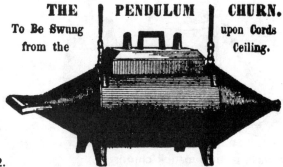

II-12.

"Piggy" style swinging churn.

"The Pendulum Churn," mfd. by Dairy Supply Co., NYC. Tin, with "no dasher, paddles, or inside work of any kind to injure the grain of the butter — surpasses all dash and crank churns. ...Takes up no floor room and is hung up out of the way when not in use." 1879 ad. **$200.00-$400.00**

II-13.

Side crank churn.

"Blanchard," mfd. by Porter Blanchard's Sons, Concord, NH. Came in 7 sizes, for from 2 to 150 gallons. With pulleys, could be empowered by animals or windmills. 1875-76 flyer states that it can be operated whilst sitting down. "Women have not been as much benefitted as men by the invention of labor-saving machines for the farm," said flyer, comparing sit-down Blanchard with tiresome "old upright dash churn ... which tasks the whole upper portion of the body." (Aerobically speaking, the dash provided a much superior exercise, as the Blanchard worked only "the muscles of the arms.") **$50.00-$200.00**

II-14.

Tabletop cylinder churns.

Wood, in two popular styles. (T) Cedar, on shoe feet, marked "R.W." with an anchor; sold through Montgomery Ward, 1890s-1910 or so. (B) "The Lightning," mfd. by Porter Blanchard's Sons, Rutland, VT, late 19th to early 20th C. Both in several sizes. **$45.00-$100.00**

II-15.

Butter machine.

The "Premier" Two Minute Butter Machine, Culinary Mfg. Co., c.1910. Square glass jar with original label, wooden paddle inside, cast iron frame & gears. **$50.00-$75.00**

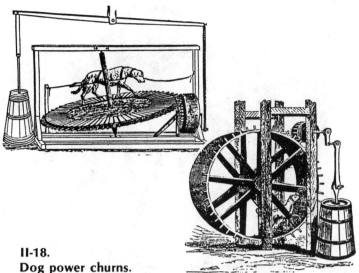

II-18.
Dog power churns.
Both are homemade versions of more "expensive" tread-power churns. American Agriculturist, *4/1876.*

II-16.
Tabletop churn.
All metal, painted blue, cream or other colors. Natural wood top, wood dashers, cast iron gears & crank, 18"H. "Dazey", pat'd 12/18/1877, but sold for many years, at least 20 years into 20th C. #'s 100 to 1600, holding from 1 to 16 gallons. Photographed stock of Country Basket, West Dennis, MA.   **$85.00-$125.00**

II-19.
Tabletop churn & butter worker.
"Julien" — "The standard churn of our country," Julien Churn Co., probably Dubuque, IA. Three sizes: holds 8 gallons (churns 5), holds 10 (churns 7), holds 13 (churns 10). Wood & metal. American Agriculturist, *1/1869.*   **$60.00-$140.00**

KAN-U-KATCH

II-17.
Skimming device from cream separator—
in its "mechanical washer" — a tin box used for washing it. Last edition I called this a "marshmallow beater," which is what collector was told. Someone else said "potato peeler & masher." Glen Thomas, mystery solver from Dwight, IL, sent full documentation of this part of a #14 or #15 U.S. Cream Separator, 1909. Oddly textured slotted cylinder or drum, vertical in separator, is put into box, and soapy water added. Turning drum gets it clean inside and out. Collection Meryle Evans.   **$40.00-$100.00**

II-20.
Whisk-like game piece called "Kan-U-Katch."
I found this picture in a c.1916. St. Nicholas *children's magazine, and put it in last edition as a confusable. Sure enough, I later saw one at a fancy antique show marked "old whisk'. I told dealer but she wasn't convinced.*

II-21.
Cream whips,

egg beaters, or batter mixers. (L) not marked; probably same as one on (R), which is a "Fries". (R) 8"H x 6" x 4 1/2". Ex-Keillor Collection. Note differences in lids, and the wood grip on crank. Linecut ads I have show strap handles, but the fancy turned grip. One calls it the "Economy" cream and topping beater, and gives 3 sizes: 10"H x 6" x 5 1/2"; 10 1/2"H x 6 1/2" x 6 1/4"; and 12 7/8"H x 7 1/2" x 8 1/8", holding from 6 to 16 pts. Other sizes appear in other ads. An electric one, the "Dumore", looks like these, but has crankshaft hooked up to a pulley with a small electric motor. Late 19th to early 20th C, over many years. **$50.00-$75.00**

II-22.
Whisks for the baker, the chef, the candyman.

Clockwise from coiled wire: (1) "Egg beater wire," for replacing whisk wires, c.1906. (2) Candy makers' "sugar spinner," 15"L, 1927. (3) c.1870s, with chained ring to adjust ballooning of bows to suit the job. (4) Long flat one with bound handle is called the "Sensible Egg Whip," and made in sizes from 9" to 15"L, over a long period. Note central wire which is soldered to others and stabilizes them. Next 3 are cream whips from Germany, c.1904. (5) "W.H.T. Patent Egg Beater," sold through candy makers' suppliers, c.1908. (6) is 16"L, big ballooned bows. c.1927. (7) Wood handle steel (or brass) whip, c.1908. (8) "Mayonnaise Whip," 5 1/2" diameter x 13 1/2"L with "four foot pole attached." c.1927. **$5.00-$30.00**

II-23.
Eggbeater trade card.

"Surprise," Cragin Mfg. Co., Cragin, IL. "An Egg Beater that beats the Whites of Eggs better than any other. Cranks will not be tolerated in Egg Beaters any more. Five Dollars offered for a better Egg Beater for the Whites of Eggs. All first-class Cooks recommend them. Take one home and TRY IT, and if not convinced it is the best bring it back." c.1870s card; sold at least 30 years. In separate cut below, note difference in handle from similar ones shown in next picture and II-26. The card: **$4.00-$7.00**

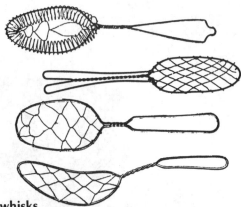

II-24.
Egg whips or whisks.

Tinned wire, various gauges. One has spring wire coiled around rim, inner network of thin wire. Two variations of the "Surprise" are in what the trade called "diamond pattern" wire-weaving. Other one is "checker" pattern. All about 8 1/2" to 10"L. Late 19th to early 20th C. **$8.00-$18.00**

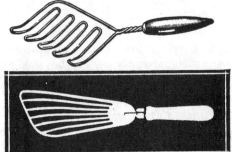

II-25.
Egg whips or batter beaters.

Five fingered one is tinned iron wire "Whipster", green wood handle. "Especially good for Angel Food Cakes." Washburn, 1936. Other is a "batter whip", for eggs, batter or cream; choice of Blutip, green, blue or yellow wood handle. 11 1/4"L. A & J Mfg. Co., Binghamton, NY, 1930. **$4.00-$12.00**

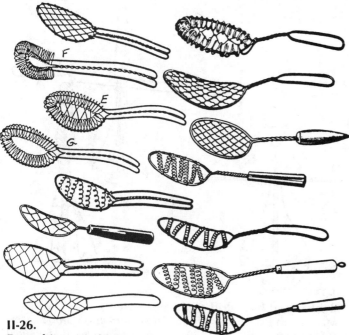

II-26.
Egg whips or whisks.

The 'chicken-wire' type is called "diamond"; closer-woven wires are "checker". Such standard names helped retailers order from different mfrs. Four are "coiled spring" pattern, two have wire lacing holding springs in place around rim. Criss-cross smaller springs is the "cross cut" pattern. Ones marked with letters are: "F" for "Flexible"; "E" for "Electric" (earlier known as the "Electra"); "G" for "Gem" — all Washburn Androck catalog, 1927. Wire Goods Co., Worcester, MA, apparently had earliest patents on these; later Washburn made same or similar designs. **$8.00-$18.00**

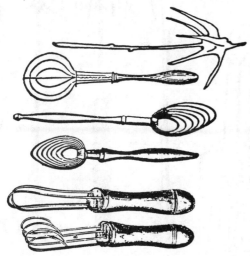

II-27.
Swizzle stick & egg whips,

some also called **spoon egg beaters.** (T) is small branched twig, peeled of bark, and used by rolling shaft between hands. (2) is a "Flat egg-whip, the best shape and easily cleaned." American Home Cook Book, 1854. Next "spoon" one, 10 1/2"L, has long maroon wood handle; Wire Goods Co., 1915. Another, by Lalance & Grosjean, came with tin or wood handle, 1890. Two like garden tools with thick handles, are homemade ones "greatly superior to the common fork or table spoon". 10"L overall. American Agriculturist, 6/1876. An American Agriculturist article on beaters said "several wire beaters are only forks in a modified form." A pear-shaped wire whisk was called "a refinement on bundles of twigs long used by confectioners and bakers." **$8.00-$35.00**

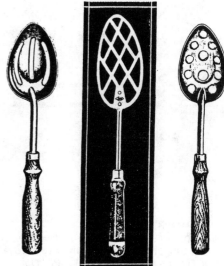

II-28.
Cake whip & mixing spoons.

Also vegetable servers. Slotted & perforated steel spoons with shellacked wood "antique oak" finish handles, 11"L, Wire Goods Co., 1915. Earlier version of perforated one was called the "Perfection Cake Spoon," and sold c.1900. Center one is cake whip, stainless steel, handles in ivory with blue band or green with ivory band, 12 1/2"L. A & J Mfg., 1930. Many variations exist. **$4.00-$15.00**

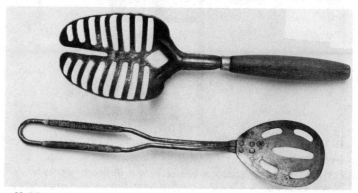

II-29.
Cake or mixing spoons.

Skeletal, rib-cage-like "Ideal" is tinned steel, in a deep bowled shape, and is for "beating eggs, cream, pan cakes, and all other kinds of cakes and batters. For mashed potatoes it can't be beat. Can also be used for lifting vegetables from the pot or eggs from the pan. Unsurpassed for mixing or stirring of fruits." Says 3/30/1908, marked "Mfd. by —ster." March 30 was on a Tuesday in 1909. In 1908, it would have been March 31; in 1903, also the 31st. Others (earlier? later?) mfd. by Stuber & Kuck, Peoria, IL. Wire handled one, 10 1/4"L, has "Rumford. The Wholesome Baking Powder" stamped into flattened part of handle. **$5.00-$25.00**

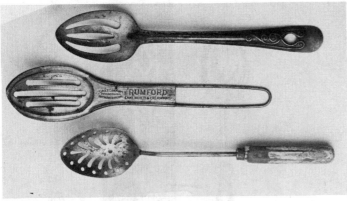

II-30.
Cake or mixing spoons.
Slotted spoons of 3 types. Rumford advertising one, 12"L, is worth most. It's stamped "Saltsmans Improved Royal Pat'd Oct 6 08 RUMFORD Cake Mixer & Cream Whip." Dark one is stamped tin, possibly German. Slotted & perforated one probably A & J, c.1930s-40s. **$5.00-$22.00**

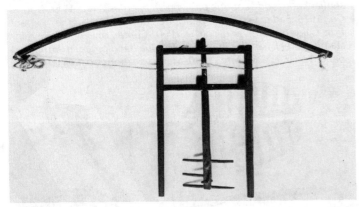

II-31.
Bow drill eggbeater.
Earliest type of mechanical beater, bow drill beater works when bow is sawed back & forth. A cord passing through two small holes in support frame turns beater first one way, then the other, as it winds & unwinds on central shaft. American, probably very early 19th C. Picture courtesy of the National Museum of American History, Smithsonian Institution.

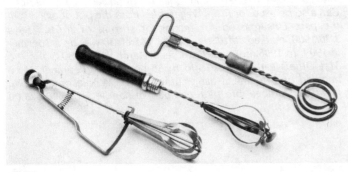

II-32.
Eggbeaters.
Squeeze action one is "One Hand 'WIP'," by Eagle Precision Mfg. Co., chrome & red plastic, 12 1/2"L, 20th C. Others are 2 types Archimedean drill action. Middle beater has black wooden handle, 13 3/4"L, early 20th C. Note swiveling button for holding it in center of bowl. Fold-flat "Bryant's Patent," from 1886, 12 7/8"L (see II-35-5). Collection of Meryle Evans. **$18.00-$35.00**

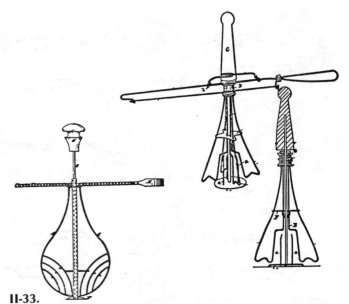

II-33.
Mechanised bow drill eggbeater patents.
(M) and (R) are two views of Howard M. Brittain's (Martin's Creek, PA) egg beater, pat'd 4/12/1892. Action is same idea as aboriginal bow drill fire-starting tool: beater is set firmly in bowl, gripped and held in place by vertical handle, while horizontal wire bow and its spooled cord is moved back & forth to turn beaters this way then that. (L) pat'd 7/7/1863, by Timothy Earle, then of Smithfield, RI. He invented a number of eggbeaters over a long period.

II-34.
Egg beaters & drink mixers.
All Archimedean drill. Far (L) is Horlick's drink mixer in glass tumbler, 9 1/4", c.1910. (2) Tin, wood, wire, 12 1/4"L, German, c.1900. (3) A. & J. Mfg. Co., wire & wood, 12 1/2"L, October 1907. Note little brass swiveling cap to be centered in bottom of bowl to help keep beater in place. A smaller size was for nursery & sick room use. (4) Tin, wood, wire, 11"L, English, no maker's mark. (5) The "Up To Date Egg & Cream Whip," 11 3/4"L, marked April 10, 190-? (either 1900 ro 1906). **$18.00-$40.00**

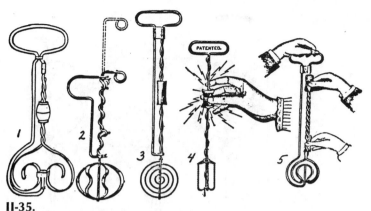

II-35.
Eggbeaters & patents.
All Archimedean drill. (1) Pat'd 6/2/1885, by Charles A. Bryant, Wakefield, MA. (2) Pat'd 5/27/1890, by Alvin Judd Austin, Shelby, NE. Entirely of "wire, whereby a very cheap, simple, and durable egg-beater is produced." (3) "Dudley-Bryant" patent beater, c.1888. (4) "Lightning Chain" eggbeater, mfd. by B.P. Forbes, successor to Tarbox & Bogart, Cleveland, OH. 1903 ad. (5) "Bryant's Patent," with much tighter twisting of vertical rod that forms beater screw. The claim was made that you could achieve 3200 revolutions a minute, i.e. 4 times up & down per second. 1888 ad.$18.00-$35.00

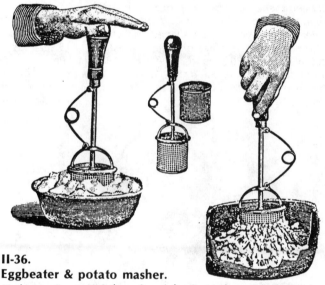

II-36.
Eggbeater & potato masher.
"Lebanon Beater," Seltzer Specialty Co., Lebanon, PA. Two interchangeable perforated cylinders (coarse or fine holes), with cast iron plunger that fits within the cylinder, and is attached to lower end of handle rod. Black wood handle. Looped wire adds spring action. 13"L x 2 3/4" diameter. Tinned or nickel plated. 1892 ad.
$50.00-$75.00

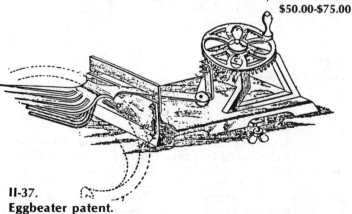

II-37.
Eggbeater patent.
Pat'd 6/16/1891, by David A. Wilkinson, St. Louis, MO. A mechanical double fork, horizontal gear.

II-38.
Eggbeater.
"Express," malleable cast iron, tinned wire, 11 1/2"L, 3" gear wheel, A.E. Rayment Supply Co., c.1910-1920. **$35.00-$65.00**

II-39. Eggbeater — prototype or patent model?
Handmade, machined brass and iron wire, wooden handle, screw clamps to table or shelf edge, modest little back-and-forth or wigwag movement of the dasher to "enable a person to perfectly beat an egg in 35 seconds." 9 1/4"L. 19th C. We thought this was homemade and a one-off contrivance. Dealer Bob Cahn who sold it to me found patent for it. Pat'd 4/22/1873, by Nathaniel C. Miller, Stroudsburg, PA. On 2/1/1870, Miller patented a horizontally-geared eggbeater resembling this one only in its wigwag "vibratory instead of rotary motion." **$150.00-$200.00**

II-40. Eggbeaters & cream whips.
The inventive debate over best eggbeating motion included strong arguments for turbine beaters. Turbines, which stir fluids, including gas, and impart a circular motion to them (providing power in some instances), have been known at least since Hero of Alexander built a small steam-driven turbine in 120 B.C. For eggbeaters & cream whips, turbines are used to cause liquids on bottom to circulate upwards where they can be whipped. (L) Tinned steel, 10"L x 2 1/4" diameter of slotted turbine. Wire Goods Co., 1915. (M) Nickeled steel, wood handle is green. Washburn Co., 1936. (R) Note handle on this "Whirlwind". Ivory white knob. 10 1/2"L. Washburn Co., 1927. **$15.00-$30.00**

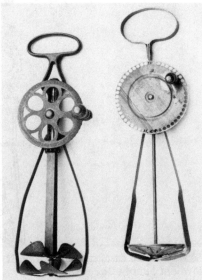

II-41.
Eggbeaters & cream whips.

(L) "Lyon No.2", double turbine blades. Iron & tin, note outer frame & 6-holed gear wheel. 10"L, mfd. in Albany, NY, pat'd 9/7/1887. (Very similar is the "Perfection," with double blades, a 4-holed gear wheel and no frame; it was pat'd 2/22/1898.) (R) Tin, wire, Cassidy-Fairbank Mfg. Co., Chicago, IL, marked "patent allowed", dates to 1910. Note simplicity of the gear wheel, with round perforated holes meshing with the teeth of the small horizontal gear not visible here. Great collecting pleasure is found in ingenious gear wheels. Collection of Meryle Evans.   **$35.00-$50.00**

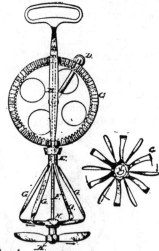

II-42.
Eggbeater & cream whip patent.

Pat'd 11/14/1882, by James T. Carley, Greenport, NY. I don't know if this one was made, but it seems — except for short shaft & overlarge gear wheel — to be an ideal combination of turbine with revolving blades.

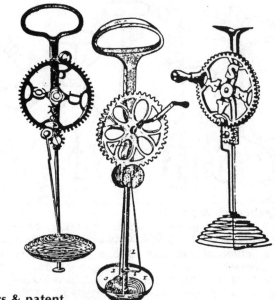

II-43.
Eggbeaters & patent.

(L) The reality: with cast iron gear wheel that spells out mfr's. initials: "P.D. & Co." (Paine, Diehl & Co), Philadelphia. Note flying saucer-like wire dasher: "a double or compound dasher, having its two parts vibrating in opposition to each other upon the egg between them, and also reciprocating up and down against the egg in the bottom of the dish. ...It automatically fits itself to and gathers up the egg from any shaped dish whether spherical or flat bottomed inside. It whips one egg in a teacup in 15 seconds, 6 eggs in a bowl in 70 seconds." Pat'd 12/1/1885. (M) Probably the patent for first one. Pat'd 12/1/1885, by George H. Thomas, Chicopee Falls, MA. (R) The "Easy", sold through Montgomery Ward, c.1895.   **$70.00-$125.00**

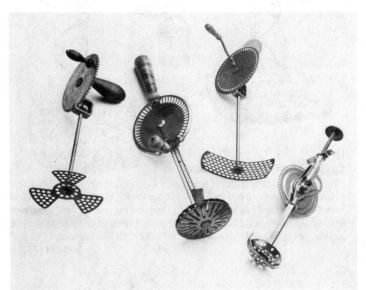

II-44.
Eggbeaters & cream whips.

More turbines. (L) "The NECO," M.P. Hougen, Minneapolis, patent pending. (2) "WHIPPIT" Cream & Egg Beater, Duro Metal Products Co., Chicago. Pat #1,705,639, white & teal blue marbled wood handle, 2 slotted dished blades & upright scraper, 13 1/2"L. 1929. (3) "Dunlap's Sanitary Silver Blade Cream Whip," Casey Hudson Co., Chicago, pat'd 1906-1916. Curved perforated blade fits dimple in bottom of "Non-slip" glazed earthenware mixing bowl which came with the beater. (4) "Quik-Whip", patent pending, nickel plated, 11"L. Unusual action: you fitted your palm to top, then used forefinger to pull up spring-tension hook, which, when released, caused perforated turbine blade to spin.**$25.00-$45.00**

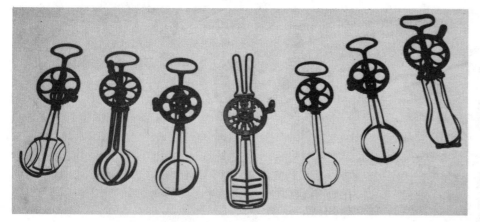

II-45.
Eggbeaters.
All fold flat — a particular love of these collectors. (L) to (R). (1) "Standard" egg beater, 10 1/4"L, pat'd 6/29/ & 9/21/1880, and 3/8/1881. (2) "Dover", 10 1/4"L. (3) "Family", 10 1/4"L, pat'd 9/26/1876. (4) "The Hill," over 12"L. Note that name is spelled out in the cast iron gear wheel, below the rabbit ear handle. Pat'd 11/5/1901. (5) Marked "USA". 9 1/4"L. (6) 10 1/2"L, pat'd 6/29/1880. (7) "Centripetal," pat'd 6/13/1887. Collection of Phyllis & Jim Moffet.

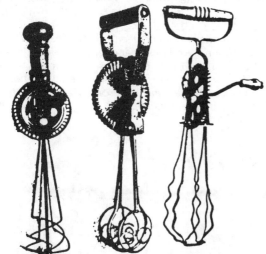

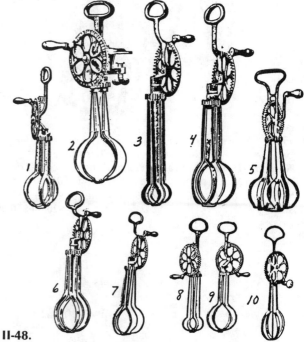

II-46.
Eggbeaters.
(1) Stamped metal gear wheel with holes around perimeter, wire dashers. "Mayonnaise Toujours — Creme Chantilly — Reussis Le Roides Batteurs - CBM - Brevete SGDG." French, 12"L. (M) Spade handle, double circle 'soap bubble blower' dashers. "K.C. USA" Pat. # 1,992,564, 1934. (R) Zig Zag, "Le Tourbillon," French, early 20th C. Pictures courtesy Bob Cahn. **$100.00-$200.00**

II-48.
Dover eggbeaters — the Classic!
Dover Stamping Co., Boston. "Dover" was, for a long while, a generic term for "eggbeater". Patents of 5/31/1870; 5/6/1873; 4/3/1888; and 11/24/1891. Three handle styles are shown here; a fourth is rectangular. Sizes in picture not proportional. (1) "Extra Family Size," 9 3/4"L, Dover Cookbook, 1899. (2) "Mammoth." 1899. (3) "Tumbler", 10 3/4"L, marked "Taplin Co., Wire Goods Co. 1915 catalog. (4) "Hotel", 12 1/2"L, handle & wheel "chestnut bronzed" or tinned. 1915. (5) Center drive, wide flared dashers, 10 1/2"L, bronzed finish. 1927 catalog. (6) 10 3/4"L, 1927 version. Note handle of these later ones. (7) "Small", 8 1/2"L, chestnut bronzed" wheel & handle. 1915. (8) "Tumbler," 10 3/4", 1899. (9) "Family", 9"L, 1899. Blades from 1890 one start higher and describe bigger circle. (10) "Family", from c.1904-1910 catalog. Note wheel knob. **$25.00-$125.00**

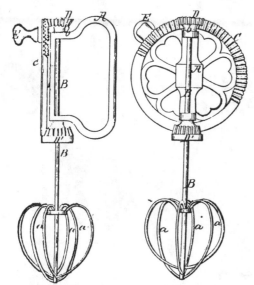

II-47.
Eggbeater patent.
Pat'd 4/24/1866, by Timothy Earle. If this one was made, the value would be sky high what with hearts and elegant compact styling.

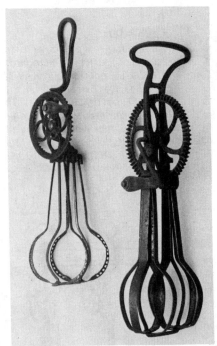

II-49.
Eggbeaters.

(L) "Cyclone," Browne Mfg. Co., Kingston, NY, perforated flanges, cast iron (some are nickel-plated), 11 3/4"L (some are 11 1/2"). 6/25/1901 and 7/16/1901. (R) Taplin "Light Running" center drive, 12 1/4"L, Taplin Mfg. Co., New Britain, CT, pat'd 1908. Note handle, which is like the handle in II-48-5. This one came in a 10 1/2" size also. **$20.00-$50.00**

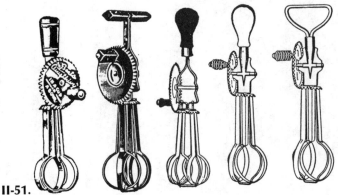

II-51.
Eggbeaters.

(L) to (R). Nickeled steel, wood, 7 1/4"L, "Beats anything in a cup or bowl." A & J, mfd. by Edward Katzinger Co. (which took over the original A & J). (2) An 8-wing, nickeled steel beater with "extra large drive wheel." Red or green angular handles. This and next 3 from Washburn "Androck" catalog, 1936. Note differences in handles and frames. (3) Also 8 wings, with green, yellow or red handle. (4) Four wings, nickeled steel, coiled wire knob, wooden handle in green. (5) the same, with somewhat longer straight part to wings, and different handle. **$20.00-$35.00**

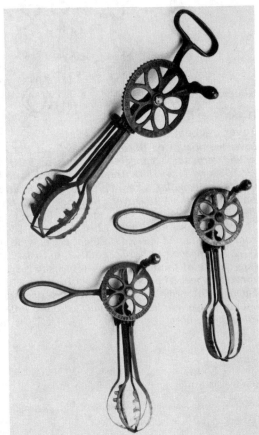

II-50.
Eggbeaters.

(T) "Holt's Egg Beater," pat'd 8/22/1899, iron & tin, 12 1/2"L. Has the so-called "flare dashers." Lower (L) is a side-handled "Holt's Pat'd Flare Dasher," 8 3/4"L, iron & tin. One on (R) has the same name, much less flair! and not so well made. Collection of Meryle Evans. **$35.00-$85.00**

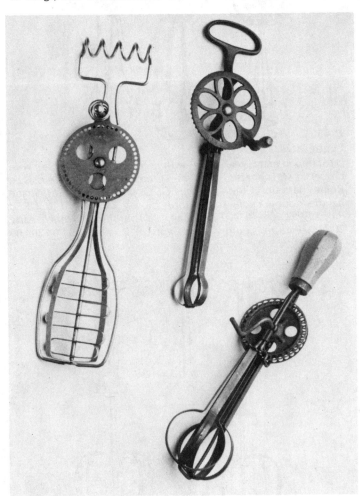

II-52.
Eggbeaters.

(L) "Ram Beater" with wiggly fingerhold grip that looks like crown. Chromed, 12"L. (M) A Dover, 11 3/8"L, iron & tin, with teensiest wings ever — the narrowest tumbler, or perhaps you mixed something down inside a bottle. (R) "Whip Well," yellow wood handle, no knob on crank handle, 11"L, pat'd 3/23/1920 and 5/2/1921. **$25.00-$135.00**

II-53.
Eggbeater.
The incomparable "Aluminum Beauty." Sometimes marked "Aluminum Beauty Beater VIKO Instant Whip." Ullman Aluminum, Division, NY. 10 3/8"L, cast & sheet aluminum. Pat'd 4/20/1920.   **$20.00-$35.00**

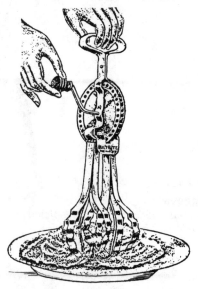

II-54.
Eggbeater.
The "Biltrite," mfd. by Stuber & Kuck Co., Peoria, IL. Tinned steel, center drive wheel, nameplate is a "locking device holding blades permanently in place," waved beater blades "result in 50% quicker results," and the blades are "so close to plate that one egg is drawn up from a flat plate ... impossible with other makes." 1919 ad _House Furnishing Review._   **$25.00-$40.00**

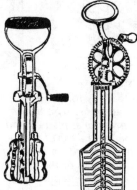

II-55.
Eggbeaters.
(L) Another waved-blade type with center drive. This is the "Flint Mixer 'Rhythm Beater,' " mfd. by Ekco Products Co., 1958. (R) Unnamed eggbeater mfd. by F.W. Loll Mfg. Co., Meriden, CT. 1/1909 _House Furnishing Review._ **$5.00-$12.00 and $100.00-$150.00**

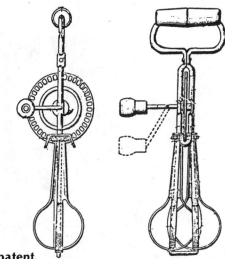

II-56.
Eggbeater patent.
Pat'd 1/13/1931, by Henry J. Edlund, Burlington, VT, #1,789,224. Mfd. by Edlund Co., Inc., Burlington.   **$18.00-$30.00**

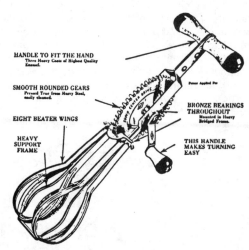

II-57.
Eggbeater.
"No. 75 Super Center Drive," nickeled steel, wood handles in Blutip, green, blue or yellow. A & J Mfg. Co./EKCO, Edward Katzinger Co., Chicago, 1930.   **$20.00-$30.00**

II-58.
Wallmount eggbeater.
"Silver Wall Style No.6", mfd. by Silver & Co., Brooklyn, c.1910. Black japanned cast iron, tinned spring wire bows. "For hotels and restaurants. Very quick in operation, and very easily cleaned." Has a "suspended arm to which is cast a socket which fits into a corresponding pocket socket ... which may remain permanently affixed to the wall and the beater portion be removed. In use large bowls or large glasses or pails or deep dishes or any other similar article may be used as a receptacle." **$100.00-$200.00**

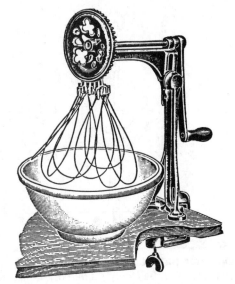

II-59.
Eggbeater.
"Silver Hotel Egg Beater No.5," Silver & Co., c.1910. "Framework ... is heavy cast iron retinned with pure tin which ... makes it sanitary. The beater portion is constructed of heavy steel piano wire and will stand a great deal of hard usage. Shown ready to attach to table. Excellent for large cake mixtures, or where a large quantity of doughy mixture, eggs or mixing of any liquids or light dough is desired. It is splendid for hotels, bakers, boarding houses, and other similar places. For convenience, it disjoints at upper portion of the arms, and is adjustable for height." Note wheel's quatrefoil cutouts. **$100.00-$200.00**

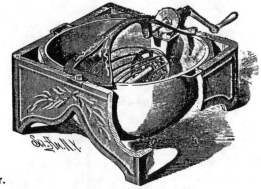

II-61.
Eggbeater.
With pan and frame, this is almost a mixing machine. "Newcomer's Improved," with a chain-drive "rotary egg whip consisting of a shaft, having skeleton heads, and wires which are so curved as to make the exterior of the whip conform very nearly in shape with the hemispherical bottom of the pan. By coming very near the surface of the pan, small quantities of eggs can be whipped." Iron frame secured to wooden stand, obviously decorated. The small continuous chain goes from the small wheel seen fully in drawing down to a small sprocket wheel which turns the beater. Mfd. by inventor, J.L. Newcomer, Baltimore, MD. 1885 article in Scientific American. *Pat'd 5/26/1885.* **$200.00-$400.00**

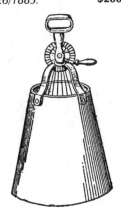

II-62.
Eggbeater.
A small "petite batteuse," depicted in Urbain Dubois' La Patisserie d'Aujourd'hui, c.1860s. **$100.00-$200.00**

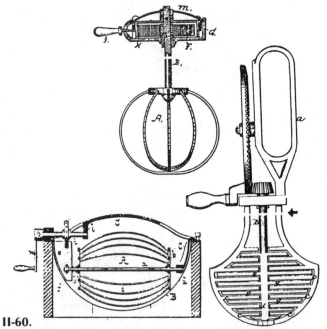

II-60.
Eggbeater patents.
All bowl-fitting. (T) Pat'd 6/19/1877, by Eustache R. Dulje, Newark, NJ. Lower (L) Pat'd 5/26/1885, by Jacob L. Newcomer, Baltimore, MD. See II-61 for finished piece. (R) Pat'd 5/8/1877, by James H. Scofield. With side handle and compact design. Small arrow points to break in drawing — original drawing had some unspecified length cut from it at that point.

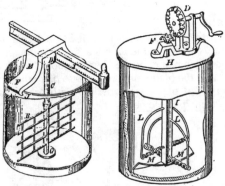

II-63.
Eggbeater patents.
(L) Pat'd 12/15/1857, by John B. Heich, Cincinnati, OH. The "net work" beater is activated by a bowing action. Central gear disk is described by inventor as made of India rubber, "or other elastic material, attached to the top of the rod. ...The beater is operated by the pressure produced upon the elastic disk by the motion backwards and forwards of the grooved bar" bow. From Patent Commissioner's Annual Report, *1857. (R) Pat'd 5/21/1867, by Marvin T. Williams, Milwaukee, WI. Note litte coils on bottom horizontals of beater wings.*

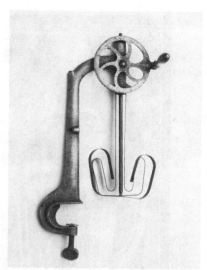

II-64.
Eggbeater.
Clamps to table, nickeled cast iron, tin, 10"H, removable beater blades. No mark, no date. Collection of Meryle Evans.
$45.00-$75.00

II-66.
Eggbeater or drink mixer.
Cast iron horizontal gear in lid, wire handle & beaters. Glass embossed "J E W E L BEATER, MIXER, WHIPPER & FREEZER. MANF BY GRAVITY TWINE BOX CO. CLEVELAND, OHIO." Called the "Household Jewel" in advertisements of the period, c.1893. Photo courtesy Phyllis & Jim Moffet.
$150.00-$250.00

II-65.
Eggbeater or drink mixer.
"Standard Specialty Co., Milwaukee, WI," with Root Mason fruit jar. The beater is fixed to the lid, but obviously other jars could replace this one. Cast iron, tin, green glass, 12"H x 3 7/8" diameter. Pat'd 6/11/1907.
$75.00-$125.00

II-67.
Eggbeaters & original vessels.
(L) A & J with its original beating bowl. Pat'd 1923. (R) a Liquid mixer marked with an intermingled monogram of "AD", pat'd 1915. Archimedean drill for one-handled mixing.
$30.00-$50.00

II-68.
Eggbeater.
"Silver Egg Beater No.4," with a "receptacle made of heavy lime glass graduated for dry or liquid measuring. The dashers or beaters are made of extra heavy bessemer steel, retinned bright, the air tube is made of XXXX tin. The valve adjustment at the base of the tube is made of german silver. The tinplate cover is heavily nickelplated and polished. The handle of enameled wood." One quart capacity only. 11 1/2"H x 4 1/2" diameter. Silver & Co., Brooklyn, c.1910. A few years later, the style of the wooden handle was slightly changed to be more angular, and with more turnings.
$35.00-$55.00

II-69.
Eggbeaters or drink mixers.
(L) Originally the "Silver No.3", Silver & Co., c.1910, with japanned cast iron top, nickeled gears, tinned steel piano wire bows, glass, enameled wood handle. Used also for mayonnaise or butter-merging. This one marked "The New Keystone Beater," Culinary Utilities Co. Top still same as the Silver. Measures embossed on sides of glass — 1 qt. liquid (worked 3 cups); "coffee cups full" on another; Flour and sifted flour; liquids in ounces. Collection of Meryle Evans. (R) "E-Z Mixer," National Mfg. & Supply Co., Pittsburg, PA. Pat'd 6/30/1903. 32 oz., 13"H. Cast iron top with flat padlike knob for pressing against heel of hand while mixing. No marks in metal. Lid has oil funnel hole for making mayo. Courtesy Bob Cahn. **$75.00-$150.00**

II-71.
Eggbeater & pitcher set.
Pat'd glass pitcher with interior (see inset) that's supposed to "do half the work" of making the liquid move around. It's "marked by a series of vertical ridges gaining in depth as they go downward and forming, on the inside bottom, a serrated cup. These vertical ridges act as passive beater wings and help to break up and beat the contents." Green or clear glass, and to fit the Sr. or Jr. beaters, which had Blutip or green wood handles. 12 1/2" overall. A & J, 1930. **$50.00-$80.00**

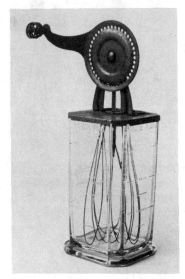

II-70.
Eggbeater & liquid mixer.
"New Keystone Beater 'Even Full'", Culinary Utilities, c.1929. Note simple top and perforations instead of gear teeth. **$65.00-$90.00**

II-72.
Eggbeater & pitcher sets.
Also A & J, in pint size glass pitchers. Edward Katzinger catalog, 1940. **$25.00-$40.00**

II-73.
Larding needles — or "Beef a la Mode" needles.
(T) Brass & steel needles in tin fitted case. F.A. Walker catalog, 1870s, but sold for at least another 30 years. Other is a mechanized larding needle with wooden handle, sort of like a latchhook for making rugs. c.1906-07 catalog. **$20.00-$30.00**

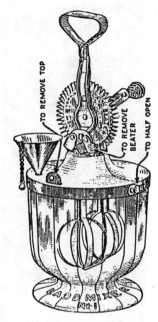

II-74.
"Mixing churn,"
or mayonnaise maker or eggbeater. "Ladd #1 in quart size footed paneled bowl, showing oil funnel. 1914 ad, but sold for at least another 15 years. **$55.00-$95.00**

II-76.
Water power beaters.
Can be attached by a hose or directly to faucet. Turbine action of water coursing through pear-shaped lid causes beaters to turn. Discharged water apparently came out tube below the lid. Fit a quart canning jar with a screw top. Not marked except for "patent pending," although clunkier painted one on left once had a round paper label. Right one highly polished brass. I wonder if a company that made lawn sprinklers didn't make this beater. Thanks to Glenda Clark and Phyllis & Jim Moffet for information & picture. **$100.00-$200.00**

II-75.
Mixers, Beaters.
(L) Electric "Challenge," mfd. by CEM Co., Tyre Avub (??). Simple single dasher blade, works perfectly, even hums. 3 cup capacity, 8 1/2"H, 110-120 volts. (R) "Ladd Beater #1," as in II-74. Pat'd 7/7/1908, 2/2/1915. Beater can be dismantled from lid. 13"H. (R) Collection of Meryle Evans. **$15.00-$25.00 and $55.00-$75.00**

II-77.
Mixer & mixing bowl.
"The Silver", one size only — 2 pts. Note oil-funnel with drop stopper for making mayonnaise. "Imported bone china" bowl, chestnut wood cover, nickelplated brass beater. Blade is sort of half-moon shape with a few bentup fingers. Silver & Co., Brooklyn, c.1910. **$75.00-$125.00**

II-78.
Electric food mixer.
"Dormeyer", mfd. by A.F. Dormeyer Mfg. Co., Chicago. American Cookery magazine, 1930. **$20.00-$45.00**

II-79.
Mayonnaise mixer.
Blue painted cast iron with heart cutout gear, large handle, glass jar, oil funnel hole. Original blue paper label reads "VITESSE-MAYONNAISE." Trademark appears to be a diamond with "FUPA" inside. French, c.1900. **$75.00-$125.00**

II-81.
Egg beater, drink mixer, cream whipper
and mayonnaise mixer. Two views of "Air-O-Mixer", patent pending, mfd. by Bentley-Jones Inc., Montgomery, AL. Glass embossed with directions. Perforated conical beater is of type used by makers of mixer churns for at least 75 years before. It appeared in Wesson Oil "make your own mayonnaise" ads from late 1933 through 1934. See II-91. **$45.00-$75.00**

II-80.
Mayonnaise mixers.
(L) "Universal Mayonnaise Mixer & Cream Whipper," Landers, Frary & Clark, patent applied for. Nickeled iron top, nickeled dashers with long fingers, lid has swivel cover for oil hole. 2 1/2 to 3 cup capacity, approx. 9 3/8"H, late 19th C. (R) "S & S No.1", or "Scientific & Sanitary". The "S & S" forms casting design of gear wheel. Glass lid with oil funnel built in. Regular eggbeater blades. 9 3/4"H overall. This one marked "patent pending." It was patented 9/2/1913, and was used for omelets, salad dressings, desserts & beverages also. Collection of Meryle Evans. **$100.00-$200.00**

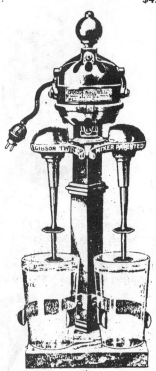

II-82.
Soda fountain drink mixer.
Gibson "Twin-Mixer", H.B. Gibson Co., NYC, hooked up to a Hamilton-Beach motor, Racine, WI. Could be had quadruple silver plated, or nickel plated. 6/1919 ad in *The Soda Fountain*. **$100.00-$400.00**

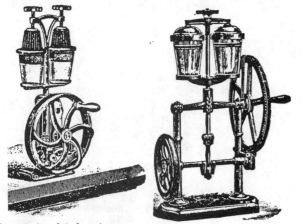

II-83.
Soda fountain drink mixers.
Hand-powered cranked, not electric. (L) "Quick and Easy" shaker, possibly Conant Co. Nickeled & painted cast iron, 22"H, for all beverages. c.1905 catalog. (R) "Philadelphia" milk shake machine, 24"H, 7 1/2" x 12" base. "Each turn of the crank-wheel gives ten distinct shocks to the liquid." T. Mills, 1915. Maker not known.
$250.00-$600.00

II-84.
Drink mixer.
Electric "Arnold Sanitary Mixer No. 12", nickeled.
$45.00-$65.00

II-85.
Mixing bowls.
(T) is wood, ranging from 12" to 37" diameter. Jaburg Brothers, who sold supplies to confectioners, advertised that they would **"strap Bowls and repair same."** *Meaning to fix cracked ones with iron bands, etc. That was in 1908. (B) footed bowl is heavy tin, from about 7" to 15" diameter. Sold by German company, c.1904. Jaburg sold seamless steel mixing bowls, from 25" to 34" diameter, finished black or galvanized.* **$10.00-$200.00**

II-86.
Mixing bowls for eggs.
Called schneekessel. *German nickel plated, copper, tin and glass bowls. Generally between 8" to 15" diameter. "D" is glass; "A" and "B" are copper.* **$10.00-$100.00**

II-87.
Mixing bowls.
(T) White semi-porcelain with wide blue band and blue pin stripes. "Heavily glazed." 4" to 13" diameter, holding from 6 oz. to 7 qts. c.1895 ad. Lower (L) is "heavy yellow stoneware, rolled edge, neat blue band ad. (R) "Yellow bowl," earthenware, holding from 1/4 to 12 qts. Duparquet catalog, c.1904-1910. **$20.00-$120.00**

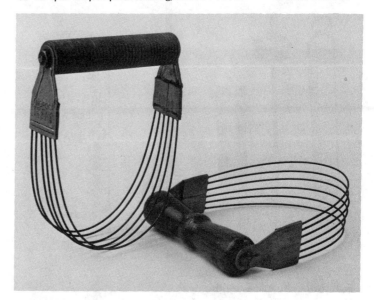

II-88.
Pastry blenders.
Wire, steel & wood, 5 3/4" x 4". Both are Androck, pat'd 1/12/1929. Note there are 6 wires. In ads from catalogs, there are always 7 wires. One lying down is oldest, other is newer. In a 1936 catalog, the handle of green or red is made of Catalin plastic. **$7.00-$12.00**

II-89.
Cocktail shaker.
Realistic bell-shape. Nickeled brass, wood handle. 11"H, 20th C.
$35.00-$55.00

II-90.
Cocktail shaker set,
in rocket ship shape. For more see price listings under "Cocktail," 12"H, c.1930s (?). Photo by Leslie Harris. **$750.00-$1000.00**

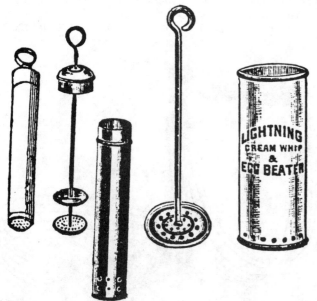

II-91.
Syllabub churns & eggbeaters.
Very old type, called a **whip churn.** *All have perforated dasher. Similar-looking ones might use another kind of dasher. (L) was for making whipped cream or syllabub, and is from* American Home Cook Book, *1854. (2) and (3) are parts of the Matthai-Ingram syllabub churn, 8"L, 1 3/4" diameter. c.1890. (4) and (5) is the "Lightning Egg Beater," also Matthai-Ingram. "The white of an egg can be beaten in one minute to a froth stiff enough to cut with a knife." c.1890.* **$35.00-$75.00**

II-92.
Spurtles.
Idiosyncratically-shaped wooden stirring paddles, adapted to various uses. Scottish word, but tool universal.

A. PREPARING
III. SEPARATE, STRAIN, SIFT & DREDGE

In the last chapter we mixed things; here we separate them. This preparation category encompasses all the implements that assist the cook either by allowing wanted food stuff to be retained (in a sieve, colander, skimmer, etc.), or for wanted liquids or solids to be cleared of unwanted particles too large to slip through the holes, or for lumpy food to be pushed through a perforated (or screened) surface in order to render the lumps smaller, or to make them uniform in size. When used with a pestle, a strainer is a form of mortar, so see Potato ricers in Chapter I.

Colanders, both foot-fast and foot-loose, are among the most popular utensils in this category, collected for the material from which made (especially enameled iron), for their shape, and for the variety of perforated patterns. A single colander can be a thing of great beauty, probably because its form tells the whole story of its simple function; but a collection of different colanders, each with its particular tattoo of holes, is spectacular.

For this edition, I have moved cheese drainers to the Mold chapter, because although they look like colanders, and their method is to strain the whey from the curds, their ultimate function is to mold the cheese once the whey has dripped out. Another change involves funnels; I have included here funnels with built-in sieves (mostly vintners' or brewers' types); the other funnels are in the chapter on Measuring & Weighing.

The most popular category in this chapter is flour sifters. Mechanically, they are satisfying because of the variety — cranks, squeeze handles, shakers. The single most necessary sifter for a collection is the Hunter, described fully in its entry.

Bean sizing sieve, wood frame with wood slats, adjusts by going from square shape down to very elongated diamond shape so that the spaces between the slats narrow down too, American, 18'' x 18'', 19th C. **$110.00-$135.00**

Bean sorting frame, also called a <u>bean sizer</u>, criss-crossed wood slats in frame of 4 equal length sides, all movable in relationship to one another because not permanently fixed at corners or where slats cross. Openings or interstices adjust in size & shape by moving the 2 opposite sides of frame to change the configuration of the parallelogram formed by the sides. American, 18½'' x 19'', 19th C. **$125.00-$150.00**

Colander, also spelled in old inventory records <u>cullender</u>, <u>collander</u>, or <u>colender</u>, this one of pewter, wide flared sides, fixed foot, ring handles, scalloped pattern of small perforations. American (?), 11'' diameter, late 18th C or early 19th C. **$500.00-$650.00**

Colander, aqua enamelware, 11''D, 20th C. **$30.00-$40.00**

Colander, brown & white swirled enamel, probably "Onyx", Columbian Enameling & Stamping Co., 10''D, late 19th or early 20th C. **$85.00-$115.00**

Colander, dark blue enamelware, black rim & handles, elegant bowl shape with high fixed foot, prob. European, 7''H x 7½'' diameter, late 19th C. • **Foot or Base?** I have tried to consistently use the term "foot" (or sometimes "footed base"), in the singular, when I am talking about a sort of fixed flared or convex ring that serves as the base of a vessel, utensil or other object. I took the term from the old catalog designations, as a matter of fact, for the two types of colanders: foot loose, and foot fast. The former meaning a ring separate from the colander, and used (like that ring put over the burner when you use a wok; the latter means a ring fixed or soldered in place, stuck "fast" to the colander. Some writers and antiques cataloguers call this type of fixed ring foot a "gallery foot." • A foot may also be barely visible, a very narrow band that allows a round-bottomed piece to stand. •More exact terms include <u>spreading foot</u> for the widely flaring incurved foot; <u>molded foot,</u> for one with beading, reeding or ogee curves or other moldings used in wood carving and cabinetry; <u>round foot</u>, for a simple convex or outcurved foot. • Descriptive terms haven't been codified or standardized to any degree concerning kitchen wares, so some applicable terms must be borrowed from fields of collecting such as silver, pewter, porcelain, & furniture, as well as wood- and metal-working tools. **$60.00-$80.00**

Colander, dark cobalt enamelware flecked with white, wire handles, footed, American (?), 8'' diameter, TOC. **$75.00-$100.00**

Colander, dark cobalt & white graniteware, riveted strap handles, rounded ring foot, American (?), 12'' diameter, TOC. **$60.00-$90.00**

Colander, gray graniteware, American or German, 9½''D, late 19th or early 20th C. **$55.00-$85.00**

Colander, gray graniteware, ear handles, short feet & attached drip tray, 19th C. • **German vocabulary** — <u>Durchschlag</u>, <u>Seihe</u> or <u>Sieb</u>, the first is a noun from the verb for "slip through"; the other words mean strainer & sieve. **$100.00-$150.00**

Colander, green speckled enamelware with cobalt blue rim & ear handles, foot fast, lovely color, 10⅞'' diameter, 19th C. **$145.00-$170.00**

Colander, mottled green graniteware, strap handles, foot fast, American (?), 10''D, late 19th or early 20th C. **$75.00-$100.00**

Colander, perforated sheet iron, foot fast, commercial though it looks handmade, good condition, 10''D, late 19th or early 20th C. **$15.00-$25.00**

Colander, perforated tin, flat bottom has radiating holes lining up with every 3rd row of holes in sides, deeply flared, strap handles, foot fast, American, 4¼''H x 12''D, late 19th or early 20th C. • At Thomas Jefferson's home, Monticello, in Charlottesville VA, there is an artifacts exhibit in an alcove of the underground tunnel connecting the kitchen with the dining room in the opposite wing. Of great interest to colander collectors is the remnant of a badly rusted tinned iron colander, which is being exhibited as dating to Jefferson's time (and he died in 1826). About a third of this colander is present, and shows that it was widely flared, had at least one inch-wide strap handle, and had relatively small holes only in the rounded bottom. The remnant's size indicates the piece was about 13'' diameter. I'm not convinced it's that old; Monticello was inhabited for a century after Jefferson's death. **$18.00-$30.00**

Colander, pewter, fast foot, heavy & beautifully made, American or English (?), 12⅝'' diameter, very early 19th C, even late 18th C. **$700.00-$1000.00**

- **Metal Drives in Revolutionary & Civil Wars.** — There is probably plenty of documentary evidence, so far unexplored, touching on the necessity for metal or scrap drives during (and perhaps preceding each of) the first four wars of the U. S., viz. the War for Independence, 1775-1781, the War of 1812, 1812-1815, the War Between the States, 1861-1865, and the Spanish-American War, 1898. Such documents presumably would be found in the National Archives, the Library of Congress, and in privately- or publicly-held collections of family papers, letters, newspapers, broadsides, perhaps even court-ordered seizure records. The wars swallowed an incalculable number of sound household wares and tools, as well as scraps of same, pooled to recast or forge as cannon, musket balls, soldiers' canteens, army horseshoes, ironclad vessels, guns, pistols and bullets. Basically we are talking about iron, lead and pewter, with some brass and copper. I can't now search primary or secondary sources, but will quote from Ledlie Irwin Laughlin's *Pewter in America*, 1940, to hint at the scope of the loss. Anything said about pewter is true in spades about iron. Laughlin writes, Vol. I, p. 109, "During the [Revolutionary] war the country was combed for everything containing lead to supply munitions for the Continental troops. Little beyond the absolutely essential, and probably new, pewter would have escaped the melting-pot." Laughlin, Vol. II, p. 69, we read that "It has been said that the dearth of Southern pewter may be chargeable to confiscation by agents of the Confederate Government of all available metal that could be used in the manufacture of munitions during the Civil War."
- Inexplicable to me, so far, is the vast supply of 17th, 18th & 19th C iron, pewter, brass & copper wares found today all over Europe, which has been ravaged by more war than have we. • **Meltdowns in the Pursuit of Commerce.** — Easily reviewed old newspapers, or "gleanings" of ads done by Dow and Gottesman, give ample proof that most if not all metal artisans in the U.S. solicited and bought "old iron, pewter, brass, copper, lead & tin" for melting down or reworking into new objects in more fashionable or necessary forms. • These two kinds of "metal drives" have left only written descriptions and incidental pictures of countless old pieces. It early colander marked by American pewterer, worth much more.

Colander, pierced tin, flat bottom, foot fast, tinned iron loop handles, sold through F. A. Walker catalog, 3¾"H x 9¾"D, 1870s-80s. **$18.00-$30.00**

Colander, rounded bowl body, pierced tin, iron loop handles, nice rolled edge foot ring, separate or loose, Matthai-Ingram, 13"D, 1890s. • This is a hypothetical entry. Although the catalogs offered foot loose as well as foot fast colanders, the chances of a foot ring surviving with its separate colander bowl are slim. **$18.00-$25.00**

Colander, sheet iron, very large with good size holes, crudely soldered foot ring, primitive & imposing, American, 14"D, mid to end of 19th C. **$30.00-$40.00**

Colander, tinned pieced sheet metal, hollow ear handles, small flat bottom has many holes, lower part of sides not perforated, then band of several rows of holes partway up sides, American, 14" diameter, late 19th C. **$25.00-$35.00**

Colander, white enamelware, blue rim, strap handles & foot, TOC. • **"Cauliflower Fritters.** — Boil the cauliflower until perfectly tender, drain and cool; break carefully into flowerettes, season with salt and pepper, dip into fritter batter and fry in deep fat. (If cauliflower has been served with a white sauce at dinner, cut into small pieces and dip in batter, and fry.) Serve very hot or put in a shallow baking dish, sprinkle freely with parmesan cheese or other cheese and bake in hot oven." *Woman's Home Companion*, June 1899. **$28.00-$35.00**

Colander, wire mesh in tin & wire frame, wooden ear handles, also used as a puree sieve, Androck, Rockford, IL, 1936. **$12.00-$18.00**

Colander, yellowware, footed, rather thick walls with pierced bottom, American, 10" diameter, 19th C. **$175.00-$250.00**

Colander, yellowware, small foot, nice pattern of holes, 2 eyeholes near rim for hanging cord, English, 10¾" diameter, mid 19th C. • Very small crack lowers price by 25% or so. **$120.00-$140.00**

Colander or strainer, dark brown stoneware, smallish roundish body with rim & base the same diameter, thick arched handle like a basket, rather large holes piercing sides & bottom, Pennsylvania German, 8"H including handle x 6¼" diameter, mid 19th C (?). • Robacker May 1989 price: **$350.00**

Colander scoop, pieced & perforated tin, missing its wooden handle, 6"L, 19th C. **$10.00-$13.00**

Drainer or strainer, a sort of perforated metal half-lid that fit into cooking vessel & held back the beans while pouring off liquid, "Drain-a-Way," 20th C. **$6.00-$8.00**

Draining pan, or sink drainer, aluminum in triangular shape, for corner of sink, "Wearever Aluminum", 1920s-30s. **$12.00-$18.00**

Dredger, also called a dredge box, tin, with double lid, the inside one is pierced, "Steele's Dredge Box," New Haven, CT, 3¼"H x 2"D, pat'd Dec. 27, 1870. **$25.00-$30.00**

Dredger, for flour, heavy old dark tin, footed like a goblet, domed pierced lid, big strap handle on side, American, 6"H, early to mid 19th C. **$18.00-$25.00**

Dredger, for flour, japanned (asphaltum) tin, small handle, domed lid, American, 4"H, late 19th C. **$20.00-$25.00**

Dredger, for flour, tin cup with handle & snug snap-on domed lid with perforations; also called a dredge, dredging box, or drudger. American (?) — prob. impossible to tell unless marked, c.1880s. • What appears to be identical is a tin Pepper Box (also made in Britannia metal), with small, closely spaced holes. It was advertised in the retail catalog of Harrod's Stores, Ltd., in 1895. **$15.00-$25.00**

Dredger, milk glass, metal screw-on lid, the word "Flour" painted on side, American, 4½"H x 2½"D, early 20th C. **$12.00-$15.00**

Dredger, or dredge box, japanned tin cup with mug handle & slightly flared base, domed pierced lid, American or imported, in F. A. Walker catalog of 1870s.
• **Reproduction alert.** — Possibly this has been made continuously since the 1870s or 1860s, or whenever the style of dredger with the wide flared concave foot (I've seen this called a "gallery base") was first made. But we know it was being reproduced at least by 1974. An ad placed by Williams & Sons Country Store, Stockbridge, MA, in the Aug. 1974 *Early American Life*, pictures a well-made somewhat shiny tin dredger, with a 5 point star perforation pattern on the lid, and a dark tin foot. The copy reads "Grandmother never baked a pie, cake or loaf of bread without her old tinware flour dreger [sic] at her

side." The repro is 5"H x 4½" diameter at widest part of foot, and cost only $5.25 ppd. **$18.00-$22.00**

Dredger, or flour shaker, green custard glass, "McKee," Pittsburg, PA, 1930s. **$15.00-$18.00**

Dredger, or <u>muffineer</u>, tin cup with pierced convex top, mug-type handle, 2 tier base, used for flour, or sugar & cinnamon, for dredging meat to make gravy, or dusting pastry boards before rolling, sprinkling cookies or muffins before baking (which is where it got its name), American (?), 7"H, 19th C. **$45.00-$60.00**

Dredger, probably for cinnamon sugar, shapely pigeon breasted glass container that looks something like a fire hydrant in profile, one flat side to fit against back of stove shelf, screw-on tin lid, American, 6"H, prob. late 19th C. **$18.00-$22.00**

Egg detector, for bad eggs, heavily tinned stamped & pieced metal, very shallow but wide mouthed funnel like contrivance with a curved sharp shell-breaker ridge from the rim down to opening of the narrow neck, which forms a sort of crook-necked double elbow "S" curve, the whole raised high on 3 tall legs, sold by, possibly mfd by V. Clad & Sons, Philadelphia, early 20th C. • The advertising in the V. Clad catalog, c. 1914, says "You," meaning mostly restauranteurs, "no doubt, in breaking eggs have many times come in contact with and broken a bad or musty egg, and in most cases have spoiled quite a number of good ones, by letting the bad one fall among them. With this Detector the chances of losing eggs by this cause will be avoided, as it contains but one egg, therefore you can only spoil one, and not from one to six or ten dozen, as the case may be, by breaking them the old way.

"By this machine you cut your shell; you do not smash it and get your batch full of small pieces. You get all out of the egg in your vessel, as there is no chance for part of each egg to run on the outside, as in the old way. You do not make a mess on your table or bench; besides, you can break eggs much faster than in the old way, thereby saving valuable time." **$35.00-$45.00**

Egg separator, 2 parts, enameled cast iron, cup is blue, slotted shallow yolk catcher that sets into it is enameled white, T. S. Ceeton, 4" diameter, pat'd Oct. 8, 1891. **$95.00-$135.00**

Egg separator, aluminum, 2 large ear handles, each with hanging hole, 2 slots in shallow cup, 3¾" diameter, 6⅜"L overall, c. 1915. **$5.00-$8.00**

Egg separator, stamped aluminum, advertising "Watkins," 20th C. **$8.00-$12.00**

Egg separator, stamped, slotted tin, advertising "Nathan Fletcher's Soda," American, 20th C. **$8.00-$12.00**

Egg separator, stamped tin, advertising "Cinderella Stoves," 20th C. **$10.00-$15.00**

Egg separator, stamped tin, advertising message "Do You Know Kemo?" on rim, early 20th or late 19th C. • Egg separators advertising dairies or egg farms, stamped of tin or aluminum, are so far an under-appreciated collectible. **$7.00-$12.00**

Egg separator, stamped tin, advertising "Excelsior Stove Works", early 20th C. • Added value because of stove. **$18.00-$25.00**

Egg separator, stamped tin, prettily-shaped thumb handle, "Jewel Stoves & Ranges," 3⅜"D, TOC. **$10.00-$15.00**

Egg separator, stamped tin, thumb handle, advertising a dairy on rim, 3¼"D, early 20th C. **$7.00-$10.00**

Egg separator, white enamelware, single thumb grip tab handle, hanging hole, early 20th C. **$12.00-$18.00**

Fish drainer, or some kind of grater (?), <u>whitesmithed</u> (hammered, filed & highly polished) wrought iron, large slightly concave bowl in elongated tulip shape, many holes punctured rough side down, relatively short twisted iron handle, American, 15⅝"L, 18th C. **$150.00-$185.00**

Fish slice, perforated tin with wooden handle, <u>called a slice but not for slicing</u>, it's for lifting cooked fish from a fish cooker and is perforated so juices drain out. The word "slice" relates to the elongated but broad shape (on which a typical fish would fit), American, 12½"L, 19th C. • **German vocabulary** — <u>Fisch-heber</u>: fish lifter. **$65.00-$95.00**

Flour bin & sieve, tall tin cylinder, paint enameled finish, ornamented with wheat sheaf design & name, tight fitting lid with knob on top, wire & wood crank ⅔ way down, pull out curved-front drawer near bottom, "Perfection", mfd by Sherman, Tangenberg & Co., Chicago, IL, 25 lb capacity (also made for 50 lbs and 100 lbs), 1890s. • "Does away with barrels, sacks, pans, scoops & seives. A few turns of the handle and you have enough for baking." Ad, March 1890. **$55.00-$80.00**

Flour bin & sifter, metal, probably for store, "Superior," 3 feet H, 20th C. **$200.00-$225.00**

Flour bin & sifter, tall tin cylinder, painted white at some date, has tin divider halfway down, into which is set a sifter, cranked from outside front. The lower compartment has hinged door that swings out to reveal handled pan that catches sifted flour, possibly Geuder, Paeschke & Frey Co., Milwaukee, WI, 14"H x 11¼" diameter, early 20th C to c.1930. • <u>Added value.</u> — If this were in its original baked-on enamel finish, with stenciled decoration and word "FLOUR", it would be worth at least twice as much. **$20.00-$30.00**

Flour or sugar sifter, tabletop, wooden box frame with pointy bootjack legs (and sides), open top, wooden rocker crossbar handle moves the 2 connected wooden roller blades across wire screen bottom, to sift flour or sugar. It comes apart for cleaning, a pan to catch the sifted sugar (or flour) was slid on table underneath, paper label reads "Blood's Patent," A. E. & J. B. Blood, Lynn, MA, 8¾"H, with approx. 10½" x 9" space underneath for pan to catch siftings, pat'd Sept. 17, 1861. They patented improvement on Jan. 9, 1866. • In the 1869 catalog of the Dover Stamping Co. (which was beautifully reprinted by the Pyne Press, Princeton, NJ, 1971, in their historical catalog series), two pages are devoted to the <u>Blood's Patent Sifter</u>, about which it was said, " ... its greatest superiority is not as a flour sifter. In preparing Squash, Apple or Pumpkin for Pies, or other Fruits for Jams or Jellies, its value is increased a hundred fold. ... [also] stewed tomatoes, currants, grapes. ... Molasses is seldom clean enough for use, — Blood's Sifter Cleanses It Thoroughly. In the West it is used to strain Sorghum as it comes from the Mill. Those who do much with CREAM TARTAR find it invaluable. Druggists find it indispensable in sifting and straining their various Medicines. So with Glaziers, in sifting Whiting. ..." The catalog copy goes on to say that imitators don't dare to use Blood's patent "vibrating rollers" so they have "substituted various contrivances in hope to answer the purpose. Among these are Cranks, India Rubber, Bristles, Leather, Stationary

Wood, &c., &c.'' They add that the objections to these things is that they impart odors, wear out, get sour & filthy, and even ''crumble and become incorporated with the bread or pies, constituting a violent poison.'' Whew! Thank heaven I can use my Blood's to make muffins.

$175.00-$225.00

Flour sifter, commercial size one for bakery or hotel, wooden with brushes & screen, mfd by J. H. Day & Co., #100, 20th C. **$100.00-$125.00**

Flour sifter, dark tin cylinder with ''scoop'' rim, fat tubular handle from which wooden knobbed crank sticks out, wire mesh sifting screen, ''Hunter's Sifter, Standard of the World,'' mfd. by The Fred J. Meyers Mfg. Co., at that time in Hamilton, OH. Toy version (See under toys), made in Covington, KY, 6½''H x 4¾''D x 11½''L (including handle and to tip of knobbed crank), pat'd Aug. 5, 1879 by Jacob M. Hunter. (Toy pat'd earlier). Sold for decades. • Classic. — This is a must have for a kitchen collection. It was advertised as combining '' ... 12 kitchen utensils in one. It is a Mixer, Scoop, Measure, Weigher, Dredger, Rice Washer, Starch, Tomato, Wine, and Fruit Strainer. It is the most useful kitchen utensil made.'' A *Ladies Home Journal* ad in Sept. 1889 reads: ''Tomato-sauce, tomato soup and tomato catsup are favorite compounds. .. In no other way can they be so easily and quickly strained as with the Hunter Sifter. Owing to its construction, it can be placed in the tureen and the soup strained while boiling hot, losing little or none of its heat in the process. Bean, pea, potato, and mixed vegetable soups are strained with equal ease and rapidity.'' (So much for truth in advertising.) • An ad in the Jan. 1879. *American Agriculturist* said that this ''Hunter's Perfection Rotary Flour & Meal Sifter'' is the ''only sifter in the world that can be taken in four parts to clean. 75,000 sold in 180 days. 200,000 now in use. Send 65¢ for small or $1.00 for large sample, or stamp for catalog.'' The ''small'' is possibly the miniature one, though it doesn't say that. If 1/5 of a million were sold in 2 years; and they were still selling 10 years later, it's a wonder we don't all have at least 10 in our collections! After all, there are only an estimated 150,000 collectors of kitchen collectibles.

$20.00-$30.00

Flour sifter, double ended, snug lid on each end, funny looking sifter, white painted tin with name stenciled in blue, almost size of oatmeal carton, out of center of cylindrical body is a tube with a wooden plug that supports a wire crank, screen ball inside, ''The Swan's Down Sifter'' in blue on body, ''R. E. P.'' embossed on both lids, mfd by Repath-Carver Co., Los Angeles, CA, 9½''H x 4½'' diameter, 20th C. **$40.00-$50.00**

Flour sifter, double ended tin, yellow wood handle, ''KWIK,'' holds 5 cups, 20th C. **$15.00-$20.00**

Flour sifter, metal, ''The Miracle Electric Flour Sifter. Do not immerse in water.'' Mfd by Miracle Mfg. Co., Chicago, IL, 20th C, patent pending. **$30.00-$40.00**

Flour sifter, scoop shaped tin, wire mesh at bottom, side handle with squeeze action, ''Sift-Chine'' (''Sift-ing Ma-chine''), mfd by Meets a Need Mfg. Co., Seattle, WA, c.1931. **$8.00-$15.00**

Flour sifter, scoop shaped tin, wire mesh, wooden side handle, knobbed side crank, ''Savory Sift-Chine,'' about 6½''H x 4¾''D , c.1910-20s. **$8.00-$15.00**

Flour sifter, tin, ''Hook Aston Milling Co., Flour & Feed, Mills & Elevators,'' Zanesville, OH, 2 cup size, early 20th C. • **German vocabulary** — Mehlsieb: flour sifter.

$20.00-$30.00

Flour sifter, tin, 2 cup, squeeze tubular tin handle & it pulls sifting grid across screen, not marked except for date, American, 2 cup size, pat'd Dec. 1, 1914. **$20.00-$25.00**

Flour sifter, tin, 3 layers of screen, ''Three screens for triple sifting'', squeeze action, but the best part of this sifter is the kitchen scene depicted on side: mother & daughter with doll, & son with baseball mitt. She's serving pie she's obviously just made with this squeeze sifter, utensils hang above, we see canisters, checkered floor, venetian blinds on the window, fruit in a bowl on top of the refrigerator, all in red, yellow, white with a little green, ''Androck Handi-Sift'', late 1940s patent #2607491.

$12.00-$15.00

Flour sifter, tin body, cast iron legs, body painted green, 3 feet painted black with gold pinstriping, paper label, 3 cranked blades, screening on bottom of body, label reads ''To use this sifter press down upon the crank; while putting articles in the sifter to be sifted always let the wheel rest upon the bottom.'' No maker's name, American, 9¾''H exclusive of crank, 19th C.

$150.00-$180.00

Flour sifter, tin bucket with 3 long cast iron legs painted black, crank in open top, 3 iron paddles go around against iron screening in bottom, ''The GEM Flour & Sauce Sifter'', Wells' Patent, Brooklyn, NY (where J. Wells lived, not necessarily where sifter was made), bucket about 6''H x 8'' diameter, legs about 5''H, pat'd Dec. 26, 1865. **$75.00-$90.00**

Flour sifter, tin canister, screw clamps to shelf edge, perforated mesh bottom, spring tension dasher, 6''H, early 20th or poss. late 19th C. **$20.00-$35.00**

Flour sifter, tin, crank in side, ''Brite Pride Visible Measure'', 20th C. **$7.00-$10.00**

Flour sifter, tin, double lid (top & bottom) so you can sift twice without removing flour, turned wooden handle painted turquoise, ''Duplex Sifter,'' mfd by Uneek Utilities Co., 6¾''H, pat'd 1922. **$15.00-$20.00**

Flour sifter, tin, has tubular handle enclosing a squeeze action mechanism like a strength test machine (which it may have become after a few minutes of using it), sifter grid in bottom is slotted, ''The Foster,'' 7''H, pat'd Dec. 1, 1914. **$20.00-$25.00**

Flour sifter, tin, lithographed advertising, wooden handle, shaking one-hand action, ''Arenzville Bank ... able to do for its customers everything that a good bank ought to do.'' mfd. by Erickson, Des Moines, IA, 2 cup capacity, early 20th C. **$15.00-$25.00**

Flour sifter, tin, mug style with side crank, green wooden knob on crank, ''H. & Hodges,'' 6½''H x 6'' diameter, with 4½''L handle, late 19th or early 20th C. **$10.00-$15.00**

Flour sifter, tin pail shaped body, brace inside & crank, 2 paddles inside, 3 cast iron legs, no mark, American, 10''H x 7½''D, 1870s or 1880s. **$50.00-$70.00**

Flour sifter, tin scoop shape, flat bottom, vertical turned wooden handle with wire up out of top of handle & going down inside to bottom of sifter to make the grid to rub the flour through mesh, shaking action — left & right in whichever hand. Ads stated ''You have heard of flour sifters that require two hands to operate! That have a round bottom which cannot be repaired! That grind through the sieve any impurities which may be in the flour! That give a handle which interferes with the use of the sifter as a scoop! But have you heard of the new ... sifter which is free from these objections? Shaking the sifter gently with one hand works the internal mechanism." Shaker Sifter, "Best In the World", mfd by Sidney Shepard & Co., Buffalo, NY & Chicago, IL, pat'd July 14, 1885. **$14.00-$20.00**

Flour sifter, tin, squeeze handle type like old strength testers, "Foley," 20th C. **$10.00-$12.00**

Flour sifter, tin & wire mesh in saucepan shape with tubular tin handle & wire crank, "Banner Sifter #15," Saranac, MI, early 20th C. **$18.00-$22.00**

Flour sifter, tin, with green side handle, lids at each end, work it by shaking it back & forth with one hand, "Bromwell's Multiple," Saranac, MI, 7"H, 20th C. **$15.00-$20.00**

Flour sifter, tin with side crank, "New Standard," 7"H, pat'd Oct. 15, 1918. **$10.00-$15.00**

Flour sifter, tin, wood crank knob, Bromwell, 3 cup size, 20th C. **$5.00-$10.00**

Flour sifter, cheap tin saucepan style, woven mesh in bottom, rather nifty spiraling wire in bottom is cranked with knob on open top, American, 9¼"D, very early 20th C. **$7.00-$12.00**

Flour sifter, heavy tin, perforated tin mesh, iron crank handle turns paddles on inside, nice crossbar wooden handle, "Eddy's Patent," 14¾"H x 8¼"D, pat'd April 20, 1880. **$50.00-$65.00**

Flour sifter, tin, bracket for attaching inside Hoosier style kitchen cabinet, maker not marked, American, TOC or early 20th C. **$45.00-$55.00**

Flour sifter, wood bin with bootjack legs at each end, screen bottom, rubber-tipped paddles, crank action, American, 10"H x 9"L, 1860s. **$100.00-$150.00**

Flour sifter, wooden with metal crank, bin shape, crank in side, "Tilden's Patent," pat'd by H. Tilden, who first lived in Philadelphia, then in Boston, pat'd Mar. 28, 1865; Tilden's other 3: May 16 & June 13, 1865; Jan 2, 1866. **$145.00-$160.00**

Flour sifter, grater & holder combined, metal & wood scoop shape, on remnant of paper label: "Improved Combination Sifter, F. Bucknam," (possibly P. Bucknan), Portland, ME, pat'd May 15, 1866. **$85.00-$100.00**

Flour sifter & scoop, fine wire mesh with rim, scoop lip & strap handle all of tin. This is an oval basket elongated into pronounced scoop shape at one end, opposite which is a strap handle, "Handy", Handy Mfg. Co., Chicago, IL, about 7"L, c.1880. **$10.00-$15.00**

Flour sifter & scoop combined, tin, shaped like a square-cornered scoop, strap handle at back, with paddles inside cranked with wire crank on right side, "Earnshaw's Patent," J. Earnshaw, Lowell, MA, 8½"L, pat'd July 25, 1865. **$75.00-$85.00**

Fruit press — See Cut & pare chapter.

Funnel, copper, with filter & brass thumb piece, American, 7"L x 4"D, late 19th C. • See Funnels in Measure & weigh chapter. **$28.00-$35.00**

Funnel, with attached strainer, which hinges & folds into bowl of funnel, the strainer being fine wire mesh in tin frame like the funnel, used with or without the strainer in place, unmarked, American, 9"L x 3⅝"D, pat'd Aug. 24, 1875. **$15.00-$20.00**

Funnel for vintner, copper, dovetail seam, brass hanging ring, fine gauze to strain out cork debris or whatever might appear in the bottle, stamped "G. E. R.", 9¾"L, 19th C. • The 3 initials are made with individual letter stamps, which I understand indicates it is probably an owner's initials, as a maker would have a stamp in one piece with his own 2 or 3 initials. **$100.00-$125.00**

Gravy strainer, tin & wire mesh, cylindrical or tubular handle with ring hanger, American, 6⅞" diameter, c.1890s. **$10.00-$15.00**

Jelly bag, unseamed strip of crash (a heavy, coarse cloth used for towels), attached by metal rings at each end to the 2 turned wooden "jump rope" handles. Put very liquid jelly in cloth, hold handles & twist to squeeze out excess liquid. possibly Shaker manufacture, American, 24"L fully extended, 19th C. **$65.00-$80.00**

Kettle strainer, pierced tin & wire, used to strain contents of preserve kettle when pouring from it, American, 16"L x 10"W, pat'd 1898. **$15.00-$18.00**

Lard skimmer, heavy tin, 10"L, 19th C. **$10.00-$12.00**

Maple sugar skimmer, galvanized pierced tin cup with wooden handle, quite beautiful, long handles were needed because these were used to skim large pots of boiling maple sugar, American, 55"L, 19th C. **$65.00-$90.00**

Meat press — See Cut & pare chapter.

Milk skimmer, stamped tin, perforations form diamond pattern, rim is crimped & turned, American, 6⅛"L x 5⅝"W, 19th C or early 20th C. **$10.00-$15.00**

Milk strainer, stamped tin, shallow perforated dish, advertising "Forbes Quality Coffee" in raised letters around rim, 3¼" diameter, 4⅜"L overall with tab, early 20th C. **$7.00-$12.00**

Milk strainer, stamped tin, small perforated shallow dish with tab handle, stamped with legend "Keep Coming to Fuller's Less Expensive Store", American, 3¼" diameter, 4⅜"L overall with tab, early 20th C. **$7.00-$12.00**

Molasses skimmer, homemade, aluminum sheeting formed & folded to scoop shape, then nailed to wood heel, nail puncture holes filed smooth, long wooden handle whittled to fit into hole of wooden heel of scoop-like skimmer. Dealer had 3, all from same place; one was made from an oil can, partly cut off & nailed to a wooden handle, the other was a large rusted tin can. From old farm home in Campbell County, VA, near Lynchburg, 29⅞"L, skimmer bowl 5" x 5", c.1920s or 1930s. • "**Molasses,** or melasses, the gross fluid matter, which remains after refining sugar; and which cannot by simple boiling be reduced to a more solid consistence than that of common syrup, vulgarly called treacle ." Anthony Florian Madinzer Willich, *The Domestic Encyclopedia; or A Dictionary of Facts & Useful Knowledge ...*, 1st American edition, Philadelphia: W. Y. Birch & A. Small, 1803-04. • **Molasses faucet.** — Another molasses-related item is a suction faucet used to draw off amounts of molasses. It is geared and made of metal, and when the crank was turned it would in effect pump the gooey mess, "winter and summer, directly into a jug or bottle, without the use of a funnel. ... Free from flies and dirt." Enterprise Mfg. Co., Philadelphia, c.1885.

• **Molasses can.** — This container of japanned tin was a half cylinder with a flat back to fit against wall, and came in 10 and 20 gallon sizes. It has a spigot close to the bottom for measuring out smaller quantities. Matthai-

Ingram made these in the late 19th C. Both articles were probably more for the use of grocers than housewives.
$15.00-$20.00

Muffineer — See Dredger.

Pea skimmers or vegetable lifters, fanciful wire twistings, some with wood handles, American, vary from about 13''L to 14¾''L, c.1870s to 1900. **$16.00-$25.00**

> I eat my peas with honey,
> I have did it all my life.
> Not because I like it,
> But it keeps 'em on my knife !
>
> — A child-tickling ditty recited by
> my grandmother, Grace Campbell Franklin,
> Memphis, TN, every time we had peas

Potato ricer, flimsy tin & painted iron, prob. 1940s.
$7.00-$10.00

Potato ricer, or food press, zinc coated or plated cast iron frame & levered handles, heavy tin perforated cup, "Genuine Kreamer Press," 4''H x 3⅜'' diameter x 11''L including handles, c.1930s. • Zinc coatings have a peculiar dark gray silvery look quite different from tin coating (which when new is very shiny and silvery), or from nickel plating or chroming. When corroded (by salts in a liquid or air) a powdery white deposit will occur on the surface. See also page 63. **$10.00-$15.00**

Potato ricer — See Cut & pare chapter.

Pureer, nickeled iron, no maker's name, marked only "MIL. WISC." and "Pat. Appl." **$15.00-$20.00**

Salad washer, or lettuce basket, wire globe in 2 halves, hinged & with 2 twisted wire grips to hold while swinging around head (is this apocryphal?) or shaking over sink, American, 9½'' diameter (but they came smaller and larger), early 20th C. **$18.00-$25.00**

Sieve, 2 part tin, like a ricer, perforated concave cup, the presser is convex, has tubular tin handle with a hanging loop, odd & attractive, American (?), about 7''D, 19th C.
$35.00-$45.00

Sieve, tin with brass screen, prob. American, tapers from 9½'' diameter down to 2½'', TOC. • **German vocabulary** — Sieb: sieve. **$10.00-$15.00**

Sieve, woven horse hair, all white, in bentwood frame, possibly Shaker, 9'' diameter x 4'' deep, 19th C.
$125.00-$150.00

Sieve, woven horse hair & bentwood, fastened with copper nails, pale ivory hair, probably Shaker manufacture, 6'' diameter, 19th C. **$125.00-$150.00**

Sieve, woven horse hair in black & white plaid, heavily (recently?) varnished wooden frame, unfortunately the varnish even dripped on the horsehair, Shaker-style, 7'' diameter, 19th C, though varnish more recent.
$140.00-$190.00

Sieve, woven horse hair mesh in 2 fingered bentwood frame, Shaker-style, 4½'' diameter, 19th C.
$125.00-$175.00

Sieve, woven horse hair sifter, plaid black & ivory horse hairs, in bentwood frame with original old dark green paint, Shaker-style, 6'' diameter, 19th C. • Most valuable are those with the plaid effect achieved by weaving dark & light or white horse hairs. Checkered patterns valued

about the same. • From the collection of Greg & Linette Salisbury, sold at a James D. Julia auction, Aug. 23, 1989, for $500.00. To me, the catalog description of condition is odd in that it stated that it "*appears* to be excellent throughout, even horsehair webbing is all intact and original." I have seen them with broken or missing strands (they do look as sad as old guitars or violin bows with broken sproingy strings). As has been proven over and over in 1988 and 1989, original old paint on a supposedly Shaker piece adds a so-far incalculable amount to value. **$400.00-$600.00**

Sieve or riddle, iron wire screening in bentwood frame, fairly crude in construction, possibly used like winnower for separating out chaff, or for mincing cooked root vegetables or potatoes, 12''D, late 19th C. • "Purees are fashionable nowadays. A coarse and a fine sieve are needed for puree. The frame may be of wood or strong tin; the strainer of strong wires — coarse neeting — being strenthened by two cross-pieces of coarse wire. Substance placed in sieve and rubbed through with wooden vegetable masher." Maria Parloa, *Kitchen Companion*, Boston: Estes & Lauriat, 1887. The sieve depicted in her book is quite large, perhaps 24'' in diameter, and is set up on wooden frame with short legs, apparently with center cut out so the "catching" pan could be slid underneath.
$18.00-$20.00

Sieves, perforated tin, shallow with slightly sloped sides, look like gold miners' pans, various perforations from coarse to fine, American, various diameters, from about 8'' to about 12'', late 19th C. • Recently I've seen in an 1849 business directory a sieve company advertising gold miner's pans. I guess you might find one; look for heavy tin, and details in the edging and construction that relate to mid 19th century construction of other tinwares.
$12.00-$20.00

Sink strainer, green enamelware with attached brass plate, "Sanitary Under-the-Sink Strainer," by Kitchen Katch-All Corp., Greenwich, OH, 1930s. **$40.00-$55.00**

Skimmer, brass bowl, copper rivets to iron handle, American, 11''L handle, 4''D bowl, 19th C. • I have searched for a place to put this next piece of historically interesting information, and might as well put it here. The "Magic Mop", mfd by Pro Diet Mop, Inc., of Belle Chasse, LA, which is of a special plastic that "attracts grease from food like a magnet." It was developed to use in ocean oil spills. It was made into mops used to stir soup and other food from which grease has to be skimmed or removed. Patent No. 3,748,682. **$50.00-$65.00**

Skimmer, brass bowl with iron handle, very nice looking as are most bi-metal skimmers & other implements, American or English, 28''L, 19th C. **$90.00-$125.00**

Skimmer, brass & forged iron, handle has heart cutout, copper rivets, American, 17¼''L, early 19th C (?).
$500.00-$600.00

Skimmer, brass & iron with only one copper rivet holding handle on, no mark, English (?), 24½''L, early 19th C.
$65.00-$80.00

Skimmer, brass with wrought iron handle, 12½''L, early or mid 19th C. • Actually, brass and iron skimmers & other utensils were made well into the 1880s, probably the 1890s, so you have to judge workmanship, details, wear, style, thickness of brass, etc. **$165.00-$200.00**

Skimmer, cast aluminum, flat bowl with many small perforations in concentric rings, long tapered handle with center rib, hanging hole, marked "WSuCL", computer can't find this in American companies, poss. German, 14"L x 4⅜" diameter bowl, c.1920s. **$15.00-$22.00**

Skimmer, finely worked forged iron, somewhat deep beautiful bowl with pierced pattern of holes, shaped handle with hook, signed "W. Werntz", Lancaster County, PA, bowl is 5⅜" diameter, with 13½"L handle, 2nd to 3rd quarter 19th C. • Robacker May 1989 price: **$475.00**

Skimmer, large, very shallow brass bowl with simple large pierced design of tripartite tulip, tapered & polished forged iron handle with hook at end, the hook on same plane as handle, rather than turned under on back of handle, Pennsylvania, bowl 6⅜" diameter, with 13⅞"L handle, early 19th C. • Robacker May 1989 price: **$700.00**

Skimmer, oak handle, imperfectly cut galvanized sheet metal disc, American, 22"L, mid to late 19th C. **$130.00-$145.00**

Skimmer, perforated enameled tin, "Cream City Ware," Geuder, Paeschke, or Geuder, Paeschke & Frey, Milwaukee, WI, c.1890s to 1930. **$20.00-$35.00**

Skimmer, pieced tin, long tapered tubular tin handle, American, 15"L, 19th C. • This kind of utensil, with the tapered tubular handle, is usually advertised as "Shaker," although that may or may not turn out to be accurate. Many Shaker pieces with this kind of handle also had a fitted brace (called a boss) at the junction of handle and whatever kind of utensil it was, from dustpan to scoop. • The term pieced is not a typo for pierced. By "pieced" I mean composed of pieces, in this case pieces of tin. **$55.00-$75.00**

Skimmer, pierced brass, marked on iron handle, "W. R. Boston," which is probably maker's initials plus place name, Boston, MA, 22"L, 19th C. **$150.00-$225.00**

Skimmer, pierced & engraved brass pan, iron handle, 22"L, 19th C. **$160.00-$200.00**

Skimmer, pierced iron with brass trim, long narrow coffin shaped handle, spoon is quite pear shaped, handle attached to fat pear bottom end, American, 12"L, early 19th C. **$95.00-$125.00**

Skimmer, shallow perforated brass bowl, riveted to forged iron handle which widens at end & finishes off with rat-tail hanging loop, American, 16½"L with 5½" diameter bowl, 19th C. **$135.00-$160.00**

Skimmer, tin bowl with iron handle, 18"L, late 19th C. **$30.00-$40.00**

Skimmer, tin bowl with long turned wood handle, 21"L, late 19th C. **$55.00-$60.00**

Skimmer, for milk or cream, perforated & stamped tin, with perforations in a diamond pattern, hanging hole in thumb handle, Geuder, Paeschke & Frey Co., Milwaukee, WI, 6" x 6", 19th C. • A much older implement for the same purpose, was a fleeting dish or flit, a shallow dish with a ring handle. **$6.00-$8.00**

Skimmer, wrought iron, big bowl, with relatively short handle looped at end for hanging, 9½"L, late 18th or early 19th C. **$65.00-$80.00**

Skimmer, yellow spatter enamelware with brown handle, American (?), prob. 20th C as color doesn't belong to late 19th C. **$25.00-$40.00**

Skimmer & dipper, matched pair, brass bowls, brass shafts, delicate tapered turned wooden handles, American, 15⅛"L, early 19th C. **$250.00-$300.00**

Skimmer & dipper, matched pair, wrought iron, marked "W. Werntz," Lancaster County, PA, 19"L, 19th C. **$250.00-$350.00**

Skimmer or butter paddle, hand-carved, figured chestnut wood, graining perfectly placed for great visual appeal, deep bowl, American, 5" across, mid 19th C. **$200.00-$225.00**

Skimmers, blue enamelware or gray graniteware, in good condition, about 18" to 20"L, TOC. **$30.00-$60.00**

Skimmers, for sorghum, perforated tin with long wooden handle, American, about 45" to 49"L, 19th or early 20th C. • These are often homemade, and those I like best. Look for nice details or idiosyncracies in the tin scoop part, or carving on the wood, or nifty ways of attaching the skimmer to the handle, or for skimmers made from old cans such as coffee cans or oil cans. • See also Molasses skimmer. **$25.00-$65.00**

Skimmers & dippers, 5 pieces, all signed, brass bowls with narrow wrought iron handles tapered at hook or hanging hole ends, some pitted or split, "J. Schmidt" or "John S. Schmidt," Pennsylvania, 19" to 20"L, all are dated: 1844, 1849, 1853, 1854 & 1854. •At Garth's Auction of several collectors' consignments, April 1986, this achieved: **$1050.00**

Soup strainer, cobalt enamelware, elongated bowl, TOC. **$35.00-$60.00**

Spout strainer, tin & wire, for teapot or coffee pot. Perfectly made deep bowl fine mesh strainer hanging from a sort of springy long hairpin that sticks into end of spout. See also chapter on Coffee & Tea. 2" diameter, c.1890s. **$12.00-$15.00**

Strainer, also called a pea ladle, wire with crude wooden handle, bowl made up of concentric spiralling rings of wire, not criss-crossed, American, 13"L x 4⅜"W, early 20th C • This type of strainer or skimmer with the long handle was used for serving vegetables out of pot likker. They were made from about the 1870s well into the 20th C. Some had interwoven wires done in various basketweaves, many had beautiful turned wooden handles, others had simple wire handles which were an integral part of the strainer's outer rim. Really nice ones might bring $10.00 more than price of this crude one. **$12.00-$18.00**

Strainer, blue graniteware with white enameling inside, 2 handles, American, late 19th C. **$40.00-$60.00**

Strainer, brown marbleized enamelware, 8" diameter, late 19th C. **$45.00-$65.00**

Strainer, dark blue & white speckled graniteware, with hook on rim for hanging, American, 7¾" diameter, late 19th C. **$65.00-$90.00**

Strainer, extremely unusual, large perforated shallow bowl with long, bird beak pointed spout off side & 40 degrees further around circumference, turned wooden handle, American (?), 13¼"L, 19th C. **$175.00-$225.00**

Strainer, for milk, tin with brass mesh, meant to fit into milk can top before pouring in contents of milking pail, American, 10¾" diameter, late 19th or early 20th C. **$15.00-$20.00**

Strainer, gray graniteware, tab feet, 7½" diameter, 19th C. **$45.00-$60.00**

Strainer, pierced tin, conical bowl, tubular tin handle with ring hanging loop, could be used with pointed wooden pestle to push through cooked tomatoes (for example), leaving seeds & skin inside strainer, American, 17"L x 8½" diameter, late 19th C. **$25.00-$38.00**

Strainer, pierced tin, handmade, 11" diameter, 19th or early 20th C. • Country, handyman pieces such as this are extremely difficult to date. Only when something like a dateable coffee can, with the lithographed label left on, has been used for the sheet metal, can a confident dating be given. **$20.00-$30.00**

Strainer, probably used in dairy, white glazed Delftware, figural bird of type seen in PA German folk decoration, Holland, 6"L, early 19th C. • These are rarely found. Other forms include fish & hearts. **$1200.00-$1600.00**

Strainer, tin with wooden handle, "Wheat -?- for Breakfast," American, 13"L w/ handle, 20th C. **$20.00-$28.00**

Strainer, tin with wooden handle, "Ajax," at least two sizes, 5"L and 8"L, early 20th C (?). **$6.00-$10.00**

Strainer, turquoise green & white swirl enamelware, poss. "Chrysolite", late 19th or early 20th C.• **German vocabulary** — Seiher, Seihe, seib or Filtriertrichter: strainer. **$65.00-$80.00**

Strainer, white enamelware with wire mesh bottom, 10" diameter, TOC. **$20.00-$30.00**

Strainer or skimmer, called a pea skimmer at the time, spiralled wire with wooden handle, sold by, but not necessarily made by Dover Stamping Co., c.1870s. **$25.00-$30.00**

Sugar shaker, copper container with pierced brass screw-on lid, interesting slanted sides almost look Arts & Crafts Movement, American (?), 9"H, 19th C. • See also Dredgers. **$40.00-$50.00**

Sugar shaker, decorated ceramic, "Cleminson's Girl", The California Cleminsons, CA, mid 20th C. **$20.00-$25.00**

Sugar shaker, or muffineer, tin cup with slightly domed perforated lid, strap handle on side, marked "Fries" on bottom, 4"H x 2½" diameter, late 19th C or early 20th. **$18.00-$22.00**

Sugar sifter —See Flour sifter.

Vegetable strainer, called a cabbage strainer by manufacturer, a sort of combination colander & press: a handled pan with perforated bottom, & pressure plate with handle which is pressed against watery vegetables to press out pot likker, then pivoted to other side while dumping food into serving dish, heavily tinned, "New Process", Silver & Co., Brooklyn, NY, c.1890. **$18.00-$25.00**

Whatzit sifter, some sort of sifter, poss. an ash sifter, cast metal with odd finish, almost as if it were a baked-on brownish gray paint, 3 short peg feet with cork tips, looks like an old style something or other made of modern materials, a sort of dustpan pan with 3 walls, scoop-like handle, 15"L, 20th C. **$15.00-$20.00**

**III-1.
Colanders —**
foot loose and foot fast (soldered on). Four sizes, from 9 7/8" to 13" diameter. Matthai-Ingram, c.1890. **$15.00-$35.00**

**III-2.
Colanders.**
All tin, with old-fashioned styling, and possibly the cuts were already 40 years old when used in Harrod's Stores, Ltd., catalog of 1895. Top (L) is deep bowl type 9", 10" and 12"; (R) is stamped, with riveted handles. Lower (L) is pieced, with riveted strap handles, 8" to 10 1/4". c.1895. **$15.00-$35.00**

**III-3.
Round bottom colanders or cullenders.**
All foot fast, as most are. (L) to (R) from top. (1) "Greystone" graniteware, from 9 7/8" to 13" diameter. Matthai-Ingram. (2) 3 1/2" to 4 1/2" deep x 9 3/8" to 12"W. D.J. Barry, 1924. (3) White "Sterling" enameled, 4 7/8"H x 9 1/2" to 6"H x 12" diameter, Central Stamping Co., 1920. (One below it is tin.) (4) Stamped tin, of large size for hotels mostly — 4 3/4"H x 13" diameter up to 7 5/8"H x 19" diameter. Lalance & Grosjean, 1890, and same cut used in catalogs of 30 years later. (5) Hotel colander in 3 big sizes. "Puritan", Central Stamping, 1920. (7) Tin, in 4 sizes from 3"H x 9 1/2" to 4 1/2"H x 13 1/4". Lalance & Grosjean, 1890. **$15.00-$35.00**

**III-4.
Colander.**
Perforated tin, ring foot is soldered on — foot fast, 3 3/4"H x 9 3/4" dimater. Late 19th to early 20th C. Collection Mary Mac Franklin. **$15.00-$30.00**

**III-5.
Slant-sided, flat bottom colanders.**
(1) "Greystone" graniteware, 9 3/4" and 10 7/8", Matthai-Ingram, c.1890. (2) Called the "Eastern Pattern," wrought iron (though not handmade) handles, 10" to 12". Offered by many companies, this one from Geuder, Paeschke & Frey, 1925. (3) Heavy pieced tin, soldered strap handles, 11 1/2" and 13 1/2", Shapleigh Hardware, 1914. (4) Flat-bottom & footless, strap handle, in 14", 16", 18" and 20", and four hole size choices: 1/8", 1/4", 3/16" and 5/16". Jaburg, 1908. (5) Tinned steel, from 5 3/4"H x 13 3/4" to 7 5/8" x 19 1/2". Pick-Barth, 1929. (6) Planished tin, 9 1/2" to 15" diameter, Albert Pick, 1909. (7) 9 3/4" and 11", Matthai-Ingram, c.1890. (8) Widely flared, another "Eastern" style, 12", GP & F, 1925. **$15.00-$35.00**

III-6.
Colander.
Flared sides, brightly tinned, foot fast. 4 1/2"H x 12" diameter. Late 19th to early 20th C. Collection Mary Mac Franklin. **$15.00-$28.00**

III-7.
Colanders.
Both made of copper; the left one sold in sizes from 10" to 18", Duparquet, Huot & Moneuse, c.1902-1910. One with small ball feet is tinned in and out, in 5 sizes from 10" to 14". Henry Rogers, Wolverhampton, England, 1914. **$20.00-$45.00**

III-8.
Colander.
Copper, with large handles making it usable with many size bowls or other vessels, on whose rim the handles would rest. 9" diameter, bottom is flat and joined to sides with dovetail seam. Ex-Wiggins Tavern Collection of Northampton, MA. Photograph courtesy of Luella McCloud Antiques, Shelburn Falls, MA.

III-9.
Confusable —
not a colander but a dip basket. Pressed fiber dip basket for brass foundries, nickel-plating works, etc., mfd. by United Indurated Fiber Co., whose agents were Cordley & Hayes. The Metal Worker, 11/8/1890.

III-10.
Colander-strainers
of saucepan style. (T) "Mirro" aluminum, with steel hollow handle, 6 1/4" to 8 1/2" diameter. Aluminum Goods Mfg. Co., Manitowoc, WI, 1927. (B) Pieced tin, large holes in bottom only. Tubular handle, c.1870s-1900. Courtesy Lar Hothem. **$5.00-$35.00**

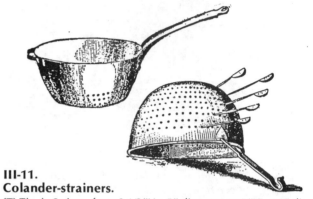

III-11.
Colander-strainers.
(T) Tin, in 9 sizes, from 2 1/2"H x 5" diameter to 5"H x 11" diameter. Saucepan style, with strap support for resting within a pan. Matthai-Ingram, c.1890. Identical pictures appeared in Lalance & Grosjean 1890 catalog, and Duparquet catalog, c.1904-1910. (B) Stamped metal (quite possibly tinned copper) colander depicted in Urbain Dubois' La Patisserie D'Aujourd'hui, Paris, c.1860s-80s. The colander is being used as a support for glazed orange segment stuck on skewers to air dry. **$10.00-$35.00**

III-12.
Drink strainers.
(T) Shaker strainer, nickel silver. Cherry-Bassett, 1921. (R) A Julep strainer, with shell-shaped perforated bowl, with star cutout in handle. Duparquet, Huot & Moneuse, c.1904-1910. Lower (L) Coiled spring wire strainer, "fits all sizes of mixing glasses. Made of 18% nickel silver heavily silver plated." D.J. Barry, 1924. **$3.00-$15.00**

III-13.
Dredgers or shakers.
(1) Sugar dredger, polished brass or nickel-plated brass. Jaburg Brothers, 1908. (2) Unidentified, probably English handled dredger, c.1870s. (3) Lightweight "Mirro" aluminum salt or flour shaker in paneled "Colonial" pattern. 2 5/8"H x 2 3/8" diameter. 1927. (4) "Dredge box," with or without handle. Tin, or nickeled tin, or nickeled stamped brass. Jaburg, 1908. (5) Flat-top (others had convex top) salt and flour shaker, "Mirro, 4"H x 3", 1927. (6) Stamped and polished tin, high domed top, two sizes. In very old style, at least back to 1850s, this picture from Jaburg catalog of supplies for candy-makers. **$3.00-$45.00**

III-14.
Egg separators.
Top (R) "Degerdon's Improved Egg Separator & Savor. No loss of albumen. No waste in yolk or white." Jaburg, 1908. Lower (R) "Perfect" separator. Albert Pick, 1909. Lower (L) "The 1892" spun aluminum, 4 1/2" x 3 1/2", with four slots around center part. (Other companies made them with two slots ringing the center.) American Aluminum Mfg. Co., Lemont, IL, 1911. **$3.00-$25.00**

III-15.
Flour sifter.
"Tilden's Universal." Wood on little legs, woven iron screen sifter, leather sifter blades. 11 3/4"H x 9 1/2"L x 7 3/4"W. Pat'd 3/28/1865. Collection of Meryle Evans. **$135.00-$175.00**

III-16.
Flour sifter.
"Eddy's Patent." Heavy tin, perforated tin mesh, iron crank handle turns paddles on inside against the mesh. 14 3/4"H x 8 1/4" diameter. Pat'd 4/20/1880. Collection of Meryle Evans. **$50.00-$100.00**

III-17.
Sugar or flour sifter.
"Blood's" patent, patented as a flour sifter by A.E. and J.B. Blood, Lynn, MA. Two patents, I don't know which one this is — 9/17/1861 or 1/9/1866. Wood with bootjack ends, 2 wooden roller blades and wire screen bottom. Comes apart so you can clean. Body stands 8 3/4"H, with space for tray pan beneath about 9" x 10 1/2". Rocker action, pivoting at center. Collection of Meryle Evans. **$135.00-$200.00**

III-18.
Flour scoop & sifter.
Cranked, handheld "Earnshaw's Patent." Tinned sheet iron, iron crank, woven wire mesh, strap handle. 8 1/2"H. Pat'd 7/25/1865 by J. Earnshaw, Lowell, MA. This picture from F.A. Walker catalog, 1870s. See how closely the catalog cut resembles the real thing seen in III-20, **$50.00-$100.00**

III-19.
Flour sifter.
Tin and cast iron, woven wire mesh in bottom, 2 paddles on inside. 10"H x 7 1/2" diameter. Late 19th C. Collection of Meryle Evans. **$60.00-$100.00**

III-20.
Flour scoop & sifter.
"Earnshaw's". Picture courtesy of the National Museum of American History, Smithsonian Institution.

III-21.
Flour sifter bin.
Japanned and decorated tin, in assorted background colors. "Cream City" line of wares by Geuder, Paeschke & Frey, Milwaukee, 1925. **$20.00-$50.00**

III-22.
Flour sifters
of the basket type. (T) The "Handy" scoop, sifter and measure. "The Ladies are Delighted with its Convenience." Handy Mfg. Co., Chicago, 1882 ad. Lower (L) "Mystic Sifter," with crossbars and agitator. "Press the Sifter lightly into the flour, at the same time twist it and it will fill." 6 1/2" diameter. Wire Goods Co., Worcester, MA, 1915. (R) Called the "Magic" in turn of century catalog. Obviously same maker. No agitator. **$7.00-$20.00**

III-23.
Barrel or trough flour sifters.
Also for sugar or starch sifting. (L) Oblong, wood, to fit any size trough. Fitted with brushes attached to revolving cylinder. Slanted box hinged and lifts off sieving screen. Duparquet catalog, c.1904-1910. (R) "Middleby's Imperial No. 1," to fit "top of a flour barrel," or to fit "top of a sugar barrel". Brass screen. Joseph Middleby, Boston, 1927. Identical one, of "poplar wood" or "ash wood with heavy sieve," was advertised by T. Mills & Brother, another supplier to confectioners. **$10.00-$30.00**

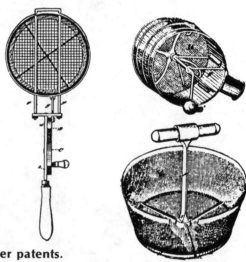

III-24.
Flour sifter patents.
(L) Flour & meal sifter, pat'd by C.O. Peck, Pittsfield, MA, 2/13/1877. "A combined scoop and sifter, with crank, reciprocating bowl and sieve, suspended from rods" (the parallel ones going across top). Upper (R) Pat'd by Willoughby F. Kistler, Cleveland, OH, 12/9/1884. Lower (R) Pat'd by C.F. Wickwire, Cortland, NY, 1/30/1877. This one was almost undoubtedly made because Wickwire was the name of a wiregoods company.

III-25.
Flour sifter & fruit strainer.
"The Standard," mfd. by Washington Stamping Co., Washington, OH. Detachable bottom and agitator. Pat'd 3/12/1878. 1882 ad in The Metal Worker. **$20.00-$45.00**

III-26.
Flour sifters.
All showing innards. (1) "Victor", with tin strap handle, showing crank and the tripart agitator. Joseph Breck catalog, 1905. (2) and (3) are same sifters, 6 1/4"H x 5" diameter, one with wood, one with strap handle. (4) Copycat of Hunter sifter (see III-29). (5) "Shaker Sifter Best In The World," mfd. by Sidney Shepard & Co., Buffalo. Ripply wires on bottom move back and forth over sieve wire when you shook the sifter from side to side. 1892 ad. (6) Another shaker sifter — also called a one-hand sifter. (2)-(4) and (6) all from Savory, Inc., Newark, NJ, c.1925-28 catalog. **$10.00-$35.00**

III-29.
Flour sifters.
(L) Savory sifter, cranked, 1910s-20s. (R) Famous "Hunter's Sifter," pat'd by Jacob Hunter, Cincinnati, OH, 8/5/1879. Mfd. by The Fred J. Meyers Mfg. Co. after a while, but first by J.M. Hunter, Cincinnati. Inventor described it as a "Perfection Rotary Flour & Meal Sifter, Mixer, Measure, Scoop, Weigher, Rice Washer, Egg Beater, Tomato, Wine, Starch, and Fruit Strainer." 11-in-one. Inventor claimed shortly after patenting that in six months 200,000 were in use. Obviously made before patent came through. **$10.00-$15.00 and $20.00-$40.00**

III-27.
Flour sifters.
Three with tubular handles. Top (L) "Reliance", with back handle, side crank. 5 1/2" x 6 1/2" x 5". Excelsior Stove & Mfg. Co., Quincy, IL, c.1916. (R) Very similar one, from Geuder, Paeschke & Frey catalog, 1925. Lower: "Nesco", with crank in handle like the Hunter. **$10.00-$20.00**

III-30.
Flour sifters.
Both double-ended, for doing double sifting for lighter cakes. (Triple and even more multiple sifters were available in professional styles of sifters). (L) "Duplex," light turquoise wood handle, 6 3/4"H, holds 5 cups. Author's collection. (R) "Bromwell's Multiple," patent pending. Medium green wood handle. This one works by shaking back and forth in one hand. 7"H. Collection of Meryle Evans. **$15.00-$35.00**

III-28.
Flour sifters.
(L) "Triple" sifter, 4 cup capacity. (R) "Twin-Sift", with double screen to "sift flour two times in one operation." 2 cup capacity. Both are tin, decorated with black bands & handle, yellow & black label. "Androck," mfd. by Washburn, 1936. **$6.00-$15.00**

III-31.
Flour sifters.
(L) Cheap tin saucepan style, woven mesh, spiraled wire agitator with crank. 9 1/4"L overall, turn-of-century. Author's. (R) Tin with mesh bottom, spring tension to crank so that it presses flour through the mesh, screw clamps to shelf. 6"H, early 20th C. Collection of Meryle Evans.   **$5.00-$15.00 ; $15.00-$35.00**

III-32.
Flour sifter & scoop.
"Universal" Scoop with sifter attachment, advertising "Pillsbury's Flour." Sheet iron, wire mesh, wood, in perfect condition. Photograph courtesy of Phyllis & Jim Moffet.

III-33.
Gravy & soup strainers.
Enormous variety of handled strainers, some with perforated bottoms, some with wire mesh of different grades. (1) Gravy (L) and Soup strainers, from American Home Cook Book, 1854. (2) Gravy, from Warne's Model Cookery & Housekeeping Book, 1868. (3) Copper, for gravy, flat bottom, 7 sizes from 5 1/2" to 8" diameter. Henry Rogers, England, 1914. (4) For soup, tin, 3 1/2"H x 8", tubular handle, Geuder, Paeschke & Frey, 1925. (5), (6) & (7) are "Sterling" enamelware, for gravy, "Handy," and "Soup or culinary," 4 1/4", 4" and 7 3/8" diameter, Central Stamping, 1920. (8), (10) and (12) are similar gravy strainers, about 4 1/2", with wood handles, from Matthai-Ingram, Central Stamping and Buhl, c.1890-1912. (9) "Large soup strainer," tin, perforated bottom, wire handle is 4 1/2"L. Butler Brothers, 1899. (11) Soup or culinary, 7 3/8", graniteware by Central Stamping. (13) Copper gravy strainer, conical, 5 1/2" to 8" diameter. Henry Rogers, 1914. (14) Deep-footed gravy, 4 1/8" or 5 1/4", looks like strainer part has own handle and lifts out. Matthai-Ingram, c.1890. (15) Tubular bent handle, tinned wire, 4 3/4" to 8" diameter, note hook. Sexton Stove & Mfg., c.1930s. (16) Soup, pieced tin, 6" and 10", Matthai-Ingram. (17) Gravy, tin handle, 4 1/4". Buhl. (18) Another deep-footed one, with perforated tin bottom — fine, medium or coarse, in 4 sizes from 4 1/4" to 7". D.J. Barry, 1924. (19) Soup, tin, braced tubular handle, 5" to 10", 12" & 14" diameter, Duparquet, c.1904-1910. Enamelware ones in perfect condition might bring a lot more than high figure here.   **$10.00-$50.00**

Wringing Sauces through the Tammy.

Rubbing Sauces through the Tammy.

III-34.
Tammy cloths.
Both pictures from Mrs. A.B. Marshall's Cookery Book, *London, c.1900 edition. Captions are from the book. So named "tammy" for a type of woollen or cotton and woollen cloth.*

III-35.
Tammy cloth or jelly bag,
with wooden handles. Unseamed strip of heavy coarse crash cloth, possibly woollen & cotton, linen, or linen & cottom. Two metal rings hold it to 2 wooden "jump rope" like handles. Put very liquid jelly, sauce or other food in cloth, hold handles and twist to squeeze out excess liquid (if making jelly), or the usable liquid (for sauces needing straining). Fully extended it's 14"L. Beautiful stained color. Late 19th C. Collection of Meryle Evans.
$65.00-$90.00

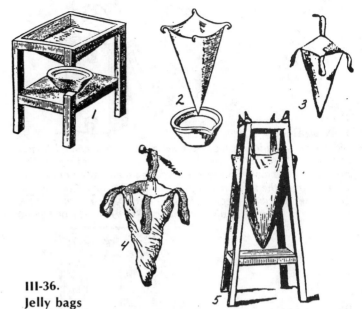

III-36.
Jelly bags
plus one filtration bag. (1) and (2) are drawings from Frenchman Antoine Lavoisier's book on chemistry, late 18th C. He describes the conical bag as made of "very close and finely woven woollen." The 'point' of the conical bag was to concentrate the draining liquid so that it could easily be caught as it dripped. (3) "Felt" jelly bag, "seamless and strains jelly handsomely." Note ties to attach it to stand such as in (5). Picture in American Home Cook Book, 1854. (4) Very similar, from Warne's Model Cookery, London, 1868. (5) Jelly bag & stand, from catalog of William S. Adams & Son, London, c.1860-61.

III-37.
Jelly bag & stand.
More elegant, with wooden stand having turned knobs at top for easier fitting of the loops of the cloth bag. Called for in making calves foot jelly and other dishes. Urbain Dubois, La Patisserie D'Aujourd'hui, Paris, c.1860s-70s.

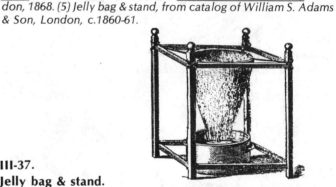

III-38.
Jelly bag strainers.
Modern types. Wire with cloth. (L) Two sizes, 6" and 8" diameter, with 3 or 4 legs, removable rim holds cloth. "Androck" by Washburn, 1936. (R) Two sizes — 12"H or 7"H, both 5 1/4" diameter. Wire Goods Co., 1915.
$8.00-$15.00

III-39.
Jelly strainer.

Pieced tin, with inner conical strainer frame for bag, and lid. Spigot at bottom. It "is made double and filled in with hot water, this heat keeps the mass limpid and a much greater amount of jelly is made from the same materials." <u>American Home Cook Book</u>, 1854. The identical linecut was used in the Duparquet, Huot & Moneuse hotelier's supply catalog, c.1904-1910. **$50.00-$85.00**

III-44.
Milk strainer buckets or pails.

(T) "The Gem Combination," mfd. by Gem Bucket Co., St. Louis, MO. Steel, with "fine brass cloth strainer which fits into a swag just below the wire in the spout, and is also held in place by the wire clasp at the back of the strainer." It has a "dairy pail bottom," which I take to mean a recessed bottom that protects the bottom from being punctured or dented. 1892 ad. Similar to many such strainer-pourer buckets. (B) "The Perfect", which "preserves milk from specks and lumps of dirt and dung, and from the atmosphere of the stable, which give the so-called animal odors. It's a seat for the milker; holds 14 quarts; cannot be stepped in nor kicked over by the cow". Dairy Supply Co., NYC. <u>American Agriculturist</u>, 7/1879. **$10.00-$30.00**

III-40.
Lard strainer.

Two part, tin, with cup with spout and perforated tin strainer. Catches the cracklins. V. Clad & Sons, Philadelphia, c.1890-1900. **$10.00-$25.00**

III-41.
Cream skimmer.

Perforated tin, turned wood handle. Nine sizes, from 6 1/2" to 10 1/2" diameter in 1/2" increments. Henry Rogers, Wolverhampton, England, 1914. **$15.00-$45.00**

III-45.
Molasses skimmer.

Homemade, 29 7/8" overall, with 5" x 5" aluminum bowl made from oil can. Campbell County, VA, near Lynchburg, c.1920s-30s. **$15.00-$22.00**

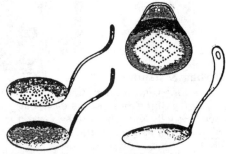

III-42.
Milk skimmers.

Top (R) with thumb handle is pierced with diapered or diamond pattern. Although surely other patterns exist, I found only this one in old catalogs of several makers. 5 3/8" x 5". Both of the other two companies here made this skimmer pattern. The two skimmers (L) with perforated and plain bowls, both with curvy iron handles are 4 1/2" diameter. Geuder, Paeschke & Frey, 1925. Lower (R) plain skimmer is described as having a "deep bowl," but that's relative. 4 5/8" diameter. Matthai-Ingram. **$7.00-$15.00**

III-46.
Syrup skimmer.

"For sugar planters." Perforated stamped tin, tubular socket handle meant to be fitted with long wood handle. 11 1/2" diameter. Matthai-Ingram, c.1890. **$15.00-$22.00**

III-43.
Milk strainer.

Tin bowl, foot fast, with brass wirecloth bottom. 8 1/4", 9" or 10" diameter, also plain one with iron wire, 10 5/8". Central Stamping Co., 1920. **$7.00-$15.00**

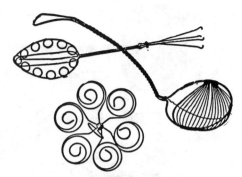

III-47.
Wirewares.

Lower (L) is a folding 6-egg rack, for boiling & serving. Top (L) is a combination whisk or vegetable skimmer and 'grapple' for dishcloth to clean lamp chimneys or bottles. Curved across is a vegetable skimmer or server, also called a pea skimmer. Several sizes, from 4" to 5 1/2" diameter bowl. All late 19th or early 20th C. **$15.00-$25.00**

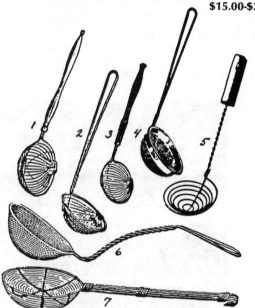

III-48.
Vegetable skimmers.

(1) Wire, enameled wood handle, 4 1/2" bowl. Matthai-Ingram, c.1890. (2) This one 9 1/4"L, "Sherwood," Wire Goods Co., 1915. Other companies made nearly identical ones. (3) Red handle or maroon handle, 9 1/4"L, also Sherwood. (4) Wire handle 10"L, wire mesh bowl. Sherwood. (5) Stubby wood handle & spiraled wire, 13 3/4"L, c.1920s-30s. (6) Wire handle, two sizes — 12" or 18"L, wire mesh bowl. Sherwood. (7) With bound-wire handle. Called by some dealers a "scroll wire skimmer" for oysters, croquettes & potatoes, in five sizes, from 5" diameter x 16"L to a 14" diameter "pretzel lifter." S. Joseph, c.1927, also Sexton, c.1930s. **$15.00-$25.00**

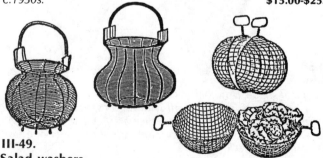

III-49.
Salad washers.

Clockwise from (L). Called a "salad shaker" for lettuce, 8", 9", 10", 11" and 12" diameter. Duparquet, Huot & Moneuse, c.1904-1910. (T) is "French Salad Washing Basket," in 7 sizes from 6" to 12". S. Joseph, c.1927. Next 2 are popular, longlived ball, 7", 8", 9" to 10" sizes. First made by Wire Goods Co., c.1915 Advertised in a 1924 catalog, and in a 1930 magazine subscription premium ad. The ball kind is worth the least. **$20.00-$100.00**

III-50.
Sieve-makers.

Unidentified early 19th C. illustrations for a book of trades. Man on left is making the bentwood hoops; man at right is sewing and weaving the hair (or whatever material he is using).

III-51.
Sieves.

(1) Flour sieve, tinned wire bottom, 11" or 12" diameter. D.J. Barry, 1924. (2) Sugar sieve, brass or iron mesh, 14" diameter. (3) Footed "hotel purrie sieve," brass mesh bottom, tin frame, 16" or 20" diameter. D.J. Barry, 1924. (4) Stack of flour and fruit sieves, with cross wires to support the iron or brass mesh, 18" and 20" diameter. (5) Stamped tin, perforated bottom, 2 3/4"H x 12 5/8" diameter. Excelsior c.1916. (6) Copper sieve "for Puree") with tin frame, 12" to 16" diameter. Duparquet, Huot & Moneuse, c.1904-1910, hoteliers' supply catalog. (7) Wood rim flour sieve, wire mesh, 11" or 12" diameter. Butler Brothers, 1899. (8) Wood frame, iron mesh, 20", Jaburg, 1908.

III-52.
Sink strainers.

The best one didn't show well in picture, but it has a press that pivots at bottom and pushed water out of the gooky garbage left inside. Clockwise from (T) "Mrs. Vrooman's", blue enamel ware, wire stand, 8" x 9". Next is a Mrs. Vrooman's with wire hangers. She invented these in late 19th C. Best to find with the labels! Washburn Co., Worcester, MA, 1927. Dark one (really white enamel!) also Washburn. White one with petal-like perforations, in white. 2 3/4"H x 9 3/4"L or 3 1/4"H x 11"L, Reed Mfg. Co., 1927. Wire mesh one in various combos of galvanized wire and tin, or white enameled, from 2 3/4"H x 9 1/4"L to 2 1/2"L x 10 1/2"L. Also blue enameled. Wire Goods Co., 1915. **$10.00-$45.00**

III-53.
Reproduction skimmers.

Bronze, in ancient designs found in first century Pompeian ruins in 19th C archaeological digs. These made by Fonderie Artistiche Riunite, J. Chiurazzi & Fils — S. De Angelis & Fils, Naples, Italy, 1910-11. One at (L) is about 15 3/4"L; one at (R) is about 12 1/2"L. Very easy to get fooled by such things.

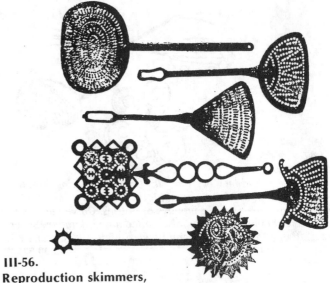

III-56.
Reproduction skimmers,

all of brass in antique styles. Lengths from top: 23", 19", 19", 22", 19" and the sun face is 22"L. These were also sold as chestnut roasters. Mfd. by Pearson-Page, Birmingham, England, 1925.

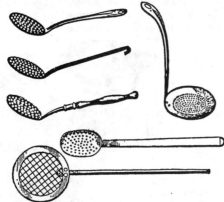

III-54.
Perforated skimmers & egg poachers.

Three dark ones at top (L) are all flat, with different handles. Ridged one at top is a "threaded" handle; next is a hooked "flat" handle; next enameled wood on "long malleable shank." All in four sizes, from 4" to 5 1/8" diameter bowls. Matthai-Ingram, c.1890. (R) with curved handle is a "threaded handle egg poacher," 4 1/4" diameter, Lalance & Grosjean, 1890. One with perforated oval bowl is a "croquette spoon," and at bottom, with coarsely woven wires in metal frame is a "fried oyster skimmer. Last two from V. Clad catalog, c.1890-1900. **$10.00-$35.00**

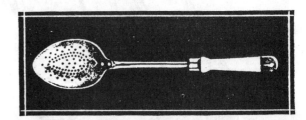

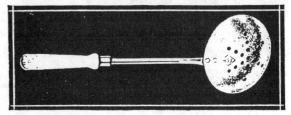

III-57.
Strainer spoon & ladle.

Perforated bowls, with choice of handles. 11 1/2"L spoon has Blutip (cream with blue tip), green, blue or yellow handle. 11"L ladle the same choices. A & J Mfg. Co., 1930. **$4.00-$12.00**

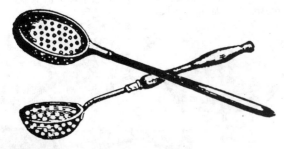

III-55.
Perforated ladle & spoon.

One with apparently bigger, oval bowl, is a "peculiar dipper, made of a round shallow tin pan, with a long handle, the tin being perforated to drain off the liquid." It is for putting eggs down gently into bath of pickling brine to keep for months. <u>American Agriculturist</u>, 10/1878. Lower one is a perforated ladle with long malleable shank and turned wood handle, in 4 sizes, from 3 7/8" to 4 7/8" diameter. Matthai-Ingram, c.1890. **$10.00-$30.00**

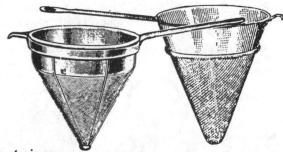

III-58.
Chinese strainers,

in conical shape. (Another is shown in group of gravy strainers.) Many companies had these, all with tin rims, iron handles, and in fine mesh. Sizes from 5" to 9" diameter. One at left has wire braces, from D.J. Barry, 1924 catalog. At right is older one from V. Clad, c.1890-1900.

III-59.
Combination salad washer & bowl strainers,
showing how two special bowl strainers with triple hooks opposite handle can be, in effect, hinged together to make salad washer. Two sizes — 2 3/4" deep x 5 1/4" diameter or 3 1/4" deep x 6". One shown made up as washer has wire-reinforced bowl. Wire Goods Co., 1915.

III-60.
Strainers.
Two more types by Wire Goods Co. (T) Round bottom, rigid rest, 1 3/4", 2 1/8", 2 1/2", 3 1/8" and 3 7/8" diameter, fine mesh. (B) Flat bottom, rigid and reinforced, 2 1/2", 3 1/8" or 3 7/8" diameter.

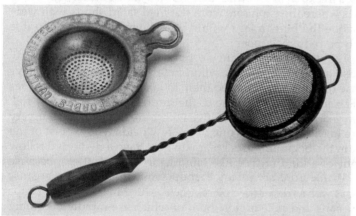

III-61.
Strainers.
(T) Stamped tin, "Forbes Quality Coffee." (B) Wire mesh, tin & wood. Both turn-of-century. **$3.00-$10.00**

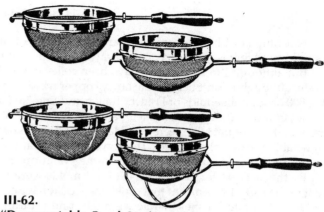

III-62.
"Demountable Bowl Strainers,"
with handles and wire frames, shown here with plain and rein-forced bowls, maroon wood handles. 5 1/4" diameter for all bowls, which you could also buy separately. Wire Goods Co., 1915.

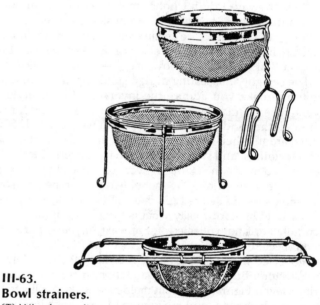

III-63.
Bowl strainers.
(T) Wire frame fits over "pan rim." In 4 sizes, from 3 7/8" to 6" diameter. Wire Goods Co., 1915. (M) 7" and 8", in simple 4-legged wire frame. Washburn, 1936. (B) Extension strainer with sliding wire frame, in 5", 6" or 8" diameter. Also Washburn.

III-64.
Vegetable or cabbage strainer.
"New Process", mfd. by Silver & Co., Brooklyn, NY. This is rather like a ricer for cooked potatoes, which was supposed to be in this chapter but isn't. When the press was inverted, and the press part folded back over, the food fell out onto serving dish in a sort of vegetable cake layer or huge puck. **$20.00-$35.00**

A. PREPARING:

IV. FORM, MOLD, SHAPE, & DECORATE

Not only am I late in coming to an appreciation of molds, so were molds late in coming to kitchens. I can't think of a single mold that is necessary, in the way a knife, pot, fireplace or stirring stick are. They are for pretty; they gussy food up.

But although I'm late, others have been collecting all kinds of molds for many years. The Rennaissance had decorated foods, although I don't believe the fancy copper molds typical of the late 18th and early 19th centuries were yet in existence. By 1800 or so, households of French, Italian and English (and probably German and Russian) nobility could count hundreds of copper molds (or shapes) in their batteries de cuisine. When there was a surplus of money, food and servants, and hours spent at the banquet table were considered hours well-spent, no decoration was considered excessive, no frou-frou wasteful. So what if guests only nibbled? The servants could eat the leftovers. Confined to noble households until the early 19th century, highly decorated food became fashionable among wealthy merchant and professional classes.

By the last quarter of the 19th century, molds were necessary in every middle class kitchen. Chromolithography's advent in the early 1880s meant that cookbooks could have sumptuous, scrumptious full-page pictures of food, showing towering molded, decorated dishes. While we might find it intimidating to face a foot-high molded aspic, quivering on its crystal stand, pictures would lead you to believe that the Victorians loved it. It's my feeling that labor-intensive manipulated food was inevitable ... philosophically related to a fervent Christian belief in the beauty of an ordered universe, within which humans were only doing God's leftover work by forcing everything (animals, furniture, children, clothing, buildings, landscapes...and food) to take on shapes, appearances and functions that were unnatural, though "inspired".

Well anyway, I didn't notice molds because at antique shows they were in with the finer things that I never looked at (furniture, glass, porcelain), and besides, it was the more active mechanical things that attracted me. It's as if molds, including copper molds, ice cream molds, chocolate molds, etc., had to wait until my attention wandered! If you are a generalist collector, like me, you will probably have experienced this kind of delayed reaction too. The unanswerable but nagging question that's raised is "How many —?— did I miss?!"

The category has lasting intrigue and appeal because some of the tools used to shape food are clever mechanical inventions that make you admire the inventors (for example ice cream dishers), and others are next to useless without the inventiveness and artistry of the cook (such as jaggers for cutting out pastry shapes to decorate pies). I used to be very aware of how clothes and people wearing them were related. Some people wore clothes, put their own stamp on them, the folds swirled around their bodies, the sleeves draped from their shoulders. Then there were people who couldn't put an impression on their clothes, and were no better than hangers. Clothes horses in expensive clothes. The clothes didn't move with them, they moved inside the clothes. (Ever see those old jungle movies where the explorers wore starched safari shorts with wide legs, which seemed to glide motionless across the landscape while the human legs within were busy busy busy?) So it is with molds — the active type does all the work, the passive type requires a user.

It would be hard to say what is the most popular subsection in this chapter. Fancy copper molds have been seriously accumulated, if not collected, for at least 70 years, partly because of their house-decoration potential. Cookie cutters have been collected for at least 50 years, in a way for 100 years, because the women who used them to make fancy holiday cookies also collected them. Cutters have recently gained widely publicized attention because of the interest in them held by folk art collectors. Butter molds got a real boost from a book a few years ago by Paul Kindig, who took the subject to a very serious level. Figural ice cream molds are widely collected; here in the U.S., this is one of the few fields where most of the pieces are European, and are known to have been imported from the beginning. Ice cream dishers have a dedicated following; astounding prices are paid for rarities, but these aren't one-of-a-kind rarities like handmade cookie cutters, because dishers or scoops were mass-produced in the last 80 years or so. Waffle irons are yet another upcoming field, mainly because of strong interest in all cast iron goods — hollowware for cooking as well as decorative pieces such as hitching posts, doorstops and architectural.elements. Related to this are cast iron muffin pans and cake molds, both of which are rapidly becoming part of an established market with strong resale potential.

Ableskiver, or Aebelskiver pan—See Ebelskiver pan.

Angelfood cake pan, spouted, gray graniteware, American, 9"D, TOC. **$35.00-$50.00**

Bake mold, 2 parts, tin, a sort of pie pan, and to set down in it a very shallow 'pork pie hat' inset, pan says "sponge mixture." You can put inset pan in 2 positions: "This way up for flans" with inset all the way down & rim part placed crown up. The 2nd way, crown down, is marked "This way up for sandwiches". "Green's Two-Way Tin," English, 8¼" diameter, registered design #77660. • See also the Cake pan for making "Mary Ann base". **$30.00-$40.00**

Bake mold, cast aluminum, 12 turk's head cups, American, 20th C. **$20.00-$30.00**

Bake mold, cast iron, 8 shallow cups: leaf, house, rooster, spade, 6 point star, petalled flower, crescent moon & club, plus 3 small diamonds between the rows, newly made but

not a reproduction of an old design, sold through Cumberland General Store, possibly marked, 14"L x 6"W, 1980s. **$7.00-$10.00**

Bake mold, cast iron, fat fish with overshot under-jaw, especially fat in tail, appears from picture to have hanging hole in tail end tab, maker not known, found in catalog of Cumberland General Store, 8½"W, shipping weight (with pkg) 8½ lbs, 1980s. • **New or Old?** — I include a few pieces like these because in a very short time they may, if they've been well made, look old. I can't order these things, not wanting them or affording them. **$8.00-$12.00**

Bake mold, for cookies or little cakes, 12 heart shaped cups made of rolled-edged strips of tin, each cup separate & riveted to blued steel flat sheet iron, no handle, prob. American, 13½"L x 6¼"W, each heart is 2½"L, late 19th C. **$35.00-$45.00**

• "**Royal Hearts.** — 1 lb. Valentia almonds, 1 lb. 8 oz. beat sugar, 8 oz. flour, 10 eggs and 6 yolks. Beat the almonds fine with yolk of egg; then add the sugar; mix it well with a spatter; keep adding one egg at a time; when beat well up, mix in your flour gently; set tin rims in the shape of hearts, neatly buttered, on paper placed on an iron sheet; fill the rims three parts full, and bake them in a slow oven." Joseph Bell, *A Treatise on Confectionary*, Newcastle, England, 1817. • A spatter is a stirring implement described by Bell as "made of ash or elm, resembling a large wood spoon, only flat on each side." *Ibid.* What is almost undoubtedly the same wooden tool is the Scottish spurtle. • "**Queen or Heart Cakes.** — One pound of sifted Sugar, one pound of Butter, eight Eggs, one pound and a quarter of Flour, two ounces of Currants, and half a Nutmeg grated.

"Cream the butter as in "Twelfth Cake" ("Put the Butter into a stewpan, in a warm place, and work it into a smooth cream with the hand"), and mix it well with the sugar and spice, then put in half the eggs, and beat it ten minutes — add the remainder of the eggs, and work it ten minutes longer, — stir in the flour lightly, and the currants afterwards, — then take small tin pans of any shape (hearts the most usual,) rub the inside of each with butter, fill and bake them a few minutes in a hot oven, on a sheet of matted wire, or on a baking plate, — when done, remove them as early as possible from the pans." William Kitchiner, *The Cook's Oracle*, London, 1827. • By the way, "Queen or Heart Cakes" is correct, although a cardplayer might suspect the "or" should be "of".

Bake mold, tin, 6 triangular troughs, for rolls, 13½"L x 3½"W, 19th C. **$15.00-$22.00**

Baking mold, professional bakery size, heavy blackened tin, 24 heart shaped shallow cups in flat tin frame, American, 29"L x 17" W, 20th C. **$55.00-$70.00**

Baking pan, also called a baking tin, stamped tin, "Independent," Davenport, IA, 20th C. **$7.00-$10.00**

Baking pan, tin, rectangular, stamped "Free 49 cent pan with your initial purchase of new Py—O—My Pastry Mix," 20th C. **$12.00—$18.00**

Baking pan, tin, small square, "Py—O—My," 1" deep x 7" x 7", 20th C. **$10.00-$15.00**

Biscuit cutter, gray graniteware with strap handle, 2½" diameter, 19th C. • "**Cheese Biscuit.** — 2 oz. of butter; 2 of flour; 2 of grated cheese; a little cayenne pepper, and salt; make into paste, and roll out very thin; cut into shape desired; bake a very light brown, and serve as hot as possible." *Treasure House of Useful Knowledge*, compiled by Henry Scammel, 1891. **$55.00-$65.00**

Biscuit cutter, rotary style, tin with wire handle, "Chicago Rotary Cutters," pat'd May 1892. **$35.00-$45.00**

Biscuit cutter, tin, long fat cylindrical handle, closed on top & stamped: "Rumford Yeast Powder", 4"H x 2" diameter, TOC. **$18.00-$22.00**

Biscuit cutter, tin, tubular handle, stamped "Rumford" on top of handle & around top of cutter itself, 4 ½"H, TOC. **$15.00-$20.00**

Biscuit cutter, tin & wire, "Cottolene" (a cottonseed oil shortening), Chicago, IL, early 20th C. **$8.00-$10.00**

Biscuit cutter, tin with scalloped or fluted edge, strap handle. Older ones are composed of 3 separate pieces: cutter body, its soldered-on corrugated cutting edge, & a strap handle. Newer ones have stamped one piece body &

soldered-on strap handle, various makers of these in 19th C, including most big tin houses, but most aren't marked, American, between 2" and 3" diameter, came in various sizes, c.1870s to 1910s. **$8.00-$12.00**

Biscuit cutter, turned wood, knob handle, very thin cutting edge, traces of original white paint, American (?), 2½" diameter x 5½"L, could cut 3" thick dough, 4th quarter 19th C. **$18.00-$25.00**

Biscuit cutter, tin with wire finger loop, stamped with advertising message, "White Lily Flour Has No Equal," Metal Specialty Mfg. Co., (the flour from Conrad Becker Milling Co.), Chicago, (mill in Red Bud, IL), 2¾" diameter, early 20th C. **$6.00-$10.00**

Biscuit cutters, nested set of 3, stamped aluminum, they snap together thanks to the 2 nifty little half-round tabs punched up on top of each one as handle, "Calumet Pastry Cutter", mfd. by Wearever, 1½", 2¼" and 3¼" diameter, 1931 patent #1797859. **$18.00-$22.00**

Biscuit cutters, nested set of 9, crinkle edged cutters, in tin box stenciled in blue, "Veritas. Made in Italy for G. M. Thurnauer Co., Inc.", a big wholesale house, in NYC, that sold mostly imported European kitchenwares, from 1" to 3" diameter, TOC. **$25.00-$35.00**

Biscuit or cake cutter, pieced tin, outer cylinder has inner cylinder with screw-on cap, spring wire coiled loosely around that, pusher plate on bottom, high arched strap handle. The pusher plate retreats up inside depending on the thickness of dough, but spring serves to push dough out. Cap screws off to fill inner cylinder with flour so that it continually dusts cutter as you sproing your way through a sheet of rolled dough. (Nice home for insects if you didn't clean it often.), marked "D. S. Co.", Dover Stamping Co., Boston, MA, 2⅞" diameter & almost that deep, pat'd, poss. May 19, 1868. **$30.00-$45.00**

Biscuit or cookie cutter, rolling kind that cuts multiples, stamped aluminum with turned wire handle, advertises "Louella — The Finest Butter in America" as well as "Gold Seal Flour — For Best Results", American, 6½"L x 2⅞"W, c.1920s or 30s. **$10.00-$18.00**

Biscuit or cookie cutter, stamped, pieced tin, round deep cutter with great 3-D egg shaped knob handle that's as long as cutter's diameter, 3 air holes, embossed "Egg Baking Powder" on the egg, Chicago, IL, 2¾"H overall x 1¹⁵⁄₁₆" diameter, cutter itself is 1¼" deep, (also found 2"H x 2" diameter, 1" deep), c.1902-1905. **$65.00-$80.00**

"**Common Gingerbread.**

— A pint of molasses. One pound of fresh butter. Two pounds and a half of flour, sifted. A pint of milk. A small tea-spoonful of pearl-ash, or if it is strong. (Sic. No indication what is the choice if "it" be strong.) A tea-cup full of ginger. — Cut the butter into the flour. Add the ginger. — Having dissolved the pearl-ash (an early baking soda, with which the molasses would react) in a little vinegar, stir it with the milk and molasses alternately into the other ingredients. Stir it very hard for a long time, till it is quite light. — Put some flour on your pasteboard, take out small portions of the dough, and make it with your hand into long rolls; then curl up the rolls into round cakes, or twist two rolls together, or lay them in straight lengths or sticks side by side, and touching each other. Put them carefully in buttered pans, and bake them in a moderate oven, not hot enough to burn them. If they should get scorched, scrape off with a knife, or grater, all the burnt parts, before you put the cakes away. — You can, if you choose, cut out the dough with tins, in the shape of hearts, circles, ovals, &c. or you may bake it all in one, and cut it in squares when cold. — If the mixture appears to be too thin, add, gradually, a little more sifted flour." Miss Leslie, of Philadelphia, *Seventy-Five Receipts for Pastry, Cakes, and Sweetmeats*. Appended to *The Cook's Own Book and Housekeeper's Register....*, by a Boston Housekeeper. Boston, 1833.

Biscuit or cracker cutter & pricker, heavy tin with nail-like prickers inside, slightly convex cap to fit comfortably in palm, one mfd by Fries, other tin houses made them too, American, 1½" deep x 2" diameter, late 19th or early 20th C. **$15.00-$25.00**

Biscuit or cracker pricker, wooden knob handle with sturdy metal teeth in pattern, American, 4" x 3½", 19th C. • A notice in the 1837 *Journal of the American Institute* (NY: T. B. Wakeman) about Pierce's patent kitchen range, manufactured by Lockwood & Andrews, NYC, and awarded a premium at the 9th annual Fair (Oct. 1836) of the American Institute, includes a biscuit treat: "This article (the range) attracted a great attention at the Fair, and was kept in constant operation. On the sixth day of the Fair, Mr. Pierce (S. Pierce of Troy, NY) provided a dinner, and cooked in it for between fifty and a hundred gentlemen, at Niblo's. Among the articles presented at this repast, were several fine biscuits, made and stamped in twelve minutes from the sheaf! That is, the wheat in sheaf was threshed, winnowed, ground, kneaded, baked, rolled, stamped, and pricked, in the incredibly short space of twelve minutes! " **$65.00-$95.00**

Biscuit pan, & matching cutter, rectangular brown & creamy white enamelware tray with raised edge & 12 round slight depressions, also enameled biscuit cutter with strap handle, "Onyx", Columbian Enameling & Stamping Co., Terre Haute, IN, 10"L, c.1915. **$85.00-$100.00**

Blancmange mold, high tin structure consisting of very pointed central pinnacle surrounded by 2 tiers of lower pointed peaks, European or American, 11"H, c.1870s. **$140.00-$160.00**

"**Ground Rice Flummery**: boil 1 quart milk, except that portion which you have reserved to wet a heaping teacup of rice. Stir this in when the milk boils up; put in 1 teaspoon of salt. When it has thickened, stir in a table spoonful or two of dry ground rice, let it boil up again all around, and take it off the fire as soon as you think the dry rice has become scalded. Have ready a bowl or blancmange mould, wet with a spoonful of milk or cold water, into which pour it. If it is of the right consistency, it will turn out after 15 or 20 minutes in good shape. Eat with sugar and milk or cream. For this an all similar milk preparations, peach leaves are better than any spice. (That's to add an almondy flavor.) Boil in the milk ½ dozen fresh leaves from the tree. Remember to take them out before you stir in the rice." Mary Hooker Cornelius, *The Young Housekeepers Friend*, Boston, 1846. • NOTE: Some flummery recipes use gelatin, but their distinguishing ingredient was always rice meal or flour. I don't know if corn meal was ever used.

Blancmange mold, relatively thin pieced copper with tinned interior, 8 sided, very architectural, English (?), only 6"H, late 19th C. • **Why for "blancmange"?** I don't know. These copper food molds are called food molds, jelly molds, blancmange molds, and they are all for jellied or gelatinized food. **$140.00-$160.00**

Blancmange molds, a pair, tin, deep scalloped base with octagonal "lighthouse" structure atop, tightly fitted lids on bottom, poss. English or French import, poss. American, 11½"H x 5" diameter at base, c.1870s. • These were also used for ice cream or Flummery. The tall tiered architectural types were also called ice-cream pagodas or ice cream towers. Most are so tall that I can't imagine how they were served. Would you like to divide a tapering tower of frozen flummery into 12 portions before it all melted or toppled? (Aspiration T. Agnew might like to try.) **$55.00-$70.00**

Border mold, copper, heavily tinned inside, geometric oval, makes an oval food "frame" for other food — say rice around peas. 7"L, late 19th C. **$175.00-$200.00**

Border mold, or ring mold, stamped tin, marked "KREAMER 2", 9½"L x 6¼"W oval, early 20th C. **$25.00-$28.00**

Border mold, tin, deep design of 13 connected hearts, American (?), 8½" diameter, prob. early 20th C. **$100.00-$135.00**

Bouche iron, also what was later called a patty or timbale iron, cast iron with iron shaft ending with wood handle, at right angles to shaft is screw-on bouche iron, shaped like a small cupcake (fluted, corrugated or plain). The iron was used by dipping it in bouche batter to coat the iron, then quickly dipping it in deep hot fat to make a little fluted shell for stuffing with crab meat salad or other ladies' delicacies, American, or French import, about 8" to 10"L, c.1870s-1890s. Much more recent ones were made at least into 1950s. • The older ones had nicely turned wooden shafts, decorative ferrules, nice turned wooden handles, everything seems carefully machined and decoratively designed. The later ones, including some from the 1920s and later, have the simplest forms, most conspicuous is the iron rod shaft with a right angle bend and machine screw threading on the end. These are often seen at fleas, but the old ones are the real prizes. •

Bouche or Dariole Batter. — "Take two tablespoons of flour, drop two eggs into it, and mix with enough milk to make a batter, similar to fritter batter. Heat iron in boiling lard; then dip Iron into batter, take out and leave on Iron till batter drops off." Recipe accompanying the linecut of a tool that appears twice in an 1886 F. A. Walker catalog, under the names Bouche Iron as well as Dariole Iron. • From Thailand comes a similar device, with longish wood handle & 2 brass heads (one a small fluted cup, one a corrugated cup) which are dipped in hot oil, then in batter, then back in boiling oil. The 2 little pastry cups "float away" from the mold, according to The *International Cooks' Catalog*, NY: Random House, 1977. Skilled users could immerse entire mold in the batter, and get 4 cups at a time. • New ones ¼ price of old ones: **$35.00-$50.00**

Bread baking mold, deliberately blackened tin, small isinglass window, hinged double loaf pan looks like 2 bombs or blimps lying side by side, or some kind of odd bivalve mollusk, "Ideal," mfd by Matthai-Ingram Co., Baltimore, MD, 3¼"H x 12 ½"L x 5"W (twice that for the double ones), stamped with patent date near little catch: Aug. 3, 1897. • This also came in single loaf size. Original advertising claimed "Makes a crisp, moist and wholesome loaf a certainty....The bread is more nutritious, more tasty, and more digestible. Professor Morse, of Westfield, NJ, says bread baked in the Ideal...is a remedy for dyspepsia and of the highest nutritive value.'' **$35.00-$45.00**

Bread pan, oblong blackened sheet iron, called <u>Russia iron,</u> folded corners, rolled rim, slanted sides, very substantial, ring handle at both ends, one kind was ''Beaman's Patent'', mfd by Matthai-Ingram Co., 4'' deep x 18''L x 12''W at top, late 19th C, into early 20th. • **Russian iron,** or russia iron is a form of planished wrought iron used for roasting, baking and dripping pans. According to Elsie Hutchinson, in a book to instruct department store employees, titled *The House Furnishings Department*, 1918, it is a ''special grade of sheet iron with a glossy black, slightly mottled appearance due to oxide adhering to the surface; it is produced by passing a pack of heated sheets back and forth under a steam hammer, the bit and anvil of which have indentations on their surfaces.'' It originated in Russia, and had an almost purple appearance, according to 19th C books. **$10.00-$18.00**

Bread stick pan, cast iron, makes 22 bread sticks, 11 x 11 side by side, design based on old pan, sold through Cumberland General Store catalog, but I don't know if this is marked, American (?), 12½''L x 7''W, 1980s. **$8.50-$10.00**

Bride & groom cake dolls, bisque, painted & dressed in real cloth clothes, American (?), 4''H, 1940s. • **Futurewatch.** — This is an undervalued collector field, offering a huge variety over a period of at least 100 years. A nice addition to a collection of them would include the arches and altars, as well as photographs of decorated wedding cakes in bakery windows. In the Jan. 25, 1989 *Antique Trader*, there was an appealing ad for 50 plus sets from the 1920s on. They were from Japan, Occupied Japan & the U.S., and the dealer, Shirley Rice, had them priced $15.00 to $35.00 per set, or $650.00 for all of them. Many bakeries and pastry shops seem to have the same old brides and grooms year after year. Keep an eye on them; you might be able to buy old pieces, or trade for some brand new ones. **$35.00-$45.00**

Bride & groom cake dolls, molded plaster of Paris, painted with black, white, pink, also pearlized white paint on bride's headdress & bodice, American (?), 5''H, dated 1948. **$5.00-$12.00**

Bun cutter, rolling pin cutter, tin, turned wooden handle, 18 iron blades set in large diameter cast metal roller, cuts 18 buns with each revolution of the sectioned drum, ''Millers Bun Divider'', (possibly mfd by Charles E. Miller Co., see the meat tenderizer in the cutting chapter), Milwaukee, WI, roller 7'' diameter, blades 6''W, pat'd Feb. 1907. • A similar implement, on a smaller scale, is a <u>Revolving Chip Cutter,</u> with 2 turned wooden handles and a 3''W tin revolving cutter divided into eight sections, 3'' x 2''. **$65.00-$80.00**

Bundt cake mold, also called Bundt pan, spouted, redware with green & orangey red glaze, American, 7''D, 19th C. • **German vocabulary** — <u>Keramik-backform:</u> ceramic baking mold, or cake mold, etc. (Iron baking mold would be qualified with <u>Eisenguss</u> (the double ess, when printed in German, is a single character that looks sort of like a capital B — like <u>EisenguB</u>). I've also seen <u>gusseisen.</u>• Bundt: I think the word relates to the word for band or bundle, and relates to the banded effect of the flutes (such as would be found in a wheat sheaf or straw wreath, tied

at intervals with twine), and probably originated as a harvest celebration cake. **$150.00-$175.00**

Bundt cake mold, cast iron, bail handle of type called a stop bail, a sort of ear that would would allow the bail to fall only on one side and on the other side to be held rigid for pouring. This would make it much easier & safer to tip pan over to release cake. A stop bail of one form or another was used on many kinds of heavy cast hollowwares. Frank W. Hay & Sons, Johnstown, PA, pat'd Mar. 10, 1891. **$65.00-$90.00**

Bundt cake mold, cast iron, enameled in cobalt blue, American, 10'' diameter, early 20th C. **$95.00-$125.00**

Bundt cake mold, cast iron, large scallops alternating with sharply defined zigs (zags?), conical spout, American, 12'' diameter, 19th C. **Lookalike alarm.**— Lehman's Hardware & Appliances, 4779 Kidron Rd., Kidron, OH 44636 offer a spouted bundt pan, 10'' diameter, with 2 handles, in their 1989 ''Non-Electric Good Neighbor Amish Country'' catalog, which costs about $2.00. They say that all their cast iron is ''produced in a family foundry — Lodge, in South Pittsburgh, TN — dating back to 1896'', and that all are sand cast and ''finished by hand.'' **$75.00-$100.00**

Bundt cake mold, cast iron, scalloped, solid tapered cylinder in center where a closed spout or open tube would be, German or other European origin, 10½''D, 19th C. • The well-known cast aluminum bundt pan, alternating 8 large scallops with 8 small pointed flutes, first made in 1949 by Northland Aluminum Products of Minneapolis, MN, was a reproduction of a 19th C European cast iron bundt pan, brought over — reportedly — by a European immigrant to Minnesota. Northland has now registered ''Bundt'' for their own use. **$110.00-$140.00**

Bundt cake mold, cast iron, tubed, very exaggerated flutes & scallops, very deep, signs of real wear, not marked, American (?), about 11'' to 13'' diameter, 19th C. **$65.00-$125.00**

Bundt cake mold, earthenware with brown glaze, spouted, fluted sides, crack mended with twisted wire, wire all around rim too, German or Austrian, late 19th C. • From the looks of the wire around the rim, you might almost assume that these pans were sold with wire bindings, to hold them together in case of bustin' in the oven. What a mess! **$35.00-$45.00**

Bundt cake mold, gray & white mottled graniteware, American (?), 13''D, 19th C. **$25.00-$35.00**

Butter hands, also called <u>Scotch hands,</u> corrugated wood, usually maple, well-made & usually satiny from use, American, between 8'' and 9''L and 2 ½'' and 3'' W even 4''W, 19th C. • I used to think these were pretty much all the same. But I can report differences. Although most are within small size range, there are things the connoisseur of Scotch hands can look for. Instead of a lighter weight, dull wood, wide grooves, seek out heavier wood, pale golden satiny patina; instead of machine carved regular corrugations, look for carefully handcarved grooves; instead of pattern-cut simple paddle handles, look for more artistically formed ones, especially those that are flat on corrugated side where they must fit together, but are curved on their backs. I even like slightly mismatched pairs, perhaps perversely. <u>Nice wooden butter hands are still being manufactured.</u> Price for pair of hand carved ones: **$40.00-$60.00**

Butter hands, finely corrugated sycamore, backs of paddles convex in section, good patina, handmade, American (?), 8 9/16"L, mid 19th C. • "A pair of creased wooden hands, for making butter balls, should be included in the outfit of the kitchen. With a little practice, butter may be shaped in many pretty forms, so that the dish will look very nice on the table. Be particular to select hands with fine grooves — much better results than coarse." Maria Parloa, *Kitchen Companion*, Boston: Estes & Lauriat, 1887. • **"How To Use Butter Hands.** — Let stand in boiling water for five minutes. Next put in cold water for five minutes or longer. Must be cold when used. Have large bowl half full of cold water. Cut some firm butter into pieces about the size of a hickory nut. Roll these pieces between the butter-hands into any shape you please — grooved balls, little pineapples, scrolls, etc. Dip the hands frequently in ice water." *ibid.* **$25.00-$35.00**

Butter hands, machine made corrugated wood paddles, for rolling butter balls, American, 9"L, late 19th or early 20th C. • **Man & Machine Made.** — Factory-made butter hands are relatively cheap — they look machine-made too, with fairly crudely finished off beveled edges and perfectly regularly spaced corrugations. They also are flat-backed. Handmade ones have the appearance of being lovingly made, carefully smoothed and finished, and often with somewhat convex backs. Pairs don't tend to match exactly. They bring three to four times as much money as factory made ones. Price range is for machine made pair. **$15.00-$20.00**

Butter mold, acorn & oak leaves, plunger type, factory-made, lathe-turned case & plunger, American, 1 7/8"D, late 19th C.• **Reproduction alerts.** — So far at least, nowhere near all the designs of machine-made butter molds or stamps have been reproduced. **Alert I.** A company (mfr? dlr?) in Atkins, VA, began (?) advertising in early 1989 "wooden butter molds: ½ lb. round reproductions. Starburst design." They were priced at six for $34.50 ppd. **Alert II.** Another company, with "Antique" in their name, advertised in May 1989 (possibly before too) *Southern Antiques* a wholesale deal: "Wooden Butter Molds, ½ lb. size Two Piece, Round Shell or cup Type Stamp. Cow, Wheat, Pineapple, Starburst, Swan. Great Repro. Sample $16 each, per dozen $145 ppd." Sounds like the same repro molds. **$35.00-$45.00**

Butter mold, bee, large carving on round stamp, fits into turned wood mold, plunger type, turned & carved wood, marked "Germany", 3½" x 1½", 20th C. **$25.00-$35.00**

Butter mold, box & plunger type, wood with nickeled brass hardware, imprints "JERSEY," early 20th C. **$85.00-$100.00**

Butter mold, cow, 2 parts: round glass (very pale greenish blue) case, molded disc or plunger prints simple standing cow, the disc is molded on top with threaded hole for screwed-in turned wooden handle, "Bomer," American, round, 4½" diameter, 8¼"L overall including handle, marked "Pat Apld for," very late 19th C. • **Reproduction alert.** — New ones are sold through catalogs of "country" wares; the glass has no faint tint of green in the new ones, and they tend to be a bit light for what they look like they'll weigh. Look for signs of wear along bottom edge of glass and on wooden handle. • A presumably much rarer glass cow plunger mold, depicted in Kindig's book, and belonging to him, has four cows molded on the case, as decoration. His does not have the name "Bomer." **$55.00-$75.00**

Butter mold, cow, incised carving, cylinder with pewter bands, hexagonal shape, American, 4½"H x 3" diameter, 19th C. **$200.00-$300.00**

Butter mold, cow, pleasantly abstracted lathe-turned case & plunger in one pound size, a craftsman-shop production of pointy-leg cow resembling what Paul Kindig calls the "Vigilant Cow," written about extensively in *Butter Prints and Molds* (see Bibliography), American, 2nd half 19th C. • **Machine made?** — You can see the concentric rings, especially inside the case, that are the mark of the tools used with the lathe. • Craftsmen in shops making butter molds were highly skilled, and bridged the world of the one of a kind completely hand carved or whittled butter stamp (much less likely to be a mold, as the cases were hard to do by hand), and the dime-a-dozen (though still attractive to us as collectors today) completely factory-made stamps, with templates and jigs guiding the cutting. **$200.00-$275.00**

Butter mold, flowers, 4 with four petals & 4 eight pointed stars, box type, wood, marked "Porter Blanchards Son's Co.," Nashua, NH, 19th C. **$100.00-$130.00**

Butter mold, goose, deep carved, plunger type, American, ½ lb. size, 3¾" diameter, late 19th C. • **Reproduction alert.** — Not this mold specifically, because I don't have the catalog, but Nettle Creek Industries advertised in early 1976 that they had "superb quality reproductions of authentic ships figureheads, scrimshaw, buttermolds and dozens of other interesting items for the collector." They seem to have missed the point: collectors don't collect reproductions. **$135.00-$150.00**

Butter mold, no pattern, wood box with iron fittings including frame & handle, 1 lb. press, American, 5¾"L x 3 5/8"W, 19th C. • This is a nice mold, and there is one in the collection of the Smithsonian. However, it is not worth $300.00 because it is "in a museum", as a dealer in Staunton, VA, told a collector in 1988. • **"In a museum"** and **"in the book"** are explanatory phrases used when raising prices, but it's pretty much meaningless, especially when the museum (Smithsonian) and book (mine in particular, and some others) are known for including a wide range of things for study. **$55.00-$85.00**

Butter mold, no pattern, wood, very small, marked "Munsing," American. • **Butter Mold Manufacturers.** — I couldn't find "Munsing" but in the 1905-06 Buyers' Guide, of *Thomas' Register of American Manufacturers,* I found a few butter mold makers listed under molds. And though not broken down that way, there are probably others to be found in Thomas' section on woodenware too. • The makers are: Robert E. Turner, Lebanon, CT; Creamery Package Mfg. Co., Chicago, IL; Freeman Mfg. Co., Kalkaska, MI; Ludington Woodenware Co., Ludington, MA; A. H. Reid, Pittsburg, PA; Vermont Farm Machine Co., Bellows Falls, VT; Moseley & Stoddard Mfg. Co., Rutland, VT; and Cornish, Curtis & Green Mfg. Co., Fort Atkinson, WI. **$18.00-$22.00**

Butter mold, rose & other flowers in center design, carved wood, square with fluted sides (unusual), Pennsylvania (?), 5¼" x 5½", mid to 3rd quarter 19th C. • Robacker May 1989 price: **$210.00**

Butter mold, wheat ear, 2 parts, very small rectangular box, motif carved inside, string holds halves together, paper label reads: "Wheat-Ear Moulds. Directions for Use. First, thoroughly soak the mould in water and then with a table knife fill in both halves of Butter Mould. Then lay a clean straw in the centre of one half, then press the two halves evenly together. Take away the top half and lift out wheat-ear on the straw.'' No manufacturer's name, English, overall size is 1¼''H x 4''L x 1⅝''W, with 3¾''L wheat-ear carving, TOC, from looks of label. **$18.00-$22.00**

Butter mold, star design, cast aluminum,. R. Hall, Burlington, NC, ½ lb size, about 3½'' diameter, prob. c. 1930s to 1950s. • I saw one of these marked almost $60.00, but that's way too much. **$15.00-$22.00**

Butter printer, flower designs, rolling type, carved wood, English (?), 5½''L, 19th C. • Dealer R. C. Bowen explained to me that rolling butter printers were used to make border prints at a dairy store. The large tray of butter, an inch thick or whatever, was divided off into sections, square-by-square of designs, so that so many squares could be cut off for so much poundage. • Carl W. Drepperd, in *A Dictionary of American Antiques*, makes a nice distinction between the oft-used terms stamp and print. He says that the tool used to mark the butter is the stamp; the marked butter is the print. This makes eminent good sense. • In an 1890 cookbook, *On the Chafing Dish, Compliments of the Meriden Britannia Co.*, by Harriet P. Bailey (NY: G. W. Dillingham), there is a recipe for ''Eggs With Macaroni'' to which Mrs. Bailey adds this genteel note: ''Note: — For cooking on the chafing dish, I advise always using print butter. It may seem a little extravagant. But surely when one in evening attire prepares a dish which proves to be above reproach, one may say with the March Hare, 'It is the best butter,' without losing the reputation of being an economical as well as a good housekeeper.'' Neither Bailey nor Drepperd, unfortunately, commented on rolling ''stamps'', so I have opted to call them printers. **$90.00-$120.00**

Butter printer, rolling type, carved wood (ash?), roller prints a thistle & 2 star-like flowers & a leaf, English (?), 4½''L x 1⅞'' diameter, 19th C. **$200.00-$225.00**

Butter slicer, nickel plated iron, 11 thin cutting wires, porcelainized cast iron base, cuts a pound block of butter into quarters, then slices them into pats, probably for hotel or restaurant use, worked by pushing wire-strung frame down using thumb tab, ''Elgin #48,'' mfd. by Cleveland Faucet Co., 8½''H x 8½''L, pat'd Dec. 31, 1901 in Canada, Sept. 1911 in U.S.A. **$45.00-$55.00**

Butter stamp, 4 petaled rosette, hearts on one side; stars on other, carved wood, PA (?), 19th C. • Robacker May 1989 price: **$140.00**

Butter stamp, armadillo or strange turtle, carved wood, crescent shape with knobby handle, looks old except for new-looking handle, subject matter makes me wary of age, 6¼''W, 20th C (?). • Dealer's asking price: **$60.00**

Butter stamp, bird in the grass design, carved wood, corrugated border, much detail in carving, American, 3'' diameter, 19th C. **$240.00-$300.00**

Butter stamp, cow, detailed handcarving of unusual rearing bovine surrounded by more typical combination of gate, overhanging branch & long grass, cable border, long handle, American, 19th C. • Teri Dziadul, who has probably had more beautiful butter molds and stamps pass through her hands than anybody except Paul Kindig who wrote THE book, offered this for $195.00 in 1984. Price range is mine not hers. **$250.00-$350.00**

Butter stamp, cow with fence behind her, eager expectant horns, nice little tail, pointed udders, well-defined hooves, hair on flanks, body of mold worn, but well carved figure is perfect, American, 4½'' overall x 2½'' deep, stamp itself 3⅝'' diameter, 19th C. **$245.00-$300.00**

Butter stamp, cow with pointy legs, ears and horns, in Kindig's ''Vigilant Cow'' style, well-cut, knob handle, American, 2nd half 19th C. **$225.00-$300.00**

Butter stamp, deer, with bent corn stalk (which he may have been eating!) overhanging him and long grass, piecrust border, American, 4'' diameter, 19th C. **$275.00-$400.00**

Butter stamp, donkey, with wonderfully bent front legs, slogging along on a sort of rayed ground, probably a plowed field, and with bursts of something, like leaves or flowers, filling the sky, deeply carved wooden disc, chip out of one side, age cracking, very unusual motif, American, 3¾'' diameter, 19th C. • Sold for $625.00 at a 1984 James D. Julia auction, Fairfield, ME. **$700.00-$900.00**

Butter stamp, dove on one side, a vase of flowers on other, 3¼'' diameter, 19th C. **$150.00-$200.00**

Butter stamp, eagle, carved wood, American, 4½'' x 4¼'', 19th C. **$325.00-$360.00**

Butter stamp, eagle, deep carved abstract figure with corrugated border, lathe-turned one-piece blank, lathe marks evident, American, 4½'' diameter, 19th C. **$450.00-$500.00**

Butter stamp, eagle, hand carved wood in half moon shape, very beautiful carving of benign but spread-winged eagle, wide-eyed & looking over his right wing (left wing in the printed butter), the details of breast and wing feathers done with genius, little chips perfectly spaced for visual appeal, and long parallel curving lines to follow sweep of ruff, back of head, tail and ends of wings, two spaces filled in with rayed suns (one a moon?), initials, and a few 4 point stars between letters just inside the piecrust border. • Clarence Spohn, in catalog, quotes Robacker as stating in his 1965 *Touch of the Dutchland*, that ''The eagle pictured here has been called the most important piece of its kind in primitive woodcarving.'' Border has initials ''S. M.'', PA German, 3¾''H x 7⅝''L, 19th C. • Robacker May 1989 price: **$6000.00**

Butter stamp, eagle with an 8 point ''star'', American, 2¾'' diameter, 19th C. • After eight points, I'm not sure the pointed motif is a star, but it probably is meant to represent or allude to a star, so instead of thinking up some new word like octopunctus let's just continue calling it a star. You'll encounter this shape, sometimes reminiscent of a compass rose, on quilts too. N. B. Even with 12 points, some writers still call this a star. **$175.00-$220.00**

Butter stamp, eagle with shield body, deeply carved, the words ''JAMES HOFMAN - SHIP BUILDER,'' around the border, American, 19th C. • Sold in early 1982 for $800.00, most likely because of relationship to ship building. Would probably bring at least that much today. • Also ship-or marine-related, is a whale ivory butter stamp, with a very large knob handle, that was part of the Jeffrey Cohen Collection auctioned by Richard Bourne on July 31, 1989 for $2750.00. (It appears in Flayderman's *Scrimshaw and Scrimshanders: Whales and Whalemen*, 1972) Lita Solis Cohen, writing in the Oct. 1989 *Maine Antique Digest* said that the auctioneer said it was the only example known of a whale ivory butter stamp, but Lita's unnamed seatmate told her that wasn't so because she had one too. More may surface. **$700.00-$1000.00**

Butter stamp, fish, 3 large ones facing same way & 2 smaller, piecrust border, handle on back, poss. New England, 3½"W, mid 19th C. **$300.00-$375.00**

Butter stamp, fish, very fat (croppie? sunfish?) with several regularly patterned lines of waves, dentil border, 2 part, very finely carved, with separate carved and inserted knob handle (partly chewed — by piranha?), American, found in barn in Dresden, ME, 3¾" diameter, mid 19th C. • The detailed, well-ordered, and patterned appearance reminds you of classical Greco-Roman tiles or wall murals, especially the compact puddle-sized water body hovering just behind the lower fin. Perhaps the carver's inspiration was in some recently published account of an archaeological dig in the 1840s or 1850s. • This stamp (or "butter print", as it is called in the catalog), from the collection of Greg & Linette Salisbury, was sold at a James D. Julia auction, Aug. 23, 1989, for $950.00 plus 10% premium. The presale estimate was $400.00-$700.00. It was by far the most outstanding mold among the ones offered. **$700.00-$1200.00**

Butter stamp, fleur-de-lis pattern, round glass with screw-in wooden knob handle, French Canadian (?), 3½" diameter, 20th C. **$75.00-$85.00**

Butter stamp, fox, running, big tail brush, overhead branch, pointy enough to be a "vigilant fox" as Kindig might term it, dense, faintly yellow wood with wormholes, American, 2nd half 19th C. **$300.00-$400.00**

Butter stamp, geometric curved-ray design, saltglazed stoneware with large knobby handle, deeply molded, poss. OH, mid 19th C. **$1000.00-$1500.00**

Butter stamp, half moon shape, heart & leaf design, attached handle on back, good patina on carved wood, which means a lot with butter stamps & molds, PA (?), 6¾" L x 3¼" diameter, mid 19th C. • Robacker May 1989 price: **$650.00**

Butter stamp, lollipop type & also double sided, carved wood, has unusually long handle; designs are a double heart on one side, a pinwheel or fylfot design on other, Pennsylvania German, 11"L overall with handle, stamp only 4¾" diameter, mid 19th C. • Robacker May 1989 price: **$1175.00**

Butter stamp, lollipop type, carved from one piece of wood, double ended with 2 prints: a square print with chipcarved eagle & 4 stars separated by shank a hand's breadth long from a round print carved with 8 point snowflake-like design, American, prob. 2nd to 3rd quarter 19th C. **$600.00-$900.00**

Butter stamp, lollipop type, carved with 6 petal flower, serrated border, elongated shield shaped handle ending in heart, American, 10"L, 19th C. • Sold for $685.00 at 1982 auction. **$400.00-$700.00**

Butter stamp, lollipop type, double carving of an abstract hex-type flower, & a fern leaf, American, 8½"L, 19th C.• This stamp was offered for sale at $325.00 by Teri Dziadul in 1984. **$400.00-$500.00**

Butter stamp, lollipop type, one piece carved wood, unusual because of handle angled somewhat to side instead of joining disc at right angles, simple 6 petal star flower (with small ellipses between each point) carved on

both sides, simple bead border, American, 8½"L, approximately 3¾" diameter stamp, prob. 3rd quarter 19th C. • This was $500.00 at Garth Auction, May 5-6, 1989, Delaware, OH. Another showed up at Garth auction, Nov. 10, 1989, with same 6 petal flower & ellipses. This may be an uh-oh item.) **$325.00-$550.00**

Butter stamp, lollipop type, separate turned wooden handle, nice carving of bulky cow standing on groundline that looks like cable, the words being TRADE MARK, above & below cow, maybe mid 19th C. • Sold for $700.00 at James D. Julia auction in 1984. **$750.00-$1000.00**

Butter stamp, Masonic building trade symbols, carved wood, carved handle, American, 4⅞" diameter, ¾" thick, late 19th C. • Value here is tied to the **Masonic symbols**, assuming they *are* Freemason symbols. The Freemasons are usually dated back to the 17th C in England, and 1733 in (Boston) North America. The 1804 English Encyclopedia traces the • **Freemasons** back to the 6th C in England, but this may be romanticizing loose guilds or fraternal orders of masons and stone-and brick-workers. • The **Odd Fellows** don't seem to be as old an order, so values are slightly, shall we say, younger. They were around by 1745 in "isolated lodges" in England and found countrywide by 1812, according to one expert.. In America, the two dates given are 1806 and 1819, the latter — for a lodge in Baltimore — generally being the accepted date. Then in 1850-51 the Odd Fellows-related Degree of Rebekah was established for women. **$1200.00-$1300.00**

Butter stamp, name in very nice serif lettering around border, oval sunburst design in center, carved wood, reads "G. Haughton" and "A. Southington", New England (?), oval 5"L x 3½"W, 19th C, prob. 2nd to 3rd quarter. • Brought $325.00 at Garth Auction, May 5 6, 1989, Delaware, OH. Good old patina, but hard to explain price when it's hand carved but not figural, unless the buyer was a Haughton or Southington. **$200.00-$325.00**

Butter stamp, name & legend around edge, geometric design in center, carved wood with knob handle,"J. CARRINGTON PAVE CASTEL", 5⅛" diameter, early 19th C (?). • This was offered by collector & dealer Teri Dziadul of Enfield, CT, in early 1980s. Anything with a name I try to include, even if I've not seen it, because by having this all on computer I can cross reference, or at least look things up. The only other J. Carrington in my records is James Carrington, of Wallingford, CT, who patented a coffee mill in 1829. Possibly the same man, this being about the right age. Teri was asking $225.00 in her catalog. The price range here is mine. **$225.00-$250.00**

Butter stamp, palm tree with stars & little amoebic odds & ends floating in sky, hand carved wood, large slightly concave (warped?) disc with short all-in-one knob on back, very unusual stylized design, dark patina, American, prob. PA, 5" diameter, mid 19th C. • **Palms & Xmas Trees.** — There are two sacred trees in the Christian religion, the palm and the evergreen. The palm generally symbolizes the birthplace of Christ; more specifically His entry into Jerusalem on Palm Sunday. • If you, like I, always thought that "Xmas" was a slangy and incorrect way to write "Christmas", you'll be as relieved as I was to find out that it is many hundreds of years old, the X standing for "criss-cross" or Christ's cross. I wonder if the common early decorative use of an X (often between straight lines above and below like a Roman numeral), wasn't used (especially by blacksmiths with their chisels and files) to signify a criss-cross, a sort of secularly-awarded religious blessing on the object. Taking this idea further, the lines may represent heaven and earth. The mark is found, sometimes in multiples, on many 17th, 18th & early 19th C forged iron and carved wood utilitarian objects. On the other hand, because decorating hot iron with a chisel or file was not the easiest thing to do, it is possible that an X and some straight lines was just the easiest form of decoration. **$225.00-$275.00**

Butter stamp, pineapple with geometric border design, fairly crudely-carved thick pine (a nice soft wood for amateurs to attack!), with no handle, American, 19th C.
$100.00-$120.00

• According to Mary Earle Gould, in her book on woodenware, these handleless stamps were actually cookie stamps, while the ones with handles were for butter. Is this true, you expert collectors out there?

Mushroom Biscuits. — 8 oz. of butter, and 3 lb. 8 oz. of fine flour. Rub the butter and flour together, and mix them into a stiff paste with water; it must be made very smooth and fine; then make it into biscuits, about two ounces each; to be made round, and stamped in the middle with a butter print; prick them in the hollow with a fork to prevent blistering; bake them on iron plates in a good oven." Joseph Bell, *A Treatise on Confectionary.* Newcastle, England, 1817.

Butter stamp, rooster, probably carved shop piece on machine-turned blank, American, 3½" diameter, latish 19th C. **$65.00-$80.00**

Butter stamp, rooster with leaves on branch, in mid crow, lathe-turned blank, screw-in handle, craftsman-shop production, nicely & competently carved wood, with simple corrugated border design, American, 3½" diameter, 19th C. **$150.00-$175.00**

Butter stamp, rose, craftsman-shop production, lathe-turned blank with hand carving, very late 19th C or early 20th. **$35.00-$40.00**

Butter stamp, rose, fullblown, with rosebud & leaves, craftsman-shop carving but very nice, on machined blank, American, 2" diameter, late 19th C. **$55.00-$65.00**

Butter stamp, rose & leaves design, for single pat, carved wood, American or imported from Europe, 1⅞" diameter, late 19th or early 20th C. **$45.00-$65.00**

Butter stamp, rose, thistle, & 3 leaf clover, single pat size, 3 finely carved designs, only 1¾" diameter, 19th C. **$90.00-$110.00**

Butter stamp, rosette with 4 radial petals, craftsman-carved, common abstract design, American, 2" diameter, 19th C. **$45.00-$55.00**

Butter stamp, snowflake design, for single pat, 1⅞" diameter, late 19th or early 20th C. **$45.00-$65.00**

Butter stamp, strawberries, 2 wild ones with viney leaves, deeply carved wood, American, 1½" diameter, 19th C. **$85.00-$95.00**

Butter stamp, swan, dense wood, longish handle, simple but well-carved, English, 3⅛"H, mold is 2⅝" diameter, 19th C. **$35.00-$45.00**

Butter stamp, tulips, 3 of them with stars, hand carved wood, marked on handle "C. I.", with date, Pennsylvania (?), 3¼" diameter, dated 1827. • Robacker May 1989 price: **$300.00**

Butter stamp, wheat sheaf, ear of corn, grapes & leaves, a rose & leaf, 4 carvings for 4 separate prints, factory-made, with box case, American, 4½" x 4⅛", early 20th C. **$55.00-$75.00**

Butter stamp, wheat sheaf, rayed or piecrust border, pressed glass disc, knob handle, M'Kee & Brothers, Pittsburgh, 1868. **$175.00-$225.00**

Butter stamp & butter paddle combined, cow & 2 acorns on the stamp, one piece of wood, hand carved, American, paddle is 14"L overall, stamp is 4" diameter, 19th C. **$600.00-$900.00**

Butter stamp & paddle combined, star with 6 points on stamp, carved of one piece of wood, with a small shaped shovel scoop or paddle at one end, and the other end of the "handle" widening out to a large disc, about the size of a child's sand shovel, PA German (?), 9½"L overall, with stamp 2⅞" diameter, mid to 4th quarter 19th C. • Robacker May 1989 price: **$475.00**

Butter stamp & pastry jagger combined, with wheel making leaf design, very unusual, PA German (?), 5⅛"L overall, stamp is only 1⅝" diameter, mid to 4th quarter 19th C. • Robacker May 1989 price: **$260.00**

Cake board, 2 sided, carved wood, one side has plant & pot with big berries, obverse depicts old woman, a cat & little dog, prominent in her costumes is a big bonnet, and a pocket tied to the waist of her dress, hung from her belt, with slit opening, European, 1" thick x 4" x 7", early 19th C. **$375.00-$425.00**

Cake board, basket of flowers on one side is typical of late 18th of early 19th style, tulips on other side, deep carved cherry wood, thick board, beautiful patina, 7"L x 6"W, prob. early 19th C, c.1810-30. **$175.00-$210.00**

Cake board, cat wearing collar, tabby striped & sitting, carved board, 10"H x 6½"W, 19th C. **$450.00-$550.00**

Cake board, corrugated, very finely, with a center line so that you could break cookie in half, for sugar cookies, lightweight wood, American (?), 13⅛"L, makes a 3⅝"W cookie, 19th C. **$60.00-$70.00**

Cake board, dressed-up dandy, perhaps a Yankee Doodle, on horseback, with flowers, high boots, knee britches, roll brim hat with feather, carved wood, slightly warped plank with 2 small age or dryness checks and a drilled hole in each corner, nice dark patina, American (?), 1⅛" thick x 10⅝"H x 8⅜"W, 2nd quarter 19th C. **$300.00-$375.00**

Cake board, fish on one side, on the other a stylized flower, American (?), 10⅜"L x 3¾"W, 19th C. • This was in an auction catalog in 1982, without the more critical measurement, the thickness of the wood. It was estimated to go between $125.00-$175.00 but reached $200.00. Original estimate still seems close to correct, as this wasn't very distinguished. **$150.00-$200.00**

Cake board, harlequin figure or possibly Pero, carved wood, Dutch (?), 9"H, proba. early 19th C. • **Lookalike alarm.** — The most commonly found images on carved wood cookie molds are single figures in peasant or old military costume. Many are reproductions, but in the strictest sense, most are just lookalikes "in the style of." A 1967 ad in McCall's Needlework & Crafts magazine, has photos of two long skinny boards, one carved with a man and woman, arms akimbo, both standing on little tufts of ground; the other with five images including a basket, bird & branch, windmill, and two that can't be identified.

The ad reads: "Dutch Cookie Molds sent directly from Holland with foreign stamps. All the charm of old Holland is captured in these charming hand-carved cookie molds. It's a double Dutch treat for not only are they the most enchanting decorations for anywhere in the house, but they make the most delightful cookies, including farmer and wife, windmills, baskets, etc. (Recipe and history of boards included.) They will make a cherished and unique gift for every woman on your Christmas list. Antique brown elm wood, 15½'' x 2¼''. $3.00 ea. 2 for $5.50. 4 for $10.00.'' *Brochure of Cookie Mold Collection* 10¢. I have no idea if they are still in business, but the company (which probably was but one of several that produced these molds that were exported and also sold in Holland to tourists and housewives) was Holland Handicrafts, P.B. 74 Ridderkerk, Holland. Remember this is a 1967 ad, so don't try to order from it. **$150.00-$200.00**

Cake board, heart shaped flower for molding a single small cookie, in middle of large board, carved pine, early 20th C (?). **$45.00-$60.00**

Cake board, horse & sleigh, lion, flower pot, courting couple, 3 carvings per side, European, 22½''L x 4½''W, 19th C. • With container load imports, particularly from cookie countries in Scandinavia, and with the continuing appeal of *emmerlinguistication* (or recountrification) in America, you will see many many carved cake or cookie boards around, many with equestrian figures, flowers in baskets, roosters, cats, pigs, etc. Dark brown Min-Wax• coloration, unsubtle gouges to ''age'' the board, and a thickness conforming to modern mill practices (often ⅞''), and the use of pine are strong clues to modern work. **$135.00-$165.00**

Cake board, man in kneepants & fancy hat, Holland, 18''L, mid to 3rd quarter 20th C. • **Reproduction alert.** — Wood is stained dark brown, to resemble a harder wood, but is carved from pine. Edges of this only 1¼'' thick board show saw marks, and the back shows no evidence of hand-planing. Finally, no signs of wear, and the design is not so intricate as the really old ones (texture of fabric, etc.) — couldn't be, because it's carved of softish pine, not hard dense walnut, mahogany or fruitwood. **$45.00-$65.00**

Cake board, owl & rabbit on one side, parrot & songbird on other, carved wood, signed ''T B. W. W. 20'' along one side edge, prob. European, 11½''L x 3¼''W, 19th C. **$140.00-$165.00**

Cake board, pears & leaves on one side, flowers on other, deep carved cherry wood, prob. American, 7''x 5'', early 19th C. **$180.00-$220.00**

Cake board, pickup truck from 1920s, spare tire, possibly depicts a common sight in the Great Depression, of a family moving all belongings in an old car or truck, carved wood, definitely unusual, American (?), 23½''L x 9½''W, 1920s or 30s. • Unusual image, but the fact of its existence, with fairly good & detailed carving, forces you to look warily at many other cookie boards with undateable images such as flowers and animals. Auctioned by Garth's in 1986 for only $150.00. Estimated price range a few years later is higher, because of image, which has crossover appeal. **$165.00-$225.00**

Cake board, woman sitting in chair spinning thread or fine yarn, carved wood, English (?), 1'' thick x 2⅝'' x 3⅛'', early 19th C. **$120.00-$140.00**

Cake board, wreath of leaves, deep carved maple (?), American (?), 4½''D, 19th C. • **''New-Year's Cake.** — Seven pounds of flour, sifted. Half a pound of butter. Half a pound of lard. Two pounds and a half of white Havanna sugar. — Having sifted the flour, spread the sugar on the paste-board, a little at a time, and crush it to powder by rolling it with the rolling-pin. Then mix it with the flour. Cut up in the flour the butter and lard, and mix it well by rubbing it in with your hands. Add by degrees enough of cold water to make a stiff dough. then knead the dough very hard, till it no longer sticks to your hands. Cover it, set it away for an hour or two, and then knead it again in the same manner. You may repeat the kneading several times. Then cut it into pieces, roll out each piece into a sheet half an inch thick. Cut it into large flat cakes with a tin cutter. You may stamp each cake with a wooden print, by way of ornamenting the surface.

''Sprinkle with flour some large flat tin or iron pans, lay the cakes in them, and bake them of a pale brown, in an oven of equal heat throughout. These cakes require more and harder kneading than any others, therefore it is best to have them kneaded by a man, or a very strong woman. They are greatly improved by the addition of some carraway seeds worked into the dough.'' Miss Leslie, of Philadelphia, *Seventy-Five Receipts for Pastry, Cakes, and Sweetmeats*. Appended to *The Cook's Own Book and Housekeeper's Register*. By a Boston Housekeeper. Boston: Munroe & Francis, 1833. For board: **$125.00-$150.00**

Cake boards—See Cake or marzipan board; also Springerle mold.

Cake decorations, candle holders, 10 pieces (probably a full set), stamped tin, each ''petaled'' holder for small birthday candles has thin, long tapered point for sticking in cake, somewhat rusted overall. Very like Christmas tree candle holders, but with spikes not clips, and probably made by same people. American (?), each about 1¼''L overall, TOC. **$15.00-$22.00**

Cake decorations, candle holders, painted iron flowers on spikes, American, late 19th or early 20th C. **$25.00-$35.00**

Cake decorations, set of 4 Beatles figures, plastic, in original package, 1965. **$15.00-$20.00**

Cake decorator set, or frosting tubes, plunger or syringe type, 12 different inserts or nozzle tubes to make frosting come out in stars, rosettes, pointed pixie caps, etc., with instruction book, in original box, ''Ateco,'' mfd by The Thomsen Co., NYC, NY, pat'd 1925, but sold in that form for many years. • A full page 1931 ad, in the *Boston Cooking School* magazine, showed an Ateco set as a premium for getting a new subscriber signed up; it included a three-tube boxed set, called ''Special Set No. 700. — Aluminum syringe with three assorted Standard Brass Ornamenting Tubes ... in its attractive display box. The satin-finished barrel with its highly polished caps and brass tubes produce a fine contrast in metals which harmonize with the color combination of the box.'' The ad also depicted the 99 other tubes you could get, ''any eight as a premium'' or $1.00 a dozen — ''each (tube is) worked out to produce a certain line, scalloped border or rosette, etc., when icing is forced through them.'' • This is still being sold, though in different package. I think the metal may be discernably different too. • Price for 12 tube boxed set. **$15.00-$20.00**

Cake mold, 12 parts, tin, the 12 parts put together form a heart, from F. A. Walker catalog, they mostly imported wares, in the 1870s and 1880s. • Cakes, with each part apparently equal in crumb count, could be made in other multi-part molds: floral crosses (for christenings, Easter and Christmas), a horn of plenty (for Thanksgiving), rounds and diamonds. **$30.00-$40.00**

Cake mold, also called a sponge cake mold, brown glazed earthenware, fluted, spouted, with side handle, American, prob. PA or Shenandoah Valley of VA or WV, 3⅛''H x 9½'' diameter, 19th C. • **Sponge Cake.** — A. H. Rice and John Baer Stoudt, in *The Shenandoah Pottery*, first published in Strasburg, VA, by The Shenandoah Publishing Co. in 1929, and reprinted in Berryville, VA in 1974, call this kind of glazed earthenware spiral fluted spouted mold a ''Spiral sponge cake mould'', in their catalog of Alvin Rice's huge personal collection. • **The meaning of sponge cake** may differ from region to region, and from period to period, because while I can find Pennsylvania German (closely related to Shenandoah Virginian) recipes for sponge cake, they are all to be baked in square or oblong loaf pans. It is angel food cake which calls for the spout. And in one book, something called ''Glory Cake'', which is like angel food cake except that the yolks are used also, separated from the stiffly beaten whites. This cookbook is Ruth Hutchison's *The New Pennsylvania Dutch Cook Book*, NY: Harper & Bros., 1958. It was originally published in 1948. • In William Woys Weaver's scholarly, entertaining *Sauerkraut Yankees*, which is based more directly on historic 19th C German American cookbooks, rather than on housewife cooks in Pennsylvania like the ones Hutchison depended on, there is no Angel Food Cake, but a Sponge Cake very similar to the ''Glory Cake'' in the earlier book. It calls for a square tin pan, with the batter an inch deep. In *Sauerkraut Yankees*, no cake recipes call for a spouted mold. In Weaver's book *America Eats* (1989) there is a picture of an 8¼'' square pan with spout, and envelope ends captioned ''Original angel food cake pan''. (p.140) • Any piece with clear provenance from a known potter, would be worth much more. **$140.00-$180.00**

''Pennsylvania German'' or Pennsylvania Dutch''. — Hutchison writes an interesting explanation of the ''Pennsylvania Dutch'' (or Germans) which I have not read before, but then I've not read that much. ''The first of the Plain Sects to sail for Philadelphia in 1683 (from the Low Countries) were the Mennonites. These were followed by the Amish, Seventh-Day Baptists, Dunkards, Schwenkfelders, and Moravians. Later came the Lutherans and Reformed, so that by the time of the Revolutionary War there were so many Germanic people (emphasis mine) in Pennsylvania it was feared they outnumbered the English. Strictly speaking, there was no Germany in that day, but emigrants from the Low Countries were loosely called Germans, most of them spoke Low German, and the first of their American settlements was called Germantown.'' p. xi.

Cake mold, cast iron, ''Krum Kake,'' Andresen, Minneapolis, MN, 20th C. **$45.00-$55.00**

Cake mold, fluted tubed redware with yellow glaze, marked ''John Bell,'' Waynesboro, PA, 19th C. • The earthenware & stoneware made by John Bell & his brother Samuel Bell is possibly, taken as a whole, the most desirable pottery in the history of America. John's figural pieces, dogs, and especially lions, bring many many thousands of dollars the rare occasions they come to auction. Most Bell pieces are probably safely (alack alas but fortunately) in museum or private collections. • I have termed this tubed, meaning a closed or capped tube, because I have several times seen such redware molds with an old cork stuck in the end of the tube. For some perhaps now arcane reason, apparently it was deemed useful to have both a tubed and a spouted mold for different baking jobs. I suppose a mold set down in water might be corked, so that water wouldn't percolate up the spout and splish splash on the food. Gosh! there's a lot to learn! **$250.00-$350.00**

Cake mold, glazed earthenware, a mottled brown finish, conical spout, large swirled flutes, stamped ''John Bell'', Waynesboro, PA, 4''H x 10'' diameter, c.1860s-70s. **$600.00-$750.00**

Cake mold, heart, cast iron, ''Griswold #2,'' Erie, PA, 3'' deep, 20th C. **$20.00-$30.00**

Cake mold, heart shaped with slightly slanted sides, ring hanger, bright tin, American, 7'' x 7'', c.1920s. **$15.00-$22.00**

Cake mold, hearts, 3 on long oblong tray, tin, Ekco #52, American, 29''L overall, each pan 9''H x 8''W, 20th C. **$45.00-$60.00**

Cake mold, lamb, cast iron enameled green outside, white inside, very unusual, about 9''L, TOC. **$135.00-$200.00**

Cake mold, lamb, couchant (lying down with head up), cast aluminum, along bottom of base reads ''Bakers Coconut'', 20th C. **$65.00-$85.00**

Cake mold, lamb, couchant, cast iron, 2 part, Wagner, 7¾''H x 11¾''L, late 1920s on. **$125.00-$135.00**

Cake mold, lamb, couchant, cast iron, 2 parts, American, 7''H x 13''L x 4''W, late 19th or early 20th C. **$100.00-$130.00**

Cake mold, lamb, couchant, cast iron, large ring ear handles at neck and tail, 2 part, protrusions as steadying 'feet', backside flatter than front, has 3 small holes (for escaping steam?), no mark, 17''L, 19th or early 20th C. **$300.00-$375.00**

Cake mold, may be thought of as some kind of muffin mold, made of heavy tin, oblong shape, 6 ''troughs'' side by side, triangular in section, for making ''Waldorf Triangles'', or ''Golden Rod Cake'', or ''Orange Slice Cake'' and many other fancy cakes, not marked, about 9''L, .c1920s. **$15.00-$22.00**

Cake mold, rabbit, cast iron, Griswold #862, Erie, PA, c.1920s on. **$75.00-$225.00**

Cake mold, rabbit, sitting (horizontal) 2 piece redware mold, American, mid 19th C. **$250.00-$350.00**

Cake mold, rabbit, vertical sitting, heavy cast aluminum, 10''H, 20th C. **$40.00-$55.00**

Cake mold, Santa Claus, cast iron, marked ''Hello Kiddies'' on base at Santa's foot, mfd by Griswold, Erie, PA, 12''H, mid 20th C. • Best thing about this one, to my mind, is the original instruction to bake him on his face for 25 minutes, then on his back, as if he were at the beach. I think the asking price range is ridiculously high. **$225.00-$275.00**

Cake mold, Santa Claus from waist up, climbing out of brick chimney, heavy stamped aluminum, 2 piece, about 9''H, c.1960. **$4.00-$7.00**

Cake mold, Santa Claus head with floppy liberty cap on Santa, tin, slightly slanted sides, 6"H Santa head within 9" diameter pan, 20th C. • I never thought about it before, but the Santa Claus we know and feed cookies to often wears a cap very like Phrygian liberty cap, and because the jolly fellow's appearance is derived from a combination of Thomas Nast late 19th C cartoons, and the Coca-Cola Santa in ads, and therefore American, it is possible that his cap may have been deliberately designed by Nast as a patriotic symbol. Harrumph. Of course, it could be that the typical cap worn by skaters and skiers, were the inspiration for Claus's headgear. **$45.00-$55.00**

Cake mold, "Savarin" mold, after famed chef Brillat-Savarin, for cakes at first, then for other dishes too, ring-shaped, tin, large center opening, rounded "bottom" (which becomes cake's top), no mark, European or American, 9" diameter, late 19th or early 20th C.
$20.00-$25.00

Cake mold, tin, fluted, tubed with closed end, American, 7"D, early 20th, late 19th C. • Lots of cake and pudding molds turn out cakes or puddings with open centers. The tube or spout in the center of the mold allowed the heat (dry, steam or hot water) to cook the contents more evenly. •If the opening has one closed or capped end it's **tubed,** if it's open it's **spouted.** You can remember this (maybe better than I can), by the mnemonic device of alliteration: Tubed is Topped. **$25.00-$35.00**

Cake mold, tin, round with low sides, top stamped with very swirly design, sometimes called a "trois freres" mold after 3 French pastry chefs, French, 2" deep x 7½" diameter, late 19th C. **$20.00-$35.00**

Cake mold, Turk's head tubed mold, redware, American, 7¾" diameter, 19th C. **$140.00-$160.00**

Cake mold, Turk's head with spout, creamware, American, 9" diameter, 19th C. **$70.00-$90.00**

Cake or gelatin molds, graphic detail of body parts, stamped copper, for "adult cake", chocolate, ice cream cakes, ice sculpture, & "punch bowl frozen centerpiece" (guaranteed to thaw out party?), "Eroti® ", mfd by Delectable Fantasies, Inc., Ft. Lauderdale, FL, 12½"L x 2½"W; 10⅛"L; 11"H; 10" x 7½", 1983. **$6.00-$12.00**

Cake or marzipan board, carved mahogany (according to dealer, although some other similar boards are American black walnut), large oblong plank with elliptical carving filling most of width & length, central round medallion with horse and rider, flanked by 2 vertical ellipses with flowers, rest of space filled in with leaves & fruits of the vine, very Eastern European-looking, Slavik or Czech, but possibly carved by J. Conger. Marked "J. Y. Watkins", NYC, NY, 25½"L x 13½"W. **$750.00-$900.00**

Watkins was in business as a tinsmith in NYC, and listed in city directories beginning in 1830. His son, James Y. Jr., joined the firm in 1852 (or at least "& Son" was added to the firm's name in the 1852-53 *Rode's Directory*) James Y. Watkins & Son, Inc., were listed variously as house furnishings or tinware dealers, who by 1866 was listed as dealing in "house furnishings and bakers' utensils" (what at least one person has interpreted as being baking, candy & ice cream trade supplies).According to one note I've seen recently, they also made ice cream molds; but maybe most of them were imports? • The board in this entry is carved with early traditional motifs, and in an early style, but could have been made in mid

century, either by John Conger, or by an American or European imitator of his work, whose carvings were also handled by Watkins. • **New York State Cake or Marzipan Molds.** — This closely resembles the J. Conger cookie or so-called marzipan boards, all of which I have seen only in pictures. They all look very European. This one was advertised in *Main Antique Digest*, February 1989, by Byron & Craig White, of Sterling, PA. The Whites cite Bishop's *American Folk Sculpture*, and Lipman's *American Folk Art in Wood, Metal, and Stone* for mentions of Conger, but mentions are all they are — no real information on him.

The most recent work on Conger was done by Louise C. Belden, a research associate at the Henry Francis du Pont Winterthur Museum, Winterthur, DE. Her article, "Cake Boards," in *The Magazine ANTIQUES*, December 1990, depicts many Conger boards and related cake boards. Earlier, food historian William Woys Weaver wrote an article in *The Clarion*, the magazine of the Museum of American Folk Art, in New York City. It is "The New Year's Cake Print. A distinctively American Art Form," (Fall 1989). He also researched Conger for an exhibition, and an accompanying cookbook and history, entitled *America Eats. Forms of Edible Folk Art.* (Harper & Row, 1989). Weaver wrote that Conger used "stock motifs" (which would include cornucopias, low baskets or urns of flowers or produce, Indians, Revolutionary War soldiers, garlands of flowers or fruit, militia men on horseback, ladies and gentlemen in faux rusticant garb (a la Marie Antoinette playing dairymaid), eagles, roses, thistles, Scottish folk, and other romantic, even then old-fashioned, designs.

In constructing the following 'dramatization' of Conger's New York City in the late 1820s and 1830s, one of the most readable, useful and absorbing books that I consulted was Sean Wilentz' *Chants Democratic. New York City & the Rise of the Ameircan Working Class, 1788-1850.* It was published by Oxford Universtiy Press, 1984, and in paperback, with corrections, in 1986. Wilentz' book provided some of the wage figures relating to carteers, and the characterization of many Reverends of the period.

Pictures of some Conger cake boards begin on page 209.

CATCHING JOHN CONGER

I hated for this book to go to press without finding out more about carver John Conger (probably pronounced kon'-ger, with a hard "g", like the eel), who had been so elusive, and about whom I could find nothing in standard books on folk art carvers. Most dealers advertising a signed Conger cake board, or an attributed board, said "New York State." An occasional rebel would say "Probably Pennsylvania." For all the information I was able to get, I can thank my computer (with its cross-referencing capabilities), and the wonderful microfiche collection of New York City directories at the New York Public Library, long a favorite and fruitful haunt of mine.

The first lead came in an ad for a mold which was marked both "J. Conger" and "James Y. Watkins, NYC". At least this placed Conger in New York. After a few useless references to Conger in a couple of books on folk art sculpture, I found my second lead in *Folk Artists Biographical Index*, edited by George H. Meyer. He cited a mention of Conger in Pauline A. Pinckney's *American Figureheads and Their Carvers* (NYC: W. W. Norton, 1940), and one in Kenneth L. Ames' excellent *Beyond Necessity. Art in the Folk Tradition*. (Exhibition catalog, pub. by Winterthur Museum, Winterthur, DE, distributed by W. W. Norton, 1977). Pinckney's book, on a subject I had already superficially researched in hopes of finding Conger, has a lengthy list of shipcarvers and *possible* shipcarvers, a list on which John Conger appears with a "flourished" date of 1830. The directories I later consulted all included both "carvers" and "shipcarvers" and from that I concluded that Conger did not describe himself as a shipcarver, and probably was not one. On the other hand, *Beyond Necessity* confirmed the lead to Watkins given by an advertiser some years ago of an attributed Conger board, that was marked only with Watkins' name.

Catalog item 143 in the Winterthur exhibition, was a cake board stamped "J. Conger", as well as "J. Y. Watkins, N.Y." It is in the Winterthur collection, acquisition #55.48.60, but I don't know if I will be able to get it for reprint here. Watkins is described as a "tinsmith and owner of a kitchen furnishing warehouse", and Conger as a "carver and baker".

Thanksgiving week, 1989, I spent mostly in the lofty embrace of reading room 315 North in the New York Public Library, a room whose virtues I have extolled in previous books. I huddled over a microfiche machine, peering at a bright screen, to skim-read hundreds of thousands of names in NYC directories from 1815-16 through 1873-74. This collection of directories, which could be the primary source book behind a hundred books on the social history of NYC, on early trades, on the plight of widow women in the 19th C, and a host of other subjects, includes the first that was published, in 1799.

I not only tracked Conger, but also James Y. Watkins. William Woys Weaver, in two publications cited above, was apparently a year ahead of me into Conger and Watkins, and confectionery in America. I read in *America Eats* that Conger was not only a carver, but also baker (making his own New Year's cakes in his own molds), and that the Watkins firm "remained in business into this century" *op cit*, p. 116, and until "at least 1900" was responsible for the continued manufacture of Conger designs." *loc cit*. Weaver also states that Conger worked in Philadelphia "for a time as a furniture carver." *op cit*, p.115.

Below, with a few side trips, is a skeletal chronology of John Conger, based solely on the city and business directories available through a microfiche collection, and not on any census records, jury lists, or other valuable, supplementary sources also on microfiche and available at NYPL. This microfiche collection is also at the Library of Congress, and a number of large metropolitan libraries throughout the country. If you've got about $5000.00 you can buy a set of these directory microfiches yourself.

The name John Conger appeared first in the 1818-19 *Longworth's Directory*, but he was an edge tool manufacturer, who stayed in the directory for the next 32 years, and was then replaced by his son or son-in-law, who was called either John Conger Berry or John Congerberry. In the 1819-20 book, a John Conger, carpenter at 5 Provost Street, appeared, but he disappeared the next year. Using the directories only, it is impossible to determine if perhaps these two wood-related artisans were related — to each other, and/or to our Conger. After one appearance, the carpenter's place was "taken" by the long-lived John S. Conger, physician, who stayed in the directory for many decades. The edge tool maker and the doctor appeared year after year as the only John Congers until suddenly, in Longworth's 1827-28 book, we find him; our man:

John Conger, carver, 121 Hester (a street in the poorest part of the lower eastern part of NYC, a city then of about 175,000 people). Conger lived — probably as a boarder, or at least a space-sharer — at the corner of Forsythe and Hester, according to what was termed a "Runners' Vade Mecum", an address finder or guide which appeared every year in the directories. This guide was to help people locate addresses on streets which were not that infrequently renumbered, or even renamed, as the city grew and the centers of population expanded northward. (James Y. Watkins, tinsmith, was not to appear at 16 Catharine Street, not far from Hester, for another four years.)

Having become somewhat obsessed with the directories, and the glimpse of life in the city where I have lived for a quarter of a century myself, and knowing Hester Street just a little from the 1975 movie "Hester Street", set at the turn of the century, I made my first side trip: a short list of other occupants of the street, within a block or so of Conger. Next door at 123 Hester, for example, lived the Reverend John W. Gibbs, a man who may or may not have had a congregation in a church. His calling was not common at that time and in that area of New York, where self-styled preachers, and irreligious laborers were much more easily found. Across the street at 120 lived Jacob Bolmore—no occupation given in the 1827-28 directory. (In the next year's directory, Benedict Bolmore, printer, was listed at 120, with Jacob as a clerk at the same address. Also next year, although John Conger had moved on to 1 Hamersley, and carried on his business on Sullivan Street, J.D.P. Champlin & Co., business unknown, stayed on at 121 Hester, where, under some arrangement, they had shared a roof with Conger.)

It is tempting to docu-dramatize the city-life of the time, but there is no evidence, beyond the baldest, on which to base speculations. Drama requires a protagonist (here we have Conger), and people, places, things, or social forces against which there is some kind of struggle. If a movie were made of his life, we'd have to know if he were married, who his clients were, his friends, exactly what characterized his struggle (we assume now) to leave Hester Street. We don't know if the man ever had more than a few minutes a day to leave his work, or if he frequented one or more of the numerous porter houses or taverns, or if it took him four grueling days or a week to finish a cake board, or what else he might have spent most of his time carving. But just to indicate who his "neighbors" were, we will imagine that Conger might have stepped out the doorway of 121 to turn right a few doors to see John G. Hughes, a carpenter at 113, about some mahogany or walnut wood scraps. If he went on a few more doors, maybe he encountered the whitesmith, Peter C. Cortelyou; at 110; he may have bought an apple from John Lyon, the grocer at 93; or stopped to talk to Clarissa Adams, the widow who ran a boarding house at 87, about a room; or perhaps he needed to ask David Coit, shoemaker, at 73 Hester, about fixing the only boots he had. If he turned left when he left his abode (which was also his workplace that first year in the directory, and which may have housed several home-work artisans, or other workers), maybe he saw Thomas Gedney, the combmaker who lived and worked at 132. (Next year, the clock-manufacturer and brass founder Engell Friend also lived at 132.) Margaret Wilcox, a carpet weaver at 140, possibly working in the cellar, trying to make the $2.00 or $3.00 a week she needed for the most frugal living, and because she was not listed as a widow, it is likely she was pretty much on her own.

Did John Conger, in fact, know any of these people the year he lived on Hester? He carved fancy cakeboards with formal, traditional European images of militia men and bounteous flowers; but did he do them this early? Where would he have gotten his inspiration? Did he, in fact, come to NYC from Pennsylvania, where a European folk tradition was beginning to flourish, and where many carvings and graphics comprised similar motifs? The prosaic, not to say squalid, images surrounding him in everyday life seem not to have influenced his work at all, except perhaps to make him work harder to get out. Not that there were many "good" neighbors at the time in NYC; only wealthy merchants and bankers lived somewhat within their own enclaves, down around Wall Street, where there were fancy retail shops as well as financial institutions having to do with banking and insurance.

In the area way below what is now called the "Lower East Side", where Conger lived throughout his time in the city, also lived most of the day laborers, jobless, and desperately poor people of New York. Pigs wandered the streets, actually performing a sort of service by eating garbage, but creating a nuisance of more than one kind on the pavement. Hundreds of cartmen clogged the streets, pushing wooden wheelbarrows or hand barrows, or pulling hand carts, laden with whatever had to be transferred, hoping to pick up a job that would bring them from 12½ᶜ to 25ᶜ a half mile. The noise—from the squealing of pigs, the crying of children, the shouts of people selling services or food, the clang and crash of hammers beating on everything from gold (to make *foil*), steel (to make tools), brass (to make vessels or trims or decorations), leather and nails or pegs (to make shoes), iron nails and wooden boards (to make houses, coffins, more carts, barrels, ships), or chisels (to make carvings), and the clatter of horseshoes on cobblestones or the rattle of looms—must have been close to deafening.

By the next year, 1828, probably on May 1 (traditional moving day in NYC for 100 years or more, because *all* annual leases, as well as the quarter spring leases, were up that day) Conger had moved and was doing well enough, we suppose, to have a workplace separate from his home.

There was a lot of competition in the carving trade. Although the directories do not make much differentiation between the types of carvers, a computer study of addresses of all carvers, as well as the carver-gilders, along with the addresses of cabinet makers, chair makers, and furniture makers, would probably tie together some of the unknown craftsmen. Men with the dual trade of carving and gilding often worked on picture or looking-glass frames; a very few probably carved trade-signs (some of which may have been freestanding figures). In the 1827-28 *Longworth's Directory*, simple <u>carvers</u> were apparently slightly in the majority; <u>shipcarvers</u> were the rarest of all the carvers. One interesting entry I found was William Alcock, <u>calico-print cutter</u>, 8 Watts. Later I was glad to have found him and his job description, when after three years out of the directory (see below), John Conger (I believe the same one as our man) reappears as a <u>printcutter</u>. Cake boards, for printing New-Year's Cakes, were widely known as <u>cake prints</u>. The job description "printcutter" may have referred specifically to cake prints, or it may mean that John Conger made carved wooden printing blocks either for a cloth-printer or a publisher — of books, broadsides, or perhaps even wallpaper.

The main publishers of the directories I used were Thomas Longworth (*Longworth's Annual Almanac. New-York Register & City Directory*); John Doggett, later John Doggett, Jr., later Doggett & Rode, later Rode alone (*Doggett's The New York Directory* or *Doggett's New York Business Directory*; later *Rode's Directory of New York City*); and John F. Trow, compiler H. Wilson (*Wilson's Business Directory of New York City, later Trow's New York City Directory*).

All addresses are streets except where noted. An occasional "skipped" date indicates a break in the city directories, not absence of listing.

DATE	NAME	OCCUPATION	WORK	—ADDRESSES—	HOME
1827-1828	John Conger	carver	121 Hester		121 Hester
1828-1829	John Conger	carver	65 Sullivan		1 Hamersley
1829-1830	John Conger	carver	15 Stanton		29 Stanton
1830-1831	John Conger	carver	15 Stanton		23 Stanton
1831-1832	John Conger	carver	222 Greene		222 Greene
1832-1833	John Conger	carver	242 Greene		117 Fourth Ave.
1833-1834	not listed	-0-	-0-		-0-
1834-1835	not listed	-0-	-0-		-0-

For 1834-1835 only, a John Conger, baker, appears .

DATE	NAME	OCCUPATION	WORK		HOME
1835-1836	not listed	-0-	-0-		-0-
1836-1837	John Conger	printcutter	211 Orange		211 Orange
1837-1838	John Conger	printcutter	211 Orange		211 Orange
1838-1839	John Conger	printcutter	211 Orange		211 Orange
1839-1840	not listed	-0-	-0-		-0-
1840-1841	John Conger	printcutter	25 Marion		25 Marion
1841-1842	John Conger	printcutter	25 Marion		25 Marion
1842-1843	John Conger	printcutter	25 Marion		25 Marion
1843-1844	John Conger	printcutter	23 Marion		23 Marion
1844-1845	John Conger	printcutter	23 Marion		23 Marion
1845-1846	John Conger	printcutter	23 Marion		23 Marion
1846-1847	John Conger	printcutter	23 Marion		23 Marion
1847-1848	John Conger	printcutter	23 Marion		23 Marion
1848-1849	John Conger	printcutter	foot of Bank St.		foot of Bank
1850-1851	John Conger	printcutter	Bank		Bank
1851-1852	John Conger	printcutter	Bank		Bank
1852-1853	not listed	-0-	-0-		-0-
1854-1855	John Conger	printcutter	181 Bank		101 Bank
ditto	a John Conger	carver	138 Bank		101 Bank

At this point, 1854-55, the new (or renewed) listing John Conger carver suddenly appears with John Conger printcutter, both listings with same home address, but different work addresses. The only way to find out more information would be to turn to Census records or other more detailed records that are probably available in New York or Washington D.C. on microfilm or fiche. Because this is the only year when two listings with the same name and related occupants are given, it is quite possible that the names are evidence of an error in information - gathering by the compiler of the directory (Trow's at this point), or that one is father, one son, and that one or the other (probably the printcutter, who I assume was the elder) died that year. The listing resumes in 1856-57:

DATE	NAME	OCCUPATION	WORK		HOME
1856-57	John Conger	cutter	138 Bank		101 Bank
1857-58	John Conger	cutter	138 Bank		101 Bank
1858-59	John Conger	cutter	138 Bank		101 Bank
1859-60	John Conger	carver	138 Bank		-?-
1860-61	John Conger	carver	138 Bank		131 Bank
1861-62	John Conger	cutter	138 Bank		131 Bank
1862-63	John Conger	carver	525 Hudson		131 Bank
1863-64	John Conger	carver	525 Hudson		131 Bank
1864-65	John Conger	carver	-?-		131 Bank
1865-66	John Conger	carver	525 Hudson		131 Bank

In 1865, for one year only, a firm appears called Conger, Smith & Heath, Tin Ware & House Furnishing Goods, at 580 Hudson as well as 400, 402, and 404 W. 15th St. The Conger in questions is Walter M. Conger, of unknown relationship to John. Conger's carvings have been tied, by marks, to the house furnishing establishment of James Y. Watkins (by 1865, James Y. Watkins & Son), who, after years of having at least two business establishments, including the one at 16 Catharine Street where James Y. Watkins started his NYC business life as a tinsmith in 1830, is back to only one address — the place on Catharine.

DATE	NAME	OCCUPATION	WORK		HOME
1866-67	John Conger	carver	214 W. Houston		

In the 1866 edition, Walter Conger shows up as a maker of trays.

DATE	NAME	OCCUPATION	WORK		HOME
1868-69	John Conger	carver	at the rear of 94 Charlton		
1870-71	not listed	-0-	-0-		

Because John Conger was not listed in the next three directories, I assumed, although lacked the time to check another five years or more of listings, that he was now gone for good. (Whichever Conger he was.) It was a rather strange moment when I found him missing for four years. I had avidly followed his progress (and apparent decline), making somewhat romantic assumptions about the rise and fall in fortune as his skill — his artistry — fell out of favor, so that his last address was in the rear of a building not far from where he began 41 years earlier. Conger's disappearance from the directories was accompanied by a sense of real personal loss for me. James Y. Watkins and his son, who had been joined, for one year only, by another son, were still working out of 16 Catharine, but the elder was living at 450 Lexington, which was up between 44th and 45th Streets, and his son was making the daily commute down to Catharine from the increasingly fashionable if rather bucolic West 128th Street near Fifth Avenue.

There really is nothing like these directories to give you a sort of Wellesian time trip. What is ironic, as it often is when you consider the income of the artisan, and the market value 50 or 100 or 200 years later, is that the current market price of one really outstanding board carved by Conger could be more than his total life income. It is also possible that the date chart given here will cause a re-evaluation and a certain amount of back-pedaling on prices. NOTE: If it is correct, as William Ways Weaver writes, that Watkins bought Conger's old stock, and continued to sell either Conger or Conger-like prints until 1900, then surely the market value will drop somewhat.

Cake or marzipan board, carved mahogany board, elliptical overall carving barely fits within oblong bounds, no separate medallions, gracefully draped Columbia figure, surrounded by laurel (olive?) wreath, holds striped shield with legend "America" at top; spread winged eagle holds arrows in foot, & scales of justice (left pan has trade symbols & barrels, right has plow, rake, pitchfork) in beak over backs of 2 horses; other figure is American Indian in plumed headdress and cape, holding staff with Old Glory flag with 16 stars, topped by the Phrygian cap or liberty cap (originated in French Revolution), further decorated with cornucopia full of fruit, many flowers, grapes, 10 large stars, sunflower, acorns, wheel, wheat, etc. An extraordinary carving. Not signed, but as fine as the "J. Conger" boards, American, 27¼"L x 15½"W, c.1800. • Although there was **never a flag with 16 stars,** the 16th state was Tennessee from 1786 to 1803. • This was sold by John Zan, Washington, NJ, in 1979, and again at auction, by Sotheby's, June 23, 1988. A good photograph appears in the catalog (Lot 307). Price range given is not Zan's or Sotheby's; it reflects the value of American patriotic motifs to collectors. **$7000.00-$9000.00**

Cake or marzipan board, carved rectangular piece of wood, elliptical carving with round center medallion with horseman, flanked by vertical ellipses with figural carvings within, marked "Old Rough and Ready", American, 18"H x 24"L, c.1815-? • The name "Old Rough and Ready" refers to Zachary Taylor, who fought in the War of 1812, and who was president in 1849-50. • NOTE: In *The Magazine ANTIQUES,* Aug. 1953, appeared a picture of a carved mahogany board, slightly rectangular, large round medallion nearly filling surface, with frontal standing figure of man with deer behind him, a memorial of Andrew Jackson, inscribed "New Orleans Jany 8", the 1815 battle, in the War of 1812, won by Jackson. This pastry mold was from the collection of Mrs. Edward R. Ferriss, St. Charles, IL, formerly in the collection of George Horace Lorimer. I don't know where it is now. • "Rough & Ready" was offered for sale in 1985, by unnamed seller, who was asking $2500.00 or best offer. **$3500.00-$4500.00**

Cake or marzipan board, carved walnut, nearly square board with round carving with central figures of man & woman in round-brimmed hats, flowers & reeded border around outside, fully carved, dealer says "attributed to John Conger", NYC, NY, size not given, date estimated as "c.1810", which is probably at least 15 years too early and possibly as many as 40 or more years too early. • In Nov. 1989, Axtells advertised a "signed carved J. Con-

ger's two-handled roller with intricately carved roses and leaves." It is a springerle roller, with carved drum (or barrel) apparently under 3"L, with turned handles about 3¾"L. It also is the only example of this form, signed by Conger, that I have record of. The other appears on page 110 of *America Eats* by William Woys Weaver. That one belongs to the Henry Frances du Pont Winterthur Museum, and the design is also of roses and leaves, with a decorative edging motif on both ends of the barrel comprised of a sort of lacy border on either side of a narrow band of dots. That one is 12⅜"L overall, 3" diameter. • Dealer Peter Axtell, Pound Ridge, NY, advertised the square board in 1986, no price given. Price range mine. **$3200.00-$3500.00**

Cake or marzipan board, carved walnut, square with chamfered & truncated corners (probably to make room for a finger to lift), round carving. Design of 5 point star in center (unusual because only 5 points), flanked by cornucopia with flowers & fruit. Above is small shield flanked by busts of 2 Revolutionary War-period military men, one has "H" next to him, other has (backwards) "P". This may be a centennial or 50-year commemorative for the Battle of Bunker Hill of June 5, 1775, and the "P" may be Colonel William Prescott, said to have commanded "Don't shoot until you see the whites of their eyes", and the "H" may be the British commander, Major General William Howe. Also in the design is a sort of barge-like ship with a flag (possibly lying off in Boston harbor). A lacy finely-scalloped border surrounds a cartouche reading "M. Hall" below the ship. It does not seem possible that this could be the name of the baker Michael Hall, who appeared at least as early as 1820 and as late as 1827-28 in NY directories, not because a baker's name would not appear but because it is so prominently featured. Board is American, probably NY, 12" x 12", c.1820s-30s. This politico-military cake board was in the Schorsch collection sale at Sotheby's, May 1-2, 1981. Price range mine: **$2000.00-$3500.00**

Cake or marzipan board, carved walnut (?), square with round medallion depicting a boy & girl and tulips, not the sort of subject expected from the carver to which the board was attributed by the dealer. The ad says "N. Y. State carved Conger's Cookie Board", but probably not signed since not mentioned in ad, NYC, NY, 11½"H x 11"W, the medallion about 7" diameter, 1st half 19th C. • **Marzipan For Christmas — Springerle For Easter.** — Jean Lipman, in *American Folk Art in Wood, Metal & Stone* (NY: Pantheon, 1948), wrote briefly about "carved marzipan and springerle cake molds (that) made it possible for thin Christmas and Easter cakes to be stamped in low-relief designs. The hard-wood springerle boards were carved in intaglio, most often in composite groups of two to twelve patterns enclosed in separate squares, to mark the cutting lines for small individual cakes; while the marzipan boards were often designed for a single large cake. ... The finished cakes could be kept for months and, though they were so hard that it has been said it was as easy to eat the board as the cake, they were evidently a popular delicacy." (p.144). According to William Woys Weaver, the marzipan molds were for New Year's, a tradition borrowed from Germany, and were used to make a so-called "water marzipan" which was a cheap non-almond version of the real thing (p. 116, *America Eats*). • This one advertised by Axtell Antiques, The Rookery, Deposit, NY, July 1989 in *Antique Review*. Price range my estimate, not Axtell's asking price.

$3200.00-$3700.00

Cake or marzipan board, carved wood, oblong with rounded corners, horseman with lance & plumed helmet, banner behind him reads "New York Lancers", flanked by cornucopias and floral sprays, piecrust border, of the "Conger" type, American, in style early 19th C, but could be mid 19th C. • **Marzipan, Marchpane or Matzabaum**. — The words are, respectively, German, English and Pennsylvania German. Marzipan is sort of a cross between a cookie and a candy, and always has two main ingredients: confectioner's (or finely pounded) sugar and almond paste, made from ground (or pounded in a mortar) blanched almonds. I think you can buy it already ground into a paste. A typical recipe would call for one pound of confectioner's sugar, one pound ground almonds, one teaspoon almond extract, and a little rosewater (which I assume you can buy in some specialty shop, rather than distilling it in an alembic yourself) to make the sugar and almonds into a paste which can be molded. Probably a little plain water would be just as good; I've never tried making marzipan. Traditionally the paste has been treated two ways: either colored and then molded by the fingers into little animals, fruits, flower forms, various shapes, and browned slightly in the oven; or impressed with springerle or marzipan molds, after being flattened with the palm of the hand and lightly floured. These are also browned in the oven. Leaving them in a little bit longer results in a really wonderful toasted marchpane. • This mold was auctioned in 1985 by Litchfield Auction Gallery in CT. • Price range is not realized but estimated range, from catalog.

$2800.00-$3500.00

Cake or marzipan board, carved wood, rectangular, with elliptical carving, nice but simple, depicting a large St. Bernard dog being ridden by small bonneted child carrying whip stick, the prognathious dog panting, and with tail awkwardly curved upwards, a single tulip growing up from teardrop chip carved border, nearly to dog's belly; figures surrounded by stems with many leaves & with 15 stars, somewhat haphazardly placed, the whole resembling Conger's work only in that there is a carved ellipse, but nevertheless "attributed" to Conger; his name does help sell cake boards. William Woys Weaver says the Conger "touchmark" — a stamped intaglio mark, "is now being counterfeited." NYC, NY if Conger, but there's a Germanic (Pennsylvania German?) look to it. I sometimes wonder if Conger didn't use popular prints and graphics

for design motifs — possibly from old books? 6¼''H x 11¾''L, 19th C. • Pictured in *Maine Antique Digest*, Feb. 1982. Price range is my estimate, not Spring Valley Antique's asking or selling price. It would be higher if signed.

$2200.00-$3500.00

Cake or marzipan board, carved wood, with one side depicting large man with beard & hat riding on a highstepping horse, other side depicts a rooster and a soldier on horseback (a very common archetypal image, found also in American pieces), edge marked "I. W.,''prob. European, 13½''H x 10¾'', 19th C.

$235.00-$250.00

Cake or marzipan board, rectangular walnut board with elliptical carving composed of 3 parts. In a round medallion in center is a basket of fruit, background heavily carved with flowers, flanking this are 2 vertical elliptical cartouches, within one is man with shepherd's crook & hat, other has woman with sheaf of wheat, signed "J. Conger" in two places, for John Conger, NYC, NY. 25½''L x 15½''W, 1st quarter19th C to 1860. • This was auctioned by the Hesse Galleries, Otego, NY, in Sept. 1986. Since that time, a few other similarly-carved boards have come up, and are described in ads as "attributed to J. Conger".

$3400.00-$3900.00

Cake or marzipan board, round carving centered on rectangular walnut board, neat sawtooth edge frames low basket, ribbed flared sides, a lively flower arrangement of roses, tulip, leaves, composition filled in with leaves under the basket, signed "J. Conger", catalog writer speculates "possibly PA", but provenance is actually NYC, NY, 15¼''L x 9½''W, diameter of circle is about 6¾'', 19th C. • Sold at the Richard A. Bourne Co. (Hyannis, MA) auction of the Cushman Estate of Duxbury, MA, November 25-26, 1988. Price realized:

$1500.00

Cake or marzipan board, round shape, for marzipan or springerle type cookies that take molding well, deeply carved mason's tools, a square, hammer, mallet, pointing tool, compass, bead design around border, possibly a Masonic piece, carved with initials "I. D." which are probably not the maker's initials; if they are, "I" could be old style "J", American, ⅞'' thick wood, 5½'' diameter, 19th C. • The dealer said this was for "butter cookies" but in my experience, butter cookies spread so much during baking that any form or molded design would be lost. All cookies have some shortening in them.

$1200.00-$1400.00

Cake or marzipan board, square pine (?) board with round carving, beaded edge, features eagle standing on shield with 4 flags, grapes and leaves in woven border, decorated in background with 45 stars, signed "J. Conger", NYC, NY, 13''H x 12''W, 19th C. • A carved "mahogany" cake board, very like the work of "Conger", is in Figure 159, Jean Lipman's *American Folk Art in Wood, Metal & Stone*, 1948. In the collection of the NewYork Historical Society, NYC, it is oblong, 14⅜''L x ⅞'' thick, with an elliptical cartouche with wheat ear border, with a depiction of a fire engine being pulled by three long coated firemen, with boots & hats, the first one blowing a horn. The engine has "17" on cistern & boiler. I thought that research into early 19th C fire companies might reveal a specific engine & engine company. I proposed to investigate 3 lines of enquiry: identification of the (1) style of engine; (2) style of firemen's coat; and (3) style of firemen's hat, all very detailed and distinctive. • But after contacting several historical societies and fire engine museums, the only conclusive information is that it is a "goose neck" and side stroke engine, with an air chamber in the back, the main body being a water cistern. It is of a type dating probably to the 1820s, possibly the 1830s. In addition, in a cartouche above the engine is the word "SUPERIOR". • Charles Radzinsky, the former curator of the American Museum of Fire fighting, in Middletown, NY, wrote me that " 'SUPERIOR' could be a pet or nickname given to the company and/or engine, such as 'Water Witch', 'Good Intent', 'Excelsior', etc. The rather high number, 17, would indicate that the company was an urban rather than a rural community." I conclude from the best book on fire fighting equipment, *Enjine! Enjine! A Story of Fire Protection*, by Kenneth Holcomb Dunshee (NYC: Home Insurance Co., 1939), that the pieced hats with brim worn by the 3 firemen carved on the board are of the four comb type, c.1812 to 1830. Finally, the long skirted, belted coats appear to be from the 1820s. Below the corrugated road the engine is being pulled over is a long fire ladder; in the sky surrounding the engine are six 9 point blazing stars. I conclude that the board is c.1820 to 1830. The provenance given in Lipman (& probably the *Index of American Design*, from which the picture was taken [?]), is "Pennsylvania"; boards marked or attributed to Conger are from New York State, and I believe this may be a Conger. Value is difficult to assign to the fire engine board; the subject matter is highly collectible, with many thousands of dollars customarily paid for early chief's horns, ceremonial helmets, decorated fire buckets, etc., so I would estimate the engine board to be at least twice the main board in this listing. • The eagle star board in the heading of this price listing was advertised by NYC dealers Herrup & Wolfner in 1985. Price range for it is mine not dealers': **$3200.00-$4000.00**

Cake or marzipan boards, carved bass wood with hanging hole in back that doesn't show on front, offered in at least 6 designs, viz. large round with wheat sheaf, heart with tulip and daisies on large square board, pineapple and laurel wreath on small round, seated cat on small oblong, woman & man in "native" (European) costumes, woman has basket, man has sword, each on oblong boards, these were made "using authentic European cookie molds and incorporating Pennsylvania Dutch designs", but they are rather hokey, especially the man & woman who are called "George and Martha" in the catalog I saw. They are carved by Don Dillon, and possibly signed on back by him, Camp Hill, PA, 12" diameter; 6½"H x 6"W; 8" diameter; 6"H x 4"W; and the two figures are 10½"H x 3¼"W, c.1983-1984. • New retail prices were between $12.00 for cat, $38.00 for wheat sheaf. You know from the retail price, making the wholesale half that, that these were created on a machine, not hand carved. Value now might be same as 1984 retail, or less. They won't appreciate in real value for a very long time, although there's no estimating sentimental value. **$12.00-$38.00**

Cake pan, angel food cake, octagonal blue & white swirled enamelware, with spout, no mark, American or European, TOC. **$75.00-$120.00**

Cake pan, angel food cake, pale aqua & white enamelware, spouted, American (?), 9" diameter, early 20th C. **$25.00-$40.00**

Cake pan, angel food cake, with sliding door in side for loosening cake, tin, spouted, advertising "Swan's Down

Cake Flour," American, small, only 6½"D, c.1920s. • **Slots & Slides**. — This pan, like the Van Deusen, has a slide in the side. The VD has two, and the slide ends extend way up above rim, whereas the SD has but one, the slot is bigger, and it does not extend up beyond the rim. The SD slot and slide looks rather like little slot on front of file cabinet drawers where you slide in a card with name of what's in the file. **$15.00-$18.00**

Cake pan, angel food or regular layer cake, stamped tin, 4 parts to make either spouted or plain, mfd. by Perfection, c.9" diameter, late 19th C. **$15.00-$20.00**

Cake pan, gray graniteware, with cast iron handles, 13" x 9", 19th C. **$35.00-$45.00**

Cake pan, octagonal with tube, factory blackened tin, American, 13" diameter, 19th C or early 20th. • Collectors sometimes ask if it's safe to use such pans for baking, even if they have a bit of rust. It's safe to the user, not quite as safe for the pan, but only if you don't carefully wash and dry thoroughly after use. The solder used in such late pieced pieces is not dangerous, and rust only adds a bit of extra minerals to your cake. If you use such pieced tin pans — cake pans or muffin pans, etc. — don't scour vigorously with steel wool or a brass pot brush. Try to use a stiff fiber brush and very very hot soapy water. Hot water won't melt the solder. My rule is: If I buy an old pan with some rust and the baked-on crud that happens when fat and flour and sugar are baked, especially over a gas flame, and if I keep this pan a month before using, not only the pan but the crud too becomes mine, and harmless. It's all a matter of rationalization. **$20.00-$30.00**

Cake pan, pieced & hammered tin, side wall has very graceful flare with 10 generous scallops & folded rim, slightly conical seamed spout soldered to bottom. This is unusual because it was made in only 2 pieces instead of 3. Starting with a large round tin "doughnut" with a hole only 1⅞" diameter in center, it was hammered or beaten up into pan with flat bottom & scalloped sides. Usually there is a seam or two on the side, as well as a seam around the bottom where the sides were joined, then a separate spout soldered on too. American, poss. VA, 3½" deep x 10¼" diameter at top, 7¾" at bottom, 1870s, poss. earlier. **$45.00-$55.00**

Cake pan, pieced tin, 6 point star, spouted, hexagonal flat bottom with very angular points, rolled rim, for individual littel cakes, Jaburg Brothers, NYC, NY, about 1⅞" deep x about 4" diameter, early 20th C. **$20.00-$55.00**

Cake pan, pieced tin, spouted, American, 9 3/4"D, late 19th, early 20th C. • Price is determined by shape (an octagonal or hexagonal mold usually costs more than a simple round one), apparent age, condition, general look, and workmanship, if handmade. **$20.00-$55.00**

Cake pan, round, 3 part, deep tin cylinder, on which fits either a bottom with built-in tapered spout, or a plain bottom, "Gem", mfd by American Machine Co., Philadelphia, PA, pat'd July 29, 1890. • **A Clean Sweet.** — "The broom splint has occupied a prominent position among aids to cooking for an indefinite time, and housekeepers who are immaculate in other matters ... often take a splint from a broom with which they have, perhaps, swept the kitchen. ... A much better way is to buy a cheap little brush-broom, and keep it for this and no other purpose; one will last a lifetime." Emma Babcock, Household Hints, 1881. **$14.00-$22.00**

Cake pan, round spouted, blue & white swirl enamelware, 11''D, 19th C. **$60.00-$75.00**

Cake pan, round spouted mold, highish sides, 2 wide slides, like sliding doors, opposite each other in sides, which you would pull up & insert palette knife or spatula into revealed slot to loosen cake from mold, "being made solid, they will not get out of order & leak batter, as the loose bottom pans do", heavy tin, "Van Deusen Cake Molds", mfd by C. A. Chapman, Geneva, NY, 3 sizes, up to 12'' diameter, 1910s. • **They stood under their pans.** — Chapman also made the "Van Deusen" molds, with slides in the sides, in oblong, square and round layer cake sizes. The original ads said "The slides are made long to act as rests to turn the mould on while the cake cools, allowing the air to circulate under the cake to keep it from sweating. The cake, being stuck to the mould, will hang in it until loosened." **A 1903** ad reads "SOME FACTS ABOUT CAKE MAKING. The old way was to grease the cake tin to keep the cake from sticking, then add flour until the cake would not settle, until it was stiff enough to stand alone, like bread. The new way is to discard the grease, and at least ¼ of the flour, make a delicate batter and let it stick to the mold, which will support the cake while baking; and when baked invert the mold and allow the cake to hang in it to cool, which is the only way known to keep a delicate cake from settling; and when cold, loosen the cake … with a knife." **$10.00-$13.00**

Cake pan, round, stamped tin, embossed "Free 49 cent Pan with Py-O-My Pastry Mix," 9½'' diameter. • Another is embossed " 'Py-O-My' Puddin' Cake". **$12.00-$18.00**

Cake pan, round, stamped tin, advertising "Calumet Baking Powder," American, 20th C. • Others embossed "Up & Up Flour," Buffalo, NY & "George Urban Milling Co.," Buffalo, NY. **$12.00-$18.00**

Cake pan, round, stamped tin, straight sides, "Swans Down Cake Flour," 9''D x 1¼''D, 20th C. **$8.00-$12.00**

Cake pan, round, stamped tin, Turk's head, spouted, 9'' diameter, 20th C. **$15.00-$18.00**

Cake pan, round, tin with spout, side handle, "Vanity Co.," American, 10'' diameter, 20th C. **$15.00-$20.00**

Cake pan, spring cake pan, heavy tinned steel, with ring side, open in one place, with little clamp, and with 3 different bottoms — plain flat disc, bottom has large spout & what was called a "Mary Ann" base, which looks like a wide-lipped pie pan, but inserted upside down, so that when cake was baked it would have a big open depression in top for putting in fillings, like strawberries and whipped cream, "Cream City Ware", mfd by Geuder, Paeschke & Frey Co., Milwaukee, WI, about 9'' across, c.1930. • Other companies made spring cake pans. One I saw, made of heavy tin, has the same kind of wire pin going through sort of hinge knuckle & barrel joints, that some ice cream and chocolate molds have. **$15.00-$22.00**

Cake pan, spring form cake pan, heart shaped, 3 part heavy tinned steel, ring opens at point, heart shaped flat bottom fits inside ring, plus clip or clamp to hold sides. "When the baking is finished and cake has cooled, all you have to do is remove the simple little clamp and the sides spring off the cake." "Cream City Ware", about 9'' **$12.00-$18.00**

Cake pan, spring form heart, tin, spout also heart shaped, American, 3'' deep x 9'' diameter, 20th C. • **German vocabulary** — Springform: spring form. • **"The London Way of mixing Cakes,** used by Pastry Cooks. — Weigh down the flour and sugar on a clean smooth table; make a hole in it; and bank it well up; in this hole put your eggs; cream the butter in an earthen pan; then put to the flour and sugar, the eggs and butter; mix all together, and beat it up well with both your hands; you may work it up this way as light as a feather; then add the currants, spices, &c. Put it up in pound or two pound hoops, neatly papered at the bottom and sides; to be baked on iron sheets, in a slow oven." Joseph Bell, *A Treatise on Confectionary.* Newcastle, England, 1817. **$35.00-$40.00**

Cake pan, square, stamped tin, wire loop handle, marked "Fries", 12'' x 12'', 20th C. **$10.00-$15.00**

Cake pans, a pair, tin in colorful cardboard box, with recipes too, "Kate Smith's Bake-A-Cake Kit," 9'' diameter, 20th C. **$18.00-$20.00**

Canape or truffle cutters, at least that's the fancy name. I think I've seen the same thing in a 1950s box labeled "cookie cutters", corrugated tin circles, 9 nested cutters, in tin box, lid stamped "242" and also either "9" or "6", probably 9 for the 9 cutters inside, "Made in Germany", box 4 15/16'' diameter, 20th C. • Dealer had this for $55.00, priced too high because they aren't old, and are still made. See Vegetable cutters, p. 40. **$18.00-$25.00**

Candle mold, crimped tin, strap handle, square base & top, makes 4 candles, PA, 5''H x 6⅛''W, 19th C. **$350.00-$400.00**

Candle mold, japanned tin, 3 tubed, strap handle, American, 6½''H x 3''W x 5''L, 19th C. **$175.00-$200.00**

Candle mold, redware & fruitwood, bench type with bootjack ends, 24 redware tubes (actually 1 missing), American, 14''H x 24''L, c.1830s-1850s. **$1300.00-$1500.00**

Candle mold, tin, 2 rows of 6 tubes each, 2 strap handles, American, 11''H, 19th C. • **Reproduction alert I.** — A 6 tube mold of "pewter-finish" (in other words, rather dark and dull, imitative of old tin) tin, set 2 x 3 with almost flat bottom and top, very small strap handle near top, was advertised by Sturbridge Yankee Workshop, Sturbridge, MA, in the Oct. 1975 *Early American Life.* • **Alert II.** — The same issue had a very similar (identical?) 6 tube mold, 2 x 3, with nearly flat bottom & top, small strap handle, advertised by Hawthorne Products Co., Bloomington, IL. They also offered 8 & 12 tube molds. Both companies were selling the molds in candle-making kits. • **Alert III.** — Another ad in same issue presents a 6 tube mold, arranged 2 x 3, somewhat deeper rectangular base with incurved sides, top piece deeper too, and strap handle comes further down end. This was a "Lucky Eleven Americana Reproduction", made for "over 12 years" by tinsmith Irvin Hoover, Irvin's Craft Shop, Mt. Pleasant Mills, PA. **$75.00-$120.00**

Candle mold, tin, 2 strap ear handles, 2 rows of 5 tubes each, American, 10''H, 19th C. **$125.00-$200.00**

Candle mold, tin, 4 angle feet, small handle, makes 4 candles, American, 6⅛''H, mid 19th C. • **Added value.** — If it's odd, huge, small, signed, proveably old, etc. — it's worth a lot. **$250.00-$300.00**

Candle mold, tin, for one candle, 1 tube with ring strap handle ⅓ way down from top, has very wide, ribbed flat lip, American, 5½''L, mid 19th C. **$250.00-$300.00**

Candle mold, tin, long fat single tube, top is soldered to large square flat lip, which serves also as stand for mold when not in use, strap handle connects tube to edge of lip, American, 21''L, mid 19th C. **$250.00-$300.00**

Candle mold, tin, round, wire handle, makes 8 candles, on plaque on front it reads "MASON'S", English (?), 6⅜"H x 4⅜" diameter, mid 19th to early 20th C. **$125.00-$180.00**

Candle mold, tin, strap handle, 6 tubes in single row, arched bracket base, American, 10½"H,19th C.
$75.00-$120.00

Candle mold, wooden frame, 16 pewter or Britannia tubes fitted in frame, dealer (Hardings of Hancock) says this is marked by maker "K. Webb", American, prob. first half 19th C. • K. Webb was not known to Ledlie Laughlin, who does give a W. Webb, of NYC, "probably after 1810", as having signed two known pewter candle molds.
$1200.00-$1500.00

Candle mold, wooden frame with 18 pewter tubes, called by the inventor an "Improvement in Candle-Mould Apparatus", marked "Humiston," patented by Willis Humiston, West Troy, NY, patent #13,334, pat'd July 24, 1855. • *American Agriculturist* reprinted this tip (from a journal called Exchange) on homemade candles in October 1850: "If you manufacture your own candles, immerse the wicks in lime water, in which a little nitre, (saltpetre,) has been dissolved, and dry them before dipping. The light from such is much clearer, and the tallow will not 'run'."
$1200.00-$1400.00

Candle mold filler, ladle with long spout to bowl, forged iron with applied handle, American (?), 25⅝"L overall, bowl is 2⅝" deep and 4¾" diameter, early 19th C.
$125.00-$140.00

Candy crimper, a sort of fluter or mangle for candy, cast iron & brass, an oblong iron box with hinged lid revealing horizontal brass crimper drums, and brass gears, crank in side, L. T. Yoder, Pittsburgh, PA, 9"H x 15"L x 10"W, pat'd Dec. 3, 1883. **$170.00-$225.00**

Candy cutter, a sort of rolling pin, plated steel, barrel or drum set with 15 fixed sharp disc blades, fixed handles at both ends, used for cutting strips of candy for sticks or rolls, Sethness Co., Chicago, IL, barrel 12"L , blades set ¾" apart, handles 2½"L. (Choice of blades fixed at ⅞", 1", 1¼" & 1½".) 1st quarter 20th C. • Sethness also made rolling cutters with "brass revolving handles", and made to order with 24"L barrels with fixed blades set in same choice of intervals as above. They also made adjustable cutters, with "revolving brass handles", packed with 12, 15, or 20 disc blades, plus washers to separate the blades, 2 cast iron wrenches for assembling, and extra blades. The Dec. 1925 *Sethness Candy Maker*, part catalog, part recipe book (for professional confectioners), also shows a corrugated wooden rolling pin, with turned handles, 18 sharp edged ridges set at ¾" intervals, overall length 15", with the drum or barrel 4" in diameter. It is called a wooden marker, and used to mark off rows for cutting with a knife, or for breaking apart. • For more See What're the Ridges For? in a rolling pin entry, this chapter. **$15.00-$25.00**

Candy cutter, for hoarhound, licorice or other hard chewy candies, looks like a miniature garden tiller or farm tool. Nickeled iron frame fitted with sharp disc blades, with a turned wooden handle. Used by rolling across spread-out pan or cooled puddle of candy to make long "sticks" of candy. Shorter pieces, even small lozenges, could be made by cutting across the original rows. American, last half 19th C. • **"Hoarhound Candy.** — 7 lbs. sugar, white or brown; ¼ oz. cream of tartar; 1 qt. water; ½ pint strong hoarhound tea; boil to the feather; grain against

the sides of the pan with spoon, 2 or 3 minutes; then pour out onto slab; form into flat sticks, rolls or drops, with a hoarhound cutter, which are made in two styles, with movable knives or with fixed divisions." Henry Scammel, compiler, *Treasure House of Universal Knowledge,* 1891. "If, when the sugar is boiled, the skimmer is dipped in and shook over the pan, and then given a sudden flirt behind, the sugar will fly off like feathers; this is called the feathered stage." *ibid.* **$22.00-$35.00**

Candy mold, boy riding slim free range pig, (an image dating back at least to early 18th C presumably from an old nursery rhyme or song, and found in pen & ink calligraphy drawings too) one half missing, grainy wood stained dark. Looks like a modern fake. — distressing on edge looks fake, too dark, it's pushing credulity to have the half that's remaining be the one with the value-adding signature initials, particularly since 2 other half-molds with the same troubling qualities have the same signature, "V. E.", on back, supposedly PA, but looks European (motif Eastern European or Dutch), 4½"H x 4⅝"W, supposed to be mid or early 19th C; poss. 1970s or 80s. • **Wormhole test.** — Back in the 1950s, "wormy chestnut" was the wood leading the pack when it came to the framing wood of choice. Lots of what was holey was actually fake. But since then, and probably for decades before, one kind of distressing done to make wood look old was the drilling of wormholes. Fake wormholes are straight; you can put a piece of paperclip wire in and it keeps going, whereas a real worm hole will wiggle around starting right under the surface, so a wire poked in will be stopped before it's gone a 16th of an inch. Sold at Garth's Auctions, Delaware, OH, April 11-12, 1986, for $255.00. • Read carefully: Probable value range now, if wrong, under $25.00; if right, much higher: **$250.00-$400.00**

Candy mold, dense, heavy yellowish wood, carvings include 2 well carved human figures, front & back views, front of figures carved at very bottom of board so the little feet could actually stick out, may be Robinson Crusoe & Man Friday — a bearded sailor with dotted pants, and a caricatured thick-lipped "native" in short grass skirt. Dealer Teri Dziadul says these figures were used on cakes. Above are something like a corset cover or camisole, a dagger and two other small weapon-like things. On the back, the only really 3-D carvings are a pair of tiny wings! There's also a longish border design, a simple aeronautical balloon, and a sort of connect-the-dot geometric shed or hut, which probably was practice carving or a child's addition, English (?), 9¾"L x 3"W x 1" thick, mid 19th C. • Daniel Defoe's *The Life and Surprizing Adventures of Robinson Crusoe* was first published in 1719, but has been a classic ever since, so it does not really assist in dating this mold. **$400.00-$600.00**

Candy mold, dog, carved heavily grained wood, one half only, curly hair on body & legs, long & down-hanging curly haired ear, short bobbed tail, probably a retriever (a popular dog in the decorative arts), this one looking rather like full figure Pennsylvania chalkware, carved wood and pottery dogs of the period, but because of fortuitous "coincidence" of the remaining half having a signature, plus the fact that in same auction another mold bearing same fakey faults & signature was bought, I doubt that this is what its maker hoped it would look like. Supposed maker's initials carved on back, "V.E." looks "Pennsylvania"; may be Dutch, or an American or European fake, 3¾"H x 5⅞"L, supposed to look mid 19th C; I'm afraid it's a fake from 1970s or 80s. • **Old? What do you think?** — The bothersome things about this one are the wood used, which is inconsistent with the dark color of its finish; it is awfully distressed around edges, in an unrealistic manner (and you really have to do a sort of method acting approach when examining wear and distress marks. It also just begins to approach cuteness, a deadly sin! But maybe the artisan was sentimental about the model. • Garth's pictured all the "V. E." molds in their catalog for the April 11-12, 1986 sale, and made no representations about the molds as to age, authenticity, etc. That is an auction house to love, with apparently hundreds of neat things appearing monthly; but the buyer has to do some of the work for him- herself. Better than always having to depend on a cataloguer's opinion. • Garth's Auctions, Delaware, OH, sold this for $135.00. At the time the price was somewhat low. Probable value range now, if wrong would be under $25.00; if for sure it's right, much higher.   **$150.00-$175.00**

Candy mold, dogs, seated, pewter, 19th C.   **$35.00-$45.00**

Candy mold, eagle pair, pewter, late 19th C.   **$35.00-$50.00**

Candy mold, man & woman, full length front views, he in long-skirted mucho-buttoned coat, with walking stick, and she in long-waisted corseted dress, one half only, looks European — Polish or Czechoslovakian, 5"H x 5¼"W, 19th or 20th C; the look looks older than the mold is I'm sure. • Even when only one part is present, these candy molds can be distinguished from similarly carved wooden cookie molds by the fact that the bottom of the carving is flush with the bottom of the board. A sort of built-in funnel is formed if both halves are placed face to face & is carved so that the molten candy could be poured in. Sometimes there are small holes on background, for fitting the two halves together with small pins or pegs. When both halves are present, the value may be more than doubled. • Sold for $105.00 at Garth's Auctions, Delaware, OH, April 11-12, 1986.   **$90.00-$145.00**

Candy mold, or some other kind of mold?, cast aluminum, fairly thin but nicely made, 2 rows of 4 egg shaped cups each, hanging hole at one end, no mark at all, American?, 13"L x 4½"W, 20th C.   **$22.00-$28.00**

Candy mold, pair of hands, flat, nickel alloy, 20th C.   **$35.00-$40.00**

Candy mold, sheep, couchant, 2 part, redware, with good detail, orange glaze inside, outside of mold follows form inside, with a 2¼" peg handles sticking up from both rumps, thought by Robacker to be "the only redware candy mold thus far reported" (that is, the 1960s), PA German, 5⅝"H x 8"L x 4½"W (when both halves put together), 19th C. • Robacker May 1989 price: **$500.00**

Candy mold, swan, carved wood, 2 piece, European or English, 3⅛"H x 4½"L, 19th C. • **Reproduction alert.** — In *House Beautiful,* in 1973, I found an ad from The Studio Barn in Wilton CT, for a pair of "Aspic Mold Fish Sconces." Are you ready? The copy goes on: "A whim-sical fish — deep-carved by early American seafarer — reproduced in Arrowood® with wrought iron candle holders. Rich, dark finish, hand-done — initialled by proud craftsman. Each 4"W x 12"H." First of all, these were never aspic molds, and if there was an original two-part candy mold with a fish, it probably wasn't carv-ed by an "early American seafarer." Arrowood® is a fake

compo wood like Syroco® , that is molded and can have a lot of detail, including wood graining, but probably wouldn't fool anyone. The mold has the "funnel" like carving on the edge of both halves, and there's a peg in corner of one and a hole in its facing half, so that the two halves could be fitted together and the melted candy poured in the "funnel". The black iron candleholder is fixed at the tail end of both halves. The combination is a pretty desperate one, but still beats other make-intos I've seen. While this pair of sconces cost $19.50 ppd in 1973, they shouldn't bring a fourth of that now. For the swan mold: **$185.00-$225.00**

Candy mold, swan in pleasingly plump shape, well-detailed uplifted perky wings, carved wood in 2 peg-fit parts, English (?), each part is 3⅛"H x 4⅝"W, last quarter 19th C. • $210.00 at Garth's Auctions, Delaware, OH, April 11-12, 1986.   **$200.00-$285.00**

Candy mold, top hats, 10 on flat metal tray, 14½"L x 1¼"W, 20th C.   **$25.00-$30.00**

Candy mold, various designs: nickeled cast iron, shapely concoction of scrolls, curling around each other, with runnels for candy or other confection. These curled & scrolled runnels, teardrops & "S" forms are not all connected; the manufacturer's instructions say "It can be used for casting, moulding as well as baking. ... When all the pieces are casted, moulded or baked, stick them together with icing or caramel to the desired shape... The most attractive ornament can be made out of caramel of different colors, also out of nougat, fragrant paste, gelatine paste, macaroon, sponge cake, plaster of paris(!), etc." H. Hueg, *The Little Confectioner,* pub. c.1921. This mold was used to make showy pieces for bakery win-dows. H. Hueg & Co., Long Island City, NY, 14"L x 10"W x about 1" thick, pat'd 1896, but sold for decades thereafter. • Hueg made another nickeled cast iron mold that is round and has 5 concentric channels surrounding a circle in the middle. Confectioners bought these molds in various sizes, in sets of a dozen, and packed the "fragrant paste" or whatever they were molding into the circles, baked the rings, and assembled baskets, pyramids, cor-nucopias, bowls, etc..   **$55.00-$70.00**

Candy pattern molds, cast plaster of Paris, various small simple shapes — buttons, lumps, elliptical discs, hearts, little bananas, lozenges, leaves, diamonds, etc., — mold patterns, used with trays of corn starch. I've never seen one that I know of, but next week? Anyway, now you'll know those cast plaster "ornaments" you occasionally see may not be architectural, but possibly are candy mold pat-terns, used as described below. A supplier of candy tools and ingredients, Sethness Co., Chicago, in their Dec. 1925 catalog, offered a page full of "Plaster of Paris Starch Mould Patterns", sold in dozen lots of one kind only — "plain, per dozen - 75¢" or "fancy, per dozen - $1.00". • They are interesting because of method of use - one maker in 1920s-30s was J. Frauenberger & Co., Philadelphia, American, European, probably ½" to 4" or 5"L, 19th & early 20th C. • **"Bon Bons.** — This name is given to cream goods, as described (below) in the manufacture of chocolate cream. Different varieties of shape, color & flavor are nearly all produced from the same formula. - It is necessary to have an apparatus to mould the forms of the different varieties. The impres-sions are made in fine pulverized starch, which is put on boards usually two feet long by sixteen inches wide, having sides one and a half inches high, which are filled with the light starch and struck off even with the edges by a straight flat stick. The models of the bon bons are usually made from plaster of Paris, and are glued on a flat board about one or one and a half inches apart. When starch is ready the impressions are made by gently pressing the moulds (mold patterns) that are fastened to the board their full depth in the starch until all are full. Now, having all ready, the cream must next be prepared to pour in the impressions. • **"Chocolate Bon Bons.** — 2 oz. finest assorted gum arabic, 2 lbs Icing sugar, 4 oz. Chocolate, 2 Whites of eggs. Flavor with vanilla. — Dissolve gum in a gill of hot water & strain through a piece of muslin; add the essence of vanilla; add icing sugar until the mass is quite stiff. - Melt chocolate with a tablespoonful of water. Work it very smooth with a spoon, stir in the 2 egg whites & icing." (Then follows a method of making bon bon drops on sugar paper sheets, squeezed from a funnel in plops.) • **Vanilla Cream Bon Bons**. — Pour a sufficient quantity (of the cream above) in a small copper pan & put it over the fire. Stir it until melted; add the vanilla. It is now ready to pour in the moulds. Confectioners use a funnel shapped vessel holding about a quart, with a handle at the upper end & a hole ¼'' in diameter at the small end, a long plug with a sharp point is fitted that can easily be moved up or down to regulate the flow of the cream. This is filled with cream, the plug prevents its escape or dripping, and by gently lifting the plug the cream is poured in each depression and shut on & off until all are filled. Let the cream remain until hard enough to handle without crushing, then empty the moulds, starch and contents in a sieve, and gently agitate until all starch is removed. Lay the bon bons in a moderately warm place for two or three days to harden, then they may be crystallized." All quotes: H. Hueg, *The Little Confectioner*, n.d. (c.1896). Each worth about: **$3.00-$10.00**

Charlotte Russe mold, small, stamped & pieced polished tin, bottom has small disc-like flat foot, rest of bottom is fluted, not actually distinguishable from jelly molds or blancmange molds, and often in old catalogs you will see the same linecut used on different pages, to depict different items! These came in small individual sizes & in larger sizes more suitable to the recipe given below. French, English or American, 3½'' deep x 3'' diameter, late 19th C. • **"Charlotte Russe.** — Whip one quart rich cream to a stiff froth, and drain well on a nice sieve. To one scant pint of milk add six eggs beaten very lightly; make very sweet; flavor high with vanilla. Cook over hot water (ie. in a double boiler or bain marie) till it is a thick custard. Soak one full ounce Cox's gelatine in a very little water. When the custard is very cold, beat in lightly the gelatine in a very little water. When the custard is very cold, beat in lightly the gelatine and the whipped cream. Line the bottom of your mold with buttered paper, the sides with sponge-cake or lady-fingers fastened together with the white of an egg. Fill with the cream; put in a cold place, or in summer on ice. To turn out, dip the mould for a moment in hot water. In draining the whipped cream, all that drips through can be re-whipped." Miss Neill, in Gertrude Strohm's *The Everyday Cook-Book*, 1888. **$6.00-$15.00**

Cheese drainer, basket, large interstices, traces of blue paint, American, 4''H x 11''D, 19th C. **$200.00-$230.00**

Cheese drainer, basket, tightly woven sides connecting square bottom with round top, 2 handles, Windsor style, American, 6''H x 12½'' diameter, 19th C. **$225.00-$250.00**

Cheese drainer, natural wood with arrow-shaped slats leading from square base up to round hooped top rim, in so-called Windsor style, because general construction resembled that of Windsor chairs, American, fairly small example, only 5''H x 9½'' diameter, early 19th C. **$300.00-$350.00**

Cheese drainer, skinny peeled hickory or ash spindles from square base (integral part of ladder stretchers) up to large round hoop, Windsor style, American, nice and big, 10'' deep x about 22'' diameter, late 18th or early 19th C. **$400.00-$500.00**

Cheese drainer mold, basket, beautiful weave forming 6 pointed stars, American, 3''H x 15''D, 19th C. **$200.00-$300.00**

Cheese drainer mold, heart shaped, punctured tin, with presser plate, and — very unusual to find — heart shaped lid, the punctures in the bottom start as triangle in center and as each concentric row was added it got more & more swirly & rounded, American, prob. PA, approx. 6'' x 6'' x 2'' deep, c. 3rd quarter 19th C. • **"Lemon Cheese-Cake.** — 1 pound cottage cheese, 4 eggs (separate), 1 cup granulated sugar, 2 rounded teaspoons flour, grated rind and juice of a large lemon, 1 teaspoon cinnamon, almost ¼ of a nutmeg, 1 tablespoon butter. — Cream the butter, add the sugar and egg yolks, and cream until light; next add the spices, flour, rind and juice of the lemon, and the cheese rubbed through a sieve or squeezed through a potato-ricer. Beat the whites to a stiff froth, stir them in lightly, and pour the mixture into a large pie-pan lined with rich pastry. Bake in a rather quick oven." *Womans Home Companion*, Jan. 1901. **$500.00-$700.00**

Cheese drainer mold, heart shaped, very wide at top lobes, tin, punctured and slit or slotted design of starbursts and holes, the holes nowhere near so close together as in more common slit & punctured heart molds, 3 strap feet, PA, pint-size, late 19th C. **$120.00-$150.00**

Cheese drainer mold, heart shaped with 3 short feet, little hanging ring, pierced tin, nice old dark tin, proba. PA German, 19th C. • **Reproduction alert**. — Because of the shape and origin, this is very desirable. It is widely reproduced, not for the purpose of fakery but for decorators, and is sold in gift shops around the country. The "country look" in new kitchens, which began the tail end of the 1970s and continues now into the 1990s, has encouraged this kind of reproduction. Study any drainer offered you carefully. Heavier dark tin is older. Idiosyncracies in curlicue feet or evidence of hand punching are indications of age too. New ones may not necessarily be shiny — they can be distressed. • **Marked Reproductions.** — Too few reproductions or "replicas" are marked at all, or marked with anything besides a stock or model number. To my mind, this is proof positive that the maker of the piece has the willingness, if not the intent, to deceive, by having his reproduction misrepresented and sold as the old thing it is a modern copy of. There are makers of cast metal wares, who have names and numbers cast into the metal only to have a future seller file them off. Unfortunately very few collector periodicals have stringent rules, or any enforced rules at all, about advertising reproductions. • One notable exception is *Antique-Week,* Knightstown, IN, with regional offices in Leesburg, VA, and Mechanicsburg, PA. They publish in every issue a ''NOTICE ON REPRODUCTIONS'', which tells all that ''Items advertised in (this paper) are supposed to be old or antique unless it is stated that they are clearly and permanently marked reproductions. ... Please advise of cases where you received reproductions that are not advertised as such. There will be honest mistakes, and we will, therefore, not necessarily take one complaint as proof that an advertiser has been unethical or is in violation of postal regulations that forbid misrepresentation.'' **$250.00-$400.00**

Cheese drainer mold, lobed form, rather shallow sides, 6 lobes with 3 pointed rays & three rounds, intricate concentric rings of slits, some wavery to give effect of hot sun, triangular hanging ring of wire, punctured & pieced tin, extremely unusual, PA (?), 19th C. • This one appeared in a picture in an interesting article by Mildred T. Bohne, ''Tin Cheese Strainers'', in *Antique Review* (formerly *Ohio Antique Review*), Feb. 1985. It is the only one I've ever seen with such unusual shape; the most common being round, the second most common being heart-shaped. Bohne writes that ''Although they have been described as having been made for draining cottage cheese (smearkase), they were really made for ... pressed egg cheese, tsierkase.'' The value given is not Bohne's. **$400.00-$550.00**

Cheese drainer mold, pierced copper, heart shaped, 3 short feet, European (?), 19th C (?). • This entry taken from an ad. It could be authentic antique, or fairly recent ''decorator'' take off on traditional PA German heart shaped tin molds for cheese curds. ''Copper'' in this form sends alarm signals. Dealer asked in 1989: **$225.00**

Cheese drainer mold, round, tin cylinder, 3 small tin peg feet, alternating rows of vertical slits & large round pierced holes, American, 4''H x 4¼'' diameter, mid 19th **$125.00-$145.00**

Cheese drainer mold, round & simple, but possibly handmade as spacing is inaccurate, punctured tin hoop with flat bottom, design on bottom & sides are 5 circles of concentric rings of holes; on sides are 8 circles, marked ''Weiss'', American, early 20th C. **$45.00-$55.00**

Cheese drainer mold, round, tin 2 strap handles, has wooden cheese ladder with it to rest over crock, American, late 19th C. **$65.00-$80.00**

Cheese mold, cow, round, carved wood, American, prob. WI, 10'' diameter, early 20th C. **$45.00-$55.00**

Cheese mold, various carved wood motifs: dogs, cows, chickens, pigs, WI, three sizes: 10''D, 12''D, 14''D, 19th C. **$60.00-$80.00**

Cheese press, round, handmade, tin cylinder with 3 short conical legs, holes in bottom and first 2'' around bottom sides, foller or press with little handle is tin, ring handle on side of cylinder, American, 7⅛''H with 1¼'' legs, 6⅜'' diameter, 19th C. **$120.00-$140.00**

Chocolate mold, alphabet, cast metal tray type with heavy tinning, all letters, numbers 1 - 0, and name, ''AUERBACH'', 12'' x 6'' x¾'' thick, making chocolate wafers ³⁄₁₆'' thick, 20th C. **$40.00-$60.00**

Chocolate mold, Army truck with tied- on canvas covering on back, ''Vormenfabriek #15371'', Tilberg, Holland, 1940s (?). **$60.00-$75.00**

Chocolate mold, baby standing with finger in mouth, very tubby, steel alloy, Anton Reiche, #17197, sold by T. C. Weygandt of NYC, Dresden, Germany, 6'' x 3⅛'', early 20th C. **$65.00-$80.00**

Chocolate mold, baby, stark naked, one hand to mouth, one to belly, 2 part, heavy stamped tin or steel alloy, marked ''Kunzig 17499,. C. Weygandt'', NYC, USA, Made in Germany, 12''H, early 20th C. **$115.00-$130.00**

Chocolate mold, birds in flight, cast aluminum, ornate, somewhat oxidized (with white powdery film), American (?), 7''H, post World War II. **$22.00-$30.00**

Chocolate mold, boy, small & fat, metal alloy, mfd by Gesetze Geschutz, imported by Van Emden Co. of NYC, German, 2½'' x 4¼'', c.1900 or early 20th C. **$65.00-$75.00**

Chocolate mold, bugle, stamped alloy, LeTang Fils #3919, 8¾'' x 3½''. **$50.00-$65.00**

Chocolate mold, Bugs Bunny, double standing figures, 2 halves hinged, within heavy frame, with old clamps, marked ''Warner Bros. Productions, Inc.'' in molds, so name would appear on finished chocolate Bugs, each rabbit 9½''H x 3¾''W, mid 20th C. **$90.00-$120.00**

Chocolate mold, bull dog, 2 parts, wide flange, Weygardt Co., NYC, but ''Made in Germany'', 5¼'' x 5'', 1920s-40s. **$60.00-$70.00**

Chocolate mold, bull dog, sitting, tin plated nickel alloy, J. G. Laurosch, #4102, German, 5¼''H, 1920s-40s. • There are many bulldog chocolate molds — something to do with Teddy Roosevelt, who died in 1919, and was sometimes caricatured (because of his teeth) as a **bulldog** or because he was a Harvard man? A popular dog of the period — maybe from a cartoon strip? See an entry under andirons in another chapter. **$55.00-$65.00**

Chocolate mold, candy bars, cast metal tray type makes 14, ''Wilbur Candy Co.,'' 20th C. **$18.00-$22.00**

Chocolate mold, cartoon character Jiggs, nickel silver, tinned, American, 20th C. **$30.00-$40.00**

Chocolate mold, Charlie Chaplin figure, well-stamped metal alloy, marked ''Dépose'' (deposited or registered), French, 6'' x 3½'', c.1920s (?). • I have never seen this, nor heard of it until browsing catalogs from dealer Teri Dziadul in Enfield, CT. Her 1986 asking price: $195.00. Price range is mine. **$195.00-$235.00**

Chocolate mold, chicken, tin, marked with dolphin stamp and #2031, 4''H, TOC. **$28.00-$35.00**

Chocolate mold, chicks standing on rim of nest, 2 figures, tin plated nickel & copper alloy, Anton Reiche, #6543, Dresden, Germany, approx. 4½'' across, early 20th C. • Little 'nipple' in the edge of this & many molds is a ''locater'' to line up fronts and backs. **$75.00-$90.00**

Chocolate mold, chimney sweep on roof holding his ladder, alloy, no marks, 4½'' x 2¾''. **$95.00-$115.00**

Chocolate mold, cigars, makes 5 of solid chocolate, good details of wrapped leaves, when 2 parts are closed, there are 5 tubes to fill, may need special funnel, American (?), 5⅛''H x 4½''W, 20th C. **$32.00-$40.00**

Chocolate mold, dirigible, nickel silver, marked with name on dirigible, ''Los Angeles,'' and #1, German (?), 20th C. **$110.00-$130.00**

Chocolate mold, dog — poodle or water spaniel with poodle cut, sitting, heavy tinned nickel alloy, 2 part mold with clamps, Sommet #1306, Paris, 9''H, (also made 6⅝''H), 1900 to 1950. **$200.00-$235.00**

Chocolate mold, Dutch boy, nickel alloy, tinned, Anton Reiche, #24247, 6''H, 1930s. **$55.00-$70.00**

Chocolate mold, egg & grapes, tin plated "nickel silver" alloy, Eppelsheimer & Co., #5024, 3¹⁵⁄₁₆''L, early 20th C. • According to Judene Divone (see Bibliography), Eppelsheimer used an alloy "very high in nickel". **$65.00-$80.00**

Chocolate mold, egg with design of jumping pig on side, heavy tin, no mark, 20th C. **$15.00-$18.00**

Chocolate mold, egg with image of Man in the Moon smoking his pipe, metal alloy, E. & Co. (Eppelsheimer), NYC, 4¼'' x 3''. **$50.00-$60.00**

Chocolate mold, electric iron, heavily tinned stamped metal, 2 parts with clamp, "Vormenfabriek", (reported once as Vormenfaberier — meaning mold manufacturer (?) Tilberg, Holland (often reported as, perhaps seen as, Tilbury or Tilburg), 4''L, c.1930s-40s. **$85.00-$100.00**

Chocolate mold, elephant, 2 part hinged, Anton Reiche #8306, also #20, TOC. **$35.00-$45.00**

Chocolate mold, Father Christmas on donkey, early Santa character has traditional peaked cap & long robe with short jacket, 2 piece tin, German (?), 7''H, 19th or early 20th C. **$75.00-$115.00**

Chocolate mold, fish with many fins, huge & slightly stylized, dark gray nickel alloy with partial tinning, somewhat flimsy for the length, probably for making a confectioner's showpiece, German (?), 26''L, 19th C. • Unlike fish molds for jellies or aspics, which are curved, this mold and other fish chocolate molds are straight. I don't know the significance of the fish; obviously it's a Christian symbol, but usually having to do with Lent, which is hardly a time to be eating a 26'' long chocolate fish! **$165.00-$200.00**

Chocolate mold, girl with watering can, 2 piece tin plated nickel alloy, Mistress Mary, quite contrary, English or German, 7½''H, 19th C or early 20th. • Good for a watering can collection! **$50.00-$70.00**

Chocolate mold, girl with watering can & large hairbow, "Little Jane," Anton Reiche, #24222, Dresden, Germany, 3''H, c.1930s. • Little Jane is cute, but fortunately not so cute as the terminally-precious "Mary Jane" little-girls-with-big-bows also made by Reiche in the same period. **$40.00-$50.00**

Chocolate mold, half old man, half egg, pewter, 1¾'' x 2½'', 19th or 20th C. **$25.00-$30.00**

Chocolate mold, half old woman, half egg, pewter, 1¾'' x 2½'', 19th or 20th C. **$25.00-$35.00**

Chocolate mold, hen on her nest, white metal alloy, Eppelsheimer & Co., #4688, NYC, 5½'' x 5'', TOC. **$50.00-$65.00**

Chocolate mold, horse, Anton Reiche #6872, 4'' x 3'', early 20th C. **$40.00-$55.00**

Chocolate mold, horse, extra soldering to make a little clip with wire, horse's legs are separate, not joined or filled in, 2 part, Anton Reiche #8, and #8760, 3¼''H, TOC. **$30.00-$40.00**

Chocolate mold, hotdogs or sausage links, 5 in tray form, heavy metal, marked "Supe & Busch", "Dresden", Germany, 7¼'' x 3¾'', early 20th C (?). **$55.00-$65.00**

Chocolate mold, Jack & the Beanstalk, tinned copper, good detail, no mark, 8¼'' x 5¼'', TOC (?). **$120.00-$140.00**

Chocolate mold, lamb, lying down, metal alloy, 2 part, Kanter Mfg. Co., Cleveland, OH, 8''H x 12''L, 20th C. **$35.00-$45.00**

Chocolate mold, lamb lying down, or — in heraldic terms — couchant, meaning lying down with head up. Front legs are visible, longish tail curled around, lots of stylized detailing of wool, tin plated nickel alloy, Anton Reiche, #6638, 7¼''L, early 20th C. **$125.00-$140.00**

Chocolate mold, lamb, standing (which is unusual), steel & copper alloy,.C. Weygandt, #381, NY, 2⅜''L, mid 20th C. • Another company using copper and steel was the American Chocolate Mould Co., in business in the 1930s & 1940s. Their molds were made of copper-plated steel that was tinned. **$40.00-$55.00**

Chocolate mold, lion, "Anton Reiche #6869'', 2½'' x 4½'', early 20th C. **$60.00-$70.00**

Chocolate mold, lion, sitting, slightly rusted metal, B.V. Vormenfabriek, #15281, Tilberg, Holland, 4⅝''L, mid 20th C. • **Collector hint.** — Rust isn't necessarily a sign of age; neither are distress marks and dings. Before you buy something, look around the dealer's stock carefully. If there are a number of very similar things, especially if they are all rusted, weathered, or otherwise distressed, the stuff is probably new and may be reproductions. **$35.00-$45.00**

Chocolate mold, locomotive, white metal alloy, Reiche, #9959, 4¾''H x 6¼''L, early 20th C. **$125.00-$145.00**

Chocolate mold, man's striped tie with looped knot, stamped heavy tin, very flat rectangular frame, marked only #12680, American, 11½''L, tie itself is 9''L, 20th C. **$30.00-$40.00**

Chocolate mold, monkey in hat, very impish, with round object (coconut?) between feet, stamped alloy, marked "H. Walter", Berlin, Germany, 5¼'' x 3¼'', early 20th C (?). **$60.00-$72.00**

Chocolate mold, monkeys, 3 sitting in a row, but they aren't "Hear no evil, See no evil, Speak no evil," just heavy metal monkeys, NYC, 3¾''H x 7''L in frame, TOC. **$50.00-$70.00**

Chocolate mold, mouse boldly climbing cat's leg, 2 part stamped alloy, perhaps a reference to a fairy tale, marked "G. DeHaeck Gand", Holland, 20th C. **$80.00-$100.00**

Chocolate mold, nesting hen, stamped alloy, marked "Ger. Fontaine et -?-" (et Fils?), French, 2½'' x 1¾'', early 20th C (?). **$40.00-$50.00**

Chocolate mold, nursing bottle with baby's face on front, stamped alloy, setting (?) sun behind mountains mark, #2050, 5'' x 2¾'', 20th C. **$55.00-$70.00**

Chocolate mold, owl on branch, tin plated nickel alloy, Letang Fils, #1599, Paris, France, 2''H, TOC into mid 20th C. • Made over a long period, in different alloys; hard to find. **$85.00-$120.00**

Chocolate mold, patties, heavy cast metal tray type makes 28, "Wilbur Candy Co.," American, 20th C. **$18.00-$22.00**

Chocolate mold, penguin with top hat & spectacles, nickel alloy, Anton Reiche, 20th C. **$50.00-$65.00**

Chocolate mold, rabbit, a blacksmith occupational mold he's got one tool in his apron pocket & is standing at anvil, hammer at the ready, not marked, late 19th or early 20th C. • From catalog of dealer Teri Dziadul in Enfield, CT. Her asking price in 1986 was $190.00, and she called it a very rare subject. • Price range mine. **$190.00-$235.00**

Chocolate mold, rabbit, crouched down, metal alloy, Eppelsheimer, #6183, NYC, 7¾'' x 3½'', 20th C (?). **$80.00-$95.00**

Chocolate mold, rabbit, high sitting with basket on back, steel & copper alloy called Platina,. C. Weygandt Co., #238, NYC, NY, 17½''H, c.1950s. **$85.00-$100.00**

Chocolate mold, rabbit, high sitting with basket on back, tinned metal, hinged at top, Eppelsheimer & Co., NYC, 9''H x 4''W, Dec. 1935. U.S. Pat. No. 948146. **$45.00-$60.00**

Chocolate mold, rabbit, high sitting with one paw on basket, tinned nickel alloy, Heris, #417, Nuremberg, Germany, 12''H, pre-1950. • **German vocabulary** — Formen fur Schokolade: mold for chocolate. Also found as Schokoladeform. This one, a rabbit, is an Osterhasen Formen fur Schokolade: Easter rabbit chocolate mold. **$60.00-$70.00**

Chocolate mold, rabbit, hiking with basket backpack, very detailed basket and features, marked ''O. Darchambeau'', 7¾''H x 4''W, TOC. **$45.00-$58.00**

Chocolate mold, rabbit in landscape, clothed & pulling wagon full of Easter eggs, ''5 Miles to Go'' signpost, houses, Eppelsheimer & Co., NYC, entire rectangle 5''H x 7½''L, early 20th C. **$40.00-$55.00**

Chocolate mold, rabbit, lady ready for church with parasol, wicker basket on back is supported by arm held behind body, beautiful curved body, apron has flipped hem, hinged on side and with 2 clips, marked #14037 and #2, Anton Reiche, 7¼''H, late 19th C. **$90.00-$120.00**

Chocolate mold, rabbit pulling cart, cast aluminum, single hinge, flat bottom, American? 9''H, 20th C. • One dealer, noted for selection of chocolate molds, says these were also for making cakes **$25.00-$38.00**

Chocolate mold, rabbit, sitting & looks surprised, rigid silvery alloy, Eppelsheimer & Co., NYC, NY, 10''H, (this rabbit came in several sizes), mid 20th C. **$65.00-$80.00**

Chocolate mold, rabbit, sitting with basket, shiny alloy, J.G. Laurosch, #4032, German, 15''H, 1930s-40s. **$50.00-$65.00**

Chocolate mold, rabbit, standing, pewter-like cast metal, heavy straps in sort of protective bridgework case around outside. American (?), prob. c.1930s. • Dealer Don Appelquist, of Suckasunny, Morris County, NJ, explained that in a candy shop, ''when finished with a particular shape, having made as many as they wanted, they'd just toss the mold into a corner until needed next time.'' Most collectors remove the straps. **$110.00-$125.00**

Chocolate mold, rabbit, striding on hind legs over clump of ferns, heavy stamped tin 2 parts, marked ''Anton Reiche #24353'', Dresden, Germany, 21½''H x 11⅞''W x 5'' deep, early 20th C. **$350.00-$450.00**

Chocolate mold, rabbit with backpack, well detailed, for making solid chocolate — has clipped-on lid on bottom, unused and looks new, no mark, American (?), 20''H, early 20th C. • Dealer Don Appelquist explains that many of ''those that look new are actually old. They were never used, and never had the edges cut or trimmed, and were never mounted in protective strapping.'' **$120.00-$150.00**

Chocolate mold, rabbits on 4 eggs, for hollow chocolate, white metal alloy, American (?), 10⅜''H, 20th C. **$45.00-$55.00**

Chocolate mold, rooster, steel & copper alloy with small rust spots, C. Weygandt #62, NY, 10''H, mid 20th C. **$125.00-$145.00**

Chocolate mold, roosters, 4 of them, steel alloy,.C. Weygandt, NYC, 4''H, 20th C. **$55.00-$65.00**

Chocolate mold, Santa Claus, ''solid nickel silver'' marked ''B-M #44'', 7¼''H, TOC to c.1920s. **$100.00-$120.00**

Chocolate mold, Santa Claus with backpack, deeply-stamped metal alloy, clips on edges, American (?), 20th C. • **Reproduction alert.** — Two Santa chocolate molds, imported from Holland, were advertised in 1983. They are supposed to be ''replicas'', and are nickel-plated stamped metal. Both are 2 part, have wide flanges and 3 spring wire ring clips. The 6½''H Santa, or Belsnickle, has long fur-trimmed coat, and soft bag over one hip, into which he reaches for gifts. The flange is stamped ''Holland Handcrafts'' and #15554. The 4½''H Santa has short belted fur-trimmed coat, high boots, jolly elfin face. Number illegible. They sold for $27.00 and $23.00 in the catalog. **$35.00-$45.00**

Chocolate mold, spaceship or rocket, shiny alloy, 2 parts, relatively flat, American, 9½'' x 6''W, 1960s-70s. • Don't mistake this, which has 2 rocket boosters on either side, for the rocket-shaped dirigible mold, one of which is embossed on airship ''Los Angeles,'' and dates from the late 1920s-30s. **$35.00-$50.00**

Chocolate mold, squirrel with acorn, very bushy tail curled up over head, dark pewtery nickel silver alloy, fairly thin & light in weight, 2 parts, 15''H, c.1880s to1920s. • **Prices of Chocolate Molds.** — Just to be old isn't enough. • Size has a strong effect on value: large, and very large molds (over 15''H, or over 20''H) seem to get about 250% more than the 5'' or 7''H molds of the same subject, condition, and approximate age. Tiny molds may also command more money than the run of the middle ones, but only if the subject is desirable. • **Subject** is very important, although chocolate mold collectors seem to have a slightly different idea of what's ''special'' than does the outsider amateur. Some subjects are predictable, because any collectible in that shape sells well: Scotties, Teddy Bears, Kewpies, Santas (Kris Kringle, St. Nicholas, Belsnickel, Father Christmas), Automobiles, Poodles, Bears, Pigs, and especially Rabbits Dressed in Clothes. • **Scarcity** is the other main ingredient of value. And only if you are an avid and active collector of the molds will you get a feel for what's rare. • **Condition** and **Completeness** almost go without saying, for most chocolate molds on the market today are in fine condition. **$150.00-$175.00**

Chocolate mold, St. Nicholas forms in high mitred hats, multiple 3-D old-fashioned type in hinged rectangular frame, called by collectors a ''book mold'', metal alloy, 6¼''W x 13''L, individual figures are about 6½''H, early 20th C. **$140.00-$170.00**

Chocolate mold, St. Nicholas on horseback, with rooftop above him, 2 parts, with clamps, Dutch, 8''H x 6''W, TOC. **$185.00-$225.00**

Chocolate mold, stag, standing with left leg poised, heavy weight tin, marked ''France 1313,'' with a fish and #48 in a diamond lozenge, probably made by Sommet, French, 12'' x 10½'', late 19th or early 20th C. **$250.00-$300.00**

Chocolate mold, stars, 6 in a row, tray type, bronze-finished heavy metal, ''A. F. Tool Co.,'' NYC, NY, 6''L x 1½''W, 20th C. **$75.00-$85.00**

Chocolate mold, steam locomotive, lots of exterior detailing and wonderful high smokestack, pewter, 2 parts with clamps, American, TOC. **$185.00-$225.00**

Chocolate mold, swan, 2 part heavy stamped tin, marked Thos. Mills & Bro., Inc., Philadelphia, 8½"H x 10½"W, TOC. **$110.00-$140.00**

Chocolate mold, swan, nickel alloy, tinned, Sommet, "#1756," with koi or catfish or sculpin fish mark, Paris, France, 3¼" x 3½," 20th C. **$75.00-$95.00**

Chocolate mold, swan, sitting (swimming), tin plated nickel alloy, Eppelsheimer & Co., #6212, NYC, 3½"L, 1919 to 1972. • According to the excellent book by Judene Divone on *Chocolate Moulds* (see Bibliography), this rather undistinguished looking mold (my judgment, not hers) was made over a very long period — 1919 to 1972. **$35.00-$42.00**

Chocolate mold, teddy bear standing (waiting to be picked up), stamped alloy, marked with new one on me, "E. I. Metro, -?- Anver", French, about 4½"H, early 20th C. **$215.00-$235.00**

Chocolate mold, television, alloy looks like stainless steel, American (?), c.1960s. • There are several really modern forms in these less-appealing molds. Radios and telephones are two that come to mind. Still, collectors pay rather high prices. **$40.00-$60.00**

Chocolate mold, toy soldier with high hat, tinned nickel alloy, Randell & Smith (?), the only English firm, or poss. American, 4"H, 20th C. **$18.00-$22.00**

Chocolate mold, turkey, tinned nickel silver, H. Walter, #8635, Berlin, Germany, 4½"H, c.late 1940s, early 50s. **$35.00-$40.00**

Chocolate mold, turkey, every feather shows, metal alloy, "Vormenfabriek, #15292," Tilberg, Holland, 4" x 4½"L. **$55.00-$65.00**

Chocolate mold, turkeys, a pair posed tail-to-tail, alloy, American, 6"H x 9⅝"W, 20th C. **$50.00-$60.00**

Chocolate mold, violin, stamped alloy, Anton Reiche #40034, 10½"L x 3¾"W, 20th C. **$125.00-140.00**

Chocolate mold set, champagne bucket & bottle, stamped alloy, only bucket is marked: "Eppelsheimer #4580", bucket 2¾"H x 2¾" diameter; bottle 4¾"H, early 20th C. **$70.00-$80.00**

Chocolate (?) molds, figurals, described by dealer in ad as "nickel plated cast iron," with "6 figures in each" of the various molds, marked "Letang Fils", Paris, 6¾"L x 3¾"W x ½"thick, early 20th C. • Although this manufacturer made chocolate molds, I don't know if these are chocolate molds, having not seen them. Am reporting to you to add to database. "Cast iron" seems odd to me. Subjects as described in ad: child behind hi-button shoe marked "BeBe"; small girl, fancy dress, high button shoe, "Elegante" on bottom; "Jockey" in riding clothes, crop, spurs, "Chasseur". **$75.00**

Chocolate molds, figures of stamped metal, tray type rows of repeat images, 20th C. • Figures include sitting rabbits, turtles, ducks, roadsters, to cigars, men in the moon, kewpies, frogs and beetles. Prices vary widely according to appeal of individual subjects, as well as determined rarity. This is too esoteric a field for me. Prices range below for 5 nicely detailed frogs (seen from above) to 4 army trucks in a row. **$85.00-$145.00**

Confection mold, cast brass, round with 2 loop handles, 13 small, finely detailed cups in traditional Chinese shapes, including butterfly, chrysanthemum, koi (carp), lion head, and other flowers and forms, very rough casting on underside. Received with the bottom "packed very hard with sand that appeared to have grease soaked into it."

This mold was reported by collector Jim Holroyd, who has shared many things with me over the years. bought in Singapore, 9" diameter x 2" deep, looks 19th C. • Price range mine, not Holroyds'. **$80.00-$100.00**

"Cookie" anyone? or "Cake"? — Once there was a clear difference, related to size, kind of dough, and effect of baking. Diminutive suffixes -ey or -y or -ie, indicate a cooky or cookie is a small cake (Dutch *koekje*). • **English Usage.** — The English (but not always the Scots) call crackers *biscuits* — small, dry, flat bread or cakes; cookies are cakes — (according to *Oxford English Dictionary* "a comparatively small flattened sort of bread" (no mention of sugar); and a cookie is "a small flat sweet cake" — a term "applicable" only in the U.S. (says the *OED*). Just for fun, and not part of the discussion here, a very funny term for a tea party is quoted in the *OED*, from the 19th C English novelist Charles Reade: "cooky-shine".

American Usage. — In Noah Webster's *American Dictionary*, 1858, a biscuit is a "kind of bread, formed into cakes, and baked hard for seamen" or "a cake, variously made, for the use of private families." According to the same American wordman, a cake is "a small mass of dough baked; or a composition of flour, butter, sugar, or other ingredients, baked in a small mass" or "something in the form of a cake, rather flat than high, but roundish." Finally, Webster says that a "Cooky" is "a small cake moderately sweet" and adds that it's a "familiar word in New England". Pennsylvania was not part of N.E. • Authors of 19th C American cookbooks called cookies "cakes", and the cutters were "Cake cutters". Some of the cakes were thick, some thin, so that is no clue. In the 1920 catalog of The Central Stamping Co., NYC, there are a number of shallow edge cutters with flat backs and handles called "Cake Cutters." These were offered in animal shapes or assorted "fancy" shapes with corrugated edges, and small inset marking designs. Marks would not stay on cookies (or cakes) that were thick or would rise and puff out in the oven. Another shown is suitable for a cookie that rises, has a deep cutting corrugated or fluted edge round cutter & a bracket strap handle, single air hole, available in four sizes from 2½" to 4" diameter. It's termed a "Cookey Cutter", while one called a "Biscuit Cutter" is slightly shallower & doesn't have the flutes. • The 1914 catalog of Shapleigh Hardware Co., St. Louis, shows several very shallow flatbacks called "Cake Cutters", with small air holes, no apparent strap handles though the catalog copy says "Flat tin Handle", possibly referring to the overhanging flat backs (?). Their cake cutters have corrugated edges, with & without insets. Fancy inset ones could be ordered "extra fancy" (and weighed 25% more & cost accordingly). Shapleigh also offered animals, birds, fish, and a tantalizing unidentified "etc." in their assorted sets of "Cake Cutters". They were shallow cutters with large roughly trimmed flat backs; no handles mentioned. Shapleigh showed simple round deep cutters with strap handles & termed them "Biscuit or Cake Cutters". Shapleigh's only cutter called a "Cookey Cutter", also for biscuits, was a simple wire and tin rotary or rolling cutter, for thick dough.

Cookie baking set, Dick Tracy motif, in original box, Pillsbury's "Comicooky," 1937. **$28.00-$35.00**

Cookie board, animals — carved wood with figures on both sides, oblong with regal lion, head at right, tail curled up over rump, one front leg on double arch tombstone, on other side is seated cat, dark color to wood, stone marked "Koning Van Dieren". Dutch? or NY or other Dutch-settled state? 8¾"H x 14"L, 19th C look; poss. 20th C. • $365.00 at Garth's Auctions, Delaware, OH, April 11-12, 1986. **$350.00-$450.00**

Cookie board, "gingerbread mold" say ads for the reproduction. Hand carved poplar wood board, figure of periwigged Punch, in fancy striped knee britches and fitted coat, holding walking stick, exaggerated nose and chin of the famous puppet, lots of details in buttons and pattern in textile of clothing, supposed to be a replica of an "18th century original now in Van Cortlandt Manor", NY, apparently not available in cast metal as was their other replica cookie board, ad is for American Heritage Museum Collection ... from Sleepy Hollow Restorations, NY, 28"H x 10"W, advertised in July/Aug. 1978 *Americana*. • Original price was $165.00 plus shipping. The value has not gone up, but has instead gone down, even though it was nicely carved. **$20.00-$35.00**

Cookie board, St. Nicholas with his miter hat decorated with a cross, long beard, bishop's crook, ecclesiastical alb or surplice, bands, and chasuble, with basket of 3 baby dolls in bunting, "hand carved" wood, reproduction or "replica of an 18th century Dutch colonial mold...in Van Cortlandt Manor", American (?), 26"L x 11"W, the figure being 24"H, advertised in 1978 *Americana*. • **Reproduction alert**. — This reproduction was "also available in a polished cast metal version", which was 24"H x 8¾"W. The description comes from the Sept. Oct. 1978 *Americana* magazine's American Heritage catalog. The wooden one originally cost $165.00; the metal one (looks like cast aluminum) was under $50.00. The unfortunate realities are that some people will have bought these on the secondary market thinking they were getting a real antique; the value has gone down, not up, unlike a real antique. A copy or reproduction, at least a nameless one, can not be expected to rise in value. Reproductions by Wallace Nutting and the Stickleys excepted. **$20.00-$35.00**

Cookie & candy mold, cat, a new, large reddish brown mass-produced stoneware mold for making flat cookies or shortbread, finely detailed striped tiger cat with bow around neck, the outer rim of the mold almost follows the cat's outline, hanging hole at top, "Le Chat", mfd by Hartstone, Inc., Zanesville, OH, 9¾"H x 5¼"W, (and also in larger size, 11¼"H x 6½"W), 1980s. **$12.00-$15.00**

Cookie cutter, angel, shown from side, with large wing, mutton chop sleeve, long dress, tiny feet, mounted on oblong tin back, but overlaps considerably, marked only "Germany", 9½"H x about 5"W, c.1891-1915. • **German vocabulary** — Ausstechform: form or shape cutter. This one, for Christmas, is fur Weihnachtsgebackerie: for Christmas Eve cookies. **$125.00-$170.00**

Cookie cutter, automobile of 1930s type, tin, flat back, strap handle, American, 4"L, 20th C. • Automobiles were a fairly popular motif for early 20th C cookie cutters and ice cream molds. I have also seen carved wooden cookie boards with the open top roadster type of car and a spiffy driver. **$25.00-$30.00**

Cookie cutter, bird, a small distelfink (gold finch or "thistle" finch — favorite food for all types of finches is thistle seeds), tin, flat back, prob. PA German, 3"L, late 19th C. **$12.00-$15.00**

Cookie cutter, bird, backward-looking, of type found in Pennsylvania German fraktur & other decorated paper documents as well on decorated stoneware, dark tin, flat back, PA (?), 4½"L x⅝" deep, 19th C. • **Some Hints On Determining Age**. — In cookie cutters look for old dark tin, rather thick gauge, spotty soldering, irregularly trimmed flat backs usually without rolled edges, and other signs of hand manufacture. Spotty soldering used to be considered de facto proof of age, because it was adduced that solder in the good old days was too expensive to make a continuous solder seam. However, if a cutter was given a lot of use, and solder spots came loose, repairs at some later date would change the character of the soldering and throw off calculations of age dependent on the appearance of the solder. If solder got cheaper, why could not a repaired old cutter have new continuous solder? • In the early popular studies (and many of the more serious studies) of old kitchenwares, mainly in the 1920s and 1930s, many assumptions were made about many kinds of cooking utensils and tools based on hearsay, and highly colored by sloppy sentiment. Myth cannot be made Fact without direct evidence. • In the case of cookie cutters, **two avenues of research need exploring: (1)** Recipes for cookies or "cake" (50 and more years ago these cutters were called cake cutters), which would predicate the need for cutters in contrast to molds (for springerle, marzipan, etc.); and **(2)** Diaries, journals, receipt & account books, in which might be found reference to such mythologized figures as the itinerant tinsmith who created cutters to order for a meal.• Many figural cookies dating back to the 16th C in Europe were created in carved wooden molds, not with cutters. Ad hoc cutters of some kind, such as canister lids or tumbler rims, were called for in 18th C American cookbooks, but we don't know now at what point cutters made for the specific purpose, especially fancy and decorative shapes, were in widespread use. • A useful start could be made using the extensive Bibliography of Published and Manuscript & Unpublished Sources in William Woys Weaver's *Sauerkraut Yankee. Pennsylvania German Foods & Foodways*, Philadelphia: University of Pennsylvania Press, 1983. However, before your mouth starts to water, note that there is only one cookie recipe, and that related to Anglo-American culinary heritage, and it's for Hard Gingerbread. Apparently food historian Weaver either found few cookie recipes or decided they were outside his purview. **$70.00-$85.00**

Cookie cutter, bootjack, tin, flat back, American, 3¼"L, TOC. **$35.00-$45.00**

Cookie cutter, bugler on horseback, in military charge position, tin, flat back, one of a very popular subject group, the genesis of which probably goes back to 17th C carved cookie boards found in several European countries, PA German, 7"H x 6¼"L, prob. 4th quarter 19th C. • Robacker Collection, auctioned by T. Glenn Horst, Farmersville, PA, May 26-27, 1989 (first of 4 two-day sales). Prices achieved at this auction are hard to translate meaningfully because of the extraordinary cutters sold. Measurements are taken from Clarence Spohn's catalog descriptions for the sale; other descriptions are from my personal observation or from photographs appearing in one or the other of the Robackers' books, or articles from publications of the Pennsylvania Folklife Society. • The first day of the first auction was a heart stopper; if you didn't faint over the beauty of some of the never-dared-imagine cookie cutters, you did over the prices people paid. **$550.00**

Cookie cutter, cartoon character figural of Blondie, yellow plastic, part of original set with Dagwood, etc., Educational Products Co., Hope, NJ, late 1940s. **$15.00-$18.00**

Cookie cutter, cat, sitting, tin, no handle, stamped "Davis Baking Powder",⅞" deep cut x 4"L, early 20th C. **$18.00-$22.00**

Cookie cutter, cat, slightly pregnant, suspicious but eminently feline , short legs, shortish tail, head turned to gaze from almond eyes. The detail inset in the face created with small curls or loops of tin soldered inside outline of head, 2 very large finger push-out holes in flat back, PA German, 3¾"H x 7¾"L, 3rd to 4th quarter 19th C. • An amusing pieced tin, flat back cookie cutter, which should be called "The Owl & the Pussycat Combined", a sort of 2 legged cat with large head & round inset eyes, inset beaky nose, and a bird-like tail, appears in The *International Cook's Catalogue*, published in 1977 by Random House. The cutter, which is 4½"L x 3¼"H x½" deep, is (at least in 1970s) imported from South America, where it was used to make a *galletita* honey & cornmeal cookie, in the form of a *gatito*, or little cat. • Robacker May 1989 price for old cutter: **$650.00**

Cookie cutter, chick, simple & little, tin, flat back with several small release or air holes, American, 3"L, late 19th or early 20th C. **$12.00-$18.00**

Cookie cutter, Christmas tree, tin, no back, strap handle, with tiny narrow brace across cutter where trunk branches out, has a handmade look, but I've seen 2 exactly alike, German(?). Phyllis Wetherill writes that the brace is typically German, 1⅛" deep x 5"L, late 19th or early 20th C. • **The Christmas tree**, because it is an evergreen, has been a Christian symbol, a sacred tree, at least as far back as the early 17th C. Many people believe its pagan origins go much further back, and that the evergreen was adopted, for obvious reasons, by Christians. **$25.00-$45.00**

Cookie cutter, corncob, tin, flat back, 6"L, 19th C. **$55.00-$65.00**

Cookie cutter, cow, tin, flat back, shallow cut, American, TOC or early 20th. • **Depth Sounding**, or Dating By Shallow or Deep. — It is possible that the old rule of thumb, that a very shallow (ie. ⅜" or less deep) always meant a 20th C cutter, is incorrect. A large number of interesting and apparently old cutters were sold at the first and second two-day sessions of the Horst auction of the Robacker Collection, May and June l989. There were some extremely deep cutters with not any more apparent age than the larger number of cutters ½" or less in depth. Upon reflection, the necessary depth would depend entirely on the kind of cookie dough being cut. To save tin, and make more economic use of scraps (which might often have been long straight strips), why make a cutter for an almost paper thin Moravian ginger cookie, for example, any deeper than it had to be to raise the flat back off the dough while cutting? One of the cutters in the sale, an almost 12"H, full length figure side profile of woman in big shoes, small topknot, and long skirt with pinked hem (or fringe), which was very shallow, was thought by Robacker to be "probably oldest" in their collection. (That cutter brought $775.00.) • For the cow: **$35.00-$45.00**

Cookie cutter, dog, standing large breed — Newfoundland? St. Bernard? heavy gauge tin, with folded top edge, strap handle, deep cutter, American, 6"L, mid 19th C. • **Woodstove Christmas Cookies In the 19th Century.** — "At least a week before Christmas all the tin cooky cutters were brought from the cellar and scoured with wood ash until they shone. There were forms of every shape and description — birds, stars, hearts, horses and other animals. No one wanted to miss a chance at cutting out these lovely cookies. Usually mother would permit the children to use her thimble to cut a hole in the center of the cookies. The dough remaining in the thimble was baked into 'thimble' cookies, as the children called them. Often a dozen or more kinds of cookies were baked. The recipe book was in constant use. There were biscuits, sand tarts, ginger, and spice cookies. ... Store baskets, wash baskets, and lard cans were brought out and filled with newly-baked goodies. Many were needed, depending on how large one's family was or where they lived. If you lived in the city there was much company and many visitors to be treated. The poor had to be remembered and some cookies must be given to the friend who had lent mother a special cooky cutter." Katharine D. Christ, "Christmas in Pennsylvania", *Historical Review of Berks County*, Winter 1960-61. **$50.00-$65.00**

Cookie cutter, dog very like a Scottie, running pose, tin, flat back with strap handle, nice age, but probably all machine manufactured, American, 3"H x 4½"L, 2nd quarter 20th C (?). • **Dog Dates**. — This is the kind of cutter you could probably research to narrow down the date, if it is indeed a Scottie. When were Scotties really popular? The 1920s and 1930s, to be overtaken by Fox Terriers, then Cockers and German Shepherds began to move up the charts. Surprisingly, the most popular dog in America in the 1880s and 1890s was the huge St. Bernard, which accounts for how many of them you see on old trade card illustrations, etc. Other very popular dogs featured in decorative arts (particularly ceramic figurines), in the 18th and 19th C were (1) the little "Comforter" or lap Spaniel, with big eyes, floppy big ears, and silky hair; (2) the Pug, another small, baby-faced dog meant for lap or silk cushion; (3) an intelligent working dog, the standard Poodle, whose poodle cut was known by the 19th C at least (from France), and whose tight curls, long ears, and cocky tail made great models for works of art or craft; (4) the watersport Retriever, a large dog also depicted with ringlets or curls; and (5) the Water Spaniel, a similar looking breed. • Although some advanced collectors of cookie cutters believe strongly that dog motif cutters didn't naturally fit into the PA German repertoire of motifs, I believe that if they used dogs in watercolors, on quilts, for wood carvings (think of Mountz) and chalkware figures, why not cookie cutters? Cats may be another story; they are much less common in all decorative art, though sometimes featured in portraits of people, or paintings of kitchen or barn interiors. **$20.00-$28.00**

Cookie cutter, dromedary (one hump, not two like a camel), tin with arched strap handle from hump to belly, 2 legs, no flat back, offered as mail order premium by "Dromedary Cocoanut" which was mfd by The Hills Brothers Co., NYC, 1915 ad. **7.00-$12.00**

Cookie cutter, Dutch boy, odd small circles (that made holes) under his arms, tin, strap handle, turned edge, American (?), 5⅛"L, 19th C. **$65.00-$85.00**

Cookie cutter, Dutchman in wooden shoes & wide pantaloons, tin, strap handle, 4¾"H, 20th C. **$22.00-$28.00**

Cookie cutter, eagle with spread wings, tin, flat back, 6¼"W x ½" deep, late 19th C. **$40.00-$55.00**

Cookie cutter, elephant, possibly related to P. T. Barnum's "Jumbo", tin, flat back with strap handle, PA German, 6⅜"H x 9⅞"L, prob. 4th quarter 19th C. • Robacker May 1989 price: **$385.00**

Cookie cutter, elephant, tin, strap handle, American, 9⅛"W, 19th C, prob. 1870s. • Jumbo was probably the inspiration for this large cutter. It sold in NYC at a Pier Show for $250.00 or so in the mid 1980s. **$350.00-$500.00**

Cookie cutter, Father Christmas (one precursor of what we call Santa Claus) with toy bag on back, beard & cap, long skirted robe, small feet, mounted to but overlaps the oblong flat back, tin, marked only "Germany", 9½"H x about 5"W, c.1891-1915. **$125.00-$170.00**

• The **Belsnickel** is another Christmas character depicted in cookie cutters. By custom, the costumed Belsnickel came on Christmas Eve to decide which children had been good or bad (shades of Santa). "If one lived in the country, he expected to see ... a weird-looking hobgoblin with a long beard & a blackened or false face, dressed in old clothing ... often ... torn and ragged. In one hand the Belsnickel carried a whip or a bundle of switches, & in the other a bag of nuts, snitz (dried apples), & occasionally candy.

"The Belsnickel always asked whether there were any children living there who had been naughty. Those who had recently raided the cooky basket or forgotten some chore had real cause to be frightened. ...

"Before he left, he would open his bag & strew his nuts, snitz, and candy all over the floor. ...Invariably, as a boy tried to get the candy, the whip would come down on his shoulders. ...Sometimes...he left a switch for the parents to use... .

The origin of the Belsnickel comes from *Pelz*, meaning fur, because St. Nicholas was always represented as a person dressed in a huge fur cap and a fur-trimmed suit. He, too, carried, thrown over his shoulders, a bag in which he had presents for good children. His servant, Knecht Rupert, had a blackened face and always carried a bundle of switches which he left for naughty children.

"The city Belsnickel was a somewhat different character. Often more than one Belsnickel visited a home. Sometimes there were as many as five or six in a group, led by a leader. Their visit was much the same as to their country cousins, except that these visitors looked for cookies as a treat. The city Belsnickels were dressed in all sorts of costumes & disguises. Among the group one was likely to find clowns, Indians, harlequins & anything imaginable. Often they carried a musical instrument such as a hand organ, accordian, guitar, trombone, banjo or musical bones." Katharine D. Christ, "Christmas in Pennsylvania", *Historical Review of Berks County*, Winter 1960-61. The English counterpart of these musical characters were **Christmas Mummers**, who still parade in

Philadelphia. Many cookie cutters are found in the shape of Indians, humorous characters, & musical instruments; probably these cutters refer directly to the Belsnickel tradition. **$125.00-$170.00**

Cookie cutter, fellow blowing a pipe or horn, on back it reads "Eleven Pipers Piping", red plastic, very modernistic, ugly too, "Made by Chilton", Aluminum Specialty Co., Manitowa, WI, 5"H, 1978. **$1.00-$2.00**

Cookie cutter, female twins, tin, outline with no detail, no back, no handle, American, 3⅝" x 3⅜", late 19th or early 20th C. • Here's something to look for, a <u>Biddendens</u> "bun" mold, as described by Carl W. Drepperd in *A Dictionary of American Antiques*. He says that from the 16th to 18th C, carved molds depicting the charitable <u>Chulkhurst</u> <u>twins</u>, Elisa and Mary, of Biddenden, England, who were joined at hip and shoulder, were used to mark the buns (probably some form of cookie) that were distributed to the poor, under the terms of the twins' will. The legend, if that it is, dates back to the 12th C. **$20.00-$30.00**

Cookie cutter, fireman, poised while working, simple but effective profile, flat back, tin trimmed only approximately to fit outline. As with many cookie cutters it is hard to recognize the subject until you study it (and others), PA German (?), 7¼"H x 3¾"W, 3rd to 4th quarter 19th C. • Robacker May 1989 price is under what we expected, but there were either no "fire fighter" collectors, hence no crossover interest. **$225.00**

Cookie cutter, fish, fairly ornate, tin, square or <u>bracket strap handle</u>, rectangular flat back with turned edges, American, fish is 5½"L, makes only ½" deep cut, back is 6½"L, late 19th C. • The term bracket strap handle is easy to remember when you think of the squared parentheses-like punctuation marks called brackets [ ], which set off certain prescribed material in a sentence. Sometimes parentheses ( ) are called "round brackets", but we don't need that term in this book. **$50.00-$60.00**

Cookie cutter, fish, simple & stylized, with crimping top and bottom to represent fins, punched up half-moons as tab handle on back, tin, flat back size of playing card, American, cuts ½" deep, 4"L, late 19th C. **$35.00-$45.00**

Cookie cutter, fish, tin, flat back, American (?), vary from 4"L to about 6"L, most seem to be late 19th or early 20th C. • **Few Fish Flaunt Flair.** — I've never seen a really nice fish cutter; most are very shallow cutters, and have open mouths, top and bottom fin & tail, but nothing particularly well-shaped. Also, I don't know why, most of the ones I've seen have very poor soldering, and are coming apart. I can *imagine* a more intricate one, perhaps with nifty crimped edges to fins & tail. • Fish cookies are almost certainly Christian religious symbols, Christ having been a "fisher of men" and also because He divided the loaves and the fishes to feed the multitude. **$18.00-$20.00**

Cookie cutter, fish, very simple, shallow cutting edge, tin, flat back, American, 3"L, late 19th C. **$18.00-$22.00**

Cookie cutter, flame, very stylized, of the advertised stove, back stamped with ornate scrolled border & name, strap handle embossed with legend, stamped tin, shallow cutter in shape that looks like ruffle top tulip, "Garland Stoves & Ranges", and "The World's Best", 3⅝"W, late 19th C. **$25.00-$35.00**

Cookie cutter, gingerbread boy, a classic form, though this one a more than insipid cutter, tin, strap handle attached to flat back, American, 5"H, late 19th C. **$15.00-$25.00**

English and European gingerbread bakers from the early Middle Ages (13th C) into the first third of the 19th C often made gingerbread men as well as other gingerbread forms. In fact, according to Max von Boehn in *Dolls and Puppets,* a revised edition of which was published in Boston in 1956, "The gingerbread doll had a tenacious life ... [and] the shapes which it assumed remained the same for centuries." According to Dan Foley, in *Toys Through the Ages,* (Philadelphia & NY: Chilton Books, 1962), "So popular was gingerbread in England that there were fairs where only gingerbread and toys were sold. Each year in Birmingham, two gingerbread fairs were held until well into the nineteenth century. ... Long lines of market stalls, filled with gingerbread in every imaginable shape and form, were interspersed with booths filled with toys." He goes on, "**Gingerbread men** were called 'husbands' at the English fairs, and were often referred to as 'Jim Crows' in nineteenth century America" where they had become popular since the 18th C. Foley cites Nathaniel Hawthorne's *House of Seven Gables* as a literary source for the mention of gingerbread elephants! Another popular and historical form for gingerbread was the edible horn book, modeled like the wooden or ivory ones, a sort of abecedarian paddle, sometimes with numbers, formed in ceramic or carved wooden molds before baking. Such **gingerbread horn books** were all said to be decorated with gold leaf, and were given children as rewards, or inducements for learning.

Andrew W. Tuer, in *History of the Horn Book* (©1897, reprinted 1968 by Benjamin Blom, Inc.; & 1979, Arno Press) devotes a chapter to gingerbread horn books. He writes "**Halfpenny gingerbread** was made of flour, sugar, and treacle. In a white variety of cake stamped from the same moulds there was more sugar and the treacle was omitted. Pieces of gold foil were dabbed on both sorts. ... The white cakes being sweeter and dearer — they sold for a penny — were considered better and were ... given as ... rewards. It may be noted here that confectioners sold a white gingerbread of a better class of flour, butter, ground ginger, lemon rind, nutmeg, and loaf-sugar." Tuer believed the molds for horn books dated to the mid 18th C. **$15.00-$25.00**

Cookie cutter, gingerbread boy, shallow stamped copper anodized aluminum, on original printed card, Color Craft Co. #89, Indianapolis, IN, 5⅞"H x 3½"W, prob. 1960s-70s. **$3.00-$5.00**

Cookie cutter, gingerbread boy with barely discernible features (meant for the purchaser because the impression made on cookie dough would be fleeting to say the least), very shallow stamped aluminum, green painted strap handle riveted on, no marks, American, 5⅞"H x 3½"W, originated c.1930s, but prob. made for a long time. **$3.00-$5.00**

Collecting Attitudes, or **Why collect "ugly" new cutters?** There is more than one way to collect anything. Some of the earliest documented collectors, many hundreds of years ago, assembled oddities and curiosities of Nature and put them in curiosity cabinets. Other collectors bought (or appropriated) objects of aesthetic "merit" or intrinsic worth, including jewelry, gold decorative pieces, marble sculptures, etc. Still other collectors added only objects with religious significance (artworks and relics) to their private collections. The curiosity collectors evolved into curators of science museums; the others became connoisseurs, who based all their judgments on immutable "facts" of proportion, style, grace, finish and other establishmentarian rules (which changed somewhat with fashion, though more slowly). In the history of the United States, there have been eminent curiosity collectors like the Peale family and John James Audubon, who were scientists & artists. Also there have been many connoisseurs and pseudo-connoisseurs, of which the latter are most common. The benefactors of many of our museums were either connoisseurs or they had lots of money and good advisors. It has not been popular outside of anthropology or sociology to collect curiosities of art until the 20th C, and even now it is often looked down upon by people who believe in a good better best (and not-so-good, worse, awful) system of connoisseurship. (A joke told about Israel Sack, a knowledgable and opinionated furniture dealer who has written books on what is "good, better, and best" of each form, is that it is more truthfully "good, better, and 'in stock'".) • For the same reasons a money standard is necessary, without widely accepted rules and calibrated values, your piece of artwork might be worthless in the very marketplace you needed it to be pricey. But I mistrust any pontificant on art — fine, decorative or useful — who claims absolutes, and who says and believes "This is great; that is terrible." Absolute aesthetics are not objective, because there is no such thing; this critical dilemma lies behind the ongoing argument over folk art (ie. Yes, but is it Art?). Material culturist collectors are often as interested in the use & context of something, the *reality* of it, as in the aesthetics. This is not to say that material culturists don't judge objects within a group or class, but they factor in a good deal of value based on purpose or function (or current educational potential). Even if an old time connoisseur concedes that a thing is interesting, to him that quality is valueless in appraisals.

Cookie cutter, hatchet, with inscribed notation "George Washington's hatchet he used to cut down his Dad's favorite cherry tree", tin, signed "Robt. P. Frey", Cleona, Lebanon County, PA, 6¾"L, dated 1973. **$25.00-$35.00**

Cookie cutter, heart, deep cutter, no back or handle, homemade from old turquoise-printed tin "Maxwell House" coffee can, American, 1¾" deep x about 3½"L, c.1940s. **$7.00-$10.00**

Cookie cutter, heart design, corrugated tin, commercial bakery type, with large fat cylindrical handle that fits in palm of hand, convex cap on handle, stamped "3½" in 2 places on handle, no maker's mark, (Jaburg Brothers was one company making them, NYC), measures 3"H x 3½"W, heart itself measures 3¼" x 3¼" x ⅞" deep, early 20th C. **$20.00-$25.00**

Cookie cutter, heart, has interesting spring-action push-off rod that goes through the strap handle & is attached to the pusher plate inside, tin, American, heart is 3" from the point up to crack between lobes, late 19th C. **$95.00-$125.00**

Cookie cutter, heart shaped, corrugated around outside, with inset in center to mark design of 3 petals, tin, flat back, strap handle, lots of little holes in back, American, 3 ⅛"W at largest part, late 19th C. **$45.00-$55.00**

Cookie cutter, heart shaped, homemade pieced tin, edges rolled on cutting edge as well as flat back, no handle, American, ⅞" deep x 2" x 2¾", late 19th C. **$15.00-$22.00**

Jingling Itinerant Tin Peddler Theory. — In popular books on folk art, especially Pennsylvania Dutch, you often find the jingling itinerant tin peddler theory of cookie cutter origins, or JITPTOCCO. So far I haven't traced it to its first appearance; but somewhere someone first wrote, in effect, as Jean Lipman did in the following: "It must have been a red-letter day for the *hausfrau* when the itinerant tinsmith came by with his jingling cart and made her some newly designed cooky cutter, while the whole family watched his nimble fingers at work with shears and solder." (*American Folk Art in Wood, Metal and Stone*, 1948). • In Earl F. Robacker's booklet about cookie cutters, he says, "The tinsmith, traveling from place to place, soon exhausted his ready-made stock, and profitably extended his trip by manufacturing a variety of buckets and pots and pans at farmsteads where they were needed. ... The smaller bits which fell from the shears were used up ... in such items as children's toys ... and cooky cutters." Robacker goes on at some length describing motifs, and then: "In later years, with the passing of the tinsmith's jingling cart, a specimen set of cutters would often be put on display at a general store, and orders received there." (*Home Craft Course, Pennsylvania German Cooky Cutters and Cookies*, Plymouth Meeting, PA: 1946). • Margaret Coffin writes "In the country the tinker was apt to travel on horseback, saddlebags filled with solder, old lead, and a soldering iron, a spoon mold, a clock dial mold, and bits of tinplate ... (to repair) a teakettle, mend a hole in a pan, or cast a spoon. He made cookie cutters to order to fit the (housewife's) fancy." (*History & Folklore of American Country Tinware, 1700-1900*, NYC: Galahad Books, 1968. • Jeannette Lasansky's *To Cut, Piece and Solder, The Work of the Rural Pennsylvania Tinsmith*, (1982) includes so much in-depth information, interpreting 10 tinsmiths' account books & cutters, that it could be called a book on cookie cutters, even though it covers all kinds of tinwares. Even in the 1750s many PA smiths had a shop. An 1793 ad for "gingerbread cutters", cited by Lasansky, gives a shop address. Lasansky does not, as far as I know, mention itinerant cookie cutter makers. **$15.00-$22.00**

Age Wrinkles. — The earliest method for corrugating sheet metal was with the use of a corrugating or crimping swedge — a sort of little molding anvil to fit onto an anvil; an iron piece, cast with the requisite pattern of hills and valleys against which the metal could be hammered, thereby taking on the corrugations. • As far as I can determine, <u>corrugating or crimping machines for tinsmiths</u> were not patented until 1854. Therefore, cookie cutters (or other tinwares) that have extremely regular corrugations are almost undoubtedly from the 2nd half of the 19th C or later. These hand-operated machines (one of which a friend and I found on the streets of NYC in the 1970s) look rather like large fluting machines, or some kind of interesting laundry mangle. The two rollers have corrugated surfaces, and the distance between the rollers is adjustable. The sheet of tin (or brass or other sheet metal) is fed through while the machine is cranked. • A very simple tool, actually a pair of long-handled tongs with special jaws with diagonal grooves on the inside, was available and advertised for "tinners, stove dealers, galvanized iron and cornice makers, and all workers in sheet metal." Tedious to crimp 200 feet of cornice for a house, maybe, but just the ticket for a cookie cutter. — "Packham's Pipe & Sheet Metal Crimping Tongs", advertised in *The Metal Worker*, Aug. 12, 1882. • Packham Crimper Co., Mechanicsburgh, OH, also had a cranked crimper which did the same jobs, only faster — a machine screw-clamped to the work table, had 2 narrow rollers and so could only crimp a narrow band of metal or the edge of something — perhaps 3 or 4" W. It was also advertised in 1882. • A tinsmith from Ohio wrote the *Metal Worker*, Sept. 9, 1882: "to suggest that all my brother chips (the nickname amongst themselves for tinners & tinsmiths) buy a machine specially devised for crimping stove pipes. It costs so little money that it is within the reach of every one, and a tool of this character is far preferable to a combination tool. A machine especially designed for the purpose is expensive only in the first cost. Experience demonstrates their great utility in the tin shop. Devices of this kind are very generally sold in the trade, and may be ordered from any tinners' suppliers. It also promotes morality, for it saves a lot of swearing over ill-fitting stove pipes."

Cookie cutter, heart with corrugated edge, strap handle, 3 air holes well-placed, perhaps unintentionally, so that the cutter resembles a modern artist's mask, American, 5" across, late 19th C or early 20th. **$70.00-$90.00**

Cookie cutter, horse facing right, rectangular flat back, no handle, 2 air holes, nice & large, American, 8" x 6", c.1870s to 1880s. • **"Ginger Horse-Cakes.** — One quart of flour, one pint of best Orleans molasses, one cupful of sugar, tablespoonful and a half of ginger, two small teaspoons of soda, half a cupful of sour cream, and a heaping tablespoonful of lard. Sift the flour first, and then sprinkle the ginger well through it, add the sugar and molasses, putting in lastly the soda dissolved in the cream. Obtain from a tinner a cutter shaped like a horse, for cutting out the cakes." Gertrude Strohm, "Pies and Small Cakes," *The Universal Cookery Book*, NYC: 1888. **$150.00-$170.00**

Cookie cutter, horse, long skinny & very short, facing left, very shallow cutting edge, tin, long bracket strap handle, American, horse is 3"H x 6"L, late 19th C. **$70.00-$90.00**

Cookie cutter, horse with high rump, high head and 4 little legs like the drawings in that charming old book *The Four-Cornered Horse*, tin, small thumb size strap handle, one tiny nail hole to string on cord probably, as it's not big enough to function as air release hole, American, 5½"L, late 19th C. **$70.00-$90.00**

Cookie cutter, horse with horn-blowing rider, tin, flat back, PA German, 7"H x 6¾"W, 3rd to 4th quarter 19th C. • **Old Cookie Cutter Shapes.** — Ann Hark & Preston A. Barba, in *Pennsylvania German Cookery*, Allentown, PA: Schlechter's, 1950, give a recipe borrowed from Mrs. Robert A. Wertman, Sr., for "**Bellylaps** — An old-time Christmas cooky." Made of flour with lots of dark molasses, a small amount of butter, two eggs and some baking soda, they are rolled out to "about ¼ inch thick on a lightly floured board. In the olden days it was customary of make large cookies of this particular dough and they were cut into the shapes of hearts, stars, eagles, horses and their riders." Bellylaps were also called <u>belly-guts</u>. • Like the Civil War reenactments popular with some people today, there was an annual <u>Battalion Day</u>

held in many Pennsylvania communities between 1783 and 1862. This day of parading, training and militia exercises, included cavalry troops outfitted in uniforms at least similar to those of the Revolutionary War. So cookie cutters, or any other decorative use of the horse-riding soldier, could as easily be inspired by latter day Battalion exercises as by the War of Independence. For more, see J. Ritchie Garrison's "Battalion Day: Militia Exercise and Frolic in Pennsylvania Before the Civil War", *Pennsylvania Folklife*, Winter 1976-77, Vol. XXVI, No. 2. • The Robacker horn-blower cutter in this listing, sold in the May 1989 auction for: **$450.00**

Cookie cutter, horse with very short, slightly bent legs, tin, homemade, primitive, rather deep ¾'' cutting edge, American, 7''L, late (?) 19th C. • Full figure horses are really popular forms; less desirable are horse heads. The variety is tremendous. **$140.00-$170.00**

Cookie cutter, hunter wearing hat & holding gun, tin, flat back, American, 4½''H, prob. 3rd quarter 19th C. **$120.00-$150.00**

Cookie cutter, Indian with raised tomahawk, tin, flat back, vigorous figure called "Threatening Indian" by the Robackers, PA German, 7½''H x 4''W, 19th C. • Robacker May 1989 price: **$550.00**

Cookie cutter, "jigsaw puzzle" interlocked figural cookies, makes 14 with 2 oddly shaped scraps left over, big cheap thin shiny rectangular frame of tin, with bent strips inside form shapes, American (?), 12⅝''L x 9¾''W, mid 20th C. Related, is a cutter comprised of a round band of tin, 12'' in diameter, enclosing about 16 different outline cookie cutters ranging from a duck, a dog, and a bird on a branch to a tulip and what appears to be a daffodil. All the cutters are soldered to one another so that all the various cookies (and the oddly shaped scraps left over) could be cut in one step. A number of them were seen in the late 1970s and early 1980s, and they are almost undoubtedly 20th C. **$3.00-$5.00**

Cookie cutter, leaf, corrugated outer edge, inset marking veins, with big cylindrical palm-fitting handle with convex cap, for commercial bakery use, tin, unusual because marked: "Wood & Selig" (or "Selic"?), which could be maker, dealer or bakery, NYC, 4''L x 2¼''W, cutter ⅝'' deep, handle 2⅜''H including cap dome, x 2⅛'' diameter, TOC to early 20th. **$18.00-$28.00**

Cookie cutter, leaf, corrugated outside & 4 inset vein markers, tin, strap handle, Pennsylvania European heritage style, 4¾''L x 2½''W, shallow cut, late 19th C. **Dutch or German?** — For many years there has been an argument about whether it is more accurate to use the term Pennsylvania Dutch, or to assume that that is corruption of Pennsylvania Deutsch, therefore that is should be Pennsylvania German. • If you want to read something interesting, get Carl W. Dreppard's *A Dictionary of American Antiques*, and look up "Pennsylvania Dutch." In part, Drepperd says "More misinformation, erroneous claims, and wrong beliefs are current (book published 1952 after 10 years compilation) in respect to the meaning of this term than any other phrase pertaining to American social history and objects that survive. What is now Pennsylvania was colonized by the Swedes and the Dutch half a century before William Penn (c.1680). ... With Swedes, Dutch, and some Finns in residence on his arrival, Penn offered haven ... to French Huguenots, Swiss Mennonites, Amish from Flanders, Rhinish Palan-

tinates, Swabians, Danes, Dutch, Walloons, Swedes, and Flemings (who) arrived in the colony from 1630s to 1760s." He says that Pennsylvania Dutch is more accurate than Pennsylvania German, and accuses numerous societies of fostering the falsehood that Pennsylvania folk arts and crafts are purely Germanic. But a *Farmer's Cabinet* of 1836 relates that 54 ships' loads of German emigrants arrived in Philadelphia in just one summer, and tells of a 1750 law prohibiting "importing too many Germans in one vessel", presumably to limit overall emigration. In 1677, Penn offered refuge to Quakers in the Netherlands and Germany in what was then western New Jersey, already settled by Swedes and Dutch for decades. Before he had ever seen "Pennsylvania", he invited Quakers from England and Wales to emigrate too. The 11th edition of the *Encyclopedia Britannica*, states that "In no other colony were so many different races and religions represented. ... Dutch, Swedes, English, Germans, Welsh, Irish and Scotch-Irish; Quakers, Presbyterians, Episcopalians, Catholics, Reformed Lutherans, Mennonites, Dunkers, Schwenkfelders, and Moravians...most now merged in the general type." The *Encyclopedia* says that the language "Pennsylvania Dutch" is a "corrupt German dialect, largely Rheno-Franconian in origin." **$15.00-$22.00**

Cookie cutter, leaping deer, tail up, tin, flat back with 3 air release holes, PA German, 9⅛''H x 12½''L, 3rd to 4th quarter 19th C. • Robacker May 1989 price: **$775.00**

Cookie cutter, lion, very simple, tin, 20th C. • **Lions** may originally have been borrowed from heraldry by cookie cutter makers; or they may be a religious symbol (the lion and the lamb shall lie down together; or a symbolic representation of Christ by a lion); or they may reflect an interest in the lion seen in early menageries or circuses. Probably the first African lion brought to America was the "Lyon of Barbary", which arrived in 1716 for exhibition in New England. **$10.00-$12.00**

Cookie cutter, Maid Marian figural, tin, advertising "Robin Hood Flour," 20th C. **$10.00-$15.00**

Cookie cutter, male figure, standing strong man, arms down, feet out, heavy sheet iron or terne plate (a heavier tinplate with higher percentage of lead), flat back with air holes of 3 sizes at head, shoulders, chest, belly, thighs and ankles, unusual in that they are symetrical, which adds to visual appeal, or rather doesn't distract, as the holes in a cutter this big are very obvious, two strap handles behind knees and behind heart, American, unusually tall at 18¼''H, mid to late 19th C. • A spectacular sculptural piece with great appeal to folk art collectors, and sold as such by dealers Roger Ricco & Frank Maresca. The piece was shown a few times, and the price kept going up. I do not know what it finally sold for; I believe it was in 1987. The low price in the range below was first asking price; the other is my guess at final price to a collector, although full effect of Robacker auction prices hasn't yet shaken the market. **$2000.00-$3000.00**

Cookie cutter, man, hunched & elderly, with skinny walking stick, imagine making a cookie & not breaking off that walking stick, tin, flat back, PA German (?), 7"H x 4¼"W, late 19th C. • Robacker May 1989 price: **$275.00**

Cookie cutter, man in derby or bowler hat, full standing, soldered tin strips that form the cutting edge in 2 parts — top half of his body overlaps bottom half & solder joints are just below waist level on both sides, no strap handle, no back, "Nut Brown Product", a mark found on a number of housewares from the U.K., English, about 5"H, mid (?) 20th C. **$20.00-$25.00**

Cookie cutter, man on horse, tin, flat back, small, GHESCINERE MENIN (?), French, Belgian, German, or Alsatian (?), 19th C. • Belonged to dealer Teri Dziadul. Price range mine. **$300.00-$400.00**

Cookie cutter, man on horseback like a Revolutionary War Hessian soldier, tin, flat back, GHESCINERE MENIN (?), French, Belgian, German, or Alsatian (?), 11"H x 9"W (tail to nose), 19th C. • Belonged to dealer Teri Dziadul. Price range mine. **$400.00-$600.00**

Cookie cutter, man, standing, tin, fat cylindrical handle with convex cap on end, for commercial bakery use, marked "Germany", 5¼" diameter, c.1920s to 1930s. **$65.00-$80.00**

Cookie cutter, man, tin, flat back closely trimmed except between thighs and between back arm and back, an example of <u>Black Americana</u> called the "<u>Runaway Slave</u>" by Robackers and in auction catalog, obviously intended to be a running black man, with crimped hair on top of head, full lips. Small curl of tin for eye, another for ear, but not much detail in extremities. The figure, with its curved torso, appears naked, or at least there are no ridges or other indications of hems or cuffs. PA German (?). PA was destination for many runaway slaves. 12⅛"H x 7½"W, prob. 3rd or 4th quarter 19th C. • **Reproduction alert**. — Within a couple of months of the sale, an enterprising person created a lookalike cutter (that doesn't really look like the original). "The Tinner", without permission or consulting either the owner of the superb original or common sense, has turned out an awkwardly drawn (but perhaps well-executed) rip-off, in the same size, in "a rich, aged patina", and supposedly in a "marked and numbered limited edition" for $24.95 ppd. Thank heaven it's marked and numbered (I don't know how many are in the edition), and let's hope the marks are permanent & deep. In the original, the lines flow as if Picasso or Matisse had drawn them; in the copy, the back leg is bulging and muscular, the front one skinny, the fingers look like hooves, and the head is tiny and with a hatchet-like projection off the back, whereas the original has gorgeously simple crimped hair, and a robust face. The inset ear on the new is oversized and poorly positioned; that on the original is a sort of squiggled "C" and in good proportion. "The Tinner", of Spencer, NC, has also advertised a heart-in-hand cutter, on a square flatback that measures 6" x 5". It only costs $8.00. Well … you know what my opinion is of fakes and most reproductions. Some are close to worthless, others have utilitarian value but no value as collectibles. • Robacker

May 1989 auction price, paid by a very discriminating collector of cookie cutters who will be writing a book, cannot be used to make judgments about *any* other cutters. The high price achieved for a fine cutter cannot be useful in determining the probable market value of any but the most closely comparable cutters. **$7400.00**

Cookie cutter, man, tin, rather primitive, standing but no hat or cane, this not my idea of gingerbread man, American, 7"H, 19th C. • Some of these almost look like political figures. Humorous caricatures of people as well as animals were popular with PA German cookie makers. **$125.00-$175.00**

Cookie cutter, man with hand raised to reach for something, small curl of tin for inset eye, tin, flat back, PA German, 9⅞"H x 5⅝"W, 3rd or 4th quarter 19th C (?). • Robacker May 1989 price: **$425.00**

Cookie cutter, man with hat, interior inset strips or curls of tin making line of his arm, also eye and ear, tin, flat back, together with a simple cutter of man in hat, PA German, 7¼"H x 3⅝"W, and 7⅝"H x 3½"W, 3rd or 4th quarter 19th C (?). • Robacker May 1989 for both cutters. **$425.00**

Cookie cutter, man with hat, very primitive standing figure, tin, flat back, looks "right" & old, American, 8½"H, 19th C. • In the early 1980s, this was for sale at a good antique show for a paltry $98.00. Gadz, what a fool I was not to have bought it. These hatted men cutters are extremely desirable, particularly in anything over 6"H. Writing just a few months after the first two parts of the Robacker Collection was auctioned by T. Glenn Horst in Pennsylvania, in 1989, it is impossible to predict what will happen to general prices. Some of the **Robacker cookie cutters** were so outstanding that I doubt if any others of comparable quality and art value will ever come on the market again. So it is not so much the $7400.00 "Running Man" cutter that need worry us here; <u>it is the $300.00 to $800.00 cutters that are more likely to affect prices.</u> **$450.00-$700.00**

Cookie cutter, mermaid with upcurled tail, nice & robust, tin, flat back, PA German, 5⅜"H x 5⅝"L, prob. 3rd to 4th quarter 19th C. Robacker May 1989: **$450.00**

Early Pennsylvania German Motifs. — Frances Lichten, writing in *Folk Art Motifs of Pennsylvania*, NY: Hastings House, 1954, wrote that the early motifs, not just for cookie cutters but for all the decorated arts, Included: tulips or lilies, hearts, several birds (such as song birds, doves, cocks, parrots, peacocks, & eagles), stars, geometric shapes, stags, unicorns, urns, mermaids, cherubs, and angels. She explains that the Pennsylvania Dutch only began to make decorated utilitarian wares after several generations spent establishing their farms. "A rough guess, judging by the objects which bear dates, would place this revival of the more decorative aspects of folk life somewhere around 1765." At first traditional motifs were taken from remembered and remaining objects and furniture brought to America from Germany, Switzerland, Moravia and other countries, Lichten explains that "In the first decades of the 19th century (the Pennsylvania German craftsman's) work began to show traces of the period decoration fashionable during the previous quarter century. Although quite out of keeping with the boldness of his <u>traditional motifs</u>, he adopted these ideas, (and) used them as he saw fit. …" These <u>adopted motifs</u> included "certain ornamental details high in favor during the Empire period … great looped draperies (used) as a frame ... rococo scrolls ...'' and later "the symbols of the Romantic period — the classic column, bow-knot, rose, forget-me-not, and wreath.'' • **Fraternal orders**, such as the Odd Fellows and Freemasons, used the column motif, so lodge decorations may have influenced, over a long period of limited exposure, non-member artisans. • **Other motifs** not designated by Lichten as being "early" are flowers, pomegranates, fish, humans, horsemen, crowns and heraldic animals. These motifs, all of them, are found in 18th C decorative arts or fraktur or cut paper documents such as taufschien, etc, and that is "early" to me.

Cookie cutter, Mickey Mouse, stamped aluminum, riveted strap handle, (or Minnie Mouse, same series), Disney licensed, 4'', 20th C. **$30.00-$35.00**

Cookie cutter, or biscuit cutter, round, metal, adv'g "Malleable Range'', Engman-Matthews Range Co., South Bend, IN, 1½''D, TOC. **$6.00-$8.00**

Cookie cutter, parrot on a branch, sheet brass, very high arched strap handle on flat back, 4 holes, PA German (?), early 20th C (?). • **Parrots** are often depicted by the Pennsylvania Germans. According to Frances Lichten the Carolina parakeet, grass green with a bright red head, was once native to Pennsylvania. Unlike some other birds, the parrot was probably not symbolic. • **Symbolic Birds.** — Cock or rooster - a Christian symbol of vigilance, and Peacock - immortality & resurrection; Dove - innocence, conjugal affection or the Holy Ghost. The symbolisms were not necessarily known to or referred to by PA German artisans, but were copied from much older European traditional work. **$75.00-$100.00**

Cookie cutter, pitcher with nice shape & handle, tin, flat back, strap handle, American, 3½''H, late 19th C. **$12.00-$18.00**

Cookie cutter, rabbit, tin, only 1½''H, late 19th C. **$12.00-$18.00**

Cookie cutter, rabbit, tin, no handle, stamped "Davis Baking Powder'', ⅞'' deep cut x 4''L, early 20th C. One of an animal set that includes a horse, goose, rabbit & cat. Hoboken, NY, 1926. **$18.00-$22.00**

Cookie cutter, rolling multiple type, makes a diamond, heart, club & spade, green wood handle, body of roller & cutters are crimped & riveted tin, no maker name, makes 1¼'' cookies, overall length 6⅛'', 1932 patent #1855663. **$15.00-$18.00**

Cookie cutter, rolling multiple type, plated cast steel, 6 designs, marked D. R. G. M., German, mid 20th C. **$12.00-$18.00**

Cookie cutter, rolling multiple type, sheet metal, white wooden handle, "Rollemout'' by American Cutter Co., Milwaukee, WI, 20th C, "Patent Applied For.'' • Phyllis Wetherill, in her profusely-illustrated book on 20th C cookie cutters (see Bibliography), shows a Rollemout with a twisted wire handle. I don't know which is earliest. **$12.50-$15.00**

Cookie cutter, rolling multiple type, tin, wire handle, 3 interchangeable barrels for making diamonds, waffling, or swirls, in original box, mfd. by Guirier, c.1930s. **$25.00-$30.00**

Cookie cutter, rolling or "rotating'' type for doughnuts, with aluminum cutting blades with small tubes, for cutting 2 doughnuts in one revolution, twisted wire & turned wooden handle available in different colors. This was one of a set of 4 for making "cookies, doughnuts, rolls, scones and tarts.'' From editorial copy in *House Furnishing Review*, Jan. 1930, we learn about "rotating cutters having detachable blade for cleaning and edges flanged at a varying pitch so that the cutting edge cuts vertically, straight through the dough, leaving no dough sticking to the blades.'' "Rollemout'', by The American Cutter Co., Milwaukee, WI, being made at least by 1928. • **Marketing information** from the same editorial piece includes that the "Item (is) somewhat seasonal. Best buying months are February, March, April, September, October and November.'' ... "Six foot counter space is sufficient for demonstration'' ... and "Relative popularity of colors is as follows: Green, 60%; red, 25%; yellow, 15%.'' Apparently blue was not a choice in 1930 (or any other time?). The price for a full set, in original carton, would be about three times the price given here for only one. **$12.50-$15.00**

Cookie cutter, rooster, all carved of wood, the cutting edge also of wood. It wouldn't really cut, per se, but would smuush the form out from the rolled dough, PA German (?), 4½'' x 4⅜'', 19th C. Robacker May 1989 **$250.00**

Cookie cutter, rooster, of a type sometimes called a "maple sugar mold'' — tin with wooden back, PA German, 5½'' x 6⅝'', 3rd to 4th quarter 19th C. • Robacker May 1989 price: **$750.00**

Cookie cutter, rooster with high perky tail with 4 squared off feathers, long open beak, 2 oblong legs with no feet, round bumptious rear end, irridescence to tin (possibly coated with something?), 4 small air holes & several small holes up in tail feathers, beak & legs, old type tin flat back, marked "A. J. B.'', poss. PA, 5''H x 4''W x ⅝'' deep, dealer tag said "not old.'' Prob. late 1970s or even 1980s. **$5.00-$7.00**

Cookie cutter, round, tin with corrugated outside cutting edge, inner ring plain, for ring "sand tart'' cookies of type traditionally hung on trees, strap handle, American, 3'' diameter, late 19th C. **$15.00-$22.00**

Cookie cutter, Santa Claus, tin, flat back in oblong shape is not cutaway to follow outline, therefore not a scrap used for backing. Figure's detailed outline includes hem of greatcoat, he carries small Christmas tree on his left shoulder (our right), stands on block assumed to be the top of chimney, all in all the form & stance is very like Christmas post cards & other holiday images of Santa, this cookie would require much decorating in different colors to make form interesting. PA German, 11''H x 5½''W, late 19th C. • Robacker May 1989 price: **$850.00**

Cookie cutter, Santa Claus with toy pack on his back & what cataloguer Clarence Spohn (and the Robackers) call a tsipfel cap, a liberty cap (though that's not the translation), tin, flat back, "handle missing, solder loose'', PA German, 9½''H x 6''W, prob. 4th quarter 19th C. **$375.00**

"Syrup Kuchlein (Molasses Cakes). — Two scant cupfuls of lard, two cupfuls of molasses, one egg, one teaspoonful of ground cloves, one teaspoonful of ground cinnamon, half a teaspoonful of salt, one teaspoonful of soda, and (probably about 3½ pounds?) flour. Melt the lard; when cool add the molasses, spices, salt, and the soda dissolved in a little hot water. Stir thoroughly and add the flour, a little at a time, until the dough is very thick; roll out and cut in fancy shapes. These little cakes are always to be found on a German Christmas tree.

"Tin forms or cutters to cut little cakes into various shapes may easily be made at home. Get narrow strips of tin from a tinsmith. These strips should be about three-quarters of an inch wide; then cut off the length desired for the form. With the fingers bend and shape this narrow strip until it is the desired shape, then pinch the two ends over one another like a seam and the form is complete. These cutters do not require a handle or top; the sides alone are sufficient to cut out any animal desired. Figures of crows (sic — possibly supposed to be cows?), elephants, birds, squirrels, dogs and cats, or the figure of Santa Claus, are easily made out of these simple strips of tin. However, these forms may be secured at many stores and at a very reasonable price." Lola D. Wangner, "Christmas Cakes of Germany", *Ladies Home Journal*, Dec. 1906. • Santa cutter from Robacker May 1989 auction:

Cookie cutter, Santa Claus with very little appeal in detail or form, factory-made, tin, 3½"H, 20th C.   **$5.00-$7.00**

Cookie cutter, Santa related motif of St. Nicholas with mitred hat & long staff, tin, flat back, no handle, stamped with illegible name — MENIN is most likely, French, Belgian, German, or Alsatian (?), 11"H , 19th C. • Belonged to dealer Teri Dziadul. Teri and I think the possible variations of the visible letters are: GHESCINERE MENIN (or MERIN or MEKIN), or GHESCUIERE MENIN (or MERIN or MEKIN — note how all have same diagonals). • See also 2 man on horse cutters, and a woman cutter. • Try as we might, we still can't extrapolate prices out of the extraordinary prices achieved at Robacker auction. Price range here is not Dziadul's, but mine.   **$900.00-$1200.00**

Cookie cutter, Scottie dog, shallow stamped aluminum with green wooden knob handle, American, 1930s-40s. • **Scotties** were popular in the 1920s, and increasingly so in the 1930s, and they were used as a motif in everything from weathervanes to boot scrapers to pocketbooks and slippers. The most famous Scottie was Fala, President Franklin D. Roosevelt's favorite pet, who often traveled with the President. Roosevelt was first elected in 1932.   **$8.00-$10.00**

Cookie cutter, song bird, a small unidentifiable species, early heavy dark tin (probably terne) with satiny feel described by some writers as a "greasy" feel, flat back, no handle, prob. PA, 4¾"L x 2½"W x 34" deep, 19th C. • **Terne Plates & Roofs** — Terne, from the French for "dull", is a mixture of tin and lead, and is actually a form of pewter, according to P. W. Flower, who wrote *A History of the Trade In Tin*, 1880. Flower said that terne plates were used to line wooden packing cases of certain products that had to be kept dry or sealed from the air. • "Of the tin plates of commerce there are two general kinds: One is known as 'tin plate' or 'bright plate,' and the other as 'terne plate' or 'roofing plate.' The coating of the former is supposed to be pure tin, and the bright appearance which it presents gives it the name by which it is most commonly designated, 'bright plate.' The coating of the second kind is composed chiefly of lead, which, being dull, or dead, in appearance, gives it the name usually applied to it, 'terne,' that term being a French word signifying 'dull of appearance.' In considering tin plate for any purpose whatever, it is necessary to examine both the plate and the coating. ..." *The Metal Worker*, Sept. 23, 1882.   **$60.00-$80.00**

Cookie cutter, squirrel with small loop for cutting out eye, & inset strips for detail in tail brush, tin, flat back, solder very bright (repair? late cutter of old tin? Probably the former). PA German, 7"H x 5⅜"W, 3rd to 4th quarter 19th C. • Robacker May 1989 price: **$350.00**

Cookie cutter, star, 5 pointed, unusually deep, flat back tin, strap handle, American, 2½" deep x 4" diameter, 19th C. • The tin is so sharp and the sides so deep that it's possible these were used for something other than cookie cutting. Can't think what, though.   **$18.00-$28.00**

Cookie cutter, star, Moravian 10 point, tin, American, 2" diameter, late 19th C. • For those delicate Moravian ginger cookies, thin as cardboard and crisp as chips.   **$18.00-$22.00**

Cookie cutter, tin, round with scalloped edge, fat cylindrical handle has convex cap on end, for commercial bakery use. This one was called a Bolivar cutter by at least one company. (They also made one with inverted scallops called a Shrewsbury cutter.), maker's name not marked, but Jaburg Brothers was one maker/importer(?), NYC, NY, 4½" diameter, early 20th C.   **$18.00-$28.00**

Cookie cutter, tobacco pipe, modern briar type, tin, flat back, for Father's Day?, American, 5½"L, this one prob. 20th C.   **$35.00-$45.00**

Cookie cutter, tulip, tin. Imagine an oval doughnut cutter which would make a tulip motif center hole instead of a round or oval one. The outer cutting edge is a ribbon of tin forming an oval, with a small central tulip with curved stem, 3 petals in design we think of as Pennsylvania German. This little tulip cutter is mounted to a capped cylinder which forms the handle, and this cylinder is held in place in the oval's center by 2 strap braces on the long axis, prob. American & commercially made, not PA German, 5½"L oval, early 20th C.   **$95.00-$125.00**

"Kindergarten Sandwiches. — Remove crusts from a white and graham loaf and cut each in thin slices, lengthwise. Shape with round, round-fluted, elliptical (oval), cutlet-shaped, square or oblong cutters. Spread one-half the pieces generously with butter, which has been worked until creamy. From remaining pieces cut out shapes, using small flower, animal or fancy cutters, and refill cuts thus made with similar (matching) cuts of cheese-cloth wrung out of hot water to keep moist until serving time." Fanny Merritt Farmer, *A New Book of Cookery*. Boston: Little, Brown, & Co., 1915 edition of 1912 book. • I found the directions confusing, even when looking at the picture in the book, so will describe in other words. First, the "graham" bread, which is whole grain bread, appears as dark as pumpernickel in the picture. The fancy sandwiches shown consist, for example, of an oval of dark bread topped with an oval of white bread, out of which has been cut the shape of a three petal tulip with curved stem. A tulip insert of dark bread has been inserted into the cutout space in the white bread. It is the butter spread on the lower "background" bread that holds the 3 parts of the little mosaic sandwich together. The various cutters shown in Farmer's book are all tin, but must have different origins. Some are deep-cutting, some shallow cutting, some flatback, some backless, some with bracket strap handles, some with no handle. The most complicated one is the tulip & oval, which does two cuts at once.   **$95.00-$125.00**

Cookie cutter, tulip with curved stem with 2 small non-tulip leaves, very graceful form, strong & simple, 3 point large petals, tin, flat back, PA German (?), approx. 6¾''L x 4⅛''W, 3rd to 4th quarter 19th C. **$625.00**

Cookie cutter, Uncle Sam. Marvelous tall proud figure, with 5 little curls of tin for buttons down his coat front, one curl for the eye, a sort of E scroll of tin for the little ear, each finger delineated, unusual flat back, in that — according to cataloguer Clarence Spohn — it is the back of a tin wall sconce that was used. The edges of the backing are turned, and there is a little impressed bead molding around part of perimeter. PA German, 12¼''H x 4¼''W, 3rd to 4th quarter 19th C. • Robacker May 1989 **$3000.00**

Cookie cutter, Uncle Sam, walking tall, in swallow tail coat that projects slightly over edge of flat back, high crowned had, beard, skinny legs with heeled boots, oblong flat back, very shallow cutter, one large push-out hole in hat, 2 small air release holes in body, PA German, 12⅝''H x 3⅛''W, 3rd, 4th quarter 19th C. Robacker May 1989. **$725.00**

How & When Were Holes Made? — Evidence of how things were made gives clues to earliest possible date, if not a latest. So far, cookie cutter holes don't add dating data. Holes are made in sheet metal by (1) <u>drilling</u>, (2) drilling or punching a start hole then <u>sawing</u> with hack or band saw, (3) <u>punching</u> out or <u>puncturing</u> with something such as a nail, a small sharp-edged punch, or a die stamp (a form of punch). A hand-held hammer is needed to drive a nail or a small punch; and either a mechanical drop hammer is needed to provide the force required to strike a die stamp through a metal sheet, or a screwed or levered press must be used to perforate the metal. • Holes made with a punch or die can be round, heart shaped, diamond shaped, or, in fact, any shape. Most cutters have round holes, some big enough to stick a forefinger in to push out the dough, some quite small, say 1/16'' across. At least one cutter from the Robacker Collection had small air holes in a heart shape, which were struck with a tiny heart shaped punch. • The holes made by any method will have a slight burred edge, perhaps visible only with magnification. The burr is called a ''barb'' or ''fin'', to be filed smooth. Most familiar to us kitcheneers are barbs or fins on punctured tin or brass graters, or pie safe tins. Besides a barb, there is apt to be a distortion of the metal surrounding the hole. It may be very slight, or a pronounced warp, especially with thicker metals and larger die stamps. The larger the hole the more metal resists the strike, and if that is not delivered evenly, some distortion may occur. • Die stamps for use by tinsmiths making cookie cutters were available at least since the early 19th C. I don't know how early a simple stamping press capable of making nickel - or quarter-sized holes in tin plate was widely available to tinsmiths. In general, assume a small town tinsmith would be restricted to small punches. A ''Machine for Punching holes in metal'' was patented by J. Sarchet in 1822. Many were patented in the 1850s to 70s. Small presses were available that screw-clamped to the workbench, using a levered ratchet. ''The Little Giant'', American Tool Co., Cleveland, was capable of making a ⅞'' hole in sheet iron 3/32'' thick. It was marketed to tinsmiths for ''small work'' — just right for cookie cutters.

Cookie cutter, Uncle Sam, with flying coat tails & high

hat, wonderful profile full figure, apparently old dark tin, flat back, American, 12½''H, 19th C. • **Reproduction alert.** — These are widely reproduced, that is to say faked, now, to capitalize on the rage for folk art. You have to develop a feel. If they look too good, they are. If the drawing or outline seems just too hokey pokey folky, it is. If it's real cute, give it the boot. If it looks too distressed, it is. If the crudeness is overwhelming, it probably overwhelmed its 1970's or 80's maker too. The rotter. A real one, and you'd have to be sure of yourself, would probably bring within range: **$1200.00-$1800.00**

Cookie cutter, woman in a long dress, copper, flat back, 2 large push-out holes (bigger than air holes & useful for thin dough cookies that might not drop out of their own weight), very plain geometric female form, with a small circle for head, larger circle for upper body, large triangle for skirt, no arms. Sounds boring, it is, sort of, but still it has more zip that can be described, if you think A R T. American, 8''H, late 19th C. • <u>Copper</u> is a popular medium with modern crafts people, but was also used by cookie cutter makers in the 19th C, much, much less often than tin. **$95.00-$125.00**

Cookie cutter, woman, small, tin, flat back, GHESCINERE MENIN (?), see St. Nicholas cookie cutter above, French, Belgian, German, or Alsatian (?), 6''H, 19th C. Ex-Teri Dziadul. **$400.00-$450.00**

''**Making Moravian Christmas Cakes.** — With your sleeves rolled up & your aprons on, you and Mother begin to roll & cut out. Mother seems to get along well from the first, but at your end of the table there is more or less trouble. ... Your first tinful looks pale & ragged beside Mother's perfect, crinkly ovals ... later you get the knack. All the extra boards are needed to hold the cakes. ... While Mother tests the oven, to see if the heat is low & steady, you survey with pride the hearts, stars, crescents, diamonds, squares, circles & different geometrical shapes, but you think more fondly still of the animals & the men and women that will be made after dinner. ... The afternoon baking is somewhat different from the morning session. You have packed the cakes away in the deep can, & have run over to borrow Mrs. Reed's animal cutters. It takes all Mother's skill to move a long-eared rabbit from board to tin, & the elephant with a curled trunk is troublesome too. There are horses, dogs, cats, roosters, ducks & many others. You are quite occupied holding your breath & making Ahs! & Ohs! as each cake is successfully or unsuccessfully placed. Mother does not make as many of these delightful creatures as you could wish, & when it comes to the men & women cakes there is just one apiece for each of you children. Baking this last batch is more work for both Mother and you, but neither of you minds the extra trouble. You remove them from the tins with care bordering on reverence, & place them on top of the 'common' ones: not a few lose their limbs and have to be put in the boys' pile of 'brokens.' When the last fragile cookie is stored away and the lid closed over it you and Mother feel that the busiest, happiest and most profitable day of the year is past.'' Annie M. Stein, *Ladies Home Journal*, Dec. 1909. • This informative little fiction whimsy had a **Moravian molasses cookies** recipe, calling for 1 qt. of molasses, 12 oz. of butter & lard, 12 oz. of brown sugar, 1 oz each of soda, ginger & cinnamon, ½ oz. each of cloves & orange peel, and 4 lbs. of flour. The soda was mixed with a TBS of milk, & when all the other ingredients (except flour) were stirred into a sticky mass, the soda was added: "How the mass puffed up!" The flour was added last, mixed in, & the mixture covered & set to get cold, before rolling & cutting.

Cookie cutter set, airplane, star, heart, chicken & clover leaf, 5 miniature cutters in original cardboard & tin box, Dixon Specialities, Inc. (or Specialties?), NYC, NY, box only 1⅜" deep x 2½" diameter, c.1940s.

Cookie cutter set, animal forms — 7 small ones in simple outline, including pig, dog, cat, deer, horse, cat-like animal with large bushy tail & a pointy eared, short tailed leaping animal that isn't a deer, all tin, in box, imported or American, c.1870s or 80s. • Catalog Cutters: A. Lalance & Grosjean Mfg. Co., NYC, 1890 catalog has no biscuit or doughnut cutters. Under "Cake Cutters" is a 12-piece set of "retinned Animals", including a sitting cat, songbird, horse, lion, sheep (?), leaping rabbit, rooster, donkey or dog (?), eagle, pig, rocking horse, & standing man with cap & insets under arms. The set could be had in three sizes: small, medium and large. Wholesale prices were $11.25 to $20.00 a gross, which might mean a gross of sets (1728 cutters), or of cutters (144 cutters). The price for the small cutters, then, were either about 8¢ a set or 8¢ a cutter. For the large about 14¢ per set, or cutter. Since this was a wholesale catalog, and it was 1890, the price was probably from 8¢ to 14¢ per set, to retail at about twice that. • A 12-piece animal set of Cake Cutters is found in a 1920 Central Stamping Co.'s catalog has of a rooster, mule, parrot, cat, horse, lion, sitting dog, standing dog (?), bull (or other udderless ruminant), dromedary, a song bird, and a long-necked, up-winged bird (eagle?). This set had two catalog numbers, possibly denoting size or gauge of tin. • A 1925 catalog from manufacturers Geuder, Paeschke & Frey Co., noted enamelware producers of Milwaukee, has a page of "cooky", biscuit, doughnut and cake cutters. The only cutter called a "Cooky Cutter" is tin, round with scalloped rim, "solid" back with air hole in center, arched strap handle. It came in two sizes: 3½" and 4" diameter. The "Cake Cutters" came in a set of "Cream City Card Party" solid back cutters, rough cut to fit shape, hearts diamonds, clubs, spades, air hole and no handle. These sets came in one size, respectively by shape: 2¾" x 3¾"; 2½" x 2¾"; 2¾" x 3"; and 2¾" x 3". Also offered was a flatback star with 6 points, 3" diameter; and a heart, flatback, 3" diameter. The best set? Animal Cake Cutters, 12 different designs, are a squirrel, swan, lion, eagle, duck (?), rooster, fish, cat (?), parrot, song bird, another bird, and pig. All shallow cutters, they are flatbacks mounted to flat, very rounded oval tin backs, and are approximately 3"L. Such a set, which originally came in a paper bag, would be a nice find, worth possibly $120.00 or so, despite a relatively recent vintage. • Price range for 7-piece set described this listing: **$45.00-$75.00**

Cookie cutter set, 12 animals: bird, cat, chicken, dog, duck, goat, goose, horse, pig, pigeon, sheep, & swan, simple tin outlines, original printed cardboard box, "Barnyard Cooky Cutters", American, 1930s. **$18.00-$23.00**

Cookie cutter set, farm animals, tin, 12 in original box with color picture of farm scene, American, 20th C. • Added value. — Sets in original boxes are desired by many collectors, although, of course, boxed sets are not comparable in value to older, handmade, non-commercial cutters. **$45.00-$55.00**

Cookie cutters, animal, human & object forms, tin flat back that fits the simple outline perfectly, shallow cutting edge, a few have strap handles, factory-made, little detail. This kind of cutter is just primitive enough to look homemade, but it isn't. (Though probably they were handmade to some degree.) American, two general groups of sizes, about 3" to 4"L and about 4" to 7"L, late 19th C or early 20th. • Added value and the appeal of form. — Variables include collector interest in and charm or appeal of individual forms, detail (though for most cutters there isn't much), size, condition. Large, well-detailed popular forms always win, and bring prices 3 to 4 times as much, within this rather narrow field of factory-made cutters. For some examples, a boring eagle might be $20.00, while one of the same size with a little more zest might be $35.00; an armless long-skirted woman might be $20.00, while one with arms and a hat might be $45.00; a fat simple chicken with no cluck might be $10.00, while a rooster with a big tail or cocky head tilt might be $45.00. **$8.00-$50.00**

Cookie cutters, boy & girl twins in original box, "Avon," American, 20th C. **$12.00-$15.00**

Cookie cutters, bridge cutters or what traditionally were called hearts, rounds & diamonds, ie. heart, diamond, spade & the trifoil club, tin, set of 4 in original box, rather deep cutters, with strap handles, these were also sold as sandwich cutters, for those little crustless dainties served at bridge parties, American, approx. 3" diameter, 1920s-1930s. • German playing cards. — Suits on German cards are an acorn, a tulip-shaped leaf, a heart, and a decorated ball. The suits correspond: acorn = club; leaf = spade; ball = diamond. I don't know if the idea of bridge party cookie cutters pertains in Germany. **$22.00-$28.00**

Cookie cutters, buildings — a set of 4 deep tin backless & strapless "cookie cutters" called "Cookie Village", consisting of 4 building shaped cutters, including a hip roof & a salt box house, a church, & a meeting house (the latter 2 with steeples). Directions tell how to make 24 different buildings, by combining shapes (which you would fasten together with icing). You could make a 3-D building because you were using "firm plain cake, baked in one inch layers". Trees and bushes could be made for your cake village by using only the steeples. It was suggested that you could freeze the village, by wrapping each building in plastic, for future use. No mark on cutters, box with directions is clearly marked: "Fox Run Craftsmen", Lambertville, NJ, cutters 2¾" to 4"H, c.1960s. **$10.00-$15.00**

Cookie cutters, cartoon characters Dagwood, Blondie, the children, the dog Daisy, and her puppies, in original box, yellow plastic, Educational Products Co., Hope, NJ, c.1948. **$65.00-$75.00**

Cookie cutters, figurals — tin, new reproductions or facsimiles (?) of "Early American designs," assortment of 13 cutters: a boy, girl, rabbit, tree, star, dog, bell, turkey, owl, Santa, angel, heart, & deer. Advertised as made by "Pennsylvania craftsmen," small, 1980s. **$7.00-$8.00**

Cookie cutters, (from Robacker auction) that were small, rather insignificant in appearance or even unattractive, "late" (ie.1920s or 30s on), or not uncommon — such as simple fish, Christmas trees, flowers, ducks, chickens, dogs, birds, bears, donkeys, lions, rabbits, stars, clubs (as in bridge), hatchets, pigs, deer, etc., — were sold in lots of 2 to 6 cutters, but mostly for 3 or 6 cutters. One lot of

11 cutters (only 4 had backs) went for $150.00, and included a hippo, Santa, angel, shooting star, etc. • **Traditional New Years motifs.** — During at least the last half of the 19th C, from various items I've seen, German decorators or artisans consistently used 5 motifs: a gold horseshoe, a pig, a 4-leaf clover, a money bag, and a lady bird or lady bug. In addition, bells are frequently seen, but this is almost universally a symbol of change, including the coming of the New Year. I think we might find cookie cutters in these shapes, perhaps even a lady bug.   **$60.00-$140.00**

Cookie cutters, **hands** — 3 tin flat backs on a theme: **(1)** hand with pointing finger, **(2)** hand & heart, and **(3)** heart with hand inside. The 2nd had a handle. The subject of hands, especially those with hearts, is very desirable, and these were nice but not spectacular cutters. Prob. PA German, about 4" x 3" or smaller, prob. late 19th C. • Robacker May 1989 price for three cutters.   **$1000.00**

Cookie cutters, hands, old dark tin, flat backs with strap handle, American, from 2½"H to about 7"H, strips forming cutting edge about ¾" wide, at least, 19th C. • Hand-shape cutters are extremely desirable, as are full figure and well-detailed human forms (particularly men, because of their legs and thus more detail) and to hearts and hands together.   **$350.00-$1000.00**

Value-adding details. — Simple outlines of inanimate objects, geometric forms, and some animate forms like some leaves, flowers and fish, are worth the least. Start adding details and the value goes up, sometimes disproportionately. This more complicated detail can be in the outline itself or within the outline or both. • **The Outline Itself.** — Detail is added with a closer following of the natural outline, viz. sawtooth or serrated leaf edge, fingers on a hand, heels on shoes, a bun, crimps or curls on a head, a zigzag hem, coattails, apron strings, a tongue in the mouth, individual hairs on a tail, a nut in the paws of a squirrel, etc. • **Within the Outline.** — Details inside the outline are sometimes added with strips of tin the same depth as the outline, the ends of the strip joined, used to cut out small details or portions of the cookie. Sometimes the strips are not as deep as the outer cutting edge so that linear marks are made on the surface of the baked cookie which would, whether iced or not, make the form more readable or more interesting. Same depth cutter types include small curls of tin to cut out holes for eyes or buttons, or rounded triangles, arches and rectangles to cut out under arms akimbo, basket handles or windows. A variation of this include short meander strips cutting all the way through the cookie, used to make a strong but small mark, going all the way through the cookie, but short so as not to jeopardize the integrity of the cookie. A little "E" of tin, for example, was used to make a human ear. Shallower marking types include simple strips bent in a curve to indicate the line of an animal's back leg, or the veining of a leaf, or to give dimension to the points of a star, or define petals on a flower, or make a heart shape within a geometric or figural outline. Sometimes crimped tin strips are used • Final note: Many stark and simple cutters, with little detail, are worthy of study and collection, and can be more dramatic artistic statements than those with more detail. Beware of the cute detail. • If you want to collect cutters, study general books on folk art long and hard,

and keep referring back to them after you've been out and have seen some cutters. If you aren't born with a sense of what folk art is, you can acquire it. You can also apply aesthetic knowledge and intuition achieved by studying all other kinds of art and design — from Japanese netsuke to African sculpture to the paintings of Miro to the wire art of Alexander Calder. A successful collector has gut feelings, backed up with exercised brains!

Cookie cutters, heart in hand motif, a Shaker as well as a PA German motif. Old dark tin, flat backs with or without strap handles, air holes for releasing dough, relatively deep cutting edges, American, range from about 2½"H to 6"H, mid 19th C to 1890s or so. • This is the second most avidly sought type of cookie cutter, after the full human form (mainly men) or vice versa, depending on the collector. Look for old tin of relatively thick gauge, signs of hand manufacture such as the edges of the strap handle meticulously but not machine turned. Reproductions of the example in the Smithsonian, made by tinsmiths Bill and Bob Cukla, of Hammer Song, Boonsboro, MD, are marked on the back of the thumb "B. Cukla". Other makers' reproductions should be marked, but may not be.   **$700.00-$1500.00**

Cookie cutters, highbutton shoes, a pair, tin, flat back with trimmed edges, strap handles, prob. PA, 4½"H, c.1880s to 1900. • Shoes have been a symbolic love token for a long time (witness the old shoes tied on the back of the going away car). It's possible that these cutters were a token of love.   **$100.00-$125.00**

Cookie cutters, man, woman & child, tin, flat back, tallest is 5½"H, late 19th C. • **Old Catalogs.** — Nothing is so helpful to the collector as old illustrated manufacturers', wholesalers', and retailers' mail order catalogs. Especially nice is a small importer's catalog, c.1906, of the firm of Ritzinger & Grasgreen, NYC. Depicted in it are two of an "assortment of 12 Human Figures In Box", which sold (retail or wholesale not specified) for 80¢. They are tin outline cutters, top edge rolled, no flatback or strap handle. Two figures are depicted: the woman's ankles and heeled boots show under her hem, she wears a wide brimmed hat; the man's suit coat is just a bit longer than nowadays, with a more pronounced waist, and he wears a flat-crowned hat. They were probably imported from Germany. The company also sold a 4 piece set of Sandwich Cutters, tin, flatback, strap handles, with air release holes in the center, in bridge sets, club, spade, diamond & heart. The set sold for $1.20 — a high price then. The look of the cutters, with flatbacks only roughly trimmed to shape, makes it easy to assume that many of the cutters sold as cookie cutters today may have originally been intended for cutting crustless luncheon sandwiches. There is also a deep cutter set of Card Party Cutters, "Hearts, Clubs, Spades, Diamonds", tin with rolled top edge, heavy duty strap arched handle. Another set offered by Ritzinger & Grasgreen is an "Assortment of 12 Animals in Box" for 80¢. Depicted in the catalog are 4 cutters, tin outlines, no backs, 3 with narrow strap handles (much narrower than the strap handles for the Humans. They are: eagle, cat, dog and fish (no handle).   **$120.00-$150.00**

Cookie cutters, multiple cutters, lot of 3 made of tin. **(1)** The most unusual is the combined flour container (according to Earl Robacker), nutmeg grater & 4 cutters. The body of the grater is cylindrical, with an oblong raised grating surface along one side. With the lid on, on both ends is a fancy cutter, inside lid is a 3″ heart cutter, and finally, with the lid off, a round cookie could be cut with the cylinder's rim. **(2)** Another unusual one was a cube with different cutters on each of the 6 sides; **(3)** was a large oval cutter for making 13 different cookies at a time, American, poss. PA German, 1st is 4½″H x 3⅛″ diameter; 2nd is 4½″ square; 3rd is 11¼″L x 7½″W, the combination piece poss. 1870s to 1900; others 20th C. • Robacker May 1989 price for the lot of three cutters was $800.00. • A similar, but more complex combination cutter than (1), is depicted in Brigitte ten Kate-von Eicken's *Kuchengerate um 1900*. It consists of a japanned tin cylinder, with a perforated domed lid on one end, a fine grater and a medium grater soldered lengthwise on opposite sides of the can, with a finely crimped round fluted cookie cutter on end, a bracket strap handle going from close to the bottom to near the top, and opposite the vertical handle is a tin bracket with a fluted pastry jagger wheel. A stamped brass (?) medallion attached to the can above the jagger is not completely legible in the photo, but it appears to read ''—RGAN COMP / MANDAL6 (or MANDAL'S) / LONDON,'' with a lot more that is completely illegible. Clearly it is English. • **German vocabulary** — The author describes it as an ''Alle Hilfsgerate beim Backen in einem'' (roughly, an all-in-one baking tool), and its various functions are as a Zuckerstreuer (sugar shaker), Ausstechform (shape cutter), Gewugreibe (spice grater), Zitronenreibe (lemon grater, or zester), und Teigradchen (and pastry wheel). It looks 1870s to 1890s, and is probably the same age as the one in the Robacker sale. A collector in America says it is called a ''Kitchen Magician'', which may be a later appellation. • Price range for rather complex tin combination baking tool cutters: **$175.00-$250.00**

Cookie cutters, round, 4 graduated cutters with corrugated edges, in box with lid, all made of tin. ''Merridale Works,'' English (?), box 4″ diameter, 20th C. **$22.00-$30.00**

Cookie cutters, Santa Claus & nicely detailed Christmas tree, tin, strap handles, a pair & very well-formed, American, 9″H, late 19th or early 20th C. **$140.00-$200.00**

Cookie cutters, tin, flat backs, shallow cut, with corrugated outside edges as well as even narrower corrugated interior inset strips for marking leaf veins or little pedula designs, once thought to be indubitably Pennsylvania German, and perhaps the first ones were. But they are found in later general manufacturers' catalogs, sometimes described as ''Cake cutters.'' American, about 2″ to 4″L x ⅜″ to ½″ deep, 1870s to 1920s. • **Not So Old.** — I had once thought that these were at least 100 years old; they all look so old-fashioned, folky Victorian, dark and beat up. A very nice 3″ shallow-cutting heart ''Cake Cutter'', with flat back, strap handle, corrugated edge, and even shallower, 3 petal inset marking design, appears in the 1920 manufacturers' catalog of The Central Stamping Co., NYC, NY. Central Stamping also had an assorted set of 12 fancy cutters, the simplest of which were a corrugated oval and a corrugated hexagon. There were also a diamond, 2 rounds, a square, an oblong, a 6 point star, an egg shape, and an oval with corrugated edges, all with insets, and finally an 8 point star with plain cutting edge. It's reasonable to assume that other companies made this type of cutter, possibly only hearts, diamonds & other geometrics, but possibly leaves and other designs too.

They are probably dark because they were either scrubbed too hard, or the tin plating was very thin; the rust and the dings came from neglect or hard usage. • ''The less expensive tin cake cutters in their multitudinous designs are very inexpensive and good tools. they are keen cutting and light and durable.'' Ethel R. Peyser, *House & Garden*, June 1922. **$15.00-$25.00**

Cookie cutters, tulip, a pistol, a guitar, and a wonderful saw, which alone might have brought the price, 4 in a lot, tin, all flat back, PA German, the saw: 7⅜″L x 2¾″W, the guitar: 5⅜″L x 2⅛″W, 3rd to 4th quarter 19th C. • Robacker May 1989 price: **$775.00**

Cookie cutters, wood backs, tacked on tin cutting sides, very uncommon, but 3 showed up in first auction of Robacker Collection: bird, 8 point star, heart. PA German, 3¼″ x 4¾″; 3¼″ diameter; and 3¾″ x 4¼″, 19th C. • Robacker May 1989 prices: **$250.00; $175.00; $100.00**

Cookie cutters—See Nutmeg grater, in Cut & Pare chapter.

Cookie machine, for bakery, 28 speculas (like springerle) cookie molds on rotary drum, German, 1910. **$175.00-$250.00**

Cookie machine, for bakery, side-by-side rows of springerle-type cookie molds on rotary drum which is cranked on side, on iron frame, with long cloth conveyor belt, mfd by Hengler & Cronemeyer, German, different sizes, to make multiple cookies at a time, laid out from 2x2 to at least 6x6, dated 1905, won awards in 1903 and 1904. **$225.00-$350.00**

Cookie machine, for making Chinese fortune cookies, American (?), prob. 20th C. • I merely report this 1983 ad from the *Antique Trader Weekly*. The machine is described as ''antique,'' ie. early 20th C., or late 19th. Dealer asking price: **$1000.00**

Cookie mold, bird on branch with 5 stars, oval, cast iron, no handles, possibly a wafer mold — at least it could make thin wafer like ''cookies''. 5″ x 3½″ oval, 19th C. • **Date By State, or Star-gazing.** — The look of this piece is c.1840s to 1860s. But if you use a star chart as it relates to each state entering the Republic, it could mean this dated to 1788, when the 5th state (Connecticut) through the 11th state joined the union. **$120.00-$150.00**

Cookie mold, carved granite, 2 sided, with bird-on-branch on one side, flowers & monogram on other, very rare, 4″ x 6½″, 19th C. **$225.00-$275.00**

Cookie mold, cast iron, oval, basket of berries, gritty silvery look to iron which indicates it may be a modern cheap reproduction, American (?), 5¾″L, if old, mid 19th C; if new prob. mid 20th C. **$50.00-$65.00**

Cookie mold, cast iron oval, casting gate in back, not in middle, mostly ground down flat, Christmas holly in theorum-like low, flared sides basket, no mark, prob. American, 5⅞″L x 4″W x ¼″ deep, c.1840s to 1860s. **$125.00-$150.00**

Cookie mold, cast iron, oval, lyre, gritty silvery look to iron which indicates it is probably a modern cheap reproduction, American (?), 5¼″L. If old, mid 19th C; if new prob. mid 20th C. **$50.00-$65.00**

Cookie mold, cast iron, oval, pineapple, Albany Foundry Co. (?), Albany, NY, 6″L x 4½″, looks much earlier in 19th C than this company, which was est. in 1897. • Turn-of-century dealer Thurnauer lists seven rectangular or square molds, five oval ones and three rounds. I wonder if the oval ones are the cast iron ovals with single designs seen in such quantity at antique shows in late 1980s. • See also Springerle mold.   **$150.00-$190.00**

Cookie mold, cast iron, oval, pineapple, gritty silvery look to iron which indicates it's probably a modern cheap reproduction, American (?), 6''L, if old, mid 19th C; if new prob. mid 20th C. • **Reproduction alert.** — A very rounded oval pineapple mold, cast iron with enough matt black paint finish to hide any gritty surface (if it exists) front & back, is marked on the back with a permanent molded identification. In a small oval are initials ''OSV'' surrounded by words ''Old Sturbridge Village'', plus another mark with illegible numbers or letters, plus numbers ''5-50''. This mold has a fairly large hole all the way through near the top for hanging. It is probably cast from a mold made from an original in their collection. If you've never been to Old Sturbridge in Massachusetts, do go; it's a wonderful place.   **$50.00-$65.00**

Cookie mold, cast iron, oval with hanging hole, Odd Fellows symbols: 3 chain links (Friendship, Love & Truth), hatchet, fireman's pike, what looks like roman numeral III but are 3 columns or pillars), hand with heart in palm, crossed swords, bow & arrow, American, 6¹³⁄₁₆''L x 5''W, 19th C. • This thing looks like a firemark, but if it were it would have more than one hole, as it would have to be screwed or bolted to a building wall. • **Reproduction alert.** — There is some evidence these are being reproduced. You've got to get to know what old cast iron, and new cast iron look like. Remember, most new cast iron is not made with ''virgin'' ore, but from all kinds of scrap iron, including whole engine blocks with other metals involved. Graininess, relatively light weight, slightly ''blurred'' details, somewhat lighter metal color and no patina are signals of newness.   **$100.00-$200.00**

Cookie mold, cast iron, rectangular, intaglio design of neo-classical Greek urn with flowers; assumed to be NY state, but not marked. 4'' x 2¾'', mid 19th C (?). **$150.00-$175.00**

Cookie mold, cast iron, rounded oval, central cornucopia, with melon, pineapple, grapes, fat leaves spilling out, 2 star-like X marks, border entirely made up of small dots, rather close together, perhaps done by a stove foundry, looks like casting from Troy or Albany, NY, 4''L, c.1840s.   **$125.00-$150.00**

Cookie mold, cast iron, rounded oval, Odd Fellows symbols, almost the same as the other one, 3 linked chain, bow & 2 arrows, crossed swords, heart in palm of hand, and 3 pillars, no hanging hole. American, 6''L x 4½''W, 19th C. • The dealer, at a very fancy show, who did not specialize in cooking things, had way overpriced it at $575.00, in May 1989.   •   **$100.00-$200.00**

Cookie mold, flat cast iron oval, butterfly, Albany, NY,. 5½''L,. early 19th C.   **$150.00-$175.00**

Cookie mold, flat cast iron oval, straw bee skip or skep, prob. NY state, 19th C. .   **$85.00-$110.00**

Cookie mold, glazed redware, large bear with fur, claws & teeth all delineated, American, 3'' x 5'', early 19th C.   **$200.00-$245.00**

Cookie mold, oblong tin mold, with 3 clamps along top, in section it is the shape of a spade (as in cards), and is for making icebox cookies, the dough of which was chilled then sliced. Presumably heart-. club- and diamond-shaped molds were made too. This kind of metal mold was usually lined with paper (antique cookbooks say letter paper or parchment), to make removal easier. American, about 12''L x 2'' across, 1930's.   **$15.00-$20.00**

Sliced or Icebox Cookies. — ''These cookies cannot be mixed and baked immediately because they require thorough chilling in the refrigerator. Their great advantage for the small family which likes its cookies fresh is that the dough can be kept on hand and the cookies sliced and baked as needed. It is because the dough can be used over a period of a week or more that we suggest a fairly large recipe even for the small family. Icebox cookies are always of the crisp, buttery type.'' • **Butterscotch Cookies.** — (45 to 60 Cookies) 3½ cups flour. 3 teaspoons baking powder. 1 cup butter or other fat. 3 teaspoons brown sugar. 2 eggs. 2 teaspoons vanilla. 1 to 1½ cups chopped nuts. — Sift the flour and baking powder together. Cream the fat; stir in the sugar gradually; add the unbeaten eggs one at a time; add the vanilla; mix well; stir in the dry ingredients. The mixture will be a stiff dough.

''The cookies may be shaped in several ways as follows: (a) In butter cartons. Stand 1 pound butter cartons on end and pack the mixture firmly into the corners. (b) In a cracker box. Waxed fiber boxes need no lining; tin boxes should be lined with heavy waxed paper with the ends extending beyond the edge of the box. Pack the dough firmly into the box. (c) With floured hands shape the dough into rolls about 2 inches in diameter, wrap the rolls in heavy waxed paper, twisting the ends. The roll will settle to an elliptical shape on standing.

''Place the molded dough in an efficient refrigerator for several hours or until it is very hard. Remove the chilled dough from its wrappings; place on a molding board covered with heavy waxed paper; cut into slices about ⅛ inch thick. Place on a baking sheet (greasing is not necessary because of the large quantity of fat in the dough); bake on the top shelf in a moderate oven (375° F.) for 10 to 15 minutes. ''Marjorie Heseltine & Ula M. Dow, *Good Cooking Made Easy and Economical*. Boston: Houghton Mifflin, 1933.   **$15.00-$20.00**

Cookie mold, or <u>marchpane mold,</u> good old cast iron, elliptical shape with a narrow channel around outside, plus 20 round concave dimples framing unusual subject — child on footed chamberpot or thundermug with handle, child has small pointy feet, almost look like boots with little heels, finely modeled, iron is right: very smooth & silky to feel, finely grained, no marks, prob. American, prob. NY state, maybe Troy or Albany — stove foundry towns. 5¾''L x 3⅜''W x ½'' deep, from look of child and chamberpot, I believe c.1840s-1850s. • Most of these molds which are right, and not grainy gray repros, may have come, as popular supposition has it, from New York State, possibly an Albany foundry, or even The Albany Foundry Co., in existance only from 1897-1932, though late 19th C or early 20th seems very late. This mold found by dealer Ed Boeyink, of Hilton, NY, in Eastern New York, between Albany and Syracuse, in a long-held private collection.   **$150.00-$175.00**

Cookie mold, or possibly for something else, rough, crude light-colored fired clay, design is spreadwing eagle standing on something, slightly undercut, so how would it work as mold? Was the undercut effect the result of the edges slightly sagging or collapsing when the well-carved wood or perhaps cast metal stamp was withdrawn after being pushed into clay? Or perhaps it sagged during firing? Anything put in it for molding would have to withdraw from the sides of the deeply molded design in order to come out, found in home in Southern Ohio, ⅝" thick x 3½"H x 4"W, c.1830s to 1850s (?). **$150.00-$175.00**

Cookie mold pan, cast aluminum, very light color & bright, 18 cups with 9 tulips & 9 scalloped rounds, Wilton Enterprises, Woodridge, IL, 1980s. • *The Wilton Cookie Maker Fancy Cookies* booklet, 1984, Wilton Enterprises, Inc., includes several catalog pages of aluminum baking pans, plastic cookie cutters, tartlet molds, cookie racks & sheets, icing & pastry bags & tips, mini muffin pans, & at least 6 cookie mold pans, 5 have 18 cups, one has 16, for Viennese, Bavarian, Marseilles (16 cups), Barcelona, Venetian & Parisian cookies. **$4.00-$8.00**

Cookie or biscuit cutter, round, wrought iron, simple circle with very high arched handle. • This extremely handsome wrought iron piece is in the Kyle Goad Collection, Virginia. Price range estimates probable current market value. American, 2⅜"H x 2⅝" diameter, early 19th C. **$85.00-$135.00**

"Apees.
— A pound of flour, sifted. Half a pound of butter. Half a glass of wine, and a table-spoonful of rosewater, mixed. Half a pound of powdered white sugar. A nutmeg, grated. A tea-spoonful of beaten cinnamon and mace. Three table-spoonfuls of carraway seeds. — Sift the flour into a broad pan, and cut up the butter in it. Add the carraways, sugar, and spice, and pour in the liquor by degrees, mixing it well with a knife; and add enough of cold water to make it a stiff dough, and knead it very well with your hands. Cut it into small pieces, and knead each separately, then put them all together, and knead the whole in one lump. Roll it out in a sheet about a quarter of an inch thick. Cut it out in round cakes, with the edge of a tumbler, or a tin of that size. Butter an iron pan, and lay the cakes in it, not too close together. Bake them a few minutes in a moderate oven, till they are very slightly colored but not brown. If too much baked, they will entirely lose their flavor. Do not roll them out too thin. The top of the oven should be hotter than the bottom, or the cakes will lose their shape." Miss Leslie, of Philadelphia, *Seventy-Five Receipts for Pastry, Cakes, and Sweetmeats. Appended the The Cook's Own Book and Housekeeper's Register...,* by a Boston Housekeeper. Boston: Munroe & Francis, 1833. See page 159.

Cookie or cake cutters, floral & leaf designs, a tin box with 12 small tin cutters, from F. A. Walker catalog, c.1870s. **$35.00-$50.00**

Cookie or jumble press, or butter press, or pastry tube, pieced tin, wing like side handles, nicely buttressed, turned wooden plunger with nicely flared out top, 5 plates to insert in business end, to create cookies in different shapes, from a half moon to a 10 point star, European (?), c.1870s. • "Jumballs. — 8 oz. of Jordan almonds, 2 lb. 8 oz. of searched (sierced, sieved) sugar, about two whites of eggs. — Blanch and beat the almonds until there is not any particle of the almond to be seen; then rub in with the pestle two pounds of the sugar with whites of eggs; beat them well until smooth; that done, divide the paste into three parts, one for white, one pink, and the other yellow. The pink must be coloured with the best lake finely ground; and the yellow with strong prepared saffron; stiffen each with part of the sugar left; then put them through a jumball mould; and make them into rings about the size of a dollar. Lay them on dry paper, and bake

them in a very slow oven. N. B. A jumball mould should be made of brass, in the shape of a butter squirt, with a star at the end, half an inch in diameter." Joseph Bell, *A Treatise on Confectionary,* Newcastle, England, 1817. (Lake is lac, the same red resinous secrection of the tiny scale insects "lacs" that's used to make lacquer). **$35.00-$50.00**

Cookie or marzipan mold, carved maple, double pointed shape (sometimes called a lozenge shape, and ellipse or a boat), deeply carved geometric border in what might be called, by cut glass collectors "strawberry diamonds", center design is a 6 point star, with other tiny chip carved designs between the petals or points, flanked by 2 hearts, chamfered back, Pennsylvania or Canadian, 9½"L x 4¼"W x 1" thick, early 19th C, c.1820-1840. • One auctioned in 1983, exactly the same, was said to be from Nova Scotia. • This double-pointed shape is often called "elliptical" in ads and descriptions. Only an elliptical orbit, in astronomical terms, would have the apparently pointed ends; in geometry, an ellipse is what most of us call an oval. • When trying to describe the border design, I got out my *American Glass,* by George & Helen McKearin, which depicts hundreds of pattern glass pieces. I was struck, while looking at cup plates, how similar some patterns are to butter prints; it is to be expected, as the art of woodcarving is of primary importance in making the molds for pressed glass. The period is the same too. I believe careful study would reveal many close relationships in motif and style, perhaps even traceable to a region. The McKearins say, for example, that pinwheels are typical of Midwestern (pattern-glass) designs; we think of them as Pennsylvanian when we see them on butter prints. Study! Study! • **Butter or Cookies?** Occasionally these molds are labeled "*butter* prints", but I am pretty sure this is inaccurate. **$8.00-$1100.00**

Cookie press, fat metal cylinder with plunger, & set of 6 cutout metal inserts to form everything from stars & flowers to corrugated rounds, made by icing decorator people, Ateco, The Thompsen Co., NYC, NY, c.1940. **$15.00-$22.00**

Corn bread skillet, cast iron, frying pan shape with short handle & teardrop hanging hole, cast with 8 dividing ridges to create 8 wedges, hole in center, mfd by Lodge, South Pittsburgh, TN, 1" deep x 9" diameter, late 20th C. • **Old Ones Too.** — I don't know how long this type of corn-bread mold has been made. Lehman's Hardware & Appliances, 4779 Kidron Rd., Kidron, OH 44636, which offers the above-described mold pan in their $2.00 1989 "Non-Electric Good Neighbor Amish Country" catalog. • Price range includes the $11.00 plus cost of the new one, and supposes antique ones that are unmarked. Marked iron seems always to bring more than unmarked, because a brand name means safe, if impersonal, investment. **$10.00-$25.00**

Corn bread skillet, cast iron, sectioned in wedges, marked "Corn Bread Skillet" on back, American, 9⅛" diameter, 20th C. **$25.00-$30.00**

Corn or wheat stick pan, cast iron, 7 sticks with well-formed kernels, "Best Made Wheat & Corn Stick Pan, No. 1270", S. R. & Co. (Southard, Robertson ?), 13⅛"L x 5⅝"W, 1927 design patent #73326. **$100.00-$125.00**

Corn or wheat stick pan, cast iron, wheat pattern, Griswold #282, Erie, PA, 20th C. (The Griswold #2800 corn stick pan is valued by collectors at around $300.00.) **$60.00-$75.00**

Corn stick mold, gray graniteware, 5 cobs, early 20th C. **$80.00-$120.00**

Corn stick pan, cast aluminum, Wagner Ware, Sidney, OH, pat'd 1920. **$18.00-$25.00**

Corn stick pan, cast aluminum, "Krusty Korn Kobs," Wagner Ware, tea size, 7⅛"L x 4⅛"W, mid 20th C. **$18.00-$28.00**

Corn stick pan, cast aluminum, 7 ears alternating direction. The way they are patterned, with slight irregularities, I'm sure the original casting molds were real ears, probably of hard seed corn, Mullins Non-Ferrous Castings Corp., St. Louis, MO, 20th C. **$18.00-$25.00**

Corn stick pan, cast aluminum, odd cob shaped cups but no kernels, just 3 long ridges in each cob cup, makes 7 sticks, medallion on back with "Wearever, No. 22—", "Made in U.S.A.", 13"L x 5½"W, 20th C. **$15.00-$18.00**

Corn stick pan, cast iron, "Krispy Korn Mold," mfd by Wagner, Sidney, OH, 7⅛"L x 4⅛"W tea size, very dainty tiny ears only 4½"L x 1"W, 20th C. **$45.00-$65.00**

Corn stick pan, cast iron, Wagner Ware, Sidney, OH, 3 sizes: Tea size, 7⅛"L x 4⅛"W, Senior size, 13¾"L x 6⅞"W, and Junior size, 11⅝"L x 5 7/8"W. 1920s. **$25.00-$40.00**

Corn stick pan, cast iron, 5 ornate cobs with curly silk tassels at ends & scrolly husks, in wide bordered rectangular frame with fancy scroll handle at each end, stamped "John Wright" on back, with button affixed to one handle reading "Classic Gourmet", Wrightsville, PA, #1984. • **Reproduction alert.** — Only one of the corn stick pans I've seen has retained the tiny white porcelain button on the front, affixed to one handle, that says "Classic Gourmet". And most have been badly (and deliberately) rusted. I saw one for $82.00, which is ridiculous at least until 2084. **$10.00-$15.00**

Corn stick pan, cast iron, 7 alternating well-modeled corn cobs, in original lithographed box (sometimes found with wraparound cardboard label instead), "Junior Krusty Korn Kobs, #1319," (I've seen this reported as #1319D), Wagner Ware, Sidney, OH, Junior size is 11⅝"L x 5⅞"W, pat'd July 6, 1920, but made for many years. **$60.00-$75.00**

Corn stick pan, cast iron, 7 cobs facing same way, Griswold "Krispy Cornorwheat Stick Pan #262," also marked "825" and "13," Erie, PA, 8½"L x 4⅛"W, 1927 design patent #73326, made for many years. • **Reproduction alert.** — This pan has been reproduced fairly recently. • **Lookalike alarm.** — Lehman's Hardware & Appliances, 4779 Kidron Rd., Kidron, OH 44636 offer legitimate (not repro) cast iron 7 stick & 9 stick pans in their $2.00 1989 "Non-Electric Good Neighbor Amish Country" catalog. All sticks point same direction. Lehman's say that all their cast iron pieces, except a griddle that's the "Atlanta" brand, are "individually sand cast and finished by hand. All are produced in a family foundry — Lodge, in South Pittsburgh, TN — dating back to 1896." The Lynchburg Hardware & General Store, Lynchburg, TN, the home of Jack Daniels, sells the same 7 stick Lodge pan. They say Lodge has been in business since 1872. **$65.00-$80.00**

Corn stick pan, cast iron, 7 ears all pointing same direction, 2 little knob feet on bottom at each end, "Puritan No. 1270, also marked #1513 on bottom, 13⅛"L x 5½"W, 20th C. **$22.00-$32.00**

Corn stick pan, cast iron, 7 head to toe cobs, in original printed cardboard sleeve, advertising blurb reads: "Corn

Cake Pan, Griswold Early American Quality Cast Iron. There's nothing like iron to cook in. By the makers of Griswold famous cast iron skillets. For almost 100 years, Americans have known Griswold." Griswold Mfg. Co., Erie, PA, this one c.1953. • Only $3.50 bought a new one in 1973. **$35.00-$50.00**

Corn stick pan, cast iron, 7 sticks, Griswold "Crispy Corn," #273," Erie, PA, 14"L x 7⅝"W, 20th C. • I have seen so many of these for $20.00 to $35.00 that I don't know why so many dealers price them from $58.00 to $65.00. I must be missing something. If you are going to specialize in cast iron cookwares, you have to subscribe to the newsletter(s). See the Bibliography. **$20.00-$65.00**

Corn stick pan, cast iron, 7 well-defined ears going same way, Griswold Krispy CornorWheat Stick Pan, No. 270, also marked #636, Erie, PA, 13⅛"L x 5⅝"W, 1927 design patent #73326. **$22.00-$32.00**

Corn stick pan, cast iron, hinged, wire handles, makes 2 full cobs, Wagner Ware, closed it is 15"L including handles x 6"W, makes approx. 1¾" x 5½"L cobs, 20th C. **$25.00-$30.00**

Corn stick pan, cast iron, hinged, wire handles, makes 4 full cobs, Wagner Ware, closed it is 20"L including handle x 12"W, finished breads approximately 5½" x 1¾". late 19th C. **$30.00-$45.00**

Corn stick pan, gray graniteware, 6 sticks, early 20th C. **$70.00-$80.00**

Corn stick pan, heavy molded glass, 7 cobs alternate directions, Wagner Ware, 13"L x 6"W, 20th C (according to collector Jim Holroyd, between 1942 & 1947. This is obviously because of WWII, and the metal drives. It's probably safe to assume most of the glass ones date to the same period.) **$20.00-$35.00**

Corn stick pan, molded glass, "Beauty Bake", 20th C. **$15.00-$20.00**

Corn stick pan, molded glass, "Griswold", 20th C. **$20.00-$35.00**

Corn stick pan, molded glass, 6 ears, half of each ear made up of gracefully pulled back husk, "Miracle Maize," American, 12"L x 6¼"W, "Pat. Pend.", 20th C. **$25.00-$38.00**

Corn stick pan, **poor reproduction**, cheap cast iron, 7 cobs all pointing same way, each letter of misspelled words on back impressed separately in the casting mold, marked "No. 252 CRISWOLD CRISPY CORNORWHEAT SNICK PAN" also "625", and address "ERIE PA USA", but made in Taiwan, 8"L x 4"W, 1980s (?). • I was fortunate to see one with its original tiny gummy gold & black sticker on the front, reading "W. E. RHYNE CO., Made in TAIWAN." You would buy one of these only for your study collection. **$2.00-$4.00**

Cracker pricker, fat wooden knob with 12 iron pins or "nails," American (?), 4¼"H x 2"D, 19th C. **$45.00-$55.00**

Cracker pricker, or biscuit prick, carved wood, one piece palm fitting knob and rather elongated body, 7 thick pins or "nails," American (?), 5"H, 19th C. • These were necessary for soda crackers or biscuits & for beaten biscuits. **$45.00-$60.00**

Cracker pricker & cutter, cast iron, spring steel with wooden block that has little 2 pronged prickers stuck in it. Spring-loaded action, fat palm-fitting handle, it not only cuts out square crackers but makes the pricked marks in them essential to their success. Without the little holes, the soda crackers would swell up and be big fat pillows, instead of pleasingly tufted. American, made crackers just shy of 2'' square, marked ''Pat'd Dec. 13''. Tuesday, patent-granting day, fell on Dec. 13 only 3 times in the possible time frame — 1864, 1892 and 1904. My patent subject index goes only to 1873, and it is not in that, so — although the appearance is 1870s, I go with 1892. Now somebody else can do the rest of legwork. **$30.00-$45.00**

Cracker pricker & stamp, carved wood, 3 nails to punch holes through cracker, depicts marvelous burning house with raging flames, house has big gothic window with tiny leaded panes, English, 1⁹⁄₁₆'' x 1¼'', c.1820-30s. • ''**Crackers.** — Take a large cupful of bread dough; roll out on the molding-board; spread on it a piece of butter and lard together, as large as a goose-egg; sprinkle a little flour over it; fold it up, and pound with something heavy a long time; take a small piece at a time; roll out very thin; stamp with a clock key, and bake very quickly.'' Henry Scammel, compiler, *Treasure House of Universal Knowledge*, 1891. **$450.00-$600.00**

Cracker stamp, carved wood basket of flowers, English, 1¾'' x 1¼'', c.1840s. **$200.00-$250.00**

Cracker stamp, carved wood depicting sheep, 6 pricker nails, cracker name ''INNOCENCE'', religious symbolism for some kind of ceremony? English, 1¾'' x 1⅜'', c.1840s. **$350.00-$400.00**

Cracker stamp, carved wood, double arched top like 2 tombstones, name of cracker ''VICTORIA'', English, 2'' across, from appearance it dates to Queen Victoria's 1837 ascendency to the 1860s or so. **$250.00-$290.00**

Cracker stamp, carved wood, looks like a dumbbell, or a doggie bone, English (?), 1⅞'' across, mid 19th C. **$250.00-$290.00**

Cracker stamp, carved wood, makes 6 point star plus many pricker holes, American or English (?), 2¾'' diameter, 19th C. **$150.00-$180.00**

Cracker stamp, wood carved with rose & thistle, name of cracker carved too: ''UNION'', prob. British, the rose signifying England, the thistle Scotland, 1⅞'' x 1³⁄₁₆'', early 19th C. **$200.00-$250.00**

Crimper, cast aluminum, wooden handle, ''Dandy,'' American, 6''L, pat'd April 22, 1925. **$14.00-$18.00**

Crimper, stamped aluminum, ''Juice Tite Pie Sealer,'' 5½''L, 20th C. **$10.00-$15.00**

Crimper & grater combined, tin, tinned steel, wooden crust crimper wheel at one end, middle part punctured for grating nutmegs, probably, fatly-pointed tip used to trim off excess dough around edge & to slash steam slits in top crust, American, 6⅞''L, late 19th C. **$18.00-$25.00**

Crimper & trimmer, aluminum sealer, plastic cutting wheel, wood handle, ''Dual Purpose, American, 20th C. **$15.00-$18.00**

Crimper & trimmer, big brass wheel, black molded phenolic resin handle, steel shaft, American, 20th C. **$20.00-$25.00**

Crimper & trimmer, nickel plated shank, red wood handle, ingeniously stamped aluminum wheel, ''Vaughn's Pie Trimmer & Sealer,'' Chicago, IL, 5½''L, pat'd May 10, 1921; this one prob. c. 1940s. **$10.00-$13.00**

Crimper & trimmer, tin, wire, corrugated wide wheel, ''The Ideal,'' mfr. unknown, American, pat'd March 10, 1908. **$8.00-$12.00**

Crimper & trimmer, cast aluminum, would trim as it corrugated the pie's edges to seal the top crust to the bottom one, no mark, American (?), 4¾''L, 1920s or 30s. • The

ridged edge of the pie, after being crimped, is what gives the name piecrust edge to quite a large number of butter stamps. On the other hand, a ''piecrust table'', in furniture talk, is one with the kind of riffled edge given to a pie edge by pinching with fingers & thumb. **$8.00-$12.00**

Croquette mold, tin, conical shape, 2 halves pinned lengthwise to release molded ground meat (ham, chicken, veal, fish) form to roll in crumbs before cooking, possibly made by Silver, marked Brooklyn, NY, 4¾''L x 3'' diameter at open end, c.1880s. **$15.00-$22.00**

Cutlet molds, pieced tin, shaped like cutlets or big fat commas, deep straight sides, used to shape a mixture of minced meat, spices, onion & egg into shape of lambchop or drumstick, etc., before cooking, but not used to bake the cutlet in, American or European, about 5''L x 1'' deep, from c.1870s to 1900. • I've never seen the leg of mutton mold, made of pieced tin in the appropriate shape but with slanted rather than straight sides, but one was advertised in the F. A. Walker catalog of 1886. I suppose it is much larger, meant for forming a meatloaf for a family rather than an individual serving. **$10.00-$15.00**

Dariel mold, often spelled dariole in old catalogs, a little cup — slightly flared cylinder, flat bottom, rolled edge, side seam, for a particular kind of small cake or custard. F. A. Walker's 1870s catalog also called them ''individual jelly cups''. The same Walker's catalog also had a cut of what looks exactly like a bouche iron, but called a dariole mold — a turned wooden handle set at right angle to corrugated, flared, solid cast iron mold to be dipped in batter before quickly deep frying. That type of mold molds on the outside rather than the inside. American or European, 2''H x 2¼'' diameter, last half 19th C. • F. A. Walker, in an 1886 sales brochure, advertised three sizes, viz. 1¾''H x 1¾'' diameter; 1⅞''H x 1⅞'' diameter; and this one. Not all had equal height & diameter. • **Added value.** — Tinned copper would bring more. **$7.00-$12.00**

Dough board, slate, arrow shaped very short handle, with hanging hole, American, most prob. PA, 17½'' diameter, 19th C. • I saw several in 1983 & 1984, and only one since; it was stuck in the window of a photocopying place on lower Broadway in NYC. I wondered at the time if they were being made now? They all had a lovely mellow slate patina, thin (about ½''), were pretty much all the same diameter, but varied widely in price. • ''A Black Board should be in every kitchen, not to mark with chalk, but to place pots and kettles on when removing them from the fire. Make it about a foot square, and one inch thick. It need not be washed often merely for looks, as the corners will be unsoiled. Its use will save the tables, floor, sink, etc., from many unsightly marks.'' *American Agriculturist*, March 1865. **$80.00-$500.00**

Dough scraper, brass blade, tapered tubular handle made of tin, capped with brass, copper rivets, very small, marked ''J. B.'', 19th C. **$85.00-$100.00**

Dough scraper, forged iron, wooden handle & brass ferrule, American (?), very early 19th C. **$30.00-$45.00**

Dough scraper, forged or wrought iron, short hollow socket handle, to be fitted with jammed-on wooden longer handle, American (?), early 19th C. • **Forged or Wrought?** The terms mean fundamentally the same thing; both apply to objects that are worked (or wrought) at a forge. Because the usual understanding of ''wrought'' is of something black and turned in scrolls like a wrought iron fence, or wrought iron lampstand, I prefer "forged". It is not enough to describe something as "handwrought", because the metal must be specified. Copper, pewter, silver, aluminum — all can be "handwrought".

$40.00-$45.00

Dough scraper, forged steel with tubular copper handle, 4½"L, late 18th or up to mid 19th C. **$100.00-$125.00**

Dough scraper, forged, whitesmithed iron, the blade a sort of hillock shape, a rounded top triangle, with a tapered peg handle set (riveted?) at right angles to the blade, near the "crest" of the hill, marked "P. D." (for Peter Derr, a very desirable maker), Berks County, PA, blade 3¼"W, dated "1854", each number stamped separately. • Robacker May 1989 price: **$475.00 - $550.00**

Dough scraper, iron blade with short stubby wooden handle, quite primitive, early 19th C **$50.00-$60.00**

Dough scraper, machined brass, very beautiful tubular handle with bands of turned decoration, signed "P.D." by maker Peter Derr, Berks County, PA, dated 1848. • Others by Derr are known. Early one dated 1832 was for sale for $375.00 in 1984. **$475.00-$575.00**

Dough scraper, or cake turner or short peel, forged iron, keyhole shaped blade with punch stippled profile bust of smiling man with high arched eyebrows & standing bird, rattail handle, length of handle marked with a triple row of punched dots, Pennsylvania in appearance, 3⅛"L overall, blade is 5¾"L, appears to be mid 19th C, may be mid 20th C fake. • I suspect this only because it's too much for the money. A portrait bust? plus a bird? both done in unusual manner, with gorgeous keyhole shape & 1989 selling price of only $100.00? If real, value should be much higher: **$450.00-$600.00**

Dough scraper, polished forged iron, decorated with etched tulip, shaped & slightly curved iron handle, marked with initials "CL" on blade's front, could be maker or owner, Pennsylvania (?), blade 4¼"W early to mid 19th C. • Robacker May 1989 price; **$500.00**

Dough scraper, triangle of steel for the blade, a separate steel handle riveted on, American, 19th C. **$45.00-$60.00**

Dough scraper, whitesmith's work, polished, planished worked iron, heart cutout, beautiful detailing on hollow tubular handle, cap knob on end, design comprised of cross-hatching with lines of tiny drilled holes, American (?), 4⅛"W, prob. 2nd quarter 19th C. **$200.00-$300.00**

Dough scraper, wrought iron, like a hoe but with a hollow handle socket, probably missing a wooden handle of whatever length that was useful to the cook who owned it, American, 19th C. **$65.00-$80.00**

Dough scraper & jagging wheel combined, unID metal (this late could be brass? aluminum? some steel alloy?), wheel-to-point is 4⅛"L, pat'd May 10, 1921. • **German vocabulary** — Teig schaber und Teigrad (also seen is Teigradchen): Dough scraper and pastry or dough wheel. **$18.00-$25.00**

Doughnut cutter, 2 part, with insert for cutting doughnuts, tin, "E-A Company Flour Always All Right," Waseca, Minnesota.2¾"D.20th C. **$12.00-$18.00**

Doughnut cutter, one piece of lathe turned wood, seen from side it's like a short ninepin or beetle, hollowed inside to make a thin cutting edge plus the hole cutter, American, 4½"L x 2⅜" diameter, 19th C. **$22.00-$35.00**

Doughnut cutter, one piece of turned wood, marked "Pat. Mar. 26, 190-?" (1901 or 1907 if the Mar. 26 is correct.) **$50.00-$60.00**

Doughnut cutter, one piece of turned wood, knob handle, possibly mass-produced in the kind of craftsman factory where butter stamps were made, American (?), 19th C. • Washington Irving described these tasty treats as long ago as 1809, in *History of New York*. "An enormous dish of balls of sweetened dough, fried in hog's fat, and called dough nuts, or oly koeks ." (The latter is the Dutch term.) **$70.00-$85.00**

Doughnut cutter, stainless steel with wood T handle, "The Saturn," 1930s. **$10.00-$13.00**

Doughnut cutter, tin, fluted sides with strap handle, center hole cutter soldered on, handle soldered on, but main body is stamped, American, 3½" diameter, pat'd Oct. 1, 1889. **$10.00-$15.00**

Doughnut cutter, tin, long cylindrical handle, closed on end, marked "Rumford", 3⅞"H x 2½" diameter, TOC. **$18.00-$22.00**

Doughnut cutter, tin, strap handle, doughnut holer cylinder has 3 struts holding it to outside cylinder, mfd by Fries, 3"H overall, cutting part 1½"H x 3" diameter, early 20th C, poss. late 19th. **$15.00-$20.00**

Doughnut cutter, tin, strap handle with center ridge for strength, edges folded over, one strap goes straight across as strut for the cylindrical hole cutter, American, 1⅛" diameter, late 19th or early 20th C. **$15.00-$20.00**

Doughnut cutter & apple corer combined, tin, strap handle, the separate corer is removed from cutter's "hole" for use in making doughnuts, American, 3⅞"L x 3" diameter, TOC. **$12.00-$18.00**

Doughnut cutter & cookie cutter combined, tin & wire, round cutter with wire handle sticking out side and going through from one side to the other so that the wire supports a small doughnut hole cutter to be used with the plain cutting edge. Flip it over and it makes scalloped edge cookies, which some writers say is the traditional style of cutter for a Pennsylvania German cookie called an "Apee". (For an Apee recipe, see Cookie or biscuit cutter, page 156.) American, 6½"L x 3" diameter, c.1890s. **$15.00-$20.00**

Apees Anyone? Ann Hark & Preston A. Barba, in *Pennsylvania German Cookery*, Allentown, PA: Schlechter's, 1950, write that A. P.'s are spelled "apees, apeas, apise and apice. Marcus B. Lambert in his Pennsylvania German Dictionary enters it as Eepies, & relates it to the French epice (*pain d'epice*, spice bread or gingerbread)." Ruth Hutchinson's *The New Pennsylvania Dutch Cook Book* (1958), repeats a story from John F. Watson's *Annals of Philadelphia*, that in early Philadelphia, a "young woman named Ann Page had made the first of these cookies, her scratching her initial on each one, hence AP's."
The apee story may be yet another apocryphal pastry origin story, the most famous being about Sally Lunns. Stories: (1) They were first made by a young English woman named Sally Lunn; or, (2) They are of French origin, and because of their golden top crust & white underneath they were first called "Soleil et Lune".(sun and moon) • Hutchison gives 19 pages to late 19th & early 20th C PA German cookies. The selection includes raised & flat cookie recipes, from old cookbooks, and PA housewives' collections, including some that are not necessarily traditional, though widely adopted: **"Moravian Brown Cookie"**, chilled overnight, rolled very thin & cut with "Christmas cookie cutters — men, deer, men on horseback, etc."; **"Mandelplaettchen"** or **Almond**

Wafers, also rolled very thin & cut in shapes; **"Almond Cookies"** cut in "diamond shapes with jagging iron"; **"Lebkuchen"**, a spice cookie of a thick dough type, chilled, rolled & cut in "hearts or diamonds"; **"Spiced Ginger Cookies"**, stiff dough, rolled thin and cut in shapes; **"Molasses Cookies"**, stiff dough, chilled, "rolled very thin, & cut in animal shapes"; **"Butterthins"**, chilled, rolled thin & "cut in shapes"; and **"Sand Tarts"** (elsewhere called "Sand" or "Saint Hearts") of two kinds, both rolled very thin & cut prior to baking, the second cut in shapes — usually rounds, also hearts, stars & half moons." • The rest are either drop cookies, or spooned & squashed (with tumbler bottom, wire potato masher or fork). No gingerbread boys, no zoomorphic or figural shapes. • The thinnest, stiffest most highly spiced cookies were best suited for Christmas tree decoration, especially after icing; this was traditional in Germany, Sweden & Switzerland. Such cookies were hard & tended to be preserved by the ginger in them. **$15.00-$20.00**

Doughnut maker & cookie cutter, strainer & apple corer combined, ingeniously pieced tin and mesh, being essentially a cylinder of tin, one edge of which is corrugated or fluted, the other straight, in between a piece of mesh, and sticking out of the side at right angles is a 3"L corer tube. Further on around the edge sticks out a short tube used to cut the holes out of doughnuts. American, 6"L (including corer), 3" diameter main cutter, late 19th C. • Nothing like these interesting combination tools to get a walkin' hawker's, traveling salesman's or agent's attention. They may have cost the salesman 2¢ wholesale, and he could sell them for 15¢. What a sales pitch too! **$15.00-$22.00**

Doughnut mold, hinged cast iron, long handles with wooden grips, looks like 3 leaf clover to make 3 doughnuts, used by filling then holding in boiling fat, "Ace Cloverleaf Donut," Ace Co., St. Louis, MO, 20th C. **$100.00-$150.00**

Ebelskiver, cast iron, 7 cups & skillet handle with teardrop hanging hole, marked "Western Importing Co." on bottom near handle, imported from Norway or other Scandinavian country (?), cups 2¼" diameter, overall 8¾" diameter, prior to 1891, prob. 1880s. **$65.00-$85.00**

Ebelskiver or aebelskiver pan, cast iron, reproduction or at least new production, 7 cannonball cups, side handle, flat on top including handle, rim of pan follows outline of cups, giving it a rounded hexagonal shape, Emig Products, Inc., (but I don't know if it is marked with their name), Reading, PA, roughly 7½" diameter with 3½"L handle, weighs 3½ lbs, in 1966 catalog. • Most if not all the **reproduction cast iron** is finished with flat black paint, but this could be distressed or removed. 1966 new price for the ebelskiver: $3.50. Realistic asking price now up to $10.00, but in real life probably 2 or 3 times as much. • **Collector Hint.** — You can expect lots of reproduction pieces, not always identified as such, in booths where there are a lot of newly-made "country" pieces, or wooden cutout (or cute-out) sheep or pigs, painted in pastels, with real ribbons. This dealer is really a decorator, not an antiques dealer, and is supplying a demand for a Look. If you want more than a Look, you may find a sleeper in with the new stuff. Conversely, you may be asked to pay too much, because you are buying a Look. **$5.00-$10.00**

Ebelskiver pan, also referred to as a muffin mold or an egg poacher, with 7 round-bottomed cups set in frying pan-like straight sided frame with short handle, marked both "Griswold No. 32" and "962", Erie, PA, cups 1¼" deep, pan is 1¾"H x 9¼" diameter with 4¾"L handle, as early as c.1918 & poss. as late as the 1960s. • An ad in *House Beautiful* in 1958 shows this as a "Danish Cake Pan" or "Ebelskiver" (sic) pan for "apple pancake balls." • According to Rebecca Wood, who wrote the wonderful cookbook *Quinoa the Supergrain. Ancient Food for Today*, here is the way to make these "apple sliver pancakes". You make a smooth batter like pancake batter (she adds cardomom), then heat the ebelskiver pan (she spells it ableskiver) over medium heat. "Thoroughly oil wells. Fill each well ⅝ full of batter and allow to cook for several minutes or just until the surface contacting the pan has browned. With a bamboo skewer (or knitting needle or nut pick), pierce and lift the cooked side up to a right angle. The batter pours out to form a second surface. When the new surface browns, turn again. A total of four turns produces a round and hollow ball." She adds a small slice of apple (or other fruit) before making first turn. I wonder, would a crochet hook work? **$35.00-$50.00**

Ebelskiver pan, cast iron, 3 peg feet, 7 cups, eye ring in handle, prob. Scandinavian, 7⅜" diameter, 11"L overall, mid 19th C (?). **$100.00-$150.00**

Ebelskiver pan, cast iron, 7 cups with resting rings, "Product of Norway", 20th C. **$28.00-$35.00**

Ebelskiver pan, cast iron, 7 straight-sided, flat-bottomed cups, squared-off rim so shape is hexagonal to pan, slightly raised edge, side handle that is also raised at angle, **reproduction or lookalike** sold through Cumberland General Store catalog, maker unknown to me, prob. American, 7" diameter, handle approx. 3½" or 4"L, shipping weight 5 lbs, 1980s. Approximate price for new one: **$11.00-$13.00**

Ebelskiver pan, cast iron with gray graniteware top, 7 cups, TOC. **$20.00-$30.00**

Ebelskiver pan, heavy cast aluminum, plastic handle, 7 cups, marked on back "Ebelskiver Pan" also "Apple Pancake Balls", Northland Aluminum Products, Inc., Minneapolis, MN, 9" diameter, 20th C. • I think this is the one sold under "Nordic Ware" trade name. **$20.00-$25.00**

Ebelskiver pan, often called an egg poacher (and at least one was patented as that, by Nathaniel Waterman), cast iron, round with short "frying pan" handle, 7 cups, no feet, only mark is "8", 1½"deep x 9" diameter x 5¾"L handle, 19th C. • **German vocabulary.** — A book on 19th C cooking implements, *Kuchengerate um 1900*, by Brigitte ten Kate-von Eicken (Stuttgart: Walter Hadecke Verlag, n.d. [c.1980]), depicts one of these and gives it a choice of names: Eierkuchlein-pfanne (egg-cooking pan) or Poffertjes-pfanne, (maybe a Popover pan, although I can't find the word in any of my German dictionaries). **$50.00-$65.00**

Ebelskiver pan or muffin pan, cast iron, 7 shallow flat bottom cups, more like muffin pan, short frying pan handle with teardrop hanging hole, the bottom is the really great part — instead of being perfectly flat, it reveals the shape & position of each cup, and has interesting hollows and negative spaces. Two molds were required to cast this —

one for top and one for bottom. That in itself is not so unusual, but the shapes in the bottom are. American (?), 9¼" diameter, 6½"L handle, TOC. **$22.00-$40.00**

Ebelskiver pan—See also Plett kaker.

Egg pan, with 12 round cups, often called a muffin pan but patented as an egg pan, cast iron, marked "N. Waterman," patented by Nathaniel Waterman, Boston, MA, pat'd April 5, 1859, patent #23, 517. • This patent covered baking pans of different shapes and sizes, despite the drawing of the 4-3-4 cup pan in the *Annual Report of the Commissioner of Patents* for 1859, the design for which the patent was granted. • See article on cast iron pans, by David Smith, for more on Waterman. **$75.00-$90.00**

French pie mold, or pate mold, also called a confectioner's mold, round, stamped tin, hinged opposite the clamp, French, came in several sizes through the F. A. Walker catalog: 7", 9", 10" and 12" diameter, 1870s. • Some of these had fluted sides, some were stamped with fruit and vine designs or other designs. The ring was in 2 parts so the sometimes concave designs on the sides could be released; rings were either hinged and pinned, or pinned in 2 places. **$20.00-$30.00**

Fritter baker, cast iron, wooden handle rather like a small branding iron, American or European import, 1870s or 80s. **$12.00-$18.00**

Frosting tubes in case, pieced tin, 6 tubes, case with conical hinged lid, French (?), case 6¼"L, 1870s or 80s. **$60.00-$75.00**

Fruit or melon ballers—See entries in Cutting chapter.

Gem pan—See Muffin or gem pan.

Hoarhound cutter—See Candy cutter, this chapter.

Ice cream brick mold, tin, American, 7½"L, early 20th C. **$45.00-$55.00**

Ice cream cone baker's mold, cast iron, hinged, makes 6 cones, 19th C. **$350.00-$450.00**

Ice cream disher, a sandwich scoop, cast aluminum handle, stainless steel body, "Rainbow Ice Cream Dispenser Cake Cone Co., Inc.," St. Louis, MO, 10"L, sandwich part 2⅞" x 3⅜", 20th C. **$75.00-$100.00**

Ice cream disher, banana split type, elongated oval bowl of nickeled nickel silver, thumb piece, black painted wooden handle, "Hamilton Beach #34", actually the Gilchrist #34 after HBCo. bought Gilchrist (1931), bowl approx. 3¾"L x 1⅜"W x ⅞" deep, c.1931-1934. **$140.00-$190.00**

Ice cream disher, banana split type, long oval, nickeled brass, wooden handle, long thumb lever, "United Products Co., Inc.," Chelsea, MA, 11½"L, bowl 3¼" + L, 1930s. **$200.00-$250.00**

Ice cream disher, banana split type, nickeled brass, wooden handle, elongated oval disher, Gilchrist 81 (is this 31? just like the round one? I haven't seen one to check it in person.), 11½"L, pat'd 1915. • Auctioned by Noel Barrett in New Hope, PA, 1988, for high seeming price of: **$550.00**

Ice cream disher, bowl shape cup, nickeled brass, wooden handle, 30 dips to a quart size, "Indestructo #30," *mfd by Benedict Mfg Co., East Syracuse, NY, 10½"L, 1920s.*© **Do You Scream For Ice Scream?** Collectors who want to know more will want to join the newletter club *The Ice Screamer.* Write Ed Marks, Box 5387, 2733 Lititz Pike, Lancaster, PA 17601-1367. (• Another in same price range, that I saw ads for at last minute, & for which I have name only, is a Philcone.) **$45.00-$60.00**

Ice cream disher, cast aluminum bowl, cast metal quadrant gear & thumb lever, steel scraper inside bowl, clumsily shaped turned wood handle, no marks, prob. American, 8½"L, bowl 2½" diameter, c.1940s. **$10.00-$15.00**

Ice cream disher, cast aluminum, non-mechanical, no special fluid in handle, "Nuroll," American, 1940s. **$10.00-$13.00**

Ice cream disher, cast aluminum, smaller bowl & longer handle than the award-winning "Roll Dipper", cap on end has blue finish, probably too early to be anodized, "Zeroll", Toledo, OH, #30, 1934 patent #1974051. **$18.00-$23.00**

Ice cream disher, cast aluminum, thumb press lever to release ice cream by making little 'golf tee' prod in bottom of bowl knock it out, squared handle, made in Japan, 7½"L, 1950s. • Futurewatch: While cheaply made, these odd mid 20th C dishers are the collectibles in this field to be looking for, as they are not as exciting and well-engineered as the older ones. I must have a dozen different ones, picked up at yard sales and thrift shops, all under $3.00. **$3.00-$8.00**

Ice cream disher, cast aluminum with golf-ball dimples cast in handle, "Scoop-Rite", patent pending, c. 1940s (?). **$25.00-$35.00**

Ice cream disher, chrome plated brass, black Bakelite handle, Model #66, mfd. by Hamilton Beach Mfg. Co., Racine, WI, pat'd 1920, with these handles prob. 1930s. • Black Bakelite® looks like hard rubber and is one trade name for the generic molded phenolic resin plastic. Catalin® is another. **$22.00-$35.00**

Ice cream disher, chromed brass, wood handle, Hamilton Beach "No-Pak" #31, 10"L, pat'd 1932. (Saw a "deplated" one for $75.) **$75.00-$90.00**

Ice cream disher, cone disher, heavily nickel plated, one handed kind with fancy looking squeeze handles (like tongs) with a spring at the end. Handles look like those grip strengtheners you get at sports stores, "Kingery's Rapid," Kingery Mfg. Co., Cincinnati, OH, 8½"L, pat'd 1894. (• Another in the same price range, a last minute addition here for which I have no information beyond name, is Ergos.) **$150.00-$200.00**

Ice cream disher, cone disher, loop handle, ornate key release, tin & iron, "K W" in oval of key, Keiner - Williams Stamping Co., Richmond Hill, NY, 7½"L, pat'd Nov. 7, 1905. • **Key names.** — The only initials or monograms found on the keys of this type of disher — known to me or Wayne Smith in his excellent *first* book (he's working on a second, for mid 1990) on dippers — are: KW, W, and G. Most keys are plain open ovals, slightly fancier geometric open forms, or very fancy casting — like Delmonico's scroll. We would love to know of any other initial keys. I'd like to say also that although I read books, and talk to collectors, and try to learn, any mistakes I make here are probably due to too little knowledge on my part. **$35.00-$45.00**

Ice cream disher, cone disher, metal, "Safe-T," American, early 20th C. **$8.00-$15.00**

Ice cream disher, cone- or cornet type, with key mechanism, key is letter "G," nickeled brass, loop handles, Gilchrist Co., Newark, NJ, 7½"L, 1920s to 1931. **$30.00-$45.00**

Ice cream disher, cone or "pyramid" shaped disher, nickeled brass, concealed reciprocating gear & notched rod atop the pyramid, thumb lever like the #31, Gilchrist #33,

Newark, NJ, 10½"L, pat'd Sept. 1, 1914. • This one came in 6 sizes: 6, 8, 10, 12, 16 and 20 scoops per quart. I don't know how Gilchrist's numbering system, using odd numbers, worked with the general rule of the number being the number of scoops to the quart. **$60.00-$85.00**

Ice cream disher, cone shape, nickeled brass, spring on top of cone, pulled by pressure on long wide thumb lever, turned wood handle, "Quick and Easy #486," Edwin Walker's patent, mfd by Erie Specialty Co.,Erie, PA, 10½"L, pat'd May 11, 1915, but inventor filed application 5 years earlier. • This "Quick & Easy" was advertised as being made of cast aluminum ("near-silver") in 1909, and it came with a tiny little tray #487, used while filling cones, that looks like a miniature griddle with frying pan handle. **$65.00-$85.00**

Ice cream disher, cone shaped nickeled "seamless pressed copper cup", german silver knives, nickeled malleable iron handle, thumb lever operates rod atop cone which pulls knife or scraper around inside cone, ad states "This Disher is used at the St. Louis Exposition", "Walker's No. 186", Edwin Walker, mfd by Erie Specialty Co., Erie, PA, six sizes of scoops-to-the-quart: 5, 6, 8, 10, 12, 16. By 1907 it was made up to size 20, advertised 1904. See listing for his pat'd 1915 brass disher. • Walker's dishers also included a shallow round cup one, #386, with levered thumb piece, almost like this one, and a simple key top conical one of tin (#184), and cast aluminum models. **$65.00-$85.00**

Ice cream disher, conical bowl, plated brass, "N. & Co., Delmonico," 8"L, TOC. **$65.00-$80.00**

Ice cream disher, conical disher, tin with heavy wire handle, key-scraper, no mark, American, 7⅝"L, TOC. • Wire handle is unusual, as most have a sheet metal or cast handle. **$22.00-$30.00**

Ice cream disher, conical disher with vaguely heart- or valentine-shaped key, tin with tubular steel handle with brass cap on end bearing name & date, "Clewell's V. Clad Maker," mfd by Valentine Clad Co., Philadelphia, 8½"L, pat'd May 3, 1876. • Molds too. — By at least 1932, ice cream molds were being made by Victor V. Clad, Phila.. **$35.00-$50.00**

Ice cream disher, conical, heavy tinned sheet metal, stamped sheet metal handle with long hole, key release/scraper is relatively big oval, American, 7⅜"L, late 19th C. **$25.00-$35.00**

Ice cream disher, conical metal dish, squeeze action handle, "Squeeze Action," early 20th C. **$65.00-$80.00**

Ice cream disher, conical, what was called a cornet disher in the old parlance, key wind, heavy tin & galvanized metal, key at top turns the cornet itself rather than the scraper inside (reverse is true on most if not all other conical dishers), #10, American, about 8"L, pat'd 1883 (?). **$30.00-$35.00**

Ice cream disher, German silver, heavy wooden handle, makes half a slab, "Sanitary Mould Co.", c.1930s. **$245.00-$300.00**

Ice cream disher, heart-shaped bowl, nickeled metal, shaft, & thumb lever, simple turned wood handgrip is stained red, makes heart-shaped servings, mfd by the inventor, John Manos, Toronto, OH, 11"L, pat'd Nov. 17, 1925. Marked "Patented Nov. 1925" on back of heart-shaped pusher plate. Mr. Manos had molded glass heart-shaped dishes made in New Moundsville, WVa (a big glass center) to go with the ice cream; I don't know what the

value of them are, but they would have suffered from use much higher casualties. • Price has skyrocketed for these, and Wayne Smith, who actually had the great honor and pleasure to talk with Mr. Manos himself, reports directly from the inventor's mouth that there were only 1000 made. • One of my concerns is that as the price goes up, it'll be profitable for a very skilled person to make fakes. After all, it's not platinum, so the material cost would be small, and it's not even really all that odd, except for that beautiful heart-shaped dipper bowl. One man in 1987 advertised his standing offer for $2500.00 for one. One sold at a Gaithersburg, MD auction in February 1988 for $3000.00. At a Noel Barrett auction in New Hope, PA, in April 1988, someone paid (including 10% premium) an astounding $4620.00. At an auction in St. Louis, MO, in 1989, one brought $5500.00. Wayne Smith has been carefully tracking the prices of these dishers; he said in late Nov. 1989 that 15 had been sold since Gaithersburg, and the prices of the latest two seemed to be hovering around $3500.00. But it is impossible to say now whether this is a temporary stall in a price rise, or a signal of a downturn.

If Manos' recollection is true, that only 1000 were made, this situation offers an almost unparalleled opportunity in collecting to track the market for an appealing, attractive, strongly-designed durable item over a period of years, not that similar situations would probably ever occur so that the knowledge could be applied! We know that 1000 could not have survived. To be neither optimistic or conservative, say that between 1925 and 1940 half, or 500, were lost, melted for scrap, destroyed, or thrown out by accident. Then there would have been, in 1940, 500 awaiting disposition. Maybe 50 of those are accounted for. If you collect ice cream implements, specializing in dishers, you would see that old pool of possibles drying up in the sun, like a rain puddle in August. So my feeling is, the price hasn't really started to go down yet. Wayne tells me that there are over 400 *known* collectors now in this field, which is rapidly expanding. A small percentage of those people would be able to afford to pay so much money for something. So who knows what the price range might become? And who knows how long it will take an entrepeneur with criminal intent to make, say, 10 copies? The price is really crazy, but it's hard to know what to say or if there's an absolute rule to apply to what you will be asked to pay, or what you "should" pay. • Probable range into mid '90s: **$3000.00-$6500.00**

Ice cream disher, lever activated roll-over type, aluminum with German silver plated bowl, "Unique", Mosteller Mfg. Co., Chicago, IL, c.1909. • There was a white metal version with German silver bowl. **$70.00-$90.00**

Ice cream disher, metal, "Double Flip", Dover Mfg. Co., early 20th C. **$120.00-$140.00**

Ice cream disher, metal, "Dover Springless", 20th C. **$65.00-$75.00**

Ice cream disher, nickel plated brass, bowl-shaped disher, 2 levers: one for thumb, one for fore- or middle finger that returns the scraper to starting position, called "The Perfection" in trade advg, marked on thumb lever "Dover Mfg. Co." with patent & place, Dover, NH, 10 15/16"L, pat'd 1928. • The dipper was sold through Perfection Disher Co., of Boston. **$185.00-$225.00**

Ice cream disher, nickeled brass, square disher, nice big cog gear wheel, small thumb lever, wooden handle, "The 'Polar-Pak' Disher," mfd by Philadelphia Ice Cream Cone Machinery Co., Phila. 10 ½"L, pat'd July 26, 1932. • Production started upon or before patent application was filed in 1928, as disher is marked "Pat. Apl'd For." **$180.00-$225.00**

Ice cream disher, nickeled brass, fat wood knob, round cylindrical disher part has central vertical shaft, worked by pushing down on knob with palm, Fro-Zon Mfg. Co., Schenectady, NY, pat'd Feb. 24, 1925. **$700.00-$900.00**

Ice cream disher, nickeled brass, round bowl disher with scraper, spring & small thumb lever, flat, knurled metal handle embossed with patent date, manufacturer & trade name, "Clipper Disher," mfd by Geer Mfg. Co., Troy, NY, 9¼"L, pat'd Feb. 7, 1905 by Rasmus Nielsen. • Nielsen went on to patent several more, some of which had conical dishers, some round. **$115.00-$175.00**

Ice cream disher, nickeled brass, round disher, marked "Dairy Fresh," American, 20th C. • According to Wayne Smith, this is a fool-the-collector item made in Taiwan (so noted on a removeable paper label), that can be detected by its shoddy workmanship. **$9.00-$12.00**

Ice cream disher, nickeled brass, round disher, knurled metal handle that looks borrowed from a screwdriver, spring-operated with thumb lever, marked: "Myers Deluxe Disher," Chicago, IL, pat'd May 19, 1936 by Louis Myers. **$25.00-$40.00**

Ice cream disher, nickeled brass, shaft screwed into end of red painted wooden handle, not well made but interesting for the extreme simplicity of the gearing. There's a tight spring inside handle, the thumb piece has 5 holes & a little gear has 5 teeth; as you push thumb lever against teeth they move the scraper, Japan, 8"L, 20th C. **$7.00-$10.00**

Ice cream disher, nickeled brass, with small gear, rack & spring halfway up shaft to bowl, wooden handle, quite simple, even modern in look, hard to find, mfd by Gem Spoon Co., Troy, NY, 10½"L, 20 dips to the quart, pat'd by Bernice J. Noyes, May 7, 1895. • This predates the similar Gilchrist #31, which was a decided improvement since the mechanical part was moved farther from the ice cream itself. **$60.00-$85.00**

Ice cream disher, nickeled brass, wood handle, lever action, "Trojan No. 16," by Gem Spoon Co., early 20th C. **$20.00-$35.00**

Ice cream disher, nickeled brass, wooden handle, Geer Mfg. Co., #A21, early 20th C. • Price from George Haney Collection at Barrett auction April 1988: **$300.00**

Ice cream disher, nickeled brass, wooden handle, 60 scoops to a quart, Hamilton Beach, #60, 1930s. **$25.00-$38.00**

Ice cream disher, nickeled brass, wooden handle, thumb lever with tiny gear, rack and concealed spring, providing "alternate rectilinear motion ... to the rack-rod, by the continuous revolution of the...spur-gear, the spiral spring forcing the rod back to its original position on the teeth of the gear, quitting the rack," from Mechanical Movements, first published in 1868, renewed in 1896, reprinted in 1933 in a "Century of Progress" special edition, #31, mfd. by Gilchrist Co., 11"L, pat'd March 23, 1915. • This is the most common make & common size (#31) of all dippers — reflective of its great popularity when made. It was not patented until 7 years after Raymond Gilchrist filed for a patent, but was sold for many years beginning in 1908.

The bowl in this model came in 6 sizes: 6, 8, 10, 12, 16 and 20 scoops to the quart. • Related collectible. — Look for the Saturday Evening Post, June 27, 1953, with a colorful cover by American artist Amos Sewell. The genre depiction of an outdoor children's birthday party shows a harrassed mother holding what appears to be a Gilchrist #31. • Added value. — Smallest & largest are most desirable. • Watch out for highly polished ones, stripped of their original nickel on shaft & gear, meant for non-purist decorators, not serious collectors. You'll really pay for "real brass" — I've seen 'em for $100.00, which is Way Too Much. **$25.00-$45.00**

Ice cream disher, nickeled metal, makes small cube of ice cream, "Prince Castle", cube would be 1½" square, 20th C. **$200.00-$250.00**

Ice cream disher, nickeled metal, wood handle, big lever, long cylinder makes a tube of ice cream, 20th C. • Price from George Haney Collection at Barrett auction April 1988: **$700.00**

Ice cream disher, non-mechanical, cast aluminum with colored anodized aluminum cap at end of tubular handle, disher filled with liquid that is supposed to chemically keep it warm enough to help scoop out very cold ice cream. This was chosen by the design curator to be in the Museum of Modern Art's Design Collection, NYC. designed by Sherman Kelly, mfd. by Roll Dippers, Inc., 7"L, c.1935. **$10.00-$13.00**

Ice cream disher, non-mechanical, cast aluminum with ridged cigar-shaped handle & a bowl clunkier than similar "Roll Dipper", marked. "PROGRESSUS," made in Italy, 7½"L, c.1935-1950s **$5.00-$12.00**

Ice cream disher, non-mechanical, metal with wood handle, "Arnold," pat'd 1928. **$20.00-$30.00**

Ice cream disher, one piece scoop, with spring action thumb button in bowl's center, cast aluminum, Decatur Lloyd Disher Co., IL (?), 1940. **$25.00-$35.00**

Ice cream disher, original nickel plating, thumb lever has only mark: "16-to-a-Quart", 20th C. **$12.00-$15.00**

Ice cream disher, pewter-like alloy & unID metal, Bohlig Mfg. Co., St. Paul, MN, #16, pat'd Oct. 6, 1908. **$85.00-$115.00**

Ice cream disher, plated brass, wooden handle, "Trojan #20," by Gem Spoon Co., early 20th C. • There was also a company, by the early 1930s, named New Gem Mfg. Co., Newark, NJ, (affiliated with C. T. Williamson Wire Novelty Co. — the corkscrewers) who made ice cream dishers. From the same period was Nicol & Co., of Chicago, and Daly Brothers, of Schenectady, NY. I don't know what their dishers looked like, but found the names in a 1932 Thomas' Register of American Manufacturers. **$35.00-$45.00**

Ice cream disher, sandwich disher, nickel silver (alloy), long shaft, wide-set thumb lever, wooden handle, marked on square disher just with maker's name, ads called it "Mayer's Handy Ice Cream Disher," marked on front "Mayer Mfg. Corp," Chicago, IL, 12"L, "Patent pending". • Very like the Jiffy Dispenser dipper, but doesn't have slightly curved disher, wooden handle is slightly different proportion, and the thumb lever is not just slightly bent, it is cast and machined. The "Jiffy" (see below), which was sold by a Chicago company, and pat'd in 1925, is undoubtedly closely related. **$95.00-$150.00**

Ice cream disher, sandwich or pie a la mode disher of nickel silver alloy, with wooden handle, "McLaren's ICYPI," McLaren Consolidated Cone Corp., Dayton, OH, 10"L, 4" x 4" slab, 1929. • According to Wayne Smith, in his outstanding first book *Ice Cream Dippers* (see Bibliography), this particular ICYPI dipper was mfd by the Automatic Cone Co. of Cambridge MA, who made other ICYPI dishers too. I don't know why — perhaps some kind of licensing deal. **$80.00-$135.00**

Ice cream disher, sandwich style, "german silver" (old name for nickel silver, which was an alloy of copper, zinc and nickel, used for flatware and some hospital equipment), nearly square, slightly bowed disher, wood handle, thumb lever, "Jiffy Dispenser Co.," distributed or possibly mfd by Jiffy Sales Co., Aurora, IL (Jiffy Sales in Chicago), 12½"L, pat'd Feb. 17, 1925. • Ice cream sandwiches (like Dove Bars® today) were very popular in the 1920s. People could make their own at home with waffles and by slicing a brick of ice cream, which was slightly larger than an unquartered pound "brick" of butter or lard. Until bulk ice cream was available, these dippers were not especially useful in a home kitchen; sales pitches were directed to soda fountains and ice cream shops. **$130.00-$165.00**

Ice cream disher, sandwich type, nickel silver (alloy of copper, zinc & nickel), wood handle, square disher, "ICYPI," Automatic Cone Co., Cambridge, MA, 10"L, makes a 4" x 4" slab, trademark pat'd 1926. • An early ad for this dipper gives the manufacturer as the Pioneer Ice Cream Cone Mfg. Co., possibly related to the wafer itself, not the dipper. **$135.00-$185.00**

Ice cream disher, sandwich type, nickeled brass scoop, rectangular & slightly curved or bowed, turned wood handle, thumb lever action, no marks, American, 12½"L, c.1930s. • This is like a cross between a Jiffy & the uncurved Mayer sandwich dishers. The wooden handle is shaped differently, as is the position & shape of the thumb lever. **$85.00-$135.00**

Ice cream disher, sandwich type, square disher, nickeled brass, lever, "Reliance," American, 20th C. **$100.00-$135.00**

Ice cream disher, nickeled brass & copper, squeeze action moves scraper inside bowl, Gilchrist #30, 10½"L, 1930s. •-The Gilchrist ice cream servers have been the victims of nickel strippers for more than a decade. It's a real bugabear of mine, the stripping of the original nickel plating from cast brass dippers. It's like taking the old finish off furniture. The price of these dippers goes up and UP. Dealer ads reflect the trend towards stripping, and unabashedly say "brass ice cream scoop." Such is the power of the golden-glow metal; brass glisters like gold, whereas nickel has no glamour unless it's on an old stove. I've often seen a Gilchrist #31 in its original, if somewhat worn, condition for $28.00 to $30.00. In the next booth, a highly polished, buffed, stripped one for as high as $75.00. It is NOT a good investment to buy one like that. **$35.00-$85.00**

Ice cream disher, nickeled brass, turned wooden handle, one lever moves scraper inside bowl, Dover #20, Dover Mfg. Co., 10½"L, c.1930s. **$35.00-$45.00**

Ice cream measure, pieced heavy tinned sheet iron, footed goblet shape with generous strap handle on one side, key (which is hidden in concave base or ring foot) turns 2 scrapers that go all way up inside of cup. Opposite the handle is a medallion, unfortunately rather smashed & illegible, "Clewell", mfd by Valentine Clad, Philadelphia, 5½"H x 3½" diameter, "Mar...07" seems to be the date on medallion. Perhaps 1876 or 1882? • Could it be the same patent date, May 3, 1876, as the disher? • The "Perfection Ice Cream Measure", which was essentially the same as the Clewell except it was "made of hard spun metal, silver plated inside and nickel plated outside" with a "tempered nickel-silver" blade inside, was advertised by Thomas Mills & Brother, Inc., of Philadelphia, along with the "Clewell" cornet ice cream disher, in their Catalog #31, from the late 1920s. The measures came in 1 pint & 1 quart sizes. **$35.00-$50.00**

Ice cream mold, airplane, pewter, E. 1132, mfd by Eppelsheimer & Co., c.1930s. • From a letter to the editor of *The Magazine of Domestic Economy*, July 1838: "Mr. Editor, — Can you give me any practical **directions for making Ice creams?** I have this year an opportunity of procuring ice in a rough state, but being unacquainted with the management of it for cream, &c., I shall be obliged by your giving the necessary directions through your valuable Magazine; also as to what vessels are necessary for the general use of ice in a small family." The editor replied: "Sorbetieres or moulds for cream or fruit-ices, are made of two sorts of materials, block-tin and pewter; of these, the latter is the best, the substance to be iced congealing more gradually in it than in the former; an object much to be desired, as when the ice is formed too quickly, it is very apt to be rough, and full of lumps like hail, especially if it be not well worked with the spatula; the other utensils necessary for this operation are, a deep pail, with a cork at the bottom, and a wooden spatula about nine inches long; being so far provided, fill the pail with pounded ice, over which spread four handfuls of salt; then having filled the sorbetiere, or mould, with cream, & put on the cover, and immerse it in the centre of the ice-pail, taking care the ice touches the mould in all parts; throw in two more handfuls of salt, and leave it a quarter of an hour; then take the cover from the mould, and with the spatula stir the contents up together, so that those parts which touch the sides of the mould, and consequently congeal first, may be mixed with the liquid in the middle; work this about for seven or eight minutes; cover the mould, take the pail by the ears, and shake it round and round for a quarter of an hour; open the mould a second time, and stir as before; continue these operations alternately, until the cream, or whatever it may be, is entirely congealed, perfectly smooth, and free from lumps. Take care to let out the water, which will collect at the bottom of the pail, by means of the cork, and press the ice close to the sorbetiere with the spatula. When the cream is iced, take it from the pail, dip the mould in warm water, but not to let it remain an instant; dry it quickly, turn it out, and serve it as soon as possible." **$45.00-$55.00**

Ice cream mold, American flag, pewter, 2 part, 20th C. • **Unmarked molds — uncommon makers.** — I looked in the 1932-33 *Thomas' Register of American Manufacturers* under ice cream molds (moulds), and found Cherry-Burrell Corp., Chicago; Reproductions Co., Boston; Fr. Krauss & Son, NYC; James Y. Watkins & Son, NYC; plus August Kreamer, Brooklyn, who made kinds of kitchenwares, but I had not been aware of ice cream molds. • Known companies were Epplesheimer & Co., Brooklyn; and Victor V. Clad, and Thomas Mills & Brother, Inc., both Philadelphia. **$40.00-$45.00**

Ice cream mold, apple, pewter, 2 part, E. & Co. (Eppelsheimer & Co.), NYC, early 20th C. **$35.00-$42.00**

Ice cream mold, apricot, hinged 2 part, pewter, only mark is a gouged X in hinge, late 19th C. **$35.00-$40.00**

"How to put Ice Cream into Moulds. — Rub your moulds very bright; then fix on the tob and bottom with writing paper; take off the top, and fill the mould with the frozen ice cream already prepared; it must be forced in very tight that no holes may appear when turned out; then lay on the writing paper, fix on the top, and immediately cover it well over with salted ice, go on in the same way until the whole is put into moulds; then lay them on one side, upon ice, in a tub with two bottoms; cover them well over with salted ice, which must be pressed tightly down; and in one hour it will be hard enough to turn out; but should it be wanted in a shorter time, a little salt petre beat small, and mixed with the salt, will be of great advantage to it. To put Ice Cream into Shapes, to represent ripe Fruits. — Your apricot moulds being ready for use, open them, and colour the inside a pale yellow, with a small brush; then take another brush, and dip it in lake finely ground, colour the sides of the mould, in part, with it; then take a small bit of whisk, dip it in the lake, and spot the mould a little with it; after which, fill both sides very full, and put them together; wrap the shape in strong brown paper, to keep the salt from penetrating the opening of the mould; then immerse it well in salted ice. N. B. Peach, pear, or pine apple, must all be coloured in the same manner, well bedded with ice, beat small, and salted properly, as before." Joseph Bell, *A Treatise on Confectionary*. Newcastle, England, 1817. • **"To turn Ice out of Shapes.** — When you wish to turn out your shapes, have every thing in readiness to receive them, and never turn it out before the moment it is wanted; take each mould and wash it well in plenty of cold water; then rub it dry with your towel; take a strong knife, and force off the top; rub the top very clean; then take away the paper, and place the top on; do the same with the other end; after which, take the mould between both your hands, (having previously taken off both top and bottom) and let the shape of ice drop on to the dish you serve it up to the table upon; repeat this with every mould, do it in as short a time as possible, and serve it to the table immediately. N. B. The ices in natural shapes must be turned out in the same way, and laid upon the dish, when you may put a natural stalk into each, garnish with their own leaves." Ibid

Ice cream mold, baby shoe, pewter, 20th C. **$35.00-45.00**

Ice cream mold, banana, pewter, hinged 2 parts, smaller than life size, #157, American, c. 1920. **$45.00-$60.00**

Ice cream mold, battleship, pewter, E. & Co. 1069, Eppelsheimer & Co., NYC, NY, 20th C. **$90.00-$120.00**

Ice cream mold, bell (wedding? Liberty?), pewter, #285, mfd by Krauss Co., Milford, PA, 20th C. • This may be the same company — in the 1932-33 Thomas' Register of American Manufacturers, there is an entry for Fr. Krauss & Son, in NYC, NY, making ice cream molds. **$45.00-$50.00**

Ice cream mold, black-eyed susan or fancy daisy, 10 big petals, rosette center, 2 part hinged pewter, marked "#240", late 19th C. **$30.00-$40.00**

Ice cream mold, bride & groom, pewter, "#627-K", mfd by Krauss, Milford, PA, 20th C. **$40.00-$48.00**

Ice cream mold, bust of Admiral Byrd in his parka, 2 part tin, Eppelsheimer & Co., No. 1165, NYC, NY, 8 per quart size, 1930. • South Pole Crossover. — A sales letter from Eppelsheimer, dated June 1930, reads: "THE BYRD ANTARCTIC EXPEDITION RETURNS TO THE UNITED STATES DURING JUNE. It is expected that Admiral Byrd will tour the entire Country, giving lectures about his Expedition to the South Pole. There will doubtless be Banquets in his honor in every City he visits. Be prepared to supply Fancy Forms of Ice Cream of the BUST OF BYRD in his 'Parka' (fur-coat), mold No. 1165 and BYRD'S SHIP 'THE CITY OF NEW YORK', mold No. 1164. Molds for making the Fancy Ice Cream Forms, capacity 8 per quart, price $3.00 each, Display Models 60ᶜ each, less your usual discount. ORDER YOUR SUPPLY NOW." The "display models" mentioned were molded composition figures that showed how the ice cream in a particular mold would look; they'd be extremely collectible; I don't think I've ever seen one for sale. **$100.00-$120.00**

Ice cream mold, bust of General Grant, surrounded by laurel wreath & crossed bullets motif, heavy pewter, 2 parts, no marks, American (?), 3½"H, prob. last quarter 19th C. **$85.00-$110.00**

Ice cream mold, calla lily, pewter, 3 part, #210. **$35.00-$45.00**

Ice cream mold, chubby bride with veil & short skirt, cast white metal, Eppelsheimer #1148, quarter pint size, c.1929. • In the Jo-Lo (Joe Lowe) catalog, c.1930s, this same pair is shown, with the same numbers as Eppelsheimer. **$30.00-$40.00**

Ice cream mold, chubby groom with tails & top hat, cast white metal, Eppelsheimer #1149, quarter pint size, c.1929. **$30.00-$40.00**

Ice cream mold, clover, hinged 2 part mold, with one half fluted pan shape, like cake mold, the other half with well-defined 4-leaf clover to make design on top only, heavy pewter, "E & Co. #1039", TOC. **$55.00-$75.00**

Ice Cream mold, cow, head turned, low haunches, hinged 2 part centerpiece mold, "L. G." in oval, mfd by Maison Letang Pere & Fils, Paris, France, late 19th C. **$175.00-$200.00**

Ice cream mold, crescent moon with face of Sphinx, pewter, marked "32nd Degree Shriner" dated 1905. **$40.00-$55.00**

Ice cream mold, crusader with cross & sword, pewter, #320, early 20th C. **$45.00-$55.00**

Ice cream mold, cupid & fat heart, pewter, #573, TOC. **$38.00-$50.00**

Ice cream mold, cupid pewter, E 992, Eppelsheimer. **$30.00-$35.00**

Ice cream mold, daisy with perfectly detailed petals and center, hinged 2 part, pewter, no mark, 2½" diameter, late 19th C. **$40.00-$50.00**

Ice cream mold, dog (retriever? poodle?), large & seated on oval plinth, with very deep tightly curled mane, long ears, body shaved close except for muffs on front feet, mane and tale, huge head, ponderous (or patient?) visage, pewter, small stamped maker's mark of old cranked freezer (resembles a well), "C C" & "Marque Fabrique", according to catalog #13 in the 969 series, mfd by M. Cadot et Cie, Paris, France, 3 pt. capacity, prior to 1900 (?). • I have a c. 1900 catalog of ice cream molds made by E. Compiegne, successor to Cadot. It says that "tous les moules portent ma marque C. C." — all molds marked C. C. • They had a poodle couchant, with curly ears — much more obviously a poodle, which was originally bred as a retriever. Also a very short haired hound dog, lying down with head pointed up. **$75.00-$100.00**

Ice cream mold, donkey head, pewter, 3 part mold, early 20th C. **$35.00-$45.00**

Ice cream mold, eagle, standing & looking over his left shoulder, lead, 2 part with 5 pinned clamps, linecut in F. A. Walker catalog shows mark of a tiny castle stamp, imported, c.1870s or 1880s. **$65.00-$75.00**

Ice cream mold, eagle with shield & swords, pewter, #517, early 20th C. **$55.00-$65.00**

Ice cream mold, eagles, a pair, pewter, hinged, German (?), early 20th C. • **Figural, Animalistic, Zoomorphic.** — In art-talk, something made in the shape of a human figure is called figural; if it's an animal or bird form it's animalistic. I use the term figural throughout because it is the more widely (mis)used term, it is easier than zoomorphic, and because animalistic is sometimes used to describe something sensual or even bestial, as opposed to what is "spiritualistic" in humans. Read the daily news for your dose of human spiritualism. **$55.00-$65.00**

Ice cream mold, elephant, pewter, E. & Co., TOC. **$45.00-$55.00**

Ice cream mold, engagement ring with floral decoration & set diamond, ring mold type, cast white metal, Eppelsheimer #1141, individual mold, a little more than ¼ pint, c.1929. **$25.00-$30.00**

Ice cream mold, Eskimo figure, pewter, 20th C. **$25.00-$35.00**

Ice cream mold, George Washington & shield, pewter, early 20th C. **$60.00-$70.00**

Ice Cream Molds in 1803. — In Ledlie Irwin Laughlin's massive, instructive *Pewter In America*, 3 volumes in one, American Legacy Press, 1981, there are but two references to ice cream molds. The first is in Vol. II, p. 54, and refers to the 1798 will inventory of pewterer William Will of Philadelphia. Laughlin was surprised to find the listing, and said that the actual form itself, with a Will touch (mark), had not been found as of then (1940). In Vol. III, p. 111, Laughlin transcribes a July 25, 1803 newspaper advertisement placed by NYC pewterer, George Coldwell. It reads: "Ice Cream Moulds, a few pair of offered for sale at the subscriber's work-shop No. 7 Beekman-street. They contain one gallon, are well made of the best materials, very strong and infinitely more durable than those made of Tinnned Iron..." Coldwell then enumerated his other products. Laughlin again states that as of the time of publication (1970) of Vol. III, he had yet to read of any other pewter ice cream molds, nor had he seen any (to recognize, we must add). Such molds may so differ from what we might assume such a mold would look like (for example, it may look like a pudding mold, or a pail with a lid) that we may never know if we've seen one or not. • **Fruit Ice Cream Recipe.** — "Ice-cream is prepared by mixing three parts of cream with one part of the juice or jam of raspberries, currants, etc. The mixture is then well beaten; and after being strained through a cloth, is poured into a pewter mould or vessel, adding a small quantity of lemon-juice. The mould is now covered, and plunged into a pail about two-thirds full of ice, into which two handfuls of salt should be previously scattered. The vessel containing the cream is then briskly agitated for eight or ten minutes, after which it is suffered to stand for a similar space of time; the agitation is then repeated, and the cream allowed to subside for a half hour, when it is taken out of the mould and sent to table." Anthony Florian Madinzer Willich, *The Domestic Encyclopedia; or A Dictionary of Facts & Useful Knowledge...*, 1st American edition, Philadelphia: W. Y. Birch & A. Small, 1803-04. **$60.00-$70.00**

Ice cream mold, George Washington's hatchet, marked "G. W." in case you thought it might be Carrie Nation's, #243. **$32.00-$40.00**

Ice cream mold, George Washington's profile bust, cameo-like on a hatchet shape mold, pewter, 2 part hinged, S & Co. 336, Schall & Co., NYC, NY, 4"H x 3½"W x 1½" thick, early 20th C. **$55.00-$65.00**

Ice cream mold, grape bunch, E 278, Eppelsheimer & Co. **$30.00-$40.00**

Ice cream mold, grape bunch, cast metal, "W. Hart," American (?). **$38.00-$45.00**

Ice cream mold, grape bunch, pewter, S 159, Schall & Co. **$30.00-$40.00**

Ice cream mold, hearts, 2 fat ones embossed with word "LOVE" and flames, almost like a religious symbol, Hearts Aflame #300. **$36.00-$50.00**

Ice cream mold, Irish gent, pewter, #387, American. **$32.00-$40.00**

Ice cream mold, Kewpie, pewter, E. & Co. 1913, Eppelsheimer & Co., 6"H. **$150.00-$165.00**

Ice cream mold, Kewpie-like figures, 2, very fat bellied, pewter, T. C. Weygandt Co., 9½"H x 7"W, 20th C. • Kewpie Krossover interest. **$170.00-$200.00**

Ice cream mold, lady's slipper with back of shoe & heel, pewter, (there was also a backless slip-on mule with heel), #899A, 20th C. **$35.00-$45.00**

Ice cream mold, lily, pewter, 3 part, 5¼"L when closed, 20th C. • **German vocabulary** for ice cream, or ice "bomb" mold — Eisbombeform. Another word used is the diminutive Eisformchen, although the word for ice cream is eis speise. I could find no use of eis speise form anywhere. The German for this exact mold — Zinnform fur Marzipanblume zur Tortendekoration Lilie: pewter mold for marzipan flower or "Lily" cake decoration, according to auction catalog for Technical Antiques, June 10, 1989, published by Breker Auction Team Koln, Koln, West Germany. No mention of ice cream at all, but I don't know if they know something we don't. **$35.00-$45.00**

Ice cream mold, lily, well-defined details, 3 part hinged pewter, #472, early 20th C. **$35.00-$45.00**

Ice cream mold, lion, standing, 2 part lead mold with 6 pinned clamps, F. A. Walker catalog linecut shows mark of a tiny castle & some illegible initials on this mold, European (?), c.1870s, 1880s. **$65.00-$75.00**

Ice cream mold, Masonic compass & square, crossed to form a diamond inside, pewter, #323, American, early 20th C. **$35.00-$45.00**

Ice cream mold, Miss Liberty (not the Statue, but Miss Columbia), hinged 2 part pewter, American, individual, TOC. • **Evaluating Molds.** — When looking at ice cream molds, remember that any damages (holes, small cracks, hinge damage) reduce value dramatically. Pewter is soft and easily damaged. Look for really good condition and fine interior detail. Interesting shapes or "cult" subjects add value too. **$40.00-$50.00**

Ice cream mold, Miss Liberty (sometimes called Miss Columbia), be-draped & standing on globe and wearing crown, hinged 2 part centerpiece mold, pewter, marked "Joh: Reinohl" for Johannes Reinohl, Ulm, Germany, c.1860s-70s. (This is not Statue of Liberty.) **$200.00-$250.00**

Ice cream mold, Odd Fellows chain links, 3 — representing Friendship, Love and Truth, #577. **$28.00-$32.00**

Ice cream mold, orange, hinged 2 part, pewter, #357. **$20.00-$25.00**

Ice cream mold, peach, in section, with almost a half cut away to reveal pit or stone, hinged 2 part pewter, marked #13, late 19th C. **$30.00-$40.00**

Ice cream mold, pineapple, with lots of outside detail, 3 part hinged, heavy cast pewter, marked Harton & Son, London, c.1870s-80s. **$65.00-$80.00**

Ice cream mold, potato, hinged 2 part pewter, "E. & Co. 244", mfd. by Eppelsheimer & Co., NYC, NY, c.1910s. **$25.00-$30.00**

Ice cream mold, pretzel, pewter, the form being a religious symbol for arms folded in supplications across the chest, #577, early 20th C. **$30.00-$40.00**

Ice cream mold, question mark — top part of 2 part hinged mold, bottom part is shallow oblong pan or tray with flared sides, top very high relief, heavy cast pewter, no numbers or marks on it, 3¾"L x 2¼"W, exclusive of hinge, 20th C. **$30.00-$40.00**

Ice cream mold, rabbit, standing, with basket backpack, Eppelsheimer & Co., NYC, NY, about 12"H, 1934 patent #1948148. • **Old Style or Reproduction?** — Tantalizing evidence exists in the 1932-33 *Thomas' Register of American Manufacturers*, that old-style ice cream molds were being made by a company called Reproductions Co., Boston, MA. Alas, when you turn to the manufacturers' alphabetical listing, this company is not given. I tried "Ice Cream Mold Reproductions Co." and "Boston Reproductions", to no avail. **$80.00-$100.00**

Ice cream mold, roast turkey, pewter, marked 364 on turkey; D & Co. on hinge — to me unknown maker's mark. Another was marked S 364 (Schall.) 20th C. **$45.00-$55.00**

Ice cream mold, rose in small posy bouquet, 2 part, pewter, marked #554, late 19th C. **$30.00-$40.00**

Ice cream mold, rose, pewter, #193, early 20th C. **$25.00-$32.00**

Ice cream mold, Santa Claus, pewter, E 991, (Eppelsheimer), 20th C. **$45.00-$55.00**

Ice cream mold, Santa Claus, pewter, one hinge, E. & Co. #166, NYC, NY, 4¾"H, late 19th C or early 20th. **$60.00-$70.00**

Ice cream mold, Santa & toy bag, plus wicker back pack, pewter, S. & Co. 427, mfd by Schall & Co., NYC, NY, late 19th C. **$55.00-$65.00**

Ice cream mold, seashell, stamped tin, conical helical shell design, with screw-on tin lid & strap handle, marked "GE #920", Austria, 9"L, lid is 8" diameter, early 20th C. **$45.00-$65.00**

Ice cream mold, shoe, pewter, 3 part, late 19th C. **$40.00-$50.00**

Ice cream mold, sitting hen has egglike body, uplifted head on elongated neck, perky tail, pewter, single serving, early 1900s. **$35.00-$45.00**

Ice cream mold, skull & crossbones, pewter, hinged 2 piece, #508, 3¾"W x 4½" with hinge, 1¾" thick, 20th C. **$80.00-$95.00**

Ice cream mold, spade (as in bridge), pewter, American, 1920s-30s. • There were also much more elaborate "bridge" ice cream molds of individual face cards with the Queen, etc., and the suit embossed. For someone with the time or the maid, these could be gaily colored just like a playing card. **$30.00-$35.00**

Ice cream mold, squirrel, sitting, pewter, TOC. **$120.00-$140.00**

Ice cream mold, stamped tin, marvelously detailed figure of 19th C German folktale bad boy "Struwelpeter", literally shock-headed Peter, with a shock of long straw like hair sticking out all over in a bush. Everything Struwelpeter was told not to do he did; he was used in morals & manners tales as an example of what happened if you didn't behave. Marked "A. Bertuch #564", Berlin, Germany, 1 litre capacity, TOC. • This same company did a mold of another pair from cartoon & book fame, Max & Moritz. The mold has a sort of "soap bar" plinth, with the 2 boys from the waist up. Mold #573. **$75.00-$100.00**

Ice cream mold, Statue of Liberty on pedestal, metal, 2 part, #150 Jo-Lo, Joe Lowe Corp., Brooklyn, NY, 10 pt. capacity, c.1930s-40s. • In their catalog, they also offered this mold (for sale or rental) with a 26 pint capacity. It was 37"H. The mold was $30.00; for $10.00 you could get a display model made in it. **$175.00-$225.00**

Ice cream mold, steam locomotive, pewter, #477, 20th C. **$65.00-$80.00**

Ice cream mold, stocking, very detailed knitted pattern, or maybe a long sock, hinged 2 part, pewter, "S & Co. #590", TOC. **$55.00-$75.00**

Ice cream mold, straw basket, pewter, 3 part, #598, early 20th C. **$30.00-$40.00**

Ice cream mold, teddy bear, little eyes, nose and every one of his hairs show perfectly inside, "E & Co., #3311" (?), or, because stamped backwards, may be #1133, NYC, NY, late 19th C. **$45.00-$55.00**

Ice cream mold, turkey, pewter, E 650, mfd by Eppelsheimer & Co., NYC, NY. **$32.00-$35.00**

Ice cream mold, wheat sheaf, stalks forming pedestal base, with the top very rounded, 2 part, Biertumpfel & Hepting, with Maltese cross & orb mark, London, design registered July 22, 1868. **$40.00-$50.00**

Ice cream mold or freezer, pressed glass cylinder, domed glass lid, perhaps has inner cylinder (?) of glass, wire clamp frame, exactly like the Fox mold, but advertised as is the Dazey as a "freezer", and not described well enough to know if there is an inner chamber. Ad reads "No cranking, no gear, no dasher, no rust, no crank, no metal, no wood, no labor, just VELVET ICE CREAM." Reassuringly, it "Makes Ptomaine Poisoning impossible." "The Sanitary", mfd by Consolidated Mfg. Co., Hartford, CT, probably about 9"H, advertised Jan. 1909, s.i.b. 1915. **$125.00-$150.00**

Ice cream mold or freezer, pressed glass cylinder with slightly domed lid, footed base, tin inner chamber open at both ends, false bottom has small hole fitted with white glazed stoneware stopper & rubber washer, which is where you would use wooden dowel pusher to push ice cream out the open top. Wire clamp, which is also handle, holds lid & stopper on, marked "G. H. Fox" and patent dates, invented by George H. Fox, Bangor, ME, 8½"H x 3½" diameter, pat'd Feb. 14, 1899, and July 15, 1902. See also Chapter XV. **$125.00-$150.00**

Ice cream mold or freezer, pressed glass cylindrical vessel, inner vessel (possibly tin, less probably glass, unclear from old ad picture), wire clamp to hold lid on & wire pusher to push round ball of molded ice cream out of inner cylinder for slicing, called a "freezer" in ad, "The Dazey Glass Freezer" — "The Freezer that Freezes Without Motion", probably mfd by the churn people, probably about 9''H, depicted in *House Furnishing Review* as a "latest model" in 1911. **$125.00-$150.00**

Ice cream old, thistle (?) is what it appears to be on inside, stamped metal, letters say "20th Century" — possibly for a railroad?, mfd by D. & Co., 3½''H, 20th C. **$20.00-$30.00**

Ice cream wafer mold, cast iron, 3 piece, patterned to make a waffled design, with ICYPI MADE IN USA in pattern, ICYPI, mfd by Automatic Cone Co., Cambridge, MA, 1920s. • These molds were not necessarily used by each soda fountain owner, because already prepared & baked wafer sandwich "holders" could be bought in large quantities already made. They are open on one end only to receive a slab of ice cream made using the ICYPI mechanical ice cream dipper. (ICYPI is pronounced I-Cee-Pie & usually spelled IcyPi by company.) **$350.00-$400.00**

Jagger, brass shaft, small brass cutting wheel, big crimping wheel is cast iron, American, 6½''L, late 19th C. **$75.00-$90.00**

Jagger, brass shaft & small brass wheel, cast iron sealing & trimming wheel, no marks, 6''L, late 19th C. **$20.00-$30.00**

Jagger, brass shank & fancily fashioned wheel, turned wood handle has original hang-up ring, American or English, 7½''L, 19th C. **$125.00-$140.00**

Jagger, brass shank, steel wheel, large but delicate, turned wooden handle, American or English, 9''L, 2nd quarter 19th C. **$75.00-$90.00**

Jagger, brass wheel, forged iron shank, wooden handle, American, 8''L, 19th C. **$35.00-$50.00**

Jagger, brass wheel & shank, black painted wood handle, Alfred Andreson & Co., Minneapolis, MN, 20th C. **$20.00-$25.00**

Jagger, butterscotch yellow molded plastic handle, cast aluminum shank, bronze or copper well-defined corrugated wheel, "American, 7½''L, 20th C. **$20.00-$25.00**

Jagger, carved bird's eye maple, handle & wheel, American, 4½''L, late 19th C. **$30.00-$40.00**

Jagger, carved whale bone with whale tooth wheel, mermaid with long wavy hair, smiling, slightly Negroid features so she almost resembles African carving, 3 brass nails hold on arms, American (?), 9⅝''L with 2¹/₁₆'' diameter wheel, early 19th C. **$1700.00-$2000.00**

Jagger, cast brass, nickel plated & very heavy, piece looks like machinists' work, American, 6¼''L, TOC. **$75.00-$85.00**

Jagger, cast iron shank with knops & effect of turning, forged iron wheel, turned wooden handle, probably a one-off blacksmith's piece, American, 5''L, 19th C. • A knop is like a knob only it's not on the end or top of something, but somewhere in the middle. **$35.00-$50.00**

Jagger, cast iron, wooden handle, quite simple, American, 9''L (which is exceptionally long, and indicates this may have been used in a bakery), late 19th C. **$15.00-$22.00**

Jagger, forged iron with file-decorated shaft & faceted ball knob end, one wheel, sometimes called a gigling iron in very old cookery books, American, 8⅛''L, late 18th C. **$200.00-$245.00**

Jagger, grain painted wood handle, metal, "Ridgely," American, late 19th C. **$22.00-$28.00**

Jagger, hand carved & turned wooden shank, with original dark worn red paint, steel jagging wheel, American, 8''L, late 18th or early 19th C. • To identify these really old ones, study books on furniture styles, candlesticks & andirons, as they will give you a feel for the look of late 1700s turnings. Here, it's partly old red paint, partly magisterial (as in sceptre) look that increases value. **$300.00-$400.00**

Jagger, heavy copper or bell metal wheel and shaft, turned wooden handle, very pretty, wheel drilled out with 4 holes, English (?), 6''L, 2nd quarter 19th C (?). **$110.00-$125.00**

Jagger, nickeled steel wheel & shaft with black-painted turned wood handle, American, 6''L, late 19th C. **$60.00-$70.00**

Jagger, or pie wheel, elephant ivory not whale or walrus ivory, inset with ebony pins, metal hook on end, nothing special, 7''L, mid 19th C. **$900.00-$1200.00**

Jagger, pewter wheel, heavily carved wooden handle with old old red paint, possibly old green paint underneath, American (?), 6¾''L, early to mid 18th C, or even older. **$375.00-$425.00**

Jagger, scrimshaw piecrust edger in form of horse with an elongated, curved fish or whale's tail, the head is fairly small & as abstract as Cycladic art from over 3000 years ago, the front legs arch downwards & grasp a jagging wheel, the 6 spokes of which are cut in such a way to create 6 hearts, American, 5¾''L, early 19th C. • At early 1980s auction of Barbara Johnson's scrimshaw collection, the jaggers, many architectural or geometric in style, went for fabulous prices, from $750.00 to $1700.00. Others, highly ornamental but not figural or animalistic, ranged $275.00 for one with a broken prong on the pricker part, to $1550.00. At another auction about the same time, some whale ivory and walrus ivory jagging wheels, none of them figural, realized between $225.00 and $650.00. Geometric was in, figural wasn't. Depending on the subject, values have risen 100% to 1000%. • At Richard A. Bourne Co.'s auction in July 1989, of the Jeffrey Cohen Collection of maritime antiques, two scrimshaw unicorn jaggers, long bifurcated horn pricker, front legs straddle wheel, sold for $8,000.00 & $10,000.00, plus 10% premium for buyer. **$1500.00-$2000.00**

Jagger, scrimshaw, with detailed horse's head with bridle, leg-like extensions grasping wheel, the spokes of which are the 5 points of a star, American, 6''L, early 19th C. • This one sold for $500.00 at auction a few years ago. **$850.00-$1200.00**

Jagger, simple, forged or possibly drawn wire rod in square shape (nail stock?), which has been split at one end to admit brass jagging wheel with 4 drilled out holes, and pinned through, handle end bent into sharp hook for quick hanging, very utilitarian, American, 5⅞''L, poss. early 19th C. • I cannot figure out why the holes are cut in the wheels, Surely not for decorative purposes. The only thing I can think is that even that little bit drilled out would mean saved brass (the filings or dust could be melted) or saved weight for shipping. **$45.00-$55.00**

Jagger, steel shank with very architectural turnings & planes, small-toothed wheel, turned wooden handle is possibly 19th C replacement, American, 7½''L, 1st to 2nd quarter 19th C. • **"Dough-Nuts.** — Three pounds of sifted flour. A pound of powdered sugar. Three quarters of a pound of butter. Four eggs. Half a large tea-cup full of best brewer's yeast. A pint and a half of milk. A tea-spoonful of powdered cinnamon. A grated nutmeg. A table-spoon ful of rose-water. — Cut up the butter in the flour. Add the sugar, spice, and rose-water. Beat the eggs very light, and pour them into the mixture. Add the yeast, (half a tea-cup or two wine-glasses full,) and then stir in the milk by degrees, so as to make it a soft dough. Cover it, and set it to rise.

"When quite light, cut it in diamonds with a jagging-iron or a sharp knife, and fry them in lard. Grate loaf-sugar over them when done." Miss Leslie, of Philadelphia, *Seventy-Five Receipts for Pastry, Cakes, and Sweetmeats. Appended to The Cook's Own Book and Housekeeper's Register...,* by a Boston Housekeeper. Boston: Munroe & Francis, 1833.   **$75.00-$85.00**

Jagger, turned brass, large wheel, extremely wide crimper piece at other end, English (?), 4¼"L, 1⅝"W with 1¹⁵⁄₁₆" diameter wheel, mid 19th C.   **$70.00-$90.00**

Jagger, turned fruitwood with ebony wheel, French (?), 4¾"L, c.1880s. • Added value. — One with really nice turning might bring a few dollars more, but this is a commonly found variety, and may even be made today.   **$22.00-$32.00**

Jagger, turned maple with bone wheel, 4½"L, 19th C.   **$40.00-$55.00**

Jagger, turned rosewood handle, with porcelain wheel, English (?), 19th C.   **$45.00-$60.00**

Jagger, turned steel handle shaped like wood handles, brass shaft, nickeled brass wheel, American, 7⅜"L, late 19th C.   **$75.00-$85.00**

Jagger, turned wood shank, wrought iron wheel, American, 6"L with 2" wheel diameter, early 19th C. • **"Rhubarb Pies.** — Gather a bundle of the leaf-stocks, sufficient quantity — cut off the leaf and peal (sic) the stock of the thin epidermis — cut in quarter inch pieces, and lay them into the crust — cover well with sugar, and add nutmeg, orange peel and spice to taste. The flavor is equal, and many deem it preferable to gooseberries. The pie-plant is perennial, herbaceous and very hardy. A dozen plants will afford a family a constant supply." *The Farmers' Cabinet,* Philadelphia, Aug. 1, 1836.   **$60.00-$85.00**

Jagger, turned wood with bone wheel, steel pin, American, 5"L, 19th C.   **$28.00-$38.00**

Jaggers, cast brass, wheel at one end, curved semi-circle cutter at other, turned brass shank, English or French, and imported in the late 19th C, between about 4½"L and 7"L, 19th C. • An all brass jagger, 4¾"L, with a slightly knobbed shank, curved stamp at one end and small jagging wheel with 4 drilled holes, was auctioned by Garth's in Sept. 1989. It was marked "Germany" — first I've heard of. • **Brass Jaggers from India (?)** — There are, upon examination, a great variety in these, even though most have the knob or thickening in the center of the shaft, and the smallish corrugated or jagged wheel, and the cutter or stamp at the other end. I have seen some rather crudely cast and finished ones, with extremely flimsy pins holding the wheels in place, that appear to be of recent manufacture. With all the brass coming in from India, that's my suspicion, though I've not seen "Made in India" marked on any of them. The best ones, most to be

desired, have leaf stamps instead of simple corrugated curves. These stamps were used to cut out pastry leaves to be applied to the top crusts of tarts or pies. The curved pieces could be used to cut out circles or ovoid shapes, as well as sawtooth-edged elliptical leaves.   **$28.00-$40.00**

Jagger, figural, steel, **replica** of early 19th C jagging wheel in the collection of Metropolitan Museum of Art, NYC, and created by them in their workshops. Roughly "S" shaped shank, with a simple bird at one end, a fishtail at the other, 10½"L, 1980s. • **Reproduction alert.** — Sold through the beautiful Metropolitan Museum (NYC) catalog in the early 1980s for $170.00. Very hard to figure a resale value for this, as it is a reproduction, not an original. The price had to be high for the reproduction because of the work involved in making it, but my feeling is that it is like new furniture in an old style, after you've had it a day it's simply "second hand furniture" and it'll take a generation or more to become valuable again. I'd be very wary of such pieces, as the price for an original of this type might be in the high hundreds. I believe the Museum marked theirs. Carefully examine anything offered you with a magnifying glass — standard collector equipment. Get as powerful a one as you can find.   **$75.00-$100.00**

Jagger, lathe turned wood, 2 wheels of different corrugations, one at each end, American, 8"L, mid 19th C. • "The handsomest way of ornamenting the edge of a pie or pudding is to cut the rim in large square notches, and then fold over triangularly one corner of every notch." Miss Leslie, of Philadelphia, *Seventy-Five Receipts for Pastry, Cakes, and Sweetmeats. Appended to The Cook's Own Book and Housekeeper's Register.* 1833.   **$70.00-$90.00**

Jagger, marbleized asparagus green plastic handle, with carved "ivory" plastic jagging wheel, steel pin, American, 5¼"L, 1930s. • The rage for interesting and well-designed plastic, partly fueled by the book *Art Plastic*, by Andrea DiNoto (Abbeville Press, 1985), has caused prices for especially nice, or particularly interesting plastic kitchen wares, to rise considerably.   **$18.00-$35.00**

Jagger, whale bone scrimshander work, sailor with hands on his midriff against his double-breasted buttoned jacket, straddling large fluted wheel (looks like he's riding a unicycle), wears little black cap, a skimmer, eyes appear set in of ebony, but are possibly carved & painted, American, 6½"L with 1¾" diameter wheel, c.1850s.   **$1800.00-$2200.00**

Jagger, whale bone scrimshander's work, determined-looking mermaid, arms nailed on with tiny nails, long hair down back, American, 6"L, early 19th C.   **$700.00-$900.00**

Jagger, wooden handle, jagging wheel is a copper coin, Quebec, CAN, 1852.   **$85.00-$100.00**

Jagger, wrought steel, lathe turned, American or English, 7³⁄₁₆"L, mid 19th C. • Sometimes you will see the term engine turning, but strictly speaking this is lathe turning done on an eccentric lathe, one that could turn designs not merely concentric to the center axis. Spiral turned borders, fancy rosette-like turnings, etc., are engine turned.   **$250.00-$300.00**

Jagger & crimper, brass, American, pat'd 1871.   **$40.00-$55.00**

Jagger & crimper, heavy brass handle or shaft, 2 brass wheels at one end plus steel edge sealing stamp or edger at other end, patented as a "pie rimmer" by J. Stephen and W. Zeller, Womelsdorf, PA, 5½"L, pat'd Sept. 11, 1866.   **$95.00-$120.00**

Jagger & pastry stamp, cast & machined brass, turned beechwood handle, cruciform with 2 stamps and wheel, English, 11''L, 2nd quarter 19th C. • "Almond Filberts. — 1 lb. of Valentia almonds, 1 lb. searched (sierced or sieved) sugar, about 2 yolks of eggs. — Blanch and beat the almonds very fine with yolk of egg; mix in the sugar and yolks, and beat them into a smooth paste with the pestle; roll the paste out thin, and cut it up with a proper cutter in lengths; then cut it so as to leave three points on each side; place a small almond on the middle point, and one opposite (being previously made wet with yolk of egg and water); roll them up, and put two across each other, and one on the top, which will form a filbert. Work up all your paste in this way; place them on a clean iron plate dusted with flour: bake them in a slow oven. NB. — A proper cutter for filberts must be made of tin, in a zig-zag shape, with nine points on each side; when the paste is cut by it, it will make three nuts." Joseph Bell, *A Treatise on Confectionary*, Newcastle, England, 1817. Imagine an oblong of pastry with 9 points of a zigzag on each side; cut this in thirds. And that's as far as I can get with this. If rolled up, with crosswise almonds sticking out, I imagine it looking rather formidable. Bell was Confectioner to the Prince of Wales and the Duke of York, before writing his book.   **$120.00-$140.00**

Jagger & pastry stamp, cruciform baker's tool, cast brass, includes jagging wheel, diamond shape stamp with 16 points laid out in rows of 4 x 4, round stamp also has 16 points, English, 7⅝''L x 3⅞''W, c.1810s. **$300.00-$350.00**

Jagger & pastry stamp, carved wood, very smooth satiny patina, abstract flower incised on shank, stamp at one end is serrated, poss. American, more prob. English, 6⅜''L, 19th C.   **$165.00-$200.00**

Jaggers, scrimshaw whale bone or walrus ivory, figural forms, American, 5'' to 8''L, 19th C. • Prices start at about $400.00.. Especially prized are pieces with double wheels and a pricker (sometimes a unicorn horn). **$400.00 on up.**

Jagging wheels, 8 different ones, forged iron, wheels of different "gauges" of teeth, very simple rod handles, a few with half circle cutters on one end, two with faceted knobs at end, American or European, 6'' to 8''L, with wheels 1'' to 1¼'' diameter, early to 3rd quarter 19th C. • A dealer at a York, PA show, May 1989, had all of these, a beautiful if spare and simple collection, priced low.
$125.00-$200.00

Jelly mold, 2 parts: fluted conical mold & lid, creamware with colorful underglaze flower painting, very delicate, English, 10''H, late 18th C.   **$2300.00-$2500.00**

Jelly mold, copper, simple, besides the makers' mark, another mark is an 8 point star. The numbers 11/11 are also scratched in, probably a personal inventory number, perhaps meaning this mold was number eleven out of a set of eleven, Maltese cross and orb mark, and #458, Birmingham, England, 4''H, mid 19th C. • Quoting dealer William Davis, of Wilmington, DE, the molds were marked because "they were very expensive when they were new. I have one with the coat of arms of the Duke of Bedford, one with those of the Earl of Selburne; these molds were marked and had inventory numbers too. Very frequently on the Birmingham ones, you'll find a star stamped in the side. This was a craftsman's signature, but I've not been able to identify the maker." He showed me

another signature comprised of a cluster of 4 periods, a half moon and a tiny 8-pointed star.   **$165.00-$200.00**

Jelly mold, copper, tinned inside, stamped & pieced with zigzig edge, marked with Maltese cross and orb, and number "198", Birmingham, England, 19th C.
$250.00-$300.00

Jelly mold, dovetail-seamed copper, scroll-petaled flower on top, round edges, slightly dented, stamped in mold, at least the top, marked only with #15, English, 6½''H, mid 19th C. • In an 1838 copy of *The Magazine of Domestic Economy*, published in London, is this query and answer: "Sir, — Every housekeeper, however practical, must, if candid, admit many failures in practice; one of my greatest is, that my jelly, of which I have to make much, never turns well or tolerably from the mould; though it is filled from cold water, of white stone ware, of each figure, & yet it never takes any form. The jelly is as invariably stiff, clear, and good, but some witchery always spoils its appearance. Can you help? — "We do not quite understand what our correspondent means; but we believe the sum of her complaint to be that her jelly does not turn out well from the mould. **A jelly-mould** may be made either of common tin, block tin, or of white earthen or stone ware. (Note no mention of copper!) If of one or other of the two first-mentioned materials, before the jelly is turned out, the outer surface of the mould should be rapidly wiped with a napkin dipped in hot water; if the mould is of earthenware, it should itself be dipped for an instant up to the edges in hot water. The jelly will then turn out well, provided it be well set, cold, and stiff."
$165.00-$200.00

Jelly mold, heart shaped, stamped aluminum, marked "Jell-O," American, 20th C.   **$12.00-$15.00**

Jelly mold, individual size, stamped aluminum cup with rolled rim, slightly flared sides, & large embossed block capital letter in bottom, mfd by The Barnard Co., Boston, MA, ¼ pint size (also came 12 to quart), c.1910. • Added value. — A single one wouldn't be worth much, but a set of six or 12 would be nice. Value would be affected also by the particular initial, whether or not it suited you. Originally you could order whatever initial you wanted.
$8.00-$15.00

Jelly mold, round, pieced tin, sides or base made in 3 parts, soldered to top, interlinked crabapple design on top, scored lozenges on sides, marked near ring hanger, initials that look like a capital N superimposed on a C, also numbers 32 and 6, no country of origin, 3½'' deep x 8⅛'' diameter, late 19th C.   **$15.00-$25.00**

Jelly mold, round, stamped & pieced tin, 4 pieces soldered — the skirt & the simple fluted side or base made of 2 pieces, and the top, which is an embossed shell design, bordered by rope, marked "France 296," 4'' deep x 6¼'' diameter, TOC.   **$15.00-$25.00**

Jelly mold, scroll shape, stamped tin, marked "SCT Co.", German, about 5½''L, 20th C.   **$12.00-$18.00**

Jelly mold, stamped & pieced tin, pineapple top, drape or "peacock eye" sides or base, simple skirt, American or English, mold depth 4⅞'', skirt is 6'' x 7'', TOC.
$15.00-$25.00

Jelly mold, stamped & pieced tin, round with castle turrets around sides & a pattern of blocks in the top, also called a town mold, because of its resemblance to an abstract medieval walled town, in a F. A. Walker catalog, most of whose things were French & English imports, 1870s or 1880s.   **$55.00-$70.00**

Fancy Molded Food. — Each of the finely detailed nooks and crannies (stamped or formed by piecing small pieces of tin) in these molds could be filled with a piece of food or a spoonful of differently-colored gelatin so that when turned out the surface of the fancy dish would be beautifully patterned. Little slices of carrots or lady fingers or olive slices or biscuits all had their places. Very contrived artifice, but in its way attractive — at least in chromolithographs of period cookbooks. In an interview in the *Washington Post*, Dec.12, 1974, William Rice was talking to Richard Olney about his new cookbook, *Simple French Food*. Olney told Rice:"...to be appetizing as well as attractive, food should always look like food, and we may be grateful that the chilly bits of baroque architecture with sumptuously inlaid facades of jewel-cut truffle, egg-white, and pimiento mosaic belong largely to the past. The grace of a field bouquet touches us more deeply to-day than the formal splendor of a funeral wreath."

Jelly mold, stamped tin, bunch of grapes design not well-defined, small, 1870s. **$15.00-$22.00**

Jelly mold, stamped tin, shape of stack of corn cobs, American, 1870s. **$40.00-$55.00**

Jelly mold, tin, thistle design on top fairly well-defined stamping, sides stamped in unnamed pattern, could be called "peacock eye" or "drape", made of 3 parts soldered together — the sides or base, the skirt or protective raised edge around fancy stamped top, and the top, American or English, mold depth 3⅜'', skirt 5¼''L x 3¾''H, c.1880s. **$15.00-$25.00**

Jelly molds, set of 5, copper-toned stamped aluminum, most with fluted or pleated or scalloped sides, all with wire ring hanger, in various shapes with rather mushy-formed "soft" stamped design, viz. pentagram with bunch of grapes, heart with 3 cherries and twig, square with pear (hey! a pome, if not a pomme), diamond with seahorse (huh? the one inedible motif), and a triangle with a crab. "Add a unique touch of beauty to your kitchen with these smart, new...molds...and the charm of decorating with copper color will be only part of the fun. You'll love them just as much for those distinctive gelatin salads and desserts they mold so beautifully. They're 'specially formed to hold more of that fancy topping, too'', reads the ad. West Bend Aluminum Co., West Bend, WI, c.1958. • These have a certain value for a study or nostalgia collection, and they add interesting sidelight to the decayed art of making fine food molds. But they won't ever really be the "antiques of the future" as they look so ... well, awful. **$7.00-$12.00**

Jelly molds, stamped & pieced tin, oval, fluted base or side wall, simple rolled-edge "skirt" or raised edge ringing the design in the top, so that the mold would stand steady (upside down) while the gelatine set. Well-defined, deeply-stamped designs include flowers, fruits, vegetables & animals, as well as geometrics, imported in the late 19th C from France, Germany or other countries, various sizes, holding ½, 1, 1½, and 2 pints, and 2 quarts, 1870s or 1880s, prob. before and after too. • These are usually found rather darkened, and with little bright tinning showing. Similar molds are made all of tin except for the top where the decorative motif is stamped; some of these are made of copper, which presumably took a deeper and more detailed stamp, and would avoid any tendency to rust in the creases or "cracks." **$55.00-$125.00**

Kugelhopf mold, spouted, stamped copper with tinning, European, 4'' deep x 10'' diameter, late 19th C. **$30.00-$40.00**

Lady finger cutter, stamped tin, strap handle, 2 air holes, American (?), 2⅞''L x 1''W, 19th C. **$28.00-$35.00**

Lady finger or madeline mold, sheet tin, rather crudely made, 6 elongated ovals, corrugated at each end, riveted to flat sheet, handle on one end, American, 9''L, each cup 4¼''L, 19th C. **$30.00-$40.00**

Lady finger pan, tin, stamped with elongated peanut shape cups, "Kreamer," Brooklyn, NY, early 20th C. **$18.00-$25.00**

Loaf pan, gray graniteware, c.1930s. • "**Apple Bread**. — Boil a dozen good-sized apples that have been peeled and cored, until they are perfectly tender. While still warm, mash them in double the amount of flour, and add the proper proportion of yeast. The mass should then be thoroughly kneaded without water, as the apple juice will make it sufficiently soft. It should be left to rise 12 hours, then formed into loaves, and baked when quite light. Apple Bread was the invention of a scientific Frenchman, and it has always been highly commended for its healthfulness." *Ladies Home Journal*, Sept. 1896. **$8.00-$12.00**

Loaf pan, white enamelware with cobalt trim, 8''L, 20th C. • Sometimes these look suspiciously like some kind of sterilizing container from a medical supplier. **$15.00-$22.00**

Lollipop mold, cast iron, makes 5 octagonal lollies, with room for stick, American, 5⅝'' x 10½'' x⅜'' deep, late 19th C (?). **$55.00-$70.00**

Lollipop or sucker mold, 2 part stamped metal, rough square with image of hen on basket, place for round stick in bottom, American (?), 3'' x 3'' square, c.1930s (?). • **Reproduction alert.** — For a while in the 1980s, lollipop molds were advertised as being a warehouse find of 1940s-50s vintage, although they appeared to be brand new. By spring 1989, a company in Vermont, started advertising "Profitmaking Lollipop Molds! ... genuine antique recreations" originally made up to 30 years ago. ... Each one-piece mold is made of heavy gauge tin for good detail and measures 2'' to 6'' high. Our assortments contain a wide variety of popular holiday designs and themes that Sell — for Easter, Mothers Day, Wash. B'day, Valentines, Thanksgiving, Halloween and Christmas, plus...animals galore...in addition to Santas and a clown. 30 different designs are included in our profitmaking assortments. Sugg. Ret(ail) up to $4.95 each." Wholesale price for 25 assorted was $55.50; and $189 for 100 of them. I will add only that "genuine antique recreations" is an oxymoron. So be careful, and don't be a ... you got it, a sucker. • In June 1989, another company, in Illinois, advertised "Old Metal Sucker/Candy Molds. Warehouse Find ca. 1950's ($4.00 Retail Value). They are stamped metal, and can be ordered in a surprising variety of forms, angel in flower; baseball player; boy in sunsuit; car; cat on ball, Halloween cat, and playful cat; chicken; covered wagon; cowboy; daisy; doll head; 2 different elephants; Father Time; fish; four leaf clover; heart; horse; 3 different Indians; Jiggs; jumping clown; owl; pumpkin; Statue of Liberty; several rabbits doing things; several Santas; a real and a toy soldier; a squirrel; a submarine; and a witch. **$5.00-$10.00**

Madeline molds, stamped in tin in geometric, natural & figural shapes, individual serving sizes, used for baking the rich small cakes, rather like poundcake, served plain or ornamented with frosting, nuts or fruit. Also called a dariole mold. no mark, French (?), a few inches wide, 1870s-1880s, poss. earlier, but known from F. A. Walker catalogs. • A horse's head, a rose, shells, a bunch of grapes, and a fluted flaring cup are among the forms known. **$18.00-$30.00**

Maple sugar mold, all tin, with corrugated cups riveted to rectangular tin pan, American, 9''L x 6¼''W, small cups. 19th C. **$45.00-$65.00**

Maple sugar mold, carved block of wood set into tin stand or frame that holds it up as if on an easel, mold is heart shaped, American or Canadian, 6¼''H with frame, mold itself is 4¼''W, 19th C. **$135.00-$150.00**

Maple sugar mold, carved maple, 2 part, makes 6 barrel shaped candies, late 19th C. **$45.00-$60.00**

Maple sugar mold, carved wood, 2 hearts & a crescent moon, American? 15''L x 3½''W, 19th C. **$120.00-$140.00**

Maple sugar mold, carved wood, a blue jay with crest, American or Canadian, 5½'' x 6¾'', 20th C. **$12.00-$15.00**

Maple sugar mold, carved wood, beaver design, Canadian (?), 8 ½'' x 3¼'', early 20th C. **$25.00-$55.00**

Maple sugar mold, carved wood, geometric forms, 8¾''H, early 20th C (?). **$45.00-$50.00**

Maple sugar mold, carved wood, heart, diamond, spade, American? 16''L x 4''W x 2''thick, 19th C. **$140.00-$165.00**

Maple sugar mold, carved wood, squirrel with thick curled tail, 6½'' x 5¼'', 20th C. **$15.00-$30.00**

Maple sugar mold, carved wood with 3 designs — sunburst, heart, tulip, American or Canadian, 17''L x 5''W, 19th C. **$185.00-$250.00**

Maple sugar mold, carved wood with 3 stars, 15''L x 3½''W,late 19th, early 20th C. **$125.00-$150.00**

Maple sugar mold, chip carved thick wood, one end cut away except for wedge shaped handle (large part out), 3 cakes made in shallow fluted cups, Canadian or American, 11''L x 2''W, mid 19th C. **$55.00-$70.00**

Maple sugar mold, deeply carved wood, oblong plank, 3 hearts, with sides & bottom of cups further decorated with carving, Canadian (?), doesn't look American, 22''L x 7''W, early 19th C. **$300.00-$375.00**

Maple sugar mold, for making sugar pyramids, very tall & narrow, all wood, 4 side pieces are acute triangles held together with simple wooden clamp: a square cut out of oblong piece of wood, meant to fit down over assembled sides & be wedged in place, so mold could be filled at big open base end. The wedge also served as a sort of flange so the mold could be put in a rack or frame to harden, Canadian, about 10''H x 4½'' square at base, 19th C. **$50.00-$65.00**

Maple sugar mold, hand carved, long & skinny, makes 14 hearts, 42''L, makes 2''H hearts, 19th C. **$125.00-$150.00**

Maple sugar mold, heavy terne plate tin, prints 12 figures, viz. cornucopia, fleur-de-lis , pear, heart, daisy, oak leaf, shell, bell, fish, moon, flag, automobile & strawberry, ''Jaburg Bros.,'' NYC, NY, 6'' x 6½'', c.1930s (?). **$125.00-$150.00**

Maple sugar mold, large house, carved wood, 19th C. **$120.00-$140.00**

Maple sugar mold, long trough of wood, makes 5 oblong blocks of sugar candy, American, 18''L x 2½''W overall, one block is about 4½''L x 1'' deep, other 4 are about 3½''L x 1'' deep, late 19th C. **$40.00-$50.00**

Maple sugar mold, oblong of wood, 14 carved figures, including horse, diamond, 6 pointed star, hearts, houses, anvil, etc., very precisely & carefully cut, in contrast to many observed maple sugar molds with rather crude carvings, American, 32''L x 7''W x 2'' thick, 19th C. The houses add particular interest. (Even more valuable are the rare house shaped molds in 3 dimensions. These are in 2 or 4 parts; inside carving includes doors, windows, chimneys, etc. They're probably earlier than flat ones, and may be Canadian.) This one offered by the Jorgensens of Hallowell in 1983. Price range mine. **$300.00-$450.00**

Maple sugar mold, or muffin pan, tin, 12 star shaped cups with 6 points, riveted to rectangular pan, with round holes in bottom, of the type of pan often called a maple sugar mold, but possibly used for muffins, American, 15''L x 13''W, marked only with illegible patent date, ''Pat'd Dec. 11, 19—''. • If the Dec. 11, 19— was stamped accurately, or read correctly, that is if the 11th was a Tuesday in early 20th C, then the only years in right period would be 1900, 1906, or possibly as late as 1917 or even 1923. • Robacker May 1989 price: **$160.00**

Maple sugar mold, sheet tin, 7 individual shallow cups with hexagonal exteriors, round interiors, riveted together (this is the reason for the hexagonal edges) & giving the appearance of a piece of honeycomb, thin strap handle, (I identified this as a muffin pan in last edition), American, 9⅛'' diameter, 19th C. • Maine collector Joanne Wilson wrote to tell me that hers was ''given to me by a lady who said it was used as a maple sugar mold on the farm where she grew up.'' I accept this new attribution, as it does seem too shallow for muffins, though not for some kind of small cake or cookie. **$28.00-$40.00**

Maple sugar mold, strawberry, carved wood, American, 9¼''L x 5½''W x 1¾''thick, 19th C. **$135.00-$145.00**

Maple sugar mold, stamped tin, fluted shallow pan, small enough for doll tarts, American or import, late 19th or early 20th C. **$3.00-$5.00**

Marzipan mold, also called a marchpane mold, tin plated, hinged, German, 19th or 20th C. **$30.00-$40.00**

Marzipan mold, heavy tin plate, 2 hinged sections, 3'' x 3'', late 19th C. **$25.00-$35.00**

Marzipan mold—See Cake or marzipan board.

Mold, armadillo design, white vitreous earthenware, ''Shelley,'' Longton, England, c.1922. **$175.00-$200.00**

Mold, brown glazed pottery, slightly oval, fluted sides, very detailed swan, high tipped up tail, with reeds, English (?), about 7''L x 6''W x 3'' deep, late 19th C. **$75.00-$90.00**

Mold, brown glazed redware, an unidentifiable, slightly curved, scaly fish with pleasant smile & pronounced double caudal or tail fin, no other fins, very primitive, somewhat lumpy ungraceful form, PA German, 11⅝''L x 4½''W, 19th C. • Robacker May 1989 price: **$350.00**

Mold, buff glazed heavy ceramic, deep molded bunch of grapes in top, American, 3¾''H x 8''L x 7''W, mid 19th C. **$70.00-$80.00**

Mold, cast iron, oval, ''M. & H. Schrenkeisan'', NYC, NY, about 2½'' deep x 7½''L, late 19th C. **$40.00-$50.00**

Mold, cauliflower design, cream colored earthenware,'' Alcock, ''English, 8''L, last quarter 19th C. **$75.00-$100.00**

Mold, cobalt enamelware, melon type with flat tin lid, last quarter (?) 19th C. $45.00-$60.00

Mold, copper, 3 tier, fancy looking with petal-like top, no mark, English, 10"H x 8" diameter, c.1860.
$1000.00-$1200.00

Mold, copper, 3 tiered, the 2nd tier is fat columns into which lady fingers would fit nicely, top tier of fat turban twists, stamped with numeral "1", also initials of owner, "J. A. C.", English, 9"H x 8" diameter, c.1860s.
$800.00-$900.00

Mold, copper, pieced & stamped, dovetail seam, tinned inside, high base or sides shaped like a fez, couchant lion on top, looking up, simple skirt, no discernible mark, English (?), 4¾"H exclusive of low lion, 7"L, c.1850s.
$550.00-$600.00

Mold, copper ring mold, stamped, tinned inside, rustic & exaggerated twiggy bird's nest design, English (?), 6½" diameter, late 19th C. $175.00-$200.00

Mold, copper & tin, ear of corn deeply embossed on copper top, tin sides & skirt, American (?), 5¼"L. 19th C.
$135.00-$150.00

FOOD MOLD PARTS. — The naming of parts of many collectible kitchen things is difficult, because sometimes manufacturers' terms are too technical or can't be understood intuitively, or because collectors and writers have used terms (which may or may not be accurate) for so long that they are understood widely. The parts of a food mold, which is called a shape in England, in order of importance to the value, are the top, the part with the stamped design, which will be on top of the finished molded food, exclusive of some kinds of ice cream, chocolate or candy; the sides or base, which is the deep part forming the walls of the mold, and which may or may not be stamped or hammered with their own designs or shapes; the skirt, which is a sort of shallow mirror image of the base, and which rims the top so that the mold may be set upside down while the food congeals or becomes firm; and, in some molds, a ring hanger; feet or similar projections that perform same function as the skirt, to make the mold stable while the food is setting (these are found almost always on fish molds); and lid. In the middle of some molds you may find a tube or a spout, the former is capped or closed, the latter is open. As a mnemomic, think of a closed mailing tube and an open coffee pot spout. $135.00-$150.00

Mold, copper & tin, lion design, deep tin sides, shallow tin skirt, English, 7"L, 19th C. $175.00-$210.00

Mold, copper, tin skirt, corn design, oval 4" deep x 4" W x 6½"L, 19th C. $125.00-$140.00

Mold, copper, tinned inside, crown-like with chain link effect on top, 5 lobes to sides, stamped "M 443", English, 5½"H x 5" diameter, c.1860. $300.00-$350.00

Mold, copper, tinned inside, flared sides, tubed turk's head, poss. American, prob. European, 11" diameter, mid to late 19th C. • Practically at the last minute, after reading 60 years' worth of NYC directories on microfiche, I found an extremely important listing in *Trow's Directory* for 1866-67, which is confirmation of what seems logical — that some copper molds were made in America. The expanded listing in question is for Louis Ottenheimer, at 404 E. Houston, and 295 Second Street "near Union Market", NYC. It reads: "Ottenheimer Louis, tin, brass and copper works. Copper tea kettles, stew pans, sauce pans, confectioners' pans, the only manufacturer in this country of

Copper Sponge Cake and Jelly Moulds; copper and brass urns for porterhouses, various styles; brass and copper drainers, copper funnels; tin, brass and copper measures." $85.00-$125.00

Mold, copper, tinned inside, oval, makes hearts at the top of columns, pieced, with dovetailed seam, no mark, English, 6"W oval, c.1870s to 1880s. $250.00-$300.00

Mold, copper, tinned inside, oval ring, gothic arches, stamped with the #198 and a maltese cross and orb, sign of a Birmingham works, English, 2¾"H x 6"W oval, c.1870s to 1890s. • **Birmingham, England** was a great copper mold manufacturing center from about 1840 to about 1910, according to mold dealer William Davis, of Wilmington, DE. Traditionally, Birmingham has been known for several centuries for brass working. $250.00-$300.00

Mold, copper, tinned inside, oval & tubed, 4" deep x 8" L, late 19th C. $125.00-$145.00

Mold, copper, tinned inside, rose design stamped in top, 7"L x 5"W, late 19th C. $65.00-$80.00

Mold, copper, tinned inside, shallow oval mold in 3 tiers, diamonds on top, marked "Moulton Paddocks" and with initials E. C, possibly the owner's initials, English, 2"H x 6½"L, mid 19th C. $115.00-$125.00

Mold, copper, with small cast brass pedestal screw-on base, brass ring handle on snug-fitting copper lid, tinned inside, looks like a lifesize upside down artichoke, marked "F. W. & Co. #1100", English, about 7"H overall, late 19th C. • See also a couple of entries under Pudding molds, with similar bases. $165.00-$180.00

Mold, copper with tin sides & tin skirt, rose design, 4" deep x 4"W x 6½"L, 19th C. $135.00-$150.00

Mold, corn design, cream colored earthenware, English, 6"L, late 19th C. $60.00-$80.00

• **No More Breaks** — "To prevent Glass, Earthen, Potter's and Iron(stone) Ware from being easily broken... put dishes, tumblers, and other glass articles into a kettle; cover them entirely with cold water, and put the kettle where it will soon boil. When it has boiled for a few minutes, set it aside, covered close. When the water is cold, take out the glass.
"Treat new earthen ware the same way. When potter's ware is boiled, a handful or two of bran should be thrown into the water, and the glazing will never be injured by acids or salts." Mrs. Cornelius, *The Young Housekeepers Friend or, A Guide to Domestic Economy and Comfort*, NY or Boston, 1846. $55.00-$75.00

Mold, figural duck head, copper, tinned inside, used for chocolate, not jellies, "Harrod's Store, Ltd.," English, 3¾"H, TOC. $18.00-$30.00

Mold, figural wheat sheaf, tinned copper, used for chocolate candies, "Harrod's Store, Ltd.," English, 3"H, TOC. $15.00-$18.00

Mold, fish, stamped copper, tinned inside, "Kreamer," Brooklyn, NY, early 20th C. $50.00-$65.00

Mold, fish, stamped tin, for congealed (jellied, or gelatinized) dishes, although at least one dealer said it was for baking Lenten bread. American or German, 19th C.
$25.00-$30.00

Mold, floral design, tan earthenware, oval, footed base, English or American, 19th C. $60.00-$75.00

Mold, fluted gray graniteware, American (?), 2½" deep x 7" diameter, late 19th C. $28.00-$35.00

Mold, for blancmange, gray glazed pottery, very decorative molding with recipe for the pudding printed on side, adv'g "Brown & Polsons Corn Flour", English, 7" x 5½" x 5", TOC. **$35.00-$45.00**

Mold, for gelatin dish, called a jelly mold, oval, clear glass, paneled sides, English, 3½"H x 7"L x 4"W, late 19th C. **$12.00-$15.00**

Mold, frame with 10 wonderful stamped fat well detailed fish in 2 rows, all facing same direction, brass & tin, probably for individual fish mousses, English or American, each fish 5"L x 2"W, overall dimension is 10½" x 10", late 19th C. **$145.00-$160.00**

Mold, fruit pattern on top, copper, tinned inside, round shape, fluted sides, short rolled-edge skirt, late 19th C. **$45.00-$60.00**

Mold, geometric, copper with tinned inside, oval ring mold, 9"L x 3"D x 5½"W, 3rd quarter 19th C. **$130.00-$150.00**

Mold, glazed pottery, oval with flutes inside & scalloped rim, design is a tall footed urn, 4 feet on mold formed as flower petals, English, only 2"H x 6¼"L x ¼"W, early 19th C. **$65.00-$75.00**

Mold, glazed stoneware, rectangular, wonderful design made up of concentric borders of round tennis balls with cross tennis rackets on top, "Copeland", English, TOC. **$75.00-$100.00**

Mold, grape cluster, brown ringed earthenware, English, 7"L, 19th C. **$60.00-$75.00**

Mold, gray enameled iron, fluted melon mold , footed to hold it stable, lid not made for this one, prob. European, late 19th C. **$95.00-$125.00**

Mold, gray enamelware, with tin lid, marked "L & G. Mfg. Co. No. 60, Extra Agate", Lalance & Grosjean, late 19th C, early 20th. **$60.00-$80.00**

Mold, gray graniteware, spouted turk's head, only 6½" diameter, late 19th C. **$40.00-$48.00**

Mold, hammered copper, spouted, marked with a "P" over a 2-step mark, also #205, 20th C. **$25.00-$35.00**

Mold, heavy cast iron, amazing finny detail on curved fish, American, 2⅜" deep x 12¹³⁄₁₆"L at widest, mid 19th C. **$120.00-$145.00**

Mold, heavy copper, pieced & hammered, spouted, Masonic hammer mark and a "5S" over a "C", American (?), 19th C. **$230.00-$250.00**

Mold, heavy copper, tinned inside, well-defined thistle design, only mark is "194", 1" deep x 2⅛" diameter, late 19th C. **$12.00-$18.00**

Mold, heavy gauge copper, tinned inside, tubed oval, fluted sides, top has turk's head effect, looks as if it has been wire brushed, marked "LAGRE 448 M. TEBE. DE", Belgian or French?, 19th C. **$550.00-$600.00**

Mold, heavy pieced tin, very carefully made, tubed, 8 pronounced scallops, large diameter tube, ring hanger, American (?), 2" deep x 6½" diameter, 1890s. **$18.00-$22.00**

Mold, heavy thick cast iron, in bath tub shape without legs, dealer thought it was a chocolate mold for cream eggs, cast on bottom is only "1 lb", American, late 19th C. **$18.00-$22.00**

Mold, ironstone, large size oval, fluted base, rare image of cow with man milking , English, 19th C. **$165.00-$200.00**

Mold, octagonal, cobalt enamelware, spouted, American (?), TOC. **$25.00-$35.00**

Mold, pear, copper, tinned inside, 3½"L, late 19th C. **$38.00-$45.00**

Mold, pieced copper, dovetail seams, tinned inside, oval with swirled lobes, English (?), 4" deep x 4 ½" x 7", c.1850s. **$145.00-$160.00**

Mold, pieced & seamed copper, tinned inside, braided border & 8 tall fluted risers, unpolished old patina, only mark is #435, stamped in so it's either maker's mark or inventory mark from large kitchen, English, 6"H x 5½" diameter, c.1840s to 1860s. **$250.00-$300.00**

Mold, pieced & stamped copper, tinned inside, each tier soldered together, tall 'chef's hat' effect, 6 lobed top with swagged sides or base, marked only with stamped number 38, probably an inventory number, English, 8½"H, c.1860. • The dealer had this at $1000.00 in fall 1987. Seems awfully high, although it is quite handsome. **$700.00-$1000.00**

Mold, pieced & stamped tin, oval, "picket" flutes around sides, seamed at each end, top is very high profile stamped copper lion couchant but looking over left shoulder (couchant sinistral? as opposed to couchant dextral) with distinctly bewildered expression, this lion polychromed in old paint, metallic gold, shades of deep yellow, black, with red inside mouth & red border, very unusual, English, 5"H x 7¼"L, mid (?) 19th C. • The paint, which I believe is original, accounts for about half the probable market value. **$300.00-$375.00**

Mold, possibly a cake mold, redware, Turk's head, orange & brown glaze, a few flaky chips, 7" diameter, 19th C. **$140.00-$165.00**

Mold, possibly for ice cream, pieced tin, straight sides with rolled edge, clumsy but charming corrugated cup in center with 6 small very pointed cones, one in each of the 6 large scalloped compartments around the center, American, 19th C. **$100.00-$125.00**

Mold, pottery with medium brown glaze, wheel thrown, fluted and spouted afterward, spout is corked with what is obviously contemporaneous cork, American, 3¾"H x 7½" diameter, 19th C. **$55.00-$65.00**

Mold, rabbit design, earthenware, "Meakin," English, 19th C. **$60.00-$75.00**

Mold, red stoneware not glazed on outside, pale yellow glaze inside, green around chipcarved edge, figural of baby (Baby Jesus) in swaddling clothes, face rather well detailed, bundling has pattern of flowers. Although this is a newborn baby (which seems like Christmas), the bread baked in it is for Easter, or perhaps Lent, at least in Germany. Several versions of the ceramic "Wickelkinder" (swaddled babies) are depicted in German books on old kitchenwares. One has curly hair, a fluted ruff, and the swaddling is criss-crossed with a ribbon tied with a bow. A stamped tin one shown in one book, which looks like a chocolate mold, & dates to the end of the 19th C. Southern German, 12"L x 5½"W, c.1830s-40s. • **German vocabulary** — Fatschenkind (Lenten child?) or Wickelkinder: babe in swaddling clothes. • The mold in this entry was auctioned for $155.00 at Garth's, July 28, 1989. **$135.00-$200.00**

"Yule-Dough, or dow (sic), a kind of baby, or little image of paste, was formerly baked (in England) at Christmas, and presented by bakers to their customers, 'in the same manner as the chandlers gave Christmas candles.' They are called yule cakes in the county of

Durham. Anciently, 'at Rome, on the vigil of the nativity, sweetmeats were presented to the fathers in the Vatican, and all kinds of little images (no doubt of paste) were to be found at the confectioners' shops.'·My correspondent, Mr. Brand, who mentions these usages, thinks, 'there is the greatest probability that we have had from hence both our yule-doughs, plum-porridge, and mince-pies, the latter of which are still in common use at this season. The yule-dough has perhaps been intended for an image of the child Jesus, with the Virgin Mary,' he adds, 'it is now, if I mistake not, pretty generally laid aside, or at most retained only by children.' '' William Hone, *The Every-Day Book*, Vol. I, n.d. (1825 or 1826). Lesley Gordon, *A Pageant of Dolls*, (NYC: Wynn, 1949), says that in the Yorkshire district of England, a ''bread doll'' was made ''as nearly as possible to look like a real baby, with fingers and toes marked on it and a small dab of dough for a nose; this doughy infant was lightly baked and dressed in real white babyclothes.''

Mold, redware fish, slightly curved with bifurcated short tail, no body fins, large exaggerated scales & smiling expression, American, poss. PA (?), 19th C. June 1989 asking price: **$345.00**

Mold, redware glazed inside with dark brown, lots of detail, rooster with squirrel-scroll tail, small feet underneath hold it steady, American, rooster is 11½''H x 11''W, mid 19th C. • From the Jacqueline Hodgson Collection; offered for sale in 1986 by Rich & Kelli Bucher, Hartland, VT. Price range mine. **$800.00-$1100.00**

Mold, redware spouted turk's head, with ''swirled fluted sides & finger crimped rim'', palpably handmade, prob. PA, 9½'' diameter, 19th C. • Only $25.00, because of ''old chips & hairline'' cracks, at Garth Auction, May 5-6, 1989, Delaware, OH. Worth four or five times as much in better condition. **$25.00-$175.00**

Mold, rose design, stamped copper, tinned inside, 4½''D, late 19th C. **$90.00-$120.00**

Mold, round with 2 handles, 9 shaped cups, very Oriental in feel, a fish, shell, leaf, melon, etc., sold as ''French'' but a new one bought in China was shown me recently, 12¼'' diameter, dealer said c.1760; I think prob. late 19th C to recent times. • The dealer's price of $1400.00 was based on belief it was ''18th C European''. Price range is based on belief it is much newer. **$45.00-$75.00**

Mold, saltglazed stoneware, grape bunch, American, 19th C. **$45.00-$60.00**

Mold, seashell design, copper, tinned inside, 3½''L, late 19th C. **$35.00-$45.00**

Mold, shallow tin skirt with tin plated copper mold, thistle pattern, almost as common as the pineapple, English or American, 19th C. **$75.00-$110.00**

Mold, so-called ''crown mold'', cream glazed ceramic, very deep molding, English, 3¾''H x 5¾''L x 4¼''W, mid 19th C. **$60.00-$70.00**

Mold, sometimes called a ''jelly mold'', 3 tiers, very architectural, copper, tinned inside, stamped ''N & G 529'' 4''H x 4'' diameter, late 19th C. • Dealer William Davis said that manufacturers used some very fine contemporary designers to design the molds, and that they also used architects. He said he had one mold that looks like the top of the Crysler Building in NYC! **$165.00-$200.00**

Mold, spouted, copper, tinned inside, stamped turban-like pattern makes it look like a Bundt pan, small metal ring for hanging, no mark, German, English or American, 5''H x 10½''D, late 19th C.• Aspics, and what were called ''jellies'' and other congealed or jellied foods were made in such molds; very small ones were used for fancy little individual jellies or cakes. **$125.00-$175.00**

Mold, spouted, copper, very simple fluted design, no marks at all, 10½'' diameter, mid 19th C. **$35.00-$45.00**

Mold, spouted, with 6 fluted cap-topped towers, heavy pieced copper, tinned inside, English, 5''H, c.1830s to 1850s (?). • For collectors, the apparent aristocrats of copper molds are the architectural ones, the more sky-reaching and cloud-breaking the more fun, but actually these are later than the highly prized molds from early Victorian times. Extreme gothic aspirations, and thin copper, date English molds to the 1880s or 1890s. **$185.00-$225.00**

Mold, stamped or beaten into form, each of 4 tiers pieced & soldered together, copper, tinned inside, tall & with a sort of scalloped Jell-O mold look on top, marked ''206 C'', English, 8''H x 6½'' diameter, c.1860. **$375.00-$400.00**

Mold, stamped & pieced heavy tin, 3 tiers, architectural in appearance, hanging ring at rim, poss. American, 9''H, 19th C. **$55.00-$75.00**

Mold, stamped & pieced tin, grape bunch design, 3¼''L x 2¾''W, late 19th or early 20th C. **$15.00-$20.00**

Mold, stamped tin fish, simple head, wide flat edges, wire leveling leg, stamped ''CF'', also numbers ''499'' over ''3'', ''AUSTRIA'', 2¼'' deep x 9⅛''L x 4¼''W, c.1900 to 1920. **$15.00-$25.00**

Mold, stamped tin, fish-shaped, fancy head, ''G. M. T. Co., Czecho-Slovak,'' 1⅝'' deep x 9¼''L x 3¾''W, c.1900 to 1920. **$15.00-$25.00**

Mold, stamped tin, fish-shaped, stamped on leveling 'leg' at tail end is ''Germany'', 2¾'' deep x 13½''L x 5½''W, c.1900 to 1920s. • **''Fish Jelly.** — Take a two-pound haddock, one onion, and half rind lemon; just cover with water, and boil; remove all the bones and skin; flake the fish, or pound it in a mortar, with a tablespoonful of butter, pepper and salt to taste. Put back the bones, reduce the liquor to one pint, add a quarter of a packet of gelatine (previously dissolved in a quarter of a tumbler of cold water). Make some veal forcemeat, without suet, roll in small balls, and drop into boiling water; they will cook in seven minutes. Decorate a mould with the balls and rings of lemon, mix the strained liquid with the pounded fish, and, when nearly cold, pour into the mould. Hard-boiled eggs may be made over in this way.'' Gertrude Strohm, *The Universal Cookery Book*, 1888. It you do not like the idea of veal, for humanitarian or any other reasons, you can use ground turkey, or decorate the mould with mushroom caps and forget the meat except for the fish. **$15.00-$25.00**

Mold, starflowers, copper, tinned inside, individual size, 3¾''D, late 19th C. **$45.00-$65.00**

Mold, tin, 2 part, with strap handle on lower section, strawberry, cherry, apple, pear, grapes & plum design, obviously for a congealed fruit salad! ''Kreamer,'' early 20th C. **$35.00-$50.00**

Mold, tin border mold, extraordinary form composed of 7 swirled (like soft ice cream) & pointed cones, wire hanging ring, German, 9'' diameter (these came in various sizes with different numbers of cones), TOC. **$55.00-$75.00**

Mold, tin, oval with short skirt, 6 point star design, an individual mold size, for a fancy jellied dish, English or American, 2½''H x 3⅞''L x 2¼''W, 19th C.   **$28.00-$35.00**

Mold, tin, sharp edges almost as if it were to be a cutter, shape is outline of pineapple, bottom is separate & pushes through the shape, no mark, 2¹³⁄₁₆'' deep x 7¼''L, TOC.   **$125.00-$140.00**

Mold, tin sides & skirt, copper top with rose design, sides formed in a sort of cathedral arch design, ''J. A. & Co.'', 1 pt. capacity, 1½''H skirt, mid 19th C.   **$95.00-$120.00**

Mold, tin sides & skirt, deeply embossed copper top, grape bunch, 5½''L, late 19th C.   **$85.00-$100.00**

Mold, tin, spouted with 9 sections shaped like Mr. Softee ice cream cones, the flat-bottomed kind, hanging ring, American or imported, 9'' diameter, 19th C.   **$150.00-$200.00**

Mold, tin with tinned copper mold part, nice wheat sheaf & sickle, prob. American, 19th C. • Motif adds value.   **$125.00-$135.00**

Mold, a set of 8 individual, stamped aluminum, fluted sides, for congealed salads or iced desserts or even Jell-O, American, 3½'' deep x 4'' diameter, 1930s or 40s. • We have two tall wire racks to hold four filled individual molds on for the refrigerator.   **$12.00-$18.00**

Mold, brown glazed ceramic, celebrating the American Centennial, molded mark ''1776-1876'' inside, American, 1876.   **$100.00-$125.00**

Mold, copper with heavily tinned inside, fluted sides, cornucopia in top, oval, 1½'' deep x 4½''L x 3½''W, late 19th C.   **$55.00-$60.00**

Mold, individual mold for ''Jell-O,'' ad said ''copper'', which is unusual because most are stamped aluminum, ''Jell-O,'' 20th C. • This mold is probably anodized aluminum with a copper finish, not really copper. Some of these entries I get from ads, feeling that even with incomplete information they are possibly first clues that lead to other discoveries for you and me. It is possible that there are real copper Jell-O molds; can anyone enlighten me? Anyway, the aluminum Jell-Os go for about $5.00-$8.00 each, a copper anodized one would be less than that, being newer, but if there really is a real copper one, value would be about: **$12.00-$15.00**

Mold, white ceramic, asparagus bunch, Minton #41/6, English, mid 19th C.   **$120.00-$130.00**

Mold, white glazed ceramic elephant, white body clay, English, 2'' deep x 6½'' x 4¾'', mid 19th C.   **$175.00-$225.00**

Mold, yellowware ceramic, oval with flat inside bottom, fluted sides, recessed inside foot, drippy Rockingham glaze outside, stamped clearly on bottom, L. B. Patterson Fire-Clay Ware Manufactory, Pottsville, PA, almost 4'' deep x 9''L x 7''W, 19th C.   **$165.00-$185.00**

Mold, yellowware, ear of corn, American, 4¾''H x 8''L x 6''W,19th C.   **$75.00-$120.00**

Molds, set of 4, stamped aluminum individual molds, anodized copper on outside, patterns stamped on tops are acorn & oak leaves, daisy or sunburst, 4 leaf clover, thistle & leaves, maker not known, offered as premium by Knox Gelatine, 5 oz. size, 1972.   **$6.00-$10.00**

Muffin baker, cast iron, 7 very shallow straight-sided indentations rather than cups, as this was for making muffins of the English muffin type, not the delicatessen bran muffin you may have visualized. Iron is heavily encrusted from use (a good sign when dating pieces), ''JOHNSON'' cast on handle, American, 10½'' diameter with 6¼''L handle, 19th C. • These have often been called ''pancake pans'' as small flapjacks could be made in the cups. I am calling it a muffin baker after seeing a nearly identical one pictured in the 1872 *The New Cyclopedia of Domestic Economy*. Such a pan took the place of separate muffin rings (tin hoops sort of like tuna fish cans with both ends open) which were laid upon a hot griddle, and the batter poured in. The all-in-one version was both more and less convenient.   **$40.00-$55.00**

Muffin, gem or popover pan, cast iron, only 6 cups, ''Griswold No. 18,'' also #6141, 9½'' x 5½'', TOC into 1930s or later. • ''**Gems.** — These are the simplest form of bread, and if properly made are certain to be light and sweet. A hot oven and hot pans are prime essentials, and there must be no delay between making and baking. The coldest water, ice-water preferred, should be used. Use either whole-wheat or Graham flour, three parts of flour to one of water. ... For a dozen gems allow one large cup — a half pint — of ice water, one even teaspoon of salt, and three cups of flour. Stir in the flour slowly, beating hard and steadily, not less than ten minutes. The pans should have been set on top of the stove, and oiled or buttered. Fill them two thirds full, and bake about a half hour.'' Mrs. Helen Campbell's recipe, in *Good Housekeeping Discovery Book, No. 1*, 1905.   **$65.00-$85.00**

Muffin mold or gem pan, cast iron, shapely oblong with 13 variously shaped shallow cups, including 2 hearts, one at both ends, a 6 point star next to both hearts on the long axis, 4 rounds in corners plus one in the center, & 2 scalloped cups on each side, cutout tab handles at both ends, looks right, nice satiny smooth dark iron, no marks, American, 16½''L x 8½''W x ¾'' deep, late 19th C (?). **''Cleaning New Iron-Ware.** — I do not remember to have seen directions anywhere for preparing new cast-iron utensils for service in cooking. I know I had a deal of trouble with my first stove furniture, and whenever I have anything of the kind to deal with now I wonder if there is not some better way than I have learned. I have just been tackling a new set of iron gem-pans. I filled them with ashes and water and left them standing during the forenoon. I heated them on the stove before emptying them, and then gave them a good washing and rinsing. I think they will do for use to-morrow morning. I usually scour new kettles with ashes, then rub them over with a little grease, and wash them well with suds. To-day a lady told me that it was a good way to wash new irons with sour milk. I had no sour milk to use, but I do not see the philosophy of it. It is not rust with which we have to deal in cleaning new iron, but a fine sand, used in the casting.'' Correspondent to Editor, *American Agriculturist*, June 1874.   **$150.00-$200.00**

Muffin or cookie pans, cast iron, fancy cups, in wide-bordered rectangular frame with fancy scroll handles, (a) 5 toy soldiers in same frame, (b) a number of small figural cups, ''Classic Gourmet Series,'' mfd by John Wright, Wrightsville, PA, © 1984.   **$10.00-$15.00**

Muffin or gem pan, actually patented as an egg pan, cast iron with gray graniteware on inside of 8 oval cups, N. Waterman, (Very unusual to find enameling inside a marked Waterman piece.) Boston, MA, pat'd Apr. 5, 1859. (When ill-cast or worn, date looks like 1853 or 1858.)   **$125.00-$165.00**

Muffin or gem pan, cast iron, 11 shallow cups in 3 rows, curved handles at ends, ''R. & E. Mfg. Co.,'' Russell & Erwin Mfg. Co., Nathaniel Waterman patent, 13''L x 8¾''W, each cup is 3¼'' diameter x 1'' deep, pat'd April 5, 1859, but made by R & E some years after that. • This was actually patented as an **''Improved Egg Pan''** and described as a ''new or improved manufacture of baking pan, or arrangement of cups, and a handle at each end of the series, all connected together and cast or founded in one solid piece of metal and with heat passages between the cups.'' This pan was not only made by Russell & Erwin, but also Hibbard, Spencer, Bartlett & Co. H,S,B & Co. made two sizes: **(1)** 11 cups 2¾'' diameter, and **(2)** 11 at 3¼'' diameter. • See article on cast iron muffin pans by David Smith is this volume. **$45.00-$60.00**

Muffin or gem pan, cast iron, 12 round bottom cups, what Griswold called a ''golf-ball pan'', tab handles, cutouts between each cup, Griswold No. 9, 10⅛''L x 7''W, c.1920s-30s. • Gary M. Smith and his wife, collectors and dealers in New Jersey, tried making a gem recipe in one of these. ''Used the lil' darlins as door stops. As my wife said, 'It sure sticks to your ribs!' We have a theory that it could also do double duty as mini-cannon ball mold,'' wrote Gary back in 1984. • Griswold also made a 6-cup golf-ball pan, the No. 19, which brings $15.00 to $20.00 more than the 12-cup. **$35.00-$50.00**

Muffin or gem pan, cast iron, 12 very shallow fluted turk's head cups, cutout tab handles, Griswold #14, 13⅛''L x 8½''W, c.1920s on. **$55.00-$70.00**

Muffin or gem pan, cast iron, 5 hearts surrounding single star, has one short, holed, handle with opening for a pot-lifting tool. Griswold's ''Heart-Star'' #100, 7¾'' diameter, c.1926 or later. • The game of bridge became extremely popular in the 1920s, and all sorts of kitchen- or cooking- or serving-related things used bridge motifs. Yes, I know; stars aren't taken from playing cards. A smaller version of this pan was also made, #50, only 6½'' diameter and only ½'' deep cups, which is valued by avid collectors between $275.00 to $350.00. The smallest — and the largest — are often worth the most. **$65.00-$75.00**

Muffin or gem pan, cast iron, 6 fluted cups arranged 3 x 3, small handle at each end with small hanging hole, American, 8''L x 5''W, late 19th C or early 20th. **$65.00-$85.00**

Muffin or gem pan, cast iron, 8 cups arranged 3, 2, 3, with 2 clubs, 2 diamonds, 2 spades and 2 hearts, called a ''Grand Slam'' mold. Shallow flat-bottom cups, almost square pan has cutout handles inside outer rim, rather than projecting out. About 9½''L x 7½''W. Not marked, American, early 20th C (?). Collector Jim Holroyd says some variation of this was made by most major foundries. **$80.00-$100.00**

Muffin or gem pan, cast iron, 8 figural fruit & vegetable cups, viz. pear, squash, apple, beet, turnip, cherries, & unidentifiable ones, and scrolled handles, 13''L x 8''W, 20th C (?). Collector Jim Holroyd sent me a picture of his, which has 3 very small holes drilled (?) down the center of the long axis. • A page from a c.1900 Schofield Mfg. Co. brochure depicts a similar one, called **''Our Ornamental Gem Pan''**, ''made of finest gray iron.'' The oblong pan shown has 8 cups (they also made a 6 Gem pan): quince or pear, peach, cherries, leaves, rosette, and something like a pomegranate (?). The makers state ''They

need no recommendation, as all housekeepers know that thin cast-iron bakes more evenly than tin or sheet iron, and the beauty of the design sells the 'gem.' The poor man's table, neatly arranged, is more appetizing than the richest luxuries improperly placed.'' The cut shows a pan with flat top, 8 neatly & deeply-molded fruits in roughly round form, the outside long edges of the whole mold pan scallops around the 4 cups. There are no handles, per se, only sort of triangular cutouts, on at each end, between the end cups. This is how you tell the new ones, which I believe all have the scrolled handles. Lodge may have made one with scrolled handles, I'm not sure. • **Reproduction alert.** — These have been almost exactly reproduced in the last 20 years. An ad in *McCall's* magazine (date unknown, c.1970s-80s), shows an 8 cup mold, and gives its dimensions as 1¾'' deep x 7½''W x 15''L, including scrolled handles. They claim it is an ''1850's style''. New it sold for $16.95; value about same now I suspect that most molds of this type found now are no older than the late 1950s, or even the 1970s. • New cast iron looks entirely different from old wares, even after use, or even if old piece with which you make comparisons was never used. New: grayish, and grainy, poor casting edges, etc. And it doesn't 'cook' well either.

Old Gray Iron. — I don't know how literally we can take it, but there were companies casting at the end of the 19th C who advertised ''cast gray iron''. But the older gray iron wasn't so terribly grainy or gritty. I don't know all (any?) of the secrets of making gray iron, but here's something on the subject from the Mar. 22, 1890 Metal Worker • ''Aluminum in Cast Iron turns the combined carbon to graphite — that is, (it) makes the white iron gray and also (closes) the texture of the metal. (Aluminum) makes the metal...more fluid and susceptible of taking a better polish and retaining it. Aluminum will also increase the tensile strength of many grades of cast iron and aids in obtaining sound castings free from blow-holes. It has been used in preparations from $\frac{1}{10}$ of 1% to 2%, with good results, with various grades of cast iron.'' • Price for new about ⅙ for old. **$120.00-$150.00**

Muffin or gem pan, patented as an ''egg pan'', sold as gem pan by R & E, cast iron, 12 round cups, interesting to examine handle ends, as slight roughness at 2 ''bulge'' points, both ends, make you think these could have been cast in long rows & snapped or chiseled apart at the handles. Is this possible, you cast iron experts? Nathaniel Waterman patent, mfd by R & E Manfg Co. (Russell & Erwin), #6, 10¾''L x 7⅛''W, pat'd April 5, 1859 — often looks like ''1858'' or ''1853'' • Collector Beth Kidder, of Normal, IL, wrote in 1988 reporting that she had three similar cast iron molds, one each with round, oval, and oblong wells, all shallow, and all bought at local antique stores. She reports that the one with oblong wells ''appeared not to have been used for baking, but it did have a light allover coating of a whitish substance which behaved like soap. The insides are pretty rough. .. I first heard these pans (all three styles) called soap molds in spring 1987,'' writes Beth, ''at a privately operated museum called Little Norway, Rte 1, Blue Mounds, WI. The museum is a preserved pioneer homestead, built by the Norwegian immigrant Austin Haugen. I questioned the guide about the pan, and she was quite definite in her identification of it as a soap mold. I have since heard them called soap molds someplace else ... possibly a local antique shop, I can't remember." Beth's husband suggests that people may have used baking molds, or gem pans, as soap molds because they worked so well for that purpose. Waterman's patent itself was granted under the name **Egg-pan,** but was described also as a **Baking pan.** **$45.00-$60.00**

Muffin or gem pan, stamped tin, 12 cups soldered into frame, ring in one corner to hang up, no discernable mark, late 19th C. **$15.00-$20.00**

Muffin or other bake pan, cast iron, skillet shape with 6 heart shaped cups, one center cup in shape of 6 point star, raised rim, side handle with pointed end and elongated hang up hole, Emig Products, Inc., but I don't know if marked, Reading, PA, 8½" diameter with 6½"L handle, weighs 4¾ lbs, from 1966 catalog. • **Egg 'O My Heart.** — F. A. Walker, the NYC supplier and importer of housewares, showed a cast iron "egg fryer" in an 1870s catalog. From the linecut picture it appears to be exactly the same as this Emig pan. Walker's catalog also had a stamped tin "egg fryer", with no handle, very shallow rolled rim, and cups for 18 eggs. Price for the recent ones: **$8.00-$12.00**

Muffin or popover pan, cast iron, 11 cups, Griswold spelled it "Pop-Over," Griswold #10, Pattern #949 (sometimes reported as 949-B), Erie, PA, 11⅛"L x 7⅝"W (given in company catalog as 11¼" x 7½"), 20th C, ads for the pan in 1973 look just the same as earlier ones. • In 1919, Griswold's full page ad in *House Furnishing Review* depicted one 11-cup pan with two large holes in both handle ends, and stated "Griswold cast iron gem and muffin pans are made in 17 different shapes. Being heavier and thicker they retain the heat more evenly and longer than ordinary pans." In 1973, the price was only five dollars! **$35.00-$50.00**

Muffin pan, blue & white mottled enamelware, 8 cups, "Iris," Hibbard, Spencer & Bartlett, Chicago, IL, early 20th C. **$100.00-$150.00**

Muffin pan, cast aluminum, 6 cups shaped like Texas, no maker's mark, c.1970s or 1980s. **$15.00-$20.00**

Muffin pan, cast aluminum, very lightweight, 12 cups, marked "GRISWCLD" (sic), also "No. 9" and "809," not Griswold Mfg. Co., a cheap fake, prob. made in Taiwan or Japan, 20th C. **$10.00-$15.00**

Muffin pan, cast iron, 12 cups, "Paterson No. 11" marked on handle, 12¾"L x 7"W, late 19th C. **$22.00-$30.00**

Muffin pan, cast iron, 12 cups, many smoothed off casting marks on back, marked with either a "9" or a "6" on back, also patent date, 12"L x 7$\frac{3}{16}$"W, pat'd April 8 (1913 or 1919?). **$22.00-$30.00**

Muffin pan, cast iron, 12 cups, nicely formed interstices between cups, rather than the rough & sloppy ones found on repros, only mark is "F" on back of handles, 11"L x 6¾"W, late 19th C. **$22.00-$30.00**

Muffin pan, cast iron, 12 fluted cups in frame with handle, American, 14"L x 10"W, 20th C. **$75.00-$95.00**

Muffin pan, cast iron, 13 cups include 2 hearts, 2 six point stars, 5 rounds & 4 fluted rounds, "Reids Patent," 16½"L x 8⅝", sometimes reported to have been pat'd Dec. 1870. But the design patent #5132 that I have a copy of says "pat'd Jul. 18, 1871" by Adam Reid. Collector Jim Holyroyd's pan is marked with the July date on one handle, and "Reids Patent" on other. Jim says this is called the "Four Seasons" pan. • In 1824, in a Charlotte, NC newspaper, as gleaned by James H. Craig (*The Arts and Crafts in North Carolina, 1699-1840*), an advertisement placed by Edward M. Bronson, who had a sheet iron and tin plate factory in Charlotte, reads "... Batter pans, of every description, Hearts, Diamonds, Scollops, &c. &c. ..." I suspect these were individual muffin molds, and as such would be the earliest I've found evidence of. Gosh! Get me one of those Jules Verne time machines! So many places to go; so little time. Muffins, of course, were known much much earlier, but were rather like what we know as English muffins, and were cooked in muffin rings on a griddle. Similar, or perhaps even identical, were flan rings, tin hoops set flat on a cookie sheet or flat pan and used for baking flan (custard). See "Royal Hearts" recipe. **$250.00-$275.00**

Muffin pan, cast iron, 6 long cups, set side by side in threes, with tab handles at ends, for muffins but they look like rolls (in fact, Wagner made one very like it, with 12 cups, that made what they called "small sticks"), Griswold #17, 7½"L x 6"W, c.1920s. • Another very similar one, Griswold #16, had deeper cups. **$38.00-$45.00**

Muffin pan, cast iron, 8 cups — leaf, clover, crescent moon, chicken, spade, 6 point star, house, scalloped — plus 3 smaller diamonds down center, heart shaped handles at each end, 14"L x 6"W, mid 20th C to 1980s. • **Reproduction alert & Lookalike alarm.** — The gift & accessory trade wholesale catalog of Upper Deck Ltd., New Bedford, MA, which you may have seen advertised in the late 1980s in collector papers, has a selection of cast iron shallow cup figural muffin pans which they call "trivets". The cups on (A) and (B) are flat bottomed and probably ½" deep; Cups on (C) and (D) are dimensional and somewhat deeper. **Designs: (A)** "Heart Trivet", 4 points-in hearts, with short frying pan handle. 5½" diameter, 3"L handle. **(B)** "Folk Art Trivet", oblong with 8 cups in club, spade, star, rosette, round, house, X-mas tree & rooster shapes, scrolly handles at ends, with heart cutouts. 14"L x 6"W. **(C)** "Cookie Man Trivet", 6 cups of cookie boys with striped pants, star pendents, in 2 feet-center rows, joined like paperdolls. Scrolled handles, much openwork & only one that looks something like a trivet (which has lots of air flowing through it to cool the object put on it). 9"L x 6"W. **(D)** "Christmas Trivet", 6 detailed jolly squat Santa figures smoking pipes, rectangle with 2 simple arched handles at ends, 11"L x 8¼"W. Wholesale prices are extremely low, all below $5.50; the heart pan one 2 for $5.00. The pictures look good; I can't tell what kind of graininess there might be **$10.00-$12.00**

Muffin pan, cast iron, 8 shell-shaped muffins or gems, rather shallow, 19th C (?). **$30.00-$40.00**

Muffin pan, cast iron, bar handles, "G. F. Filley #10," mfd by Excelsior Stove Works, St. Louis, MO, late 19th C. **$75.00-$90.00**

"Giles F. Filley, Pioneer In Stove Trade. — Mr. Filley was born in 1815, and went to St. Louis from Connecticut, in 1836. "Upon his arrival he sought employment with his brother, O. D. Filley, who was then conducting a tinsmith's shop. ... Later Giles F. Filley was taken into partnership with his brother, assuming a third interest in the business. In this connection he remained until 1841, at which time he (decided) that there was not enough in the business for two, and so he retired. In that same year he came to NY with the intention of buying trinkets to take to Oregon for the purpose of trading with the Indians. It was his original intention to take one of Astor's boats from NY to Astoria, OR, but changing his mind he purchased a stock of crockery, which was shipped to St. Louis, where he opened a crockery store in 1842, remaining in that business until 1849.

"In 1848 he concluded to engage in the business of manufacturing stoves, and in December of that year ground was broken for a stove foundry, the molding floor of which was 80 x 100 feet, and the warehouse 30 x 100 feet. The first casting was made in the foundry on Sept. 1, 1849. ...

"The first stove made by Mr. Filley was what is known as a step stove, called the Prize Premium, and was sold to Stark Mauzy of Brunswick, MO. The first Charter Oak stove was turned out on March 18, 1852, and was purchased by a man who, coming along the street and seeing the stove standing on the sidewalk, asked Mr. Filley if it was for sale. Informed that such was the case, he purchased the stove and took it home to his farm, some miles back of Clarksville, MO. The first bill of Charter Oak stoves was afterward sold to C. G. Jones of St. Louis, MO, who was then conducting a stove store. ... At the time Mr. Filley took up his residence in St. Louis that city had a population of about 7300. The first theatrical performance was given in the upper part of an old salt warehouse, the entrance being by an outside stairway. The chandelier for this theater was made in Mr. Filley's shop and Mr. Filley personally superintended the work of putting it in place. It was a tin chandelier with petticoat lamps." *The Metal Worker*, Feb. 27, 1892. **$75.00-$90.00**

Muffin pan, cast iron, cutouts between each shallow flat-bottomed cup, not for puffy kind of bran or corn muffins you buy at a deli, probably for English-style muffin, Wagner #1322, 11⅜"L x 7¾", inside of cups only ⅝" deep, early 20th C into 1920s. **$25.00-$35.00**

Muffin pan, cast iron, makes 12 cakes or muffins in troughs, mold almost identical to 19th C Nathaniel Waterman patent "French Roll" pan, made for many years by Hibbard, Spencer, Bartlett & Co., This one "Griswold #11", Erie, PA, 12⅛" x 6⅛", 20th C. • **Griswold Collectors.** — In a way, compared to all collecting fields except stamps and coins, and maybe dolls, new heights have been attained in knowledge of details and minute differences by collectors of Griswold (and to a much lesser extent, Wagner). It is way way beyond me, partly because my cataloguing instincts are more than satisfied by working on these books. So you won't find details like "slant TM" (meaning slanted trademark, or very much detailed notation of pattern numbers, especially what they signify (like "the 400 series indicates this was a ______", or "the 866 didn't appear on earlier ______", etc.) • If you are a specialist collector of Griswold, or Wagner, or Wapak, or other marked, catalogued, listed manufacturers, you will have to subscribe to *Cast Iron Cookware News*, ed. by Steve Stephens since 1988. His address is 28 Angela Ave., San Anselmo, CA 94960. Write him for rates and information on available back issues. **$35.00-$50.00**

Muffin pan, cast iron, round with 7 cups: 2 plain, 2 fluted, 2 hearts, one star cup in center, maker not stated in catalog, 9" measured across handles, 8" measured diagonally without handles, 20th C. • **Lookalike alarm.** — A new, interesting looking pan, sold through (among other places I'm sure) Cumberland General Store, Crossville, TN 38555. In 1983 they were selling it for $7.00. It seems to be going in the secondary market now for much more. • Another, actually more attractive, with 9 heart shaped cups (outside rows both go one way, inside row goes opposite direction, so all 9 fit neatly together, shaped sides, handles at both ends. It is 9⅛"L x 7½"W, and is seen in the Lehman's Hardware & Appliances (4779 Kidron Rd., Kidron, OH 44636) $2.00 1989 "Non-Electric Good Neighbor Amish Country" catalog,. It is possible that the Lodge foundry makes them; they don't say. Lehman also offers a 13"L x 7⅜"W muffin pan with ribbed handles at each end, design of what looks like 11 interlocking animals, mostly rather exotic ones. Yet another has 8 teddy bears, and is 15¼"L x 7½"W; another is the 8 cup one of fruits and vegetables, offered by other companies too, which is 15⅛" x 7½"; yet another, which contains 26 highly decorative letters of the alphabet, is 14⅝"L x 7⅝"W, and is for making "cookies". Finally, one more, with that same pair of handles, but double-sided, has a "durable no-stick coating", is 13¾" x 6⅞", and allows you to make a gingerbread house & a gingerbread man & woman. One side makes a "Victorian home" and the spicy couple; the other side makes a log cabin, and 2 more folks. **$20.00-$35.00**

Muffin pan, cobalt swirl enamelware, 8 cups, early 20th C. **$140.00-$160.00**

Muffin pan, cobalt & white swirl enamelware, 8 shallowish cups stamped (before enameling) in rectangular sheet metal, rolled rim, small hanging hole at one end, 1880s or so. **$185.00-$200.00**

Muffin pan, gray graniteware, 12 cups, joined by metal strips, marked "Agate Nickel Steel Ware", Lalance & Grosjean, TOC. **$55.00-$75.00**

Muffin pan, interesting raised rectangular tin tray has wire end handles, sides ventilated with penny-size holes, 6 shallow round cups set into holes in tray, Delphos Can Co., Delphos, OH, c.1905. **$15.00-$18.00**

Muffin pan, or corn bread pan, cast iron in shape of frying pan with handle and 3 short triangular legs, 7 cups, one in center, casting gate in center on bottom, no marks, prob. American, 7" diameter with 4¼"L handle, c. mid 19th C. **$150.00-$225.00**

Muffin pan, or madeline pan, stamped tin, 7 scallop shell cups riveted together within circular frame, still rather brightly tinned, American, 9" diameter, 19th C. **$28.00-$40.00**

Muffin pan, pieced tin, 8 cups held together in thin flat tin frame, mfd by Geuder, Paeschke & Frey, 1" deep x 14¼"L x 7¼"W, TOC. **$10.00-$15.00**

Muffin pan, rusted cast iron, overall shape is a sleigh, interior cups are in Christmas motifs: gift stocking, Santa's head, star, tree, snowman, toy soldier, no marks, possibly John Wright, Wrightsville, PA, 7"H at highest point x 15¾"L, c.1970s or 1980s. • This may look great, but it sure isn't worth the $350.00 the dealer had on it at Brimfield in fall 1987. **$35.00-$50.00**

Muffin pan, sheet iron, 12 cups, "Lockwood," Cincinnati, OH, early 20th C. **$25.00-$30.00**

Muffin pan, soapstone block with 9 cups, from a Vermont dealer, prob. VT, 1¾"H x 11¾"L x 7½"W, late 19th C. **$100.00-$125.00**

Muffin pan, stamped heavy tin, 7 scalloped cups riveted together, crude strap frame, American, 9" diameter, TOC. **$40.00-$50.00**

Muffin pan, tin, 12 cups, "Minute Maid," American. **$15.00-$20.00**

Muffin pan, unusual glazed earthenware, handle on each end, 12 cups, ochre yellow glaze inside & on top, green glaze on bottom, minor chipping, touched up glaze on rim. Not very attractive, but an earthenware oddity. iPA, 16¾"L x 11"W, 3rd to 4th quarter 19th C. • Robacker May 1989 price is amazingly high. I just don't know enough about pottery to know every factor in this price, but suspect much of it is size and rare form. **$650.00**

Muffin tin, "Pillsbury Health Bran", 20th C. **$12.00-$15.00**

Noodle cutter, called a Pot Pie Noodle Cutter & Lifter by dealer, corrugated tin wheels with wire handle, rolls along & cuts ruffled-edge lasagna-like noodles, pat'd by FELDT, Jamestown, NY, 8"L, no date, but looks c.1880s or 1890s. **$30.00-$35.00**

Noodle cutter, iron, wood & brass, mechanical, "Teek 1," German, TOC. **$65.00-$85.00**

Noodle cutter, metal, wood, crank action, "A A L Werke," & "Mark AAL," German, 20th C. **$250.00-$300.00**

Noodle cutter, or noodle pin, a noodle cutting turned wooden rolling pin with sharp edged corrugations. German (?), 14"L, late 19th C (?) or early 20th? • **German vocabulary** — Nudelrolle aus Holz: noodle roller of wood; also simply Nudelholz. Mostly these words seem to be applied to ordinary smooth rolling pins, although in one book, Ulrich Kelver's *Alte Kuengerate, Backen und Kochen* (Munich: Wilhelm Heyne Verlag, 1979) a ribbed rolling pin, with extremely shallow and close set corrugations, hardly sufficient for cutting noodles, is captioned "*Nudelrolle aus Holz*". **$22.00-$35.00**

Noodle cutter, rolling type, wire handle and frame, 14 sharp blades with plate to push cut noodles off blades as it is turned, "The Ideal", Toledo Cooker Co., Toledo, OH, c.1910. **$12.00-$15.00**

Noodle cutter or candy cutter (?), tin & wire, hand held & rolling, 10 blades, German, 20th C. **$7.00-$9.00**

Noodle cutter & pasta maker, cast iron frame with 4 long legs, mounted to wooden base, iron crank, kneading rollers like a mangle or wringer action, white rubber on axle of cutter attachment, set with blades, "Vitantonio Mfg. Co.," Cleveland, OH, 7"H x 7"W, pat'd Feb. 13, 1906, March 2, 1920. • I saw great ad in 1983 *Gourmet Retailer*, for Vitantonio, depicting Angelo Vitantonio and his "first American pasta machine." The company is in Eastlake, OH now, still importing and manufacturing Italian cookery items — pizzelle irons, ravioli makers, cavatelli & gnocchi makers, tomato strainers. **$65.00-$85.00**

Noodle pin, for ravioli, carved wood, long body has 10 spool-like sections with corrugations around circumference and 4 long ridges end to end, 2 short turned handles. Two flat pieces of dough with the filling in blobs inside were rolled with this to seal the filling in the little squares of pastry. After drying a little they were broken apart & cooked in roiling boiling water, Italian, 24"L, 20th C. **$18.00-$25.00**

Pastry board, oak covered with tim, T. Mills & Brother, Philadelphia, PA, 23" x 14", late 19th or early 20th C. • Mills made confectioners' and candy makers' tools. **$75.00-$90.00**

Pastry board, thick plank cut slightly oval, very slightly warped, but beautiful dark patina from all the butter rolled on it, small hanging handle with hole, American (?), 19"D, 19th C. • **German vocabulary** — Bachmulde: dough tray. **$165.00-$200.00**

Pastry board & rolling pin, a set that could be hung on the wall. The board is wood, with a working surface of tin. According to the 2 partial paper labels on the back, "The metal plate _____ _____ the manufacture of th_____ is a special composition _____ finished in pure palm of _____ therefore necessary before using the first time to wash it with soap and warm water to remove any oil that may have been left on the surface. The _____ of the board is made of _____lv _____ veneer, with the grain _____ crossed, and then _____ saturating entirely (with) pure boiled oil, this _____ it from spliting (sic) or _____." At the bottom is a wooden ledge, sort of like found on a blackboard, with 2 metal spring clips to hold the wooden rolling pin. The pin has 2 spool-turned handles. The American Bread and Pastry Board Co., Cambridge, OH, c. 25" square, TOC. • The all sheet tin pastry "board" or cookie sheet, curved at one end to hold the tin-covered wooden rolling pin when the set was hung on the wall, was the only kind I knew about, and that is very hard to find. In July 1989, I walked into Paula Lewis' Court Square antiques & quilt shop, in Charlottesville, VA, and she showed me this beauty ... the first I've ever seen. **$200.00-$350.00**

Pastry board & rolling pin, all sheet tin, ring loop at center top for hanging on wall, bottom edge turned up to hold tinned pin (wooden handles), paper label reads "Union Manufacturing Co.", Cambridge, OH, 19th C. **$200.00-$350.00**

Pastry board & rolling pin, also called a cookie sheet, tin with tin rolling pin, partial label on back: "The Metallic Board — Only All Metal Bread & Pastry Board" American, 21½"L x 8½"W, pat'd 1893. **$200.00-$350.00**

Pastry board & rolling pin, white enamelware, mounted to wall with iron brackets, board hinges down out of way & brackets fold inward, pin has turned wooden handles, Barnes Mfg. Co., Mansfield, OH, 27" x 28" with 6"H backplate, c. 1914. **$350.00-$500.00**

Brown, Then Serve. — Even a scrap of newspaper found in a box can provide tidbits to spice up your general knowledge. A very yellowed piece torn out of a January (!) issue of an unidentified Richmond, VA paper, dated probably c.1900-1905, has this delightfully odd tip: "**A Brown Luncheon.** — Just to vary the monotony of life there is the 'brown' luncheon. The creamed lobster is served in cups covered with brown tissue paper, the browned chops, browned fried potatoes, and browned rice croquettes on plates decorated with a design of brown oak leaves and acorns. The ice cream is chocolate frozen in shape of large English walnuts and the little squares of white cake bear the design of a leaf in tiny chocolate candies. The courses are served from large wooden trays ornamented in pyrographic work decorated in brown leaves and the water is poured from a little brown jug. All the decorations are brown, shading from seal to orange. The candles are yellow with autumn leaf shades. The name cards are placed inside little boxes decorated with pyrographic work and suitable for jewel boxes. The hostess wears a gown of panne velvet in the shade of brown known as 'burnt onion' and the maid's apron and headdress are decorated with brown bows."

Pastry sheet, tin, wooden back, trough of wood at bottom to hold rolling pin, which is missing, paper label on back "The Non-Absorbent Bread & Pastry Board", American,

21''L x 21½''W, c. 3rd quarter 19th C. • If this had the tin & wooden rolling pan with it it would be a lot more expensive. **$150.00-$175.00**

Pastry stamp, cast & lathe-turned brass, like a small meat tenderizer with 6 small pyramidal points on head, turned wood handle with original hanging ring, very heavy, English, 7⅞''L x 4¼''W, c.1820s to 1830s. **$275.00-$325.00**

Pastry tube, also called a pastry syringe, or cookie press. White metal cylinder & funnel nose, wood plunger, German (?), late 19th C. • **German vocabulary** —Teigspritze: pastry syringe. **$25.00-$35.00**

Pastry tube, or cookie press, tin cylinder with wooden plunger, star shaped opening, American, 10½''L, late 19thC. **$30.00-$40.00**

Pastry tube, or cookie press, tin, small cylinder, with side wings used to hold it up while pressing the plunger. Could be fitted with several different flat tin discs that have cutouts in various shapes — stars, rosettes, etc. through which the dough was expressed in fancy shapes for making drop cookies in something besides blobs. Also used as a butter press for fancy pats, American, c.1870s. **$25.00-$35.00**

Pate mold —See French pie mold.

Patty bowl, cast iron, bail handle, pouring lip, Griswold "Deep Patty Bowl", #72, 2⅝'' deep x 5'' diameter. **$25.00-$30.00**

Patty iron set, cast iron, with long handle, 4 molds: 2 deep cups, 2 lacy open ones, in original box, Griswold Mfg. Co., Erie, PA, about 9''L with handle, early 20thC. **$55.00-$75.00**

Patty irons, cast iron, in original box, "Mrs. Wheelock's", American, 1920s. **$25.00-$35.00**

Patty irons, cast iron, set of 2 deep cupped ones in original box, with one screw-in heavy wire handle. One cup heart shaped, one fluted round. These were cooked & then filled with cold or hot, savory or sweet fillings — very nice for luncheons! Mmmm, wish I had me one right now. Griswold, Erie, PA, round cup: 2¼''D; heart about 2⅞'' across, c.1926 on. **$30.00-$40.00**

Patty mold set, cast iron, in original box, cast iron, little kettle with thin wire bail handle for boiling oil, just right size for dipping in the batter-coated rosettes & patty irons, also a cast iron rosette, a mold with concentric rings with 4 spokes, a heart, & a patty shell mold, 2 screw-in threaded wire rod handles, chromolith inside box lid shows kettle on little electric hot plate, Griswold, oil kettle is 2½'' deep x 5⅛'' diameter, c. 1940s-50s from box image. **$85.00-$135.00**

Pie crimper, turned wood handle in unvarnished pale wood, blue & white Meissen wheel, Dutch (?), late 19th C. **$75.00-$85.00**

Pie crimper, turned wooden handle, brass ferrule, wire axle with wide corrugated wooden roller wheel, American, TOC. **$30.00-$40.00**

Pie crimper & trimmer, cast aluminum, relatively large wheel with corrugations & cutting edge, short pointed handle with large hanging loop, "Ateco", mfd by August Thompsen & Co., NYC, NY, c.1920s. **$15.00-$22.00**

Pie divider, tin, rim turned up, big strap handle, looks like a huge cookie cutter that cuts wedges, cuts only 5 pieces in an 8'' pie, no maker's mark, American, about 4¼''L, 20th C. **$20.00-$25.00**

Pie or cake pan, tin, round, slightly flared sides & wide rim, embossed "PY-O-MY Dutch Apple Cake Mix Baking Pan", 1½'' deep x 9'' diameter, early 20th C. **$10.00-$14.00**

Pie pan, cobalt blue & white agate enamelware, 10'' diameter, early 20th C. • Another, only 8½'' diameter and with all white interior, about same price. **$12.00-$15.00**

Pie pan, green & white swirl enamelware, 9''D, 20th C. • A cobalt & white swirl, 8'', is same price range. **$12.00-$16.00**

Pie pan, pale blue & white swirl enamelware, 12'' diameter, early 20th or late 19th C. • In turquoise, a bit more desirable. **$12.00-$15.00**

Pie pan, stamped tin, "Goldblatt Brothers," 20th C. **$8.00-$12.00**

Pie pan, stamped tin, shallow very slightly slanted sides, attached metal cutter pivots from center, to cut pie out of pan, "Clipper Pie Plate", L. E. Brown & Co., Cincinnati, OH, 8'' diameter, c.1880s. **$5.00-$7.00**

Pie pan, tin, "Mrs. Smith's," early 20th C. **$3.00-$5.00**

Pie pan, tin, flared sides, embossed "Manning" in script, 7¾'' diameter, early 20th C. **$8.00-$11.00**

Pie pan, tin, slanted sides, embossed "New England Table Talk Flaky Crust — Mother's Only Rival", 1¼'' deep x 9⅝'' diameter, early 20th C. **$10.00-$14.00**

Pie pan, tin, slanted sides, advertising would make you think it a cake pan, "Presto Self-Rising Cake Flour," pat'd 1924. **$12.00-$15.00**

Pie pan or pie plate, stoneware with brown glaze, corrugated edge, American, 9'' diameter, 19th C. • **"Shrimp Pie.** — Take a quart of shrimp, clean picked from the shells; if they are very salt in the boiling, season them only with a little cloves and mace; but if they want salt, shred two or three anchovies very fine, mix them with the spice, and season the shrimps. You may make a good crust, because they do not want much baking; put a pretty deal of butter over and under them, one glass of white wine, and sent it to the oven." Eliza F. Haywood, *A New Present for a Servant-Maid; Necessary Cautions and Precepts to Servant-Maids for Gaining Good-Will and Esteem*, Dublin, Ireland: 1771. **$80.00-$90.00**

Pie pan or pie plate, (usually the ceramic ones are called plates), PA German redware, with message in yellow slip, "A Good Apple Pie is the Best of All," PA, 9'' diameter, late 19th C. **$650.00-$800.00**

Pie plate, spongeware pottery, "The Pure Food Sanitary Cooking Ware," American, early 20th C. **$125.00-$135.00**

Pie plate, stoneware, bright blue glaze inside only, maple leaves molded along sides, outside not glazed, "Cookin Ware", Neu-Deel Economy Health Cookin Ware, Canadian (?), 9'' diameter, "Patent Office R & G", prob. 2nd quarter 20th C. **$25.00-$32.00**

Plett kaker or pancake pan, cast iron, like griddle with 7 extremely shallow cups that are bigger than the ebelskiver cups, slightly raised edge, short upcurved handle with hanging hole, Griswold Mfg Co., after a Swedish type of pan, 9½'' diameter, with cups only ¼'' deep, each cake 3'' diameter, made c.1918 on, for many years. **$40.00-$55.00**

Popover pan, cast iron, 11 deep, slightly slant-sided flat-bottomed cups, Wagner Ware #01 B, Sidney, OH, cups are 1⅞'' deep, 11'' L x 7½''W, late 19th or early 20th C. • **One Alarm Reproduction alerts.** — A credible new popover pan is being made by Iron Craft Inc., Freedom, NH, 2 sizes — 6- and 11-cup. They are cast iron, but cups are only 1⅜'' deep. Two ''flower petal'' cutouts at each handle end, presumably serve not only as decorative touches, but also to slightly cool the iron just where a per —son would pick it up. • Lehman's Hardware offer 6-cup and 11-cup ''2 petal'' hole handled popover pans, made by the Lodge foundry **$18.00-$30.00**

Popover pan, cast iron. Because Griswold bought Wagner in 1957, for a while both names appeared on some pans. marked both ''Griswold'' & ''Wagner Ware'', c.1957-58. **$40.00-$50.00**

Popover pan, cast iron, tab handles, 2 casting gates on bottom, no mark, 8'' x 12''L, TOC. **$40.00-$50.00**

Popover pan, or gem pan, cast iron, tab handles solid not cutout, 11 cups, Wagner Ware, marked ''B'' on center cup on back, Sidney, OH, 11¼''L x 7⅝''W x 1⅞'' deep, late 19th C (?). **$35.00-$45.00**

''Graham Gems. — To one quart of Graham flour add one half pint fine white flour; enough milk or water, a little warm, to make a thick batter; no salt or baking powder; have the oven hotter than for biscuits; let gem-pans stand in the oven till you get ready; beat batter thoroughly; grease your pans; drop in while the irons are smoking hot; bake quickly a nice brown.'' Henry Scammel, compiler, *Treasure House of Useful Knowledge*, 1891. • **Graham flour** was named after the Reverend Sylvester Graham (1794-1851), an American who was the first to recognize the value of eating whole-wheat flour, bran and all. He spent a lot of his life trying to encourage housewives and cooks to use his flour, which we now welcome as high fiber. He was ridiculed as a mad faddist by some, but did attract a large, enthusiastic following. Many 19th C recipes called for graham or ''entire wheat'' flour. **$35.00-$45.00**

Pudding mold, beehive type, brass screw-on base, ring handle on snug lid, concentric lines inside are tinning lines, according to dealer William Davis, no mark, 5¼''H x 4½'' diameter, 1840s to 1860s (?). • I asked Delaware dealer William Davis about the tinning, and he said that in some instances the makers ''began with tinned sheet copper; in others they were dipped. Frequently you'll find them tinned both inside and out. I had an eagle mold, the exterior was originally tinned but in the cleaning I had it removed — much more attractive.'' If ALL jelly or pudding molds had been tinned outside, I'd take the same purist stance on removing tinning that I do on 'brassifying' ice cream dishers, which were tinned for health reasons. The molds did not have to be tinned on the outside, and if the housekeeper was willing to devote the time to polish them, because of their beauty, fine. **$175.00-$225.00**

Pudding mold, ceramic, glazed & handpainted, apple design in relief, fluted sides, spouted, American (?), small size, only 3¾'' x 4¾'', 20th C. **$20.00-$25.00**

Pudding mold, copper, cylinder with slightly slanted shape, bayonet mounted lid with bracket strap handle, tinned inside, marked only with the Birmingham orb and Maltese cross, and #195, English, 5⅜''H exclusive of strap handle x 5½'' diameter, 1840s to 1860s (?). **$175.00-$225.00**

Pudding mold, copper, tinned inside, hanging ring, marked ''Christian Wagner'', German, 11'' diameter, TOC. **$65.00-$110.00**

Pudding mold, dark brown & white mottled enamelware, European, 2'' H x 12½'' diameter, TOC. **$38.00-$45.00**

Pudding mold, earthenware, spouted, has handle, American, 9½'' diameter, mid 19th C. • **''Brown Betty Pudding.** — Take a cup of grated bread crumbs, 2 cups fine-chopped tart apples, ½ cup brown sugar, teaspoon cinnamon, one tablespoon butter, cut into bits. Butter a deep pudding dish, and put a layer of apples on bottom; then sprinkle with sugar, cinnamon and butter and cover with bread crumbs. Put in another layer of apples, and proceed as before until ingredients have been used, having a crumb layer last. Cover the dish and bake for ¾ hour in moderate oven, then remove the cover and brown the top. Serve with sugar and cream.'' Maria Parloa, *Kitchen Companion*, Boston: Estes & Lauriat, 1887 **$100.00-$150.00**

Pudding mold, grape bunch design, yellowware, English or American, 19th C. **$65.00-$85.00**

Pudding mold, gray & cobalt blue agate enamelware, slope sided, possibly Columbian Enameling & Stamping Co.'s ''Dresden'', Terre Haute, IN (?), 11'' diameter, late 19th C or very early 20th. **$20.00-$25.00**

Pudding mold, gray graniteware, a melon mold with plain tin close-fitting flat lid, 7''L, 19th C. • Very attractive, and much less common than all tin mold. **$145.00-$175.00**

Pudding mold, gray graniteware, spouted Turk's head, American (?), 19th C. **$28.00-$38.00**

Pudding mold, heavily tinned, so-called melon style (imagine half an elongated acorn squash) with close-fitting flat lid that has an oval wire ring handle that folds flat, some of these are found marked ''Kreamer,'' others unmarked, American (poss. also English), various sizes, typical one is 6½''L x 5''W x 3¾ '' deep (stamped 3 on lid), another is 7''L x 5½''W x 4'' deep, another 10''L x 5⅝''W, late 19th C to early 20th. • The handles are sometimes missing, and the molds are sometimes found still brightly tinned outside, but rusted inside, where dampness was trapped by the tight-fitting lid. Most have an oval wire loop soldered to the body of the mold so that you could grasp lid and body with your left and right hand and pull apart. If the ring was once there and is now missing (you can see the evidence by bits of solder in a roughly rectangular shape), subtract about $5.00 to $7.00. Extra large sizes cost the most. **$20.00-$40.00**

Pudding mold, heavy tin, hinged lid with clasp, German or American, 19th C. **$65.00-$85.00**

Pudding mold, melon shape, tin, 3 clips, marked only with 14 in a diamond and 127 on other half, 5½'' deep x 6'' diameter, 19th C. • I got the sparse description from an ad, so this is a **hypothetical entry.** I imagined a flat-top mold until reading that Henry Eppelsheimer, of the famous ice cream mold company, had patented a full-round ''pudding and ice-cream mold'' on Nov. 10, 1885. His patent drawing looks like tops of 2 flat-lid melon molds fitted together, both with elongated oval wire handle. • I think this one isn't Eppelsheimers (theirs have no need of clips), although it is possibly a full round. **$45.00-$55.00**

Pudding mold, melon type, gray graniteware, flat tin lid, ''L & G,'' mfd by Lalance & Grosjean, Woodhaven, NY, 19th C. • An 1898 ad reads: ''Cooking Utensils are Safe is stamped with trademark (''AGATE nickel steel ware). Because to each article is attached chemist's certificates (a blue label), guaranteeing that it is free from arsenic, antimony, lead or any other poisonous ingredient.'' **$75.00-$90.00**

Pudding mold, melon type, tin, 2 part, flat lid with ring handle, "Kreamer," Brooklyn, NY, late 19th C. **$25.00-$35.00**

Pudding mold, so-called <u>beehive mold</u>, large rounded copper bowl on disproportionately tiny pedestal foot of tooled brass that screws on so it can stand upright, snug-fitting lid with ring handle, marked only #6, English, 6½"H, mid 19th C. • One similar to this had a bayonet fastening for the lid. **$90.00-$125.00**

Pudding mold, thick glazed ironstone, fluted sides, pineapple motif, English or American, 7"L, 19th C. **$38.00-$45.00**

Pudding mold, tin skirt to support mold upside down while gelatin setting, tinned copper oval mold with slightly slanted sides, fairly common pineapple design, English or poss. American, 6½"L x 5"W x 5"D, late 19th C or early 20th. **$65.00-$85.00**

"The Accolade of the Pudding Mold. — Every year the harassed interior decorator is driven well nigh distracted in a vain endeavor to find some new idea in decoration. What shall it be? Eagerly he searches London, Paris, Berlin and Vienna in the chance hope of discovering some novelty that will fit in with the general furnishing scheme and make one room look different from a hundred others. ... Now an enterprising few, instead of scouring the foreign marts and exhibitions have stayed at home and looked around their own homes for inspiration. And at last they have found it. ... Strangely enough, the kitchen has been the chief source of inspiration; so the following suggestions for decoration are well within the reach of the slenderest purse.

One of the most amusing of these ideas is the way in which the ordinary tin pudding molds can be used for decorative purposes. ... (Especially) interesting is the use of large jelly or pudding molds as mural decorations. For this purpose the molds selected should be rather important in design. Fortunately many enchanting patterns are obtainable. Some show fruit nestling in beds of vine leaves, while others reveal fantastic looking fish, such as one sees in old Japanese prints. Then there are animals — rabbits, chickens, and even squirrels — charming accessories for a child's room. More novel are the molds patterned in geometrical designs — a type particularly well suited to rooms furnished in the modernist taste. Hung upon the wall or above the mantlepiece, gleaming like dull silver and covered with unusual designs, they look like native masks or ... modern sculpture." Derek Patmore, *House & Garden*, Aug. 1928.

Pudding mold, redware with unusual black glaze, Turk's head or turban design, spouted, widely-canted sides, American, 11" diameter, 19th C. **$140.00-$175.00**

Pudding mold, stamped tin, flat close-fitting lid with round turban or turban squash mold, American or imported, about 6" or 7" diameter x 4" deep, c.1870s or 1880s. **$25.00-$40.00**

Pudding pan, blue & white swirl enamelware, rectangular, 12"L, late 19th C. • **"Indian-Meal Pudding.** — One cup of yellow Indian meal, one quart and a cupful of molasses, one generous tablespoonful of butter, one teaspoonful of salt, one pint of boiling water, half teasponful each of cinnamon and mace. Scald the salted meal with the water. Heat the milk in a <u>farina-kettle</u> (a double boiler); stir in the scalded meal, and boil, stirring often, for half an hour. Beat the eggs light; put in the butter and molasses, stirred together until they are several shades lighter than at first; add the spice; lastly, the batter from the farina-kettle, beaten in a little at a time, until all the ingredients are thoroughly invorporated. Grease a pudding-dish; pour in the mixture, and bake, covered, in a steady oven, three-quarters of an hour. Remove the lid, and brown. This is the genuine, old-fashioned New-England 'Indian' pudding. Eat with sauce, or with cream and sugar. It is very nice." Marion Harland, *Universal Cookery Book*, 1887. **$30.00-$35.00**

Pudding pan, gray graniteware, shallow, slightly flared sides, "Chef-ette Enameled Ware" on red paper label, American. **$25.00-$30.00**

Rice ball, large perforated 2-part spun aluminum ball, clip fastening, chain to hang off pot's side, American, 7" diameter, 20th C. **$10.00-$16.00**

Rice ball, tin & wire screening ball, 2 parts unscrew, wire handle locks over edges to hold halves together, chain & hook for edge of pot, American, 5¼" diameter, marked with date, pat'd June 17, 1930. **$10.00-$16.00**

Rice boiler mold, stamped & pieced tin, flat-bottomed, tubed with slanted out fluted sides, close fitting slightly convex lid with big strap handle, small wire ring catches to attach lid, American or European import, about 5" to 7"H x about 3" to 4" diameter at top, c.1870s to 1880s. • These look like pudding molds, and may have been used as such, but adv'd by F. A. Walker in their catalog as rice boilers. **$45.00-$50.00**

Rice cake mold, carved wood paddle, good luck symbol & calligraphy, Chinese, 7"L, poss. 19th C, more likely a 20th C sort of export "souvenir". • These started showing up, in vast quantitites, about 1982 or 1983. Many of them do not have Chinese characters carved in them, but typically Chinese motifs such as koi (goldfish/carp), butterflies, chrysanthemums and fruit. They come in a sort of butter paddle shape, or in truncated and elongated ovals, often with hanging hole with leather thong tie. The first wholesaler ads for them listed them in six styles: **(1)** a long narrow one, 12"L x 1¾"W with 10 small images; **(2)** 8½"L x 3½"W paddle, with sort of flower clam design; **(3)** 8"L x 3"W, paddle, irregular head, with curvy fish design; **(4)** 12"L x 2½"W board with four fruity designs; **(5) (6)** 12"L x 3½"W boards with either 2 strange flower-fruit butterfly carvings, or 2 fish. Nothing in ad identified them as being Chinese, but they were called "Molds, 75-100 years old", and were priced $23.00 to $32.00 each, with 50% discount if you bought 10 or more, which meant that a dealer could then resell them for about the wholesale for one. It didn't take many months before they began appearing. The resale price is often very high, if there is but one on display, as much as $85.00 or $95.00. Asking price usually at high end of range. **$15.00-$35.00**

Rice cake mold, large oblong paddle with smallish handle, probably used for some kind of rice confection, 6 carved out cups including 3 different fish, a bird, also 2 plant-like flowers, Chinese, 13"L x 6"W, late 19th C (?). • **CAUTION:** This is the largest of the so-called Chinese rice cake molds, which are being sold all over the United States since about 1983 as, variously, maple sugar molds, cookie molds, or candy molds. This is not to say they are not nice molds, but you could be paying a premium for "early American" when it's probably "late Chinese". **$30.00-$40.00**

Roll cutter, brass & iron, it rolls with 2 handles, like a rolling pin, cuts dough into oblongs, English, 4¾'' diameter rolls or biscuits, English patent #16798 (19th C, prob. c.1880s). **$85.00-$100.00**

Roll pan, cast iron, 10 long troughs, 2 lengthwise casting marks, filed down, catty-corner on back, no maker mark, 13¼''L x 9¼''W, 19th C. **$22.00-$30.00**

Roll pan, cast iron, 6 cigar shaped cups, many cutouts in frame, marked in cups:''Vienna Roll Bread Pan No. 6,'' early 20th C (?). **$70.00-$85.00**

Roll pan, cast iron, makes 12 French rolls in trough-like cups rounded on bottom & oblong in outline, in 2 rows 6 x 6, very similar to what Griswold called a muffin pan. American, dated 1850. • No U.S. patent that year for bake pan, roll pan, muffin pan, gem pan or bread pan.
$25.00-$30.00

American Agriculturist, Jan. 1868, had one of these illustrated, with a short article called ''**Gems or Aerated Rolls**. — The only convenient article for cooking Gems is a French roll pan for baking, and we cannot warrant success in anything else. The pans are made of cast iron, and can be had at the large hardware and furnishing stores in the cities at about $4.50 per dozen, and 75¢ single. Put the pan upon the stove, heated nearly to redness. Take one cup of water, one cup of milk, and three cups of flour, of the best quality. Stir in the flour gradually, and with a spoon beat the mixture five minutes briskly. The object of the beating is to get as much air as possible into the batter. Put a piece of butter of the size of a pea into each of the moulds, and fill about two-thirds full with the batter. Put immediately into a very hot oven, and bake for 20 minutes, or until nicely browned.

''This form of unleavened bread is the best article for breakfast or tea we have ever found in that land of good housekeepers, Eastern Connecticut. It is exceedingly light, palatable, and nutritious, excellent for invalids and dyspeptics, and quite as good for people in sound health. They are so nice that we hope our readers will try the article for themselves. We bear no ill-will to hop growers, or venders of soda, saleratus, and other salts, but we have no doubt that the Gems once introduced into a family would greatly diminish the use of these unwholesome articles in cookery, and help to promote health and good digestion.'' (What I don't understand, is how you take this ⅔ full red hot pan weighing 4 pounds or so and get it quick into the hot oven.)

Roll pan, cast iron, very shallow, makes 8 rolls, only mark is ''No. 5'' on back, 7⅜''W, TOC. • **Confusable.** — What looks in pictures like a roll pan for making 4 oblong rolls, and may look like one in real life (or it may be much smalelr), is a solder mold. It is oblong with flat long handle coming from one end, the pan divided into 4 shallow oblongs. It is marked ''C. S. Osborne'' on the handle. I found it in Alfred Revill's *American Plumbing*, NY: Excelsior, 1984. The resemblance in picture is striking enough to make me add it in here. (Also very similar to baking pans, and approx. the same size, are cast iron molds with conical cups; these are assayers' slag molds, and have various numbers of cups (often 6) in an oblong frame. One has 'frying pan' handle off one end, and 2 rows of 3 cups. Another has a long single-file row of 6 conical cups; it has a wooden handle at one end. These molds were used as crucibles to melt finely-ground ores to

determine the percentage of gold or silver in a particular prospector's sample. Collector Jim Holroyd told me about them, sharing information he'd got from Jack Ward.)
$22.00-$30.00

Roll pan, flat tin sheet with 6 curvy roll cups riveted to sheet, Silver & Co., Brooklyn, c.1916. **$12.00-$20.00**

Roll pan, for Vienna rolls, cast iron, 6 cigar-shaped cups set rather farther apart than usual, Griswold #26, about 12½''L, TOC or early 20th C. • Wagner's was almost the same, 12''L x 6½''W. **$35.00-$45.00**

Roll pan, cast iron, ll shallow cups set 4 x 3 x 4, handle brace at each end, W & L Mfg. Co., 19th C. **$22.00-$35.00**

Rolling pin, aluminum, ''Mil-Bar Co.,'' Canton, OH, 20th C. **$25.00-$35.00**

Rolling pin, amber glass, freeblown, knob ends — one with pontil, prob. American, 16''L, 19th C. **$85.00-$120.00**

Rolling pin, amethyst glass, freeblown with 2 knob handles, American, 15½''L, 19th C. **$90.00-$130.00**

Rolling pin, blue & red spattered opaque white glass, white glass inside so possibly of a type called Nailsea, freeblown, double ball-knobbed, English, 14''L, 19th C.
$200.00-$265.00

Rolling pin, blue & white china, with blue painted wooden handles, ''T. G. Green & Co., Ltd.,'' English, 18''L, late 19th C., early 20th. • ''**Shrewsberry Cakes.** — 1 lb. butter, 1 lb. sugar, 2 lb. flour, and a few caraway seeds.— Rub the butter in with the flour; then put in the sugar and seeds, and mix them up into a paste, with a little milk; roll them out thin, cut them with a small round cutter, and bake them on iron plates in a good oven.'' Joseph Bell, *A Treatise on Confectionary*. Newcastle, England, 1817.
$85.00-$100.00

Rolling pin, blue & white Delft faience barrel with windmill scene, very heavy, has turned wooden handles & rod, English, German or Dutch, 9⁹⁄₁₆''L (overall 17⅞''L), c.1870s. **$285.00-$325.00**

Rolling pin, blue & white loopy Nailsea glass, English, 20''L, 2nd or 3rd quarter 19th C. **$250.00-$270.00**

Rolling pin, blue & white sponge decorated saltglazed stoneware, wooden handles, American (?), 15''L x 5¼''D, 19th C. **$165.00-$180.00**

Rolling pin, blue-decorated white pottery, with Dutch windmill scene, turned wooden handles, English or Dutch, 15''L, 19th C. • Caution: Sometimes the handles have been replaced. If the pottery shows wear, even small chips or hairline cracks, but the handles look unused, you shouldn't have to pay as much. **$175.00-$225.00**

Rolling pin, bottle green, very dark, freeblown, tapers to small knobs, lots of wear scratches show up on this very utilitarian but handsome pin. English or American, 14''L, 19th C. **$95.00-$125.00**

Rolling pin, Bristol glass, beautiful translucent blue with ship & other decorations in gilt, poss. Bristol, England, or other English glass center, 14''L, prob. early to mid 19th C. • Practically all these rich cobalt blue rolling pins with traces of enameled decoration, are called Bristol glass. According to Hampden Gordon (*The Lure of Antiques*), painted blue, emerald green and purple glass were all done at Bristol, Sunderland and ''a number of other places''. It's a field in which too little knowledge can do you in. Over a period of more than 100 years, the blue color was achieved several different ways, according to the supply of varying qualities of the cobalt mineral (or substitutes) with which a blue color could be created in glass. • The opaque white glass that is found with enameled and gilded decorations are also called by what is almost a generic term — Bristol glass, but was made probably at even more places than the decorated blue glass. **$120.00-$135.00**

Rolling pin, "Bristol" type opalescent white glass, turned wooden handles, Imperial Glass Mfg. Co., Cambridge, OH, 19"L, pat'd July 26, 1921.

Rolling pin, carved tiger maple all one piece, with 2 long handles, American, 21" L including both 4" L handles, 19th C. • I've seen several, and of course maple was the best wood after lignum vitae for rolling pins, because of weight & dense grain, which meant protection from moisture and cracks, and both resisted absorption of ingredients that might make the pin smelly or unsanitary. **$80.00-$115.00**

Rolling pin, ceramic, "Petit Point Rose" design, has original stopper, Harker China, American, 20th C. **$45.00-$55.00**

Rolling pin, clear glass, blobs of cobalt with blood red and brown glass blobs too, big knob ends, salt still inside, cork intact, prob. Nailsea, England, 14"L, prob. 2nd or 3rd quarter 19th C. **$250.00-$280.00**

Rolling pin, clear glass, metal axle, turned wood handles, "Gem," 19½"L, 20th C. **$65.00-$90.00**

Rolling pin, cobalt blue glass, enameled ship design, English, 13¾"L, dated 1854. • You see so many with ships and flowers, you have to wonder how the decorative painting survived on so many. These pins, reported to be sailors' love tokens, were probably never actually used in the kitchen, but were decorative parlor pieces. **$120.00-$135.00**

Rolling pin, cobalt blue glass, freeblown knobbed "salt bottle" type, with corked end, English, 16"L, 19th C. **$175.00-$200.00**

Rolling pin, crockery, advertising "Robert F. McAfee, Dealer in Groceries," Augusta, IL, late 19th or early 20th C. • Others noted: adv'g "John M. Merriot" (possibly John H.), Mt. Vernon, Iowa; adv'g "J. F. Reily Groceries, Hardware, Implements, Buggies & Wagons," Seaton, IL; adv'g "Dawson Furniture," Ziegler, IL (that one with blue stripe); adv'g "Thompson's General Store," Grand Junction, IA, (brown stripe); adv'g "Killian's", Wahoo, NE (brown stripe); adv'g "Peterson & Anderson", Pomeroy, IA; adv'g "Joseph Reuter, General Merchandise," Gilbertville, IA, Price is for main entry; full range would be $115.00 to $235.00 (most $150.00 to $185.00), mostly based on desirability & subject of advertising, meaningfulness of place, and condition & decoration, is range for others noted. **$160.00-$175.00**

Rolling pin, crockery, advertising maxim "Save Your Dough," late 19th or early 20th C. **$120.00-$130.00**

Rolling pin, crockery decorated with wildflowers, type found from Rodman, Iowa, also Milwaukee, WI, late 19th, early 20th C. **$145.00-$155.00**

Rolling pin, custard glass with aluminum screw-on cap, American, 1930s. **$70.00-$85.00**

Rolling pin, double rollers with oval-ended frame & simple turned handles, maple, beautiful patina, paper label "Taylor's Patent Combination Rolling Pin," pat'd by A. L. Taylor, Springfield, VT, rollers 11¾"L x 1¾" diameter, overall length 20½", pat'd July 16, 1867. • This pin, because of the simplicity of form and shape of turned

handles at each end has been incorrectly attributed by other writers to the Shakers. • As the original spiel had it, "The Advantage of this Roller is, it will do the work in half the time it can be done with the single roller. It is worked with the greatest ease, as the Combination Rollers give double the surface bearing, and one roll following the other — making the Pastry of uniform thickness, and perfectly smooth and even finish." Original price was (you'll have to dust yourself off now!) only 50¢. **$175.00-$225.00**

Collector Hint: Keep On Reading. — Some antiques people think that out of a given number of collectors, a very few are graced with "the eye", an ability to see and know what is good, to pick the treasure from the dross. Furthermore, some of the antiques experts firmly believe that you're either born with it or you'll never have it. I don't believe that. Lots and lots of studying, of subjects as diverse as Japanese woodblock prints, African masks, Fauvist paintings, Egyptian jewelry, Shenandoah pottery, Victorian valentines, Thonet chairs, and Christmas glass ornaments, will never be wasted. But you must absorb yourself in each subject, sit on the sofa with a pile of library books on art and antiques shelves, and look at all of them, back & forth. Don't say, "I don't like African masks." Look at pictures of them, or best, real ones in museums, until you do like them. Don't say, "Fiesta Ware is cheap and ugly." Look at it until you appreciate what there is about it that's perfectly done. This is not to say you have to like everything, or that everything is worthy of praise. But everything you study, go in with a Zen "don't know" mind, the open mind, will teach you something you can apply to your butter molds, churns, tin trays, copper tea kettles, cast iron griddles. You will find yourself choosing, and knowing why. • I used to think that to study a piece (or to analyze your motive for wanting it) took the fun out, spoiled it, maybe even prevented its purchase (to question is to doubt). Now, because I know there are **many ways to study a piece or a field: aesthetically, socially, historically, functionally,** that it can only add to the pleasure. Harry Rinker wrote in a column on "Collectibles" in early 1989 that the "fun" of collecting is in the chase, not in the piece itself. If he really means that, I am diametrically in opposition. In collecting, a little (or no) knowledge is not only the dangerous thing, the foolhardy way, it's self-defeating in the long run, because the fun of the chase is diminished by a lack of awareness of the other hunters, as well as the hunted. Then, after it's up on the wall, mounted with the other trophies, there would be nothing to reflect on, no new way to re-appreciate, or re-evaluate. • So keep on reading and looking, and exercise your own "eye".

Rolling pin, glass bottle type, with white painted screw-on metal cap, "Roll-Rite," with Good Housekeeping Institute Seal of Approval printed on cap, American, 14"L x 2½" diameter, 20th C. **$22.00-$25.00**

Rolling pin, glass with cork stopper, American, 20th C. **$22.00-$32.00**

Rolling pin, glass with wooden axle rod & turned wooden handles, this one not a bottle, American, says pat'd July 28, 1921, but the 26th was Patent Tuesday that year. **$25.00-$40.00**

Rolling pin, gray white saltglazed stoneware with blue circumferential rings, Clinton, OH, late 19th C.
$170.00-$200.00

Rolling pin, green glass, fat & short, with small knob ends, European or American, 5½''L, 19th C. **$60.00-$80.00**

Rolling pin, green glass, freeblown, lots of bubbles, American, 15''L, 19th C. **$75.00-$85.00**

Rolling pin, green & white Nailsea glass, big thick white swirls, freeblown, knob ends, prob. really from Nailsea, England, 14''L, 2nd or 3rd quarter 19th C. **$275.00-$300.00**

Rolling pin, hardwood with turned bone handles, prob. American, 15''L, 19th C. **$175.00-$200.00**

Rolling pin, heavy purple blown glass, knob handles, English or American, 15½''L, 19th C. **$225.00-$250.00**

Rolling pin, heavy, thick lignum vitae which is the hardest of all woods & nearly as dense as iron, meant to last forever. Probably a commercial baker's pin, American (?), 16''L, 4½''D, 19th C. **$85.00-$100.00**

Rolling pin, heavy wood with heavy frame & 2 vertically-held handles at ends, the type called by the PA Germans, draalhus, American, 11''L x 6¾''H including upright handle frame, prob. late 19th C, and prob. patented. • **German vocabulary** — Wellholz, Rollholz, or Teigrolle. With various meanings, the last word most directly translating as dough roller. Nudelholz, and Nudelwalze are for the circumferentially ribbed rolling pins. • **Pennsylvania German vocabulary** — Draal Huls or Draalhus. **$35.00-$55.00**

Rolling pin, ironstone, long turned wooden handles, American (?), 9½''L x 3¾''D pin, 4''L handles, 19th C. **$130.00-$150.00**

Rolling pin, maple with handles on axle rod, probably bakery or hotel kitchen ware, American, 27½''L, early 20th C. **$40.00-$50.00**

Rolling pin, marble, all one piece including handles, very heavy & cold, 16''L, 19th C. **$35.00-$50.00**

Rolling pin, marbleized or swirled cobalt blue & white glass, knob handles, American, 17½''L, mid 19th C. **$145.00-$175.00**

Rolling pin, marbleized or swirled pink & white blown glass, knob handles, American, 16''L, mid 19th C. **$150.00-$200.00**

Rolling pin, milk glass, 2 smallish knobs, one rough, English, 19th C. • May have had some stenciled paint decorations, flowers and the like, but completely worn off now. **$50.00-$65.00**

Rolling pin, milk glass, knobby ends, painted flowers & green leaves, had name on it, mostly rubbed off, English, 19th C. **$85.00-$100.00**

Rolling pin, milk glass, wooden handles, advertising ''Pekin Coal Fuel Co.,'' Pekin, NE, 19th C. **$120.00-$140.00**

Rolling pin, milky, almost opalescent white Bristol glass, English (?), 13''L, 2nd or 3rd quarter 19th C. • Nineteenth C opaque white glass (often called ''milk glass'', a term a lot of glass collectors don't like), is sometimes called Bristol glass, although it was made, wrote Hampden Gordon (*The Lure of Antiques*), ''... in London & Stourbridge, Sunderland and on the Tyneside as well as at Bristol.'' **$275.00-$300.00**

Rolling pin, milky pastel green ''Jadeite'' glass, American, 1930s. • June 1989 asking price: **$350.00**

Rolling pin, molded plastic, fixed handle arched across from one side to other, round red frame set with 8 white rolling cylinders, like cigar tubes of different lengths, side by side at right angles to the handle, which was held to push multiple rollers to & fro', ''Magnus New Style Rolling Pin'', mfd by the Magnus Harmonica Corp., Newark, NJ, about 10'' diameter, c.1940s (?). • Yep, the harmonica-makers made this. The copy on the colorful box states ''Like Magic. Rolls the Dough with one Hand. Fluffier, Tastier Pies and Pastries.'' It doesn't have a lot of heft, but all those rollers, and the pressure of the hand directly above the center, does work. **$25.00-$35.00**

Rolling pin, Nailsea glass, blue with white loopy stripes, English, 15''L, 19th C. **$120.00-$135.00**

Rolling pin, Nailsea glass, red with white loops, knob at each end, unusual & very desirable in red or cranberry, English, 14½''L, prob. mid to late 19th C. • **''Best Scotch Bread.** — 1 lb. butter, 1 lb. sugar, 1 lb. 8 oz. flour, 4 oz. cut almonds, 4 oz. lemon. — Cream the butter; then mix the other ingredients with it into stiff paste; you may cut it in different shapes; put caraway comfits and citron on the top; and bake it in a slow oven. *** **Scotch Bread, another Way.** — 1 lb. 8 oz. butter, 1 lb. sugar, 2 lb. flour, a little mace. — The butter to be rubbed very fine with the flour; then add the sugar and spices; make it into stiff paste, with a little cream; roll half of it out, and lay upon it cut almonds, citron, and caraway comfits; then roll out the other half, and lay it upon the top; press it down; mark it in diamonds; cut it any shape you please; and bake it in a slow oven. It is most commonly cut in small diamonds, and mixed with rout biscuits.'' Joseph Bell, *A Treatise on Confectionary.* Newcastle, England, 1817. **$125.00-$150.00**

Rolling pin, Nailsea-type glass, aquamarine with white loopy swirls, a handle at each end, remnant of ribbon hanger, prob. English, but poss. American, 9½''L, prob. mid 19th C. **$200.00-$250.00**

Nailsea Glass. — British antiques author, Hampden Gordon, wrote a no-nonsense, easy to follow, small book, *The Lure of Antiques. Looking and Learning Today,* published first in 1961 by John Murray, London. The chapter ''Variety in Old Glass'' gave tips on Nailsea and Bristol glass, invaluable to those who fancy glass rolling pins. Nailsea glass is ''... but a species of bottle glass, which was taxed at a lower rate ...,'' writes Gordon. Then, with but one passing reference to rolling pins, he explains that the glass-house at Nailsea was founded in 1788 by J. R. Lucas (a bottle maker from Bristol), and that typical ''early work'' was dark green with ''splashes and loops of white.'' He goes on, ''The style was changed in 1810 ... (with a new owner), and ''clear glass took the place of green with loops and stripes in white and pink and blue and other popular colours. ... About 1830, came the style in which the coloured loops are massed closely together, concealing the clear glass. Dating is very difficult; for the later Nailsea patterns, and particularly the quaint conceits such as walking-sticks and pipes and rolling-pins with inscriptions — great favourites on the fairgound — were still immensely popular in late Victorian days.'' He goes on to say that the term ''Nailsea'' is almost a generic term for the white-swirled novelty glass that was made not only at Nailsea, but at Warrington, Stourbridge, and other glass-making towns.

Rolling pin, opaline glass, painted with ship & prayer, English, 14½''L, 19th C. **$110.00-$130.00**

Rolling pin, opaque ''black'' or extremely dark green 'Nailsea' glass with what appears as light blue & white splashes throughout, knob ends, prob. English, 12"L, prob. 2nd to 3rd quarter 19th C. **$150.00-$175.00**

Rolling pin, pale tan or buff saltglazed stoneware, black eagle mark, turned oak handles, 9¾"L pin, 4½"L handles, late 19th C, maybe even early 20th. • Very handsome, but somehow doesn't look quite right with the eagle. Perhaps this is a much later 20th C piece for the "country look" market. **$135.00-$150.00**

Rolling pin, pale turquoise opalescent glass, English, 14½"L, 19th C. **$100.00-$125.00**

Rolling pin, robin's-egg blue freeblown glass, 29"L, 19th C. **$125.00-$135.00**

Rolling pin, saltglazed stoneware with blue border with flowers, wooden handles, advertising message "Compliments of Berks County Democrat, a Newspaper", Boyertown, PA, 8½"L excluding handles, late 19th C. • This one has extra appeal to crossover collectors because it advertises a newspaper. **$275.00-$300.00**

Rolling pin, saltglazed stoneware with blue flower design, European or American, 16"L, late 19th or 20th C. **$135.00-$165.00**

Rolling pin, saltglazed stoneware with orange bands, Red Wing pottery, 20th C. **$120.00-$140.00**

Rolling pin, saltglazed stoneware, wooden handles, motto "May peace and plenty/ Dwell on England and shore/ And there remain/ Till time shall be no more." English, late 19th C. **$225.00-$250.00**

Rolling pin, Stourbridge glass, turquoise color, English, 13"L, 19th C. **$135.00-$145.00**

Rolling pin, tapered wood, name marked in pyrography or hot poker burned letters, "Pie Maker," Harrisville, NH, late 19th or early 20th C. **$40.00-$50.00**

Rolling pin, turned maple, button or mushroom knob at one end, American, 12½"L, 19th C. • I believe these dense wooden pins, with one knob only, could also be used as pestles of a sort for such things as cooked apples or potatoes, although this is just a hunch. **$35.00-$50.00**

Rolling pin, turned maple, nylon ball bearings, length marked off in centimeters & inches, Rowoco Inc., Elmsford, NY, 18"L x 3½" diameter, early 1980s. **$20.00-$30.00**

Rolling pin, turquoise green Bristol glass with gold & red painted floral decoration, cork missing, English or French Bristol, 15"L, c.1870s to 1880s. **$185.00-$220.00**

Rolling pin, very heavy glass, old style fat drum with fat knobby short handles, filled with bath salt crystals, "Clean Bath Salts", mfd by the Clean Perfume Co., Chicago, 13"L, TOC to c.1915 (?). **$35.00-$45.00**

Rolling pin, blue & white china, Blue Onion pattern, nicely turned wooden handles, 19th C. **$145.00-$175.00**

Rolling pin, clam broth glass (off-white murky mottled color, faintly tan), American or English, 19th C. **$50.00-$65.00**

Rolling pin, glass with screw-on black-painted metal lid, step-down ribbed glass handles, meant to be filled with ice water, American, 14¼"L x 2¾" diameter, c.1920s-30s. **$15.00-$20.00**

Rolling pin, marble with no handles, very smooth (but not finished like a statue would be), American (?), 17"L x 3" diameter, prob. 19th C. • **Reproduction alert.** — Repros, or rather new marble ones, often have turned wood handles & highly polished finish. **$35.00-$45.00**

Rolling pin, nickeled metal pin, turned wooden handles, plus something inside that makes it rattle, perhaps lead shot to make it weigh more?, American, 15½"L, c.1920. Another similar one, same value, has green stained wooden handles and is 15¾"L. **$15.00-$22.00**

Rolling pin, white opaque "milk glass", plump, with very small knob handles, like little mushrooms, 16"L, 19th C. **$150.00-$170.00**

Rolling pin, white & blue pottery, "Ernest Nelson Sells the Flour that Makes the Dough Hump Great," American, late 19th C. **$135.00-$150.00**

Rolling pin, white "milk" glass, well-turned wooden handles have plain wood knob close to pin with gripping part stained green, National Mfg. Co., Cambridge, OH, patented but I can't read date. Presumably late 19th or ealry 20th C. **$38.00-$45.00**

Rolling pin, white porcelain, with painted ship, "The Harkaway" & painted motto reading "A present for my cousin Rose Godsmark, 1861" ... also "When this you see, remember me, and bear me in your mind. Let the world say what it will, speak of me as you find." (NO, it did not say "... as your friend."), open at one end, English, 1861. • Retyping this into the computer, something about the ship's name makes me wonder if this was sort of a generic seaman's gift, that he could get painted with his lady's name. "Harkaway" sounds more like a romantic story than a ship ("Hark! I'm away."). Can anyone out there report another pin like this one? Or news of a real ship by that name? **$125.00-$140.00**

Rolling pin, white pottery, "Kelvinator" — yes! the fridge people, the pin to be chilled before using, American, 20th C. **$45.00-$65.00**

Rolling pin, white pottery, lavender & blue flower decoration, turned wooden handles, American or English, 19th C. **$120.00-$135.00**

Rolling pin, white saltglazed stoneware with blue floral & scroll bands near ends, T. G. Green & Co., Ltd., English, 18"L, 19th C. **$200.00-$225.00**

Rolling pin, wood with iron rod, turned handles painted green, set at right angles to pin itself, marked only "D. R. G. M.", German, 10⅛"L with 5½"L handles, pre-1918, prob. early 20th C. • The initials D. R. G. M. are found on some German collectibles — prior to 1918 — and stand for Deutsches Reichs-Gebrauchsmuster, which meant that any trademark shown was a registered trademark of Germany. After 1918, and until the division of Germany after WWII, I believe at least one official mark used was D. R. P., or Deutsches Reichspatent. **$65.00-$85.00**

Rolling pin, wood, with pyrographic, or hot poker work, adv'g Custers Mills, Milton, PA, late 19th C. **$75.00-$90.00**

Rolling pin, wooden pin with wooden rod & handles, also wood & mesh self-dusting compartment above, "Harlowe's Do Not Stick," American, 20¼"L, pat'd Dec. 1903. **$75.00-$120.00**

Rolling pin, yellowware, oak handles, English or American, 11¼"L pin, 3½"L handles, 19th C. **$200.00-$250.00**

Rolling pin confusables, 2 types: **(1)** Wooden pin, with 6 corrugations & tapered ends, an axle & 2 handles, about 24"L. It is a very old leather tanner's tool for working the "bloom" off hides. **(2)** All-wood or wood & hard rubber pins with a waffled pattern, about 16"L; which are antique "spot reducers" or massagers. American, late 18th or early 19th C & late 19th C respectively. **$200.00-$300.00 and $45.00-$100.00**

Rolling pin for candy makers, cast iron, wood handles, American, 24"L, early 20th C, or late 19th. **$35.00-$50.00**

Rolling pin whatzit, hard wood, ridged or corrugated lengthwise rather than around the pin's circumference, this one carved of one piece of wood including handles at each end, nice patina, American, 14"L, this one poss. as early as mid 19th C. • **What're the Ridges For?** In *Tri-State Trader* of Aug. 5 & Sept. 3, 1985, collector William Baader and Ralph & Terry Kovel had a rolling pin fight about what this was for. • Is this (the one with ridges around circumference) for crushing crackers or stale bread to make crumbs? • The Kovels, using Doreen Yarwood's *The British Kitchen* as their source, say it is for rolling out oat cakes (and allows "a current of air to pass beneath the oatcakes" Yarwood). • Baader claims it is for crushing oats to make oatmeal, using Edward Pinto's *Treen & Other Wooden Bygones* as his expert source. • I say it is what it's used for. Many of us (at least in the 1950s) rolled graham crackers for pie crusts, or wheat cereal flakes for fried chicken or even Saltines for topping tuna casseroles. I've seen these pins used to pound meat (and therefore it could be called a tenderizer). Pins with the lengthwise ridges are also used for making croissants or other pastry with lots of butter that has to be layered into the dough. • Pierre Franey's column on Kitchen Equipment in the New York Times , 2/21/79, describes one thus: "The French-made Tutove pin, which has (longitudinal ridges the length of) its barrel and is excellent for distributing butter in puff paste, costs four or five times as much as...(another pin selling for $10 then)." • **Ridges around circumference.** — An ad in the July 1897 *Woman's Home Companion,* depicts a rolling pin with a barrel about the same length as either of the two handles, ridged circumferentially. The ad copy reads "Noodles now made easily by the Lightning Noodle cutter. 'Cuts 'em quick and fine.' The cooks delight. Sent to any address for 35¢ Household Supply CO., Toledo, O". • See also Noodle cutter; also one Candy cutter entry this chapter.
$45.00-$85.00

Rolling pins, turned wood, handles or knobs all in one with pin, interesting woods & knob shapes, unusual lengths, American, from about 14"L to 20"L, 19th C. • Look for variations of turned maple, for example, with particularly nice knobs. These may have mostly been one-off turnings meant as gifts. Some were commercially produced. • **Added value.** — Add another $20.00 or so if some feature is extra ultra — for example, extra long, or extra thick, or with extra nifty turning details, or great patina. • **Reproduction alert.** — At least 2 forms of new ones are being made and sold through Cumberland General Store. One is based on a "1907 design from Garland County Arkansas ... made up in sassafras and various fruit woods from Cumberland County, TN, about 19"L x 2¼" diameter". The other is a "standard Old World style ... made of smooth hardwood, 18"L" with short very ball-y knob handles, turned all-in-one. About $7.00-$9.00 for new ones. **$50.00-$85.00**

Rosette iron set, cast iron in original box, the star and wheel molds were dipped into thinnish batter, then plunged quickly into a deep pot of very hot cooking fat, cooked for a minute, dropped off the molds and drained on paper, making light crispy confections in the same shape as the molds, and served after dusting with powdered sugar, "Manufactured for Alfred Andresen & Co.," Min-neapolis, MN, this one, from the box's design, is mid 20th C. They are a much older form. • An Alfred Andresen ad in *Ladies Home Journal,* Dec. 1906, shows "**Rosette Wafers**" being cooked in a steaming stovetop sauce pan. They are described as the "daintiest, crispest little morsels that ever tempted an epicure, or delighted the fastidious. Light as a summer zephyr, and delicious as ambrosia. You can make forty of them in 20 minutes at a cost of ten cents with this simple little iron and the thinnest batter. A distinct novel delicacy for breakfast, luncheon and after-noon tea ..sold by leading dealers at 50 cents per set." They offered to send a free recipe booklet, "illustrated in eight colors", plus an "interesting catalog of culinary novelties", and all you had to do was send your dealer's name. I wish it would work now; I'd love to have a catalog (which itself, incidentally, would be worth about $35.00 to $50.00). See patty irons. **$20.00-$25.00**

Rosette irons, cast iron, set of 2 in original cardboard box, the "shallow pattern" openwork rosette irons, heavy gauge wire screw-in handle with wooden grip, Griswold, (there were several makers of these), Erie, PA, round rosette is 2 5/16"D; scalloped one (which looks like 4 hearts, arranged points in) is 3"D, c. 1926-1960s (?). **$20.00-$28.00**

Rosette & timbale mold combined, cast aluminum molds in set, screwed onto Y shaped handle that looks like slingshot or wishbone, simple hotdog-shaped turned wood handle, meant that 2 could be dipped at once. One fluted round & one fluted square timbale or patty shell mold, plus one star & one wheel-like rosette mold. The patty shells could be filled with anything from fruit or custard to creamed chicken, very popular for luncheons, American, molds each about 3" diameter, 1960s. • **Modern maker.** — Shown in an early 1980s kitchenware catalog is a cast aluminum dessert rosette set, for making "waffle cookies & fruit filled patty shells", shrink wrapped on printed card, mfd or imported by Fairgrove, place illegible. It consists of slightly bent rod with handle, a patty iron with heart, spade, diamond & club, a butterfly & an 8 petal flower, the three things to be screwed to handle. **$15.00-$20.00**

Sausage stuffers—See Cut & pare chapter.

Sealer or crimper, turned varnished wooden handle, chrome plated or stainless steel metal bracket and wheel, which has double tread design, for making fancy "tea and open sandwiches, delicious canapes for your luncheons, teas, and meetings ... helps make turnovers, ravioli, pierogi, kreplach, strudel, dumplings. Free recipes fur-nished." "Krimpkut Sealer", mfr unknown, adv'd by Gemini House, Buffalo, NY, 1968 ad. • Originally this tool, guaranteed to make you a "Sandwich Queen", cost only $2.15 ppd. **$2.00-$5.00**

Snow cone set, molded plastic & metal, snowman figure of white on white snowbank base, red plastic foller goes in hopper in top of head, eyes, nose & teeth of plastic "coal", red plastic shovel & funnel, red crank in back turns perforated metal cylinder against ice cube, shaved ice supposed to come out front & cascade picturesquely down front into snowbank so it could be shoveled into cups; set includes red & yellow squeeze bottles with flavoring syrup, small Dixie conical cups, in original box, with illustrated instruction folder, "Frosty Sno-Man Sno-Cone Machine", marked Hasbro, mfd by Hassenfeld Bros., Inc., Central Falls, RI, 9¼"H, c. 1952. **$10.00-$15.00**

Souse mold, for pork head-cheese, dating back in America to at least 1801. Cast iron, round with 2 handles, scalloped border design with sow's head including ears, in good detail, American, prob. PA, 11'' diameter. • **Reproduction alert.** — Dating is hard to do. I believe I have seen one old one; all the rest, in that easily-detected orangey powder-rusted state, are either reproductions, or something somebody came up with in the mid 20th C. I have never seen reference to a souse mold, and am still not convinced they are 19th C in origin. But, if this one was old the value would be high. $15.00 ought to be enough for new ones. **$150.00-$175.00**

Souse mold, painted cast iron, pig's sad face, ears down, natural pink tones, scalloped frame, loop handles cast in top & bottom, American, 8¾'' diameter plus 1¼'' handles, late 19th C. • The worst thing I've seen in a grocery store ever is an arrangement of styrofoam trays with pigs' heads under the shrink wrap. It almost made me sick. I wouldn't eat pork, or beef, or lamb, or veal, or mutton, and haven't for 13 years, if you paid me a million dollars. Think about it: a pig is more intelligent than a dog, by far, and can be trained and housebroken (even to use a litter box), can be affectionate and naturally clean. Why not try soy protein ''bacon'' ... it's very good. **$75.00-$100.00**

Sponge cake tin, stamped tin, oblong tray with 6 elongated peanut shaped, or as the catalog says, ''finger shape'' cups, in Harrod's Stores catalog, London, England, 11''L, late 19th C. **$18.00-$25.00**

Springerle board, carved birch wood, depicts horse, ram & boar, prob. European, 19th C. • *Springerle* is said in many sources to be the German word for a ''small jumping horse''. **$235.00-$250.00**

Springerle board, carved hard wood, vertical rectangle with 12 designs, including woman in gathered skirt, holding 3 part burden on head; rooster; woman sowing seeds from apron; an arch of some kind with tree; cherry or current branch; bird on fruit tree branch; 2 handled posset cup or tyg with odd plant (?); alert deer; sprightly flower; man with whip, probably a wagoner; hunting horn with 2 tassels; and woman in native costume with brimmed hat, and multi tiered gathered skirt, next to tree. The individual cookies have very narrow frames, separated by a narrow channel or runnel — the type to be cut apart before drying & baking. European, about 6¾'' x 4'', 19th C, prob. 3rd quarter. • **Sources for Springerle Designs.** — It is hard to find identification of, or exact sources for, the designs, but if you keep your eyes open all the time, serendipity and diligence will sometimes give you clues. I picked up a Dover Publications book called *Catchpenny Prints 163 Popular Engravings from the Eighteenth Century*, originally published in London by Bowles & Carver, in the late 1780s and early 1790s, (reprint published in 1970). A man with a whip, seen on one mold, is identified as a waggoner (sic), in one very similar picture in this book. A man with a tall ladder stumped me until I found a cut of a man with a ladder entitled ''Lamp-lighter''. **$110.00-$140.00**

Springerle board, carved maple wood, 8 patterns laid out in 2 x 4 formation, including animals, fruit, flowers, German or poss. German American, 8¾''L x 3¾''W, 19th C. **$120.00-$150.00**

Springerle board, carved walnut, large ornate wreath design of flowers & birds, ''Harman's Bakery'', Brunswick, ME, 20th C. **$250.00-$350.00**

Springerle board, carved wood, 6 designs: rooster, house, fruit compote, dog, shore bird, grape bunch, European (?), 7''H x 3¼''W, late 19th or early 20th C. **$100.00-$120.00**

Springerle board, cast pewter mold mounted to wooden back for stability, 12 rectangular designs include people, plants & animals, European, 7½'' x 4½'', 19th C (?). • **Using a Springerle Mold.** — Although it might seem that a springerle board would be used lying flat on a work surface, with the rolled dough pressed into it. It is used the other way: the dough is rolled out and the mold is pressed down on the dough, and lifted off before the individual designs were cut apart with a jagger or knife, or baked whole to be broken apart, depending on the kind of dividing line between each design. **$165.00-$175.00**

Springerle board, hand carved wood, images on both sides (as they usually were), designs include angel, pecking chicken, steamboat, castle, tricorn hat, unusual and small, 19th C. **$145.00-$165.00**

Springerle board, machine carved wood, 4 squares on pale maple wood, American or European import, early 20th C. **$35.00-$45.00**

Springerle board, or confectionary mold? carved wood, long & skinny, on one side is a woman carrying water, a ship, a mermaid, & a lion, on other side are 37 small carvings, mainly fish, some people, a dog, birds, griffin, European, 18''L, board is 1⅝'' thick, looks c.1800 to 1820. **$200.00-$250.00**

Springerle board, worm eaten fruitwood, carved on both sides, rooster, boar, squirrel & heart on one side, a cat, dog, horse & lion on the other, European, 5'' x 9'', prob. very early 19th C, though poss. late 18th C.

Springerles — ''The beauty of [these baked springerle] cookies, with their detailed designs in high relief, veritable cameos in dough, charms young and old,'' writes Ann Hark & Preston A. Barba, in *Pennsylvania German Cookery*, Allentown, PA: Schlechter's (''Publishers for the Pennsylvania Germans since 1810''), 1950. They go on to say that the word springerle means ''charger or horse'' in ''South German'', but other sources say it means leaping deer. Hark & Barba note that ''the man on horseback is a familiar figure among our old Christmas cooky cutters'' and the image is common on cake boards and springerle molds too. They write that the ''beautiful designs (are) delicately engraved into pearwood or some other hard or close-grained wood. Most of them are imported from Germany and are occasionally for sale in our large department stores.'' • **Springerle Cookie Recipe.** — A basic recipe for these cookies, requires 2 eggs, a cup of sugar, grated lemon rind, 2 cups of sifted flour with about a half teaspoon of baking powder, and 2 teaspoons of aniseed (it is this and the lemon that give the distinctive and fragrance). All the recipes suggest beating the eggs first, then slowly beating in the sugar and adding the lemon rind. Then you start adding the flour and baking powder. Finally add the aniseed. The dough shouldn't be too soft; if it seems soft, stiffen by kneading in a little more sifted flour, and roll out thin (a quarter inch thick) and lightly flour the surface. The mould has to be pressed onto the dough carefully to leave its impression. you can cut the cookies apart before baking, especially if you use a mold that doesn't have the dividing lines. Some molds are so made that the whole set can be baked whole and broken after being baked and cooled. The ones with a groove between each design probably should be cut before drying; the ones with a ridge, sometimes relatively wide, between each design can be left until after baking. Carefully lift the printed dough with a couple of spatulas or cake turners, and shift to greased then floured tin baking sheets. Cover with a dry towel overnight, so that they have a chance to set and dry out. They will bake in about 15 minutes at 325°, and should not be allowed to get brown.

Springerle mold, carved boxwood (?), 6 images laid out 2 x 3: foamy beer mug (?), long-skirted bustled lady with fan, a cupboard, a pig, a boy bowling or playing or playing bocci, with 3 balls in pile behind him, & finally a stepped thing like a plant stand with tiny unreadable objects on the 3 shelves, European, 5⅞"H x 4⅛"W x 1" thick, 1870s when bustles were "in" or skip to mid or late 1880s. • **Costume fashions.** — I don't have & can't find a good reference book on costume, including hair styles, shoes and hats, but it would be very valuable for collectors who specialize in decorated pieces or figural items.
$160.00-$185.00

Springerle mold, cast metal plate, probably zinc, attached to oak board. This one has 12 designs laid out 3 across by 4 down, is unusual because the designs show **tradesmen or craftsmen & their tools** & products. Amazingly detailed images of Butcher (sausages, cleaver & chopping block); Cooper (barrel); Tailor (sitting cross-legged, 'tailor' fashion, on his table, scissors); Wheelwright (wheel & plane); Blacksmith (horseshoe & anvil); Stone Carver (blocks, pick & square); Druggist (scales & apothecary chest); Fisherman (net); Lamp-lighter (ladder); Carpenter (adze & sawbucks); Shoemaker (boots & shoes); Clockmaker (carrying case clock reading 10 to 2). All with dividing ridge, & herringbone chip-carved edges, American (?) or European — nothing here to rule out either. Measures 7⅝"L x 4⅜"W. Cookies are 1¹⁵⁄₁₆" x 1⅗". Metal is ⅛"- thick, mounted to board almost ⅝" thick, 19th C, prob. 1840 to 1860 or repro from 1970s-80s. • Crossover interest from tool collectors. (This one was bought with the mold entry that has an explanation of zinc.) • **Reproduction alert.** — I had quite a start when I found an ad in Dec. 1973 *Early American Life* for a "Beautiful springerle cookie mold...an exact reproduction of 18th century Pennsylvania German original. Makes 12 cookies picturing 12 different craftsmen. Mold is of heavy metal mounted on hand-finished cherry-wood. Also serves as a handsome and indestructible kitchen wall plaque. History and our own springerle recipe included; $15.00 ppd. The House-On-The-Hill, So. Strafford, Vermont 05070." Now. **Do I have a repro?** The small, dark & rather sharp ad photo shows the same 12 images, but there appear to be slight differences in the shapes of things, esp. the Fisherman's net. And mine is not mounted on cherry, and there are no signs of a once-attached hook for hanging on the kitchen wall. It's scary and very maddening; you buy something because it looks so right, then a bully kicks sand in your face with a 1973 ad. • House-On-The-Hill has been moved by collector Caroline Kallas to River Forest, IL (POB 221, 60305). I bought her catalog ($1.00 ppd) to check if my trades mold were a recent reproduction. The most helpful thing she told me, in a letter, is if you find screw heads in the back of the wooden plaque, this indicates the metal face is screwed on and old. Newer, pot metal molds, are first copper- then nickel-plated. Kallas's good-looking springerle molds include the "Guildsman" (or Trades) mold (7½ x 4½"); "Musical & Variety" mold , flowers & trades & musical instruments (7½ x 4½"); the "Swan" mold, swan, bird, boater, fruit, churner & house (6" x 3½"); "Petite", house, dog, church, church, bird, grapes, fruit, bee skips, goat on rocks, swan, peacock, flowers (5¾" x 4"); "Cornucopia", with cornucopia, flower, game beater, goat; "Heart", heart design with lovebirds & flowers (3½" square); "Der Kinderbringer (The Child-bringer)", winged angel with baby (4" x 2⅝"); 6 round designs — grapes, birds, flowers, birdhouse, female gardener (6" x 4"); 6 ovals designs, anchor, house, lovebirds, etc. (6" x 3½"); "Architectural", 9 churches, buildings (6" x 6¼"); 15 designs, animals & people (8¾" x 4¾"); and others (mostly religious) imported from Europe. • Price range is for an authentic old one; divide by 5 or 10 for value of repro..   **$200.00-$275.00**

Springerle mold, cast metal, probably zinc, with 12 designs, L to R: crossed guitar & cornet; 3 berried plant; squirrel on stump eating nuts; lyre & laurel wreath; clump with 3 flowers; bird (magpie, mockingbird or nightingale?) on branch; dairymaid in long gathered skirt with ruffled bottom, carrying 2 pails; wild flower with 6 leaves and single stalk with tiny flowers; woman in long 2 tiered gathered skirt, possibly arranging flowers in pot on 3 legged stool; man (lamp lighter?) with tall ladder, hand in belt; lily of the valley type plant; & man in skirted hunting coat with gun under arm walking toward tree. Each design has chip carved herringbone frame, and was meant to be cut apart before baking. European, 6⅛" x 3¾", mid 19th C (?). • **Bird Watching.** — Catchpenny prints and chapbooks for children are full of birds. The Dover reproduction of 1780s-90s catchpenny prints, in one book, must have 100 bird pictures, tail up, tail down, straight beak, finch or parrot-like beak, open beak, closed beak. Each bird is labeled, but it is very difficult to decide which bird was used by the springerle mold carver. Some birds are more likely to have been used than others because of fable and song, viz. swan, peacock, turkey, sparrow, magpie, robin, wren, nightingale, magpie, swan, duck, & goose. More unusual waterbirds such as cranes (herons?) and sandpipers are found on some items, like decorated stoneware.   **$150.00-$175.00**

Springerle mold, cast metal sheet with 12 rectangular designs, 3 across by 4 down with dividing ridges & chip carved edges, mounted to oak board. The very heavy dark gray metal is not lead or iron, but probably cast zinc, as the detail is very good, and zinc was similarly used for electrotyping & printing plates. Designs, L to R: log church & pine tree; peacock (?) on shed roof (?); 2 grape bunches; strawberry plant; table with 2 bee skeps & 6 bees; downhill mountain goat; swan on pond; wild turkey (?); branch with 5 five petal flowers (jasmine?); man in hat, gun under arm & dead rabbit; butcher with sausages & butcher's block; short-skirted woman (man in skirted coat?) in kitchen with posnet, dead fowl & a fish in each hand & utensil rack (?). American (?), or European for American market, 3⅝"L x 4⅞"W 1⁵⁄₁₆" x 1¼" cookies. Metal is ⅛"- thick, mounted to board almost ⅝" thick, prob. 1840 to 1860. • The originals of these molds were probably carved wood, used to make casting models for metal molds. The cast metal ones, whether zinc or iron, reveal their carved wood origins. Price range for old ones: **$150.00-$175.00**

Springerle mold, ceramic block, flat with 35 separate small impressed images, German, mid (?) 20th C. reproduction. **$30.00-$35.00**

Springerle mold, heavy cast metal, probably zinc, makes 15 individual cookies to be cut or broken apart, designs are laid out 3 across x 5 down, & include house with well; dog; church; another church; bird; grapes; raspberries; 2 bee skips on outdoor table; elk (?); duck in pond; heron; berries; hunter with gun & rabbit; man cooking over gypsy kettle with hanging implements; woman holding something in one hand (broom?) & something unidentifiable in other hand, motifs could be English, American or German, 5¾''H x 3½'', mid 19th C (?). • **Lookalike Alarm, Modern Springerle Molds.** — In a 1984 catalog of Maid of Scandinavia Co., Minneapolis, appeared a cast aluminum springerle mold with 12 designs, laid out three across, four down, with flowers, birds, fish, a ship, a windmill, fruit. It measures 8¼''H x 4½''W and cost $16.25. The old one is not cast aluminum. **$240.00-$270.00**

Springerle mold, or marzipan mold, cast iron, 12 squares laid out 3 across by 4 down, each square slightly irregular in outline, depicts basket with 3 apples; pear with 2 leaves; turkey or peacock; cornucopia; bird in branch; oak leaves with acorn; fruit tree branch; horseshoe with blacksmith's hammer; large bird (parrot?) standing on branch; tall bushel basket with apples; grape leaves, a high cross; a stunning collection of images, European or American, each cookie would be about 1⅛'' x 1¾'', mid (?) 19th C. **$185.00-$220.00**

Springerles Wood to Iron. — I have read in various sources that these were sometimes cast from patterns made from original carved wooden springerle molds. Would be especially good for bakery which could soon wear out a wooden mold. These metal springerle molds are also found in a heavy cast metal something like lead that is probably zinc. A book by Katherine Morrison McClinton states that marzipan molds were first made in carved wood, then of tin and cast iron. • **Iron to Pewter?** Garth's auctioned a similar one, Sept. 22-23, 1989, for $65.00 It was "heavy cast pewter or other white metal" (zinc?). It was 7½'' x 4⅝'', no wood mount, with 12 images, 3 across x 4 down, Not all images clear from picture, but include in 2nd row from bottom a tall basket with 3 apples and hoop handle, a building, a cat, and on bottom row twig with cherries, -?-, lion (?). Several other buildings, & a swan. • **What do you make of this?** The Smithsonian was offered a puzzling mold with these same images. It is cast iron but with strange variegated irridescent color appearing on underside that make you suspect impurities or unorthodox casting methods. On the mold's top are 3 x 4 sections with intaglio images *identical* to those described above. On the underside of this relatively thin metal slab, in relief, are the same images, backwards so to speak. Furthermore, four short peg feet, almost like casting sprues, extrude from the four corners. There is considerable "damage" to the underside image of the tall basket where the peg leg is joined, and also to the cross cookie. Overall dimensions are slightly larger than the one described above, viz. 8³⁄₁₆''H x 4¹³⁄₁₆''W; each cookie about 1¹⁵⁄₁₆'' H x 1⁷⁄₁₆''W. The collection from which the mold came was rather old and select, so if this is a reproduction, it has some age. My suspicion is that the upper and underside images are somehow indicative of the exact method of production, a method that remains elusive.

Springerle mold, unidentified heavy cast metal, rectangle divided into 6 pieces including 2 birds on branches; perky flower; odd domed building; building with thing on top like TV aerial but possibly a lighthouse; and something like a mug on top of a drum; all these descriptions are based on a picture in a 1917 ad of imported metal molds brought into NYC by Otto Thurnauer, German, c.1917. • Turn-of-century dealer Thurnauer lists seven rectangular or square molds, five oval ones and three rounds. I wonder if the oval ones are the cast iron ovals with single designs seen in such quantity at antique shows in late 1980s. • See also Cookie mold. **$50.00-$65.00**

Springerle rolling pin, carved wood, relatively fat short barrel divided into 16 segments with flowers, animals, butterfly, fruit, other designs, yellow painted wood handles, American or European import?, c.1930s. (With original cookbooklet, maybe a bit more.) **$25.00-$35.00**

Springerle rolling pin, carved wooden wheel in slingshot-like handle, pineapples & leaves, with metal pin axle, German (?), 5½''L, 19th C. • Look for well carved designs, in unusual subjects, just as you would for butter molds. Rarest are those with 4 or 5 different designs, not a band of repeats. Look also for well-formed handles, old patina (butter & age contribute), condition, and size. Almost all seen at recent shows are repeat patterns, rather simply (that is to say quickly & commercially) carved, and in pale unpatinaed wood; these are 20th C, perhaps country-look reproductions. Cumberland General Store has one with 16 pictures "deeply carved," and a "hard maple barrel with natural polished lacquer finish. Enameled handles...ivory or yellow." This new one about $10.00. Old ones: **$55.00-$80.00**

Stick mold pan, riveted tin, 12 compartments, "Kreamer," mfd by August Kreamer & Co., Brooklyn, NY, early 20th C. **$15.00-$20.00**

Sugar cubes, white sugar cubes decorated in colorful sugar frosting, include candlestick, angel, snowman head, white wreath, green wreath, Christmas star, Star of Bethlehem, bells, Christmas tree, poinsettia, candy cane, praying angel & full-figure snowman, 1940s (?). **$4.00-$7.00**

Tart pan, fluted sides with ring holder, gray graniteware, only 3¾''D x 1¼''deep,19th C. **$35.00-$45.00**

Tart pan, sheet metal, "Parkersburg Iron & Steel Co., WV, TOC. **$18.00-$22.00**

Tart pan or muffin pan, cast iron, 7 shallow cups in 4 shapes, including plain, fluted and with star in center, rounded hexagonal in shape with side handles, called a "four season pan," but there don't seem to be leaves in the design or snowflakes, don't know maker, sold through Cumberland General Store catalog, 9'' diameter, 1980s. **$7.00-$10.00**

Tart pan or muffin pan, cast iron, 11 shallow turban mold cups, cut out between cups, maker or mark not known, sold in Cumberland General Store catalog, 9½''L x 6''W, 1980s. **$7.00-$10.00**

Tart sealer, cast aluminum with wooden knob, spring-loaded action works scalloped inner ring to seal the tart while outer ring cuts round outline. Could be used for ravioli or tortellini too. "Tart Master", approx. 4'' diameter, pat'd 1938. • A new "Tartmaster" was being made in the 1970s (still may be); looks the same except that knob is now a metal cap. Directions read "Roll out a sheet of dough, place small mounds of filling at regular intervals, cover with a second layer and then, with a quick push of plunger, punch out tarts or ravioli." **$8.00-$12.00**

Tortilla iron, looks like a cast iron stovetop waffle iron, low frame with very flared base, cutout short side handle like a skillet's, hinged press with long iron rod handle, used like a waffle iron only it bakes a thin cornmeal batter to make one tortilla at a time, not marked, American, or poss. Mexican?, 1870s to 1900. **$200.00-$300.00**

Utensil rack & pastry sheet, tinned sheet iron, holds rolling pin in curved bottom edge, hangs on wall from little wire ring, American (?), 16" x 23", 19th C. **$150.00-$185.00**

Vegetable cutters, for garnishes, small round tin box with 10 tiny, very fancy tin cutters with reinforced edges, designs include fleur-de-lis, rosettes, scrolls, & forms that look heraldic, "J. Y. Watkins", possibly an importer of European kitchen items, "NY", can only 4½" diameter, c.1870s-90s. • Importer F. A. Walker advertised a single deep-cutting vegetable cutter, tin, flat back, in one of the almost figural "heraldic" designs found in the Watkins box. No size is given, but Walker was in business from the 1870s probably to c.1900. **$35.00-$50.00**

Vegetable or rice mold, pieced tin, an assemblage of pointed spires, almost spikes, the overall outline fitting into a cone shape, meant for molding cooked mashed root veggies or cooked rice, from F. A. Walker catalog, European (?), probably about 6" to 8"H, probably came in 2 or 3 sizes, late 19th C. **$30.00-$45.00**

Vienna baker, or very shallow cake pans, heavy tin, 9 oval shallow cups set in frame, with end handles, mfd by Lalance & Grosjean Mfg. Co., late 19th C. **$10.00-$15.00**

Wafer iron, cast iron, hinged, on base, plates decorated with flowers & cornucopia, Wagner, 6½"D iron, 9"D base, 1892. **$100.00-$125.00**

Wafer iron, for hearth, cast & forged iron, intaglio design of heart within rectangular frame of criss-crossed lines, long handles called reins, marked "S. M. /ID ED," American, 5" x 8" head, 31½"L overall, dated 1787. Originally in the Keillor Collection. **$600.00-$800.00**

Wafer iron, for hearth, cast & forged iron, round head has design of eagle & shield with 13 stars for original 13 colonies, American, head: 5¼" diameter, overall length 27½", 18th C, between 1790 (13th state RI joined Union) & 1791 (VT joined). **$350.00-$400.00**

Wafer iron, for hearth, cast iron, eagle & shield design with 16 stars, long handles, American, poss. TN, c.1796 to 1803. **$1200.00-$1500.00**

Dating by the Stars — Antiquastrology. There was never, officially, a flag with 16 stars, but at one time there were only 16 states. The state was Tennessee, and it was the 16th state from 1796 to 1803, when Ohio became the 17th state. There were 13 stars to the first American flag, under the First Flag Act of 1777 and back to 13 stars on coins from the 1820s, 1830s, 1850s, 1860s and 1890s; there were 12 stars in the Bon Homme Richard flag of 1779; there were 15 stars in the flag under the Second Flag Act in 1795 and 15 stars on 1794 and 1797 Liberty coins ; and 20 stars in the design under the Act of 1818. This is useful information so far as it goes. Check a world almanac or encyclopedia if you are trying to determine origins or dates from the number of stars on a piece. Even then it could be a commemorative or patriotic piece that

refers back to a date or period.

Wafer iron, for hearth, cast iron plates (sometimes called lips), long forged iron handles (called reins) with figure 8 loop attached to one, a knob on other, the plates with finely detailed eagle & striped shield with 16 stars, "E Pluribus Unum" in ribbon banner in eagle's mouth, one foot holding 8 arrows, one holding olive branch, American, 6½" diameter, 31⅞"L, c.1796 to 1803. **$1150.00-$1300.00**

Wafer iron, for hearth, cast iron with forged reins, flower surrounded by concentric rings, American, 28"L, c.1800. **$250.00-$300.00**

Wafer iron, for hearth, cast with long forged iron handles, makes a heart shaped wafer, American, poss. PA (?), 23½"L, 19th C. **$250.00-$300.00**

Wafer types. — We are accustomed to seeing pictures of round wafer irons with ecclesiastical or eagle & star motifs; the former probably used for religious ceremonies or occasions. Political or patriotic ones are harder to relegate, and yet there are proportionally many of them. (Perhaps skilled 1876 reproductions?). • Albert H. Sonn, in his three-volume *Early American Wrought Iron*, NY: 1928, wrote that wafer irons were "used in making of holiday or wedding wafers." Heart-shaped ones were probably for weddings. • Dr. Henry Mercer's "Wafer Irons", an article in Vol. V, Bucks County Historical Society publications, 1920, outlines six types of wafers: **(1)** ecclesiastical, **(2)** domestic, **(3)** documentary, **(4)** medicinal, **(5)** fish, and **(6)** confectioner wafers. This was related by Richard H. Shaner in his fact-filled article "Waffles and Wafers", *Pennsylvania Folklife*, Summer 1962, Vol. XII, No. 4, pp. 20-23. Shaner adds that the ecclesiastical ones were probably most common, because they were still being used in the 20th C. He wrote that in 1920, "there were still Catholic churches in the area [Pennsylvania Dutch country] which were stil making wafers from 18th century styled wafer irons."

Wafer iron, for hearth, forged iron, long handles, also called an oble iron (which may be from the German, or else an example of a phenomenon in the English language, of a dropped "n" word, in this case noble iron. Another example is the word apple, which was originally napple), American or English, 17½"L, 18th C. • **German vocabulary** — Oblaten-Backzange: wafer bake tongs. In some German books, no distinction is made, in vocabulary, between a waffle iron and a wafer iron, and both are called Waffeleisen. **$135.00-$160.00**

Wafer iron, for hearth, forged iron with brass stamps inside the 'lips' to ensure very fine detailing in finished wafers, & fast even heating, American or English, 2½" x 4½" wafer disks, and 14½"L handles, 18th C or very early 19th C. **$250.00-$300.00**

"Sweet Wafers. — Two ounces of butter, half a pound of sugar, half a pound of flour, five eggs, beaten separately. Bake in wafer-irons well greased, and roll over a knife." Mrs. A. P. Hill, *Mrs Hill's New Family Receipt Book*, NY: 1870. • **Almond Wafers**— Ingredients, ½ lb. of sweet almonds, ¼ lb. of sifted sugar, 1 oz. of flour, and 2 eggs. Blanch and cut the almonds small, moisten them with the yolks and whites of eggs previously beaten. Sift into them the sugar and the flour, and mix the whole together with two drops of essence of lemon baking pan), and spread the mixture over it as thin as possible. Bake it a light brown, and cut it with a knife, before it is cold, into long squares; roll them immediately on pieces of wood, to make them round and hollow. They are usually served to garnish creams.'' Webster & Parkes, *An Encyclopedia of Domestic Economy* 1848 NY edition of 1845 English book.

Waffle iron, nickeled cast iron, floral design inside plates, Wagner, Sidney, OH, 1892. **$60.00-$80.00**

Waffle iron, cast aluminum, handle replaced with piece of heavy black insulated cable, lid has smiling sun face, waffling pattern comprised of 6 stars & a crescent moon in each waffle, slightly corroded, ''Mazie Lee,'' 8⅛'' diameter, 20th C. **$70.00-$90.00**

Waffle iron, cast aluminum high frame, multi-purpose outfit that makes waffles & if you use the frame with omelette pans, it cooks eggs too. Wagner Ware #8, Sidney, OH, 20th C. **$140.00-$165.00**

Waffle iron, cast aluminum, oblong, makes 2 rectangular waffles, very simple grid with squares with a dimple in each, short stubby black painted wood handles, ''Waffle Iron For Armstrong Table Stove'', S. S. Co., Huntington, WVa, 6¼'' x 5¼'' exclusive of handles, which are 3''L, early 20th C. **$30.00-$40.00**

Waffle iron, cast iron, Giles F. Filley, St. Louis, MO, prob. 3rd quarter 19th C. • Here's what Mrs. S. C. Lee of Baltimore, wrote in her 1884 *Practical Housekeeping* about waffle irons: ''The waffle iron is a very peculiar machine. The waffle is put in, locked up, baked on one side to a lovely brown, turned over, prison and all, until the other side is a still lovelier brown, and then released steaming hot ready for the table.'' **$65.00-$95.00**

Waffle iron, cast iron, mfd by Bridge & Beach Stove Co., dated 1865, but poss. made over long period. **$65.00-$80.00**

Waffle iron, cast iron, 2 parts, hinged iron fits over range eye, makes 5 sectioned waffles, marked only ''No. 14'', American, 11½'' diameter, makes 8¼'' waffles, 19th C. **$50.00-$65.00**

Waffle iron, cast iron, 2 piece with bail handle, Wagner Ware, 1920. • An ad in the Dec. 10, 1892 *The Metal Worker*, claims that Wagner had just brought out in November the ''only bailed and detachable hinge waffle iron in the market'' Depicted in ad is a low frame mold, the socket joint hinge opposite the 2 handles, arched bail crosswise. **$25.00-$35.00**

Waffle iron, cast iron, 3 pieces, low frame with extra decorative frying pan handle, the 2 part waffle iron has openwork casting to dissipate heat, Majestic Mfg. Co., No. 885M, St. Louis, MO, 16''L with handle, pat'd 1908. **$30.00-$40.00**

Waffle iron, cast iron, design of little girl & garden (Mistress Mary? not contrary enough to not get her waffles?), 2 hinged round plates, 20th C. • Friend & collector Linda Fishbeck of Texas found this, the dealer said it was a waffle iron, and she didn't buy it, feeling there was something wrong about it. Sounds to me, some years later now, that it was probably just missing its frame, and that it possibly could even be late 19th C. In the future, one sure thing to look for would be the two side ''pegs'' that would fit into slots in the frame. **$35.00-$45.00**

Waffle iron, cast iron, flower, heart & diamond design waffling plate, 2 part with stand, Francis Buckwalter & Co., Boyer's Ford, PA, pat'd Aug. 9, 1910. **$45.00-$65.00**

Waffle iron, cast iron, frame has 2 high arched handles, hinged 2 part mold fits down in, has marvelous recipe for potato waffles in pretty hand printed-looking letters cast intaglio on flat lid: **''Kartoffel Waffeln''**. A translation of recipe: ½ lb. cooked grated potatoes, ¼ lb. meal, ½ litre warm milk, 3 eggs, 50 grams butter, 20 grams yeast. Recipe is only marking, American, thus PA German, or German (?), 11'' diameter, 19th C. **$175.00-$200.00**

Waffle iron, cast iron, high frame, Wapak #8, mfd by William H. Howell Co., Geneva, IL, 20th C. **$100.00-$125.00**

Waffle iron, cast iron, high frame, Harwi #8, American, early 20th C. **$25.00-$35.00**

Waffle iron, cast iron, high frame or base with bail handle, coiled heat-dissipating handle on 2 part mold part, heart & star waffling pattern, Griswold #88, ''928,'' pan: 7¾''D, pat'd May 18, 1920. **$150.00-$170.00**

Waffle iron, cast iron, low frame, Wagner Ware #8, TOC. **$90.00-$115.00**

Waffle iron, cast iron, low frame, Favorite Piqua #8, Favorite Stove & Range Co., Piqua, OH, late 19th or early 20th C. ''Favorite'' line introduced 1892. **$145.00-$160.00**

Waffle iron, cast iron, low frame, 2 part hinged round mold fits into it, simple grid pattern, Dover Stamping Co., about 8'' diameter, c.1870s. **$55.00-$75.00**

Waffle iron, cast iron, low frame, 2 parts, hinged, 2 side handles on frame, mold divided into 4 wedges, design is fleur-de-lis & crosses, Norths, Harrison & Chase, #7, 8, Phila., late 19th C. **$55.00-$80.00**

Waffle iron, cast iron, low frame, 2 piece mold, coil handles, ''American No. 8,'' also 885-B, Griswold Mfg. Co., pat'd Dec. 1, 1908. • **WWI Waffles.** — It was your patriotic duty during WWI to eat waffles. Early ads in 1918 & 1919 really pushed them as food, so that they could sell more waffle irons. What I don't understand is how they managed to get the iron to cast the waffle irons with; what about metal drives? In Sept. 1918 trade publication, *House Furnishing Review*, a Griswold ad stated ''With housewives all over the country absorbed in menu problems, this is the time to feature your kitchen-ware!'' Since this was aimed at retailers, they added ''Our advertising, appealing to 550,000 readers, stimulates waffle-hunger.'' Stover, meanwhile, claimed that people were ''Living on waffles.'' **$45.00-$55.00**

Waffle iron, cast iron, low frame with slightly up-angled frying pan handle, hinged round waffle mold set down inside, you would need an extra tool, perhaps some kinds of stove lid lifters would work, to open it up, oh bother it all, must we have waffles again? Lid of waffle mold has beautiful crisp design of small daisy-like flower in center and a half inch band of radiating lines around outside, not marked, American, frame is 9½'' diameter with 5½''L handle, makes 6½'' diameter waffles, c.1870s or even 1860s • **From the look of the casting,** my hunch is this was cast by a stove maker, probably in Troy or Albany, NY, and possibly as early as the 1850s. There was a waffle patented by C. Swartwout of Troy, NY, Aug. 24, 1869. A really early waffle iron patent was a design patent granted Nathaniel Waterman of Boston, on July 5, 1853. • There were, I believe, no more than 5 waffle iron patents, including a design patent, granted before 1873. But I'm sure that many waffle irons were made, especially simple ones to go with specific ranges or stoves, without a pat'd design. **$135.00-$160.00**

Waffle iron, cast iron, low frame with very wide flange to accomodate a variety of range eyes, frying pan handle, 2 part, hinged mold has no handles but for a little tab with hole for lifting tool, dealer called "Deck of Cards" pattern, but it wasn't, instead there are hearts, diamonds, rosettes, circles and Xs, Orr, Painter & Co., No. 6-7, Reading, marked No. 7-8, with broken hinge, was priced $25.00. What use is a broken one? **$35.00-$45.00**

Waffle iron, cast iron, low frame with wide flange, longish "frying pan" handle, mold is hinged, 2 part with no handle, 4 designs: heart with 3 small diamonds inside; simple scrolls with 3 small diamonds between; 5 radiating broken lines; and a pattern of rather widely spaced small diamonds. Top mold has same 4 designs, only they're rotated 90° on the axis so that each waffle would have different patterns front & back. Lid has small iron ring near edge for lifting with small pot hook, unfortunately this has no mark at all, but see "Augur & Lord" one (6 entries down), American, 8" diameter, 9½"L handle on frame, mid to 3rd quarter 19th C. **$120.$150.00**

Waffle iron, cast iron, low frame with wire bail handle, coiled wire "Alaska" handles that kept cool by dissipating heat, simple waffling pattern. Base also was available with short cast 'frying pan' handle. Griswold #8, Erie, PA, 2-part pan with 7¾" diameter, frame 10" diameter, makes 7¼" diameter waffle, c.1926. **$45.00-$60.00**

Waffle iron, cast iron, medium high frame with 2 part waffler, makes 4 small waffle wedges with pattern of fleur-de-lis & crosses, North, Chase & North, #6, 7, Philadelphia, 5¾" diameter, 11¾"L with handle, late 19th C. **$65.00-$80.00**

Waffle iron, cast iron, range top, very low frame with flat rim, frying pan side handle, 2 part hinged mold fits into it, nice casting of scrolly wreath around center design of concentric rings on lid, American, 8" diameter, 14"L overall, marked "8/9/1910". **$40.00-$50.00**

Waffle iron, cast iron, range top, very low frame with frying pan handle, 2 part hinged mold, Orr Painter & Co. 7 & 8, Reading, PA, makes 6¾" diameter waffle, 13"L overall with handle, 19th C. **$65.00-$75.00**

Waffle iron, cast iron, round, 3 parts: flanged frame, hinged mold making 4 wedge waffles decorated with small: hearts, diamonds, scrolls, ridged rayed lines. Augur & Lord, Chester, CT, 8" diameter mold, mid to 3rd quarter 19th C. **$190.00-$225.00**

Waffle iron, cast iron, round, 3 parts, wide flanged low frame with "frying pan" handle, hinged mold making 4 waffles in different patterns: small outlined hearts, small diamonds, small squares with pattern that could be interpreted as "SS" on surface, & small circles with pebbled surface, John Savery's Son & Co., NYC, NY, c.1880s. **$45.00-$65.00**

Waffle iron, cast iron, round (despite measurements given in their catalog, as transcribed below), 3 part with low frame with side frying pan handle, 2 part hinged mold fits into it, Matthai-Ingram Co., came in 4 sizes: 6" x 7", 7" x 8", 8" x 9" and 9" x 10", c.1890s. **$45.00-$55.00**

Waffle iron, cast iron, round head with 6 pointed PA German flowers on one side & waffled grid on other, no maker mark, prob. PA, 20th C. **$20.00-$25.00**

Waffle iron, cast iron, round high frame, Wagner Ware #8, TOC. **$115.00-$125.00**

Waffle iron, cast iron, short handled, makes 5 heart-shaped waffles, riveted-on leather handles probably replacements, marked "MUSTAD #4", European, inside diameter 6¼", handle 7"L prob. early 20th C. **$150.00-$165.00**

Waffle iron, cast iron, small flared, wide-flanged frame, hinged 2 part mold, wood handles, "Buster Waffle No 8" cast in script on lid, depicts Buster Brown facing his dog Tige, who sits up to get treat. Mfd. by Andrew M. Anderson & Co., Chicago, pat'd 11/13/1906. • One is depicted in Steve Stephens' "Cast Iron Cookware News," Nov. 1990 issue; it has coiled-wire, heat-dissipating handles. **$175.00-$250.00**

Waffle iron, cast iron, star inside heart, American, 19th C. **$125.00-$150.00**

Waffle iron, cast iron turntable style, heart pattern waffling plates, Alfred Andresen & Co., 20th C. **$45.00-$55.00**

Waffle iron, cast iron, very low, hinged 2 part mold, the lower being also the frame, with frying pan handle, John Savery & Sons, NYC, NY, 8" diameter x 15"L with handle, mid to late 19th C. **$45.00-$65.00**

Waffle iron, cast iron with 4 different waffle designs, Griswold #1. • "Among **iron goods used in the kitchen** are frying pans, waffle-irons, roll-pans, griddles for batter cakes, large iron pots, etc. Sometimes some of these things are so highly polished that they only require to be washed in soap and water and rubbed dry. ... Griswold's American Waffle-irons are most satisfactory. They are comparatively new." Maria Parloa, *Kitchen Companion*, Boston: Estes & Lauriat, 1887. The text illustration is of a cast iron waffle iron, low frame with short "frying pan" handle with hanging hole, and hinged mold, with very short handles, the baking surfaces divided into four parts with a simple waffling pattern made up of small raised square blocks with dimples. **$200.00-$225.00**

Waffle iron, cast iron, with hearts, clubs, spades & diamonds waffling pattern, marked only #7, American, 20th C. **$95.00-$120.00**

Waffle iron, cast iron, with stand, Shapleigh #8, 20th C. **$28.00-$35.00**

Waffle iron, cast iron with stand, "National," American, 20th C. **$22.00-$30.00**

Waffle iron, cast iron with stand, hearts & diamonds waffling pattern, Abbott & Lawrence, 8½"L, late 19th C. **$45.00-$55.00**

Waffle iron, cast iron, with wonderful logos forming waffling pattern for 4 pie-wedge waffles, "Keen Kutter No. 8," E. C. Simmons Hardware, St. Louis, MO, 20th C. • **Reproduction alert.** — There are repros of this. Look closely, because it's a pretty good copy. **$120.00-$150.00**

Waffle iron, commercial use, cast iron, makes 12 waffles, I have no idea what this looks like, having only read about it in a trade journal of 1892, "The Hotel Mammoth", mfd by Stuart & Peterson Co., Philadelphia, advertised Sept. 24, 1892, *The Metal Worker*. • **Hypothetical entry.** — Value range may be way off, although as a rule large commercial wares don't get the same attention from collectors as regular family sized, or toy sized. **$50.00-$100.00**

Waffle iron, electric, aluminum base, chromed lid, shaped wood handles painted black, 3 Bakelite® or hard rubber feet, temperature dial in lid has mica covering, "Bersted Model 242", Bersted Mfg. Co., Chicago, IL, 12" overall diameter, 8¼" diameter grid, 1930s. **$40.00-$50.00**

Waffle iron, electric, chrome all over except plastic side handles on octagonal base & hinged lid, various controls on base, "Wafflemaster", Waters-Genter Co., Minneapolis, MN, 1931. **$45.00-$55.00**

Waffle iron, electric, nickeled cast metal, hinged mold raised off simple flat base, turned wooden spade handle on side, huge outlets in top & bottom plates for electric cord, General Electric Co., about 9" diameter, maybe a bit more, 1922-1923. **$45.00-$55.00**

"Gingerbread Waffles. — 2 cups flour, 1 tsp ginger, 1½ tsps cinnamon, ½ tsp salt, 1 tsp baking powder, ¾ tsp soda, 1 cup molasses, ⅓ cup butter, ½ cup sour milk or buttermilk, 1 egg, well beaten. — Mix the dry ingredients. Put molasses and butter in a saucepan, let come to boil and remove from heat at once. Cool, then add milk and egg. Add mixture to dry ingredients and beat until light and smooth. Bake immediately on an Electric Waffle Iron which is not quite so hot as for ordinary waffles, for molasses burns easily. Serve with honey or sweetened whipped cream." Recipe from "*Waffles*", Brooklyn Edison Co., Inc. Bureau of Home Economics, n.d. (c.1935 to 1940). Included in this little booklet was information on: Saturday morning junior misses' cooking classes; how to arrange a waffle party for your club; and even Lamp Shade Making Classes. In those days, they had to urge the surge. **$45.00-$55.00**

Waffle iron, electric, nickeled metal, fancy cutout pedestal base, side lifting handles, another handle for domed top plate of mold, "Universal," Landers, Frary & Clark, c.1920s. **$35.00-$45.00**

Waffle iron, electric, plated metal, pedestal base, Bakelite or other phenolic resin handles, Manning-Bowman, Meriden, CT, early 20th C. • **"A New Piece of China.** — The waffle plate is a great addition to the table ware. It may be had in plain china or handsomely decorated; the former costs one dollar, the latter from two to three dollars. The perforations in the top admit the escape of the steam so that the cakes may be kept warm yet free from moisture. the deep bowl gives ample space for the half-dozen circles of delicious brownness." The Housewife, NY, July 1891. This is a deep, widely flared bowl or dish, with perforated flat china top with knob handle. **$24.00-$30.00**

Waffle iron, for hearth, cast iron heart shaped head, forged reins & catch to hold ends together while baking, heart shaped waffles, no mark, American, 21½"L x 5¼"W, early 19th C. **$275.00-$350.00**

Waffle iron, for hearth, cast iron, hearts, diamonds, flowers, low frame, 2 part mold, long forged iron handles, Warnick & Leibrandt "8, 9", Philadelphia, PA, 3rd quarter 19th C. **$75.00-$100.00**

Waffle iron, for hearth, cast iron, hinged 2 part with long handle, one part has small ⅛" lip that holds other half more securely in place, head is lovely 12 scallop edged circle, which when waffles are broken apart reveal that they form 6 hearts, simple waffling pattern, American (?), 10⅝" diameter head, 20½"L overall, 19th C. **$75.00-$100.00**

Waffle iron, for hearth, cast iron with forged iron handle, the iron is star shaped, with small stars within the waffling grids. These small stars look punched; iron collector Joel Schiff believes they were swaged, that is, while the cast iron was hot (or after reheating), the waffling grid was hammered on a <u>swage block</u> with a small star design. I'm not sure the apparent accurately placed stars could have been achieved that way. American, prob. PA German, 6½" diameter waffle, 34¼"L overall, late 18th C. • Robacker May 1989 price: **$1550.00**

Waffle iron, for hearth, cast iron with long forged iron handle, bottom part is pan-like, flattish lid, nice arrow-like hinge details, unusual patterns — top & bottom both have 4 different waffling patterns, almost a sampler of waffle patterns, no marks, American (?), waffling iron is 6⅛" x 8¼" and bottom section is about 1¼" deep, overall length with handle is 27⅛", early 19th C. **$250.00-$325.00**

Waffle iron, for hearth, forged handles, cast rectangular iron, simple grid, American (?), 31½"L, early 19th C. **$185.00-$200.00**

Waffle iron, for hearth, forged iron handles, cast iron mold, beautiful decoration along top edge of one half of the mold's back depicts 2 Hessian soldiers on horses, & a pine tree, inside is a simple waffling grid, no maker's mark, American. Head is 6"W x 4¼"H, overall 26"L 18th C. • **German vocabulary** — <u>Waffeleisen</u>: waffle iron (but <u>waffel</u> also means wafer). **$550.00-$700.00**

Waffle iron, for hearth, forged iron long handles, cast iron plates with simple waffling criss-cross design, 23"L, 19th C. **$75.00-$100.00**

Waffle iron, for hearth, heart-shaped cast iron head or mold, long forged reins with very small knobs on ends, simple waffling pattern, no mark, American, 31"L x 7"W, 18th C. **$350.00-$500.00**

Waffle iron, for hearth, long forged iron reins & rectangular plates with diamond waffle grid, "scissor" or pivot point levered handles rather than type with hinged head. Marked "Chatham," (probably B & W Co., or B. W. Co.), Chatham, -?- (Chathams in GA, CT, IL, IA, KY, MA, PA, NY, NC, VA), 24½"L, early 19th C. • **"Rice Waffles —** Boil half a pint of rice and let it get cold, mix with it one-fourth pound butter and a little salt. Sift in it one and a half pints flour, beat five eggs separately, stir the yolks together with one quart milk, add whites beaten to a stiff froth, beat hard, and bake at once in waffle-irons." Mrs. S. C. Lee of Baltimore, in *Practical Housekeeping*, 1884. **$135.00-$150.00**

Waffle iron, for hearth, rectangular cast iron head has rows of small dimpled squares for grid (looks like aerial view of city streets, from 10 miles up), set at right angles to long wrought reins, one ending with knob, other with free-moving loop to work as catch, marked "B. W. Co.", "Chatham" (see another above), approx. 15"L overall, head 6" x 4", early 19th C. • "At auctions kitchen furniture is popularly supposed to go for a song ... these things are usually sold in lots and a person needing a waffle-iron and muffin rings may find himself in possession of coal skuttles and dish-pans." *Appleton's Home Books*, 3 volumes, NY, 1881, 1884. **$135.00-$160.00**

Waffle iron, for hearth, though modern, cast iron, with long handles, rectangle with diamond pattern waffling, Baccellieri Brothers Mfg. Co., Philadelphia, 20th C. **$20.00-$25.00**

Waffle iron, for hearth though modern, cast steel, rectangular, long handles, Ciunta Brothers, Philadelphia, 20th C. **$20.00-$25.00**

Waffle iron, hinged waffle part only, frame missing, cast iron, turned black painted short wood handles, grid of 4 simple parts, "Crescent Waffle #8", Fanner & Co., Cleveland, OH, late 19th C. **$25.00-$35.00**

Waffle iron, rectangular 2 part hinged mold that sets into 4 legged frame with side handle, makes 3 waffles with patterns of little squares, little diamonds & little hearts, maker not marked, American, 5"H x 8"L x 5"W, c.1870s. **$125.00-$140.00**

Waffle iron, sits over range eye, 2 big looped bail handles, 4 waffling patterns, hearts, stars, diamonds & rounds, hinge is gorgeous cast leaf, New England Butt Co., Providence, RI, 9¾" diameter, makes 7" diameter waffles, mid 19th C. **$175.00-$225.00**

Waffle iron, stove top, cast iron, bail handle on frame, coiled heat dissipating handle on hinged mold, Griswold #18, Erie, PA, pat'd May 18, 1920 & July 11, 1922. **$175.00-$200.00**

Wafflet molds — according to manufacturer the pieces in this set are "combination rosette and patty shell" molds, includes rod handle that screws into the 8 cast iron heads — club, heart, diamond or spade rosette or patty — also available in a scalloped edge cup or flower, "Century", mfd by U. S. Utilities, Chicago, IL, c.1933. **$20.00-$30.00**

Whatzit cutter or mold, stamped & pieced tin, partly corrugated deep sides, shaped like horseshoe & looks like a mold or some kind of cutter, "Acme Potato Implement Co.", Traverse City, MI, 1⅞" deep of which ¾" is corrugated, 5"L, TOC. **$8.00-$12.00**

IV-1.
Baking mold.

or Backform . Leering man's head — mythological character. Copper, 10 5/8" diameter, German, mid to late 19th C. Picture courtesy Waltraud Boltz Auctionhouse, Bayreuth, Germany.
$200.00-$400.00

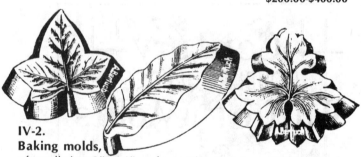

IV-2.
Baking molds,

of small size, 3" to 4" — for patties or tart cases. Stamped tin. See others farther on in chapter. From A. Bertuch catalog, Berlin, Germany, c. 1904.
$5.00-$15.00

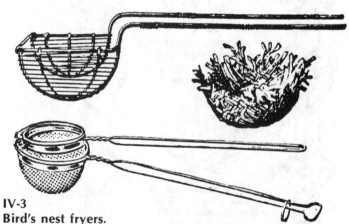

IV-3
Bird's nest fryers.

For molding cooked noodles or shredded raw potatoes into shape of bird's nest, and then deep frying them. Tinned iron wire, 2 nesting baskets with long handles. (T) four sizes, 3 1/2" to 6 1/2" diameter. S. Joseph Co., suppliers in NY, c. 1927 catalog. (B) Two sizes — outer bowl 3 1/4" or 4" diameter. Washburn Co., Androck line, 1936 catalog. NOTE: Length of this chapter means shorter captions. Catalog references will be full only in first citing. This is particularly important for jobbers' and wholesalers' catalogs, where the maker is unknown
$7.00-$25.00

IV-4.
Biscuit cutters.

All stamped or pieced tin except 2nd row left, which is "Mirro" aluminum. All are between 1 1/2" and 3" diameter. (L) to (R), row by row from top, #1 to #10. (1 & 2), 1 1/2" to 2 3/4" diameter, S. Joseph, c. 1927. (3) Savory Tinware, Newark, NJ, c. 1926-28. (4) Aluminum Goods Mfg. Co. Manitowoc, WI, 1927. (5) Geuder, Paeschke & Frey, Milwaukee, WI, 1925. (6) Sexton Stove & Mfg. Co., Baltimore, c. 1930s. (7) and (9) Fluted edges & plain circle, Matthai-Ingram, Baltimore, c. 1890 catalog, pat'd 10/15/1889. (8) Pick-Barth jobbers' catalog, 1929. (10) Deep, commercial one, 2" or 2 1/2" diameter. Pick-Barth.
$5.00-$15.00

IV-5.
Biscuit cutter & roll cutter.

(L) Tin, rolls out 4 biscuits with each full revolution of wheel, wire handle, 8 3/4"L, early 20th C. Author's collection. (R) Tin roll cutter with wooden handles, to cut rolled dough into long rolls. Makes 14 rolls each revolution. Roller is 11"L overall and makes rolls 5"L. From Mennonite boarding house, Olley Valley, PA, 19th C. Collection of Meryle Evans.
$18.00-$45.00

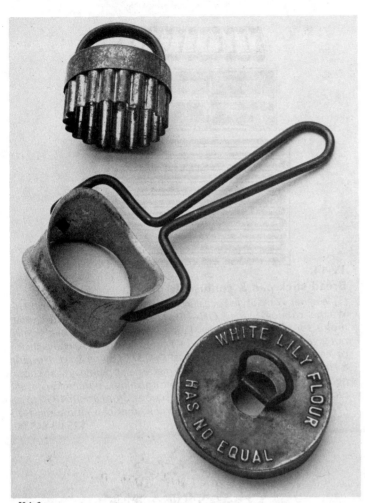

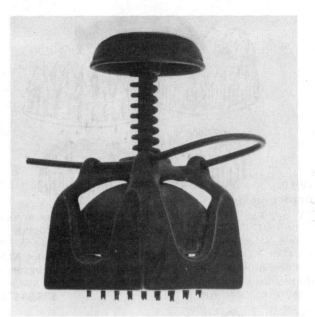

IV-7.
Biscuit or cracker stamp.
Mechanical, cast iron, spring steel with wooden block fixed with little 2-pronged prickers. Spring-load action, this knocks out pricked biscuits or crackers just short of 2" square. Stamp is 3 3/4". Pat'd December 13, no year marked, but patent Tuesday the 13th came in 1870, 1881, 1887, 1892 and 1898. I think probably 1880's. Collection of Meryle Evans. **$30.00-$50.00**

IV-6.
Biscuit cutters.
From top: (1) Scalloped pieced tin, heavy duty strap handle, 2" diameter, late 19th or early 20th C. (2) Rolling aluminum & wire one, advertises "Loella — the Finest Butter in America" and "Gold Seal Flour — For Best Results." Words embossed. 6 1/2" x 2 7/8"W, c. 1915. (3) Embossed stamped tin, wire handle. "White Lily Flour Has No Equal." 2 1/4" diameter, mfd. by Metal Specialty Mfg. Co., Chicago, c. 1910. **$8.00-$20.00**

Plain Border Mould.

Concave Border Mould.

Savarin Mould.

Corenflot Mould.

IV-8.
Border molds,
*Also called **ring molds**. For forming rings of one kind of food (such as rice or a salmon mousse) around another kind or color. These are all pieced tin. "Plain" came in rounds from 5 1/2" to 9 3/4" diameter, and in ovals from 6 1/4" to 10 1/4"L. "Concave" in similar but slightly smaller dimensions. "Savarin" came in rounds, from 6 1/2" to 11 3/4" diameter, and in ovals, 6 1/4" to 11 3/4"L. It was used for making a Savarin cake, soaked in spirits while still warm, but served cold with a cold sauce. Hexagonal "Corenflot" came 3 1/2" to 10" diameter. All from the Duparquet, Huot & Moneuse jobbers' catalog, c. 1904-1910.* **$15.00-$35.00**

IV-9.
"Breton" border mold.
Six lobes, offered in two sizes (not given, but probably about 7" and 10" diameter). One page of "moulds for entrees, sweets, savouries, &c.," Mrs. A.B. Marshall's Larger Cookery Book of Extra Recipes, London, c.1902. Mrs. Marshall, in addition to writing cookbooks, had a cooking school, and a large shop for culinary tools. Her books all have advertising pages in the back, all identified as coming from her "Book of Moulds" — a catalog. One mold dealer in NYC has seen a large book of moulds; cookbook dealers here and in England have turned up only one much smaller one. The search continues. For the mold: **$25.00-$45.00**

IV-10.
Border molds.

All "imported tin." Clockwise from top (L): (1) Came in rounds, 8" or 8 3/4" diameter, or ovals, 10 1/4" or 11". (2) Rounds in 7", 8" or 8 3/4" diameter, or ovals, 7", 8" or 22"L. (3) Oval only 5 1/2", 6 1/4" or 7"L. (4) Round only, 7", 8" or 8 3/4" diameter. Note in last one, especially, how one color of food can be pressed into the knurled knobs on top. All from Duparquet, Huot & Moneuse catalog, c. 1904-1910. **$35.00-$75.00**

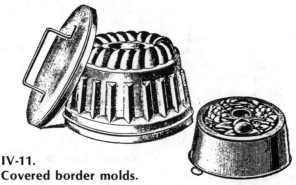

IV-11.
Covered border molds.

Metal not mentioned — could be stamped tin or stamped copper with tinned inside; probably copper. (T) 2-quart. (B) 3 1/2 quarts, fruit wreath design, lid not shown. S. Joseph Co., c. 1927. **$45.00-$75.00**

IV-12.
Bread dockers.

Used to mark bread before baking. (T) Tin & wood, in 6 sizes, from 2 1/2" to 5" diameter. (B) "We make our bread dockers of a very heavy grade of tin, so that the letters will positively stay in place. We make these dockers in any shape and of any number of letters. They cost according to the number of letters." Both from Jaburg Brothers catalog, NYC, 1908. **$15.00-$50.00**

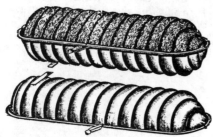

IV-13.
Bread pan.

"No. 140," in corrugated spiral shape "which gives the finished baked loaf a peculiar but appetizing appearance, the bread or cake may be sliced through the indentations." XX imported tin plate, 12 1/2" x 3 1/2" diameter. Silver & Co., Brooklyn, c. 1910. **$45.00-$65.00**

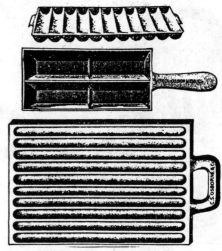

IV-14.
Bread stick pan & confusable molds.

(T) Wagner Ware Style E, cast iron, for 11 bread sticks. From 1915 Wagner catalog, Sidney, OH. (M) and (B) Both of these are solder molds for plumbers to use. Made of cast iron, and while size is not given they are about 7" to 14"L, and were used to make sticks of lead solder. Both apparently cast by C.S. Osborne & Co., Newark & Harrison, NJ. That foundry also made can openers, meat choppers, tools, oyster knives, kitchen furnishings, nutcrackers, nutpicks, sardine scissors and cheese scoops, from about 1890 to c. 1920. Found pictures in Alfred Revill's American Plumbing, NY: 1894. **$25.00-$45.00**

IV-15.
Bride and groom figures.

One of many fancy designs shown in a confectionery tools & supplies catalog. Materials not given, but probably silk flowers, molded & painted plaster or bisque figures & base. Dressed in cloth & paper clothing, 9"H x 4"W. From Joseph Middleby Jr., Inc., Boston, catalog, 1927. They also had designs with the couple in autos or blimps, also birds, bells, bowers and clasped hands. **$35.00-$75.00**

IV-16.
Kewpie groom & bride.
Pink celluloid or other plastic, paper & real cloth clothing. From Middleby catalog, 1927. **$30.00-$50.00**

IV-17.
Bundt cake mold.
Cast iron, spouted, 10" diameter, Wagner Ware, c. 1915. All bundt pans are similar; the earliest were imported from Europe in the 19th C. Value depends on size and quality of casting — and sometimes on the "name brand." **$45.00-$125.00**

IV-18.
Butter curler.
Nickel-plated, wooden handle, 8"L. From Ritzinger & Grasgreen catalog for traveling salesmen, c. 1906-07. **$5.00-$12.00**

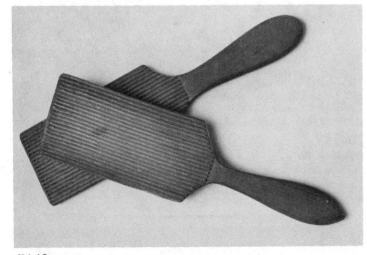

IV-19.
Butter hands.
*Also called **Scotch hands**. Corrugated French boxwood, or rock maple, commercially made, and this is not a matched pair. 9 1/2" x 2 1/2" W. Late 19th or early 20th C.* **$20.00-$30.00**

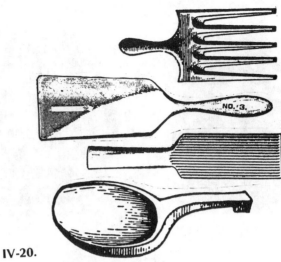

IV-20.
Wooden butter tools.
*(T) "Mrs. Bragg's" **butter fork**, maple, 12" x 5". Montgomery Ward catalog, 1895. (M) **Butter spades**, plain & grooved. The grooved one is the same as a butter hand. Joseph Breck agricultural supply catalog, 1905. (B) **Butter ladle** with hooked handle. Duparquet, Huot & Moneuse, c. 1904-1910.* **$10.00-$35.00**

IV-21.
Butter mold.
Paddle shape. Cow in elongated oval, rope border. Note pine tree, flower and the cow's bell. 11"L x 4 1/4"W. According to auction catalog, this was one of Harold Corbin's "most highly regarded" carved molds. Photo courtesy Litchfield Auction Gallery, Litchfield CT. Ex-Harold Corbin Collection, auctioned 1/1/1990. Price realized: **$750.00**

IV-22.
Butter molds,
or stamps. Both quite small. (L) Miniature with swan. 1 1/4" diameter. (R) Rooster with 2 bees or stars. 2" diameter. Photo courtesy Litchfield Auction Gallery, Litchfield CT. Ex-Harold Corbin Collection, auctioned 1/1/1990. Prices realized: **$275.00, $250.00**

IV-23.
Butter molds.

or **butter stamps.** (L) Pennsylvania style heart-shaped tulip with leaves. 2 3/4″ diameter. (M) Cow under tree branch, piecrust border. Note cow has deer-like 2-point antlers. 3 3/4″ diameter. (R) Civil War soldier's bust in profile, with beard and cap. Concentric ring border. 3 1/2″ diameter. Photo courtesy Litchfield Auction Gallery, Litchfield CT. Ex-Harold Corbin Collection, auctioned 1/1/1990. Prices realized seem odd to me as I would have valued the very unusual soldier stamp much higher:

$350.00, $355.00, $300.00

IV-24.
Butter mold.

Deeply carved ram with tree branch. Piecrust edge. 4 1/4″ diameter. Photo courtesy of Robert W. Skinner Inc., Auctioneers, Bolton, MA. **$350.00-$500.00**

IV-25.
Butter mold.

Cow with tree branch and tall grass. Piecrust border. Courtesy Joe & Teri Dziadul, Enfield, CT. **$175.00-$275.00**

IV-26.
Butter mold.
*Demilune stamp, cow & tree, cross-hatched border with wear.
Collection & photograph of James E. Trice, author of Butter Molds,
Collector Books, 1980.* **$275.00-$400.00**

IV-27.
Butter molds.
*(L) Finely-detailed anchor with line. Long handle. 3 1/4" diameter.
(M) The sheep or ram here (see IV-24) appears on a brass mold
rather than a carved wooden one. 4 1/4" diameter. (R) Cow under
tree, facing right and with raised or repouse design rather than
intaglio design of a carved mold. 3 1/2" diameter. Redware;
probably made by impressing damp clay with a carved wooden
mold. Butter printed with this one would have intaglio design.
Photo courtesy Litchfield Auction Gallery, Litchfield CT. Ex-Harold
Corbin Collection, auctioned 1/1/1990. Prices realized:*
$325.00, $775.00, $750.00

IV-28.
Butter mold.
*Leaping hare or rabbit, with log & grass. Very unusual. 19th C.
Collection & photograph James E. Trice.* **$300.00-$500.00**

IV-29.
Butter mold.
*Elongated oval with heart & flowers, thickly carved wood. 6"L.
Ephrata Cloister provenance, Pennsylvania. Photo courtesy
Litchfield Auction Gallery, Litchfield CT. Ex-Harold Corbin
Collection, auctioned 1/1/1990. Price realized:* **$700.00**

IV-30. Butter mold.

Sitting squirrel, with nut in paw. Unusual zigzag border. Courtesy Joe & Teri Dziadul **$250.00-$350.00**

IV-31.
Butter mold.

Very unusual big-footed baby armadillo or tortoise on demilune stamp. Notched border. Fancy carved handle seems out of sync with mold. 6 1/4"L, age hard to judge because style is old, but subject is perhaps unique. Courtesy Bonnie Myers, B & J's Unclaimed Treasures, Dillsburg, PA. **$150.00-$300.00**

IV-32.
Butter mold.

Spotted deer with corn plant curved over head — which he may have been eating! Piecrust border, 4" diameter. American, 19th C. Picture courtesy of Robert W. Skinner Inc., Auctioneers, Bolton, MA. **$275.00-$350.00**

IV-33. Butter mold.

Demilune, carved wood with pineapple & leaves. Rope border on curve only, meaning it could be used to create a round print, without a line across the center, which would mark off the half-pound division. 7"W. American, 19thC. **$300.00-$450.00**

IV-34. Butter mold.

Demilune, with abstract flower (tulip?) and curved leaves. 4"H x 7 1/4"W. Picture courtesy of Robert W. Skinner Inc., Auctioneers. Bolton, MA. **$250.00-$375.00**

IV-35. Butter mold.

Carved eagle with dairyman's name "A.F. Thompson, New York." Star above eagle's head matches star in piecrust border, 4 1/2" diameter, American, 19th C. This was cracked and has repair of some age. Picture courtesy of Robert W. Skinner Inc., Auctioneers, Bolton, MA. **$350.00-$500.00**

IV-36.
Butter mold.
Eagle stamps are among the most sought-after designs. This eagle, with odd baby-bird lip-like beak, appears to be holding clutch of arrows. No stars. Collection and photograph of James E. Trice.
$275.00-$400.00

IV-37.
Butter molds.
All eagle motif, finely carved. One, 3-5/8" diameter, is mounted on old paddle board. One with shield body is 4-3/4" diameter; other is 3-3/4". 19th C. Picture courtesy Christie, Manson & Woods International Inc., NYC. All from 1980 Brooke sale.
$300.00-$500.00

IV-38.
Butter molds.
All eagle designs, with handles. (L) Tulip-like eagle with graceful leaf-like wings, crosshatched body, narrow piecrust border, a single star. 4-1/4" diameter. (M) Eagle facing left, with shield body, long neck, flanked by laurel (?) leaves. Concentric ring border, 5" diameter. (R) Eagle & large 8-pt star, leaves. 3-3/4" diameter. Photo courtesy Litchfield Auction Gallery, Litchfield, CT. Ex-Harold Corbin Collection, auctioned 1/1/90. Prices realized.
$350.00, $225.00, $300.00

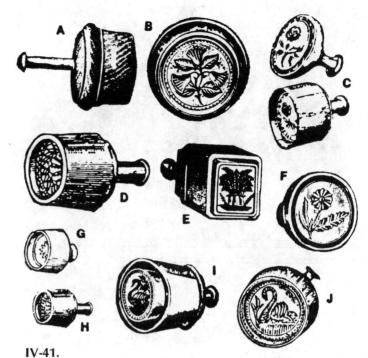

IV-39.
Butter molds.
Acorn motifs. Courtesy James E. Trice.   **$200.00-$300.00**

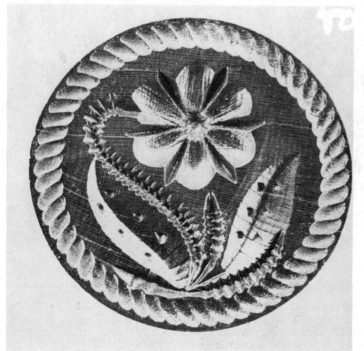

IV-40.
Butter mold.
Flower with curious curved stem, rope border. Courtesy James E. Trice.   **$150.00-$200.00**

IV-41.
Butter molds.
All machine-carved wood. (A&B) Two views of what seller called individual "butter prints," in "Hollywood" pattern. Three sizes, for 1/2 oz., 3/4 oz. and 1 oz. pats. (C) Two molds "by which butter may be put up in pound or half-pound cakes for the market. They are made of soft wood, as white-ash or soft maple, and are generally kept for sale at all country stores where willow-ware is sold. The manner of using them is as follows: when the butter is ready for making up, it is weighed out into the proper quantities, and each piece is worked in the butter-dish with the ladle into flat round cakes. These cakes are either pressed with the mold shown in the upper picture, or are made to go into the cup of the lower mold. Inside the cup is a mold with a handle which works through a hole in the upper part of the cup. The cup is inverted onto the table, and when this handle is pressed down it forces the mold on to the butter, which is squeezed into a very neat ornamental cake. By pushing down on the handle and lifting the cup, the cake is pushed out of the mold. This makes a very favorite mode of putting up fine butter for market, and is also well adapted for preparing butter for the table in houses where neatness of appearance is studied. The molds when in use should be kept wetted in cold water to prevent the butter from sticking." American Agriculturist, 5/1872. (D) Flower pattern in four sizes: 1 oz., 3 oz., 1/2 lb. and 1 lb. From Duparquet, Huot & Moneuse catalog, c. 1904-1910. (E) Wheat sheaf in square design, Valentine Clad & Sons, Philadelphia, c. 1890-1900. (F) 3" to 4" stamps, Joseph Breck catalog, 1905. (G) "Butter pat in Case. — This gives the butter a handsome form and print at the same time." American Home Cook Book, 1854. (H) Same as (D). (I) Swan in case, 1 oz. and 2 oz. Jaburg Brothers, 1908. (J) Swan in 1/2 oz., 3/4 oz., 1 oz., 2 oz. sizes. Ritzinger, Grasgreen, c. 1906-07. **$40.00-$125.00**

IV-42.
Butter mold.
Rayed flower with dandelion-like leaves. Courtesy James E. Trice.
$150.00-$200.00

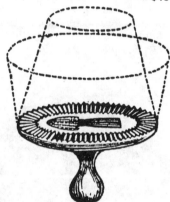

IV-43.
Butter mold "hand stamp."

" 'Fancy Butter' packages are, of course, of many forms, as each maker wishes his butter to be both attractive and unique. All '**print-butter**' or butter in small packages marked with the name of the maker, is properly regarded as 'fancy,' whether it bring a higher price than other good butter or not. Still, it ought to be good enough to sell higher than good **tub or firkin butter.** Philadelphia has long been famous for its excellent print-butter. This is generally put up upon the common hand stamps in pound 'pats,' which may have either of the two forms represented by the dotted lines. Simple devices, such as a sheaf of wheat, roses, pineapples, acorns, and oak leaves and nondescript leaves are common. Monograms or single letters are not rare, with occasionally a more elaborate device. These 'pats,' for they are patted into form upon the stamps*, are marketed in what are known as Philadelphia tubs, which are oval tubs of cedar, lined with tin, and having ice chambers in each end, having a nearly rectangular space in the center, in which the butter is packed upon shelves 2-1/4" to 3" apart. A good deal of butter is now made in rectangular, square or brick-shaped prints, and shipped in these Philadelphia tubs, or in square packages, with provision of ice in hot weather." It goes on to extol round butter boxes that are an "ingenious application of the new kind of veneering, but into a continuous ribbon round and round the log" and then sewing the ribbons of wood at seam. *American Agriculturist,* 1/1880. *Patted with a butter spade or paddle.

IV-44.
Butter molds,
*so-called **lollipop** style. Simple geometric carvings from single. pieces of wood. Probably Pennsylvania German, early 19th C. Photograph & collection of James E. Trice.* **$300.00-$500.00**

IV-45.
Butter stamp.

Hand carved from one piece, with unusual handle. Zinnia-like flower with leaves. 5-1/4" x 4-3/8" diameter. 19th C. Courtesy Joe & Teri Dziadul. **$400.00-$600.00**

IV-46.
Butter mold.

"In reply to readers who say they can not procure the butter molds which we described in a former issue, we give directions for making them at home. The difficulty lies in getting the stamp made. Anyone who can work a foot lathe, can turn the mold and the plain stamp with the handle, but the device which ornaments the stamp troubles them. To make this, take a piece of wood free from grain — a piece of soft maple or birch-root is very good — and have it turned or dressed the proper size, and a smooth face made on it. Then either draw on the face, the wrong way, or cut out letters from a printed bill or newspaper, and paste them on to the face of the mold, the wrong way and make a border to suit the fancy, in the same manner. Then take a small, sharp gouge, like the one shown, not larger than a quarter of an inch in diameter, and smoothly cut away the wood beneath the letters, making them deep enough to show well when printed on the butter. About a quarter of an inch would be right. The depression should be neatly smoothed out, so as to make a neat, smooth print. A pretty border for the mold is a quantity of clover leaves; they may be pasted on, and the wood then cut out as before, or any other leaves would answer." American Agriculturist, 12/1872.

IV-47.
Butter stamp.

Anchor & line with some odd berry-like motifs. Minor cracks and handle missing, 3-3/8" diameter. American 19th C. This was estimated to sell from $350.00 to $450.00 at a 1980 auction, but it realized only $75.00, despite very good carving. Picture courtesy of Robert W. Skinner Inc., Auctioneers, Bolton, MA. I agree with a higher estimate of value. **$75.00-$350.00**

IV-48.
Butter stamp.

This was described by the auction house as being a "highly stylized eagle." I feel the resemblance to an anchor is much greater. 3-1/2" diameter, American, 19th C. Estimated to sell between $300.00 and $400.00, but didn't sell some 10 years ago. Picture courtesy Robert W. Skinner Inc., Auctioneers, Bolton, MA. **$250.00-$400.00**

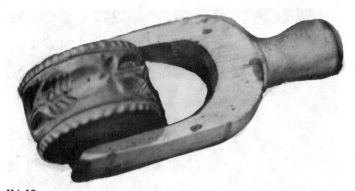

IV-49.
Rolling butter printer.
Simple botanical motif & border. 5 1/2"L. Courtesy R.C. Bowen. See also IV-340 for a cookie roller which is quite similar — perhaps interchangeable. **$85.00-$150.00**

IV-50.
Butter mold.
Carved wood in four parts, with holding pegs. Simple star motif. Maker's (?) mark are initials "H.Y." Block of butter would be 3 3/8" x 2" x 2 3/4". Collection of Meryle Evans. **$125.00-$200.00**

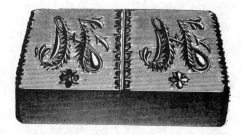

IV-51.
Butter stamp.
"There is rivalry amongst fancy butter makers to excel, not only in quality, but also to offer their product in the most acceptable form, and in attractive, convenient packages. The favorite method of putting up butter for immediate sale, is that of pound cakes, ornamented with a stamp, and marked in the center, so that each can be divided into half pounds for use on the table. For this, moulds and stamps are used. This illustration shows a stamp bearing the maker's initials. Being square, the prints may be packed upon the shelves in any butter-carrier without loss of space." American Agriculturist, 9/1878.

IV-52.
Butter molds.
Box molds of more mechanical type than the one in IV-50. Note how closely the carving and styles resemble springerle boards. Perhaps they were interchangeable. (T) Carved wood "Blanchard" butter mold, by maker of churns. Brass latches. Came in three sizes: 1/2 lb., marked to make two 1/4 lb. prints; 1 lb., for four prints; and 2 lb., for eight prints. This company also sold a cheaper version, which they claimed was the "same pattern as Blanchard." (B) This box did not come apart. It came in 11 sizes, making 3, 4, 6, 12, 16 and 24 "cakes," from 1 1/4" x 1 1/3" (one ounce cakes) up to 3 1/2" x 3 1/3" (8 oz. cakes). From Breck catalog, 1905. **$45.00-$100.00**

IV-53.
Butter mold & butter stamps.
A hinged box mold, that comes apart completely. Makes a 4 or 5-lb. brick, marked off by grooves made by stamps. The technique differs from others, and is as follows: "A pound of butter is weighed and packed into the end of the mold by means of the stamps, one of which presses the side, and the other the top, the latter having the packer's initials or trade-mark. Then another pound is weighed and packed in the same manner, and so on. In the packing, grooves are left in the butter, marking the divisions between the pounds, by which the retailer may cut it up into pieces of exact weight, each piece having been weighed previously." The finished cake with divisions at (R). American Agriculturist, 5/1876.

IV-54.
Butter mold.
After the butter is worked to removed excess moisture, it is packed into a mold. The one shown here is "made of lignum vitae (an extremely hard wood), in the manner of a pair of bullet-molds. Each half being filled with the finished butter, the handles are forcibly squeezed together, and the butter is compressed firmly into a solid roll (note curved interior), which drops from the mold when it is opened. The mold is kept wetted with cold water during the operation." These rolls, which were then wrapped individually in muslin, were made to fit vertically into a large trunk-like butter box which held 30 rolls. American Agriculturist, 3/1876. **$40.00-$55.00**

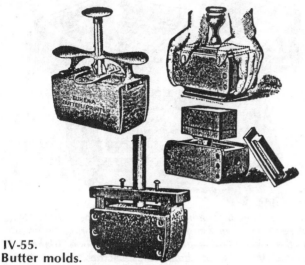

IV-55.
Butter molds.

All are of "close-grained hard wood," and all have a "hand carved sheaf of wheat" printing block. Upper (L) "Eureka," with a self-gauging attachment. Prints pounds or half-pounds, by adjusting a collar on the upright standard, which is kept in place by a clamp and screw. Nickel-plated brass. (R) "Philadelphia," made of cherry, screwed together with brass screws. Block has wooden stem, and mold's top is fitted with hardwood moveable cap. Pound or 1/2-pound sizes. Lower (L) "Economy" self-adjuster. Brass screws. "Cut the butter from the churn batch on the table, press the hopper full, cut surplus off smoothly with handle paddle, press block from printer by pressure on the wood stem of block, extending through the printer head block." Cherry-Bassett Co., Baltimore dairy supplier, 1921. **$55.00-$85.00**

IV-56.
Cake mold,

or **cake board.** *Square, two-sided. One side has three men in hats, two in sort of pugilist pose, or perhaps they're fighting to gain control of a handgun, while a third looks on. Lots of stars in a circle. Verso has a bird and a dog. 8 1/2" square. Photograph courtesy Litchfield Auction Gallery, Litchfield, CT. Ex-Harold Corbin Collection, auctioned 1/1/1990. Price realized:* **$850.00**

IV-57.
Cake board.

Elliptical lozenge shape on oblong board, with female equestrienne in center floral circle, flanked by small ellipses with Colonial man (L) and American Indian (R). Cornucopias below. John Conger's mark. Auctioned by Clarence Pico, Litchfield Auction Gallery, Litchfield CT, 3/25/1990. American, 19th C. **$2500.00-$3500.00**

IV-58.
Whatzit butter worker? cracker crumber?
It seems much too large for a coggling tool used by a potter to make a corrugated design on damp clay. Hand-carved wood with roller, 17 3/4"L; roller 3 1/2" diameter; paddle-handle is 1 3/4" thick. Courtesy Alice Solomon, Schnectady, NY.

IV-59.
Cake board.
"New Year Cake Board," of carved wood, with round medallion filled with horse & rider, flowers, stars and deep decorative border. Came in two sizes, "large" for a one-pound print, and "small" for a half-pound print. Also offered, though not depicted, were one-pound size metal cake boards. Design & style is early to mid-19th C, but this picture is from Jaburg Brothers catalog of 1908.
$100.00-$300.00

Photo © 1989 Sotheby's, Inc.

IV-60.
Cake board.
Mahogany oblong board, design within ellipse. Many symbolic and patriotic motifs, including American Indian, holding a staff with the American flag, topped with the Phrygian "liberty" cap, borne in cornucopia-shaped chariot, drawn by horse toward the figure of Columbia, wearing flowing dress and holding a shield and laurel wreath aloft. The shield, with stars & stripes, is inscribed "America." Above is the American eagle with an olive branch in one talon and with a pair of balance scales in its beak, the left one bearing small kegs or barrels, and the right one with a plow, rake and pitchfork. Large cornucopia at left, many grapes, leaves, stars fill background. 15 1/2"H x 27 1/2"L. Typical in execution and motif, though more elaborate than others known, of John Conger's work. Unsigned. Photo courtesy of Sotheby's, NYC. Auctioned 6/23/1988. Value range below is the catalog estimate; realized price probably lower. **$8,000.00-$10,000.00**

IV-61.
Cake board.

Mahogany, elliptical carving typical of Conger's boards. Central round medallion has footed urn or fountain with 2 doves and many flowers. Flanking figures are a Colonial man (L) and milkmaid-type woman in knee-length dress and apron (R). Typical cornucopias below, roses above. 15"H x 26"L. Used for making "New Year's Cakes." Signed "J. Congers" twice. New York City, 19th C. Photo courtesy Litchfield Auction Gallery, Litchfield, CT. EX-Harold Corbin Collection, 1/1/1990. Price realized: **$2950.00**

IV-62.
Cake boards and sugar mold.

Carved wood. (L) In vertical ellipse is Indian bearing bow in one hand and feathered staff in other. 8"H x 5 1/4". (M) Maple sugar mold, for two cakes, each bearing large heart and 2 stars. 10 1/2"H x 4"W. (R) Two sided board, with pistol on one side, tobacco pipe on other. 8 1/2" x 4". American, late 19th C. Photographer courtesy Litchfield Auction Gallery, Litchfield, CT. Ex-Harold Corbin Collection, auctioned 1/1/1990. Prices realized: **$375.00 and $350.00 and $300.00**

IV-63.
Cake board.

Square with round medallion decorated with an American eagle, shield body with stripes & stars, clutching arrows, surrounded by wreaths of leaves. 10 1/4"H x 11". Photograph courtesy Litchfield Auction Gallery, Litchfield, CT. Ex-Harold Corbin Collection, auctioned 1/1/1990. Price realized: **$525.00**

IV-65.
Cake board,

or cookie mold. Carved wood, great detail of sporty gent in plaid or checkered suit, bearing a pig on his head. In some ways he resembles a Scotsman. 19-1/2" x 7-7/8"W. Late 19th C. Collection of Mary Mac Franklin. **$150.00-$350.00**

IV-64.
Cake board.

"Ancient Carving. It represents the letters A, H, C (backwards) in the centre, surrounded by this legend, viz. 'An harte that is wyse wyll obstine from sinnes and increas in the workes of God.' As this legend reads backward, and all the carving is incuse, it was evidently intended to give impression to something; I imagine pastry." William Hone's The Every-day Book. Vol. II, n.d. (1827 or 1828). Hone also reproduces part of a letter from the Lord Chancellor Thurlow dated 1778, from Bath, England, regarding this mold, which he had received from a farmer from Norfolk.

IV-66.
Cake board.
Carved wood with wormholes, two-sided (see other side under springerle molds, IV-332.) Heart with flowers growing from small heart. Pennsylvania German or European. 9 1/4"H x 6 1/4"W. Signed "F.G." Ex-Keillor Collection.   **$500.00-$1000.00**

IV-67.
Candy curling machine.
For making candies (probably hard?) "known to the trade as 'Opera Curls.'" Thomas Mills & Bro., Philadelphia, 1930 catalog.
$55.00-$75.00

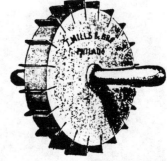

IV-68.
Candy cutters.
(L) "Circular batch cutter...especially useful in handling caramel batches." Steel knife revolves between 2 wooden handles. (R) Handy chip cutter...used for cutting chips (hard boiled candy pulled thin as paper) made in a variety of colors and highly flavored. This will cut them into uniform pieces about 1 1/2" square, while at the same time permitting them to keep flat and glossy." Two sizes: 8" block, 1 1/2'W, and a 12" block with set-in steel blades 2"W. Mills, 1927.   **$15.00-$25.00**

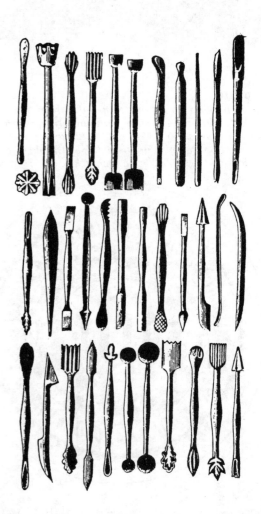

IV-69.
Candy & confectionery-modeling tools.
Carved boxwood with great detail. About 4-1/2"L. Especially good for marzipan candies and modeling leaves and flowers for cake decorating. A full set included 34 tools. Bertuch catalog, Berlin, c.1904. Value range given is for a small mixed collection of, say, 10 tools.   **$30.00-$50.00**

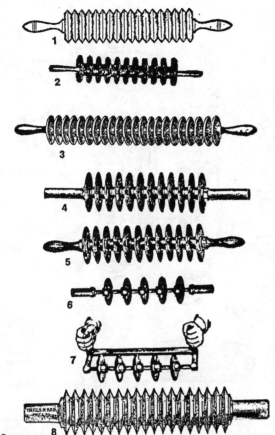

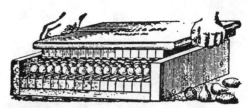

IV-72.
"Ball or Gooseberry cutter,"

being a hand-operated machine for cutting and rolling a "perfect round Ball or Gooseberry." Wood, with top part tracking along sides of lower part, rolling out candy balls. Stock sizes to make 5/8", 11/16", 3/4", 15/16", 1-1/8" and 1-1/4" balls. They also made them to order for larger balls, and for forming almond paste (marzipan). Mills, 1927, but made for many years before that. Value would depend on patina and general appeal of appearance. Many people pay premiums for good lookin' wood. **$15.00-$50.00**

IV-70.
Candy marker & cutters.

Most are metal, and therefore not confused with rolling pins. From top: (1) Turned wood corrugated pin, called a "marker." 15"L x 4" diameter, marking off 3/4" divisions. Sethness Candy Maker, 1925. (2) Caramel cutter, steel blades or "knives." Could be had "adjustable," meaning you could get one with 8, 12 or 15 knives, and set them as close as desired; or "stationary," meaning with fixed blades, from 1/2" to 1" apart in 1/8" increments. Duparquet. Huot & Moneuse, c. 1904-1910. (3) Bonbonschneidewalze (candy cutting roller) with tempered steel blades 3-1/4" diameter. You could order with 12, 18, 26 or 35 blades. (also, cheaper, one with 26 tinned iron fixed blades.) Catalog of A. Bertuch, Berlin, c. 1904. (4) Brass revolving handles, 12 blades with spacers, for cutting caramels and other candies. Also could be had with 6" diameter blades. Mills, 1927. (5) Adjustable steel blades, 4" diameter, with spacer rings. Mills. (6) and (7) Movable steel cutters, for marking or cutting lengths of horehound sticks, butterscotch, peanut cakes or bars, taffies, etc. Five 4" diameter knives, with provision for adding blades. (7) has iron frame and is presumably for added weight bearing. (8) Horehound stick cutter with brass revolving handles & steel blades. "Designed to meet the demand for a cutter which will cut horehound and peanut sticks and add the beveled side and rounded top to the goods." 18"L plus handles. Last three all Mills, 1927. **$15.00-$35.00**

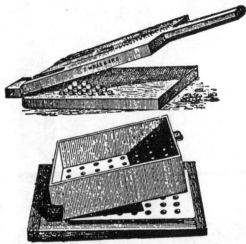

IV-73.
Candy press & dropper.

(T) Mint cake press, for "pressing balls into kisses." Wood lined with tinned iron. 24"L x 12"W. (B) Chocolate wafer dropper, wood, 10"x14". Wood with hinged upper box. Both T. Mills & Bro., 1920s, but probably made much earlier. **$15.00-$50.00**

IV-71.
Candy & confectionery-modeling tool.

Carved boxwood, double-ended, 4 1/2"L. Bertuch, c.1904. **$5.00-$8.00**

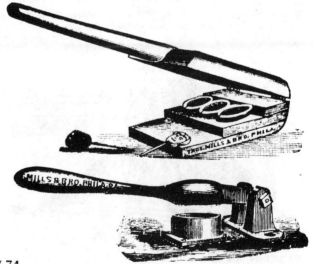

IV-74.
Confectioners' presses.

(T) Sucker press, for making lollipops. Seven styles, including making 3 "faces on a stick," a lemon slice, an oval, and a heart. Sizes of suckers varied from about 1-1/2" diameter to 2-3/8". (B) Pop Corn Ball hand press, to make popcorn & caramel balls from 2" up to 4" diameter. Also had one for making egg shaped balls. Both these appear to be plated cast iron with wood. Mills, 1927. **$15.00-$50.00**

IV-75.
Fruit-drop frame.
Cranked machine with patterned rollers, for imprinting boiled sugar fruit-drop candies. Fully adjustable, and with scores of patterns, all interchangeable. You had to buy the frame before you could order the rollers. Rollers were from about 3-5/8"L up to 6"L, and all 2" diameter. Mills, 1927 catalog, but made earlier. Good condition, with interesting rollers would increase collectible value. **$50.00-$125.00 +**

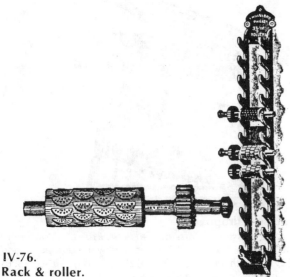

IV-76.
Rack & roller.
A cast iron wall rack to hold pairs of rollers. Could be had to suit longer rollers and from 3 to 6 pairs. A cast bronze roller with steel shaft, 5"L x 2" diameter, to make watermelon slice-shaped boiled sugar candies. Mills, 1927. **$50.00-$125.00**

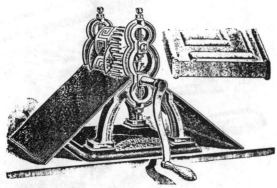

IV-77.
Stick candy machine.
"Five-Cent Stick" size, and adjustable for different candy thicknesses. See example of what the candy looked like. Cast iron with cast bronze rollers. This one has a hand crank, but others could be had hooked up to an electric motor. Mills, 1927.
$50.00-$125.00

IV-78.
Patterns for fruit-drop rollers.
Shown is a selection from many pages of patterns in Thomas Mills' 1927 catalog. The detail is probably greater than what came out embossed on the candy itself. They were all identified by name, and by how many of the fruit-drops it would take to make a pound of candy. These probably weren't even big enough to be penny candies. Of particular interest to me are the heart and hand (200 to the pound), the bowlegged clog dancer (there were 146 of these to the pound), the face drop above the fish at left, the Boy Scout, and the delightful Yellow Kid (big ears & nightgown), the first beloved comic strip character, originated by Richard Outcault about 1896.

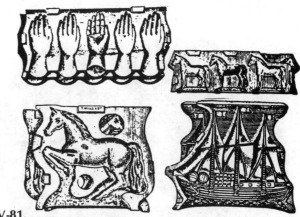

IV-81.
Clear toy candy molds.
Hinged metal, making from 3 to 6 candies in the small molds, and singles in the larger ones. Sizes not given, but the small candies come out about 1"H; the larger ones up to about 3"H, or even bigger. The large ones were not made to be eaten, and were more likely to be saved (if possible) as holiday ornaments for a tree or table centerpiece (or shop window). Mills, 1927, but most of these are also found in late 19th C Mills' catalogs. **$20.00-$40.00**

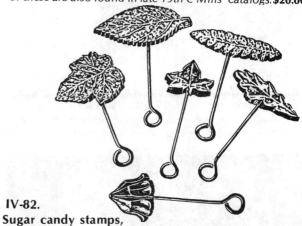

IV-79.
Patterns of sugar toys,
that could be made by the electric-powered "Universal" **sugar toy machine,** *used to make transparent, brightly-colored, hard sucking candies, or decorations. "The animals turned out in this machine stand erect as if made in moulds, and run 65 to the pound." The machine was not like the stick candy one. The candy actually passed between two revolving wheels, both of which had the pattern cut into its smooth face. The candy toys went through 'standing up', so to speak, making their bottoms flat and smooth. Actual size of the candies ranges from 1 1/4" to 1 1/2"H. If a hoard of these candies, perfectly preserved, were to be found — in an iceberg, say — they would be collectible, and could probably be freeze-dried for permanent preservation. Mills, 1927 (but patterns found in late 19th C Mills' catalogs also).*

IV-82.
Sugar candy stamps,
for making leaves & flowers. Embossed cast lead wire handles with loop for hanging. Bottom one, looking like fairy parasol, is a flower mold, the deepest one. Several companies made them, main differences are in the handles. These from A. Bertuch, Berlin, Germany, c. 1904. **$5.00-$12.00**

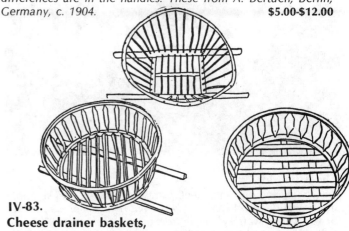

IV-80.
Molded nougat,
meant to resemble a small footed bulge pot full of potatoes. A pretty little confection from Urbain-Dubois' La Patisserie D'Aujourd'hui, *Paris, c. 1860s-70s. Nougats are a sugar paste candy mixed with chopped fruits or nuts (in this case, almonds.)*

IV-83.
Cheese drainer baskets,
one type of cheese mold. These "Windsor"-style baskets were lined with cheescloth and the wet cheese put in. The basket was then set over a container to catch the whey. Some had built in "ladders", others needed a separate ladder or pair of sticks. When completely drained, the cheese was formed into round shapes. (T) Drawn from unidentified ad in Maine Antique Digest, *ash & hickory, 10" deep x about 23" diameter. (L) Drawn from ad of Evelyn Rue in* M.A.D., *1981. (R) Drawn from ad of Jerard Paul Jordan in* M.A.D., *1982. Value range mine.* **$375.00-$700.00**

IV-84.
Cheese mold.
*Very fine pierced tin heart-shaped drainer-mold. With hanging ring.
About 12" H. American, c. 1850s-70s. For making tsierkase,
or "pressed egg" cheese, not so-called cottage cheese (smearkase).
Photograph courtesy Gail Lettick, Pantry & Hearth, NYC.*

IV-86.
Cheese molds.
*Also called **cheese strainers**. Pierced tin. (L) Diamond shape, with
4 small feet, wire hanging loop. 3 3/8"H x 7 7/8" x 5 1/4". (R) Slanted
sides, strap handles, 4 round feet, wire hanging loop. 5"H x 7-1/8"
square at top. Ex-collection of Earl F. & Ada F. Robacker, auctioned by T. Glenn Horst, Horst Auctions, Farmersville, PA,
6/23-24/1989. Prices realized:* **$100.00 & $750.00**

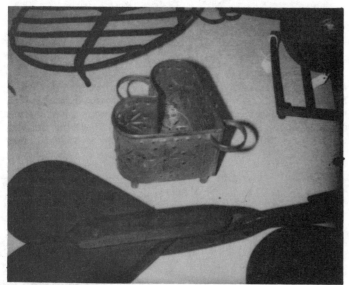

IV-85.
Cheese mold.
*Pieced tin heart on 3 small feet, 2 strap handles, pierced in simple
star-flower design. 4-1/2" x 5-1/4". Pennsylvania German, 19thC.
Heart-shaped waffle iron in foreground went for $525. Ex-
collection of Earl F. & Ada F. Robacker, auctioned by T. Glenn
Horst, Horst Auctions, Farmersville, PA, 6/23-24/1989. Price
realized for mold:* **$775.00**

IV-87.
Cheese mold.
*Pierced tin, round, with 6-point star and concentric rings. Wide
strap handles. Slightly domed lid with strap handle. 4-1/4"H x
9-3/8" diameter at top. Ex-collection of Earl F. & Ada F. Robacker,
auctioned by T. Glenn Horst, Horst Auctions, Farmersville, PA,
6/23-24/1989. Price realized:* **$975.00**

IV-88.
Cheese mold.

Very unusual shape — a cloverleaf overlying a triangle. Drawn from picture in enlightening article by Mildred T. Bohne, "Tin Cheese Strainers," in (Ohio) Antique Review, 2/1985. Bohne calls these strainers a "specialized form of colander," which explains them very well. Value probably **$500.00-$800.00**

IV-91.
Chocolate mold.

Heavy tin in protective frame. Hinged, marked #34882. Weygandt Co., NYC, but made in Germany. They are just 3 monkeys — not hear no evil, see no evil, speak no evil, or eat no evil. Collection of Meryle Evans. **$50.00-$75.00**

IV-89.
Cheese mold.

Handmade tin, perforated on bottom and lower sides of cylinder. Three short conical feet. Has round tin "foller" or presser, shown at left. Both have loop handles. 7-1/8"H with 1-1/4"H legs; 6-3/8" diameter. Pennsylvania, late 19th C. Courtesy Jean Hatt, Hatt's Hutt, Denver, PA. **$150.00-$225.00**

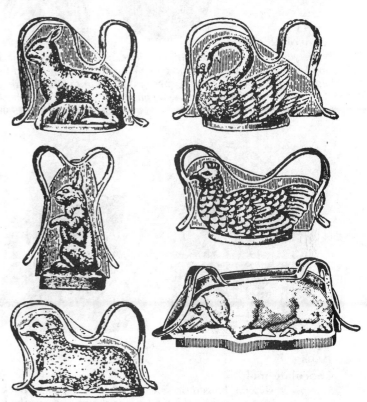

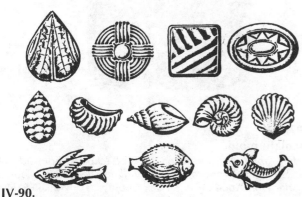

IV-90.
Chocolate or marzipan molds.

Also meant for fondants. Stamped tin. Upper ones are the "large" size, which came mounted "in plaques containing 6 moulds, all of one pattern" or with 12 the same. Size probably about 1" or 1-1/4". Lower set is "small" size, mounted same way. Probably about 3/4" to 1". From Mrs. A. B. Marshall's Larger Cookery Book, *London, c.1902. Note flying fish — it and the dolphin, lower right, would probably bring the most.* **$4.00-$10.00**

IV-92.
Chocolate molds,

"or pudding molds. Can also be used for cheese." Imported tin, with ribbony spring clips. Rabbit top (L) made in 5 sizes, from 1/8 pint to 2 pts. Lamb at bottom (L) made in 1-1/2 pint and 4-1/2 pt. sizes. Swan made only in 3 pint size. Worst and most unappetizing is the unhappy dead pig at bottom right. How anyone could think the agonized grimace on the intelligent face of an animal more easily trained than a dog would be fun to eat beats me. All from S. Joseph Co. catalog, c.1927. **$40.00-$150.00**

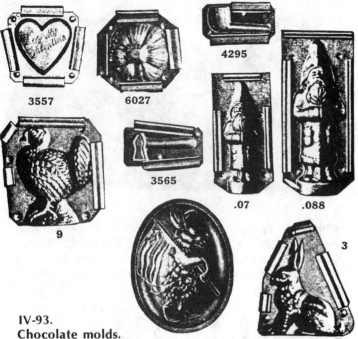

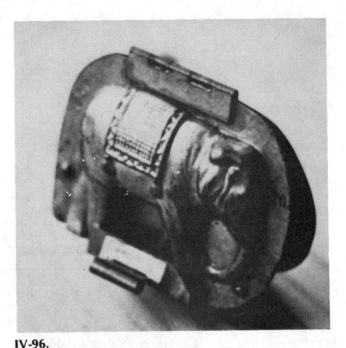

IV-93.
Chocolate molds.
Variety of 2-part stamped tin molds with clips, including two standing Santas and a standing turkey. The rabbit with flag could be used to celebrate a patriotic Easter I guess. All from Mills' catalog, 1927. I left numbers on in case you find molds stamped with those numbers. **$20.00-$45.00**

IV-96.
Chocolate mold.
Elephant in hinged mold. Stamped #8306 and also #20. Anton Reiche, Dresden. About 4-3/4"H. Collection of Margaret Upchurch & Kyle Goad.

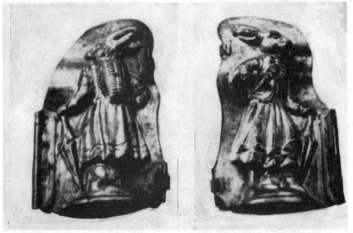

IV-94.
Chocolate mold.
Stamped heavy tin, hinged on side, with 2 clips opposite. Back and front views of female rabbit, ready for church and a potluck afterwards, with parasol, wicker basket on back which she supports with an arm behind her back. Apron has flipped hem. 7-1/4"H. Beautifully detailed. Marked #14037 and #2 down by bottom clip. Anton Reich. Collection of Margaret Upchurch & Kyle Goad.

IV-97.
Chocolate mold.
Standing rabbit with apron and wicker backpack. Both sides the same. Hinged with one large clip. Well-detailed, 20"H. Courtesy of dealer Don Appelquist, Sussex County, NJ. **$125.00-$160.00**

IV-95.
Chocolate mold.
Stamped tin, 2 part, makes chocolate blacksmith's tool. 5"L, no mark, late 19th or early 20th C. **$20.00-$35.00**

219

IV-98.
Chocolate mold.

Man holding small ginger beer bottle; probably a Dutchman, because he's wearing a sailor's cap, with a leather bag under his long coat, and has a typical Van Dyke (also spelled Van Dyck) beard and a deep Dutch collar. His right hand is extended but holds nothing; maybe when they finished the chocolate they stuck something in his hand? 9-3/8"H. Marked #84, and partial name "—zerhey & Co., Rotterdam." Collection of Margaret Upchurch, Kyle Goad & Amanda Carrotluv.

IV-99.
Chocolate mold.

Stamped tin chicken, with large clip. Standing type, marked with small dolphin, and #2031, 4"H. **$25.00-$35.00**

IV-100.
Chocolate mold.

I've finally decided to call it a chocolate mold. 4-3/8"L. Looks like an egg's bathtub. Heavy cast iron with 3 legs. Something similar is shown in IV-102; I saw a depiction of that one with two halves joined. Late 19th C. **$15.00-$22.00**

IV-101.
Chocolate mold.

Santa in two parts, with registration dimples or bumps and 2 clips. Marked #76(?). 7"H, heavy tin, early 20thC. Picture courtesy of the National Museum of American History, Smithsonian Museum, Washington, DC.

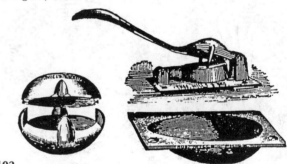

IV-102.
Cream egg molds.

At top is "lever press for making handmade cream eggs." This came in nine sizes, making eggs that would require from 3 to 22 to make up a pound. (L) Cast brass mold, with some resemblance to mold in previous picture. Made eggs of 5 sizes, from 25 to the pound up to 2 to the pound. Next is a cast iron mold, in 9 sizes, making eggs from 5 to 1 per pound. Last is a white metal, or "composition" metal, like Britannia or pewter, hinged and making multiple eggs. All from Mills catalog, 1927. **$15.00-$50.00**

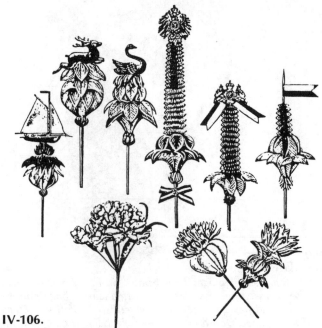

IV-103.
Cake ornamenting stamp,
and a design that could be made using it. *"These little stamps (probably nickeled brass, with wooden handles) enable any person to make the most difficult designs such as scrolls, console, valutes, etc. They are stamped direct on the cake"* and were then traced over using an icing bag or ornamenting tube. At bottom, the clasped hands, lyre, and scrolls all done with simple star or plain tubes. *"A few flowers and leaves will finish the cake, however the designs will look considerably better when other tubes are used such as the star ruffler, crimper, rope, etc., especially when the shoving, swinging or pushing motion is used."* Hueg's *The Little Confectioner*, 1921.

IV-106.
Paper decorations,
on sticks. For use with confections, and for roasts and joints of meat. Sailboat, buck, swan, flowers and various towers. Bertuch, c. 1904. **$5.00-$15.00**

IV-104.
Decorating stencils
for cakes. Unidentified metal (probably brass, like most other stencils), 10" diameter, but others made to order. 12 designs, with which *"a boy can ornament six layer cakes in one minute. DIRECTIONS: Place the Stencil on top of a layer cake iced with either chocolate or white icing, then sift a little xxxx sugar on top of the stencil and remove stencil carefully."* Child labor! Hueg, *Book of Designs for Bakers & Confectioners*, 1896 **$15.00-$30.00**

IV-107.
Baker decorating cake.
Statue of Liberty cake, on revolving stand. Note how baker supports his right hand to steady it as he makes a fancy border with the icing tube. From Hueg's 1896 how-to book.

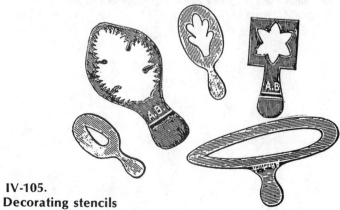

IV-105.
Decorating stencils
or *schablonen*. Unidentified metal. These were very like the full cake-top stencil above, but with more freedom. The biggest one, at bottom, was for making palm leaves; the fancy big one for making grape leaves. Bertuch, Berlin, c. 1904. **$7.00-$25.00**

IV-108.
Decorating bulb & ornamenting tubes.
(L) Rubber bulb with threaded mouth. Various tubes and exten-sion tubes could be used with it; it was supposed to make it easier to squeeze out the icing. (R) The "Boss" ornamenting bag and tubes (bag not shown, but it was a rubber bag). Cloth bags also used. Before the turn of the century, the tubes, and the threaded bag screw were silverplated brass; later they were nickeled. Hueg, 1896.   **$8.00-$20.00**

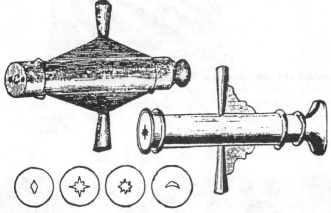

IV-109.
Jumble machines,
or jumble syringes. (L) Syringe in four sizes, with 2, 3, or 4 insert discs. Jaburg, 1908. (R) Pieced tin, wood plunger, various fancy-holed inserts. F.A. Walker import catalog, c.1870s. This style of jumble press required both hands (to hold the side handles) and a belly to push against it, which was achieved by eating jumbles.
                                                              $25.00-$65.00

IV-110.
"French butter forcer."
Tin with insert disc with star cutout, wooden plunger. Virtually identical to those in IV-109. "There are 12 different forms to each that give an infinite variety to this decorative manner of serving butter." American Home Cook Book, 1854.   **$25.00-$65.00**

IV-111.
'Kiss machine.'
Tin syringe with wooden pusher and various insert discs, for mak-ing candy kisses. Jaburg, 1908.   **$25.00-$65.00**

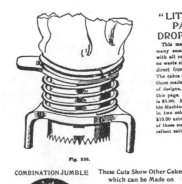

"LITTLE WONDER"
PATENT CAKE
DROPPING MACHINE

This machine is invaluable where a great many small cakes are made. It does away with all rolling and cutting, and there is also no waste of flour. The cake dough is deposited direct from the machine on the baking pan. The cakes will be found lighter and better than those made by hand. It will make any number of designs, and we illustrate some of them on this page. The price of Star Jumble Machine is $5.00. Extra attachment for the Star Jum-ble Machine cost from $1.00 up. To make cakes in two colors the attachments cost $5.00 and $10.00 extra for each design. A large number of these machines are in daily use and give ex-cellent satisfaction.

IV-112.
"Cake dropping machine."
A little metal stand with bag. Spring action. Came with various inserts to make all the different jumbles and cookies shown. Jaburg, 1908.   **$25.00-$45.00**

IV-113.
Syringes for cake dough & garnishes.
(L) A "Queenspritze," for cake dough. Crank action, 12 inserts. 14"L x 3 1/2" diameter. (R) A "Garnierspritze", only 3 7/8"L, and could be worked with one hand (the thumb pushing the plunger). Bertuch, c.1904.   **$15.00-$35.00**

IV-114.
Ancient molds,
in **reproduction**. Cast bronze cake molds, the originals of which were found buried under the volcanic debris at Herculaneum (L), and at Pompeii (R), almost 1800 years after the eruption of Vesuvius destroyed the towns in minutes. (L) Scallop shell-shape. Original 2" deep x 8 1/4" diameter. (R) Scalloped with more detail. 2 7/8" deep x 8 3/4" diameter. They both have simple round bot-toms, and the reproductions were only made with a polished finish. From catalog of the Fonderie Artistiche Riunite, of J. Chiurazzi & Fils and S. De Angelis & Fils, Naples, Italy, c. 1910-11.

IV-115.
Decorated cakes.

Clockwise from top (L) the names of the cakes are: Gâteau aux fleurs; Gâteau Venitien au sucre; Gâteau Jeanne-d'Arc; Gâteau Palestine; Gâteau Moucey; and Gâteau moscovite a l'ananas. From Urbain Dubois' La Patisserie, c.1860s-70s.

IV-116.
Angel cake pan.

Loose bottom with spout that projects an inch above sides of pan, which is 4 1/8"H x 10 1/2" diameter; 3 legs assist when you turn the mold upside down to get cake out. Savory Inc., Newark, NJ, c.1925-28 catalog. **$5.00-$15.00**

IV-117.
Baba cake,

shown in the Ryzon Baking Book, 1916. Advertising cookbooklet for baking powder maker.

IV-118.
Spouted cake molds,

*all called **turban molds**, or **turk's head molds**, despite differences in the fluting. Top (L) Stamped tin, made in six sizes, from 3 3/4"H x 7 1/4" diameter to 4 1/4"H x 11" diameter. Matthai-Ingram, c.1890. (R) Similar one with less-angled flutes, to be had with or without the spout. Stamped tin, 4 sizes, all somewhat smaller than the previous one. Savory, Inc., c.1925-28. Bottom: Unusual ovoid flutes, stamped & pieced tin, made in 3 sizes, from 7 7/8" to 10" diameter, holding 2, 4, 5 and 6 quarts. Lalance & Grosjean, 1890.* **$15.00-$35.00**

IV-119.
Baba cake mold.

Stamped & pieced copper, heavily tinned. Another name for this, from the German, is "Old German pound cake mold." Came in 8 sizes, in 3/4" increments, from 6 1/4" to 11 3/4" diameter. Bertuch, c.1904. **$85.00-$135.00**

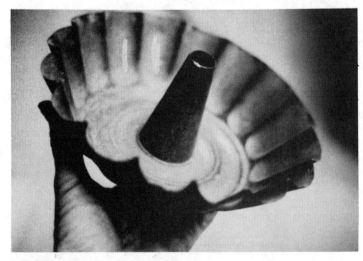

IV-120.
Fluted mold,

with spout. Stamped tin, with spout soldered on separately. 7 1/2" diameter. Late 19th or early 20th C. **$20.00-$35.00**

IV-122.
Dessert made in "biscuit mold,"
which you might think could mean an unglazed ceramic mold, or one in which biscuits or cookies (or cakes) were made. Many copper molds are called "biscuit mold." In French catalogs, similar-looking molds were described as being "pour biscuit ou pour glaces." A particular type of frozen dessert was called an "iced biscuit," made of different colors and flavors of a frozen meringue, pureed fruit & whipped cream, put into the various nooks or compartments of the biscuit molds. I believe from my reading of the catalogs that some biscuit molds were meant for a cake-like dessert. This picture from Urbain Dubois, La Patisserie, c.1870s.

IV-123.
Sandtorten molds.
These have similar tops (or bottoms) for almonds, but one has high plain sides, one has low "fancy" sides. Both from 8" to 13" diameter, pieced tin. S. Joseph Co., c.1927. **$35.00-$75.00**

IV-121.
Kugelhopf or gugelhupf cake mold.
Two views. Stamped copper with tinned inside, 4" deep x 10" diameter. Probably German, late 19th C. A gugelhupf cake has a yeast dough mixed with seedless raisins, grated lemon peel, chopped almonds. The mold is first greased with butter, coated with chopped almonds & bread crumbs, filled about half full, put in a warm spot to raise the dough, then baked. Served sprinkled with powdered sugar. Collection of Mary Mac Franklin.**$85.00-$135.00**

IV-124.
Spouted mold.
Redware, glazed inside & out. Handle on one side. 3 1/8" deep x 9 1/2" diameter. American, 19th C. Ex-Keillor Collection.
$200.00-$300.00

IV-125.
Cake mold.

Copper, 2 halves. Called a "copper cake form — To bake cake for icing." *American Home Cook Book*, 1854.   **$250.00-$350.00**

IV-126.
Cake mold.

Cast iron rabbit, 2 halves, 12"H, Griswold Mfg. Co., Erie, PA.
                                                    $150.00-$250.00

IV-127.
Cake pan,

for small cakes. Six-point star, pieced tin, spouted. Three sizes, plus the smallest one, probably about 5" across, came 12 fixed on a frame. Jaburg, 1908. The sizes of many of these cake and candy molds were described in the early catalogs by the retail price of the cake or candy baked within. For example, this one came in penny, five and ten cent sizes, referring to the little cake's price.   **$15.00-$35.00**

IV-128.
Cake pans.

(L) "Perfect," with removable bottom, available with or without spout. Stamped tin, two sizes, 3" deep x 9 5/8" diameter, or 3 1/8" deep x 10 1/2" diameter. Also made square with upside down legs (like those in IV-116, but called lugs). Central Stamping Co., 1920 (R) "Perfection," removable bottom, 1 5/8"H x 8 3/4" square or 2 5/8"H x 9 1/8" square. Savory, c.1925-28.   **$10.00-$20.00**

IV-129.
Twelfth-Day scene outside a Confectioner.

Probably similar to the scene outside pastry shops in America for New Year's Cakes (see the cake boards by Conger et al). This one in London. "From the taking down of the shutters in the morning, the pastrycook and his men, with additional assistants, male and female, are fully occupied by attending to the dressing out of the window, executing orders of the day before, receiving fresh ones, or supplying the wants of chance customers. Before dusk the important arrangement of the window is completed. Then the gas is turned on, with supernumerary argand-lamps and manifold wax-lights, to illuminate countless cakes of all prices and dimensions, that stand in rows and piles on the counters and sideboards, and in the windows. The richest in flavour and heaviest in weight and price are placed on large and massy salvers; one, enormously superior to the rest in size, is the chief object of curiosity; and all are decorated with all imaginable images of things animate and inanimate. Stars, castles, kings, cottages, dragons, trees, fish, palaces, cats, dogs, churches, lions, milkmaids, knights, serpents, and innumerable other forms in snow-white confectionary, painted with variegated colours, glitter by 'excess of light' from mirrors against the walls. This 'paradise' of dainty devices is crowded by successive desirers of the seasonable delicacies." William Hone, *Every-Day Book,* Vol. 1. London: (1825-26). The scene above with disconcerted customers pinned together in the front, illustrates the typical London boys' Twelfth-night tricks of nailing gentleman's coats to the door frame, or pinning stranger ladies and gents together.

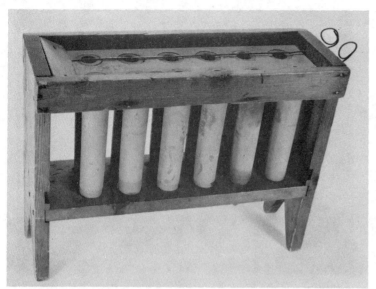

IV-130.
Candle mold,
redware, 12-tube in wooden frame. Impressed mark by maker,
Alvin Wilcox, West Bloomfield, NY. 15"H x 10"L. Photo courtesy
Litchfield Auction Gallery, Litchfield, CT. Ex-Harold Corbin Col-
lection, auctioned 1/1/1990. Price realized: **$1200.00**

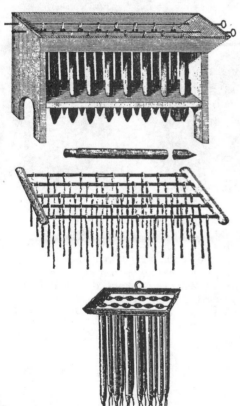

IV-131.
Candle molds.
Top three pictures show a set of tube molds, possibly pewter, set
in wooden frame. Note wire rods with wicks, in place in tubes,
ready for pouring the melted tallow. Note also the rack strung
with many wicks. Engravings from unidentified book, dated 1820,
found at a print shop. Bottom picture shows a typical pieced tin
mold, for a dozen candles, with hanging ring, and the wicks in
place. From American Agriculturist, 11/1876.

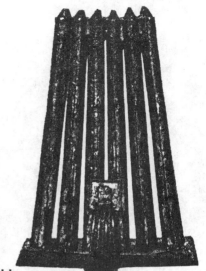

IV-132.
Candle mold.
Pieced tin, for making 6 candles. Ribbed strap handle. Shown 'upside down,' as they were stored if they didn't have a hanging ring.
10 1/4"H x 7"W. Early to mid 19th C.   **$125.00-$175.00**

IV-133.
Cookie cutter.
Tin, strap handle, flat back with large hole. Hand motif very
popular. 2 3/4"H, American, late 19th C. Picture courtesy of the
National Museum of American History, Smithsonian Institution,
Washington, DC.

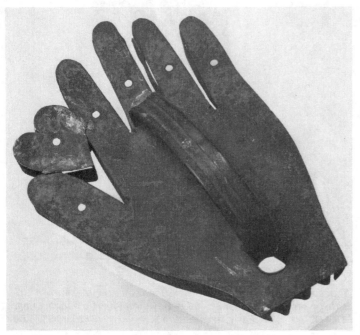

IV-134.
Cookie cutter.
Old dark tin, corrugated at wrist, folded-edge strap handle, small holes neatly placed in each finger and the heart. Heart-in-hand, 4 3/4"H x 3 1/2"W. Picture courtesy of Museum of History and Technology, Smithsonian Institution. Note: Copies of this cutter have been made in quantity by tinsmiths Bill and Bob Cukla, Hammer Song Country Tinware, 221 S. Potomoc, Boonsboro, MD, 21713. Each copy is conscientiously and responsibly marked on the back of the thumb with "B. Cukla." Too bad more skilled artisans don't sign their work; when they don't, they are in partnership with the person who passes the item off as "antique."

IV-135.
Cookie cutters.
*Varieties of heart shapes in tin. Clockwise from top (L). (1) "Card Party" cutter, for cookies or sandwiches, in sets of four including club, spade & diamond. Ritzinger, Grasgreen catalog, c.1906-07. (2) Actually a heart **mold**, not a cutter. 3"L x 2 1/2"W, fairly deep, with flat bottom, no handle of course, and no holes. D. J. Barry jobber catalog of housefurnishings, NYC, 1924. (3), (4) and (5) Commercial bakery types, with thick palm-fitting handles. (3) is 3" across, with interior trefoil design. Central Stamping Co., 1920. (4) Three sizes, 2 1/2", 3 1/2" and 5 1/2" across. Jaburg, 1908. (5) Another scalloped one, 2 3/4" x 3" or 3" x 3 1/2", Jaburg. (6) Nested set of 7 cutters. Bertuch, c.1904* **$5.00-$25.00**

IV-136.
Side view of cutter in IV-137.

IV-137.
Tin hearts.
(L) Pieced tin, carefully made, appears to be handmade. Perhaps is a small heart mold, as in last picture, or a cutter with a rolled edge. Only 7/8" deep x about 2 3/4" across. Late 19th C. (R) Commerical bakery cutter with scalloped edge. One advantage of big handle is extra air intake to drop those cookies out faster. Stamped 3 1/2 in two places on handle. Measures 7/8" deep x 3" x 3 1/2", although heart is really only 3 1/4" x 3 1/4". Late 19th or early 20th C. **$10.00-$25.00**

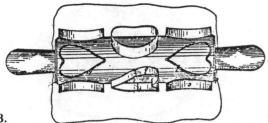

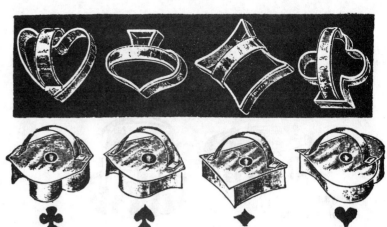

IV-138.
Cookie cutter rolling pin patent.
Pat'd 10/31/1865, by Isaac N. Pyle, Decatur, IN. "I have invented a new and improved combined cake-cutter and rolling-pin." The pin was an ordinary rolling pin, with all-one-piece handles, or rigid handles. The cake cutters are made on a cylinder that will "envelop or partially envelop" the rolling pin, which you provide. "It will be understood that the roller is to be used as an ordinary roller for rolling out dough into sheets; that it can be then be rubbed off and enveloped in the case. This can then be rolled over the sheet of dough, and the cakes will be cut out quickly and accurately. The cakes so soon as cut drop out of the cutters more readily than when ordinary flat-surfaced cake cutters are used." Official Gazette. In the picture, the odd oblong shape represents the rolled dough. Pyle said that of course it was understood that "several different cases, bearing different designs" could be used in succession, providing many varied cookies.

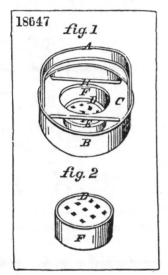

IV-139.
Cake cutter patent.
Pat'd 11/17/1857, by G. R. Peckham, Worcester, MA. Has a separate section in center. Official Gazette.

IV-140.
Cookie cutters.
All stamped aluminum, with riveted handles. "Mirro," mfd. by Aluminum Goods Mfg. Co., Manitowoc, WI, 1927 catalog.
$2.00-$6.00

IV-141.
Sandwich cutters,
or large cookie cutters. Pieced tin. (T) Simple strap-handled backless set of card suits, from S. Joseph catalog, c.1927. (B) Flat-backs with air holes. Ritzinger, Grasgreen catalog, c.1906-07. Value range for singles: **$4.00-$10.00**

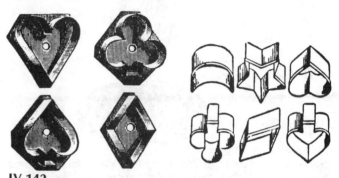

IV-142.
"Bridge set" or "card party" cookie cutters,
all pieced tin. (L) All approximately 2 3/4" x 3", but the heart is the biggest at 2 3/4" x 3 3/4". Flat backs, trimmed roughly to follow outline. (R) Card party set plus a star and a crescent moon. About 2 1/2" x 2". Savory, c.1927-28. **$4.00-$10.00**

IV-143.
Cookie cutters.
Flatbacks all cut round, with rolled edges. For making tea cookies. A. Bertuch, Berlin, c.1904. **$4.00-$10.00**

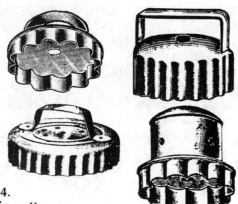

IV-144.
Cookie cutters.
All with scalloped edges. Clockwise from top (L). (1) Tin, flatback with strap, 3 1/2" or 4" diameter. Buhl Sons hardware, c.1919. (2) Seamless stamped tin, bracket handle, 2 1/2", 3", 3 1/2" or 4" diameter. Central Stamping Co., 1920. (3) Baker's style, called by Jaburg a "Bolivar" cutter. 1908 catalog. (4) Aluminum with riveted handle, 3 1/4" diameter, Aluminum Goods "Mirro." **$4.00-$15.00**

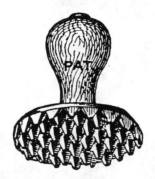

IV-145.
"Rock Cake" stamp.
"The Handy," nickeled cast iron, wooden handle. "This little stamp is a great time and labor saver, it makes the cakes all alike, uniform and prevents burnt edges; it does away with the fork, and is invaluable to any bake shop." Hueg, c.1927. **$15.00-$25.00**

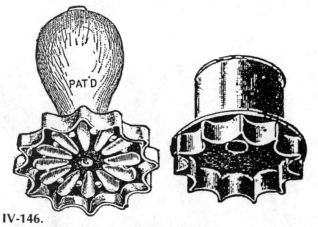

IV-146.
Shrewsbury cake mold & cutter.
(L) inverted scalloped edge, with almond-shaped flower design inside. Wood knob handle. "This Patent tool will cut, crimp and finish a Shrewsbury cake at one operation, and as fast as Sugar cake can be cut out; have them all perfect and uniform far superior to hand work. For very stiff doughs this tool may be used as a mold by simply unscrewing the handle." Hueg and Jaburg both sold it, c.1908 through 1920s at least. **$15.00-$25.00**
(R) Tin, 3 1/2" diameter. Note inverted scallops and fat handle. Jaburg, 1908. **$10.00-$20.00**

IV-147.
Nested cookie or cake cutters.
Leaves, flowers, and a few useful abstracts. Tin, in tin boxes. Sets of 1, 2 or 3 dozen cutters. A. Bertuch, Berlin, 1908. **$25.00-$50.00**

IV-148.
Nested cookie or cake cutters.
Hearts, 6-point stars, etc., ten cutters per box, sizes range from 1 1/4" to 4". S. Joseph, c.1927. **$20.00-$40.00**

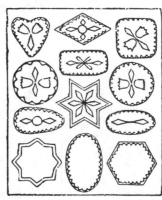

IV-149.
Cake cutters.
Assorted fancy shapes, crimped or corrugated edges, flat backs. Some with interior flower shapes. Central Stamping Co., 1920 catalog, but using much older linecut that may date to 1860s. **$10.00-$20.00**

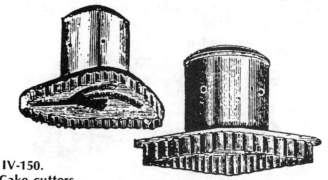

IV-150.
Cake cutters.
Bakery type. (T) Leaf cutter with interior design, made in 2 sizes: 3 3/4" x 1 3/4" and 4 5/8" x 2 1/4". (B) Diamond, 4 1/2" x 2 1/2". Duparquet, Huot & Monesue, c.1904-1910, pictures from much earlier catalog. **$10.00-$25.00**

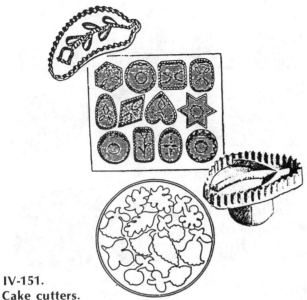

IV-151.
Cake cutters.
From top: Fancy leaf with tulip inside, from Henry Scammell's Treasure-House of Knowledge, *1891. An assortment that shows "a few of the many designs in cake cutters made of tin, to give fancy forms to cakes. They may be had of all house furnishings stores, and are among the luxuries of the kitchen — very nice where they can be afforded, and they are not very costly. The effect is pretty when different or even a single fancy form is used."* Scammell's, *1891. Next is a bakery version with fat handle. Two sizes: 1 3/4" x 3 3/4" or 2 1/4" x 4 5/8". Joseph Middleby, Boston, 1927. Round box of assorted flower shapes. Sometimes these are mistaken for toy cookie cutters. F. A. Walker catalog, c.1970s.*
$10.00-$60.00

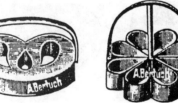

IV-152.
Cake cutters.
Pieced tin with strap handles. Pretzel cutter, 3 7/16", and almond-cookie cutter, 3 1/4" diameter. Bertuch, c.1904. **$30.00-$60.00**

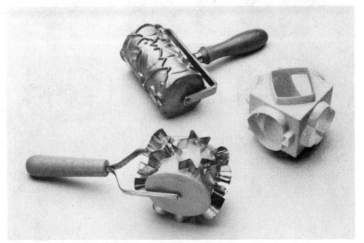

IV-153. Multiple cake cutters.
Top rolling cutter: heavy cast metal drum, many contiguous designs, bird on branch, elf, bear, bell, rabbit, chicken, chick, Christmas tree, etc. Natural finish wood handle, 7 3/4"L, no marks, c.1960s-80. Plastic cube at right is EKCO, with 4 bridge club motifs (heart, spade, diamond, club), plus half moon and star. 3 1/2" square, 1980. Bottom roller has yellow plastic drum on which are a cross, 6-pointed star, shamrock, circle, heart and a whatsit. 9 3/4"L, yellow wood handle. Marked "Made in Hong Kong." Early 1980s. **$5.00-$9.00**

IV-154.
Cake cutters.
Top (L) is combination tool: apple corer, biscuit cutter, doughnut maker, fluted cookie cutter, strainer. You made doughnuts by first cutting with plain round, then cutting center with small tube seen at top. 6"L x 3" diameter, late 19th C. Top (R) is deep star-shaped tin cutter, 4" diameter, 3 1/2" deep overall, cutter itself an unusal 2 1/2" deep. Bottom is lathe-tuned wooden doughnut cutter, 4 1/2"L x 2 3/8" diameter. Late 19th or early 20th C. All Collection of Meryle Evans. **$15.00-$35.00**

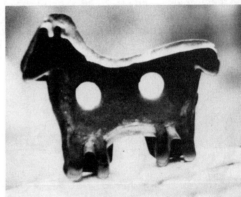

IV-155.
Cookie cutter.
Farm draught horse, old tin, flatback, 5 1/2"H x 6 1/8"L, 19th C. **$75.00-$100.00**

IV-156.
Cookie cutter.
Tin horse on rough-trimmed conforming flatback. One of assorted animal, bird & fish forms in Montgomery Ward catalog, c.1895. $.04 original cost! **$25.00-$45.00**

IV-157.
Cookie cutters.
Three tin flatbacks with small air holes offered by Joseph Middleby, in jobber's catalog, 1927. A "large man" cutter was 10 1/4"H; a "small" was 5 1/2", whereas a large animal was only 5"H. **$20.00-$45.00**

IV-158.
Cookie cutters.
Assorted fancy animals and geometerics, flatback tin. They could be had with "fancy centers," as most are here, or plain. Animals (like the lion & horse at top) came in 3 approximate sizes: 2 3/4"H, 3 1/2"H and 4"H. Matthai-Ingram, c.1890. **$20.00-$55.00**

IV-159.
Cookie cutters.
Four of the 12 assorted "fancy animals" that were offered in a box for $.80. Strap handles. Ritzinger & Grasgreen, c.1906-07. **$10.00-$25.00**

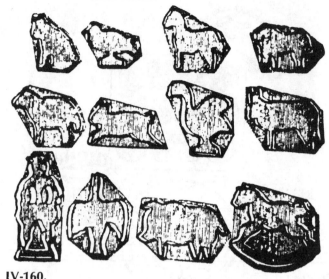

IV-160.
Cookie cutters.
Tin, flatback with backs cut roughly to conform to contour. Sold in 3 sizes, small, medium, & large. Lalance & Grosjean, 1890. **$15.00-$35.00**

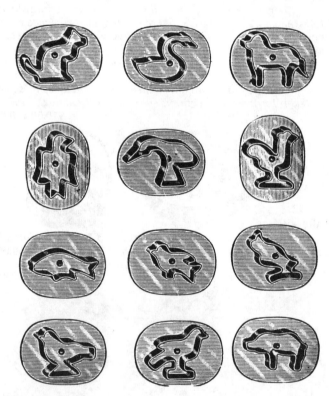

IV-161.
Cookie cutters.
Tin, solid oval backs, small air holes, about 3 1/2". Packed a dozen in a paper bag. Geuder, Paeschke & Frey, 1925. **$15.00-$35.00**

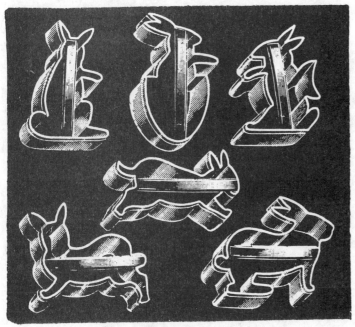

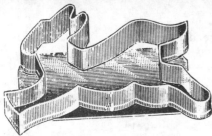

IV-162.
Rabbit cookie cutters.
All tin. Strap handle, backless ones at top are about 3 1/2"L. Bottom one, with flat tin back, was about 6"L. It was offered in sitting, running & standing positions also, and was called a "gingerbread rabbit cutter." S. Joseph, c.1927. **$15.00-$35.00**

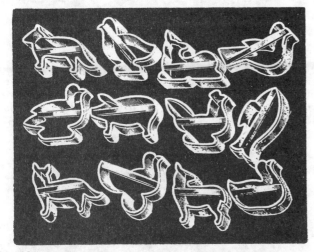

IV-163.
Animal cookie cutter.
Assorted set in two approximate sizes—1" and 2 1/4". Tin, no handles, boxed. S. Joseph, c.1927. **$10.00-$35.00**

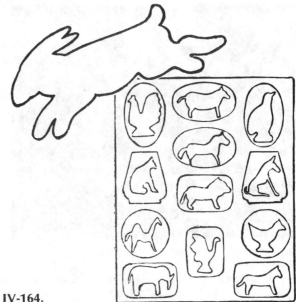

IV-164.
Animal cake cutters.
Large leaping rabbit was only one of many backless cutters offered by Jaburg, which included in "small" a horse, basket, scissors, pitcher, trumpet, bear, parrot, star, camel, and cat. A "small rat" and a "large man" were offered side by side. Also "Jumbo" (elephant), horse & rider, Liberty Statue, Men and Women, watch, padlock, and eight sizes of hearts. The boxed set shown under the rabbit was also sold, and possibly made, by Central Stamping Co. The same cuts were used over and over, and by several manufacturers at the same time. These pictures, Jaburg Brothers, 1908. **$15.00-$55.00**

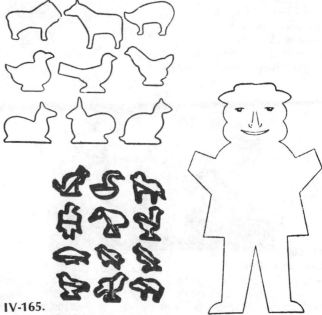

IV-165.
Cake cutter sets.
Above is a "Noah's Ark Set" of 1" deep x 3"H cutters that came in an "attractive cellophane wrapped box." Standing tall is the "Ginger Bread Man," who was 9 1/2"H x 5 3/4"W x 2" deep; the features are the artist's improv. Savory, c.1925-28. Small set, with 12 designs about 3"H or long, from the Buhl Brothers Hardware Co., Detroit, c.1919. **$10.00-$55.00**

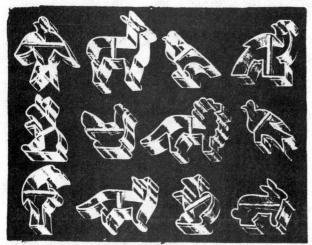

IV-166.
Cake cutter set.
"Noah's Ark" assortment, 3 1/2"L. Could be had with or without handles. Shown here with what appear to be braces across body for strength. (They also made the rabbit set, which shows handles clearly). S. Joseph, c.1927.   **$10.00-$35.00**

IV-169.
Gingerbread boys.
(L) Shiny thin tin, fairly recent manufacture, 8"H. (R) Stamped aluminum, with details that probably wouldn't show on finished cookie. Has strap handle created by slitting back. 5 3/4"H, 1940s.   **$3.00-$7.00**

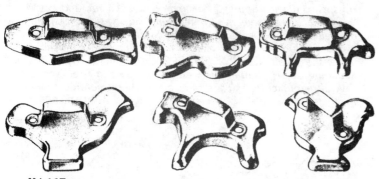

IV-167.
Cookie cutters.
Stamped aluminum with riveted bracket handles, about 4". "Mirro," Aluminum Goods Mfg. Co., 1927.   **$3.00-$8.00**

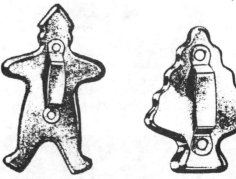

IV-170.
Gingerbread boy & tree.
(L) Similar to one above, but here the bracket handle is riveted on, and there are no features. 6" x 3 3/4". The tree is about 3 1/4", and the catalog pictures were not to scale. "Mirro" Aluminum Goods Mfg. Co., 1927.   **$3.00-$7.00**

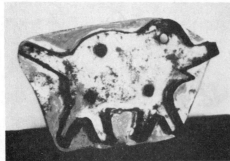

IV-168.
Cookie cutter.
A large flatback tin elephant, probably "Jumbo." Strap handle. Shallow cutter, exuberant trumpeting position. 9 1/8"W, 19th C. Collection of Charismatic Studio.   **$200.00-$400.00**

IV-171.
Santa Claus & Angel.
Tin profile cutters with rolled top edge (for stablity) and bracket handles. Santa is 4 1/2"H; not-to-scale angel is 5"H. S. Joseph catalog, c.1927.   **$10.00-$30.00**

IV-172.
Men & women cutters.
(T) Part of what Ritzinger & Grasgreen refers to as an "assortment of 12 human figures." 3"H, without handles. About 1908. (B) Tin man & woman with brace handle, 3"H. S. Joseph Co., c.1927. Slight variations from top one, but essentially the same.

IV-174.
Cookie mold.
Cast iron, oval, intaglio impression of flowers and leaves in a basket. Casting gate on back is mostly ground down. 5 7/8"L x 4"W x 1/4" deep. Possibly Albany or Troy, NY, 19th C.
$125.00-$150.00

IV-173.
Cookie cutters.
Molded light blue plastic with fine interior details. Santa is 5"H; Christmas tree, 4 1/2"H. Stanley Rome Products, 1950s-60s.
$1.00-$3.00

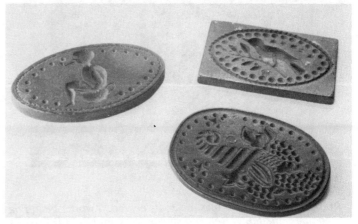

IV-175.
Cookie or marchpane molds.
"Marchpane" is the English equivalent of marzipan. Cast iron, elliptical or oval intaglio designs. Upper (L) Unusual design of boy with pipe in his mouth, sitting on chamber pot. 3 1/2" x 6". Border design of dots. The author's version is quite similar, though 1/4" smaller, and the child has no pipe. Mary Mac Franklin mused whether or not these molds might have been used for making sweet rewards for successful toilet training—the pipe version for a boy. Top (R): Songbird on branch, dotted elliptical border. 3 1/4" x 5 1/4". Bottom: Cornucopia, grapes, dot border, 5 3/4" x 4 1/4". Photo courtesy Litchfield Auction Gallery, Litchfield, CT. Ex-Harold Corbin Collection. Auctioned 1/1/1990. Prices realized:
$275.00 and $170.00 and $185.00

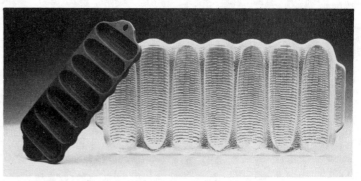

IV-176.
Cookie molds.
Swan in a circle, surrounded by dots, on oval mold, 4 3/4" x 5 3/4"; pineapple in Pennsylvania German style, though probably New York State. 6" x 4 1/2"; and oval with acorn leaves, 4" x 5 3/4", the last being the thickest of all six molds auctioned. 19th C. Photo courtesy of Litchfield Auction Gallery, Litchfield, CT. Ex-Harold Corbin Collecion. Auctioned 1/1/1990. Prices realized:
$180.00 and $85.00 and $160.00

IV-179.
Corn stick pans.
(L) Cast iron, "Griswold Krispy Cornorwheat Stick Pan -262, "Erie PA. 8 1/2"L x 4 1/8"W. Makes 7 one-way sticks. (R) Molded heavy glass, Wagner Ware. 13"L x 6"W. Makes 7 which-a-way sticks. Which makes me wonder out loud, why did muffin and roll pans always make odd numbers? For luck? Collection of Meryle Evans. Two value ranges: **$22.00-$32.00 and $20.00-$35.00**

IV-177.
Cookie mold.
Round, deeply carved mason's tools carved in wood, including a hammer, mallet, chisel, and square. Also initials "I.D." 5 1/2" diameter x 7/8" thick. Dealer thought it might be a butter mold instead. I disagree. **$150.00-$250.00**

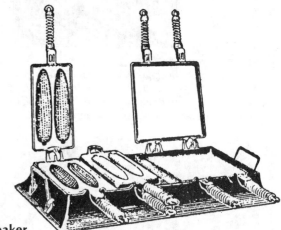

IV-180.
Corn dog baker.
"Krusty Korn Dog" baker, also sandwich toaster (grill) or steak fryer. "A big money maker! For use on gas, gasoline, oil or coal stoves. "Krusty Korn Dogs" are novel and delicious. The hot dog is baked inside the corn batter, which as it bakes, moulds itself to resemble an ear of corn 6 3/8"L and 1 1/2" diameter. Easy to make: Red hots are first fried in butter, then placed in 'korn dog' sections together with required amount of batter, they are then quickly and thoroughly baked together. Baker is made of cast iron, smooth japanned finish, with heavy, sturdy wire coil pan handles. Heavy lifting handles at each end." Frame is 2 1/2" x 10 1/4" x 21 1/4"; fryer pan (R) is 3/4" deep x 8 1/2"H x 8 3/8". You bought the frame and a fry pan (griddle), and a pair of the "Krusty Korn Sausage Dog Pans," each of which made two, separately to suite your business. In Pick-Barth wholesale catalog of many makers' hotel and restaurant supplies, 1929. **$40.00-$150.00**

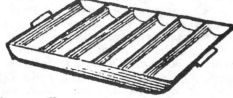

IV-178.
Corn cake or roll pan.
Called a "Russia Iron Roll, or corn cake pan. — Gives a handsome brown soft under-crust." Russia iron is heavy sheet iron, not cast iron. This appeared as a kitchen necessity in American Home Cook Book, 1854. **$50.00-$75.00**

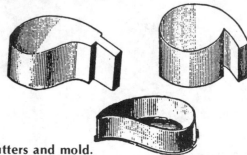

IV-181.
Cutlet cutters and mold.
Two punctuation marks-like cutters, pieced tin, from F.A. Walker catalog, 1870s. I don't know if they had a flatback. Two sizes, probably about 4" and 6"L. Bottom one is a mold, in same catalog as the heart mold in with heart cookie cutters. Tin, 4"x 2 1/4". The top ones might be used to cut shapes from whole, as opposed to ground, meat. **$10.00-$15.00**

IV-182.
Dough scraper.
Wrought iron, polished and worked by a whitesmith to take on an appearance of steel. Socket handle. About 3 3/4" overall x 3"W. Early to mid 19th C. Not an uncommon type, and very simple. Collection of Mary Mac Franklin. **$50.00-$65.00**

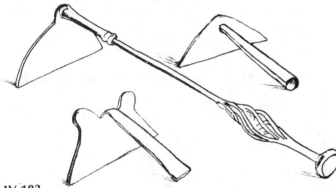

IV-183.
Dough scrapers.
Long-handled one is wrought brass and iron, about 12"L, with split and twisted cage handle, with three marbles inside. Drawn from story on a March 1990 Pook & Pook sale at Chester, PA. One in foreground is drawn from memory of one seen at Pennsylvania show, about 4 1/2"W. It was made from one wrought piece, the handle being bent back between the 'ears' of the blade. One in background is simple triangle with separate tapered tubular socket handle riveted through hole in blade. Also about 4"W. Price realized for big one, then range for other two, the higher value being if signed. **$935.00 and $150.00-$450.00**

IV-184.
Doughnut cutters.
Clockwise, from (L). Tin, strap handle, deep cutting, no top, one size only, 3" diameter. Marked "Fries". From Sexton Stove & Mfg. catalog, c.1930. Next is heavy tin one with rounded palm-fitting top, deep cutter, for bakeries. 3". Pick-Barth catalog, 1929. Next, combination Cookie and doughnut cutter, with detachable center cutter. Aluminum, white painted wooden handle, 3"H overall x 2 3/4" diameter. "Mirro," Aluminum Goods Mfg., 1927. Last, the solid back tin one, either 3" or 3 1/2" diameter. Geuder, Paeschke & Frey, 1925. **$8.00-$15.00**

IV-185.
Doughnut cutter,
top and underneath view. Fluted or crimped & pieced tin, strap handle, pat'd 10/15/1889. Matches a similar biscuit cutter. From F.A. Walker catalog, c.1890. **$10.00-$20.00**

IV-186.
Ebelskiver or aebelskiver pan.
Also called a muffin pan, or an egg cooker, but really for ebelskivers, which are apple-chip pancakes. Cast iron, Griswold No. 32, #962, Erie, PA. Seven cups, 1 3/4"H x 9 1/4" diameter, with 4 3/4"L handle. Cups are 1 1/4" deep. **$35.00-$60.00**

IV-187.
Ebelskiver pan,
or egg poacher. Cast iron, 7 cups, no feet. Only mark is "8". 1 1/2"H x 9" diameter with 5 3/4"L handle. I like this one much better than the Griswold, especially its bottom. Courtesy Jean Hatt, Hatt's Hutt, Denver, PA. **$45.00-$65.00**

IV-188.
Detail of IV-187.

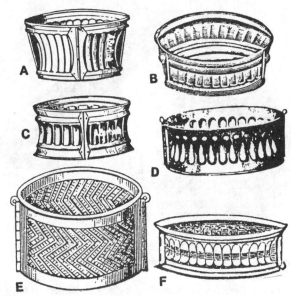

IV-190.
French pie or pâte molds.

All hinged, most relatively shallow compared to diameter. (A) German hinged mold, simple flutes, in 5 sizes, from 5 1/2" to 8" diameter. (B) Similar, with ring border, ranged from 5 1/2" to 8 3/4" diameter. (C) Another German one in 8 sizes, from 4 3/8" to 9 3/4" diameter. All Bertuch, Berlin, c.1904. (D) Oval "pie mold," planished tin. 11 1/2", 12" and 13 1/2" diameter. John Van Range Co., Cincinnati, 1914. (E) Round, herringbone design, two sizes. English, from Mrs. A.B. Marshall's Cookery Book, *c. 1887-1900. (F) "French Oval Meat Pie Mould. — Opens at one end."* American Home Cook Book *1854.* **$20.00-$75.00**

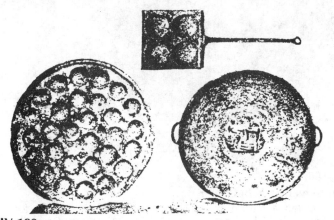

IV-189.
Egg poachers & basin.

Cast bronze **reproductions** *of cookwares found at Pompei, during excavations at different times in the 19th C. (The basin at right, with bas-relief decoration of swimmers, was excavated June 5, 1880). Large pan at left has 29 cavaties for eggs; and measures 19 1/8" in diameter. The long-handled pan for four eggs measures 17 1/4"L. They were offered in the "Pompei or the Herculaneum" finishes. J. Chiurazzi & Fils & S. De Angelis & Fils, Fonderie Artistiche Riunite, Naples, Italy. Catalog from 1910-11.*

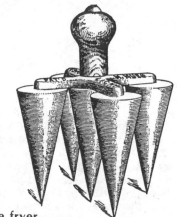

IV-191.
Ice cream cone fryer.

Cast & plated iron, wooden knob handle. **Batter:** *1 lb. soft flour, 4 oz. confectioners sugar, 3/4 pt. beaten eggs, 3/4 pt. milk. Mix flour, sugar and eggs with an egg beater very good, then add milk gradually. In meantime have your oil heated to 370° to 375°. Put your spring iron in the oil, allow to get hot; then dip the iron into the mixture, but don't let the mixture run over the iron. Then take the iron out and put in the heated oil; in a few seconds the cake (cone) is baked. Take out and give it a knock on a piece of wood to remove the cakes from the iron. Put the iron in the oil again for a few seconds. Knock the adhering oil off, and continue the same way as before. If mixture gets thick, add a little more milk and eggs. A nice showy cake which has a fine taste if eaten fresh, but it will be dry the next day." H. Hueg, pat'd 1910 (?).* **$45.00-$100.00**

IV-192.
Ice cream cone baker.

Called a "Standard Cone Oven," used on any style stove. Came with wooden conical roller for rolling into cone as soon as taken off the baker. T. Mills, 1915. **$50.00-$75.00**

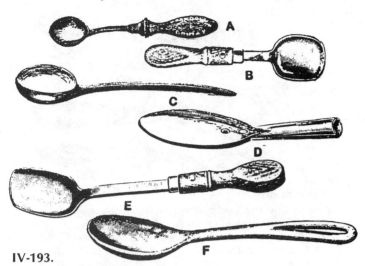

IV-193.
Ice cream dishing spoons.

Also called **ice cream spades.** *From top: (A) nickeled metal with wood handle. Round bowl. Marked "Crandall & Cudahy" on handle, in Duparquet, Huot & Moneuse catalog, c.1904-10. (B) Tinned steel, shank riveted to wood handle. 2 sizes: 10"L and 12"L. From Pick-Barth, 1929. (C) All metal, round bowl. D, H, & M, c.1904-10. (D) Oval paddle, tin, D, H, & M. (E) Long-handled, "spade bowl," 10", 12", or 14"L, D. J. Barry catalog, 1924. (F) Spade bowl, all metal, nickel-plated cast metal (brass?). 11 1/2"L. Pick-Barth, 1929.*
$5.00-$15.00

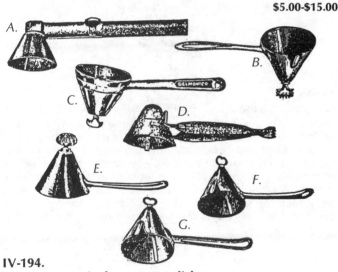

IV-194.
Ice cream conical or cornet dishers.

The simplest mechanical types: the **'key scraper,"** *with a blade (sometimes called a knife) inside that is scraped around inside of cone by twisting the "key." And two with a* **spring-loaded scraper,** *one activated by thumb, one by squeezing double handle. This type seems odd now because the conical scoop of ice cream faces the wrong way to fit into the cookie cone. From top: (A) "Chicago" disher, nickel plated, one size only, 16 to the quart. (B) "Clad's Improved," of seamless drawn steel, German silver knife, 4, 5, 8, 10, 12 and 16 to the quart. (C) "Delmonico Improved," cast iron handle, heavy spun brass bowl, all nickeled, interior cup removable. 6, 10 and 12 to quart. (D) "Rapid," one-hand squeeze type. Nickel-plated spun brass bowl & blade, "Bessemer steel spring," in 4, 5, 6, 8, 10, 12, and 16 to quart. First four from Albert Pick catalog, 1909. (E) "K-W-Cone" disher, mfd. by Keiner-Williams Stamping Co. Tinned bowl, malleable cast iron handle, with long slot. Several sizes. Cherry-Bassett catalog, 1921. (F) & (G) Two versions of the "Clewell" disher & measure. (F) Tin bowl, cast iron handle with small hanging hole, German silver knives, made in "standard sizes." Mfd. by V. Clad, Philadelphia. This one pictured in 1892 ad. (G) Bowl is seamless drawn steel. Note handle with long slot opening, like in "E". 4, 5, 6, 8, 10, 12, 16 and 20 to quart. In 1915 and 1924 catalogs.*
$15.00-$75.00

IV-195.
Ice cream key scrapers.

Two types, tin with capped tubular handles. One has conical bowl, braced to handle. Other makes rounded serving. Bertuch, Berlin, c.1904.
$25.00-$45.00

IV-196.
Ice cream measure.

"Perfection" was one name used; "Philadelphia" was a later name. Actually a Clewell patent, mfd. by Valentine Clad, Philadelphia. Picture shown is from a 1915 catalog. Spun brass, nickel plated outside, silver plated inside (probably meaning German silver), with nickel-silver blade. In cutaway linecut you can see the key in the base. Two sizes, 1 pint and 1 quart. An 1892 V. Clad ad mentions only German silver. The Cherry-Bassett Co., called it a "Philadelphia," has two versions—one "heavily tinned," and one silvered inside, nickeled out.
$35.00-$50.00

IV-197.
Three types of mechanical ice cream dishers.

(T) Cast aluminum, thumb-lever spring action prod knocks ice cream out of bowl, 7 1/2"L, made in Japan, 1950s. (M) Longest one is a Dover Mfg. Co. #20, wooden handle, nickeled bowl. This has a leveling cutter that flattens scoop before it comes out. 10 1/2"L. (B) Cornet disher with key-wind, heavy tin, marked "#10." In this case, the key at the top turns the cornet-shaped bowl, not the scraper inside, although the reverse is true of most (or all?) others. Pat'd 1883 (?). Last two collection of Meryle Evans.
$7.00-$55.00

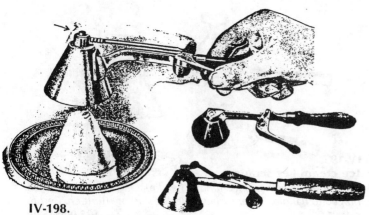

IV-198.
Mechanical cornet dishers.

All with thumb levers that move the blade within. Large one is "Gilchrist's No. 33 Pyramid" disher. "Bowl and scraper all made of German silver (nickel). Phosphor bronze spring fully concealed. Press button (arrow points to it) to take entire thing apart for cleaning or repairing. Six sizes: 6, 8, 10, 12, 16 or 20 to the quart. Disher under the hand is C. L. Walker Co.'s "Quick and Easy" disher, formerly made by the Erie Specialty Co. Nine sizes: 6, 8, 10, 12, 14, 16, 20, 24 and 30 to the quart. First two from 1919 ads in The Soda Fountain trade magazine. Bottom disher is the "Dan- Two qualities — silver plated or tinned, with wood handle. 8, 10, 12, 16 to the quart. Pick catalog, 1909. **$22.00-$45.00**

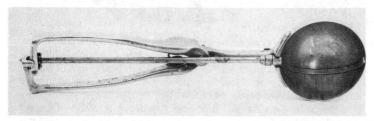

IV-199.
Ice cream disher.

"Gilchrist #30," with squeeze action. Nickeled brass & copper, 10 1/2"L, c.1930. **$35.00-$55.00**

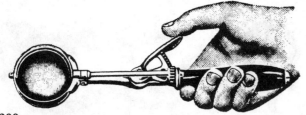

IV-200.
Ice cream disher.

Classic #31, thumb lever. Made in nine sizes: 6, 8, 10, 12, 16, 20, 24, 30, 40 to the quart. Also sold for dishing out mashed potatoes! Nickel-plated "bronze metal." From 1930s catalog. Caution: These are the ones dealers like to "engolden", by removing necessary nickel plating. **$35.00-$55.00**

IV-203.
Ice cream disher.

"Unique," mfd. by Mosteller Mfg. Co., Chicago. "A perfect cone filler and dispenser, made in sizes 6, 8, 10, 12, 16 and 20 to quart." Two styles, one of white metal, one of aluminum, both with German Silver bowls. 1909 ad in Iron age. **$35.00-$65.00**

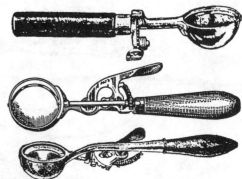

IV-201.
Ice cream dishers.

(T) "Arnold," with nickel plating. End of handles marked with code colors for size. (So you could see them when they sat immersed in that bucket of disgusting bath-water scummy mess). (M) Identified as a "patent chromium plated disher," in Jaburg catalog, 1915. Only in small-scoop sizes, 12, 16, 20, 24 and 30 to quart. (B) "Gem" disher, with bowl made of "aluminum bronze, heavy nickel plated." Rosewood handle. From 6 to 20 to the quart sizes.

IV-202.
Ice cream disher.

"Service" disher. The distinguishing feature is the pointed piece on top, and their ads are filled with word play on "the point." But it's a great idea: "Make a hollow in the top of the cream with the point on the back of the disher. Serve the syrup on the top of the cream where it will do the most good. Make every drop count. A little less fruit and syrup served this way looks like more and gives better satisfaction." Heh heh. Service Commodities Mfg. Co., Chicago. 1919 ad in The Soda Fountain. **$35.00-$65.00**

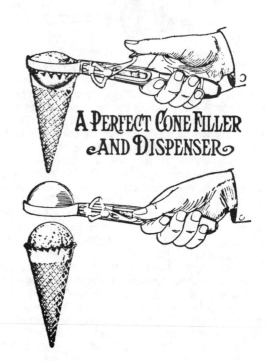

A PERFECT CONE FILLER AND DISPENSER

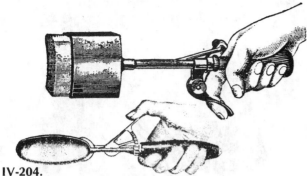

IV-204.

Ice cream dishers.

(T) Slice molder, "Handy," mfd. by Mayer Mfg. Corp., Chicago, c.1910s. Not actually a thumb lever as I've said, but a forefinger lever, as shown. (B) Banana split disher Gilchrist #34, long oval, 3 3/4"L x 1 3/8"W, 20 to the quart. Both in MIlls catalog, 1915. **$100.00-$175.00**

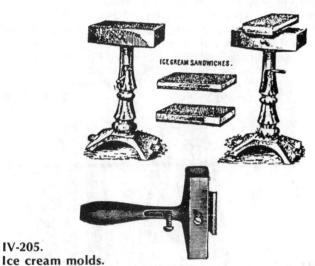

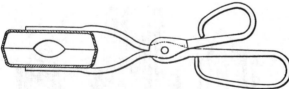

IV-205.

Ice cream molds.

"Pan-American," for "the very latest form in which Ice Cream is sold at Soda Fountains, Cafes, etc., is the Ice Cream Sandwich, composed of two oblong Biscuits with a thin cut of Ice Cream between them." Style One is shown above with fancy cast iron base; style Two below, appears to be handheld. Apparently the "mold" holds the wafer or biscuit in place while ice cream slab is put on and topped. I assume the size to be about 7" to 8"L. Thomas Mills, 1915 catalog. **$50.00-$125.00**

IV-206.

"Mold for Ice-Cream, Jellies, &c." patent.

Pat'd 8/19/1873, by Edgar Mason May, Fond Du Lac, WI. What is seen is a sectional view of the scissor-action mold. The mold is a round "pan or cup" with open ends facing each other. "Each cup has a curved piece cut from one side, so that when they are closed together they resemble a round box with an opening in the periphery." It was to be used by holding open and dipping in the cream, "or other substances to be molded, taking up as much as can be held. They are then forced together, pressing the cream into a compact mass, the surplus passing out through" that hole in the periphery! Cast or sheet metal, inner surfaces "corrugated, carved, or ornamented in any mannner." <u>Offical Gazette.</u>

IV-207.

Bomb or bombe molds.

All for iced dessert dishes—ice cream, iced pudding, etc. I don't know what made this style so popular, maybe it was some exciting anarchist movement, but it goes back at least two centuries. Clockwise from upper (L): (1) "Bomb", tinned copper, two sizes—1pint and 1 quart. Note the fuse opening. Pick-Barth, 1929. (2) Tinned copper, from William S. Adams, London, C.1860-61. (3) "Bombe Enflammee" mold, A. Anthoine, Paris, c.1900. (4) "Boulet," in four sizes, holding 1/2 litre, 1, 1 1/2 and 2 litres. Anthoine, c.1900. Note: An invaluable book for research into dishes is <u>Hering's Dictionary of Classical and Modern Cookery,</u> trans. by Walter Bickel, published in Germany. I have 1974 edition. There are almost seven pages of recipes for Bombe, "a special ice concoction moulded...and deep frozen. The mould is lined first with plain ice cream and the center filled with a bombe mixture of different flavor, to which may be added diced fruit and other ingredients. (Just like iced biscuit). Fruit should be macerated in liqueur and sugar before being added to prevent it freezing too hard. Bombe mixture is made by whisking egg yolks with a syrup of 28 deg. first hot and then cold, blended with whipped cream and the desired flavor." Just one for example: "Zamora: lined with coffee ice: filled with Curacoa-flavored bombe mixture." **$50.00-$200.00**

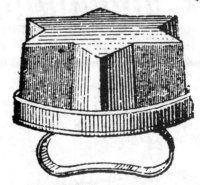

IV-208.

"Bombe Sarah Bernhardt" mold.

Not all bombe molds are shaped like bombs. Some are conical; this one is a 6-point star, made of tin, with a close-fitting lid. It appears in Urbain Dubois' <u>La Patisserie d'Aujourd'hui,</u> published over long period, with illustrations from early editions, c.1860s-80s. A Sarah Bernhardt bombe, named after the French actress of the last half of the 19th C., had peaches, maraschino cherries, and vanilla mousse. (It is not in Hering's.) **$40.00-$70.00**

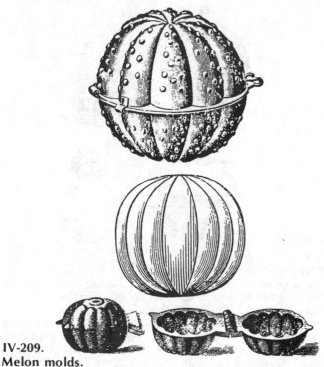

IV-209.
Melon molds.

Used for iced desserts and puddings. (T) The warty "Musk Melon" mould is tin, hinged, and made in 4 1/2", 5 1/2" and 6" diameters. S. Joseph, c.1927. (M) Plain melon, holding 1 1/2 pints. Mrs. A. B. Marshall's The Book of Ices, c.1900-02. (B) Two views of hinged pewter ice cream melon mold, for "fruit glaces." Urbain Dubois, c.1860s-80s.   **$60.00-$100.00**

IV-210.
Ice cream mold.

Shown in 1 pt. and 2 pt. sizes. Looks like a quonset hut. Tin. "An entirely new idea is worked out in the Silver Ice Cream mold. The housewife may send the receptacle to the cream saloon, and have the ice cream packed in ready to use, or it may be packed at home. In each instance it assumes the shape of the pan and makes a splendid appearance. The cream can be sliced at the sections. The results are very dainty and appetizing...It can be used also for gelatine, custards, etc."   **$20.00-$40.00**

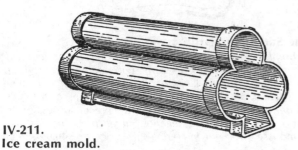

IV-211.
Ice cream mold.

Tin, long "bridge party" motifs, for slicing. Cherry-Bassett, 1921.
$30.00-$60.00

IV-212.
Pyramid ice cream molds.

None look like the Egyptian pyramids, but the influence is there from the exciting archaeological digs in Egypt at various times in the 19th C. (L) Fancy patterned mold, 1 litre or 2 litre sizes, Anthoine, Paris, c.1900. Top (R) Looking like a stack of witch's hats, this was made round (as here), square and octagon, with 1, 2 and 3 rings. Jaburg, 1908. Bottom: Swirled like soft ice cream, with lid. Imported, possibly from England. 1 1/2 quart size: 6"H x 6 1/2" diameter; and 2 1/2 qts.: 8 1/2"H x 8" diameter. Joseph, c.1927.   **$20.00-$60.00**

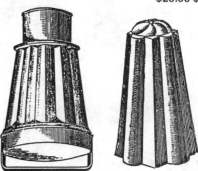

IV-213.
Ice cream or ice pudding mold.

(L) is the mold, balanced on its bracket strap handle. The cylinder at top is the protective ring for the stamped copper ornamental top. At right is the "shape produced." Mold made in 1, 1 1/2, 2, 3 and 4 pint sizes. Mrs. Marshall's Book of Ices, c.1902.
$30.00-$60.00

IV-214.
Ice cream or ice pudding molds.

All "pillar molds," of tin, possibly with stamped copper tops. (L) "Fruit Top," in 1, 1 1/2, 2 and 3-pt. sizes; (M) "With plinth" is sole description. 2 and 3-pts. (R) "Cherry top" in 1, 1 1/2 and 2 pts. Made to put maraschino cherries in. All Marshall's Book of Ices.
$40.00-$90.00

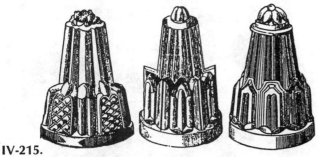

IV-215.
Ice cream or ice pudding molds.
Various tin ornate molds, 1 quart size with nooks for fruit, lady fingers, etc. Probably all imported from England, c.1870s-90s.
$60.00-$110.00

IV-216.
Jelly & Cream molds.
Copper, with lining inserts, so that a different color or flavor could be put into center of mold. (T) "Alexandra", in 2 sizes, and (R) "Brunswick Star", in 2 sizes. Mrs. Marshall's Book of Ices, *c.1902. Design registered in England in 1890s.*
$150.00-$250.00

IV-217.
Ice cream molds.
Transportation themes. The detailed drawings from catalogs are idealized versions of what ice cream would look like when molded. There was lots of exaggeration allowed the artists— although many molds have great detail, not all of it shows on the ice cream. Things like wheels, flags, canes, etc., had to be added, and were made of paper, wood or metal. Top two pewter molds, for 1 1/2 and 1 1/3 litres, from Bertuch, Berlin, c.1904. Bottom two, in individual sizes of 7 to a quart are pewter, pictures from Duparquet, Huot & Moneuse catalog, c.1904-1910. Bike one also made in large 4-pint capacity.

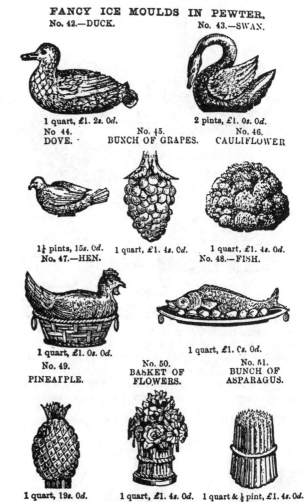

FANCY ICE MOULDS IN PEWTER.
No. 42.—DUCK.   No. 43.—SWAN.

1 quart, £1. 2s. 0d.   2 pints, £1. 0s. 0d.

No 44.   No. 45.   No. 46.
DOVE.   BUNCH OF GRAPES.   CAULIFLOWER

1¼ pints, 15s. 0d.   1 quart, £1. 4s. 0d.   1 quart, £1. 4s. 0d.
No. 47.—HEN.   No. 48.—FISH.

1 quart, £1. 0s. 0d.   1 quart, £1. 0s. 0d.
No. 49.   No. 50.   No. 51.
PINEAPPLE.   BASKET OF   BUNCH OF
                FLOWERS.   ASPARAGUS.

1 quart, 19s. 0d.   1 quart, £1. 4s. 0d.   1 quart & ½ pint, £1. 4s. 0d.

IV-218.
Ice cream molds.
SPECIMEN PAGE FROM 'BOOK OF MOULDS.'
Pewter, various designs from a sample or "specimen" page of Mrs. Marshall's advertised Book of Molds. *Late in 19th C.*

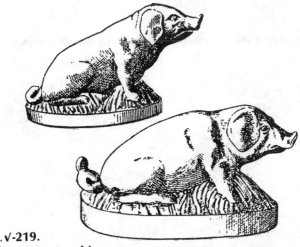

.√-219.
Ice cream molds.
Two tin pig styles on bases. (T) 1 litre #22, and 3/4 litre #1149 From Fabrique Speciale de Moules en Etain...Marque c.c., *Paris, France catalog, 1900. The "C.C." mark had a well with bucket and the initials "c.c." I will refer to molds from that catalog as "Marque C.C." from here on out. (B) This tin mold is from the same catalog, but you can see the design is different. It is advertised as #832 "1/2 Glace" style; which I assume may mean there's dimensional modeling on only one side? Price range for all animal molds:*
$35.00-$150.00

IV-220.
Ice cream molds.

Horses. Top (L) appears to be the sea god Neptune, borne on the waves in a chariot. It and the large one at (R) are 1 3/4 and 1 1/4 quart sizes. The jockey on left is 7 to a quart. First three tin molds all sold through Duparquet, Huot & Moneuse, early 20th C. Jockey lower right is pewter, 1 1/8 litre is about 9/10 of a quart; a liquid litre is just over 1 quart. Ice cream must be halfway between). Bertuch, Berlin, c.1904.

IV-222.
Ice cream molds.

Dogs, mainly poodles or retrievers. Top (L) #13, glace, entière, tin. Marque C.C., 1900. (M) #3 in Series No. 969, tin, glace entière for 9 centilitres. Marque C.C. (R) #83, Anthoine, c.1900. Bottom (L) #8, Series No. 969, tin, glace entière, Marque C.C. (M) "Chien loup," No. 82, Anthoine. (R) Poodle with ball, #52, demi-glace, Anthoine.

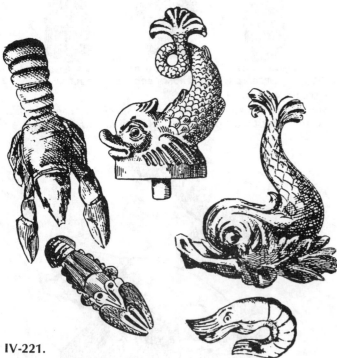

IV-221.
Ice cream molds.

Lobsters, dolphins and a shrimp. The dolphin, or dauphin, molds, a symbol of French royalty, were probably used for "Crownprince" bombes, with a hazelnut and kirsch mixture. Big lobster was described in catalog as a "Glace entiere" as opposed to a "Demi-glace" (or half glace) mold. Anthoine, Paris, c.1900. Small lobster found in Duparquet, Huot & Moneuse c.1904-10 catalog, in very small sizes, from 9 to 20 to the quart, and in a 5 pint size. Shrimp is #1090 in Marque C.C. catalog, 1900. Upper dauphin, #1180, is 2, 1 1/2 and 1 1/4 litres. Marque C.C. Large dauphin, #101, in 1 litre size. Anthoine, c.1900.

IV-223.
Ice cream molds.

Cats. Top (L) Pewter Cats' Quartet, the cats and platform, holds 2 1/2 litres. Complete with music stand. Apparently instruments were extra. Bertuch, c.1904. (R) #14 in Series No. 969, glace entière. Marque C.C., 1900. Bottom (L) and (M), #74 and #75. One on left is a wild cat. Both Anthoine c.1900. (R) Cat with ball, small size — 11 to quart. Duparquet, Huot and Moneuse, c.1904-10.

IV-224.
Ice cream molds.

Squirrels. (L) #18, Series No. 969, glace entière, Marque C.C., 1900. (M) #84, Anthoine, Paris, 1900. (R) Small one in several sizes, from 7-10 to the quart, 20 to quart, and 2 pints. Duparquet, Huot & Moneuse, c.1904-10.

IV-225.
Ice cream molds.

Chickens Top (L) Hen on high basket, #818, Marque C.C. (R) Hen on basket nest #55, demi-glace, Anthoine. Bottom: Rooster, #49, sold glace entière and demi-glace. Anthoine. I left out one that shows rooster mounting hen — hey! what occasion was that one for?

IV-228.
Ice cream molds.

Lions. Top (L) Lion couchant, with paw on ball (globe). #10, 9 centilitres. Marque C.C. (R) Another regal lion, #103, holding 1 1/2 or 3 litres, Anthoine. Middle (L) # 84, Anthoine. (R) More realistic cut of a mold, showing the two hinged parts and the clamps. Lead or pewter mold, from F.A. Walker import flyer, c.1880s. Bottom (L) Box mold, tinned sheet iron, holding 1 1/2 liter. Bertuch. (R) Two sizes, 9 to quart, and 3 1/2 quarts Duparquet, Huot & Moneuse.

IV-226.
Ice cream molds.

Rabbits. Top (L) 12 and 20 to quart; also 3 pint size. Duparquet, Huot & Moneuse. (R) Pewter, 2 pint size, Mrs. Marshall's <u>Book of Ices</u>. Middle (L) #16 in Series No. 969, glace entière, Marque C.C. Bottom (L) #78, Anthoine. Standing rabbit in cabbage patch, pewter, 1 1/4 litre size. Bertuch.

IV-229.
Ice cream molds.

Eagles. (L) Small, 7 to a quart. Duparquet, Huot & Moneuse. (R) #0256, lead or pewter, with clamps. F.A. Walker, 1880s.

IV-227.
Ice cream molds.

Elephants, perhaps Jumbo. (L) #559, pewter, 2 3/4 litre. Bertuch. You could also order a canopy accessory. (R) #73, Anthoine.

IV-230.
Ice cream molds.

Baskets. Clockwise from top (L): Basket of Fruits, with split pomegranate on top. 3 pint capacity. Wheatsheaf, 8"H, 1 quart. Smaller fruit basket, only 1 1/2 pints. Basket of flowers, 1 1/2 pints. All from Mrs. Marshall's <u>Book of Ices</u>. English, late 19th C.

IV-231.
Ice cream molds.
Flowers, including lily. Hinged pewter. Beautiful detailing in 3-part lily mold. 5 1/4"L closed. No marks. Author's collection. Two-part chrysanthemum and tulip molds, collection of Meryle Evans. Late 19th into early 20th C. Made for long time. **$35.00-$50.00**

IV-232.
Ice cream molds.
Pewter gnomes. #633, two of them at tavern table, holding 1 litre in all. #632, gnome pushing a large nut, holding 1 1/8 litre. Bertuch, Berlin, c.1904.

IV-233.
Ice cream molds.
More fantasy figures in hinged pewter molds. (L) #578 Snowman in 1 1/4 litre size. Broom & hat extra. (M) #591 Bachus, holding 1 1/2 litre. (R) #564 Struwelpeter, or Shock-headed Peter, the anti-hero of cautionary morality stories used to teach children manners and behavior. 1 litre. All Bertuch, c.1904.

IV-234.
Jagging iron.
Probably all metal, maybe cast and sheet iron, or brass. Drawn from tiny sketchy engraving in original kitchen interior print in Bartolomeo Scappi's Opera di M. Bartolomeo Scappi, a 1570 Italian cookbook. There's a trestle table holding a mound of dough or flour, rolled-out paste with a long slim rolling pin resting upon it, a carved wooden tool like a big molar tooth, used as a dough marker, and a clumpsy, large jagging iron with serated wheel and relatively short shaft, with knops at center and end.

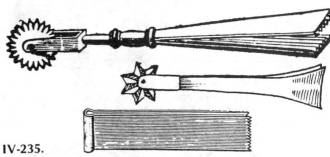

IV-235.
Jaggers & pastry pinchers.
(T) a "paste jigger," with smallish wheel and long pincers, corrugated lengthwise on the inside. Hard to say what material, both brass and iron could be springy. From Warne's Model Cookery, London & NY: 1868. (M) Drawing adapted from the paste-pincher depicted in Mrs. Beeton's Everyday Cooking, 1872 edition. (B) A spring steel pincher, from Duparquet, Huot & Maneuse catalog, c.1904-10. Value range for jaggers only. **$35.00-$100.00**

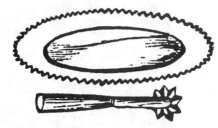

IV-236.
Jagger & Pie.
Simplified jagging iron with a pie crust showing serrated edge, taken from Henry Scammell's Treasure House of Useful Knowledge 1891, a book compiled, often without credit, from all existing books available to the editor. The style of this engraving seems very old, even 18th C, and it is possible that the jagger was meant to have a pincing end, rather than what appears to be a horn or wood handle.

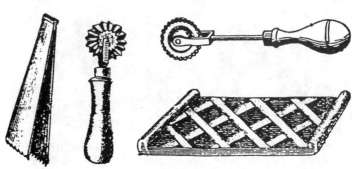

IV-237.
Jaggers & pincer.
Top (R) is a wood-handled jagger, from Lalance & Grosjean, 1890, as well as Duparquet, Huot & Moneuse, c.1904-10, catalogs. Other three pictures from chapter on little cakes and petits fours, in Urbain Dubois, La Patisserie, pictures c. 1860s-80s.

IV-238.
Jagger with ornamenter.
A very old style, back to the 1600's, wheel with a cutter that worked like a cookie cutter to make pastry leaves. Such leaves ornamented the top crust, or were baked, then laid upon the filling. Probably brass, English or French. Note knop (a mid-shaft knob) in center. F.A. Walker, Boston, import catalog, c.1870s.

IV-239.
Jaggers.
Cast iron long ones from Italy, 17th C, many tiers of turned knops and rings. In center is smaller brass one, 18th or early 19th C. Note the drilled holes in the brass one; this is often found, and I can only assume it had something to do with a cost-per-ounce, either making or shipping costs. Iron ones 8 1/4"L; brass one is 5 1/2"L. Courtesy Hillman Brooks. **$125.00-$200.00**

IV-240.
Jaggers.
Top one is cast brass, with long curved paste cutter for making circles, ovals, ellipses, leaves, etc. Five knops in center of shaft. This picture is from the 1908 Jaburg Brothers catalog for confectionery supplies. The style is very old. Similar ones, differing in workmanship, number of knops, length of cutter, style of serrated blades, and style of the straddling shaft for the wheel. The lower picture is from John Van Range, Cincinnati, catalog of 1914. Similar one-knoppers appear in 1865 catalog of Russell & Erwin Mfg. Co., New Britain, CT, and Lalance & Grosjean, 1890, as well as a 2-knopper made by Ekco, with 1" wheel, about 1925, and many modern cheap imports. Caution: These are often way overpriced. **$15.00-$45.00**

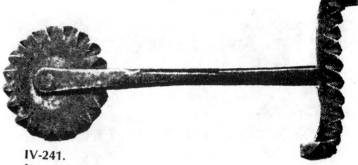

IV-241.
Jagger.
Brass, with unusually curved cutter at one end. 6 1/4"L. Mid 19th C. **$15.00-$45.00**

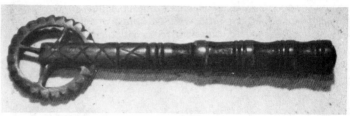

IV-242.
Jagger.
Cut pewter wheel, 4 spokes, set in turned and carved wood handle in old red paint, possibly overpainted on old green. 6 3/4"L, probably American, early to mid 18th C. **$375.00-$450.00**

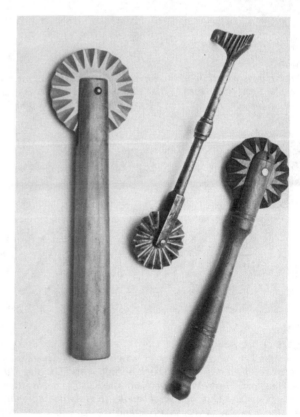

IV-243.
Jaggers.
(L) "Ivory" colored plastic wheel, asparagus green shaped plastic handle, beautifully simple, c.1915-20s. (M) Machined brass, commercially made, possibly the Russell & Erwin one mentioned in IV-240. 3rd quarter 19th C. (R) Turned wood with ebony-like wheel, 19th C. All between 4 1/2" and 5 1/4"L. The most valuable is the plastic one. **$25.00-$50.00**

IV-244.
Jaggers.
A pair of double-wheeled ones, cast with substantial knopped shaft, wheels not drilled out; other with sheet brass wheels, 4 holes each (which may have had something to do with diecutting technique of making the wheels), and with much thinner shaft — actually brass rod split at each end to accommodate wheels. 4"L each. 19th C. Courtesy Barbara Canter, Livingstone, NJ. **$35.00-$55.00**

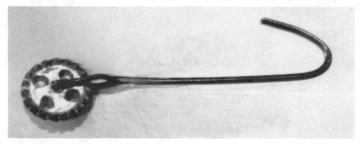

IV-245.
Jagger.
Stamped brass wheel, like those in previous picture, set into split iron square rod (nail stock?), that's hooked at end for easy hanging up. 5 7/8"L, 19th C. **$35.00-$45.00**

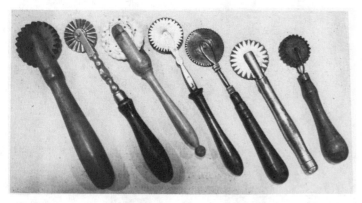

IV-246.
Jaggers & pie sealer.
Left to right: Fat wood handle, thick, machined steel wheel, 6 1/4"L; Nickeled steel shaft & wheel, black, turned wood handle; Blue & white Meissen or Blue Onion porcelain wheel, light-colored handle, possibly boxwood, Dutch (?) Steel handle, steel shaft, architecturally cut, steel wheel with very small serrations — possibly not a jagger but bookbinder's tool. Next, very heavy cast brass, nickel-plated. Dealer thought a machinist might have made it for his wife; last, pie sealer, turned wood handle, brass ferrule, wire axle, corrugated wood crimper roller. This might be potter's coggler. Courtesy dealer Lenny Kislin, Bearsville, NY. **$40.00-$125.00**

Jagger.
Carved whalebone, 6"L, early 19th C. **$100.00-$175.00**

IV-247.
Commercial jaggers.
For bakeries. (T) Brass wheel, drilled holes, long shaft, turned wooden handle. 7 1/2"L with 1 1/8" wheel. (B) Shorter, stubbier, 6 3/4"L, 1 1/8" wheel with finer serrations. Both S. Joseph catalog for bakers, c.1927. **$20.00-$35.00**

IV-248.
Scrimshaw jagger.
Sailor of carved whalebone, with ebony hat, high button shoes, pupils and buttons. He straddles the jagging wheel like a unicycle. 5 3/4" H. Courtesy Neil Blodgett, Higganum House, Higganum, CT. Value range mine, not Blodgett's. **$2000.00-$2500.00**

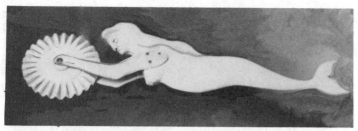

IV-249.
Scrimshaw jagger.
Mermaid holding large wheel. Carved whalebone. Arms nailed on with tiny nails. Courtesy Sidney Getler, American Folk Art, NYC.
$2000.00-$2600.00

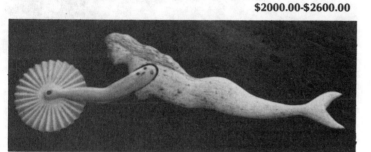

IV-250.
Scrimshaw jagger.
Carved whalebone mermaid holding large wheel. Flowing hair, lots of face detail. Slightly Negroid features on smiling face. Three brass nails holding on arms. 9 5/8"L, wheel 2 1/16" diameter. Courtesy Neil Blodgett, Higganum House, Higganum, CT. Value range mine, not Blodgett's.
$2000.00-$2600.00

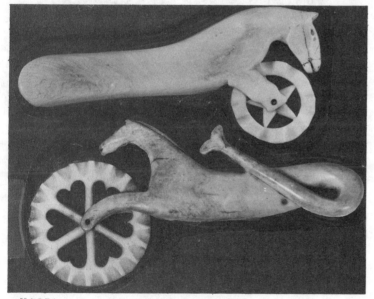

IV-251.
Scrimshaw jaggers.
Sea horses (T) Carved whalebone, star-shaped 'spokes' to wheel. 6"L, early 19th C. Picture courtesy of Robert W. Skinner, Inc., Auctioneers, Bolton, MA. (B) Carved whalebone, fishy tail, heart cutouts on wheel, 5 3/4"L. Picture courtesy of the National Museum of American History, Smithsonian Institution.
$1000.00-$2500.00

IV-252.
Jagger.
Cast pewter rabbit or leaping hare, resembling cast pewter chocolate molds made by 19th C. makers such as Anton Reiche, Dresden, Germany. Charming, almost feminine look, 6 1/4"L. I wouldn't be surprised if this was made as a sideline by a chocolate mold manufacturer in Europe. **$200.00-$350.00**

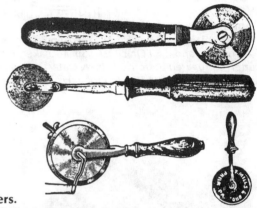

IV-253.
Pastry cutters.
Sharp steel blades, in a variety of wooden handles. From top: (1) From Jaburg, 1908. (2) Long shafted one, in 3 sizes: 7 1/2"L with 1 1/2" wheel; 8"L with 2 1/4" wheel, 8 3/4"L with 3 1/4" wheel. S. Joseph, c. 1927. (3) Lower left, a large-wheeled cutter, 6" diameter, with gauge and (4) right, a 4" or 6" diameter cutter, larger sizes to order. T. Mills, 1930. For candy, pizza, bread, dough, etc.
$5.00-$15.00

IV-254.
Pie crimper & ornamenter.
"Cinderella," invented & mfd. by Mr. G.J. Capewell, Cheshire, CT. Face of wheel used for printing rosettes; and also crimping, on the other side, opposite the wheel...is a set of blades which cut ventilating holes in the crust in star shape. American Agriculturist ad, 12/1876. **$35.00-$45.00**

IV-255.
Pie rimmer, crimper & pastry cutter.
Pat'd 9/11/1866, 5-1/2"L, brass. Mfd. by J. Stephen & W. Zeller, Womelsdorf, PA. Illustration is from flimsy printed broadside that advertised the rimmers. Note the little footstool the infant stands on. **$85.00-$125.00**

IV-256.
Combination tool.
Pieced tin, japanned finish, brass medalion appears to say "-organ —— Comp. Mandal 6 LONDON." Sugar shaker or dredger, shape cutter (corrugated bottom), nutmeg grater, lemon grater or zester, and pastry jagger. Late 19th C. Probably "Morgan." **$65.00-$115.00**

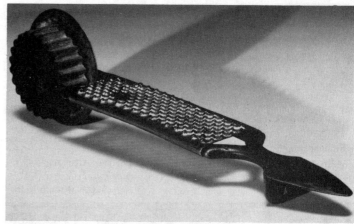

IV-259.
Crimper & grater combined.
Tin, wood and cast metal. The grater was probably used for nutmeg. The pointed end may be a can opener, or for making slashes in top crust before baking. 6-7/8"L, American, late 19th C. Picture courtesy of the National Museum of American History, Smithsonian Institution.

$35.00-$45.00

IV-257.
Crimpers & jagger.
(L) to (R): Large all wood wheel, set in wooden handle, 7"L, homemade? Collection of Meryle Evans. Next is galvanized tin sealer with plain wood handle, 6 1/2"L, possibly homemade with kitchen tool handle, late 19th C. Next is cast aluminum, very cheap, 4 3/4"L; Cheapest of all is "Vaughn's Pie Trimmer & Sealer," pat'd 5/10/1921. Aluminum wheel, green painted wood handle. 6 1/2"L. **$8.00-$25.00**

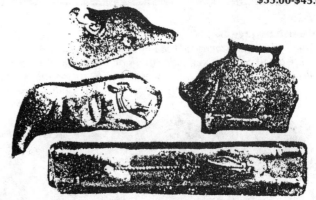

IV-260.
Ancient animal-shaped molds.
*Pictures not to scale. These are cast bronze **reproductions** of pastry and other molds found in excavations at Pompei during the 19th C. Two at (L) are a leg of ham, 13 1/2"L, and a whole dead pig, 20 1/2"L. At right is a pig with handle, only 7 7/8"L. At bottom is a horrible flayed hare, each detail of its poor backbone dotting the length of the mold. 26 1/2"L. All made at Fonderie Artistiche Riunite, by J. Chiurazzi & Fils & S. De Angelis & Fils, Naples, Italy. From catalog, 1910-11.*

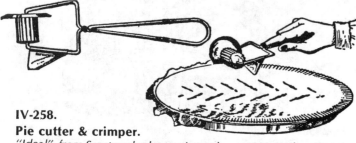

IV-258.
Pie cutter & crimper.
"Ideal", from Seastrand salesmen's catalog, c.1929. "Why not save time by using the Ideal? The only perfect pie cutter and crimper; it not only makes a cleaner cut and a neater crimp, but it presses both crusts firmly together, thus preventing the rich juices from boiling over." Wood and wire and tin, with edging trimmer.

$10.00-$20.00

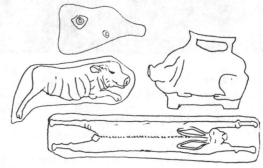

IV-261.
Outline drawings of molds in 260.

IV-262.
Nineteenth Century Pastry Kitchen with Molds.
Unidentified highly-detailed print, showing kitchen layout similar to those found 300 years before and today. From the (L) traveling around the wall: cupboard with rolling pin, dredger, pan with scoop; range with 3 grated openings, above which are bracket shelves loaded with molds and sieves. In the middle of the back is an oven. Then more molds, with a balance scale on the table at right rear, and a large dresser with molds. Then a churn. Probably English or French, probably about 1870-80.

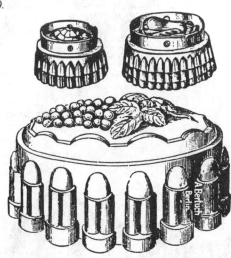

IV-263.
Biscuit, creme or jelly mold.
Stamped copper, tinned inside, oval, 7 1/4"L. Bertuch, Berlin, c.1904. **$125.00-$175.00**

IV-264.
Jelly molds.
Two at top have protective rims, to keep designs from being banged, and also to enable the mold to stand firmly, upside down, to be filled and while setting. Tin with fluted skirts. Sizes from 1/2 to 2 pints, and 2 quarts. F.A. Walker catalog, 1880s. Bottom mold, with grape bunch on top, is also oval, in 2 sizes — 8" and 8 5/8"L. Bertuch, c.1904. **$65.00-$125.00**

IV-265.
Photogravure plate of copper molds, etc.
which is #XXIX plate, in unidentified 19th C. German book. The
molds are probably early 19th C. Note especially the turtle mold
at bottom.

IV-266.
Small molds,
for dariols and one bouche cup (center). Stamped & pieced tin.
Mrs. A.B. Marshall's Larger Cookery Book, 1902. **$10.00-$20.00**

IV-267.
Jelly mold.
Stamped & pieced tin, pineapple design, rim. Mold depth 4 7/8";
Overall 6"H x 7"L. Ex-Collection of Grace Manney, NYC food
stylist. **$40.00-$55.00**

IV-269.
Jelly molds.
Stamped & pieced tin. (L) Round, interlinked crabapple (?) design
bordering top, scored lozenges on skirt. Skirt in 3 parts, soldered
to top. Marked near hanging ring, looks like capital N superimposed on a C or H, with "32" and "6". No country of origin, could
be pre-1892 if imported, or turn-of-century if American. 3 1/2" deep
x 8 1/8" diameter. (R) Round, tin, shell design bordered by rope.
Simple fluted skirt of 2 pieces soldered. Marked "France 296,"
4" deep x 6 1/4" diameter. Ex-Collection of NYC food stylist Grace
Manney. **$40.00-$55.00**

IV-268.
Jelly molds.
Sampling from ad of stamped tin molds sold by J. & C. Berrian,
NYC. Ad in History of Prominent Mercantile & Manufacturing
Firms in the U.S. Boston: 1857. **$45.00-$150.00**

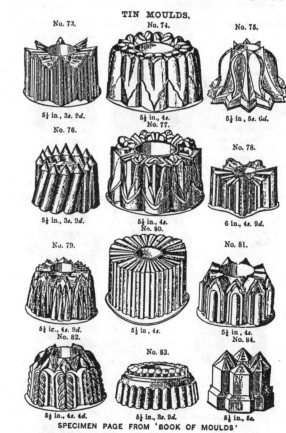

IV-270.
Specimen page from Marshall's 'Book of Moulds."
Tin molds in fancy shapes, mostly for jellies, from Mrs. A.B. Marshall's Cookery Book, London, c.1900 edition.

TIN MOULDS.

No. 72A. No. 72B. No. 72C.

5¼ in., 5s. 5¾ in., 5s. 5¾ in., 4s. 9d.

No. 72D. No. 72E. No. 72F.

5¼ in., 5s. 5¼ in., 5s. 5¼ in., 5s.

No. 73. No. 74. No. 75.

5¼ in., 3s. 9d. 5¼ in., 4s. 5¼ in., 4s. 6d.

No. 76. No. 77. No. 78.

5¼ in., 3s. 9d. 5¼ in., 4s. 6 in., 4s. 9d.

IV-271.
Specimem page from Marshall's 'Book of Moulds.'
From *Mrs. A.B. Marshall's Larger Cookery Book of Extra Recipes*, London, c.1902 edition.

MOULDS FOR HOT & COLD ENTRÉES & SAVOURIES.

No. 215B. No. 215C. No. 215D.
BUTTERFLY MOULD. FANCY MOULD. FANCY MOULD.

Copper tinned, Copper tinned, Copper tinned,
10s. per doz. 10s. per doz. 10s. per doz.

No. 215E. No. 215F. No. 215G.
FANCY MOULD. FANCY MOULD. FANCY MOULD.

Copper tinned, Copper tinned. Copper tinned,
10s. per doz. 10s. per doz. 10s. per doz.

No. 215H.—COPPER BOMBE.

No. 217.—FLUTED FLEUR RING.

9s. per doz. 1s. each. Plain Fleur Rings, 6d. & 9d. each.

No. 215I.
WALNUT MOULDS.

No. 209.—2s. and 3s. per doz. For Petits Fours, etc., 2s. per doz.

IV-272.
Specimen page from Marshall's 'Book of Moulds.'
Molds for hot & cold entrees and savories, as well as a copper bombe mold. From *Mrs. A.B. Marshall's Cookery Book*, London, c.1900 edition.

IV-273.
Mold.
Stamped tin scroll, hanging ring, marked "SCT Co., Germany." 7"L, 20th C. Ex-Collection of NYC food stylist Grace Manney.
$25.00-$35.00

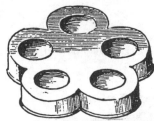

IV-274.
Piccolo mold,
for making a fancy jellied dish called Little Piccolos. "Line molds with 1/8" thick lemon jelly, and after lining, fill up the top parts with 2-colored creams, using forcing bags and plain pipes for the purpose, and partly fill up the bottom part of the moulds with finely-shredded blanched sweet almonds and pistachio nuts; in the centre of each put a little liquid jelly, then close up the moulds, place them on ice till set, and turn out on wet foolscap paper." Serve on a little plate, with chopped jelly around edges, and pour over a pale green cream made of whipped cream mixed with lemon jelly, rum, "Noyeau" syrup, and coloring. From *Mrs. A.B. Marshall's Larger Cookery Book*, c.1902. Picture from her 1900 book.
$45.00-$65.00

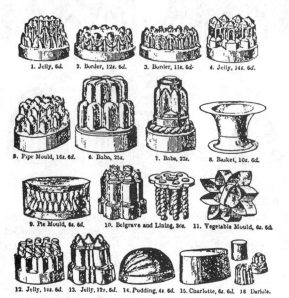

1. Jelly, 6d. 2. Border, 12s. 6d. 3. Border, 11s. 6d. 4. Jelly, 14s. 6d.

5. Pipe Mould, 16s. 6d. 6. Baba, 25s. 7. Baba, 22s. 8. Basket, 10s. 6d.

9. Pie Mould, 6s. 6d. 10. Belgrave and Lining, 30s. 11. Vegetable Mould, 6s. 6d.

12. Jelly, 14s. 6d. 13. Jelly, 12s. 6d. 14. Pudding, 4s. 6d. 15. Charlotte, 6s. 6d. 16. Dariole.

IV-275.
Jelly molds, and others,
from William S. Adams, & Son, London, ad in *Francatelli's Cook's Guide Advertiser*, c.1860-61.

IV-276.
Molded gelatin (jellied) dessert,
made with Rich's "Tryphosa" brand jelly mix. They had great flavors, including mint and coffee and wine (like Madeira). Turn of century booklet.

ORANGE TRYPHOSA WITH RICH'S PRESERVED CUMQUATS

IV-277.
Dessert jelly ad.
"Bro-Man-Gel-On," mfd. by Stern & Saalbert, NYC. Ladies' Home Journal, 11/1902.

IV-278.
Molds for biscuits, cremes, etc.
Copper. Many of these made in several sizes. All sizes range from 4" to 8" diameter. Bertuch, c.1904. **$25.00-$150.00**

IV-279.
Jelly molds.
Ovals with various designs. 6 1/2" to 7 1/2"L. Material not mentioned, possibly stamped steel as some others on same page, or possibly copper with tin lining, or maybe just tin. S. Joseph, c.1927. **$35.00-$50.00**

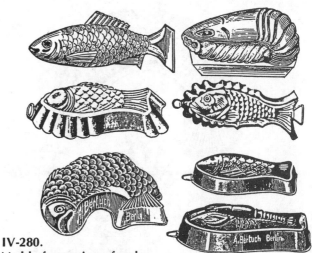

IV-280.
Molds for various foods,
including iced, jellied and biscuit. Most of these probably for fish-flavored aspics or mousses. All about 7 1/2" to 13"L. Top two are from Mrs. Marshall's cookery book, c.1902; one in second row (R) is from S. Joseph, NYC, c.1927. Rest from Bertuch, Berlin, c.1904. **$35.00-$75.00**

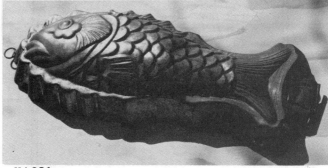

IV-281.
Fish mold,
for aspics, etc. Stamped tin, leveling 'leg' at tail end, marked "Germany," c.1900-1920. 2 3/4" deep x 13 1/2"L x 5 1/2"W. Ex-collection of NYC food stylist Grace Manney. **$20.00-$35.00**

IV-282.
Fish mold,
for aspics, etc. Stamped tin, simple head, wide flat edges. Wire leg at tail end. Stamped "Austria", and "CF" (?), also #499 over a #3. 2 1/4" deep x 9 1/8"L x 3 3/4"W. Ex-collection of NYC food stylist Grace Manney. **$20.00-$35.00**

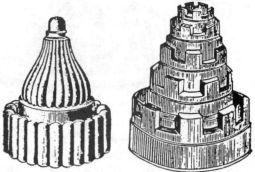

IV-285.
Macedoine molds.
Imported copper, 6 1/4" and 6 3/4" diameter at bottom. A macedoine is chopped fresh fruit, soaked in kirsch and maraschino cherry juice, mixed with cream and chilled. Duparquet catalog. **$100.00-$200.00**

IV-283.
Fish molds.
Curved fish. Dark one at top, with hanging ring at center, is stamped tin, 8" or 11" diameter, size from S. Joseph, NYC, c.1927. Lighter one in 11" and 12" diameter, from Bertuch, Berlin, c.1904. **$25.00-$45.00**

IV-286.
Cornucopia or Horn of Plenty molds.
For various foods. All are hinged. In center is a dessert, decorated with a molded cornucopia, from Urbain Dubois' La Patisserie. Simple mold at top, made in 4 sizes, from 5 1/2" to 10 1/4"L, Duparquet, Huot & Moneuse, c.1904-10. Decorated one at bottom (L) is copper, 6 3/4"L, and imported (from Germany?), also D, H & M. Bottom (R) is "French Horn of Plenty," 10 1/2"L with 7" opening, for ice cream. S. Joseph. **$25.00-$55.00**

S. JOSEPH CO., INC. 24 EAST 22ND STREET, NEW YORK, N. Y.

STAR MOULD	TURTLE MOULD
No. 900	No. 901

LOBSTER MOULD	CORN MOULD
No. 902	No. 905

STRAIGHT FISH MOULD	MELON MOULD
No. 906	No. 907

IV-284.
Ceramic molds.
A page from the S. Joseph catalog, c.1927.

IV-287.
More cornucopias,
a popular form because it symbolizes bounteous harvests, plenty, prosperity. Ribbed one upper (L), 6 3/4"L. One with flower horn is much larger, about 10 3/4"L. Smaller one made in 4 sizes, from 4 3/4" to 11"L. All Bertuch, c.1904.

255

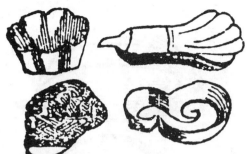

IV-288.
"Fancy Patty Pans
*for baking ornamental tea cakes." American Home Cook Book,
1854.*

IV-289.
Madeline molds.
Small molds of stamped tin. S. Joseph, c.1927. **$5.00-$8.00**

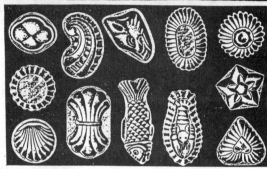

IV-292.
Madeline molds.
Top set, stamped tin, from Pick-Barth catalog, 1929. A few sample sizes: top left one is 4" x 2 1/8"; the star one at right is 2 7/8" diameter. Lower set, imported tin molds, from G.M. Thurnauer & Bro., NYC dealers & importers. House Furnishing Review ad, 1/1903. **$5.00-$10.00**

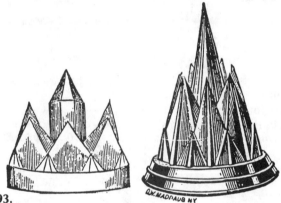

IV-293.
Hall of the Mountain King molds.
Stamped, pieced tin. Actually (L) is a "Jelly or Blanc Mange Mould", also for ice cream. American Home Cook Book, 1854. (R) is a "Vegetable and Rice Mould," #229, for making decorative spires of cooked, mashed root veggies or rice. F.A. Walker catalog, c.1890. **$55.00-$100.00**

IV-290.
Madeline molds.
Stamped tin, from F.A. Walker catalog, c.1890. Probably imported **$7.00-$15.00**

IV-294.
Rice boiler,
or pudding mold. Fluted, tubed, closefit lid with strap handle. Tin. F.A. Walker, c.1890. **$35.00-$50.00**

IV-291.
Petits fours molds.
Small, and pretty much indistinguishable from madeline molds. S. Joseph, c.1927. **$5.00-$12.00**

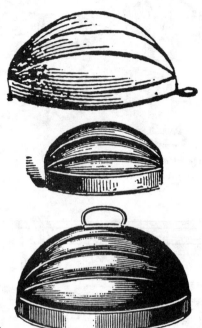

IMPORTED TIN FORMS.
For Glace, Nougat ou Sucre.
Many other designs kept in stock.

Corbeille cannelee.

No. 128. { Round 9¼ ins. diam., 8½ ins. high.
         { Oval 21 " long, 9½ " wide.

Corbeille cannelee.

No. 124. { 9¼ ins. diam.
         { 8½ " high.

Vase.

No. 394—11 ins. high.

Piece Montee.

No. 406—12 and 14 ins. high.

Moule de Cascades.

Tin Buisson d'Ecrevisses.

No. 117—18 and 24 ins. high.
Other sizes to order.

No. 120—12½ ins. high.
Other patterns 13 to 23 ins. high.

IV-295.
Molds for glace, nougat, etc.
Tall urn and fountain "forms" for a variety of fancy desserts. Page from Duparquet, Huot & Moneuse, c.1904-10. **$200.00-$350.00**

IV-297.
Melon molds.
Tin, oval. Three versions (you'll note that some never did have handles on the body). (T) "Pudding Mould.—Who likes boiled pudding can have it dry and light if cooked in one of these moulds." American Home Cookbook, *1854. (M) "Fancy Quart and Two-Quart Ice Cream Mould." Cherry-Bassett, 1921. (B) With wire handle. Four sizes: for 2, 3, 2 1/2 and 4 pints. From 6 1/2" x 4 3/4" x 3 1/2" up to 8" x 6 1/8" x 4 1/8". Central Stamping Co., 1920. An even larger range of sizes, from 2 to 8 pints, was offered by Duparquet, about 1904.* **$25.00-$45.00**

IV-296.
Melon mold.
Very unusual mold with ribbed copper body, wrought iron handle. 18"L overall. Ex-Wiggins Tavern Collection, Northampton, MA. Photograph courtesy of Luella McCloud Antiques, Shelburn Falls, MA. Value range mine not McCloud's. **$400.00-$600.00**

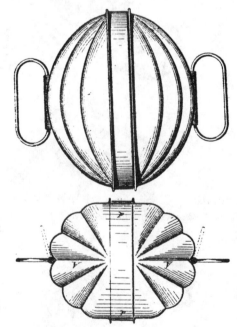

IV-298.
"Ice cream & pudding mold" patent.
Pat'd 11/10/1885, by Henry Eppelsheimer, NYC. He, of course, was connected to the well known American ice cream mold firm. This melon has two convex halves with one serving as the 'lid' to the other Official Gazette.

IV-299.
Pudding mold.
Round tin "Turk's Head" or turban mold. (Could also be a turban squash — related to a melon!) I call this one the laughing jockey. F. A. Walker catalog, c.1890. **$25.00-$45.00**

IV-301.
Pudding molds.
(L) Stamped & pieced tin, imported by Duparquet, NYC. 4 3/4" diameter. Big flat bracket handle on lid. Hearts add value. c.1904-10.
(R) Heavy tin, spouted, showing bayonet mount clearly. Four sizes, from 1 1/8 to 2 3/4 litre. Bertuch, c.1904. **$35.00-$50.00**

IV-300.
Steamer molds,
for pudding and bread. All three, with spouts or plain, are for steaming pudding or brown bread. Bottom two have so-called "bayonet" mount (put on and twist to secure) lids. Tin, in many sizes. Spouted ones, mainly for pudding, are for 1 to 4 quarts. Plain one, from 1 1/2 pint to 4 quart, from 4" x 4" to 8" x 6 1/2". Top one, made by Dover Stamping Co., c.1899 (and before & after); others from D. J. Barry, 1924. **$15.00-$30.00**

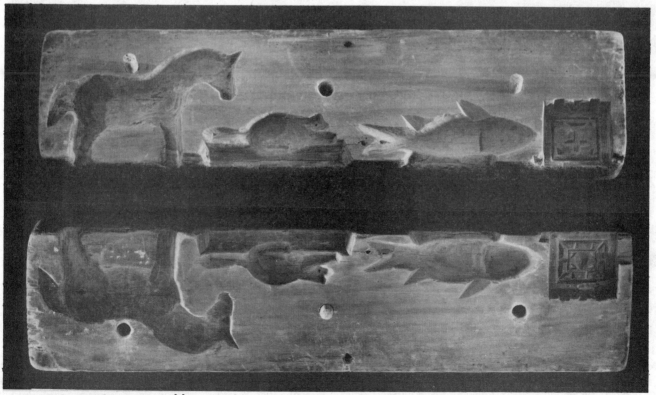

IV-302. Maple sugar mold.
Carved wood, 2 halves. Horse, beaver, fish and little square cake with a cross. Note pegs & holes, for holding halves together. Each half is 18"L x 4 1/2"W x 1 3/4" thick, American or Canadian, late 19th C. Photo courtesy of Jeannine Dobb's Country/Folk/Antiques, Merrimack, NH. Value range mine. **$500.00-$750.00**

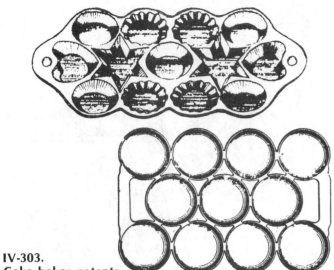

IV-303.
Cake baker patents.

Both designed to be made of cast iron. (T) Design pat'd 7/18/1871, by Adam Reid, Buffalo, NY. Hearts, stars, plain & scalloped cups. (B) "Egg Pan & Cake Baker," pat'd 4/5/1859, by Nathaniel Waterman, Boston, MA. His objective was to invent "a new or Improved Egg-Pan or Article for Cooking or Baking Eggs." Eleven cups, with flat bottoms. He believed that the design of cups was necessary in order to allow for a strenghtening (and convenient) handle at each end. "Open spaces are left between the cups to allow the currents of heat to pass upward between them so as to equalize the heat against their surfaces. The metallic connections of the cups serve as conveyors of heat from cup to cup." Official Gazette.

IV-304.
Cake or egg baker.

This one follows almost exactly the design of Waterman. Cast iron, marked "W & L Mfg. Co.," pat'd 1867. Picture courtesy of the Smithsonian Institution, Museum of History & Technology.

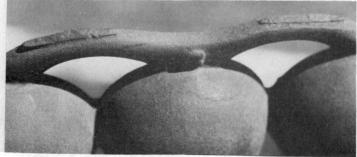

IV-305.
Closeup of baking pan edge.

Cast iron, R & E. Mfg. Co., pat'd April 5, 1858. "6" on back. Detail shows one end, the handles' edges, which look as if the pans were cast in long strips and snapped apart at the handles, then cursorily filed down. Pan has 12 cups, 10 3/4"L x 7 1/8"W. Ex-collection of NYC food stylist, Grace Manney.

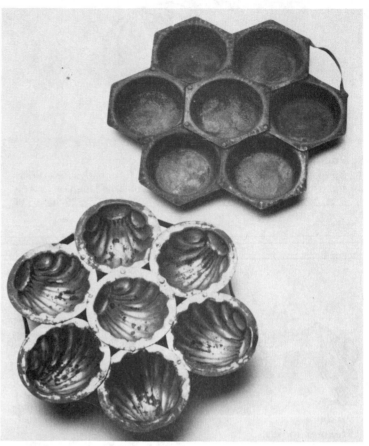

IV-306.
Baking molds,

although the darker one, sort of honeycomb pattern, has been called a maple sugar mold. (T) Seven shallow flat bottom cups riveted together with bent tin strap handle, 9 1/8" diameter, 19th C. (B) Seven scallop shells in circular form, 9" diameter, stamped tin. Collection of Meryle Evans. **$40.00-$60.00**

IV-307.
Baking pans,

of stamped tin. (T) "Turk head pan," in 3 sizes: 11" x 7 1/4" with 6 cups; 14 1/2" x 7 1/4" with 8; and 14 1/4" x 11" with 12. Cups all same size. Geuder, Paeschke & Frey, 1925. (M) Unusual round "biscuit pan," on frame. Plain cups, 2 1/4" x 1 1/8" deep. Only one size, with 9 cups, 9 1/2" diameter. Central Stamping Co., 1920. (B) Oblong pan with detachable shallow flat bottom cups. Stamped tin. Delphos Can Co., Delphos, OH. A company that made oil cans and dustpans. Ad in House Furnishing Review, 1/1906. **$20.00-$35.00**

IV-308.
Melon pans.
Size not given, but a commerical bakery pan, stamped tin. The melons are probably about 5"L each. Jaburg, 1908. **$30.00-$45.00**

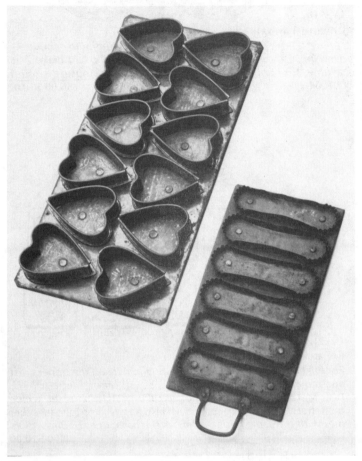

IV-309.
Baking pans.
Sheet tin. 12 hearts riveted to oblong blued steel sheet. 13 1/2"L x 6 1/4"W, each heart is 2 1/2"L. Maker unknown. Other one makes 6 Lady Fingers, with fluted ends. Mold 9"L exclusive of handle; cups 4 1/4"L. Both late 19th or early 20th C. Collection of Meryle Evans. **$75.00-$125.00; $30.00-$55.00**

IV-310.
Timbale sheet.
Twelve cups riveted to sheet metal tin, made in four sizes. Sheet 8" x 6" with cups 1 3/4" x 1 1/2" up to 10" x 7 1/2" with cups 2 1/4" x 2". Sold through D.J. Barry catalog, 1924. **$25.00-$40.00**

IV-311.
Noodle cutter.
Hand-cranked, table top. "Vitantonio Mfg. Co., Cleveland, OH." Pat'd 2/13/1906 and 3/2/1920. Cast iron, tin and wood, roller attachment shown here, the "Zigzag #6," is iron, tin and has white rubber around axle. Pasta maker is screwed to piece of wood which would be clamped to table top. 7"H x 7"W. Company still in business. **$65.00-$85.00**

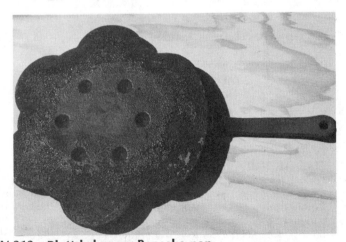

IV-312. Plett kaker, or Pancake pan.
Also referred to as a "muffin baker" in the 1872 New Cyclopedia of Domestic Economy. "Muffin" as in the flat "English" muffin. Cast iron, 7 very shallow cups, with "JOHNSON" cast on handle. 10 1/2" diameter with 6 1/4"L handle. Lower picture shows interesting appearance of bottom. Note heavy incrustation. Ex-collection of NYC food stylist, Grace Manney. **$75.00-$125.00**

IV-313.

Plett kaker, or Pancake pan.

Cast iron, 7 shallow flat bottom very shallow cups, 3 legs. From ad of NYC dealer, J. & C. Berrian, in a book on prominent manufacturers of the U.S., 1857.

IV-314.

Pancake griddle iron.

"U Like 'Em" multiple griddle. Polished cast iron that "will not absorb fat." Reversible so "no turning of cakes required." Each 6" diameter pan works independently. Made in 3 sizes, for 4 cakes (originally $.49), for 6 cakes ($.71) and 8 cakes ($.97). Albert Pick catalog for hoteliers, 1909. **$75.00-$125.00**

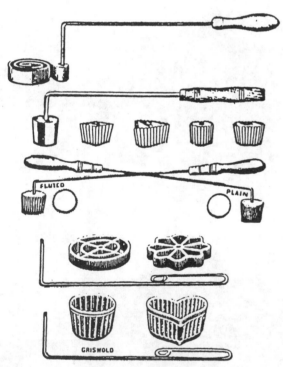

IV-315.

Timbale, patty, rosette or bouche irons.

For making little pastry cups, about 2"H, that could be filled with cremes, mousses, and savouries. Top one with spiraled iron is a **Coiled Spring Cake"** *or sprungfedern iron. Turn-of-the-century catalog. Second down, with a plain and 4 fluted cups or "case fryers," is nickel plated, from S. Joseph, c.1927. Crossed timbale irons, also nickeled, could be had as plain or fluted rounds, oval, hearts, diamonds, spades, or clubs. From Sexton Stove & Range Mfg., c.1930s. Last sets from Griswold. These you often find in original boxes.* **$20.00-$60.00**

IV-316.

Rosette-Timbale set.

"Enjoy 'Old World' pastry treats!" Cast aluminum, about 3" diameter. Double stemmed handle meant you could make 2 at a time. Probably A. Andresen. Gift shop in <u>House Beautiful,</u> *4/1964.* **$5.00-$10.00**

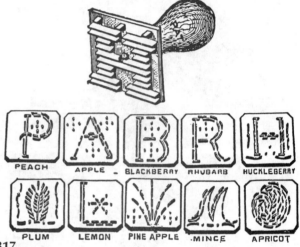

IV-317.

Pie markers.

For bakeries. (T) Pie stamp, for putting initials on the upper crust and puncturing it to let steam escape. Full set of 7 letters: A, H, L, R, M, C, P in H. Hueg catalog, c.1900-1921. (B) This set, which has letters (P, A, B, R, H, L, and M) also has designs to mark other pies with the same initial letters as the basic ones. Jaburg, 1908. **$8.00-$20.00**

IV-318.

Pie pans or plates.

Shallow, with slanted sides (layer cake pans have straight sides). From top: (1) Scalloped, stamped tin, in one size, 8 9/16" diameter x 1 1/8" deep. Savory, c.1925-28. (2) Perforated tin, 9 3/4" x 1 1/16", Also Savory. (3) "Greystone" gray graniteware plate in 5 sizes, from 7" to 11" diameter. Also came in slightly deeper versions, 9" to 11" diameter. Matthai-Ingram, c.1890. Bottom one is a "Greystone Lebanon" referring to an area of Pennsylvania. Also Matthai-Ingram. **$5.00-$25.00**

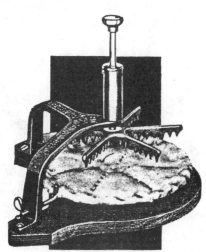

IV-319.
Cake & pie marker.
For professional bakers. Screwed to wooden base, spring-loaded punch. Nickel-plated, or polished cast aluminum. It marked a dotted line where to cut pieces, and could be fitted with markers for from 4 to 12 slices for different sizes of pie or cake tins. D. J. Barry, 1924.   **$15.00-$35.00**

IV-320.
"Cottage stamp."
"In place of moulding the Cottage in six pieces, mould them in one piece, place same in pans, when half raised dust them lightly with Rye flour and stamp with this tool." In Hueg and Jaburg catalogs, early 20th C. "Cottage" is hard to track down. It's probably the same as "Cottage Pudding," a cake-like confection, which Marjorie Heseltine, in Good Cooking, from early 20th C., says to bake in a pan and cut into squares. The stamp is for bakeries.   **$15.00-$22.00**

IV-321.
Popover pans.
Actually these are referred to as a "corn bread" pan in Hibbard, Spencer, Bartlett's catalog showing "Waterman's Cast Bake Pans," and as a "Gem Pan," in Griswold's catalogs. (T) #10, 11 pans, 2 3/4" diameter each. 1880s. (B) #10, cakes 2 1/2" x 1 3/4". Griswold, early 20th C.   **$35.00-$75.00**

IV-322.
Rice ball boilers.
Top (R) "Wire pea or vegetable boiler, for beans, rice, boils dry and when taken out no grains are left in the pot." Small one at right is a "tea boiler". American Home Cook Book, 1854. (L) For balls of "fried" farina, from Urbain Dubois, c.1860s-80s. Lower Tinned screen or wire gauze, in one size, 5 1/2" diameter. Washburn "Androck" line, 1936.   **$10.00-$25.00**

IV-323.
Rice molds from China.
Carved wood paddles, with typical Chinese motifs of fish, butterfly and lotus flower. Usually called "sugar molds" by dealers who don't know. These are actually imported from China, and may be old in some instances. Photograph courtesy of Mary Colborn, Murrysville, PA.   **$15.00-$45.00**

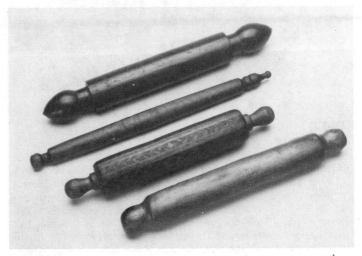

IV-324.
Rolling pins.
Fancy carved wooden pins, well-turned from one piece of wood. One with variegated wood, third from top, with bulbous handles and thick barrel, is possibly a Shaker piece. Note the 2 different ends on the long French pin—undoubtedly made to order for a cook with special needs. From about 15 1/4"L to 18 1/2"L. 19th C. Collection of Meryle Evans.   **$50.00-$115.00**

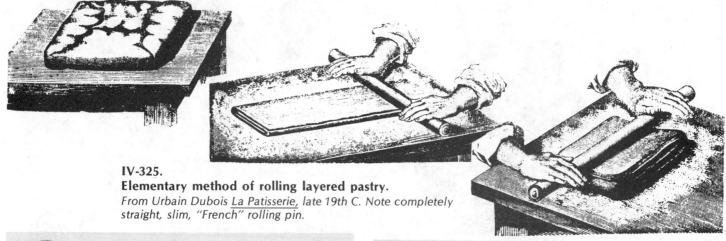

IV-325.
Elementary method of rolling layered pastry.
From Urbain Dubois La Patisserie, *late 19th C. Note completely straight, slim, "French" rolling pin.*

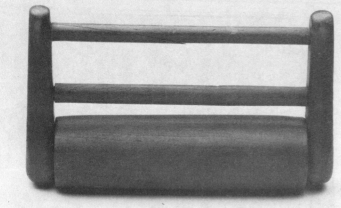

IV-326.
Rolling pin.
Heavy wood with double-barred handle for extra strength and good grip. 11"L x 6 3/4"H as shown. 19th C. Collection Meryle Evans, as are two below. **$55.00-$100.00**

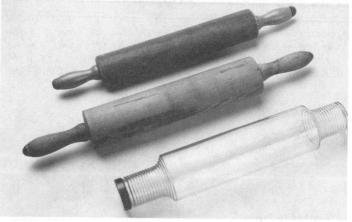

IV-328.
Rolling pins.
Two wooden ones, with separate turned handles and an axle rod. 16 1/4"L and 18 1/2"L. Glass bottle pin has screw-on metal cap, and was meant to be filled with cold water or shaved ice. Many old pins were glass—they could be chilled and this makes rolling fine pastry easier. c.1900 for wood; 1930s for glass. **$15.00-$35.00**

IV-327.
Rolling pins.
Two patented ones. Upper one has its own compartment of dusting flour above in mesh cylinder. 20 1/4"L. This is Harlowe's "Do No Stick" pin, pat'd 12/1903. Other one, with double barrels or rollers, and beautifully formed handles, is 20"L, with rollers 11 3/4"L x 1 3/4" diameter. It is "Taylor's Patent Combination Rolling Pin" pat'd 7/16/1867. June Sprigg says it is a Shaker pin. The instructions sheet reads "The advantage of this Roller is, it will do the work in half the time it can be done with the single roller. It is worked with the greatest ease." Courtesy Meryle Evans. **$125.00-$200.00**

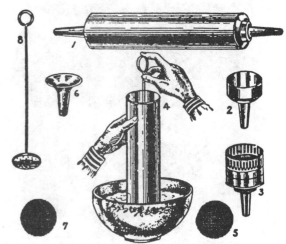

IV-329.
Rolling pin combination tool.
Pieced tin, with everything needed to cut cookies, churn syllabubs, funnel, strain, and squirt. From Seastrand catalog, c.1912. **$55.00-$75.00**

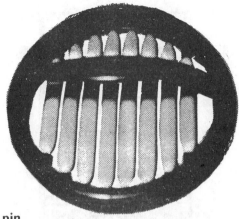

IV-330.
Rolling pin.
Really odd red & white plastic one. The "Magnus," mfd. by Magnus Harmonica Corp., Newark, NJ. Arching handle across the 8 rollers. One handed—great conversation piece. Or use for duet performances with a harmonica player. Photograph & information courtesy of great cookie cutter collector, Evelyn King.
$45.00-$65.00

IV-332.   *See also IV-66.*
Springerle board.
Carved fine grained wood, 9 1/4" x 6 3/4"W signed, "F.G." American, Pennsylvania German, 1860s-70s. Note great variety of motifs, including man playing pipe while sitting on bench under a tree with curving branch (think of those butter molds), and the St. Nicholas, and his reindeer. Ex-Keillor Collection.
$500.00-$1000.00

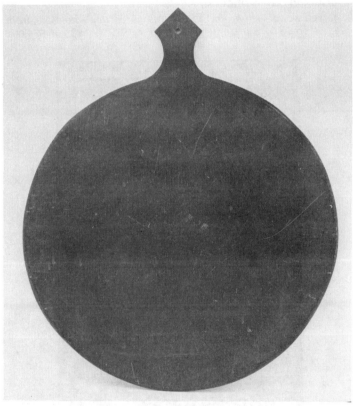

IV-331.
Pastry "board" made of slate.
*Also called a **dough board**. This beautiful thing with arrow tab handle is made of slate not wood. Hole for hanging cord. 17 1/2" diameter, American, probably Pennsylvania, possibly early 19th C. Bigger than most I've seen. Picture courtesy of Robert W. Skinner Inc., Auctioneers, Bolton, MA.*   **$400.00-$600.00**

IV-333.
Metal faced springerle boards.
Modern manufacture, both from ads of The House-On-The-Hill, Vermont, or Minnesota. Make puffy little cookies. "Heavy metal mounted on hand-finished cherry-wood." With hanging rings to serve as "kitchen plaques." (L) Ad from Gourmet, 10/1967; (R) ad from Early American Life, 1975. Company has been bought and revived, so these are still being made. It's easy to pay too much thinking they're old. I did it several times, alas.   **$25.00-$65.00**

IV-334.
All cast metal springerle mold.
Heavy metal like pewter. Makes 15 individual designs, measures 5 3/4" x 3 1/2". House with well, dog, church, another church, bird, grapes, raspberries, 2 beeskips on bench, elk (?), duck in pond, heron, berries, hunter with gun & rabbit, man cooking over gypsy kettle, woman holding a boot (?) in one hand. Courtesy Lenny Kislin, Bearsville, NY. **$200.00-$250.00**

IV-335.
All cast iron springerle mold.
12 squares, slightly irregular, each cookie would be about 1 1/8" x 1 3/4". Basket with 3 apples, pear with 2 leaves, turkey or peacock, cornucopia, bird in branch, oak leaves with acorn, fruited branch, horseshoe with blacksmith's hammer, large bird on branch, tall basket with apples or peaches, grape leaves, a cross. Courtesy Lenny Kislin, Bearsville, NY. Now in Joel Schiff collection. **$225.00-$350.00**

IV-336.
Commercial springerle,
carved wood. With from 1 to 12 pictures, costing wholesale, from $2.50 to $8.64 a dozen!!! S. Joseph, c.1927. **$35.00-$75.00**

IV-337.
All cast metal springerle.
Probably cast pewter. 7 1/2"H, with musical, fruit, and household scenes. Note woman arranging flowers, 3rd down on far right. Late 19th C. **$100.00-$150.00**

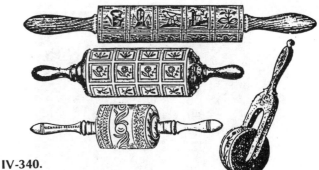

IV-340.
Springerle rolling pins & cake marker.
Some called "New Year's or Springerle Rolling Pins." Top one has 12 designs, from Middleby, 1927. Next one has many designs, this one has 24, the picture cheats a bit on perspective. Jaburg Bro., 1908. Others from Germany. All 20th C. **$100.00-$150.00**

IV-338.
Commercial quality carved wood springerle
(L) "Wooden cake prints or Springerle Moulds," 6 prints to block, available "plain" or "fancy" (don't know which this is), Ritzinger, Grasgreen c.1906-07. (M) One of several designs, which could be had on boards with from 2 to 12 designs, for from 15¢ to 80¢ each. (R) More fully detailed round designs on bigger board, but price still under 80¢. Both from Jaburg catalog, 1908. Prices higher than they should be for something mass-produced and machine carved. **$35.00-$150.00**

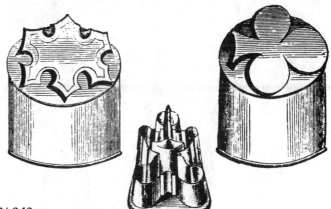

IV-341.
Whatzit press mold — for tortillas?
All wood, bent & carved. 16"L x 6 7/8" diameter. Practically without mark or stain, none inside, so probably not used. No drainage holes for cheese. No bloodstains, so not for meat patties. Collection of Meryle Evans. **$7.00-$15.00**

IV-342.
Vegetable cutters.
In this chapter instead of Chapter I, because while they are cutters, they are meant to create special shapes. Pieced tin. The pictures are primitive, as are many old catalog linecuts, but they show that you can cut a shamrock or 6-point star from a slice of root vegetable. Came in 20 styles, used for decorative veggies for inside molds, or for soup. F.A. Walker catalog, c.1890. Julienne cutters are similar — they, by accident of book composing by author, are in Chapter I. **$12.00-$35.00**

IV-339.
Souse mold,
for a kind of spiced, pickled pork-head dish, yuck. Cast iron, 8 1/2" diameter x 2 3/4" deep. Photo & collection of David G. Smith.

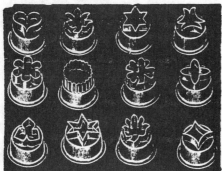

IV-343.
Vegetable cutters.
Set of tin cutters, showing available designs (note 4-leaf clover). Came in three sizes: 7/8", 1" and 1 1/4" diameter. Ordered as "macaroon cutters," the same set was made in 2" and 2 1/4" diameters. S. Joseph, c.1927. For a set: **$20.00-$55.00**

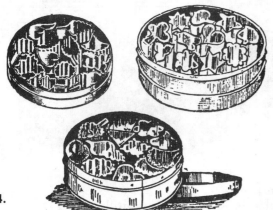

IV-344.
Vegetable cutters.
Three more sets, in round tin boxes. Top 2 sets are from S. Joseph. 1 1/2" cutters; and 2" cutters. Bottom set of 12 cutters, very like others, is in a tin box only 3 1/2" across. "Can use either end of cutters." Subscription premium for 1930 American Cookery *magazine.* **$45.00-$65.00**

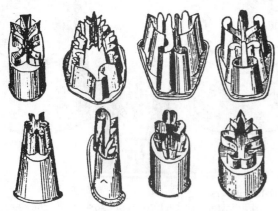

IV-345.
Vegetable or "garnishing" cutters.
Also for pastry. Came in 50 patterns, in sizes 1", 1 3/16", 1 5/8", 1 3/4" and 2 1/8". Duparquet catalog. Per cutter: **$10.00-$20.00**

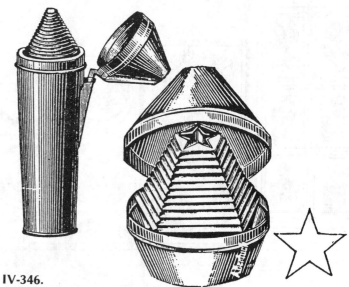

IV-346.
"Column cutters" or corers.
Nested, tin, made in various shapes. Only about 7"H overall. F.A. Walker, c.1890s, but made before. **$40.00-$60.00**
Nested cutters.
Many shapes, all geometrics. This shows the star set. For vegetables or pastries. Bertuch, c.1904. **$50.00-$75.00**

IV-347.
Vienna roll stamp.
for making vienna rolls the right way, marked in 5 sections. "May also be used for hot cross buns." Used when the yeast dough is "half proved." you mark them, turn them over, wash with water, and bake. Hueg, c.1905.

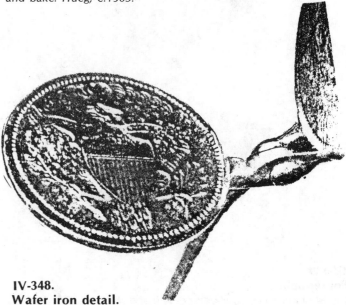

IV-348.
Wafer iron detail.
Cast iron, wrought handles. Eagle with shield body and 13 stars, possibly as early as 1800. 27 1/2"L x 5 1/4" diameter, American. Ex-Keillor Collection. **$350.00-$500.00**

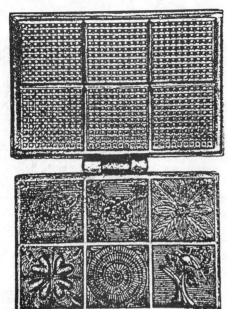

IV-349.
Waffle-wafer iron detail.
Showing mold or head only. Cast iron, forged iron handles. About 22"L. Commonly found, but quite appealing, an iron with rectangular heads for making a sort of waffled wafer combo. Thicker than wafers. 6 designs. Note bird in tree and various flowers. This one marked "H. & M". Others have been brought back from German trips, and found with no marks, or with name of Werle Iron Foundry, Ottweiler. **$125.00-$175.00**

IV-350.
Wafer iron detail.
Cast & wrought iron. Used to make thin, crisp cookies called wafers. Note design with wreath of leaves around border, and the sort of urn or vase design with stylized flowers. Compare with next picture. This photograph courtesy of the National Museum of American History, Smithsonian Institution. **$150.00-$200.00**

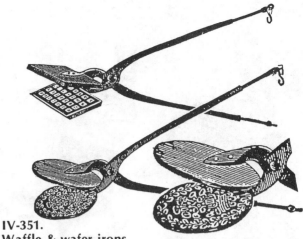

IV-351.
Waffle & wafer irons.
Cast heads, wrought handles. Note clips at end. Simple waffle iron at top, 6" x 3 1/2" head. Lower one particularly interesting because by blowing up the small, small picture in the Duparquet catalog, c.1904-10, I saw that the design of wreath and urn is the same as the Smithsonian one. **$100.00-$200.00**

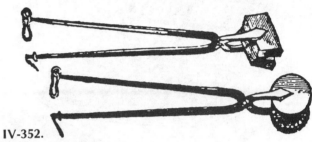

IV-352.
Gauffre & wafer irons.
Probably similar combination as the previous picture, the rectangular one making a waffle, or "gauffre." William Adams & Son, London, c.1860-61 ad. **$100.00-$200.00**

IV-353.
"Waffle furnace."
Of type familiar today. Cast iron, with removable iron and handled low frame. Range-top. This one is "A very ingenious article, making four good-sized waffles with less labor than is required in making one with the ordinary iron." (i.e. the long handled kind.) From American Home Cook Book, *1854.*

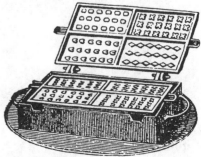

IV-354.
Slightly later stove top waffle iron.
Cast iron 4 designs. Note hearts! Maker unknown. Ad of J. & C. Berrian, wholesalers & retailers of house furnishings, NYC. 1857 ad.

IV-355.
Waffle irons.
One in "new style," with fleur de lys designs, low frame for range or stove top, others on legs, and called "patent revolving" designs, probably by Nathaniel Waterman. From Russell & Erwin catalog, 1865. **$200.00-$350.00**

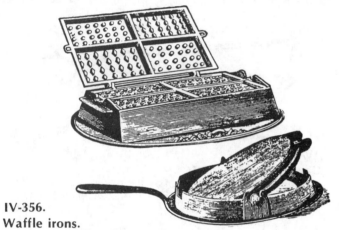

IV-356.
Waffle irons.
Top is a "square" iron, for stove tops. For 1, 2, or 4 cakes. Bottom one, is round, low frame, flipped with lid lifter tool. Four sizes (6" x 7", 7" x 8", 8" x 9" and 9" x 10" — sizes which I think refer to the diameter of the iron and then the frame) were offered by Stuart Peterson, 1875 and Leibrandt & McDowell Stove, 1861. **$100.00-$200.00**

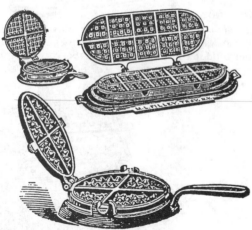

IV-357.
Waffle irons.
Stove top styles, cast iron. Big one from M.L. Filley, Troy, NY, c.1880. Small one from Matthai-Ingram, c.1890, in sizes "6x7" to "9x10". Bottom one, with fancy face, from unidentified 1880s cookbook. **$100.00-$200.00**

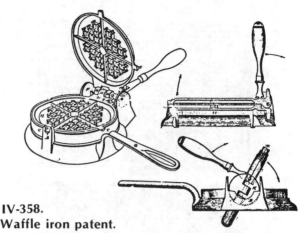

IV-358.
Waffle iron patent.
Pat'd 8/23/1881, by Alexander S. Patton, Columbus, OH. Shows in several pictures the particular type of "hinge journal" used for turning the mold in the frame, and the upright handle. Official Gazette.

IV-359.
Waffle irons.
Griswold. High or "deep" frame & low frames with round pans. Low one came in "8" and "9", with pan diameters 7 3/4" and 8 5/8", and the deep ring, "specially adapted for vapor stoves," came in one size, "8D", with pan 7 3/4" diameter. Buhl catalog, c.1912.

IV-360.
Waffle irons.
Everybody wanted in on the heart act. These are Griswold's "heart & Star Waffle irons," low and high frame. Cast iron, from c.1925 with recipes.

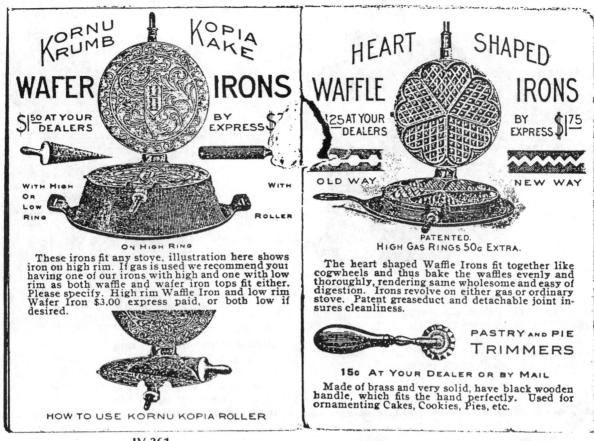

IV-361.
Wafer & waffle irons.
For stove top. Wafer in high or deep frame, making fancy quasi-religious old-fashioned design, and the waffles being heart shaped. Note wooden rollers that came with the wafer iron, to roll the wafers into cones or cylinders, for filling. Alfred Andresen & Co., Minneapolis, booklet, c.1905. **$150.00-$250.00**

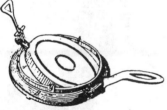

IV-362.
Waffle iron patent .
Pat'd 4/17/1877 by J.T. Lambert, Detroit, MI, assignor to the Detroit Iron & Brass Mfg. Co., "Handle may be used to lift lid or reverse position of the iron." Official Gazette.

IV-363.
Waffle iron.
Griswold "French Waffle Iron," for doing four pairs at a time. Hotel or restaurant (or large family) model. Ad in The Metal Worker, *6/20/1890.*

IV-364.
Waffle irons.
All multiple range eye frames. Top (R) by John Van Range Co., Cincinnati, made "to fit on all our Pacific, Maggie, Chimney Corner, and No. 130 Single Oven Ranges, but no other range." 8" and 9". (L) is Griswold, in 3 sizes, from 17 3/4"L to 21"L, with cakes from 4 7/8" x 2 3/8" to 5 1/2" x 2 3/4". 1909 catalog. Bottom one possibly Griswold, or Shapleigh (it's in Shapleigh catalog 1914). Pan length only 9 3/4"L, which hardly seems possible.

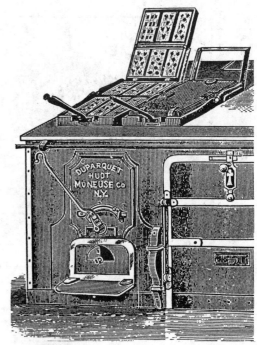

IV-366.
Waffle irons built into range.
This is a "griddle & waffle range combined," all sheet iron and cast iron. Range itself 4 feet long, with 2 waffle irons (one shown here closed, one open) and a griddle 21" square (you see corner at right). Duparquet, Huot & Moneuse, NYC, c.1904-10. Note heart design of some waffles.

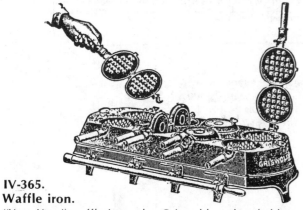

IV-365.
Waffle iron.
"Yum Yum" waffle iron, also Griswold, and probably not their name but the cataloguers' (Albert Pick, 1909). While the "French" one sat over a stove, this one has its own stove. Other irons, like from the French, would fit this frame also. Three sizes: 2 pans, 4" diameter, frame 14 1/2" x 11 1/2"; or 3 pans, 4" pans, 20"L x 11 1/2" frame; or 4 pans in 22 1/2" x 11 1/2" frames.

IV-367.
Electric waffle iron.
One of the earliest, very early 20th C. General Electric #293079. Cast iron frame and waffler. Note the spiral "cool" handles, and the two sets of screw-in power plugs. Photo courtesy of General Electric Corp. **$200.00-$300.00**

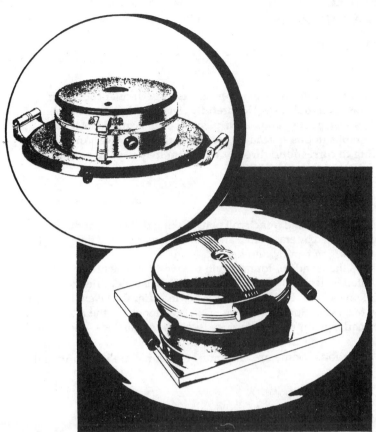

IV-368.
Electric waffle irons.
(T) "Westchester Automatic, Catalog #149Y183," by General Electric. Chromed finish, black enamel stripes, "old ivory marblette" handles and pendent drop handle. Fibre feet. Detachable cord. 11 3/4" diameter base. The rim you see is to catch batter overflow — great idea! From 1935-36 catalog. (B) The "Handy-hot" iron, No. 4704-H. Square overflow tray. 7 1/4" cast aluminum grids, chromium finish on outside, "rich looking walnut finished" handles. Chicago Electric Mfg. Co., 1938. Really cool Deco look.
$80.00-$120.00

IV-369.
"Hot Dog" patent.
This picture is from the June 1930 issue of Science & Invention, in their "Yankee Brains at Work" column about new inventions. This is Patent #1,742,945, issued to Peter S. Banff. "Relates to an electrical cooking device designed primarily for that type of sandwich termed 'hot dog'. However, it may be adapted for producing any article of food to which it is applicable. The invention consists of an electrical cooking device with an open bottom upper casing and an open top lower casing, each adapted to contain a heating unit," and 2 facing molding plate detachably connected to the lid and the lower part of mold. Wow! Bow Wow! Wonder if it was ever made? See IV-180.

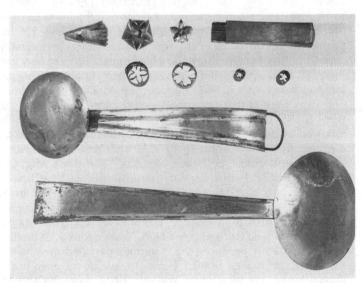

IV-370.
Wax-flower modeling tools.
Pieced tin. This is an example of the kind of confusable item often mistaken for a cooking tool. Shown are dippers for molten wax, plus forms for cutting out petals. 19th C. Picture courtesy of the National Museum of American History, Smithsonian Institution.

A. PREPARING
CAST IRON BAKING PANS
By David G. Smith

DAVID G. SMITH
11918 Second Street
P.O. Box B
Perrysburg, NY 14129

Advanced collector David Smith has a spectacular collection of old cast iron cookware. He carefully cleans, weighs, measures, catalogs and photographs each piece as it is acquired. All the photographs in this special article were taken by Dave. Anyone wishing to correspond directly with him may use the address at left. Please use an SASE.

Muffin pans, gem pans, popover pans, breadstick pans, cornstick pans, and french roll pans; baking pans with numerous compartments are called by many names. The names of the pans were influenced by era, culture and cookbook recipes, and then designated by the manufacturer. A *muffin* pan by one maker might be called a *gem* pan by another.

Cast iron baking pans were made in many hundreds, perhaps thousands of foundries in the world. Some of the largest and most notable foundries that manufactured baking pans in the United States are **Wagner,** Sidney, OH; **Griswold,** Erie, PA; **Favorite Stove & Range Co. (Favorite Piqua),** Piqua, OH; **Wapak,** Wapakoneta, OH; **R & E** (Russell & Erwin) **Mfg. Co.,** New Britain, CT; **G.F. Filley** (Excelsior Stove Works), St. Louis, MO; and **Lodge Mfg. Co.,** South Pittsburg, TN. The identity of the makers of the baking pans illustrated in this article has been determined by markings on pans, reference to old trade catalogs, and/or design characteristics.

Shown here are dozens of styles and sizes, with many variations. Some are common, and some are very unusual.

Nathaniel Waterman & R & E Mfg. Co.

If any one person influenced the design and manufacture of baking pans, it was Nathaniel Waterman of Boston, MA. Waterman established in September 1825 a large kitchen furnishings jobbing house that sold many kitchen items—including French-style coffee biggins, waffle irons, water filters, tea kettles, "ventilated refrigerators," and gridirons—under the name "Waterman's Patent. He received patents for these and several other inventions. In 1858 he designed and patented a series of roll pans to be used "for baking bread in small rolls." That patent was followed by his patent for "Improved Egg Pan" which had openings between the cups "in order to allow currents of heat to pass upward between them, so as to equalize the heat against their surfaces." This patent was dated April 5, 1859. Subsequent production of Waterman Roll Pans were of this "egg pan" modification, and display the April 5, 1859 date. Waterman designs set a standard which was followed by many foundries. The most common series found today are numbered from #1 to #11, and are marked either "Waterman-Boston," or "R & E Mfg. Co." The R & E Mfg. Co. was the Russell & Erwin Mfg. Co. (later Russwin) of New Britain, CT, which specialized in building hardware. As was common in the 19th C, indeed in the 20th, inventors either sold sole rights or licensed other companies to manufacture their inventions. Designs were (and still are) pirated too. Notable foundries besides R & E apparently produced the Waterman patented designs but they were not marked as such. Some of these are included in the illustrations of the Waterman Series in **CIBP-1 through CIBP-11.** Marked "Waterman"pans are not as plentiful as those marked "R & E Mfg."; therefore the former are more desirable to a collector.

Numbers which were standard with many manufacturers are #3 (See **CIBP-3, -63 and -81**); #5 (**CIBP-5, -70,-79**); #9 (**CIBP-9, -52**); #10 (**CIBP-10, -42** through **-44, -72**);and #11 (**CIBP-11, -48, -49, -73**). For the most part, foundries participated in this standardization of style numbers. Two major exceptions were Wagner, which preferred a letter designation; and G.F. Gilley, which, with the exception of one pattern, was very creative with their designs and therefore did not follow the norm. Filley's one pan that did conform was their #5 (See **CIBP-70**).

Roll pan.   **CIBP - 1**
"R & E Mfg. Co.#1." Also marked "Patent April 5, 1859." Eleven round very shallow cups. 12½" x 8 5/8"; cups, 3 1/8" x 5/8" deep.
This photo and all the 120 plus that follow were taken by the author, David G. Smith. Values have not been given for the pans. Generally speaking, the value range for old original pans (not reproductions) is wide—from about $50.00 to upwards of $250.00

273

Roll pans.   **CIBP - 2**

Top: Underside of an otherwise unmarked "#2". Eleven round cups. 12½" x 8 5/8"; cups, 3 1/8" x 5/8" deep. Bottom: "Detroit #6," with same handle as other. Eleven shallow cups in openwork frame. 12 5/8" x 8½"; cups, 3" x 5/8" deep. Other makers call this a "#2" as above. Note: Appearance of same size in pictures does not mean pans are same size. Always read measurements.

Roll pan.   **CIBP - 4**

"R & E Mfg. Co. #4." Other handle marked with patent date. Eight elliptical cups. 13 7/8" x 7"; cups, 4 1/8"L 2¾"W x ¾" deep.

Roll pan.   **CIBP - 5**

"N. Waterman Boston" #5. Also marked with April 5, 1859 patent date. Eight rounded oval cups. 12¼" x 7 3/8"; cups 4 1/8" x 2¾" x ¾" deep.

Roll pan   **CIBP - 6**

"N Waterman Boston" #6. Also has patent date. Twelve rectangular cups with rounded corners. 12¾" x 7 7/16"; cups, 3¼" x 2 1/8" x 9/16" deep.

Roll pan.   **CIBP - 3**

Underside of a "#3," showing small round 'foot' to each cup. Eleven round cups. 12 3/15" x 8 11/16"; cups, 3 1/8" x ¾" deep.

Roll pan. CIBP - 7

"R & E Mfg. Co. #7." Also marked with patent date. Eight rounded rectangular cups. 11¾" x 7 11/16"; cups, 3½" x 2½" x 11/16" deep.

Roll pan. CIBP - 8

"N. Waterman Boston" #8. With patent date. Eleven oval cups. 13 9/16" x 6 11/16"; cups, 3 3/8" x 2 5/8" x 5/8" deep.

Roll or muffin pan. CIBP - 9

"R & E Mfg. Co." #9 'golf ball' pan. Also marked with patent date. Twelve round cups. 10½" x 6 5/16" diameter x 1¾" deep.

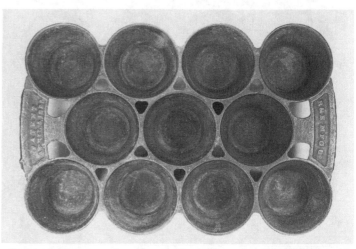

Popover pan. CIBP - 10

"R & E Mfg. Co." Marked with patent date, that appears to say 1858, not 1859. Eleven cups with flat bottoms and flared sides. 12 3/8" x 8 1/8"; cups, 2¾" diameter x 1¾" deep.

French roll pan. CIBP - 11

"#11." Marked on handles with "Patent Apr. 5, 1859." Twelve trough-shaped cups. 13¼" x 7¼"; cups, 3 3/8" x 2" x 1" deep."

Wagner

Wagner Mfg. Co. of Sidney, OH, used a lettering system to identify their styles. In addition, they used a four-digit catalog number. Though the pan may not be marked with their name (Wagner, or Wagner Ware), the letter or a combination of letters and numbers identify the piece as Wagner. The illustrations from **CIBP-12 through CIBP-22** were all listed in Wagner's 1913 and/or 1924 catalogs.

Gem pan,   **CIBP - 13**
*commonly called a **popover pan**. "Wagner Ware," style "B". Note small hanging hole at both ends. 11 15/16" x 7 11/16"; cups 2 ¾" x 1 ¾" deep.*

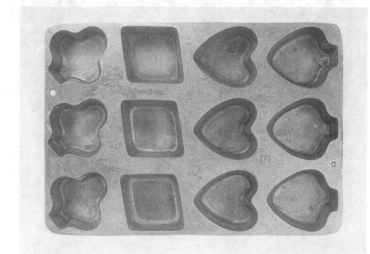

Vienna roll pan.   **CIBP - 14**
"Wagner Ware Sidney," style "I", also marked "Vienna Roll Pan" and with a 4-digit catalog number. Six fat cigar-shaped cups in solid frame. There is also one with an open frame. 11½" x 6½".

Gem pans.   **CIBP - 12**
Top: "Wagner Ware" - "Little Slam Bridge Pan". Twelve figural shallow cups with three in each card suit. Widely spaced in solid rectangular pan with no handle, but with small hanging hole. 10¾" x 7 5/8"; cups, 2" x 2" x 1¼" deep. Bottom: Another very shallow cup pan. Wagner, style "A". Eleven flat bottom shallow cups. 11 3/16" x 7 5/8"; cups, 2¾" x 5/8" deep. Note: Appearance of same size in picture is misleading. Read measurements.

Gem or popover pan.   **CIBP - 15**
"Wagner Ware," style "Q". Five flat bottom cups. Note recess for stove lid lifter. 7½" x 5 5/8"; cups, 2½" x 1½" deep. These are easy-cleaning cups; where the sides join the bottoms is slightly rounded.

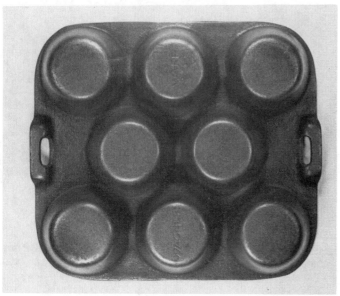

Gem pan.   **CIBP - 16**

"Wagner Ware," style "R" Eight flat bottom round cups. 8½" x 7 3/8"; cups, 2½" x 1½" deep.

Gem pan.   **CIBP - 18**

"Wagner Ware," style "T," commonly known as a "turk's head" ot "turk head" pan, for the supposed resemblance to an ancient Turkish-style turban. Twelve cups in openwork frame, with handles. 14 7/8" x 10"; cups, 2¾" x 1" deep.

CIBP - 17

Gem pans.

Left: "Wagner Ware," style "S", pattern #1428. Eleven flat bottom round cups in solid frame with stove lid lifter recesses. 10¾" x 7¼"; cups, 2½" x 1½" deep. Right: "Wagner Ware" - "Little Gem", style "C". Marked "pat. pending" on underside. Twelve round flat bottom cups in openwork frame. 9 5/8" x 7 1/8"; cups, 1¾" x 1¼" deep.

Generally speaking, the value range for old original pans (not reproductions) is wide — from about $50.00 to upwards of $250.00.

Gem pan.   **CIBP - 19**

"Wagner Ware," style "K", with five swirl-fluted cups, also sometimes called a "Turk's head" pan (more accurately, costume-wise, than the other, because the swirls more closely resemble the turban referred to). Unusual because of almost nonexistent frame. 7" x 5"; cups, 2½" x 9/16" deep.

Gem pan.   **CIBP - 20**

*Wagner Ware, style "L." Six bowl-like round cups. This style is usually **not** marked. 6¾" x 4½"; cups, 2¼" x 1" deep.*

Gem pan or French roll pan.   **CIBP - 21**

Wagner, style "O". Five trough-shaped cups. 9 3/8" x 3 1/8"; cups, 3½" x 1¾" x 7/8" deep.

Gem pan,   **CIBP - 22**

with a short handle. Wagner #2. Three flat bottomed cups like the popover pan cups. Including handle: 6 5/8" x 5 3/8"; cups, 2½" x 1½" deep. (Ed NOTE: This looks like a cloverleaf, and is most charming pan that I've ever seen. LCF.)

The 1924 Wagner catalog had this to say about the "Krusty Korn Kob" mold **(CIBP-23):** "One of the most delicious and popular hot breads today is the 'Krusty Korn Kob' made in the Wagner mold. This mold produces delicate, crisp, golden brown cornbread, shaped just like an ear of corn, but infinitely more delicate and appetizing than old fashioned cornbread."

Cornstick mold,   **CIBP - 23**

*also called a **cornbread mold**. "Wagner Ware Sidney" - "Krusty Korn Kob" - "Reg. in U.S. Pat. Off." — "Pat'd July 6, 1920" and with the catalog number 1318, plus the little outline cross. Seven well-delineated cobs, alternate directions. Tab handles with hanging holes. The "Senior" size: 13¼" x 6 7/8".*

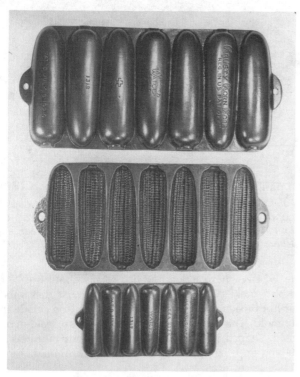

Cornstick molds,   **CIBP - 24**

comparing the three sizes of "Krusty Korn Kob" pans. From the top: the "Senior" as depicted in CIBP-23; the "Junior," 11 5/8" x 5 7/8"; and the "Tea Size," 8½"x 4¼". All with seven alternating cobs. Wagner Ware.

Lodge

The Lodge Mfg. Co. has been located in South Pittsburg, TN, since 1896, and is still producing cast iron cookware (and other items) today. While Lodge did use a catalog numbering system, not all their baking pans are numbered. Some are marked with a letter.

There are two significant differences between the letters used by Wagner and those used by Lodge. The letters used by Wagner are usually located in the middle of the pan and are *intaglio*, that is, they give the effect of being incised or indented into the surface because the casting mold had raised letters. The letters on a Lodge pan are, in most cases, raised, or embossed, usually on the end or in a corner, and they also appear to have been placed at random. I do not know the purpose of the Lodge letters, and cannot find any references in their catalog to them. The following illustrations, from **CIBP-25 through CIBP-33,** are all Lodge pans.

NOTE: At least one source says Lodge Foundry has existed since 1872. See page 157. *Editor.*

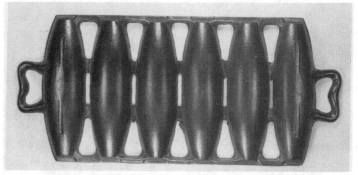

Gem pan, or Vienna roll pan.   **CIBP - 25**

Lodge Mfg. Co. #18. Six fat cigar-shaped cups or sections in open frame. Handles almost like truncated hearts. 13¾" x 6¼". (See also CIBP-14.)

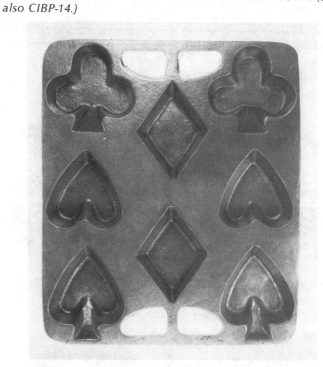

"Bridge" pan,   **CIBP - 26**

for making gems or little cakes in shape of card suits. Lodge #26, style "D". Eight flat bottom shallow cups, hearts, diamonds, spades & clubs, in rectangular solid frame with generous cutouts for fingerholds at both ends. 9 7/8" x 8 3/8".

Muffin or gem pan   **CIBP - 27**

Lodge, style "R" turk's head pan. Six deeply fluted cups in solid, flat-top frame, with tab handles with hanging holes. 9¾" x 5 3/8"; cups, 2½" x ¾" deep.

Muffin or gem pan.   **CIBP - 28**

Another Lodge turk's head mold, the #19. Six fluted cups in open-work recessed frame with the 'truncated heart' handles. 13¼" x 8"; cups, 3" x 1" deep.

Muffin or gem pan.   **CIBP - 29**

Lodge's largest turk's head pan, #20. Twelve fluted cups in open-work recessed frame. 16 1/8" x 11"; cups, 3 9/16" x 1 1/16".

Muffin or gem pan.   **CIBP - 30**

Lodge turk's head pan, marked "R" on raised circle on back. Six fluted cups in solid, recessed frame, with bifurcated "T" handles. 12" x 7".

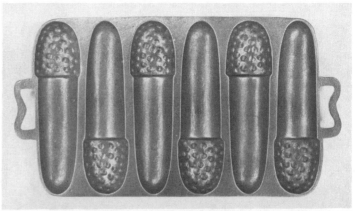

Stick molds.   **CIBP - 31**

Top: The Acorn pan, which is popularly known as the "penis pan" among collectors, and supposedly was withdrawn from manufacture for that reason. Six cups in the form of the typically elongated acorns of the magnificent southern Live Oak tree. This example is a particularly fine casting. Caution: reproductions are being made of this pan. 11¾"x 6 3/8"; cups, 6 1/8" x 1 5/8" x 5/8" deep. Bottom: Cornstick mold. Lodge, "V". Five cobs facing same direction in solid rectangular frame with arched handles the full width of the frame. 9" x 5 3/8". NOTE: Appearance of same size in picture is misleading. Always read measurements.

Cornstick molds   **CIBP - 32**

Both Lodge, but not marked. Identified by the typical Lodge handles. Both have cobs all facing same direction. Nine stick pan: 15 5/8" x 5½". Seven stick pan: 12½" x 5½".

Cornstick mold.   **CIBP - 33**

No marks, but handles, casting texture, and pan shape are indicative of Lodge. Seven square-end cobs — neither alternating, nor same way. 11 3/4"L x 6 1/8"W; cobs, 5 7/8" x 1 1/4" x 5/8". Since picture taken, one almost identical found, marked "CAHIL" in diamond cartouche; also "1507". Slightly smaller: 11 1/2" x 6"; cobs themselves are same size. A Cahill Co., a foundry specialzing in fireplace, was in Chattanooga, TN, in 1930s. See also CIBP-78 to 80.

Griswold

The Griswold Mfg. Co., Erie, PA began manufacturing hollowware (the trade's name for cooking utensils, and found spelled as one or two words) in 1884. Early Griswold baking pans were marked "Erie", but many Griswold baking pans were not marked either "Erie" or "Griswold". They are identifiable as Griswold however by a three-digit pattern number. Many of these pattern numbers appear to have been inscribed by hand in the mold (**CIBP-53**). Griswold identified their baking pans by two methods: a style or catalog number, and a pattern number. For example, a #22 Breadstick pan is also identified by pattern number 954.

Of all the manufacturers, Griswold produced the greatest number of patterns, including variations. It is the variety that make their molds so interesting and challenging to collectors.

Variations of the Griswold cornstick pan took several paths. First, there is a difference in the designs of the kernels and the cobs (**CIBP-34 through CIBP-38**). Notice that all the cobs face in the same direction, with the exception of pattern #270. Size is also a variable. Most of Griswold's cornstick patterns came in two sizes: 13 3/4" x 5 3/4", and 14" x 7 5/8".

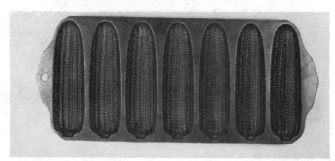

Cornstick mold,   **CIBP - 34**

called the "Crispy Corn Stick Pan." Griswold pan with seven cobs all facing same direction, and hanging hole in only one handle. This type came in three sizes. #273: 13 1/4" x 5 3/4"; #283: 14" x 7 5/8"; and #262: 8 1/2" x 4 1/8".

Stick mold,   **CIBP - 35**

called the "Crispy Corn or Wheat Stick Pan." Griswold pan with seven sort of all-purpose cups (neither much like ears of corn nor wheat) all facing same direction, and hanging hole in only one handle. This type came in two sizes. #272: 13 1/4" x 5 3/4"; and #282: 14" x 7 5/8".

Stick mold,   **CIBP - 36**

called the "Crispy Corn or Wheat Stick Pan." Griswold pan with seven all-purpose corn or wheat ears, alternating directions, and hanging hole in only one handle. This type came in two sizes. #270: 13 1/4" x 5 3/4"; and #280: 14" x 7 5/8".

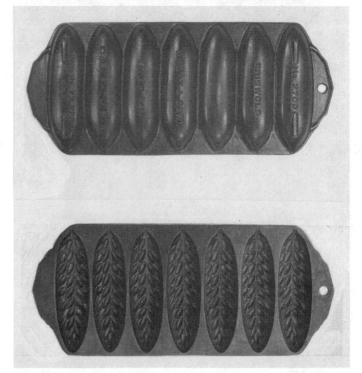

Stick mold,   **CIBP - 37**

called the "Wheat and Corn Stick Pan." Two views, of cups and of the bottom. Seven eliptical ears facing same direction. 13 1/4" x 5 3/4". Came with two pattern numbers, #2700 and #1270, the latter of which is not marked "Griswold," but rather "S.R. and Company Best Made," and was reportedly made for Sears, Roebuck & Co.

"Wheat Stick Pan,"   CIBP - 38

marked "Griswold." Six ears of wheat, all facing same direction in open frame. One hanging hole. This pan came in two sizes: #27 is 10 3/8" x 5 7/8"; and #28 is 12 5/8" x 7".

Griswold also made "Puritan" wares. The kernal design of the Puritan (**CIBP-40**) is almost identical to that shown above in **CIBP-37**. The shape of the Puritan pan's handle is different from the other cornstick pans, and the pan is also slightly smaller.

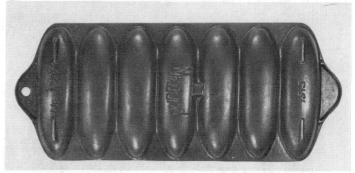

Stick pan,   CIBP - 40

in "Wheat and Corn Stick" pattern, #1270. This one made by Griswold, but marked with a name they used, "Puritan" and "1533". Rounded tab handles, one with hanging hole.

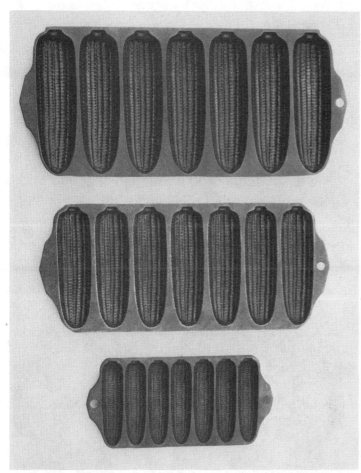

Cornstick molds.   CIBP - 39

Griswold's "Crispy Corn or Wheat" stick pans, showing comparison of the three sizes. All have seven cobs facing same direction. 14" x 7 5/8"; 13 1/4" x 5 3/4"; and the "tea size" (pattern #262), 8½" x 4 1/8", which is a quarter of an inch narrower than Wagner's "tea size."

The Griswold patterns #27 and #28 "Wheat Stick Pan" vary in size, and in marking. Both sizes may be marked either "Wheat & Corn," or "Whole Wheat." Judging from the quality of lettering, I believe the "Whole Wheat" marking is earlier. **CIBP-41** illustrates both the size and lettering variations.

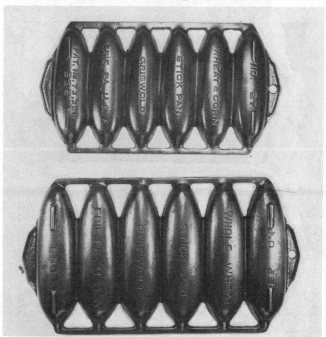

Stick pans,   CIBP - 41

by Griswold. They show size and marking variations. Both have six sticks in open frames. Smaller one, pattern #638, is #27, "Wheat & Corn Stick Pan" - "Griswold" - "Erie, PA, U.S.A." - Pat. No. 73, 326. It measures 11" x 6"; cobs, 5 3/8" x 1 1/2" x 1/2" deep; larger one, pattern #639, is #28, and is marked "Whole Wheat." It is 12 5/8" x 7"; cobs, 6 3/8" x 1 3/4" x 5/8" deep.

Without a doubt, the most common style muffin pan, whether by Griswold or any other company, is the #10, eleven-cup popover pan. Griswold made several variations, of which **CIBP-42, -43, and -44** illustrate but three.

There were also variations in Griswold's #18, six-cup popover pan (**CIBP-45, -46, -47**).

Popover pan.   CIBP - 44

"Griswold" - "Erie, PA U.S.A.", #10, pattern #949B. Eleven flat bottom cups in mostly solid frame with large fingerholds at both ends — note the difference in their shape and those of CIBP-43, top. 11 1/8" x 7 5/8"; cups, 2 1/2" x 1 3/8" deep.

Popover pan.   CIBP - 42

"Griswold's Erie" #10, pattern #948A. Eleven flat bottom cups in openwork frame. 11 1/4" x 7 3/4"; cups, 2 1/2" x 1 5/8" deep.

Popover pan.   CIBP - 45

"Griswold's Erie No. 18" marked on handles. Six flat bottom cups in openwork frame. 8 1/2" x 5 1/2"; cups, 2 1/2" x 1 5/8" deep.

Popover pans.   CIBP - 43

Top: *"Griswold" - "Erie, PA, U.S.A.", #10, pattern #948. Eleven flat bottom cups in mostly solid frame with large fingerholds at both ends. 11 1/4" x 7 3/4"; cups, 2 1/2" x 1 5/8" deep.* **Bottom:** *"Best Made No. 10" - "S.R. and Co." Pattern #1253. Eleven flat bottom cups in openwork frame with large fingerholds. This was made by Griswold for Sears, Roebuck & Co. 11 3/16" x 7 1/8"; cups 2 9/16" diameter x 1 1/2" deep. NOTE: Appearance of same size in picture is misleading. Always read measurements.*

Popover pan.   CIBP - 46

"Griswold's Erie No. 18." Six flat bottom cups in openwork frame that differs substantially at handle ends from previous page, therefore in length. 9 1/8" x 5 1/2" cups, 2 1/2" x 1 5/8" deep.

Popover pan.   **CIBP - 47**

"Griswold," #18. Pattern #5141. Six flat bottom cups in openwork frame with yet another handle style. 9 1/8" x 5½"; cups, 2½" x 1 5/8" deep.

Many foundries produced a #11 muffin or roll pan. Griswold — being true to form — had its own variations (**CIBP-48, -49**). Another variation was a so-called half-sized version (**CIBP-50**). A larger version of their #11 was the #15 (**CIBP-51**). (They also made a #16 — a "half-size" of the #15 — and not illustrated here).

French roll pan.   **CIBP - 48**

Griswold #11. Twelve closely-regimented trough-shaped cups. 12 7/8" x 6 1/8"; cups, 2 7/8" x 1 ¾" x 7/8" deep. Frame is closed rather than partially cutout as in CIBP-11 (the early one from 1859, which overall seems more delicate and graceful).

French roll pan.   **CIBP - 49**

Griswold #11. This version has a dividing 'aisle' of a half inch between the two rows of six trough-shaped cups. 12 7/8 x 6 5/8"; cups, 2 7/8" x 1 ¾" x 7/8" deep.

French roll pan.   **CIBP - 50**

Griswold #17. So-called "half-size" version. Six troughs. 7½" x 6"; cups, 2 7/8" x 1 ¾" x 7/8" deep. (Ed NOTE: Although I haven't seen this in the flesh & bone, so to speak, it looks very lumpen prol to me compared to other Griswold pieces. LCF.)

French roll pan.   **CIBP - 51**

Griswold #15, pattern #6138. Twelve rather deep troughs, narrowly separated. 14 3/8" x 7½"; cups, 3½" x 2" x 1¼" deep.

Often referred to as the "golf-ball pan" is Griswold's #9, pattern #947 pan. In this instance, Griswold made design variations with the same pattern number. **CIBP-52, -53, and -54** are all marked with the same pattern number, 947. **CIBP-53** is one of Griswold's early pans. **CIBP-54** is probably made for a chain store's distribution.

"Brownie Cake Pan,"   **CIBP - 52**

also familiarly called "golf ball muffin pan." Griswold #9. Twelve bowl-like cups in skeletal frame. No hanging hole in handle, but none needed with those cutouts. 10 3/8" x 7"; cups, 2" diameter x 1" deep.

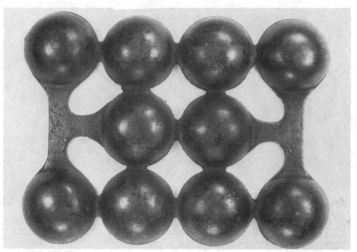

Muffin pan.   **CIBP - 53**

Griswold pattern #947, marked at both ends crosspieces in what appears to be hand-drawn numerals. Ten bowl-like cups in open frame. 9½" x 7 1/8"; cups, 2" x 1" deep. (Ed NOTE: I wonder why they didn't go ahead and make an 11-cup mold? There was certainly room for one more cup in the center row. But then, I'm always speculating as to why they made 11-cup molds, which seems such an odd number, divisible only by one or eleven. Also, although David doesn't say so, this sure does look an awful lot older than the others. LCF.)

Muffin pan,   **CIBP - 54**

another in the "golf ball" pattern #947. Griswold. Twelve cups. 10 3/8" x 7 1/8"; cups, 2" x 1" deep.

Even the plain #22 Breadstick pan is interesting because of variations **(CIBP-55).**

Breadstick pans.   **CIBP - 55**

Top: Griswold #22, pattern #954. Eleven long troughs. 14½" x 7 5/8"; cups, 7 1/8" x 1 1/8" wide. Bottom: Marked "Corn Bread Pan" on bottom. Griswold, "E", pattern #954. Eleven long troughs. 14½" x 7 5/8"; cups, 7 1/8" x 1 1/8" wide. (Ed NOTE: This is the type of baking mold that bears close resemblance to cast iron molds with series of thin (or fat) troughs used by plumbers to cast lead sticks. I saw one just before this book went to press, and it was marked "LEAD" on one of the troughs, which may or may not even have been customary. LCF)

A fancier Griswold pan is the "Heart and Star." See Griswold's and another company's versions in **CIBP-56.**

Another Griswold variation to look for are two pans with the same pattern number but different style numbers. The #6 Vienna Bread pan, pattern #958 was later designated style #26, with the same pattern #958 (**CIBP-57**). To add to the confusion, there was also a #26 Bread Pan (**CIBP-58**). This however, was pattern #960.

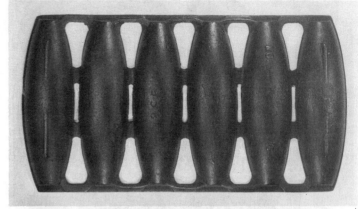

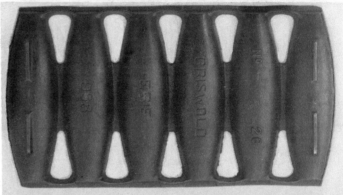

Baking pans,   **CIBP - 56**

in two versions of a "Heart and Star" design. **Top:** *Griswold #100, pattern #960. Five fat hearts with star in center. Short tab handle. 7¾" across including handle. Cups, about 2" x 1" deep.* **Bottom:** *This one is not Griswold, and is an unmarked pan with skillet handle with teardrop hanging hole. Six hearts surrounding 6-point star, recessed in round frame. 9" diameter plus 6"L handle; cups, approx. 2½" x 2½" x 1" deep; star is 3½"W.*

Roll pans,   **CIBP - 57**

in the Vienna roll pan style. **Top:** *Griswold #6, pattern #958. Six fat cigar-shaped cups. 12½" x 6 7/8"; cups 6¼" x 1 5/8".* **Bottom:** *Griswold #26, pattern #958. Six fat cigar-shaped cups. 12½" x 6 7/8"; cups, 6¼" x 1 5/8".*

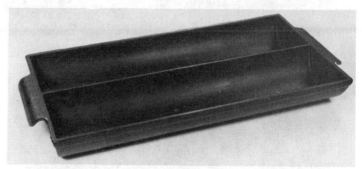

Bread pan,   **CIBP - 58**

"Griswold Erie" #26, pattern #960. This bread pan is listed in a 1905 Griswold catalog. Two long trough-like sections for two loaves. 13 7/8" x 6½"; loaves, 12 1/8" x 3"W x 1 3/8" deep (if they didn't rise!). Note undercurve of the handles at both ends.

Muffin or gem pans.   **CIBP - 59**

Top: *Griswold #8, pattern #946. Eight flat bottom shallow cups in openwork frame. 12¾" x 6 3/8"; cups, 3" x 7/8" deep.* **Bottom:***Griswold #2, pattern #941. Eleven flat bottom shallow cups in openwork frame. 12½" x 8½"; cups, 3" x 5/8" deep.*

Muffin or gem pans.   **CIBP - 60**

Top: *"Erie #8, mfd. by Griswold. Pattern #946. Eight flat bottom cups in skeletal frame. 12¾" x 6 3/8"; cups, 3" x 7/8" deep.* **Bottom:** *Griswold #1, pattern #940. Eleven round flat bottom cups in openwork frame. 11½" x 8½"; cups, 2 9/16" x 5/8" deep.*

Muffin or gem pans.   **CIBP - 61**

Top: *Griswold #7, pattern #945. Eight flat bottom rectangular cups with rounded corners. 11¾" x 7 7/8"; cups, 3½" x 2¼" x 5/8" deep.* **Middle:** *Another Griswold #7, pattern #945. Eight rectangular cups, openwork frame. Note difference in measurements: 11¾'" x 7 5/8"; cups, 3 9/16" x 2 3/8" x 5/8" deep.* **Bottom:** *Griswold #6, pattern #944. Twelve rectangular cups with rounded corners. 11¾" x 7¾"; cups, 2 7/8" x 1 7/8" x ½" deep. Note lettering style of name "Griswold." NOTE: Appearance of same size does not mean pans are equal in size. Please read measurements.*

Gem pan.   **CIBP - 62**

Griswold #12, pattern #951. Eleven flat bottom, straight sides cups in interesting rectangular frame that conforms to 4-3-4 arrangement of cups. 11" x 7¼"; cups, 2¼" x ¾"

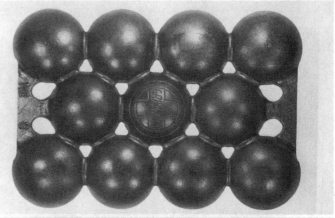

Gem pans.   **CIBP - 63**

Top: *Griswold #3, pattern #942. Eleven bowl-like cups in open-work frame. 12½" x 8½"; cups, 2¾" x ¾" deep. Note trademark.*
Bottom: *Griswold #19, pattern #966. Six cup "golf ball" pan in very openwork frame. 7¾" x 4 5/8"; cups, 2" x 1" deep.*

Gem pans,   **CIBP - 64**

in turk's head design with fluted cups. **Top:** *Griswold #130, pattern #634. Six cups in solid frame. Marked on underside of one large tab handle; hanging hole in other. 10" x 5½"; cups, 2 5/8" x 7/8" deep.* **Bottom:** *Griswold #14, pattern #641. Twelve cups in open-work frame. 13½" x 8 5/8"; cups, 2¼" x 7/8" deep. NOTE: Appearance of same size is misleading; read measurements.*

Muffin pans.   **CIBP - 65**

Top: *Griswold #20, "Turk Head" pan, with swirled flutes. Eleven cups in openwork frame, the outer corners round to encompass the corner cups. 10 3/8" x 7 1/8"; cups, 2" x 3/4" deep.* **Bottom:** *"Detroit #33." Eleven turk's head cups in openwork frame. 10 3/8" x 7 1/8"; cups, 2 1/4" x 3/4" deep. (Ed NOTE: If I were a patent examiner, I would have been sure that Griswold copied "Detroit," or vice versa. LCF.)*

CIBP - 66

Muffin pan.

Griswold #140 "Turk Head" or "Queen Cake" pan, pattern #835. Twelve fluted flat bottom cups (they actually look just like the stamped aluminum Jell-O molds). 12 5/8" x 8 1/4"; cups, 2 5/8" x 7/8" deep. This pattern also came in the #240 size, which is 14 5/8" x 10"; cups, 2 3/4" x 7/8" deep.

G.F. Filley/Excelsior/W.C. Davis

Baking pans marked "G.F. Filley" were manufactured by the Excelsior Mfg. Co., St. Louis, MO. The Excelsior Stove Works, incorporated in 1865 as the Excelsior Mfg. Co., was founded by Giles F. Filley. This explains the pans being marked with his name. Excelsior also made "Charter Oak" stoves and ranges.

Excelsior's 1884 catalog illustrates a line of "Excelsior Baker's or Gem Pans," in #1 through #8, and #11, and #12. It lists no #9; does one exist? The catalog also lists a #15, but with no illustration.

For the most part, Filley designs (CIBP-67 through -73) were very creative and did not follow the trade's standardization. The exception is their #5 (CIBP-70). Filley pans are highly desired by collectors.

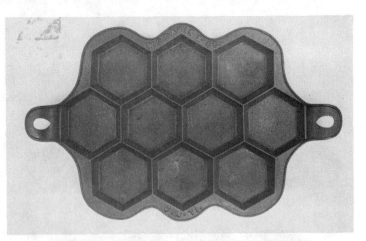

CIBP - 67-B

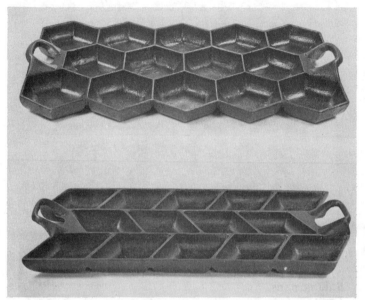

Muffin or gem pans.   **CIBP - 67-A**

Top: *G.F. Filley #2, mfd. by Excelsior Mfg. Co. Hexagonal honeycomb design, quite possibly used for some kind of honey cake. Fourteen cups in oblong shape with zigzag sides. Two upraised handles with large openings. 12 3/8" x 7"; cups, 2 1/4" x 1/2" deep.* **Bottom:** *G.F. Filley #1. Fourteen diamond-shaped cups set in sort of herringbone pattern. 13" x 6 5/8"; cups, 2 1/4" x 2 1/8" x 3/4" deep.*

Gem or muffin pans.

More in the honeycomb hexagonal pattern. These by W.C. Davis, Cincinnati, OH. Top: Ten cups in roughly rectangular frame. Elongated tongue-like tab handles. 14½" x 9 1/8"; cups, 3 1/8" x 1" deep. This pan was also made with thirteen cups. Bottom: Seven cups in roughly round pan, with elongated skillet handle with teardrop hanging hole. 9 5/8" diameter, plus 5"L handle: cups, 3 1/8" x 1" deep.

Muffin or gem pan.   **CIBP - 68**

G.F. Filley #4. Eight uniquely-shaped 4-petaled oblong cups, with edge of frame conforming to edge of side cups. 14 3/8" x 6 5/8"; cups, 4 5/8" x 2 3/8" x 5/8" deep.

Muffin or gem pan.   **CIBP - 71**
G.F. Filley #8. Eleven rectangular flat bottom cups with canted sides. 13 1/8" x 6 1/8"; cups, 3 1/8" x 1 7/8" x 1" deep.

Muffin or gem pans   **CIBP - 69**
Top: *G.F. Filley #3. Eight simple rectangular flat bottom cups with rounded sides and corners. Same angled upwards openwork handle grips. 11 3/4" x 7 5/8"; cups, 2 1/4" x 1/2" deep.* **Middle & bottom:** *Two views of G.F. Filley #7. Eleven ribbed rectangular cups. 12 1/2" x 6 3/8"; cups, 3" x 2" x 9/16" deep.*

Baking pans.   **CIBP - 72**
Top: *G.F. FIlley-12. Fourteen bowl-shaped cups in solid frame. 12 1/4" x 6 5/8"; cups, 2 1/4" diameter x 7/8" deep.* **Bottom:** *G.F. Filley #10. Eleven round cups with raised bottoms, in solid frame with cup-conforming outer edge. 12 1/2" x 8 1/2"; cups, 3" x 3/4" deep (Ed NOTE: Probably used for making a small shortcake or spongecake that would be served upside down, the shallow depression caused by the raised bottom in the mold to be filled with berries. In today's grocery store, you'll see packaged spongecakes of this type sold with strawberries. LCF.)*

Muffin or gem pan.   **CIBP - 70**
G.F. Filley #5. Eight flat bottom oval cups; with Filley's typical upraised handles, and cup-conforming sides to the pan. 11 5/8" x 7 1/8"; cups, 3 5/8" x 2 3/8" x 3/4" deep.

Baking pans.   **CIBP - 73**
Top: *G.F. Filley #11. Eleven round cups (with bowl-like bottoms and a rounded molding ring around top half of cup that will result in a sort of 'foot' or ring around the cake, that would be served upside down. LCF) 12 1/4" x 8 1/2"; cups, 3" x 3/4" deep. There is also a G.F. Filley #6 with eleven oval cups with same molding ring. It is 12 1/2" x 6 1/2"; cups, 3" x 2 1/4" x 9/16" deep.*

Generally speaking, the value range for old original pans (not reproductions) is wide — from about $50.00 to upwards of $250.00.

Other Foundries

The following baking pans (CIBP-74 through -91) are from various other foundries. Some have marks identifying the company, some do not. Some companies were prominent, some obscure. Encouraging to collectors is the fact that the variety goes on and on.

Popover pan. CIBP - 76

"Favorite" "pop-over pan," mfd. in Piqua, OH. This is the largest of the popover pans. Nine cups in openwork frame with side handles. 10 1/2" x 10 1/2" plus handles that extend from edge of frame about 1 1/2". Cups, 3 1/8" diameter at top x 2 1/2" deep. Weight, 8 lbs., 12 oz.

French roll pan. CIBP - 74

Unmarked. Unusually large, with twelve trough-like cups with interesting cutouts in the 'aisle' between the rows. Handles look like the ends of draughtsman's T-squares. 16 1/4" x 8 1/4"; cups, 3 3/4" x 2 1/4" x 1" deep.

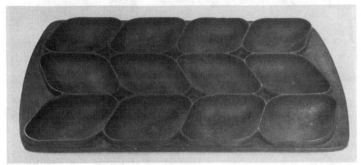

Muffin pan. CIBP - 75

This example unmarked, but other known examples have been marked "Barstow Stove Co.", which was a 19th and early 20th C stove foundry in Providence, RI. Twelve parallelogram cups set in an interesting pattern, and with sides raised almost 1/4" above top surface of solid frame. No real handles, but because of angling of the cups, two cattycorner handles are effected. 11 1/2" x 7 1/2"; cups 2 1/2" x 2 1/2" x 1" deep.

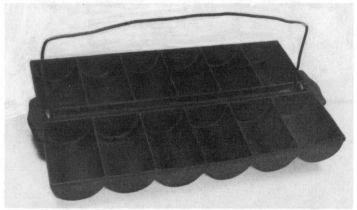

French roll pan. CIBP - 77

Barstow Stove Co., Providence, RI. Twelve trough-like cups with bracket-shaped wire bail handle, hooked into holes in the 'aisle' between the rows. Note handle shape. 14 1/8" x 8 1/4"; cups, 3 3/4" x 2 1/8" x 1 1/4" deep.

Muffin or gem pan. CIBP - 78

A #2, identified by fellow collector Chuck Wafford as made by "Chattanooga Iron." Eleven flat bottom cups with rounded sides and cup-conforming frame edge. 12 5/8" x 8 5/8"; cups, 3" x 5/8" deep (Ed NOTE: There was a Chattanooga Iron & Coal Co., in Chattanooga, TN, that made cast iron radiators; there was also a Chattanooga Stove & Foundry Co. In addition, see CIBP-33 for information on Cahil Co. LCF).

Muffin or gem pan.   **CIBP - 79**

A #5, identified by fellow collector Chuck Wafford as made by Chattanooga Iron. Eight oval flat bottom cups with rounded sides; solid frame whose outside shape conforms to the layout of the cups. 12 1/4" x 7 1/4"; cups, 3 3/4" x 2 1/2" x 3/4" deep. (Ed NOTE: Talk about restrained design and pure elegance. If the Japanese can be attracted to antique American kitchen utensils as a hot new collectible for the 1990's, this pan and the next, also by Chattanooga (?), may do the trick. LCF.)

Muffin or gem pan.   **CIBP - 80**

A #8, identified by fellow collector Chuck Wafford as made by "Chattanooga Iron." Eleven oval flat bottom cups in simple frame. 13 1/8" x 6 5/8"; cups, 3 1/8" x 2 1/4" x 3/4" deep.

Muffin or gem pan.   **CIBP - 81**

Unmarked #3, but from its appearance, probably from a Southern foundry. Eleven round flat bottom cups in solid rectangular frame with oval handle openings (note raised edges). 13 1/8" x 9"; cups, 3" x 3/4" deep. This design is found also in a smaller size, the #6, also with eleven cups. 12" x 8 3/8"; cups, 2 5/8" x 1/2" deep.

Ebelskiver or applecake pans.   **CIBP - 82**

Top: Hollow iron socket handle to accommodate a long wooden handle. Marked "NAC & Co." Seven bowl-shaped cups set in round recessed pan frame. 9 3/4" diameter with additional 7 3/4"L handle. Cups, 2 1/2" diameter x 1 1/4" deep. **Bottom:** This example is exactly the same size, and is also marked "NAC & Co.," It has a rigid bracket handle of heavy steel wire, and was cast with reinforcements, specifically for taking this handle. Otherwise it is the same as the one above. (Ed NOTE: "NAC & Co." has not been identified. It is possibly some precursor or variant of Northland Aluminum Co., Minneapolis, MN, even though this pan is made of cast iron and Northland is known for their cast aluminum ebelskivers. LCF.)

Gem pan.   **CIBP - 83**

Unmarked and maker unknown. Crudely molded (or perhaps only crudely cast) oblong pan with eight oval cups with the stepback ring that will form a 'foot' when the cake is turned and served upside down. Simple tab handles. Cloverleaf cutouts are interesting. 14 7/8" x 8 1/8"; cups, 4" x 2 1/2" x 3/4" deep.

Vienna roll pan. CIBP - 84

Unmarked. Four very fat cigar-shaped cups in openwork frame. No handles. 12 1/2" x 6 1/2"; cups, 5 7/8" x 2 5/8" x 1 1/8" deep.

Muffin and roll pans. CIBP - 85

Top: *Marked only "#14" under handle. Twelve rectangular flat bottom cups in very modern-looking frame with slotted openings between the cups. 12 1/2" x 6 5/8"; cups, 2 1/2" x 1 7/8" x 3/4" deep.* **Middle:** *Roll pan. "Shepard" - "Buffalo", #12. Twelve rectangular flat bottom cups in frame with vent slots. Note recess in one handle that accommodates stove lid lifter. 15 3/4" x 6 3/4" cups, 2 3/8" x 1 3/4" x 3/4" deep.* **Bottom:** *Marked "French Roll Pan No. 11". Twelve trough-shaped cups in ventilated frame. 12 3/4" x 7 1/2"; cups, 2 3/4" x 1 7/8" deep.*

Roll pan. CIBP - 86

Unmarked. Six oblong flat bottom cups with canted sides, tab handles. 10 7/8" x 9 1/4"; cups 4 1/2" x 3" x 1" deep.

Muffin or roll pan. CIBP - 87

Shepard Hardware, Buffalo, NY, #7. Mfd. c.1880. Eight oblong cups with rounded corners, in openwork frame with square recesses at ends to accommodate a stove lid lifter. 11 1/2" x 7 1/2"; cups, 3 5/8" x 2 3/8" x 5/8" deep.

Roll pan. CIBP - 88

Unmarked. Unusually large pan, with ten oblong cups with canted sides. Note fancy raised handles. 15 1/2" x 9 1/4"; cups, 4" x 1 1/4" x 1 1/4" deep.

Muffin pan.   **CIBP - 89**

Schofield Mfg. Co., NYC, c.1890. Rare fruit and vegetable pattern, with figural cups in openwork frame. 9 1/8" x 6 5/8".

Gem or cake pan,   **CIBP - 90**

or possibly a candy mold? Unmarked. Nine cups with crosshatched or "waffled" bottoms, fancy, sort of pleated sides, joined to form the largest possible open spaces between cups (which is probably a clue to use). Cups, 2 1/2" x 2 1/4" x 1/2" deep; handle, 2 1/2"L. (Ed. NOTE: I don't think it's a candy mold, having seen nothing like it in any of the numerous trade catalogs I've searched. The cups are too big anyway. LCF)

Gem or muffin pan.   **CIBP - 91**

Unmarked. Rounded oblong frame with handles; twelve cups, with 9 flutes instead of the more usual 10 flutes. 15 3/4" x 10 1/2"; cups, 2 3/4" x 1" deep.

Reproductions of Baking Pans
by David G. Smith

Reproductions and copies are increasingly a problem in today's antique and collectibles market, as originals become more difficult to find. Unfortunately, reproductions are sometimes sold as originals. For the novice, and sometimes even the experienced collector, it is difficult to recognize the difference. There are some indicators which can help determine an original from a reproduction.

•Rust. — Many originals, even if rusted, will have an accumulation of years of burned-on food and grease. Also, rust on an old piece will probably be uneven. This is caused by the protection the encrusted food has given parts of the metal. Rust on a new reproduction will usually be even, and often is bright orange.

•Casting quality. — Craftsmen who cast the originals were proud of their work. Their products were precise. Today's repros, for the most part, are mass-produced in great quantities, and do not get the attention of human hands.

•Patina. — The illustration, **CIBP-A,** below, shows a forgery of the Griswold #262 Tea Size Corn Stick Pan. Note how grainy the iron of the reproduction is (right), in comparison to the original (left). Older iron has a patina, a satiny smoothness, which new castings don't have. In, **CIBP-B,** note the difference in the detail of the kernels between the reproduction (right) and the original (left).

Stick pans.   **CIBP - A**
Left: Authentic *Griswold #262 "Crispy Corn Wheat" pan.* **Right:** Reproduction *of same pan.*

295

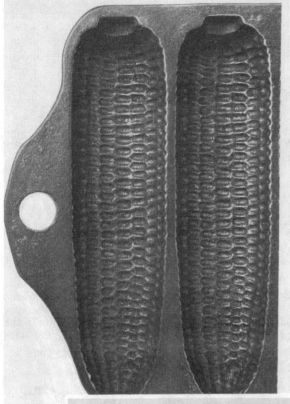

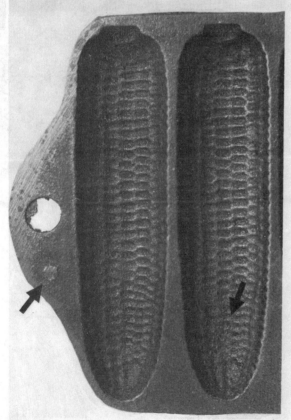

• **Modern casting technique.** — Note the excess left by the breathing hole pin **(CIBP-B).** In one modern method of casting, breathing holes are punched into the cast to allow air to escape when the molten iron is poured into the mold. When the air escapes, the molten iron rises in these holes. These pins are then broken off or ground down.

•**Inaccurate copying.** — CIBP-C illustrates an attempted copy (possibly of Far Eastern manufacture), not a reproduction. This pan is marked "CRISWOLD" (with a "C" not a "G"), and says "SNICK" (with an "N" not a "T"). It also has the pattern number 252 (with a "5") not 262 of the Griswold original. This pan is commonly seen; there may be others. Buyer beware!

Stick pan,   **CIBP - C**
laughably inaccurate **reproduction.** *Note misspellings in "Criswold" and "Snick" as well as incorrect pattern number. These are not uncommon.*

                                            CIBP - B
Details of previous stick pan.
Top: *Detail of two cobs from* **authentic** *Griswold #262 from previous illustration. Note sharp detail of kernels, clean hanging hole, relatively smooth surface of frame and handle.* **Bottom: detail of two cobs from reproduction** *Griswold. Note fuzzy kernel delineation, the ground off breathing hole pin, the evidence of other grinding on the handle, and the partly filled-in sloppy hole.*

296

•**Grinding and finishing.** — Older, original castings were, for the most part, precise, therefore required very little "cleaning" — filing or grinding. Shoddy molding of repros is compensated for by grinding off excess metal, but sometimes the reproduction-maker doesn't even bother with that. CIBP-D shows the edge of an original casting compared to the edge of a repro.

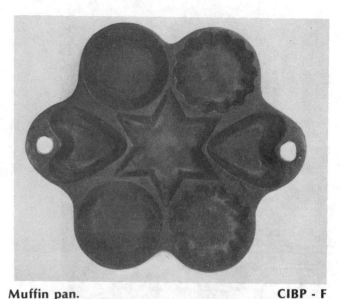

Muffin pan. CIBP - F

*An **authentic**, half-size version of Reid's Pat. However, it is not marked or dated. The casting quality is the same as the large original pan. Seven cups: 2 fluted, 2 hearts, 2 plain rounds, surrounding a single 6-point star. 9 1/4" x 8 1/8"; weighs 2 lbs., 4 oz.*

Details of cup edges, CIBP - D
*comparing an **authentic** pan (**top**) and a **reproduction** (**bottom**).*

Muffin pan. CIBP - G

*This is an **authentic** original of the twelve-cup heart pattern pan. 13 1/4" x 8 3/8"; weighs 4 lbs., 12 oz.*

The nine-section heart pattern is the most commonly reproduced heart pattern. I have no original for comparison.

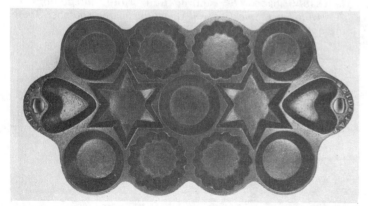

Muffin pan. CIBP - E

*One of the most famous. An **authentic**, original "Reid's Pat.", dated "July 18, 1871. It is 16 1/4" x 8 3/4", and weighs 4 lbs., 11 oz. The reproduction of this pan is not marked and dated.*

Muffin pan ·   CIBP - H

*This is an **authentic** original of the often-seen eight-cup fruit and vegetable pan. 16 5/8″ x 8 1/4‴ weighs 4 lbs, 9 oz. One of the reproductions is found with a tiny white enameled button identifying it.*

•**Signs of wear.** — Wear is a good indicator of an original. Being pushed in and out of an oven over a period of years polishes high points on the bottom of a muffin pan. **CIBP-I** illustrates these wear points on the bottom of the eight-cup fruit and vegetable pan.

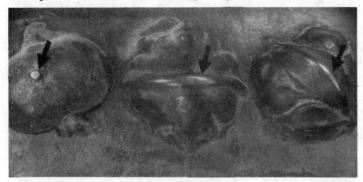

Detail of previous muffin pan,   **CIBP-I**
showing bottom of the fruit and vegetable pan cups. Notice how wear polishes the high points.

Just one of the eight indicators of an original (encrusted food, uneven rusting, high quality casting, patina, weight, or signs of wear) is probably not sufficient to positively determine what is an old original from what is a reproduction, although the newer the repro, the easier the task becomes. Complicating the issue are old reproductions, from 50 or 60 years ago, which have been heavily used. However, a combination of several of the indictors or clues is a good guide.

Cleaning and Preserving Iron
By David G. Smith

It is no easy task to clean a muffin pan, or any other iron cooking utensil, which has an accumulation of many years of burned-on grease, or rust from years of neglect. The result, however, is worth the effort. There are two basic elements needed to initiate the task: optimism and perserverence. If you have these, the rest is elementary!

The first consideration is to not destroy the patina of the metal. In cast iron, the patina is the natural smoothness of the surface, smoothness which has developed through years of use. To preserve the patina, do not use anything abrasive. Especially, DO NOT SANDBLAST. Sandblasting destroys the old finish and the value, and often gives a pitted grainy look which is no better than that of reproductions.

•**Soften & remove burned-on food.** — The first step of the cleaning process is to soften and remove the burned-on grease. This can be accomplished by applying an oven cleaner. Apply it as directed on the product, with plenty of fresh air, and let it set for several hours. Oven cleaner can burn your skin, so wear rubber gloves. After a few hours, wipe the deposit off and apply another coat. Repeat the process until all the burned-on grease is removed. Stubborn spots can be scraped with a putty knife or spoon. Be careful not to dig into the iron. *(Ed. Note: Some collectors will not use anything chemical on their old iron, and advise using wood or glass (like a heavy shard from a bottle) to scrape the metal. (LCF).*

After removing burned-on grease, you may discover rust underneath.

•**Remove the rust.** — The most difficult task is removing the rust. The best way to remove rust is with a wire brush. If you have an electric drill, many shapes and sizes of brushes are available. Power brushing is much easier than hand brushing. A word of caution: Do not use a coarse brush on a smooth surface. A coarse brush will scratch the surface, and destroy the patina. Use a fine brush first. If this is not adequate, cautiously try a coarser brush. *(Ed. Note. Again, many collectors hate wire brushes in all forms and descriptions, but particularly the big unwieldy coarse ones often used to refinish (i.e. ruin) old furniture. I have seen experienced people use a fine wire brush mounted on an electric motor, with beautiful results. I would advise practicing — maybe on a few of those repros you wish hadn't bought. I tried using a fine brass-wire brush on heavily rusted old andirons, and ended up with a sort of golden sheen. LCF).*

Severe, crusted rust may not come off with brushing. Crusted rust pods resemble barnacles. Rust pods can be broken by scraping them with a spoon or putty knife; then use the brush to remove them.

I do not like to use a rust-removing chemical because it leaves the iron a dull gray and destroys the patina. I have used it in several cases; it does work. After removing the rust, I scrub the pan in detergent with a brass brush to remove iron dust and the remainder of the grease. After thoroughly drying the iron, you are ready to cure and preserve it.

•**Cure the iron.** — There are several methods you may use to cure and preserve the iron. Some use vegetable salad oil, some peanut oil, and some mineral oil. All of them will protect against rust.

I prefer curing the pan with solid Crisco, which works better than Crisco oil. Apply it to the pan and put it into the oven at about 225°, and leave in for about 30 minutes. Remove the pan and wipe off excess grease. Replace in the oven and leave for another 30 minutes. Then shut off and let it cool. I think you will be pleased by the results. Vegetable oil, like corn or peanut oil, tends to leave a sticky film on the pan, making it unsuitable for curing pieces meant for display.

Considered only from the viewpoint of rust prevention, I have found that mineral oil works best. Wipe it on liberally and let it soak in for a few days, then wipe off. The mineral oil accents the patina and also tends to darken the color of the iron. It is also consumable, so you can cook with the pan later if you choose.

•**Care after use.** — After you have baked with a cured pan, don't scour it. Merely rinse it in clear hot water and wipe it out with a paper towel. Stubborn deposits may be dislodged by scraping with a spoon. After the pan is clean and dry, apply a protective film of Crisco; it doesn't take much.

Clocks and scales are the best-established categories in this chapter, but not necessarily from a kitchen collector's viewpoint. In fact, kitchen clocks of old or new vintage are hardly collected at all. I think a **futurewatch** on kitschy figural kitchen clocks might be in order for the 1990s.

Scales relating to food handling have a well-established market. Those with polished brass faces, or interesting cast iron bases, lead the category. However, scales are, for most advanced scale collectors, the only dip in the ocean of kitchen collectibles that they've ever taken. Scales are seen primarily as an important specialty in the Scientific instrument collecting field and have been featured as "men's antiques" for decades. Egg scales are virtually ignored by most scale collectors, but with kitchen collectors they are very popular, and — it is nice to report — relatively inexpensive.

Many cupboards and pantries have been raided by collectors who have preferred (at least until very recently) to not acknowledge kitchen antiques as a serious and worthy field. The contents that have been "kidnapped" this way include most decorated tin (sometimes appropriately called "tole") wares, most *polishable* brass and copper wares, and all woodenwares which could be attributed to the Shakers, or which could be given the name treen (also trein), which is a Scottish word for something made of wood. Although there is much disagreement about what "treen" includes, it usually applies to objects of turned wood, sometimes called turnery. Anyway, the way you will find turned and carved cider funnels, or fine old scoops will be to conduct your own raid into the Treen Market, which is altogether more posh than ours.

Another category in this chapter that has enjoyed a good deal of cachet is measures. Most particularly liquid measures of copper (remember the rule about polishing = decorative value) or pewter. (I have not done pewter measures here because that field of collecting is long-established and requires years of specialized study.) Green Depression glass measuring cups are also borrowed from Glass — a specialist collecting field about which I know little. I don't do glass.

Asparagus buncher, cast iron, painted dark red, mounted to board, has end plate, a U-shaped cradle for stalks, & spring loaded hinged piece to form bunch, "The Philadelphia Buncher", 5½"H x 8½"L exclusive of board, looks late 19th or early 20th C. **$35.00-$45.00**

Asparagus buncher, cast iron top of frame, slightly scrolled cutout wood adjustable for bunching the asparagus, brass spring clips & ratchet thumb catch, (probably "The Philadelphia" model), mfr unknown to me, "PHILA." is only mark, buncher hoop is 4¾" diameter, base is 11⅝" x 10", 3rd quarter to late 19th C. • A simpler one, mostly of wood, with springy brass partial hoops in a wooden cradle, flat wood end piece against which to thump the bottom of the stalks, is depicted in the Feb. 1876 *American Agriculturist*, as "Conover's Asparagus Buncher". They give advice on sorting by size & washing before bunching, and to stand the finished bunches (held in the buncher until they can be tied in 2 places with string) on wet hay if they have to be "kept for some hours before packing" for market. • This magazine was full of advice on marketing, and said once that it was easy to grow the food, but hard to market it. For example: a delicious juicy watermelon couldn't be sold in NYC markets because it was too hard to carry under your arm, too big for a market basket, and New Yorkers "refused to" hoist them on their shoulders to carry home! After several years of disappointing sales, someone finally came up with a sort of bookstrap device with a wooden handle (shades of those nifty things we used to get attached to suit boxes), to provide what nature had neglected to provide — a way to carry a watermelon. • In another article, in 1873, the editor noted that if one wanted to sell produce one had to "conform to the customs of that market. ... If a lot of loose asparagus, or strawberries in the large trays used in Cincinnati, were sent to the New York market, they would probably find their way into the garbage-cart." This is probably still true. I am dismayed by huge trays of strawberries (such as are found 125 years later in Charlottesville, VA), and wish for the small box style of NYC. **$80.00-$100.00**

Bean sizer or **Bean sorting frame** — SEE Sift & Strain chapter.

Beer measure, copper slant-sided pitcher-like container with long "V" neck lip or spout originating at bottom, flared foot, strap handle, inset panel with 4 small arched glass windows down one side, hinged lid with small perforated hatch in middle, mfd by E. Ketcham & Co., NYC, NY, 2 qt. capacity, c.1877. **$125.00-$165.00**

Candy scoop, japanned tin, tapered sides, small with braced tubular handle, late 19th or early 20th C. **$12.00-$15.00**

Candy thermometer, tin with brass face, marked "Spirit, Boil, Simmer, Heat, Temple, Freezing" (stages for sugar cooking), mfd by J. Kendall & Co., 6½"L, 19th C (?). **$30.00-$45.00**

Clock, alarm clock, not for the kitchen but here because of related subject, animated scene of woman working at her moving spinning wheel, Lux Clock Mfg. Co., Waterbury, CT, mid 20th C. **$75.00-$100.00**

Clock, battery, decorated china plate, 6 herbal bouquets, Arabic numerals, General Electric, 9½" diameter, c.1960. **$12.00-$18.00**

Clock, ceramic, Black Americana, Aunt Jemima, works' mfr not known to me, pottery by Red Wing, MN, 20th C. **$75.00-$125.00**

Clock, electric, blue & white Delft china plate, Dutch scene, English, German or Dutch, 20th C. **$35.00-$45.00**

Clock, electric, colorful yellow china octagonal plate with blue & green flowers in border, center is clock face, Arabic numerals, insignia of windmill, "Cretonne", by Irving Miller & Co., NYC, NY, 9" diameter, 1930. • **Time Isn't Ageless.** — "To the casual observer, today's smart kitchens seem perfect in their charm. Gay, sparkling, they are a whirl of matching color ... harmonious in every detail ... except the offending clock! Sometimes a crude, ungainly alarm. Often a makeshift relic of other days. ... Miller has created an enchanting array. Clocks, bright as butterflies ... perky-fresh and in perfect tune with the kitchen scene. Designed in a cheerful 'cottage-y' mood, these delightful time pieces are of gleaming porcelain ...

so charmingly right for the kitchen, so easy to keep twinkling and clean. ... Either with the 8-day lever movement (which does away with the pendulum nuisance) or the new electric movement (which need never be wound or regulated)." Sept. 1930 ad, *House & Garden*.

$12.00-$18.00

Clock, electric, for wall, depicts Elsie the Cow, adv'g "Borden's Ice Cream", 20th C. **$50.00-$65.00**

Clock, electric, molded avocado green "antiqued" plastic, in shape of hutch cupboard, with 3 little metallic plastic "copper" plates on top shelf, a pot & 2 candlesticks on 2nd shelf, clock face on front of lower doors, Arabic numerals, mfd by Spartus, 12"H, 1960s? • More charm than you'd think. I saw another version of this in wood tones, with blue & white plastic "Delft" wares, plates, etc., on the shelves & wonderful blue & white coffee pot. I wonder how many versions Spartus did. **$7.00-$12.00**

Clock, frying pan, a real one, key wound, for Pan American Exposition of 1901, 17"L including handle, c.1901.

$250.00-$450.00

Clock, frying pan, black painted cast iron, sides have hammered look with bronzed finish, outside bottom of pan cast with raised numbers, painted white, electric or battery (?), unclear from catalog, Emig Products, Reading, PA, 8" diameter x 12"H overall, c.1966. • Wholesale price then was $13.00. Asking price now isn't much higher.

$15.00-$22.00

Clock, frying pan, cast iron, quartz battery motor, loop hanging hole, 2 pouring lips, 4 Arabic numerals & 8 dots as well as hands finished brass, second hand, sold (& mfd?) by Clock Wise, Inc., Andrews, NC, 6" diameter frying pan bottom or clock face, advertised 1983.

$10.00-$22.00

Clock, frying pan, electric, enameled iron & tin, white pan, red screwed-on handle, red knife & fork (minute) hands, modern-looking sans serif Arabic numerals in white on white, "Made in Great Britain", c.1950s (?). **$40.00-$55.00**

Clock, frying pan, electric, molded plastic with copperoid finish, "Model 504," Herold Products Co., Chicago, IL, c.1950s. **$30.00-$40.00**

Clock, frying pan, electric, stamped tin, Sessions, Forrestville, CT, c.1920s. **$35.00-$55.00**

Clock, frying pan, inset clock. A cast iron promotional piece for dealers. Made to be hung by hole in short handle, with the bottom of the skillet facing out. Cast with large-letter legend around clock, "ERIE UP TO TIME" and "We Sell Hollow-Ware", Griswold Mfg. Co., Erie, PA, early 20th C. High price because it's Griswold

$2500.00-$3200.00

Clock, frying pan, keywound with regulator, a real stamped sheet steel frying pan, decal image of North & South America as voluptuous women's figures, mfd for Expo in Buffalo, NY, a "Cold Handle Acme" pan, mfd for the Pan-American Exposition Co. by the New York Stamping Co., NYC, 26"L including handle, 13" diameter, clock itself 1899 for 1901 fair; but pan pat'd Nov. 14, 1876.

$400.00-$600.00

Clock, frying pan, sheet metal, with knife & fork hands, this one German, early 20th C. **$75.00-$150.00**

Clock, milk can figural, battery-operated, molded plastic, finished in a sort of brushed pewter or old tin look. Great thing about casting is it successfully imitates a banged-up old milk can, with dents. Face with large Arabic numerals

is on a flattened front, has sweep second hand. Called the "Milkmaid" clock in ads, "Seth Thomas" on face; inside, cast into plastic, it says "Ronthor R 60 3464," & "Seth Thomas 2436," NYC, NY, 11"H x 7¾"W, 1973 ad.

$10.00-$15.00

Clock, pumpkin, stamped 3-D tin, round face has some 3-D dimension & modeling, painted in shaded orange, with black Arabic numerals, 2 hands. I saw this in an ad only, which doesn't mention works — probably some form of 7-day windup. Advertises in bold lettering on face: "None Such Mince Meat [&] Pumpkin-Squash Like Mother Used To Make", American, 10" diameter, early 20th C.

$400.00-$600.00

Clock, refrigerator in shape of Monitor Top, electric works, heavy cast metal, painted white, black "hinges" on 2 doors, clock face on doors, Warren Telechron Co. mfd this Electron clock for The General Electric Co., Ashland, MA, 8¾"H x 5"W x 3⅛" deep, made from 1928 to early 1931. • According to refrigerator collector Russell Wilson, there were **four types of these GE Monitor Top clocks** made in 1928, 1929, 1930 and part of 1931, alike at a cursory glance, but differing in case, movement and numerals. For example, he said that the nameplate above the clock shrank on later models from 3⅜"L to only 1⁹⁄₁₆"L; the condensor "monitor top" went from 16 down to 14 coils and vertical fins were added; numerals changed size too; and later movements were marked "Model No. M-1, with a serial number prefix "A". • Wilson also said that a cast iron pennybank that is 4¾"H also exists.

According to Edwin P. Mampe, writing in the National Association of Watch & Clock Collectors Museum's *The Bulletin*, at least two versions of the clock were made — an earlier one with longer nameplate, larger Arabic numerals, legs "indented" at the joint with box so they appear separate, and the 16 condenser coils on top permanently affixed to the case. A later type has no indentation where the legs join, and has a 14 coil condenser bolted to case, and thus removable. There are other differences. • Russell Wilson adds that these clocks were "an exclusive premium item given to managers (dealers) of G.E. appliance stores selling the 'Monitor Top'. There were, according to G.E. only 21,460 made altogether during the years 1928 to 1931." **$200.00-$225.00**

Clock, shelf, gingerbread oak case, brass works, key wound, William L. Gilbert Clock Co., original paper label "Tiger," Winsted, CT, 19th C. **$165.00-$200.00**

Clock, teapot, chubby figural, stamped metal, electric movement, Arabic numerals, came in white, green, red or blue finish, Sessions, 7"H x 8½"W, c.1940. **$15.00-$20.00**

Clock & inkwell combined, cast brass with cast round face, decorated with flour sacks, brooms, barrels or kegs & groceries, advertising 50th anniversary (1863 to 1913) of Joseph Spidel Grocery Co., mfd by Mercedes, American, 1913. **$150.00-$175.00**

Coffee measure, metal, with sliding backwall to adjust capacity for 2, 4 or 6 cups, "Dix Coffee Meter", pat'd 1908. **$30.00-$40.00**

Coffee measure, tin, Bokar, 20th C. **$5.00-$7.00**

Dinner chimes, mahogany rectangular base with molded edges, 4 bell metal oblong keys mounted to base, raised above it a little, to be hit with little wooden ball on a stick. My grandmother, Grace Campbell Franklin, had one of these on her sideboard, and when we visited it was the greatest thing to be asked to ring the dinner chime. I usually played a version of "My dog has fleas"; originally such chimes came with booklets showing different tunes, even "bugle calls", be played on the chimes. Who knows — one might mean "Liver Tonight, Stay Upstairs", another "Buttered Biscuits Going Fast", another "Soup's On, Come Immediately". One company, Kohler-Liebich, made "Liberty" chimes, Chicago, IL, 1910s & 1920s. Prob. much earlier. **$15.00-$25.00**

Dry measure, bentwood, handforged lap nails, painted old gray, American, 9¾" diameter, 19th C. **$40.00-$55.00**

Dry measure, bentwood, turned wood side handle, copper rivets & nails, American, 3½"H x 5½" diameter, 19th C. **$55.00-$70.00**

Dry measure, bentwood with copper rivets, for measuring dry weights as opposed to liquid amounts, "C.A. Wilkens," Henniker, NH, 8¾"D, 20th C. **$50.00-$70.00**

Dry measure, bentwood, with cover, supposedly Shaker, Maine, 8" diameter, 19th C. **$90.00-$120.00**

Dry measure, bentwood with old red paint, wire bail handle, American, 19th C. **$20.00-$30.00**

Dry measure, bentwood with tin binding, American, 5¼" diameter, 1 quart size, mid 19th C. **$50.00-$60.00**

Dry measure, dark green painted bentwood, 9"D diameter, late 19th C. **$55.00-$70.00**

Dry measure, for grain, marked "Dry 4 Quart, Frye," American, 20th C. • **"Dry measures"** may be marked with some of same quantities — pint, quart, gallon, barrel — as a "wet or liquid measure," but the weight & cubic inches to be filled differ. One dry pint, holds 33.6 cubic inches; one wet pint has 28.875 cubic inches; a British pint is equal to 1.03% of a US dry, & 1.201% a US wet pint. Other dry measures are a peck (8 qts) & a bushel (4 pecks). A barrel varies from 31-42 gallons! **$18.00-$25.00**

Dry measure, for grain, wood with old mustard paint, American, 19th C. **$28.00-$35.00**

Dry measure, oak bentwood, "Daniel Cragin," Wilton, NH, 11½" diameter, 19th C. • Another by same maker, only 5¾" diameter: add 10% to 20%. **$40.00-$45.00**

Dry measure, bentwood, copper nails, looks like a saucepan with exaggeratedly uptilted handle, American, 6½" diameter, 19th C. **$85.00-$100.00**

Dry measure bucket, tin, with handles, "Franklin", ½ bushel capacity, late 19th C. **$12.00-$18.00**

Dry measure bucket, wood with old green paint, American, 2 gallon capacity, 19th C. • "BUCKET. The term is applied, in the South and West, to all kinds of pails and cans holding over one gallon." John Russell Bartlett, *Dictionary of Americanisms. A Glossary of Words and Phrases usually regarded as peculiar to the United States*, Boston: 2nd ed. 1859 (1st ed. 1848). **$45.00-$55.00**

Dry measures, for grain, nested set of 4, old blue painted bentwood, American, 6"D to 12"D, late 19th C. **$160.00-$190.00**

Dry measures, set of 4 round graduated measures, bentwood, American, 6", 7", 9" and 11" diameter, late 19th C. **$60.00-$75.00**

Egg alarm timer, aluminum insert, in original box with instructions, whistles when egg is done, 20th C. **$15.00-$18.00**

Egg tester or candler, pierced tin cylinder with strap handle, resembles a drinking cup, has hole in top for holding eggs to be candled using candle inside, "The Family Egg-Tester," American, 3"H, pat'd March 13, 1876. **$28.00-$40.00**

Egg timer, Black Americana, tin with color lithographed "Mammy", 3 hooks for potholders, 3 minute timer, American, early 20th C. **$25.00-$30.00**

Egg timer, cast iron frame with pedestal base, shaped like a cheval mirror, with small glass bulbs pivoting inside, from F. A. Walker catalog, American (?), or European import, about 4"H, c.1870s to 1880s. **$45.00-$55.00**

Egg timer, Mauchlin ware (wood with red plaid finish), simple square top and bottom with 4 corner columns, glass hourglass bulb inside this "cage", Scottish or imitation from Germany, early 20th C. **$35.00-$45.00**

Egg timer, turned wood frame with old red paint, small glass bulbs inside, American, 4"H, 19th C. **$25.00-$35.00**

Egg timer, cast white metal, painted, Amish woman with churn, glass bulbs off to side on pivot, John Wright Inc., Wrightsville, PA, 2"H x 3"W, c.1963. **$16.00-$20.00**

Egg timer, wall mounted, figural milk bottle backplate of enameled tin, attached flip timer with small glass bulbs, American, 6"H, TOC. **$45.00-$55.00**

Egg timers, or egg glasses, figure-8 "hourglasses" within frames of cast iron or turned wood, sold through F. A. Walker catalog, prob. European import, probably about 3" to 5"H, c.1880s. **$35.00-$55.00**

Folk art sculpture, saxophone, made up of soldered together tin kitchen utensils: funnel, flour sifter, grater, and lots of tin ice cream spoons as the buttons & plates, almost full size, probably for hardware store display, American, very early 20th C. (Lavines say 1910). • Dealers Jim & LuAnn Lavine in Geneseo, IL, advertised this in early 1989. Price range mine. **$350.00-$500.00**

Fruit jar filler or funnel, mottled gray graniteware, TOC. **$18.00-$22.00**

Fruit jar funnel, for canning jars, enamelware, with wide untapered neck, no mark, American (?), 5"L, late 19th or early 20th C. **$10.00-$15.00**

Fruit jar funnel, green sponged yellowware (unusual form for ceramic), small handle, American, 3"L x 5"D at top, wide neck, 19th C. **$80.00-$95.00**

Fruit jar funnel, large size for canning jars or bulk meals & grains, also called a grocer's funnel, wide neck & mouth, cobalt & white swirled enamelware, late 19th C. **$175.00-$200.00**

Fruit jar funnel, pieced tin, ring handle, 20th C. **$4.00-$8.00**

Fruit jar funnel, for canning jars, spun aluminum, coffee cup like handle, wide cylindrical neck to fit into top of canning jar, 4½"H x 5" diameter, late 19th C. • **Tunnel Funnel.** — "Three tunnels [sic] are needed — a grocers tunnel for filling preserving jars, and one large and one small for filling bottles, jugs and cruets." Maria Parloa, *Kitchen Companion*, Boston: Estes & Lauriat, 1887. **$4.00-$8.00**

Funnel, amethyst glass, flared sides, rolled lip, American (?), 5"L x 10"D, early 19th C. **$150.00-$190.00**

Funnel, blue & white mottled enamelware, white interior, small strap handle, 5"L x 4" diameter, TOC. **$35.00-$45.00**

Funnel, blue & white swirl enamelware, 4½"D, TOC.
$25.00-$32.00

Funnel, brewers', copper with wire hanging loop, Eastern Bottlers Supply Co., 11"L x 9¼"D at top, c. 1880s-1900.
$45.00-$60.00

Funnel, cider, carved from one piece of wood, American, 18" x 8½" oblong x 3½" deep, with 1"D hole in center of the oblong bowl, early 19th C. • These cider funnels are very unusual looking, often primitive in style. They were meant to fit across the top of a cider keg. Prices range considerably, not so much because one is that much nicer than another, but because of knowledge of dealer, demand of collector, and general market conditions. A few cider funnels have dates or initials carved on them, which adds considerably to the value, as do any "finishing touches."
$135.00-$180.00

Funnel, cider, carved from one piece of wood, American, 20" x 8½" oblong x 4" deep, prob. c. 1825-1850.
$125.00-$150.00

Funnel, cider, carved from one piece of wood, oblong with rounded corners, separate wooden spout or neck fitted into center of bottom, American, 18½" x 9" oblong x 4½" deep, early 19th C.
$125.00-$150.00

Funnel, cider, carved from one piece of wood, oblong wooden trencher with hole in bottom center, American, 21" x 8" oblong x 3" deep, early to mid 19th C.
$120.00-$140.00

Funnel, copper, "Lash's Bitters", late 19th, early 20th C.
$65.00-$85.00

Funnel, copper & tin, large tumbler-shaped cup with rolled rim, abruptly narrowing neck, "Schuyler's Improved Safety — Statis Proof Filtering Funnel No. 1," Schuyler Mfg. Co., Springfield, OH, 8½"H x 5½" diameter, cup is 5"H, early 20th C "pat. pending".
$20.00-$28.00

Funnel, copper, tinned inside, American (?), tapers from 6½" D at mouth down to 2" at neck, late 19th C. • This is lovely, but it's the kind of puff 'n' buff piece which is as much Brasso® as anything else! I know I sound crazed on the subject of stripping and over-polishing brass and copper, but it drives me crazy. On the other hand, if a dealer has just retinned an old copper piece, I will pay extra because it now costs over $1.00 a square inch to have it done. By the way, an old-fashioned way to polish copper was to keep a little saucer of sour milk (or butter-milk) near the stove, for wiping the copper pots every day. It tends to make a pinkish finish, at least at first. Try it; it almost always works, at least after more vigorous first-time cleaning.
$25.00-$30.00

Funnel, copper, with brass spout & stopper, "Straiter," Boston, MA pat'd Dec. 5, 1893.
$45.00-$55.00

Funnel, copper with brass thumb piece that closes funnel, bulbous shape, "Straiter," Boston, MA, holds almost a quart, pat'd 1890. • SEE also strainer funnels in the Sift & Strain chapter.
$65.00-$75.00

Funnel, for maple sap, barrel construction with iron band, American, 12"H x 11½"D with 6"L cylindrical neck, 19th C.
$180.00-$225.00

Funnel, for maple sap, hand carved from maple, American, early 19th C.
$75.00-$110.00

Funnel, glass, bottom of neck is quite sharp, somehow looks like laboratory equipment, and it's not marked "Pyrex," which you would expect if it were a kitchen piece, 20th C (?)
$5.00-$8.00

Funnel, gray graniteware, crimped bottom, small side handle, 6"H, early 20th C.
$25.00-$35.00

Funnel, gray graniteware, elliptical mouth, 6"L, TOC.
$40.00-$50.00

Funnel, gray graniteware, loop handle, 5"L, late 19th or early 20th C.
$12.00-$18.00

Funnel, handwrought copper, dovetail seam construction, American, 10½"L, 19th C.
$50.00-$60.00

Funnel, pieced tin, interesting "around the corner" shape, 2 elbow joints that allow funnel to fit into hole otherwise unaccessible, looks like a Dogpatch hearing aid for Mammy Yokum, no mark, 14½"L measured sort of diagonally, 5½" diameter, late 19th C.
$20.00-$30.00

Funnel, spun aluminum, fat bowl, ring handle, shapely neck, about 4½"H, late 19th C.
$5.00-$8.00

Funnel, tin, with long cylindrical handle, capped & hooked, possibly for filling candle molds, American, 6" deep x 4¾" diameter, overall length 13¼", early 19th C.
• **German vocabulary** – Trichter: funnel.
$95.00-$115.00

Funnel, turned wood, with nice lip, rather deep nicely rounded bowl, tapered neck, American, 5¼"L, early 19th C.
$100.00-$135.00

Funnel, white enamelware, small with relatively long neck, 4"H, early 20th C.
$5.00-$10.00

Funnel, wide-mouthed, for fruit jars (?), unusual brass in oval shape, American, mouth is 5" x 6⅛", neck is 2" x 3", funnel is 7"H, 1860s.
$35.00-$45.00

Funnel, corer, cookie cutter & grater combined, pieced tin, the funnel having a scalloped mouth for cutting cookies, the small end having sharp points for coring, the strap handle partly punctured for grater and with one edge with sawteeth, maybe for scaling fish. American, 5¾"L x 3½" diameter, "pat. appl. for" c.1890s to 1915 (?). • Collection of Carol Bohn. Price range mine.
$35.00-$55.00

Funnel & dipper combined, tin, with 6 parts that fit together in various ways to create a funnel, sifter, dredger, measure, tea or coffee strainer, colander, ladle, clothes sprinkler, egg poacher, or funnel cake maker — considerably more than its name implies. The 6 parts are (1) main body or bowl, with handle, and bottom with screw threads, (2) funnel neck soldered to flat plat that fits hole in bottom of bowl, (3) screw threaded ring, like a canning jar ring, (4), (5), & (6) discs of perforated tin or wire mesh to provide various porosities. "Five-in-One," American, 5¼"H x 4 3/8" diameter x 8½"L including long handle, c. 1890s into 1910s.
$16.00-$22.00

Hourglass, glass funnel-like bulbs in wood frame, with gilt & blue paint. (SEE also Egg timers.) American (?), 7"H, early 19th C.
$180.00-$250.00

Hourglass, simple 6 corner wooden cage-like frame, turned wooden "columns" at each corner, 2 glass flask shaped bulbs fastened at waist with chamois leather, sometimes called a bottle glass, American (?), 8⅝"H, early 19th C or late 18th C.
$135.00-$160.00

Hourglass, wood frame in old blue paint, glass with sand, American, 19th C. • Added value. — Old blue color more $$ than red; this one has nice detailing besides and a certain lopsided charm.
$55.00-$75.00

Hourglass, wooden frame with rounded glass bulbous "funnels" joined at the small ends, 7½"H, late 18th, early 19th C.
$150.00-$185.00

Lamp funnel, copper, embossed with name, a store premium or giveaway, for filling lamps with kerosene. (Coleman lamp funnels known in tin too; worth something less.) "Coleman Lamp & Stove Co." with paper label for "Steve's Furniture," TOC. **$30.00-$45.00**

Liquid measure, brass can, strap handle, American (?), 1 pint capacity, mid 19th C. **$45.00-$60.00**

Liquid measure, copper, flared complete wraparound lip, strap handle with semi-cylindrical inset for better grip, dinged, "Fleming Apple Distillery", Fairmount, NJ, 7½"H, late 19th C. • Only $35.00 at the Garth Auction, May 26-27, 1989, Delaware, OH. **$35.00-$60.00**

Liquid measure, copper, wraparound pouring lip, strap handle, American or English, 1 quart capacity, 19th C. • Sets of these were sold by candy makers' suppliers, at least as late as 1925. Copper ones were offered in six sizes, from 1 pt. to 1 gal., by the Sethness Co., Chicago. Theirs had a completely wraparound lip that was wider at the pouring "front" than over the handle. The largest one, which sold for only $2.50 in 1925, also had a strap handle with part of the loop filled in to make a hand grip. **$70.00-$80.00**

Liquid measure, gray graniteware, "NESCO," St. Louis, MO, 1 gal. capacity, 20th C. **$45.00-$65.00**

Liquid measure, gray graniteware, graduated stepped thirds, wire handle, American, 1 cup capacity, TOC. **$22.00-$35.00**

Liquid measure, gray graniteware, pouring lip, slanted sides, 2 qt. capacity, 19th C. **$45.00-$55.00**

Liquid measure, gray graniteware, riveted handle & lip, American, ½ pt. capacity, TOC. **$45.00-$50.00**

Liquid measure, gray graniteware, straight sides, applied flaring wraparound pouring lip, strap handle, American, 2 qt. capacity, TOC. • (Pint size about ⅓ the price, quart about ½.) **$50.00-$55.00**

Liquid measure, pieced tin, stepped sides, upside-down truncated cone, strap handle, marked "Kellerman's" (the mfr ?), & "U. S. Standard," also "J. Coover", Harrisburg, PA marked on measure, (Coover from Chambersburgh, PA), 6½"H, marked 1 qt, 1 pt, ½ pt & 1 gill, pat'd Oct. 22, 1872. • Coover was inventor of method for forming sheet-metal measures. **$35.00-$45.00**

Liquid measure, tin, bail handle, shaped like a small coal scuttle, marked "Pour Chaque Litre" & "Canneleure Correspondante", French, 1 decilitre capacity, 19th C. **$40.00-$50.00**

Liquid measure, tin, flared wraparound lip, strap handle with brace, American, 8"H, 8 cup capacity, 19th C. **$18.00-$22.00**

Liquid measure, tin, high pouring rim, blobs of spelter or solder on it with marks stamped in the blobs, size on a brass plate, & words "JOB" under, square or bracket strap handle, strangest marks are letters stamped near handles, front & back: "Y Q A R C D F G H K M N P Q", only 2"H x 2" diameter, marked "1 deciliter", 19th C. • As to the meaning of Y Q A R C D F G H K M N P Q, I wonder if it indicates that the measure had been inspected 14 times, and each time the inspector used a different letter punch to indicate it had passed inspection? **$40.00-$50.00**

Liquid measure, tin, wraparound lip, generous strap handle, can part is perfectly cylindrical, marked with 3 ridges to divide it into fourths, looks like a coffee can, Matthai-Ingram was one mfr; I'm sure many others made similar wares, American, 4 sizes: 1 pt, 1 qt, 2 qts & 4 qts. The 1 quart size is 5"H x 3" diameter, c.1890 to 1910. **$15.00-$20.00**

Liquid measure, varnished, dark reddish brown wood fiber & glue composition, rather thick-walled, cylindrical with raised edge for pouring lip opposite tin strap handle, bound with thin wire in 3 places, Indurated Fibre Ware, Cordley & Hayes, NYC, 9"H, late 19th or early 20th C. **$35.00-$45.00**

Liquid measure, copper, simple cylinder with strap handle, close-fitting lid with strap handle, "Stevens & Duncklee," Concord, NH, 5½"H x 5" diameter, holds 52 oz, an odd amount, neither here nor there, being 6½ pints or 3¼ quarts, prob. last quarter 19th C. **$45.00-$60.00**

Liquid measures, copper & brass, elongated necks & widely-flared bodies (like skirts), English (?), 1 qt. & 1 gal. capacity, 19th C. • Price for pair: **$200.00-$250.00**

Liquid measures, set of 3, tin lined copper with small attached brass labels & brass strap handles in rounded rectangular shape, English (?), ½ pint size is 3⅜"H x 3⅛" diameter; 1 pt. — 3⅞"H x 3⅝" D; 2 pts. — 4¾"H x 4½" D, 19th C. • Price range is for each, the way measures are usually found. **$40.00-$55.00**

Liquid measures, set of 6, pieced tin, slightly conical, wraparound lips, large strap handles, only one of which (the 2 gallon size) is reinforced, from F. A. Walker catalog, American or imported, ¼ pt. to 2 gal. capacity, that is, approx. 3"H to 15"H, c.1870s to 1890s. **$18.00-$30.00**

Liquid or dry measure, stamped tin, "Kreamer," 4 cup capacity, TOC. **$7.00-$12.00**

Liquid or dry measures, set of 4 graduated cups with thumb tab handles, stamped tin, "Maryann's Accurate Measure," Chicago, IL, ¼ cup to 1 cup, 20th C. • For the set: **$12.00-$18.00**

Measure, for vinegar, 9"L, pat'd Feb. 1889. **$25.00-$30.00**

Measure, tin, with scrolly cast iron side handle, upside down conical shape with stepped divisions marking off 1 gill, ½ pint, 1 pint, 1 quart, big flared fixed foot, prob. English, as on one 2-day trip to PA I saw at least a dozen of them, 6¾"H x 5½" diameter at top, late 19th C. • **Collector hint.** — Keep track of how many of a form you see in one group shop, one market, one show, one antiquing trip, especially if it's something you don't think you've seen before. You can often tell when a container-load has just arrived, and from other things in the booth or show, maybe even where it was from. **$35.00-$45.00**

Measure, wooden, "Best Sealer," Henniker, NH, 6"D. **$15.00-$20.00**

Measure & funnel combined, called in catalogs a utility measure, a slightly tapered vessel, with strap handle hand grip, fitted with most of a funnel instead of pouring lip, copper, tinned on inside, American, 1 gallon capacity, late 19th into 2nd quarter 20th C. • A similar one was sold in pieced tin in 5 sizes from ½ pint to one gallon by the Matthai - Ingram Co. The funnel attachment, as they called it, made it easy to fill small mouthed vessels or to direct the stream in a particular place in a larger mouthed vessel. The tin ones would bring only about half what the more "decorative" copper one would bring. **$50.00-$75.00**

Measure or pitcher, copper, tinned inside, wraparound lip, reinforced strap handle, big dent in one side, no marks, American or English, 7½"H, 1 quart capacity, 19th C. **$28.00-$40.00**

Measuring cup, cobalt blue & white mottled enamelware, "McClary", Ontario, CAN, 1 pt. capacity, early 20th C. **$75.00-$100.00**

Measuring cup, embossed green Depression glass, Kellogg's, American, 1930s. **$22.00-$30.00**

Measuring cup, embossed green Depression glass, 3 way pouring lips, straight sides, Hazel Atlas, 1 cup capacity, c.1930s. **$10.00-$12.00**

Measuring cup, embossed green Depression glass, one pouring lip, sides flare up slightly, Hazel Atlas, 1 cup capacity, c.1930s. **$9.00-$12.00**

Measuring cup, embossed green Depression glass, sides flare, modernistic or Art Deco stepped angular handle, rather tall, 3 pouring lips, c.1930s. **$17.00-$22.00**

Measuring cup, for coffee, "Harrington Hall," 3½"H, 20th C. **$8.00-$12.00**

Measuring cup, glass, "Faultless Diamond Starch," American, 1 cup capacity, 20th C. **$5.00-$7.00**

Measuring cup, gray graniteware, heavy, applied pouring lip, strap handle, "Granite Iron Ware," mfd by St. Louis Stamping Co., St. Louis, MO, 1 cup capacity, pat'd May 30, 1876, May 8, 1877. **$30.00-$50.00**

Measuring cup, heavy colorless glass, no pouring lip, marked on one side ¼, ½, ¾ & 1 cup; on other side ⅓, ⅔ & 1 cup, "Sellers," to go with cabinet, pat'd Dec. 8, 1925. **$10.00-$16.00**

Measuring cup, spun aluminum, "Swans Down Cake Flour Makes Better Cakes" embossed on one side, American, 1 cup capacity, 20th C. **$12.00-$15.00**

Measuring cup, stamped tin, "Rumford Baking Powder," 20th C. **$15.00-$20.00**

Measuring cup, stamped tin, "Cottolene" (shortening made from cottonseeds), American, 1 cup capacity, early 20th C. **$8.00-$12.00**

Measuring cup, stamped tin, embossed advertising message "Drink Barrington Hall Coffee," 1 cup size, 20th C. **$4.00-$6.00**

Measuring cup, tin, deep wraparound lip, strap handle, American, 5"H, 2 cup capacity, late 19th C. • **German vocabulary** — Messbecher (looks like MeBbecher): measuring cup. **$12.00-$18.00**

Measuring cup, turned maple, double ended with cups at each end, American, only 3⅝"H, late 19th C. **$55.00-$75.00**

Measuring cups, set of 4, Jadite glass, American, 20th C. **$18.00-$28.00**

Measuring cups, small tin flared side cups with tab handles, set of 4, "Mary Ann's Accurate Measure", mfd by Katzinger Co., Chicago, measure ¼ C, ½ C, ⅓ C, and 1 C. c.1930s-40s (?). **$6.00-$9.00**

Measuring pans. — I have seen cooking pans, of bell metal & possibly sheet iron (I can't recall now) with concentric rings on the inside bottom, as well as the sides. I thought it was some "accident" of the manufacturing process. But when I read in one of Soyer's cookbooks about frying, and read to "place into the pan any oleaginous substance [viz. butter, lard], so that, when melted, it shall cover the bottom of the pan by about two lines …", I realized that the lines, even on the bottom, might be used for measur-

ing. (It is also possible that a "line" is a unit of measurement, somehow related to line as a measure of length equalling 1/12 of an inch. In that case Soyer would mean covering the bottom of the pan with large enough to be 1/6 of an inch deep when melted.) 19th C. • There are measuring lines in the bowl of some kitchen spoons, used for measuring liquids. Measuring pitcher, pieced tin, Dover Mfg. Co., 1 qt. capacity, 19th C. • "Measuring pitcher" is one name for a liquid measure with tapered body, wraparound lip & strap handle. **$10.00-$15.00**

Measuring pitchers, copper, set of 6, "D. M. Smith," English or American, early 19th C. **$500.00-$650.00**

Measuring spoon, 4 way flip over action, stamped metal, 2 spoon bowls measure 1 TBS and 1 tsp, flip over & small concavities on back of bowls measure ½ tsp and ¼ tsp, adv'g "Dr. Price's Baking Powder," 4⅜"L, "patent pending," 20th C. **$12.00-$18.00**

Measuring spoon, aluminum, peculiar instrument with flat center handle strip, with propellor-like swiveling spoons at each end, measures ¼ and ½ tsp, 1 tsp, and dessert spoon, "Level Measuring Spoon", mfd by Barnard Co., Boston, MA, "patent applied for" c. 1920s. **$5.00-$8.00**

Measuring spoon, silver plated metal, beading around handle, with hanging hole, bowl of tablespoon-like spoon engraved with concentric oval rings for different measurements, with "Armour's Extract of Beef" engraved on bowl, picture of can of beef extract on handle, with label engraved "Armour & Co.", Chicago, U.S.A., c.1905. **$15.00-$18.00**

Measuring spoon, tin, "A & P," 20th C. **$6.00-$10.00**

Measuring spoons, stamped tin of extremely simple construction, the handles of the 3 sort of riveted together with an open brass ring like a grommet, "Original," American, measured in teaspoons and drops: ¼ teaspoon or 15 drops; ½ teaspoon or 30 drops; and 1 teaspoon or 60 drops, pat'd 1900. • I have rarely seen old measuring spoons, & believe this may be a very early example, perhaps even the "original", of what we now take for granted. **$10.00-$15.00**

Oven thermometer, 2 part, heavy stamped brass-finished (or brass?) sheet metal with asbestos on bottom, & tilted upright frame with mercury thermometer, in original box, chromolithograph picture on front shows turn-of-century aproned woman putting food in oven with her thermometer, & legend "Always Use a Taylor Thermometer for Uniformity in Cooking & Baking". Also is an illustrated cookbooklet, *Taylor Homeset Cookbook. Bake & Cook the Thermometer Way*, with recipes. Woman on cookbook is of later date, but same box was probably used over a long period. Taylor, model #5928, Rochester, NY, c.1920s. • Added value. — If the box were in good condition, with vibrantly colored, instead of faded & scuffed, picture, the set would sell for two or three times as much. **$5.00-$9.00**

Pie bird, Black Americana figural "Mammy" with exuberant bandana turban, ceramic, American, about 4½"H, c.1920s-30s. **$20.00-$40.00**

Pie bird, ceramic, figural blackbird, in original box. The bird was positioned in the pie, a slit was cut in the top crust & it was put, serape-fashion, over the bird. Steam was supposed to be vented from within the pie, although it is possible that they didn't work as well as they were supposed to. This bird is marked "Royal Worcester," English, 4½"H, 20th C. • <u>Four & Twenty Blackbirds</u>. — There are at least 20 blackbird figures, most of which look fairly similar; few are marked. They come from potteries in several countries. • My friend Lillian Cole, and a friend of hers, have started a **newsletter for pie bird collectors** in 1990. Lillian has about 150 different birds (or other animals), most of which she believes are American-made. She probably knows more about them than anyone — partly because she has had incredible luck in tracking down people and potteries who have made them. For information please write her at 14 Harmony School Rd., Flemington, NJ 08822, and enclose a SASE. **$20.00-$35.00**

Pie bird, figural goose, pink ceramic, English, 20th C.
• **Huge Pie.** — The following appeared in the *Newcastle Chronicle*, 6th January 1770, in England: "Monday last was brought from Howick to Berwick, to be shipp'd for London, for Sir Hen. Grey, bart., a pie, the contents whereof are as follows: viz. 2 bushels of flour, 20 lbs. of butter, 4 geese, 2 turkies, 2 rabbits, 4 wild ducks, 2 woodcocks, 6 snipes, and 4 partridges; 2 neats' tongues, 2 curlews, 7 blackbirds, and 6 pigeons: it is supposed a very great curiosity, was made by Mrs. Dorothy Patterson, housekeeper at Howick. It was near nine feet in circumference at bottom, weighs about twelve stones [204 pounds], will take two men to present it to table; it is neatly fitted with a case, and four small wheels to facilitate its use to every guest that inclines to partake of its contents at table." For the pie bird: **$19.00-$30.00**

Pie bird, pink ceramic figural of the "Pillsbury Twin", Pillsbury, 20th C. **$25.00-$35.00**

Pie bird vent or funnel, also called a <u>pie chimney</u>, white china, marked "Gourmet Pie Cup" with a crown, English, 19th C. • There are several white pottery or stoneware pie vents, from England, Germany and the United States. Some names to look for are "Roe's Rosebud Patent; Cascade; The Improved Pie Funnel. There are also glass & aluminum funnel vents.
$30.00-$40.00

Room thermometer, stamped & painted tin, shaped like an urn, American, 20th C. **$8.00-$12.00**

Room thermometer, wall mounted, stamped sheet metal painted red, shaped like round teapot, has 2 simple hooks at bottom for hanging potholders, "Tel-Tru," Tel-Tru Thermometer Co., Rochester, NY, 5"H x 7"W, c.1930s to 1940s. **$10.00-$15.00**

Scale, balance, equal arm balance type, tin & iron, center post like a dinner horn, closed end is possibly weighted with plaster or sand, beam is cast and appears European, 2 tin pans hung with string, probably homemade of assorted parts, American, 21"H, mid 19th C.
$800.00-$1000.00

Scale, bathroom, iron & brass, clock face style standing on dimpled platform, spring balance type, "John Chatillon & Sons", NYC, NY, 1905. **$275.00-$325.00**

Scale, beam, cast iron, Dearborn Patent, 19th C.
$35.00-$55.00

Scale, beam or balance, <u>equal arm balance</u> type, very elegant, decorated with restraint, cast brass, nickeled brass, sheet brass, marble base, adapted Byzantine central column of brass, weight pan attached to brass rods, goods scoop pan set on odd one sided support, both rods &

supports on hooks, mfd by one of finest American scalemakers, Henry Troemner, Philadelphia, PA, early 19th C. • **Scientific Instrument Collecting,** for Gents. — Scales of this class are probably not for foodstuffs. They form a collecting field, along with microscopes, quadrants, telescopes and other precision scientific instruments, that exists in rather rarified air, and has been considered by realists as well as chauvinists, as of interest to men only. It's true, until recently, few women have collected such pieces. But then, many fewer women became scientists or pilots or astronomers, too. • **Collectors society**. — If you desire information about the International Society of Antique Scale Collectors, founded in 1976, please send SASE to Bob Stein, ISASC, 111 N. Canal St., Chicago, IL 60606.
$600.00-$850.00

Scale, beam or balance, iron, chain hangers, tin pan, American?, 14" x 24", 19th C. • This is from the class of scales known as equal arm balances. **$12.00-$18.00**

Scale, candy, cast iron, painted black, with gold pinstriping, with brass pan, weights missing, no mark but date, 1915. • So-called <u>candy scales</u>, or <u>countertop equal arm balances</u>, are the most collectible scales at this time because of the decoration & form of the cast iron part, and the presence of a polished brass or interesting pieced tin pan or scoops.
$65.00-$90.00

Scale, candy, countertop, cast iron with brass pan, set of cast iron weights, "Dayton Style No. 166," (possibly Dayton Standard Scale Co., Dayton, OH), late 19th C. • Most candy scales are of the class called **equal arm balances**. They have a calibrated beam with arms of equal length, one end supporting a pan or scoop or platform for the thing being weighed, and a platform on which to pile weights that will counterbalance exactly that which is being weighed. Instead of being suspended from a hook, the calibrated beam is, in effect, suspended on its fulcrum, like a teeter totter, a see saw. When you are trying to remember just what kind of scale is a candy scale, visualize eating candy while playing on a see saw.
$75.00-$100.00

Scale, candy, for countertop, cast iron, brass pan, counter top, "Brandon," American, about 14"L, pat'd 1867.
$40.00-$50.00

Scale, candy, plated metal, "National," American, 19th C.
$300.00-$350.00

Scale, candy, tin base, brass pan, white enameled dial, Hanson Brothers, Chicago, IL, 12"H, late 19th C.
$45.00-$60.00

Scale, candy or confectioner's, unequal arm balance type, black painted cast iron, abstract fishtail or bird foot base, with 3 toes, brass pan, Fairbanks & Co., Philadelphia, PA, 1870s-1880s. • Fairbanks also used a lot of red paint on cast iron bases. **$65.00-$90.00**

Scale, candy or confectioners, cast iron stepped base, flat pan at one end, interesting half-circle horizontal graduated arc with a sliding weight on bar below arc, Buckelew & Waterman, Philadelphia, PA, prior to 1867, but I can't find patent. • This one is an **equal balance arm scale** but the platform or pan for what is being weighed is balanced by a permanent weight which causes a pointer to show the weight on the calibrated arc. In addition, below this arc is a small calibrated beam with a small sliding poise, which is used to weigh the bottle or jar or small container that is to be filled. This prior weighing "automatically" adjusts the pointer on the arc. It really is quite ingenious, but I'm glad we don't have to use them at salad bars!

The advertisement states that "this novel invention combines with Utility, both Beauty, and Convenience. Its primary object is to save the annoyance and expense attendant upon the loss of weights. It works upon knife heads, as in ordinary Counter Scales, but in lieu of the plate for the reception of weights, has a graduated Arc, with a Permanently Attached Weight, through which an Index [pointer] is passed, which latter, moving over the Graduated Arc, denotes with great accuracy the commodity in the opposite dish [on the opposite platform]." **$125.00-$175.00**

Scale, counter top, sometimes called a country store scale, black finished cast iron with red & gold trim, tin pan, brass beam, an equal arm balance scale, American, late 19th C. **$65.00-$85.00**

Scale, countertop, equal arm balance type, red painted cast iron base, tin pan, with 1 lb & 2 lb weights, very handsome, Southwark Hardware Co., Philadelphia, PA, late 19th C. • "No kitchen outfit is complete without scales. Two kinds come for use in the household. The old-fashioned is the better, as there is nothing to get out of order. These scales [the equal arm balance type, with cast iron base] are more cumbersome than the dial scales, but the latter are likely to require repairing." Maria Parloa, *Kitchen Companion*, Boston: Estes & Lauriat, 1887. **$175.00-$215.00**

Scale, countertop, sometimes called a platform scale, equal arm balance type, cast iron base with 'fishtail' that keeps base stable, flat platform (for putting basket, box, bag or pieced brass pan of goods), oval brass pan with fixed ring base, sold through Montgomery Ward catalog, American, ½ oz to 25 lbs capacity, dated 1892. • Platform scales of this type are **unequal arm balance scales,** & have a long calibrated bar sticking out to the side, with a hook at the end from which a weight can be hung, plus a movable sliding weight that slides along the bar (like the scale at the doctor's office). The most commonly seen base design has an exaggerated fishtail sticking out at the bottom in the same direction as the bar; it helps keep base stable. **$40.00-$50.00**

Scale, egg grading, cast iron weight & balance painted red, cast iron base painted sky blue, aluminum egg pan & scale, brass pointer, very sculptural & aerospacey, "Zenith Egg Grader, #1002," also marked "1-F", Earlville, NY, 8"H, early 20th C. • Thanks to collector David La Duke for correcting place name spelling from last edition. **$22.00-$33.00**

Scale, egg grading, galvanized metal, stamped tin, "Oake's 'Sanitized' Equipment for every poultry need," Oakes Mfg. Co., Tipton, IN, 6½"H x 6½"W, 20th C. **$25.00-$30.00**

Scale, egg grading, metal, "Mascot," American, 20th C. **$12.00-$18.00**

Scale, egg grading, metal, "Val-A," American, 20th C. **$12.00-$18.00**

Scale, egg grading, metal, "Montgomery Ward," American, TOC. **$18.00-$25.00**

Scale, egg grading, metal, (could this be Toledo Scale Co.?) — all I know is they were made in Toledo, OH, 20th C. **$15.00-$20.00**

Scale, egg grading, metal, "Unique," possibly made by the Steel Edge Stamping & Retinning Co., Boston, MA, 20th C. **$15.00-$20.00**

Scale, egg grading, painted heavy tin, Oakes Mfg. Co., Tipton, IN, 7"H x 7"L x 3½"W, 20th C. **$22.00-$28.00**

Scale, egg grading, painted sheet metal, red, green & white, a spring balance scale, "Jiffy-Way," "World's Largest Manufacturers of Egg Scales," Owatonna, MN, 5¾"H x 7⅛"L, pat'd 1940 & still being made. • This is the other commonly found egg grading scale. It is a **spring balance scale** like many postal scales. The weight of the egg depresses a spring which makes a pointer move to the calibration mark. New they cost about $18.00; "old" ones, if you can recognize them are also: **$18.00-$25.00**

Scale, egg grading, polished metal, mounted on wooden board, has clip to hold egg, no mark, 20th C. **$55.00-$70.00**

Scale, egg grading, sheet metal base with spun brass egg cup, very simple modern frame, thumb screw adjustment, beautiful engraving of numbers on the scale, no marks, 9⅞"H, 20th C. **$55.00-$70.00**

Scale, egg grading, stamped aluminum, wonderful soft slithery sound of the fulcrum as the egg is weighed, "Acme Egg Grading Scale," Specialty Mfg. Co., St. Paul, MN, 4½"H x 10½"L x 3½"W, pat'd June 24, 1924. • Some egg grading scales, like this one, are very much like some postal scales, and are classed as pendulum balances. **$15.00-$22.00**

Scale, egg grading, tin box mounted to wooden base that's painted green, cup for egg, directions printed on it "It is necessary that this scale is set level to weigh correctly. Clamp furnished is used when definite grade is desired. Place clamp on dial at grade wanted, and it will act as a stop to indicate for any .. [weight]. This speeds up grading." "Reliable, Automatic Dial Egg Scale", Reliable Incubator & Brooder Co., Quincy, IL, 13"L, early 20th C. **$20.00-$28.00**

Scale, egg grading, painted sheet metal, extremely simple with cast metal counterweight, something like a Jiffy-Way, American, c.1910 to 1940. **$15.00-$20.00**

Scale, hanging spring balance, brass face, "Landers, Frary & Clark," New Britain, CT, 19th C. **$30.00-$40.00**

Scale, hanging spring balance, brass face, "Royal," TOC. • **Hanging spring balance scales** use a spring, but the weight hangs off the spring (with a hook) rather than being place on top of it to depress it, as in a dial scale. The face or dial of the scale, on which the pointer registers the weight, is usually long and rectangular and often brass, but it can be round, like a dial scale's face. There has to be a hanging ring at top, so the scale can be conveniently hung near where it's to be used, and from the bottom comes a hook from which is hung the food to be weighed. A complete set might also have a round platform with a fixed bail handle to hang off the hook (some of these have porcelainized platforms and nickeled brass frames & bails), or a pieced tin pan with chains to hang off the hook. **$25.00-$30.00**

Scale, hanging spring balance, brass face, iron, "Eagle Warranted," American, 19th C. **$15.00-$22.00**

Scale, hanging spring balance, brass face, iron, "Excelsior," Sargent & Co., 50 lb capacity, 19th C. **$18.00-$22.00**

Scale, hanging spring balance, brass face, iron hook, steel spring, "Landers Improved #2 Balance," mfd by L.F. & C., New Britain, CT, early 20th C. • In Albert R. Eaches' Technical Leaflet #59, "Scales and Weighing Devices", he writes "a spring balance is a weighing device which utilizes the physical distortion of a piece of metal." In this case it's a steel spring, inside the cylindrical scale body, that is "distorted" or pulled to a looser spiral by what is hung from it, causing a little pointer to move on the calibrated face. **$16.00-$22.00**

Scale, hanging spring balance, brass, iron, "Frary's Improved Balance #2," mfd by Landers, Frary & Clark, 50 lb capacity, late 19th C. **$20.00-$30.00**

Scale, hanging spring balance, brass & iron, "Chatillon," NYC, NY, 8"L x 1⅜"W, with 25 lb capacity, pat'd Dec. 10, 1867, Jan. 6, 1891, Jan. 26, 1892. **15.00-$18.00**

Scale, hanging spring balance, brass plate, steel & iron, "Excelsior Improved Spring Balance", mfd by Sargent & Co., American, about 6"L, 25 lb capacity, late 19th or early 20th C. **$15.00-$18.00**

Scale, hanging spring balance, brass plate, steel & iron, weighs up to 60 pounds, "For industrial use only", mfd by Henry Boker, German, about 6"L, late 19th or early 20th C. **$15.00-$18.00**

Scale, hanging spring balance, cast steel, brass base & iron pan, "Class Two, Salters Improved Family Scale, No. 50," Silvers Patent, English, 14"H, late 19th C. **$90.00-$110.00**

• *Asher & Adams' Pictorial Album of American Industry*, published in 1876 as a gala advertisement & history for the Centennial, has a piece on the New York scale manufacturer Thomas Morton, in which they surveyed the **"origin" of [hanging] spring balances,** or hook balance scales. "Since the invention, nearly half a century ago, of the spring balance by one George Salters, of West Bromwich, England, we suppose no article of a mechanical nature in itself has obtained so universal a practical character as this. Scarcely a butcher or grocer in any country ... but finds its utility second only to his knife and hatchet. ... When spring balances were first introduced in America our people had but little confidence in them. The principle of springs was deemed unreliable, but they soon began to work their way forward. As soon as their real value was known, competitors in the field...sprang up with great rapidity, and the market was flooded with unreliable scales and balances. ... In 1842, in conjunction with Mr. A. A. Bremner, Mr. Thomas Morton introduced to the American public the first domestic made spring balance, the construction of which was based upon Salter's method. This was a hook balance scale to weigh up to 24 lbs. From that day to this the principle [of these scales] has remained intact, though the number of varieties of spring scales now made by Mr. Morton amounts to more than 150, rising from balances that will weigh a ten cent stamp — whose weight by the way is only a quarter of a dram — up to heavy instruments capable of weighing accurately 2000 lbs. at a time. ... Mr. Morton's goods rank with the best. None but the very best iron, steel and brass that can be bought are used in his manufacturers.... As a striking evidence of their excellence it might be remarked that one of the Morton & Bremner spring scales has been in use in the Boston market for the last twenty years, and has

never faltered or required any repairs whatever. ..." One of the scales pictured with the above is a jockey chair, a very elegant armchair without legs, hanging from a large round dial decorated with an eagle and the date 1866.

Scale, hanging spring balance, for ice, iron with brass face, (Landers, Frary & Clark, as well as Wilson Mfg. Co., made ice scales of this type), American, c.1900. **$25.00-$30.00**

Scale, hanging spring balance, green painted steel case, "The Viking #8910", mfd by Hanson Scale Co., 13"L, 100 lb capacity, 20th C. **$30.00-$40.00**

Scale, hanging spring balance, iron ring, iron hook, brass face engraved with measurements, "Salter's Improved Spring Balance," mfd by Salter & Co., West Midlands, England, 50 lb capacity, 2nd to 3rd quarter 19th C (?).
• **"Salter's improved Spring Balance.** — A very neat form of the instrument [known as the spring steelyard] has been recently brought before the public by Mr. Salter, under the name of the Improved Spring Balance. The spring is contained in the upper half of a cylinder behind the brass plate forming the face of the instrument; and the rod is fixed to the lower extremity of the spring, which is consequently extended, instead of being compressed, by the application of the weight. The divisions, each indicating half a pound, are engraved upon the face of the brass plate, and are pointed out by an index attached to the rod." Captain Henry Kater, *The Cabinet Cyclopaedia*. Conducted by the Rev. Dionysius Lardner. Volume on *Natural Philosophy. Mechanics.* London: Longman, Rees, Orme, Brown, & Green, 1830. The engraving in the book looks exactly like the Salter's scales so often seen. It should be noted that the hook is forged iron; on later examples, the hook would be a heavy drawn wire, cut into a point and bent. **$25.00-$38.00**

Scale, hanging spring balance, iron with brass face, "Peck's", (Peck, Stow & Wilcox), TOC. **$10.00-$12.00**

Scale, hanging spring balance, iron with large brass face, another brand of feed advertisement, legend reads "FEED KASCO FEEDS, weigh the milk, weigh the feed", Kasco Mills Inc., Waverly, NY, about 11"L, 20th C. **$125.00-$160.00**

Scale, hanging spring balance, iron with large crested brass face, decorated with checkerboard design top and bottom, legend reads "COW CHOW MAKES MORE MILK AT LESS COST, Don't guess — Use this Purina Milk Scale", Ralston Purina, (coincidentally there was a Ralston Scale Co.), American, face is 10½"L x unusually wide 4½"W, weighs to 30 lbs, 20th C. **$145.00-$175.00**

Scale pan, pieced tin, oval with its own foot ring attached to the flat platform of balance scale, American (?), 4" deep x 14⅛"L x 8"W, late 19th or early 20th C. • Hard to evaluate because it is part of something else, & might be worth a lot to someone trying to set up a scale. **$12.00-$22.00**

Scale, spring, also called a dial scale, the boxy kind with pan or platform on top, meant for kitchen or household use, & sometimes called a family scale, green painted iron, red & white enameled face, red pointer, tin pan, "American Family Scales," TOC to 1920s. **$22.00-$35.00**

Scale, spring, for kitchen or household use, cast iron & stamped sheet iron, "Simmons Hardware Co.," 20th C. **$22.00-$35.00**

Scale, spring, kitchen balance with large brass dial face, Ariosa Coffee, 20 lb capacity, early 20th C. **$65.00-$90.00**

Scale, spring, <u>kitchen or family scale</u>, also called a <u>dial scale</u>, the boxy base with a large dial face on front, with the weight pan or forked support (almost like an upraised hand with fingers outspread) that holds a scoop or pan on top, sheet iron, partly painted, "Winchester," TOC. • **German vocabulary** — <u>Küchenwaage</u> or kitchen weighing machine. **$45.00-$55.00**

Scale, spring, kitchen or household type, iron base, "Cat Tail," sold through Sears & Roebuck, American, TOC. **$45.00-$55.00**

Scale, spring, metal with white face, red pointer, "Pelouze," 12"H x 6½"D dial, 20th C. **$15.00-$22.00**

Scale, spring, red, black & green finished iron, with white enamel face, 2 pointers, marked "Hanson Dairy" (perhaps a "dairy scale" by Hanson Scale Co.?), American, 6¾"D face. **$25.00-$35.00**

Scale, spring balance, brass face, iron, "Excelsior Spring," 50 lb capacity, late 19th C. **$20.00-$28.00**

Scale, spring balance, cast iron 3 legged frame, round cast iron face plate, very finely cast with calibrations, weighing platform on top, "Novelty Scale", "Turnbull's Patent", American, 7¾"H, 12 lb capacity, pat'd July 24, 1877. **$175.00-$215.00**

Scale, spring balance, countertop, (despite brand name this is not the standard old fashioned "family" style scale), heavy sheet iron, finished black, very fancy dial plate, legs, flat platform, "Novelty Family Scale," sold by Montgomery Ward, Chicago, IL, late 19th C. **$65.00-$80.00**

Scale, spring balance, family or dial scale, metal, "Perfection," pat'd 1906. **$15.00-$18.00**

Scale, spring balance, family or dial type, painted sheet metal, square base, round dial, square flat platform, American Family Scales, 9¾"H x 6" square, pat'd 1898, mfd for years. **$18.00-$28.00**

Scale, spring balance, family scale type, sheet metal painted black with fancy trim, brass dial, tin pan, "Columbia," Landers, Frary & Clark, 24 lb capacity, TOC. **$55.00-$75.00**

Scale, spring balance, family type, cast iron with brass front, American, dated 1877. **$55.00-$70.00**

Scale, spring balance, family type, fancy cast iron, "Sutler #49," 12½"H, TOC. **$75.00-$90.00**

Scale, spring balance, family type, slanted dial, stamped steel body enameled blue with pin striping, tin scoop fits on claw, " Triner Perfection," mfd by Allsteel Scale Co., Inc., NYC, 24 lb capacity, 10"H x 6"W, pat'd May 1, 1906. **$28.00-$35.00**

Scale, spring balance, family type, very graceful minimalist cast iron base, round deeply engraved brass face, beautifully formed shallow bowl is the attached weighing pan, "Salters Family Scale, No. 50, Class II Improved", about 13"H, weighs to 15 lbs, late 19th or very early 20th C. **$85.00-$115.00**

Scale, spring with beam, countertop, cast iron, brass scoop, 2 iron weights, includes scoop, 20th C. **$50.00-$65.00**

Scale, steelyard, iron & brass, "Detector," American, 23"L, late 19th or early 20th C. • A **steelyard scale,** from the class of scales known as unequal arm balances, is the oldest type of scale, & examples from many parts of the world are known. It consists of a long flattened beam suspended from a hanger hook attached close to the thicker, shorter arm of the beam. There is a hanger hook underneath the short arm, from which the thing to be weighed is hung. The long arm of the beam is calibrated, in pounds or ounces, or metric units, and has on it a weight called a poise which can be slid along the long arm to balance whatever is hung from the hook at the other end. The poise may be cast iron and somewhat decorative, and a steelyard scale might have several different poises. According to Albert R. Eaches, who wrote the invaluable Technical Leaflet #59 *"Scales and Weighing Devices"* for the Association of State & Local History, these unequal arm balance scales got the name steelyards "when steel was first imported into England." He also explains that another type of unequal arm balance scale very like a steelyard, and sometimes even called a steelyard, should actually be called a <u>weighmasters beam scale</u>. These can be identified by the rather large swooping hooked end (looks almost like an antique iceskating blade) of the short arm of the beam, and by two sets of calibration and two "separate poises to correspond" to these calibrations. **$35.00-$45.00**

Scale, steelyard, iron, with an iron weight that has a raised star design cast on it, American, 25 lb capacity, late 19th C. • **Caveat emptor.** — Being imported now from Turkey are a steelyard scale with single hanging dished pan, & an equal balance scale with two pans hanging from the beam, which is suspended by a chain & hook. All the pans are hung with three chains, and are made of copper & iron. Three sizes of each are being imported: of the first type, a 21"H with 8" pan; a 24"H with 10" pan; and a 27"H with 12"pan, ranging from $60.00 to $125.50 in price. Of the second type, a 17"H with two 5" pans; a 20"H with 8" pans, and a 27"H with 10" pans, ranging from $67.50 to $142.50 each. The ads of one of the two import companies never mentions country of origin, and explains that "Some items have minor dents and old repairs that do not reduce their value." This company also sells various straight-sided pots, round-bottom pots, waisted pots with bails, flared sided shallow pans with covers (all preceding have 2 handles); also 3 sizes of copper "egg pans" with round cups, also plates, bowls, frying pans & long-handled pans with braces. In many sizes. One company sells by the piece; the one that mentions "Turkey" sells by weight. • Price for old, very plain scale: **$15.00-$20.00**

Scale, steelyard, or <u>stillyard</u> type, wrought iron, long rod with weight, hook at other end for the goods, nice detailing. When not in use, steelyard scales tend to look like a pile of iron bars & hooks. They only really come to life when they are hanging up & have the movable poise placed so it can balance the weight of the end with the hook or hooks, or when actually weighing something. For display, some scale collectors hang a heavy weight from the hook meant for the goods. According to Carl W. Drepperd, a small steelyard scale is called a <u>steel foot</u>. American, 25"L, 18th C. • **German vocabulary** — <u>Schnellwaage</u>: literally quick scale. **$95.00-$125.00**

Scales, countertop, an equal arm balance type sometimes referred to as a "balance scale", cast iron base with hexagonal pyramid flanked by lyre shapes, pieced tin pan with fixed ring base, full set of 7 cast iron weights, in F. A. Walker catalog, American or import (?), about 6"H excluding pan, c.1880s. • A **countertop equal arm balance**

scale has a base that supports a sort of see saw beam each end of which has a platform. On one platform (or four-"fingered" support) goes the pan with the goods; on the other goes a weight or selection of weights in pounds & ounces, until the two platforms balance. This type is also sometimes called a platform scale, a country store scale, a countertop scale, or (if it's small enough) a candy scale. It should not be called simply a "balance scale" because all scales are balances — they are equal arm balances; unequal arm balances; spring balances (either platform or hanging); and pendulum balances. See the technical leaflet *"Scales and Weighing Devices"* that Albert R. Eaches wrote for the American Association for State and Local History. **$150.00-$200.00**

Scales, countertop, or grocery scales of the equal arm balance type, green painted cast iron, brass scoop pan, Fairbanks, 11"L x 6½"H, dated 1877. **$75.00-$85.00**

Scales, spring balance, or dial scale, red painted cast iron base, brass pan & glass dial face, "Eureka," style C, 18"H x 15", pat'd Oct. 5, 1869. • These spring balance scales have a base below the weighing platform or pan, and a large clock-like dial on the side of the base with an index pointer that indicates the weight. These usually have a little fine tuning wheel for resetting Zero. **$225.00-$250.00**

Scoop, adjustable, tin, has lever you push to shove backplate out, works very smoothly, American (?), 10"L x 4"W, 19th C. **$135.00-$160.00**

Scoop, adjustable, tin, inventor must have been still working on this one when he quit. You have to sort of wriggle the backplate out with your fingers, like the backplate in a really old style filing cabinet drawer, no marks, American (?), 13½"L x 4⅞"W, 19th C. **$75.00-$100.00**

Scoop, apple butter, carved wood, all one piece, open "D" handle, American, 4½" x 11½", late 19th C. **$135.00-$175.00**

Scoop, candy, a crude measure, pieced sheet brass, attached handle, small in size, late 19th C. • Some of these were made by candy scale manufacturers, & match the pieced sheet brass scale pans. **$25.00-$30.00**

Scoop, candy, molded glass including handle, American, 6"L x 4"W, early 20th C. **$25.00-$45.00**

Scoop, carved & stained wood, probably walnut, folk art piece with largish oblong bowl, the handle being a gorilla with a snake twisted around it, supposedly made by an elderly black sailor, coastal New Jersey, 9⅛"L, mid 20th C. • I tried a number of times to contact the dealer, who claimed she had information at home about the identity of the carver, but to no avail. I also bought a box with a sliding lid by the same man, a master carver with a sense of humor. **$175.00-$200.00**

Scoop, carved wood, long bowl & longish handle, huge check in wood mended with tacked-on strap iron, bowl mended with waxed string, American, 12"L, 19th C. **$30.00-$40.00**

Scoop, cast aluminum, fairly smooth, rounded handle, marked "Wagner Ware" on handle, 11¼"L x about 4½" deep, c.1930s (?). • **Lookalike alarm.** — Somebody is making these cast aluminum very streamlined scoops today. Lehman's Hardware & Appliances, 4779 Kidron Rd., Kidron, OH 44636 offer 5 sizes in their 1989 "Non-Electric Good Neighbor Amish Country" catalog, which costs about $3.00. • Old ones (of any type of scoop) will show

damage to the lip of the scoop, the front edge that pushes against whatever is being measured out. I saw a picture of one in a turn-of-the-century magazine that was said to have measured "over two and a half tons" of coffee beans during the preceding year or so, and the long "lower lip" of the scoop had been worn down so that essentially the scoop was a can with a handle at one end. **$12.00-$16.00**

Scoop, cast iron, sharply truncated cylinder with longish handle, meant for measuring a quantity of a washing or cleaning compound, marked "4 ounce OAKITE", mfd by Oakite Products Inc., NYC, NY, 6"L, late 19th C. **15.00-$22.00**

Scoop, coal, pieced brass, riveted-on wooden handle, nice curvy body, Brasscrafters, Syosset, NY, 16¾"L, 1980s, poss. before. • **Lookalike alarm.** — So nicely made & good-looking, as well as being old-fashioned in design, that it could easily be mistaken for an antique. I don't know if it is marked. It is always a good idea to get on the mailing list of such catalog houses as Yield House (which specializes in the country look), and keep a clip file of info on new pieces. That's why I never turn down even a 1950s or 1960s magazine such as *Good Housekeeping* or *House Beautiful*; I search the back pages for small display ads showing items which are likely, just 20 or 30 years later, to be taken as antique. New about: **$20.00-$30.00**

Scoop, coffee beans, cast aluminum, Barrington Hall Coffee", 20th C. **$5.00-$9.00**

Scoop, coffee, probably for grocery use, cast aluminum, "Blue Diamond - Sunbeam Best Coffees", 12"L x 4½"W, 20th C. **$22.00-$28.00**

Scoop, flour, carved from one piece of wood, rounded short handle, American (?), 6½"L, late 19th C. • Small hole at end of handle, as well as handle's rounded shape are evidence that this was at least partly lathe-turned, therefore probably from a manufactory. **$15.00-$22.00**

Scoop, flour, carved maple, nice long oval bowl with curved handle, American (?), 12½"L, early 19th C. **$85.00-$125.00**

Scoop, flour, carved wood with fingerhold grip, primitive, very smooth finish, American (?), 7"L, 19th C. **$60.00-$70.00**

Scoop, flour, metal bowl with thick wire handles, handles stamped "Airy Fairy Kwik Bis-kit Flour", also "Airy Fairy Cake Flour," American, 7½"L early 20th C. **$15.00-$18.00**

Scoop, flour, tin with turned wooden handle, American, 7"L, late 19th C. **$12.00-$16.00**

Scoop, gray graniteware, 7"L, late 19th C. **$50.00-$60.00**

Scoop, heavy, galvanized crimped sheet iron, brass rivets, cast iron heel, wooden handle, 8"L, early 20th C. **$15.00-$20.00**

Scoop, tin, strap handle, American, 3¾"L, TOC. **$8.00-$10.00**

Scoop, tin with tubular handle, braced underneath at attachment. (This brace was called by tinsmiths the boss.) American, 9"L x 4½"W, 19th C. **$22.00-$30.00**

Scoop, turned wooden handle, bentwood cup is enlonged half-round, brass nails like are used for pantry boxes, Shaker 14"L x 6¾"W, 19th C. **$125.00-$150.00**

Scoop, dry measure, carved wood, very shallow and long bowl, very short hooked handle, marked "Tollard," American, 15¼"L, prob. last quarter 19th C. **$45.00-$65.00**

Scoop for coffee beans, tin, "Martinique Coffee Scoops Them All," Oct. 19, 1897. **$35.00-$45.00**

Sorghum meter or faucet, to be fitted into a keg, metal, pat'd 1878. **$30.00-$40.00**

Spigot for cider barrel, wood with pewter key, marked "John Sommer's Best Block Tin Key," English (?), 19th C. **$8.00-$15.00**

Sugar scoop, stamped metal, "Trisco Flour," 5⅜"L, early 20th C. **$12.00-$18.00**

Thermometer, cast iron corncob, cast in 2 or possibly 4 part mold, painted black, hand engraved brass face along length is flat, rest of cob is full dimensional, American, 10½"L, c.1870s. **$200.00-$235.00**

Thermometer, for candy & jelly, long palette-knife shaped calibrated metal plate with glass tube, and with marks giving stages in candy-making, tapered turned wooden handle with large hanging loop at end, Taylor Instrument Co., Rochester, NY, Toronto, Canada, mid 1930s. **$5.00-$8.00**

Thermometer, for candy & jelly, metal with light green wooden handle, "Taylor," c.1940s. **$13.00-$18.00**

Thermometer, for oven, modeled almost exactly like the "Bake-Rite", but available only in white porcelainized metal, tombstone shaped vertical face with glass tube, set on stamped round base marked with maker's name, registers from 200 degrees to 800 degrees, & is also marked from "slow" (at 300) to "hot" (at 500), with the extra 300 degrees for people who fire pottery in their ovens? Taylor Instrument Companies, mid 1930s. **Handy Oven Thermometer.** — "Many test their ovens in this way: if the hand can be held in from 20 to 35 seconds, it is a quick oven, from 35 to 45 seconds is moderate, and from 45 to 60 seconds is slow. 60 seconds is a good oven to begin with for large fruit cakes. All systematic housekeepers will hail the day when some enterprising, practical 'Dixie' girl shall invent a stove or range with a thermometer attached to the oven so that the heat may be regulated accurately and intelligently." *Practical House-keeping*, 1884. • Thomas Masters of London invented what was probably the **first oven thermometer** about 1850. It was a glass ring, with mercury, and an indicator guide telling what to put in the oven when the mercury reached a particular point on the guide. **$5.00-$8.00**

Thermometer, for ovens, porcelainized iron in white, light blue, light green or orange, tall vertical tombstone shape set on flat round base, glass tube with degrees from 100 to 600 marked off, "Bake-Rite Portable Oven Thermometer No. 115", mfd by American Thermometer Co., St. Louis, MO, 5½"H, late 1920s, early 1930s. • **Futurewatch:** This is certainly an unexplored collecting area, as far as I know. There is a great variety available, including candy, meat, deep fat and oven types, as well as kitcheny motif wall hung room temperature thermometers. Other companies to look for include: "The Acme" oven thermometer, mfd by Evans Stamping & Plating Co., Taunton, MA, early 20th C; oven thermometers by Ingram - Richardson Mfg. Co., Beaver Falls, PA, and Rochester Mfg. Co., Rochester, NY, both from the 1920s-30s; **$5.00-$8.00**

Thermometer, painted wood, "Occident Flour," Russell-Miller Milling Co., Minneapolis, MN, early 20th C. **$35.00-$45.00**

Thermometer, printed metal, "Ward's Vitovim Bread," Ward Baking Co., NYC, etc., early 20th C. • A store thermometer, although no doubt some would have been found just outside the kitchen door, maybe on the icebox porch, **$100.00-$125.00**

Thermometer, & skewer set, in original box, metal, Westinghouse Betty Furness set, American, 20th C. **$12.00-$15.00**

Thermometer, candy, copper, "Moeller Instrument Co.," Brooklyn, NY, TOC. **$55.00-$65.00**

Timer for toaster, green marbleized plastic, chrome, green cord, to be hooked up to a Hotpoint toaster, "Hotpoint", Edison General Electric Appliance Co., Chicago, IL, 1930s. • An interesting explanation for the name The General Electric Co., is found in Orra L. Stone's *History of Massachusetts Industries*, 1930. He says **THE** is a formal part of the name and is an acronym for Dr. Elihu **T**hompson and Dr. Edwin J. **H**ouston, who were co-founders of the American Electric Co., est. 1879 in Philadelphia, and a predecessor to GE, plus Thomas Alva **E**dison, whose Edison General Electric Co., est. 1881, merged with American Electric to become The G. E. Co. This may be an apocryphal tale. **$125.00-$140.00**

V-1.
Asparagus buncher.
Cast iron, hinged, wooden base. Joseph Breck & Sons catalog, 1903-05. **$35.00-$100.00**

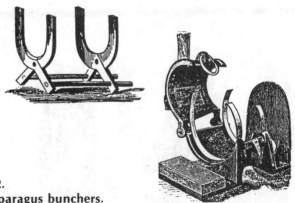

V-2.
Asparagus bunchers.
(L) Oldest of French bunchers, consisting of "Two pairs of wooden scissors with curved blades, to each short arm of one of these is fixed a wooden rod, which passes through a hole in the corresponding arm of the other, allowing the two to be placed at the desired distance apart." A string is used to hold the rods in place after the 'scissors' are opened to the right size. (R) Conover's buncher, wood, hinged with lever (partially visible in vertical position), with brass strips inside. The fattest butt end of the stalks are pushed against the enboard at right. Both pictures from American Agriculturist, 5/1876; and 2/1876. **$35.00-$100.00**

V-3.

Beer measures.

Copper, with glass viewing or indicator window, hinged flat lid with vent holes, strap handles. (L) A 2 quart size form Duparquet, Huot & Monuese hotel & restaurant supply catalog, c. 1904-1910. (R) One with a braced handle from the Manning & Bowman catalog, 1892. It came in 2, 3 & 4 quart sizes, either planished copper or nickel-plated copper. The catalog says it has a "strainer for pouring from bottom." These are found in other TOC catalogs. **$100.00-$165.00**

V-4.

Teapot electric clock.

Stamped steel, finished in choice of colors: ivory, white, green, red or blue. 7"H x 8 1/2"W. with 4" dial. Manufactured by Sessions. Advertised in various ladies magazines in 1941. **$5.00-$20.00**

V-5.

Egg timers.

At first glance, these appear identical. Both are obviously plaid, probably Mauchlin ware. (L) Called an "egg glass," in "Scotch Wood," glass bulb. From 1870s-80s F. A. Walker catalog. (R) 3"H, in c.1909 A. Pick catalog. **$30.00-$45.00**

V-6.

Egg timers.

(L) Japanned cast iron pedastal-based frame with swiveling glass bulb, imported or American. Could be anywhere from about 4"H to 7"H. From F.A. Walker catalog, 1870s-80s. **$40.00-$55.00**
(R) Three turned wooden posts, wood disks for top and bottom, glass bulb. Virtually identical linecuts found in F.A. Walker and c. 1909 Duparquet, Huot & Moneuse catalogs. **$15.00-$35.00**

V-7.

Egg timers.

Also called in latter years "telephone timers," to hang on kitchen wall. (L) Heavy printed fibre board with glass bulb containing fine white sand. Printed marks. (R) Brooklyn Egg Timer "is made of Bohemian glass with a sifted clear yellow imported time glass sand, that is absolutely reliable, never clogging, never stopping, and always indicating the correct time at the graduated points on the enameled board." 8 1/2"H x 1 1/2"W. These two are from the c.1910 catalog of Silver & Co., Brooklyn **$5.00-$15.00**

V-8.

Egg timers.

Though similar in form, (L) is of turned wood, with portholes for viewing the sand bulbs, and (R) is of pieced tin, japanned with background color and a few sprigs. From S. Joseph catalog, c. 1927, and Ritzinger & Grasgreen import catalog, c.1906-07. **$15.00-$45.00**

V-9.

Egg timer.

This was found in the 2/1882 American Agriculturist. "A short while ago we (the editor) visited Messrs. Baldwin & Co., Murray Street (NYC), for novelties. Among other things...is the Signal Egg-timer. In this the sand-glass is suspended in a frame;...and when sufficient sand has run into the lower part of the glass, its weight turns the glass and the hammer, shown at the top, falls down and strikes the bell below, informing the cook that the time is up. Below is a wedge-shaped counterpoise; by moving this, the alarm will be given at the end of two, three, or four minutes." **$45.00-$65.00**

V-10.
Egg testers.

(L) Turned wood with cup for egg, encircled by a sheet tin or cardboard "frame" with a hole in the center about the size of the eggs tested. Black cloth or ribbon fills in space around edge of egg. The idea is to completely block light from escaping around edges of egg, in order to intensify the effect of the light shining through it. "A fresh or infertile one (is) perfectly clear, while a fertile one that has been incubated two days will show the embryo, as in the engraving. Infertile eggs may then be taken from the nest." *American Agriculturist*, early 1870s. I always had thought egg candling was done prior to selling the eggs. This implies that it's done when gathering, to leave fertile, viable eggs with the hen.

$4.00-$15.00

(R) Pieced tin with lamp. Called a "Prairie State," in Joseph Breck 1905 catalog.

$30.00-$50.00

V-11.
Egg detector.

Pieced tin, wire. Note arched piece at left of "dish"–this is the cutting edge. "By this machine you cut your shell; you do not smash it and get your batch full of small pieces. You do not make a mess on your table or bench; besides, you can break eggs much faster than in the old way, thereby saving valuable time." V. Clad & Sons pamphlet, c.1890-1900.

$20.00-$40.00

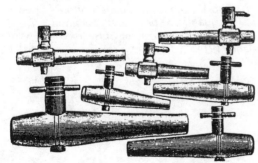

V-12.
Faucets.

Turned wood faucets, leather-or-cork-lined. For use with coopered vessels. J. Breck catalog, 1905.

$2.00-$5.00

V-13.
Fruit jar funnels.

Top (L) is plain, pieced, strap handle, shortish neck, 4 3/8" diameter cup with 2" diameter neck. Top (R) "Greystone" graniteware, same dimensions. Both Matthai-Ingram catalog, c.1890. Bottom is spun & polished aluminumn, riveted handle, with 1 pint capacity. 5 3/8" diameter cup; 2 1/8" diameter neck. "Mirro," Aluminum Goods Manufactured, 1927.

$5.00-$22.00

V-14.
Measuring funnel.

"Improved candy funnel," heavy tin, spiral spring ("no stick needed"), originally for confectioners. "Lately it found its way into restaurants and hotels for laying out griddle, wheat and buckwheat cakes." Henry Hueg, *The Little Confectioner*, c.1900-1921.

$10.00-$25.00

V-15.
Cider funnel.

Turned wood, with 5 1/4"L neck. From 1983 Linden sale at Christie, Manson & Woods International Inc.

$100.00-$135.00

V-16.
Measuring funnel patent.

"Combined graduated measure and funnel," pat'd 10/2/1877 by Simon Schippert, Burlington, IA. Has a stop valve to plug the mouth of the neck (seen within cutaway), activated by the thumb lever. Pieced tin. *Official Gazette.*

V-17.
Measuring funnel,

called a "Combination Funnel Jigger," quadruple silverplated Britania. Graduated inside to show 1/2, 1, 1/2 and 2 ounces. "Produced by one who has many years of experience in dispensing drinks, and he found a constant need for an article that would combine both all the uses of a graduated jigger and Pousse Cafe and Float making contrivance...It will make one dozen Pousse Cafes as easily as one. It is almost instantaneous in making a brandy, or other float...and dispenses with the old-time method of using a spoon in order to float a liquid." A. Pick, 1909.**$10.00-$25.00**

V-18.
Measuring funnel.

"Burke's Patent," copper that's tinned inside, strainer piece inside pouring nozzle. Two sizes: to measure from 1/2 pint to 1 quart; and 1/2 pint to 1/2 gallon. 1920s. **$10.00-$25.00**

V-19.
Percolator funnel,

to put in top of coffee pot so that the flange held it in place. Cloth filter inside. 4 1/2" diameter. Graniteware manufactured by Matthai-Ingram, c.1890. **$20.00-$50.00**

V-20.
Funnels.

(L) Graniteware with large riveted side handle with grip, in 1 quart and 1/2 gallon sizes. Available through the Sethness Co. candymaker's catalog, maker unknown. 1925. (R) White enameled steel without a seam, imported from Czechoslovakia. Five sizes: 3", 4", 4 3/4", 5 1/2" and 7 1/8", with capacities from 3 to 32 ounces. Pick-Barth catalog, 1929. **$20.00-$50.00**

V-21.
Combination funnel.

Aluminum. This has long handle, and the neck is a different shape. Maker unknown, but from the Ritzinger & Grasgreen import catalog, c.1906-07. **$15.00-$22.00**

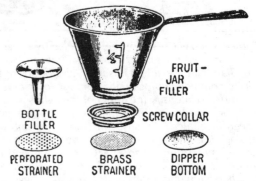

V-22.
Combination funnel.

Another, this one in pieced tin, with one brass strainer. Also Ritzinger & Grasgreen. **$15.00-$22.00**

V-23.
Funnels.

Deep one at (L): Copper or brass, with strainer, in two weights — "light" and "strong" and six sizes from 1/2 to 2 pints. Top—a large brewers' funnel, "brown" copper, with shapely bowl, in five sizes from 1/2 to 4 gallons. (R) Copper or brass, with strainer, in six sizes from 1/4 to 2 pints. Bottom — pewter strainer funnel, in two qualities: "best" and "common," five sizes from 1/4 to 2 pints. All four from catalog of Henry Rogers, Wolverhampton, England, 1914. **$15.00-$65.00**

313

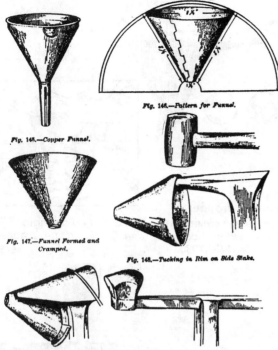

Fig. 146.—Pattern for Funnel.

Fig. 145.—Copper Funnel.

Fig. 147.—Funnel Formed and Cramped.

Fig. 148.—Tucking in Rim on Side Stake.

V-24.
Fig. 149.—Putting in Wire.   Fig. 150.—Bright Head on which Funnel is Planished.

Steps in making a funnel.
From a series on the "Art of Coppersmithing" by long-time coppersmith John Fuller, Sr. in The Metal Worker, 6/14/1890. His book was published first in 1889. "Copper funnels were generally made brown, in size from pint to gallon; that is one into which a half gallon of liquor may be dumped without running over. It will be found that an 8" cone whose slant height is equal to its diameter will hold approximately a half gallon, Imperial measure. Funnels have always been of one style, and formed of one-half a disk whose radius is equal to the diameter of the mouth of the funnel." After assembling, it was scoured, tinned inside, and the outside rubbed with "Spanish brown." Note the dovetailed seam; also fluted or furrowed neck providing air-escape route. **$15.00-$30.00**

V-25.
Funnel with stove polish.
You bought it with a quarter pound of C.W. Hart & Co., Troy, NY, paste stove polish inside. "All will readily perceive the convenience of the tube of the funnel, which serves as a handle, thereby making it possible to polish a stove without soiling the hands." You certainly didn't rub the funnel on the stove, and would need a brush too. "After the Polish is out of the Funnel, it can be used as a household article, always ready and convenient; therefore we utilize all, both the box and the blacking." Ad in The Metal Worker, 10/7/1882. Collector value now would be related to finding one with the marked tin cap or lid. Otherwise it's just a tin funnel with fluted neck. **$5.00-$25.00**

V-26.
Custard dippers or pie fillers.
Top is from Duparquet, Huot & Moneuse, NYC, catalog c.1904-1910, and has extremely pronounced spouts. It came in 1, 2 and 3 quart sizes. Bottom has braced tubular handle, and was available in 1 and 1 1/2 quart sizes. It's from the Jaburg Bros. candy-making supply catalog, 1908. Both probably made of heavy pieced tin. **$35.00-$55.00**

V-27.
Droppers for candy-making.
Sort of a cross between a measuring funnel and a ladle, but put in this chapter because of relationship to droppers and fillers seen in the coming pictures. Top (L) is a "copper sugar dropper," in sizes from 5 to 10" diameter, tapered tubular socket handle
Bottom (L) is a "copper mint dropper, with one or two lips," 4" to 10" diameter, also tubular handle. They are in the Duparquet, Huot & Moneuse c. 1904-1910 catalog. Top (R) is one of Lavoiser's chemistry instruments—made of copper or silver, for making a solution of salts in water. It dates to the 18th century. Bottom (R) is from a German confectioners' supply catalog of c.1904, a "Giesspfannen" (pouring pan) with two lips. A Bertuch, Berlin. It is probably the same as the 2nd one described above. **$45.00-$125.00**

V-28.
Pumpkin Pie filler.
Pieced tin, with braced handle, two spouts, and a flared funnel-like hopper at top; 2, 3 & 4 quart capacity. The catalog had absolutely no explanation of how it's used, but at least you'll recognize one if you see it. Jaburg Bros., 1908. **$20.00-$55.00**

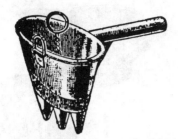

V-29.
Three-nose funnel,
for making butterscotch wafers. Pieced copper, with valve control ring visible coming up out of mouth. Braced tubular handle. Thomas Mills confectioners' catalog, 1930. **$20.00-$55.00**

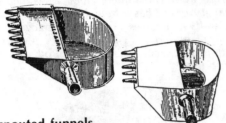

V-30.
Multi-nose or spouted funnels,
also "A.B. Runners," "Candy Droppers," or in German, **Giesspfannen,** *or pouring pans. Five-to-8 spouters were depicted in several confectioners' supply catalogs. A c.1904 Bertuch catalog from Berlin offered them with 4, 6, 8 and 10* **feststehenden Rohren,** *but depicted only a 5-spouter. Duparquet, Huot & Moneuse (c. 1904-1910) also had a 5-spouter (with a beveled front edge like Bertuch's in the picture above) and 4, 6 or 8 spouters. The 1925 Sethness candy-making catalog picture (L) actually shows a Thomas Mills' runner with 8 spouts; Sethness offered only 5-spouters, but a 1930 Mills' catalog says they could be had with 4, 5, 6 or 8 spouts...or "any size to order." An antique dealer's ad in 1990 called one of these a "rare candlemould filler," which it isn't.* **$65.00-$115.00**

V-31.
Multi-nose or spouted funnel,
or "dropper for cream work," to be used in filling cream-filled pastries. Pieced tin, bail handle, seen curving around just above the 10 spouts. Turned wood handle above operates the bank of rubber stoppers. This could be had in "any size to order." Thomas Mills, 1930. **$25.00-$50.00**

V-32.
Funnel droppers.
All pieced tin. Top (L) one from Sethness 1925 catalog, apparently manufactured by C. & B. S.(ethness). Co., with braced handle. 6" diameter at top, 3/8" opening. Came with a funnel stick similar to one Lower (L) with Thomas Mills' c.1915 one Lower (R). The cone of that one came in four diameters and heights: 6 1/4" x 7"; 7 1/2" x 8 1/2"; 7" to 10"; and 10 1/2" x 12". The funnel stick is used to push the creme material through the hole. The biggest one in the picture is also Mills'—from 1930. It has a spring-lever built-in funnel stick, and was advertised as useful also "for cordial work." **$20.00-$30.00**

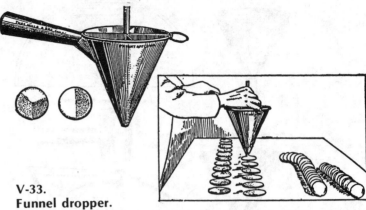

V-33.
Funnel dropper.
For making cream wafers in 2, 3 or 4 colors (note dividing partitions within body of funnel). Pieced tin, capped tubular handle. Mills, 1930. **$15.00-$25.00**

V-34.
Cake filler,
or cream puff filler. Screw clamped to work table, tin. For a small set-up. Jaburg Bros., 1908. **$20.00-$45.00**

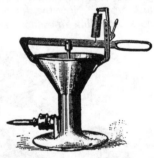

V-35.
Cake filler.
The great headline in the catalog is "THE ANGER FILLER," which sounds like a short story by Ray Bradbury! A cream puff filler which would "deliver large portions" or could be "regulated down to the smallest, which is 60 parts to a pound." I suspect it was about 16"H. Jaburg Bros., 1908. **$20.00-$45.00**

V-36.
Measures.
(L) "Straight ale measure" in choice of "best pewter" or "common pewter," and in 1/2 pint, 1 pint or 2 pints. (R) Wine measure, in "best" or "common" pewter, and in "gun-metal." Many more sizes here: 1/16, 1/12, 1/8, 1/4 and 1/2 pint, 1 pint and 2 pints. Henry Rogers, Sons & Co., Wolverhamptom, England, 1914. A full set of seven would be a good find, and would be over $100, despite lack of age. **$18.00-$50.00**

V-37.
Measuring device patent.

Pat'd 8/2/1887 by Elijah Truman, Parkersburg, WV. "The measure provided with a chamber closed on all exterior sides and partially covering the top of the measure, and having a discharge-nozzle, and a (spring-controlled) hinged cover to that portion of the top of the measure not covered by said chamber." Truman claimed as worthy of a patent "the combination of a measure having pins or axles below its center of gravity, and a support having standards provided with notches at different heights to receive the axles of the measure." The drawing alone makes this worth putting here. It's as surreal as a Man Ray or other Dada drawing. Patents were granted for many useless things; sometimes it seems as if patent examiners were charmed by the drawings as much as anything! Official Gazette.

V-38.
Measures.

Copper, tinned inside, with brass handles. Tinned inside. From 3 3/8"H to 4 3/4"H. 1/2 pint to 2 pints, marked on small brass plates. Collection of Mary Mac Franklin. Value range for the three: **$60.00-$90.00**

V-42.
Measure.

Heavy tin, shown in 3 sizes: 1 pint(R), 1 quart, and 2 quarts (L), with beautiful curved and reinforced handle. Flared wraparound high lip. A gallon size, with similar handle 2-quart, was also available. Notice the rib or ridge denoting divisions within. Lisk Manufacturing Company, 1896. **$25.00-$50.00**

V-39.
Spirit measures.

Both brown-finished copper many sizes: 1/8, 1/4, 1/2 and 1 pint, 2 or 4 pints, 1, 2, 3, 4 or 5 gallons. The (L) one is termed a "bottle necked" measure. H. Rogers, 1914. The value here is not in real age, but in the ancient form. **$20.00-$120.00**

V-40.
Measures.

Pieced tin, wraparound lips, braced or reinforced handle for largest, 2-gallon, size. Smallest is 1/4 pint. F.A. Walker catalog, c.1890; same cut used to depict "Old Time" measures of heavy tin plate in the Matthai-Ingram catalog also c.1890. **$18.00-$35.00**

V-41.
Measures.

Quite similar to those in V-40, except that they are made of heavy tin with copper lips, and all, including the smallest, have reinforced strap handles. Sizes 1 gill, 1/2 and 1 pint, 1 quart, 2 quarts and 1 gallon. Duparquet, Huot & Moneuse, c.1904-1910. Extra value is for the "decorating" value of copper. **$25.00-$75.00**

V-43.
Measures.

Graniteware, gray & white. Completely wraparound lip, reinforced strap handle. Maker unknown, but was available in 4 sizes from Sethness: 1 pint, 1 quart, 1/2 gallon and 1 gallon. 1925 catalog, but probably virtually unchanged for 30 years before that. **$45.00-$70.00**

V-44.
Vinegar measures & funnel.

Cut from one piece of wood, which was not identified in catalog of Joseph Breck, 1905. All pieces look like much older examples. A set consisted of a pint, quart 1/2 gallon measure and the funnel. Approximate value range for measures might tend to be higher than that for a funnel, which was probably about 7"H. Much of asking price would be based on patina and condition, and the assumption of great age. **$35.00-$70.00**

V-45.
"Utility" measures,

or combination measures, described in various catalogs as being a measure with an attached funnel. These appeared in several catalogs from about 1890 well into the 1920s (and probably later). Top one, shown being used to fill a bottle, is of pieced tin, in 5 sizes: 1/2 and 1 pint, 1 quart, 2 and 4 quarts. Matthai-Ingram, c.1890. Lower one is of polished tinned steel, with "tinned steel rests" on the bottom, reinforced handle. It came in 3 sizes: 1, 2 and 4 quarts. "Puritan" line, Central Stamping Co., 1920. Another one, almost identical but made of copper and available only in the 1-gallon size, is found in the Sethness publication of 1925. Value range for tin only; add from 50 to 100% for a copper one. **$25.00-$45.00**

V-46.
Measure.

Stamped & pieced tin, wraparound lip, strap handle, embossed graduations of 1-quart size. 5"H x 3" diameter. Maker unknown, TOC. **$12.00-$20.00**

V-47.
Measure.

Copper, 5-gallon size only, with two tipping strap handles near the bottom, flared wraparound lip-rim or flange, swinging strap handle with reinforcement at center. Graduated with ribs. Sethness, 1925. Original price was $9.75. **$40.00-$70.00**

V-48.
Measuring Cup.

Molded lime glass, "annealed to prevent breaking from extremes of heat or cold." Graduated in thirds and fourths. Style called the "Brooklyn." "One may hold it up to the light and see just the exact measurement." Silver & Co., c.1910. **$12.00-$18.00**

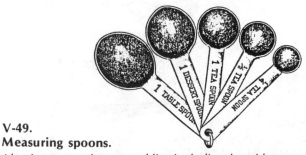

V-49.
Measuring spoons.

Aluminum, on a ring, a set of five including the midway measurement "dessert spoon," widely known in England, but not here. Mfd. by the E.A. Fargo Co., Taunton, MA. An ad in House Furnishing Review, *5/1915.* **$15.00-$20.00**

V-50.
Measuring spoon.

A nickel-plated stamped steel mixing spoon with built-in measuring graduations marked on bowl. Green pastic handle. Two sizes: 8 1/2"L and 10 3/4"L. "Androck" line, Washburn Co., 1936. **$5.00-$10.00**

V-51.
Pie birds.

Pastel-colored glazed china, the (R) one in the form of a baby bird asking for food is much heavier than the other. (L) 5 1/8"H; (R) 5 3/8"H. 20th C. For those of you who wondered if you would recognize a pie bird vs. a bird figurine: note the cutouts in the base. Ex-collection Lillian Cole. The value range for these is very wide, depending on where you find them. **$15.00-$35.00**

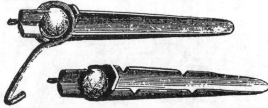

V-52.
Sap spouts.

Above: galvanized cast iron Eureka sap spout of 1869; below "improved" Eureka from 1870, mfd. by inventor, C.C. Post, Bùrlington, VT. "In the improved one, the bucket hangs by two points, so that it cannot swing like a pendulum, and in two narrow notches, so that it cannot twist nor wabble (sic)." W.J. Chamberlain, Hudson, OH, wrote in "Maple-Sugar Making," American Agriculturist, *2/1871: "Last year I recommended a wooden sap spout...because it was, on the whole, better than any metallic one I had then seen. I find four or five different kinds are used in Vermont, but only one appears to me preferable to the turned, bored, and notched-in-three-places one in general use (in Ohio). That is Post's Eureka." The marble-like "hemisphere 'hugs' against the outer edge of the hole" in the tree.* **$3.00-$8.00**

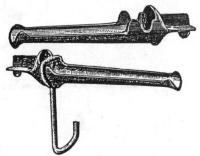

V-53.
Sap spouts.

Here are C.C. Post's Eureka spouts after another 13 years! "The Sugar Maker's Friend. Over 6,000,000 sold, to replace various kinds." About 3 1/2"L. Note that he went back to the wire hanger for one style. The price in 1871 was described by Mr. Chamberlain as "high" at $4 for a hundred spouts. By the time of this ad, in American Agriculturist, *3/1883, the price was $4.25 and $4.50 per hundred. You could order a sample for three 3¢ U.S. stamps.* **$3.00-$8.00**

V-54.
Sap spout.

Galvanized malleable iron, the "Breck" spout—"the invention of a practical sugar maker." Guaranteed not to break from being driven into the bored sap hole in the tree, and the cast-in hooks were made to "withstand the strain of high winds" which often caused buckets to twist off the hooks. They also sold the "Concord," "the common spout used largely in New Hampshire and Vermont, made of wood and steel." Joseph Breck, 1905. **$3.00-$8.00**

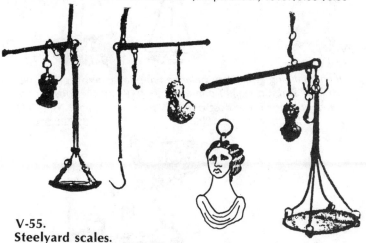

V-55.
Steelyard scales.

Excuse the poor quality of the picture: it is adapted from a 1910 catalog with shadowy photographs, of a foundry in Naples, Italy, that specialized in reproductions of ancient bronzes found at Pompei and Herculaneum. Cast bronze. 2 have hanging pans, 1 has a hook. This type of scale has changed little in 2000 years; the weights **have** *changed. In this lengthy catalog, the date the archaeological find was made, and measurements of the originals are given. These steelyards were found the 31st of July, 1888, at Pompeii. (L) 45 cm or about 17 3/4"L; (M) 40 cm or about 15 3/4"L; (R) 50 cm or about 19 3/4"L. J. Chiurazzi & Fils - S. De Angelis & Fils, 1910-11. They were available in 2 finishes: blackened cast bronze (Herculaneum) or verdigris or green (Pompeii). Line drawing is done from figural weight of steelyard at right. Cast bronze, in form of woman's bust, with waved hairstyle and draped bodice. It appears that a hook was cast on top of the heads (this one represents the weight of the (R) scale, which hooked through a ring that hung from a chain fixed to the steelyard beam. The size is probably about 5 1/2" to 6"H. My drawing adapted from J. Chiurazzi.*

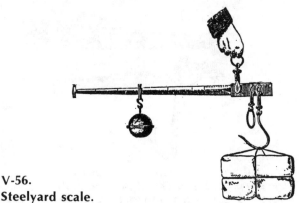

V-56.
Steelyard scale.

The round moveable weight is at (L), the package being weighed at (R). The illustration, taken from a schoolbook of 1905, entitled *Natural Philosophy*, explains that the steelyard scale, also known as the **Roman balance**, *"has no great sensitiveness"* and is based on the principle of a lever. The fulcrum is the pivot point on the beam below where the hand is holding the hanging ring. The arm or beam to the left of the fulcrum is *"graduated into equal parts,"* and the weight is moved along the sharp edge of the arm until a position is found in which it just counterbalances the load. The weight of the lever itself is allowed for in the graduations. For this type of manufactured scale the value is much less than that for a comparably-sized hand-forged one. **$10.00-$20.00**

V-57.
Spice scale.

Of the hanging equal arm balance type. Japanned & pinstriped cast iron arm, tin weight pan and scoop (R) for the loose spice being weighed. These cost only 75¢ for small size, or $1.25 for large, in Jaburg catalog, 1908. **$25.00-$50.00**

V-58.
Counter scale.

Japanned cast iron, bronze pinstriping, one type of so-called "fishtail" base, tin scoop pan, single beam, 25-pound capacity. Possibly a "Howe" scale; offered in the A. Pick catalog, 1909. The price then was only $3.60. **$75.00-$120.00**

V-59.
"Union scales,"

platform countertop, with single beam and slotted cast iron weights that slip over hanging weight rod. Painted and decorated cast iron, with pieced scoop (tin? brass?). Capacity from 1/2 ounce to 240 pounds. Jaburg catalog, 1908. The original cost was only $4, which seems absolutely impossible. **$125.00-$250.00**

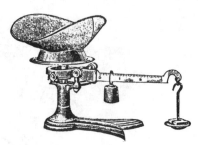

V-60.
Spice scale,

or candy, grocers' or counter scale. At any rate, an unequal arm balance scale with a single beam. Black enameled cast iron with gold pinstriping, brass beam, cast iron weights and poise (the moveable weight along the beam), and choice of brass or tin scoop (pan). Note the one in the picture has a high flared foot; the thing looks almost like a fancy hat. Round plate upon which the scoop sits is 8" diameter; scoop is 18"L x 8 1/4"W. Mfd. by Fairbanks — a high quality scale, and the price in the 1910 Norvell-Shapleigh catalog reflects that: $15.50 with the brass pan; a buck and a half less for tin. **$95.00-$150.00**

V-61.
Counter scales,

unequal arm balance scales with single beam. (L): "Little Detective Pattern," probably Fairbanks, black japanned cast iron with brass beam. Tin scoop 12" x 6 ¾". Capacity 25 pounds. Norvell-Shapleigh 1910 catalog. (R): Painted and striped cast iron columnar base, capacity to 36 pounds, available with tin or brass scoop for the round plate. Available through, and possibly manufactured by, the John Van Range Co., Cincinnati, 1914. **$95.00-$150.00**

V-62.
John Wanamaker's Candy Department,

"from a photograph—showing four National Cash Registers in use", but also an unequal arm candy scale in foreground. From ad in *Century*, c.1880.

V-63.
Cake scale,

or platform scale with dial. Decorated cast iron, with oblong marble platform. Wonderful fluted columns. It came in three sizes: capacity 5 pounds, measured in 1/2 ounce increments; capacity 10 pounds, measured by 1 ounce; and capacity 20 pounds, by 2 ounces. Mfd. by John Chatillon & Sons, NYC; sold through Jaburg, 1908 catalog. **$175.00-$275.00**

V-64.
Scale,

called a "ball scale" by Thomas Mills & Bro., in 1930 catalog. It is impossible to read the name plate because it wasn't engraved as real words, but it may have been made by Mills—and from the looks of it, long before 1930. Ornate cast iron with ball shaped poises. Nickel-plated brass scoop. It could also be had with a plate (or platform) instead of a scoop. Capacity five pounds by quarter ounces. 1930 price with scoop was $22. **$175.00-$275.00**

V-65.
Counter scale,

a "double graduated 'arc scale' " that "combines with Utility, both Beauty, and Convenience. Its primary object is to save the annoyance and expense of the loss of weights. It works (like) ordinary counter Scales, but in lieu of the plate for the ...weights, has a Graduated Arc, with a Permanently Attached Weight, through which an Index is passed, which moves over the Arc and denotes with great accuracy the weight of the commodity in the opposite dish. The scale is peculiarly adapted to Druggists, by having upon the Arc, a scale of Apothecaries' weights along with the ordinary Avoirdupis scale...with an outer and inner index...The scale is also manufactured for Grocers, Tea Dealers & Confectioners." Buckelew & Waterman, Philadelphia, c.1804s-60s **$175.00-$350.00**

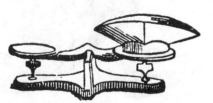

V-66.
Counter scale,

equal arm balance type. Cast iron, meant to be used with weights piled on plate at left. The picture, of an "improved weighing balance," comes from the 1854 <u>The American Home Cook Book,</u> which had many illustrations of recommended kitchen equipment. **$150.00-$200.00**

V-67.
Counter scale,

equal arm balance with plate, weights and scoop. Black japanned cast iron with fancy lyre-like Federal-inspired design. Weights ½ ounce to 4 pounds. This illustration from the F.A. Walker catalog, c.1890s. An identical linecut appeared in the 1875 Stuart, Peterson & Co.'s manufacturer's catalog, so they may have made them. Either this was the most popular style of scale at the turn of the century and several firms made them, or the artists doing the linecuts for catalogs all drew the same one just a bit different. **$150.00-$250.00**

V-68.
"French scales,"

equal arm balance, with brass plate and index pointer. Capacity 4 and 5 kilograms. Imported from France, and sold by Duparquet, Huot & Moneuse, NYC, through their 1904-1910 catalog. **$150.00-$200.00**

V-69.
Counter scales,

equal arm balance scales with the lyre base, almost identical to the Stuart, Peterson/Walker scale. Top: "Hatch Pattern Even Balance" from the 1910 Norvell-Shapleigh Hardware Co. Catalog. "A low priced scale for family use." 8-pound capacity, japanned cast iron frame 12 1/2"L, tin scoop is 16 3/4"L x 9 1/4"W. Original price only $4.20. Bottom: "Iron Bearing Bakehouse Scales," cast iron. With the weights, in the 1908 Jaburg catalog, this was only $2.75. Hard to believe. **$150.00-$250.00**

V-70.
Counter scales

Japanned and decorated cast iron frame, seamless stamped brass scoop 13"L x 6"W, rubber tips on the "fork" that holds the scoop. Thomas Mills catalog, 1930. **$90.00-$150.00**

V-71.
Counter scales,
or even balance trip scales. Enameled or japanned and decorated cast iron bases, weight plate, seamless brass scoops. Top one is described as being "without tare beam," which means that you could not adjust it to take the weight of the commodity's container into account when weighing for contents. It came in four sizes. The bottom one has a tare beam, and came in three sizes. Both from the 1908 Jaburg catalog for professional confectioners and bakers. **$120.00-$175.00**

V-72.
Cake scale,
of equal balance "trip" type. Japanned and decorated cast iron with 8" x 10" cool marble plate for the cake (or fudge?) being weighed. Jaburg, 1908. **$75.00-$120.00**

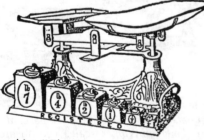

V-73.
Scale,
or "weighing machine." The "Registered" style, in three sizes, 1/4 ounce to 14 pound capacity; 1/4 ounce to 7 pound capacity; and 1 ounce to 4 pound. Cast iron, ornate, japanned base, octagonal scale plate, slightly dished pan. Harrod's Stores catalog, London, 1895. **$125.00-$200.00**

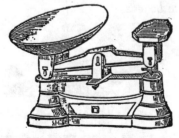

V-74.
Scale,
or "weighing machine." in "Family" style. Very simple cast iron frame, octagonal weight plate. Same three capacities as the "Registered" in V-73. Also Harrod's, 1895 catalog. **$125.00-$200.00**

V-75.
Scale,
with weights arrayed along front of cast iron frame. "As one of the great elements of success in cooking is preciseness in the proportions of ingredients, the cook should never be without a good pair of scales, and she should keep them in thorough order. In delicate dishes an unequal proportion of an article inserted only to impart a certain flavor, will ruin the dish. The necessity as well as use of scales is therefore obvious." Picture and quote from *Warne's Model Cookery and Housekeeping Book*, compiled by Mary Jewry. London: 1868. **$125.00-$200.00**

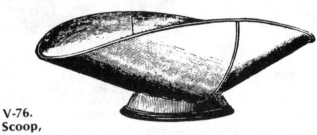

V-76.
Scoop,
for bakehouse scales. Heavy tin, pieced construction, footed. Came in three sizes: medium, large and extra large. 1908 Jaburg supply catalog. **$15.00-$25.00**

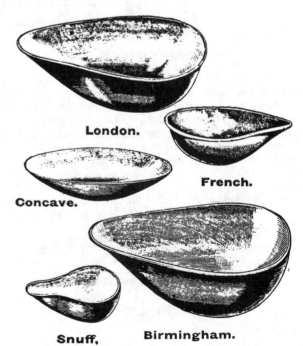

V-77.
Scale pans or scoops.
All obviously unseamed (which means stamped) and probably brass. The five styles—London, Birmingham, French, Concave, and Snuff—were all offered in the 1914 Henry Rogers, Wolverhampton, England, catalog. Collectors will pay extra for brass pans, even if originally the scale had a tin pan, or if the brass pan was nickeled. **$20.00-$60.00**

FAIRBANKS' STANDARD SCALES.

BUY ONLY THE GENUINE.

V-78. Trade card,
for Fairbanks scales, NYC. Chromolithograph depicting the showroom, with several gents looking over various sizes and types. Card from 1880s. **$8.00-$16.00**

V-79.
Weights,
for bakehouse scales. Five materials, available singly or in sets of 8 or 9, from 1/2 ounce to pounds or 1/4 ounce to 4 pounds. The five were nickel-plated brass, solid brass, cased brass, zinc, or cast iron. 1908 Jaburg catalog. Value mostly for sets of matching weights, even if the sets are incomplete. Per weight, with maybe a bit added for solid brass weights depending on metal market. **$1.00-$8.00**

V-80.
Weights,
of two types. (L): "Nest of Brass French Weights" in wooden box, in kilograms. (R): "Nest of Iron American Weights," stacked, 1 ounce to 8 pounds. Duparquet, Huot & Moneuse, c.1904-1910. A full set of 10 French ones would be worth between $40 to $60. Individually, any of them. **$1.00-$8.00**

V-81.
Weights.
Cast iron. (L) Flat weights, beveled edge, 9 in a set, from 1/4 ounce to 4 pounds. Top (M) Convex edge weights, same 9. Bottom (M) Plain flat weights. (R) Bell weight, in 10 sizes, from 1/4 ounce to 7 pounds (skips 5, 6 pounds). All in Henry Rogers, Wolverhampton, England, 1914 catalog. **$1.00-$15.00**

V-82.
Egg scale.
"Acme Egg Grading Scale," mfd. by Specialty Mfg. Co., St. Paul, MN, aluminum. 4 1/2"H x 10 1/2"L x 3 1/2"W, pat'd 6/24/1924. This one doesn't seem to get the price that the Jiffy-Way does, though to my mind it's far more desirable aesthetically and aurally. **$15.00-$25.00**

V-83.
Egg scale.

The most commonly found kind—mainly because it's been made continuously since being patented in 1940. "Jiffy-Way," green & red painted heavy sheet metal, 5 3/4"H x 7 1/8"L. Patent No. 2205917. Jiffy-Way Inc., Owatanna. MN — "World's largest manufacturers of egg scales." 1 1/2 ounces to 2 1/2 ounces. **$18.00-$25.00**

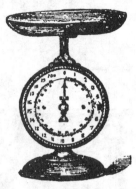

V-85.
Family scale.

Stamped sheet iron, white painted dial, 11"H with 8" diameter pan or tray attached on top, "The Daisy", maker unknown. Subscription premium ad in The Housewife, 7/1891. **$55.00-$90.00**

V-84.
Family scales,

*also called **dial scales**. Both enameled and decorated sheet iron with flat platforms and round dials on front, all weigh to 24 pounds. (L) "Columbia," mfd. by Landers, Frary & Clark, New Britain, CT. In six models: black enamel; white enameled dial, square steel top; white enameled dial, steel top, tin scoop; brass plated scale; brass plated with white enameled dial and steel top; and the most desirable one—brass plated body, brass dial, brass scoop, steel top. Joseph Breck catalog, 1905. (R) "Favorite," mfd. by John Chatillon & Sons, pat'd July 16(?), 18—, "silver-plated" brass dial, "handsomely ornamented." 24-pound capacity. In 1924 D.J. Barry catalog.* **$20.00-$120.00**

V-86.
Family scale

Cast steel or iron with brass base and iron pan. "Class Two, Salters Improved Family Scale, No. 50," 14-pound capacity, about 14"H. English, late 19th C. Salters is one of three big names in scales, the others being Chatillon and Fairbanks. **$90.00-$135.00**

V-87.
Hanging spring balance scale.

Fancy japanned cast iron case with large white enameled dial, 7" diameter, with graduations enameled in black. 13" diameter pan suspended from tinned bow and swivel. Overall 31"H. 10 pound capacity. Norvell-Shapleigh, 1910 catalog. **$50.00-$90.00**

V-88.
Hanging spring balance scale.
This is the most commonly found type of old scale; at least one appears at every show and flea market. This one is iron with brass face to the spring-housing, steel spring, white-enamaled dial in front. Mfd. by Morton & Bremner (formerly Thomas Morton), NYC. In Asher & Adams Pictorial Album of American Industry, 1876. **$35.00-$70.00**

V-89.
Hanging spring balance scales.
(L) "Sargent Armored", black japanned steel case for spring, nickeled dial on both sides, steel spring, tinned steel hook & ring, 9 1/2"H x 2 1/2"W, overall length 14", 200-pound capacity in 5-pound graduations. Norvell-Shapleigh Hardware Co., 1910 catalog. (M) Chatillon's Balance No. 2", iron cast with curved back and nickel-plated brass front; also available with flat back and much broader index pointer. 25-pound capacity by 8-ounce increments. D.J. Barry catalog, 1925. **$18.00-$40.00**

(R) Called a "German Crab" scale in the Norvell-Shapleigh catalog, which refers to the side hooks, because its capacity is 300 pounds, in 5-pound graduations—not the thing for weighing crabs. Spring steel frame 3 3/4" x 3 1/2", overall 10 1/2"L, polished brass demilune face with stamped lines & numbers, polished wrought steel hooks and ring. **$22.00-$40.00**

V-90.
Candy scoop
Molded glass. From D.J. Barry 1924 catalog. **$18.00-$28.00**

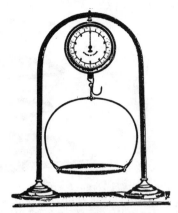

V-91.
Spring balance scale,
and standard. Nickel-plated brass. Maker not shown, but probably Chatillon. Could be had with a double-faced dial, and the arched standard could be bought separately. Jaburg 1908 catalog. **$120.00-$170.00**

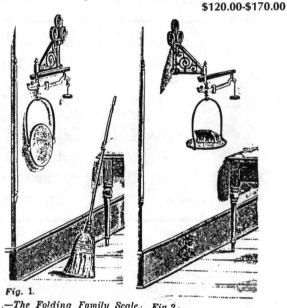

Fig. 1.
.—The Folding Family Scale.
Folded Flat Against the Wall.
Fig. 2.
—Scale Unfolded and Ready for Use.

V-92.
Fold-away scale
Called in the Metal Worker article about it a "folding family scale", but the term "family" is most usually associated with spring scales with platforms or pans above the dial. Ornamental cast iron bracket, brass pan, unequal arm balance type with poise and loose weights, 50-pound capacity by 1/2-ounce graduations. Mfd. by folding Scale Co., Beloit, WI. "Heretofore persons having a family scale have been troubled by having no regular place for it that would not at times make it an inconvenience. This new device overcomes that difficulty, as the scale can be folded up against the wall or door to which it is attached." The Metal Worker 5/31/1890. **$120.00-$170.00**

V-93.
Scoop.
Flat-bottom, pieced brass, which could be had nickeled for a quarter extra. Tubular capped handle. Sizes 00, 0, 1, 2, & 3 (measurements not given, but probably ranging from about 5"L to 10"L). Jaburg 1908 catalog. **$15.00-$30.00**

V-94.
Scoops

From the top: (1) "French sugar scoop", from <u>American Home Cook Book</u>,1854. (2) Thumb scoop, tin with ring handle, in 2 sizes: 5"L x 3"W and 6"L x 3 1/4"W. Buhl Sons c.1919 catalog. (3) Spice scoop with ring handle, tin, in 3 unstated sizes, and (4) Tea or candy scoop with tubular handle, tin, in 2 sizes. Both from 1924 D.J. Barry catalog. **$3.00-$15.00**

V-95.
Scoops

The struggle to find a catchy advertising phrase has long been with us. (Now we would probably say "scoop this up". Brass scoops in set of four, tubular capped handles, crimped back plate, apparently flat-bottomed self-balancing. These were manufactured by William Wrigley, Jr., & Co., Chicago & Philadelphia, the chewing-gum makers! They were offered as a "necessity in every retail store", and available as a free premium when the dealer sent in order for 120 five-cent packages of gum. Advertising card, printed in blue, c.1900. The scoops, singly: **$10.00-$20.00**

V-96.
Looks like a scoop—

but it's a banker's **money shovel**. Copper, flat bottom, steel lip like certain dustpans, tubular handle of copper (available also in turned ebony), protective heel like a shoe! The size is not given, but presumably about 10"L or longer. English. Henry Rogers, Wolverhampton, England, 11914 catalog. This is sure to show up in the containerloads from England. Now you will know what it is! **$30.00-$60.00**

V-97.
Tea scoop.

Seamed brass with big rounded bowl, turned ebony handle. Four sizes that measured from 2 ounces to 1 pound of loose tea leaves. Henry Rogers, Wolverhampton, England, 1914. **$25.00-$45.00**

V-98.
Flour scoop.

Pieced tin. braced tubular capped handle, reinforced upper rim. Came in 2 sizes — small and large. Jaburg, 1908 catalog **$15.00-$25.00**

V-99.
Sugar scoop.

Cast solid aluminum, 3 sizes: 11"L x 4"W; 12"L x 5"W; and 14"L x 5 1/2"W. Thomas Mills 1930 catalog. **$10.00-$22.00**

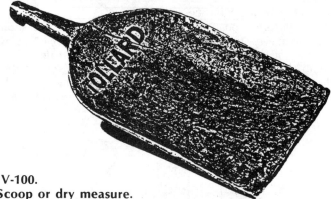

V-100.
Scoop or dry measure.

Carved from one piece of wood. Marked "TOLLARD"— which could as easily have been the store in which it was used as the maker. Short hooked handle. 15¼"L. c.1860s-80s. Picture courtesy of Christie, Manson & Woods International Inc. (NOTE: Here, as elsewhere throughout the book, you will see that the value range given with the picture differs from that given in the regular price listing. The picture captions were done almost a year later than the price listings, and while many price corrections were made in the listings, it is always impossible to make a please-everyone price guide. Prices change with whims in collecting fashion). **$45.00-$80.00**

V-101.
Room thermometer

Red-painted, stamped heavy tin in teapot shape. "Tel-Tru" Thermometer Co., Rochester, NY. 7"W, c.1930s-40s. For you who are looking for backgrounds for photos—this is water-spritzed chipboard, an excellent mottled background for dark objects. **$10.00-$18.00**

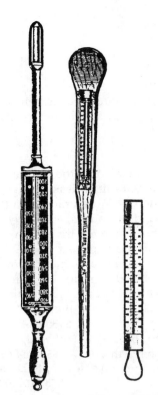

V-102.
Candy-makers' thermometers.

(L) Copper-cased with glass, 12"L, 14"L or 18"L. (M) "Improved boiling thermometer", turned wooden handle, in 2 sizes. First, for caramels, hard candy, etc..., has a 14"L stem and is 32"L overall. Second, for hard candy, with 5"L stem, 14 1/2"L overall. (R) "Wood stirring paddle with thermometer", this one at least we know was mfd. by Thomas Mills. 36"L. All from 1930 Mills catalog. **$10.00-$30.00**

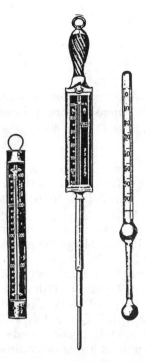

V-103.
Thermometers.

All mercury stems. (L) Confectioners' thermometer, copper case. 12"L. Mfd. by something like W.L. Inhagen & M. Espe, NYC. (M) Dough-mixing thermometer, turned wooden handle. 7"L case, approx. 21"L overall. Pat'd April 24, 1894. Made by Homann & Maurer (sp?), Rochester, NY. (R) Syrup hydrometer, also known as a saccharometer. Glass. Also Homann & Maurer. (L) and (R) from Sethness 1925 catalog. (M) from Jaburg, 1908. **Price: $15 to $35**

Coopered Wares — How Big?
Or, Twenty-nine Firkins of Beer on the Wall

In everyday 18th C. life, a knowledge of such exact measures as barrel, hogshead, tub or firkin was vital to any citizen who bought, sold or bartered grain, butter, ale, soap, tallow, cider or any other dry or liquid stuff that was measured out in supposedly uniformly-sized coopered (staved & bound wood) containers. Many of these containers (at least the smaller ones) are found in kitchen and country store collections today.

In America's earliest days we used British standards of measure. Later the legal capacity of coopered vessels differed (and still do) in England and America. To take just one early 18th C. liquid product — ale or beer — and give its rounded off old time British measures: one **tun** of ale equaled about four **hogsheads** or almost seven and a quarter **barrels,** or fourteen and a half **kilderkins,** or close to 29 **firkins.** A tun of ale held about 259 gallons, a firkin held only a little over nine gallons. A **keg** was a small ale or beer cask that held 10 gallons or less, so it was an inexact measure that might easily coincide with a firkin. (A **cask** usually referred to a generic coopered container, just as today we often use "barrel" to generally mean a big coopered container, or "keg" to mean a small one.) A **kilderkin** and a **runlet** had the same measurements — almost exactly 16"H x 20" diameter; a **firkin** was half that in both dimensions; a **butt** was twice as big.

The word "trivet" is most commonly used for the often three-legged stand meant for sadirons, but the ones here are for cooking utensils — inside or under. For the most part they are like hot pads, and most are technically stands, not trivets. See also page 445 and 446.

Hot mat, variegated woods in pinwheel design, supposed to be Shaker because of the variegated woods (used for rolling pins & table mats), 8" diameter, came in other sizes, 1920s. **$20.00-$25.00**

Jelly maker's stand, cast iron, sort of like a trivet bench, 4 legs, top has 2 large holes — for 2 kettles, American, about 26"L (?), 19th C. **$150.00-$175.00**

Stand, cast iron, sand casting of real hand, hanging (?) hole in wrist, American, 18th or early 19th C. • This was seen in a dealer's (Rose W. Olstead, Madison, NJ) ad in *The Magazine ANTIQUES*, July 1962. I suspect the price was under $100.00; possibly under $50.00. If you found such a piece now, if it was determined to be old, the price would be much higher. **$250.00-$500.00**

Stand, for hot dishes, round, tight spiral of thin wire, reinforced and soldered by eight spokes radiating from center, with 8 little loops underneath as feet, several makers among the wire novelty companies, American, about 6¼" diameter, late 19th or early 20th C. • **Reproduction alert.** — This type has some variations, sometimes unsoldered and held together only by little twists of wire at each intersection of spiral and spoke. I have seen them as large as 8" diameter; others may be larger. This and other types of twisted wire stands have been heavily reproduced, and sold to "country" dealers. I don't know what to tell you about telling the difference between new and old. I would say that the soldered are much more likely to be new, because no modern worker would spend the time twisting the tiny wire around some 90 to 100 intersections. • Other variations of thin twisted wire stands include some that look like daisies, with each petal having its own little bent loop foot, and some with many spokes or rays but without the spirals, and using heavier wire, twisted sometimes from two strands. **$15.00-$20.00**

Stand or trivet, for pots, and <u>combination tool</u> including meat tenderizer, tack hammer, stove lid lifter, pot lifter (hook fits around bail handle), pie crimper, candleholder (the last 2 dubiously efficacious), found in cast iron and cast bronze-like metal. Basically round, with 4 deep ridges (the tenderizer) shooting off at an angle, 2 round candle- or finger-sized holes, one longish curved piece (lid lifter), 3 short hooked pieces off bottom, the whole thing can be seen as a caricature of Groucho Marx. This is almost always found at fleas and shows on the tables of people dealing in knives, guns, Nazi memorabilia, camo junk, etc., and is usually labeled "brass knuckles", which it most assuredly isn't. "6-Way Trivet" is one; another is the "Seven Way Kitchen Aid", pat'd by W. H. Thayer, American, Thayer's pat'd May 24, 1881. **$30.00-$45.00**

Trivet, also called a <u>dish rest</u>, cast iron, round with side handle, 3 legs, heart motif with radiating spokes, heart end to handle, American, 11⅜"L x 6½" diameter, dated 1829. **$275.00-$325.00**

Trivet, brass, fire bar type that hooked onto the fire bar that went between 2 andirons, stylized thistle design, English (?), 19th C. • **Reproduction alert.** — A decorative hearth-side trivet type frequently found nowadays, especially with English imports, is the brass lyre-top trivet with wrought iron legs or base, with heavy turned wooden handle, and penny feet. Much to my amazement, I found a 1937 *House Beautiful* ad for a $4.50 reproduction, offered by H. Wiener, on Allen Street in NYC, the brass capitol of America in the late 19th C & 20th ... up to the 1960s! **$150.00-$175.00**

Trivet, cast brass woman's head, Bradley & Hubbard, Meriden, CT, 3rd to 4th quarter 19th C. **$50.00-$65.00**

Trivet, cast iron, round with heart & rays design, 8"D, late 19th C. **$75.00-$100.00**

Trivet, expands, for hot dishes, copper & brass, probably originally nickel plated, "Manning-Bowman," American, 1st half 20th C. **$20.00-$25.00**

Trivet, for kettle or pot, cast iron square, 4 legs riveted on, at the knee of each leg is a flattened oval medallion with a relief profile of a Roman warrier in helmet, all 4 the same, openwork top plate spells out name, "Houchin's Patent", NYC, NY, but T. W. Houchin lived in Morrisania, NY, 2¼"H x 5⅜" square, prob. 1870s to 1890s. • Another Houchin trivet, probably for portable kettle or other little vessel, has very delicate cast iron top, probably brass plated or bronzed, is only 3¾" square with 3 shaped 1¼"H brass legs, round cutout design in top spells out H O U C H I N. It is worth only $5.00 to $7.00. **$75.00-$100.00**

Trivet, for pot, beautiful cast iron in interesting flat top piece with large hole cut in center, outside edge basically round with projections where 3 legs attached, largish tab handle (shaped like a porringer handle) has a hanging hole, English (?), only 2⅝"H x 4½"W at widest part, mid 19th C (?). **$35.00-$50.00**

Trivet, for pot, cast iron, advertises "Cinderella Stoves", early 20th C. **$25.00-$35.00**

Trivet, for pot, cast iron, letters form openwork design, J. R. Clark Co., Minneapolis, MN, late 19th C or early 20th. **$25.00-$35.00**

Trivet, for pot, cast iron, pattern of round holes, "Griswold #204," Erie, PA, 12"D, TOC. **$20.00-$35.00**

Trivet, for pot, cheap metal cast to resemble bamboo, back bears motto "East or West - Campbell's Soups Are Best", Campbell Soup, c.1970s (?). **$10.00-$15.00**

Trivet, for pot, enameled cast iron, very ornate openwork, the center a sort of flowerette composed of 6 hearts joined at the points, the outside frame composed of 12 looped and rococo scrolls arranged so that 2 form a unit, all surrounded in delicately scalloped edge, peg feet,

American, 18″ diameter, prob. 1860s-1880s. **$75.00-$90.00**

Trivet, for pot or kettle, a real wrought iron horseshoe welded to sheet iron, 3 feet, American, 19th C. • I'm sure there are enough of these, all one of a kind, to make a very handsome collection. **$100.00-$145.00**

Trivet, for pot, wrought iron, heart shaped, with a scroll & heart inner design, 3 boot shaped feet, like riding boots, stamped with a small eagle punch mark & a flower on the handle, maker's name marked too, ''J. English'', Pennsylvania (?), 10¾″L x 4¼″W, early 19th C. • Robacker Collection. Sold at T. Glenn Horst Auction, June 1989 for $1600.00. • **The Composition of Price.** — Why did this sell for so much? Surely a record for a trivet or stand. There are many elements that went into the price, which may or may not be the secondary market value for this trivet. (1) It came from a famous, published collection, the Robacker Estate, and gains value from association, and from the fact that it had presumably been bought by a knowledgeable couple who wouldn't have bought a reproduction or fake. (2) It was sold at auction, where the pace and fever of selling are conducive of high realized prices. (3) It is marked. It not only had a maker's name, ''J. English'', but also an American eagle with a shield & banner and a clutch of arrows. So far, nothing is·known about the maker. (4) There was a valuable multiplier motif in the design, in this case cutout hearts — usually good for multiplying price by 5X to 10X or more, meaning that without it, the price might be 1/10th to 1/20th. (5) There was a figural element in the design. For me, personally, the most enchanting factor (thanks to my 12AAAA understanding) are the boot feet. I already own one nice trivet with cast boot feet. I saw another trivet or stand, probably Pennsylvanian, in the Keillor Collection, when I was doing my first book; the Keillors' was 13″L, with a cutout cock or rooster, a very graceful & shaped handle and is truly the most wonderful of the three, and I wish I owned it. I also wish that I could see all three next to each other; it'd be useful to compare the shape and exact size of all the boots. (6) Size is the most easily overlooked factor in the composition of price, whether a piece is unusually large or small. In this instance, it is largeness. This is a good sized trivet, quite impressive. • I believe that factors (1) & (2) probably contributed to the price realized in June 1989, but that the real market value ought to be lower. I believe the current market value for the Keillor trivet, which sold at auction in 1976 for an unknown amount, is more likely to be $1600.00. The Robacker one, because of the marks, the hearts & the boots: **$700.00-$900.00**

Trivet, for pot, wrought iron pony shoe mounted to black painted copper plate cut to fit shape, 3 wrought booted feet with rounded toes and heels, the boots resemble riding boots, American (?), 1¼″H x 4⅞″ x 4⅞″, early 19th C. **$175.00-$200.00**

Trivet, for pots, cast iron, this one also called a simmering cover, to use on cookstove, Walker & Pratt Mfg. Co., ''W & P,'' 7¾″D, 19th C. **$18.00-$22.00**

Trivet, for utensil, or kettle, forged iron, with hearts in center, plus a 2 hearted handle, American, 12″L, date difficult to call. • **Old Hearts.** — With the heart motif's popularity, and proliferating fake forged iron pieces of all kinds, this could be as recent as a year ago. This one has convincing signs of wear, cleaning, polishing, use, both on bottoms of feet, and on surface, and may be early 19th C. **$120.00-$150.00**

Trivet, heavy wrought iron in a tight coil, with handle, 10″L including handle, early 19th C. **$65.00-$80.00**

Trivet, orange painted cast iron, advertising ''Grain Belt'' beer, early 20th C. **$25.00-$35.00**

Trivet, real forged iron horseshoe, backed with disc of sheet metal from which a large V has been cut, with 3 forged short peg legs, American, 4½″L, late 19th or early 20th C. • I bought this for $2.00 from a dealer who said it was an ''ashtray'', but that is way under the money. And, no, I didn't argue. **$18.00-$25.00**

Trivet, spiraled wire, cross pieces form legs with a rivet, American, 6″ diameter, c.1890s to 1910s. **$15.00-$18.00**

Trivet, wrought iron, round long triangle outline, with pointed piece almost like steeple from point of trivet up into open space, topped by cutout bird form (like a weathervane), 3 feet in shape of boots, all pointing away from slightly curved skinny handle. This was in the Keillor Collection, auctioned in 1976, and may be one of the finest trivets ever seen on the market, American or poss. French, 2″H x 13″L overall, early 19th C. **$700.00-$1600.00**

Trivet or stand, probably for pot, cast iron with bronzed finish, skeletal triangle with 3 longish feet, marked on underside ''Thos. W. Houchin Co. 1898'', NYC, 1½″H x 4¼″ sides, TOC. **$14.00-$18.00**

VI-1.

Trivet

Called a "farrier's whimsy" in the auction catalog. Steel and brass; a horse (or pony) shoe, fitted with three high laced boots as feet and decorated with miniature farrier's tools–anvil, tongs, hammer, etc... Approximately 5 3/4″W by about 1 ½″H. Photo courtesy of Litchfield Auction Gallery, Litchfield, CT. Ex-Harold Corbin Collection, auctioned 1/1/1990. Sold for low **$350.00**

VI-2.
Trivet for pot
Intricate cast iron, japanned finish. In style, like the ones that were enameled. Russell & Erwin, mid-1860s. **$15.00-$20.00**

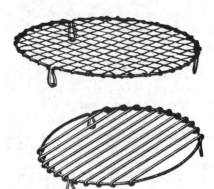

VI-5
Kettle bottoms & meat rests
*A form of trivet, and often identified as such. They were meant for the **inside** of a pot or kettle. Both are tinned iron wire. The upper mesh one, with wires welded to the round frame, came in 6", 7", 8", 9" and 10" diameter. The bottom one was only made 7" and 8½" diameter. The Washburn Co., Worcester, "Sno-Cap" catalog, 1927.* **$3.00-$6.00**

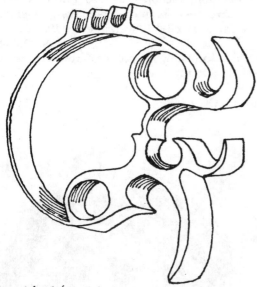

VI-3.
Stand or trivet *for pots,*
and combination tool. This is the one patented May 24, 1881 by W. H. Thayer as a "seven-way" tool. The functions are (1) trivet, (2) stove lid lifter, (3) pot bail hook, (4) meat tenderizer, (5) pie crimper, (6) bottle opener, and (7) candleholder. It is found most commonly in cast brass, sometimes in cast iron. **$30.00-$45.00**

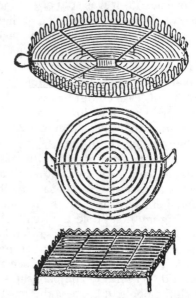

VI-6.
Grates
Much older than the previous wire stands are these three pastry or confectioner's grates, meant for cooling baked goods. The top one came in sizes from 6" to 16" diameter. The simpler center one made 5½" to 15¾" diameter (or any size to order"). The bottom one, 9"x 13", 10½"x 15", and 12"x 16", although any size could be ordered. From professional suppliers Duparquet, Huot & Moneuse, NYC, c.1904-1910. The form, and probably the linecuts, are from the 1870s. **$10.00-$45.00**

VI-4.
Trivet patent
Pat'd 12/8/1885 by Joseph P. Hurley, Philadelphia, PA. No. 332,201. Called a "Kitchen utensil" by Hurley, and claimed to be "a new article,...a metallic stand for kitchen utensils, consisting of two plates with connecting legs, all cast in one piece." **Official Gazette.** **.$25.00-$35.00**

VI-7.
Pot stand
Twisted iron wire, originally tinned. Probably French, but could also have been made by Sherwood of Worcester, MA. Called also a "teapot stand" (see others in Coffee & Tea Chapter). **American Agriculturist,** *11/1872.* **$15.00-$25.00**

C. HOLDING & HANDLING:

VII. STORAGE & CONTAINERS

This is a catch-all chapter in many ways; inevitable perhaps because of the subject. It has been said that women are great collectors of containers — boxes, jars, trunks — and there may be some psychological basis for what is often an obsession!

Variety is great, as is the quantity. As was said about sifting out the important matters from the flood of legislative work in the Congress, it's "like trying to use a straw to drink from a fire hydrant", as some wag said about Congress and its legislative agenda. It all comes at you so fast. Probably half the stuff at any flea market or antique show might be classified as a container of some kind. Open or closed.

I have quite a few cookie jars listed, but nothing conclusive can be said about price trends following the Andy Warhol auction, except that there was no real leap in prices, merely an upward motion. The jar market is well-organized, and its devotees avid; I am an outsider trying to whet any receptive appetites with a short report on a few representative examples. Lunch boxes form another highly specialized, one might say 'regulated' market. The market value of lunch boxes has been artificially manipulated by one or two artful collectors. The man who wrote the book on them admitted that he looked around for something which had not yet received much attention, and determined to buy everything he could, write a glossy book, then sell. Not my way of operating, and it sounds terribly Wall Streetish. Salt & Pepper Shakers appeal to me; and although a beautiful big book was done about them, and there are three collector clubs, there's a homey, mosey-around cadence to the collecting of them. Write them, with SASE, for info. • Salt Shaker Collectors Club, Dottie & Bill Avery, 2832 Rapidan Trail, Maitland, FL 32751. • Art Glass Salt Shaker Collectors Society, Jackie Mills, 348 N. Hamilton St., Painted Post, NY 14870; and • Novelty Salt & Pepper Shakers Club, Clara McHugh, RD 2, Box 2131, Stroudsburg, PA, 18360.

Some areas are ripe for attention, but may be too limited in scope for a broad following. If there isn't enough variety (in price as well as appearance or material), there's no fun. Christmas tree stands and fences (included here because I think they go with the other stuff in this book), Collapsible cups, and String holders are all of interest, but I think probably only the latter might have enough variety to sustain a collector market.

Apple butter jar, stoneware, dark brown Albany slip glaze inside, mug shape with round lip & slightly limp applied "mug" handle, impressed mark, "F. H. Cowden" with place, Harrisburg, PA, 7"H, c.3rd quarter 19th C. • This was catalogued & sold at the Garth Auction, May 26-27, 1989, in Delaware, OH. I had not been aware of such a vessel. It looks very much like a stoneware chamberpot, except that the mouth is slightly smaller than the largest circumference of the vessel's body, whereas in a chamberpot, the mouth widens out slightly. I would rather collect apple butter jars than chamberpots. In "The Shape of Stoneware", an article by James Mitchell, of the William Penn Memorial Museum (Harrisburg, PA) in *Early American Life*, Oct. 1978, we are told that "Sanitaryware is generally not found made from stoneware, but chamberpots are sometimes encountered. There are at least three marked examples. ... One is dated 1776 and was excavated from the site of the James Morgan Pottery in Cheesequake, Middlesex County, NJ. ... Another is marked 'Charlestown' and belongs to the Smithsonian. ... The third is marked 'Hawthorne Pottery Co. (Hawthorne, PA)' and is in the ... William Penn Memorial Museum." Memorial Museum." **$85.00-$135.00**

Apple tray, painted tin, square bottom with widely-slanted arch-topped sides, good condition with original paint in red, green and yellow, on dark asphaltum background, prob. CT, 19th C. **$175.00-$225.00**

Apple tray, tole, oval shape with amber crystalized inner bottom, large hand hold cutouts at both ends, simple flowers & leaves in red, salmon, pink, yellow, green, black & white, American, 2¾" deep x 12⅝"L x 7¾"W, mid 19th C. • $4450.00 at Garth Auction, May 5-6, 1989,

Delaware, OH. The color is beautiful and rich. **$3000.00-$4600.00**

Basket, for fruit, on sideboard or dining table, delicate, lacy twisted wire, sometimes found painted dark green or very dark red, 3 ply wire pedestal base, handles, very attractive, & seen sometimes with a display of painted carved stone or cast plaster or "chalk" artificial fruit from the same period or from 1920s-30s, French or American, 14"H, 1870s-80s. • Like the wirework egg stands or baskets, meant for table use, these could be imports from France rather than the product of an American company, even if the USA had a number of good wiregoods companies. **$165.00-$200.00**

Basket, tin, woven, 10th Anniversary piece, high handle, American, 5" diameter, 19th C. • **Perhaps a Futurewatch?** — On Jan. 1, 1988, the Litchfield Auction Galleries, CT, sold the James & Nancy Clokey collection of folk art, including their extensive assemblage of 10th Anniversary tin pieces. I wish I'd been there. The *Maine Antique Digest* reporter summed up the disappointing take by saying that the Clokey's "enthusiasm never rubbed off on others." I, and everyone else who might have smidges of the Clokey's *joi*, so overestimated what the pieces would bring that I (we?) didn't bid. A square basket of woven strips of tin, with a fancy wrapped hoop handle and edges, and four sproingy loops at each corner, filled with polychromed stone fruit (which alone should have brought the price) sold for only $425, plus 10% premium. A punch decorated pudding mold sold for $900 (plus 10%), and the decoration probably accounted for most of the money. A life size Windsor chair, all made of tin, went for an astonishingly low $525 (plus 10%). A cake box, round with slanted sides, domed lid with nifty funnel finial and applied 3-D tin flowers, which *MAD* reported the Clokeys paid over $4000 for when they bought it, went for a paltry $1200 (plus 10%). I don't know what this bodes for the future of Anniversary Tin, but surely that isn't true market value.   **$175.00-$200.00**

Basket, wire, woven in form of chicken, very intricate weaving, wires are close together, painted tin trim, viz. red comb, yellow eyes, with wooden beak, carrying handle of heavier wire, prob. American, 8½"H x 12"L, 19th C. • This is not the mid 20th C chicken basket frequently seen, perfectly rounded & made from somewhat heavy wire not too close together, soldered joints. That kind should not be priced higher than $20.00 or so. This one:
$350.00-$400.00

Basket, woven splint, miniature melon, Tennessee, only 5¾" across, c.1850s.   **$300.00-$325.00**

Basket, woven splint (& reed?), large, straight-sided, colored green, blue, orange & yellow with potato stamp designs, American, 20"H x 24" diameter, 19th C.
$500.00-$700.00

Bowl, burl, deep, waxy feeling wood, 2 small checks (dryness or age cracks, naturally occuring as wood dires out), one check was filled with some kind of repair composition material, bowl slightly warped, American, 4¼"H x 11" diameter at widest part, late 18th or early 19th C.
$750.00-$900.00

Bowl, burl, heavy wood, probably maple, American, 5¼"H x 12¹⁄₁₆" diameter, early 19th C.

Burls, the abnormal protuberant wartlike growths occuring on the trunks & large limbs of trees, are usually found on hard- or semi-hardwood trees, although they can occur on all species of trees. The cause is "imperfectly understood", to use Albert Constantine, Jr.'s phrase. Speculations as to cause include injury (fire, frost, nail holes or other violent physical contact, and irritation from bacteria, fungi or viruses, says Constantine. I have heard people explain them as the effect of wasp stings; Constantine relates the belief that woodpeckers may cause burls to form. • Different writers list different trees as most probable to have burls, especially those burls valuable to wood turners or cabinetmakers. Most lists include walnut, oak, cherry, sugar maple, mahogany, myrtle a.k.a. acacia, thuja (or thuya), various types of ash, yellow poplar, olive, acacia a.k.a. mountain laurel, arbutus a.k.a. madrone burl, birch, Norway burl birch, English elm, redwood, and box. Not only did the early settlers and 19th C artisans in Europe and the United States prize the highly figured burls, especially for making bowls. American Indians used burls to make bowls, some with handles carved in figural or animalistic forms. • According to Constantine, some species of burls check and warp easily, maybe even requiring repair before using. This may explain why some burl bowls are so decidedly warped & cracked. Most burl wood can be very highly polished, sometimes without the addition of any wax or oil. • To read more about wood, and to better understand color and figure (pattern of eyes, swirls & loops) of all woods, I recommend *Know Your Woods*, by Albert Constantine, Jr., (NY: Charles Scribner's Sons, 1959; revised by Harry J. Hobbs, 1975). Constantine is a name well known to 20th C wood artisans, because the firm has supplied woods, veneers & other materials for many years. • "In the back country... cups, bowls, and trenchers were cut out of wood and served everyday table purposes. White ash knots were used for... bowls and constantly the woodworkers were grubbing around the forests for knots in old sugar maples, soft maples, ash, beech, and birch trees. A single large knot would make a whole nest of bowls. Such wood was referred to as 'dish timber'." Richardson Wright, *Hawkers & Walkers in Early-America*, 1927.

Bowl, burl, large, well-figured oval, 2 small handles are part of rim, very good patina, small crack with old repair done with metal staple or brad (when I use the term staple in this context, please do not imagine Swingline®), not signed, but known to be from Bergen County, northeastern NJ, 6½"H x 19"L x 15"W, early 19th C. • $2300.00 at Garth's Auctions, Delaware, OH, April 11-12, 1986.   **$2000.00-$2700.00**

Bowl, burl, lathe-turned bands on outside, cracks fixed with solder, American, 15" diameter, early 19th C.
$1500.00-$1800.00

Bowl, burl, lathe-turned decorative bands, American, 10¾" diameter, early 19th C.   **$600.00-$700.00**

Bowl, burl, looks like birds'-eye maple, 2 bands turned around top, American, 5¼"H x 13⅜" diameter, early 19th C.   **$700.00-$900.00**

Bowl, burl, oval shape, finely figured, old iron staple repair of short age check, American, 19"L x 15"W x 6½"H, late 18th or early 19th C.   **$2300.00-$2800.00**

Bowl, cast iron, American, unusually deep, 7" deep x 9" diameter, 19th C.   **$85.00-$125.00**

Bowl, cast iron, deep, with rounded rim and ring base, American, 9"D, 3½" deep, 18th C. • You see very few of these advertised for sale.

Bowls, cast iron, most without foot, some with ring base, slanted straight sides or slightly rounded sides, earliest have round sprue marks on bottom, later ones (late 18th, early 19th C) have straight sprue gate mark. no recorded marks known, American, varying heights from about 3" to 4¾"H, varying diameters from about 7" to 12", 18th or 19th C. • I want to buy some of these before this 3rd edition hits the bookstores! They are fabulous. One dealer in Pennsylvania labeled hers a "slave bowl." Another dealer there described one of hers as having "a ring like bell metal." Clara Jean Davis of Hopkinton, NH, has described her offerings as being nicknamed "poor man's pewter." Solely on the strength of her avid and appreciative descriptions have I acquired a taste for these heavy black perfect forms. Oooooooh!   **$75.00-$165.00**

Bowl, probably for fruit, painted turned wood, tulip on grayish old rose background, probably Lehnware, named for Joseph Lehn (also found spelled Lehne), Lititz, Manheim Township, Lancaster County, PA, 5"H, mid 19th C (Joseph Lehn lived 1798-1892, & worked c.1856-1892). • For comparison, See the entry for a turned wooden Sugar bowl made by Pease.   **$675.00-$800.00**

Bowl, turned wood, rather thick, old gray paint on outside, American, 17½" diameter, mid 19th C. • I have an idea about all the old gray paint seen on 19th C pieces: when you mix lots of colors together and add white, it is some shade of gray. Perhaps old batches of mixed paints were used up in painting utilitarian pieces. Otherwise it seems odd to pick gray, unless it was because it didn't show dirt. For modern collectors, it's a boon, as the grays seem very contemporary and cool and allow form to lead.
$250.00-$275.00

Bowls for mixing—See Mix & Beat chapter.

Box, bentwood, straight lap with copper tacks, constructed with wooden pegs, wire bail handle with wooden grip, original varnish in golden color, stamped "Weston Sherwin & Co.", Winchendon, MA, 2¾"H x 4¾" diameter, 19th C. **$550.00-$625.00**

Bread box, a sort of quonset hut, with rollup lid, painted tin with little design of long-skirted woman with parasol, painted ivory with green trim, ivory with red, or white with red, "Betsy Ross Roll-A-Way", mfd by E. M. Meder Co., c.1935. **$12.00-$20.00**

Bread box, enameled white with stencil "BREAD", American, TOC. **$30.00-$35.00**

Bread box, for restaurant, holds 4 loaves stacked on end, tin, and with baked-on white enamel, lid has knob and holde, word "BREAD" stenciled on, motto reads "The All Welded, Rigid, for strength and durability. Built like a bridge", English, provisional patent #29069/24. • The dealer had several, white, green, a white one with no stenciling. *In my now-defunct newsletter, I once published & sent out 400 + copies reading "Built like a bride." I got quite a few queries from that one. You are on your toes, I can tell. **$30.00-$50.00**

Bread box, green graniteware, late 19th C. **$75.00-$125.00**

Bread box, hinged lid, green & white enamelware, American, 19"L, c.1920s. **$85.00-$135.00**

Bucket, composition wood fiber & glue, wire & wood, bail handle, "Indurated Fibre Ware," agented by Cordley & Hayes, later called "Fibrotta", NYC, NY, 9¼"H, 1883, 1884, 1885 and 1886 patents, s.i.b. 1915. • After years of thinking Cordley & Hayes were manufacturers, I read in *The Metal Worker* that they were agents for The United Indurated Fibre Co., Lockport, NY. I don't know under what agreement the Cordley & Hayes name was the one most used on the wares. • "A good substitute for wooden pails is what is called wood-pulp ware. Pails, dishpans, wash-bowls, etc., are made of this. [It is] light; no hoops to rust or loosen, and can be kept dry and clean easily." Maria Parloa, *Kitchen Companion*, Boston: Estes & Lauriat, 1887. Other products were fruit bowls, keelers, slop jars, commode pails, spittoons, cuspidores, mats and trays. • Other fibreware companies were The Standard Fiber-Ware Co., Mankato, MN, who made a line of pails and basins, etc., of flax fiber c.1891; and Delaware Hard Fibre Co., Wilmington, DE, c.1905. The wares varied considerably, and included things to be left outside, filled with water! Anything in this somewhat vulnerable pressed wood-pulp composition, which first lost its protective varnish after long exposure to water and hot sun, and then would crack, is rather rare. • An especially odd & rare item is a deep straight sided basket with high hoop handle, the entire body being perforated. This was made in the 1890s for industrial use. They were called "dip baskets" and meant for use by brass foundries, nickel plating works, etc. They replaced stoneware baskets, because they were thought to be more durable. **$45.00-$55.00**

Bucket, coopered wood painted with diagonal smoke graining, iron bound at bottom, middle and near top, the bands daubed with paint, falling wire bail with simple wood grip with beading at each end — a subtle detail that probably translated into a few hundred $ of the total, perhaps the punctum, or telling point. Joseph Lehn, 9½"H, 19th C. • Sold by Christies East (NYC), at April

26, 1989 auction of the property of Violette de Mazia, for the low figure:. **$4800.00-$5500.00**

Bucket, emerald green & white enamelware, bail handle with wooden grip, TOC. **$165.00-$200.00**

Bucket, extraordinarily bold, handsome small wooden bucket, painted dark green, with 3 wide lapped fingers in rather high relief, 2 large arched lugs for the pegged bentwood bail, said to be Shaker, about 7"H x about 7" diameter, 19th C. • The buyer of the bucket, George Morrill, a collector and an auctioneer in Maine, said "When you find impeccable color, you just have to go for it." • The price below (no buyer's premium) is what George Morrill paid at the April 23, 1988 Mike True auction, held incidentally at Morrill's auction room at Gray, ME. **$3050.00**

Green Paint. — Cornelius Weygandt wrote in his 1944 book *The Heart of New Hampshire; Things Held Dear by Folks of the Old Stocks* (NY: Putnam's), a delightful chapter entitled "Why Woodenware is Painted Green: for Leslie Joy." He searches, wonders, and asks all around; he notes that "Most cooperage is left unpainted, fully three-quarters of it. If twenty-five percent is painted, fifteen of that ... is green, five madder red, and five a blue so light it is almost gray, a blue even lighter than the Amish blue of barns and houses in Pennsylvania Dutchland." He describes many pieces of painted "cooperage" in his collection, some "painted the characteristic dark green." One is a "spice box seven inches long, five inches broad, and three inches high. It is oval in shape and redolent of ... spices. ... Its top and bottom are pumpkin pine and the sides of both base and cap look and feel like brown ash. The sides are pegged to top and bottom. Each is one piece of thin brown ash bent around on itself and sewed together with linen thread. ... Some folks would write it down as Shaker made, but there were good artisans aplenty in the long ago outside the Shaker communities as well as within them. Its sides, rubbed in places, reveal a green much lighter in color than the characteristic dull dark green traditional for such pieces. This lighter green is, perhaps, a priming coat." Finally, Weygandt talks to a "lady of Newbury across the Connecticut in Vermont" who says "There has never been any question in the matter. Since Vermont has been Vermont it has been proper to keep white sugar in green buckets, brown sugar in red buckets and soft maple sugar in unpainted buckets." He concludes by suggesting "Though one can give no cause for it, there seems, somehow, a rightness in green for cooperage."

Bucket, for sugar, japanned tin, stenciled "SUGAR", American, 19th C. **$28.00-$35.00**

Bucket, for sugar, pine staves with wire bail, flat cover with wooden knob, 19th C or early 20th C. **$40.00-$50.00**

Bucket, for sugar storage, not to hang on a maple tree, slanted sides with fitted & turned staves, 3 decoratively painted bands, lid has rounded edge, turned bands on flat top, possibly original white porcelain mushroom knob with screw, painted with orangey salmon background, white, red, yellow, green & black leaf & vine decoration, what is now called "Lehnware", made by Joseph Lehn, Lititz, Manheim Township, Lancaster County, PA, 8½"H x 7½" diameter at top, mid 19th C. **$775.00-$900.00**

Joseph Lehn's Turned Wooden Wares. — Lita Solis-Cohen, in her *Maine Antique Digest* report on the Musselman auction of 1985, says that Lehn was a "farmer-woodworker from Hammer Creek Valley,

Elizabethtown Township, Lancaster County, ... active from 1850 to 1890." However, I can't find any Gazetteer that locates an Elizabethtown Township in Pennsylvania. Carl W. Drepperd, in an article in the May 1954 *Spinning Wheel* speaks of Lititz (or Litiz), as an "old Moravian Community", and furthermore places Joseph Lehn at a hamlet called Clay, "some four miles north of Litiz", where he made a "fairly scrumptious living as a wood turner, selling plain turned things. Then he had the idea of painting the woodenware somewhat after the manner to tinware painters of an earlier day." He also used Staffordshire wares and the "Gaudy" wares for motifs. Drepperd tells us that Lehn's special favorite, was his own design of pussy willows. Mildred T. Bohne, in the *Ohio Antique Review* (now *Antique Review*), June 1984, wrote that Lehn settled in Clay, "close to Ephrata", and that he started making barrels about 1856 to supplement his farm income, and also small turned woodenwares. She goes on to say that "his small shop was at the back of the house he built at Hammer Creek, a little south of Clay." (Notice how we keep inching south?) Spohn describes many of the forms, from buckets to small covered spice & saffron containers and trinket containers in the shape of footed goblets, and also explains that Lehn "had trouble keeping up with his decorating" and resorted to a combination of paint and decalcomania, and that he also "contracted out some decorating to William Helich, an Ephrata chairmaker, and to John Sechrist."

Butter box, pine bentwood, bentwood strap handle, iron hardware locks when box is lifted! American, 12"D, 19th C. **$100.00-$135.00**

Butter carrier, round bentwood with original old blue paint, wire bail handle, wooden grip, American, 9¾" D, TOC. **$150.00-$165.00**

Butter carrier, with cover, red painted wood, with wire bail handle, 12"D, 19th C. **$100.00-$125.00**

Butter carrier, with cover, wooden, unpainted outside, with pegged-in wooden swing handle, 6"H x 9"D. **$125.00-$150.00**

Butter crock, also called a butter pot, saltglazed stoneware with indigo blue on bluish gray, depicts Utica's characteristic bird on branch, marked "White's Utica", Utica, NY, 3 lb. size, 3rd quarter 19th C. **$250.00-$375.00**

Stoneware Investment. — The most valuable American or Canadian saltglaze stoneware dates to the late 18th or early 19th C, and has incised decorations filled in with cobalt blue or brushed with blue before the stage in the firing when the salt is thrown into the top of the kiln. These pieces are very rare. Not so rare are stoneware forms with elaborate "quill traced" cobalt decoration (liquid slip applied through the narrow opening of a quill fitted as a sort of funnel into the mouth of a "slip cup", a small, squushed-sided bottle filled with liquid slip, powdered cobalt mixed with a flux and a binder and some water, and used sort of like modern day tubes of fabric decorating fluids, by drawing with the tip of the quill, leaving a trail of blue slip. The commonest cobalt decorated wares have brushed decorations. They are distinguishable because the lines tend to be broader, softer and reveal strokes of the stiff brushes used. Birds, animals, flowers, anthropomorphized suns, moons & stars, and often humorous portraits of people are all found in all 3 types of decoration, though mainly the 2nd

& 3rd types. While collectors like crocks and jugs that have the maker's stamp impressed in the clay before firing, or marked in blue under the glaze, wonderful stoneware forms can be found that are unmarked. It is advisable to study books that offer advice, and to pick up and look at and think about stoneware that is available for sale at antique shows, auctions and flea markets, and always to ask questions. • The best book to my mind is Donald Blake Webster's *Decorated Stoneware Pottery of North America*, Rutland, VT: Charles E. Tuttle, 1971. It will be hard to find, and worth whatever you have to pay if you intend to seriously collect stoneware. **$250.00-$375.00**

Butter crock, apricot saltglazed stoneware, with original lid & wire bail handle, 9"D, late 19th C. **$175.00-$215.00**

Butter crock, blue & cream saltglazed stoneware, original lid, wire bail handle, 10½" D, late 19th C. **$65.00-$85.00**

Butter crock, blue & gray saltglazed stoneware, original lid, word "Butter" on side in blue relief, American, 4" deep x 9" diameter, late 19th or early 20th C. **$50.00-$70.00**

Butter crock, brown "Rockingham" glazed pottery, with original lid, 8½" D x 6½"H, 3rd to 4th quarter 19th C. **$60.00-$85.00**

Cake box, also called a cake tin, chromolithographed tin, round with close-fitting lid, marvelous trio of extremely collectible images: Santa Claus holding a bird toy, with a teddy bear & a Golliwog in his toy pack, border of holly leaves, one of the best ever, "Rich Iced Christmas Cake", Debus Bakeries, 3¾" diameter, c.1910s to 1920s. **$125.00-$300.00**

Cake box, for Christmas fruitcake, lithographed tin, depicts an Art Deco Santa Claus, American, 1930s. • **Added value.** — The most collectible boxes have Santa images, especially if the art is in a very pronounced style, such as Art Deco, where the image of Santa has been manipulated to fit the art style. **$25.00-$65.00**

Cake box, for Christmas fruitcake, lithographed tin, depicts cherub, American, 8" diameter, 1930s. **$25.00-$35.00**

Candle box, heavy tinned sheet iron, in cylindrical shape with hinged lid, not of common storebought style (such as the one with the shield-shaped back), American, 18"L, early to mid-19th C. • **Reproduction alert.** — A "handcrafted reproduction of box used in 1800's", made in copper (natural or burnished), plain tin, "pewter finished tin", or "raw tin for toleware painting" were all available from Craft House in Tiverton, RI. This candle box was a long cylinder with hinged, pierced lid with single hasp, 2 tabs with holes for hanging on wall, and was 13½"L x 4½" diameter. They were offered for $16.00 and $9.25 in Dec. 1973, and $20.75 and $12.00 in the Oct. 1975 editions of *Early American Life*. **$300.00-$350.00**

Candle box, japanned tin, long simple cylinder with hinged lid, 2 unusual wedge shaped, high hanging pieces, with large holes, near both ends, American, 13¾"L, 19th C. **$325.00-$400.00**

Candy box, heart shaped cardboard, top is chromolith of exuberant roses in turquoise vase, gilt paper on edges, box maker unknown, contained Schrafft's candy, Boston & NYC, 2 lb box, 13" across x 1" deep, 1940s. **$15.00-$22.00**

Candy boxes, cardboard, some covered in printed or colored paper (desirable motifs include "pretty ladies" & certain animals like cats, pigs, bunnies), some have satin or other cloth or paper ribbons, some are shaped (hearts probably best), some with paper-hinged lids, some retain-

ing paper lace flaps inside, various candy makers, but not all have a name & were possibly identified with paste-on paper label, American, German, English, French, Swiss. Sizes from miniatures (like little Whitman Sampler® boxes) to large 10 lb. chocolate boxes, late 19th C to 1950s.
• **Futurewatch**. — As far as I know, there is little collector activity in this field, but it may be one of the most attractive collecting fields. Some of us may have candy box collections without realizing it because old candy boxes have been used as the perfect containers for trinkets, buttons, pencils, greeting cards, etc., and have often been just too good to throw away. Candy box manufacturers' catalogs and old candy advertisements would round out a collection. Price range for boxes only. **$3.00-$45.00**

Candy bucket, miniature turned wooden bucket with flat lid, bound with wire, with wire bail handle, originally filled with maple sugar hearts, "Sap Bucket", Maple Grove Candies, Inc., St. Johnsbury, VT, 21 oz. capacity, c.1930. **$10.00-$14.00**

Canister, embossed stamped tin with stylized overall chrysanthemums in *Japonisme* style, truncated conical top with close-fitting lid, japanned in bronze color, American, 6¼"H, 19th C. **$18.00-$25.00**

Japonisme. — This French word describes a style of decorative arts (or the decoration on useful objects) that show the direct influence of various arts of Japan, as well as China and the rest of the exotic Orient. "Japanese" motifs such as chrysanthemums, butterflies, fans, parasols, & bamboo, are found on Japanese screens, kimono cloth, inlaid metalwork, and other domestic goods; the same motifs can be export to Europe and the U.S. since the mid 19th century. These imports were further westernized & interpreted (diluted or exaggerated) by Western artisans who used them as models for making goods for their consumers. *Japonisme* as a movement is usually dated from the 1870s to 1890s, although some people push up the tail end of it as far as WWI; a design movement with some similarities is "The Eastlake Style", named for aesthetician Charles Eastlake, whose influential theories about good design and applied decoration were widely subscribed to. Both correspond somewhat in period & inspiration to the flowering of Art Nouveau. •
Activating the "Japanese Movement" — Nineteenth century American interest in Japanese-like decorative motifs actually began with Commodore Perry's 1850's voyages to Japan, which were meant to open trade with Japan. This interest became a very popular fashion in the 70s, long before Gilbert & Sullivan wrote *The Mikado* (which was first seen, in London, in 1885); the musical only fanned the flames. The Centennial Exhibition in 1876 also added to the interest in the Japanese style. • By 1890, such a huge manufacturer as Manning-Bowman satisfied popular demand for the look with a large selection of enamelware designs influenced by Japanese motifs; at about the same time, David Block, a New York manufacturer of stamped tin housewares, sold "Chinese Pattern Embossed Goods", which were Western forms the surfaces of which were covered with a dense Westernized hodgepodge of Oriental motifs. Many late Victorian artisans in all fields adopted the coloration of *Japonisme*, especially vivid colors against dark backgrounds. Examples are seen in black velvet crazy quilts & chromolithographic commercial arts such as trade cards or greeting cards. By WWI, the

"Movement" was over, having been supplanted by the Arts & Crafts Movement, and early stirrings of Art Deco.
• **Japanning Is Something Different.** — Japanning is much older than *Japonisme*, and it is another thing entirely, though much of it is characterized by vivid coloring against a dark background. By the early 1600s, imported Chinese Coromandel screens & lacquered furniture were known in the West, including Britain, where some of the finest early japanning was done. Many of these Oriental wares had dark (black or brown) or "Chinese" red backgrounds, with decorative motifs in color & gold or bronze, plus inlays of colored stone or mother of pearl. Imitation "Japan" finishes were applied to papier mache & wooden furniture & trays, as well as sheet metal coal vases, trays, coffee urns, etc. In the 18th century, fashionable ladies in England and America (and probably in Europe) took up japanning — that is, "the Art of covering bodies by grounds of opake colours in varnish, which may be either afterwards decorated by painting or gilding, or left plain...", according to Robert Dossie, in *Handmaid to the Arts*, published in 1758. Ground (background) colors were browns, reds, maroons & blues. • By the mid 19th C, the term "japanning" mostly meant semi-translucent, heat-resistant lacquers on tin, like most pieces in this book. Oxidized tinted linseed oil or baked-on asphaltum (a sort of petroleum) were used. Dark maroon-y brown is commonest color.
• **Chinoiserie or de Chine.** — These are French terms used in the decorative arts to describe Western decorative motifs considered or supposed to be typical of, or related to, Chinese arts. Western artisans and artists got inspiration from Chinese porcelains (some of which were made by Chinese potters in designs and with decorations, ordered by Western importers (especially those in Holland). Jewelry, clothing, screens, scrolls, paintings, rugs, and other works were admired and imitated by the Western world for several centuries. • For the most part, the *Chinoiserie* motifs are only "supposed" — that is, they are often not authentic, but are based on exotic decorations taken more from European engravings in travel books about China than from real Chinese arts. The term is related to *Japonisme* (See that under a Canister entry in this chapter). • In applied decorations, there are many Chinese and Japanese motifs common in name, if not completely in appearance. They included depictions of Nature and of manmade objects; among the motifs are and forth, as well as the cross cultural influences between China and Japan and the rest of the "Orient" (including India) is common to both decorative movements — *Japonisme and Chinoiserie*. (Western furniture, on the whole, is a more direct borrowing, and shows the close influence of intrinsic aspects of Chinese furniture and decorative arts. The purer design of furniture is easily contrasted to the superficial, apply-it-to-anything borrowing from Oriental arts, used for surface patterns and ornament. Thomas Chippendale, an English cabinetmaker and furniture designer, whose book of designs, *The Director*, was published first in 1754, made chairs, tables, etc., copied from Chinese models, furniture which came to be called "Chinese Chippendale", as opposed to other of his borrowed styles.)

Canister or pantry set, 10 emerald green glass jars, slanted ribs, rectangular, metal screw-on lids, name labels for Cereal, Flour, Sugar, etc., mfd by Owens Illinois Glass Co., Toledo, OH, c.1920s or very early 1930s. • A Greenie's Dream Set !   **$200.00-$250.00**

Canister set, also called a cereal set, decorated earthenware, sort of ovoid rectangles, domed lids with huge hand grips, glazed with light cream background with a sort of happy go lucky plaid effect in blue and black in horizontal band near tops, entire set has 15 pieces, often you find just the big 6, marked on the fronts: "Tea, Coffee, Sugar, Rice, Barley, Farina", or maybe 7, with the "Salt" box with hinged wooden lid. Jug-like cruets are marked "Vinegar" and "Oil". Six half-size smalls are for spices: "Ginger, Cloves, Nutmeg, Cinnamon, Allspice, Pepper". imported from Czechoslovakia, early 1920s.
$125.00-$150.00

Chamberstick, white enameled stamped steel, blue edge, saucer base with small ring handle, short candleholder with wide flared flat rim, marked underneath with a medallion with balance scales, "KJAB", the "Scale Brand" mfd by the Kockum Enamel Works, imported by Markt & Co. of NYC, made in Sweden, 6¼" diameter, TOC. Kockum factory (established in 1859, and also maker of "Flag Brand" wares) is as high as 20,000 vessels." *House Furnishing Review*, Feb. 1907.   **$60.00-$80.00**

•"When the vessels in the stamping works are of the right shape they are sent to the magnificent enameling department. It is here that the ware receives its ornamental, porcelainous (sic) appearance. The various utensils are first placed on large carriages and run into the enormous ovens, in which process a quantity of oil and other matter is thrown off. They emerge from this heat black and ugly, and are then dipped into tubs of stain and are afterward boiled and washed quite clean. They are now ready to receive their first coating of enamel, and afterward to be enameled white or blue. In order to receive the first coating the vessels are dipped in a thick, creamy enamel paste, but this first coating however, must be burned in, and for this purpose, after being thoroughly dried, they are placed on iron cars and run into red-hot ovens, in which they remain from eight to ten minutes.

"The wares are then once more placed in the enamel to obtain the outer coating; the edges of white wares are coated blue, the handles of water cans, etc., are coated and all the other articles are given their proper appearance. By a most ingenious method the so-called granite effect is obtained in the coating. This is brought about by the vessel being dipped in enamel, the specific gravity of which is different, so that when the vessel is lifted out the enamel runs off, gets hard and certain attractive markings appear. When the vessels have been fully enameled they are once more burned, this time becoming quite hard and glossy. They are then assorted and sent to the warehouse. The daily output from the Kockum factory (established in 1859, and also maker of "Flag Brand" wares) is as high as 20,000 vessels." *House Furnishing Review*, Feb. 1907.   **$20.00-$28.00**

Cheese baskets—See Mold chapter.

Cheese cradle, tole with birds & flowers in ochre, white, gray, made to hold a small "wheel" of cheese, or part thereof. Sort of like an upside down old car fender, with footed base, New England, 14" x 6"W, c.1840s.
$250.00-$325.00

Collapsible cup, also called a <u>collapsion cup,</u> divided into telescoping sections of nickel plated brass, engraved with scrolls, 5 telescoping bands, marked on top in fancy script "Vest Pocket Cup," Scovill Mfg. Co., Waterbury, CT, pat'd Feb. 23, 1897.   **$15.00-$20.00**

Collapsible cup, metal with depiction of couple on tandem bike, these are also called <u>cyclist cups</u>, American, late 19th or early 20th C. • **Why Go Thirsty?** — Michigan laws forbid the use of public drinking cups. Probably you have noticed that when traveling, and made pointed remarks about the lawmakers, which didn't relieve your thirst in the least. No one need go dry. An aluminum collapsible drinking cup that will slip into a handbag, a traveling bag, or a coat pocket, solves the thirst problem, and enables the possessor to laugh at the laws. We can furnish these cups in any desired quantity at figures that will net you a comfortable profit." *Hardware News*, published monthly by Buhl Sons Co., Detroit, MI, April 1912.   **$35.00-$50.00**

Collapsible cup, nickel plated Britannia, 3 narrow & one wide telescoping band, footed base like a wine goblet, engraved, Meriden Britannia Co., Meriden, CT, 1886-87.
$20.00-$30.00

Collapsible cup, nickel plated metal in heavy leather fitted case, cup has little fold-out wire handles, no lid but presumably case was its protection, marked with "R" within a tiny keystone mark, probably C. F. Rumpp & Co., Philadelphia, PA, late 19th or early 20th C.
$13.00-$18.00

Collapsible cup, nickeled brass, pat'd by John Lines, mfd by Scovill Mfg. Co., Waterbury, CT, pat'd Feb. 23, 1897.
$15.00-$20.00

Collapsible cup, nickeled brass, very small — good for one shot, embossed flowers & scrolls on cover, American, only 1"H, perhaps a traveling medicine cup? pat'd Dec. 23, 1896.   **$25.00-$30.00**

Collapsible cup, satin finished nickel plated Britannia, 3 telescoping bands, side cup handle, snug lid, decorated with applied stamped flowers, called "Collapsion Cups" by mfr, Meriden Britannia Co., Meriden, CT, late 1880s to 1890s.   **$15.00-$20.00**

Collapsible cup, tin, 3 telescoping bands, engraved lid, name "Clement" engraved on lid, which could be owner, late 19th C. • There was a Clement Mfg. Co. that made cutlery, etc., in Northampton, MA.   **$17.00-$22.00**

Comb pocket, wall hung, heavy embossed brass, with flowers, scrolls & sentiment "Remember Me," arched top with 2 holes for hanging, American, 13"L, 19th C. • Nice to think of this as a love gift, given by a person courting a cook or a maid!   **$125.00-$150.00**

Cookie jar, ceramic boy's head, Cardinal Pottery Co., mid 20th C.   **$20.00-$35.00**

American Ceramic Cookie Jar Makers. — There have been many companies making these containers over the last 50 years or so. They include: Abingdon Pottery Co., American Bisque Co., American Pottery Co., Art Pottery Co., Brush Pottery, Brush McCoy, California Originals, Cardinal, Doran, Fredericksburg Art Pottery Co., Gilner Pottery, Hall China Co., Layne Co., Ludowici Celadon Co., Mar-crest, Marcia of California, McCoy Pottery Co., Metlox, Morton, Nelson McCoy, Pan American, Pearl China Co., Pottery Guild, Purinton-Esmond, Red Wing, Regal China, Robinson Ransbottom, Shawnee, Sierra Vista, Stanfordware, Twin Winton, and Vantellingen.

Cookie jar, ceramic Mickey & Minnie turnabout, licensed by Disney, marked "The Leeds Co", distributer, Chicago, IL, 1940s. • **Too Pooped to Pop.** — Anyone who expects to find the prices for the Andy Warhol cookie jars sold at auction in 1988 will be disappointed here. Those outrageous prices do not signal anything except that even Andy Warhol's cookie jars had their 15 minutes of fame. **$75.00-$90.00**

Cookie jar, ceramic Mickey Mouse on a drum, Disney licensed this; possibly to Ludowici Celadon Co., Chicago, IL, 20th C. • Really a Mickey Mouse collectible. **$75.00-$90.00**

Creamer, injection molded plastic, Black Americana "Mammy", red dress, white painted apron, teeth & kerchief, black painted face, head & top of kerchief is hinged lift-off lid, some paint missing, "F & F Mold & Die Works", Dayton, OH, 6½"H, c.1930s. **$40.00-$50.00**

Creamer, injection molded plastic in 2 parts, Black Americana Aunt Jemima "Mammy", painted face, white painted teeth, paper glued on for apron, hinged lid with thumb piece, head & part of kerchief lift off, marked "F & F Mold & Die Works", 5⅜"H, c.1940s. **$25.00-$35.00**

Crock, saltglazed stoneware, 2 applied ear handles, flat rim with slight lip, pale ochre or tan glaze with black and cobalt blue decoration, of bosomy bustle-y young woman, from knees up, walking small black dog, who has just made his contribution to the footpath, with large very pretty script remark, "Oh my?" (question mark rather than exclamation mark), a wonderful example of humor, though of course a strange subject for a food crock, although possibly this was for vegetable scraps bound for the compost heap, also stamped "J. B. Pfaltzgraff & Co.", with place, York, PA, 7¼"H x 8" diameter, last quarter 19th C, prob. late 1880s. • Robacker May 1989 price. Here you don't have to know that Pfaltzgraff is a Big Name to Collectors (began as Pfaltzgraff Pottery c.1840 (?) and still in business too); it's the humorous figures that brought most of the money. **$19,000.00**

Crock, saltglazed stoneware, blue quill-traced, very calligraphic decoration of bird, Millers, Boston, MA, 3 gal. capacity, mid to 3rd quarter 19th C (?). **$500.00-$550.00**

Crock, saltglazed stoneware, leaf decoration, one of several makers in this stoneware town, Lyons, NY, 1 gal. size, late 19th C. • **"Apples, in small quantities, may be preserved** by the following. First, completely dry a glazed jar, then put a few pebbles at the bottom, fill it with Apples, and cover it with a piece of wood exactly fitted, and fill up the interstices with a little fresh mortar. The pebbles attract the moisture of the apples, while the mortar excludes the air from the jar and secures the fruit from pressure." Anthony Florian Madinzer Willich, *The Domestic Encyclopedia; or A Dictionary of Facts & Useful Knowledge...*, 1st American edition, Philadelphia: W. Y. Birch & A. Small, 1803-04. **$100.00-$125.00**

Crock, saltglazed stoneware with 2 flowers in blue, marked J. Fisher & Co., (Jacob Fisher), Lyons, NY, 3 gal. capacity, late 19th C. **$160.00-$185.00**

Crock, stoneware, gray with blue band ⅝ of way down side, with legend, "WESSON OIL — For making good things to eat." 5½"H x 4¼" diameter, 20th C. **$75.00-$85.00**

Cutlery tray, also called a knife box or cutlery box, this one a bentwood oval with copper nails, straight lapped, original (?) light green paint, bent nail or wire hinges for the 2 center-hinged lids, 3-arch centerboard has handhold cutout, possibly Shaker, 2⅞"H handle, body is 3"H x 12¾"L, c.1870s (?). **$185.00-$200.00**

Cutlery tray, bentwood with border decoration of cutout holes, bottom edge cut so as to form 4 feet in middle of sides, turned wood "curtain rod" grip handle, lapped ends fastened with nails and turned balls of wood, green baize lining of both compartments, highly decorative, American (?), 4¼"H at center x 11"L x 7¼"W, 19th C. **$65.00-$80.00**

Cutlery tray, bentwood with turned wooden handle on centerboard, probably Shaker, 4¾"H at handle, 13"L, late 19th C. **$95.00-$135.00**

Cutlery tray, natural finish wood, slightly canted sides, nice cutout central handle, American, 1⅞"H (3¾"H at centerboard) x 12"L x 7¾"W, 19th C. • Cutlery trays (also called knife boxes, knife & fork trays, cutlery trays, flatware trays, knife carriers, silverware trays or spoon boxes) from the 19th & early 20th C all seem to be divided into only two compartments. Rarely can an old one be found with three sections, though the 20th C plastic or wooden cutlery trays we keep in our kitchen drawers often have 4, sometimes 5 or 6 sections. Certainly knives, forks and spoons were all in wide use during the 18th and 19th Cs. In the 17th C, forks were rare, considered devil's tools, but I don't know of a 17th C cutlery tray anyway. • Another item entirely is the lidded knife box that holds knives (sometimes also spoons & forks) upright in separate padded slots, often very fancy, with inlaid woods, sometimes with a slant front lid, sometimes in an urn shape with the lid fitted on a rod so that it pulls up out of the way for removing a knife. This type of knife box or knife urn from the 18th C, was made in pairs & kept in the dining room on the sideboard or serving table. **$35.00-$45.00**

Cutlery tray, oak with red paint, American, early 20th C. **$20.00-$25.00**

Cutlery tray, painted pine with imitation graining, very fanciful with knots & extreme grain pattern, what is called "folk art," American, 19th C. • **Caveat:** Folk art is a catch-all term meant to describe a certain naivete in vision or execution, and it's sometimes used to lend distinction (and extra $$) to things better or more accurately described as "handmade" or "crude" or "old magazine craft project style." Folk art is the exceptional not the ordinary artwork of "folk"; the emphasis is on art. It is practically impossible to come up with an all-purpose definition. You must develop your own taste and eye for it; conjure up a vision of all the handmade objects you have (or have seen) which were made by people who considered themselves craftsmen or artists but whose work doesn't fall into the mainstream of academic art of the period in which they worked. Then sift out what you believe to be the very best examples—the pieces that are definably art, which have something about them you may not be able to describe in words. You probably have a few pieces that qualify as folk art. The secret is to refine your own taste even if you can't define it out loud. When someone else, like me, tells you it's folk art, never take our word for granted. Start at beginning & figure out why. **$125.00-$150.00**

Cutlery tray, walnut with slanted sides carved into "tiles" or quilted squares, rope-carved grip on centerboard, American, 5"H at handle x 10"L x 5½"W, 19th C. **$90.00-$110.00**

Cutlery tray, with fairly unusual 3 sections, dovetailed walnut, with original brass handle (perhaps "borrowed" from drawer hardware), American, 19th C. **$85.00-$100.00**

Dinner pail, tin, 4 stacking compartments that set down into each other, high wire rack handle, from F. A. Walker catalog, c.1890s. • "The tin pail is a badge of work, generally honest work, always productive work, and work is the root of all that we have. We, the people, the rich, the society people, the literary people, the talkers and writers who make so much fuss in type and pretend to rule — or ruin — the world, all depend on the workers who are represented in force in 'the tin pail brigade.' " *The Metal Worker*, Sept. 2, 1882. **$25.00-$35.00**

Dish cover or fly screens, called fly walks by the Shakers. Wire screening, stamped into dome shape, with narrow japanned tin frame & disc for black-painted turned wood knob, made in rounds or ovals, to fit plates, dishes, pans, etc., Japanning was red, green, blue or asphaltum brown, perhaps other colors I've not seen, Matthai-Ingram was one manufacturer, American, Matthai-Ingram's nested sets all about 5"-7"H; ovals 8" to 18"L ; 6" to 14"D rounds, c.1870s to 1910s. • Other manufacturers of the period were: Bromwell; Gibbert & Bennett; Frederick J. Myers; Joseph Scheider; W. H. Sweeney; Wickwire Brothers. All the products probably were very similar. These have gone up incredibly in price. Range covers most asking prices: **$20.00-$65.00**

Firkin, tapered sides, bail handle, for liquids, 12"H, 19th C. • "A firkin is an English liquid measure which is the 4th part of a barrel, and containing 8 gallons of ale, soap or herrings, and 9 gallons of beer. Two firkins make a kilderkin (18 gallons)." Anthony Florian Madinzer Willich, *The Domestic Encyclopedia; or A Dictionary of Facts & Useful Knowledge...*, 1st American edition, Philadelphia: W. Y. Birch & A. Small, 1803-04. • A **firkin** is also a cask that measures one fourth of a barrel, from the diminutive of the Dutch *vierdel*, meaning "a fourth part", and is kin to our own word fourth. **$80.00-$90.00**

Firkin, wood, painted mocha, finger-lapped, American, 9½"H, 19th C. • **History in Small Things.** — "I embrace the common, I explore and sit at the feet of the familiar, the low. Give me insight into today, and you may have the antique and future worlds. What would we really know the meaning of? The meal in the firkin; the milk in the pan; the ballad in the street; the news of the boat; the glance of the eye; the form and the gait of the body." Ralph Waldo Emerson, "American Scholar", 1837. **$60.00-$75.00**

Firkin, wood with dark green paint, finger-lapped construction, probably for liquids, American, 12"H, 19th C. **$50.00-$60.00**

Firkin, wooden staves, painted putty color, 4 wood bands with copper fasteners, wooden bail handle, made by cooper, probably Shaker manufacture, American, 9½"H x 9½" D, 19th C. **$230.00-$250.00**

Ginger beer bottle, or pop bottle, grayish tan stoneware with blue glaze inside intaglio name stamp, "W. Pendleton, Jr. POP", 10½"H, 19th C. **$55.00-$75.00**

Ginger beer bottles, tan saltglazed stoneware, banded in ochre (usually top half is ochre), thick flat mouth, rather roughly finished. Used for holding explosive homemade drinks that built up pressure and needed to have the corks tied down. The overhanging lip serves to anchor the string or twine. These bottles are a common type often seen at flea markets. American, English, about 7" to 9"H, 19th C. **$7.00-$12.00**

• **"Ginger Beer (superior).** — To six quarts of water add one ounce of cream of tartar, and two ounces of white Jamaica ginger; boil it ten minutes. Strain it; add to the liquor a pound of loaf sugar. Put it on the fire; let it simmer until the sugar is dissolved. Pour into an earthen vessel, into which has been put two ounces of tartaric acid and the rind of one lemon. When lukewarm, add half a tumbler of strong hop yeast. Stir all well together, and bottle; tie down the corks tightly. Use in a few days." Mrs. A. P. Hill, *Mrs. Hill's New Family Receipt Book*, NY: 1870. • **"Imperial Pop.** — Three ounces of cream of tartar, an ounce of bruised ginger, a pound and a half of loaf sugar, half a tumbler of lemon juice, a gallon and a half of water, a wineglass of yeast. Shake well together; bottle, and cork well." (ibid.) • **Ginger Beer.** — Boil together four gallons of water, one pint of hops, twenty races of ginger, beaten. Boil briskly half an hour; keep the vessel covered; strain; sweeten with good molasses. When tepid, add a pint of brisk yeast. Cover it closely with a thick cloth until morning; then bottle, and cork tight. Scald the corks, and drive them in, and tie down with twine. Keep in a cool place. It will be ready for use the third day. Less yeast may be used if the taste is not liked." *Ibid.* **$7.00-$12.00**

Implement rack, wood, scrolled crested top, forged iron hooks, prob. not American, a bit too ornate along top, 24½"W, early 19th C, perhaps late 18th C. **$150.00-$175.00**

Implement rack, wooden framed round plate-like wall hung piece with round Delft tile in center, wooden piece at bottom has 6 holes for handles of tools, including skimmer, ladle, spoons, etc., German, c.1904. • What is broadly referred to as Delft ware, is named for the protypical blue and white, tin-glazed earthenware, sometimes called *faience,* which originated in the Netherlands. This type of ceramic ware was made from the early 18th C on in Lambeth, England and Liverpool, England, and also in Dublin, Ireland. The word faience is a French word referring to the Italian pottery center, Faenza. **$65.00-$85.00**

Implement racks—See also Utility racks.

Jar, earthenware, glazed with a reddish brown, cream body clay, charmingly marked in nice big letters on side "PLUMBS" (sic), English, 5¼"H, mid 19th C. **$120.00-$150.00**

certain flowers, birds, fans, kimonos or robes, stools, bamboo shoots, etc. One marked difference is that Chinese arts have more motifs which appear geometric or abstract, although Japanese arts may have more even, allover patterns. • Cross pollination, ie. the influence upon Oriental art by Western arts, and vice versa, back

Jug, gray saltglazed stoneware with cobalt scrolling & leaves, "New York Stoneware Co.," Ft. Edward, NY, 2 gal. capacity, c. 3rd quarter 19th C. • Added value. — A hand carved wood jug stopper can be worth more than the jug itself, if it's good folk art and figural. Some to hope for are a black man's head, a dog's, a cat's or mule's head, or a coiled snake (perhaps made from a root). Doris Axtell, dealer in Deposit, NY, advertised one in may 1989 that sounds great: "carved wooden hand & wrist jug stopper, old natural patina, well-defined sculpture, 7¼"L overall." She had it at $750.00, and if you had the right jug (as sculpture base), you'd really have something. It is exceptionally large. **$165.00-$190.00**

Jug, gray saltglazed stoneware with quill-traced cobalt eagle with shield body, NY, 2 gal. capacity, 19th C. • **"How to make Perpetual Yest.** — Take a pound of fine flour, make it the thickness of gruel with boiling water, add to it half a pound of loaf sugar, mix them well together, put three spoonfuls of well purified yest (sic) in a large vessel, upon

Jug, saltglazed stoneware, applied handle at neck, 2 peg-like projections on either side, halfway down body, that fit into cast iron swing frame, so that the jug can be tipped to pour without picking it up, rather like modern whisky-pouring bottles in frames, "Brackett's Revolving Jug", American, c.1880s (?). • Sold at auction by Sanders Auctioneers & Appraisers, Wilton, NH. **$350.00-$400.00**

Keeler, staved wood, with 2 handles, low sided tub for cooling liquids, American, 5½"H x 12½" D, very early 19th C. • **German vocabulary** — Zuber: tub; and Kleine Zuber: small tub. **$165.00-$200.00**

Knife box—See Cutlery tray.

Lard jar, gray saltglazed stoneware with funnel top, American, ½ gal. capacity, 19th C. • **"Miss Matilda's Ginger Cakes.** — Three quarts of flour, one teacup of lard, one quart of molasses, one tablespoonful of soda beat into the molasses, half a teacup of sour milk, the same of water, and three tablespoonfuls of ginger. Roll half an inch thick; cut in any shape, and brush over with the white of an egg." Mrs. A. P. Hill, *Mrs. Hill's New Family Receipt Book*, NY: 1870. **$45.00-$55.00**

Lunch box, called a *tine*, medium-colored wood, bentwood strap handle on lid, design of rosettes & geometric florals, plus hearts is burned in, Norwegian, 4½"H exclusive of hoop handle, 19th C. • Norwegian *tines* came in various shapes, from slightly oval to very oval, to round and rectangular. Most were decorated with a hot poker in stylized designs. Some were colored. Some were painted then carved through to the light wood underneath.
$160.00-$180.00

Lunch or dinner pail, tin, with wire bail handle, 2 compartments, plus lid is a flask for hot coffee (or tea), the opening is capped with a tin mug, "cup-top kettle", American, late 19th C. **$25.00-$35.00**
    Dinner Pails. — In the 1850s & 60s, "the dinner pail was a simple two-quart tin pail, with a cover. The food was packed in it as well as the space would permit and the skill of the housewife allow. And sometimes it was a queer mess when lunch time came around. The bread-and-butter slices at the bottom of the pail, and the corned-beef sandwich that made the next layer, were saturated with the juices of the applie pie and mince pie on the top, which had gradually settled and become compressed by the joltings of carrying, and the entire dinner tasted of a conglomeration of flavors that only exactive hunger could render palatable. No provision was made in this miscalled dinner pail for the reception of drink or the carrying of a knife and fork and spoon. If these were carried, they were bestowed in pockets in the clothes, as was also fruit, or else were made up into a separate parcel.
    "The first true dinner pail came years after this makeshift had proved inadequate. It was a pail with removable compartments — or at least one removable receptacle. About half way from top to bottom was a projection to redeive a cup fitting the interior of the pail, the cup to hold coffee or tea, while the lower space received

the solid food. On top of the cover was a cylindrical ring that was a receptacle for salt, or salt and pepper in desirable proportions, and this ring was covered with a half-gill cup, with handle, into which the coffee or the tea might be poured. Subsequently were added a plain disk or diaphragm of sheet tin to separate the bread from the pie, or the dry from the moist..., and on the outside of the pail were fixed tin straps that served as sheaths to a fork, spoon and knife.
    "But a still more important advance has been made....If one will take a run west of New York to Paterson, NJ, and beyond, and can spend time at prominent railroad centers, or the mining regions of Pennsylvania, he will observe workmen departing in the morning carrying a tin trunk of considerable size. With some curiosity he will inquire what these peddlers are vending, and will be told that these tin trunks contain rations for one and sometimes two days. These trunks are arranged for hungry men. They are divided into partitions, each with its cover, and each cover nearly air-tight. At one end is the removable receptacle for drink." *The Metal Worker* Sept. 2, 1882.

Match holder, wall hung, crimped tin resembling pair of scallop shells under cylindrical pockets for matches, striking surface below, originally japanned or painted, often found in sort of salmon color; one sold by big catalog house, Butler Brothers, at the turn-of-the-century, had a crested stamped backplate with striking panel between 2 pockets with a scalloped top, and scallop shells underneath. It was called the "Twin", and came in assorted colors of "enameled" tin. Another type had the 2 shell decorated open pockets, mounted to a back plate of brass-finished tin, which I think was probably a transparent yellow japan or varnish. This one, pat'd in 1859, is the most valuable of this style. American, 4½"H x 7"W, another is 4"H x 8"W, c.1860s-1910. The fairly common scallop shell match pockets are a *de riguer* classic for kitchenarians, often unrealistically priced $100.00 or more.
    $30.00-$60.00

    "The History of Matches. — The 50th anniversary of the invention of matches by three Austrians was recently celebrated in Vienna. The inventor of the lucifer match lives in every country under the sun, so Austria will do as well as another. Fifty years ago, in England, matches had only reached the stage known as 'lucifers', and were clumsy and inconvenient. Fox, Burke & Dr. Johnson used to light their candles with flint & steel, though practice probably made them more skillful than we would be at such an operation. About the beginning of the century long brimstone matches took the place of tinder. About 6 inches long, tipped with sulphur, they caught fire easily from the spark of a flint. In 1825 an apparatus called the 'eupyrion' was used in most cities. This was a large-mouthed bottle containing sulphuric acid, soaked in fibrous asbestos, and the matches, about 2 inches long, were tipped with a chemical combination, of which chlorate of potash was the principle ingredient. When the match's end was dipped in the acid & rapidly withdrawn, fire was produced, but the acid was inconvenient, the matches easily spoiled by damp. Next came the 'pyrophoros', pneumatic tinder-box, and Doberlenier's hydrogen lamp. In 1832 the first friction match was made. It was jokingly called a lucifer. Lucifers were substantially the same as present matches, pulled through a piece of sandpaper. Since then, it has been altered from a silent to a noisy match, and the safety fuse, which ignites only when rubbed upon chemically-treated paper. This safety match was patented in England in 1856.'' *The Metal Worker,* Nov. 4, 1882. • The **first American friction matches,** or lucifers, were made by Daniel Chapin & Alonzo Dwight Phillips of Massachusetts. Phillips received a patent on phosphorous friction matches on Oct. 24, 1836. Their nickname was apt: the head was coated with a composition of powdered chalk, phosphorous, brimstone & glue. • **Boon or bonfire** — The friction match saved trouble except when two of them accidentally rubbed together and caught on fire. Safety matches, which required a special striking surface, meant that open-top match holders (as differentiated from match safes) could be considered safe.

Match holder, wall hung, cut out wooden cat, green with black trim, metal furniture leg skids for eyes, American, 20th C. **$18.00-$25.00**

Match holder, wall hung, iron finished in brass color, 19th C. **$35.00-$45.00**

Match holder, wall hung metal, depicting Abe Lincoln, an axe, tree & goat — sounds like they mixed metaphors! ''Kindling Wood,'' on a barrel, 5¼'' x 4¾ '', TOC. **$50.00-$75.00**

Match holder, wall hung, redware, decorated with cream & green acorns & leaves around border of pocket, very unusual, American, 6¾'' D, 19th C. **$135.00-$150.00**

Match safe, blue japanned tin with golden pinstriping, American (?), 3'' x 4'', 19th C. • A match safe is a match holder with a lid, especially a self-closing one. **$55.00-$65.00**

Match safe, cast iron, ''Self Closing,'' mfd by D. M. & Co., New Haven, CT, 19th C. **$35.00-$45.00**

Milk pan, redware with brown glaze, relatively shallow compared to diameter, slanted sides, American, 16½'' diameter, 19th C. **$165.00-$200.00**

• **Earthenware vs. Stoneware.** — ''Before the glorious Revolution ... here and there were scattered Potteries of Earthen-ware, infamously bad and unwholesome, from their being partially glazed with a thin, cheap washing of Lead. The best of Lead-glazing is esteemed unwholesome, by observing people. The Mischievous effects of it, fall chiefly on the country people and the poor everywhere. Even when it is firm enough so as not to scale off, it is yet imperceptably eaten away by every acid matter: and mixing with the drinks and meats of the people becomes a slow but sure poison.

''It is wished the Legislature would consider of means for discountenancing the use of Lead in glazing Earthenware, and encourage the application of the most perfect and wholesome glazing, produced only from Sand and Salts....A small bounty, or exemption, on this might be sufficient to the end. But, what if public encouragement was to be given on homemade Stone-ware, rather than on Earthen-ware? In Stoneware, Lead is never used; no other glazing need be used for stone than what is produced by a little common salt strewed over the ware, which operates as a flux to the particles of sand that stick on the sides of the Ware, whilst it is in the furnace.

''Stoneware is now scarce and dear amongst us, as the housewife knows. This is owing to its great bulk and low value, that scarcely affords to pay the freight.'' *Pennsylvania Mercury,* Feb. 4, 1785.

Napkin rings. — Made of many materials, viz. carved wood, molded plastic, woven straw, but most spectacularly, Victorian silverplate, especially figural ones, little sculpturinos with animals and/or people cleverly disporting themselves on a platform (sometimes wheeled), including a cylindrical holder for the cloth napkin. This is a highly specialized field, especially the silverplated figurals, which I will not attempt to include in this book. Look for Dorothy Rainwater's books on silver & silverplate, some published by Schiffer, and Victor Schnadig's *American Victorian Figural Napkin Rings,* Wallace - Homestead, 1971, out of print. American, European, Oriental, c.1850s (?) through present time. • ''Napkins are never supposed to appear a second time before washing, hence napkin rings are domestic secrets and not for company.'' Todd S. Goodman, *Domestic Cyclopedia of Practical Information,*NY: Henry Holt, 1877. **25¢-$500.00**

Newspaper rack, not for a newstand like I always thought, but for the man who buries his face in the paper at table. ''Keeps the daily news out of the breakfast butter. So good-looking that even wives like it. In English bronze, or brass and copper'' reads the ad. A tabletop easel of wire, with a cutout silhouette of a cock, & word ''NEWS'', Chase Brass & Copper Co., Waterbury, CT, mid 1930s. **$35.00-$50.00**

Pail or bucket, enamelware, flared sides with flared ring foot, wire bail with wooden grip, tiny ring ears for bail, white enamel inside, white with cobalt chicken wire pattern on outside, European, 13''H x 10½'' diameter, TOC, perhaps back to 1880s or 90s. **$125.00-$165.00**

Pails—See also Buckets.

Pantry box, bentwood painted robin's egg blue, 2 finger laps, 5½''L oval, 19th C. **$100.00-$125.00**

Pantry box, bentwood, deep green paint, 3 finger laps, 1 finger lap lid, 7'' diameter, 19th C. • Price is all those finger laps. **$500.00-$600.00**

Pickle bottles, mold blown green or aquamarine glass, all with collared mouths, molded in the Gothic arch sided style called ''cathedral'' jars, ranging from pale green to rather dark green, collection of 5, as follows: **(1)** short squat one with 3 arches, extra decoration on front, plain arch in back has columns on either side, 8¼''H; **(2)** 4 sides, 3 arches with extra designs, 8½''H; **(3)** 8 sided jar with arches, 11''H; **(4)** dark green, 4 sides with upside down crown around neck of jar, very simplified designs on body, 11⅜''H; **(5)** large version of first one, crude mold, lots of bubbles, 4 sides, 3 arches filled with designs, 14¼''H. Quite extraordinary range of sizes. American, mid 19th C. • According to Steven Van Rensselaer, who wrote *Check List of Early American Bottles and Flasks* (Southampton, NY: Cracker Barrel Press, 1921), ''It is probable that most of the glass works made them, but it is known at they were made at the Willington Glass Works (in) East Willington, CT.'' • Individual prices might range from $250.00 to $800.00. This set was $2000.00 in 1985. Now more likely to fall within higher range: **$2200.00-$2500.00**

Pickle jar, stoneware glazed inside and out, levered bail clamp-on lid, Weir Pottery Co., Monmouth, IL, 14''H x 8'' diameter, 19th C into early 20th C. • In a 1902 ad in *Ladies Home Journal,* a note was added at bottom of ad that ''Heinz, the pickle man, has just ordered 500,000 Weir Jars.'' The H. J. Heinz Co., by the way, founded in 1867, has a museum of artifacts and memorabilia numbering in the thousands. It is at company headquarters in Pittsburgh, but is so far not open to the public, alas.

$40.00-$50.00

Picnic basket, tightly woven ash splint over reed, a bit of unravelling on swing handle, not seriously affecting value, Shaker style, 10"H x 16"L, 19th C. **$200.00-$235.00**

Picnic basket, wicker, fitted out with knives and forks, tumblers, napkins, collapsing cup, tin canister, tin plate, wine bottle & pickle jar, has lock and key, English (?), 7"H x 12" x 8", TOC. **$125.00-$150.00**

Picnic basket, wicker with plywood top, zinc lined, stained dark brown, 20"L x 11"W, early 20th C. • **"For Autoists and Picknickers.** — One of the problems confronting the auto driver or the chief of a picnic party when in an out-of-the-way place is to provide drinking accommodations for the guests. Theoretically, drinking from one cup is an expression of good fellowship. In actual practice it presents objections that need not be enumerated here. It was with this fact in mind that the Buhl No. 10 nested aluminum drinking cup was devised. The outfit consists of six stamped aluminum drinking cups, nesting one in another in such a manner that they really take up but a trifle more room than a single receptacle, with a tightly fitting cover rendering them dust proof. The set can be put in a pocket to an automobile or tucked away in one corner of a lunch basket, and is always ready for use. We will supply the trade with these nested cups for $6.00 a dozen sets." *Hardware News*, published monthly by Buhl Sons Co., Detroit, MI, April 1912. **$30.00-$40.00**

Picnic or automobile lunch kit, blackened tin, in wood case, "Model 4 Auto-Cook-Kit," by Prentiss-Wabers Products Co., Wisconsin Rapids, WI, 5"H x 16½"L x 9"W, early 20th C. • Automobilia collectors are probably well aware of such things, but it's a new branch of kitchen collecting.

$28.00-$35.00

Pie carrier, plywood, homemade, 7 tiers of cutout "C" pieces of plywood, plus full circle top & bottom pieces, American, 20"H x 10" diameter, c.1950s. **$12.00-$15.00**

Pie rack, 4 tiers, twisted wire, not painted black (as some repros are), no mark, problematic to date. Could be late 19th C — could be 1908s. **Reproduction alert.**— I see them advertised all the time, but haven't examined any. Common sense would tell you to look for signs (using a magnifier) of wear — pie pans scraping in and out for years, scuff marks on bottom from being moved, polishing marks. From other repro wire pieces, I know they use wire of the same guage for uprights and rests. Don't pay for a descriptive tag that tries to assure you "early" or "old", unless you are sure. **$25.00-$30.00**

Piggin, for liquids, staved pine, ash "buttonhole" hoops top and bottom, overlapped & fastened with wooden button-like peg, the distinguishing feature making this a piggin is the one elongated stave handle, this one beautifully shaped like long-stemmed mushroom, to give the hand a good purchase, has unusual flat cover with flange inside, finished outside & in with dark brown stain, possibly walnut stain (?), New England (?), or poss. Canadian, 6"H x 9" diameter plus 4"L handle stave, early 19th C. • **Piggins** are described sometimes as small wooden buckets. The elongated stave for the handle, for most of them, is quite simple & it may have a hanging hole in it. They are not often found with their lids.

$200.00-$250.00

Pitcher, Bennington-type brown glazed stoneware, originally one of the pitchers with molded old man's face under lip. Handle broken off, repaired neatly with wide tinsmithed bands (with turned edges) forming a sort of harness around the body of the vessel, with a wide braced tin strap handle. Prob. VT pitcher, with New England (?) repair, 12"H, pitcher maybe 1840s to 1860s, repair poss. 1860s to 1880s. **$300.00-$400.00**

A July 1885 note in *American Agriculturist* is headed "**Handles for Pitchers.** — A jug or pitcher without a handle is often considered past its usefulness. An economical person, believing a few pennies saved are equal to so many earned, may re-handle a jug or a pitcher with great ease, in the manner shown in the engraving...." (which shows a thin tin harness around neck & under belly, vertical strap in front, strap handle connects top & bottom band.) prob. VT pitcher, with New England (?) repair, 12'H, pitcher maybe 1840s to 1860s, repair poss. 1860s to 1880s. • Repaired pieces are in great demand. A book, *Waste Not, Want Not: The Art of the Make-Do* was published in 1986 about the broken goblets, lamps, pitchers, etc., repaired or fitted out with new parts of different materials; such pieces are called fractures or make-dos. In the book there is heavy emphasis on pincushions made from broken goblets or hurricane lamp bases, and not a lot of other types of things. The book is still available (?) for $10.95 plus postage from the author, Don Naetzker, 205 S. Main St., Fairport, NY 14450. • The name "make-do" comes from the thrifty ditty: "Use it up, Wear it out, Make it do, Or do without." I think the repaired piece, or the one made into something else (maybe, "make it do a new service"), has a very long, perhaps ancient lineage. The mid to late Victorian urge to make some kickshaw out of every possible material object, from acorn to felt scraps, from ribbon to cut paper scrap, fed into this lineage & added such things as the pincushions mentioned above. (I bought one recently with a goblet foot & stem, ground off at top of stem, & fitted with a human hair-filled pillow in old patterned silk.) • The *American Agriculturist*, a journal for farm families published in NYC, had an article in March 1875 on "**How to Make a Catch-all.** — Some clever person has contrived a use for broken goblets. They were so popular near last Christmas, that crockery stores were beseiged for broken goblets, and when none were left, it is hinted that some store-keepers were so obliging as to break them on purpose. Here (a picture of the goblet top and its broken off stem & foot, and a picture of a sort of crocheted hanging basket on a wall hook) you have a picture of the fractured article — the bowl and the foot. Of course you all know how to make a pincushion of the base of the glass; and now I am going to tell you how to utilize the upper part. Take a strip of silver perforated cardboard, 9 holes deep (cutting it through the 1st and 11th row of holes). Measure the top of the goblet, and allow the strip to lap over 1 or 2 holes. Fit it snugly, now (needle) work upon the cardboard in any colored worsted you like, the 'Roman Key,' or any other pattern ... through the holes." Then you crochet the bag and make a tassel, and you can "hang it up by your bureau or other convenient place for burnt matches, bits of thread, paper, etc." sort of like a small wall wastebasket. Hmmm.

Porringer, cast iron, fanned or ribbed openwork short handle, shallow recess underneath bottom edge, long casting gate on bottom, "Kenrick #0" marked on bottom, along with size, West Bromwich, England, 4⅛" D, ½ pint, the smallest size, early 19th, late 18th C. • Many porringers marked "Kenrick" are found in this country, as well as coffee mills & a few other ironmonger wares. Alex Ames, in his book on old iron, definitely identifies the first "Kenrick" maker as Archibald Kenrick, of West Bromwich, who established his foundry in 1791, and is still in business as A. Kenrick & Sons. • The distinctive openwork fan-ribbed handle style was probably copied by American founders. **$95.00-$120.00**

Porringer, cast iron, openwork ribbed fan handle, "Kenrick," English, 6¾" D, early 19th C. **$135.00-$175.00**

Porringer, cast iron, pierced tab handle, handle marked "Bellevue", bottom marked "E & T Clark" with size, English, one pint, prob. 2nd quarter 19th C, **$50.00-$75.00**

Porringer, cast iron, very rounded bottom, longer handle than usual on porringer, with round hanging hole fitted with mysterious chain with 6 elongated oval links, American (?), chain 24"L, porringer approximately 8" diameter, 18th C. • This was from the Roger Bacon Collection, and was for sale by dealer Anne Serra of Cuba, NY, for $350.00 around 1985. Now: **$350.00-$425.00**

Porringer, cast iron with white porcelainized interior, fanned openwork handle, not marked, English or American, 19th C. • Carl W. Drepperd, in *A Dictionary of American Antiques*, says the crest-shaped pierced tab handle is the "conventional American" porringer style. **$50.00-$75.00**

Portable pantry, also called a "security safe," painted tin, bins for staples, lockable compartments, coffee grinder, American, 19th C. **$750.00-$1200.00**

Portable pantry, black japanned pieced tin, countertop, with almost turret-like bins on either side of large central rounded "silo" part which contains 5 stacked spice containers, lids out, coffee mill on right side, compartments in bottom with white porcelain knobs, center bottom door labeled "The Kitchen Secretary", American, about 40"H, 19th C. **$750.00-$1000.00**

Portable pantry, black japanned tin, wheat design stamped in the tin, big bins on top for coffee, flour & corn meal, coffee grinder on right side, flour sifter in center works by moving lever left & right back & forth, 6 spice canisters with double lids, including inner shaker lid, in "stacked" position, lids out, down center, 2 heavily encrusted compartments at bottom, almost as if used as an oven, but that couldn't be, mark so worn & rubbed it can't be read (except by infrared maybe?), probably "Queen Safe", 50"H x 36"W, 19th C. **$750.00-$1200.00**

Portable pantry, called a tourist kitchen, meant for fitting to the running board of a touring car, for fixing picnics, painted tin chest with fold down front, hinged top, revealing neatly stacked tin boxes & containers of varying rectangular sizes, ranging from big cereal box size to baby shoebox size, each one labeled for contents, American, early 20th C. **$175.00-$250.00**

Portable pantry, dark asphaltum japanned tin with ochre stenciling in Japanese-derived (*Japonisme*) bamboo and birds and butterfiles motif, basically straight sides with front slanted out at bottom, usual bins for flour & coffee beans, with built in flour sifter & coffee mill (crank on side), 5 vertically stacked spice canisters in center, compartments below for flour, sugar & meal, marked "Manufactured for the Standard Cabinet Co. by B. Hunt Stamping Works", Kansas City, MO, 34"H x 26"W, pat'd 1893. • Collector Mike Murrish of California sent me the information on this one. **$600.00-$800.00**

Portable pantry, japanned black tin, with stenciled letters & bouquets of roses, also containers or canisters stenciled GINGER, CLOVES, CINNAMON, SPICE, MUSTARD, TAPIOCA, RICE, HOMINY, BARLEY, and one that's unreadable, crank on side for coffee mill, lower bins labeled CAKE & BREAD, the 2 above those for SUGAR and MEAL, with flour sifter in center, "Security Safe", 38"H x 31"W, pat'd 1900 and 1901. **$900.00-$1200.00**

Portable pantry, japanned & stenciled tin, sort of *Chinoiserie* designs, top has 2 half-round bins with hinged lids on top that reveal compartments for flour sifting & coffee grinding with pans to catch the grounds, doors in bottom section reveal 2 sifters (flour & sugar(?)), center section has vertical row of spice canisters with screw-on tops, divided compartment below has 2 small pans like miniature loaf pans, originally there was a mirrored door covering the spice containers, there seems to be storage for baking pans or implements too, stenciled in script on lower doors is "Globe Cabinet", 41"H x 27"W, on wooden base possibly added later with 8"H legs, 1880s-1890s. • Collector Geraldine Hoven is to be thanked for her description and pictures of this heretofore unknown portable pantry. This one belonged to her grandparents in Iowa. Of special note is the mirrored door, which I have never seen, and which is unfortunately missing on this one.

$900.00-$1200.00

Portable pantry, japanned tin, painted with flowers, butterflies, etc., compartments for all staples — flour (with sifter), sugar, etc. — spices, coffee (with grinder), unusual swing-out scale on side, missing the clock. scale marked "F & C" on face; cabinet marked "The Standard Cabinet Co., B. Hunt Stamping Co., Kansas City, (KS or MO?),early 20th C. **$800.00-$1200.00**

Portable pantry, set on table, or well-braced shelf, not hung on wall, japanned & flower stenciled tin with name on 2 lower doors covering shelves, bins or containers for flour, corn meal, sugar, built-in coffee grinder on right side with crank sticking out side, white porcelain knobs on doors & spice canisters, clock in center top, "Perfect Pantry Co.," St. Louis, MO, about 50"H, pat'd 1904. **$800.00-$1200.00**

Portable pantry, simple black finished tin with stenciled labels for various compartments, 2 tall side "silos" flanking center section with 6 stacked spice containers with double lids (one for shaking), topped with opening for clock (I've never actually seen one with the clock intact; maybe you had to furnish your own? or maybe you put a portrait of the cook in it!), 2 match safes, lower compartments for flour, meal & sugar, coffee grinder on right, bottom compartment like most of the portable pantries has hinged lids with curved fronts that make base larger & steadier, stenciled "Portable Pantry" on front, 42"H x 31"W x 21"D, 19th C. **$900.00-$1200.00**

Portable pantry, simplest most economical kind, white painted metal chest with hinged cover, compartments inside hold 5 lbs sugar, 5 lbs flour, 3 lbs coffee, on front are 3 pull-out small catch drawers, with crank for flour sifter,

Salt box, blue enamelware with wooden hinged lid, prob. imported in 1880s-1900 from Germany, late 19th C. **$65.00-$95.00**

Salt box, blue & white saltglazed stoneware, relief design of birds, European or poss. American, very late 19th C. **$20.00-$35.00**

Salt box, floral decorated ceramic, wooden lid, German (?), or Czechoslovakian, early 20th C. **$15.00-$25.00**

Salt box, glass with wood lid, wall hung, lid has moisture-absorbing sponge fixed to it, word "SALT" molded on side, 3¾"H, TOC or early 20th C. **$28.00-$40.00**

Salt box, gray & cobalt saltglazed stoneware, wall hung, round with flattened back, the German "SALTZ" written on front, German, late 19th C. **$50.00-$65.00**

Salt box, gray graniteware with tin lid, round shape, to hang on wall, paper label: "Haberman's Steel Enamelled Ware," with trademark of diamond around a tea kettle, late 19th C. **$95.00-$135.00**

Salt shaker, known by collectors as a Christmas Salt because of patent date, a bright blue clear blown molded glass honey pot or barrel shaped jar, screw-on pewter or Britannia lid with high acorn knob that you twist to turn the inside agitator device, like little metal fingers, some pointing down, some up, to break up damp salt, marked on lid, "Dana K. Alden. Boston." Glass by Boston & Sandwich Glass Co.; agitator by Alden Salt Caster Co., Sandwich, MA, and Boston, MA, respectively, 2½"H, pat'd by Hiram J. White, Dec. 25, 1877. • These came in different colors, some much more rare than others, and in a taller panelled shape. There were sets with a pepper shaker too, sometimes found in a little caster with ring handle. There are other versions, patented by other inventors **$275.00-$400.00**

Slop jar, gray graniteware, slightly rounded body, with wire bail & wooden grip, lid. Kept in the kitchen next to the sink, these held dish scrapings & veggie juice & parings used to "slop" the pigs, although there was disagreement about how much "garbage" was really good for a pig. 12"H, TOC. **$55.00-$75.00**

Slop pail, probably from a toilette set, rather than a kitchen slop pail, made of pieced tin, with lid, mustard grain painted finish, American (?), 11¼"H including lid, c.1870s to 1890s. **$60.00-$80.00**

Soda glass holder, also called a zarf, nickeled brass, open-work with cup handle, used in soda fountains, American, about 3½"H, late 19th C through mid 20th C. **$3.00-$10.00**

Soup tureen, stamped & pieced tin with ornate cast iron finial & handles, lid has a "bite" opening in edge for ladle, from F. A. Walker catalog, American, or English (?), came in several sizes: 3, 4, 6, 8 and 10 quarts. One example seen is 10"H x 15½"L x 9½"W oval, c.1870s. • Soup Tureen Museum. — The Campbell Museum, Campbell Place, Camden, NJ 08101, has hundreds of American & European tureens, ladles, spoons, trays, etc., made of ceramics, pewter, silver, etc. Call ahead for further information. • Finials or knobs for tea or coffee pots, were shown in the 1869 Dover Stamping Co., which had many supplies for tinsmiths, as well as housewares. They offered a "bright bird", a simple dovelike bird on grass; a "bright acorn", a pair of acorns sticking up from leaf; and several round, and rosette models offered "black" or "bright" finish. I suppose the bright was tinned. **$125.00-$150.00**

Spice box, 6 containers inside, all tin, "Kreamer," Brooklyn, NY, TOC. • Most Kreamer pieces are not so interesting. This is hard to find. **$45.00-$60.00**

Spice box, 6 round cans, oblong japanned heavy stamped tin box, cast iron handle on hinged lid, hasp closing, American (?), 9"L x 6⅛"W, c.1890s. **$65.00-$80.00**

Tin Origins & Tin Tariffs. — It's hard to tell the provenance of some tin items because until the early 20th C there were virtually no tinned iron or steel "plates" (or sheets of what we call tin) manufactured in the U.S. We didn't have the rolling mills for it, and probably 999% was imported as the raw material for the hundreds of stamping or piecing tinware factories in the U.S. Virtually everything from canned peaches & pie pans to pails & pudding pans were made of imported plates or sheets of tinned iron (or steel). And many tin housewares were imported from Europe or England ready to sell. William McKinley, a Republican Congressman who became president in 1897, introduced a protectionist tariff bill which passed in the fall of 1890 and went into effect March 1, 1891, and had at least three provisions of interest to collectors. (1) country of origin must be marked on all imported items. (2) imposition of a higher tariff on import tin plate, which occasioned long editorials & heated fights in the House because it would raise prices of finished goods made by Americans by an estimated 5% to 25%. Republicans wanted the tariff to encourage the infant industry of rolling tin plate in this country. Democrats argued that the increase of prices on canned goods & housewares would be an "unfortunate burden for the working man." (You might say here, what else is new?) One of many long *The New York Times* pieces in 1890 laid out a chart of examples of how prices would rise. A 4 quart coffee pot now costing 20¢ would cost 18¢ with no tariff at all, but 23¢ with the new tariff. An 11¼" colander costing 15¢ would be 14¢ or rise to 17¢. A 4" pie plate now 5¢ could cost 4¢ or rise to 7¢. (3) a huge tariff on import enamelwares. For more on (3) see a Coffee & Tea chapter entry. • An 1890 ad for Wanamaker's, Philadelphia, said "Tinware is advancing in cost, and very soon the manufacturers (!) will have their way and you and we will have to pay very much more. In view of this... we made some time since a large purchase of kitchen tinware at what was a low price then and would be far lower now...Bread Raisers, 10 qt., with cover & ventilator in lid 58¢; tin-frame Flour sieves 9¢; tubed Cake molds 10¢; small Tea Kettles 20¢; Japanned Nutmeg Graters 1¢; Japanned Nests of spice Boxes 30¢..." Letter to the Editor, *New York Times*, Oct. 1890. **$65.00-$80.00**

Spice box, dovetailed pine with arched "gravestone" back plate for wall hanging. Hinged lid slants down, 2 drawers with 6 compartments below, dealer says "Shaker," 19th C. **$350.00-$450.00**

Spice box, japanned & pinstriped tin, 2 hinged lids on either side of center handle, each open to reveal 3 compartments, Dover Stamping Co., 19th C. **$75.00-$90.00**

Spice box, japanned & pinstriped tin, oblong two-tier chest, with small collapsing cast iron handle on top, 10 almost square drawers — 5 on each side (3 above, 2 slightly larger below), all stenciled with name, the bigger drawers for commonly used spices like salt, pepper, sugar, etc., Dover Stamping Co., 6½"H x 9½"L x 6½"W, 1860s to 1880s. **$120.00-$150.00**

Spice box, thin quarter sawn maple bent into round, tin rim to lid and bottom, 7 round canisters with spices marked on lids, largest, for Cloves, in center, bottoms of canisters marked Patent Packing Co., Newark, NJ, pat'd Aug. 31, 1858. • This is one of at least three versions of "bentwood" boxes with seven canisters. **$150.00-$175.00**

Spice box, tin, punched (not punctured) tin design on hinged lid, inside are 4 compartments with largish round open center for nutmeg & grater, tin ring legs, very delicate & pretty, American, 3¼"H x 6³⁄₁₆"L x 3¹¹⁄₁₆"W, mid 19th C. **$175.00-$200.00**

Spice box, tin with asphaltum japanning, domed lid with brass knob, inside partitioned into wedges for 6 loose spices, nutmegs & grater fit in hole in center of wedges, American, 6½" diameter, 19th C. • Here's what Miss Eliza. Leslie wrote in her *Housebook* in 1840: "For spice boxes, it is best to keep different sorts in small, separate painted tin boxes, each with tight lid and handle to hang it by, to nails driven along the edge of dresser shelf. Each box to have name painted on side. These are better than large boxes, in which, not withstanding the division, the spices are very apt to get mixed." **$125.00-$150.00**

Spice box, tin, with stamped design of morning glories, 4 spice compartments & 2 graters for bread & nutmegs. American (?), late 19th C. **$75.00-$120.00**

Spice box, tin-banded varnished round bentwood box with 8 individual bentwood boxes inside. Stenciled SPICE on lid of outer box & names of spices on containers, American, 3½" deep x 9" diameter, 3rd quarter 19th C. **$150.00-$200.00**

Spice box, varnished thin wood with metal bands, black stencilling on lid of outer box, lids & sides of all 8 inner boxes, American, 9" to 9½" diameter, supposedly dated 1858 (one report said 1856). • I tried to track this one down in the patent subject indices, but nothing listed under Spice-Boxes were this early. I recall when these used to go for $45 and it seemed like an awful lot of money! **$275.00-$320.00**

Spice cabinet, maple, 6 drawers with white porcelain knobs & whitish pewter-like or Britannia labels which could have penciled identifications wiped off, American (?), mid 19th C. **$250.00-$325.00**

Spice cabinet, oak, 16 drawers, wall hung, late 19th or early 20th C. • **Reproduction alert.** — A Wisconsin firm advertised in 1983 four "solid pine" versions, "exact copies of original models" and all nailed "no staples", stained & finished, all with white knobs and incised ring around knobs. Four drawer (not seen in antique ones) :7"H x 9½"W; six drawer with shaped backplate, 13½"H x 9½"W; eight drawer same backplate, 16"H x 9½"W, all three 4½" deep; nine drawer "counter top" is 9½"H x 14"W x 5" deep. These sold for $15.00 to $23.00 each, with quantity discounts. • The old TOC one, overpriced but gets... **$150.00-$250.00**

Spice cabinet, or spice chest, dark green painted wood, dovetail construction, 8 drawers, countertop not wall hung, American, 19"H x 27½"L, 19th C. **$550.00-$700.00**

Spice cabinet, pine painted green & red, 8 drawers in simple frame, a nice country piece with early paint, American (?), 11"H x 9"W, 19th C. **$220.00-$250.00**

Spice cabinet, red painted tin, 8 drawers, scalloped top edge, wall hung, late 19th C. **$135.00-$175.00**

Spice cabinet, yellow varnished natural wood, marvelously shaped & engineered, wall hung, with 6 tin & wooden drawers, paired 2 x 2 with centerboard between, making a double bow front, shaped backplate, pin goes through from top to bottom on both sides & round drawer compartments pivot out on the pin, pat'd by J. T. Carter and J. Park, Lowell, MA, about 9" to 10"H, pat'd Dec. 10, 1867. **$250.00-$325.00**

Spice cabinet or chest, wood, outside grain painted dull brown, with gold pinstripes, inside (surprise!) red &

green with yellow varnished drawer fronts, 2 doors with one remaining knob of turned ivory, lock missing, 12 drawers inside, 10 with paper labels with ink handwritten names "Cinnamon, Pudding Spice, Nutmegs, Carraway Seeds, Black Peppers, Mace, Cloves, Cayenne Pepper, White Pepper, Long Pepper", English, 10½"H x 12⅝"W, c.1840s to 1860s. • **"Currie** — Imitation of the India Currie. — 3 ounces coriander seed, 3 ounces turmeric, 1 ounce black pepper, 1 ounce ginger, 1 ounce mustard, ½ ounce lesser cardamoms, ¼ ounce each of cayenne pepper, cinnamon and cummin. Pound fine and mix well." Mrs. Cornelius, *The Young Housekeepers Friend, or, A Guide to Domestic Economy & Comfort*, Boston & NY: 1846. **$500.00-$600.00**

Spice can, tin, Silas Pierce Nutmeg, late 19th or early 20th C. **$18.00-$20.00**

Spice chest, and Pasta 'n Pizza Rack. Wall hung, Philippine mahogany chest with crested backplate, 2 long earthenware-fronted labeled drawers full width at bottom, for linguine & some other spaghetti, above that 2 half-width drawers for macaroni & noodles, 4 small spice drawers at top for oregano, bay leaf, rosemary & basil. All "hand-painted under glaze with Venetian gondolier designs", European for American market, 13"H x 11"W, c.1960. **$18.00-$23.00**

Spice & condiment containers, glass with PA German designs, possibly an incomplete set with only 5 pieces: marked "Cocoa, Salt, Spice, Sugar, Nutmeats," American, 4¾"H, 20th C. **$35.00-$45.00**

Spice rack, with 12 milk glass square shaker jars with black metal lids, Griffith Laboratories, Chicago, IL, each jar 4⅜"H, patent #2,107,697 (1938), being advertised in early 1940s. • This also came with green lids & lettering; Griffith made a set with little honeypot-shaped jars with lift-out shaker piece under lid. **$35.00-$45.00**

Spice shakers, molded plastic Black Americana, Aunt Jemima, painted, head & top torso come off, shaker top is at figure's waist level, labeled "Nutmeg, Paprika, Cinnamon, Cloves, Ginger & Allspice," F & F Mold & Die Works, Dayton, OH, 4⅛"H, 20th C. • I saw two of these with paper aprons printed with Allspice and Paprika. Under the Allspice paper apron was molded "Pepper", under the Paprika one it still said "Paprika". **$15.00-$22.00**

Spice tower, 3 sectioned varnished turned wood, decal labels are light yellow with black engraving, this one for "Mace, Cloves, Nutmeg", English, about 6"H, 19th C. **$170.00-$220.00**

Spice tower, turned wood, lovely light yellowy color, stacked powder box size containers, all screw together, one on top of the other. This particular tower has Cloves, Nutmegs, Cinnamon, Allspice & an undesignated box, English, different sizes & number of boxes, this one 9½"H, with each container 1½" deep x 2½" diameter, 19th C. Also called spice turret. **$175.00-$250.00**

Spice tower, varnished wood, lid & base painted red, green paper labels engraved with black, stripes on lid & base, 3 tiers, for Mace, Nutmegs, Cloves. Very unusual for coloring. English, 19th C. **$150.00-$175.00**

Spice tray, 6 cans in handled tray, adv'g "Grand Union" grocery chain, early 20th C. **$45.00-$55.00**

Spice tray, japanned tin, 6 canisters with slightly convex shaker lids in carrying tray with low sides & strap handle, English (the flat-topped set, very similar, was American), c.1860s-70s. **$30.00-$40.00**

Spice tray, japanned tin, strap handle, 6 small round cans with snug lids, American (?), tray is 5½" x 4¾ ", cans are 2⅞"H x 1¾" diameter, late 19th C. $35.00-$50.00

Storage containers, mostly for the refrigerator, molded polyethylene plastic the inventor first called "Poly-T", with snap-on lids, also other forms, "Tupperware", originally called "Wonder Bowl", named after inventor Earl Silas Tupper, Orlando, FL, 1931 to present. • An entertaining *Washington Post Magazine* article, Jan. 22, 1989, written by Vic Sussman ("I was a Middle-Aged Tupper Virgin"), tells about Tupperware **International's Museum of Historic Food Containers,** where, he says, "you can inspect everything from prehistoric vessels to the latest in Tupperware." Tupperware World Head-quarters, Box 2353, Orlando, FL 32802. Call ahead for fur-ther information. • Price range for resale "collectible market" not new Tupperware® .   50¢-$4.00

Sugar bowl, gray graniteware, with Britannia mountings, nice round body, high domed lid with finial, 19th C. • What is often called "pewter" in modern dealers' ads is either an unnamed white metal (as described in the mfrs' own catalogs) or Britannia (sometimes seen spelled Brit-tania), which was a British, and later American, white metal substitute for pewter (and very close to it in com-position & appearance), that contained no lead, but rather tin, antimony & copper. An American white metal com-pounded of the same 3 metals, invented about 1825 by Isaac Babbitt, of Taunton, MA, was known as "Babbitt Metal." $175.00-$190.00

Sugar bowl, milk glass in shape of Monitor Top refrigerator, adv'g General Electric, c.1930s. $65.00-$80.00

Sugar bowl, nickeled stamped metal base with 3 stamped cabriole legs, side ear handles, bowl is molded glass, rather like a melon with scalloped flutes, flat top, sliding lever in base releases sugar, "Sanitary", mfd by Ideal Sanitary Sugar Bowl Co., NYC, NY, 2 lb. capacity, c.1915. $12.00-$20.00

Sugar bowl, painted tin, double stepped foot ring, slightly domed lid with 3 small tin cylinders for the knob, black ground with red, yellow & green flowers, super looking, American, 3¾"H x 4" diameter, 19th C. $400.00-$500.00

Sugar bowl, robin's-egg blue enamelware with black trim, including knob, rim & handles, probably Lisk Mfg. Co., Canandaigua, NY, 4½"H x 4"D, 20th C. $85.00-$125.00

Sugar bowl, turned maple, nice fat (sugar-loaded) shape, lid has finial, American (?) or English, 3½"H x 6½" D, 19th C. • The charm of these lies in the turning, the plump-ness & the little details like the finial. Some are found with paint, or color staining on outside. $175.00-$200.00

Sugar bowl, with fitted lid, beautifully patinaed turned wood in bulbous shape, nice finial, called Peaseware, made by Hiram Pease, (& other Peases ?), Painesville, Lake County, OH, 4½" x 5", worked c.1850-1890. • The **turned wood containers** made by Pease(s) closely resem-ble woodenware covered bowls by other makers such as Paine. Some are footed goblet shapes, like the Lehnware trinket & saffron containers, and open eggcups. Some, with small flared footed base, have thin wire falling bail handles with simple wooden grips, with slightly convex lids with (mostly) acorn finials of wood. At some point, the company was Pease & Brown. Products of this part-nership are rising in value, especially large lidded pieces, which may bring up to $900.00. • Added value. — At this time, collectors value more the distinctive, colorfully

painted decoration epitomizing its Pennsylvania-European heritage, turned & footed woodenwares of Joseph Lehn of Lancaster County, PA, which can bring more than $2500.00 for certain covered forms. • This Pease bowl: $200.00-$250.00

Sugar bowl, with lid, turned & grain painted wood, wire bail handle, either New England or PA, 7⅝"H to top of finial, c.1870s. $1000.00-$1300.00

Syrup jug, called simply "syrups" by collectors, gray graniteware, trim in white metal (also came in nickel plate) — lid, belly band (called a "protection band") & handle, finial is woman's head with partly tied-back hair. (She resembles a Valkyrie, or perhaps was copied from a Liberty head coin from the late 18th or early 19th C, with Greco-Roman nose & same hair.) These jugs were adver-tised as "air-tight & ant-proof." "Perfection Graniteware", Manning-Bowman, late 19th C. • They also made a very fancy one with acanthus leaf-molded metal part with enameled round bottom decorated with flowers in color, same sort of Valkyrian head finial. Also a series in their "Pearl Agate", in choice of colors (brown, laven-dar, green, blue — all with white pebbling or mottled finish), with very narrowed neck and high hinged lid. $175.00-$235.00

Syrup jug, quadruple silverplate, rounded bottom & gently sloping sides, high domed hinged lid, with chased engraved design of springs around fat "belly" at bottom, high cylindrical lip inside domed lid as typical for their syrups, late 19th C. $1250.00-$155.00

Syrup pitcher, black (asphaltum) japanned tin, with stenciled gold flower design, conical shape, hinged lid, shell-shaped finial, very rare, early 1800s. $165.00-$195.00

Syrup pitcher, die molded colored plastic, Aunt Jemima Black Americana, F & F Mold & Die Works, 5½"H, c.1940s. $30.00-$35.00

Syrup pitcher, gray graniteware, tin lid, late 19th C. $145.00-$160.00

Syrup pitcher, hammered copper with brass details, dovetailed seam construction, Arts & Crafts Movement, American, late 19th or early 20th C. $45.00-$50.00

Syrup pitcher, pink Depression glass, metal lid, 1930s or 1940s. $25.00-$35.00

Syrup pitcher, sky blue color enamelware, white inside, 19th C. $125.00-$175.00

Syrup pitcher or jug, dark turquoisey green & white loopy swirled enamelware, rounded belly (bottom is but ⅙ of total body height) has protective pewter ring at widest part, slanted sides, the pewter domed lid & decorated rim are like those found on German steins, pitcher handle, "Chrysolite" TOC. • Sold at Helen Greguire Collection "Graniteware" auction, July 30, 1989 for: $1625.00

Tea bin, tin, slanted lift-up lid, "Lee & Cady Green Tea," 90 lb size, 19th C. $100.00-$145.00

Tea caddy, brass box, simple round lid, large stamped medallion with stars and wheat sheaf mounted on front, no mark, American (?), 7"H x 6"W x 3" deep, 19th C. • A sheaf of wheat was often used in the 18th and early 19th Cs as a patriotic motif. $275.00-$325.00

Tea caddy, for grocer's counter, japanned & decorated tin box, looks like a rounded upright piano in shape, with portrait medallion of woman, tea is scooped out at bot-tom, from hinged horizontal cylindrical base, Sidney Shepard & Co., Buffalo Stamping Works, Buffalo, NY, 5 lb. size, 9¾"H x 8"W x 8¾" deep, (Came in six sizes, viz. 2, 5, 10, 25, 50 & 75 lb.), late 19th C. $125.00-$160.00

Tidy rack, embossed tin, design of Japanese fans & ribbons, 3 pockets & a mirror set on angle in center, hung on wall, sometimes simply called a "tidy", American, 6¾" x 7", TOC. • See also Comb rack. **$30.00-$40.00**

Tidy rack, for comb or oddments, carved & painted wood, with relief motif of horse in pasture, and young girl, on other side of fence, some painting, American, 16"W, TOC. **$150.00-$185.00**

Tray, hammered aluminum, round, large side handles riveted on, made of 2 slender rods of aluminum, twisted & with tendrils and bud-like or tulip terminals, marked "B. W." flanking a castle turret, & "Buenilum", Made in U. S. A., 16½" diameter, c.1940s. • This tray was also made in a smaller size, 14" diameter, which brings slightly less money. • A newsletter, *The Aluminist*, was begun in Oct. 1986. Whether or not it will survive into the 1990s (many collector newsletters have a three-year lifespan), you may want to know about it. For information, send a SASE to Dannie Woodard, POB 1346, Weatherford, TX 76086. **$20.00-$25.00**

Tray, or <u>waiter</u>, tin, with crystalized center and japanned, stenciled and painted border design of large grape leaves, spiral tendrils, outer border is a chain of comma or teardrop shapes, elongated octagon (rectangle with truncated ends to make 8 corners or sides) or coffin tray, no handle cutouts, could be NY, CT or PA, 32"L x 17"W, 2nd quarter 19th C.

Crystal Gazing — Provenance of this waiter, or serving tray, is hard to know because <u>crystalization</u> used by tin decorators in 3 states. Grape leaves (vineyards?) may be clues. Earl Robacker, who thinks Pennsylvania, wrote that "the effect of crystals (is) obtained by washes such as aqua fortis and sal ammoniac before the varnish was applied in japanning." • "<u>Moiree Metallique</u>, called in this country (U.S.A.) **crystallized tin-plate,** is a variegated primrose appearance, produced upon the surface of tin-plate, by applying to it in a heated state some dilute nitro-muriatic acid for a few seconds, then washing it with water, drying, and coating it with lacker. The figures are more or less beautiful and diversified, according to the degree of heat, and relative dilution of the acid. This mode of ornamenting tin-plate is much less in vogue now than it was a few years ago. "Andre Ure, M.D., *A Dictionary of Arts, Manufactures, and Mines; Containing a Clear Exposition of Their Principles and Practice.* NY: Appleton & Co., 1854, in 2 volumes reprinted from the "last" corrected English edition. "Less in vogue *now*" may be 1830s or 40s. • Ure explains chemical aspects of this decorative technique in his "Tin-Plate" entry: "It seems that the acid merely lays bare the crystalline structure really present on every sheet (of tin plate), but masked by a film of redundant tin. Though this showy article has become of late years vulgarized by its cheapness, it is still interesting...to practical chemist. The English tin-plates marked F answer well for producing the Moiree, by the following process. Place the tin-plate, slightly heated, over a tub of water, and rub its surface with a sponge holding one part of common salt or sal ammoniac in solution. Whenever the crystalline spangles seem to be thoroughly brought out, the plate must be immersed in water, washed either with a feather or a little cotton (taking care not to rub off the film of tin that forms the feathering), forthwith dried with a low heat, and coated with a lacker varnish, otherwise it loses its lustre in the air. If the whole surface is not plunged at once in cold water, but...is partically cooled by sprinkling water on it, the crystallization will be finely variegated with large and small figures....A variety of delineations may be traced, by playing over the surface of the plate with the pointed flame of a blowpipe." Ibid . **$850.00-$1000.00**

Tray, tole, with flowers, Pennsylvania-European heritage motifs, not strictly PA Dutch, 18"L, late 19th C. • **Collector hint.** — If you are going to buy painted or decorated objects of household decoration, especially things made of tin, elegant enough to be termed tole in this country, you must carefully read a how-to & history book long out of print. It is Esther Stevens Brazer's *Early American Decoration*, Springfield, MA: Pond-Ekburg Co., 1940, 1947. It is an extraordinarily fine and useful book on painted decoration on tin, papier mache, wood, etc., used to make trays, chairs, floors, apple trays, bellows, candle sconces, coffee pots, dower chests, etc. Brazer covers subjects such as gold leaf and "floating" color, various kinds of graining — smoked, feathered, sponged, feathered or brushed, and has especially valuable information on "How to collect designs" (in order to reproduce them yourself), "searching for an old design beneath outer prints", "faint traces", etc. This book was intended to assist the skilled home crafts person to successfully decorate the surface of many kinds of decorative accessories as well as furniture, and has detailed drawings and patterns, which might help identify a piece you aren't sure of. Remember the things done then are now 50 years old, and with ordinary wear and cleaning could look quite old and fool just about anybody. **$100.00-$125.00**

Water pitcher, blue & white mottled enamelware, ice lip, TOC. **$75.00-$125.00**

Date By Weight — One clue in dating enamelware is the weight of the underlying steel or iron. <u>Reproductions or lookalikes</u>, as well as most regular wares made since the end of WWI, are rather considerably lighter in weight than older pieces. If you recall, in the 1970s a lot of bright new wares, in very colorful blue, turquoise, green, red, orange or yellow, were imported and sold in warehouse stores specializing in fun, inexpensive, household wares. If you have such a piece, compare its heft with that of a piece you are trying to date. New pieces also seem to make a sort of tinny scratchy sound when pulled across a stainless steel sink or other resonating surface. You can develop a list of sensory tests for many categories of collectibles — <u>sound</u> (when struck with wooden spoon, tapped with fingernail, dragged on a metal surface); <u>feel or touch</u> (the surface, especially when you can run your thumb opposing your middle finger on the inside and outside of something; <u>appearance of magnified surface</u> examined with high power loupe or magnifier); <u>weight or heft</u>; and even <u>taste and smell</u> sometimes.

VII-1.
ABC plate.
Stamped tin, round (though depiction is oval), Jumbo, an elephant famed in the 1880s. 5" diameter. Central Stamping Co., 1920 catalog. **$35.00-$50.00**

VII-4.
(L) Peach basket,
standard Jersey & Delaware" type. Wood veneer with 3 hoops, came in 2, 4, 6 & 8 quart sizes. From D. J. Barry & Co. catalog, 1924, but old type. **$15.00-$25.00**
(R) Bushel basket.
Elm staves, oak bottom & handles, galvanized iron hoops. Originally cost $4.00 per dozen! D. J. Barry & Co., jobber's catalog, 1924, but old type. **$25.00-$40.00**

VII-2.
ABC plate.
Stamped tin, 6" diameter, Cock Robin depiction. This one probably late 19th C. This design offered in mail order catalog of Butler Brothers, 1899. It was offered in other catalogs through the 1920s, along with "Hi-Diddle-Diddle" nursery rhyme. Butler also offered an undescribed one called "Harvard." **$75.00-$125.00**

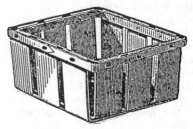

VII-5.
Fruit basket.
"Mellish" patent, for berries, peaches, etc., in various sizes. Wood bark with unusual appearance. Illustration from David Lyman ad in American Agriculturist, 7/1968 and later. Mellish baskets also manufactured by Baird, Roper & Co., Norfolk, VA, and advertised in same magazine after May 1870. **$100.00-$140.00**
Square, veneer with nailed rim, meant for strawberries. "Thoroughly ventilated, remarkably attractive when filled with fruit — and can box." Capacity one quart; they also made crates to hold from 12 to 96 quart baskets! American Basket Co., New Haven, CT. American Agriculturist, 6/1865. **$20.00-$30.00**

VII-3.
Produce basket.
Wood splints woven in flared shape almost like standing cornucopia. About 25"H. **$150.00-$225.00**

The Rochester Berry Basket.
[Patented 1870.]

1 quart.   1 pint.   ½ quart.
The best ventilated and neatest Basket made.
Fits in Beecher Crates.

VII-6.
Berry baskets.
Interesting wood veneer construction, nailed rims, pat'd 1870. Collins, Geddes & Co., Moorestown, NJ. Ad in American Agriculturist, 5/1872. **$20.00-$50.00**

Beecher Baskets.

Star Basket.

QUART.   PINT.
PATENTED DECEMBER 17, 1872.

IMPROVED Square Basket.
Patented Feb. 26, 1878.

VENEER BASKETS. Patented May 31, 1864.
For circular of description, &c., address
THE BEECHER BASKET COMPANY,
Westville, Conn.

VII-7.
Berry & fruit baskets.

The baskets in the last picture were advertised as fitting "in Beecher crates." Here are some real Beecher Basket Co. baskets. Various shapes and sizes, pat'd 5/31/1864; 12/17/1872; and 2/26/1878. Westville, CT. American Agriculturist ad, 5/1878. Thirteen years before, C. Beecher & Sons, advertised their widely-acclaimed "Veneer Fruit Basket," being "neat, stylish, durable and cheap." As well as close-nesting when empty. It was similar to the 1864 patent basket shown at bottom, only sides didn't curve at all. **$20.00-$50.00**

The above cuts show the form and some of the uses of the Sugar-trough Gourd. They grow by the acre to hold two bucketfuls each, and I have raised them to hold over eleven gallons each. My Catalogue tells how to grow them, and illustrates and describes over 200 varieties of choice vegetable and flower seeds. Send stamp for Catalogue, or 25 cents for it and package of the Gourd seed.
Address WALDO F. BROWN, P. O. Box 2, Oxford, Butler Co., Ohio.

VII-8.
Useful gourds.

Ad placed by Waldo F. Brown, Oxford, OH, to sell his gourd seeds and a booklet. Note two baskets made from the gourd, which he said could be grown to hold 2 gallons! American Agriculturist, 2/1892. Basket made from gourd: **$20.00-$40.00**

VII-9.
Berry basket.

Wood veneer, wood bottom, sheet metal rim. Type often called a "Shaker" basket. Many marked "D. Cook's," or "L. Cook & Co." or "Union Manufacturing, New Haven, CT." Pat'd 7/12/1859, but made over long period. 4 3/4"H. **$85.00-$125.00**

VII-10.
Berry basket.

Wood splits, galvanized metal rim & hoop at bottom. 3 1/8"H. Courtesy Mickie Carpenter. **$130.00-$150.00**

VII-11.
Wire baskets,

and fruit compotes, cake stand, flower-holder centerpiece. The linecuts are all "Sherwood's Standard White Lustral Wire Ware" from the catalog of Woods, Sherwood & Co., Lowell, MA, as it appeared in a book from 1876. In 1872, the same linecuts were used in an article on "tinned twisted wire" household goods, based on French originals, in 11/1872 American Agriculturist. **$35.00-$125.00**

The Convertible Basket

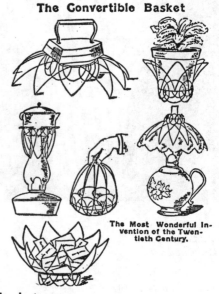

The Most Wonderful Invention of the Twentieth Century.

VII-12.
Convertible basket,

made of nickeled iron wire, and used as a lamp shade, flower stand, egg boiler, hanging lamp, ladies' work basket, (sad) iron stand, card holder, cake stand, fruit basket, etc. Novelty catalog of A. E. Rayment Supply Co., Rockford, IL, c.1910-20s. **$12.00-$30.00**

VII-13.
Beer pot or pitcher.
Graniteware, reinforced strap handle, wire bail handle with turned wood. From Lalance & Grosjean Mfg. Co. catalog, NYC, 1890.
$40.00-$60.00

VII-14.
Market basket.
Dyed straw, 14"H x 14 1/2"L, 1930s-40s. Collection of Mary Mac & Robert Franklin.
$25.00-$35.00

VII-16.
Pen & ink drawing.
"The Warm Weather — Terrific explosion of a Ginger Beer Truck." Signed K. Gregory (?), c.1880. 11 1/8"H x 8 1/4"W. A primitive, spirited drawing. Note corkscrew in vendor's hand, and the exploding stoneware ginger pop bottles tan & ochre thick ginger beer bottles, about 7" to 9"H.
$60.00-$85.00

VII-15.
Birdcages.
(T) Enameled iron wire & stamped & perforated sheet metal, 18"H x 11 x 7 3/4". (B) Wheel cage with painted iron wire and stamped tin front & trim. 19"H x 13 1/4" x 6 1/2" body (tray base is 16 1/4" x 12") Both in catalog of Norvell-Shapleigh Hardware Co., St. Louis, 1910.
$90.00-$125.00

NOTE: Dozens of birdcages will appear in my upcoming book on garden collectibles.

VII-17.
Stoneware bottles.
Middle one is a root or ginger beer bottle, big lip, initials in cobalt blue "D B", 10"H. (L) A Gin bottle, with handle, made by Wingender, in NJ, cobalt blue flower & bands, 10"H. (R) Another Wingender. Photo courtesy Litchfield Auction Gallery, Litchfield, CT. Ex-Harold Corbin Collection, auctioned 1/1/1990. Prices realized:
$175.00 and $120.00 and $130.00

VII-18.
Pickeled food bottle.
Green glass in the so-called "Cathedral" shape with gothic arched hexagonal sides. 13"H, American 19th C, mold-blown. Photo courtesy of Robert W. Skinner Inc., Auctioneers, Bolton, MA.
$300.00-$400.00

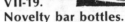
VII-19.
Novelty bar bottles.
All are molded figurals with etched details. From (L) to (R): (1) Mermaid; (2) Portrait bottle of champion heavyweight pugilist Jim Jefferies, who boxed from 1896 to 1904, and 1910 to 1921. This design shows "champion ready for an engagement," probably was done after his first retirement. Bottle has etched tights, body painted flesh color. Catalog states "best and only representation of a pugilist made in the form of a bottle." (3) "Never Rip" decanter..."They like to pour from it." A touch of soft porn, as in many late Victorian things. (4) Elephant's head & trunk, "cleverly gotten up for back bar display." All from the hotel & bar supply catalog of Albert Pick & Co., Chicago, 1909 (with some items going back to 1905). **$100.00-$500.00**

VII-20.
Burl bowl.
Old, original red paint on exterior, about 16 1/2" diameter but slightly warped as usual. First half 19th C. Photo and information courtesy Jeannine Dobbs' Country/Folk/Antiques, Merrimack, NH. A sublime form. **$2000.00-$2800.00**

VII-21.
Burls still growing on tree.
This particular tree is near Mt. Crawford, VA, in the Blue Ridge area. But in many places in Virginia and New Jersey (two states I know of) there are huge trees growing with a full supply of burls.

VII-22.
Bottle carrier.
Tinned iron wire, made for 2, 4 or 6 bottles. From F.A. Walker catalog, 1870s-80s. **$90.00-$125.00**

VII-23.
Bread box.
"Roll-A-Way" style with choice of decorations. This one is "Early American Girl Moderne," in ivory with red trim, or white with red. "Betsy Ross Moderne" was not shown in ad. Mfd. by E. M. Meder Co. 1935 ad. **$10.00-$20.00**

VII-24.
Bread raiser.
"With ventilated cover." Heavy tin, riveted strap handle, 4 sizes in same odd-seeming choice of quart capacities — 10, 14, 17 and 21. Central Stamping Co., 1920. **$30.00-$60.00**

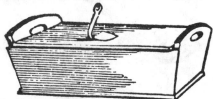

VII-25.
Bread trough & scraper.
Oblong wooden box with slanted sides. This was used the way the raisers were later used. This picture from American Home Cook Book, by an American lady. NY, 1854. The scraper is not described, but is probably wood, and has a crooked handle. **$125.00-$250.00**

VII-26.
"Dutch bucket."
Pieced tin, footed, japanned on outside, 4 sizes from 8 to 14 quart capacity. Matthai-Ingram Co., Baltimore, c.1890. **$20.00-$40.00**

VII-27.
Butter boxes.
"Bradley's" patented boxes, made of spruce or oak veneer "sewed together", tin bands at top and bottom. Used after scalding, by packing tightly with butter, overlaid with a disc of wax paper. American Agriculturist, 1/1880. **$10.00-$35.00**

VII-28.
Butter jar or crock.
Stoneware, with applied ear handles, slightly domed lid with knob. Made in 11 sizes: 1/4, 1/2, 1, 2, 3, 4, 5, 6, 8, 10, and 12 gallons. Also made in bigger sizes, from 15 to 50 gallons. Also made in bigger sizes, from 15 to 50 gallons, for meat. These did not have lids. Duparquet, Huot & Moneuse, hotel supplier, c.1904-1910 catalog. **$30.00-$150.00**

VII-29.
Butter chip holder.
You're right, it looks like a poker chip holder. We don't know which came first. Wood, holding 6 stacks of butter chips or patties on what appear to be little pans or saucers. From V. Clad & Sons, Inc., c.1800-1900 pamphlet. **$10.00-$20.00**

VII-30.
Butter dishes.
Both in "Perfection" granite ironware with choice of white metal or nickel plated mountings & protection bands. Both have two small hooks on lip to hold butter knife. Manning, Bowman & Co., c.1892 catalog. **$70.00$120.00**

VII-34.
Candlesticks.
Japanned stamped tin, all with black finish. At (L) is a "save-all" with the bottom of the candle accessible to the saver of scrap candles. Top (R) is 6 1/2" diameter with deep saucer base for runny candles. Bottom (R) came in two sizes — 4 7/8" and 5 1/2" diameter. Central Stamping Co., 1920 catalog. **$15.00-$30.00**

VII-31.
Cake box.
"The japanned tin boxes keep cake, bread, &c., perfectly fresh without the undesirable moisture of the stone jar." American Home Cook Book, 1854. **$40.00-$60.00**

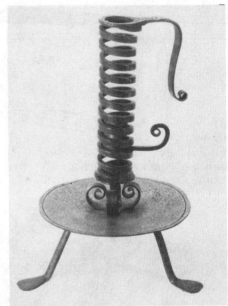

VII-32.
"Pastry closet" or cake safe.
"Model" round corner, black or white japanned stamped tin, 6 compartments. 15 1/2" x 11 1/4" x 10 1/8". Central Stamping Co., 1920 catalog. **$10.00-$20.00**

VII-35.
Candle holder.
Forged iron "pigtail" holder, on tripod base. 10"H. Maker's mark on rim of underside of base, "Samuel Yellin." Philadelphia, early 20th C. (Yes, the 1900s, not a misprint.) Photo courtesy Litchfield Auction Gallery, Litchfield, CT. Ex-Harold Corbin Collection, auctioned 1/1/1990. Price realized: **$2100.00**

VII-33.
Cake & pie box.
"A new idea in making a receptacle for pie and cake. In this box may be placed pie and cake in separate compartments perfectly safe form insects of all kinds, and yet thoroughly ventilated and aerated by its patented construction." One size only: 8"H x 12 1/2" square. Three finishes: brown japanning with gold stenciling; oak grained with gold; white enamel with gold. Silver & Co., Brooklyn, NY, c.1910 catalog. **$40.00-$60.00**

VII-36.
Candlesticks.
These five styles are also from the 1925 Pearson-Page **reproductions** catalog. Clockwise from top (L): (1) Pan type of sheet brass, riveted handle, 5 5/8" diameter. (2) 7 1/2" diameter pan. Note thumb rest on curled handle. (3) 7" diameter pan decorated with chased designs around floor of pan and on handle. Shallow sides have perforated design. (4) 8 1/2" diameter pan, probably a new art style, not a reproduction. (5) Version of chamberstick, 6 1/2"H x 7" diameter pan. Could be had plain or with chased decoration. **$20.00-$60.00**

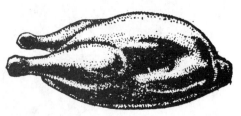

VII-37.
Candy box.
Papier mache turkey, "colored to represent a roasted turkey." Bottom opening. 4"L. From Slack Mfg. Co. novelty catalog, c.1925. Originally cost $9.50 for a gross. **$50.00-$70.00**

VII-41.
Canister set.
Yellowware "Dandy-Line", mfd. by Brush-McCoy Pottery Co., Zanesville, OH. Included spice containers (on top row), those for sugar, salt, butter & flour, tea & coffee, and also bread & cereal & cake jars, rolling pin, mixing bowls, milk pitchers, and nappies (the smallest bowl on table). Various kinds of knobs and handles, not really matching. Ad in House Furnishing Review, 8/1915.

VII-38.
Candy boxes,
for Christmas. Lithographed cardboard, frosted with mica sprinkles for snow. Candy fits into opening in bottom of each. Originally cost $5.00 a gross. From Slack Mfg. Co. novelty catalog, c.1925. **$40.00-$100.00**

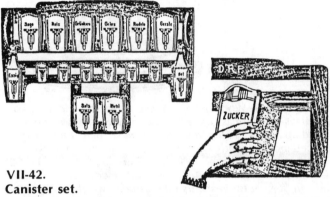

VII-42.
Canister set.
Decorated china with patented rack with built-in metal lids. Made in Germany and imported by housewares wholesaler G.M. Thurnauer, NYC. House Furnishing Review, 8/1910. **$100.00-$150.00**

VII-39.
Candy boxes.
For fancy chocolates or candy assortments. All were oversized for actual contents held — meant to fool recipient. Chromolith paper covers in "beautiful assortment of art pictures," with real ribbon. One at left, 15 1/2" x 9", has classy deep flange. Catalog says "This is positively the biggest flash on the market." Two at right came in 3 sizes: 1/2 lb. box, 10 1/2" x 4 1/2"; 1 lb. box, 10" x 6"; and 18 oz. box, 12 1/2" x 5 1/4" which "looks like a 2 lb. box." From Slack Mfg. Co. novelty catalog, c.1925. **$5.00-$15.00**

VII-43.
Table caster patent,
for small bottles — oil, vinegar, perhaps a bottled catsup or sauce too. Pat'd 11/10/1874, by Daniel Sherwood, Lowell, MA, assignor to Woods, Sherwood & Co., who were huge manufacturers of wire goods. **$50.00-$75.00**

VII-40.
Candy boxes,
for Hallowe'en. All in orange & black, cardboard & tissue. The ones in the top row are small size; the lower row has big ones. From Slack Mfg. Co. novelty catalog, c.1925. **$30.00-$100.00**

VII-44.
Cheese cradle.
Tole, with birds & flowers in ochre, white and gray on dark ground. 14" x 6". Courtesy The Abrahams, Langhorne, PA. **$250.00-$350.00**

VII-45.
Christmas tree holder.
"The Crown," mfd. by North Brothers, Philadelphia. Painted cast iron, tripod. Two sizes, for 2" or 3" trees. 1912 catalog cookbook, "Dainty Dishes For All the Year Round," by Mrs. S.T. Rorer.
$50.00-$75.00

VII-46.
Christmas tree stand.
With music box. Wooden base, 5 feet, nickel top, clockwork inside plays 2 Christmas carols. "Patented attachment which when pulled up makes the tree revolve and music play. Music can be stopped independently while the tree continues to revolve. Any sized tree can be placed in holder. Stand is 9" high x 13 1/2" diameter. This is just the article for show windows and family use and can be kept for years. Its total carrying weight is about 100 lbs." From Butler Brothers mail order Christmas catalog, 1899.
$100.00-$150.00

VII-47.
Cookie jar.
"Baker" jar, light tan & brown glaze, Red Wing Pottery, Red Wing, MN. These are real specialty category, and I don't have room to compete picture-wise. This one I chose because the figural theme is also cooking-related.
$50.00-$60.00

VII-48.
Cracker or pretzel jar.
Sponged decoration in blue on white ironstone. Nickeled copper bottom & top rims, and nickeled brass hinged lids. 7 1/2"H x 12 1/4" diameter. Late 19th C. Courtesy The Abrahams, Langhorne, PA.
$120.00-$160.00

VII-49.
Creamery vessels.
(L) Milk jug or ewer for 3 quarts of milk, earthenware, unglazed outside. German type; made also in 19th C. US. Lid fit into top like butter crock top. (M) Large milk vessel. "Filled with milk and set into water in pans or tubs — or other crocks...Water is renewed as often as ...convenient. The outside is so porous that the water, if it once wets the surface, is continually drawn up by capillary attraction. It evaporates all the time, thus notably cooling the milk." (R) Process called "Slipping the cream," whereby "after the milk is two days old, in ordinary weather, the cream may be loosened from the sides of the pan," and slips from the pans into a cooler that has a spigot at the bottom. _American Agriculturist_, 5/1880.

VII-50.
Stoneware crock.
Pale gray glazed stoneware, 10"H, wire bail handle with turned wood grip, 10"H, c.1900.
$20.00-$35.00

VII-51.
Public drinking cup,

as depicted for c.1908-1910 campaign to improve sanitation in public places. Such pictures helped companies like Dixie Cup, who made one-use throw away cups, as well as the collapsion cup companies, who made cups for each person to carry around with them. This from an "Educational Sheet" distribution by the Minnesota State Board of Health, published by Pioneer Press, St. Paul, MN.

VII-52.
"Pocket drinking cup."

Stamped metal, nickel-plated. "Indispensible for fishing and picnic parties, tourists, etc." Rayment catalog, c.1910-20s.
$15.00-$20.00

VII-53.
Collapsion cups.

(L) "Pure white metal, finished in the finest style; warranted non-corrosive; holds half-pint; incased in screw top nickel case." Robert H. Ingersoll & Bro., NYC. Turn of the century ad.
(R) Embossed aluminum, polished finish, 2 1/2" diameter at top. "Mirro" made by Aluminum Goods Mfg. Co. **$10.00-$20.00**

VII-54.
Cutlery tray.

Cutout thin wood, fancy centerboard handle, scalloped base, canted sides, typical Deco decoration of greyhounds, but possibly earlier. Four dogs on long sides, 2 on short. 13"L x 7 3/4"W. From booth of The Silver Flag, folk art dealers. **$250.00-$400.00**

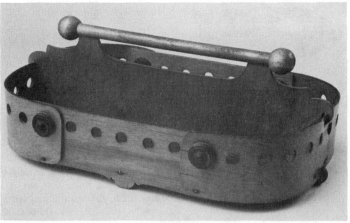

VII-55.
Cutlery tray.

Cutout bent veneer finish in silky honey-color, turned wood grip and bull's-eye knobby decorations, green baize bottom lining, 2 1/2"H exclusive of handle & centerboard x 11 1/4"L x 7 1/2"W, c.1890. Since the publication of the last edition, the Smithsonian has acquired a wonderful sewing stand made like this. If any of you have seen other pieces which seem to be of the same type, please let us know! **$65.00-$100.00**

VII-56.
Cutlery tray or knife box.

Japanned tin, hinged lids on either side, handle with reinforced grip. "A knife box should be large enough to hold the knives and forks in every day use, and nothing more...The handle should be large and sensible, and the partition through the middle of the box always separate the knives from the forks; there should be a lid to each side, to keep out the dust." American Agriculturist, 8/1879. **$55.00-$85.00**

VII-57.
Cutlery tray.

Wood, slanted sides, well-shaped centerboard handgrip, painted in bright colors like a game board. 14 3/4" x 7 3/4". In booth of Stephen Score, Essex, MA. Value range mine, not Score's.
$1200.00-$1500.00

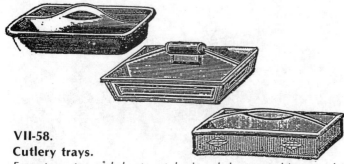

VII-58.
Cutlery trays.
From top: stamped sheet metal; pieced sheet metal japanned & pinstriped, with tubular grip; and wicker work, lined with tin. All from 1895 catalog of Harrod's Stores, Ltd., Brompton, England.
$30.00-$50.00

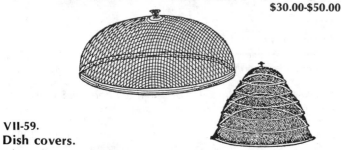

VII-59.
Dish covers.
*Also called **fly screen** or fly covers. People who have these always price them very highly, but the price is unwarranted. They were made over a very long period. The top picture, of a cover in oval shape is made of "closely knitted wire, blue steel coloring." It was "especially adapted to Free Lunch Counters," and came in 10", 12", 14", 16" and 18" lengths. Round ones came in a series from 8" to 14" diameter. From Albert Pick catalog, 1909. At right is a stack of "wire dish covers. — To cover meats, pastry, milk, butter, &c., from dust, flies, &c., in the pantry or on the table." The picture is from the American Home Cook Book, 1854. Value range usually seen may be double this:***$20.00-$75.00**

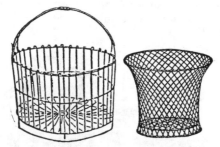

VII-60.
Egg baskets,
for gathering. (L) Iron wire, in 5 sizes (6", 7", 8", 9" nad 10" diameter), from Duparquet, Huot & Moneuse catalog, c.1904-1910. (R) Retinned wire, looks like wastebasket, even in dimensions — 15"H x 12" diameter at top. "Keeping eggs in our wire basket has the advantage of locating broken ones instantly." From Albert Pick catalog, 1909.
$20.00-$40.00

VII-61.
Flour bins.
Japanned tin, with more or less decoration, in gold. (L) Black background with gold Japanese-influenced motifs, c.1880s. (M) Japanned brown, 50 lb. capacity. Buhl Brothers, c.1919. (R) Black with simple border design, in three sizes: 15"H x 10 1/2" diameter; 21 5/8"H x 12 1/2" diameter; 27 1/8"H x 15". Central Stamping Co., 1920.
$50.00-$70.00

VII-62.
Food holder.
"Crystal," mfd by Ware-Standard Mfg. Co, NYC. For sugar, coffee, rice, salt, Indian meal, hominy, etc. Clear glass in metal bracket. This one shown with wall bracket; also was made to slide into brackets mounted to underside of shelf, so that they would hang down from the shelf. Made in 3 sizes, for 3 1/2, 7 and 14 lbs of dry food. "Turn the knob and the food runs out." Ad in House Furnishing Review, 5/1905.
$15.00-$22.00

VII-63.
Flour canister,
3-part, with sifting tray inside. Tin-lined copper, 7"H x 6 3/4" diameter, wooden knob. 19th C. Collection of Mary Mac Franklin.
$70.00-$90.00

VII-64.
Lehnware goblets.
Carved & painted wood. (L) Red & green paint, with snake wrapped around it, 3"H. (R) Flowers & vines, typical of Joseph Lehn, Lancaster County, PA. 2 1/2"H. Photo courtesy Litchfield Auction Gallery, Litchfield, CT. Ex-Harold Corbin Collection, auctioned 1/1/1990. Prices realized: **$550.00 and $400.00 Prices**

VII-65.
Herb tray.
Japanned tin, iron central handle, compartments. Picture from ad of William S. Adams & Son, London, in Francatelli's Cook's Guide Advertiser, c.1860-61. **$50.00-$70.00**

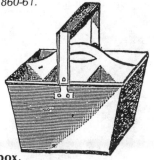

VII-66.
Housemaids' box,
for carrying little cleaning tools, polishes & rags, pieced tin, high handle in addition to the centerboard with the handgrip cutout. Japanned to resemble oak. From Harrod's Stores, Ltd. 1895 catalog. **$30.00-$40.00**

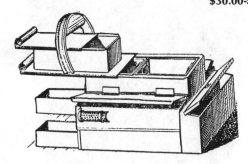

VII-67.
Housekeeper's safe patent.
Pat'd 2/10/1880, by Ebenezer H. Sturges, Wing's Station, NY. It has many compartments, not only for cleaning tools for cooking tools too. The top box is for knives. Spices were apparently meant for the hinged compartment in the front, where the nutmeg grater is mounted. Official Gazette.

VII-68.
Implement hook,
bought with ladle probably not original to it. Heavy brass, cutout in large-eyed bird form. Oval plate to be mounted to wall or woodwork of fireplace surround. 7 1/4"H x 8"W. 19th C English. Collection of Mary Mac Franklin. **$225.00-$275.00**

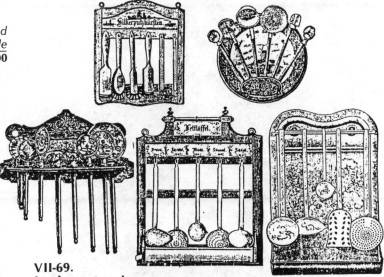

VII-69.
Implement racks.
All imported from Germany, about 1904. "German manufacturers of house furnishings have devised a great variety of racks or sets for holding articles of kitchen utility. They are decorative and practical, some bearing appropriate designs in the panels, while others are plain, the panels finished in Delft tile. The woodwork is of grained oak or of a softer wood heavily enameled in white...The vogue for these sets has gained great headway abroad, and the demand is also extending in this country. The sets pictured retail for from $4.50 to $6.50, with all the accessories." The only metal one is at lower right, with the curved dripping trough at bottom. Though the article, in House Furnishings Review, doesn't mention Thurnauer, it was probably that NYC firm that imported these. The German words for spices and staples didn't seem to deter sales. **$100.00-$200.00**

VII-70.
Make-do "Bail for a Water Jug."

Drawing in American Agriculturist, *4/1881, showing how "a jug, having lost its handle, was provided with a substitute in the form of a bail, as follows: Two wire 'rings' were made, one to go below the largest part of the jug, and the other and smaller one near the neck. These were held together by four wires passing between them. 'Ears' were put on opposite sides of the upper ring, and a stout wire bail attached; this bail was provided with a wooden handle through which the wire passed. From experience we can say it is more convenient to carry than a jug with the ordinary, one-sided handle."*

VII-72. Jug.
Redware with brown crackle glaze, wonderful lady's leg in high laced boot forms the angled handle. 8 1/2"H. 19th C, New England. Photo courtesy Litchfield Auction Galleries, Litchfield, CT. Ex-Harold Corbin Collection, auctioned 1/1/1990. Price realized:
$450.00

VII-71.
Jug with frame.

"Brackett's Revolving Jug," stoneware jug in cast iron frame making it easy to pour from. A beautiful, elegant form. Probably 1870s-80s. This was sold way under the money to my mind in 1985, for only $150.00. Photo courtesy Penny Sanders, Sanders Auctioneers, Wilton, NH.　　　**$150.00-$250.00**

VII-73. Jug.
Definitely a plumber's whimsy, as it's made of lead. Softened lead worked like clay to make decoration around neck and handle. I forgot to measure it, but seem to recall about 7" or 8"H. From stock of Lenny Kislin, Bearsville, NY.　　　**$145.00-$175.00**

VII-74.
Jardiniers.
Stamped, heavily-embossed sheet brass, with cast brass handles & feet. (T) is 10 1/2"H x 10 1/2" diameter, with fruit grouped around a pineapple. Lion's head drop handles. (B) 10 1/2"H x 11 3/4" diameter, ring foot. Decoration of bowl of fruit. These are from Pearson-Page catalog, Birmingham, England, 1925. **$30.00-$50.00**

VII-75.
Jugs.
(L) Shoulder jug, for liquor. Four sizes, from 1 qt. to 2 gal. capacity. (M) "Common shape" jug, "the kind that has been in use for many years. The demand for this old-style jug is ever increasing." In 7 sizes, from 1 qt. to 5 gal. (R) Bailed jug, "a new style." 2 1/4" diameter opening, 3 sizes — 1/4, 1/2 and 1 gal. From Albert Pick catalog, 1909. Makers unknown. **$30.00-$45.00**

VII-76.
Keeler.
Staved shallow tub, made in pine or cedar. Came in 4 sizes: 9 3/4", 12", 15" and 16 1/2" diameter. Duparquet, Huot & Moneuse, c.1904-1910 catalog. **$20.00-$50.00**

VII-77. Tine.
A Norwegian lunch box, bentwood oval, 10"L, painted black then carved through to make design. Lid swivels. Courtesy R.C. Bowen. Value range mine not Bowen's **$250.00-$350.00**

VII-78.
Lunch satchel.
"In outward appearance it is not to be distinguished from any other Leather Satchel for the use of working men and women, bookkeepers, clerks, engineers, conductors, drivers, school-teachers, dressmakers, seamstresses, excursionists, and all persons whose business requires their absence from home during the dinner-hour. It will hold a sufficient quantity of meat, vegetable, bread, and pie, coffee, tea or milk for one person's dinner, properly secured in their places, without napkin or paper, perfectly ventilated, and with an independent arrangement for heating them. They are made in different colors and in two sizes." Disguised brought-from-home lunches seem to be important at the time. Peck & Snyder ad in Century Monthly, 3/1883. **$25.00-$35.00**

VII-79.
Folding lunch box patent.
Pat'd 11/4/1884, by Alfred Brown & Alvin Lightener, Kansas City, MO. Sides and end are hinged, and the cover has slots for the straps of the handle. Official Gazette.

VII-80. (L) Dinner carrier,
in style called "decked". That is, the compartments (2, 3, or 4) stack. Tin. From F.A. Walker catalog, 1890s. **$30.00-$50.00**
(R) Dinner pail.
"New England" style. "Sterling" gray enamelware, by Central Stamping Co. Wire bail with wooden grip, and lid, which "shuts over outside" has wooden knob. Three sizes, holding 1 3/4 qts, 2 1/2 qts or 3 1/4 qts 1920. **$50.00-$75.00**

VII-81.
Lunch box,
another disguised one. This looks like a book, and is japanned in assorted colors, all in "imitation of Morocco Leather." 2 1/4" x 7 3/8" x 4 7/8". Lalance & Grosjean catalog, 1890. **$50.00-$75.00**

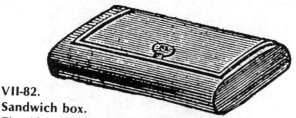

VII-82.
Sandwich box.
Tin with hinged lid. I'd like to find a source for these, newly made. They would be very useful. From Harrod's Stores 1895 catalog.
$20.00-$35.00

VII-83.
Lunch kit.
Black finished steel box with sliding compartment, steel & aluminum bottle, tinned steel drinking cup, with extra nested aluminum food trays to fit inside. 7 1/2"H x 10"L x 5"W. D.J. Barry catalog, 1924.
$20.00-$35.00

VII-84.
Dinner pail,
with trays & pie plate. "Saulson," in 2 sizes, 6 1/2" x 6", and 6 3/4" x 7 1/8". Central Stamping Co., 1920.
$20.00-$35.00

VII-85.
Lunch box.
Chromolithographed tin, oval, close-fitting lid, swing strap handle. This small box pictures characters from Peter Rabbit, as illustrated by Harrison Cady. Mfd. by Tindeco in the 1920s. A similar, more commonly found box has square corners. This one is 2 1/4"H x 4 1/2" x 3 1/2". Photo and collection of Robert Carr. Value range mine, not Carr's.
$65.00-$110.00

VII-86.
Lunch box.
Mickey Mouse, color lithographed tin, with "Bull Dog" wire handles, mfd. by Geuder, Paeschke & Frey, Milwaukee, in 1935. 4 3/4" x 8 1/4"L x 5"W. This is the earliest known comic character lunch box, and while it has an interior tray, it never had a thermos bottle. It was made by a firm that had specialized in tin — and enamel— wares of many kinds for at least 55 years. Photo and collection of Robert Carr. Value range mine, not Carr's.
$125.00-$250.00

VII-87.
Make-do "catch-all."
A hanging repository for "burnt matches, bits of thread, paper, etc., made from the broken top part of a footed goblet. All the rage in 1874-1875, so much so that "crockery stores were beseiged for broken goblets, and when none were left, it is hinted that some store-keepers broke them on purpose." _American Agriculturist,_ 3/1875. The article said that after you made a pincushion of the bottom half, you could use the top part too, with bits of cardboard, silver paper, crocheted tassels & bag.
$25.00-$50.00

VII-88.
Spill cups,
an early version of match holders, only these don't predate striking matches. Embossed, pieced sheet brass, with fleur de lys, Adams' wreath, heraldic device. All 10 1/2"H x 5"W. From Pearson-Page 1925 catalog. **$20.00-$30.00**

VII-92.
Match holders.
All wall-hung, and all stamped tin, japanned in variety of colors, (L) type called a "twin," with scalloped bottom. (R) Two with lids, and properly called match safes. One at bottom is "self-closing." Sizes: 5" x 4 1/2" x 1"; 3 3/4" x 2 1/2" x 1 5/8"; and 4 1/4" x 2 3/8" x 3". Central Stamping Co., 1920. **$10.00-$30.00**

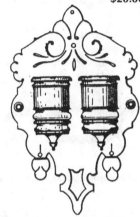

VII-89.
Match holder patent.
Pat'd 3/13/1877, by J.A. Kratt, Buffalo, NY. Wall-hung, carved wood, fancy backplate, 2 turned half-cups. The feature claimed by the patentee is the fact that the "box plate" is hinged to a backplate, and is "provided on the rear side with a friction-surface." I can see the spilled matches now. <u>Official Gazette</u>.

VII-93.
Match safe.
"Lusk," with choice of oxidized copper, nickel plated, or brushed brass finish. Two advertised features were a "spark guard" along side that protected against flying sparks, and also that a "Lusk will save its cost many times over in keeping the wall paper and polished woodwork from being marred by matches, as the scratcher is always handy." In traveling salesman's supplier catalog put out by F.W. Seastrand, c.1910s. **$20.00-$35.00**

VII-90.
Match holders.
These were advertised as "safety match safes" because of the "round receptacle at the bottom to hold" burnt matches which was effectively closed by turning the inner cylinder. The term match safe usually refers to a fireproof receptacle in which the unburnt matches are kept, with a lid that would contain fire if by rubbing together they ignited. These japanned and decorated tin ones were pat'd 8/6/1895, and sold by Dover Stamping Co., Boston. **$20.00-$30.00**

VII-94.
Match holders.
(L) Fry pan wall-hung holder, black-enameled cast brass, with egg given oxidized "silver" finish. Owls on stone wall a popular Victorian motif. Both from Montgomery Ward catalog, c.1895. **$35.00-$55.00**

VII-91.
Match holder.
Stamped sheet steel enameled in "dull gunmetal finish." 5 3/4" diameter. The Washburn Co., Worcester, MA, 1927. **$10.00-$15.00**

VII-95.
Matchbox holder.
"Just out and the funniest novelty of the season. A perfect pair of miniature pantaloons, but five inches in length, made from the finest cassimere. A pair of silk suspenders attached to the buttons on pants can be used to hang it on the wall. It will hold a full box. "Sandpaper patches 1 3/4" across. A.E. Rayment Supply Co., c.1910-1920s. **$8.00-$12.00**

VII-96.
Matchbox holder.
Cutout plywood, green with black trim, furniture leg skids for eyes. Typical of home craft project holders, usually animals or people. 1920s-40s. **$15.00-$25.00**

VII-97.
Milk bottle.
"Warren," pat'd 3/23/1880, mfd. by Warren Glass Works Co., NYC. Advertised American Agriculturist, 1882. **$10.00-$18.00**

The *Milk Can Server* is simple to operate. Cut or tear away paper label where spout closes, place can in container (see illustration), clasp tightly in one hand, bring spout to place with quick, firm motion and close down top. This action punctures a vent hole in top of can and locks spout in place, ready for instant service.

VII-98.
Milk can server.
Provided an "attractive pitcher that harmonizes with the most richly appointed table service." Pat'd 1915 & 1916. Liquid Container and Server Corp., Los Angeles, CA. **$10.00-$18.00**

VII-99.
Milk pail & teapot.
Pail in plain gray enamel, turned wooden knob, bail handle, about 10"H. Teapot cobalt blue with gold trim & white flowers, hinged lid. Courtesy Mainland Antiques, Mainland, PA. **$60.00-$135.00**

VII-100.
Milk pail holder.
Hoop iron with riveted knee pieces, homemade, not commercially sold. American Agriculturist, 7/1873.

VII-101.
Molasses pitcher.
Japanned pieced tin, holding either 1 or 2 pts. Central Stamping Co., 1920. **$20.00-$50.00**

VII-102.
Nappies.
Lipped, 'square' and round, all earthenware. "Very neat milk pans, made of yellow or white ware, are sometimes used and are by far the best round shallow pans. They are called by the trade **'nappies,'** *and are round or oval. The convenient sizes hold 4 to 6 quarts; the 8-quart ones are heavy to handle. The round ones with a lip were formerly made extensively for the southern trade, but less so now. Square dishes of the same ware are called* **'puddings'***; they are rectangular with somewhat rounded corners, and in common use as pudding dishes, but are admirable milk-pans when small quantities of milk only are kept." American Agriculturist, 5/1880.* **$30.00-$100.00**

VII-103.
Nappy or nappie.

Yellowware, in 10 sizes, from only 3" to 12" diameter. Note slanted sides. In all my searchings I have yet to find a definitive description of a nappie, or any idea of where the word came from. Some sources say they are for cooking, and some nappies have fluted bottoms or sides. Obviously, from the quote in the last caption, to some people nappies were milk pans of a fairly large size. 20th C ads show glass nappies, but most are ceramic. This cut from Duparquet, Huot & Moneuse hotelier supplies catalog, c.1904-1910. **$30.00-$100.00**

VII-104.
Nursing bottle.

Burr patent "medallion feeder," glass flattish bottle, glass 'straw,' rubber tube & nipple. Embossed eagle in medallion, M.S. Burr Co. From Butler Brothers 1899 catalog. This type of flask-like nurser, though not this brand, dates to at least the 1830s. The tubes may have been made of bone or pewter or porcelain. Nipples were bone, wood, ivory, pewter (hopefully without lead) and finally rubber in the last half of the 19th C. **American Collectors of Infant Feeders,** *SASE to Jo Ann Todd, 5161 W. 59th St., Indianapolis, IN, 46254.* **$20.00-$40.00**

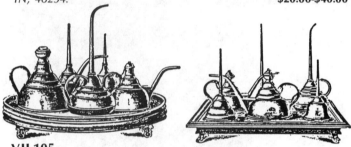

VII-105.
Oiler sets.

Here because they're as elegant as cruet sets for the dining room, and possibly confusable. (L) Engineers' oiler set with oval tray and set of 4 oiler cans. Two sizes: trays 14" x 8 1/2" and 16" x 11 1/2", the larger having 5 cans. They could be had in brass or nickeled brass finishes. Note little wheeled casters on the trays. (R) set on either 14" x 9" tray with 4 cans or 17 1/4" x 11" with 5. Both McNab & Harlin Mfg. Co., NYC, 1898 catalog. **$50.00-$120.00**

VII-106.
Pails.

(L) Staved wooden pail of cedar (10, 12 or 14 qts) or pine (12 qts only). Iron bound, wire bail, wood grip. Duparquet, Huot & Moneuse 1904-1910 catalog. (R) Graniteware water pail in 12 qt. size only. From Sethness Co. catalog, 1925. (M) Pieced tin, flared sides, wood grip, in 6 qt. (6 1/4"H), 8 qt. (6 3/4"H) and 10 qt. (7 7/8"H) sizes. Savory, Inc., c.1925-28. Tin one least valuable, although even rusted sometimes are priced high. **$20.00-$120.00**

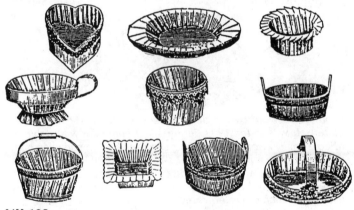

VII-107.
"Milk-Jug and Water-Pail."

A cautionary morality fable in the form of a conversation:
MILK-JUG.

> Water-pail, how can we two agree?
> What are you, pray, sir, compared to me?
> You'd better be gone, to drudge about,
> *For, if you stay, I shall turn you out.*

WATER-PAIL. My dear little jug, mind what you do;
> Fine things are brittle, and so are you.

———

> The milkjug thought always of his worth,
> He look'd so handsome upon the hearth;
> But the cook she crack'd him, which made him leak,
> And he lay on the dust-bin that very week;
> But the plain old water-pail held his own
> Full three years after the jug fell down.

———

Picture Fables, drawn by Otto Speckter, translated from German rhymes of F. Hey. NY: Appleton, 1858.

VII-108.
Paper cases,

or cups for candy or other small confections. Fluted colored paper in a variety of forms. Note the heart; the keeler at right of 2nd row; the coffee cup; the low pail or firkin; the washtub; the basket! All from Duparquet, Huot & Moneuse catalog, c.1904-1910, from which hoteliers and shops bought supplies. **$3.00-$15.00**

Pepper Box.

VII-109.
Pepper boxes & salt box.

(L) Made in pieced & stamped tin, or better, in Britannia metal. From Harrod's Stores, Brompton, England, 1895 catalog. (R) Top is a relatively flat-top salt box, 3"H; bottom is dome-topped pepper box, 3 3/4"H. Both in Duparquet, Huot & Moneuse catalog, c.1904-1910. **$10.00-$30.00**

VII-110.
Pepper bottle.
"A Charming, life-like representation of a funny, knowing little pug dog. It is entirely of frosted silver, and will never fail to receive admiring attention. The pepper is shaken out through the tiny holes in the top of the dog's head." Original cost only $2.00, c.1883-84. Value range assuming bottle really made of silverplate.
$30.00-$65.00

VII-111.
Picnic or market basket.
Called a "chip-basket," which is "made of neatly interwoven wooden splits, with strongly-framed flat covers, which shut down closely, and are fastened by catches." Rounded corners. *American Agriculturist*, 5/1871.
$40.00-$60.00

VII-112.
Hanaper.
I found this word by accident, along with the hard-to decipher picture. It was in the 1903 <u>Century Dictionary Encyclopedia</u>. A Middle English word, hanypere, or Old French word hanapier, hannepier, etc. meaning "a case for a hanap or drinking-cup, or for other vessels...It was often made of wickerwork, and sometimes covered with leather." It is obviously where the word **hamper**, used for a picnic basket, came from.

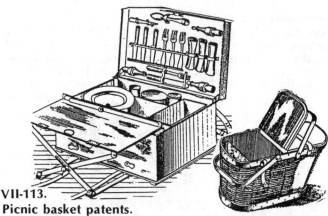

VII-113.
Picnic basket patents.
(T) "Lunch-box," pat'd 7/26/1881, by Sarah A. Hoskins, Bangor, ME. With a "hinged & folded table, each leaf of which has a pair of hinged legs crossing one another." Fitted compartments. (B) "Refrigerator-basket," pat'd 10/28/1884, by John R. Hare, Baltimore, MD. "A waterproof bag (is) placed between the felt filling and the wicker-work casing" to act as an insulator. <u>Official Gazette</u>.

VII-114.
Picnic baskets.
(T) Refrigerator basket, made of rattan, with layer of asbestos (!) and layer of felt between rattan body and inside metal lining. Ice compartment shown at near end, which is removable for cleaning. Called the "Everybody," and came in 2 sizes: 12"H x 21" x 10", or 14 1/2"H x 22" x 10". (B) is woven of ash, plywood top, lined of material, and "made for the sole purpose of keeping out sand and dirt." 11"H x 19 1/2"L x 11"W. Both in 1930s Abercrombie & Fitch catalog of outdoors goods.
$30.00-$50.00

VII-115.
Picnic basket.
Handsome form, said to be Shaker. Tightly woven ash splint over reed. 10"H x 16"L, 2 lids, woven handle slightly unravelled. Late 19th C probably.
$200.00-$350.00

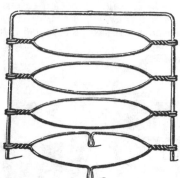

VII-116.
Pie holder & cooler.
Tinned wire, made in 5 styles. The 4 plate style made in lightweight wire and heavy wire. Others all heavy wire, for 6, 12 even 24 plates!! The latter for a bakery. From catalog of Wire Goods Co., 1915. Caution: Some **reproductions** of these are sometimes hard to tell, being of heavy wire. Most are painted dull black, but then so are some of the old ones. Ones with bright orange rust are undoubtedly repros. I can't guarantee a description of an old one, but I'd say if you have one you've had for at least 20 years, maybe longer, it's probably old.
$20.00-$100.00

VII-117.
Piggin,
with lid, which is unusual. 9 1/2"H overall. Early 19th C, either North American or European. **$200.00-$400.00**

VII-118.
Pitcher,
without a handle, economically repaired with soldered tin. Picture sent to American Agriculturist, 7/1885, by C.F. Alkire, Madison County, OH. Value depends on artfulness of repair, as well as original interest of the pitcher. **$60.00-$400.00**

VII-119.
Porringer.
Cast iron, half-pint size and so-marked on underside. Mfd. by ubiquitous West Bromwich, England, founder, A. Kenrick, with fanlike tab handle. 4 1/8" diameter, long casting gate. Some in this size are marked "No. 0" but this one appears to be marked "No. 3". Photo courtesy of Oveda Maurer Antiques, San Anselmo, CA. **$85.00-$120.00**

VII-120.
Salt.
Turned and chip-carved wood in abstract form of pineapple or osage orange, perhaps even a sort of inside-on-outside pomegranate. Green paint on outside, red inside, 5"H. Photo courtesy Litchfield Auction Gallery, Litchfield, CT. Ex-Harold Corbin Collection, auctioned 1/1/1990. Price realized: **$750.00**

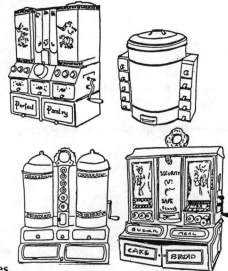

VII-121.
Portable pantries.
Clockwise from upper (L). (1) "The Perfect Pantry," pat'd 1904. Some have a clock frame on top, although I believe the user supplied the clock. (2) Maker unknown, flour compartment in center, with sifter built in, spice containers along sides. (3) "Security Safe," pat'd in 1900 and 1901, 38"H x 31"W. Japanned dark brown with flowers and gilt stenciling. (4) Possibly a "Globe Cabinet," though similar in some respects to the 'Queen Safe." 42"H x 31"W x 21" deep. Note opening for a clock, and also curved fronts of lower compartment. What's different from named examples I've seen are the two different-sized spice compartments down center. Value goes down, and identification is hard, when pantries have been painted. **$500.00-$1200.00**

VII-122.
Salt box.
Two colors of turned wood, with bull's-eye backplate hanger, hinged lid. Word "Salz" in little ribbon design on front. Imported from Germany by G. M. Thurnauer, NYC. Ad in House Furnishings Review, 1/1911. **$40.00-$90.00**

VII-123.
Salt boxes.
(L) Turned wood, no lid, painted to simulate ceramic mocha ware (which may have been what some graniteware designs were meant to resemble), with gilt rim. Only 3 1/2"H. Photo courtesy Litchfield Auction Gallery, Litchfield, CT. Ex-Harold Corbin Collection, auctioned 1/1/1990. Price realized: **$175.00**
(R) in form of **piggin**, with one long stave forming the hanger/handle. Iron hoops. Norwegian, 12"H overall x 4 3/4" diameter, 19th C. Picture courtesy of the National Museum of American History, Smithsonian Institution.

VII-124.
Salt box & match safe.
Red & white checkered enamelware, probably German, possibly French, late 19th C. From booth of Steve Smith, Country Bumpkin Antiques. For the pair: **$185.00-$250.00**

VII-125.
Salt & pepper shakers,
originally meant for lunch kit or picnics. Spun aluminum, 2"H x 1 5/8" diameter, "Mirro." Mfd. by Aluminum Goods Mfg. Co., 1925 catalog. **$4.00-$8.00**

VII-126.
Salt shaker.
"Crown," with device that prevents clogging. Heavy glass, with silver-plated brass embossed top. H. & H. Mfg. Co., NYC. House Furnishings Review ad, 5/1907. **$15.00-$20.00**

VII-127.
Salt & pepper shakers.
Cactuses of molded plaster, painted green, with red and yellow flowers. 2"H, they sit in base made of real cactus wood. Souvenir of Benson, AZ, c.1940s. Value may increase slightly with renewed interest in Western motifs. **$10.00-$15.00**

VII-128.
Salt shaker.
Another anti-clogging one called the "Kant-Klog." Crystal and "non-corrosive white metal." Humboldt Mfg. Co., Brooklyn, NY. House Furnishings Review ad, 10/1915.

VII-129.
Salt & pepper dispenser.
Glass containers screwed into green plastic stand. Two buttons: push white one to release salt; black one for pepper. 2"H x 2 3/8"W. Imperial Metal Mfg. Co., pat'd 8/5/1939, #1,772,041.
$12.00-$18.00

VII-130.
Salt & pepper shakers.
Novelty plastic power lawnmower in original box. Red & white plastic, black rubber-like wheels. "Tiny Power Mower," but no maker's mark. When you push mower, the eccentric axle underneath alternately pushes up the pepper then the salt. 1950s.
$12.00-$20.00

VII-131.
Slop jars.
All "Greystone" enameled ware by Matthai-Ingram, c.1890. (L) Tin lid, bail, tipping handle near bottom. (M) Two handles; (R) bailed. "Slop" was not contents of chamberpot. It was, in the toilette set, for the used wash water from the basin. In the kitchen, it could be the soggy remains on a plate, to be "slopped" to the pigs, or more discretely, it could be only leftover vinegar, wine, apple or grape juices, which could be distilled into vinegar. **$40.00-$60.00**

VII-132.
Syrup dispenser.
"Ward's Lemon-Crush," ceramic lemon with metal pump, colorfully decorated. Pumped lemon syrup into soda water. c.1920s.
$1500.00-$2200.00

VII-133.
Syrup dispenser.
"Buckeye Root Beer," urn, with dancing fauns and price 5¢. Cleveland Fruit Juice Co., Cleveland, OH, ad in The Soda Fountain, 6/1919. **$1200.00-$1800.00**

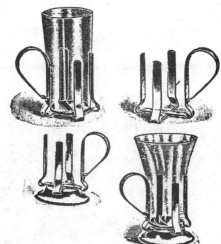

VII-134.
Soda glass holders,
also called **zarfs.** Both are adjustable, and made of nickel plated spring brass. Bottom one has a base. From Cherry-Bassett Co., Baltimore & Philadelphia, 1921 supply catalog. **$3.00-$8.00**

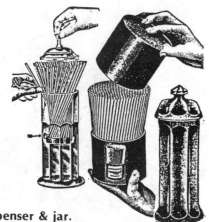

VII-135.
Soda straw dispenser & jar.

In the center is a carton of 500 of Stone's soda straws. (L) A straw dispenser, "fool proof, sanitary, ornamental." (R) A paneled straw jar. Clear glass jars or dispensers are not worth anywhere near as much as are colored ones, such as blue or green. I recently saw a green one advertised for $650.00. These are from the Cherry-Bassett catalog, 1921.   **$100.00-$175.00**

VII-136.
Soup tureen.

"Patent Perfection Granite Iron," round tureen with nickel-plated or silver-plated mountings. 6-pint or 8-pint capacity. Manning, Bowman & Co., c.1892.   **$250.00-$350.00**

VII-137.
Soup tureen.

Tin, with cast iron handles and lid finial. "Bite" out of lid for ladle. 10"H x 15 1/2"L x 9 1/2"W oval. Ex-Keillor Collection. The exact same tureen, even with the vertical lines on the body (which I thought were shading), appeared in the F.A. Walker catalog from 1870s. It was available in five sizes — for 3, 4, 6, 8 and 10 quarts.
$125.00-$160.00

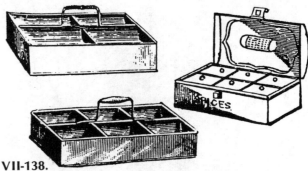

VII-138.
Spice boxes.

Top (L) " 'Cooks' tin spice boxes, with 4 and 6 compartments.' ". Duparquet, Huot & Moneuse, c.1904-1910. (R) "The Spice Box. — Has six separate boxes that take out, so that whole or ground spices may be kept nice and separate." Note the nutmeg grater in the lid. <u>American Home Cook Book</u>, 1854. Bottom (L) heavy XXXX tin, highly polished, heavy wired edges top and bottom." 3"H x 9 1/2" x 12 1/2" with 4 compartments, or 15"L with 6. Pick-Barth catalog, 1929.   **$60.00-$125.00**

VII-139.
Seasoning box.

Japanned tin, hinged lid, cast iron handles. Harrod's Stores, Brompton, England, 1895 catalog.   **$60.00-$125.00**

VII-140.
Spice caddy patent.

Pat'd 10/14/1879, by William B. Hartley, Washington, DC. "The invention consists in a caddy consisting of a main or stock receptacle or vessel constructed of suitable material, and of any desired capacity, to hold the articles (tea, coffee, spices) in bulk, (and) being provided at the bottom with a series of hoppers, each with a sliding partition or cut-off, beneath which are arranged a series of removable drawers of varying sizes." <u>Official Gazette</u>.

VII-141.
Spice box.

Japanned tin, hinged hasp-closing lid, iron finial. Round box with 7 containers, all stenciled: "Ginger, Cloves, Pepper, Allspice, Mace, Nutmeg, Cinnamon." F.A. Walker catalog, c.1880s.**$145.00-$175.00**

VII-142.
Spice boxes.
(L) Japanned tin with gold border, radiating compartments, hinged close-fit lid with cast iron finial, hasp. Center hole, where axle would be in a wheel, is where nutmeg grater fit. (R) Open spice basket-type carrier for canisters. Decorated in "art colours with gold border." Both from Harrod's Stores, Brompton, England, catalog of 1895. **$125.00-$155.00**

VII-143.
Spice boxes.
Both from Silver & Co., Brooklyn, catalog of c.1910. Spice & condiment box, with hinged lid and drawer has 12 spice boxes and a compartment for 6 bottles of extracts for flavoring. Tin, finished brown & gold, oak-grained & gold, or white and gold, with white porcelain knobs and 2 handles. 8"H x 10 1/2" x 11 1/4". Round spice box is "neat, roomy" and has 8 small canisters. 3"H x 10" diameter in brown japanning with gold, oak grained with gold, or white with gold. A smaller one, 8" diameter, was offered in brown only. **$95.00-$175.00**

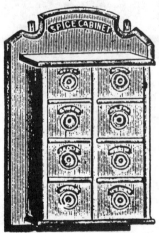

VII-144.
Spice cabinets.
(L) Ash with oil finish, 8 small marked drawers, shaped backplate for wall-hanging. 18"H x 12"W. Sold originally through Montgomery Ward, c.1895, for only 90¢ **$150.00-$200.00**
(R) Wooden with carved fancy arched pediment. Eight marked drawers. Imported by G.M. Thurnauer, NYC, 1903. **$150.00-$200.00**

VII-145.
Spice cabinet.
Simplest wooden type, 6 marked drawers, varnished finish. 13"H x 9"W x 5" deep. D.J. Barry catalog, 1924, maker unknown. **$50.00-$70.00**

VII-146.
Spice cabinets.
Another imported carved wooden one, this with 4 small feet, to set on top of sideboard or counter. G.M. Thurnauer & Bro., NYC, House Furnishings Review, 1/1911. **$135.00-$200.00**

Japanned tin, bronzed or "fancy decorations." Made in 2 sizes, with 6 or 8 drawers. Jobber's ad in House Furnishings Review, 8/1913, maker unknown. This is the kind of tin cabinet sometimes described, inaccurately, as "Pennsylvania German" or "early tin." **$125.00-$165.00**

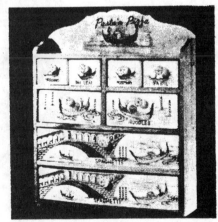

VII-147.
Spice & pasta cabinet,
advertised as a "pasta 'n pizza rack." Philippine mahogany, earthenware drawers are hand-painted. 13"H x 11"W. This is hard to value. On the one hand you can say "it's only 30 years old" (advertised in House Beautiful, 9/1960), and think of it as rummage sale material worth under $25.00. Or you could say, "it's already 30 years old, and awfully neat looking." The 21st C isn't that far off, so let me upgrade value from price listing to: **$40.00-$60.00**

VII-148.
Spice tower, or spice turret.
Stacked spice boxes, turned wood, light hardwood. Decalcomania labels in light yellow with black engraved letters for Cinnamon, Ginger, Cloves, Nutmeg. 7 1/8"H. English, 19th C. Courtesy R.C. Bowen. **$175.00-$250.00**

VII-149.
Spoon dripper.
A wall rack for hanging ladles & tasting spoons & basters. Copper, 28"H x 21"W. Mfd. by Henry Rogers, Sons & Co., Wolverhampton, England, 1914 catalog. Likely to be sold as older than it is. **$90.00-$150.00**

VII-150.
String holders,
or **twine boxes.** (L) Brass ball, nickeled, on stand. (M) Nickeled brass with embossed design. (R) Cast iron, on stand. Finished with copper or with japanning. All from Jaburg Brothers catalog, makers unknown, 1908. **$115.00-$200.00**

VII-151.
String holders.
Two hanging types, two counter tops types. All are cast iron, either japanned or finished in black paint. The only one with a name is the "beehive" lower (R), 4"H x 4 1/2". The others are about 3 3/8" diameter. Top two from Albert Pick catalog, 1909; others from D.J. Barry catalog, 1924. Considering lack of age on these, I think they are overpriced usually unless very unusual. **$9.00-$150.00**

VII-152.
Sugar bucket.
Staved wood, bentwood hoops and handle. Fitted lid. 9 3/4"H x 10 1/2" diameter at base. From Massachesettes, 19th C. Photo courtesy of the National Museum of American History, Smithsonian Institution.

VII-153.
Sugar bowl.
"Sanitary," with lever to release measure of sugar. Holds 2 lbs. Clear glass with nickel-plated base. Ideal Sanitary Sugar Bowl Co., NYC. 1915 ad. **$35.00-$50.00**

VII-154.
Tin containers.

(L) A mini top hat, painted tin, and not a container except when upside down. 3 1/4"H. (R) Pieced tin in form of farrier's anvil, the lid having a horseshoe-shaped handle. Decalcomania transfer shows horseshoeing scene. English tea container, 6 1/2"H. Photo courtesy Litchfield Auction Gallery, Litchfield, CT. Ex-Harold Corbin Collection, auctioned 1/1/1990. Prices realized. **$425.00; $450.00**

VII-155.
Syrup pitchers.

Also called simply **syrups.** *All but first have "patented central spout and cut-off," from Manning, Bowman c.1892 catalog. Clockwise from top (L): (1) Decorated enamelware one, with separate drip plate, with nickeled or silvered mountings. (2) "Pearl Agate" in assorted soft tints in mauve, brown, green, etc. (3) "Decorated Opal," with Grecian finial. (4) Chased quadruple silver plate. (4) Another chased design, nickel or silverplate.* **$150.00-$250.00**

VII-156.
Child's tray,

for clipping to table edge. Assorted colors and fancy designs on chromolithographed stamped tin, spring steel clip. This one shows children playing outside on lawn, somewhat dangerously with bows and arrows. 15 3/8" x 10 1/2". Central Stamping Co., 1920, in design from 19th C. **$30.00-$100.00**

VII-157.
Tea caddies.

(T) Lightweight one, for "use of spice dealers in putting up goods for the trade." Could be had in 5 sizes, from 8 7/8"H x 7 3/4"W to 19 1/2"H x 13"W. When the druggist ordered it, he was to "state name of tea, coffee, or spice to be marked on caddy." (L) "Lillibridge's Patent Base Delivering, Self-Feeding, Flavor Preserving" caddy, in 6 sizes, from 8"H x 4 1/4"W to 21"H x 14 1/2"W. (R) Heavyweight one, in 6 sizes, from 12 1/2"H x 9 3/4"W to 21 3/4"H x 16 3/4"W. All from catalog of Sidney Shepard & Co., Buffalo Stamping Works, Buffalo, NY, 1870s. **$60.00-$200.00**

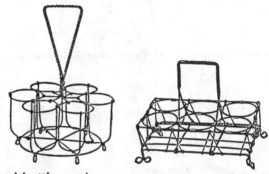

VII-158.
Tumbler and bottle carriers.

Made of tinnned wire, plain with twisted handle at (L), for 4, 6 or 9 bottles, or all twisted construction (R) for 2, 3, 4, 6, 8 or 12 tumblers and ranging in size from 6 1/2" x 3 1/2" up to 12 3/4" x 9 1/2". Wire Goods Co., "Sherwood" products. 1915. **$30.00-$65.00**

VII-159.
Vegetable dish,

to match the soup tureen in VII-176. "Patent Perfection Granite Ironware," with white metal mountings. Came in 3 sizes, 11"L, 13"L and 15"L. Manning, Bowman & Co., c.1892. **$250.00-$350.00**

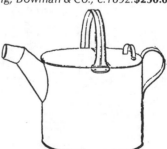

VII-160.
Water can.

Not a watering can for gardens, but a hot water can for adding hot water to wash basin, or for other uses. Enameled sheet iron, white inside & out. Harrod's Stores, Brompton, England, 1895 catalog. **$115.00-$150.00**

VII-161.
Water pitchers,

for hot and cold water. Wild designs, "painted in bright and subdued colors; superb adjuncts to summer or city houses." F.A. Walker, 1886 catalog supplement. **$50.00-$200.00**

VII-162.
Wine coolers.

Bottom (L) is oldest. It is japanned tin, with cast iron handle. From American Home Cook Book, 1854. Other two are from Duparquet, Huot & Moneuse, 1904-1910 catalog. Top one is japanned tin; other is galvanized sheet metal for one bottle. **$30.00-$150.00**

VII-163.
Oooops!

Main picture is from a humorous story in Century, 6/1878. The officer from the War of 1812 has fallen backwards "plump into the sour-tub." The term **sour-tub** does not appear in any dictionary of Americanisms I have. I suspect it may be the same as yeast tub, one of which is shown at right, from the Duparquet, Huot & Moneuse catalog, c.1904-1910. It was made to hold 12, 16, 24, 30, 35 and 40 gallons. Top left is a yeast pail, holding 10, 12, 14 or 16 quarts. Both of oak staves.

C. HOLDING & HANDLING:
VIII. OPEN & CLOSE

In this chapter are the ingenious devices used to open bottles having caps or corks, cans, and a few jars. Arguably, the most elegant group is corkscrews, which have been collected for many years, whether not it is true today, corkscrews have gained their cachet because of the wine within most bottles with corks. Anybody who would pay $4000.00 or $20,000.00 or even more for an historic aged bottle of wine (whether or not it would be drinkable), would want the very finest antique corkscrews. If you are interested in joining the Canadian Corkscrew Collectors' Club, write Ron MacLean, 4201 Sunflower Dr., Mississauga, Ontario, CAN, L51.

The aristocrats are the mechanical ones from the early 19th C; next in desirability would be rigid iron or other metal ones dating back to the 16th or 17th century — pure functional form. Least costly, widely and popularly collected, are the late 19th C and all 20th C corkscrews, figural and mechanical. In any mechanical corkscrew collection, the patient and patented search for improvement is evident. Therefore, while handmade and one-of-a-kind screws are valuable additions to a collection, the patented examples excite the most interest. The Englishman William Lund was probably the most prolific inventor of corkscrews and his designs vary considerably in mechanical principle. The entire field, American and European, is vast, and only a hint of the range is given in this chapter. One of the most select of all collector societies is devoted to these clever metal pigtails: The International Correspondence of Corkscrew Addicts, whose international membership is limited to 50. Their president is called the "Right", as in "I'd rather be right than president".

The only jar openers here are a few meant for pickle jars or peanut butter jars, etc., with tightly screwed-on lids. Jar *wrenches*, on the other hand, are usually considered a "go-with" for collectors of canning or fruit jars, and other related canning equipment, and are to be found in the Can & Dry chapter XVI, in the Preserving Section.

Can openers are probably more popular with American collectors than are corkscrews. The variety in mechanical types is very great — from one moving part to a series of gears. There are many rigid openers also, of which the majority look like tools, the minority have figural handles. As more collectors specialize in can openers, prices rise, and more and more unknown types are discovered setting off a search for multiple examples. It is a good field for a beginning collector because of the quantity, and there is also an opportunity to trade up and to specialize. I expect there will be a book on them by 1992 or so. There is a book on beer can openers, by Don Bull; this is a very specialized field whose devotees seek out those marked with rare breweries.

Bar set, molded white plastic & metal, skeleton & bone figurals, including bottle opener, corkscrew, 6 drink stirrers, motif is skull on top of long femur bone, "Name Your Poison", 1950s (?). **$10.00-$18.00**

Bottle capper, cast iron, lever action, countertop, "Big Ben", English (?), late 19th C (?). **$20.00-$30.00**

Bottle capper, iron finished black, 1926. **$30.00-$35.00**

Bottle capper, turned wood, 2 part, with copper insert in bottom cylindrical part, fitted over bottle with a cap, then punched down to secure cap, not marked, 10¼"L when completely closed, 19th C. **$20.00-$25.00**

Bottle, jar & screw cap opener combined, rubber gripper to protect & assist hand, "EZY GRIP", Sieberling Latex Products Co., Akron, OH, early 20th C. **$4.00-$6.00**

Bottle opener, adv'g "Rumford", early 20th C. **$15.00-$18.00**

Bottle opener, "Baltimore Cork & Screw", MD, 1908. **$25.00-$30.00**

Bottle opener, alligator, polychromed cast iron, 20th C. **$35.00-$40.00**

Bottle opener, automobile jack figural, iron, American, c.1915 to 1925. **$15.00-$20.00**

Bottle opener, baseball cap, cast metal, painted black & orange, souvenir of "Mets," NYC, NY, 20th C. **$15.00-$18.00**

Bottle opener, billy goat with great horns, sitting atop opener, polychromed cast iron, 20th C. **$35.00-$40.00**

Bottle opener, brass with antler handle. prob. 20th C. • **Antlers or Tusks.** — An antler is a renewable resource; people walking through the woods in early spring can find deer antlers wherever deer live. A tusk — whether it's an elephant, walrus, rhinocerous, or boar tusk — as well as a buffalo or cattle horn, is not renewable, and requires the savage mutilation, and painful death, of the animal from which it is taken. For me, it is bad karma to have anything obtained in the brutal way all tusks are obtained. Doing research in 19th C business directories for the city of NY, and other cities, I found horrifying and truly sickening illustrated ads for ivory, showing "natives" fighting with elephants, blood and gore pouring from wounds in the elephant, the native triumphant in his fight to obtain the ivory tusk for the decorative trades in the Western and Eastern Worlds. The old directories list many men whose occupation is described as "turner, in ivory and wood". I think it is imperative that the vast numbers of people who make up the collecting world become responsible and respectful "harvesters". • **Plastic.** — Although 30 or 25 years ago I absolutely hated plastic, thinking it beneath consideration because it was a fake for something else, I believe that the reason I have come to appreciate plastic objects so much in the last decade is because they may represent a saved elephant, a spared tree, a cow that wasn't turned into a pocketbook. Think about it. **$12.00-$15.00**

Bottle opener, cast iron, "Arcadian," early 20th C. **$7.00-$10.00**

Bottle opener, cast & plated iron, mounted with 2 screws to wall, "The Starr X", pat'd 1925, made well into 1930s, poss. even early 1940s. **$4.00-$6.00**

Bottle opener, cast steel, "Anchor Opener," 4"L, c.1910. **$7.00-$12.00**

Bottle opener, clown's head with open mouth as opener, cast iron, painted colorfully with polka-dotted tie, wall mounted, poss. made by John Wright Inc., or maybe earlier by another company, 4½"L x 4"W, weighs 14 oz, when worn looks like 1930s piece. Same design in Wright's 1963 catalog. • See the lobster bottle opener for remarks on evaluating new things. • Double or triple value if it can be proved to be old (ie. 1920s or 30s). In fact, one was advertised in the late 1980s for $75.00, but I didn't see it and can't judge. 1963 wholesale price was 60¢. Asking price now is much higher. **$18.00-$22.00**

Bottle opener, dachsund, cast brass, no mark, 20th C. **$45.00-$65.00**

Bottle opener, dachsund, nickeled-iron, adv'g "Medford Lager Beer," German (?), 20th C. **$40.00-$55.00**

Bottle opener, dog with open mouth, cast brass, 20th C. **$15.00-$18.00**

Bottle opener, donkey, cast iron, 20th C. **$30.00-$45.00**

Bottle opener, donkey handle, cast iron, 20th C. **$20.00-$22.00**

Bottle opener, double-ended, flat steel, adv'g "Stone Malt Co.," 7½"L, 20th C. **$3.00-$6.00**

Bottle opener, drunk or lovelorn cowboy embracing a cactus, cast iron, painted, souvenir type, 20th C. **$20.00-$25.00**

Bottle opener, drunk & palm tree, cast iron, painted, 20th C. • I hate these things, not finding drunks funny, but they are collectible. The palm tree drunkard is rarer than the lamppost ones. While the original price might have been a dollar, now the asking price is much higher. **$20.00-$25.00**

Bottle opener, drunkard leaning on signpost, colorfully painted cast iron, poss. made by John Wright Inc., Wrightsville, PA, 4"H x 2½"W, weighs 7 oz, in 1963 Wright catalog, but poss. theirs is repro of earlier one. • Souvenir type, and the sign was painted with different placenames, such as St. Petersburg, FL, or Hershey, PA. A more common variation is the drunk on lamp post, which usually did not have a place name. That one weighs only 6½ oz. The 1963 wholesale price of either was 40¢. Asking prices now are partly dependent on place name. **$12.00-$20.00**

Bottle opener, duck's head, painted cast iron, American, early 20th C. **$45.00-$60.00**

Bottle opener, dachsund, cast brass, no mark, 20th C. **$45.00-$65.00**

Bottle opener, dachsund, nickeled-iron, adv'g "Medford Lager Beer," German (?), 20th C. **$40.00-$55.00**

Bottle opener, dog with open mouth, cast brass, 20th C. **$15.00-$18.00**

Bottle opener, donkey, cast iron, 20th C. **$30.00-$45.00**

Bottle opener, donkey handle, cast iron, 20th C. **$20.00-$22.00**

Bottle opener, double-ended, flat steel, adv'g "Stone Malt Co.," 7½"L, 20th C. **$3.00-$6.00**

Bottle opener, drunk or lovelorn cowboy embracing a cactus, cast iron, painted, souvenir type, 20th C. **$20.00-$25.00**

Bottle opener, guitar heavy metal, with opening in body of guitar, Japan, 20th C. • The English call these openers **crown cork openers,** after the shape of a bottle cap, which within living memory was lined with cork for a tight seal. (Remember making badges or pins of Coca-Cola caps by prying out the cork, and pressing the two halves back together with a thin layer of clothing in between?). The **crown cap** (crown cork) was invented by William Painter of Baltimore, in 1894. For some reason, Americans call the double-ended can & bottle opener a **church key,** but I don't know of anyone who calls other can and/or bottle openers that. Do you? **$12.00-$15.00**

Bottle opener, hunting dog, cast iron, 20th C. **$30.00-$40.00**

Bottle opener, lizard (or baby alligator?), realistic small figural of cast bell metal or bronze painted in shades of brown; curled tail with a loop near end works as the cap lever, looks European from fineness of detail, poss. Austrian? (Vienna?), 4¾"L, early 20th C. • If this were a Vienna Bronze, and the dealer knew it, the price would be four times the asking price of $50.00. Price range here is what I've seen for 3 offered examples at big shows. **$45.00-$125.00**

Bottle opener, lobster, red painted cast iron, possibly a reproduction of a late 19th C or early 20th C opener, poss. made by John Wright Inc., Wrightsville, PA, 3½"L x 2¼"W, Wright's weighs 7 oz., shown in 1963 Wright catalog. • The difference in real value and asking price for reproductions is very difficult to determine. By now, those Wright pieces which are assumed to not be repros, that were made in 1963, are over a quarter of a century old, easily qualifying under any criteria as collectibles. The difficulty comes when a piece is a reproduction, for it would take much, much longer than 25 years to become valuable in its own right. 1963 wholesale price was 30¢. **$18.00-$20.00**

Bottle opener, metal, adv'g Coca-Cola's "Sprite Boy," late 20th C. **$10.00-$12.00**

Bottle opener, metal, "East Tennessee Brewing Co.," pat'd by F. W. Lyons, Louisville, KY, 3⅛"L, pat'd Feb. 19, 1901. **$5.00-$10.00**

Bottle opener, nude with arms stretched above head, cast brass & steel, 4"L, 20th C. **$15.00-$20.00**

Bottle opener, nude with upstretched arms, white metal, plated with brass? marked "Herbert," prob. mfd by Herbert Specialty Mfg. Co., makers of toys & novelties, Chicago, IL, 4½"L, 1st third 20th C. **$25.00-$28.00**

Bottle opener, pelican, painted cast iron, souvenir type, 20th C. **$20.00-$28.00**

Bottle opener, pointing hand, flat sheet metal, "Effinger Beer", Baraboo, WI, 20th C. **$20.00-$25.00**

Bottle opener, reclining nude, chromed iron, 20th C. **$35.00-$50.00**

Bottle opener, rhinoceros, cast iron, 20th C. **$80.00-$100.00**

Bottle opener, shark, cast aluminum, American, 1930s. **$15.00-$20.00**

Bottle opener, spaniel dog, painted cast iron, early 20th C. **$30.00-$40.00**

Bottle opener, steel business end, nicely tooled, with turned wood handle, "Havell," Irvington, N.J, 5"L, c.1900. **$20.00-$25.00**

Bottle opener, steel with green painted wood handle, dated 1933. **$6.00-$10.00**

Bottle opener, steel with horn handle, sterling silver applied decoration, American, 7¼"L, pat'd 1864. • The trade in buffalo hides, horns, etc., may have encouraged the creation of these things. Somebody had to think what to do with the horns. See entry above on Antlers and Tusks. **$30.00-$35.00**

Bottle opener, steer head, handsome very Cubist sculptural form somehow goes with Picasso's "Guernica" painting, cast iron with bronzed finish, no mark, 7"L, 1920s 30s. **$50.00-$75.00**

Bottle opener, swordfish, painted cast metal, 20th C. **$20.00-$35.00**

Bottle opener, parrot or Macaw on perch, cast iron, painted in bright colors, may or may not be reproduction, poss. made by John Wright Inc., 5"H x 2½"W, weighs 7½ oz, 20th C. • **Reproduction alert?** If there was an "original," that may date to 1920s or 30s, but there is one in Wright's 1963 catalog. Wholesale price from 1963 was 40¢.
$18.00-$22.00

Bottle opener, wall mounted, tinned iron with red lettering: "Coca-Cola," by Starr X, pat'd 1925. • **Reproduction alert.** At one time these were hot; then someone claimed to have found a huge warehouse supply, and then (or simultaneously, or instead of finding them) someone started reproducing them, so the value hasn't risen. In early 1989 I noticed an ad for a repro, which may have first been offered long ago. A company in Clarksville, AR, adv'd "Coca-Cola cast iron wall type bottle openers $21 doz.", but we don't know if this is a new repro, or by now a "Warehouse find" of an old cache of old repros. Arggh. Many collectors are not in a position to watch one particular item over the long crucial period between, say, 1960 and 1990...either because it's not their specialty, or they aren't old enough! I've never wanted one of these openers, but used to see at least 10, in original boxes, every Saturday during the 1960s that I went to Englishtown Flea Market in south central NY. To see them still for sale, for the same price or a little more, is proof that when something is available in large quantities, and has nothing going for it beyond the name, it just won't increase in value. **$10.00-$15.00**

Bottle opener & cake server combined, possibly for weddings? wire and sheet metal, the most peculiar combination ever, 11⅝"L, pat'd Nov. 24, 1914. **$22.00-$28.00**

Bottle opener & can opener combined, fish, cast metal, adv'g "C. G. Richardson Oils, Gas & Machinery," Patten, ME, late 19th C. **$18.00-$22.00**

Bottle opener & corkscrew combined, adv'g "Green River Whiskey," 20th C. **$18.00-$22.00**

Bottle opener & corkscrew combined, fish, cast brass, German. • The 1989 address for the **Figural Bottle Opener Collector's Club** is: c/o Phyllis Eisenach, 13018 Clarion Rd, Ft. Washington, MD 20744. Or contact Bonnie Bull, 20 Fairway Drive, Stamford, CT 06903. Always use an SASE. **$12.00-$18.00**

Bottle opener, knife sharpener & glass cutter combined, cast iron, "Apex", TOC. **$8.00-$12.00**

Bottle opener & slotted spoon combined, wire & sheet metal, 10½"L, pat'd Feb. 23, 1915. **$15.00-$18.00**

Bottle opener & spoon-stirrer combined, iron, "Firestone". **$2.00-$3.00**

Bottle opener, wrench & meat cleaver combined, iron, "Kitchen Klever Kleever," American, it's gotta be. Late 19th, early 20th C. • As in Leave it to Klever Kleever — a short of homey horror show. **$12.00-$15.00**

Can & bottle opener, "Riswell". **$12.00-$16.00**

Can & bottle opener, iron, Mirvalle Mfg. Co., early 20th C. **$3.00-$5.00**

Can & bottle opener, steel with black painted wooden handle, "Peerless", 8¾"L, pat'd Oct. 29, 1912. **$12.00-$15.00**

Can & bottle opener & corkscrew combined, also knife sharpener & glass cutter, cast iron, American, pat'd Aug. 17, 1875, as marked on frame. • This combo tool is a mirror image, almost, of one in next entry, and is owned by collector John Lambert. **$12.00-$15.00**

Can & bottle opener & corkscrew combined, also knife sharpener & glass cutter, cast iron, fish skeleton type, no maker mark, marked "Pat. Aug. 24, 1875". • Collector Mark Bornfreund wrote me about this some time ago and said that he could not find a can opener listed for that patent date. It is strange that it is almost identical to one marked with a patent date a week earlier. It is possible that the maker received advance notice of the patent being granted, but the date was wrong. **$12.00-$15.00**

Can & bottle opener, knife sharpener combined, hooked iron blade with knife sharpener sticking up sort of like wings above, wood handle, Boye Needle Co., Chicago, about 7½"L, pat'd Sept. 10, 1912 & Dec. 18, 1917 (?). • Boye also made nutmeg graters, apple corers, screwdrivers & various needles. **$12.00-$18.00**

Can & bottle opener, knife sharpener combined, steel, "Norlunds 3-in-l," O. A. Norlund, Williamsport, PA, 4½"L, c. 1915. **$12.00-$18.00**

Can & bottle opener, knife sharpener combined, wood handle, iron top, "Sharp Easy," Premier Mfg. Co., Detroit, MI, pat'd 1922. **$12.00-$15.00**

Can & bottle opener, knife sharpener, glass cutter combined, cast & sheet iron, long & very neat with 2 knife - sharpening emory wheels at tip, the eyes of the insect, less like a fish than the other combo openers, this is more like a 6½" length of skeletal insect or backbone segment, "The Improved Peerless," Austria, "patent pending" in U. S. c.1900-1915. **$18.00-$22.00**

Can opener, knife sharpener & glazier's tool combined, mostly cast iron, American, 5½"L, pat'd June 8, 1869. • Marion Levy believed what I identified on p. 412 of 2nd edition is not a can opener but a glazier's tool with these parts, left to right: tiny roundel glass cutter at tip, tapper, 2 nippers (top edge), knife sharpener, putty knife with spacer pins, and corkscrew to pull cork on linseed oil bottle to be mixed with whiting to make the putty. **$12.00-$16.00**

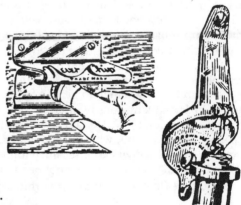

VIII-A.
Bottle openers.
(L) Nickel-plated "Never-Chip" opener for crown caps, to be screwed to table, cabinet, wall or [wooden] refrigerator. 2 1/2"L. (R) Combo "for removing crwon caps and corks from bottles." Nickeled cast metal, Monel™ corkscrew. 5"L x 1 7/8". Both Pick Barth, 1929. **$1.00-$2.00**

A Brief History of Canning
or, Bully Beef For You, Too!

You can't find two histories of canning that give all the same names, dates, and information. I am footnoting this article (which first appeared in my newsletter, *Kitchen Collectibles News,* Jan/Feb 1985), to facilitate retracing the various authors' research. See footnotes following article and table of patents.

It is agreed, however, by all sources, that in 1809 in response to General Napoleon's challenge to find a way to keep food fresh, or safe to eat, for his fighting troops, the concept of the supposedly longterm, airless preservation of food became practical. The French confectioner, chef, pickler and bottler Nicholas Appert won a 12,000-franc award by devising a way to put food up in glass containers. In 1810, he published the results of his studies, to fulfill the stipulations of the awarders. At the same time, the Englishman Peter Durand was awarded a patent for his technique of putting food up in glass containers, but he included <u>tin cannisters</u> in his patent.[1]

These early glass, wide-necked canning jars or bottles were filled with food, immersed up to the neck in a bath of boiling water until the contents were also boiling, then corked with waxed corks. The corks were then secured with wire. But these bottles cracked easily during the boiling process, or were broken later, and they were not perfectly sanitary because of the porous corks, which would admit bacteria (a danger unknown to Appert or Durand). Certainly not a handy way to preserve food for soldiers in the field or sailors on the high seas.

In 1811, Englishmen Bryan Donkin and his partner John Hall (mentioned in a few sources) patented a similar technique, and then in 1813 or so[2], they changed to handformed tin canisters. Through a smallish hole in the top, minced or diced food was put into the cans, the cans were set in boiling water baths (like a French *bain marie*) until the food boiled. A little cap-like disc was set on the hole and soldered in place. though Donkin and Hall worked about the same time as Appert and Durand, it was this unheralded pair who actually set up the first factory for canning meat; in 1818, the products were being sold — including to career officers who could afford this luxurious new convenience food.[3]

Meanwhile, in America, tin-canning of fish was begun in New York City about 1819[4], and glass jar "canning" was patented in 1825[5] by Ezra Daggett and Thomas Kensett. If the reported dates are fuzzy, the two men's names are known for sure, as is that of William Underwood, who about the same time began putting up vegetables in glass jars. One source[6] says that all three changed from glass to tin in 1839.

Can-makers, who frequently were also the food processors who filled the cans, went from small enterprises that could turn out a few score cans a day, by hand, to factories that could produce hundreds of cans. The Winslow Brothers of Portland, ME had a can factory in the 1840s[7] that made cans with a filling hole 1½'' across. Each worker could make about 60 cans a day. By the end of the 1850s, there were machines involving stamping of one-piece blanks that boosted production to 1000 cans a man (though not necessarily in the Winslows' operation). A man named Colonel Silas Ilsley made cans in Brooklyn[8] in the 1860s, as did Joseph Campbell (Soup's on!), and Abram A. Anderson in Camden, NJ[9]. Two Libby Brothers and their partner Archibald McNeill moved from Portland, ME to Chicago where the stockyards were, and began canning corned beef and other meats in 1872. Business was booming in canned goods, and the early pioneers of canning often became big names in canned goods later — names still known today from the grocery store shelves!

But there's more to the story between the 1830s and the '60s and '70s. One reason for the popularity of canned foods before the Civil War was the huge number of people travelling westward, including Gold Rush miners. About 30 years after the gold-panning Forty-Niners rushed across the American continent, Philip William Flower wrote his *History of the Trade in Tin*—[10], and described huge rusting dumps of empty tin cans left by the miners and other westward-ho'ers. He also told of the astounding number of tinned goods leaving the major canning city of Baltimore in just one year: 45-million one-pound cans, primarily of oysters and peaches!

Different ways of opening cans were possible, using simple tools, or even no tools at all. Early hole-and-cap cans sometimes had rings soldered on with the cap, and when pulled they were able to cut through the relatively soft solder and reopen the hole. (The problem was then to get the food out of the hole. To digress: once on an ill-planned trip from New Orleans to Memphis, in my adventurous twenties, all we had in the car were a couple of cans of baked beans, a heavy jackknife, and no money even for 15¢ McDonald's. But we had a nice roadside picnic by punching a hole in the cans and drawing out the beans, one at a time, with September-stiff weed stalks. Very ad hoc, very subsistence.)

Some cans were opened with a chisel and hammer in the early days. But by 1858[11] there was probably a usable can opener; a patent model exists, production has not been proved, of Ezra J. Warner's can opener of January 5, 1858. By the 1870s, some cans could be opened by cutting the thin tops off with a knife, or by pulling a tin strip a lã Quaker Oats boxes off to loosen a cap.[12]

Invented can openers worked on two principles: either Stab-and-Saw-Open; or Stab-Twist-and-Behead. Collector Joe Young wrote up a list of the first 10 can opener patents granted in the United States for an article in my newsletter.[13] I have combined his list with one that I had assembled in an earlier issue of the newsletter.[14]

First Ten Years of U.S. Patented Can Openers

INVENTOR'S NAME,	RESIDENCE,	DATE,	NUMBER
1. Ezra J. Warner	Waterbury, CT	Jan 05, l858	19,063 **
2. William C. Dick	New York, NY	Nov 01, 1864	44,856
3. Charles A. Ruff	Providence, RI	Mar 07, 1865	46,709
4. Eben T. Orne	Chicago, IL	Mar 13, 1866	53,173 ***
5. W. K. Baldwin	Chicago, IL	May 15, 1866	54,668
6. O. J. Livermore	Worcester, MA	Jun 26, 1866	55,878
7. Seth P. Chapin	Atlantic, NJ	Jul 17, 1866	56,368
8. John Willard	Norwich, CT	Aug 21, 1866	57,422 ***
9. J. Osterhoudt	New York, NY	Oct 02, 1866	58,554 **
10. William McGill	Cincinnati, OH	Jan 08, 1867	61,080 ***
11. S. O. Church[15]	West Meriden, CT	Jan 15, 1867	61,161
12. S. E. Totten	Brooklyn, NY	Jan 22, 1867	61,484
13. T. A. McFarland	Meadville, PA	May 21, 1867	64,891
14. W. L. Hubbell	Brooklyn, NY	Oct 22, 1867	69,996
15. W. H. Forker	Meadville, PA	Oct 29, 1867	70,188
16. G. A. Dickson	Woodcock Twnsp, PA	Dec 24, 1867	72,464
17. M. T. McCormick	Meadville, PA	Apr 07, 1868	76,490
18. N. F. Stone	Chicago, IL	Apr 14, 1868	76,669
19. C. F. Ritchel	Chicago, IL	May 12, 1868	77,916
20. F. S. Wyman	Chicago, IL	Jul 28, 1868	80,326
21. G. C. Humphrey(s)	Washington, DC	Nov 17, 1868	84,122

**Patent model for this is known to exist.

*** Examples of these can openers are known to exist.

NOTE: The listings, which cover the first 10 years, were patented under various names, most commonly "Can opener" or "Tin can opener". My original failure to check under "Tin can" led me to miss several early patents.

[1]. Bragdon, Charles R. *Metal Decorating from Start to Finishes*, Freeport, ME: Bond Wheelwright Co., 1961. Page 81.

[2]. Clark, Hyla. *The Tin Can Book*, NYC: New American Library, 1977. Page 13.

[3]. Ritchie, Carson I.A. *Food in Civilization. How History Has Been Affected by Human Tastes*, NYC/Toronto: Beaufort Books, 1981. Page 144.

[4]. Clark. Page 11.

[5]. Bragdon. Page 81.

[6]. Bragdon. Page 82.

[7]. Bragdon. Page 82.

[8]. Clark. Page 11.

[9]. Bragdon. Page 83.

[10]. Flower, Philip William. *History of the Trade in Tin*. London: G. Bell & Sons, 1880.

[11]. Young, Joe. "Some Notes on Early Can Openers", *Kitchen Collectibles News,* March/April 1985. Page 23.

[12]. Clark. Page 19.

[13]. Young. *Loc. cit.*

[14]. Franklin, L.C. "Bully Beef for You, Too!" *Kitchen Collectibles News,* Jan./Feb. 1985. Page 8.

[15]. *Is it possible that the expression* Church Key *came from this?*

Can opener, alligator & black man, cast iron, obnoxious racist <u>Black Americana</u>, undoubtedly <u>American</u>, alas, and even worse, it's 20th C. • **Collectibles That Offend.** There's no "right way" to deal with these things. For a collector, many things do not come with intrinsic moralities or value judgments. I just know <u>what I wouldn't want around the house</u>, and that includes offensive racist things, Nazi collectibles, animal traps of all kinds (you'll note I have never put a mousetrap into one of my books; I hate them), and meat-tools of the kitchen, such as cleavers, meat grinders, etc. *De gustibus non est disputandum;* it's your choice, of course. **$25.00-$35.00**

Can opener, black painted cast iron, thick ring at business end, longish handle with large hangup hole (or, as dealer Nancy Schlegel says, "handle holed for hanging"), circular blade, marked only "MARVEL", 7¼"L, blade is 2⅝" diameter, TOC. **$45.00-$60.00**

Can opener, black painted cast malleable iron, all vertical, loop handle, double blades in arrowhead shape, "Heysinger's", 5¼"L, pat'd Oct. 24, 1876. **$55.00-$65.00**

Can opener, bull's head handle, cast iron (sometimes nickel plated), American or English? Usually about 6" to 6½"L, last quarter19th C. • One early major canned food was tinned beef, also called "bully beef" (at least by the British Army), but surprisingly, the first known patented can opener shaped like a bull, was pat'd in 1875 by J. A. Wilson, of Chicago, IL. His and others of these openers — strong as a bull themselves — utilize a play on words. There are many variations in expression, eyes, horns, hair detail, collar (not often present), tail, body shape. Because they are included in present-day containerloads of "smalls" from England, I assume that many of them are English. Perhaps they were exported from the US to England? An example depicted in Evan Perry's *Collecting Antique Metalware* (London: Hamlyn, 1974) has a spike cast with the head, and the steel blade is marked with an undecipherable work's name, plus "Sheffield", which I assume was, as usual, England. There may be an avenue of exploration: evidence that American manufacturers pirated the word "Sheffield" to imply fine-quality cutlery steel. **$35.00-$50.00**

Can opener, bull's head & partial body, cast iron in 2 halves, spike & blade one piece screwed in to head, not much detailing in casting, English, 6"L, late 19th C. **$40.00-$50.00**

Can opener, bull's head & partial body, cast iron in 2 halves, spike cast in top of head, nice round eyes & ears, long hairs go straight back in line with body, English (?), 6"L, late 19th C. **$40.00-$50.00**

Can opener, bull's head & partial body, cast iron in 2 halves, very pronounced horns, particularly when seen from front, upper jaw's crosswise ridges look like teeth from side; blade & spike are one piece & screw in; interestingly, while the horns & ears are the same, the hair on the 2 halves is different, evidently the mold maker didn't use the same carving technique for both sides, little details like this make this small area of collecting very interesting, spike is marked "H L 43", English, 6"L, late 19th C. **$40.00-$50.00**

Can opener, bull's head with very curly hair, cast iron, 6"L, 19th C. **$50.00-$55.00**

Can opener, cast iron, "Yankee," TOC. **$12.00-$15.00**

Can opener, cast iron, "Indestructo," early 20th C (?). **$5.00-$8.00**

Can opener, cast iron, "King," pat'd 1895. **$15.00-$18.00**

Can opener, cast iron, Vaughn's "Open-All," Chicago, IL, 20th C. **$8.00-$10.00**

Can opener, cast iron, "A. S. & Co., Columbia", NY or PA or CT, pat'd July 25, 1899. • There were many towns & villages named Columbia all over the U.S. by this time, the most likely manufacturing center being in NY, PA or CT. **$65.00-$70.00**

Can opener, cast iron, adjustable blued steel blade, round ridged wheel with crosspieces (looks just like miniature steering wheel), center pin was punched into can's center, then cutting blade moved to position at edge of can — whatever the can's diameter (within reason) name & date cast into crosspieces: "Hopper's Can Opener," about 4⅜" diameter, marked "Pat. Dec. 22, 1896". **$65.00-$85.00**

Can opener, cast iron, cigar-shaped wood handle stamped with name, "Keen Kutter," Simmons Hardware Co., c.World War I. **$35.00-$45.00**

Can opener, cast iron, counter top, possibly for a restaurant, maybe a big family's kitchen, with an eagle on the top, mounted to heavy block of wood. This is a double opener that will open short cans on the side, taller cans in the back. Long curved lever works a small blade in the front to open a tuna fish size can, while the back blade is large & sort of heart shaped, not in turn-of-century catalog, I suspect this is Enterprise, because of the eagle, 7½"H; lever is 12"L, c. 1880s 90s. **$150.00-$200.00**

Can opener, cast iron, handle has cross-hatch knurling pattern like Disston tools, adjustable blade, no mark, maybe Disston, 5½"L including blade, late 19th C. **$18.00-$22.00**

Can opener, cast iron, longer steel blade with greater adjustability, looks pretty much same as earlier version, slightly finer-looking casting of outer "Wheel", marked on crosspieces "Hopper's Can Opener", with date, pat'd Oct. 3, 1899. • Another that looks just like it, and could be a rip-off or just a later edition, with a snappy new name, is the "Safety First". **$45.00-$60.00**

Can opener, cast iron, looks like an abstract fish, contains tiny sharpening stone in groove, no mark, American, 5⅜"L, 1901. **$18.00-$22.00**

Can opener, cast iron loopy handle with tool steel blade, "Peerless," 6½"L, pat'd Feb. ll, 1890 (same patent date as "Delmonico"). **$7.00-$10.00**

Can opener, cast iron, mechanical, "Bunker Clancy", late 19th or early 20th C. **$7.00-$9.00**

Can opener, cast iron, mounted on its original card, "Vaughn's Safety Roll Junior," Chicago, IL, 20th C. **$8.00-$10.00**

Can opener, cast iron, openwork handle has sliding blade to adjust to different can sizes, "World's Best," Pittsburgh, PA, 6¾"L, TOC or late 19th C. • Very similar to the U.S. Can Opener, and because both are made in Pittsburgh, possibly one is an improvement on the other. **$20.00-$30.00**

Can opener, cast iron ring, with ratchet clamp to hold can, separate cutter on another pivoting ring, long loopy handles, "Champion," pat'd 1873. **$75.00-$100.00**

Can opener, cast iron, skinny short snake of curved metal with blade, with screwed on simple cutting blade, "The Delmonico," 7"L, pat'd Feb. 11, 1890 (same date as one of "Peerless"). **$10.00-$12.00**

Can opener, cast iron, sliding blade adjusts to fit different size cans, not very spectacular to look at, but still a nice one, "U.S. Can Opener," Pittsburgh, PA, 6"L, pat'd May 7, 1895. **$20.00-$30.00**

Can opener, cast iron; the knob at end opposite sharp pointed blade serves as place for tapping with hammer to drive point in before starting to cut, very graceful & interesting, unmarked, American,7⅝"L, late 19th C. **$30.00-$40.00**

Can opener, cast iron & tool steel, vertical mechanical type, 2 blades one rounded, one straight for sardine cans, lever attaches to either of 2 pivot points, "Blakeslee" (?) or "Blakesley" (?), American, about 16" to 18"H, pat'd May 1888 (?). **$120.00-$140.00**

Can opener, cast iron wheel-like ring,with 4 "spokes," and sort of scalloped edges like worn gear teeth, has wingnut in center to tighten cutter into correct position to fit radius of can being opened, "Safety First," American, 4½" diameter, 19th C, prob. around 1885 to 1890. See also the Hopper above. • Owner Peggy Wainscott found hers amongst woodworking tools at a flea market, so it proves you should look everywhere, and leave no box unturned. **$28.00-$40.00**

Can opener, cast iron with 2 long, openwork, loopy pivoting handles, one of which has adjustable blade in it, to fit the size of the can, poke tip in center, adjust blade to match the radius of the can lid, and while holding one handle stationary as a sort of lever against which you can push, you swivel the other handle with the cutting blade around, American,7¾"L, marked only "patent applied for, c. 1890s. • See the Lehman, Bolen lookalike 3 entries below. **$30.00-$40.00**

Can opener, cast iron, has adjustable blade in sliding frame, big "nail head" or spike on end to pound hole into can top, and a great screw-action works, with rat-sized 'Mickey Mouse' ears on a disc, "Baumgarten," American, 9¾"L, 19th C, poss. as early as 1880. **$65.00-$80.00**

Can opener, cast iron with gritty cast no-slip surface on handle, simple pointed blade, curved handle, no marks, 6 ¾"L, TOC. **$10.00-$12.00**

Can opener, cast & sheet iron, with 2 openwork "Loop" handles, opposite each other on the outside of the cutting blade, a full circle of sharpened iron, push down circular blade on can lid & rotate entire opener, while pushing downward, no mark, <u>looks like</u> one mfd by Lehman, Bolen & Co., of Decatur, IL, 10"L, advertised c.1890, so fits with patent date of 1889. **$28.00-$35.00**

Can opener, corkscrew, glass cutter, knife sharpener, bottle opener combination, cast iron, with wire screw, no marks, American? 5½"L, late 19th C. • Evan Perry, author of a Shire Album book, *Corkscrews & Bottle Openers* (See Bibliography), said about a similar multi-purpose tool that it was "<u>the nastiest corkscrew ever issued</u>." (His example was very like this, except that it also had a screw gauge and a 3" ruler, was 6½"L, and had a British patent.) **$15.00-$20.00**

Can opener, countertop for restaurant, cast iron with deep-blue painted spool-like wooden handle, "Heavy Duty Can Opener, No. A-123," also No. 134, mfd by Dazey Churn Co., St. Louis, MO, 12½"H x 11½"W, 20th C. **$45.00-$55.00**

Can opener, crowing rooster, cast iron, American, 20th C. **$15.00-$22.00**

Can opener, fish, cast iron, blade set in with screw to remove for sharpening, English, 5"L, late 19th C. **$35.00-$45.00**

Can opener, fish, like a sardine, with slender slightly curved body, dark-green-painted cast iron, very exaggerated and beautiful scales & front fins, gills bold too, large ring around eyes (where blade can be unscrewed for cleaning or sharpening), rather small tail ending in large ball, no mark, American or English, 4"L, c.1870s. **$60.00-$85.00**

Can opener, flat wood handle, brass ferrule, marked "T N & S", English (?), 6½"L, TOC. **$15.00-$18.00**

Can opener, flat wood handle, bulbous head, brass ferrule, marked on cutting blade, "Wynn & Timmins", English (?), 6"L, TOC. **$15.00-$18.00**

Can opener, for sardine cans, tempered tool steel blade in turned wooden handle, with distinctive & typical sardine-opener's long evil-looking blade, prob. American, about 8"L, 1870s. **$15.00-$18.00**

Can opener, green enameled wood handles, one to hold, one to turn, steel mechanism & blade, "Edlund Junior," mfd by Edlund Co., Burlington, VT, 6¼"L, pat'd April 21, 1925, May 12, 1925, June 18, 1929. **$12.00-$18.00**

Can opener, hardened steel hooked blade, simple turned wood handle, ferrule, "Handy", mfd by Handy Things Mfg. Co., Ludington, MI, pat'd June 11, 1895. **$8.00-$12.00**

Can opener, iron, "The Jewel". **$15.00-$18.00**

Can opener, iron, "Lowe," 19th to early 20th C. **$7.00-$9.00**

Can opener, iron, loop-handled, with corkscrew folded inside handle, "Dixie", 1930s. **$3.00-$5.00**

Can opener, iron, with corkscrew, "Opens All", mfd by Vaughan, 1930s. **$3.00-$5.00**

Can opener, iron, with gears, "Enbay," early 20th C (?). **$12.00-$15.00**

Can opener, iron with wood handle, "Clean Cut," early 20th C (?). **$8.00-$12.00**

Can opener, iron & wood, "A & J Miracle," Binghamton, NY, 6¼"L, 1930s. • The all metal one is slightly less. **$10.00-$15.00**

Can opener, like multi-purpose tool, has a tamper at end of handle, handle swells out in center to give good grip, blade adjusts, no mark, American, 7⅜"L, late 19th C. **$22.00-$25.00**

Can opener, malleable cast iron, with 2 pivoting loopy handles — upper one with steel cutting blade that you push in circle around can top, with lower ring as guide, the other handle, which is attached to a ring-shaped piece that roughly fits within top of can, has a point at end opposite handle. That pointed piece is a punch for puncturing the can top to start the cutting and to hold the can. Ad copy says this is a "double lever patent can opener & holder, combined. You hold the can firm with one handle, while you cut the top out with one stroke with the other." A little rickety — from age or imperfect manufacture, but terrific looking. ads identify this as "Lehman 9", mfd by G. W. Lehman & Co. (later? Lehman, Bolen (or Bowman?) & Co.), Decatur, IL, 8½"L with ring 3¼" diameter, no mark but patent date, May 7, 1889. •
Malleable cast iron.— I feel uncomfortable using this term without a clear understanding of it, especially how to look at something and know if it's plain cast pig iron or malleable cast iron, which has less carbon in it than pig

iron but more than wrought iron, which is extremely "malleable" or workable by hammering or rolling. • When I have found documentation for an object, such as an ad, booklet or flyer, and the metal is described as "malleable cast iron", I have added it to the description (of what I count as only 11 pieces in this whole book). One source describes it as an "alloy of steel". Another has a simple definition that states that "Malleable iron is able to be shaped or formed by hammering or pressure." An editorial answer to query in the May 31, 1890 *Metal Worker*, says that "The work of making malleable iron castings necessarily involves considerable time, and they cannot be turned out with the rapidity of gray castings." This was to explain the higher cost. • I believe that the more important aspect is that malleable cast iron can keep its strength and integrity when subjected to "hammering or pressure", meaning that an object with a lever action, for example, could hold up well without fracturing like ordinary cast iron might, and without tending to bend, as some wrought iron might if the pressure were great enough. An economic advantage is that casting is cheaper than forging, and scrap is an integral part of the alloy. • Many, probably most, of modern objects made of cast iron, unless otherwise noted, are made with re-founded scrap cast iron. This scrap, which is composed in great part of old cracked car engine blocks, will not be "picked over" before founding, and so will also contain small quantities of aluminum and brass. • See note on Aluminum in Cast Iron under an entry for a Muffin pan in the Mold chapter.   **$75.00-$90.00**

Can opener, mechanical, cast iron, with handle something like a skillet handle, fitted onto end with a vertical screw, & several sharp points underneath, similar to the Baumgarten patent opener, only mark is "Pat Appl For," American, 7½"L, TOC.   **$35.00-$45.00**

Can opener, metal, with little lifting spout slightly inset to catch drips, "For Karo Cans Only," very small, pat'd 1935.   **$7.00-$10.00**

Can opener, nickel plated iron, very modern-looking, with graceful curve, & relatively big head, "The Safety" marked on end of handle, American, 6½"L, patented May 12, 1914. • "Can openers are of many styles and there are few satisfactory ones." Elsie Hutchinson, *The Housefurnishings Department. Department Store Merchandise Manual*, NY: NY University, 1918.   **$20.00-$30.00**

Can opener, nickeled steel shaft, tempered steel blade, and turned wood handle, "A & J," Edward Katzinger Co., Chicago, IL, 8½"L, 1940.   **$12.00-$15.00**

Can opener, pistol-shaped, loop handle, cast iron, adjustable steel blade, American, 8¼"L diagonally, pat'd Mar. 9, 1886.   **$20.00-$25.00**

Can opener, plated & black painted cast iron, adjustable, long shaft with round head with 3 big ribs, "ABC", 7"L in closed up position, 9½"L fully extended, pat'd Nov. 27, 1894.   **$40.00-$50.00**

Can opener, rearing horse, cast iron, American, 20th C.   **$20.00-$25.00**

Can opener, screw clamps on shelf or table edge, nickeled iron works with horizontal gears, blue wood knob, "Blue Streak," Turner & Seymour Mfg. Co., Torrington, CT, 4"H x 7"L, pat'd Oct. 1, 1921, Aug. 8, 1922, & Apr. 10, 1923. Sold into 1930s. • Patented 7 years before 1st wall mount opener.   **$18.00-$22.00**

Can opener, several small triangular steel blades to puncture can, turned wood handle with mushroom-like knob, J. Kaufman, NYC, NY, 6"L x 3¼" diameter, pat'd Sept. 6, 1870.   **$85.00-$100.00**

Can opener, shaped wood handle, flat sided -- probably flattened after turning on lathe, steel blade, "Midget," American, 6⅛"L, (another reported measuring only 5¾"L), pat'd July 19, 1904.   **$10.00-$15.00**

Can opener, skeletal steel frame, point at smaller end for sticking in center of can, then the cutting blade can be moved along slide of shaft to fit can's radius, then whole thing is rotated to cut off most of lid, marked on sliding blade part "Hercules" with patent date, pat'd Aug. 12, 1902. • I wonder what the tetanus death rate was when such openers were in wide use? At least no-one tradenamed an opener "The Lockjaw".   **$12.00-$18.00**

Can opener, sort of like sardine (can) shears, a levered, 2 handle iron & steel cutter which gnawed its way through the tin after starter hole was made, tension of handles achieved with leaf spring. They claimed it could be used for cutting stove pipe also. Wheeler Patent Can Opener Co., St. Louis, MO, introduced 1890.   **$15.00-$22.00**

Can opener, steel blade & malleable cast iron, 2 parts, with long handle & toothed piece, plus a shorter handle with chisel-like blade. The tip of long piece is stuck into middle of can, then the chisel blade is moved along the teeth until the blade lines up with edge of can. It is then stuck into can top at edge, and pushed down to lock into position. Then it is pulled around the can top, presumably while turning the can counterclockwise with left hand. Could be used only with right hand, and does not live up to name at all. "Best Yet", Hasbrouck Alliger, NYC, NY, c.1890.   **$20.00-$30.00**

Can opener, steel, long black painted wooden handle, "Sterling", 7½"L, pat'd Aug. 26, 1902.   **$15.00-$18.00**

Can opener, steel, of type sold at the grocery now, a real cheapo type that actually works well, "Tilt-Top O-Matic," American, 3"L, c. 1920.   **$10.00-$15.00**

Can opener, steel with turned wood handle, and sliding piece on shaft, "Vulcan Cut Can & Bottle Opener," American, 8⅞"L, 1910. • **German vocabulary —** Buchsenoffner: tin box (can) opener.   **$12.00-$15.00**

Can opener, steel, wood handle, "Sure Cut," 1904.   **$12.00-$15.00**

Can opener, steel & wood, mark on blade is a diamond with SR inside, also a shield that says "Our Label" above it, and "M. P. B. D. BM. & S. W. U. of N. A." also "Unity Mutual Assistance and Education" inside it, mfd by S. it, and "M. P. B. D. BM. & S. W. U. of N. A." which John Lambert, a few years ago, guessed might stand for "Massachusetts Professional Bottlers and Professional Bottle-Makers Brotherhood & Skilled Workers Union of North America." Inside is motto "Unity Mutual Assistance and Education" mfd. by S. Richard, Southbridge, MA, 5⅞"L, late 19th C.   **$15.00-$20.00**

Can opener, tinned or nickel plated steel with turned wooden handle, painted turquoise, shaped like a slingshot "Y", 7½"L, 20th C, prob. 1930s.   **$12.00-$15.00**

Can opener, unusual 2 steel blades, deep V shaped, fitted to horizontal suitcase grip turned wood handle, the whole thing pushed into top of can, "One shove does the act", as the ad said. "This is not the usual or average cheap 'cut around the edges' can opener or one that 'pulls around in a circle.' The Joy Can Opener cuts out a complete circle with one shove or one downward pressure and leaves a tiny part of the opening uncut, which acts as a hinge, so that the cutout part can be pressed back again, for a covering." "Joy Can Opener", mfd by W. E. Beveridge Mfg. Co., Baltimore, MD, not adjustable for different size cans, would make cut about 4" diameter, c.1915. **$15.00-$20.00**

Can opener, wall mounted, "Dazey," by churn company, St. Louis, 20th C. **$10.00-$12.00**

Can opener, wood turned handle, steel shaft with adjustable blade & punch at end, no mark, American? 8⅞"L, c. 1895. **$15.00-$20.00**

Can opener combined tool, bottle opener, fish scaler, screwdriver, carrot slicer, etc., steel, "Ten-In-One," New Jersey Patent Novelty Co., Passaic, NJ, 7½"L, c. 1900. • Extremely clumsy & weird; if Evan Perry ever saw this one, I'm sure he'd say that it was the "nastiest" combo tool he'd ever seen. And it doesn't do windows, because there's no glass cutter on it! **$12.00-$15.00**

Can opener combined tool, steel & wood, no mark, American, 6⅞"L, 1930s. **$8.00-$12.00**

Can opener & corkscrew combined, nickeled steel, with screw folding up into space between handle loop, of a style commonly seen today, and probably being made from original design, "Browne Line None Such", mfd by The Browne & Dowd Mfg. Co., Meriden, CT, pat'd Nov. 3, 1908. **$12.00-$15.00**

Can opener & jar wrench combined, sheet steel, "4-in-1", mfd by J. C. Forster & Son, Pittsburgh, PA, about 6¾" or 7"L, pat'd Sept. 13, 1910. **$15.00-$22.00**

Can opener & knife sharpener combined, cast iron, with exaggerated fish-bird fantasy animal shape (as if drawn by an abstract artist), "Peerless," American, 6½"L, pat'd Aug. 12, 1902 and Mar. 3l, 1903. **$12.00-$15.00**

Can opener punch, red & yellow painted wood bottle-shaped tool with little metal punch to open can, "Pet Milk Irradiated Can Opener," 4"L, early 20th C. • See? People could have had to worry about "irradiated" food 50 or so years ago, but then it seemed healing, magic. I wouldn't eat it if you paid me. **$8.00-$15.00**

Cork bottling press, cast iron, painted & pinstriped, "Yankee," 13"L, 19th C. **$60.00-$75.00**

Cork driver, turned & cutout wood, highly polished finish, "Best Star of Bottling," John Sommers, Newark, NJ, 11¾"L unextended, pat'd Aug. 25, 1885. **$55.00-$65.00**

Cork driver, turned maple, "Redlich Mfg. Co.", Chicago, IL, early 20th C into 1930s. **$45.00-$55.00**

Cork extractor, iron & wood, looks much like a button hook with a T-handle. "B.J. Greely," c. 1880s. **$15.00-$25.00**

Cork press, alligator with head looking up, cast iron, hinged at chest, holes drilled in feet so that it could be screwed to countertop, would press 4 sizes of corks. By "press" is meant compression. A cork slightly larger than was needed would be put in the press to compress it so that it could quickly be inserted in the bottle before it expanded to its original cut size. English? 19th C. • **German vocabulary** — Kork-Handpresse: hand press for cork. **$175.00-$200.00**

Cork press, cast iron, "Whitall - Tatum," Philadelphia, 19th C into early 20th. • Probably for pharmaceutical bottle corks. **$45.00-$65.00**

Cork puller, nickeled iron (also found silver plated), to be mounted to vertical surface, side of cupboard, even door jamb, lever action, "Yankee", The Gilchrist Co., Newark, NJ, TOC. **$22.00-$35.00**

Cork puller, or cork extractor, mechanical, mainly for bars or restaurants, cast metal, screw clamps to bar edge, "Edie Patent", Smith & Egge Mfg. Co., Bridgeport, CT, pat'd Feb. 4, 1890 by Alexander Edie. **$60.00-$80.00**

Cork puller, screw clamps to bar edge, cast brass with lots of cupids, replica of 19th century opener, one lever clamps to bottle neck, larger one, with turned wooden handle, used to draw out cork, recorks by reversing motion, says "VINTNER" in vertical letters on main body, c.1985. • **Reproduction alert.** — a simpler version, of cast aluminum, mounted to vertical iron rod and board, instead of screw clamp, is less than half the price. Well-made enough to probably pass for old, if the wood and metal is distressed. New price from 1985 "Wine Enthusiast" mail order catalog: **$159.90**

Cork puller, screw clamps to edge, mostly for bar or restaurant use, fancy openwork cast iron, nickel plated usually, lever, "Phoenix", 1887. **$145.00-$175.00**

Corkscrew, "The Utility," English, 19th C. **$85.00-$100.00**

Corkscrew, "The Club." **$110.00-$120.00**

Corkscrew, "Plants' Magic." **$80.00-$90.00**

Corkscrew, 2 ivory handles, iron, "King's," English, 19th C. **$300.00-$350.00**

Corkscrew, advertising folding type, flimsy yellow & black printed tin, "Listerine," mfd for them by unknown novelty company, about 1½"L folded, TOC to 1920s. **$10.00-$12.00**

Corkscrew, advertising type in printed wooden tube, "Kellerstrass Distilling Co., Kansas City", 1900. **$15.00-$18.00**

Corkscrew, alligator of carved staghorn, steel worm, prob. American because of motif, 20th C. **$120.00-$135.00**

Corkscrew, antler tip handle with sterling silver fittings, very small, so may have had some kind of sheath for pocket, 3"L, 19th C. **$25.00-$35.00**

Corkscrew, Archimedean screw, steel, "Diamant J P Paris" (J. H. Perille), c.1900. **$100.00-$150.00**

Corkscrew, baby's upper torso, cast brass, French, TOC. • You have to wonder, Why a baby? unless it was the infant Bacchus. **$85.00-$120.00**

Corkscrew, Bacchus' head with wild curly hair, double lever type, the levers being arms, the body that fits over bottle neck cast of brass to look like a Greek tunic, with grapes, mfd by Godinger, c.1983. **$20.00-$30.00**

Corkscrew, bottle shape, nickeled, with brass plate showing logo & date, "Anheuser Busch," dated 1897. **$40.00-$50.00**

Corkscrew, brass barrel with turned ivory handle with black bristles, "Thomason," English, 19th C. **$600.00-$700.00**

Corkscrew, brass & bone or ivory, with dust & cobweb brush in one end of handle, Thomason type, English, 7⅞"L, 19th C. • Estimated at a 1983 Christie's sale to get $80.00 to $120.00, because such corkscrews had brought that before, this one got $440.00. Often auction prices are reported in trade papers with "Caution: Auction Price," but auctions can go anywhere — up or down — depending on the people bidding. Want a brass & bone Thomason's? Well … maybe one person bid it up. **$400.00-$500.00?**

Corkscrew, brass & iron, "Yankee Bar Screw," 1913. **$225.00-$235.00**

Corkscrew, cast iron with vines & flowers, clamps to bar, "Champion Bar Screw," American, pat'd 1896. **$175.00-$250.00**

Corkscrew, cat with screw as the tail, brass & steel, 3¾"L, TOC. **$45.00-$55.00**

Corkscrew, cheap metal, very small folding type, worm folds into handle loop, for "Carter's Ink", pat'd 1894. **$10.00-$15.00**

Corkscrew, Cheshire cat, cast brass & steel, English (?), late 19th C. **$100.00-$125.00**

Corkscrew, clown head, molded plastic, 4½"L, 20th C. **$65.00-$75.00**

Corkscrew, clutch mechanism, steel with open barrel cage, turned wooden (or fancier bone) handle, Coney & Co.'s "THE KING" (not the King's Screw), Birmingham, England, patented 1904. • Handle affects price. **$160.00-$250.00**

Corkscrew, compound lever (lazy tong or concertina) style, steel, "Zig-Zag, No. 38", also marked "Bte S.G.D.G. Fr & Et M & M. DER", French, 10¼"L fully extended, 1870s. • **Marks on French Items. — Bte** is an abbreviation for Brevete, or patentee. **S. G. D. G.** stands for _Sans Garantie Du Gouvernement_, or, registered, but without warranty by the government. In this case, it seems to say registered without warranty by the government of France and someplace else, I don't know where. The **Et** may be an abbreviation for _Etalage_, in the sense of a retail shop. In other words, "sold by", although I can't find that exact idiomatic use. **$150.00-$175.00**

Corkscrew, compound lever type, a multiplied leverage achieved by several-jointed criss-crossed arms (like a lazy tongs), "American Reliable Concertina," TOC. **$165.00-$170.00**

Corkscrew, compound lever type with criss-crossed arms with 4 lever points, also called "Lazy tongs" or concertina type corkscrew, forged steel with bronze finish, "Wier's Patent", mfd by J. Heeley & Sons, English, 14"L fully extended, patent #12804, pat'd Sept. 25, 1884. **$100.00-$150.00**

Corkscrew, disguised within World's Fair key that opens, "Century of Progress," 1939. **$15.00-$22.00**

Corkscrew, double-action mechanical type with so-called "hermaphrodite raising screw," steel screw, brass barrel ornately decorated with the fruits & plants of wine & beer making, turned bone handle. Also has intact brush at one end of T-handle, Thomason patent, English, 1802 patent. **$285.00-$350.00**

Corkscrew, elephant head, ivory handle, glass eyes, sterling silver ferrule, English, 8⅛"L, TOC. **$50.00-$65.00**

Corkscrew, flimsy lithographed metal, advertising "Welch's Grape Juice," 20th C. **$15.00-$18.00**

Corkscrew, folding, "The Davis," pat'd 1891. **$15.00-$20.00**

Corkscrew, for beer bottle, wooden cigar shaped T-handle, nickeled shaft, short bell shaped cap lifter of iron, design pat'd by William A. Williamson, for Anheuser Busch, pat'd Dec. 13, 1898. **$18.00-$25.00**

Corkscrew, forged iron, very elegant L shape, long worm, Italian, 9¼"L, 18th C. **$90.00-$120.00**

Corkscrew, Gay 90s' lady's legs, bent at knees, wearing red & white striped stockings (they also came in charcoal gray stripes), partly nickel plated, with high top laced boots, very elegantly risqué, German, 3"L, late 19th C. • **German vocabulary** — Korkzieher or Korkenzieher: cork drawer. **$85.00-$95.00**

Corkscrew, grotesque head of cast brass, steel helical worm, head is mythological hairy beast adapted from Durham Cathedral doorknocker, possibly a souvenir, marked only "DURHAM", English, 7¼"L including hanging ring on head's top, c.1930s. **$70.00-$90.00**

Corkscrew, iron, 2 parts, a plier-like lever with a bell cap to fit over cork, and with a "Worm" or screw that fits on end. The worm was twisted into the cork, and then the plier-lever was hooked on. The screw is commonly found by itself, having lost the plier part, "Lund's Lever," English, pat'd 1855. • **Classic.** — According to Watney & Babbidge's _Corkscrews for Collectors_, variations of Lund's Lever were made by "a number of firms over the years," and were sold through the "Army and Navy Catalogue as late as 1925-1926." **$100.00-$125.00**

Corkscrew, iron with curlique thick grapevine handle, 19th or 20th C. **$15.00-$30.00**

Corkscrew, key of heavy cast brass, shaped like a very old-fashioned, ornate door key, probably a sommelier's corkscrew — the key signifying his control of the locked door to the wine cellar. (Some people have speculated the key just stands for hospitality.) "G E A Bochum," European, late 19th C (?). **$45.00-$55.00**

Corkscrew, lever action, cast iron with brass maker's plate, "The Royal Club," pat'd by Charles Hull, English (?), 1864. **$300.00-$350.00**

Corkscrew, man dressed as aproned waiter or sommelier holding green bottle, looks like carved and painted wood, but is molded wood composition, head and shoulders pull out to reveal corkscrew and bell cap, "Syroco", mfd by Syracuse Ornamental Co., Syracuse, NY, 8"H, c.1930s-1950s. **$40.00-$55.00**

Corkscrew, mechanical double lever type, bronzed iron, broad-shouldered levers (in down position), wingnut-like top, steel helical worm, marked "Heeley's Patent A-1 Double Lever 1888," & "James Heeley & Sons, 5006 Patent Double Lever," English, 6½"L, 1888. • Marvelous looking — a collector's classic. **$150.00-$175.00**

Corkscrew, mechanical lever type, cast & machined brass, with cog & rachet mechanism, and wingy top that looks almost like a maple tree seed, has a collar to grasp top of cork, Rosati's patent, Italy, 6½"L, 20th C. **$45.00-$55.00**

Corkscrew, mechanical lever type, shiny tinned iron, "Magic Lever Cork Drawer," English, 5¾"L in closed position (levers down), TOC — marked "pat. appd for." **$65.00-$95.00**

Corkscrew, mermaid, cast iron, 7½"L, 19th C. **$200.00-$250.00**

Corkscrew, mermaid, molded plastic, "Geschutz," 20th C. **$200.00-$225.00**

Corkscrew, nickel plated metal, cap fits over bottle's mouth & cork, action consists of a compound lever — a "jointed extension" like a lazy tongs, with 3 crossed or zig zag arms, used by screwing in worm, then pulling on handle, which pulls cork as it extends, "Zig-Zag Corkscrew", American, late 1920s. • Probably related to the French one in more than name & works. **$10.00-$16.00**

Corkscrew, nude 'bionic' man, brass with red faceted glass eyes, looks more like a hood ornament than a corkscrew. Yuck. 20th C. • Investment tip: There's always value in camp. Heh heh. But is it lasting? **$20.00-$35.00**

Corkscrew, owl's head, with large eyes, plated metal, lever type, the 2 lever arms rather like wings, the words "HOOTCH-OWL" cast into body, pat'd by R. G. Smythe, American, pat'd 1935. **$200.00-$225.00**

Corkscrew, "peg & worm" pocket or travelling type, polished cut steel with some lathe turning, and faceted peg, English, 4"L, 19th C. • **Peg and Worm.**— The "peg" is the handle, a cross piece with a knob or handle (in this case) either plain or decorated, and the peg fits into the twist at the end of the "Worm," which is the screw. These came in a little tubular sheath, making them safe to carry about in trouser pockets. $65.00-$95.00 for really simple peg & worms. **$120.00-$130.00**

Corkscrew, pistol, chromed cast metal, 20th C. **$18.00-$22.00**

Corkscrew, pixie figure carrying lantern, cast copper, simple helical worm screw, English, 6"L, late 19th C. **$65.00-$80.00**

Corkscrew, rack & pinion mechanism, similar to famed Lund's patent screw, blued steel (some have brass barrels or cages) with lathe-turned bone-ivory handle at top, plain steel smaller side handle, "King's Screw," or with only King's capitalized. Two English makers of are Mapplebeck & Lowe, and Dowler, English, about 7"L (hard to measure mechanical in a uniform way — open, half open or closed.), 19th C. • **Classic.**— Those with double bone or ivory handles cost more. Messrs. Watney & Babbidge, in *Corkscrews for Collectors* (see Bibliography), say at least to manufacturers have been identified as making the so-called "King's Screw", which is supposed to be one of the handsomest and finest of the rack & pinion types. **$285.00-$350.00**

Corkscrew, rack & pinion type, cast iron, 19th C. **$65.00-$70.00**

Corkscrew, rack & pinion type, steel frame with turned wooden handle, brush intact, "London Rack, Lund Maker, Cornhill & Fleet Street, London", England, 19th C. **$150.00-$200.00**

Corkscrew, sailing ship, cast brass, 20th C, prob. 1950s. **$25.00-$35.00**

Corkscrew, screw clamps to table edge, for bar or butlery, nickeled cast iron, steel, wooden knob on crank, nicely eared wingnut on clamp, helical worm, "Infanta No. 8", pat'd 1895. **$290.00-$350.00**

Corkscrew, Shriner's cap, cast aluminum 6"L, 20th C. **$45.00-$65.00**

Corkscrew, sommelier, a formally-dressed wine-serving man of carved & painted wood, with steel, European (?), 20th C (?). **$30.00-$40.00**

Corkscrew, sommelier, double lever type, silver plated metal, little man's body fits over neck of bottle, modeled with wescot & sommelier's medallion on chain, shoulders are where the levers pivot, the levers are his 2 arms, round bald head with big ears, called "Pierre le Sommelier", French import, 8"H, c.1980. **$15.00-$22.00**

Corkscrew, squirrel, steel helical worm (this is the kind that is just a twist of wire, with no sharp or "bladed" edges like you'd find on auger, cast brass acorn with huge-tailed squirrel perched on nut, hanging ring at top, English (?), 6½"L, late 19th C. **$65.00-$80.00**

Corkscrew, steel in wooden tube, small, meant for the corks in flavoring extract bottles, advertising printed on tube: "Chamberlain's Pure Extracts," 19th C or shortly after. **$8.00-$12.00**

Corkscrew, steel, pump lever type, works like the handle of a water pump, marked "W.W. Tucker", Hartford, CT, pat'd Sept. 3, 1878. **$600.00-$700.00**

Corkscrew, steel with boar's tusk handle, silver & ivory trim, European, late 19th C. **$95.00-$125.00**

Corkscrew, steel with turned wood handle, with motheaten brush in handle, European, late 19th C. **$45.00-$65.00**

Corkscrew, steel & wood, with cap that fits over bottle mouth, "W. Williamson" patent, American, 5¾"L, pat'd 1887. **$30.00-$45.00**

Corkscrew, tangent lever mechanism, iron, originally enameled black, brass, separate worm is iron with metallic copper finish, "Spong & Co.", London, England, 7⅜"L, registered Nov. 4, 1873. **$120.00-$135.00**

Corkscrew, tomahawk or hatchet, wood handle, iron works, American (?), TOC. **$25.00-$30.00**

Corkscrew, town crier, brass & steel, "Southwold," maybe English, 4½"L. **$30.00-$35.00**

Corkscrew, tree stump figural handle, iron, 6"L. **$25.00-$30.00**

Corkscrew, Viking ship, cast iron, 20th C. **$20.00-$25.00**

Corkscrew, Viking ship with mythological Griffin heads, remove single sail to reveal screw, nickel- or chrome-plated cast iron, 3½"H x 4¼"L, 20th C. **$25.00-$35.00**

Corkscrew, with Archimedean drill in cage, cast iron, wood handle, 1883. • **Old Corks.**— A long article in *The Metal Worker*, Aug. 5, 1882, on the secondhand bottle market in America, includes some new (to me) information on cork-selling. "That bottles should be used again is not so much of a wonder when considered, but that old corks should be is something to marvel at. In a low, wooden building in Mulberry street old corks are made 'as good as new.' This is the only place in New York where they are dealt in. The dealer buys the corks by the barrel, and pays from $1 to $3. His trade is mostly in champagne corks. The best and cleanest of these he sorts out and sells to American champagne makers (who, the article explains, also bought used foreign champagne bottles, being unable at that time to make them strong enough in America). The bottom of the cork where the first bottler's brand appears is shaved off and the name of the second stamped on them. These corks were cut expressly for champagne bottles, and as they can be bought much more cheaply than new ones, the bottlers purchase them. The old cork dealers obtain 25 cents a dozen for them, and make a handsome profit. The broken and dirty corks go through a peculiar process. They are first subjected to a sort of Turkish bath to clean them, and after they are dried are cut down. They are put in a machine and turned, while a sharp knife runs across them and takes off a portion. They can be cut to any size, and with the solid surface removed look as bright as when new. The corks cut down are purchased by root beer and soda water makers, who use smaller bottles. They can save a considerable amount by purchasing old corks, which, as it is easy to see, will do as well as new ones. The 'old cork man' is rushed with business. The champagne and root beer and soda water bottles take all the corks that he can furnish. He gets his supply at the hotels and elsewhere....No demand has yet developed for small corks. The druggists are compelled to use new corks, but the dealer talking on the subject thought that manufacturers of ink, mucilage and the like, might use old corks as well as not." I wish the article had mentioned what they did about corkscrew holes.

$25.00-$35.00

Corkscrew, women's legs that fold out, plated metal with enameled red & black stockings, German, 5½"L, TOC.

$35.00-$45.00

Corkscrew, wooden "cigar" handle, with wire-cutter blade in one end, iron, steel, W. Williamson patent, advertising "The Lion Brewery," American, patented Aug. 10, 1897. • These are around with quite a number of breweries advertised on the wooden handles. **$18.00-$25.00**

Corkscrew & bottle opener combined, nickeled steel, looks sort of like can opener except the cap-lifter part isn't at all sharp, screw folds within open loop handle, pat'd by H. A. Chippendale, American, TOC. **$125.00-$150.00**

Corkscrew & bottle opener combined, Volstead figural, shape of stern top-hatted man (**Andrew Volstead,** who authored the **Prohibition Act**) with beaky nose, black hat, huge shoes, clasped hands, corkscrew pivots up out of tail coat in back, now and piece on chest are bottle opener, hat comes off and reveals small space — for a jigger of liquor (?), base marked "Old Snifter", mfd by Demley, American, c.1919-1933 (period of Prohibition). • There were a number of corkscrews done in Volstead's caricatured image. Similar ones have hats that do not come off. **$175.00-$250.00**

Corkscrew, bottle opener & jigger combined, chromed brass, handle unscrews to reveal screw & bottle opener, Chase Brass & Copper, with centaur logo, Waterbury, CT, 1930s. • Chase's flashy Deco home bar products (ice buckets, shakers, trays, etc.) and other kitchen-related things, are a popular separate field for collectors. Not all bright chromed cocktail accessories are Chase. West Bend, Farberware, Manning - Bowman, and a Canadian company, whose name I don't know, made similar wares.

$15.00-$18.00

Corkscrew, buttonhook & pick combined, steel frame, folding tool in harp, French or English, 3½"L, 19th C.

$20.00-$30.00

Corkscrew & can opener—See Can opener & corkscrew combos.

Corkscrew & cork combined, cork with wire passed through the cork from top to bottom, bent at ends, not as airtight as needed for wine, probably, invented by William H. Towers, possibly mfd by The Union Pin Mfg. Co., Boston, MA, 1862. • Towers also invented a machine for opening oysters, a new kind of broom, and a straight pin that wouldn't fall out. • **First American Corkscrew Patent** — Raymond Townsend wrote article, *Fine Tool Journal*, Sep/Oct 1989, saying he believed that although it has been thought that the earliest American corkscrew patent is that of Philos Blake, New Haven CT, dated March 27, 1860. (NOTE: Joe Kane, *Famous First Facts*, wrote that the first was rec'd by M. L. Byrn, #27, 615, on March 27, 1860.

Hmmm.) Actually, according to Ray, it was George Blanchard's combined nutmeg grater & corkscrew, July 15, ___ 1856 (See under Nutmeg graters). (According to Ray, Blake was a "nephew of Eli Whitney".) The claim of Blake was that "This invention is a new and improved manufacture of cork extractor, as made not only with a lever head applied on such screw and to the cap of the heck stand, in such a manner that it may rotate and screw on the lifting screw and either rotate against or within said cap." **$5.00-$6.00**

Corkscrew & jigger combined, Volstead figural of the Senator, "Old Snifter" with beaky nose, corkscrew pivots up in front when head is turned, hat comes off as jigger, "Old Snifter", mfd by Neghaur, NYC, NY, c.1919-1933 (period of Prohibition). **$175.00-$250.00**

Jar & bottle opener, sheet steel, "4-in-1," J. C. Forster & Son, Pittsburgh, PA, about 6¾" or 7"L, pat'd Sept. 13, 1910. **$15.00-$22.00**

Jar opener, cast iron, "H. L. Jenney," Greenfield, MA, undated 19th C "Pat. Appl'd For." • **"Pat. Appl'd For,"** which dealer Bob Cahn always refers to as "Pat Apple," was put on gadgets in an attempt to protect them at least for long enough for the inventor to make some money. Sometimes it wasn't even true; but usually it seems to have meant production could go on for a few months or even one or two years, *before* a patent was granted (or possibly rejected, something the inventor would hardly cast on the side of his invention). **$35.00-$40.00**

Jar opener, iron with screw-action adjustable hook, "Best", mfd by H. & E. Sanborn, Portland, ME, 3"L, "patent applied for", c.1920s (?). **$7.00-$10.00**

Jar opener, mechanical, tinned cast iron, meant to be wall mounted with (missing) bracket, vertical frame with "faucet" knob to screw one of 2 corrugated jaws to fit lid, "#A100" on moving jaw, "Speedo," Central States Mfg. Co., St. Louis, MO, 6"L, c.1900 to 1912 "patents pending". • Worth a lot more with wall bracket. **$20.00-$35.00**

Jar opener, or jar wrench, nickeled iron oblong frame for geared jaws, which are set by turning the cigar-shaped wood handle clockwise until the jaws fit the jar lid, then turning the other way to twist the lid off, handle painted red or green, or varnished, "Top Off Jar & Bottle Screw Top Opener," Edlund Co., Burlington, VT, gear moves jaws from 1⅛" to 4⅜"; width of metal part of tool is 1⅝". 1933, but made for some years, with various handles. • Works so well, I buy all I can find at yard sales, to give as gifts. **$5.00-$10.00**

Milk bottle cap opener, iron, "Jack Spratt", TOC.

$4.00-$5.00

Milk bottle opener, metal with wood handle, advertising "White Lily Milk," 5"L. **$8.00-$10.00**

Milk bottle opener, to open paper cap wires, looks like a cross between a buttonhook and a pick, embossed with the dairy's name, 1920s?-30s? • How I loved to open (with my bare fingers) the wires on those pleated paper caps as a child. The wires went in a kitchen drawer, like the twisties do now, for future repair jobs. My parents still use an aluminum pan lid that lost its ring, that Daddy fixed with two of those milk bottle wire twists. **$4.00-$8.00**

These attractive stoppers are made of celluloid and are unbreakable. They are beautifully decorated in life colors and mounted on cork. We have a large variety of different figures but space being limited we show but two designs. When more than that number are ordered we will supply a nice assortment.

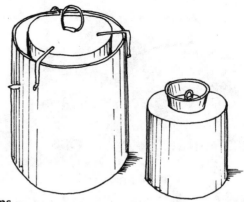

VIII-1.
Bottle stoppers.

Molded colored celluloid. Modernized version of more familiar carved & painted wooden stoppers — many of them also from Germany. Albert Pick, 1909. Most valuable in pairs; priced each.
$10.00-$20.00

VIII-2.
Bottle stoppers.

Figural heads, all mounted to corks. (L to R) A dour Uncle Sam, of "elegant china bisque...finely colored". A carved wooden bulldog, decorated with pyrography. Best: a comical colored rubber clown, whose tongue protrudes when squeezed. This might be a **Futurewatch!** I've never seen any of these. Albert Pick, 1909.
$12.00-$30.00

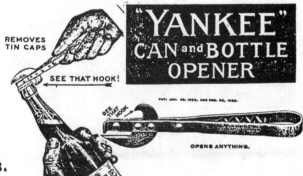

REMOVES TIN CAPS

"YANKEE" CAN and BOTTLE OPENER

SEE THAT HOOK!

SEE THAT HOOK

OPENS ANYTHING.

PAT. JAN. 28, 1902, AND DEC. 25, 1906.

VIII-3.
Bottle & can opener.

"Yankee". Nickel plated. Pat'd 1/28/1902 & 12/26/1906, and mfd. by Taylor Mfg. Co., Hartford, CT.
$1.00-$3.00

VIII-4.
Milk bottle cap lift.

Steel, handle stamped with name of dairy. Cherry-Bassett Co. catalog of supplies for dairies, 1921.
$3.00-$8.00

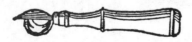

VIII-5.

Called a "sardine opener, to open tin boxes of sardines, preserved meats, preserves, &c. "Wood & steel. American Home Cook Book, 1854.
$10.00-$20.00

VIII-6.
Early cans.

Both of pieced tin plate. (L) "Cotton's Preserve Can", pat'd 12/21/1859 by P.H. Cotton, Demopolis, AL. Lid slightly concave to form recess for wax or cement poured in to make air tight. Bent wires hold lid on while cement hardens. (R) "Manley's Preserve Can", pat'd. 8/3/1858 by E. Manley, Marion, NY. According to Scientific American, no can "surpasses this one for cheapness..., simplicity and perfection." Slightly concave top is removed to put food in; can then placed in hot water to expel air from inside; cover replaced & center cup fitted into top to hold the cement. "To open the can...pour hot water into the cup, which melts the cement." Scientific American, 2/26/1859 and 9/25/1858.
$20.00-$30.00

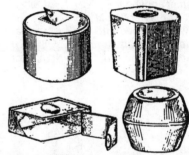

VIII-7.
Early cans.

Pieced tin; various kind of air-tight openings. Top (L) a "rip patch can" from 1875, which required a hole to be opened, and a hook to pull off squarish patch. (R) a squarish can with canted sides, called a "pyramidal can", 1879. Bottom (L) a "rip side can", 1879, and (R) a fruit can with bulge-pot sides and large opening for lid, 1879. Drawings adapted from Wonders of Modern Industry, 1938.
$20.00-$30.00

VIII-8.
Can opener patent.

Pat'd 5/21/1867 by Thomas A. McFarland, Meadville, PA. For opening oyster, fruit and other tin cans — "a cheap, simple, and effective implement for cutting an opening in a can by a single blow" by its "curved pointed teeth" which enter the lid easily, and as it is forced downward "the cutting continues, the cutting edges expand until they meet...and thus punch out a...disk or plug" of lid. McFarland wrote "I am aware that it has been proposed to open cans by the use of a single cutter operating like the single blade of a shear;...also that cutters have been used in combination with separate spring handles sliding through a ring, and thus compressing the cutters to cut a plug out of a cork." Official Gazette.
$20.00-$35.00

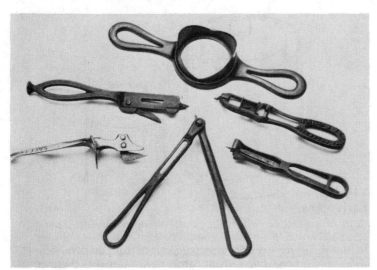

VIII-10.
Can opener.
Cast iron mechanical type, with large turning screw something like Baumgartner opener. Spikes & blade underneath. Marked only "Pat. Appl. For" on handle. 7 1/2"L. c.1890s. Collection of Peggy Wainscott. **$55.00-$75.00**

VIII-9.
Can openers.
Clockwise, starting at top: (1) Cast iron & steel, 2 handles, pushed into lid then rotated to cut off whole top. 10"L. (2) Cast iron & steel, sliding adjustment for blade, embossed "World's Best, Pittsburg, PA, "6 3/4"L. (3) Cast iron & steel, very like #2. "U.S. Can Opener, Made in Pittsburg, PA, Pat'd May 7, 1895." 6"L. (4) Cast iron, 2 pivoting handles. Poke tip in, swivel it around. Marked only "patent applied for." 7 3/4"L. (5) Nickel plated cast iron, steel, 6 1/2"L, "The Safety", pat'd 5/12/1914. (6) Cast iron, pointed tip at right was punched into can's top by tapping on little knob at other end with small hammer. 7 5/8"L. Unmarked, c. 1880s. All six located by the Primitive Man, Bob Cahn, Carmel, NY. **$20.00-$85.00**

VIII-11.
Can opener.
Cast iron mechanical type. Looks like a Nardi steering wheel! Marked "Safety First." Looks like the Hopper. No date, but about same time as Hopper — late 1890s. 4 1/4" diameter. Collection of Peggy Wainscott. **$30.00-$40.00**

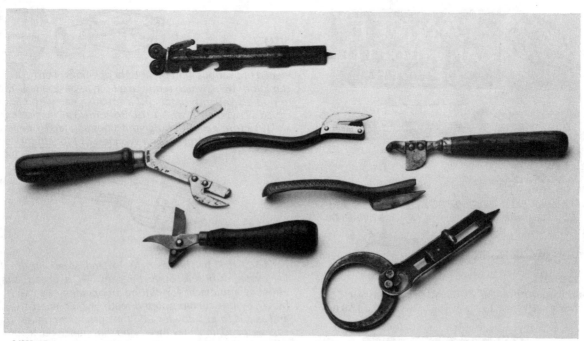

VIII-12.
Can openers.
(1) (L) Most unusual is slingshot "Y". Steel, turquoise wood handle. 7 1/2"L. (2) To me, neatest is top combo: knife sharpener between eye-like wheels, glass cutter, can & jar or crown cap bottle opener. (3) Center, serpentine handle, painted cast iron, steel blade. "The Improved Peerless, Austria, U.S. Patent Pending". (4) Just below it also with curved handle, pat'd 2/11/1890. (5) (R) Simple fat wood handle, large blade, mfd. by Cassady-Fairbanks, Chicago. (6) Combo tool with circular jar wrench, mfd. by J.C. Forster & Son, Pittsburgh." Pat'd 9/13/1910. 6 3/4"L. (7) Big blade & pivoting guide, wood handle. Collection of Meryle Evans. **$10.00-$50.00**

VIII-13.
Can opener.

Cast iron, cast eagle on top. (Mounted to wood for stability here.) This is a double opener — small short cans cut on side seen here; taller cans in the back. Snaky lever works small blade in front to open a tuna fish-size can. Large, heart-shaped blade in back. Only 7 1/2"H. Lever 12"L. Eagle makes me wonder if this is an Enterprise Mfg. Co. product. C. 1880s. Collection of Meryle Evans.
$150.00-$200.00

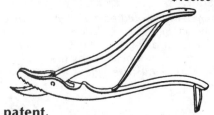

VIII-14.
Can opener patent.

Pat'd 5/29/1877 by David F. Fetter, NYC. A "pair of spring-pliers, with a slotted convex jaw, notched or serrated on either side of the slot, and pivoted therein; a curved blade having concave cutting-edge, terminating in an upwardly-turned point; the handles authoritatively thrown open by a spring, and held together, when not in use, by a wire loop at their extremities." Official Gazette. Compare this with the Wheeler in the next picture.**$15.00-$25.00**

VIII-15.
Can opener.

Cutlery steel blade, malleable iron handles, steel spring. Mfd. by Wheeler Patent Can Opener Co., St. Louis, MO, and introduced in mid 1890. Looks like the Fetter patent. Makers claimed the Wheeler "is the only can opener that will cut off the top of paint pails...It cuts stove pipe, tin pipe, &c. Also cut square cans (as seen by the corned beef can in picture). TMW, 1890.**$15.00-$25.00**

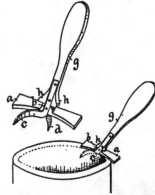

VIII-16.
Can opener patent.

Pat'd 12/18/1877 by John McWilliams, Prairie City, IA. Assigned half rights to E.B. Tilden — presumably for manufacture. "A traveling fulcrum having one straight and one curved side is combined with a straight cutter and a curved cutter, the whole attached to a suitable handle in such manner that by simply reversing that tool in the hand either a straight or a curved incision is cut, at pleasure, adapting it equally to the opening of sardine-boxes or of round cans." Official Gazette. **$30.00-$40.00**

VIII-17.
Can opener.

The Baumgartner side cutter, pat'd in Canada in 1896. According to expert Joe Young, although Mr. Baumgartner was living in Ohio when the patent was issued, he never got a U.S. patent. As shown 9 3/4"L. Ex-Keillor Collection. **$65.00-$85.00**

VIII-18.
Can opener.

One of three malleable cast iron openers pat'd 5/7/1899 by G.W. Lehman, Decatur, IL. Thi is their No. 3. After point at far side of ring was stuck into top of can near the edge, the opener is "pressed down upon the top of the can until the spur (blade) penetrates the top. Then the moving handle is rotated and the top is cut off. Mfd. by G.W. Lehman & Co., later Lehman, Bowman & Co.

$40.00-$60.00

VIII-19. Can openers.

Two Lehman top openers, with wingnuts. No 1 (L) is at top of piece of stationery dated July 8, 1890. No. 2 (R) appears on a business card. From photocopies of ephmera in the Phyllis & Jim Moffet collection. The ephemera almost as valuable as the real things.
$50.00-$80.00

VIII-20.
Can opener patent.

Pat'd 8/30/1887 by William J. Hammer, Boston, MA. A "spring clasping-holder" with handle, and a "standard extending over the top with a pointed turning rod sliding through" it, and a "knife", with a blade at each end, moved by the turning handle above. Looks extremely efficient.
$40.00-$60.00

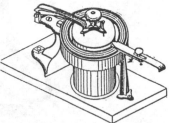

VIII-21.
Can opener patent.

Pat'd 12/29/1887 by Charles W. Acker, Watertown, NY. Patent application was accompanied by a patent model. This one includes a frame into which the can sits, while the blade is carried by a rotary ring above.
$40.00-$60.00

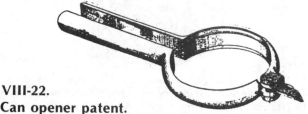

VIII-22.
Can opener patent.

Combined jar-wrenched & can-opener, pat'd 6/9/1885 by Alexander Van Slyke, Fort Plain, NY. The wrench part is easy to see, but heaven knows how it cuts can's top. More jar wrenches in Canning chapter.
$10.00-$15.00

VIII-23.
Can opener.

*Or **Tin opener**, as it would be called in its native England. Cast iron, with looped tail. Spike & blade one piece of steel, adjustable or removable for cleaning. 6"L. 19th C. There are many variations on this — enough for a herd. Many have spikes cast as part of iron body, with adjustable blade (lower "jaw") of steel.*
$25.00-$50.00

VIII-24.
Can opener.

Cast iron fish, adjustable blade & spike-in-one. Probably English. 5"L. Late 19th C.
$25.00-$35.00

VIII-25.
Can opener.

Cast iron with well-defined scales and eye, original dark green paint. Only 4"L. Meant for opening sardine tins. English. 19th C.
$25.00-$45.00

VIII-26.
Advertisement.

Franco-American can shows one version of a can ready-made for easier opening. One tactic used to complement the search for better can openers was to make cans themselves easier to open. Century, 5/1893.

VIII-27
Can opener patent model.

Cast iron, pat'd 11/15/-1887 by Walter B. Nutter. Appears to fit over top of can, and worked with rotary motion. Pieces in foreground look like size adapters — on right may be a blade. Picture courtesy of the National Museum of American History, Smithsonian Institution. **Possible value: $200.00-$400.00**

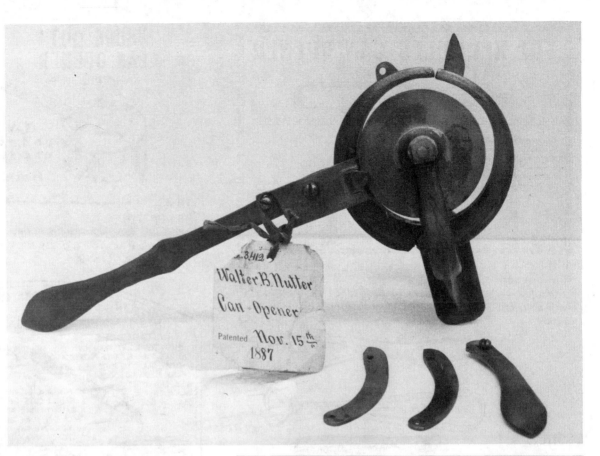

VIII-28.
Can openers.

(T) "Acme," Goodell Co., steel, not a "cheap John affair." Opened any shape can. 1890. **$15.00-$25.00.** *(M) The "Stand-by," steel blade riveted on, not adjustable. 1899.* **$2.00-$5.00.** *(B) "Peerless", nickeled, toothed gripper prevents slipping. Pat'd 2/11/1890; 1903 ad.* **$8.00-$12.00.**

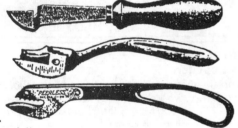

VIII-29.
Can opener.

"Best Yet", mfd. by Hasbrouck Alliger, NYC. Malleable iron, steel blade. Point is driven into the top near center, then it's levered down to almost horizontal position to force chisel-like blade into rim. Then, holding the two parts firmly in the right hand, while holding the can in the left, one "carries the two handles around in a circle" as one either cuts off one's left thumb or the can's lid. Alliger claimed "It is so shaped that the blade will not work up, and (it) has no thumbscrew...but fastens in the desired place by an automatic lock." TMW, 8/30/1890. **$20.00-$30.00**

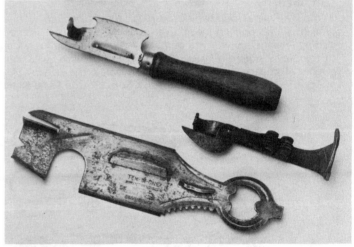

VIII-30.
Can openers.

From top: (1) Multiple use opener, crown cap opener & -?-, wood handle, c.1930. (2) Small c.1915 "Norlunds 3-in-1" with knife sharpener wheels center shaft. (3) Wide nickel plated "Ten-in-One", mfd. by New Jersey Patent Novelty Co., c.1910. It scales fish, opens bottles, slices carrots, etc. **$10.00-$18.00**

VIII-31.
Can opener.

"Handy", made of hardened steel, for round or square cans. An "improved" version of original pat'd 6/11/1895. Mfd. by Handy Things Mfg. Co., Ludington, MI, and sold originally for only a nickel! HFR, 1/1903. **$8.00-$12.00**

VIII-32.
Can opener.

"Hercules" — "A Giant of Strength". Pat'd 8/12/1902. Skeletal steel with adjustable blade position. Manufacturer unknown. HFR, 2/1904.   **$8.00-$12.00**

VIII-33.
Can openers.

At top is all-metal loop handle version of the "Never Slip"— one of many similar openers meant to give a good grip and a leveraged cutting angle. One with wooden handle is "Improved" version. In middle is simple all steel "King" combo corkscrew & can opener. A cheaper version of it (not shown) is the "Dean". All in April 1905 catalog of Joseph Breck & Sons, Boston. **$3.00-$8.00**

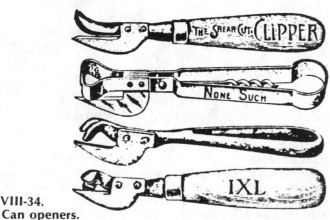

VIII-34.
Can openers.

Variety, some all metal, some with wooden handles — all made by same company, W.G. Browne Mfg. Co., Kingston, NY, who also made ice picks, potato mashers, tack hammers & "The Cyclone" eggbeater. Their best seller was "The Best", which opened crown caps & corks too. It looks like the "None Such" (second down), but with a bottle cap hook on top. Others pictured are "The Shear Cut Clipper", an all metal one with a tack puller, and the "IXL." HFR, 10/1902.   **$3.00-$8.00**

VIII-35.
Can opener.

"Sure Cut", long shank with sliding blade, wooden handle, for round & square cans. Pat'd 7/19/1904. Mfd. by Ira F. White & Son, Newark, NJ. HFR, 5/1906.   **$5.00-$12.00**

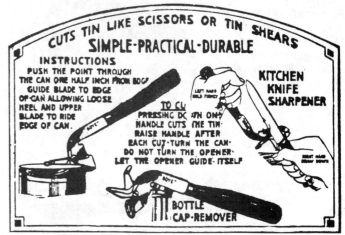

VIII-36.
Can opener.

A bottle opener & knife sharpener combo tool made by The Boye Needle Co., whose nutmeg grater is more notable. Pat'd 9/10/1912 and 12/16/1917. This is a little double-sided printed flyer that was sent out with the products.   **$12.00-$18.00**

VIII-37.
Can opener.

"Joy" — "One Shove Does the Act" (sounds like a "Columbo" episode!). Metal with wooden grip. If kept sharp, it probably worked very well. Mfd. by Beveridge Mfg. Co., Baltimore, where tin-canning got started a century and a half ago. HFR, 2/1915.   **$15.00-$20.00**

VIII-38. Can opener.
"Stork" combo can opener & jar sealer. All metal. Mfd. by the Stork Mfg. Co., Dayton, OH. HFR, 5/1905.   **$3.00-$8.00**

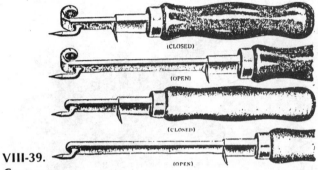

VIII-39.
Can openers.
Top one, also a bottle opener, is a "Peerless", shown open and closed. Nickeled carbon steel, turned wood handle enameled black. Below is the "So-Easy". Mfd. by Hardware Specialty Mfg. Co., Chicago, IL. HFR, 1/1914.   **$7.00-$12.00**

The Can Opener that *really* opens cans, tins, etc., without bruising the hands—it's the adjustable LOCK that does it.

Pat. Nov. 1, 1910
Quick 10, 15 and 25c. Sellers   ← SEE THAT LOCK

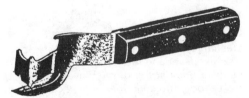

VIII-40.
Can opener.
"Slick-Ope", very similar to those in VIII-39. Adjustable, sliding blade on shank has locking device. Pat'd 11/1/1910. Mfd. by Irwin Mfg. Co., NYC. HFR, 1915.   **$7.00-$12.00**

VIII-41.
Can opener.
"Nuform", carbon steel & cocobolo wood handle, modern beveled design. Also crown cap opener; shown with the foods it would open. Its makers, The Lo-Vis Co., Kalamazoo, MI, were given the Good Housekeeping Seal of Approval. HFR, 1/1917. Probably went out of business during war, or turned to making other things.   **$5.00-$8.00**

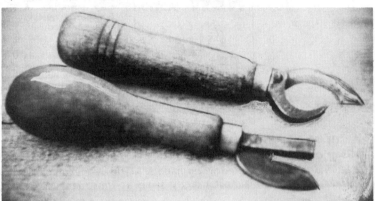

VIII-42.
Can openers.
Two with fat wood handles. Bulbous one (bottom) marked on steel cutting blade "Wynn & Timmins", which sounds English. The other is marked "TN & S". 6 1/2"L and 6"L. Early 20th C. **$10.00-$18.00**

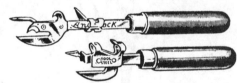

VIII-43.
Can openers & bottle openers combined.
Top one, 8"L, a 2-way type with sliding knife on long shank. Bottom, 6 1/2"L. Nickeled metal & painted handles in choice of green, yellow, red, green with ivory band, and yellow with blue band. Washburn Co., "Androck" line catalog, 1936.   **$5.00-$10.00**

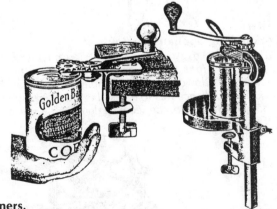

VIII-44.
Can openers.
Illustrations from c.1927 S. Joseph catalog of kitchen & bar wares, show the household size (L) and the "Hotel Blue Streak", with metal stake & adjustable platform to support large heavy cans. 4"H x about 7"L (plus crank).   **$18.00-$50.00**

VIII-45.
Can opener.
The "P-38", U.S. Army issue. Steel, hinged triangular blade. Stamped "USA Shelby Corp." 1 1/2"L. (In the 1935 <u>Thomas' Register of American Manufacturers</u>, a hinge company, Shelby Metal Products Co., Shelby, OH, was listed. I'd bet this is the one, and by WWII became Shelby Corp). Collection of Jim Holroyd, Oregon.   **$3.00-$6.00**

VIII-46.
Can opener.
Edlund Jr., steel, painted wood handle. Made over many years, and 1930 version almost exactly same as this 1944 version.
$4.00-$7.00

VIII-47.
Cork-pulling appliance patent.
Pat'd 12/2/1890 by Alfred J. Parker, NYC. Composed of a flexible strap (to put foot through) passed through a "flexible yoke" (spoked piece lower right) with a hole in center for the bottle's neck. The appliance was to be used to aid the person pulling the cork by holding the bottle secure. I doubt if it was ever produced. <u>Official Gazette.</u>

VIII-48.
Cork press.
Cast iron, wooden base, rotary motion compresses cork to reduce its diameter long enough to stick it in bottle neck. A. Pick & Co. hotel & bar supplies catalog, c.1905-09, but press may be much older.   **$85.00-$125.00**

VIII-49.
Cork-extractor patent.
Pat'd 8/9/1881 by Frederick Mann, Milwaukee, WI. A tubular sheet metal handle with long slot. Cap at left is removed & the vertical slender arm or rod on left is taken out from inside tube, passed through the slot, and cap is somehow used to fix it to tubular handle. The right arm "pivots and swings" or can be made to be detachable and kept inside also. If this looks feasible to you, you must be knocking the tops off bottles to open them now. <u>Official Gazette.</u> If it exists, the value should be quite high because of construction and material.   **$30.00-$45.00**

VIII-50.
Cork press.
Figural alligator, well-detailed cast iron. Mounted to shaped oak board, screwed through feet. Does four sizes of corks. Photo courtesy James & Phyllis Moffet.   **$300.00-$500.00**

VIII-51
Corkscrew.
Mechanical "Lund's Lever" 2-part, 2-step opener. The 2 parts are plier-like lever and the screw, the shaft of which has a hole that fits over hook at top of plier/lever. The 2 steps are: screw the 3 1/2"L worm into cork, then fit bell cap over mouth of bottle and hook lever through hole in worm. The screw part is commonly orphaned, and mistaken for small pocket corkscrew. English. In importer F. A. Walker's catalog, 1870s but pat'd 1855.
$90.00-$100.00

VIII-52.
Cork drawer or puller.

"Yankee-6", cast iron in choice of finish: bronze or nickel plate. Fancy casting of mechanism housing. Bottle is clamped into position underneath, and handle is worked up & then down. There was also a "Yankee-7", also to be clamped either to counter, shelf or work board. Its handle started in vertical down position, and was moved up only, but traveled the same overall distance as the #6. The bottle clamp was optional. Mfd. by the Gilchrist Co., Newark, NJ, early 20th C. **$90.00-$150.00**

VIII-55.
Corkscrews.

The cheapest kind, but perfectly efficient for many kinds of corked bottles. These came with single ring of wire for the fingerhole, or double ring for strength. Simple one at top could also be had with two kinds of tubes. Center one has wooden tube with no _printed_ advertising. The wholesale price was 250 of them for $3.75. At bottom is one showing printed wooden tube, meant as giveaway. They were only 25¢ more! Made at Albert Pick & Co.'s Pennsylvania factory. A. Pick, 1905-09. Value affected by advertising. **$1.00-$10.00**

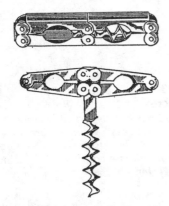

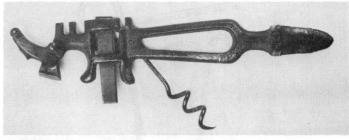

VIII-53.
Corkscrew.

Another folding type, the "Handy Pocket Cork Screw", mfd. by the Little Giant Letterpress Co., NYC. Nickel-plated. You worked it by holding the tip of the screw worm to the cork with one hand, then pulling up on upper half of handle, which "forces the screw down". It would, of course, if it worked at all, force it straight into the cork without screwing. I don't see how it would work, but it was sold. TMW, 7/28/1892. **$18.00-$30.00**

VIII-56.
Corkscrew combination.

A glazier's tool. According to the late Marion Levy, whose apple parer article appears elsewhere in this book, from L to R are glass cutter, tapper, 2 nippers, knife sharpener, corkscrew for pulling linseed oil bottle cork, and at end, the arrowhead shape, a putty knife with "two spacer bars". 5 1/2"L. Pat'd 6/7/1869. There are many variations. **$20.00-$30.00**

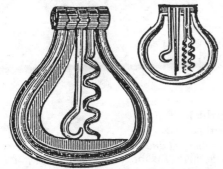

VIII-54.
Corkscrews.

Combination folding pocket types. Large one on left is a "Champagne Opener", and has button hook (nothing to do with bottle-opening) and a curved wire-cutting blade in addition to worm; smaller one has extra worm, and a pick. F.A. Walker catalog, 1870s. **$20.00-$35.00**

VIII-57.
Corkscrews.

(L) A so-called "self-puller" with cap to fit over mouth of bottle. (R) A "flat twist" helical worm, and slender wooden handle reinforced with a metal ring at each end. About 6 1/2"L. D, H & M catalog, c.1904-10 **$4.00-$10.00**

VIII-58.
Corkscrew.

A simple one with turned, stained wood handle, hardened steel wire, attached to handle by winding. More expensive versions upgraded step by step: nickeled wire, varnished wood; then tempered steel, brace, and imitation rosewood handle; then "best tempered steel", wire cutter and polished hardwood. They were mounted to a card, 12 at a time, and originally wholesale for from 30¢ a doz. to $1.75 doz. Butler Brothers catalog, 1899.**$2.00-$6.00**

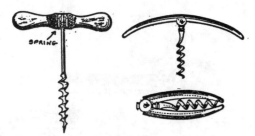

X-59.
"Captain Warren's Bachelor's Frying Pan."
Cast iron, with heavy sharp edged flutes inside to retain heat, and long rein handles. Pat'd in the U.S. by Frederick Pelham Warren, East Court Cosham, Great Britain, on 2/13/1872; pat'd earlier in England. "It shuts and can be turned over from one side to the other, as the cook pleases." Note slip ring holding handles together. From Warne's Model Cookery, *London, c1868.*
$100.00-$200.00

VIII-63.
Corkscrew.
Turned bone handle (possibly ivory), dark bristle dust & cobweb brush intact, cast & turned brass cylindrical sheath covering mechanism. Thomason type. Patented, 19th C. English. 7 3/8"L as shown. Picture courtesy of Christie, Manson & Woods International, Inc.
$400.00-$500.00

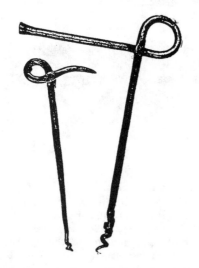

VIII-61
Corkscrews.
Called "cellar" corkscrews. Forged iron, twists at top provided leverage for turning. Italian, late 18th C. 6 3/4"L and 8 3/8"L. Collection Hillman Books.
$100.00-$150.00

VIII-64.
Corkscrew.
Another of Lund's patents from 1855. Bone crossbar handle, steel cage, helical worm, hanging ring at top, missing the dust brush. About 7 1/4"H as shown. English. Courtesy Bruce Michel.
$120.00-$185.00

VIII-62.
Corkscrews.
All forged iron, all helical worms. European, probably Italian. Folding one 2 7/8"L folded. Others 4 3/8"L, 4 5/8"L. Mid to late 18th C. Collection Hillman Books.
$85.00-$120.00

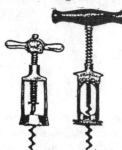

VIII-65.
Corkscrews.
(L) "The Challenge", French-style, locking "fly nut" at top, cast steel open cage, helical worm. 6 1/2"L fully extended. (R) Steel & wood "Columbus", with spring around shank between cage & turned wood handle — referred to as a "sprung shank" type 6 1/2"L. The "Challenge" worth $20 to $40 more than other. Full range or value:
$85.00-$165.00

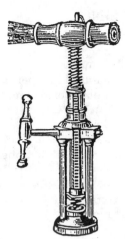

VIII-66.
Corkscrew.
Double lever corkscrew with ratchet wheel, and side turning handle, in the style of the King screw. Probably steel with bone or wood handle, fitted with dust brush. From F.A. Walker import catalog, 1870s. **$200.00-$300.00**

VIII-67.
Corkscrew.
A modern figural: Bacchus, mfd. by Godinger, cast brass. C. 1983-84. **$25.00-$35.00**

VIII-68.
Corkscrew.
Figural "Old Snifter" caricature of Senator "Prohibition" Volstead. Corkscrew tail, bottle opener hook under chin. Hat removes — purpose not known, not big enough to hold much but a sniff. Painted cast metal (brass?). Many versions of this, some without cap opener or removable hat. c.1920s. **$85.00-$150.00**

VII-69.
Bawdy corkscrews.
(L) "Leg puller". Enameled striped stockings in red & white, blue & white, etc. Crucible steel worm. 2 1/2" folded; 5"L open. One example of popular type. Original wholesome price was $7.25 a doz.
(R) Folding female. "An imported novelty, beautifully enameled in colors." Tempered crucible steel worm. Both <u>A. Pick</u> catalog, 1905-09. **$45.00-$85.00**; **$65.00-$125.00**

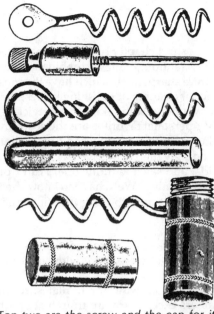

VIII-70.
Corkscrews.
For "vest pocket. Top two are the screw and the cap for it, to be assembled by putting the rod through hole and using as handle to twist. Nickeled steel, 3"L. Next is simple heavy twisted nickeled steel wire & metal tube, 3 1/4"L. At bottom is a neat one with screw kept inside, then fitted into position for use. Nickeled steel. 2 3/4"l in tube. A. Pick, 1905-09. **$15.00-$22.00**

VIII-71.
Corkscrews.
And crown cap opener combined. Protrusion is a wire breaker. Pocket advertising type, shown with & without printed wooden tube. (Also came with metal tube). A. Pick, 1905-09. **$4.00-$10.00**

VIII-72.
Jar opener.
Malleable iron, thumbscrew adjusts tension. Paper label "Best", Portland, ME. 3"L. "Pat. Appl.", early 20th C, maybe 1920s. **$7.00-$12.00**

This short chapter has the tools and racks that are used for washing dishes and draining them dry, others for sharpening knives (although a few combination can openers and knife sharpeners are found in Open & Close, Chapter VIII.

Knife sharpeners, which have the most variety, are probably the most popular tool in here. If you include the contrivances used for cleaning or polishing knives, there's something for everyone — from an 18th C knife-cleaning box to a strange revolving wooden drum, like some magician's trick machine, with slots for the knives.

My personal favorites are the soap savers, but I'm afraid the field is quite small. A surprise field, closely related to advertising collectibles, and just a tiny bit out of my purview, are the small flat chromolithographed tin pot scrapers. Some astoundingly high prices were achieved at an auction where a number of them were sold in April 1988. I have said about other fields, and say about this one, I can't put a market range on something which has achieved astronomical prices with not much warning. We'd have to know the full story about the buyer(s) of the scrapers. If it was one person, aiming for a book along about now, buying the "illustrations", so to speak, it was a smart move.

Cutlery trays-—See Storage & Container chapter.

Dish drainer, 2 piece, wire with sheet metal soap tray, TOC. **$18.00-$25.00**

Dish drainer, all wire, for 12 plates, resembles today's dish drainers except for wire trough at end for cutlery, "Loop Weld Model No. A#4", by Marlboro Wire Goods Co., 3⅞"H x 18¾"L x 12"W, c.1910. • A child's toy version was made exactly the same way & just as well, differing in the number of loops & plate arches. It is 6⅛"L x 3⅝"W. It's value is about $30.00-$35.00. The bigger one: **$20.00-$30.00**

Dish drainer, blackened tin & wire, with fold-down cutlery draining trough with 8 drain holes along gutter of it, wire rack lengthwise down center for plates & saucers, Androck No. 199, 3⅞"H x 19½"L x 12"W, early 20th C. • Rusts like crazy! There was, in the 1870s or so, a wire rack that looks like a dish drainer, but was advertised as a dish warmer, pictured sitting over 2 range eyes, lids on. This one would have served well to warm plates, but then it wouldn't have had the cutlery compartment. **$35.00-$45.00**

Dish drainer, pine with woven wire screen & wooden dividers, American, 1880s. **$35.00-$45.00**

Dish drainer, round dish drainer, very substantial heavy plated wire, wide metal rim to help hold shape, round cutlery basket in center, Utility Mfg. Co., Baltimore, MD, about 15" diameter, c.1920s. **$12.00-$18.00**

Dish drainer, round, open woven wire, detachable cutlery holder suspended in center has much finer wire mesh bottom, Androck, Washburn Co., 5¼"H x 15" diameter, c.1930s. • When I first saw one of these I mistakenly thought it was just a discard from an old dishwashing machine, and by "old" I meant, say, the 1950s. **$30.00-$40.00**

Dish drainer, soldered wire, T shape with cross bar for flatware, or tumblers if tall narrow loops used, longer piece has loops for plates, American, 16"L, c.1890s to 1910s. **$25.00-$40.00**

Dish drainer, water- & soap-bleached pine, 2 rows of nearly vertical dowel pegs to hold plates, a third of the drainer has cross pieces of dowels for flatware, small white rubber knobs on 4 feet, American, 2¾"H x 17¾"L x 11½"W, 1890s to 1920s (?). **$25.00-$35.00**

Dish mop, cotton thrum with slender broomstick handle, Shaker construction, 9"L, 19th C. • **Thrum** is the word for loose ends of warp threads, left when the finished weaving is cut off the loom, and hence for short pieces of scrap thread or yarn. **$35.00-$55.00**

Dish mop, turned wooden handle, cotton mop head tied on. In 1904, *House Furnishing Review* commented "Not one housewife in 25 knows how useful a ... dish mop is in the kitchen. ... Women who as girls were taught to immerse their hands in hot, greasy dish water are not prone to leave the beaten path of drudgery. They say the old way is good enough. As most of us have graduated from the tallow candle and the stage coach to the electric light and trolley car, why not improve in the same ratio in minor things?" According to the same magazine, the largest American mfrs were J. H. Estes & Sons, Fall River, MA, with 4 styles, 5 sizes each. This company began making them c.1900. • We often see dish mops at antique shows labeled "Shaker". Indeed, the Shakers made dish mops, using cotton thrum or the warp weaving threads cut off the looms. The simple turned wood handles and the bound cotton threads used in all the early ones would make it hard to know which were Shaker, which were J. H. Estes or other company. **$3.00-$6.00**

Dish or plate scraper, hard white rubber, green rubber handle, "Daisy", mfd by Schact Rubber Mfg. Co., Huntington, IN, 5¾"L, 1933 patent #1898690. **$4.00-$5.00**

Dish or plate scraper, rubber with wood handle, "A & J", but mfd. by company that took over A & J, Edward Katzinger Co., Chicago, IL, c.1940. **$4.00-$5.00**

Dish pan, blue & white mottled enamelware, TOC. **$25.00-$30.00**

Dish pan, dark blue & white agateware, ear handles, 12" diameter, 19th or 20th C. **$15.00-$18.00**

Dish pan, gray graniteware, 12" diameter, 19th or 20th C. **$15.00-$18.00**

Dish pan, or basin, green marbleized enamelware, 8½"D, late 19th C. **$22.00-$28.00**

Dish pan, royal blue & white swirl enamelware, "F. W. Morse, Omega", 19th C. **$35.00-$45.00**

Dish warmer, usable also as a drainer, all wire oblong trough-shaped rack, made so it's flat on top, with vertical slots for a dozen or so plates or shallow dishes, to be set over 2 lidded range eyes for warm air to rise & dry or warm plates, American, 15"L, mid to late 19th C. **$22.00-$40.00**

Dishcloth holder, wire, 4 hooked fingers, the handle end is a coil and twist of the wires, a slip ring makes the fingers hold cloth in a tight grasp, American, 10¾"L, c.1890s. **$9.00-$15.00**

Dishcloth holder & cork puller combined, wire & wood, slip ring & 4 wire prongs which grasp cloth, American, 12"L, c.1880s to 1910.

$9.00-$15.00

Dishcloth holder & vegetable skimmer combined, wire, with 4 hooked prongs at one end, an openwork twisted wire spoon at other end, slip ring to tighten prongs, American, 12"L, TOC.

$12.00-$15.00

Dishwasher, tinned sheet iron, wooden lever handle, basket inside, "Whirlpool Sanitary Dishwasher", mfd by Hershey-Sexton Mfg. Co., pat'd July 28, 1914. • A "Whirlpool" washer was being made by the Nineteen Hundred Corp., of Binghampton, NY, in early 1930s. I can't find any better clues to maker.

$65.00-$85.00

To Wash Dishes

Dishes should be rinsed in clear, hot water after having been washed in soap suds. It is necessary from a sanitary point of view (because) the caustic alkali is corrosive and unwholesome, and the grease often impure. A rack made of narrow strips of half-inch board is a device frequently used for draining dishes, thus saving the trouble of wiping them. this rack placed on a shelf inclining towards and adjoining the sink holds the dishes securely while they are drying. Milk is a substitute for soap in the kitchen. A little put into hot water will soften it, give the dishes a fine gloss, and will not injure the hands. China and glass (when very dirty) are best cleaned with finely powdered fuller's-earth and warm water, afterwards rinsing it well in clean water. All china that has any gilding upon it may on no account be rubbed with a cloth of any kind, but merely rinsed, first in hot and afterwards in cold water, and then left to drain till dry. Cups and saucers which have become stained with coffee or tea can be easily cleaned by scouring them with baking soda." Henry Scammell, *Treasure-House of Knowledge*, 1891.

Dishwashing brush, glass cylindrical bottle to be filled with soapy water, one threaded end has a turned wood handle that is hollow but has remnants of red rubber — probably a squeeze bulb; the other threaded end has screw-on zinc cap with small perforations on top, & a wood doughnut-shaped brush set with tampico fiber bristles, embossed on glass "CLIMAX Dish Dash Washer", American, 10"L, "pat. pending", c.1920s. • Collection of Carol Bohn. Price range mine.

$30.00-$45.00

Draining pan for sink, royal blue & white enamelware, 12"D, TOC or early 20th.

$15.00-$20.00

Draining pan for sink, white enamelware, triangular to fit into sink corner, 3 short legs, TOC. • An idea which has proved "most reliable in my own home,.. I send along. A round piece of tin which one can easily procure, when punched full of holes (which you can easily do with hammer and nails) makes a capital arrangement to put in the opening of the pipe which leads from the butler's pantry sink. This of course prevents many things from going down and stopping up the drain." *The Housewife Magazine*, Feb. 1910, NYC: A. D. Porter.

$10.00-$15.00

Gloves, "India rubber", gauntlet style, apparently stitched together, Goodyear's India Rubber Glove Mfg Co., NYC, NY, advertised 1870. • I don't know if any of these could have survived, but if you thought gardening or dishwashing rubber gloves were fairly new, look at the date on these! • At least by 1901, Faultless Rubber Co. of Akron was making molded rubber gloves, which you could order by glove size, and finger length — long or short. • "Rubber gloves for kitchenette and kitchen use save the hands and are worth their weight in radium. If more women used them the housework problem would be less like martyrdom. They preserve the hands' health and beauty." Ethel R. Peyser, "Tinware, Rubber and Paper for the Kitchen", *House & Garden*, June 1922.

$7.00-$12.00

Knife cleaner, cast iron square frame screw clamps to table. A crank at side turns 2 geared & cranked felt covered rollers, making them rub together; they adjust for even snugger contiguation with 2 set screws. The device is used by inserting tip of knife blade between rollers, then turning crank, probably while pushing blade all the way through. I imagine the felt rollers were possibly dressed with some kind of scouring material too, pumice or brickstone. This scouring powder probably fell off the rollers into the bottom of the device, which has sides that form an inch deep well. The felt was in round discs, like washers, put on (like beads on a string) the rollers' axles. I guess so that individual ones could be replaced if badly cut or worn. pat'd as a "Machine for Scouring Knives, Etc." by G. M. Morris and J. Newton, Watertown, CT, base 4⅜" square, rollers approx 2" diameter and 2½"L, overall height 7½", including screw clamp, only mark is the patent date, Dec. 4, 1855. • **Detective Serendipity Identifies Whatzit.**— I got this at auction, and thought it was a pea sheller — that pea pods were cranked through the presumably once-soft felt rollers, popping them open so the peas would fall in the well. Oh dear, such fantasizing. The patent date would not help for an 1855 patent, as the Official Gazette didn't start until 1873. The thing wasn't listed under Pea Shellers in my subject index to patents up to 1873. By chance, browsing in a Patent Office book, outlining agricultural and mechanical patents of 1855, I found this knife scourer, and it immediately made perfect sense! Nice to identify a Whatzit.

$30.00-$50.00

Knife cleaner, polishing-stone blade, green wooden handle, probably A & J, 7"L, c.1930s to 1940s.

$4.00-$6.00

Knife cleaner, tabletop style, cast iron frame with wooden drum slotted for inserting knives so several can be done at once. Inside, a rubber roller (like wringer) polishes blades, with aid of a polishing powder, "Kents", London, England, various sizes for different numbers of knives, pat'd 1882; Kents' common "Improved Patent" was pat'd 1890. • In *Knights' Cyclopaedia of the Industry of All Nations*, (London, 1851), appears this: "... a machine has been invented to perform the operation of cleaning table-knives; in which the cleaner has simply to turn a handle, instead of bestowing arm-movement in a somewhat laborious way. There are two rival patented machines for this purpose, Kent's and Masters'; both relate to a machine which was invented by an American, and was introduced into this country (England) ... by the parties above-named. The machine consists of a flat cylinder, or drum, in the inside of which are brushes placed in contact; holes are made round the drum, in which are placed from four to twelve knives, according to the size of the machine. The blades of the knives pass between the brushes; and when the brushes are made to roate by a handle worked from without, the blades of the knives are exposed to an amount of friction sufficient to clean their surfaces.'' **$165.00-$200.00**

Knife cleaner & polisher, cast iron frame, screw clamps to table edge, other screws adjust distance between white rubber fat rollers, works like a mangle, ''Spong's UneeK'', English, about 9''L, 19th C. • **''Slow Tunes and Quick Tunes.** — I have heard the anecdote attributed to Rowland Hill; who, being annoyed at his footboy singing profane songs whilst cleaning the knives and forks, ordered him, under the penalty of dismissal, to sing hymns. But as the work proceeded only to the tune of the solemn yet slow measure, Mr. Hill was compelled to tell the boy to return to his old style of profane music, otherwise his knives and forks would not have been ready for dinner.'' Alfred John Dunkin, British periodical *Notes and Queries*, 3rd Series, Volume VII, April 8, 1865. **$85.00-$100.00**

Knife & scissor grinder, japanned cast iron, screw clamps to table edge, ''sapphire'' carborundum wheel is turned by crank, & with each turn passes through cooling water compartment below. Both of the 2 wire clips, one on each side, are put in position for one side of knife blade (but are raised out of way when doing scissors). 3 toothed gears ''gear up'' action so that one turn of crank turns wheel 6 times. ''Clipper'', mfd by Montgomery & Co., NYC, wheel 4'' diameter x 1'' thick, entire grinder about 7''H, 1890. **$15.00-$30.00**

Knife scouring board or box, also called simply a knife board, used for cleaning blades, painted wood with bath brick in compartment, heart cutout at top end, prob. PA, 38''L x 5½''W, mid 19th C. **$200.00-$250.00**

Knife scouring box, simple pine, late 19th C. **$75.00-$100.00**

Knife scouring box, pine with original green paint on outside, simple box attached to footed scouring platform, American, mid 19th C. **$250.00-$300.00**

Knife scouring box, wood, long board with compartment at one end for bath brick powder or other abrasive that was spread on board so that when the flats of the knife blades were rubbed up & down, sort of a la razor stropping, they would be polished. American, 34''L x 5½''W (they vary in length from about 30'' to 40'', and in width from about 4½'' to 6''), 19th C. • Added value.— Those with old painted surfaces outside, fancy cutting to sides of compartment, or hangup hole in fancy cutout (especially a heart), bring up to five times as much as this: **$85.00-$120.00**

Knife sharpener, bentwood drum, vertically mounted (like a one man band's drum beat with the foot pedal) on iron frame, iron crank, with leather polishing leaves inside on a wheel. Used with polishing powder, mildly abrasive, ''Self-adjusting Stag'', mfd by Spong & Co. Ltd., English, tabletop model, (others floor standing and more expensive), late 19th C. • Spong also made the earlier ''The Servant's Friend Patent Knife Cleaner'', circa 1880. **$165.00-$200.00**

Knife sharpener, cast iron with 3 legs, spring steel in bottom allows adjustment of the 2 bars that sharpen, American, 6''L, pat'd Oct. 1891. **'5.00**

Knife sharpener, for scissors too, cast iron fishtail-like piece at one end with sharpening stone, attached to a longish pointed ''steel'' (a rod with very fine surface texture) for sharpening large chef's or butcher's knives, mfd by Goodell Co., about 13''L, TOC. **$10.00-$13.00**

Knife sharpener, homemade tools with 2 squares of steel screwed to wooden handle, resembles a patented sharpener of same type, American, 5½''L, late 19th C. **$20.00-$25.00**

Knife sharpener, iron & carborundum, ''Winchester'', New Haven, CT, early 20th C. **$65.00-$75.00**

Knife sharpener, iron with wood handle, ''Eversharp'', Tungsten Tool Co., NYC, NY, early 20th C. **$15.00-$18.00**

Knife sharpener, large bench style, has 6 carborundum sticks in a wheel at top, adjustable, red painted cast iron with black & yellow pinstriping, oil can attached, ''Blankner's Knife Sharpener'', mfd by Blankner Knife Sharpener Co., Cleveland, OH, 9½''H x 11''L, ''patent pending'' (c.1880s), and marked on wheel 0-5-4-3-2-1. • These numbers may work like the number used to designate printings in books, and which are removed one by one each time book goes back to press. Don't know why this would be desirable here. **$250.00-$285.00**

Knife sharpener, looks homemade, brass with some iron, stamped with individual letter stamps to read ''M A R Y E Z I L'', 3⅝''L, 19th C. **$15.00-$20.00**

Knife sharpener, metal, adv'g ''Crescent Hill Milk'', 1920s. **$12.00-$15.00**

Knife sharpener, metal, ''Sharpeit'', mfd by Dazey Churn Co., St. Louis, pat'd 1925. **$20.00-$25.00**

Knife sharpener, metal, ''Lil Sharpy'', mfd by Milwaukee File Co., WI, late 19th or early 20th C. **$7.00-$9.00**

Knife sharpener, nickeled cast metal, 2 sharpening stones, screw clamps to table, lever works the 2 upright ''Y'' sharpening stones mounted to metal, H. L. Johnson, 6⅞''H, pat'd July 24, 1888 & Sept. 2, 1890. **$45.00-$65.00**

Knife sharpener, nickeled steel with wooden knob handle, J. B. Foote Foundry Co., Fredericktown, OH, about 5''H, 1906. **$20.00-$30.00**

Knife sharpener, simple turned wood handle with screwed-on adjustable steel pieces, brass tip, American, 7¼''L, late 19th C. **$30.00-$35.00**

Knife sharpener, steel frame & ''roof''-like housing, ''corundum'' wheel, wall mounted, access through 2 guide slots on top, crank turns wheel, ''Wulff Knife Sharpener'', Hone-Rite, 1941 patent #2257407. **$3.00-$5.00**

Knife sharpener, tabletop, iron frame with iron water trough to catch the water used to cool as it worked, cranked grindstone, mounted on wooden plank base, American, 8'' diameter grindstone, (other sizes from 6'' to 12'' diameter), TOC. • **Stove & Knife Sharpener Combined.**— A candidate for most unusual, although very logical, combination tool is F. & L. Kahn's c.1890 range or stove top of cast iron, with a special beveled edge in the front to be used like a knife sharpening steel to clean up burry edges of a knife. Sturdy — that's for sure. The ads claimed ''Always ready. Always Sharp! Always useful.'' Kahn, I believe, sold rights to stove companies to manufacture their own stoves or ranges with the Kahn's patented edge. **$35.00-$50.00**

Knife sharpener, turned wood handle & frame, partly cut through from use, 2 small square iron plates bolted in position to create a V opening for sharpening knife, loosen them & rotate edges of plates, American, 5⅜''L, mid 19th C to 1870s. **$20.00-$25.00**

Plate scraper, white rubber blade in stamped metal holder, turned wooden painted handle, marked ''WB/W'', probably Waterbury Button & Mfg. Co., (thought by Don Thornton to be Washburn Bros.), Waterbury, CT, 5¾''L, c.1925. • A number of hard rubber & metal plate scrapers were made by different companies. Lasher Mfg. of Davenport, IA, made one around 1909-1910 with turned wooden handle, half moon metal plate with rubber scraper part, called the "Kitchen Kumfort". around 1915 Cassady-Fairbank Mfg. of Chicago made the "Foskett" scraper, almost identical in form. **$6.00-$8.00**

Polish, for aluminum, paper canister with silvery printed label, "Silver-Seal Polish, esp. prepared for Silver-Seal Kitchen Equipment", mfd by Century Metalcraft Corp., Detroit, MI, (Chicago office named on label), early 20th C. **$5.00-$7.00**

Pot cleaner, stamped sheet steel, parallelogram almost square, with short handle from one corner, 2 corrugated edges, one edge with bristles set along it, "The Korker Sink & Pot Cleaner", about 4" square, TOC. **$25.00-$30.00**

Pot cleaner, wire rings like chain mail, wire loop handle, some have iron loop handle, made in the late 19th C, but now widely reproduced. • "The 'chain-cloth' a net work of steel rings resembling an old fashioned reticule is of great service in cleaning burned kettles." Todd S. Goodholme, *Domestic Cyclopedia of Practical Information*, NY: Henry Holt, 1877. **$16.00-$40.00**

Pot mender, tube holding a small sharp metal reamer and white metal (relatively soft) rivets. Only a hammer was needed. Paper label on tube reads: "For tin, enamelled & Aluminum ware. Saves money — double life of ware. Directions. Rivets in the handle. Ream hole to fit rivet. Hammer in place. ..." Arco Sanitary Mender, 7"L, 1910. **$9.00-$15.00**

Pot menders, soft metal patches with tiny rivet or bolt, small triangular wrench, mounted on chromolithographed card, "Mendets", Collette Mfg. Co., Amsterdam, NY, different sizes & different number of patches, pat'd 1922, still being made. **$5.00-$8.00**

Pot menders, wooden box with little metal discs and special "wrench", "Mendet's", pat'd 1922. **$5.00-$8.00**

Pot scraper, green & white & black printed sheet tin, advertising type, "Mount Penn Stove Works, Penn Pots & Pan Scraper, Fits any corner of pot or pan", W. D. Beach Co. (mfr? printer?) Mount Penn Stoves was in Reading, PA, Beach was in Coshocton, OH, TOC. • Of all the pot scrapers, this is the only one I run into fairly often. Still — this, like anything else — won't get less rare with time. **$15.00-$37.50**

Pot scraper, lithographed tin, "Royal Granite Ware", 19th C. • This one achieved at the George Haney auction in April 1988, just a bare six months after Black Monday's crash, an amazing $225.00. I don't like to think high auction records set future market prices, but they sure affect them. **$225.00**

Pot scraper, lithographed tin, "Ruby Grand Coal Burner", • Price is from Haney auction. **$175.00**

Pot scraper, lithographed tin, depicts flour sack with big red wing, "Red Wing Milling Co., Red Wing, MN", 19th C. • Another Haney piece, with a lot of crossover interest because of "Red Wing". It brought what may be "fair market value". **$275.00**

Pot scraper, nickel plated steel, shaped to fit crevices & corners of pots and pans, marked "Jack the Scraper", mfd by Bauer Utensil Mfg. Co., Cleveland, OH, c.1914. **$12.00-$15.00**

Pot scraper, tin, triangular with hang up hole, no advertising — possibly scoured off long ago, 19th C. • "A clam

shell is more convenient for scraping kettles and frying pans than a knife. It does the work in less time." Emma Babock, *Household Hints*, 1881. **$12.00-$15.00**

Pot scraper, color lithographed tin, nice depiction of dairy maid entering stone-floored dairy house, carrying her bucket, and preparing to use the advertised cream separator, near the door, "Sharples Tubular Cream Separator", 19th C. • (Other prices from Haney auction: "Wards Extracts", $110.00, "Henkels Flour", $80.00.) **$100.00-$120.00**

Scissors sharpener, adv'g "Monarch Malleable Ranges", TOC to 1920s. **$10.00-$15.00**

Sink brush, tin, steel wire bristles, simple wood handle, fan-shaped, also for cleaning crevices in pots & pans, marked "Y/R", mfd by Rice Mfg. Co., New Durham, NH, 9¼"L x 4"W, pat'd Feb. 27, 1900. **$8.00-$12.00**

Soap cleanser canister, green paint enameled metal canister with shaker holes in top, side embossed with image of Dutch Girl, screw-on bottom is black, "Old Dutch Cleanser", 20th C. **$15.00-$20.00**

Soap cleanser canister, tin, color lithographed, "Bon Ami" 12 oz. capacity, 1940s. • When I was about 2½, I started a combined scrapbook and sketchbook. The color ads for the Bon Ami chick — "Hasn't scratched yet" — were my favorite, and the scrapbook is full of Bon Ami ads. **$20.00-$25.00**

Soap saver, homemade sheet steel, nice perforated box with long handle, fill with soap scraps to swish in dishpan, American, 13¾"L, TOC. **$15.00-$22.00**

Soap saver, or suds whipper, woven wire like a bustle making 2 fat pillows with a long wooden handle, American, 10⅝"L, early 20th C. **$20.00-$25.00**

Soap saver, round perforated tin box , 2 equal parts held together with slip ring on long spring wire handle, Matthai-Ingram Co., about 11"L, pat'd Sept. 14, 1875, but sold for decades. **$12.00-$20.00**

Soap saver, spring steel wire with stamped mesh holder for soap scraps, 2 biscuit-shape halves of the soap compartment clamped together by slip ring on long wire handle, American, 19th C. **$12.00-$15.00**

Soap saver, tin frame with twisted wire handle & hanging loop, wire mesh container for the soap, 3½" x 2½" with 7"L handle, TOC. **$18.00-$25.00**

Soap saver, wire mesh box, wooden handle, box is hinged 2 parts, with little hook closing that slips under ring on shaft of handle, 10"L, c.1920s to 1940s. **$12.00-$15.00**

Soap shaver, tin with wire arch handle, looks like a vegetable grater but the openings are like little crescent moons or smiles, embossed "Sunny Monday — Saves Soap & Labor", 10¾"L x 4"W, c.1900 to 1920. **$15.00-$20.00**

Stove blacking brush, iron handle, black bristles, "People's", TOC. **$18.00-$25.00**

Stove polish can, colorful lithographed tin, depicts devils cavorting on black iron cookstove, "X-Ray Stove Polish", TOC to 1910s. **$5.00-$8.00**

IX-1.
Kitchen interior with sink & stove.
Charmingly exaggerated spaciousness. Note slanted sink drain. Hot & cold running water. Mosely Folding Bathtub Co., Chicago, IL, 1896 catalog. "We have heard of a dish-washing machine, and seen an engraving. After it was invented, and pictured in one of the papers devoted to inventions, that was probably the last of it, for we never heard of one in use, and never expect to. The great trouble about a machine is that it can not think, and will give the same treatment to a delicate China saucer that it would to a large heavy platter. Dish-washing does not demand a high order of intellect, but it requires some thought." American Agriculturist, 7/1875.

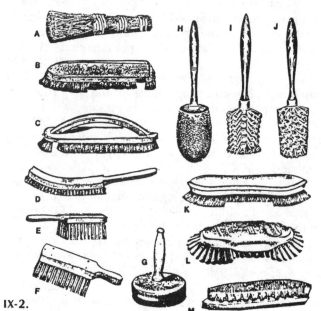

IX-2.
Brushes, mostly for cleaning.
(A) Sink brush, bound natural fibers. (B) Scrub brush, wooden back. Note gap between bristles & different angle & set of bristles. (C) Stove brush, arched wood handle. Note gap. (D) Curved plate brush, made with 2, 3, 4, or 5 rows. (E) Baker's wash brush. (F) Steel wire brush for kitchen tables & butcher blocks. (A) - (F) all from Duparquet wholesale supply catalog, c.1904-1910. (G) Puree sieve brush. Looks like sign-painter's stencil brush. Jaburg Bros., NY, 1908. (H) Glass-washing brush, of "best Russia boar's bristles, drawn with copper wire." (I) Another, of horsehair, for tumblers. "Each little bunch ... bound with copper wire." (J) Another for tumblers, also Russia bristles. These 3 styles came in 3 sizes: "pony", **$6.00-$22.00**

IX-3.
Dish drainer.
Water & soap-bleached wood with dowel pegs, 2 3/4"H x 17 3/4"L x 11 1/2"W. White rubber feet. American, 1890s. **$25.00-$40.00**

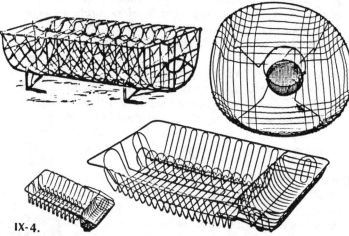

IX-4.
Dish warmer, drainers.
Top (L) Galvanized iron wire rack, to hold plates, and "set upon stove or in front of a fire, or over a hot-air register." American Agriculturist, 3/1872. Top (R) Round, wire, with mesh cutlery drainer in center. 5 1/4"H x 15" diameter. Pat'd in 1901 by Marie L. Price, Chicago, who assigned on third rights to Bertha A. Price. Pat. #646,128. Similar one with detachable silverware basket, was sold through Washburn-Androck in 1936, as something "good for country trade as drainer will fit inside round dish pan for draining dishes." (B) Full-size and toy. "Loop Weld" iron wire, Marlboro Wire Goods Co., 3 7/8"H x 18 3/4"L x 12"W. Child's sample version, on original cardboard mount, 6 1/8"L x 3 5/8"W. Both c.1910-15.

$28.00-$50.00

IX-5.
Dish Dryer.
"Androck" #199." 3 7/8"H x 19 1/2"L x 12"W, with fold-down perforated cutlery drainer tray. From Washburn Co., Andrews Division, catalog, 1936. A similar blackened "charcoal" tin one had an attached wire cutlery basket instead of tray. **$30.00-$40.00**

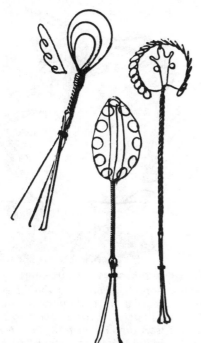

IX-6.
Dish towel holders & vegetable servers.
Twisted wire, slip-ringed prongs. Longest one is 13 1/2"L. No perfect chapter for these. See others in Chapter III. One at (R) collection of Meryle Evans. **$15.00-$30.00**

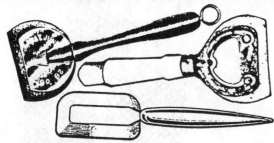

IX-7.
Dish or plate scrapers.
(T) "Foskett's," wood, tin, rubber, 5 3/4"L, pat'd 6/26/1906. Sold through Wire Goods Co., Worcester, MA, 1915 catalog. (M) Wood handle, tin riveted clamp for rubber blade. Marked "WB/W." 5 3/4"L, c.1925. (B) Rubber with green wood handle, 9 1/2"L. Androck, 1927. **$4.00-$8.00**

IX-8.
Dish swab.
Type often described as "Shaker". Turned wood handle, cotton strings. "The swab may be used on any smooth round stick, about a foot long, and an inch in diameter. About two inches from one end cut a groove; take candle-wicking, white carpet-chain, or even strips of strong cotton cloth, and cut or fold about eight inches in length; tie this material firmly into the groove at the middle, and turn down and tie firmly at the end of the stick, and you will have a 'machine', which will last many weeks, and go into boiling soap-suds, or even lye, without cringing." The one shown was store-bought at a "house-furnishing store," but the description was for a homemade one. **$20.00-$35.00**

IX- 9.
Rubber glove.
From 1870 *American Agriculturist* ad, of Goodyear's I(ndia) R(ubber) Glove Mfg. Co., NYC, in business at least since 1866. I don't know if you'd ever find a pair not dried out or shrunk in on themselves and sticky, but a collector of rubber bathtub toys & hot water bottles suggests treating them with Neat's Foot Oil and carefully stuffing with polyester fiber fill. **$5.00-$20.00**

IX-10.
Knife cleaning boxes.
A bath brick or other suitably fine grit was kept in the box-like part; knives were laid on the long part of (1), or slanted part of (2) and (3), and rubbed with rag, brush or large cork. Knives polished by moving back & forth between leather-covered hinged parts of (4), while pressing down to make tight fit. All between about 16" to 26"L. (1) and (2) F.A. Walker catalog, c.1870s. (3) from *American Agriculturist*, 6/1876; (4) from *American Agriculturist*, 8/1875. It was advised to "wipe knives with woolen cloth after rinsing." This was to impart a bit of anti-rust lanolin to the metal. **$40.00-$150.00**

IX-11.
Rotary knife cleaners.
(L) Cranked machine (the interior moved, not the outer part with the knives stuck out of holes), on table-like frame. "Knife-cleaning machine. — By the use of which knives need never be put in water, and are kept bright with less time or trouble than in the old fashioned way." *American Home Cook Book*, 1854. (R) "Kent's" patented rotary cleaner, originally pat'd in England. Made to hold 3, 4, 5, 6, 7, 8, 9, or 10 knives, including a carving knife. This one is tabletop style with cast iron frame and wooden drum. Very similar one mfd. in England by Spong & Co. ˙ ˙ vell into 20th C for hotels and restaurants. This picture from V. Clad catalog, c.1890. **$165.00-$250.00**

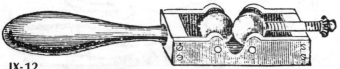

IX-12.
Razor sharpener.
"Expeditious," modification of American table-knife sharpener of 1830s. Two smooth cast steel balls in brass frame with ivory handle; blade was drawn between the balls, which were 3/4" to 1" diameter and had a hole drilled through the center. Screw at right "added for the purpose of keeping the balls in contact, and if the pivots are ... a little loose in frame, the balls may be turned and again fixed. The balls are made as hard as possible, and polished in a direction opposite to that of their axes." *Journal of the Franklin Institute*, 1837. **$50.00-$100.00**

IX-13.
Knife sharpeners.
Top (L) has 3 cast iron legs, and spring steel in bottom allows adjustment of 2 crisscross sharpening bars. 6"H. Pat'd 10/1891. One in foreground is turned wood with 2 crisscrossed, adjustable steel sticks. 7 1/4"L. One at rear is homemade, wood handle with 2 squares of steel screwed to wood, the wood almost cut through by many sharpenings. 5 1/2"L. Late 19th C. **$15.00-$55.00**

IX-14.
Knife sharpeners.
(L) "Silver Duplex," silver & Co., Brooklyn, c.1910. Small screw-clamped cast iron frame, 2 steel sharpening sticks. (R) Nickeled steel with knobby wood handle. J.B. Foote Foundry Co., 1906. **$15.00-$30.00**

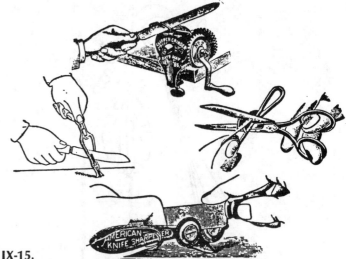

IX-15.
Knife sharpeners & scissor sharpener.
Clockwise from top: (1) "Clipper," for the knives & scissors. Shown with wire clip for doing knives. Cranked, screw clamped to table, pat'd 5/18/1886. Widely advertised 1880s to 1910s. (2) "Handy" sharpener for scissors. Eastman & Co., NYC. 1895 ad. (C) "American," mfd. by Mossberg Wrench Co., Mfrs. of Novelties, Attleboto, MA. Pat'd 2/23/1892. Two discs between which blade was pulled. (4) "Peerless" combo sharpener & can opener. Early 20th C. **$6.00-$45.00**

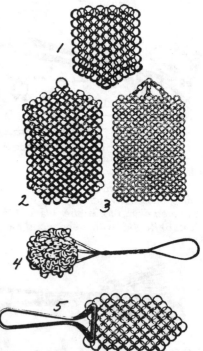

IX-16.
Pot chains or pot scrubbers.
Not shown to scale; assembled from various catalogues. All chain mail — iron rings linked into flexible pads (or ball with a handle). (1) double rings, 4 sizes, from 3 1/2" x 5 1/2" to 8 1/2" x 11", with 1/2" or 3/4" rings. Washburn Co., 1936. (2) 13" x 7", double mesh, hanging ring. Matthai-Ingram, c.1890. (3) "In some parts of the country, a pot-scrubber made of iron rings, as shown, is used, but it is by no means so well known as it ought to be. We do not know who the manufacturer is, bu it is for sale at some of the hardware stores in New York City." *American Agriculturist*, 7/1877. In the 1980s, some were being made in midwest by an elderly man who made them in a factory ages ago. (4) also Matthai-Ingram. (5) "Sensible", all nickel plated, iron handle is also a scraper. 5/8" double rings, 5 1/2" x 3 1/4". Excel c.1916 catalog, and Washburn, 1936. **Caution:** *Various styles are* **being reproduced.$15.00-$40.00**

IX-17.
Pot menders.
"Mendets," Collett Mfg. Co,. Amsterdam, NY. A metal patch, a tiny 'bolt', and a small triangular wrench, mounted on chromolithographed card. This one c.1940. Fun is to collect a variety from different periods; in 1908 they called them "Collette's Patent Patches." By 1910 they had name "Mendets." They're still sold, but card graphics are ugly. **$6.00-$10.00**

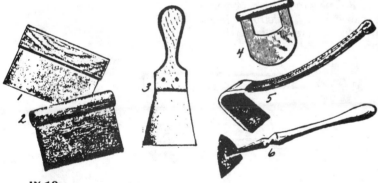

IX-18.
Scrapers.
(1) and (2) are dough scrapers. (1) Wood handle, 5", 6", 7", or 8"W; (2) Tubular handle, all iron, 4" 5" or 6"W. Duparquet, Huot & Moneuse, c.1904-1910. (3) Crystallizing pan scraper for candy-makers. Sethness, 1925. (4) often sold as chopper, but is kettle or pan scraper, all steel, tubular handle. T. Mills, 1930 catalog of candy-makers' supplies. (5) Butcher block or bench scraper, all steel. (6) Broiler scraper, triangular blade, wood handle. (5) & (6) look quite old; but are c.1904-1910. **$15.00-$40.00**

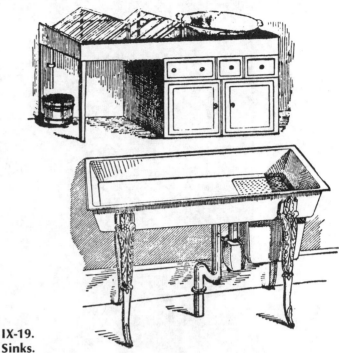

IX-19.
Sinks.
(T) "Wash Sink for Kitchen," suggested to improve the "unpleasant features" of a dish washing. Sink is "lined with sheet-iron instead of zinc, and is made with two divisions." Removable wooden racks. American Agriculturist, 4/1883. (B) "Sanitas" kitchen sink, fancy cast legs. From Alfred Revill's American Plumbing, NYC, 1894.

IX-20.
Sink brush.
Wire with wood handle. Marked "Y-R," pat'd 2/27/1900, mfd. by Rice Mfg. Co., New Durham, NH. 9 1/4"L. **$6.00-$18.00**

IX-21.
Soap saver.
Wire mesh box, twisted wire handle with slip ring, wood grip. 10"L, c.1920-40s. Collection of the Disshuls. **$10.00-$15.00**

IX-22.
Repaired pieces.
No hard feelings, but this is probably my favorite picture in the book, and I wish I owned them all. This was from an exhibition of repaired pieces "On the Mend," held by Bonnie Grossman, The Ames Gallery of American Folk Art in 1988. As she wrote, "examples are leather-patched, tin-patched, gut-sewn, stapled, and glued with sawdust paste." Also as Bonnie wrote, these are very "endearing" pieces, with which it would be wonderful to live. Photograph by Ben Blackwell. All objects courtesy Ames Gallery of American Folk Art, Berkeley, CA.

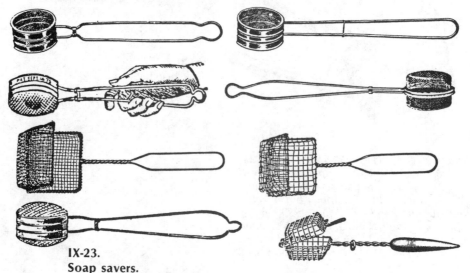

IX-23.
Soap savers.
Soap scraps are put into the boxes or cups, and tool is swished through dishwater to make suds. Works great. (L) to (R) from top: (1) to (2) Tin with fine wire mesh, 2 different handles. Both are 1 1/2" deep x 2 3/8" diameter x 12"L. Wire Goods Co., 1915. (3) Matthai-Ingram, pat'd 9/14/1875. c.1890 catalog. (4) "New Standard," from unidentified c.1900 flyer. (5) & (6) Tinned wire, different meshes offered. (5) came in 4 box sizes, 11"L or 16"L. (6) Only in wide mesh, 8 1/2"L overall. (7) with "cups of wire gauze," was described in American Agriculturist, *1881. (8) Welded wire, tinned, green handle, 10 1/2"L. Washburn, 1936.* **$10.00-$40.00**

403

The following article was written for the second edition of this book by collector, dealer and author Karol Atkinson. She and her husband Phil, specialize in what is widely known as ''country store'' and advertising collectibles — a variety of objects meant for improving commerce, usually extra-colorful and often exaggerated in form or claim.

When the article was first written in the early 1908s, there were perhaps 20 known examples; Atkinson believes (as late as summer 1990) that there may be 60 different pot scrapers, including a small percentage of plain chrome or tin ones. The biggest change in the market has been a huge increase in prices. The scrapers with lettering only, which might have once sold for under $5.00 are going for between $115.00 and $135.00. Those with lithograph illustrations are up at least to $200.00 and often more. Two types mentioned in the article have escalated in market value to over $350.00 because of crossover collector interest. They are: the NESCO (sought by graniteware collectors) and the Red Wing Milling flour one (desired by Red Wing ceramics collectors). In 1984 or thereabouts, Atkinson had a short list of scrapers available but not in her collection; since then she has acquired all the ones on that list and a number of others. One that eludes her is a lithographed tin one depicting Buster Brown, and advertising ''Buster Brown Bread'', made by Schmidt's Bakeries, Harriburg, PA.

If you wish to correspond with Karol Atkinson regarding these scrapers, her mailing address is 903 Apache Trail, Mercer, PA 16137. Please be sure to enclose a SASE (self-addressed stamped envelope) if you wish a reply.

ADVERTISING POT SCRAPERS

By Karol Atkinson

''Pot what?'' This is the standard answer received in the search for these elusive little kitchen helpers of the past.

The tin advertising pot scraper is not to be confused with the circular chain-mesh version which is relatively easy to find. (See IX-16).

Most examples are in the shape of the DOVE Brand pictured here. The JUNKET shape is seen less frequently. Actual measurements of the JUNKET are 2 9/16''H x 3''W.

Dating the scrapers is difficult. An estimate of manufacturing dates would be between 1900 and 1925. All but one of the scrapers illustrated dates to that period, with most of them dating before 1910. The exception is the BIG DIAMOND Flour one, whose shiny chrome-like finish and bottle cap opener (which replaces the small hang-up or finger hole) hint at a later date than 1925. Only one of my scrapers has the year of issue on it — the SHARPLES Cream Separator, dated 1909. An approximate date can be assumed on the ADMIRAL COFFEE scraper owing to the spelling of ''Pittsburg'' with the ''h'' at the end. The last time that spelling was in effect was 1890 to 1911.

The Cleveland Co-Operative Stove Co. issued scrapers illustrating their various stoves and ranges. The earliest of their three known examples is one with a pot belly stove. Next is the combination range, and finally one with a gas range.

Some of the scrapers have advertising on both sides, informing the user about everything there is to know about the advertised product. The reverse of the SHARPLES Cream Separator, 1909, is cobalt blue and depicts the tubular separator itself. The two different types of JUNKET scrapers also have advertising on both sides. Besides scraping cooking pots, the JUNKET scraper also scraped the mixing bowl, cake pan, rolling pin and moulding board!

Comical phrases, illustrations and/or verses are printed on scrapers such as the DOVE Brand Ham & Bacon.

The WARD'S Better Butter and FAIRMONT Creamery are examples of a stock item which could be ordered personalized with the company's name. This practice is similar to that used with advertising trade cards, which could be ordered from a catalog showing the decoration and the space where the name would go.

The familiar red wing logo of the RED WING Milling Co., seen so often on the crocks and jugs from that famous Minnesota town, is also present on a colorful pot scraper. For collectors in the Midwest and Northwest, anything bearing the red wing in highly desirable.

Most commonly seen of all the pot scrapers, at least in the Eastern United States, are the MT. PENN Stove Works one in cream, green and black, and the HENKEL's Flour one. As with other collectibles, the examples cited may differ in availability in other geographic areas.

Out of all my scrapers only two are marked by the manufacturer. Passaic Metal Ware Co., Passaic, NJ, and H.D. Beach Co., Coshocton, OH, made scrapers, but are much better known for their high quality lithographed tin trays.

Although when I bought my scrapers, less than 10 years ago, I paid between $2.00 and $45.00 each, these prices seem riduculously low now. In those days there were a mere handful of collectors interested in the pot scraper; now there are probably scores of collectors. It's the old law of supply and demand: while interest (demand) has increased tenfold, the supply of available scrapers has not.

APS-1.
Pot, pan and kettle scraper.

"A curious thing came by mail. It was a piece of galvanized iron, of about 2 inches length, and had attached to it a label which read: 'Pot, Pan, and Kettle Scraper. Please accept, with the compliments of the season, from John Furbish, dealer in kitchen furnishing goods, stoves, etc., Main street, Brunswick, ME. December 25, 1871.' It seems that Furbish did not, as many stupid people do, go and patent a simple thing. He had tried it, found it good, had a lot made, and gave one to every holiday customer. The piece of sheet-iron is so shaped that it will meet all possible angles, and save no end of knives and spoons...First rate, and I wish I had had one before." American Agriculturist *editor, 5/1872.*

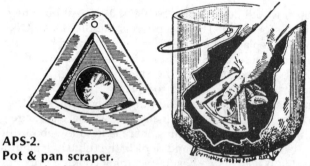

APS-2.
Pot & pan scraper.

"Instantly cleans pots, pans, pails, cake tins, cake griddles, dough boards, etc." Picture copyrighted 1909 by "Peale Hdw. Co." or possibly "Pease Hdw. Co." From door-to-door salesman's catalog, F.W. Seastrand, c.1910s.

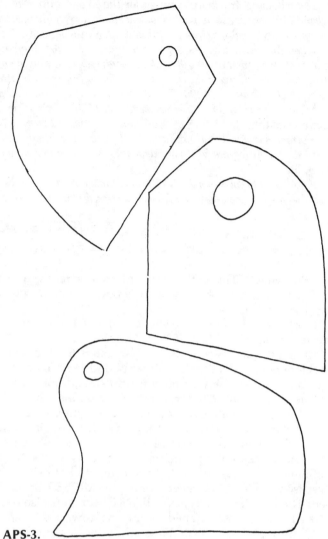

APS-3.
Pot scraper shapes.

Actual 75% tracings of three types in the Karol Atkinson Collection.

APS-4.
Pot scraper.

"Dove Brand" Ham & Bacon, Cincinnati, OH. Approximately 3 1/2" across. Picture courtesy Karol Atkinson Collection.

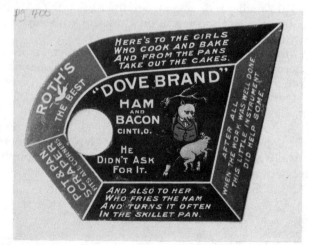

APS-5.
Pot scraper.

"Junket" dessert powders. Note how different sides describe what they are meant to scrape. Approximately 3 7/8" across. Picture courtesy Karol Atkinson Collection.

APS-6.
Pot scraper.
"Sharples" cream separator. Beautifully color lithographed scene. Approximately 3 1/2" across. Picture courtesy Karol Atkinson Collection.

APS-7.
Pot scraper.
"Red Wing Milling Co.," Red Wing, MN. A name known to many collectors of Red Wing stonewares. These are another crossover collectible, sought by two schools of collectors. Picture courtesy Karol Atkinson Collection.

D. COOKING:

X. HEARTHS & FIREPLACES

The increasing interest in practical hearth cooking and the revival of walk-in fireplaces, as well as the generally separable goals of collectors of hearth tools and those of cast iron cookware, have persuaded me to make hearth cooking a chapter on its own. Nevertheless, you will have your right ring finger stuck in the Pots & Pans chapter while reading this one, to flip back and forth and mutter to yourself "Criminently, what'd she put it *there* for.

This chapter is not only about the 18th century and early 19th century, although for the most part the hollowware is from that period. I've tried to limit them to cookwares used on the hearth or an open fire. In fact, Camp stoves are in the Stoves chapter, but Braziers and Conjurers are in the Pots & Pans chapter. Friends who are writing books on subjects which break down well by chronology find, like me, that sticking to the calendar isn't always the best way to categorize. Bear with us.

There will be some confusion, I'm sure. First, in the area of hollowwares that were made at a time when cooking ranges were just coming in, there may be some mixups over those utensils strictly for hearth use, and those which were adaptable. Second, in the area of fireplaces, I have to make excuses to include some of the things (like andirons) that I have included, because they really belong with non-kitchen fireplaces, and are mainly decorative. However, the burgeoning field of metal-collecting in general, and the spectacular purchases of certain figural andirons for example, give me enough of a reason to include them here. Some of the most interesting information about cast iron, for example, comes with the story of 19th C andirons. Implements such as flesh forks or tasting spoons, which would carry over to cook stove or range use, though they started life as hearth cooking implements, are all together in Chapter XIII.

One caution about collecting hearth-cooking tools — from whirling broilers to spiders to trammels: a good percentage (not calculable at this point, but perhaps as many as 75%) of the *old* forged iron, cast bronze, or cast iron pieces have been brought over in the last decade from Europe. The first wave of modern immigrant hearthiana came, like the *Mayflower* 300 + years ago, from the British Isles. Then came wares from Germany, Holland, Italy, France, and other areas such as Scandinavia. Then the great elephant boneyard of old iron that must lie in every cellar and outbuilding in Portugal was discovered. So there is a good deal of Portugese iron here now — much of it quite attractive and decorative. In fact, 'decorative' is the quality of much of this container-loaded old iron that enables us to recognize it as European. Where a simple curve might have been used on an American pot rack, for example, a splendiferous (splendi-ferrous?) scrolly crest would more likely have been the choice of a European artisan. As has been said about the relatively late application of decorative motifs to everyday household items made by the Pennsylvania Germans here, a delay attributed to the lengthy struggle just to meet purely utilitarian needs, so too would decoration for art's sake have come late throughout this country. If one blacksmith had to do for an entire village, pounding out necessaries like horseshoes and cranes, does it stand to reason that he would have labored an extra amount of time to add curliques and furbelows, while six horses which had thrown their shoes waited out front?

Anyway, the future for this field looks bright, partly because so many of collectors actively use their collections, partly because it's an interior decoration idea still in the ascendency. The field still needs a great deal of sorting out. We are faced, somewhat more directly than is often the case, with the questions of how much value do we place on provenance — how much are origins worth, how much extra value do we chauvinistically place on American origins, how much information will we demand from dealers who sell us old iron trammels and three-legged kettles. From a somewhat academic point of view, I think origins mean a lot, for two reasons. First, we are usually asked to pay a premium for things "made in the U.S.A." (or the American Colonies, if they predate the Revolution), and second, our clear view of the background of a thing is obscured when either we aren't told where something is from, or when its origins are deliberately misrepresented. I feel it is necessary to continually stress the substance of things because I value meaning as much as, perhaps more than, appearance — in antiques as well as everything else from dogs and presidents to cars and cloth coats. This means swimming against the current sometimes, in a country where a dozing leprechaun can become President, where a living wolf can become a bimbo's coat, and where labels and namebrands are used (and accepted) as a sort of chromium plating to gloss over the worst cases of rust and empty content.

Adapter ring, looks rather like pot stand or trivet, missing the legs. Forged iron ring with a long angled-up handle with hanging loop, meant to fit over hole or eye of an early range to support handleless utensils of different circumferences. A versatile handle, useful in late 18th or early 19th C on the ranges of the time, which had iron tops, with rows of holes (or eyes) for the utensils, set into the top of a brick structure which was the firebox. The fire was fed through doors set in the brick, and drafts and dampers were also possible. This kind of cooking range was something midway between a fireplace or hearth, perhaps with an oven set in the bricks, and a cast iron cooking stove, where the firebox too was made of iron. American or European, about 19"L overall, 8" diameter ring, late 18th or early 19th C. **$30.00-$40.00**

Ale boot, pieced copper, tinned inside, lid missing, 12½"H, early 19th C. **$150.00-$250.00**

Ale boot, sheet metal, hinged lid, nice pouring spout, American, 16½"H, early 19th C. **$300.00-$375.00**

Ale boot, shoe shaped, pointed toe, pieced copper, strap handle, pushed into hot ashes to warm ale, American, 18th C. **$240.00-$300.00**

Ale boot or shoe, pieced copper, hinged fitted lid, strap handle, tinned inside, English (?), 7½"L, late 18th or early 19th C. **$500.00-$650.00**

Copper caveat.— "When taken into the human body, copper acts as a violent emetic, and is generally considered as poisonous; though it has occasionally been prescribed by physicians, it is always an unsafe and hazardous remedy. Hence, the greatest precaution is necessary in using this metal, of which so many kitchen utensils are manufactured. Besides the most scrupulous attention to cleanliness, it is extremely improper to leave any liquid to cool in a copper vessel; for this metal is more easily decomposed by liquids, when cold, than in a heated state.

"In order to prevent the deleterious effects of copper, the vessels made of it are usually covered with tin, on the inside. Nevertheless it is justly complained, that the tinning of copper vessels is not sufficient to defend them from the action of the air, moisture and saline substances; because, even when strongly coated, they are liable to rust (sic). This may be remedied by a thicker coating of tin; and a manufacturer of this kind was established a few years hence in Edinburgh; in which...the surface of the copper is made very rough...; then a thick coat of tin is laid in, and the copper hammered smooth as before." Anthony Florian Madinzer Willich, *The Domestic Encyclopedia; or A Dictionary of Facts & Useful Knowledge*. 1st American edition, Philadelphia: W. Y. Birch & A. Small, 1803-04.
Ale shoe, pieced tin with cast white metal knob on hinged cover, English or American, 1 qt. size, early 19th C.
$300.00-$375.00

Andirons, a pair, hammered wrought & cast iron in "neo-Medieval" style, quite cute with one of them fitted out with a small swiveling crane of its own, with a hook for a little pot or tea kettle. Coincidentally, I saw this in June 1989 at Renninger's Extravaganza, and two weeks later I found a picture of a very similar one in a 1922 *House Beautiful* ad; the advertised one has a cresset cup top and a scrolled crane, but is otherwise quite similar. In the ad a small 3 legged gypsy pot is shown on the hook, and there is a hook projection on the front near the legs of each andiron, with a knob-handled long bar of iron resting there. This bar is referred to as a "Log Roller", which presumably you would remove from the hooks to use (?). No mark on the flea one, the advertised one mfd by The H. W. Covert Co., NYC, NY, the ones at Renninger were 30"H; the advertised ones 27"H, prob. early 20th C.
$100.00-$125.00

Andirons, bizarre nude female forms, from waist up, plump faces with short hair, below the waist is a sort of open flower with large petals, possibly a kind of skirt, somewhat humanoid legs, cast iron with polished finish, reproduction of some unknown original, made by Edwin Jackson, Inc., NYC, NY, 1930s from an early 19th C, maybe even late 18th C original. • I've seen a pair of cast iron women, from the waist up, much in the style of 17th and early 18th C gravestone carvings, very somber, bosoms pronounced in low-neckline gowns, hands clasped at waist in an almost prayerful position, below the waist are widely set curved legs. A dealer who had a pair for sale in December 1989 said they were 18th C; I believe they are probably 1st or 2nd quarter 19th C. They would sell in the somewhat frenetic market today for about 6 to 8 times the low figure for the 1930s pair: **$200.00-$400.00**

Andirons, black painted cast iron, a pair of tall owls, each sitting on a curved rustic branch that forms front legs of andiron, glass eyes with open casting behind so firelight makes them glow, either an original or a reproduction of an older pair, Lemee's Fireplace Equipment, Bridgewater, MA, 13"H & 17 lbs (15 lbs in later catalog), (in 1989 catalog they offer a pair 14"H & 20 lbs), advertised at least as early as 1973, and at least through 1989. • **Reproduction alert I.**— Not all figural cast iron andirons are from the mid 19th C (or earlier). There has not been enough research to identify all done since the mid 20th C. These owls, which might appear to be older than they are, are fairly light (only 8½ lbs each) for their height, and they are painted black, and the casting doesn't have an old look. In 1973 they were advertised for $17.95, plus $2.00 postage "west of the Mississippi." **Alert II.**— An earlier lookalike or repro was made in the middle 1920s. H. W. Covert Co., NYC, who made all kinds of fittings for fireplaces, advertised a cast iron owl andiron pair, the owls perched on a rustic tangle of branches, with a nice effect as "The firelight shines thru the glass eyes." Their pair was 15"H. The branches are much nicer on Covert repro than Lemee's. **$15.00-$25.00**

Andirons, black painted cast iron, very detailed casting, good surface finish, pair with identical (rather than mirror image) figures of military man from Revolutionary War — known from 1920s ad to be a General Putnam (not George Washington, as often claimed now), left hand on hip, muscular legs, high boots, big epaulettes, lots of buttons on coat. **Which Putnam was it?** General Israel Putnam (1718-1790) of Massachusetts fought in the Battle of Lexington & Battle of Bunker Hill. The more likely man is General Rufus Putnam (1738-1824), later known as the "Father" of Ohio, who was born & fought in Massachusetts. In 1796 he was made Surveyor General of the new U.S. Possibly 1920s' reproduction by Albany Foundry Co.; possibly older one from the 1870s ... maybe even 1840s? 14¾"H, early 1800s? 1870s? or 1920s repro? • Price range for pair, let's say, from 1870s. (Older much more; newer less.) **$400.00-$700.00**

Andirons, brass & cast iron, low, solid square black finished iron pilaster bases topped with low relief figures of rearing horses, cast in brass, Kenneth Lynch, Long Island City, NY, late 1930s. **$425.00-$750.00**

Andirons, cast hammered finish brass, bold fat cat's head with unhappy mouth, upright angular ears, diamond cutouts for eyes, with red glass marbles set in from behind — partially held in by a flat brass plate, which would seem to defeat the purpose of the glass eyes, which was to sparkle with the fire behind them. The heads, long neck & arched legs bolted to iron log supports also called billet bars, dealer said cast by "Ed Lynch", but possibly meant Kenneth Lynch?, American, 15½"H x 7½"W at widest point, 1920s. **$900.00-$1200.00**

Andirons, cast iron, a pair of long haired tall women, each wearing a crown, in surprisingly short, blown open, wrap front dress with low bodice & ¾ length sleeves, holding at midriff torch-like cornucopia, legs bare above knees, standing on scrolly arched stand with scallop shell behind legs, like "Venus on the Half Shell", Sandro Botticelli's Birth of Venus painting. Liberty coins designed by Saint-Gaudens, from 1907+, show a crowned maiden with long curls, holding torch & boughs out to her sides, posed on ocean waves with sun rays behind her. This would mean 20th C. Other possible sources: Tobacconist effigies of short-skirted Indian maidens; Columbia figures, which sometimes were depicted half-naked; figureheads. No mark, American, 17½"H, prob. pre-Statue of Liberty, so I guess 1870s to early 1880s. **$275.00-$325.00**

Sources of Inspiration. — I talked to a coin dealer about the image, and he suggested that it was far more likely that inspiration came from **engraved paper money,** of which thousands of designs were printed in the 19th C by federal mints, states & banks, as well as by the Confederacy during the Civil War. It is true that paper money was by far the most widely distributed "popular" art for over a hundred years. The engravers took inspiration from foreign money, wallpaper & chintz engravings, illustrations in Bibles and other books, etc. • **Figureheads** were female forms for a century or more in the United States, far outnumbering animals or men. Many were actually carved portraits of a captain's or ship owner's wife or daughter. Many figureheads have representations of waves behind them, and arms are usually folded against the body. Often skirts or draperies appear to be blown back by the ocean wind, bosoms are often partially revealed.

Andirons, cast iron, angular sawtooth-edged pine trees, like Christmas trees, bases are as big as that part of the ground covered by shade. American, mid 19th C.
$900.00-$1200.00

Andirons, cast iron, black man and woman, in semi-squatting position with knees out, hands on knees, woman in long dress with sleeves rolled up, pinned bandanna collar, necklace of fat beads, man in abbreviated tail coat with well-defined lapels, extremely well-cast Black Americana. For sale in Georgia auction in 1988, prob. from GA, mid 19th C. I don't know if these are pre- or post-Civil War. • Another pair sold at Morton M. Goldberg's auction galleries in New Orleans in April 1989 (price not known). • A pair consisting of two of male figures instead of a man & woman, sold at Dick Withington's 2000th Auction, Aug. 4, 1989, Hillsboro, NH, for $375.00. I imagine this price would have more than tripled for a man and woman pair. $1200.00-$1500.00

Early figural andirons & dogs.— According to Alice Morse Earle, *Customs & Fashions in Old New England* (Scribner's, 1893): "The andirons added to the fireplace their homely charm. Fire-dogs appear in the earliest inventories under many names of various spelling, and were of many metals — copper, steel, iron, and brass. Sometimes a fireplace had three sets of andirons of different sizes, to hold logs at different heights. Cob irons had hooks to hold a spit and dripping-pan. Sometimes the 'Handirons' also had brackets. Creepers were low irons placed between the great fire-dogs. They are mentioned in many early wills and lists of possessions among items of fireplace furnishings, as, for instance, the list of Captain Tyng's furniture, made in Boston in 1653. The andirons," she writes, in a somewhat confusing reference, and I don't think she means here that Tyng had the figurals, "were sometimes very elaborate, with claw feet, or cast in the figure of a negro, a soldier, or a dog." • **Creepers** apparently once had at least four meanings in early America that are at all related to our subject here: **(1)** A dutch oven; **(2)** "An iron used to slide along the grate in kitchens." Noah Webster, *An American Dictionary*, 1858; **(3)** "An instrument of iron with hooks or claws, for drawing up things from the bottom of a well, river, or harbor." *ibid.* ; and **(4)** "A small, low iron, or dog, between the andirons" — given as an obsolete meaning in *Webster's New International Dictionary, 1931.* (4) is the usage which Earle cites.

Andirons, cast iron cats — each seated on a splayed leg short pedestal base which is rather Chinese-looking. The cats are large eared, very well-modeled, painted, with tuxedo markings; they constitute ¾ of the total height. Mfd by S. M. Howes Co., Boston, MA, 17½"H, c.1890s to 1920s, with more likelihood of 1920s. • **Reproduction alert.**— The 1989 catalog of Lemee's Fireplace Equipment Co., Bridgewater, MA, shows a similar pair, all black. Theirs have green glass shine-through eyes, are described as "mounted on a stool shaped base", are 17"H, and 15" deep to back of log rest, and weigh 19 lbs. $300.00-$500.00

Andirons, cast iron dogs. Each with scrolled legs that terminate in a sort of fancy pedestal on which a dog (standard poodle or curly-haired retriever or water spaniel) sits, the dog forming about ⅓ of the total height, American, about 17"H, prob. 1870s-80s. • Another version.— Another pair of spaniel or retriever cast iron andirons, has simple scroll legs upon which sit dogs with collars, with large eye-rings as large as the dogs' heads cast as "finials". The dogs here are the same height as the scrolled base; the ring adds another inch or so. Overall height of this pair is 13½"H, length of log supports 13". Dealer W. M. Schwind, Jr., Yarmouth, ME, advertised these in May 1988, *Maine Antique Digest,* and suggested they were "probably made in Norfolk, VA, 1850-60." • Another version — 13"H cast iron dogs, sitting on a scrolled base, haunches stuck out, slightly curly hair, and what appears to be a ring surrounding head, with log support slipped into back in sort of dovetail slot, sold at Garth's, July 28, 1989 for only $100.00. **Reproduction alert.**— In the March 1937 *House Beautiful,* I found a picture of dog andirons, sitting on scrolled base, with flat rings haloing the dogs' heads. Made by an old fireplace firm, Edwin Jackson, NYC, the full ad copy reads "To meet a revived interest in the Victorian spirit, we present this pair of andirons. They are copies of rare original Victorian ones made about 1859, authentic even to the St. Bernard dog so often found in family portraits of the period. We consider them very much worth your notice, since it is difficult to find any andirons of that period. They are 14" high, and are made of black cast iron. $9.00, express collect." Golly! **Pricing figural andirons.** As I said before, this cannot be done now with a lot of accuracy. Figural irons have only begun to appear in any quantity since about 1987, and reflect the general and widespread interest in all kinds of figural cast iron. Each new auction price, every new discovery, all the display ads, bring more out — entirely new types as well as multiples of the biggies. $300.00-$700.00

Andirons, cast iron, figural Scottish short-haired men in kilts, sporrans & fitted coats, wearing what we now call a "golf cap", legs and feet pointed out, right hand inside buttoned coat front, left hand holding a long clay pipe. The figure seems to be a decidedly 20th C romanticized image of a Scotsman, such as might be found on a doorstop or bookend. This pair, which I've not seen "live", is on page 101 of Henry J. Kauffman & Quentin H. Bowers, *Early American Andirons and Other Fireplace Accessories,* 1974. It is attributed by Kauffman & Bowers to Joseph Webb, Boston, MA, and hence to late 18th C (?), because of some passing similarity between the irons and an engraving (see below). I believe these are mid 19th C, and have nothing to do with Webb. **Dating the Kilt.**— The Jacobean uprisings in Scotland, finally put down in the bloody rout at Cullenden, in 1746, resulted in the English outlawing clan kilts. In 1782 things were calmed down enough for them to be legalized. I find the "golf" caps puzzling; coincidentally (?) golf supposedly began in Scotland. Judging value is very difficult. The images have some appeal to lovers of Scotland. If age could be absolutely proved, they would gain much for historical interest. As it is, they do not have the strong appeal of what seems more native-born subject matter. **18th C Figural Andirons.** — According to Kauffman & Bowers, these andirons are the ones depicted and "advertised on the trade card of Joseph Webb of Boston. The card was engraved by Paul Revere." But they are *not* the same. A close examination of the small engraving on the Revere trade card for Joseph Webb, as printed in Clarence S. Brigham's *Paul Revere's Engravings* (NY: Atheneum, 1969), reveals that the figural "Cast (Fire) Dog" is similar in stance only, and is not the same casting by any means. Webb's fire dog or andiron is a small male figure, apparently wearing a wide-skirted double-breasted heavy coat over full pants that come just below the knees, and low shoes on out-turned feet. No kilt, no pipe. The engraved Webb figurals look *much* more 18th C than the Scotsman, for which the range is: **$400.00-$600.00**

Andirons, cast iron, intertwined snakes, fairly abstract and geometric, no founder's mark, American, 16"H, late 19th C. **$125.00-$150.00**

Andirons, cast iron, old blackened metal finish, no apparent trace of paint, **Hessian soldiers**. These are tall, have the cockaded hat, both striding same direction (to the right), right hand carrying curved sword which follows curve of coat front, no space between elbow & coatwaist, muscular legs in knee-high boots. Of most interest are the faces, which have long stern noses, very simplified features in a 16th C style. There are so many version of this type of andirons, and so many reproductions have been made, it is extremely difficult to pass judgment on a particular pair. This pair has fine old smooth, polished & highlighted iron surface, and looks better than any I've seen in Virginia, where so many are found even today. dealer thinks NJ or PA, 20"H x 18"L (unusual height; equal to repro (4a) below; a bit "plodding" but probably not a 20th C repro). Dealer estimated c.1820; I think c.1840s. • Price range is for the old 20"H version: **$600.00-$800.00**

Those Hessians

• **Reproduction alert I.**— Lester Beitz, *Early American Life*, Aug. 1975, in answering a query about two cast iron "Negro deckhand" andirons, told of two sets he'd seen that year. **New Iron Falsely Aged & Its Telltale Rust.**— Beitz wrote: "[Recently] I came upon sets of the renowned Hessian Soldier & General Washington cast iron andirons in the same shop — which made me mighty suspicious. ... Close examination revealed ... top quality recasts, complete with that peculiar rust effect, circa 1974, caused by immersion in a solution of vinegar & nitric acid, caustic soda, salammoniac, or car battery acid — any number of concoctions which produce the desired effects ... the overly large, thin flakes of rust resulting from such treatment are ... a dead giveaway." • **Alert II.** — *House Beautiful* in 1921, 1923, 1925, & 1936, has ads for

four repro Hessian andirons. Chronologically they are as follows:

• **(1)** "Hessian Andirons — In colors — red coat, buff breeches." B. F. Macy, Boston, MA. Macy's ad shows single andiron strides kneebent to his right, left arm bent close to body, cockade on high helmet, buttons on boots, coat tail flipped to reveal most of soldier's left leg. No indication of direction other figure faces.

• **(2)** "Hessian Andirons (Black Finish), 16½"H, Wt. 24 lbs. $6.50." Albany Foundry Co., Albany, NY. **(3)** "The Hessian Andirons — 17" H, Wt. 24 lbs. $5.00." Albany Foundry Co.. Both of Albany's pairs look the same as each other though one is ½" taller. Pairs are mirror images. More exaggerated stride, both legs hyperextended (kneecap concave), bent elbow has space under arm, no cockade, coat tail lies close along leg.

• **(4)** "A pair of fiery Hessians are ... perfect ...for a Colonial house. If your fireplace is gigantic, with Dutch oven & room to roast an ox, ... the [4-a] larger Hessian (20"H) are what you need; very superior, painted red & yellow, with touches of gilt, & cost $10; all black $6. For smaller fireplaces, the [4-b] smaller size (12"H) will do nicely. $5.50, [or if] you prefer, all black, $3.00." Edwin Jackson, NYC. The Jackson (4-a) is tallest of all the repros, a bit plodding, and cockaded like (1); Jackson's smaller pair (4-b) has short tailed coat, very bent leading leg, low helmet with fat half-ring handle cast on top of it.

• **(5)**. A half century later, in 1989, another version was offered by Lemee. Theirs stand 19"H, and are a white, red, black & gold, same-direction, cockaded pair

Andirons, cast iron owls, glass eyes, American, 16"H, dated 1887. **$300.00-$425.00**

Andirons, cast iron pair, each a figural George Washington, painted black, rust, white & blue, standing on a plinth, with left arm resting on a draped pedestal and left hand holding a scroll, his right hand at his side holding his tricorn hat, American, poss. 3rd to 4th quarter 19th C. • These are unusual because of the paint. It is hard to date these patriotic andirons. This pair could have been done originally for centennials in 1876, or 1889, or could be 1920s or 30s repros. **$700.00-$1200.00**

Andirons, cast iron pair of bulldogs, mirror images, with turned heads, made from 2 different casting patterns (not one somehow made in reverse of other), front legs, chest and angry-looking head, with so many wrinkles around neck it looks like a bandana, American, prob. c.1860s to 1880s. • I'd have to check records of **bulldog popularity** to get a closer dating. I think that these are not related to Winston Churchill, although bulldogs and bull mastiffs are both English dogs. John Bull is the British equivalent of Uncle Sam, and the expression "Boys of the bulldog breed" refer to pugnacious Britons fighting Kaiser Bill. • I could be wrong about the whole thing, and these might be 20th C. Bulldogs could also be tenuously related to Teddy Roosevelt because of Harvard. **$175.00-$225.00**

Andirons, cast iron, possibly never painted, full length figures of robust George Washington standing on pyramidal flat top plinths decorated with drapery swags & 2 crossed arrows, rather delicate casting under rust. Log supports & back of figures are charred. American, 20¼"H, maybe c.1870s, maybe mid 20th C repros. • Not enough is known about these figural andirons, and the date of manufacture is the crux of the value. <u>Reproductions are nothing but second-hand used merchandise,</u> and do not increase in value beyond the replacement value of new reproductions. The dealer in fall 1989 had these marked $350.00, but the age wasn't convincingly there. **$175.00-$235.00**

Andirons, cast iron, remarkable Ol' Sol sun faces (sometimes called <u>sunflower faces</u>), well-modeled with wide expressive lips, arched eyebrows, dimpled cheeks, each surrounded by a very formal reeded halo of rays, the vertical member is wavery and fluted, a stylized flame, the legs are also wavery in form, though thick, and are cast with deep incised lines that echo the flame. (I saw a pair with the same motif, much more timid neat little faces, in cast brass or bronze. Maker was not marked.) Mfd by Bradley & Hubbard, 16½''H, pat'd Aug. 24, 1886. • The low in the price range reflects a reasonably plentiful supply, the high will not surpass Schorsch's high (See below). I think he'll end up eating about $10,000.00 of what he paid on that New Year's Day. Although publicity is worth lots of moolah in and of itself. **$600.00-$12,700.00**

Price Burn-out.— Rarely can dates and marks be seen on andirons — either because of condition or illegible original casting. The first pair of these sun faces, known to the general public, sold at a spectacular auction of part of Harold Corbin's collection, at Litchfield, CT, January 1, 1989. Dealer David Schorsch bought this pair (missing the log holders) for an astounding $12,700.00 ($13,970.00 with 10% premium). Reportedly before the sale, Schorsch saw the ''B & H'' mark on the irons. I think he should have done some heavy investigating before bidding so high. Between Dec. 1988 when the catalog came out, and April 1989, only four months, at least seven pairs (maybe 100s by the time this book is published!) have been found, the second of which has maker's name, the log supports, and black and red — possibly original — paint, and were auctioned by Olmstead to dealer Bill Samaha, who paid $4900.00, plus 10% buyer's premium. Olmstead later said that the ultimate market value would ''depend on how common they turn out to be.'' For a while, at least, the price can't be predicted. When it seemed possible they were unique, and the maker was unnoticed, or generally unknown (and Bradley & Hubbard couldn't be more popular with cast iron collectors), any price at all seemed achievable. The price dropped since, and one dealer remarked in March 1989 that the Corbin sale seemed to have ''brought them out of the woodwork''. A pair sold at John P. McInnis' first auction, Boxborough, MA, in May 1989 for only $1750.00, plus 10%. A pair sold at Richard Oliver's Kennebunkport, ME, auction, Aug. 27, 1989 for $1200.00, plus 10% premium. • They are wonderful looking, so right now it's the buyer's decision whether to wait until the price has settled, or to make sure he or she gets one for a collection or resale.

Andirons, cast iron, short splayed legs with unidentifiable wing-like casting in center, surmounted by fluted square tapered column with wonderful oval heads, probably <u>Black Americana</u> men's heads, with old paint, Shenandoah Valley, VA, about 12''H, mid 19th C to 3rd quarter. **$850.00-$1200.00**

Andirons, figural anchors, black painted cast iron, chain connects tops of both, Anchorwares, Winchester, MA, 16''H, early 1930s. **$340.00-$550.00**

Andirons, for baking potatoes in hearth, cast iron, no upright post, mainly comprised of horizontal log supports that are actually hollow slant-sided ''tunnels'' with slide-out drawers or ovens for 4 to 6 potatoes to be pushed back within the tunnel. The drawer fronts are shaped, and have a small projection bottom front for hooking with a log hook or other tool to pull drawer out. Both bars have a high toothed ridge cast the length of the top — like a stegosaur's spine plates — to hold logs. No marks mentioned, American, about 5'' or 6''H x about 5'' or 6''W, about 14 or 15''L, poss. as early as the 1st quarter 19th C, but could be 2nd, even 3rd quarter. These unusual andirons were pictured in an article on ''Pre-Stove Cooking'', by Edwin C. Whittemore, in *The Spinning Wheel*, March 1965, and have never appeared in any other publication, nor been seen by anyone I've ever talked to. I am guessing at dimensions from the photograph. They are a wonderful idea, and somebody ought to make them now for use in living room fireplaces. **$350.00-$425.00**

Andirons, forged iron, welded and chisel cut, sort of fire god demons, one skirted female, one bearded male, arms upraised, legs in knee-out squatting position, American (?), 9¾''H, 1910s to c.1930s. • These remind you of animated Jack o'lanterns, and were probably made for a country cottage fireplace, to order. They were advertised by M. Finkel & Daughter in 1988. Price range mine. **$950.00-$2500.00**

Andirons, highly polished cast and forged iron, 2 fantastical neo-Renaissance birds, which you would call griffins if you could see any part of a lion's body in them. Serpentine curved breast & neck, ending in angry eagle-like head, widespread 4-toed bird legs, pointed small wings pointed up following line of neck, marked ''B & H'', mfd by Bradley & Hubbard, 20¼''H, late 19th C. • The price was realized at a 1989 Seaboard Auction Gallery sale, Eliot, ME. **$1000.00**

Andirons, <u>knife blade</u> type, flat forged iron retort shape uprights, urn finials in brass, brass stem between blade & legs, penny feet, marked ''I. C.'' on lower brass plate, American, 20¾''H, late 18th or early 19th C. • Garth's Auctions, Delaware, OH, April 11-12, 1986, for $750.00. **$700.00-$1000.00**

Andirons, or firedog & firecat, high relief modeled cast brass cat with tail tucked around feet, facing short tailed pug with wide studded collar, attached to iron log holders, maker unknown, American, 10''H, early 1930s. **$150.00-$175.00**

Andirons, spelled variously in old inventories, etc.: handirons, aundyrnes, and even called hand-dogs. This pair of wrought iron so-called <u>knife blade</u> type, with brass ball finials, the flat shapely blade — an elongated bulb shape — being at least ¾ of the total height, American, 17''H, late 18th or early 19th C. This is my favorite type, but they have not, until fairly recently, been considered as classy (and hence were generally less expensive) as cast brass andirons. Price ranges considerably. I saw a pair missing the brass finials for $750.00 at a fancy antique show. Hmmm. Others sold in the late 1980s have been priced in this range: **$850.00-$3500.00**

Apple butter kettle, copper, huge size with bail handle, American, 19th C. **$250.00-$325.00**

• **Apple Butter Making.**— In the Sept.1847 *American Agriculturalist*, writer E. S. notes "The large copper kettle (my kettle holds half a barrel of cider) three-quarters full of new sweet cider, made from sound apples, is set over the fire before five o'clock in the morning. I let it boil two hours, and then put in as many apples, which were peeled, cored, and cut up the night before, as will fill the kettle, and at the same time, I throw in about two quarts of nicely cleaned peach-stones, which by sinking to the bottom, and being moved about incessantly by the stirrer, prevent the fruit from settling and burning, which would spoil the whole. I take care in selecting the apples to secure a large proportion of sour ones; for, as the cider is sweet, unless this precaution be taken, the sauce will have a vapid taste that nothing can remove. ... On the hearth, around the fire, I place numerous pans and pots of apples and cider, simmering and stewing, which I empty into the kettle as fast in succession as the contents boil away enough to make room for them; but after twelve o'clock I never allow any more to be added to the mass. The boiling must be continued steadily until the whole is reduced to a smooth, thick marmalade, of a dark, rich brown color, and no cider separates when a small portion is cooled for trial.

"From the moment the first apples are put into the boiling cider, the whole must be stirred without a moment's intermission, otherwise it will settle and burn; but the handle of the stirrer must be passed from hand to hand as often as fatigue or inclination makes a change desirable.

"My kettle holds half a barrel of cider, which, with the first apples in it, begins to boil about nine o'clock in the morning, and the whole is done enough by eight o'clock in the evening, when a sufficient quantity of powdered all-spice, cloves and cinnamon may be added to season it to your taste. The apple-butter must be dipped out as soon as possible when it stops boiling; for, if it cools in the copper or brass, it is in danger of becoming poisonous, as may be detected even by the unpleasant taste imparted by the action of the acid upon the copper. I prefer sweet stone, or earthen-ware pots to keep it in, but where the quantity made is very large, a barrel may be employed."

Apple butter kettles, copper, flat bottom, side ear handles of iron, American, range from 15 or so gallons up to 40 gallons or more. Imagine lifting this, full or empty. You couldn't! 19th C.   **$250.00-$500.00**

• Anne M. Thomas, of Flemington, NJ, wrote a query to *Americana* magazine in July/Aug. 1989, about the effects of making **apple butter in cast iron.** She wrote "of the experience of a woman in this area who made apple butter in a large ironware pot, only to find that her teeth turned black after she ate the apple butter. A food scientist at Rutgers University explained that tartaric acid from the apples combined with iron from the pot to produce iron tartrate salts." Maybe all those witches depicted cooking over a pot, grinning through their black teeth, were fond of apple butter, not eye of newt.

Apple or bird roaster, sheet iron, domed shape, hooks, American, 19th C.   **$170.00-$225.00**

Apple roaster, dark heavy gauge old (?) tin reflecting oven, 3 shelves, shaped feet, 2 little strap handles on side, about the size for pippins, American, only 7⅜"H x 6"W, 19th C. These were made in 18th C and throughout entire 19th Cs.
$350.00-$400.00

Apple roaster, tin hearth reflector, on top is a bracket strap handle, 2 shelves, upper shelf is perforated with long eye- or almond-shaped slots, the only apple roaster that dealer Joe Dziadul has ever seen with perforations, American, 9⅛"H x 9⅝"W, early 19th C.   **$450.00-$520.00**

Bannock board, thick plank of wood with smooth face, set with stubby wooden handle in back that props it at about a 40 degree angle, used for making corn meal cakes called bannocks. American (?), 12"L x 8"W, handle 6"L, early 19th C, poss. later.   **$30.00-$50.00**

Recipes for Bannocks.— (1) "Into one pint of Indian meal stir a pint of buttermilk; ½ teaspoon of salt; one teaspoon of molasses; one of butter; and add two well-beaten eggs; one pint of wheat flour; thin with milk to a thin batter; last, stir in two large teaspoons of soda dissolved in hot water; pour into buttered shallow pans; bake one hour in quick oven which bakes top and bottom brown." This recipe, which sounds like corn muffins, appeared in *Treasure-House of Useful Knowledge,* compiled by Henry B. Scammel, who pirated recipes from many earlier cookbooks. (2) "To one quart sour milk, put a teaspoon of salaeratus, dissolved in water; warm the milk slightly, beat up an egg, and put in corn meal enough to make it thick as pudding batter, and some salt; grease a pan and bake it, or you may put it in six or eight saucers." Elizabeth Lea, *Domestic Cookery,* Baltimore, 1851, 1859. (3) "**Irish Bread.**— 4 cupfuls flour, ½ cupful butter, 1½ cupfuls milk, ½ teaspoonful salt, 3 teaspoonfuls Calumet baking powder. Mix the ingredients to a soft dough; roll an inch thick, shape into cakes, six inches across, with a large cooky cutter, and bake on a hot griddle. Before taking from the fire, be sure they are baked to the heart. Split in two, butter and serve hot." Sidney Morse, *Household Discoveries,* c.1909. • When I made bannocks (on a plank in front of a huge fire), I used the latter recipe, substituting cornmeal for half the flour. They were rolled to about half an inch thickness, and slapped on the board rather smartly. They cooked through, "to the heart", before they lost their precarious hold on the plank. If I tried them again, I'd experiment with using a little brown rice flour (from health food store), which is quite sticky.

Fire-Cakes. — "There never was anything that tasted better than my mother's 'fire-cake,' — a short-cake spread on a smooth piece of board, and set up with a flat-iron before the blaze, browned on one side, and then turned over to be browned on the other. (It required some sleight of hand to do that.) If I could only be allowed to blow the bellows — the very old people called them 'belluses' — when the fire began to get low, I was a happy girl." Lucy Larcom, in *A New England Girlhood,* Boston: 1890.

Basket spit, also called a <u>cradle spit</u>, forged iron, a cage-like "basket" of iron is in the center of the long spit rod, for holding something to be roasted which might come apart if just skewered to a plain spit, this one complete with hinges and pulley, English (?), late 18th C.
$200.00-$225.00

Bellows, new leather, wooden body painted yellow with stenciled & painted flower decorations, new leather, brass nozzle, American (?), 18½"L, 19th C. This pair was

$275.00 at Garth Auction, May 5-6, 1989, Delaware, OH. (At the same sale, another decorated bellows, with fruit & leaves, and the old leather, in very worn condition, reached $175.00.) **$250.00-$350.00**

Bellows, various types: **(1)** small, hand held decorative leather & painted wood, turned handles, brass trim, for parlor use; **(2)** larger, simpler wood & leather, for kitchen hearth or small blacksmith's hearth; and **(3)** mechanical bellows, keywound or cranked, wood & metal without accordian action, more like a fan. All 3 types are collected; at present, mechanicals are most desired by collectors. For example: iron fitted, wood-cased belt-drive type in 2 parts: a sort of bellows-shape body, awkwardly held in left hand by short turned wood handle or set on hearth pointing brass "hose" nozzle at embers, upper wheel cranked to motivate fan blades in lower part, drawing air in side vents & exhaling it from nozzle, French, 21"H, early 19th C. The French bellows above was for sale by Edwin Jackson in NYC in 1972. Their price at the time was $270.00; below the money now. **$400.00-$600.00**

Reproduction alert for Bellows.— A very large number of old-looking decorated bellows were sold during the heartily hearth-conscious Colonial Revival 1920s & 30s. The leather of these repro or fake old bellows were painted, studded with brass, or fitted with repousse brass in the same shape of the bellows. They cost under $10.00 usually, and worked perfectly for their purpose, so a battered bellows found now might be but 50 years old.

Bird roaster, heavy gauge tin reflecting oven with triangular sides with strap handles, looks like a pup tent, the back pivots at the crest of the "tent' and flips to cover open side, so you don't have to take the birds off the 2 hooks to turn them, you simply flip the reflecting back & turn the roaster, American, 7"H x 8"L, 19th C. **$200.00-$235.00**

Bird roaster, tin reflector oven for hearthside use, hooks for 4 birds, triangular shape with side strap handles, from F. A. Walker catalog, prob. English, c.1870s. **$100.00-$150.00**

Bird roaster, tin, very simple arched top with 4 hooks, no legs or feet, American, 10"H x 10"W x 8" deep, 19th C. **$130.00-$150.00**

Bird roaster, tin, with hooks inside, short strap legs & strap handles, American, 7"H x 11"L, 19th C. By birds they didn't mean chickens or Butterball® turkeys, but very small field birds. **$200.00-$275.00**

Bird roaster, tinned sheet iron, seen from side looks like bent over "L", generously looped strap handle, 6 hooks in pairs of 2, one pair top center, 2 pairs on lower row on either side of top pair, hooks reinforced on backside of this small oven, rimmed drip pan below, American, 11½"H x 9"W x 4¼" deep, 19th C. **$165.00-$200.00**

Age Will Out? — Just when you feel a little secure about the probable age of these old reflecting ovens, you find a copy of the wonderful 1895 Harrod's Stores, Ltd. (London) catalog, reprinted by St. Martin's Press in 1972. (The actual title, which is probably how you'd find it at the library, is *Victorian Shopping*) Over a thousand pages with terrific linecuts of everything anyone would want for house, home, body, yard, barn or buggy. • There are several tin reflecting ovens, called generically "Broilers", in the Ironmongery & Turnery department pages. (For their "Cheese Toaster" see another entry in this chapter.)

A pup tent "Game Oven", with hinged front lid, three wire hooks, and a strap handle on the two triangular ends, could be ordered 9"W, 11"W, 12"W or 14"W. Another, not pictured, but described as "strong", came in three sizes: 11"W, 13"W and 15"W. Presumably "strong" means thicker gauge tin as well as more substantial structure. Also available was an "Improved Broiler" oven with rather tall squared body, hinged domed hood with strap handle, four wire hooks, and a heavy wire hook support to hang on fender bar. It came 9"W and 12"W. Another was a "Cheese Oven", with hood and strap handle fixed to a large rectangular double pan. Another, the "American Oven", was made of tin, a large rectangular box, with a lift-out tray with wire handles, set onto a shelf, about ⅔ way up from bottom, hinged lift-off hood or lid, and the most distinguishing feature, a sheet of tin set at 15° from front to back, which reflected the heat to the underside of the shelf and tray. Behind this reflector, rather like underneath a flight of stairs, is an open space supported by side pieces of tin. Another was Harrod's "Dutch Oven", with open straight front, round back and domed lid, strap handle on top, three hooks over a reticulated removable shelf midway from top to bottom. Long pins at both ends allowed you to take this partly apart for cleaning. It came 9"W, 10"W, 12"W and 13"W. • It is hard to imagine that in the age of "kitchen pianos", those lumbering flights of cast iron fancy, that much call would come for fireplace reflector ovens, but there they are. Harrod's did ship all over the world...from Smyrna to Switzerland, from Tahiti to Tripoli. Apparently in 1895 they did not ship to the United States, as "Parcel Post [is] not in operation." Hmmm.

Bird roaster, wrought iron, dangle type which was hung on crane by its own hook, with sliding hoop with 2 hooks, poss. NY state?, 16"L, 18th or very early 19th C. • I'm glad we don't eat little birds that fly by nowadays. Imagine hooking a robin, a lark or a nice fat chicadee to such a thing. Yuck. I don't even like to eat chickens. (You never know where you'll read a plea for vegetarianism, do you?) **$290.00-$350.00**

Bird roaster trammel, wrought iron and brass, marked with stars & other punched designs, stamped all over it is "PATENTEE PATENTEE PATENTEE", French, 18¼"L at its least extension, adjusts in ½" increments, mid 19th C. **$140.00-$190.00**

Bird trammel, 2 hooks, for hanging a large trussed bird for roasting, American or English, adjustable from 16" to 23" fully extended, 18th C. **$120.00-$150.00**

Bottle jack, brass with forged iron hook, rotary action provided by a clockwork movement, spring wound, concealed within the cylindrical bottle shaped drum above the hook. The key hole for winding is in the side, near the bottom of the cylinder. "Salter's Warranted Economical Bottle Jack", mark is a mariner's knot pierced by an arrow, & the initial "S", English, 12"H, c.1820s (?). A Mr. Salter (probably the same one) made brass-faced hanging spring balance scales. **$350.00-$450.00**

Bottle jack mantle clamp, also called a jack rack, cast & worked brass, a simple screw clamp, sliding jack hook, acorn finial to screw, English or poss. American, late 18th or early 19th C. **$250.00-$375.00**

Broiler, revolving or rotary, cast iron wheel with 19 spokes with a concavity directing drippings to reservoir in handle, next to broiler, 3 legs, hanging hole in handle, handle marked only "PATENT", American, 12" diameter, 25¼"L overall, c.1830-1860. **$150.00-$250.00**

Broiler, rotary, wrought iron, long handle with rattail loop, round grill with double serpentine design, 3 footed, 18th C, American (?), 9" diameter x 18"L overall, 18th C. **$175.00-$275.00**

Broiler, rotary, wrought iron, round wavy grid, American (?), quite small, 7" diameter, 19th C. **$225.00-$300.00**

Broiler, stationary, front legs with penny feet, back legs are double-toed, beautiful long handle with rattail loop, American, 18th C. **$400.00-$550.00**

Broiler, whirling (also called rotary or revolving), alternating scalloped & straight bars, 3 legs, American or English, 3"H x 11" diameter with 11¾"L handle, early 19th C. **$350.00-$450.00**

Broiler, whirling, forged iron, very plain with neat perky upraised handle, long legs, American or English, 3¾"H x 12⅜" diameter, 14⅜"L handle, early 19th C. **$275.00-$350.00**

Broiler, whirling, grids made from square bars turned at angle so the sharp edge is along the top, English (?), 24½"L x 12¼" diameter, early 19th C. **$150.00-$250.00**

Broiler, whirling, wrought iron, quite simple with straight bars on grill, long handle, American (?), 10"diameter, 19th C. **$125.00-$175.00**

Broiler, whirling, wrought iron, tripod feet, long handle with hanging eye, American (?), 24"L, late 18th or early 19th C. **$200.00-$275.00**

Broiler, wrought iron, 4 serpentine bars, very simple feet, long handle ends in "doughnut' hole, American (?), 17"L, early 19th C. **$275.00-$375.00**

Broiler, wrought iron, horseshoe-shaped standing tripod type, American, 15¾"H x 12"W, late 18th, early 19th C. The design of the broiler face & tripod, and condition of the iron contributes to value. Added value given by penny feet & extra iron scroll. **$250.00-$400.00**

Broiler or gridiron, stationary, wrought iron, 4 short feet, ram's horn handle, American (?), 30"L x 17"W, 18th or 19th C. **$120.00-$160.00**

Broiler or grill, whirling, forged iron, American (?), 11" diameter x 24"L overall, early 19th C. **$185.00-$250.00**

Camp stoves—See Stove chapter.

Chestnut roaster, cast iron, iron legs, European or poss. American, 4" deep x 12½" diameter, 19th C. **$85.00-$120.00**

Chestnut roaster, copper pan with pierced design in cover, twisted wrought iron shaft and wooden handle, American (?), 13½" diameter, 18th C. • I cannot tell you why this is a chestnut roaster and not a bed warmer. It seems a bit big for the former, but that's what the dealer said. **$500.00-$750.00**

Chestnut roaster, copper pot with slightly flared foot, turned wood handle, hinged lid with ring knob or handle, many pea size perforations cut in lid, English, 13"H, late 18th or early 19th C. **$1200.00-$1500.00**

Chestnut roaster, like a bed warmer, sort of, hexagonal pieced brass pan with a pierced lid, long flat handle, very shapely and with cutouts, English or poss. American, early 19th C. **$275.00-$350.00**

Chestnut roaster, pierced brass, long wooden handle, prob. English; could be American, 17"L, early 19th C. • **Reproduction alert.**— Arthur Todhunter, NYC, NY, made "quaint & useful gifts", mainly for use around the fireplace, that were "reproductions of Old England and Colonial wrought iron work and fire place furnishings." In a Dec. 1921 *House & Garden* ad, we see a "chestnut roaster", which is a round brass pan, pierced lid with slight convexity to center of it, with what appears to be a simple turned wooden handle. The size is not given, but is probably about 20" to 30"L. For the old: **$225.00-$400.00**

Chestnut roaster, steel with decorative engraving, wooden handle, American or English, 12" diameter, c.1810-1830. **$275.00-$350.00**

Clock jack, brass & iron, iron weight, English, 8 ¹¹⁄₁₆"H exclusive of wheel at top, early 19th C. **$1750.00-$2000.00**

Clock jack, forged iron, spoked wheel, scrolled front plate, arched wall bracket, 3 gears and spool, American or English, 14"H, late 18th or early 19th C. **$850.00-$1200.00**
• In the *Journal of the Franklin Institute..and Mechanics' Register* [Philadelphia], of 1839, appeared a report of a patent obtained July 12, 1838 by Samuel Pierce of NYC for an "Apparatus for Roasting Meat and other Articles". The *Journal* editor writes as follows: "This apparatus is denominated the 'manifold roaster, or planetarium stove,' and the patentee says, 'the main object of my improvement is to combine together a number of spits, or jacks, each of which is to sustain a joint of meat, a fowl, or other article to be roasted; and each of which spits is to be suspended by a hook over its appropriate dripping pan, the whole of which spits may be made to revolve simultaneously by wheel work, properly geared, either before an ordinary fire, or more perfectly by being placed around a stove constructed for that purpose; in which latter case the spits not only revolve on their own axes, but have an orbicular revolution round the stove. The effect of the heat is, in either case, to be promoted by means of reflectors. When the planetarium stove is complete, and in operation, its external appearance is that of an ordinary cylindrical stove of large diameter, the external cylinder being a case (usually made double) which surrounds the stove, and which also surrounds the system of spits which revolve round said stove." Pierce went on to claim that the originality of this invention was in the multiple vertical spits revolving simultaneously.

Clock jack, steel, cast, wrought & machined brass beautifully scrolled front plate, clean clockwork, the word "jack" in the name, standing for the assistant or spit turner who is no longer necessary, English, 18th C. **$850.00-$1500.00**

Clock jack & crown spit, or spit engine, cast and machined brass, forged iron, marked "John Linwood," English (?), 18th C. • A spectacular mechanical spit was reported in William Hone's *The Every-Day Book*, 1827: **"The most singular spit in the world** is that of the count de Castel Maria, one of the most opulent lords of Treviso. This spit turns one hundred and thirty different roasts at once, and plays twenty-four tunes, and whatever it plays, corresponds to a certain degree of cooking, which is perfectly understood by the cook. Thus, a leg of mutton a la anglaise, will be excellent at the 12th air; a fowl a la

Flamande, will be juicy at the 18th, and so on. It would be difficult, perhaps, to carry farther the love of music and gormandizing.'' For the Linwood jack: **$900.00-$1300.00**

Cook pot, also called a flesh pot, cast iron, very globular body, high straight-sided neck with triangular ears, forged and twisted iron falling bail, very long splayed legs, very handsome, American, 14¼''H, late 18th or early 19th C. • A cooking pot is one form of cast iron **hollowware,** or hollow ware. Kettles, tea kettles, skillets, posnets, saucepans, porringers, spiders, Dutch ovens, the bowls of large ladles, and other wares with ''hollow'' insides are called hollowware. Some had to be cast in two, three, even four parts because the mouth or rim was smaller in diameter than the belly or middle. The term is also used for pewter, silver, brass, bell metal, copper and bronze wares. • **German vocabulary** — Eisene Hafen: iron pots; Kamin-Hangetopf: hearth- (or Fireplace) hanging saucepan. Kochtopf means cook pot. Another way of saying for the fireplace is fur di Herdplatte.
$100.00-$165.00

Crane, cast iron, simple and small, American, late 19th or early 20th C. This is not strictly a fake or reproduction but is a revivalist piece that was made to satisfy decorators' demands during a renaissance of Colonial accessories that got underway in the 1880s-90s (and again in the 1920s). •
$45.00-$70.00

Crane, forged bar iron, curved bracket, very very simple, American (?), only 19''L, 19th C. ''The **lug-pole,** though made of green wood, sometimes became brittle or charred by too long use over the fire and careless neglect of replacement, and broke under its weighty burden of food and metal; hence accidents became so frequent, to the detriment of precious cooking utensils, and even to the destruction of human safety and life, that a Yankee invention of an iron crane brought convenience and simplicty, and added a new grace to the kitchen hearth.'' Alice Morse Earle, *Customs & Fashions in Old New England,* Scribner's, 1893.   **$125.00-$165.00**

Crane, forged iron, curved brace, very simple, American or European, brace is 34''H, crane is 26''L, prob. 18th C. • The will inventory of Jacob Alleweins, Berks County, PA, who died in 1781, listed a brass crane — very unusual.
$120.00-$150.00

Crane, forged iron, simple design with ram's horn tip to tapered bar, American (?), 21''L, 19th C.   **$350.00-$400.00**
•Cranes start at under $75.00 for simple small ones of late manufacture. Added value.— The bigger, more interestingly forged cranes bring more, up to $2000.00 + if anything animalistic or figural has been done with the iron. **Reproduction alert.**— Yes, that little crane that doesn't look old *is* wrought iron, but it is easily perceived as new. The iron is merely a scrolled piece of perfectly uniform ¾''W, ⅛'' or ³⁄₁₆'' thick flat wrought iron bar. • A fireplace crane & barbecue grill set, comprised of a vertical tension bar, a fixed fire bowl of sheet iron (like a big 24'' diameter, shallow, slightly round-bottomed pan), above which is a grill (round with 10 cross bars of plated iron wire), above the grill is the scrolled bracket crane with hook, from which to suspend a cooking pot. Sold as part of this 5-piece set was a small gypsy kettle with 2 quart capacity — a cast iron 3-legged, round-bottomed pot with the old type casting band around the widest part, wire bail handle. The whole set was made by Malone's

Creative Products (formerly Malone's Metalcraft) of McMinnville, TN, prior to 1973, and sold for $49.50. The little pot or kettle could be bought separately for $8.50. The June 1973 ad states that they made ''hundreds of other items''; wish I had a catalog.

Cranes, forged iron, a pair of floor-standing cranes with penny feet, T-bar, American or English, 35''H, 18th C. Very unusual.   **$1500.00-$1800.00**

Curfew, from the French couvre-feu, or fire-cover. A sort of half dome, or quarter sphere — think of a baby buggy hood. They are usually at least 10'' across, sometimes larger, made of sheet brass, copper or iron. This one is forged sheet iron, somewhat pitted, with a vertical twisted forged iron handle from the top down to the bottom, with a curl at the bottom tail. This hearth essential was pushed against the back or side of the fireplace, with the glowing embers of a wood fire within, to shut off the air. In the morning, the curfew was removed and the fire could be quickly restarted with a few puffs of the bellows. American (?), 10''H x 13''W, late 18th or early 19th C. • Added value.— Although I prefer iron, there will probably be more brass ones shown (mostly European imports), and as their decorative value is considered greater, their price would be higher by 10% to maybe 50% over that for the iron: **$165.00-$500.00**

Dangle spit, steel, horizontal serpentine winglike governor at the top of a steel vertical rod with 6 holes at one inch intervals, with a much thinner rod with a small hook at its top and 3 very sharp bigger hooks at the bottom to hold the meat or game bird to be roasted. The small hook at the top could be set into one of the holes to adjust the height off the fire. The whole thing was suspended by a stout twine or cord from the edge of the mantle, and it was set in rotary motion by twisting, so that when released, it would twirl as it unwound, thereby winding itself up again, English or American, 16''L fully extended, early 19th C. • Added value from any file or engraved decoration, or a date or initials.   **$185.00-$225.00**

Dutch oven, cast iron, 3 footed, ear handles to use with pot lifter hooks, lid with raised edge to contain coals, lid has a few triangular ''chips'' along edge, marked only ''Baltimore'', 8½''H x 12''D, early 19th C. • Dutch ovens marked ''Baltimore'' show up fairly often. It is not known who made them, but there are three good possibilities: William Baer & Co., est. prior to 1817, or the Cast-Iron Baltimore Cast-Iron Manufactory) est. by 1803, and Hayward, Bartlett & Co., established 1844. **$200.00-$250.00**

Perhaps or Maybe: Why Ifs, Ands & Buts Are Necessary. — Throughout this book I have tried to be as accurate as possible, about provenance or dates. You will notice lots of question marks in parens after dates and places. You will also find a good number of ''looks like'' or ''possibly'' [poss.], or ''probably'' [prob.], and a few ''perhaps''. The appeal of objects with marks and patent dates obviously lies in the surety which such identification gives the collector. In fact, I believe that's why the two most popular fields of collecting worldwide, all totaled, are stamps and coins, because they have dates, provenance, and well-established histories. Our field has its marked pieces too, but probably more pieces are mysterious and require research and study.

Dutch oven, cast iron, 3 peg feet, deep raised edge on lid, small interior flange to make a good fit in kettle, very handsome, particularly in this big size, American, 11"H, early 19th C. For some comments on a utensil called a creeper, see under "Spider" further on. **$350.00-$450.00**

• **Lookalike alarm.**— Calling it a "camp oven", Lehman's Hardware & Appliances, 4779 Kidron Rd., Kidron, OH 44636 offer 5 sizes of cast iron Dutch ovens, made at the Lodge foundry, in their $2.00 1989 Non-Electric Good Neighbor Amish Country catalog. The utensils have 2, 4, 6, 8, and 12 qt. capacities all have "integral" legs, flanged lids, & falling bails. In order they are 8", 10", 12", 14", & 16" diameter, & weigh from 10 lbs. to 32 lbs. Without further explanation, Lehman's says they range from 3½" to 4½" deep, 5½" to 7½" high (which sounds like 2" & 3" legs, but in the picture they look short & peggy. They also have what they call a "Dutch Oven", which is for stovetop use, and has a somewhat domed lid with no flange. • Lynchburg Hardware & General Store, Lynchburg, TN, offer the Lodge Foundry Dutch oven with legs, in the 4 qt. size, 10" diameter; & one without legs in 9 qt. size, 13" diameter.

Dutch oven, cast iron, forged bail handle, 3 legs, high lipped lid, American, 14" diameter, early to mid 19th C. **$300.00-$450.00**

The word "Dutch" is sometimes used to indicate that something is a substitute for something else. A Dutch wife (or husband) is the long torso size or bolster pillow that you use to drape your arm about when sleeping on your side. Dutch gold is actually a cheap alloy, tombac, made of copper and zinc, which is beaten to a foil and used to gild certain toys or knicknacks. A Dutch treat is not really a treat, because you are paying for yourself. And a **Dutch oven** is a substitute for a built-in bake oven. The chief characteristic is the raised edge around the lid — meant to hold hot coals so that while the oven sat on the hearth, or in the embers, getting heat from below, it was also getting heat from above.

Dutch oven, cast iron, forged falling bail handle, 3 stubby legs, nice deep flange or raised edge on lid, American, 6¾"H x 9¼" diameter, early 19th C. **$350.00-$450.00**

"To make Yankee Bread. — Take two measures of Indian and one of Rye meal, mix with milk or water, to the consistency of stiff hasty pudding, and add yeast — bake in iron pans or iron kettles four or five hours. Eat with fresh butter, or other food, and if while warm the better. Yankee bread is very good or very bad, according to the manner in which it is made. We commend it to dyspeptics. The Indian meal should be either bottled or sifted." *The Farmers' Cabinet*, Philadelphia, Aug.1, 1836. • **What's Meant by "Iron Pan"?** — I can't guarantee what is meant by "iron pans". Although from the context it sounds as if an iron pan might be a cast iron gem or muffin pan, the recipe is way too early for that. So I believe them to be sheet iron, flat-bottomed pans, rather deeper than pie pans but with slightly flared sides, which are rarely found today. It is possible that they are cast iron Scotch or Maslin kettles of some kind, especially as the other utensil of choice is a kettle. "Iron kettles" I'm presuming to be a Dutch oven. Another possibility is that iron pans and iron kettles are the same thing, and both refer to **Dutch ovens,** because Beecher & Stowe in their 1869 *The American Woman's Home*, list among requisite iron wares, "a Dutch

Oven, called also a bake-pan." As for "bottled cornmeal" I have no notion of what it is, because cornmeal was kept in bins or closed canisters, not (so far as I know) preserved in bottles.

Dutch oven, & lid, sometimes called a braising pot, bake kettle, camp oven, or bake oven, cast iron, with 3 short legs, raised edge on lid, small interior flange to keep lid in place. "Kentucky Stove Co.", KY, 10"D, early 19th C. **$350.00-$400.00**

• This was called a **four de campagne** in French, literally country oven. Many recipes in Alexandre Dumas' classic *Le Grand Dictionnaire de Cuisine* call for such a utensil, and called for the "braising pot" to be set in hot coals with the special lid with raised edge to be piled with coals. Close reading of some recipes seem to indicate that the *four de campagne* sometimes referred to what was called a tin kitchen in America. So perhaps the confused American usage of the term "dutch oven" dates to a similar French ambivalence.

Why "Dutch"? — One reasonable explanation for the name is given by Louise Peet and Lenore Sater in *Household Equipment*, NY: John Wiley, 1934, 1940. They wrote: "Dutch ovens were brought to America by the Pilgrims. As is well known, the Pilgrims spent some years in Holland before coming to America. The Mayflower was a tiny vessel and baggage limited. The dutch oven could be used for such a variety of cookery that it took the place of several other pots and pans and was, therefore, a favorite utensil of the early settlers."

Dutch oven — See also in Pots & pans chapter.

Fireback, cast iron, cupids & flower garlands, prob. 20th C reproduction. • **Reproduction alert.**— It is a pleasure to mention some reproductions, because they are so faithful to the originals and so well done, & because old firebacks are probably by now mostly in museums. The Country Iron Foundry, POB 600, Paoli, PA 19301, makes 18 "replica" designs from American, English, Dutch, Spanish and French originals, and 17 firebacks of their own design. I have not been able to find out if they mark each fireback. You can get a catalog for about $2.50. • Another company making reproduction firebacks is New England Firebacks, POB 162, Woodbury, CT 06798. Their brochure is about $1.50 **$75.00-$100.00**

Fireback, cast iron, parrot design in a medallion, ornate scrolling, American, 19th C. **$190.00-$225.00**

Fireback, cast iron, portrait of General Wolfe in a medallion, surrounded by flags, American, early 19th C. **$900.00-$1500.00**

Fire dogs—See Andirons.

Fire kindler, asbestos-filled bulbous head, wire handle, adv'd: "100 fires with 3 cents of oil." "Yankee", American, late 19th C. **$5.00-$8.00**

Fire kindler, brass, tapered cylindrical pot with top to bottom strap handle, looks like a pitcher or coffee boiler missing the spout, flat lid with small cut in edge for the wire and composition kindler to stick out of, on its own brass tray, American Hardware Stores magazine ad, 1918. **$35.00-$40.00**

Fire kindler, cast iron elongated "gypsy" kettle, round bottom, 3 short splayed peg legs, rather large lug ears, slightly uptilted at the "elbow", with a curved lower "arm", thin wire falling bail handle, slightly domed lid, with twisted iron rod and insert of composition to soak in igniting fluid, designed by Hanson Booth, mfd by Half Moon Fire Lighter Co., Poughkeepsie, NY, mid 1920s. **$20.00-$30.00**

Fire kindler, composition & wire, "Oval", late 19th C. **$5.00-$6.00**

Fire kindler, wire, composition head, fat turned wooden handle that also plugs end of original cylindrical tin container with paper label. "Directions for using. Put in Tin, 2 inches of Kerosene Oil. In one hour it will thoroughly soak, then it is always ready for use. When the fire is well started, put it [kindler] out by a quick puff, endways, then place in Tin." "Smith's No. 1", mfd by R. P. Smith, Dubuque, IA, 8¾"L, pat'd Oct. 10, 1871. **$18.00-$25.00**

Fire kindler, wire, screen mesh, composition head molded around wire, American, 8"L, late 19th C. **$5.00-$9.00**

Fire kindler or lighter, hammered wrought iron, called by the maker "wright iron", a square container with strap handle, on footed tray, rivets in great evidence, look is definitely Mission or Arts & Crafts Movement, so perhaps the "wright" is actually meant to imply Frank Lloyd-like. "Cape Cod Fire Lighter" advertised in 1918. • This might be essential for the total Arts & Crafts look, gaining so in popularity since late 1988. **$45.00-$55.00**

Fire lighter, brass vessel shaped like a mug or measure, hinged lid with small round finial, two sets of raised concentric rings near top and bottom of body, big loopy strap handle, round flat brass tray with slightly raised rim, brass and composition lighter wand, Todhunter, NYC, NY, looks early 19th C, but is 1930s. **$18.00-$30.00**

Fireplace powder in container, chemical powder packaged in fabulous paper composition container made to look like a chunk of log with rough dark brown bark, with 2 realistic sawed off branches, one the opening with a cap, makes odd blue, green, orange & purple flames, Fireside Powder Co., Port Richmond, Staten Island, NY, about a foot high, early 1920s. The price here is for the graphics on the paper. **$30.00-$60.00**

Fireplace tool set, on rack, rustic hammered finish forged iron, tripod stand topped by large sailing ship, a cross piece under the ship, has knobs for hanging tongs, hearth brush, ash shovel and poker, a bit top heavy looking, mfd by Heather, NYC, NY, mid 1920s. **$45.00-$75.00**

Fish broiler, flips like hearth toasters, wrought iron footed frame with spikes to hold fish, even a small arch under handle to hold it up off hearth, American (?), 18th C. **$350.00-$450.00**

Fish grill, forged iron, elongated grid, long handle, prob. American, 30½"L x 3½"W, early 19th C. **$70.00-$100.00**

Fish roaster or broiler, wrought iron with wooden handle, 4 hooks, fits on fire bar in front of the fire, American (?), 16"L, 19th C. **$250.00-$300.00**

Footman, also called a <u>waiter</u>, for hearth, fancily cutout brass top and wrought iron strap legs, turned wooden handle in front, the piercing depicts a hunting scene and foliage, English (?), 13"H x 13¾"W x 8⅛" deep, 19th C. or early 19th C. **$450.00-$600.00**

Footman, brass, cabriole front legs, poss. American, prob. English, 10½"H, 19th C. • These are known as <u>footmen</u> because they stand by, usually on the hearth, holding food or drink hot until needed. They are four legged, and often have a bigger top surface than pot trivets which stood on the hearth too. **$250.00-$300.00**

Footman, for hearth, cast iron base with sheet brass top, simple flower cutout in center, the lion's paw front legs decorated with convex brass discs, English (?), 11¾"H x 14½"W x 12½" deep, c.1850s to 1860s. • Tricky to date English pieces if you're used to studying American things for style and look. Paw feet relate to pieces from the 1870s in America, but the look of the brass is 1840s. **$200.00-$300.00**

• **Stop, Look, Listen & Learn.** — The only way you can gain confidence in the antiques & collectibles market is to listen to experts, and read about things in your leisure time. Books, magazines, collector newspapers, as well as ads in contemporary lifestyle magazines, and books of related interest to your subject. You can never know too much. An early ad for *The Magazine ANTIQUES,* when it was only five years old, reads: "ANTIQUES. Everyone talks about them, but not everyone can speak with authority; almost everyone buys them, but not everyone buys wisely; everyone occasionally wishes either to acquire antique items or to dispose of things already owned, but not everyone knows what market to seek for either purpose." The ad goes on to tout the mag, but nowadays, when everything and its uncle is collected, you have to read a lot more than ANTIQUES . That magazine still lives up to its claim to be "interesting without sentimentality, scholarly without pedantry, authoritative without egotism", but I wish it had more articles on household tools, and less on furniture and the total look to aim for in a restored mansion! To my mind, it is one of the triumverate which generalist collectors would wisely read: The other two are *Maine Antique Digest,* and *Antique Trader Weekly.* Following close on, though a much smaller paper, is *AntiquesWeek,* which has become a better buyer's source for books on local history and manufacturing history (both invaluable in research) than that bible of antiquarian bookdealers, *Antiquarian Bookman Weekly.* It's also a good general source for out of print books on antiques, though the weekly selection is small. You should also look for copies of the now sadly extinct *Spinning Wheel,* which was edited by Albert Christian Revi, and is mourned by thousands of collectors and dealers. It had more articles on our field than you could dream for in any magazine now. Finally, specialist collector newsletters on individual subjects, ranging from cast iron cookware to cookie cutters, from Depression glass to lunch boxes, are very useful to specialist collectors & dealers. If you are a beginning dealer, you can't do yourself a bigger favor than to read & listen before you buy or sell.

Metal Polishing Recipes.— "Common irons may be brightened by rubbing them first with a rag dipped in vinegar and the ashes, then with an oily rag, and after that with scouring paper, rotten stone, or white brick; but, if possible, red-brick should not be used, for it makes sad work. This method of cleaning serves for all sorts of common irons or brasses, tho' some prefer goose-grease to oil, or any other sort of grease, and do not use scouring-paper to brasses. If these should be very fine steel stoves and fenders, they should be first rubbed with oil, then with emery, till clear and bright, and next with scouring paper, which is an excellent thing to rub irons with that are not in constant use, every two or three days." Eliza F. Haywood, *A New Present for a Servant-Maid; Necessary Cautions and Precepts to Servant-Maids for*

Gaining Good-Will and Esteem, Dublin, Ireland: 1771. Whew! and for a wage of a few pounds a year!

Footman, for hearth, steel straps and rods, very elegant, English (?), 12½"H x 12"W x 8½" deep, early 19th C. **$140.00-$165.00**

Frying pan, cast iron, 3 legs, American, 6" diameter, early to mid 19th C. **$28.00-$45.00**

Frying pan, cast iron, 3 legs, American, 10½" diameter, early to mid 19th C. These 3-legged ones could have been used on an early brickset range too. **$40.00-$65.00**

Frying pan, cast iron, 3 legs, forged iron replaced handle that was riveted on to chipped edge of pan, long casting gate, this isn't a new pan but there is an odd gray glittery look to the iron on the bottom, possibly because of heat from replacing handle, after pan cracked and original cast handle broke off, marked only "No. 8, 12 in." on bottom, American, actually 11½" diameter, overall length with new handle is 21⅝"L, early to mid 19th C (?). See two cast iron frying pans in Pots & Pans. **$60.00-$70.00**

Frying pan, & lid, cast iron, pan has 3 legs, lid has raised edge like for Dutch oven, marked "1 N", G. T. Glascook & Son, Greensboro, NC, 12" diameter, 19th C. **$25.00-$50.00**

Frying pan, repaired sheet iron, hand wrought handle is extremely long, the 2 repairs to pan — one a rectangle of brass, one of copper — are riveted on, American, pan 14" diameter, handle about 38"L, late 18th or early 19th C. **$200.00-$250.00**

Frying pan, wrought iron, American, 5 feet long including handle, late 18th C. I find these fascinating, especially the repaired ones. But the price doesn't seem to move off this range. Maybe because they are cumbersome, but since when did that stop anyone? **$150.00-$200.00**

Frying pan, wrought iron, rattail handle, American, 12" diameter, 14"L handle, early 19th C. • **German vocabulary** — Bratpfanne or simply Pfanne: frying pan. The word Tiegel, meaning stew pan, is also sometimes used. **$75.00-$110.00**

Frying pan, forged iron, long handle, American (?), 10"D with 11"L handle, early 19th C. • **Terminology varies.** — What started out as a clearer cut difference between a frying pan and a skillet in the 18th C, based on the form, became at some time a regional difference in language usage (in my experience Ohio and New York people say **frying pan**, Tennessee said **skillet**) not catalogued anywhere. Then there's a chronological difference; a skillet in the 18th C and early 19th C is more like what we might think of as a saucepan with legs. Besides place and age, there's trade terminology — the names used by the manufacturers. Griswold, from Pennsylvania, used "skillet" as did Ohio's Wagner. Your choice. **$50.00-$70.00**

Girdle or griddle plate, cast iron, rigid bail handle, American (?), 14³⁄₁₆" diameter, c.1830. **$40.00-$55.00**

"Flannel Cakes or Crumpets. — Two pounds of flour, sifted. Four eggs. Three tables-spoonfuls of the best brewer's yeast, or four and a half of home-made yeast. A pint of milk. — Mix a tea-spoonful of salt with the flour, and set the pan before the fire. Then warm the milk, and stir into it the flour, so as to make a stiff batter. Beat the eggs very light, and stir them into the yeast. Add the eggs and yeast to the batter, and beat all well together. If it is too stiff, add a little more warm milk. Cover the pan closely and set it to rise near the fire. Bake it, when quite light. Have your baking-iron hot. Grease it, and pour on a ladle-full of batter. Let it bake slowly, and when done on one side, turn it on the other. Butter the cakes, cut them across, and send them to table hot." Miss Leslie, of Philadelphia. *Seventy-Five Receipts for Pastry, Cakes, and Sweetmeats. Appended to The Cook's Own Book and Housekeeper's Register...*, by a Boston Housekeeper. Boston: Munroe & Francis, 1833.

Girdle plate, cast iron, half-hoop fixed handle with large ring on top end, to be hung from crane, English or Scottish, only 9" diameter, early 19th C. **$350.00-$400.00**

Some English foundry names which may appear on hollowwares or other cast iron wares, from the 18th & 19th Cs are: Baldwin, Son & Co., Stowport; "Beatrice" — John Harper; Carron Co.; Coalbrookdale Abraham Darby, Shropshire; Cockrane & Co.; A. Kenrick; Walter Macfarlane & Co., Caracen Foundry, Glasgow; Richard Rowbotham, Providence Foundry; and J. & J. Siddons, West Bromwich.

Grates, wrought bar iron and/or cast iron, or steel, left plain, polished, or with nickel trim. Simple basket grates, iron bars with short legs, were like ones sold today. More elaborate ones — called fireplaces, fireplace heaters or stoves — have decorative cast iron fronts, fancy front legs, "andirons" & "fenders". The most ornate fill the fireplace opening completely to make a smaller opening, for laying a smaller fire above the hearth floor to improve draft & economy. Some have bay window fronts "illuminated" with isinglass or mica. An 1882 ad for Open Stove Ventilating Co., NYC reads "Air Warming Grates — each one combines the radiation and ventilation of an open fire and economy of a warm air furnace." American, Canadian, English, French, etc., various sizes from about 16"W to 3 feet W. 18th C on. Height of potentially collectible ones from 1840s to 1900. **$5.00-$500.00**

A Touch of Plumbago. — "In summer, when coal and wood are banished, and the grate is a dreary mass of plumbagoed (black lead or graphite polish) iron, the fireplace is an unslightly bugbear. It is a social incumbrance, immovable, and useless. Here, then, is another opportunity for putting a little art to practical use. In most houses we find the fire-place occupied by a mass of tinted papers, shavings, or that terrible sanitary & artistic atrocity ironically termed an "ornament for the fire stove." This dreadful conglomeration of gaudily-colored tissue paper cut into strips, or stained shavings, gilt paper & artificial flowers, is a remnant of barbarism, and (fortunately) is fast going out of fashion. Its capabilities for collecting & holding dirt and dust, the liability it possesses of being easily inflamed, and its general incongruity with surroundings, all combine to render it both useless & offensive.

"A mirror, or painted panel fitting in front of the grate is an improvement on the paper & shavings, but neither are very desirable, as they close up the chimney and prevent natural ventilation. A colored Japanese umbrella, opened, and with the handle placed under the grate, is a cheap decoration and often very effective, its bright colors and curious patterns making an agreeable variety in a plainly furnished room. We fear, however, that although this combination may be gratifying to the eye, it is incongruous to the taste according to Ruskin. A small screen, about 24 or 30 inches high, with five or six or-namental panels, say 6 inches wide hinged together, forms a very neat method of concealing an ugly stove; it is, moreover, quite portable, easily cleaned and not liable to hold the dust. A miniature rockwork constructed of virgin cork, moss and ferns in pots, also looks very well, a drawback being the short lives of plants exposed to a con-fined & gassy atmosphere. Artificial plants, now made wonderfully realistic, may be substituted, but they soon get dirty, and are not easily renovated. A short curtain of tapestry or other heavy material fitted with rings to slide on a brass rod fixed under the mantel, offers itself as a means of exhibiting art needlework. More elaborate is a full-sized cabinet constructed to conceal grate and sides may be placed in front and covered with bric-a-brac; but unless the room is large this is liable to give a rather heavy appearance.'' *The Metal Worker*, Aug. 5, 1882.

Griddle, cast iron, long handle, 3 longish legs, American, 12'' diameter, legs 3¼''H, 2nd quarter 19th C.

$60.00-$75.00

Griddle, cast iron, round with short ''keyhole'' shaped han-dle with hanging hole, no legs, cool, smooth, seductive, slate-like finish, American (?), 11¾''D with 2½''L handle, very early 19th C. **$75.00-$100.00**

''**Best Batter Cakes, or Mush Cakes.**— Beat the yolks of eggs very light, add one pint milk, two pints mush almost cold, 1½ pints flour, one tea-spoonful salt, three table-spoonsful melted butter. To be well beaten together. Just before frying them, whip the whites to a strong froth, and stir it lightly into the batter. For frying all kinds of batter cakes, use no more lard than is necessary to make them turn well. But the usual mode is to boil hominy twice a week, and put it into a wooden or stone vessel, and set it in a cool place to prevent its becoming musty. When wanted for use, take the quantity necessary for breakfast or dinner, and having put a small quantity of lard into an oven, let it become hot; put in the hominy and mash it well, adding some salt; when well heated it is ready for the table. Some persons allow it to bake at the bottom, and turn the crust over the hominy when put on the dish. Be careful to have no smoke under the pot while boiling, or when frying for the table. Few things require more care or nicety in their preparation than hominy. (These pints were all measured with the common tin cup.)'' *The Farmers' Cabinet, Devoted to Agriculture, Horticulture and Rural Economy.* Philadelphia: Vol. 11, NO. 1, Aug. 1, 1837. • ''Let me suggest for the comfort of those who stir (mush) an hour or two, and then labor a great while to wash out the pot in which they boil it, that all this trouble may be saved by cooking it in a tin pail, set in a pot of boiling water, and after it has cooked, letting it cool in the same, after which it will slip out in a mass, leaving all clean behind it. Whosoever tries this plan will never try the old one again, for it prevents the possibility of burning the mush, and dispenses with all care and trouble except occasionally to replenish the water in which the pail is set to boil'' *Farmer and Mechanic*, April 1853.

Griddle, forged iron, 3 longish legs, long handle with hang-ing hole, found in Virginia, 11¹¹/₁₆'' diameter, overall length 23¼'', late 18th or early 19th C. **$300.00-$350.00**

• **1865** —''I looked over a whole batch of recipes sent in by readers, and though I don't doubt they are good of their kind, it is the kind that don't suit me. The only thing the title of which tempts me at all is **Johnny cake.** I open the recipe, and find that though the mixture may be good, it is baked in an oven ! Shade of my grandmother ! a Johnny cake in an oven ! Don't you see that when it is baked in an oven, though it may be something good, it isn't Johnny cake? That must be baked on the middle piece of the head of a flour barrel (Beach's brand preferred), with a hole in the north-east corner. The cake is placed on this, and set up against a flat iron in front of a bed of hickory coals, to bake, and nothing short of this can be Johnny cake — but as I sometime intend to make a cook-book, I won't say anything more about it. — If I do make a cook-book, I won't have any mince pies, any sausages, nor cakes, nor puddings, nor anything sweet, nor any saleratus; but just you wait and see what I do put in.'' A Bachelor, ''Household Department'', *American Agriculturist*, Feb. 1865.

Griddle, forged iron, to hang from crane, with bail handle and swivel ring at apex of arch of handle, American (?), 14½''D, 19th C. **$50.00-$75.00**

Jonakin, Jonikin or ''**Jonny Cake** derives its name from Jaunny, the name of Pequots and Narragansets for Maise or Indian Corn. As this was a new grain to the Pilgrims, they very naturally adopted the Indian name, and called the bread made of it Jaunny Cake. After these once powerful Indian tribes were destroyed and forgotten, the origin of this name was forgotten also, and from similarity of sound, became corrupted into Jonny Cake.'' *Journal of the American Institute*, NYC, March 1839, p.336. ''**Superior Johnny Cake.** — The following receipt will make a Johnny cake fit for an alderman, a mayor, an editor or any other dignitary in the land: Take one quart of milk, three eggs, one tea-spoonful saleratus, one tea cup of wheat flour and Indian meal, sufficient to make a batter to the consistency of pancakes. Bake quick in pans* previously buttered, and eat warm with butter or milk. The addition of wheat flour will be found a great improvement in the art of making these cakes.'' *The Farmers' Cabinet*, Aug. 1, 1836. (*The pans aren't further identified, although *Subject-Matter In-dex of Patents for Inventions*, has an intriguing early patent for a ''baking-iron'', records of which burned in 1836 or 1877: which was granted E. Skinner on Oct. 1, 1830 Was a baking-iron a Dutch oven with lid? a dripping pan? •

''**Journey Cake.** — Pour boiling water on a quart of meal, put in a little lard and salt, and mix it well; have an oak board with a rim of iron at the bottom, and an iron handle fastened to it that will prop it up to the fire; put some of the dough on it, dip your hand in cold water and smooth it over; score it with a knife, and set it before the coals to bake.'' Elizabeth Ellicott Lea, *Domestic Cookery*, 1859. •

''**Johnny-Cake.**— Sift one quart of Indian meal into a pan; make a hole in the middle, and pour in a pint of warm water, adding one teaspoon of salt; with a spoon mix the meal and water gradually into a soft dough; stir it very briskly for a quarter of an hour or more, till it becomes light and spongy; then spread the dough smooth and evenly on a straight, flat board (a piece of the head of a flour-barrel will serve for this purpose); place the board nearly upright before an open fire, and put an iron against the back to support it; bake it well; when done, cut it in squares; send it hot to table, split and buttered.''

Mary Stuart Smith, *Virginia Cookery-Book* (as reprinted in G. Strohm's 1888 *Universal Cookery Book*).

Griddle, rotating, wrought iron, long handle has heart shaped loop, 3 peg feet, American, 25"L, 19th C.
$175.00-$225.00

Griddle or girdle plate, also called a <u>backstone</u> (bakestone) in old inventories, forged iron, fixed bail handle with swivel ring, American, 10" diameter, 18th C.
$120.00-$150.00

Griddle or girdle plate, forged iron, fixed forged iron handle forms quarter circle hoop, swivel ring to hang from trammel or pot hook, 3 peg feet, American, 13" diameter, 18th C. • If Jonathan Winters were writing the copy for this, he'd make a crack about needing a girdle after you'd eaten a few of the flapjacks made on this, but actually <u>girdle</u> meaning <u>encircle</u> is the word origin. Transposition of letters, such as "r" and "i" to make girdle into griddle, was typical for the English language for centuries
$135.00-$165.00

Gridiron, cast iron, 3 legs, long handle, drip cup midway along handle, cast along back of handle is the name, each word looks as if it were carved on separate narrow plaques that could be used in the casting mold arranged in a horizontal line or stacked, depending on requirements of various castings, "Campbell Foundry Co.", Harrison, NJ, 28⅜"L x 16⅝"W, c.1850s. **$75.00-$100.00**

1884 Steak. — "Place the steak on a hot, well-greased gridiron, turn often so that the outside may be seared at once; when done, which will require from five to ten minutes, dish on a hot platter, season with salt and pepper and bits of butter....A small pair of tongs are best to turn steaks, as piercing with a fork frees the juices. If fat drips on the coals below, the blaze may be extinguished by sprinkling with salt, always withdrawing the gridiron to prevent the steak from acquiring a smoky flavor. Always have a brisk fire, whether you cook in a patent broiler directly over the fire, or on a gridiron over a bed of live coals....A steel gridiron with slender bars is best, as the common broad, flat iron bars fry and scorch the meat, imparting a disagreeable flavor." *Practical Housekeeping*, Minneapolis, 1884.

Gridiron, cast iron, enameled white inside, 3 legs, grease cup, "A. Kenrick & Sons", also either numeral 9 or 6, West Bromwich, England, 1½"H legs, 21¾"L including handle, mid to 3rd quarter 19th C. • **German vocabulary** — <u>Bratrost innen weiss emailliert</u>: gridiron, enameled inside. (The way the double <u>ess</u> at end of <u>weiss</u> is printed in German looks rather like a capital B.) **$75.00-$110.00**

Gridiron, cast iron, grease drip basin in back, 2 short front feet, short handle, American, 13" x 16", 19th C.
$75.00-$95.00

Gridiron, cast iron, grease trap and spouted to pour, grid is 10 runneled strips, 2 legs in front, 1 in back, shortish handle about 6"L, American (?), mid 19th C. **$35.00-$55.00**

"The Gridiron and Frying-Pan. <u>Results of their Rivalry in Domestic Cookery.</u> — Your favourite utensil,. the frying-pan, Eloise, is, without doubt, the most useful of all kitchen implements, and like a good-natured servant, is often imposed upon, and obliged to do all the work, while its companion, the gridiron, is quietly reposing in the chimney corner.

"The following scene was witnessed by those two faithful servants, the other afternoon, in a domestic establishment, where the sly dog of a gridiron often laughs between its bars at the overworked frying-pan.

"The husband...arrives home, and asks his wife what he can have for dinner, the hour of her dinner, and that of the children, having long passed. 'What would you like to have, my dear?' was her question.

'Anything you have.'

'Let's see! why — we have nothing, but I can get you a mutton chop, or steak.'

'Can I have nothing else; I am tired of chops and steaks.'

'Why, my dear, what can be better than a chop or a steak?'

'Well, let me have a steak.'

'You had that yesterday, my dear: now, let me get you a chop. I always make it my duty to study your comfort; and as I have been reading...a medical work on diseases of the skin in which it is said that nothing is so wholesome as a change of food, since which time I have made a point of varying our bill of fare....'

'Very well, send for two chops.' In about twenty minutes the servant returns, saying she could get no chops, but has got a nice piece of steak.

'Very well. That will do as well, will it not, my dear?' to her husband, who is reading a periodical.

'Yes; but how long will you keep me here before it is done?'

'Not a minute, my love. Now, Jane, do that well on the gridiron.' Jane descends (into the kitchen which is in the cellar). but quickly returns, saying, 'Please, ma'am, the fire is not fit for broiling.' 'Well, fry it,' is her answer. The husband, who hears it, exclaims, 'Drat the frying-pan, it is always so greasy.'

'Then, my dear, how would you like to have it.'

'Not at all,' was his reply, throwing down the paper, and exclaiming, 'Bother the place, there is no getting any victuals properly cooked here. I must go to the cook-shop and have it.'" Alexis Soyer, *A Shilling Cookery for the People*, London: George Routledge & Sons, 1854.

Gridiron, forged iron, almost square top with 12 very slightly concave bars, long front legs, back legs curved and much shorter, detachable grease catcher hooked along back edge, longish upcurved handle with large ring at end, American (?), grid is 11¼" x 12½", overall length 23", late 18th or early 19th C. **$350.00-$450.00**

Gridiron, forged iron, simple rectangular grid of flat bars, short leg in each corner, the hind legs are a bit shorter than the front, medium-length fishtail handle with grab bar along top, detachable grease catcher like hook-on trough along back edge, American, 17"W x 23"L overall, 18th C. **$500.00-$700.00**

Gridiron, or "<u>cooking furnace gridiron</u>" as the inventor called it. Round, has runneled (or concave) bars or ribs, gravy trough "all around, on the outer edge, having a spout on one side for discharging the gravy," handle on one side. "It may be made of cast-iron, or wrought, or sheet-iron, or any other material, and may be varied in form, size, or shape, as convenience may require, with, or without legs, for so I make them," wrote the inventor, Jonathan Powers, Lansingburgh, Rensselaer County, NY, who pat'd it Aug. 10, 1829. • The Editor of the *Journal of the Franklin Institute* commented about this gridiron: "We are again at a loss to know what is intended to be patented. It certainly cannot be a round gridiron, as these have been made by the thousand. The fluted, or concave bars, and gravy trough, we have known for upwards of forty years (ie. c.1780s): these, therefore, are not new. But, as the patentee has not chosen to tell his claim, it is not our business to do so; we therefore leave the discovery to others.'' It would obviously be hard to know if you'd found a Powers' gridiron, but I include all this as instructive of workings of the patent office, and of the infinite potential for finding interesting pieces, perhaps signed somewhere. **$150.00-$200.00**

Gridiron, wrought iron, 2 penny feet plus foot at base of long handle, fixed grid, New England, 2¼''H x 19 18/''L, late 18th or early 19th C. **$145.00-$175.00**

Gridiron, wrought iron, 4 small peg feet, long handle, American, 10½'' x 11'' rectangle, with 11''L handle, early 19th C. **$120.00-$135.00**

Grill, or broiler, forged iron, large square with shaped flat forged iron handle with rattail, the bars alternating plain with little loops & hearts, the whole giving an effect of iron ribbon cleverly tied, French or Belgian, or poss. French Canadian, about 12'' square, handle 10''L, late 18th C (?). **$800.00-$1000.00**

Grill, revolving or rotary, wrought iron with fleur de lis pattern formed by flat bars of iron making the grill's surface with unusual scalloped ''fence'' or edge around circumference, short penny feet, European, prob. French, 10'' diameter, 18½''L overall with handle, 18th C. **$250.00-$350.00**

Grill, rotating, wheel-like grill with radiating spokes fairly close together, lubricating grease cup below center pivot pin, ''Y'' handle, the 2 arms supporting the grill, plus nice long handle with grease catching cup, forged iron, 3 feet, American, 13½'' diameter, 25''L overall, 18th C. **$300.00-$450.00**

Grisette, wrought iron, long canoe-shaped rather shallow bowl, with long forged iron handle set at right angles from middle of long axis, the handle terminating in a right angle bend forming a supporting leg, this was used in the 18th C for dipping lengths of rush into melted fat, to coat the stalks as crude ''candles'', American, ''boat'' bowl is 7''L x 3''W x 1'' deep, handle 21''L, 18th C. Confusable.— This is here only because it could be mistaken for some kind of fish cooker or cooking ladle. **$550.00-$700.00**

Gypsy pot or kettle, cast iron, with 3 casting ribs around circumference, cast in part mold, American, 11¾''H x 12⅞'' diameter, early 19th or late 18th C. **"Preparing Homminy for the Table.**— It must be thoroughly washed in cold water, rubbing it well with the hands; then washed in the same way in warm water, changing the water several times. Put it into a large pot of cold water, and boil steadily eight or ten hours, keeping it closely covered. Add hot water frequently while boiling, otherwise the homminy will burn and be dark colored. When homminy beans are used, one pint to a gallon of homminy, to be put in when the homminy is put on. If it is put on the first thing in the morning, and kept briskly boiling, it will be ready for dinner at two o'clock. Season with butter and send it to the table hot. (These pints were all measured with the common tin cup.)'' *The Farmers'*

Cabinet, Devoted to Agriculture, Horticulture and Rural Economy. Philadelphia: Vol. II, No. 1, Aug. 1, 1837. **$275.00-$325.00**

Hake, forged iron, an ''S'' hook for hanging pots or kettles from crane, American (?), 6''L, 18th or early 19th C. With these, the best you could hope for would be something zoomorphic, for example, the hook ending in a snake's head or dog's head. Multiply price below by 20 if you should find such a thing. **$15.00-$18.00**

Ham hook, or meat hook, braided wrought iron, with eye at top and but one hook. Sides or large cuts of meat (such as hams) were hung in smokehouse from these. Sometimes the meat was rubbed in ashes, or wrapped in cloth. American (?), late 18th, early 19th C. • A handsome one with braided wrought iron and 4 hooks, formerly in the Keillor Collection, was found in the chimney of a house built in Plymouth, MA in 1711. It is 7½''L and the hooks reach out 10''W. It would be worth half as much without provable provenance, but probably more with solid identification. **$75.00-$200.00**

Hearth warming shelf, wrought iron bracket, hung on nails in side of fireplace, American, 9''H x 13''W, 18th C. These are extremely rare, and might be mistaken for regular wall bracket shelves. **$150.00-$185.00**

Hoes, forged iron, broad-bladed, without their long wooden handles, sometimes struck with maker's mark, American, 19th C. **$10.00-$25.00**

Looking at a modern hoe, it is not easy to imagine propping one up at such a slant in front of the fire that a corn cake could actually be slapped upon it and baked. But the 19th C had a variety of hoes, for purposes such as weeding or grubbing, with shanks set at different angles, and blades of different dimensions. Hoes varied from region to region too. I have not yet seen a perfect description of a hoe suitable for hoe cakes. **"Virginia Hoe Cake.**— Pour warm water on a quart of Indian meal; stir in a spoonful of lard or butter, some salt, make it stiff, and work it for 10 minutes; have a board about the size of a barrel head, (or the middle piece of the head will answer,) wet the board with water, and spread on the dough with your hand; place it before the fire; prop it aslant with a flat-iron, bake it slowly; when one side is nicely brown, take it up and turn it, by running a thread between the cake and the board, then put it back, and let the other side brown. These cakes used to be baked in Virginia on a large iron hoe, from whence they derive their name.'' Elizabeth E. Lea, *Useful Receipts and Hints to Young Housekeepers*, 10th ed., Baltimore, 1859 (1st ed. 1851). • E. Scott Boyce, in *Economic and Social History of Chowan County, North Carolina*, 1880-1915, published by Columbia University, 1917, wrote about this odd cooking utensil of the 1880s: ''The '**hoe-cake**' — a pone of cornbread baked on a hoe that had already lived out is usefulness as a farm utensil — in Chowan had not yet passed into the realms of fiction.'' (p.223).

Hook, forged iron, 4 points, flattened, dealer Dorothy Lyon said she was told it was used for roasting small game birds and the flattened ends were supposed to keep the juices from dripping, American, prob. Richmond, VA, 9''L, late 18th or early 19th C. **$90.00-$110.00**

Hot water kettle—See Tea kitchens.

Jack & spit, standing floor model clockwork jack, timer bell, vertical oblong housing for works, lion's paw feet to 4 short legs, carrying handle on top, cast iron & steel, cranked to wind, can motivate 3 long spits, one end hooked to jack, other supported on wrought iron stand, French, 48''H, early 19th C. • I don't know maker of this, it's not marked, but another French one, with clockworks inside a small 4 legged pedestal base, that drives a spit in a tin reflector oven with rounded back, and tapered tubular tin legs, was made in the mid 19th C by Viville of Paris. Not only did the spit turn, but some system of ''rotating spoons'' kept basting the meat as it turned. The clockwork has bells that ring when it's winding down. It was exhibited at an antique show in 1988 by Larry Melvin, Springfield, OH, who was asking $950.00 for it then.

$800.00-$1200.00

Kettle, also found spelled cettell, or kittel in old records, this one of cast iron, 3 short feet, slightly flared out sides, reinforced with one inch wide wrought iron band near top, American (?), 7½''H, 18th C. Every once in a while you see such pieces with the wrought band, which may be as narrow as ⅜''. $70.00-$90.00

Kettle, cast iron with 3 legs, heavy twisted forged iron bail handle, domed lid, 3 longish feet, circumferential ribs or ridges, type that looks like a ''gypsy kettle'', American, 6¼''H x 4¼'' diameter, late 18th C. I have read of a 17th & 18th C practice called ''kettlin the roads'', which involved dragging iron kettles and pots behind a sleigh in order to destroy the potentially dangerous slick iced-over tracks of sleigh runners on snowy roads. $275.00-$300.00

Kettle, cast iron, with 3 legs, rare in this small size, American, only 4''H, early 19th C. $125.00-$150.00

Kettle, with lid, heavy copper with wrought iron swing handle, slightly convex bottom, meant to hang on a fireplace crane, American (?), 15''D, early 19th C. •
Lookalike alarm. — Lehman's Hardware & Appliances, 4779 Kidron Rd., Kidron, OH 44636 offer a full range of hammered copper kettles with extra bottoms brazed in, cast iron or cast brass lug ears, and steel bail handles, in their 1989 ''Non-Electric Good Neighbor Amish Country'' catalog. These are ''apple butter'' and ''flat bottom'' kettles; the former come in 8, 10, 12, 15, 20, 25, 30, 40 and 50 gallon capacities, from about $150.00 to $450.00. I believe the stamped trademark is ''MAKERS'' on the side. The flat bottom kettles come in 1, 2, 4, 6, 8, 10 quart sizes, and 3, 5 and 8 gallon. They have a ''tough, tarnish & weather-resistent polyurethan coating'' which must be removed with paint remover for cooking. • Price range is for fairly small antiques; $$$ goes up in quantum leaps for large ones. $120.00-$150.00

Kettle tilter, also called a tipper or a lazy elbow, wrought iron, no marks, English or American, late 18th C.

$165.00-$200.00

Kettle tilter, forged iron, monkey-tail handle, American or English, 19½''L, 18th C. $145.00-$170.00

Kettle tilter, forged iron, nice swivel loop to hang from hook, pleasantly curved handle, American or English, hard to measure exactly, but about 8½''H x 14''L, 18th or early 19th C. $250.00-$300.00

Kettle tilter, forged iron, swivel ring and brass knob on end of curved handle, poss. American, more prob. English, 21''L, 18th or early 19th C. $325.00-$350.00

Kettle tilter, forged iron, swivel ring top with acorn finial, nice swoopy thin handle, American (?), about 13'' across, late 18th or early 19th C. $350.00-$425.00

Kettle tilter, wrought iron, used to assist the cook in pouring from a heavy kettle (especially a tea kettle or hot water kettle) suspended over a fire in the hearth, these were also called idle backs, American or English, about 13'' to 15''L, 18th or early 19th C. $300.00-$500.00

Mantel ornaments, or candle reflectors, a pair of flat easel-back cutouts in shape of milk jugs, spouts facing each other, English, 6½''H, early 19th C. $150.00-$225.00

Meat hook, forged iron with 4 graceful hooks, ring for hanging at top. Made from 2 twisted lengths of bar iron, heated & pounded together. Could be from anywhere; no stylistic details to tie to a country, 24''H; each hook 7¼''H, prob. late 1700s, early 1800s. • Hard to date. So many turn up, you wonder if somebody has a blacksmith in the backyard. • **The Smoke-house of Col. M'Allister in 1828,** Fort Turner, on the Susquehanna, above Harrisburg. ''A convenience worthy of imitation,'' reported visitor Judge Buel. ''The Smoke-house was a wooden octagon building, perhaps 16 feet in diameter, perfectly tight, except the door-way. The peculiarities of this building were, it was set a foot or more above the ground, and was perfectly dry, and bacon, hams, &c., were kept hanging around its walls all summer without becoming damp or mouldy, or being injured by flies; and in the second place, no fire was admitted into the building, the smoke being conveyed into it through a tube from the outside, where it was generated.'' *The Farmers' Cabinet, Vol. I, No. 1,* Philadelphia, July 1, 1836.

$55.00-$75.00

Mulling iron, forged iron, wooden handle, paddle-like end, American (?), 16''L, 18th or early 19th C. $75.00-$100.00

Mulling iron, wrought iron, a hook at one end, a sort of curved blade, almost a paddle, at the other end, English or American, 18''L, 18th or 19th C. $75.00-$100.00

Peels—See Implements chapter.

Plate warmer, sheet iron cabinet, tall and cylindrical with door, small chamber at bottom with air vents, but no access for putting in charcoal, so the air vents probably just helped draw hot air from hearth up into cylinder, American (?), 3 feet H x 13'' diameter, early 19th C.

$275.00-$350.00

Plate warmer, sheet iron with original red paint with flowers in ochre, cast brass side handles, elegant slim cast iron cabriole legs with penny feet, arched top, door, American or English, 32''H, c.1800 to 1830.

$400.00-$550.00

Plate warmer, wire & forged iron, concentric wire rings form platform, meant to hang in fireplace, American (?), 15'' diameter, 19th C. $175.00-$225.00

Plate warming cabinet, japanned sheet metal with domed top, shaped like a firescreen, 2 wire shelves inside, in F. A. Walker catalog, American (?), c.1870s. $150.00-$250.00

Plate warming cabinet, sheet iron with cast iron legs bolted on, brass side handles, most of japanned and painted decoration burned off long ago, 3 shelves, nice back door (facing out to room) & open of course in front though braced with bars of metal, prob. made at the Usk, Monmouthshire works in Wales, 28½''H x 13¼''W, c.1800- to 1815. $375.00-$450.00

Plate warming cabinet, tin & cast iron, 3 well shaped cabriole legs with lion's paw feet, pretty much open at top with wide inner lip, only one shelf, side handles, no door, American (?), about 28"H, early 19th C. **$275.00-$400.00**

Plate warming cabinet, japanned tin with bronzed cast iron decorative trim, high cast iron cabriole legs, lion's paw feet, English (?), 30"H x 15"W, 19th C. **$275.00-$400.00**

Plate warming cabinets, japanned tin with high cabriole cast iron legs & side handles, back (or front) open to fire or stove, plates & dishes heated on shelves inside, from F. A. Walker catalog, made by various companies, American & English, about 25" to 30"H, c.1870s. **$275.00-$400.00**

Posnet, cast iron, 3 feet, slightly upslanted side handle, no mark, American, 5"H x 5"D, early early 19th C. The way to collect these is to look for variations in handles and feet, or to get a range of sizes (maybe starting with the darling miniature ones about 2½"H), or — and this appeals most to me — to get only repaired ones. **$55.00-$125.00**

Posnet, cast iron, rather shallow, with 3 short legs and long handle, American, 3"H including legs, 7"D bowl plus 6" handle, 18th C. **$100.00-$125.00**

Posnet or skillet, bell metal, long handle, 3 peg feet, "Austin & Crocker," Boston, MA, 18th C. Sold at the 1980 Garbisch collection auction for $3100.00. I just don't believe it would make that price today, partly for lack of such a prestigous and renowned collector (at least of folk arts), but will just record the price as it was then. **$3100.00**

Posnet or skillet, cast bell metal or bronze, 3 legged with long handle, used like a saucepan, marked "Wasbrough No. 6", 7"H x 7½"D with 11½"L handle, 5¼"H legs, 18th or very early 19th C. **$375.00-$425.00**

Posnet or skillet, cast bell metal, 3 legs, longish handle, marked "Wasbrough No. 2", 15"L, early 19th C. **$325.00-$400.00**

Posnet or skillet, cast iron, 3 legs, long handle, repaired in very entertaining way: one leg seems to have dropped out, leaving hole (?) or else broke off, and hole was ground out, then a bolt was stuck through the hole with a washer, and it was all hammered up around to fit the curve of the pot, then a pin, sort of like the cotter pin idea, was driven through a hole in the bolt to hold it tightly in place, American, 5¼" diameter, with handle 11¹¹⁄₁₆"L, legs are 1¼"H, early 19th C. • I love things like this, but paid only $19.00 for it. I honestly don't know if I would have bought it if it had been much more; I have very deep pockets but very short arms when it comes to collecting. My advice is go for the old old repairs, as they are truly unique and add worlds of romance to a piece. **$30.00-$50.00**

Skillet or Posnet? Both the posnet and skillet were used rather like sauce pans. A posnet is probably the smaller of the two. You do not find clear distinctions in old inventories or even cookery books, and certainly no exact sizes given anywhere. • Alice Morse Earle, writing in a chapter called "Table Plenishings", in *Customs & Fashions in Old New England* (NY: Scribner's, 1893) has rather a lot to say about posnets: "A similar vessel (to the porringer), frequently handleless, was what was spelt, in various colonial documents, posned, possnet, posnett, porsnet, pocneit, posnert, possenette, postnett, and parsnett. It is derived from the Welsh *posned*, a porringer

or little dish. In 1641 Edward Skinner left a 'Postnett' by will; this was apparently of pewter. In 1653 Governor Haynes, of Hartford, left an 'Iron Posnet' by will. In the inventory of the estate of Robert Daniel, of Cambridge, in 1655, we learn that 'a Little Porsenett' of his was worth five shillings. In 1693 Governor Caleb Carr, of Providence, bequeathed to his wife a 'silver possnet & the cover belonging to it.' By these records we see that posnets were of various metals, and sometimes had covers. I have found no advertisements of them in early American newspapers, even with all their varied array of utensils and vessels. I fancy the name fell quickly into disuse in this country." p. 141.

Posnet or skillet, cast iron, 3 tall tapered legs, long handle, marked "N. S." (possibly Nathaniel Starbuck), American, 12"L including handle, 18th or very early 19th C. **$115.00-$135.00**

Posnet or skillet, cast iron, nice deep bowl with 3 legs, flat top handle, American, 5½"H x 6⅝"diameter plus 6½" handle, 18th C. **$135.00-$150.00**

Pot, also found spelled pott in old records, this one cast iron, bulbous body, 3 legs, with cast iron cover with generous curved loop handle, wrought bail handle, straight sprue mark on bottom, American (?), unusual heighth to width ratio: 10"H x 8"D, 18th C. This is a wonderful piece offered for sale several years ago by Clara Jean Davis of Concord, NH. She loves old iron and it shows in the pieces she finds. **$140.00-$175.00**

Pot, cast iron, with lid, oval shape with plump rounded sides, forged bail handle, English (?), or poss. American, about 11"L the major axis, late 18th or early 19th C. **$90.00-$135.00**

• A NYC importer named George Ball advertised in the newspaper in 1775 that he had just received some "useful and wholesome iron utensils, so much recommended by physicians for their safety, and so generally and justly preferred to copper, by all the best housekeepers in England, for two of the best reasons in the world, viz. that they are entirely free from that dangerous, poisonous property [verdigris], from which so many fatal accidents have been known to arise amongst those who use copper vessels, and because they never want tinning...." He goes on to enumerate the imports, including "Tea kettles from three quarts to six, four-gallon pots with covers, to five quarts, Pie pans, two gallon oval pots, stew pans and covers, of several different sizes, Fish kettles of six different sizes, with strainers, Saucepans, from six quarts to one pint. For cabin use on board of shipping, they are far preferable to copper, as no danger (however careless the cook, or long the voyage) can possibly happen from using them, as too often has through these causes, from the use of copper. They are all wrought according to the most approved pattern now used in London...." Ball had no doubt of a warm, anglophilic reception to his ad: the British used New York City as its base of operations during the Revolutionary War from 1776 to 1783. New York had been a British stronghold since the 1660s, after taking over from the Dutch; about two thirds of the population was either British or Loyalist. The New York area did become the site for many battles between Americans fighting for independence and British forces.

Pot, "gypsy kettle" type with globular body, sometimes called a bulge pot (as it was in some founders' price lists), flared rim, pitted cast iron, 2 lug handles of triangular shape with "elbows" that are almost straight out from side and partly curved inside, 3 circumferential or horizontal mold rings on belly and one around flared neck, as well as a "latitudinal" or vertical casting line from the "equatorial line" to the rim on both sides between the handles, long casting gate on bottom, 3 tapered legs that are flat on side facing in and deeply rounded on outside, this example with beautiful especially high, full half-circle wrought bail, which — when up — exactly copies the curve of the unusually large and high arched handle riveted to the flat, hammered sheet iron lid, which is probably original. No mark, American, 7⅛"H x 7¾" diameter at top, legs are 1⅝"H, late 18th or early 19th C. • For me, a good deal of the charm (and value) of this particular pot lies in the lid, and the matched arches of lid and bail.   **$60.00-$80.00**

• **The most authoritative writing** — all new books included — I've found **on dating old iron pots and kettles** was done by John D. Tyler, Curator of Science, Industry, and Technology at the Pennsylvania Historical and Museum Commission. He wrote two similar articles, one in *The Magazine ANTIQUES*, Aug. 1971, and another in the April 1978 *Early American Life*. The latter is somewhat more helpful, because it has a chart of the lug or ear handles. Both have a lot of information tying English and American technology to evidence found on the pots themselves — casting mold & seam lines, and sprues & gates (the former round and older, the latter a narrow oblong) evidence of where molten iron was poured into the molds. Tyler says that the rounded legs are typically American; the "triangular" ones English. We can all wish there were a Tyler book to read and reread.

Pot bail, wrought iron, 2 curved arms with hooks on end, forming a sort of wishbone shape, used to hook under ears of kettle or pot, for lifting. 14"L, late 18th or early 19th C. • With a huge iron pot full of boiling food, I'd hate to have to depend on a pot bail. Besides childbirth, accidents at the hearth — especially catching on fire, or other burns — caused most women's deaths in the 18th C.   **$60.00-$80.00**

"**To extinguish Ladies' Clothes, catching Fire.**— We often hear, and read in newspapers, when one of those deplorable accidents has happened, which generally deprive us of the youthful and most lovely of our kind, dry recommendations, that ladies, whose dresses may catch fire, should lie down. This, though undoubtedly the right method of extinguishing a flame, is better illustrated, and imprinted more deeply on our recollection, by the following experiment. Take two pieces of muslin, (the article which usually catches fire), or paper, or any other light ignitable substance, and having set on fire the lower part of both, hold one piece upright , as female dresses are worn; it will burn out in about one minute, blazing up to a great height, where the neck and face may be supposed to be burnt. Meantime, fling the other piece of burning muslin on the ground; it will burn slowly, the flame at no time ascending more than an inch or two, and although the burning article might not be moved — as must happen when a living person is enveloped in it — nearly ten minutes would elapse before it would be consumed. In short, it is evident that a perpendicular female dress, though fifty feet high, would burn out with a destructive flame in less time than a single yard of the same material laid in a horizontal position. It results, therefore, from the foregoing experiment, that as soon as a lady's dress is discovered to be on fire, she should instantly lie down; and she may then call for assistance, or confidently set about extinguishing the flame herself. N.B. A current of air always prevails near the floor, particularly between the door and fire-place, and therefore it must be kept in mind, not to run out of the room, nor to open a window, in such cases, as that would be fatal." *The Young Man's Book of Amusement, Containing the Most Interesting and Instructive Experiments in Various Branches of Science.* London: 1850.

Pot chain, forged iron, to hang pot over fire, hook at each end, 25 nice big round links, by using the hooks in different ways the effectual length of the chain is changed, could be American or European, 41"L, 18th C.
                    $65.00-$85.00

• A **superstition** reported in William Hone's *The Year Book* (London, 1845 edition), reports: "Professor Playfair, in a letter to Mr. Brand, dated St. Andrew's, January 26, 1801, mentioning the superstitions of his neighborhood, says: "... mischievous elves cannot enter into a house at night, if, before bed-time, the lower end of the crook, or iron chain, by which a vessel is suspended over the fire, be raised up a few links.'"

Pot hooks, also called racking crooks, forged iron "S", hooked over pot chain, trammel, crane, or other pot hook, with a bail-handle or hoop-handle kettle, pot or griddle hung from the lower crook. Alice Morse Earle, in *Customs & Fashions in Old New England* (1893), writes "In earlier days the great lug-pole (made of green wood, to withstand the heat & flames), or, as it was called in England, the back-bar, stretched from ledge to ledge, or lug to lug, high up the yawning chimney, and held a motley collection of pot-hooks and trammels, of gib-crokes (or jib-crooks), twicrokes, and hakes, which in turn suspended at various heights over the fire, pots, and kettles and other cooking utensils" (p.130). Cotrall is another term. American or European, from about 6"L to 9"L, any age up to end of 19th C. • **Reproduction alert.**— I suspect many of the ones found laid out on the hopsacking for the unwary are newly forged. Look at the "grain" of the beaten iron, the texture, and particularly the two tips, which should not look as if they'd been snipped off with very powerful cutters. The blacksmith of the past might have used pincers, but would have cut then hammered again to finish the tips. • If you ever see a pot hook with a snake's head, buy it. (And sell it to me?) • Some of Earle's terms are not to be found in 19th C dictionaries and glossaries of Americanisms, of which I have not a few. I believe croke is a corruption of crook, and a gib-croke would be a side hook. I think twicroke could be either a 2 hooked crook, or possibly a twisted hook. A hake is a kind of fish, but possibly it is here a corruption of hook.   **$6.00-$12.00**

Pot lid, copper with relatively short forged iron handle with hanging hole chiseled out, leather, wood or horn gasket to insulate iron handle where it is riveted to the lid, copper rivets, tinned inside, raised edge to fit saucepan rim, marked "M. W".; inventory numbers "226, 7225, 2573"; plus initial "E" scratched lightly on surface near handle, English, 6¾" diameter, 3⅝"L handle, early 19th C. • Another one marked "M. W".', bought at same time, is much smaller (4½" diameter with 2½"L handle), and has one number the same, "7225", with some scratchmarks under the first 2 making it look like a "5", and a small "6" under the long number, probably left over from some other time, plus the "E". • It was only when closely examining these lids, which my mother has owned for years, preparatory to photographing them and writing these descriptions, that I noticed the faint scratched inventory numbers, and the heat-insulating gasket on the larger one. <u>Close examination when you clean or draw something seems to work better to uncover unnoticed details than just looking at it</u>. That is, until you learn how to look. A Zen technique for approaching life is called a "don't know" attitude, and this open-minded, "don't know" until-you-find-it-out approach works when buying antiques or clothes or cars or anything.

$22.00-$30.00

Collector Tip. — You know those little black plastic hooks that some socks come attached to at the store? Well, don't let the cashier throw them away. They are perfect for hooking over wrought iron dutch crown pot racks to hold extra pieces that aren't too heavy.

Pot lifter, forged iron, wooden handle, early 19th C.

$55.00-$75.00

Pot lifter, wrought iron, 2 hinged arms ending in inward bent flat & wide hooks that could fit under outside lip of pot or kettle, or under some types of ear handles, American, prob. PA, 15"L each arm, 18th C.

$95.00-$155.00

Pot lifter, wrought iron, 2 hinged & slightly curved arms with hooks at ends, meant to fit any size pot or vessel with ear handles, American (?), each arm 13"L, 18th or very early 19th C.

$65.00-$80.00

Pot or kettle lifter, forged iron, 2 long arms twisted partway for tensile strength, hung on ring, arms end in curved pieces that act as your curved fingers would to fit under rim of pot, Pennsylvania, 17⅛"L, mid to late 18th C.

$165.00-$200.00

Pot pusher, forged iron, 3 legs and curled handle, semi-circle cradles pot and makes it easy to push pot steadily and farther into the hot coals on floor of fireplace, rather ornate, American (?), 5"H x 6"W, 18th C. Very simple ones, with no detailing, go for between $40.00 and $60.00. The fancier ones, perhaps with interesting long handles or good penny feet are:

$165.00-$200.00

Pot pusher, wrought iron, chiseled zigzag decoration on handle, English or poss. American, 6⅛"W at farthest reach of 2 arms, which means it wouldn't push a very big pot, early 19th C or late 18th C.

$85.00-$95.00

Pot pusher, wrought iron, pot-fitting wide open "horseshoe" of iron, with the ends bent into legs, short twisted handle supported by another leg, used to push posnets or bulge pots or other cooking vessels deeper into the coals or hot ashes. The height, of course, couldn't be so great as to push against the pot above about the lower third of its height. American (?), 3½"H x 7¼"W x 9"L including handle, 18th C or very early 19th C.

$120.00-$170.00

Potato rake, for pulling potatoes from ashes in fireplace, (or some kind of scraping tool, like for scraping out pumpkins), forged iron, straight toothed blade curved

around so it would fit inside something like a pumpkin, longish handle with rattail end, American (?), 13"L, early 19th C. In Henry David Thoreau's 1854 *Walden, or Life in the Woods*, in the "House-Warming" chapter, we read "The next winter (1846) I used a small cooking-stove for economy, since I did not own the forest; but it did not keep fire so well as the open fire-place. Cooking was then, for the most part, no longer a poetic, but merely a chemic process. It will soon be forgotten, in these days of stoves, that we used to roast potatoes in the ashes, after the Indian fashion. The stove not only took up room and scented the house, but it concealed the fire, and I felt as if I had lost a companion. You can always see a face in the fire."

$145.00-$165.00

Reflecting oven, small, tin, horizontal blimp shape, 4 V strap legs, crank for spit at one end, 2 strap carrying handles on top, oval hinged lift-down door in back to check progress of food, English or German, 12½"H x 14"L exclusive of crank, late 19th C. • The dealer had a lot of late 19th C containerload metal German stuff, all of it rusted. And I saw several of these in one 2 day antiquing trip in Pennsylvania, so am supposing that they have recently arrived on these shores and are getting out there in the antiquing boonies.

$35.00-$55.00

Reflector oven, called a <u>Yankee baker</u> by Henry Thoreau, sheet iron, has a crank spit, grease spout to pour off accumulation in bottom and 4 feet, American, 11"W, 19th C.

$250.00-$300.00

Reflector oven, heavy tin plates soldered together, with spit, strap handle and strap legs at each corner, basting door in back, American, 16"H x 20"L, late 18th or early 19th C.

$350.00-$450.00

Reflector oven, heavy tin, with spit, American, 17"H x 25"L, 19th C. If you want to read a very old-fashioned but sweet storybook, featuring as the protagonist one of these neat old reflecting ovens, look for *The Tin Kitchen*, by J. Hatton Weeks, published in New York and Boston by Thomas Y. Crowell & Co., in 1896. The protagonist — a tin kitchen — relates the job of cooking an old gander as brown and juicy as possible for the parson's visit.

$100.00-$125.00

Reflector oven, tin, meant for biscuits, with 2 shallow shelves, American, 14"W, c.1840 to 1850. **$100.00-$150.00**

Reflector oven, tin, spit and spout, 4 legs, American, 17"H x 19"W, 19th C.

$200.00-$250.00

Reflector oven, tin, with strap handles on top, 4 strap legs, spit & crank handle, "back door" for basting, American, 10"H x 12"L, 1830s-40s. In many old cookbooks, these are confusingly also called "Dutch ovens". **$350.00-$450.00**

Reflector oven or tin kitchen, heavy sheet tin, cranked spit, door in back, 4 short strap legs, pour-off grease spout at side bottom, American, 18"W, 19th C. **$350.00-$450.00**

In 1797, a Tin Plate worker by the name of Dewsbury Crawley, of New York City, advertised in the paper that "a very capital improvement (has been made) on the tin roasting ovens so universally in use, by making easy what was thought the most difficult task in using them, (the former mode of basting) which by the improvement is done on the top by means of a hopper and strainer, which causes the fat to drip gradually on the victuals roasting." I've never seen one; I'm sure we could recognize it by the built-in hopper and strainer in the top. • At the time Crawley was working, tin was imported in small plates, measuring about 8″ x 14″, from Wales for the most part. This is why really early tin kitchens are made of pieced-together plates if they are over 14″L. For more (conflicting) <u>information on sizes of tin plate</u>, look at the long entry under 2 coffee pot entries in Coffee Chapter, • Carl W. Dreppard, in *A Dictionary of American Antiques*, (Doubleday, 1952), calls the tin kitchen an "American oven", and says it was invented here in America c.1790.

Reflector oven or tin kitchen, heavy sheet tin large cylinder, on 4 high iron legs, spit crank in side, hinged door in back for basting, etc., not marked, 38″H, c.1820s to 1840s. **$450.00-$600.00**

Reflecting Ovens & Dutch Ovens. — You will find in some early cookbooks & other writings, as well as ads by some 20th C dealers, that a tin kitchen reflecting oven is sometimes called a Dutch oven. The underlying meaning of "substitute for oven" makes both uses appropriate. I use "Dutch oven" only for a cast iron kettle with a lid with raised edges. Recently I found that John Russell Bartlett defined Dutch oven in the 1889 (4th) edition of his *Dictionary of Americanisms*, whereas he did not in the 1859 (2nd) edition. Bartlett writes, **"Dutch Oven.** A tin screen placed before a kitchen range, or open wood fire, within which is the meat to be roasted." He doesn't define tin kitchen in either edition. • An English book from the 1860s, in its American edition of 1870, has three line engravings of types of reflecting ovens. **(1)** "The well-known Dutch oven" is a reflecting oven with a rounded back and sides, therefore having a half-circle "footprint". "It is usually made with a little dripping-pan in the bottom, and it has a (slotted) shelf in the middle to place anything upon that requires to be warmed or browned; a small meat cut, or a bird, may be roasted by removing this shelf, and suspending the article by one of the hooks, which are made to turn to expose the different sides of the meat." **(2)** Next "The Yorkshire oven"... differing from the Dutch in "being higher in proportion to its width, giving more room for anything suspended to be roasted; and by a slit in the handle, the meat may be moved farther from the fire, or nearer to it. There is likewise a door in the back for access to the meat. The shelf is only placed occasionally. ..." The back side of this one is flat, and it is the top that is a rounded arch from side to side. **(3)** Last is "The American oven ... an improvement on the Dutch. By means of a bottom slanting upward, and the top slanting downward, the reflection of heat is still stronger. In this case, the meat, or other article, is laid in an iron tray, which is movable, and may be lifted out by two handles, the top (of the oven) moving back on hinges; beneath the false bottom is a place for warming plates. This apparatus is coming much into use, being found extremely convenient for roasting & baking bread, cakes, &c." American collectors usually see types (1) and (3), especially the slanted one. It may not always have a slanted bottom, with a hidey-hole or sort of plate shed behind.

Reflector oven or tin kitchen, tin, angled "reflective" back, strap handle and 2 strap back legs, front legs twisted wire, extentions of the wire that went around edge of whole body, over which tin was folded at the edge, pouring spout at bottom right, forged iron spit, American, 14″W, mid 19th C. **$275.00-$350.00**

• A utensil suitable for summer, or shipboard or camp cooking, was the <u>Salisbury portable kitchen</u>, an enclosed brazier Invented in 1780 by an Englishman, William Redman. He described it thus: "For roasting, boiling, or baking of any kind of provision. The body or furnace is made oval or round, of wrought or cast iron, tin or copper. Within it is placed a grate for the fire, and in the upper part a pot for boiling with water or steam, or a plate for baking. Underneath the fire is a vacuity open in the front, serving as a receptacle for the ashes and admitting a current of air to pass through the fire, thereby carrying off any smoke or dust through a tube or funnell affixed. A front is fixed to the furnace before the fire, which joins close to a reflector, purposely to confine the heat so as to roast and boil, or do either separately with a very small quantity of fire. The reflector is made of tin, brass, or copper. A spit goes through it, and at the bottom a dripping pan is so fixed as to draw off the gravy, that the meat may be easily basted at a door which is made on the top or any convenient part. A gridiron may be fixed occasionally in the place of the spit for broiling, with an additional reflector placed obliquely underneath it, or occasionally an iron plate may be placed in the reflector for the purpose of baking. They may also be made with two reflectors, to fix to the same body, for roasting two or more joints at once." *Abridgments of Specifications Relating to Cooking, Bread-Making, and the Preparation of Confectionery A.D. 1634-1866.* London: Office of the Commissioner of Patents, abridged edition, 1873.

Revolving toaster, or <u>toe toaster</u>, so-called because instead of having to lean over to turn the toast, you could just give it a tap with your foot. Forged iron, with unusual sprouted corn stalk-shaped supports for the bread, within the double arches more commonly found, American, late 18th or early 19th C. I learned the toe toaster term by accident, watching an episode of "Reading Rainbow" in August 1987, which featured a visit to Sturbridge Village in Massachusetts. **$250.00-$350.00**

Revolving toaster, wrought iron with 2 sets of double arches, nice handle with hanging eye, American, 19″L, early 19th C. **$250.00-$350.00**

Roaster, steel, iron & brass, square shaft, fully adjustable for distance to fire, hung over grate, handle unscrews, 6 hooks, English (?), approx. 18¼″L, early 19th C. **$240.00-$265.00**

Roaster, wrought iron vertical frame with penny feet, adjustable hooked rack, brass finials, "Bainbridge", English or American, 31″H, dated June 22, 1833. • Not a patent date, because that year June 22 was Sunday, and patents aren't issued on Sunday no matter what country. The name sort of "sounds English", but lots of 18th & 19th C American names did too! A cursory search of the index to the *Official Patent Gazette*, for numbered & unnumbered patents, fails to turn up a Bainbridge. **$600.00-$700.00**

Roasting fork—See Implement chapter.

Roasting hooks, bipartite hinged curved bars, with leg at each end and one close to pivot point, with 3 hooks dependent from each bar, plus a hook as part of each of the 3 legs, called by the dealer a "bird roaster", but hard to see quite how it would work, as the ends of the hooks are too close to the bottom for much to hang off them. Can be put into sort of half circle with hooks inside, or flying-bird V, perhaps made to fit inside a certain drip pan? American (?), 9½''H x about 33''L, 18th C. • **Price Paid For Provenance.**— These are Ex-Colonial Williamsburg Foundation Collection, offered for sale by dealer Gail Lettick, in 1988. Value range below is not hers. I have not taken into account potential added value accruing from this type of provenance. While "provenance" used to mean place of origin, in today's parlance of collecting, it usually refers to what (classy) dealer or previous (famous) owner can be named, but only if — once named — that can be expected to add to the market value. This is related to the phenomenon of starshine ruboff, where the fact that some celebrity's fingerprints may have once sullied an object adds to its market value. I am always curious about deaccessioning; if they are getting rid of something, why? **$425.00-$500.00**

Rotating broiler, or whirling broiler, wrought iron, round broiler or grill has alternating straight & undulating flat bars, 3 feet, longish handle, American, Canadian or English, 13''D, 18th or early 19th C. • This type, with the wavy & straight line design, is most common, and apparently added just a touch of decorative quality to satisfy the original customer. There are many variations on the wavy straight theme. French whirling broilers or French Canadian ones tend to be fancier, and incorporate variations of fleur-de-lis for the broiling surface. When I see one with snakes, I'll buy it. **$265.00-$350.00**

Salamander, forged iron, beautiful trifed feet, English (?), 6½'' diameter disk, 34''L, 18th C. • A "wrought iron" salamander was offered in five (unstated) sizes in the Harrod's Stores, Ltd, of London, 1895 retail catalog. It is a bit thicker looking than the old ones, with a nearly round head & neck, with a thinner long handle with knob at the end. Apparently some could be ordered with a stand, and these salamanders have a different neck, with a hole through it that slips over the top of the stand. The stand has a heavy stepped base that supports a shortish vertical rod about the same thickness as the salamander's handle. You could thereby heat the salamander, slip it on the stand on your work table, and pivot it over your meringue or whatever it was you were lightly browning, and leave it there while you tended something else. • When you read catalogs, particularly those from the very late 19th C or early 20th, you cannot believe how many things you supposed long gone by then were still offered for sale and actual use. This is not the same as reproductions or fakes meant for decoration. **$250.00-$300.00**

Salamander, wrought iron, file decorated, short knee-out legs at join of disc and handle, American, 16''L, 18th or very early 19th C. **$125.00-$175.00**

• You don't see salamanders very often, and often they are very utilitarian with no decoration at all. A number of them don't seem to have the little legs either, which would support the red-hot disc over the dish to be browned. That means the cook had to heat the thing, then hold it over the dish, probably by leaning over, making the procedure much more dangerous. **"Chocolate Custard.**— Scald a quart of milk; stir in 4 heaping table--spoonsful of grated chocolate and simmer two minutes to dissolve it; beat up the yolks of 6 eggs with 1 cup of sugar; add to the milk and chocolate; stir for one minute; then add vanilla flavoring and pour into your custard cups, which should be waiting in pan half full of boiling water in the oven; cook until you see that the custards are done; let them cool and then grate sweet almonds over the top; make a meringue of the whites of the 6 eggs and a little sugar; pile it on the top of each custard; grate more sweet almonds over that; set them in the oven to brown a little, or brown by holding a salamander or hot stove lid over them." Henry Scammel, compiler, *Treasure-House*, 1891 (filled with recipes from unidentified older sources).

Skewer holder & skewers, forged iron, ring top to boldly-shaped rack, American, 8''H, 18th C. Added value.— Provenance and attractiveness are important to skewer rack values. A plain unexceptional example, relatively late, would bring $75.00-$100.00 at best. An early Pennsylvania German rack, with skewers, in some unusual or desirable design like a heart would bring lots more. One or two cautionary notes: you can't know if skewers are original to a particular rack, so shouldn't pay for this "matching", and you shouldn't expect it. Blacksmith's marks may identify maker or owner. **Reproduction alert.**— Also, there's a high probability of finding recently-made holders and skewers, made not with the intent to deceive, necessarily, but as part of Colonial Revivalism. 20th C blacksmithing craftsmen's books usually include a skewer design or two. There's no way to tell the difference if someone clever means to trick you. Some collectors feel that there's a general falling off in the buying of the simple forged iron early pieces because of this fact that they can be easily reproduced, then aged with only a little more care and skill. Such collectors go on to say that perhaps this explains the fast-track approach of later 19th C patented gadgets, etc., which cost a lot to reproduce and are therefore not. (So far.) The cost of molds and the whole casting process probably means that until antique cast iron things start selling for $1000.00 or more, we won't have many reproductions of things with moving parts, although cast iron toys have been profitably reproduced for years. For the skewer in this listing: **$700.00-$1000.00**

Skewer rack & skewers, holder is tulip pattern with wide arms, all 4 skewers have end bent for hooking to holder's arms, 2 are twisted for strength, one has very very sharpened point, American (?), holder 4''H x 4''W, early 19th C. **$400.00-$500.00**

Skewer rack & skewers, the rack also called a skewer fraime, wrought iron, familiar elongated diamond with bull's eye above, upcurving horns or arms, 5 assorted skewers, no mark, American or European, holder or rack is 6''H, skewers range from about 5¾'' to 11''L, late 18th C for rack, skewers may be 18th & 19th C. • Look for special forms & beautiful detailing in rack. Be somewhat suspicious of figural or zoomorphic or animalistic rack forms, such as open-beaked birds or eagles. Probably too good to be true. **$350.00-$500.00**

Skillet, cast iron, 3 peg feet, cast into handle is "13 IN", also "Cleveland TN", 13'' diameter, 2nd quarter 19th C. **$225.00-$275.00**

Skillet, cast iron, 3 stubby feet, long handle, shallow rounded bowl, American (?), 19th C. **$100.00-$150.00**

Skillet, cast iron, with 3 legs, American, only 6''D, 18th C or early 19th. These skillets look like what we would think of as a saucepan with legs. A **hearth skillet** has been described as a utensil shaped like a shallow kettle, that is, pretty much cylindrical with the mouth being about as large in diameter as the bottom. See notes on hollowware under Cook pot, this section. **$75.00-$85.00**

Skillet, forged iron, 3 legs, American (?), 6"H x 6½"D x 5"L handle, late 18th, early 19th C. From the size of so many of the very early skillets, the following reference would seem impossible: • "Some three families cook and bake in one skillet, called the cook-all." W. Faux, *Memorial Days*, London: 1823. **$125.00-$150.00**

Skillet, forged iron, perfectly round-bottomed, 3"L legs, long handle, American (?), 5½"H x 7½" diameter, with 3"L legs, 11"L handle, mid to late 18th C. A skillet for hearth cooking very rarely had a flat bottom, unlike a spider. **$225.00-$300.00**

Skillet, forged iron with long handle, dished bowl, 3 stubby feet, American (?), 4" diameter, 18th C. • In a fascinating book entitled *History Cast in Metal. The Founders of North America*, by Clyde A. Sanders & Dudley C. Gould (n.p.: Cast Metals Institute, American Foundrymen's Society, 1976) the authors show a cast iron pot, bellied body, triangular lug handles, three longish feet, which they describe as an English-made posnet. They go on to say that a four-legged pot was a skillet, or, in Northern England, a stufnet. I have yet to see the absolutely dependable definitive explanation of a skillet or posnet. **$100.00-$120.00**

Skillet, or is this a posnet?, wrought iron, long handle, 3 long legs, "G. W. Ibach", PA. 17½"L including handle, 5"H, 18th or very early 19th C. **$200.00-$235.00**

Skillet, ring handle, iron, W. Foster, #8, early 19th C. **$150.00-$175.00**

Skillet, forged iron with pouring spout and fixed arched handle with trammel ring, American, 12½"H including handle x 12" diameter, 19th C. **$150.00-$175.00**

Skillets, cast iron, set of 6 in different sizes, long handles and 3 legged, to use on hearth. American, late 18th C. This rare & wonderful set was sold by Lillian Blankley Cogan, one of the earliest dealers in kitchen "primitives," in 1988 for only: **$1800.00**

Sleeper, or fire cover, or curfew, wrought iron, 2 penny feet, gooseneck, American, 9½"H x 10½"L, 18th C. **$135.00-$150.00**

Spider, cast bell metal, long handle at 40 degrees off the horizon, 3 long splayed peg legs, handle marked "20 Warner", American or English, about 7"H x 7¼" diameter with 9½"L handle, late 18th or early 19th C. • $200.00 at the Garth Auction, May 26-27, 1989, Delaware, OH. **$175.00-$250.00**

Spider, cast iron, 3 short peg legs, flat bottom, American, 9" diameter with 5½"L handle, mid 19th C. • **"Poached eggs.**— Have ready a kettle of boiling water, pour it in a pan or speeder, which is set on coals; have the eggs at hand; put a little salt in water, and break them in, one at a time. Let remain till white is set and take them out with an egg spoon." Elizabeth E. Lea, *Useful Receipts and Hints to Young Housekeepers*, 10th ed., Baltimore, 1859 (1st ed. 1851). **$125.00-$140.00**

Spider, cast iron with 3 feet, long handle, straight sides and flat bottom, American, 5"H x 10¾"D pan with 9"L handle, 18th C. **$55.00-$75.00**

A "**creeper**", as described in W. Scott Boyce's *Economic and Social History of Chowan County*: "The principal cooking utensils, even of most of the best families, were a pot, a creeper (a spider) or two, a long-handle frying pan, a tea-kettle, a griddle, and two or three wornout hoes"

(p.222). It sounds the same as a Dutch oven, but is a spider according to Boyce. He writes that "most baking...was done in the creeper. ...To bake in the creeper, it was set on the fire and coals heaped on the lid. It was in this receptacle that was cooked that famous dyspepsia-producing Southern dish known as 'hot biscuit.' The much-prized apple and peach 'jacks' (kinds of pies — the New England 'turnovers') were cooked either in this or in the frying-pan" (p.223). while "some few had big ovens for baking sweet potatoes, and some were baked in creepers, but probably the bigger half was roasted on the hearth before the fire...or in the hot ashes." *loc sit*. He further describes "The creeper at this time (1880s)..as a heavy cast-iron pan some 3" or 4" deep, covered with a lid, (that) stood on three legs about three inches high. The handle was from 12" to 15" long." W. Scott Boyce, *Economic and Social History of Chowan County, North Carolina, 1880-1915*, submitted as a doctoral thesis at Columbia University, and published in NYC in 1917. It is a marvelous book, with many valuable nuggets of information.

Spider, so named for the long legs, wrought iron, 3 legs, repaired, American, prob. PA, 6"H x 6½" diameter with 10½"L handle, 18th or early 19th C. **$120.00-$145.00**

Spider, wrought iron, flat bottom, long handle, "Whitfield" marked on handle, American (?) or English (?), 8"H x 14" diameter with 17"L handle, early 19th or late 18th C. **"New England Fire Cakes.**— Make a pie crust not quite so rich as for puff paste. Cut off small pieces and roll out thin about the size of a breakfast plate, as nearly round as possible. Have a griddle over the fire, and bake a nice brown, turning it when done on one side and browning nicely on the other. When done, put on a plate and butter it well. Have ready another cake, and bake, piling one upon the other, and buttering each piece, until all you have made are cooked. Serve them quite hot, cutting down through all the layers. This is very nice if, as you butter each piece, preserved strawberries or raspberries are spread upon each layer. It is an old-fashioned New England cake, and in olden times was cooked in iron spiders, propped up before the kitchen fire; hence its name. It is a very nice short cake, to be eaten hot, for supper or breakfast." Mrs. F. D. J., in *Home Cook Book*, 1876. The spider: **$175.00-$225.00**

Spider, wrought iron with 3 legs, flat bottom, American, 7¾"D, late 18th or early 19th C. **$45.00-$60.00**

Spit, wrought iron with penny feet, adjustable vertical spit with hooks, American or English, 28"H, 18th C. **$750.00-$1000.00**

Spit engine, clockwork mechanism for driving spit, brass face, wrought iron frame, English (?), 18th C. • Appearance, workability (or at least repairable condition), completeness add value. **$1500.00-$2500.00**

Striker, for striking against a flintstone to make a spark to start a fire, would be found in an early home in a tinder box (probably tin), a stone, a piece of charred linen. This striker, slightly different from most I've seen — flat narrow bar of forged iron, bent in a very tight hairpin curve with both tips curled in at the open end, American or European, 3¾"L, 18th or very early 19th C. • Other strikers I've seen include something almost as wide open as a small horse shoe with no attempt to finish off the tips at the open end; rather loosely curved striker with one "arm" decidedly shorter than other, both tips curled; and various strikers with file and chisel decoration. The value range below would not include the decorated ones, which would add another $25.00-$50.00 to the high value.

$40.00-$95.00

Striker, forged iron, flat, form appears to be a "rocking fox", the rocker blade with both ends curled rather tightly, like old ice skate blades, incised lines to indicate the separation of 2 front legs and 2 back legs, also the eyes and mouth, brush tail out straight behind, American (?), poss. CT, VA ?, prob. not PA, 2¾"H x 4⅞"L, early 19th C (?). • This is the first figural striker I've ever seen, so don't know how to judge it. The dealer is from CT, the show in VA, a lot of very interesting iron in his booth. It is possible that this is European; some people say his wares are Portuguese; iron is getting all mixed up nowadays. **$275.00-$400.00**

Tea kitchen, a sort of kettle, also called a <u>covered cauldron,</u> copper, tinned inside, slightly round-breasted body, sturdy bail handle with pivot ring, small central opening with lid, copper and brass spigot sticks out straight from side, right at bottom, spigot as long as kettle is in diameter, to be hung on trammel or pot hook in fireplace for ready supply of hot water, English, 10"H x 10½" diameter, late 18th C. • A slightly later variation of this was adapted, or created, for use on top of a range, with the spigot sticking out off to side of range, as supply of hot water. This type is generally somewhat larger, and because it stood on its own, was made to balance more safely by being taller and having shorter spigot relative to diameter. • The 1895 Harrod's Stores catalog depicts two of these, cylindrical bodies, slightly domed top, with fitted lid with strap bracket handle, long spigot spout, falling wire bail handle. They came in cast iron and also "London Wrought Iron", and were called either Tea Kitchens or Boiler for Fire. In cast iron, there were three sizes: 2, 3 & 4 gallons; in wrought iron: 2 & 3 gallons. **$350.00-$500.00**

Tin kitchen, with bottle jack, pieced sheet iron, tall domed oven on 4 cylindrical tin legs, balloon shaped tin structure above, of strap tin, supports windup jack inside, flywheel inside has 6 counterweights, door in back for basting or checking doneness, sometimes this type of vertical tin kitchen was called a <u>niche screen roaster</u>, and the English called it a <u>meat screen for bottle jack</u>, American, about 30"H, c.1790 to 1840. **$1000.00-$500.00**

Lookalike alarm.— Just when you thought you were safe with an oldie. Harrod's Stores, Ltd., the great London department store, has one of these "Meat Screens, for Bottle Jack" in their 1895 retail catalog. It has a sort of lyre-shaped tin rack above the round dome top, that was for suspending the windup jack. It also has a lidded grease or fat well in the bottom, the tubular tin legs are braced, and it was offered in three sizes: 19"H, 21"H and 24"H. They also made one they described as "Extra strong, with enclosed Bottom for Hot Closet, to order, 21 in., 24 in." These were almost twice as expensive. I don't know what a "hot closet" is, but perhaps it means that instead of tubular legs there's a sort of warming oven compartment under there, probably with access from the back, just like the hinged door in the back of the meat screen.

Toaster, fancy brass single slice toaster for hearth use, probably for tea time in the parlor, with pivoting lazy elbow handle, scalloped-edge heavy gauge brass plate with 2 curved arches of brass rod to hold bread, English almost undoubtedly, c.1830s. **$175.00-$225.00**

Toaster, forged iron, long slightly arched handle fixed to pair of footed arches with hook support underneath for one thick slab of bread, English, 12½"L x 5"W, 18th C. **$375.00-$425.00**

Toaster, forged iron, revolving, double arch holder on frame with long handle, 2 sets of double tree-like sprays of iron within arches that hold bread fit into holes, one on each side adjusts for various size of slices, American, c.1770s. **$400.00-$550.00**

Toaster, forged iron, upside down horseshoe shape filled in with scrolly bars of iron, with bar in back to prop in front of fire, Scottish (?), 15"H x 16"W, 18th C. **$350.00-$500.00**

Toaster, pivoting, forged iron, the frame is horse-shoe shaped and is for bannocks (?), English (?) or Scottish (?), 13"L, late 18th or early 19th C. **$400.00-$500.00**

"BANNOCK. (Gaelic: <u>bonnach</u>. Irish: <u>boinneag</u>.) In Scotland, a cake of oatmeal, baked on an iron plate.

> Behind the door a bag of meal;
> And in the kist was plenty
> Of good hard cakes his mither bakes;
> And bannocks were nae scanty.
> *Scotch Songs*, II. 71. .

"In New England, cakes of Indian meal, fried in lard, are called bannocks." John Russell Bartlett, *Dictionary of Americanisms. A Glossary of Words and Phrases usually regarded as peculiar to the United States.* Boston: 2nd ed.1859 (1st ed. 1848).

Toaster, pivoting or swiveling, forged iron, 2 sets of 3 twisted arches, European (?), toaster frame 13"L with 13"L handle, early 19th C. So many of these flip-over type are appearing at fleas and shows that I believe most are probably coming in from Europe in container loads. **$180.00-$250.00**

Toaster, pivoting or swiveling, the kind you have to pick up the handle & move it to swivel the toast frame, very decorative wrought iron arches and handle, American (?), more likely French Canadian or European, late 18th C. **$265.00-$350.00**

Toaster, pivoting or swiveling, wrought iron, 4 rectangular arches, American (?), late 18th C or early 19th. • A recipe for a "**Method of Making Toast Water**" appeared in the Aug.1851 issue of *American Agriculturist*. "Take a slice of fine and stale loaf bread, cut thin, (thin as toast is ever cut,) and let it be carefully toasted on both sides, until it be completely browned all oaver, but nowise blackened nor burned in any way. Put this into a common, deep stone or China pitcher, and pour over it, from the teakettle, as much clean boiling water as you wish to make into drink. Much depends on the water being actually in a boiling state. Cover the pitcher with a saucer or plate, and let the drink cool until it is quite cold; it is then fit to be used. The fresher it is made, the better, and of course, the more agreeable. The above will be found a pleasant, light and highly diuretic drink. It is peculiarly grateful to the stomach, and excellent for carrying off the effects of excessive bile." **$165.00-$225.00**

Toaster, pivoting, wrought iron and wire, 4 pairs of arches, arched penny feet on toast frame, American or European, 40"L overall, early 19th C. **$265.00-$325.00**

Toaster, pivoting, wrought iron with 4 twisted arches on footed frame, can be flipped at swivel-hinged junction of long handle and toaster, American (?), late 18th, early

19th C. • The fancier the iron work on these, the more likely they are to be English or European. Most have iron handles; occasionally you find one with a wooden handle. **$300.00-$400.00**

Toaster, rotating type, frame has 4 sets of double rams' horns to hold 2 slices of bread, 4 little deep kneebend legs, and very unusual tiller handle rising up for convenient handling, wooden grip, signed "N. B." New England (?), 8½" x 12", late 18th C. **$400.00-$500.00**

Toaster, swiveling type with long handle, forged iron, heart design supports, from Maine coast, frame is 12⅝"W x 5¼" deep, 18⅝"L, handle, late 18th C. **$600.00-$700.00**

Toaster, rotating, wrought iron, 3 pairs of arches, penny feet, eye hole in handle for hanging, American (?), 28"L, 19th C. **$175.00-$225.00**

Toaster, wrought iron, for one slice, rotating head with 4 "horns" or antennae curving up from swivel point. Two legs under head or frame, one leg partway back on handle, reminds you of an abstract beetle or other animal, American (?), 12 ½"L x 5"W frame, 18th C. Again, this was found by Clara Jean Davis; the description is based on hers, price range is mine. **$350.00-$450.00**

Toaster, wrought iron, frame holds one piece of bread & has 2 short feet, nice shaped handle with foot or support a few inches from end, American, 14½"L x 5¾"W x 3"H toast frame, 18th C. This one was turned up by Clara Jean Davis, The Old Parsonage, Concord, NH. She wrote, in her List #146, "These are extremely rare...In all the years we've hunted for rare, early iron, have only seen a few of these...It had coats of paint on it, so old and dried it just chipped off." **$325.00-$400.00**

Toaster, wrought iron, swivel hinge, 2 front feet on frame, simple bars to hold toast, "W. H." also "N. P." (one could be blacksmith, one the owner), American, 16"W x 16"L, 18th C. **$150.00-$190.00**

Toasting forks—See Implement chapter.

Tongs, forged iron, one arm is twisted, small head, American, prob. PA, 17⅝"L, mid to late 18th C. **$140.00-$160.00**

Trammel, chain, forged iron, 50"L, early 19th C. **$50.00-$60.00**

Trammel, chain, strong twisted wrought iron hook, 70"L, early 19th C. **$50.00-$65.00**

Trammel, for fireplace, wrought & polished steel, nice filework, swiveling hook, English (?), 13" to 21", closed & open lengths, late 18th, early 19th C. **$135.00-$150.00**

"Polishing Metals.— The polishing of metals differs according to the kind of metal and the kind of manufacture; (but) there are some general principles to be attended to as being common to all, of which it is useful to have a clear idea. All polishing is begun, in the first instance, by rubbing down the surface by some hard substance that will produce a number of scratches in all directions, the level of which is nearly the same, and which will obliterate the marks of the file, scraper, or turning tool...first employed. For this purpose coarse emery is used, or pumice and water, or sand and water, applied upon a piece of soft wood, or of felt, skin, or some similar material. When these first coarse marks have been thus removed, they next proceed to remove the marks left by the pumice-stone of finely powdered pumice-stown ground up with olive oil, or by finer emery and oil. In some cases, certain polishing stones are employed, as a kind of hard slate, used with water. To proceed with the polishing, still finer powders are used, as Tripoli & rottenstone, which is still finer, and is found only in Derbyshire. Putty of tin & crocus martis are also used for high degrees of polish. But the fact is, in respect to polishing, that the whole process consists ... in removing coarse scratches by substituting those which are finer & finer, until they are no longer visible to the naked eye; and ... if the surface be examined by a microscope, it will be seen that what appeared without any scratches is covered ... with an infinity of them, but so minute that they require a high magnifier to be discovered. The operator... who understands this principle, will...vary his polishing substances according to the nature of the article he wishes to polish. ... His polishing material must be able to scratch, in a coarser or finer manner, the substance he is desirous of polishing, for wearing down is only effected by producing minute cuttings or scratches. It is evident ... that great care must be taken to have the last polishing material uniformly fine, for a single grain ... of any coarse substance mixed with it will produce some visible scratches instead of a perfectly polished surface. ... Polishing materials: coarsest are emery, sand, glass-paper, whiting, or chalk, putty of tin, & black-lead" usually mixed with oil. — Webster & Parkes, *An Encyclopedia of Domestic Economy*, 1848 NY edition of English book of 1845.

Trammel, forged iron, 2 piece flat bar iron, one with holes, one with rod to fit into any hole of other part, with hook at bottom, American, adjusts from 35"L to 60"L, so for very large fireplace, late 18th C. Unless these have some kind of spiffy form or decoration or hook or look, they are really rather dull. I like the sawtooth trammels much better, or the hand wrought chain ones. **$30.00-$50.00**

Trammel, forged iron, chain with long hook, knobbed lugpole hook, American or English, early 19th C. **$85.00-$100.00**

Trammel, forged iron, sawtooth type, simple keeper attached to hook through rattail loop, 11 usual-sized teeth, somewhat (and appealingly) different in angle and size, American, 21¼"L extends to approximately 32"L, early 19th or late 18th C. $250.00, a rather good price, at the Garth Auction, May 5-6, 1989, Delaware, OH. **$225.00-$300.00**

Trammel, possibly for a lamp, steel, English, 20⅞"L sans hook, dated with individual punches or stamps, "ANNO 1774". **$200.00-$250.00**

Trammel, sawtooth ratchet, cut out of heavy sheet brass, with a cutout flat finial decoration of a cock, English (?), extends 20" to 35"L, looks 2nd to 3rd quarter 19th C. • If it is that old, I'd have expected the mid 1989 price to be at least twice the dealer's asking price of $125.00. It's possibly a containerload piece, or maybe it was a decorative piece made in the 20th C. If as old as it looks, the range would be higher: **$200.00-$300.00**

Trammel, very heavy wrought iron chain, 86"L, and that's some fireplace! 18th C. **$175.00-$225.00**

Trammel, very large wrought iron sawtooth type, large hanging ring at top, 24 relatively small sawteeth (the 12th down broken off), decorative keeper and hook, heart cutout in crested top of the wide "blade", very unusual low relief decoration top to bottom of vines & tulips, poss. PA German, 47"L unextended, early 19th C (?). • Brought $1750.00 at Garth Auction, May 5-6, 1989, Delaware, OH. **$1500.00-$2200.00**

Trammel, wrought iron chain type with top hook, used with a separate pot hook too, American (?), 21''L, 18th or early 19th C. **$60.00-$90.00**

Trammel, wrought iron, hook & eye type, adjustable from 31'' to 47''L, early 19th or late 18th C. **$130.00-$150.00**

Trammel, wrought iron, nicely detailed and really wicked teeth, prob. European, 56''L extended, 18th or early 19th C. • Most trammels go for under $100.00. Possibly because they don't excite much visual interest unless they are very fine examples. But look again: workmanship, when you lean over and study them or clean them, begins to add up to higher value. Of course, you have to love iron. Several trammels would have been found hanging from the lug pole or crane in early kitchens, some are surprisingly long. Added value.— Some are very decorative, with scrolling curves and fanciful sawteeth or hook-and-eye elements; chains can be gussied up too. The finest go for upwards of $250.00. Containerloaded.— Many, maybe most, antique trammels for sale in the U.S. today probably just arrived on these shores from England or Europe. Is there a difference if a French trammel got here in 1780 or 1980? **$100.00-$135.00**

Trammel, wrought iron, sawtooth style with crane ring, American (?), extends from 45''L to 61''L, early 19th C. **$125.00-$175.00**

Trivet, cast & wrought iron, 3 legged hearth style for pots, also called a brandelette, brandiron or brandise, American (?), 10''H, 18th C. **$250.00-$275.00**

Trivet, for hearth, revolving, forged iron, American, 11''D & high legs, very early 18th C. • The trivet, without a handle, is much rarer than the revolving broiler. **$200.00-$225.00**

Trivet, for hearth, with adjustable fork or handle support that works on the pawl & ratchet idea, forged & twisted iron ''running man'' piece with adjustable height to hold fork or spoon, 2 long legs on either side of circle of trivet, one leg near end of handle, very handsome form that looks like what sculptor Alberto Giacometti would have done, if he'd made 18th century cooking utensils, found in house on the Connecticut-Massachusetts line, 24⁵⁄₁₆''L, trivet is 7⅝'' diameter, maybe mid 18th C. **$425.00-$550.00**

Trivet, for hearth, wrought iron with sliding support for saucepan handle, 3 penny feet, 22½''L, 18th C. **$200.00-$300.00**

Trivet, wrought iron, round with 3 legs & a long handle, for use on the hearth, American (?), 6''H x 8'' diameter with 11''L handle, 18th or early 19th C. **$125.00-$140.00**

Trivets not for hearth use—See separate Trivet chapter.

Wafer & waffle irons for hearth — See Chapter IV.

X-A.
Kitchen scenes, c.1690-1700.
English. Note pie funnel being used by woman in lower picture! Early chapbook pictures, from undated chapbook A Choice Collection of Cookery Receipts, *printed at Newcastle, England*

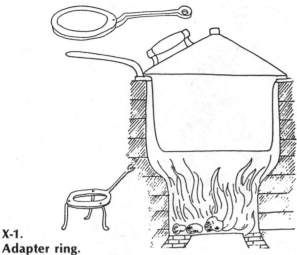

X-1.
Adapter ring.
A ring of flat iron with a long handle used to adapt the opening in an early brick raised-hearth range to a vessel somewhat smaller than the opening. What's it doing here instead of in Stove chapter? Author error. Something similar, but with legs (bottom left) was used to hold a legless cooking vessel over coals in the hearth.

X-2.
Ale or beer warmers.
Top two conical ones are of copper, with bow handle or turned wood handle. Sometimes called **ale spikes.** Henry Rogers Sons & CO., Wolverhampton, England, 1914. Other two, with and without lids, are called **ale boots,** ale shoes or ale slippers, also made of copper, although some sheet iron ones are known. The shoes were easier to use than the conical ones which had to be held, or stuck into some kind of trivet or stand. Top two came in 1, 2, 3, and 4 pt. sizes; bottom (L) about 9" to 11"L exclusive of handle; bottom (R) is 6"H x 18"L overall. It is from reproduction catalog of Pearson-Page Co., Birmingham & London, England, 1925. Only old ones worth much. **$75.00-$400.00**

X-3.
Andiron.
Cast iron, with sliding oven 'drawer' for baking potatoes or other food. This is drawn from the only picture I have ever seen of this type. It is relatively low and rather short, appearing to be about a foot to 15"L in the photograph illustrating "Pre-Stove Cooking," by Edwin C. Whittemore, Spinning Wheel, 3/1965. The brontosaurus ridge holds the logs above, and coals and hot ashes are pushed up against the tunnel. Possibly mid 19th C, although it's possible they are much earlier or much later. **$250.00-$425.00**

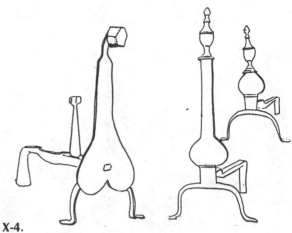

X-4.
Andirons, showing one of each pair.
Forged iron knife-blade type. (L) Pronounced inverted heart, almost humorous in its bloomer-bottomed stance. Note leg stop, also with faceted head. A very fine pair, thought to be from Hadley, MA, c.1900. Pair sold at Richard A. Bourne's auction, Hyannis, MA, 12/16/1986. For $5000.00. (M) & (R) Wrought iron and brass andirons, 24"H and 16"H. The tall pair is signed by John Constantine, NYC. Other pair is attributed to Constantine, for obvious reasons, and was auctioned by Litchfield Auction Gallery, Litchfield, CT, 12/10/1989. **$2000.00-$5000.00**

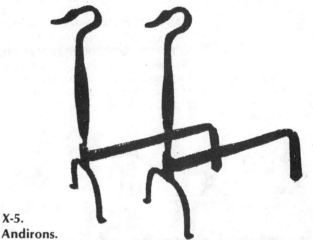

X-5.
Andirons.
Gooseneck type, forged iron, American (or English), first half 19th C. **$400.00-$700.00**

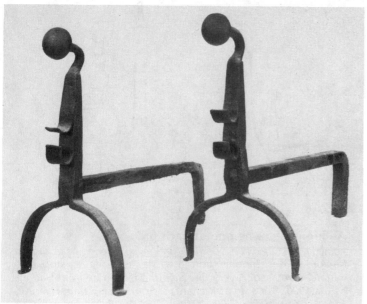

X-6. Andirons.
Forged iron, with double spit brackets, round ball finials. 18 1/2"H, probably American, first half 19th C. Auctioned at 1983 Linden sale for $500.00. Picture courtesy of Christie, Manson & Woods International Inc. **$400.00-$600.00**

X-7. "Ornamental 'Fire-dogs' " design patents.
Both pat'd by Theodore W. Lillagore, Philadelphia, PA. Design patent #1189, pat'd 1/10/1860; #1194, pat'd 1/24/1860. For cast iron firedogs of low andirons. (T) utilizes rustic look popular at the time for garden furniture. Note shield shape at base of shafts on both of them. This shield shape shows up frequently on all kinds of mid 19th C. andirons. **$65.00-$150.00**

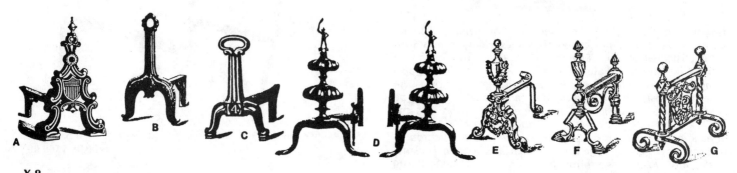

X-8.
Firedogs and andirons.
(A), (B), and (C) are heavy cast iron firedogs. (A) has brass top and bronzed iron finish, with log rests in three lengths, 12"L, 14"L and 15"L to fit shallow to deeper fireplaces, probably in a bedroom or small parlor. (B) is described as "common", and has a japanned finish, and lengths from 10" to 15". (C) is "new pattern", heavy and japanned, 12" to 18"L log rests. All Russell & Erwin Mfg. Co., New Britain, CT, 1865. (D) "Exmoor Pixie — Luck Bringer of the Moorland Wilds," in cast brass. 16"H. Pearson-Page, 1925. (E), (F) and (G) are all cast brass firedogs. Harrod's Stores, Ltd., Brompton, England, 1895 catalog. (H) "Hand wrought in antique steel finish with brass mounts, 23"H." Made by Todhunter, NYC. Advertised new, in House Beautiful, *12/1928. (I) "The Jacobean," cast brass, 19"H. Pearson-Page, 1925. Like most P-P andirons or dogs, complete matching fire iron sets and stands were also available. (J) Cast brass and wrought iron, reproductions, Edwin Jackson, NYC, advertised 10/1927. The firm, founded in 1900, is still in business. The pixie set would be worth the most — maybe up to $400.00.* **$50.00-$150.00**

433

X-9.
Andirons.
Cast iron, primly-posed if provocatively garbed goddesses of plenty holding cornucopias. 17 1/2"H, mid 19th C. Wide value range depending on where purchased. Picture courtesy Litchfield, CT. Ex-Harold Corbin Collection, auctioned 1/1/1989 for an astounding $1100.00. **$275.00-$400.00**

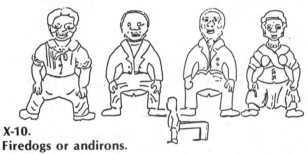

X-10.
Firedogs or andirons.
Black Americana motifs, cast iron, sometimes found with touches of paint. I've not investigated design patents after 1873, but suspect most of these are 1870s-1890s. Dealer Steve Miller, who had the (R) pair, dated them to "c.1850." If he is close to correct, it is possible they are post-1852, when Harriet Beecher Stowe's Uncle Tom's Cabin was published (and began to sell millions over the years). The woman is assuredly not Topsy, but the male figure does resemble Uncle Tom of early depictions. (L) This type, with two identical black men, dressed as sailors, possibly cabin "boys", have a remarkable amount of detail and a rather more realistic, if still caricatured, faces. Drawn from figures in stock of Rosemary Schorr & Barry Dobinsky, Bucks County Conservancy Show, 1989. Second from (L) is from pair of identical black men, dressed in tailcoats (possibly they are butlers); eyeholes through which flames can be seen. Drawn from photo at Pook & Pook Auction, at Ludwig's Corner, PA, of Monroe Fabian et alia collection, 3/30-31/1990. Sold for $700.00 Right pair, black man and woman, in late 18th or early 19th C-style clothing. Man wears waistcoat, tails, and stock at his throat. Woman has laced bodice, full skirt, pantaloons, & pinned shawl or handkerchief-collar crisscrossing prominent & perfectly round, apple-like breasts, like those of many andirons & firedogs, including English ones of the 16th and 17th C. They're not taken here as racist; we don't even know if they are sexist, strictly speaking. Note woman's mob cap & beads. Mfd. by Taylor Iron Works, Macon, GA, 19th C. Drawn from ad of Steve Miller, folk art dealer, NYC. **$600.00-$1600.00**

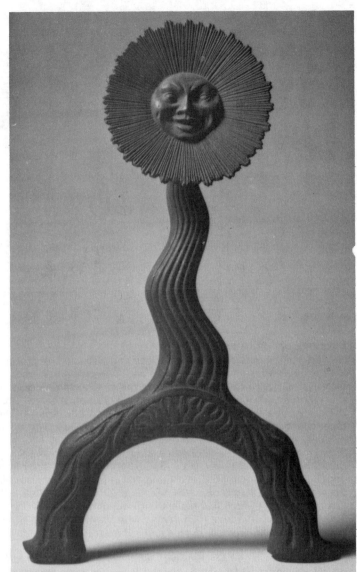

X-11.
Andiron.
Cast iron, late 19th C, possibly PA or NY state. As the cataloguer or perhaps Harold Corbin wrote for the auction catalog, the design is of "a radiant sun face seemingly rising on a wave of heat." Much more on the price history of this pattern, which turns out not to be so rare as hoped, is found in the price listings. This pair was missing the log rests. Picture courtesy Litchfield Auction Gallery, Litchfield Auction Gallery, Litchfield, CT. Ex-Harold Corbin Collection, auctioned 1/1/1989 for an astounding price: $12,700.00. Full value range as determined by the market so far (up to late 1989) is: **$495.00-$12,700.00**

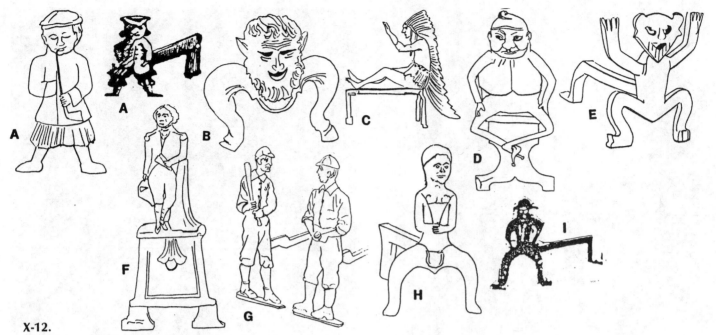

X-12.
Firedogs or andirons.

All cast iron figurals. Some are described and discussed more fully in the price listings. (A) #1 — Kilted Scotsmen, identical figures (that is, not mirror images), with caps and long clay pipes. Because Henry Kauffman, who has written extensively on all kinds of metalwares, has written that these were the same as those depicted on a 1765 tradecard, dealers have picked that up as their date. It is incorrect. (A) #2 is a "cast dog" made by Joseph Webb of Boston, on a tradecard engraved by Paul Revere in 1765. The figure is clearly not a Scotsman, as he is not wearing a kilt. Anyway, the wearing of tartans and kilts was outlawed in Scotland at the time, and not to be resumed until about 20 years later. The figure is dressed, not like an Englishman, and not like an American colonist, but sort of French soldier, of c.1715 (as far as his coat and his tricorn hat go) but with the fuller pants of 100 years or more before that. The decorative, almost cute look of the Scotsman with the pipe leads me to date him to the third quarter of the 19th C, or perhaps even later. (B) Cast iron, identical, satyr heads, cutout eyes & mouths, 11"H x 11"W. From Main Street Antiques ad, West Branch, IA. (C) Cast iron, beautifully detailed Amerindians greeting each other. Early 20th C. At a Sotheby sale, 1989, they realized $19,000.00 plus 10% premium. (D) Cast iron, disgruntled "Brownies", of type most usually associated with artist Palmer Cox in late 19th C. Identical figures, with wonderful details in tiny hands and belled slippers. Oriental-like faces, much more sullen, but much more attractive than in my awful drawing. 18 1/2"H. From ad of Patricia Anne Reed Fine Antiques, Damariscotta, ME. (E) Cast, wrought, welded, riveted and cut iron. This is the devilish male figure; his consort has teeth and a long skirt with iron "rickrack." 9 3/4"H. Front to back they're 18". Probably American, probably 1930s. From ad of M. Finkel & Daughter, Philadelphia, PA. (F) Polychromed cast iron, with white, black, blue and reddish brown. George Washington, holding tricorn and Declaration of Independence (?) leaning on draped stand. On monumental-style plinth. Sloppily painted, as is customary for early 20th C products of paint-it-yourself foundries. Maker unknown. Sold at a Weschler auction in 1987 for $1000.00. (G) Painted cast iron, baseball players — batter & pitcher. 19"H, probably 1920s. Gold-painted pair, possibly once polychromed, sold at Oliver's for $1400.00, plus 10%, 1990. (H) Cast iron, apple-busted high-foreheaded woman. On some, the tiny hands are well detailed. 11 1/2"H. Costume details look medieval. Probably 2nd quarter 19th C, but based on 16th C. English firedogs. Drawing done from ads of Vincent Mulford, Malden Bridge, NY, and June Lambert, Alexandria, VA (I) See X-92 for more on 1833 figural man.

X-13.
Firedogs or andirons.

The name "firedogs", often referred to simply as "dogs" or "dog irons" in old accounts, probably precedes the zoomorphic dog forms of many 19th and 20th C andirons. (A) Cast iron, facing pair of bulldogs, which are not exact mirror images of each other. Probably early 20th C. (B) Cast iron griffin mythological irons, mfd. by Bradley & Hubbard, marked "B & H", 20 1/4"H, late 19th C. From Martin Willis, Seaboard Auction Gallery, Eliot, ME, 1989 sale. Realized $1100.00 (C) Cast brass, beautifully detailed, crafted by William van Erp, San Francisco, mid 20th C. Drawn from San Francisco Craft and Folk Art Museum photo. (D) Nearly flat iron, 14"H, c.1930s-40s. From ad of American Primitive Gallery, NYC. (E) Cast iron, ring top, spaniels with haunches out. Collar around neck. 13 1/2"H. Possibly made in Norfolk, VA, mid 19th C. From ad of W. M. Schwind, Jr., Yarmouth, ME. (F) Seated cast iron cats on low "footstool" plinths, 17 1/4"H. Possibly mfd. by Howes (?). From unidentified clipping. **$300.00-$1000.00**

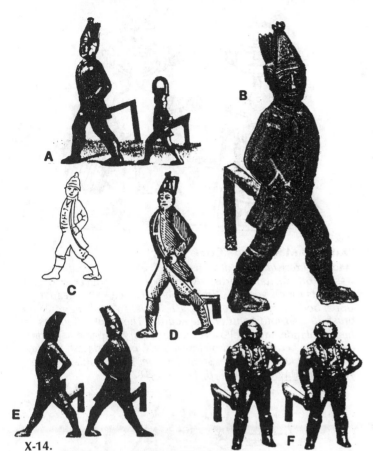

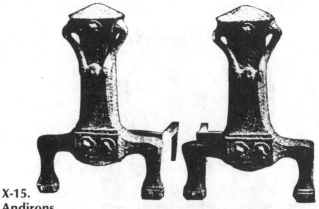

X-15.
Andirons.
Cast iron, finished black, 18"H (also offered 22"H, and also in wrought iron, 26"H). Ancient design, but this one probably has taken what may have been movable handles, and possibly some kind of drawer-like hiding place (?), and made them solid and un-movable. From hotel supply catalog of D.J. Barry, 1924.
$40.00-$80.00

X-14.
Hessian soldier andirons plus Putnam.
All cast iron, some polychromed. Named for German mercenary soldiers fighting with the British in the Revolutionary War. (A) 20"H and 12"H pair, originally painted red and yellow with "touches of gilt" or "all black." Repros from Edwin Jackson, NYC, House Beautiful, 5/1936 ad. (B) Cast iron, 20"H, well-modeled, but this doesn't prove they aren't 20th C reproductions, as Edwin Jackson did beautiful castings. (C) Sword-bearing Hessian, with boyish face and modified cap. Sloppily painted. Both figures in the pair faced same direction. Came with matched fire tool set. Probably 1920s. Drawn from ad of Candlewick Antiques, Mont Vernon, NH. Similar ones found with puttees over shoes. (D) From ad of B.F. Macy, Boston, MA, 12/1921. "In colors — red coat, buff breeches." (E) Jaunty well-cast pair, 16 1/2"H, in black finish, mfd. by Albany Foundry Co., Albany, NY, 11/1923 ad. This foundry specialized in paint-it-yourself castings. (F) Often called George Washington, actually "General Putnam" (for which one, see page 408). 13 3/4"H. Albany Foundry, 7/1925 ad.

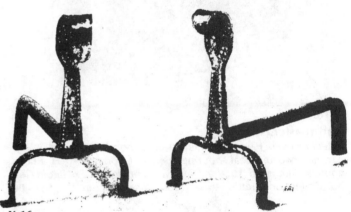

X-16.
Andirons.
Hand forged iron — "an unusual design the originals of which were found in Maine." 14"H. Reproductions from Todhunter, NYC, advertised in House & Garden, 1/1929. $22.00 at the time.
$40.00-$80.00

X-17.
Fireplace,
described in ad as "Franklin stove." Cast iron, reproduction. Note small figural firedogs, which I have blown up as much as possi-ble here, and still can't see detail of very well. There appears to be a high-forehead, an apple bosom, and a shield shape between the legs. Compare with description of X-12-H. Edwin Jackson ad, 4/1936.
$200.00-$400.00

X-18.
Bird roaster,
reflecting oven. Pieced tin, 4 hooks under hood, strap handle. Drip pan has two birdbeak pouring spouts at corners. 10"H. Photo courtesy Litchfield Auction Gallery, Litchfield, CT. Ex-Harold Corbin Collection, auctioned 1/1/1990. Price realized: **$375.00**

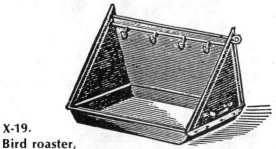

X-19.
Bird roaster,
of reversible type. Hooks for 4 birds; small bracket handles on sides. From F.A. Walker import catalog, 1870s-80s.**$100.00-$150.00**

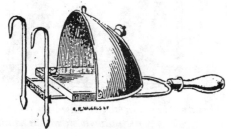

X-20.
Roaster or toaster — reflecting oven.
Hangs on fender of fireplace, for toasting cheese sandwiches (?), birds or apples. From F.A. Walker catalog, 1870s-80s. See X-38 for more on cheese toasters. They were made for melting cheese; this reflecting oven more likely was used for melting cheese on top of something.   **$125.00-$200.00**

X-21.
"Kitchen Maid" and "Cook Maid,"
made up irresistably of kitchen tools. The real master of this style was a 16th C. Italian artist, Archimboldo. See chapter on implements for his version. Kitchen Maid has tea kettle head, tong upper body, coal "skuttle" skirt, ash shovel and poker arms. Note brush tucked into band on the scuttle. The Cook Maid has lid head, colander face, bellows upper body, frying pan and gridiron arms, soup kettle or cauldron lower body, peel and flesh fork legs and I don't know what her shoulders are. From William Hone's, The Every-Day Book, Vol. II, London, 1827.

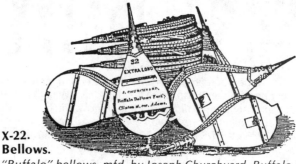

X-22.
Bellows.
"Buffalo" bellows, mfd. by Joseph Churchyard, Buffalo Bellows Factory, Buffalo, NY. Under his direction, "skilled workmen" made "warranted bellows of the Eastern, Southern and Pittsburgh Patterns...of the best materials." He also repaired them. Ad in Thomas' Buffalo City Directory, 1866.

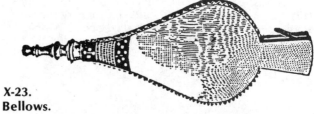

X-23.
Bellows.
"Antique oak" in six sizes, and "complete assortment of other styles." German import advertised by G.M. Thurnauer & Brother, NYC, 11/1909. Many companies made bellows in a deliberately old-fashioned style, some complete with painted boards and fancy trims.

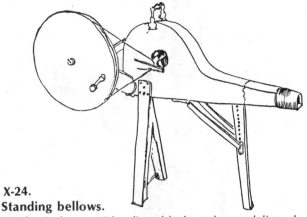

X-24.
Standing bellows.
Mechanical type with adjustable front leg to deliver the blast where it was needed. 27"H x 38"L, probably English, early 19th C. From ad of James II, in James Robinson's gallery, NYC.

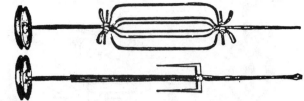

X-26.
Spits.
Iron. Basket or cradle spit & "spit with Holdfast." The basket or cradle type was used to hold small game birds or animals or joints of other meat which it was better to keep unskewered so that it would remain moist inside instead of dripping out all its juice. The one with the holdfast was supplemented with skewers, which went through the meat and through holes (which you can't see here) in the thicker part of the shaft. From William S. Adams & Son catalog, London, c.1860-61.

X-25.
Basket spit, spit-dogs & clock jack.
A clockwork jack, with heavy weight to drive it. just like in a tallcase clock. It moved the chain which moved the pulley wheel which turned the spit, the height of which could be adjusted by hooking it on at different levels of the special andirons. The cup-like tops were supposed to be for caudle cups, to heat a milk and mead or other hot drink. From an ad of the now lamented and defunct B. Altman & Co., 6/1957. Longtime buyer for Altman's antiques department was a wonderful Scotsman who traveled all over the world looking for such things. His name was Archie Keillor, of Long Island, and it was his family collection featured in my first book on old kitchen things, now out of print. I'm sure he found these items.

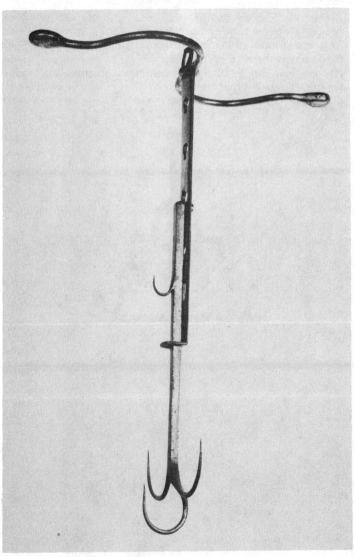

X-27.
Dangle spit.
Probably for birds. It was hung from a cord (which had to be replaced every so often), and then twisted. The longish curved wings or governors helped to keep it twisting and turning, first one way then the other. Steel, 16"L fully extended (shown here about half extended), American, early 19th C. Ex-Keillor Collection.
$175.00-$300.00

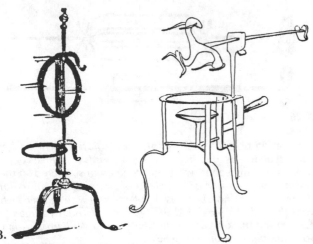

X-28.
"Toaster and Trivet,"
performing similar functions as one at right. Picture from *Warne's Model Cookery and Housekeeping Book*, London: 1868. Wrought iron, and it looks as if it may even have a brass finial.   **$250.00-$500.00**

Bird roaster or bird spit.
Wrought iron, with small drip or grease cup. Note triskellion motif of the whirling spit, and the heart at the other end. Drawn from ad of Heller Washam Antiques, Portland, ME. Value range mine.   **$600.00-$1200.00**

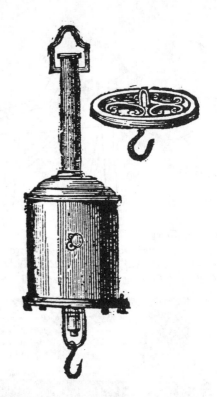

X-30.
Bottle jack.
Japanned sheet iron or brass, which were much more expensive. Clockwork inside, but named for its overall shape. From Harrod's Stores Ltd., Brompton, England, 1895 catalog. They also cleaned and repaired bottle jacks, as probably many clock repairers did too.   **$75.00-$200.00**

X-29.
Bird spit.
Tripod base with pronounced snake feet. Wrought iron, interesting 'easel' hanger with six double spits. 30"H, 18th C. Photo courtesy Litchfield Auction Gallery, Litchfield, CT. Ex-Harold Corbin Collection, auctioned 1/1/1989. Price realized: **$1600.00**

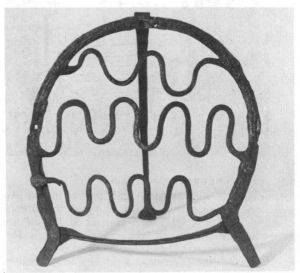

X-31.
Scotch broiler,
also called a **brander.** Easel-back upright broiler, forged iron, serpentine grids. Probably Scottish, 18th C. Photograph courtesy of Pat Guthman Antiques, Southport, CT. She has a large and very fine selection of kitchen-related antiques, almost exclusively related to hearth or early brickset range cookery, and writes a food column in Newtown Bee's "Antiques & Arts Weekly," Newton, CT. CT.

X-32.
Whirling broiler or rotary grill.
Forged iron. Note serpentine grid and rattail hanging loop. 18"L x 9" diameter, American, 18th C. Ex-Keillor Collection.

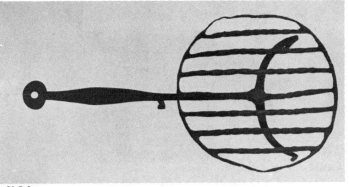

X-34.
Whirling broiler or grill.
Forged iron with unusual twisted-for-strength grids. Very nice penny diamond handle. Photograph courtesy of Pat Guthman Antiques, Southport, CT.

X-33.
Whirling broiler.
Forged iron, with upright handle in center, and hooks for hanging small birds (?) around rim of wheel. French fleur-de-lys design, probably French, or possibly French Canadian. 16" diameter, late 18th C, probably prior to the Revolution. Courtesy Sestienne Collection.

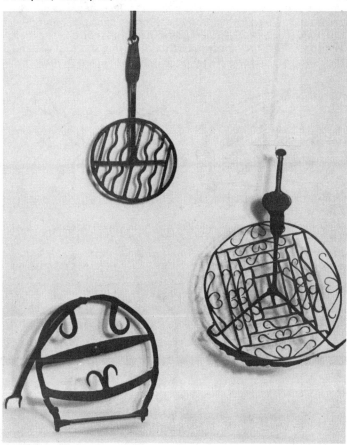

X-35.
Various hearth broilers.
All forged iron. Top two are meant to sit flat. One at right has very decorative, probably European, hearts and scrolls, and 3 legs. Bottom left is another brander or Scotch broiler, startlingly anthromorphic. All late 18th C. Photograph courtesy of Pat Guthman Antiques, Southport, CT.

X-36.
Whirling broiler or grill.
Forged iron piece, with alternating straight and serpentine bars. Late 18th or early 19th C, probably American. Photo courtesy of Oveda Maurer Antiques, San Anselmo, CA.

X-37.
Cauldron or caldron.
Riveted bronze, from ancient Ireland, 8th C. The illustration is from an article "The Old Poetic Guild in Ireland," by Charles de Kay, Century, 4/1890. The story told in the article is about a "band of poets" who traveled all around and carried with them a "large pot, or caldron, called 'The Pot of Avarice.' This was the sign of their intention to claim food from the chief they visited, although in legend it was meant for the gold and silver they expected as prerequisites...From a caldron like this one, king, poet, and hero obtained their porridge, their boiled beef and mutton, and their venison, which they ate without forks," using short knives and their fingers. This one is one of several in the Dublin Museum.

X-40.
Clock jack.
Skeletal iron frame, brass front. 8 11/16"H excluding governor or fly wheel at top. Cast iron weight. Photographed from stock of Mark & Margery Allen, Putnam Valley, NY. **$1800.00-$2200.00**

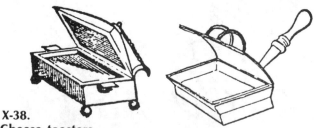

X-38.
Cheese toasters.
(L) "Cheese toaster to make Welsh Rarebits, with double bottom for hot water." American Home Cook Book, 1854. (R) Cheese toaster, with wooden handle, from F.A. Walker catalog, 1870s-80s. Both of pieced tin. **$75.00-$150.00**

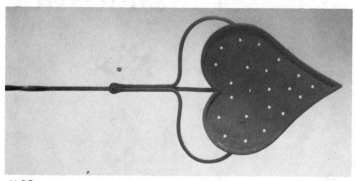

X-39.
Chestnut roaster.
In extremely unusual heart shape. Long thin handle, twisted for strength. 28 1/2"L. Pennsylvania, 18th C. Photo courtesy Litchfield Auction Gallery, Litchfield, CT. Ex-Harold Corbin Collection, auctioned 1/1/1989. Price realized: **$900.00**

X-41.
Curfew,
or couevre-feu. Used to cover hot coals in fireplace. This one illustrated an article in William Hone's The Every-Day Book, 1825-26. About it was written: "It is of copper, rivetted together, as solder would have been liable to melt with the heat. It is 10"H, 16" wide, and 9" deep. The Rev. Mr. Gostling, to whom it belongs, says it has been in his family for time immemorial."

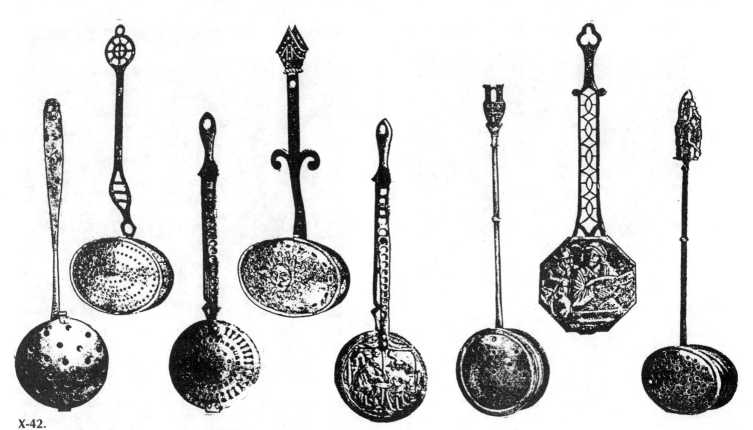

X-42.
Box chestnut roasters.
All are reproductions or meant-to-look-old decorative brass items, made by Pearson-Page, Birmingham, England, 1925 catalog. Top row (L) to (R): "The Battersea," 20 1/2"L; "The Bishop," 20 1/2"L; and "The Musician," made round square or octagon, 22"L. Like the others, you could choose a brightly polished or an "old colour" finish. Lower row: (L) to (R): "The Christy," 17"L, the oldest-looking one, "The Graham," 16"L; "The Wells" 16"L; "The Colchester," 18"L; and the oval "The Stratford," 19"L. Value range is for exactly what they were made to be — decorative items, with no claim to authenticity. $75.00-$125.00

X-43.
Dripping pan and ladle.
Placed under spitted meat to catch the drippings, which were used for making sauces, gravies, soups, or for rendering for a purer fat. Warne's Model Cookery, London, 1868.

X-44.
Double boiler.
Copper kettle inside, with bail handle, hung from hook in double arch of fixed handle of outer iron kettle. Could be used with a crane in the fireplace, and later on a range. 16 1/2"H overall x 13 1/2" diameter. 1830s.-50s. Ex-Keillor Collection.

X-45.
"Interior of Mennonite Kitchen."
In Kansas. Note adobe or brick cooking range at right, and wash or laundry range at left, and the ubiquitous huge basket of corncob fuel. What look like ovens in the ranges are "fire doors" through which fuel was added. Baking ovens are seen as dark rectangles in the back wall, which is actually part of the main chimney. According to the American Agriculturist, *12/1878, a Mennonite settler was quoted as saying "Americans burn money; we burn straw." Still true, alas.*

X-47.
Dutch oven in use.
Somewhat romanticized illustration from the 1880s of a somewhat earlier housewife piling hot coals on the dished lid of her long-legged Dutch oven, to bake something within. Note stationary crane in fireplace, with chain trammel — the most primitive kind. Also the ring atop the andiron. Its mate also had a ring, and a spit could be suspended thus between the andirons.

X-46.
"Mennonite Woman Cooking at a Hearth."
A raised hearth, almost a range. Note hams and sausages hanging high up to be smoked; also the trivet or stand on which the center utensil rests, with the fire underneath. The flat-bottomed frying pan at right has three rather tall legs and a long handle. The tall, round-bottomed pot at left also has legs. "The most primitive cooking arrangement was seen in Harvey County (Kansas). This is merely a block of adobe or masonry, 2'H, built in the base of an ordinary chimney. Cooking is done by building straw and corncob fires under each vessel, like persons camping out." Article on Mennonites, based on observances of Mr. H. Worrall, Shawnee County, KS, in American Agriculturist, *12/1878.*

X-48.
Dutch oven.
Cast iron, bail handle, 3 shortish legs, very well-fitted and undoubtedly original lid with deep flange. 8 3/4"H x 9 1/4" diameter. American, probably early 19th C. Picture courtesy of Robert W. Skinner Inc., Auctioneers, Bolton, MA. It has been claimed by at least one writer that the Pilgrims, who spent some years in Holland before departing for the new land, brought "Dutch ovens" with them and used them on shipboard. **$325.00-$400.00**

X-49.
Cooking pot,

something like a Dutch oven, but without distinctive high flange on lid. This charming illustration, is but one of at least 32, in a French book about a Monsieur Vieux Bois, Mr. Old Wood, who has many household adventures. Apparently the food cooking in this pot caught on fire, and was ruined, so Monsieur Bois carried it up on the roof so the dog could eat it. We all have known such, n'c'est pas? Unfortunately, the NYC bookshop where I found this tears many non-valuable books apart and sells the pictures as decorations. But those of us who use the pictures as part of our research, as well as those who just love an intact book, squirm at such practices.

X-50.
Dutch oven.

Cast iron, very unusual with the raised handles for the bail. Late 18th or early 19th C. Photograph courtesy of Pat Guthman Antiques, Southport, CT.

X-51.
Dutch ovens or French bake pans.

Clockwise from upper (L): (1) "French Bake Pan of wrought iron, to put fire or embers on the cover if needful." American Home Cook Book, 1854. (2) "A Bake-kettle, or Skillet." "When cooking stoves came in, the bake-kettle, or covered skillet, went out, and with it went a large part of what was good in our American cookery. How many of your readers (American Agriculturist, 9/1870) ever saw a bake-kettle? Probably only those who enjoy the blessing of a wood fire to cook by. Just send an artist down to the backwoods of Maine or away 'out west', and have a drawing made of this most capital kitchen utensil. 'Pioneers' will know what I mean; it is a shallow kettle with a lid, which has a turned-up edge, and upon which coals are placed; and the thing to be cooked is 'between two fires.' " (3) Cast iron, unground, shallow or deep pattern, in sizes from 8" to 14" diameter, from 2 1/2"-3 1/2"D for shallow and 3 1/2"-5 1/4"D for deep. National Stoves & Ranges, c.1916. Note triangular ears, generally thought to be a sign of great age. (4) "French bake kettle," cast iron, note there is no flange at all on the lid. Henry N. Clark, Boston, MA, 1884 catalog.

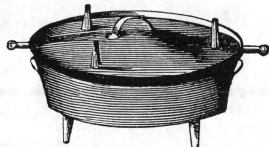

X-52.
Biscuit baker.

Cast iron, very like the Dutch oven. 12" and 14" diameter, from Stuart, Peterson & Co., catalog of cast iron hollowware, 1866. No explanation is given, time travelers are supposed to know these things. See three legs on lid, and the two little stubby knobs obviously used to flip it over. Perhaps this could be used with both parts upside down, or the way shown here. **$150.00-$200.00**

X-53.
Trivet or kettle stand.
Wrought iron, probably European. 13"H x 15"W, dated 1821. Ex-Keillor Collection.

X-54.
Footman.
Much fancier type, sometimes called a waiter, although that term is usually reserved for a type of large tray. Cast iron frame, bolted together, with highly polished brass convex knees to the lion-footed cabriole front legs. Perforated sheet brass top. 11 3/4"H x 14 1/2"W x 12 1/2"D. Probably English, mid 19th C. Collection of Mary Mac Franklin.   **$170.00-$250.00**

X-55.
Footman.
"The Weston," with perforated brass top and shelf and brass legs. (They made others with steel legs.) 11"H x 11 3/4" x 12 1/2". Pearson-Page, Birmingham, England, 1925.

X-56.
Footman.
Pieced brass and forged iron, turned wood handle. Hunting scene and foliage. Described in my 2nd edition as "probably English, late 18th or early 19th C" but since finding the Pearson-Page catalog I doubt it. 13"H x 13 3/4"W x 8 1/8"D. Picture courtesy of Christie, Manson & Woods International Inc. **$175.00-$250.00**

X-57.
Footmen or trivets.

In horseshoe shape, and type often found in containerload antique shops nowadays. (L) "The Kingsbury", cut brass with steel legs. Two sizes, 8 1/2"H x 9 1/2"H x 11" x 8". (R) "The Newark," steel legs, wooden handle. 8 1/2"H x 9 1/2" x 6 1/2". Pearson-Page, England, 1925.

X-58.
Frying pan.

Wrought iron, 50"L x 14 1/2" diameter. American, 18th or early 19th C. Ex-Keillor Collection. **$150.00-$225.00**

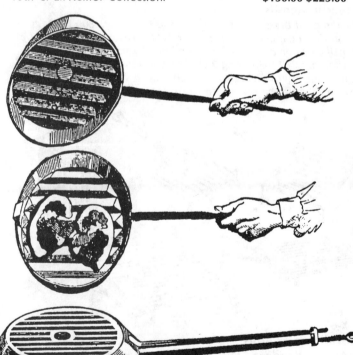

X-59.
"Captain Warren's Bachelor's Frying Pan."

Cast iron, with heavy sharp-edged flutes inside to retain heat, and long rein handles. Pat'd in the U.S. by Frederick Pelham Warren, East Court Cosham, Great Britain, on 2/13/1872; pat'd earlier in England. "It shuts and can be turned over from one side to the other, as the cook pleases." Note slip ring holding handles together. From Warne's Model Cookery, *London, 1868.* **$100.00-$200.00**

X-60.
Girdle plate or griddle,

hanging type with swiveling trammel ring. Deep rim, crudely cast iron. 16"H x 13" diameter, American, late 18th C. Photo courtesy of Robert W. Skinner Inc., Auctioneers, Bolton, MA. **$200.00-$300.00**

X-61.
Gridiron or grill.

Forged iron, with grease trough. Late 18th, early 19th C. Probably American. Photograph courtesy of Pat Guthman Antiques, Southport, CT.

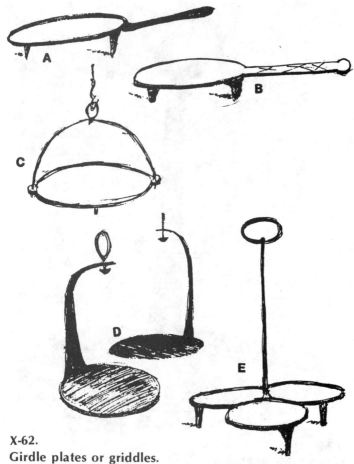

X-62.
Girdle plates or griddles.
(A) (B) Cast iron, Pennsylvania. 11" diameter, early 19th C. Three legs with leg under handle nearly twice height of other two, intentional, I'm sure to get more reflected heat when placed on hearth. Simple crisscross on handle of (B) is cast in; it had no rim. (C) Full-bailed plate, with short feet. Cast and wrought, with side ears for the bail. 15 1/2" diameter. Early 19th C. (D) Both are quarter-hoop hanging girdles, probably English or Scottish. Forged iron, with plates almost 17" diameter. One on right, missing part of the ring bolt, sold at a 1986 auction for $700.00. (E) Cast and forged iron, hearth-standing or hanging, central handle, late 18th, early 19th C. Drawn from ad of Pat Guthman Antiques, Southport, CT. **$125.00-$700.00**

X-64.
Hearth utensils.
Skimmer of brass with iron and wood handle, c.1800-1820; grill or gridiron hanging at top right, c.1790-1810. Bottom, from (L): Small cast iron bowl; large cast iron bowl; small posnet or skillet, cast iron, c.1820s-30. Long-legged cast iron frying pan, c.1830. Picture courtesy of Georgia G. Levett, Levett's Antiques, Camden, ME. Probably the bowls are worth the most. **$100.00-$250.00**

X-63.
Hearth utensils.
"The sow came in with the saddle, The little pig rock'd the cradle, The dish jump'd up on the table To see the pot swallow the ladle. The spit that stood behind the door Threw the pudding stick on the floor. Odsplut! said the gridiron, Can't you agree? I'm the head constable, Bring them to me." ("Odsplut" is very old way to swear "God's blood" without actually saying it.) <u>Mother Goose Melodies</u>, 1833.

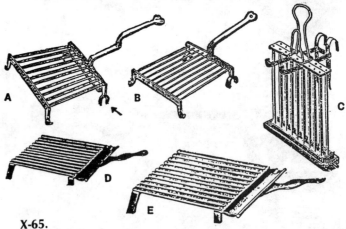

X-65.
Gridirons or grills.
(A) "Fluted gridiron," fluted steel bars, "fat pan" or grease through along back edge, under bars. Notched back feet to hook onto fender; 7, 8, 9, 10, 11, & 12 bars. (B) "London gridiron," a more economical model in same range of sizes. (C) "Double-hanging gridiron," with tinned iron wire (or with wrought iron, tinned all over "after made.") 8", 9", 10", 11" & 12" (or for wrought one, 10, 11, 12, 13, & 14 bars). (A-C) from Harrod's Stores, Ltd., Brompton, England, 1895 catalog. (D) "Heavy gridiron" in iron, 6 sizes, from 8 1/2" x 12" to 13" x 16 3/4", the smaller three for families, others for hotels. Duparquet, Huot & Moneuse, c.1904-1910. (E) Tinned sheet iron, 15 1/2" x 9 1/8" to 16 3/4" x 13". Lalance & Grosjean, 1890. **$50.00-$150.00**

X-66.
Revolving & stationary gridirons.

(T) Cast iron, 12" diameter, catches grease underneath. (R) Rectangular slightly convex, cast iron. Both Russell & Erwin, 1865. (L) "Revolving enameled gridiron with fluted bars to convey the gravy to the cup" (which is seen mid-handle). American Home Cook Book*, 1854.* **$60.00-$175.00**

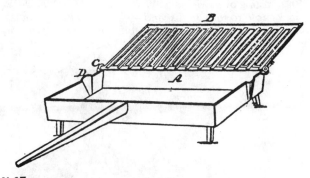

X-67.
Gridiron patent.

Pat'd 11/14/1836, by Amasa Sizer and George Sizer, Meriden, CT. "Combined gridiron and spider." "The nature of our invention consists in uniting a gridiron and spider in one instrument in such manner that both may be used together or each separately at the same time, the juices of the broiling meat being conducted into the spider or when the spider is separately used, into a receiver placed within it. To enable others skilled in the art to make, and use our invention we describe its construction as follows: The form may be square, circular, or oval when open for use, or a half square, or parallelogram, or a semicircle when folded. The model deposited in the Patent Office is semicircular when folded. The spider (A) and gridiron (B) are each cast whole in separate castings, and united in the following manner. The spider is formed with legs and a handle, and on each end of the spider around the corners of the side approaching the fire is a projecting ear (C), having a staple of wire set in the casting to receive the pintle or gudgeion of the gridiron, and on which it turns. Near each of these ears is a spout (D) on each end. The gridiron is cast with fluted bars, and rim, on the end of the bar, which joins the spider, gudgeons or pintles are extended, which when connected" form a hinge. When the two parts are used separately, and a the same time, a narrow tin pan is placed under the edge of the gridiron and within the basin of the spider, to receive the drip. When folded, the tin pan may be used as a chafing dish." Official Gazette*.*

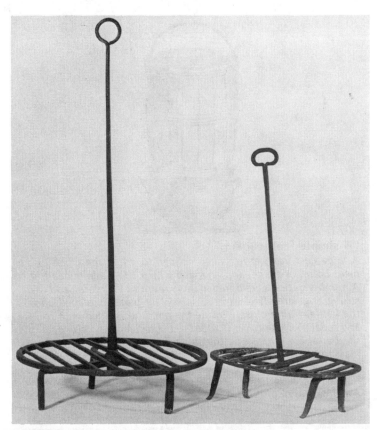

X-68.
Standing gridirons.

Wrought iron. 18th C. Photograph courtesy of Pat Guthman Antiques, Southport, CT.

X-69.
Grill.

Wrought iron, well-finished. Heart decorations add much to value. 26"L overall x 13"W. Probably English, late 18th C. **$300.00-$400.00**

X-70.
Hoe blades.

Forged iron, potentially used for baking hoe cakes in front of coals or fire. When laid down, the shank socket would serve as a little foot that would raise one end toward the fire. Blades about 6" to 8"W. (L) is a Virginia style weeding hoe; (R) is a Carolina style hoe. Both made as "plantation" hoes in Sheffield, England, c.1816.

X-71.

"A simple feed cooker."

A large cast iron kettle, "large enough to admit the chine of a meat barrel or tierce, and arranged with a fire-place beneath it. A number of holes are bored in the bottom of the barrel, and two strong rings are affixed to the sides. The barrel is placed upon the kettle, fitting closely inside the rim, and is filled with roots and meal. A close cover is fitted to the top, and the contents of the barrel are cooked by the steam from the kettle. The barrel may be lifted off when the feed is cooked, by means of a small crane and windless, and placed upon a wheelbarrow to be carried where it is to be used." Imagine doing that every day! American Agriculturist, 6/1878.

X-72.

Meat screen.

Tin, with bottle jack in place. William S. Adams & Son, London, c.1860-61 ad in Francatelli's Cook's Guide Advertiser. Note that all of these have a basin-like depression in the bottom for drippings.

X-73.

Meat screen.

Came in three widths, 19", 21" and 24". Note lid on grease trap. Harrod's Stores, Ltd., Brompton, England, 1895.

X-74.

Meat screens.

You may think I've got too many of these, but I found it fascinating that something so ancient looking could be relatively new. Both are tin, with clockwound bottle jacks in place. (L) "Roasting screen and jack. The screen in adapted to the ranges and cooking stoves in general use. The jack is wound up and runs so as to keep the meat constantly turning til cooked." American Home Cook Book, 1854. (R) "Roasting oven with jack." Two sizes — 18"W and 24"W ovens, jacks able to turn 25 lbs. and 40 lbs. Note key for bottle jack on floor. Duparquet, Huot & Moneuse, hoteliers' supply catalog, c.1904-1910.

X-75.

Meat screen,

sometimes called a **tin kitchen.** Of type specifically for a hanging jack of some kind, especially a bottle jack. This one has a dangle spit with 6 weighted rods — a flywheel — spoked out to assist the backward and forward spinning. Sheet iron with crown-like superstructure. We see it as we would from the fire, the door in back is for the cook to view the procedings and to baste. Vertical forged iron spit with hooks. Front left leg propped up on wood support indicating piece was either customized to fit, a particular hearth, or that one leg has broken, or possibly that the other three legs were lengthened. c.1790 to 1840. Picture courtesy of the National Museum of American History, Smithsonian Institution.

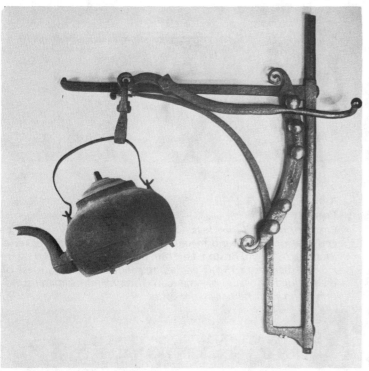

X-76.
Quadrant crane & kettle tilter,
with tea kettle. Forged iron, beautifully detailed and well-finished. Lever caught under one of six pegs (one missing). 18th or very early 19th C. Photograph courtesy of Pat Guthman Antiques, Southport, CT. Value range is solely mine, not Guthman's. If I'm way low, Pat, lemme know. . **$1200.00-$1800.00**

X-78.
Plate warmer or dish warmer.
Sheet iron with japanned finish, and with cast iron cabriole legs with lion's paws. Cast handles at sides. This kind was slightly more versitile than the closed top kind, although heat escaped out of the top. American (?), mid 19th C. Courtesy William Hodges.

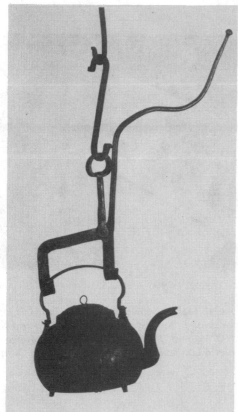

X-77.
Kettle tilter with kettle.
Forged iron with cast kettle. Photograph courtesy of Pat Guthman Antiques, Southport, CT.

X-79.
Plate warmer.
Japanned and decorated tin, most of decoration and finish burned off. With sheet iron legs bolted on. Brass decorative side handles. 28 1/2"H x 13 1/4"W, 2 inserted shelves. Other side open to the fire. Probably English, late 19th C. Photographed at booth of Jill Oltz, Mountainville, NJ, at show in NYC. **$300.00-$400.00**

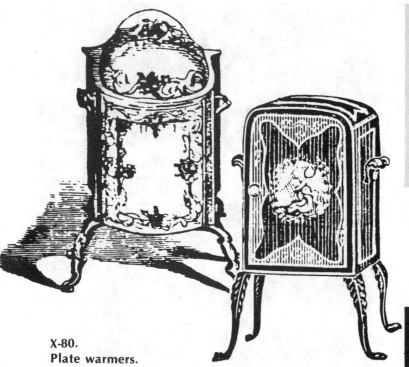

X-80.
Plate warmers.

Both japanned tin with decorative cast iron legs and handles. Both with open blocks to fire. Both probably imports from England. (L) From ad of J. & C. Berrian, NYC dealer, in History of Prominent Mercantile & Mfg. Firms in the U.S., 1857. (R) From F.A. Walker catalog, 1870-80s. **$250.00-$400.00**

X-81.
Posnet.

Cast bronze, 3 legs, one under handle longest by far so tilts forward. Long horizontal handle flat on top, half-round in section. Cast along top of handle: "W.C.: NEWPORT C (?)." 9 1/16"H x 8 1/16" diameter x 17 5/16"L with handle. Picture courtesy of the National Museum of American History, Smithsonian Institution, John Paul Remensnyder estate.

X-82.
Posnet.

Cast bell metal, 3 long legs, long flat handle slightly tapered at end, flat on top, round in section. Made by Robert Crocker & Richard (?) Austin, Boston, late 18th or very early 19th C. 8 1/2"H x 8 3/4" diameter x 19 5/8" including handle. Picture courtesy of the National Museum of American History, Smithsonian Institution, John Paul Remensnyder estate.

X-83.
Closeup of handle of posnet.

"Austin & Crocker, Boston" in floriate scroll border, which is very unusual. Picture courtesy of the National Museum of American History, Smithsonian Institution, John Paul Remensnyder estate.

X-84.
Posnet.

Cast bell metal. Maker, known more for andirons, is James Davis, who was working in the last quarter of the 18th and first quarter of the 19th C. Marked "J. Davis Boston." Photographed from stock of Jay Kohler & Louise Rozene, Sunset Mountain Farm, Amherst, VA.

X-85. Posnets.

A delightful family of cast bell metal posnets in five sizes. Note brace, which may be an old repair, to handle at far right. I find it very difficult to say with assurance, "this is a posnet," instead of a small saucepan or a skillet, which also looked like this except the skillets had rounded bottoms. Photograph courtesy of Pat Guthman Antiques, Southport, CT.

X-86.
Pot,
of type sometimes called a "gypsy kettle." Cast iron, squat bulging body, 2 vertical seams, long casting gate on bottom, 3 longish legs, 3 vertical bands in relief around circumference. Marked on side "No. 1. 2 QTS. SAVERY & Co. Philadelphia." 6"H x 9 5/16" diameter. Photo by Jennifer Oka. Picture courtesy of the National Museum of American History, Smithsonian Institution, John Paul Remensnyder estate.

X-87.
Pot,
or "gypsy kettle." Cast iron, 3 legs, twisted forged iron bail, domed lid with loop handle. 6 1/2"H x 4 1/4" diameter — beautiful small size. American, late 18th C. Picture courtesy of Robert W. Skinner Inc., Auctioneers, Bolton, MA. **$275.00-$350.00**

X-88.
Hearth scene,
with large cast iron cauldron in background on 3 long legs, cast iron tea kettle, "S" hook hanging from chane, probably hanging from lug pole rather than crane, ash shovel and tongs in foreground. The little story told in this 1858 children's book is remarkably humane. The little mouse explains she has stolen sugar to feed her babies, and the lady smiles and says "Well, Mouse, you may keep your prize; For I am going, just like you, To feed my child, who is hungry too." Picture Fables, drawn by Otto Speckter, from German rhymes by F. Hey. NY: Appleton, 1858.

X-89.
Hearth scene,
showing anthropomorphized food an utensils. Sausage is cooking in a frying pan over the coals. The covered vessels in rear are not identified. One on stand is probably made of heavy earthenware; smaller one with lid looks like a small skillet with lid, of cast iron. Also from <u>Picture Fables</u>, drawn by Otto Speckter, 1858.

X-90
Gypsy kettle or pot,
cast iron, 2 vertical seams, bail handle. A little beauty. Early 19th C. Photo courtesy of Oveda Maurer Antiques, San Anselmo, CA.

X-91.
Bulge pot, two views.
with pieced tin slightly domed lid. Cast iron, wire bail handle, 3 short feet. 9 1/2"H x 10 3/4" diameter. From stock of Jean Hatt, Hatt's Hutt, Denver, PA.

X-92.
Similar pot in use.
"To bed, to bed, says Sleepy-Head; Let's stay awhile, says Slow; Put on the pot, says Greedy-Gut, We'll sup before we go." Mother Goose's Melodies, 1833. Many of these moralistic fable books for children have delightfully detailed engravings or woodcuts, which show such things as dress and household accoutrements. Note here what appears to be either a frying pan or a bed warmer leaning against the surround. But especially note the **figural andiron** of man in tricorn hat. See X-12 for more on figural andirons.

453

X-93.
Standing crane with utensils. Cast iron pot at left, cast and wrought girdle plate, and wonderful 18th C English cast bronze pot. Photograph courtesy of Pat Guthman Antiques, Southport, CT.

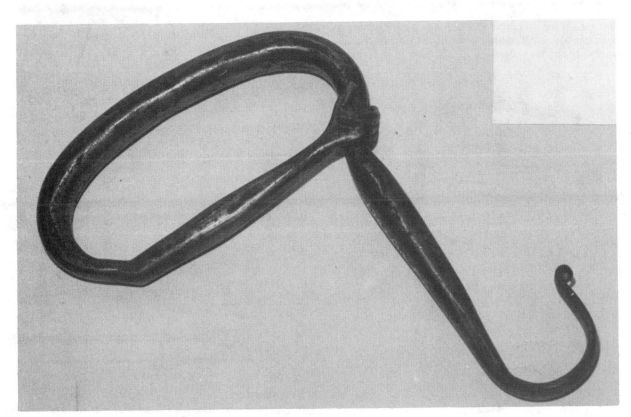

X-94.
Pot hook.

Best one ever. Finely whitesmithed steel hook with beautifully shaped long slender forearm and hand grasping where loop comes around. 5 5/16" x 4 1/4", American (?), early 19th C. Photo by Jennifer Oka. Picture courtesy of the National Museum of American History, Smithsonian Institution, John Paul Remensnyder estate.

454

A   B   C

X-95.
New England kitchen interior,

as depicted on frontispiece of Esther Allen Howland's The New England Economical Housekeeper, and Family Receipt Book. Worcester, MA: S.A. Howland, 2nd edition, 1845. Note light walls and well-lit room. This is obviously not a very old house; neither is it new or it would have a brick-set range if not a cooking stove. Note dead animals hanging on walls — yikes! At (A) is a spit leaning against work counter. She is probably going to spit the goose, and fix it with a skewer, lying on counter. At (B) far back is black cast iron kettle hanging on crane. Out some is a tin kitchen, a reflecting oven of good size. Foreground shows requisite bountiful-harvest basket with spilled veggies. At (C) are more iron 3-legged pots.

X-96.
Reflecting oven.

Called in English catalog a "Dutch oven," which was another common name for a tin kitchen reflecting oven. Came in four sizes, from 9" to 13"W. Harrod's Stores, 1895.

X-97.
Reflecting oven,

also called here a "Dutch oven for baking before the fire." Tin, boxy, not very attractive. F.A. Walker catalog, 1870s-80s.

$55.00-$75.00

X-98.
Tin kitchen.

Sheet iron, made from rectangles of tin soldered together, indicating an early date — late 18th or early 19th C. They were known and documented by the late 18th, and were considered novel and very useful. Wrought iron spit could be used at three different levels. There are tiny slots in the spit and they took the ends of skewers which secured meat to the spit. 13 1/4" x 18 5/8"L. Picture courtesy of the National Museum of American History, Smithsonian Institution.

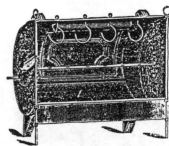

X-99.
Tin kitchen.

Tin, four hooks, spit and crank. Back door opens to allow basting. Came in three sizes, 20", 24" and 26"W. F.A. Walker catalog, 1870s-80s.

X-100.
Salamanders.

Wrought or cast iron. They were heated to red hot in the fire, then set over a dish to radiate the heat and brown a meringue, pudding, or whatever else needed it. Even in 1891, they were still being called for in recipes, although you could use a "hot stove lid" instead. (T) Wrought iron, 34"L, 6 1/2" diameter, English, 18th C. Ex-Keillor Collection. (M) Drawing to show how used. (B) Newfangled style, adjustable in height — it probably turned on a threaded post. Warne's Model Cookery, London, 1868.

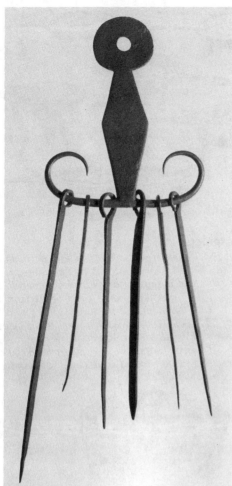

X-101.
Skewer rack & skewers.
Wrought iron, early 18th C. Picture courtesy of the Smithsonian Institution, Museum of History & Technology.

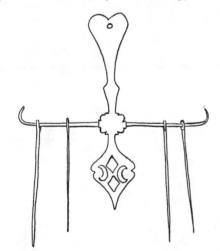

X-102.
Skewer rack & skewers.
Forged iron with very fine cutting & filing. Thought to be possibly from East Windsor, CT, c.1760. Drawn from photograph of piece exhibited at Wadsworth Atheneum. From unidentified private collection.

X-105.
Skewer pullers patent.
Pat'd 10/30/1877, by F.A. Will and Julius Finck, San Francisco, CA. Consists of a handle, a permanent jaw, a movable jaw operated by the thumb-lever. Shown with skewer stuck in it. <u>Official Gazette</u>.

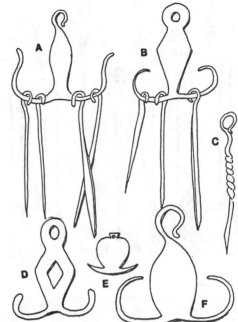

X-103.
Skewer racks & skewers.
Wrought iron, 18th & 19th C forms. Almost all skewer holders or racks are variations on two themes: a diamond shaft (B) and (D), or somewhat bulbous shaft (A) and (F) with upraised arms. The tulip-like form of (E) is very unusual, but probably wouldn't have the presence to command a top price. Value depends on age, size, and design. Don't worry about a "matched" or "original" set of skewers, because even in the 18th and 19th C a set would be a built up of various skewers made for specific purposes. Special forms and beautiful detailing, such as extra fine rattail loops or twisted (C) iron add value. **$150.00 and up for racks.**

X-104.
Skewer racks & skewers.
Even commercially ordered and relatively late sets might have well-shaped racks. (L) Iron, from Henry Adams & Son, London, c.1860-61 ad. (R) "Steel skewers. Round, 3 to 9". Oval, 3 to 11", and 4 to 12"." Look at that rack. Would you guess Duparquet, Huot & Moneuse, c.1904-1910? Although they could just have picked up an earlier linecut to use in their catalog. Still, the style looks early 19th or late 18th C.

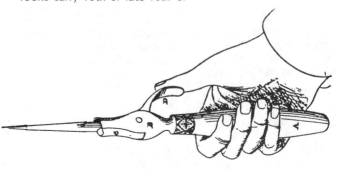

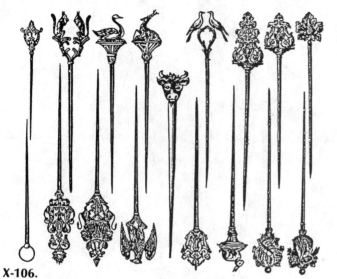

X-106.
Fancy skewers.

All are French, with possible exception of center one, the bull's-head, which came from a different catalog. That one from <u>Mrs. A.B. Marshall's Cookery Book</u>, London, c.1900. The others from Duparquet, Huot & Moneuse, c.1904-1910.

X-107.
Skillets.

Cast iron, rounded bottoms, 3 legs, long handles flat on top, half round in section. Used sitting on raked coals in fireplace. 18th or early 19th C. Picture courtesy of the National Museum of American History, Smithsonian Institution.

X-108.
Skillet.

Cast iron, long, more angular legs and handle. Longish casting gate on bottom. 4"H x 13 3/4"L overall. Picture courtesy of the National Museum of American History, Smithsonian Institution, John Paul Remensnyder estate.

X-109.
Skillets & spiders.

All cast iron. (A) "Lipped frying spider," in light or medium weight, both in 4 sizes, 8", 9 1/2", 11" adn 12 1/2" diameter. (B) "Biscuit spider with lid." Also in light or medium weight, and 11", 12" or 13" diameters. (C) "Plain cake spider." Light or medium, four sizes from 8" to 12 1/2" diameter. All from Russell & Erwin Mfg. Co., New Britain, CT, 1865. (D) "Shallow spider" in six sizes from 8" to 13" diameter. (E) "Skillet," which came nested in 3 sizes (not given); and (F) "Deep spider," in six sizes from 8" to 13". Note flat-top handles and half-round undersides of handles. Stuart, Peterson & Co., 1866 catalog.

X-110.
Skillet.

Cast iron, "plain finish, unground." "Furnished in deep or shallow patterns." Seven sizes, from 8" to 14" diameter, from 2 1/2" to 3" deep for the shallow ones, and 3" to 3 1/4"D for the deep ones. National Stoves & Ranges. c.1916. Looks just like Dutch ovens.

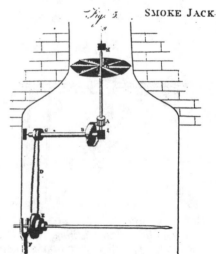

X-111.
Smoke jack.

18th C. drawing cut from unidentified book of plates. A. Bell was the engraver, this is the "Smoke" plate, CCCCLXXI, so it was a big book. Note gears. This interesting invention worked by using the heated air (smoke) updraft which caused the vanes to turn, which turned the shaft which turned the spit. Archie Keillor told me, when I worked on my first book, that you couldn't collect these — unless you caught a sight of one, peering up an old chimney in an English manor home.

X-112.
Spit driven by dog power.
"Dog-Wheel. — Both the turnspit-dog and apparatus for cooking are now nearly out of use. The example here was sketched in Glouscestershire about five years since." Hone's Every-Day Book, *1850. What a horrible thing to do to a dog. And probably breathing smoke the whole time.*

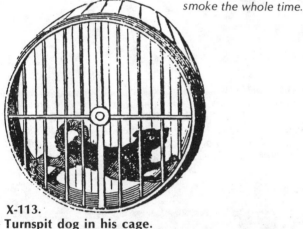

X-113.
Turnspit dog in his cage.
Depicted in The Comic Offering; or Ladies' Melange of Literary Mirth for 1835. *London: 1835. Hah hah hah.*

X-115.
"Kitchen Fire-Place at Windsor Castle."
"The open fire-place measures 6 x 8 feet in size, the products of combustion passing up the chimney in such a way as to operate a kind of fan wheel (smoke jack), which is connected by means of belting and gears and revolve with the long spits placed before the fire. On these spits are various kinds of joints and poultry, while beneath is a large pan for the purpose of collecting the drippings from the various kinds of food in process of cooking." The drawing is an engraving, made from a pencil sketch, that a "gentleman connected with the (stove-making) firm" of Rathbone, Sard & Co., Albany, NY, made on a trip to England in 1889. The Metal Worker, *4/5/1890.*

X-114.
"The Turnspit."
Illustration from the magazine Frank Leslie's Boy's & Girl's Weekly, *8/7/1869. "Not long since, a wheel in a circular box was brought from an old house to a railroad station in England, with a lot of old trumpery. The other articles attracted little attention, but this puzzled all the group. There were old men and women, too, but none remembered to have seen in use. At last, a blacksmith of a neighboring village said it was a turnspit's wheel, such as he remembered to have seen in use. It seems a hard lot for the dog to be kept at this work for, perhaps, three hours, till the joint was done, and we do not wonder the custom at last fell into disuse." Special short-legged, barrel-chested dogs were bred for this.*

X-116.
Pivoting toaster.
Wrought iron, 30"L x 13"W, possibly English, early 19th C. Ex-Keillor Collection. All you had to do was pick it up by the long handle, do a neat sort of flip with the handle, and set it down again.

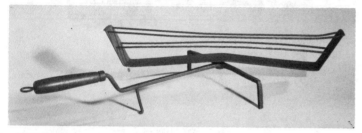

X-117.
Revolving toaster,
also called a **toe toaster,** *because instead of leaning over to turn it, you could turn it with your foot, wooden grip on handle, possibly mid 19th C. Handle is the puzzler — it just doesn't look old. Picture courtesy of the National Museum of American History, Smithsonian Institution.*

X-118.
Revolving toaster.
Wrought iron, strong spirals, extremely well-made. 3 3/4"H x 11"L overall x 7"W. American, early 19th C. Ex-Keillor Collection.

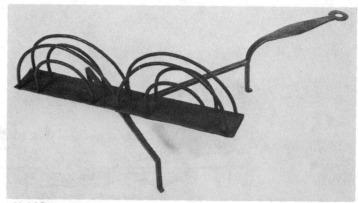

X-119.
Revolving toaster.
Wrought iron, with two sets of four arches, big and small. 19"L, early 19th C. Ex-Keillor Collection.

X-120.
Revolving toaster.
Wrought iron, with unusual "corn sprout" supports for bread, in addition to double arches. Late 18th or early 19th C. Picture courtesy of the National Museum of American History, Smithsonian Institution. A very similar one, with 3 simple legs, was offered by Oveda Maurer Antiques, San Anselmo, CA, for $595.00 in 1987.

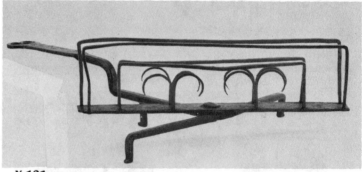

X-121.
Revolving toaster.
Wrought iron, another one with the "corn sprouts." Ram's horn handle. 17 1/2" x 13 1/2"W, American, late 18th C. Picture courtesy of Robert W. Skinner Inc., Auctioneers, Bolton, MA.

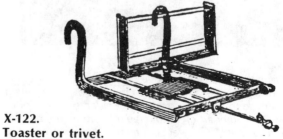

X-122.
Toaster or trivet.
Described in <u>Warne's Model Cookery</u>, *London, as an "improved revolving toaster, also available as a hanging Trivet, for Kettle, Saucepan, or Plate." Hmmm.*

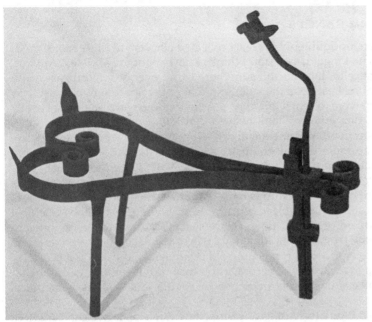

X-123.
Trivet for frying pan,
or other pan. Forged iron, heart shape. Upright piece supports handle of pan, if it tilts up. Continental European, possibly French or Portuguese. Late 18th or early 19th C. Photograph courtesy of Pat Guthman Antiques, Southport, CT.

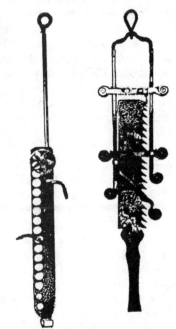

X-124.
Trammels.
Both wrought iron, 18th C, probably not American. (L) Pawl & ratchet type, with crank action. 36"L as shown. (R) Elaborate sawtooth style, probably earlier than the other one. 56" as shown. Ex-Keillor Collection.   **$200.00-$500.00**

X-125.
Trammel.
Wrought iron, finely done. Saw-tooth style with crane ring, extension 45" to 61"L. Probably American, early 19th C. Ex-Keillor Collection. The faint numbers you may see are Keillor's acquisition numbers, not a mark.   **$175.00-$250.00**

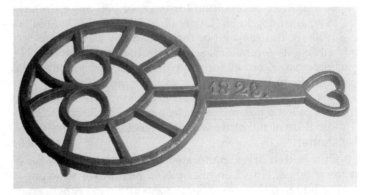

X-126.
Trivet.
Cast iron, heart design. Dated 1829, which makes it very desirable, as well as the hearts. 11 3/8"L x 6 1/2" diameter. Picture courtesy of the National Museum of American History, Smithsonian Institution.

I wrote in the last edition, seven years ago, that "stoves are undoubtedly the least collected objects" in this general field, "though only because of their size I'm sure." Arguably this is no longer true. I don't think I knew about the Midwest Antique Stove Information Clearinghouse and Parts Registry, in Monticello, IN. I'm still sure there won't ever be a Northeast ASIC & PR., in New York City, say. Or anyplace else where rental real estate is the rule, and where the space one old cast iron cook stove would take up is worth about $200.00 a month if you were to rent it out as a "spacious studio with sleeping alcove."

But for sure there are hundreds of people seriously into old stoves. Thank heaven they came along at the right time; and fortunately an adequate supply of stoves seems to have survived wartime metal drives because they were necessary fixtures in the home. Cook stoves probably have a big edge on popularity, but there are some fantastic parlor beating stoves that will get more and more attention. **Futurewatch:** A new related category is hot water radiators with built-in warming ovens, meant for cold, high-ceiling dining rooms where eating dinner took an hour or more. These are going to be the hardest things to find; they haven't been given the sort of safety net that a lot of other old things have (either because they weren't important enough to notice and throw away, or they were too useful or too noticeable to discard). Probably several million radiators, many of them attractive works of cast iron art, have been junked or melted down in the last 60 or 70 years, gone forever.

I also wrote that some people collect stove parts. This is still true. I knew somebody who used to climb into those giant dumpsters (where they throw all kinds of eminently-collectible stuff when renovating old buildings) to dig out cast iron gas-stove jet rings, which come in cast forms as varied as flowers in a garden, or coronets at a turn-of-the-century gathering of the crowned heads of Europe. I used to try to rescue all the porcelainized cast iron knobs, drop pulls and handles; sometimes I was able to get a decorated oven front.

Some people collect stove tools — from ash shovels and lid lifters to scuttles and stovepipe flue stops. I've seen enough flue stops to know that there is a satisfactory diversity and range to give a collector a run for the money. Although I can agree that a lot of stove lid lifters are competently-designed, even handsome, I've only seen one lifter that would make me want to look for more in a serious way. That's the cast iron female figural one described in this chapter, which I was fortunate enough to see listed in an *Antique Trader Weekly* classified a couple of years ago. Ah ha! I didn't even write the advertiser for five months, and for some reason it was still there. What a beauty!

Another upcoming category is camp stoves — probably because of the increasing interest in hearth cooking and portable 'stoves' from early soldiers' field braziers to a variety of stylish chafing dishes. You might find a wrought iron one at a militaria show, from a dealer in Revolutionary War or Civil War equipment. Smart collectors, no matter what their specialties are, will not depend solely on specialist dealers within that field, but imaginatively seek connections to other specialties where treasures may lie hidden. So for you, it might be a dumpster, a scrap yard, a gun show that will yield up something grand. In fact, there are many recognized "crossover collector" fields now, mainly in 20th century collectibles where cartoon characters or advertising images on objects are sought by people coming at them from three viewpoints: attracted to the image, the theme, or the object. This crossoverage has complicated pricing, because while I would like to give a price range related to the object, the buyer may find the major market is related to the theme, image or character.

Ash shovel, wrought iron, ram's horn handle, 18"L, early 19th C. **$55.00-$70.00**

Ash sifter shovel, wood & wire, instead of steel blade with the typical shovel rounded shoulder, it's made of welded heavy wires, going lengthwise and joined at shoveling edge, and at top, steel "ferrule" fasted to long wooden handle, for shoveling through ashes to clear out clinkers or unburned debris from furnaces, or perhaps even large stoves. Androck, 50"L overall, "blade" is 14"L x 8½"W, 1930s. • You see a lot of these, made by all different wiregoods companies, some with patterns of braced crisscrosses, but all for same purpose. Very graphic collectible. Even the blades only, as the handles are often found missing or broken. • A shorter version, almost identical, was called a potato scoop. Its handle was 30"L and the shoulder of the blade was solid steel, so the wires were shorter. **$9.00-$25.00**

Boot & mitten dryer, perforated & plain tin, oval box for over range, with 2 angular pieced horns over which to put the mittens, the center flat place with holes, American, 23"L x 10"W x 13"h, 19th C. **$125.00-$150.00**

Boot or shoe dryer, metal base shaped like horseshoe with 2 tin tubes on which to place shoes or boots, stovetop, "Hubbard", American, 8" x 10", pat'd 1877. **$85.00-$100.00**

Camp stove, boxy iron body, supposed to burn a special fuel, 4 squatty, fat-knee cabriole legs, adjustable air vent on side, single hole on top fitted with lid that has notch for lid lifter, wire bail handle & turned wooden grip, trademarked "Carbonite", The American Safety Fuel Co., NYC, 10"h x 10½" square, with 6" hole & lid (also came in 7" or 8"), early 1890s. **$35.00-$50.00**

Camp stove, Boy Scouts, in original canvas bag, iron, round, "Coleman", 20th C. **$15.00-$22.00**

Camp stove, one burner, cast iron, gas fueled, Griswold, early 20th C. • The 2 burner model brings somewhat less. **$150.00-$200.00**

Camp stove, round, iron with brass reservoir, Coleman, 20th C. **$12.00-$15.00**

Camp stove, small portable type called Revolutionary War soldier's stove, penny feet, sheet iron & forged iron, wood handle, for all the world like a modern day Sterno®, American, 6½"h x 5"D, 18th C or early 19th C. **$300.00-$450.00**

Camp stove, wrought iron with turned wooden handle and hanging ring, 4 small penny feet, rectangular body or firebox, with rack or grid above, plus 4 corner supports for pot, actually works as a brazier would, as a portable fire. American, 5¼"h x 6"W x 12"L, 19th C. Sold at auction in early 1980s for $375.00. **$600.00-$800.00**

Canal boat stove, cast iron, 2 burners, 3 legged, American (?), 18''h, late 19th C. **$400.00-$550.00**

Chafing dish — See page 489.

Coal carrier, brass with wood & wire carrying handle on side, like little suitcase, sheet iron bottom, called a "stoker", small knob slides in slot to regulate vent opening in top, several marks stamped on lid, "Girodon & Cie. Fabnts. Depose a Villeurbanne Lyon; Brevete en France" & "A l'Etranger Stoker S.G.D.B.'', Lyon, France, 1⅞'' deep x 7¼''L x 5½''W, c.1870s (?). • *Brevete en France* means Patented in France; *S. G. D. B.* stands for *Sans Garantie Du Gouvernement*, or, registered with, but not warranted by, the government. **$55.00-$65.00**

Coal hod, wood with tin interior, cast brass handles, English, 19th C. **$65.00-$75.00**

Coal hod or scuttle, japanned & tole-decorated heavy sheet tin with original tin liner, for the parlor, flowers & scrolls on black background, cast brass handles on side, nice feet, slanted hinged lid, this was the type of coal vase called a purdonium, back stenciled "Mfd by Sidney Shepards Co.'', Buffalo, NY, 23''H, 3rd quarter 19th C. • **Reproduction alert.**— Exactly this bin type of drop-front coal container was made by the thousands in the late 1920s & early 30s during that phase of Colonial Revivalism. They were sold as magazine holders, kindling boxes, & especially for fireside decoration. • John Fuller, Sr., author of occasional articles in a series called "Art of Coppersmithing'', *The Metal Worker*, wrote about "coal scoops and coal hods'' as well as "coal scoopettes'' (yikes), in article XVIII, Nov. 15, 1890. Some interesting terminology is used, which may either explain or confuse our notions of what's what. A number of horizontal coal containers with long "lower lips'', like pelicans or pouters, all have flared feet and he calls them all "coal scoops'' Only two designs are called "coal hods'' — one is a vertical cylinder with tipping handle, arched falling handle and a roller coaster top edge to form a scoop mouth when held horizontally; the other looks almost identical to another that is called a scoop. Finally, the little scoop shovels used to remove coal from the receptacle is called a "scoopette''. All the designs, which he encourages metal workers to make, have names. (As usual in his articles, Fuller mixes past & present tenses.) "Coal scoops were made in a number of fashions, among which, besides the common hod, were the round mouthed scoop; the square mouthed or flat bottom; the Tudor; the Florence; the Nautilus; the Royal; the Boat; and the Helmet. Some of these names are variable, according to the factories in which they are made, while others have had the same name from the time they were first designed. The hod has always been a hod, and the common round mouth shape [he calls it a hod] has never received any other cognomen.'' • He goes on to say, in the only clue I've found to dates, that "we will now endeavor to describe the manufacture of several scoops in which we participated some forty years since (ie. c.1850), and while there have been deviations made during this long time...it would seem that nothing of any marked importance has been introduced to inconvenience one from resuming work as of yore.'' Most of the designs he describes measure 12'' diameter at front, 13½'' at back, and are 18'' long. He says "the ears may be cast or wrought'' and the tubular handles are bent of ¾'' pipe, "filled and bent, then filed and burnished.''

$225.00-$265.00

Coal scuttle, hammered & pieced rounded copper body with brass base, large "gravy boat'' type pouring lip, lion's head fittings for swinging handle, blue and white Delft porcelain hand grips on back handle & large swinging handle, supposed to be a "traditional Dutch Coal Scuttle'', made in Holland, three sizes: 9½''h , 12¼''h, 15¾''h, all measured to lip, sold through the mail in 1973 ads in *House Beautiful*, etc. • **Lookalike alarm.**— So many old copper & brass things are imported from Holland, if this were distressed at all & the lacquer finish gone, it might be good enough to fool you. Take every opportunity to look at old pieces of copper & brass, that have been in collections for several decades; this will help you pick up on the little details that are wrong. The gauge of the wire of the back handle, the way the pieces and parts are assembled, all are important. This advice goes for all kinds of antiques. • The advertised prices of these three sizes, in 1973, were: $18.75, $29.75, and $39.75, all marked down about $16.00 from earlier prices.

$15.00-$25.00

Coal scuttle or vase, japanned & stenciled tin, highly decorative, cast iron feet & handle on pull-down bin front, counterweighted so as to be self-closing, holds small supply of coal for parlor heating stove, from F. A. Walker catalog, English (?), c.1870s. • Chance of finding one with japanning & stenciling intact, and without major dings & dents, equals that of finding a Model-T in factory condition. **$115.00-$135.00**

Coal scuttle or vase, pieced sheet metal, painted black, flower-like pressed white glass knob on tight fitting lid, bail handle with wooden grip, little decorative cast iron feet, American, 13¾''h, c.1870s to 1880s. **$25.00-$40.00**

Coal scuttle or vase, tole (decorated tin), footed helmet-shaped basket with high arched handle, domed lid with cast iron finial, cast brass lion's head side handles, could possibly be a chestnut urn, used to carry hot chestnuts to the table, but none depicted in book on Pontypool & Usk Japanned wares shows a handle like this one, from Pontypool or Usk, or Wolverhampton, 25''h, c.1800-1810. • **American Coal Scuttles.**— "Thomas Darby & Son, 160 Bowery (NYC), exhibited specimens of brass and copper coal scuttles, at the late fair, and obtained a premium. Mr. Darby claims to have first carried this manufacture into successful operation in this country, and offers them of as good quality and as cheap as the imported. They are articles required in almost every family. We hail the successful commencement of the manufacture of every new article of general use and necessity, as the commencement of a new era in the history of our productive industry, and the name of the pioneer should be enrolled on the catalogue of benefactors. Let any one just ask the question — what will be the difference to the country, whether a coal scuttle is made and sold here, or imported from England and sold. It is, simply, that in the one case the money is in the country, and in the other, it is out of the country. We hope every American will purchase Mr. Darby's coal scuttles, as long as he sells as good and as cheap scuttles as the imported.'' Report in the December 1838 *Journal of the American Institute* on the 11th annual Fair, October 1838, sponsored by the American Institute, NYC. **$600.00-$900.00**

Coal shovel, cast iron, for stoves, "Boss,'' TOC. **$20.00-$25.00**

Coal shovel, heavy cast iron, "DMI Co.'', American (?), late 19th C. **$12.00-$15.00**

Coal tongs, cast iron, small & decorative, late 19th or early 20th C. **$18.00-$25.00**

Coal tongs, cast iron with spring in hinge, possibly mfd by Matthai - Ingram, American, 12"L, late 19th C. **$20.00-$28.00**

Conjurers—See entries in Pots & pans chapter. Also one entry in Coffee & Tea chapter.

Cook & parlor stove, cast iron, actually a parlor stove but known as a "dining room helper" because the top is a small oven, "Oven Parlor No. 7," mfd by Newberry, Filley & Co., Troy, NY, c.1854 to 1858. • According to the 1860 census, Troy had 3 brass and bell founders, three iron works, eight stove manufacturers and 20 tinware manufacturers. That year, in the entire United States there were some 290 cast iron stove and hollowware foundries. Think how many hundreds of thousands of collectible objects were made that year alone! **$900.00-$1300.00**

Cook stove, 2 burner, cast iron, Tennessee "Gem," only 18½"h x 14½"W, TOC. • E. Scott Boyce wrote, in *Economic & Social History of Chowan County, North Carolina, 1880-1915* (NY: 1917) that in the studied area, by 1915, "probably 90% of home owners and 50% of all other families now have sewing machines; for cook-stoves, the percentage is about 98 and 75, respectively." So some people were still cooking over fires, probably still using the "creepers" Boyce wrote about (see Hearth cooking chapter). **$250.00-$325.00**

Cook stove, beige enameled cast iron, Kalamazoo, 1927. **$650.00-$900.00**

Cook stove, blue porcelainized iron, nickel trim, gasolene fueled, "Quick Meal," Ringen Stove Co., early 20th C. **$900.00-$1100.00**

Cook stove, cast iron, "Imperial Clarion 8-20," mfd by Wood & Bishop, Bangor, ME, late 19th C. **$850.00-$1200.00**

Cook stove, cast iron, completely refurbished, re-nickeled, & painted with black high temperature paint, marked "Glenwood F" and "Glenwood Range #108", c.1906. • Dealer Dave Erickson, of Erickson's Antique Stoves, at the Depot, Littleton, MA, explained to me about nickel plating. He said that the plater grinds & polishes the surface to be plated, then puts a heavy copperplate layer on & buffs that. The copper gives a warm glow to the nickel tone, & also is a "primer" to fill in minor imperfections. A good nickel-plater always puts the copper on first, then nickels the surface. Poor nickel-plating is obvious when you sight down the nickeled part from an extreme oblique angle and you see ridges, ripples, sanding & filing marks. **$1900.00-$2200.00**

Cook stove, cast iron, nickeled copper, 6 burners, oven, warming oven, hot water reservoir, and all original accessory tools, "Copper Clad," 5 feet high, 19th C. **$2000.00-$2500.00**

Cook stove, cast iron, nickeled iron decorative pieces with acorn motif, very substantial base with cabriole legs, oven above, fold-down nickeled shelves on either side of flue, refurbished, "Crown Acorn," mfd by Rathbone, Sard & Co., Albany, NY, 61"h x 64"W, pat'd April 18, 1907 & Sept. 17, 1907. **$3000.00-$4000.00**

Cook stove, cast iron, oblong box, rather fancy "bath tub" legs, 4 holes on top, oven & firebox doors on side, no maker's or founder's name, American, c.1840s-50s. **$850.00-$1000.00**

• In the *American Agriculturist* of Nov. 1847 comes the following lamentation, along with a **kudo for a new** cooking-stove. "Stoves are now so generally used all over the Middle and Northern portions of the United States for cooking, that one is to be found in almost every dwelling. Common as they are, the mass of them are defective, and in many cases very poor. We feel that we are doing a great service to our readers by recommending them to the use of proper stoves for cooking, particularly the planters of the South whose system of economy in cooking is very bad at present, incurring a vast deal of labor and expense for fuel, to say nothing of the imperfect manner in which it is often done. In fulfilment of our promise in the October (1847) number, we would now call attention to Granger's iron-witch air-tight cooking-stove ... the main object of which has been to get as perfect and convenient an implement as possible, and at the same time to have it simple and without complication of flues, dampers, &c. The front of the stove is lined with brick, which keeps up that steady even heat, which is so desirable in baking, and in which particular cast-iron ovens are found so defective. By means of the brick in this stove, the baking is more like the old fashioned brick-oven, which it is universally acknowledged bakes in the best manner. A summer-furnace on the hearth is also attached to the stove with two boiler holes on which any and all the boilers fit. The furnace will be found very desirable for summer use, when but little fire is wanted; as a few chips or charcoal will do the cooking. The furnace can also be used at the same time with the stove, giving six boiler holes. A gridiron is also well fitted to the hearth for broiling, by raking the coals directly from the fire-chamber on to the grate. The grate in the fire-chamber is omitted, and the wood is burned directly on the bed of ashes, by which means the fire can be covered up and kept over night, which cannot be done on a grate; the expense of purchasing new grates is thus avoided." • Conservation of fuel that so occupied the minds of some 19th C editors & inventors was not based on any ecological or environmental beliefs. It was a matter of supply & transport, & heavily populated areas especially needed to use as little as possible.

Cook stove, cast iron, quite simple, "Home Clarion," mfd by Wood & Bishop, late 19th C. **$700.00-$1000.00**

Cook stove, cast iron, sheet iron, 3 side-by-side large burners & oven, burns white gas. Has white porcelainized panels on doors, ornate nickel trim & on the fancy versions there are small grill work doors that flip down to reveal niches for warming a bun or two or for keeping salt & pepper shakers, or perhaps a flour dredger, or some crackers to keep them crisp. Towel rack on side. A smaller one has one oven, no storage cupboard, no salt & pepper niche. All have a japanned tin & cast iron fuel tank & filter, with 4 cocks with air intake valves, connected with rubber tubes to the burners & oven, "Quick Meal," Ringen Stove Co., pat'd Sept. 15, 1903, March 31, 1908, Dec. 21, 1909. • Thanks to collectors Marilyn Bertz, Mike Craven, Harlan Tlustos and Dewayne Ziegler for writing me. Two are from Minnesota, one from Oregon and Mr. Ziegler neglected to give me an address. Interesting that the Quick Meals may have been used more widely out west. Mr. Ziegler writes that the picture in the 2nd edition is "just the very top part of an old white gas kitchen stove. The long tubes on the end fill up with gas. Pull them out, light them, and shove them in a hole in your burner.'' Mrs. Bertz wrote that ''a picture of the back of the stove would be nice to show how the tubes run down the back.'' Thanks again, everyone.   **$1900.00-$2800.00**

Cook stove, cast iron, very ornate with lots of shiny trim, ''Atlantic Grand,'' mfd by Portland Stove Foundry, Portland, ME, 19th C.   **$1500.00-$2000.00**

Cook stove, cast iron, very square & geometric designs typical of designs on paper goods from the same period, no really rounded forms, reflects jigsaw gingerbread rather than more voluptuous hand-carving, oven, large water reservoir at side, nice hob shelf with cutout brackets, ''Happy Thought,'' mfd. by Pittston Stove Co., date 1884. • **What's In a Name?** — I suspect that there are other collectors, like me, who would pay extra, a sort of premium, because something had a really great name right on the front. Call it conversation piece or good karma, this stove has got a good collectible name.
$2000.00-$2500.00

•**Designing Stoves:** ''How Solids Suggest Modern Products. — The cube and its elastic variations, called in geometry by the incredibly awkward name of 'rectangular parallelepeds,' will probably be the most useful (in designing). Stoves, refrigerators, kitchen cabinets, even the kitchen sink, are generally variations of these forms.'' Harold Van Doren, *Industrial Design, A Practical Guide* (NYC: McGraw-Hill, 1940).

Cook stove, cast iron, with water reservoir & warming ovens, ''Blue Banquet #B'', TOC.   **$60.00-$800.00**

Cook stove, cast iron wood stove, ''Oak Jewel No. 618,'' American, TOC.   **$900.00-$1500.00**

• **Pricing Old Stoves.**— This is really beyond the scope of this book, and is almost like the antique car market. See the article Clifford Boram wrote outlining the field. Generally speaking, if you want to buy a nice looking, somewhat ornate, nickeled-and-shined cast iron stove of any size or age, rebuilt so that it all works, you can expect to pay at least between $1000.00 and $2000.00. The fanciest of these kitchen pianos may have colored enameling, fancy renickeled trimmings, overhead ovens, ornate hob shelves, the works, and if they have been rebuilt or refurbished, expect to pay between $3000.00 and $6000.00. These prices are mainly for coal or wood stoves. For early 20th C gas stoves, expect to pay up to $4000.00, depending on the features. Wood & coal stoves can also be converted to work with gas or electricity, while retaining the outward appearance of its original state. Add about $500.00 to $1500.00 for conversions. The days of finding a fabulous looking 100 year old relic from a bygone kitchen for under $100.00 (and it wasn't all that long ago) are past. • Parlor stoves, base burners, heating stoves, from the mid to late 19th C, with some of the same trim and pizzazz of the cook stoves, are generally less than cooking stoves. • **Stove Collector's Best Friend.** — If you only want one old stove, or if you want to start a collection, join the Midwest Antique Stove Information Clearinghouse and Parts Registry, 417 North Main St., Monticello, IN 47960. There are many perks, and it's worth sending your SASE for information.   **$900.00-$1500.00**

Cook stove, electric, cast iron boxy body, flexible tubes coming up from back to attach to wall mounted box with switches & dials, ancient styling for hinges on oven door, 4 eyes, the lids of which make an even or flush working

surface stove not in when not in use, oven has inner glass windowed door, ''Carron'', English, c.1912.
$700.00-$900.00

Cook stove, for gas, wood or coal. Finished in light gray blue (almost like Wedgwood) enamel over the cast iron, re- nickeled, fitted with safety pilot for gas, given fiberglass insulation. Gas oven & broiler on right above door with built-in temperature gauge, a woodstove oven below with temperature gauge in door, range eyes fueled by gas, United Premier Boston Stove Foundry, Reading, MA, c.1926. • Offered at Brimfield, Fall 1987, by Erikson's Antique Stoves, Inc., Littleton, MA. • To share with you the charm of technical journalism 100 years before this stove was a gleam in the eye of its inventor, I will transcribe a few paragraphs on an invention granted John J. Hess from an 1829 issue of the *Journal of the Franklin Institute* (Philadelphia). ''For and Economical Cooking Stove; John J. Hess, Philadelphia, March 19 (1829).'' The inventor claims ''This stove consists of seventeen pieces, or plates, independent of eight doors, and three grates, all resting upon four feet, which, when properly applied, and put together, form a perfect, whole, and entire construction, capable of performing, with rare economy, a great variety of cooking operations, together with numberless other services in housewifery, being heated by a very small portion of wood, or anthracite coal.'' The editor advises that ''The foregoing is the exordium of the specification, and the following is its peroration.'' Then back to Hess: ''With this apparatus, and attentive care in its operations, great economy must be preserved in the consuming material used for fuel. Steam is generated from the boilers, and when received into proper vessels, can be applied to all the delicate cookery of luxurious dishes, without the aid of assistants; an important advantage to families. Boiling water is always in readiness; and with the same fire, baking of meats, and bread, or fruit, roasting, broiling, stewing, frying, boiling, and fricaseeing, are expeditiously going on, at one and the same time!''

The editor adds ''There is a something so stimulating in the foregoing enumeration of properties and results, as to make us wish to anticipate the usual 'hour of prime;' and had we one of Mr. Hess's stoves, we certainly should hurry the cook. As it is impossible to describe this stove without engravings, and as most of our readers, like ourselves, are more inclined to partake of a good dinner than to study the means of preparing it, we will merely give them the address of the patentee, who resides at No. 237 North Second Street, Philadelphia, who is prepared to gratify the taste of those who will apply to him.'' For the ''United Premiere'':   **$3400.00-$4000.00**

Cook stove, for railroad car, iron, ''Stearns,'' E. C. Stearns & Co., Syracuse, NY, TOC.   **200.00-$225.00**

Cook stove, of type called a covered wagon stove, though not old enough to be, cast iron, oval with slanted sides, flat top with 2 eyes, looks sort of like bath tub with little grate in side, 4 short legs, mfd by Fischer Leaf Co., Louisville, KY, 12''h x 18''W x 12'' deep, pat'd 1879.
$250.00-$350.00

Cook stove, cast iron, small oven, 4 burners, large flat hearth, 4 legs, design of front is like 6 fluted columns close together, called a ''Summer and Winter Cooking Stove No. 4,'' pat'd by famed stove designer Philo Pen-field Stewart, Troy, NY, 41"h x 36"W, pat'd Sept. 1838 (and he was still patenting stoves 20 years later).

$3500.00-$5000.00

Cook stove, ornate cast iron, warming ovens above, urn pedestals on either side of flue, 6 holes, water reservoir on side, "Grand Windsor," Windsor Stoves and Ranges, in Montgomery Ward catalog, late 19th C. • Prices for most of these stoves reflect value for stoves that have been restored and are in good working order. • <u>Added value</u>.— Even higher prices are asked and received for stoves completely re-nickeled. **$2000.00-$3000.00**

Cook stove, water reservoir, warming ovens, center oven, 6 lids, white porcelainized cast iron, TOC. **$450.00-$550.00**

"Right and Left-Hand Ranges. — It is somewhat difficult to tell just what the custom may be in different parts of the country or among different manufacturers or dealers. Ranges are made of several kinds. Some are double ranges with a fire-pot in the center and an oven on each side. Others are single ranges with a fire-pot on the left side and oven on the right. Other single ranges are made with fire-pot on right and oven on left...<u>The one in ordinary use has the fire-pot on the left, oven on the right</u>. The question arises, is this a right or a left-hand range? As the vast majority of people are right-handed, it seems...natural to suppose that the range most widely used would be constructed so as to be most convenient for them and would therefore be a right hand range. Yet this view is not taken by many manufacturers, who curiously enough regard the range in common use as a left-hand range, insisting that the location of the fire-pot fixes the name. Fuller & Warren's catalogue, for instance, says about their Diamond B. range: 'This range has the fire-box constructed at the right side of the oven, hence it is termed a right-hand range, and for that reason it can often be used to advantage when a left-hand range or cook stove could not be used conveniently.'

"This peculiarity in naming ranges gives rise to a great deal of uncertainty in filling orders. One stove manufacturer, whose ranges are all made with fire-pots at the left, says that when he is asked by a customer for a left-hand range he invariably replies that he does not make them. While all his ranges are really left-hand, according to [Fuller & Warren's usage], he knows that his customer is seeking a range of a different type from those in common use, even if he does not use the term 'left-hand.' Other manufacturers, however, do not reason in the same way, but fill the order according to their own acceptation of the term...Among dealers it is very probable that the custom exists of calling a range right or left hand according to the oven.

"It would be most interesting to have the opinions of the trade on this question in nomenclature and their reasons for adopting the name...they regard as correct...What say you? Is a right-hand range one with the oven on the right or the fire-pot on the right, and why?" Editor, *The Metal Worker*, March 15, 1890.

Cook stove, white & baby blue porcelainized cast iron, gas, "Windsor," early 20th C. **$900.00-$1200.00**

Cook Stove Coloring.— "Retail store equipment used to be painted red in most instances and for a time there was a fad in scales and meat grinders for gold lacquer. Machine tools were painted at the whim of the manufacturer until the conglomeration of hues in factories became

absurd...When the cast-iron stove was replaced by the more modern sheet-metal variety, the industry went chiefly to white. For a period of four to five years white in turn gave way to a variety of pastel colors, applied with fancy crystal, cloud, and wood-grain effects. This fad finally ran its course, and white again became the overwhelming choice of most women." Harold Van Doren, *Industrial Design, A Practical Guide* (NYC: McGraw-Hill, 1940).

Cook stove name plate, from oven door, multicolor enameled metal rectangle, "Glenwood," 8" x 10", TOC. **$12.00-$15.00**

Cook stoves—See also Ranges.

Fireless cooker, metal box printed to look like wood, 3 holes with aluminum lining, single chest lid, "Rapid", mfd by William Campbell Co., Detroit, MI, c.1919. **$25.00-$40.00**

Fireless cooker, metal box with 2 wells containing original soapstone heater discs, 2 lids, with clip fasteners, stones were heated on range then put in the cooker, then the special deep pan was set over the disc, "Thermatic", American, TOC. • As some of these were insulated with straw, at least the homemade ones, they were also known as <u>haybox cookers</u>. **$40.00-$55.00**

Fireless cooker, oak box like blanket chest, 3 wells, enamelware kettles with lids that lock on when twisted like a bayonet mount, "The Auto Cook", mfd by Caloric Fireless Cookstove Co., Grand Rapids, MI, 17"h x 36"L x 15"W, c.1905. **$50.00-$65.00**

Fireless cooker, oak chest with 2 lids, each covering a metal lined well with a soapstone disc at the bottom, which were heated in or on the stove, plopped in, the food in cylindrical vessels put in on top, for slow cooking without fire! This one with its original vessels & their lids, "Caloric" — "Hygenic, Scientific, Economical", Caloric Fireless Cookstove Co., Janesville, WI, 14"h x 29"L x 15" deep, the vessels shy of 12" diameter, early 20th C. **$75.00-$135.00**

Fireless cooker, wooden box with all aluminum inside, including pots, pans, racks & lids, 2 holes with soapstone heater discs, "The Ideal," Toledo Cooker Co., Toledo, OH, early 20th C. **$30.00-$45.00**

Fireless cooker range, looks like small apartment stove, electric powered rather than the heated stone type, pull out drawer below with insulated box that looks like old-fashioned fireless cooker, oven above that with "Pyrex" window, hotplate style top, William Campbell Co., Alliance, OH, c.1925. **$55.00-$85.00**

Flue cover, also called a <u>chimney hole cover</u>, very decorative cast iron, probably made by a stove foundry to match a particular line of stoves, late 19th C. **$25.00-$35.00**

Flue cover, also called a <u>flue stop</u>, japanned tin, brown color, put in place when cook or heat stove was dismantled for summer, leaving hole where stovepipe would ordinarily go. The trade name reflects the marketing magic of an exciting new source of power: "Electric," American, 14½"D, pat'd Jan. 7, 1890. **$40.00-$50.00**

• **"Taking Down Stoves.**— Some people do not know when to take down a heating stove. The good wife may be one such, for a day that is warm enough to thaw out the flies is a suggestion to her that the heating stove should go. She tells her husband that the time has come to call the tinner to come at once. The husband is so full of fear that she will mention the subject of garden and ask him to bring home infantile cabbage plants, that he is only too glad to have stoves the only 'spring' subject. Unfortunately, he neglects to tell the tinner. The fire has died out in the stove and the evening is cool, so he sits by the kitchen stove.

"The next morning is rather cool, so the wife allows a fire to be made. For a few days all goes well, but then the sun come out like a Fourth of July parade, and then there is no use of talking, the stove must go. As usual, he forgets to inform the tinner, and when he comes home he is told that no further foolishness will be allowed.

"The husband hunts up an old coat and a hat that the tramps would not take as a gift. The kitchen table is used for a pedestal, and on this he stands. The wire that holds the pipe to the ceiling is removed with care, and then as the wife and hired girl stand with outstretched arms, the stove pipe is detached from its surroundings. Two joints of the upright pipe slip out, and as they fall our man tries to catch them, and in so doing tips the pipe in his hands and gives wife and hired girl a deluge of ashes. The room resembles the crater of a volcano retired from active business.

"After much tugging and lifting the stove is got as far as the back kitchen by placing a pair of roller skates under it. The carpet is swept and the table is returned to the kitchen. It is then discovered there is no stopper in the chimney; when found, it must be put in, so the kitchen table has another journey. All goes well for a few days, until a cold wave. At last the tinner is sent for, and soon the stove is again in position, where it remains until all doubts about the weather are set to rest. After ice cream has been in vogue for some time, the tinner and his men come and in a few moments take down and away the stove and its pipes. There is no dirt on the carpet, and the hired girl's hair is free from ashes. This family has concluded that the proper person to transport stoves is the stove man." Tin Chips, as quoted in *The Metal Worker*, April 23, 1892.

Flue cover, brass colored metal frame, hanging brass-color chain, picture of 2 girls in bonnets under glass, 19th C or early 20th C. **$18.00-$25.00**

Flue cover, brass frame, chromolith depiction of lovely girl in garden, German, late 19th or early 20th C. **$30.00-$40.00**

Flue cover, brass frame, chromolithograph of dancing Victorian children, music by a bug orchestra, American, litho prob. German, 9½"D, c.1880s. • This cute conceit, of the cheerful bugs playing music, is found on all kinds of color lithographed commercial art of the period. It always amazes how peculiar some Victorian art is. Dancing bug pictures nowadays would be featured in the before panel on a Raid® ad, I'm afraid. **$35.00-$40.00**

Flue cover, brass frame, color depiction of English countryside with lots of teensy flowers, only 5" diameter, 19th C or early 20th C. **$18.00-$25.00**

Flue cover, brass frame, decoratively stamped border, chromolith picture of Little Boy Blue, American, 9"D, TOC. **$15.00-$20.00**

Flue cover, brass frame, litho of 2 curly-headed little girls, clip back, American (?), 7½"D, late 19th or early 20th C. **$15.00-$20.00**

Flue cover, brass frame, litho of 2 girls on a lake, swans around the boat, clip back, German (?), TOC. • These fan-

cified brass frame flue covers (or flue stops as they were also called) were available with stove pipe collars that had matching stamped flanges. **$30.00-$40.00**

Flue cover, brass frame, lithograph of wintery church scene glued in center, American, 8½"D, TOC to 1920s. • An ad in *The Metal Worker*, April 12, 1890, shows a flue stop tradenamed the "Crystal", made by Haslet, Flanagen & Co. of Philadelphia. They were patented July 19, 1887; Sept. 4, 1888; and April 9, 1889. They were packed for wholesale trade 12 to a box, half "gold", half "silver", and were 8 3/8" diameter. The one in the ad has a gadrooned border surrounding a picture of an old mill, bridge and trees. • A c.1919 supplier's catalog put out by Buhl Sons Co., Detroit, shows several "Flue Stops". Two have stamped brass frames, with a sort of egg and dart design to the brass part, the centers, as shown, both have a snowy scene of a tall steepled church. One, "The Royal", which has a double figure-8 spring wire fastener on the back which popped into the stove pipe hole, was available either in a brass finish or "fancy assorted (lacquered) colors". The 2nd flue cover, "The Perfect", came in a brass finish, with "fancy assorted centers." This cover had two spring wire ears, sticking out both sides, which were bent into the stove pipe opening. A third type, "The Gem is a Flat Stop which can be papered over if desired. It has a Patent Fastener at the center" (the double figure-8 wire one). It came painted gray with "fancy assorted centers" — presumably the same cheap chromolith landscapes, etc., that the other(s) came with. • Any of you who have been in a store offering supplies for wood-burning stoves have seen the modern flue covers. They are stamped metal, they look brass plated rather than brass, or may have an off-white or beige baked-on paint finish, with exceedingly ugly, poorly-printed color pictures glued on the centers. You could do better with a picture cut from any magazine. **$10.00-$15.00**

Flue cover, brass frame, lithographed picture of horses & stable, American (?), 19th C or early 20th C. • **Reproduction Alert.**— A company in Missouri makes reproduction flue covers. If you collect them, I suggest you send for their catalog, which costs $2.50. Write: NUHL, 2113 Nottingham, Cape Girardeau, MO 63701. **$15.00-$20.00**

Flue cover, brass frame, picture of little boy in late 18th C shortpants outfit, American or European, 19th C. **$20.00-$25.00**

Flue cover, brass frame, reverse painting of sylvan scene on glass, late 19th C. **$18.00-$25.00**

Flue cover, brass frame, stamped & beaded border, chain hanger, well-done, "naive" handpainted snow scene in oils, depicts shed, barn, trees, lots of snow, & large black dog walking across center of scene, American, large — 12" diameter, late 19th C. **$50.00-$70.00**

Flue cover, brass frame, with beading around outside, oil painting of pug dog inside, no mark, 12"D, TOC. • You compete here with crossover dog & folk art collectors, so cheap prices (such as this one was marked) is probably because those collectors hadn't yet harvested the flue cover field. **$50.00-$70.00**

Flue cover, glass & color-tinfoil, brass chain hanger, depiction of kitchen with little girls paring apples by hand, prob. European, nice big 12½"D, late 19th C or early

20th. • Not very many flue covers have kitchen depictions, as the fancier ones were meant to cover the hole when the parlor stove was knocked down for the summer months. **$25.00-$30.00**

Flue cover, glass & colored tinfoil, brass hanging chain, religious depiction of 2 children watched over by an angel, European, 12"D, late 19th or early 20th C. **$18.00-$22.00**

Flue cover, tin frame, stamped with design, center picture painted in oils of child feeding cat, 19th C. **$45.00-$75.00**

Flue cover, tin, lithograph picture of garden girl with red roses, spring clips to hold in hole, 8" diameter, 19th C or early 20th C. **$18.00-$25.00**

Flue cover, tin, stamped & painted, with chromolith farm scene on paper center, 19th C or early 20th C. **$12.00-$15.00**

Flue cover, tinsel frame in dark blue, brass chain, center depicts young woman with water jug, Belgian, late 19th or early 20th C. • I believe that the flue covers with chains are as a rule older than the spring clip ones. They fit in better with the Victorian conceit of hanging as many decorative things on the wall as possible. **$20.00-$30.00**

Flue cover, tinsel frame, rich red color, brass chain hanger, chromolith family scene in center, European, early 20th C. **$20.00-$30.00**

Flue cover, brass frame, small blond boy's portrait bust wearing red winter cap, American or European, 8"D, TOC. **$20.00-$25.00**

Flue cover, brass with glass cover, depicts bust of young girl surrounded by flowers, 19th C. **$30.00-$40.00**

Foot warmer, blue & white saltglazed stoneware, "Logan", 12½"L, late 19th C. **$140.00-$175.00**

Foot warmer, brown glazed pottery, for hot water, American late 19th C. **$45.00-$60.00**

Foot warmer, brown glazed pottery, shaped like a dustpan for feet, "Bennington" type glaze, could be Vermont or Ohio, 9½" x 7"W x 5¼" Deep, 19th C. • Unusual form for foot warmers, & collectible type of ceramic, so rather expensive! **$250.00-$300.00**

Foot warmer, brown glazed stoneware, dome-shaped with ring handle; you heated the whole thing before use, dense stoneware holds heat a relatively long time, "C. J. Jager," Albany, NY, 19th C. **$250.00-$300.00**

Foot warmer, carpet-covered elliptical (squashed oval) sheet metal cylinder, drawer in one end. Pull out perforated drawer & it should have small inner perforated pan for the special fuel, "Carbonite", about which I can find nothing. Wire bail with turned wooden grip, "Carbonite", The American Safety Fuel Co., NYC, 4"h x 12"L x 8"W, early 1890s. **$35.00-$50.00**

Foot warmer, charcoal heated, tin, "Clark Heater No. 7D," or No. 2, mfd. by Chicago Flexible Shaft Co., IL, TOC. **$25.00-$35.00**

Foot warmer, dovetailed wood case with soapstone bar to heat, American, late 19th C (?). **$65.00-$75.00**

Foot warmer, japanned tin box in a sort of pup tent shape, ledge at bottom of one slanted side is for resting feet, screw-on cap in narrow top, wire handle, especially good for reclining person, and it would hold end of sheet & blanket up, too, "Peerless", Thompson Mfg. Co., Lansingburgh, NY, 1890s. **$25.00-$40.00**

Foot warmer, pine frame with 4 turned wooden posts on each long side, including corners, punctured tin box insert with heart-in-circles pattern, open wood foot rest crosspieces on top with room for 4 feet, wire handle, branded "E. Stone", CT, 8"h x 19"L x 8"W, early 19th C. • Dealer Sharon W. Joel, Jacksonville, FL, offered this in 1986. Price range mine. **$650.00-$900.00**

Foot warmer, pottery, "Rue Bed Stove", mfd by Rue Pottery, Matawan, NJ, mid 19th C. **$65.00-$80.00**

Foot warmer, punctured tin box inside wood frame, with turned corner posts, wire carrying handle, design of concentric rings of slits, door in side of box with wire ring handle, for putting charcoal pan inside, American, 7½"h x 7" square, early 19th C. **$240.00-$275.00**

• **Warm Feet,** Cornelius Weygandt's *The Heart of New Hampshire; Things Held Dear by Folks of the Old Stocks* (NY: Putnam, 1944): "If I could bring my little treasures of yesterday, or my junk — call it what you will, I should have with me here a foot warmer of punched tin to show you a utensil for which charcoal is needed. It is from the Hobbs place over in Effingham, an old home from which nothing had been thrown out for a century. It is almost the only foot warmer I ever came upon in which the charcoal pan was still inside. Such a contraption made the difference between comfort and discomfort in winter in churches under which there was no cellar. This is a circular foot warmer, with a base of unpunched tin laid over wood, and sides and top of punched tin. It is six inches high and ten inches in diameter, with a wooden frame around the top. It is carried by a wire handle, and the door which admits the charcoal pan is fastened with a wire catch. Four ovals punched with round holes and crosses, each five by a little less than four inches, decorate the sides. The top is punched all over with round holes, in the center of which is that six-petaled conventionalized tulip that is a symbol of well-being all over Europe and was brought to America with the first white men who settled here."

Foot warmer, punctured tin in wood frame, soapstone heating brick & oil burner, probably for whale oil, American, 4½"h x 6" x 9½"L, early 19th C. **$240.00-$275.00**

Foot warmer, punctured tin, wood frame, wire bail handle, American, 8" to 12" squarish, some more pronouncedly rectangular than others, 19th C. • The price of foot or feet warmers (also called foot stoves or foot bankes) is determined by visual appeal & designs of the punctured tin, the construction & patina of the wooden frame, which may have turned corner posts, and some nice color, & by condition (not rusted, busted or burned out). Look for wood that's finished not left rough, for heavy weight dark old tin, for interesting punching, for nifty or ingenious bail handles. Look for unusual sizes, like one for two people. Look inside for the coal pan, usually not found. If it looks too good, take heed. Most are under $150.00, but the range is considerable. **$75.00-$400.00**

Foot warmer, saltglazed stoneware, "Red Wing", one quart size, early 20th C. **$40.00-$55.00**

Foot warmer, saltglazed stoneware, "The Henderson", Dorchester Pottery Works, Dorchester, MA, pat'd Nov. 5, 1912. **$75.00-$110.00**

Foot warmer, saltglazed stoneware, long jug on its side, carrying knob at one end, corked stopper in center top, marked "Doultons' Improved Foot Warmer, Lambeth Pottery," London, England, 13"L, 19th C. $80.00-$100.00

Foot warmer, tin &wood, flowered carpet, has coal tray inside, wire bail handle with turned wood grip, American, 19th C. • These remind you of carpet bags & other carpeted things (like chairs or footstools) popular in the 1860s & 1870s. This one sounds like, except for the possibly misinterpreted "coal tray" the "Improvement in Feet-Warmers" patent, by Nathaniel Waterman (muffin pan man), #13859, of Nov. 27, 1855. It was of wood with a thin sheet metal top, entirely carpeted, and with a vessel inside for hot water. Waterman's might bring about three times as much money, because of what is becoming a Waterman Cult. The man was a very prolific inventor. $85.00-$125.00

Foot warmer, all wood case, pierced in simple design, heavy sheet metal coal tray inside, wire bail handle, little feet, American, 6½"h x 7" x 8", 19th C. $150.00-$200.00

Foot warmer, white saltglazed stoneware with spout (snout) in center of long cylinder, sometimes called the "piggy" style, American, 11"L x 5½"D, late 19th C. $45.00-$55.00

Foot warmer, wooden frame with turned corner posts, punctured tin box inside, wire bail handle, signed "J. Ballen", although few of them are marked at all, (could this be J. Beverly Allen?), New England (?), early 19th C — maybe 1830s. $165.00-$185.00

Foot warmer & lantern combined, wooden box with backside of sheet iron, round glass windows on 3 sides protected by criss-cross of iron wires, delicate iron carrying handle on top forms support when hinged lid-like top folds down to reveal carpeted foot rest. Inside is brass burner for burning the fuel which heats as well as provides light, actually patented as a Stove Lantern, but possibly adapted after patenting to another use. pat'd by D. L. Jaques, Hudson, MI, 6"h x 7¾"L x 5" deep, pat'd Mar. 14, 1865. • Although this sounds unusual, it was not the only combination lantern & foot warmer. W. F. Bartlett of Hillsdale, MI, patented one on Nov. 20, 1866, and S. M. Wirts & F. Swift, of Hudson, MI, patented one on Aug. 6, 1867. Michigan is a big ice-fishing state; I wouldn't be surprised if these were meant for fishermen sitting out on the cold, dark frozen lakes. G. A. Wells of Oskaloosa, IA patented a combined Lantern, foot-warmer & water-heater, on Jan. 29, 1867. $145.00-$170.00

Foot warmer (?) or toy stove, for inside use. One dealer claims this "Little Eva" miniature box stove, because of the hearth in front, is actually a foot warmer. Cast iron, 3 legs, 2 ovens, coal & ash doors. The manufacturer listed it as a toy coal stove. "T. Southard, Little Eva" cast on hearth, mfd by Southard, Robertson & Co., Peekskill, NY, one dealer reported 10" x 12" x 14½" another gave height as 9½", c.1860s-70s. $225.00-$275.00

Gas range, cast & sheet iron, box with fancy side valves, "The Sun Dial", mfd by Goodwin Meter Co., South Carolina Power Co., South Carolina, c.1946. $75.00-$95.00

Grate shaker, ornate cast iron tool, used to move the grate & shake out the ashes & small clinkers to the floor of the stove's firebox for cleaning. Bements Stove Co., late 19th or early 20th C. $7.00-$10.00

Grates—See Hearths & Fireplaces.

Heating stove, enameled sheet iron, best described as Arts & Crafts lighthouse shape, beautiful rich medium blue, the base & 6 short legs & the hexagonal frame of lid are black, with large & small ventilating holes, ruby glass is behind larger double row of holdes in front, hole in back near top for small stovepipe, lid has acorn finial, lifts off to reveal small surface, for a tea kettle, front embossed "Quick Comfort", lid: "Quick Meal Stove Co., Div. of Am. Stove Co.", 23½"h, TOC to 1910s. $175.00-$250.00

Kerosene stove, black sheet metal with gold fancy painting, 3 burners and lower burn at side for stovetop oven. Dealer said "possibly in working order". "New Process, No. 4," pat'd Feb. 4, 1890, Feb. 18, 1890, Dec. 30, 1890. • If not working, should be ¼ to ⅛ value of restored one. Price range for working one: $400.00-$650.00

Oven, sheet & cast iron, nickeled hinges & fittings, through glass window in drop-down door looks like 2 shelves, but is actually 2 ovens, connected by flue, "Bolo", mfd by Griswold Mfg Co., Erie, PA, about 22"h, c.1920. $75.00-$90.00

Oven door, cast iron, fancy casting, "F. Earl Landis, Brunerville Foundry," Brunerville, Land County, PA, late 19th C. $75.00-$125.00

Oven door, for a bake oven, cast iron with hinged plump heart with sliding vent & motto "Heart of the Home" cast on it, dealer Emanon Corner Antiques says it was made in Ringoes, NJ, first half 19th C. • It has high collecting value for several reasons. First, the heart and the motto. Second because it is not just decoration, as more and more colonial revivalists have bake ovens and walk-in hearths built in their 20th C homes, to use for cooking the old way. • Price range mine, not Emanon Corner's. $700.00-$850.00

Oven door, for hearth oven, cast iron, strap latch, pintail hinges, draft plate, design of 5 fluted fans, "Lincoln Foundry", Bath, ME, 11½" x 15", early 19th C (?). $325.00-$375.00

Portable stove, cast iron, tabletop gas stove with 3 burners, Griswold, early 20th C. • See also Camp stoves. $85.00-$100.00

Portable stove, folding "pocket" stove, black painted hinged and folding sheet metal 3 sided base, with stamped brass & tin fuel cup, in original box, with directions: "Use only Alcohol, pour in slowly through the wire gauze, one or two table-spoons full and light it. The Best Folding Pocket Cook Stove in the World." "Climax Patent Folding Pocket Cook Stove No. 888", Houchin Mfg. Co., NYC, NY, about 4½"H x cup 3½" diameter, trademark reg. May 18, 1875, with patents earlier & later. • Pat'd Sept. 17, 1872, May 4, 1875, July 27, 1875, Jan. 29, 1878, Mar. 20, 1883. $12.00-$18.00

Portable stove, for fishing vessels or whaling ships, cast iron wide lipped pot with inset rack for putting pot on, falling forged iron bail handle, fits on base that has 3 legs and a little hearth, American, 9½"h x 13" diameter, 19th C. $500.00-$700.00

Radiating dumb stove, polychromed cast iron George Washington figure with draped Roman toga statesman's robe worn over his ordinary 18th C clothing, right hand held like Napoleon — hidden within fold of cloth. This one mounted as a radiating stovepipe above a small stove with 4 cabriole legs, with 4 large white-painted tassels of cast iron pendent from the corners of the overhanging plinth which is the stove top & the figure's base. Patented by Blanchard as a radiating dumb stove, it was also sold as a garden ornament (at least by Mott) & probably painted only with lead or zinc-based white paint when used as the latter. Pat'd by Alonzo Blanchard, but also made, probably unofficially, by J. L. Mott, Albany, NY (Blanchard), NYC (Mott), figure: 46½''h x 15''W, (also one reported 49''h x 17''W, possibly the Mott one? or some other rip-off?). Supposedly pat'd 1841 & 1843. • I may be dumb, but I can't find an A. L. Blanchard stove or radiator patent from 1841 (only a cookstove patented by another Blanchard in NJ. Alonzo Blanchard got a Design Patent (#8) for a ''statue'' on Aug. 26, 1843. He also got a stove patent on July 25, 1846. **$17,600.00**

• **George Washington Stoves.** — A fully polychromed one, with the stove base, was bought by a folk art (mainly weathervanes) collector at a Sotheby auction in spring 1988, for $17,600.00 (including 10% buyer's premium. That same stove once belonged to Andy Warhol, and was displayed at the Museum of American Folk Art's 1977 Folk & Funk exhibition. • Beatrix Rumford, in an article in *Early American Life* in February 1976, said that these were cast by the Mott Iron Works of Brooklyn, NY, for the Centennial celebration, and were made until 1900. The Jordan L. Mott castings do not have the patent date on the back as do the Blanchard ones.

Radiator, ornate cast iron, meant for dining room with 2 compartments called <u>hot closets</u> built right into it for keeping food warm, spectacular item — and think how many are rusted out in dumps or melted down during two World Wars. American, late 1880s to 1990s. •
Futurewatch.— I predict that even as this book is being printed there will be a number of people discovering & collecting ornate old steam & hot water radiators, and the salesmen's samples of them. **$125.00-$175.00**

Range, cast iron, oblong, 3 eyes, long strap hinges in nickeled iron on double oven doors, nice bracket type short legs with ribbing, ''Treasure'', mfd by T. J. Constantine, London, England, 1880s. **$750.00-$900.00**

Range, for gas, colorful enameled cast iron, main body in white with a Chinese red trim (manufacturer called it ''Mandarin Red''), long red legs, ovens to side with heat control on inner side wall over range top, Estate Stove Co., Hamilton, OH, c.1928. • Estate also made electric ranges, and color combinations were a rich ''King's Blue'' and white, and ''Jade Green'' and white. You could get the oven and broiler on left or right side of range surface.

• **''More color in Kitchens.**— About a year ago colored kitchen utensils burst upon the horizon, pots and pans as well as the handles of flat ware assuming such gay tints as vermilion, sea green, ultramarine and daffodil yellow. As a result, kitchens bloomed, decoratively speaking. Housewives, proud of their softly tinted walls, hangings and pots and pans, brought their guests into the kitchen to demonstrate the superiority of this colorful room over the all-white interiors of yore. The cook, stimulated by all this novelty, looked contentedly around and cooked a better meal, and even the family cat blinked more conten--tedly on a hearth made of brightly-hued tiles. Now a manufacturer has gone a step further and created colored plumbing fixtures. Enameled sinks for kitchens are now available in such engaging tints as horizon blue, West Point gray, spring green, lavender, old ivory and autumn,

the latter being a deep, pinkish beige tone.'' Editorial, *House & Garden*, Aug. 1928. Just two years later, someone else was saying that ''severity should, perhaps,'' be the rule for the kitchen. The whimsy drained out very quickly. **$700.00-$900.00**

Range, for gas, looks almost like a fancy sideboard or buffet for dining room, oblong box on slightly cabriole legs, enameled in tan, with fronts of ovens & control panels in black & white marbleized enameled iron, green Bakelite® pendant pulls on all doors & utensil drawer, extremely handsome, ''Magic Chef Patrician Model'', mfd by American Stove Co., St. Louis, MO, late 1920s. • About $200.00 was the original price. **$700.00-$900.00**

Range, for gas, streamlined clean design, white enameled steel, pendant or drop pulls, broiler drawer under 6 control dials, ''Magic Chef'', American Stove Co., St. Louis, MO, c.1934. • An ad for this starts off with words sure to shrivel the heart of a collector of today: ''**The Modern Housewife discarded the old Coffee Mill Years Ago**... Isn't it about time to discard that old-fashioned range of yours? The sound of the old coffee mill is no longer heard in the modern kitchen. Progress has relegated this outmoded appliance to the junk pile. Yet thousands of women who wouldn't keep a coffee grinder in the house, except as a relic, continue to use a gas range that is just as out of date. Don't cheat the junk pile and yourself any longer. ... Replace the antiquated range with a modern automatic Magic Chef.'' Hee hee. **$200.00-$400.00**

Range, huge black cast iron range with its own enclosure, lintel and heating shelf, to be ''brickset'' into fireplace, with flues to go up chimney. David Foulis, Edinburgh, Scotland, whole assembly about 55''h x 54''W, c.1875. • A complaint aired March 1839, in the *Journal of the Franklin Institute of Philadelphia*, goes ''The greatest objection to the kitchen ranges devised by various ingenious projectors, is the want of simplicity. Cooks will not take the trouble of learning to use them, or, which is necessary, to keep in order the various novel articles by which they are accompanied.'' By the 1870s, probably most cooks were either supplied with simpler ranges, or experience as their teacher. **$1200.00-$1800.00**

Range, ivory & green enameled iron, 4 burner gas stove, ''Magic Chef'', 1939 or so. **$250.00-$300.00**

Range, peach enameled cast iron, nickel trim, 2 warming ovens above, oven & broiler below, 6 eyes with one having smaller eye in middle of lid, 2 lids in center lift out along with the fat ''I'' shaped piece between them, to open up a long, round-end oblong suitable for a 2 hole gridiron or griddle, etc. In unrestored condition. ''Copper Clad'', early 20th C. **$600.00-$1000.00**

Simmering cover, cast iron round ''trivet'' to set into range eye to reduce heat, openwork 6 wedge design, with slots for lid lifter, marked ''Simmering Cover, W & P Mfg. Co.'', Walker & Pratt Mfg. Co., 7½'' diameter, TOC. **$12.00-$20.00**

Slipper or shoe warmer, in a low-top boot shape, saltglazed gray stoneware, cork stopper, filled with hot water before inserting into shoe, no mark, American, about 6''h, mid 19th C. **$175.00-$225.00**

Stove blacking, in tin container, red, white & blue label with flag design, ''The Union Blacking,'' TOC. **$15.00-$18.00**

Stove door, cast iron, depicts man clearing wood, "Leibrandt & McDowell Stove Co.", Philadelphia & Baltimore, mid 19th C. **$175.00-$400.00**

Stove knobs, nickeled cast iron, one an elongated blimp shape with the pointed tips of metal, the middle half transparent blue glass; the round one having an orb of blue glass fitted into a metal base with 2 arms for holding bolt through glass, "Jewel", Greene & Mallett, manufacturers of stove trimmings, Troy, NY, came in 10 sizes and styles, and also in amber glass, Jan. 1892 ad in *Metal Worker*. • I have not seen these. Most knobs, pendant drop handles, and bracket handles are either nickeled cast iron, or nickeled iron wire coils (such as made by the Troy Nickel Works), or are cast iron enameled in white. I still think that if you can't save the stove, save the knobs. In NYC it is not so common as it once was to find a stove thrown out on the street for pickup that day by the Sanitation Department, and most stoves are vintage 1920s, but there are still goodies to pick up. **$3.00-$15.00**

Stove lid lifter, cast iron, design of heat-dissipating handle formed of handsome cutout letters, "ESTATE" #33, American, 10"L, TOC. **$12.00-$16.00**

Stove lid lifter, cast iron in form of voluptuous long-haired and long-gowned woman wearing a crown, which, with her upraised arms, forms part of the pot lid lifter at her head end, the stove lid lifter being at her foot, odd monobuttock rear, unmarked, American, 8⁵⁄₁₆"L, I believe this is c.1850s or 1860s. **$95.00-$125.00**

Stove lid lifter, cast iron with coiled wire loop handle, "Stover," late 19th C. • Al & Nancy Schlegel, Penacook, NH, told me in the early 1980s that a lid lifter is also known as a "Democrat." **$7.00-$13.00**

Stove lid lifter, crudely finished cast iron, marked on one "horn" with initials M A, American, 9⅜"L, TOC. **$8.00-$12.00**

Stove lid lifter, nickeled cast iron, working hook end is a bull's head, handle is tight coil to dissipate heat, hence name, "Alaska" brand, sold through Montgomery Ward as well as other stores, mfd by Troy Nickel Works, Troy, NY, about 10"L (?), late 19th C. **$18.00-$25.00**

Stove lid lifter, openwork cast iron, the central motif being a heart outline, with a sort of fish outline coming from between the lobes, & a sort of banner from the point, there being useful tips at both ends, the banner or streamer contains the initials "J P A" & date, mfd by J. P. Abbott, Cleveland, OH, 1882. **$40.00-$55.00**

Stove lid lifter, cast iron, in combination with a pot lid lifter at other end, quite simple form, made by an unknown stove company, American, 9"L, 19th C. **$10.00-$18.00**

Stove lid lifter, coppered cast iron, handle is thick tube with a number of holes cast in it to help disperse heat by helping air circulate around it, fairly straight long shank, "The Zero," sold through Montgomery Ward, late 19th C. **$12.00-$15.00**

Stove lid lifter, wrought iron bar, handle split into 6 narrow strips then loosely woven together to form heat dissipating handle, really beautiful, American, 14"L, early 19th C. **$150.00-$250.00**

Stove lid & trivet, cast iron in slightly raised design of sort of ruffly edged nautilus shell, on the underside are 2 short peg feet plus the slot where you stick in the lid lifter which forms the 3rd foot, extremely handsome piece of cast iron, marked on back "K O 118", might be Kiechle & Oberdorfer stove company, or O. K. Stove Works, 9¹⁄₁₆" diameter, 19th C. **$15.00-$20.00**

Stove ornament, brass plated cast pot or slush metal, marvelous standing Indian with feather headdress, framing him is sort of wreath of elongated pin oak leaves, stands up on round base, doesn't need to be on a stove for great effect, "Round Oak" stoves, Doe-Wah-Jack, 11"h, very early 20th C. • There are several versions of this, some with the Indian figure, some with urns or other shapes surrounded by stylized oak leaf wreath. **$160.00-$350.00**

Stove pipe plate, cast iron, "Adams," American, pat'd 1897, 15¾"D, rim 6¼"W. **$45.00-$55.00**

Stove pipe trivet, airy fine cast iron, very openwork design within round frame, of 6 stars, touching at points to each other and frame, one projection, just like a lid lifter, fits into ring that goes around pipe. Ring could hold several. no mark, American, 6⅝" diameter, late 19th C. **$35.00-$45.00**

Stove plate, from early cook stove made up of plates, rather like a prefab house. Depicts 2 tall men with guns, wearing what look like Liberty caps, and 2 bearded men in frock coats shaking hands, from the Hudson River Valley, NY, 24"h x 25½"L, late 18th or early 19th C. • **German vocabulary** — Ofenplatte: stove plate; Ofen: stove. **$1000.00-$2500.00**

Stove shovel, cast iron, hook-ended handle, said to be Shaker, 18"L, 19th C. **$120.00-$150.00**

Stove tongs, wrought iron, said to be Shaker, 16"L, 19th C. **$60.00-$75.00**

Stove tools, wrought iron, shovel, poker and lid lifter, said to be Shaker manufacture, 19th C. **$225.00-$300.00**

Stove trivet, attaches to back of stove, cast iron, deer design, American, early 20th C. **$30.00-$45.00**

Stove urns, cast iron, footed open top compote-like vessel that fit on hob shelves of some stoves, and were filled with water which evaporated, humidifying the dry kitchen. Some were enameled inside; some were nickel plated or "bronzed". No foundry mark on many of these, American, about 5½ to 6½"h, about 6" diameter, 19th C. **$45.00-$150.00**

Stoves, laundry—See Wash, Dry & Iron chapter.

Stovetop oven, aluminum with iron bottom & wire rack, with thermometer in lid, "West Bend Ovenette," by West Bend Aluminum Co., West Bend, WI, 10½" diameter, c. 1940s. • I can bake a pair of sweet potatoes in this much faster than I could clear out the cast iron wares I keep in my oven. A mouse lives in there too, sometimes, and I'd hate to disturb him. **$7.00-$10.00**

Stovetop oven, heavy tin, has heat indicator in lid, "Bake Queen", early 20th C. **$7.00-$12.00**

Stovetop oven, tin, "Princess," 1920s. **$22.00-$32.00**

Stovetop oven, tin, rack inside, looks like a cake carrier, one half of the oven, sides and top, is on a pivot and swings around inside other half, no mark, American, 6½"H x 10¾" diameter, 19th C or very early 20th. **$35.00-$45.00**

Stovetop oven, tin with copper bottom, 2 door, "Conservo," Schwarzbaugh Co., Toledo, OH, 20th C. **$22.00-$32.00**

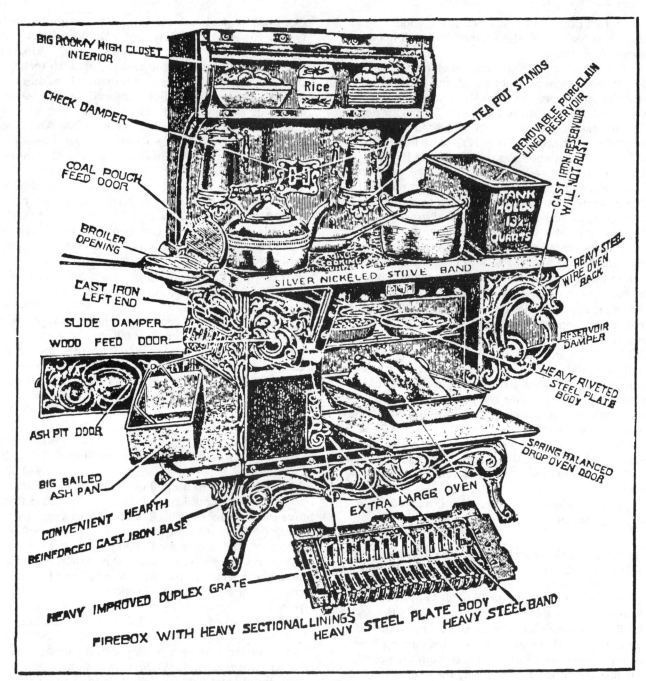

XI-21.
Cook stove with parts identified,
*on one turn of century Sear's catalog page. Was accompanied
by lots of text extolling virtues.*

XI-1.
Camp stove,
to be used like a brazier. These could be used by anyone needing a small portable stove. Wrought iron with turned wooden handle. For use with charcoal. Four resting pads on the corners of the top accommodated whatever needed heating, and raised it slightly above level of detachable grill 5 1/4"H x 12"L overall x 6"W. This type is late 18th or early 19th C; later ones were cast iron. Picture courtesy of Robert W. Skinner Auctioneers, Boston, MA. **$500.00-$800.00**

XI-2.
Brazier or camp stove.
Cast iron footed body with wire bail. Lift-out grid has heart with radiating lines (symbolizing warmth of heart). 7 1/2"H x 10 5/8" diameter. Sold at Ada F. & Earl F. Robacker auction, Horst Auctions, 7/21-22/1989, for only $275.00 **$300.00-$500.00**

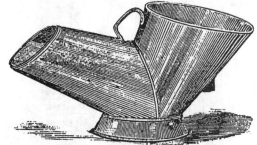

XI-3.
"Improved coal-scuttle."
For a base-burner stove or top-fed stove. Amount of effort required to raise to a pouring level (note tilting handle on right side near bottom) was much less than a conventional scuttle because it did not need to be "lifted through a large part of a circle." American Agriculturist, 2/1881. **$20.00-$40.00**

XI-4.
"Coal scoops."
I have no idea why these are scoops and similar ones are hods. The primary difference seems to be the rounded, hooded tops. These illustrations accompanied a series of practical articles, "Art of Coppersmithing," serialized in The Metal Worker, from John Fuller's 1889 book on the same subject. These copper coal containers, "considered an adornment for the parlor," were made in these traditional shapes some 40 years before Fuller related his long experience in crafting all manner of copper household articles. The names, clockwise from top (L) are "The Florence," "The Nautilis," "The Boat", "The Royal". The Metal Worker, 11/15/1890.

XI-5.
Coal vases.
Japanned and "handsomely ornamented." (L) Three cast iron fancy feet, fire iron attachment in back, and a half-cylindrical 'vase' decorated in Japanese motifs, after the high (and low) fashion of the day. The "japanned" finish, by the way, does refer to the country Japan, but only because of its attempted resemblance to the fine lacquer finish used by generations of Japanese artisans. Japoniste motifs, also imitative, decorated all kinds of minor and major decorative arts in America, beginning with the 1850's opening of Japan to U.S. trade, and then in full bloom after the 1876 world fair. Mfd. by Heinz & Munschauer, noted for their birdcages, depicted in 1882 catalog. (R) Patent self-closing vase, cast feet, from F.A. Walker import catalog, 1870s. Valuable only if finish is in very good condition. **$125.00-$300.00**

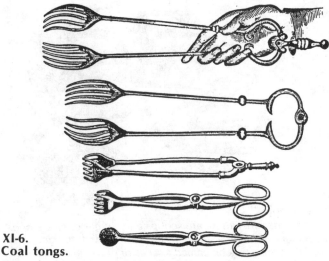

XI-6.
Coal tongs.

From the top: (1) and (2) Malleable cast iron in two patented designs. Longer one goes with fire iron set. Russell & Erwin, New Britain, CT, 1865 catalog. (3) "Claw tongs" with spring, cast of malleable iron, in choice of "japanned" or "Tuscan bronzed" finish. (4) Simple, scissor-style "claw tongs," same finishes. (5) "Flat" tongs, same finishes. c.1880s. **$10.00-$40.00**

XI-7.
"Patent Hand Revolving Pan,"

or confectioners' nut roaster (?). "It will pay the Retailer to manufacture Cream, Jordon and Burnt Almonds, which can be made fresh everyday. The goods made in this pan are more like the Hand-made goods. The sugar coating does not become so hard and brittle. This pan will also do three times the work of the old-fashioned swinging pan...Put one in your store window and set a boy to work making goods." Broadside signed by Thomas Burkhard, date unknown, but looks to be 1860s-80s. I looked under everything I could think of in the patent index to find exact date, but couldn't find anything. See also nut roasters in the next chapter. **$50.00-$200.00**

XI-8.
Radiating dumb stove figural

of George Washington in classical garb and pose. Cast iron, on stepped base, actually stove top, 46"H. This figure, or at least one quite similar, was patented by Alonzo Blanchard, 11/12/1841 and received a design patent 8/26/1843, with a cast lead model, now in the collection of the Albany Institute. (See Bibliography for excellent book by Tammis Kane Groft on old stoves). The figural dumb stove was copied later by founder J.L. Mott. This one is marked "Design Patented" on back; probably a Mott because it doesn't have the date. Blanchard's figures and/or Mott's have been found painted with white lead paint, badly rusted at the bottom; it is thought that these might have been used — perhaps even intended — as garden ornaments. A similarly garbed female statue, though certainly not of Martha, by Blanchard exists too; it is not known if Mott copied that one also. **$7000.00-$12,000**

XI-9.
Radiating dumb stove.

(L) Alonzo L. Blanchard's 1841 patent drawing of a hollow statue which, "besides being elegant in its appearance, forms a constituent part of the instrument, and exposes a large radiating surface." (R) Complete stove in very fine condition. The figure has been polychromed. Ex-Collection Andy Warhol. Sold at auction in 1988 to noted folk art collector for following price (not including 10% buyer's premium). **$16,000.00**

XI-10.
Range.

"Union Range," which won many medals and awards at the world's fair in London, and at others in U.S. and Canada. Moses Pond & Co., Boston, MA. Ad in American Portrait Gallery, *1856.*
Note ovens, large oval boiler at left of range, and huge hot water kettle. Standing at right is a hot water heater, with pipes leading to upstairs!

XI-11.
Range & stove.

Cast iron. (L) is a brickset range, probably set into old high walk-in fireplace recess. Note ornate castings on door, but simplicity of rest. (R) is a large box stove. Sanders & Wolfe, successors to A.T. Dunham & Co., Troy, NY. 1855 or 1856 ad; range pat'd 1853.

XI-12.
Box stove,

with four legs, but otherwise identical to a three-legged one that once belonged to trade-catalog-cataloguer Lawrence B. Romaine. Cast iron, 16"H x 23"L x 13"W, cast by Tyson Furnace, Plymouth, VT, dated 1839. This one was drawn from an Old Brookfield Tavern (Danbury, CT) ad in The Magazine ANTIQUES, *from 11/1929. The side view shows the ships which caused it to be referred to as the "Mayflower" stove, and the other drawing is a bird's-eye view. The 3-legged version is depicted in Josephine Peirce's* Fire On The Hearth, *published in 1951. "Very rare" in 1929 ad, and "very popular design, possibly made other places (besides at Tyson), according to Peirce.*

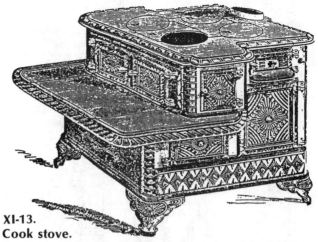

XI-13.
Cook stove.

Cast iron, ornate all over. Maker not mentioned, but I believe this is the "New World Air-Tight" cooking stove, mfd. by Vose & Co., Albany, NY. From a dealer's ad in Johnson's Detroit City Directory, 1857-58.

XI-14.
Air-tight stove,

toted by Uncle Sam-like figure, on top of advertising flyer dated 1872. C.H. Taylor, a dealer, referred to himself as "U.R. Uncle," and was located in Greenfield, MA.

XI-15.
"Anti-clinker" stove,

the "Fearless No. 8" made by Rathbone, Sard & Co., Albany, NY, 1873. Called a "plain top" cook stove, it is shown here without the reservoir for hot water and the warming closet which would be attached at the right side. Clinkers are rock-hard pieces of coal which will not ignite.

XI-16.

Kitchens of "Notable People,"

from article in The Metal Worker, 2/8/1890, detailing importance of the "French range" instead of a stove, for the wealthy. Clockwise from top (L). (1) "Fred Vanderbilt's Kitchen, showing end of servant's dining table." Frederick Vanderbilt, 459 Fifth Avenue, NYC. "This kitchen is an old-fashioned one, is below the street and is dark and damp. Gas is burning all day long. The servants when at dinner sit at two long tables in the kitchen. There is no chef here. His place is occupied by a French woman, who has the girth of a typical cook". I bet the servants of "Fred Vanderbilt" were a diseased, unhappy lot. (2) "Kitchen of W.W. Astor." William Waldorf Astor 8 E. 33rd Street, NYC. The kitchen "is comparatively small, but there is a separate dining-room for the servants, so the chef has it all to himself. Here the cooking dishes are of porcelain, the French cook considering porcelain more wholesome for use than copper. Hardwood floor, polished to the smoothness of glass." (3) "Kitchen of Cornelius Vanderbilt." 1 W. 57th St., NYC. It was the largest private kitchen in New York, and considered very fine. Floor of brown & white marble; pressed brick walls, one side and end with glass-doored cupboards. "This kitchen is beautifully lighted, as it is in the front part of the basement, on a level with the street, and has two very large stained glass windows." German chef used copper because "copper is cleaner than anything else." (4) A.M. Palmer's kitchen, 25 E. 65th St., NYC. "The most beautiful, light and clean kitchen imaginable, and in it is a cook who makes one think of the old days when in mother's kitchen at home he reveled in doughnut horses and gingerbread men...It is typical of those of New England, with its oaken floor and shining tins, and one looks instinctively for the cat that should be purring before the fire."

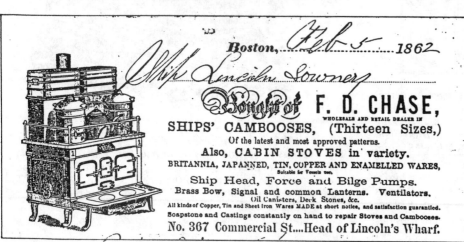

XI-17.

"Ship's camboose,"

or caboose, or cabin stove. Remaining top third of sales receipt of F.D. Chase, Boston, MA, dated 2/5/1862. Note the brass rail or gallery which would keep the utensils from falling to the lower deck.

475

OH! WHAT A DIFFERENCE!

THIS IS THE WAY OUR FATHERS USED TO COOK.   THIS IS THE WAY WE COOK.

XI-18.

Cook stove with attachments.

A drying & towel rack fits on stovepipe, and was made of walnut or maple rods. The shelves, which also were fitted to the pipe, and could be had in sets of 2 or 4, were meant for "dishes while taking up dinner," or for keeping plates warm, or for raising bread. "Always Handy" accessories mfd. by American Manufacturing Co., New Haven, CT. American Agriculturist, 12/1874. Possibly a Vose "wide oven" stove.

XI-22.

Modern cooking,

as depicted in The Metal Worker, 6/18/1892. At left is a hot old smoky wood stove, with what appear to be corncobs (now coming back as a clean fuel) all over floor, a squawling baby fallen into the coal hod, and the chauvinist husband stalking out instead of helping. A "Fire King" gas stove, mfd. by A. Weiskittel, & Son, Baltimore, with tin plate from the factory of Coates & Co., Baltimore, has made everyone happy.

XI-19.

Cook stove.

"Original Troy Charter Oak." M.L. Filley, Troy, NY. 1882 ad in The Metal Worker, reading "We offer our celebrated Charter Oak, manufactured by us since 1854. Entirely remodeled and with the improvements usually found in first-class wood stoves. In altering it we have retained all the good features that have made this stove so famous, and added those that experience has shown the trade demanded."

XI-23.

Oil cook stove.

"Rippingille's," in "large" size, with four 4 1/2" burners, cast iron top, sheet iron body. 18"H x 24"L x 14"W. The smaller size was about 10" shorter from side to side. Harrod's Stores, Ltd., Brompton, London, England, 1895 catalog.

PAW — TURN THEM CHICKENS AND LETS GO TO BED!

XI-20.

Humorous post card.

That stove is giving all it's got. But what I love are the sleeping chickens, which "Paw" has to turn to face the wall before retiring. Published by Asheville Post Card Co., Asheville, NC, in the 1950s, and an example of stove-related non-advertising paper available to collectors.

XI-24.
Gas range.
"Caloric," in pale green porcelainized finish with ivory trim, in kitchen with marbled dark forest green & white floor. *House & Garden*, 1930 ad.

XI-25.
Tabletop gas stove.
"No. 2 Junior," mfd. by Cleveland Foundry. Advertised *The Metal Worker*, 2/6/1892.   **$20.00-$30.00**

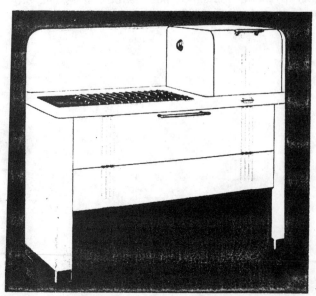

XI-26.
Oil range.
"Perfection #R-869," by Perfection Stove Co,. Cleveland, OH. *Farm Journal & Farmer's Wife*, 5/1939.

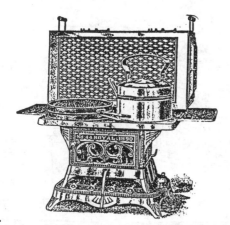

XI-27.
Oil stove.
"Royal #44," mfd. by The Perry Stove Co.'s Argand Stove & Ranges, Albany, NY. Nickel-plated cast iron. This was a small stove, but size isn't given in ad. The Metal Worker, 6/28/1890.

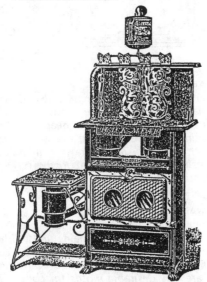

XI-28.
Gasoline stove.
"Quick Meal Cabinet Range, #924," mfd. by the Quick Meal Stove Co., St. Louis, MO. "Among the features may be mentioned glass tubes which show the dripping of gasoline when the stove is in use, German silver needle points and a rim on the gasoline burner top extending over the burner drums and tubes, thus protecting them against the dripping from cooking vessels. All the pipes are anti-rusting material. (This model) is a new pattern, nicely japanned and ornamented." The Metal Worker, 2/6/1892.

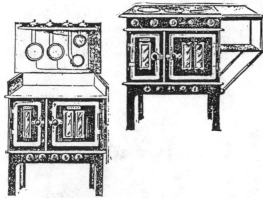

XI-29.
Electric cooker, two views.
"Gilbert", mfd. in England. (L) View with hinged shelf down at side, and top raised for work surface, showing underside of the 4 round "boiling discs." Note controls for each of discs. Two ovens, one with two heating elements, one with three — explaining the row of 5 control dials. (R) In position for cooking. Picture from Maud Lancaster's Electric Cooking, 1914.

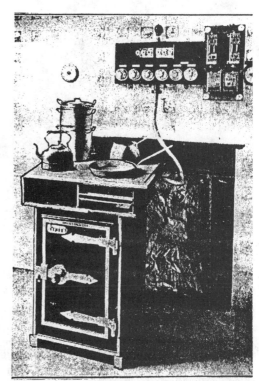

XI-30.
Electric cooker.
"Electroyl," mfd. by Purcell & Nobbs, London, England. Picture shows how it is set up in front of a fireplace, with some kind of crinkled stuffing filling the hearth opening. Cast iron frame, steel oven, with oven 23" x 16" x 16". Two 8" boiling discs flush on top, also one 6", and a griller/toaster. The area between the top and the oven is a "hot closet" or warming oven, for keeping plates and food warm. The control panel is mounted to the wall. Maud Lancaster's Electric Cooking, 1914.

XI-31.
Fireless cooker.
"Caloric — the Auto Cook." Caloric Fireless Cookstove Co., Grand Rapids, MI. 17"H x 36"L x 15"W. "solid quartered oak, furnished complete with German-made enamel ware, patent revolving bar-lock covers." On casters. Ladies' Home Journal ad, 4/1906.

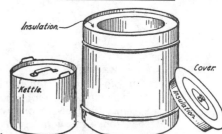

XI-32.
Fireless cooker.
"Two vessels, one inside the other, separated by sawdust, asbestos, or other poor conducting material. Foods are heated in the usual way to the boiling point or to a high temperature, and are then placed in the inner vessel. The heat of the food cannot escape through the non-conducting material which surrounds it, and hence remains in the food and slowly cooks it." Bertha M. Clark, General Science, NY: American Book Co., 1912.

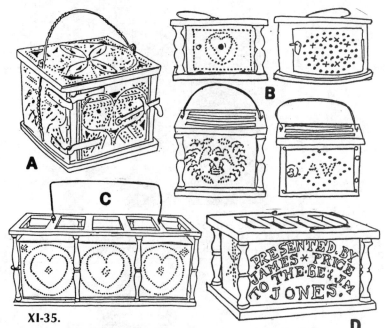

XI-33.
Flue covers,
for covering hole in wall where stovepipe (usually parlor or heating stove) goes through. Top (L) Stamped tin, with brass-like finish, cheap chromolith picture. From Lalance & Grosjean, 1890. (R) A similar one, called a "crystal flue stop...the handsomest now on the market. Gold and silver finish." Pat'd 7/19/1887, 9/4/1888, and 4/9/1889. Haslet, Flanagan & Co., Philadelphia. The Metal Worker, 4/12/1890. Lower (L) "Gold lacquered, wide flange" flue stopper, with "fancy picture." 8 1/4", with steel spring to snap into hole. Wheeling Corrugating Co., 1921.

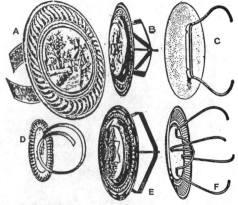

XI-34.
Flue covers,
showing different types of hoops. (A) Spring steel. Sears & Roebuck, c.1900. (B) "Higgins Perfect" flue stops, with 5/8" double hoops, brass-lacquered embossed cover, 6" diameter. (C) Androck Folding, with flat cover for papering over. Green enamel finish. (D) "Gold lacquered" disc with no picture, single coiled flat spring. Central Stamping Co., 1920. (E) A "Higgins Single Hoop Star Cover," embossed and "brass lacquered," no picture. (F) "Edward's Tip-Top" flue stop, with double folding spring steel hoop, colored pictures, embossed metal disc, brass lacquered. 9 3/4" diameter. B, C, E, and F all from The Washburn Co., Rockford, IL, catalog from 1927.

XI-35.

A. Foot warmer.
Chip-carved oak, with metal hardware and twisted wire bail handle. What looks like punctured tin is actually the nicks made by the gouge. Lines describing the heart and the petals and circle are continous incised lines in the wood. Only the round and triangular dark holes in the drawing are actually holes through to the inside. Palatin (Bavarian) origins, c.1750. Drawn from one in collection of Old Stone Fort.

B. Foot warmers.
All punctured tin in wooden frames. Top two are from the Essex Institute; the one on the (R) being unusual because it is round. The bottom two are drawn from ad of Joe & Teri Dziadul, Enfield, CT, who specialize in kitchen and hearth antiques. Eagles and hearts are very desirable motifs for collectors.

C. Foot warmer.
A triple, punctured tin with hearts within circles, pine frame (branded with name "E. Stone," probably the maker's), wire bail. 8"H x 19"L x 8"W, from Connecticut. Drawn from ad of Sharon W. Joel Antiques, Jacksonville, FL.

D. Foot warmer.
Double size, decorated tin with name. Ex-Eric Sloane collection, sold at Skinner's auction house for $1650.00 in 3/1987. Then Ex-Barbara & Gregory Reynolds' collection, sold again at Skinner's, in 10/1989, for $1870.00 Drawn from ad. **$1500.00-$2000.00**

XI-36.
Foot warmers.
Top "piggy" one is stoneware, like a sideways bottle holding two quarts, with cork on top, and handles at each end. Bottom (L) is a slanted stoneware one with cork. Bottom (R) is a slab of soapstone fitted with wire bail handle. "Those ancient and time-honored devices to remedy cold feet, the junk bottle and the stone jug filled with hot water, often led to petty disasters, more vexatious than perilous. The corks would fly out or get loose and make a bad matter worse." American Agriculturist, 1/1868.

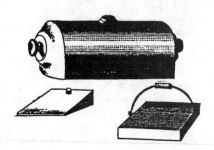

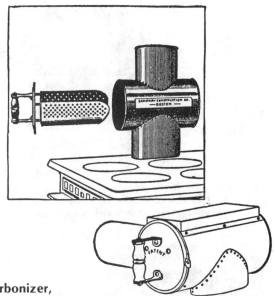

XI-37.
Garbage carbonizer,
to fit in stovepipe "between the stove and the flue of the chimney, and becomes a permanent fixture. It is a horizontal cylinder about 1/3 larger in diameter than the stovepipe. One end is removable, and attached thereto, on the inside, is a semi-circular pan or scoop, perforated along both sides and having solid ends and a tight bottom." The scoop is filled with the garbage and slid into place, where the heat eventually carbonizes it. "The carbon which remains is utilized as fuel," wrote Fannie Merritt Farmer from her Boston Cooking School, in praise of the gadget. Mfd. by New England Sanitary Co., Boston. *American Kitchen Magazine*, 4/1896.

XI-38.
Parlor stoves,
with fancy finials. From the "Madison Square Series," mfd. by Southard, Robertson & Co., NYC. While they were "very moderate in price" in 1890 when advertised, they would cost a small fortune today, at least the building-shaped one with the horse. It is spectacular. Note low-set carrying handles. Collectors for these would probably come from the folk art sector rather than the true stove collecting population. **$3000.00-$5000.00**

XI-39.
Two photographic stereopticon cards,
making visual a no-joking-matter affecting many husbands and wives in the 19th and early 20th C. Busy one shows wife admonishing husband, who's ready to throw elbow pipe on floor. Note: flue cover already in place; also ladder, mad wallpaper, coal hod. "Have patience, dear, don't swear" caption is repeated on back in several foreign languages. © 1897 by Strohmeyer & Wyman, pub'd by Underwood & Underwood. Simpler one is posed so man has stovepipe legs. "Oh, Dear! Don't Swear" is the caption. © 1892 by B.L. Singley, pub'd by Keystone View Co. How-to columns advised aiding a "felicitous putting up" by numbering both ends of each section of pipe. Several versions of the cards exist. For photographic ones: **$5.00-$10.00**

XI-40.
"Heating Stoves of 1990."

In *The Metal Worker*, 8/16/1890, was printed a teasing piece on stoves of the future, based on the un-stovelike appearance being exaggerated beyond reason by contemporary stove designers. An abridged version of a spoof newspaper account, supposedly from 1990, of the purchase of this stove in the shape of a Newfoundland dog follows: "I, being in need of a new base burner, called on Jones & Johnson for the purpose of purchasing a stove. Upon entering, I was bewildered at the glittering array of samples of artistic stoves spread before me. The place would hardly be taken for a stove store on account of the peculiarity of the designs. One would sooner imagine he was in a zoo or taxidermist's place of business, or possibly Barnum's winter quarters. There were cook stoves in the form of turtles, alligators, camels; heating stoves representing Bismarck, General Washington, Uncle Sam, dogs, cats, bears, tigers, elephants, lions, and in fact, almost every conceivable object. The huge elephant stove is for school houses and public institutions...One beautiful pattern was George Washington. Standing as he did, he looked as if he might indeed be the father of the world. He was mounted on a platform or box with the word 'Liberty' in large raised letters across the front of the ashpit section. His right hand rested on the Western hemisphere of a bronze atlas which was placed at his side. His left hand held a statuette of the Goddess of Liberty Enlightening the World. The look upon his face was that of success achieved. A gentle pressure upon his right shoulder would cause his head to fall back, exposing the top into which the fuel was put to replenish the fire." He describes this fanciful dog stove as being cast iron with glass eyes on a nickel-plated base. Don't we wish!

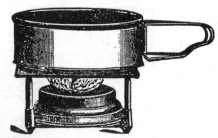

XI-41.
Pocket stove.

"Houchin's Improved Patent", with gridiron and boiler (with folding handles) holding nearly one quart, which can be used as a drinking cup. Will "boil water in five minutes to make 2 or 3 cups of Tea, Coffee, or Chocolate, Boil Eggs, Stew Oysters, etc." Fueled with 2 tablespoonsful of alcohol; "The Lamp being filled with indestructable packing will not spill or explode." Houchin Mfg. Co., NYC. 1877 ad.   **$12.00-$25.00**

XI-42.
Dining room radiator — two views.

"Perfection," mfd. by Michigan Radiator & Iron Mfg. Co., Detroit. Shown open it reveals the oven or "hot closet" above with a slotted shelf, and the smaller one below. Top "oven" is about 18"H x 21"W. Radiator came in seven sizes, from 35" to 65"L. *The Metal Worker*, 8/23/1890.   **$125.00-$250.00**

XI-43.
Stove door.

Oval, cast iron, "Liberty & Union," with 26 stars, which would date it to between 1837, when Michigan became the 26th state, to 1845. 11"H x 13"L. Photo courtesy Litchfield Auction Gallery, Litchfield, CT. Ex-Harold Corbin Collection, auctioned 1/1/1989. Price realized: **$450.00**

XI-44.
Stove handle.
"Alaska. Always Cold," mfd. by Troy Nickel Works, Troy, NY. I don't know if this is the actual appearance of one of their coiled, heat-dissipating handles, or if the lighter-shaded Egyptian, symbolizing desert heat, was an artist's eye-catcher. Note echo of the coils in the stylized hairdo. Ad in The Metal Worker, 8/6/1890.

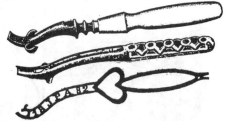

XI-45.
Stove lid lifters.
From the top: One with japanned cast iron shank, brass ferrule, and red-stained turned wood handle, 11"L. The two little arms are for lifting pails. From unidentified catalog page, c.1870s-90s. Next is a "cool handle" one, nickeled cast iron, mfd. by Cleveland Foundry, OH. 1892 ad. Finally, a heart-and-ellipse one, cast iron. Letters in cutout form are "J.P.A." flanked by "18" and "82". Mfd. by J.P. Abbott, Cleveland, OH, in 1882 ad.

XI-47.
Stove lid lifter.
Spectacular voluptuous female form, cast iron. Surely not for a housewife's cook stove; probably for the stove on a railroad caboose or the like. 8 5/16"L, c.1850s-80s. Just before this book went to press, I saw another figural lifter in the booth of folk art dealer Marion Harris. It was a woman's bent leg, in high button boots, and with garter above her knee. **$150.00-$250.00**

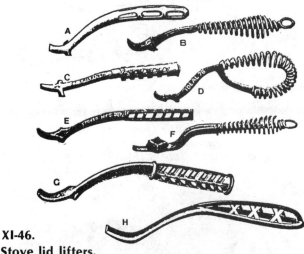

XI-46.
Stove lid lifters.
(A) through (F) are from Excelsior Stove & Mfg. Co., c.1916. (A) and (C) are cast iron with a "coppered" finish. (B), (D), (E) and (F) are nickeled cast iron. (F) is a combination lifter and grate shaker. (G) and (H) are openwork castings of cast iron, offered in "coppered" finish. Heinz & Munschauer, Buffalo, NY, 1882.

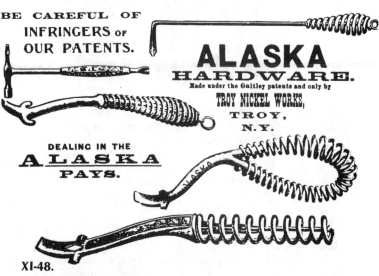

XI-48.
Stove lid lifters, etc.
Top is the entire ad of Troy Nickel Works, Troy, NY, who made the "Alaska" line. The bent tool at top is a poker. The small hammer is for tacks — note tack-pulling tip to handle. Hardware News, 2/25/1895, by made much earlier. At bottom is a coiled-wire lifter — perhaps one of those "infringers" of patents warned against by Troy. It was mfd. by L.M. Devore, Freeport, IL. He calls it a "non-heating wire handle." The Metal Worker, 1892.

XI-49.
"Improved handle for stove covers,"
Wire handle with built-in spring, allowing it to "bend down freely under any vessel placed upon the stove, and pop back up when the vessel is taken up. Pat'd by J.H. Gould, 9/13/1859. Mfd. By Gould & Hartshorn, Alliance, OH. *Scientific American*, 3/10/1860.

XI-50.
Stove polish ad.
"X-Ray," mfd. by Lamont, Corless & Co., Ladies' Home Journal, 10/1904. Blacking wasn't just a cosmetic: it was meant to protect surface from rusting.

XI-51.
Stove urns,
of stamped metal trimmed with cast handles & finials. Top (L) available from 5 1/2" to 8 1/2"H; next one 7"H; top (R) 8 5/8"H and 9 1/4"H; Bottom (L) 10 5/8"H and 11 3/4"H; (M) 11 1/4"H and 12"H; and (R) 12" and 13"H. They made more — up to 14 3/4"H. National Stoves, Ranges & Furnaces, in Excelsior Stove & Mfg. Bo., Quincy, IL, c.1916.

XI-55. Whatsit,
of slight resemblance to similarly well-cast accessories that went around a stovepipe. Cast iron, 2 parts, small 5 cupped bowl-like piece sets down into large part with center hole, lower part has 5 slots that keeps bowl from rotating, "bowl" has 5 "petals" that tilt slightly down toward cups cast at each tip, not a pronounced pouring spout on the cups, but tiny groove that might aid in pouring. (?). Marks on back of bowl look like numbers in reverse, and read from right to left 073342 or 073345, with a definite Oriental character at each end. Bowl is 6 5/8" diam. overall diameter is 19", hole in center of piece is 5 5/8", 19th C. • Dealer Lenny Kislin, who has an eye for the unusual, had this. We don't know what it is, but maybe you do? It is not a nail tray. **$45.00-$65.00**

XI-52.
Stove blacking box.
A homemade wooden box, 4"H x 7"L, with a screw-on cover with handle, and a place for a cake of polish, the brush, and the "mixing plate or dish" (E). "The cover has an opening (C), which comes directly over the mixing dish. Across this opening is placed an old knife blade, or a bit of iron filed sharp. The cake of polish is pushed across this blade until a sufficient quantity for use is scraped off, and falls directly into the dish, where it is to be mixed" — with greasy dishwater?

XI-53.
Stove polishes in cans.
"Black Silk" paste "to be mixed with naptha, benzine or gasoline." "Vulcanol," a cream ready for instant use. Offered by Excelsior Stove & Mfg. Co., c.1916.

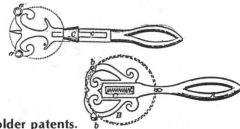

XI-54.
Blacking box holder patents.
Top one, with the round can indicated by the dotted line, was pat'd 1/13/1857, and mfd. by J. & W. Cairns, of Jersey City, NJ. It is cast iron, and has three little "feet" and was made with a figural dog head. 10"L. Bottom one, with spring, is G.W. Taylor's patent #60962, of 1/1/1867. Springfield, VT. *Official Gazette.*
$45.00-$65.00

(The following article was first published in ''The Antique Trader Weekly,'' February 8, 1984. This is a revised version. Clifford Boram and the Antique Stove Information Clearinghouse may be reached at the Monticello, Indiana, address given at the end of this article. Please Send a SASE, ED.)

''What Is My Antique Stove Worth?''
by Clifford Boram

''What is my antique stove worth?'' If someone answered your question with, ''It's worth whatever you can get for it,'' you'd think he was being evasive or flippant. But let's take a closer look at your question, to see if it's asking too much.

The question seems to say, ''I'm not familiar with the market for antique stoves, but I take it for granted there's a going price for stoves like mine, regardless of circumstances, if only I can find out what it is.'' Sorry, but the assumption is not correct. The market for antique stoves is too thin for a consensus on a going price to emerge. In a market this thin, even the experts are at sea. In the course of long experience, they've resigned themselves to the very unhelpful truth that an antique stove isn't ''worth;'' it's only worth something *to somebody.*

Time is one of the circumstances that influence a stove's price. In 1972, before the energy shortage and the suddenly renewed popularity of them, they were being sold for scrap at one cent a pound. Later, their increasing popularity happened to coincide with a period of high inflation when the price of all collectibles was being driven skyward. In 1982, when inflation appeared to be under control and a recession had made many buyers tight-fisted, the price of antique stoves edged back. Whoever wants the best price must time his sale to the economic cycle.

Time of year also influences prices. Spring is the worst season to sell your stove; demand is slight. Late August through December are the months of heavy demand. Antique stove restorer-dealers are often overstocked and short of money in July, so they're only buying at bargain prices if at all.

Time is also a factor in another way: are you in a hurry to sell or can you afford to wait for the right buyer to come along? If you have to sell the stove by tomorrow, you'll pretty well have to take whatever an antique dealer will give you for it, which is often surprisingly little. A dealer who specializes in dolls and glassware won't offer as much for your stove as one who trades in hard goods. And no dealer's offer will be even close to the price he expects to get by waiting - a year or more if necessary - for the right buyer.

Place is another circumstance impacting on the price. There's a thin but continuous stream of desirable stoves being shipped to the lucrative Pacific Coast market. Prices in the Midwest are comparatively very affordable. New England is a hotbed of interest in antique stoves. Interest is practically zero in the Deep South, and Southerners are taken aback when they hear New England prices. Although New York City is notorious for its high prices on antiques, the demand for antique wood/coal stoves is small, since New Yorkers aren't in a position to store such fuels, and the cost of firewood is prohibitive. In New York City, such stoves would only be used as decorative pieces, and their bulk and weight keep them from being popular even for that purpose.

Place also matters where restorer-dealers aren't evenly spaced in a region. A restorer-dealer in Rhode Island tells us he never has to pay more than $200 for even the most desirable unrestored stove in perfectly good condition. With no other restorer-dealers competing for stoves in his area, he has the market to himself. Farther north in New England, where there's more competition, restorer-dealers have to pay more.

Place also makes a difference when an antique stove is being sold in its own home town. A stove made by Madison Stove Works is just another out-of-state stove to a buyer in Iowa. But take it back to Madison, Indiana, and the demand will be greater for an item of local interest. The same holds true in much lesser degree for stoves sold in their own home state.

Besides time and place, there are several other things that affect an antique stove's price. A very important one is *artistic value.* There are plenty of people, especially older and less educated ones, who fail to realize the beauty (if any) in their old stove. Either they sell the stove at a scandalously low price to the first bargain-hunter who happens to come along, or they're flabbergasted to see the high price it brings at auction. By contrast, there are other people who have heard of an antique stove that brought a premium price and who are quite incensed when someone offers them a realistic price for their very plain and uninteresting one. In general, a stove that's generously ornamented with raised designs on the castings and has some nickel-plated parts is worth more than a plain one. The more mica windows it has, the better. One or more ceramic tile cameos attached to the castings are another desirable feature. And the less sheet metal, the better. Desirable options like a high warming-closet, water reservoir, and gas side attachment on a wood/coal range also add to the price.

If the stove was cast from fresh patterns, the designs will have a crispness that may add a little to the price. Many stoves were cast from old, cracked, and carelessly-repaired patterns. The traces of these defects often show on the castings, and may lead a choosy buyer to pass the stove by.

The *age* of a stove influences its price, but it's not completely true that the older a stove is, the greater its value. There was a golden age of stovemaking, say from 1870 to 1910, during which art and technology both reached a peak. An 1820 stove is interesting, but not as efficient or useful as the improved 1890 models. A 1930 stove is just as useful as an 1890, but not so pretty. Most people who admire old stoves want to *use* them too. If a stove isn't very useful, the people who would want to buy it are fewer, and the price suffers. Hardly anyone is a really serious stove collector; the great bulk of demand comes from admirers who have only a few stoves at most.

The golden age of stoves ended as stoves became smoother, plainer, and easier to wipe clean. In general, stoves with a porcelain finish are more modern, and hence less desirable, than the bare-iron ''black'' stoves, but some of the earliest porcelain stoves, still shaped in the old style, are raving beauties that will make your eyes pop. White is the least desirable color for porcelain. Chrome trim, rather than nickel, is the sure mark of a stove too modern to be interesting.

The *rarity* of a stove may have a modest infuence on its price, but perhaps not in the way you'd expect. Rarity may be undesirable to a buyer concerned about the parts situation. A kitchen range by the Majestic Mfg. Co., of Saint Louis, may command a premium over an equivalent model by the Cedar Grove Stove Co., of Cedar Grove, Wisconsin (a small and obscure manufacturer). Majestic parts are available; Cedar Grove parts would have to be made. Certain common makes, such as Glenwood and Monarch, have a reputation for quality that gives them preference over an unknown make.

The only time rarity helps the price of a stove is when the buyer is looking for a particular type or model. For years, a serious collector has been searching for a hay-burning stove, and has been willing to pay a premium price for it, since it's the only type he doesn't have. The Nott's Patent stove would be another such example. Its historic significance as the first base-burner combines with its rarity to make it prized by collectors.

Some *types* of antique stoves are more in demand than others. Base burners are the most coveted type, because of their beauty. The 1900-1915 base burners are most often seen, but once you've met an 1890 square base-burner, you'll know why it commands an even higher premium. Wood parlor stoves, cooking stoves, and the upright, steel-jacketed "oak" stoves are in the second rank of demand. Cannon ("pot belly") stoves rank third. Laundry stoves and sheet-steel "air-tight" heaters go begging, and are so common that there's some agreement on a correct price. One restorer-dealer offered to bury another's house in oval air-tights for $25-30 a piece.

Restorers prefer cast iron stoves, which are bolted together and hence easy to take apart for repair. Steel ranges, on the other hand, are riveted together. If their sheet steel panels are rusted through or otherwise damaged, most buyers just aren't interested.

As for fuel types, wood-burning and coal-burning stoves are the usual favorites in demand. A wood and gas combination range often receives a modest premium over a comparable wood-only range because of its greater utility: a wood range makes the kitchen uncomfortably hot in summertime. Gas stoves are less in demand. There has lately been increasing interest in antique gas ranges, which are at a considerable advantage in metropolitan areas, and which some cooks find more satisfactory than the modern type. Antique gas heaters are trailing behind, with only one restorer-dealer, in Texas, specializing in them. The first, tentative demand for antique electric ranges has just begun to appear in a few areas. Significant demand for antique kerosene ranges is limited to Amish country. Gasoline ranges go begging.

In evaluating a stove's *condition,* first see if its defects impair its beauty. Some buyers, who only want a stove for show, will disregard the most shocking internal damage, if only the stove *looks* good. At a 1981 country auction, a heating contractor bid the price of a 1907 Splendid Universal base burner up to $400 although several of its internal parts were horribly warped, cracked, and burnt. He didn't even object to the missing mica window. If it had also been in fine condition, someone who not only valued its beauty but also wanted to heat his home with it would have bid the price up over $1000.

To take account of a stove's condition, run down this checklist:

1) Is there rust? Are the rust pits so deep they'll be a problem to fill? Are any parts rusted through? (Remove ashes and soot to be sure).
2) Are there any cracks in the cast iron?
3) Have any hooks, tips, etc., been cracked off?
4) Are any parts warped or burnt out?
5) Is the firebrick (if any) intact and sound?
6) If there's a porcelain finish, has it been badly chipped?
7) Are there any bolt holes or mounting tabs that suggest missing accessories or controls?
8) Do all parts fit together nicely? Is anything loose? Do moving parts work smoothly?
9) If repairs have been made, are they neatly and professionally done, or are they crudely finagled with putty and incorrect substitution of materials or parts?
10) Are the correct stove tools (ash shovel, soot rake, poker, lid lifter, and grate shaker handle) included, and are they marked with the stove's name? Is there a teakettle or other hollow ware marked with the stovemaker's name? Is there an original manufacturer's catalog or official cookbook showing the stove?
11) Is the stove's history known?

Are you still wondering what your antique stove is "worth?" A better wording for the question would be, "What have stoves like mine been selling for lately?" But even this may not get you a really useful answer. The range of prices that any particular stove might sell for is just too great. Consider this: in 1981, an 1893 Columbia Oak heater by Indianapolis Stove Co. sold for $300 at auction. Its grate had a piece missing, but was usable. The tip of the draw center arm was broken, so the grate shaker handle couldn't hook on. And the very tip of the ornamental finial atop the urn was missing. The stove was worth $300 to the successful bidder (an antique dealer), and *not* worth $300 to any of the other 263 people at the auction. The following year, the very same stove came up for auction again, and only brought $210 (this time from an individual homeowner). And in 1983 an equivalent 1890 Round Oak heater with better quality castings and no defects except a badly wrinkled sheet-steel jacket only brought $50, and that was at a large auction with plenty of knowledgeable antique dealers (but no stove restorers) present. A restorer-dealer would gladly have paid $150 for the Round Oak, and could easily have retailed it for at least $750 after replacing the jacket.

Normally, the auction price is lower than the retail price. Auctions are where antique dealers get a lot of their wares, and their mark-up from the auction price often approaches 200%. But if collectors attend the auction, they may bid some prices up to the retail level, or even higher. In 1892, when the Bryant collection of 148 antique stoves was auctioned off, in Maine, estimated retail values were included on the report list of prices realized. A circa 1810 Wyer & Noble open Franklin stove estimated to be worth $300-500 sold for $75. The fact that a certain stove once sold for a certain price at a certain auction doesn't mean that's the price you should charge for yours.

Perhaps you'd like to turn to an antiques price guide to learn "the value" of your stove? In 1986, the editor of a price guide wrote me as follows: "I've been interested in antiques long enough to know that there are so many variables involved in buying and selling that I myself have problems with many of our categories such as stoves and furniture (one I especially consider to be a farce when it comes to including enough information in our scanty descriptions to make them worthwhile); if I don't my book stacks up short compared to the competition."

Here's a spectacular example. Blair Whitton (retired curator of the Strong Museum, Rochester, NY., one of America's finest antiques museums) included a price guide section in his 1984 book *Toys*, one of the Knopf Collector's Guides to American Antiques. He consulted with leading toy collectors in arriving at his appraisals. An attractive toy range by the Qualified Range Co., Fort Recovery, Ohio, is listed as being worth $150-200. In that same year, an identical Qualified toy range sold for $3,300 at a nationally advertised auction in Independence, MO. It made Whitton look like a fool, but only to people foolish enough to expect a thin-market appraisal to have predictive validity. The fact is: Whitton was right. The little range *really is* worth $150. *And* $3,300.00. Depending on the circumstances!

Perhaps you'd like to look in an antique stove restorer-dealer's shop to see the prices on restored stoves? You'll find that he's based the prices on a number of factors, including cost of restoration supplies, overhead, and hours of labor; utility value of a new stove of equivalent size and type; and the decorative/artistic desirability of the antique. Most of these factors have a going price, but the art value doesn't. And it's the one that matters most to a buyer. That's why some types of stoves aren't worth restoring.

A complication arises when a dealer is also a collector. He may like some of his merchandise so much that he really isn't particularly interested in selling it. In such cases, he may put an unreasonably high price on those items. It's his way of saying, "If you're crazy enough to pay me that kind of money for my stove, I'd be crazy not to accept; otherwise it's a keeper." Don't expect to get such an exorbitant price for your stove. You'll have to price yours to sell.

Perhaps you'd like to ask an antique stove restorer-dealer for an appraisal? Many restorer-dealers are willing to appraise a stove by mail from a photo if you tell them its condition in detail. There may be a charge of as much as $10 for this service. And how much good will it do you? Thin-market appraisals are properly used for estate tax calculation and insurance inventory valuations, where you just have to have a number, regardless of reality. They're *not* properly used to decide how much you should charge.

So what shall you do to set a correct price on your stove? The foregoing observations aren't meant to keep you from examining the market. They're only intended to keep you from being intimidated by it and to help you understand that in a market this thin, *you are the market*, to a surprisingly large degree.

Start by figuring out what the stove is worth *to you*. That is, how much worse-off would you be without it? This will be your minimum price. Be sure to take into account th stove's desirability. Next, find the right buyer: a high-incentive buyer with enough income to let her pay generously for what she wants. The amount of time and effort you put into finding her has a lot to do with how much you wind up getting. Help her decide her maximum price for the stove by asking how much better-off she'd be with it. Have her write her price on a slip of paper while you write yours on another, and then exchange papers. The correct price is half way between your minimum and her maximum; that way you'll both be pleased. This is negotiation, the most satisfactory pricing technique in a thin market. There's no reason why the burden of setting the price should be borne entirely by the seller.

A number of helpful publications are available from The Antique Stove Information Clearinghouse, 417 North Main Street, Monticello, IN 47960. They include a **Nationwide List of Antique Stove Restorer Dealers** ($1), a 60-page illustrated catalog of the Bryant auction, 1982 ($9.50), and several others on various antique stove appreciation and restoration subjects. Prices include postage. Send SASE for complete booklist and an introductory sheet on The Antique Stove Association. (ED. Note: It would be best to write first before ordering anything, because postage rates will be up in 1991, and again in 1992.)

WIMSW-1.
Wood - or coal-burning cook stove.
Example: "Valley Queen." Such a stove can retail for about $800.00 when fully restored. At a country auction, the rusty, neglected veteran, complete but with some warped and cracked parts, would bring about $50.00 (ED. note: Prices here are subject to all factors mentioned in text of Clifford Boram's article. Any discrepencies between his and my valuations should be decided in favor of Boram, with reference to actual market conditions in your community.)

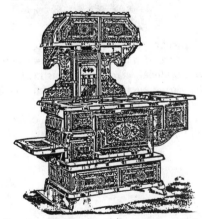

WIMSW-2.
Range.
An attractive all-cast-iron range from the 1880s will often be priced at over $2000.00 in a restorer-dealer's shop. But this 1891 "New Adonis" range, Buckwalter Stove Co., is so spectacular that it deserves a price of $3000.00 or more.

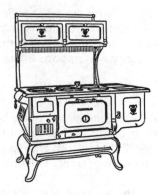

WIMSW-3.
Range.

This porcelainized cast iron range, a 1922 "Peninsular," is typical of the plain style that became the predominant favorite in the early decades of this century. Restorer-dealers often price these very common ranges well below $1000.00 in Midwest markets; below $1300.00 in New England.

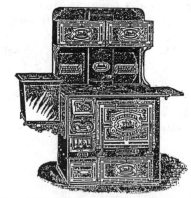

WIMSW-4.
Range.

Numerous rivet heads identify steel ranges like this 1899 Majestic #251. They're exceptionally difficult to restore, but in top condition they can bring over $1200.00 at the right auction.

WIMSW-5.
Wood-, coal-and-gas combination range.

New England restorer-dealers have lately been getting $2000.00 or more for fine combination ranges like this 1927 Magee National. In 1984, at the wrong auction in Indiana, an unrestored one in average condition sold for $15.00 because no-one in the crowd was interested in cooking. The buyer was an elderly woman who needed something to heat her garage.

WIMSE-6.
Base-burner.

Dealers have been known to ask over $5000.00 for a fully-restored square base-burner, such as the classic 1904 "Art Andes." The "piggyback" oven seen at back, is a desirable option.

WIMSW-7.
Base-burner.

The 1886 Argand round base-burner is awesome, though many round base-burners are plainer and too small to be really spectacular. Note the piggyback oven here, too. Value probably at least equal to WIMSW-6.

WIMSW-8.
Base-burner.

The 1931 "Columbian Art" reflector base-burner typifies the twilight of the base-burner era: the desirable Victorian fancywork has been smoothed away, leaving only a handsome structure that would have trouble getting $2000.00 in some markets.

WIMSW-9.
Heat stoves.

Two extremes of the oak stove desirability spectrum are shown by (L) E. Bement & Sons' 1892 "Capital Oak" and (R) Auto Stove Works' 1937 "Sun". The "Capital Oak" is blessed with mica windows, fancy ornamentation, and even a cast iron jacket — a deluxe option preferable to the "Sun's" sheet steel jacket. Larger skirt rails and a pair of nickel-plated wings beside the feed door would also be desirable in Bement's stove, but those features belong to the 1900 to 1930 era. Even though the "Sun" is now 50 years old, its Art Deco styling denies it any claim to an antique premium above its utility value. (ED. note: If truly "Art Deco" it would have value, but it seems hardly styled at all except for legs.)

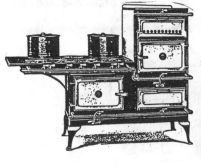

WIMSW-10.
Gas ranges.

The recent surge of interest in gas ranges has driven some prices over $3000.00 for fully-restored, top-of-the-line models. The 1928 Tappan (R) shows the routine antique gas range configuration. A price of $150.00 for a good unrestored one would be a realistic minimum price paid by a dealer. It sould be obvious that the 1921 double-oven Chambers (L) is infinitely more desirable. 1930s gas ranges with no high structure are so close in form to the modern ones that they have trouble commanding a significant antique premium.

WIMSW-12.
Cannon or "pot-belly" stoves.

*These too are considered of low value to most collectors. Popularly called "pot-belly" stoves, but termed **cannon, globe, or egg stoves** by the industry, most of these were among a manufacturer's cheaper goods — comparatively plain and simple stoves with no pretensions to the fancy, nickel-plated, mica windowed parlor stove category that antique enthusiasts admire and pay high prices for today. Plenty of first quality, heavy, and substantial cannons were made too, but they were for depots, schools, offices, and other commercial situations, rather than for homes. Only a few achieved artistic merit, despite the limitations of their type, by adopting parlor stove features.*

Within the cannon category, it's possible to distinguish differences in desirability, and hence value. Lowest in interest and value is the utterly utilitarian and totally uninteresting little cannon, picture #0 above. Such a stove's value depends entirely on its usefulness, not on the fact that it may be 60 years old. It would generally bring less than $40.00 at auction, although you might see it priced at more than $100.00 in a shop. #1, still low on the scale of desirability, is the sort of cannon most often seen. It has a bit of ornamentation, and isn't unattractive, but it lacks any features that would make it stand out from the crowd. #2, with its ribbed design and fender ring, begins to be more desirable. #3, with both foot rails and a fender ring, is a fine, handsome cannon, as cannons go, but would benefit still more from cherry mica windows in its feed door, through which to view the fire. #4, an artistic jewel among cannons, has mica windows in its feed door and three mica doors just above grate level. Its foot rail, deep ribs, and rich, angular design also contribute to its great desirability. It would be a bargain at $300.00, especially in its larger sizes.

Occasionally a sheet metal extension drum or even a cast iron extension containing a self-feeding magazine for coal would be added to the top of a cannon stove. #5 has one (not the ornamental "urn" on top, but the cylindrical part below that), and is thus a base-burning cannon. The ornate extension must be considered desirable, although it makes this stove more spectacular and odd than beautifully-proportioned.

WIMSW-11.
Various low-demand stoves.

Large black one is a kerosene range. Top row (L) to (R) are a sheet iron oval Air-Tight, a kitchen heater, and a cast iron circulator. Below them are a cast iron laundry stove and a gasoline range with its small fuel tank raised above. (ED Note: Perhaps it is the influence of collectors who want, in effect, whatnot shelves for their collectible utensils, but the kerosene and gasoline stoves are increasingly sought, and laundry stoves are considered natural adjuncts to sadiron collections.)

D. COOKING
XII. POTS, PANS & HOLLOWWARE

This brief chapter gives a simple outline of the most important shapes and forms of hollowware.

The soon to be published guide to collecting cookbooks will include, pots, pans, hollowware, and utensils called for in old recipes. It will also cover all the hollowware forms you expected to find here.

Cast iron is still an upcoming field; you can subscribe to the dedicated **"Cast Iron Cookware News,"** 28 Angela Ave., San Anselmo, CA 94960. Graniteware has been collected for decades. A well-established newsletter comes from the **National Graniteware Society,** POB 326, Alburnett, IA 52202. Use SASE when writing, please.

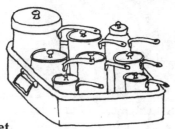

XII-1.
Bain marie set.
Tall, straight-sided pans, long handles, for setting in large pan called a "box" of water Bain marie means bath pool." This set, copper with iron handles, Mrs. A.B. Marshall's c.1900.
$200.00-$650.00

XII-2.
Broiler & fry-pan combined.
"Tracy's The Triumph," Maltby, Henley & Co., Rocky Hill, CT. Stamped steel frying pan-lid detaches. Broiler is cast iron with grooved ribs. One of many such openwork stovetop broilers. 1890 ad.
$40.00-$75.00

XII-3.
Chafing dish.
Copper & silver, 11"H, 3 standing hares — punning decoration for "Welsh rarebit" pan. Photo courtesy Michael Cable, Woodside Antiques, Greenville, NC.
$900.00-$1200.00

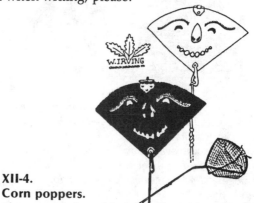

XII-4.
Corn poppers.
Sheet metal, forged iron handles with strengthening twist, wire basket. Marked with 3 oak-leaf stamp & name "W. Irving." Other living pieces include a "Saratoga Jabber" & "Saratoga Frizzler" — for fireplace cookery? Courtesy Aarne Anton, American Primitve Gallery, NYC.
$1000.00-$1400.00

XII-5.
Cruller or potato fryers for deep frying.
*Also called **frying baskets** or **double fry pans.** Heavy wire or perforated metal baskets suspended in various sizes pans. (L) pat'd 7/8/1879, mfd. by Matthai-Ingram, Lalance & Grosjean, etc. (R) Up to 20" diameter wrought steel, c.1900-1910.* **$60.00-$135.00**

XII-6.
Double or farina boilers & valved saucepan.
(T) "French Milk Sauce Pan," with valves in lid. (L) Farina boiler, for custard, corn starch, milk. (B) Sauce Pan & Potato Steamer." 3 from American Home Cook Book, 1854. Top (R) Milk saucepan, tin with earthenware inner pan. 1870s-80s import catalog.
$30.00-$100.00

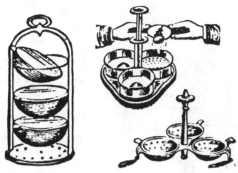

XII-7.
Egg poachers.
(L) Tin, 3-stack, <u>American Home Cook Book</u>, 1854. Top (R) "Maryland" poacher, catch at top of handle, used in stew pan or skillet. c.1890. (R) Tin with iron handle, 1870s-80s import catalog.
$25.00-$50.00

XII-8.
Frying pan patent.
Pat'd 9/20/1864, S.B. Sexton, Baltimore. Cast iron with integral venting tube/flue. Used with domed lid. Sexton mfd. stoves & utensils into the 1930s, so this probably made.

XII-9.
Frying pans.
Cast iron. (L) "Common spider, ventilated handle," 6" to 10" diameter. Henry N. Clark, Boston, 1864. (R) Idealized drawing of Wapak Ware Indian on skillet bottom. 1915 ad. **$50.00-$100.00**

XII-10.
Soapstone griddles.
Iron rims; bail & ear handles. For grease-free cooking. (L) "Hodges' Superior," William Hodges & Co., Philadelphia, c.1880s-1920. (R) From 12" to 16" diameter. Buhl Sons, c.1919 hardware catalog.
$30.00-$75.00

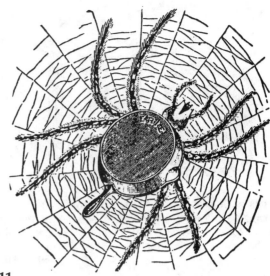

XII-11.
Griswold's "Erie" spider,
another word for frying pan. From 1890's ad in trade magazine for founders. Erie Hollow-Ware Works, Griswold Mfg. Co., Erie, PA.

XII-12.
Brass & enameled kettles & cast iron pot.
(L) Bulge pot, with bail, tipping handle, 3 short feet. "Favorite Piqua" cast iron, Favorite Stove & Range, Piqua, OH, 1890 ad. (M) Spun brass preserve kettle, 2-14 gals., iron bail, c.1900 — form & Mf'g method dates to H.W. Hayden's 12/16/1851 brass-spinning patent. (R) "Sterling" gray enamelware, 10 sizes, up to 15" diameter. Central Stamping, 1920. **$40.00-$125.00**

XII-13.
Saucepans — most age-deceptive old forms.
(L) Copper or wrought iron, tubular handle, pouring lip. Harrod's, 1895. (2) Cast iron, tinned or enameled inside, 1-20 qts., early 20th C. (3) "London" shape, iron or copper, no lip, Harrod's. (R) "Sugar boiler," tinned copper, William Adams, London, c.1860-61. Same form lasted many decades. **$25.00-$100.00**

XII-14.
Stock pots with brass spigots near bottom.
(L) "Gotham," seamless agateware, tin cover, brass strainer inside. 10 1/4" to 15 1/2" diameter. Central Stamping, 1920. (R) Choice of copper, brazed iron, or seamless steel. English, c.1900.
$60.00-$150.00

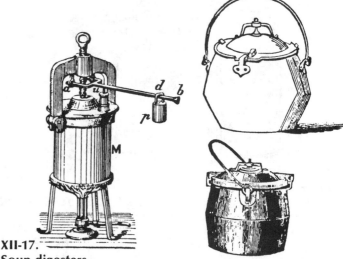

XII-17.
Soup digesters,
an early form of pressure cooker. (L) Papin's Digester, a cylindrical metal vessel "M" with a firmly screwclamped lid. "To close the vessel hermetically, sheet lead is placed between the edges of the cover and the vessel. In the cover there is a hole which is closed by a rod kept in place by a cylindrical guide "u" which presses against a lever. Pressure may be regulated by means of a weight, movable on the lever. The lever is so weighted that when the pressure in the interior is equal to six atmospheres, for example, the valve rises and the vapour escapes. The destruction of the apparatus is thus avoided, and the mechanism has hence received the name of safety valve. The digester is filled about two-thirds with water, and is heated by a large Bunsen burner." Denis Papin, French scientist, invented this digester in 1679 — over 300 years ago! Picture from D. Atkinson's <u>Natural Philosophy</u>, 1905. Top (R) The Digester produces "a larger quantity of wholesome and nourishing food" than any other. This was claimed because in it bones and gristle could be softened completely, for eating in a soup form. Arggh! Sizes given as ranging from 1-8 qts. and from 4-qts. to 8 gals. <u>American Home Cook Book</u>, 1854. Lower (R) From 2 to 6-gals., cast iron, Duparquet, Huot catalog for hoteliers, 1909. **$30.00-$400.00**

XII-15.
Utensils of blue enameled ware.
"Complete outfit...true blue." Sets sized for #7, #8, or #9 stoves. Tea kettle, teapot, coffee pot, Berlin kettle (bottom R), saucepan, pudding pan (top L), double boiler, dish pan, soap dish, basting spoon, 2 pie plates, 1 Windsor dipper (in dish pan center), soup ladle. $4.58 for all, Sears, 1908. In perfect condition, probably 100 X as much!

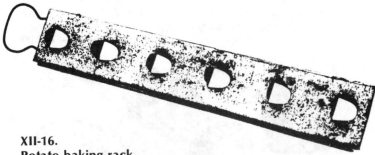

XII-16.
Potato baking rack.
Tin with wire handle, 15 1/4"L, c.1900. **$10.00-$18.00**

XII-18.
Stovetop or tabletop ovens.
Top "Gas-Saver Oven," with rack. 7 5/8"H x 11 1/2" diameter. Color printed paper band around lid. Androck, Washburn Co., 1936. Lower (L) Electric "Stanley Ovenette," Stanley Savage Mfg. Co., 1935 ad. (R) "Kantburn Kooker" or ovenless baker. Sheet metal. Also Stanley Savage. 1913. **$15.00-$35.00**

XII-19.
Stovetop toasters.
Top (L) "Worcester," tin & wire, folds up, 8 7/8" diameter. Washburn, 1936. (R) "Jim's Toaster," convex tin bottom with wire heat-throwing cone. Does 5 slices. Excelsior Stove & Mfg., c.1916. Lower (L) "Kitchen Kumfort" 2-sided. Steel, with perforated radiator base. 5"H x 8 1/2" diameter. "Sno-Cap," Washburn Co., 1927. (R) "Brooklyn Bread Toaster," heave sheet steel, wire supports on 4 sides. 6"H x 8" square. Silver Co., Brooklyn, c.1910. **$4.00-$20.00**

XIII. IMPLEMENTS THAT TURN, SPOON, FLIP & DIP

The title of this chapter says it all. These are handheld, nonmechanical cooking tools (correctly called implements, not utensils) of the most basic type. These tools are extensions of the cook's hands, that help the cook move food or food particles from one utensil or container to another. Many are variations on a spoon theme (spoon, ladle, dipper); others are forks of various types and sizes; most of the others have blades — narrow or wide, metal or wood — that will slide under cooked food so it can be turned over or retrieved from kettle, griddle or oven.

There are some things which might have appeared in this chapter but I moved them to a chapter more related to function. Butter paddles are in the Form, Mold & Decorate chapter; skimmers, as well as wire vegetable skimmers or "pea ladles", are all in the Separate & Strain chapter; scoops are in the Measuring & Weighing chapter.

In the last edition, I wrote that cake turners were the most generally popular category within this chapter. This is still true for collectors of 20th century kitchenwares. The enormous increase in collectors of metal and wooden Colonial and hearth-cooking implements has meant more interest in ladles and cooking spoons, although I know of no-one who collects them as a "category". Collectors of enameled implements are legion; primarily they are material collectors, not form collectors.

As with all the chapters up to this point, there are some problematic entries. For example, the first here is an apple butter stirrer, which could easily have found a place in the Mix, Beat & Stir chapter. But if you won't argue, I won't.

Apple butter stirrer, long wood handle set at right angles to heavy oak (?) pear-shaped blade, with curvy "X" cutout, good patina on handle, American, handle about 6 feet long, blade about 6"W and 13"L, 1840s to 1850s. • **"Apple butter.** — Stir apples and cider all the time; you should have for the purpose a stick made of hickory wood, somewhat like a common hoe, with holes in it." Elizabeth E. Lea, *Useful Receipts and Hints to Young Housekeepers*, 10th ed., Baltimore, 1859 (1st ed. 1851). **$75.00-$100.00**

Apple butter stirring paddle, long wood handle with paddle with largish cutout holes, used with handle horizontal & paddle in a vertical position, dragged back & forth across rim of the huge kettle, so that the paddle would stir the viscous liquid, American, 43"L, 19th or early 20th C. • These looked the same for at least 150 years, & were advertised for two decades into the 20th C, often with 1860s-1880s illustrations. Best choice are those that show use, with real good dark patina, handles polished with the wear of hands, worn paddles, repairs or interesting wooden or metal bracing, even a bit of warping gives character. **$50.00-$85.00**

Basting spoon, also called simply a baster, heavily tinned iron, deep bowl, possibly mfd by Lalance & Grosjean, Woodhaven, LI, NY, 19"L, TOC. **$8.00-$12.00**

Basting spoon, speckled black & white agateware, deep bowl, pointed end, American or European, 13"L, TOC. **$20.00-$40.00**

Basting spoon, though rather shallow bowl, cast aluminum, marked "Mueller & Co.", Hagen, Germany, 14"L, TOC. **$6.00-$12.00**

Butter hands—See Mold & Shape chapter.

Cake server, wide trowel-like tin blade but otherwise with same stamped embossed wire handle as the cake turner or spatula of same make, both adv'g "Rumford, the Wholesome Baking Powder", possibly mfd by Pilgrim Novelty Co., American, early 20th C. The price spread is wide because some people price it as a "Rumford" collectible, and some as a simple cake server. **$12.00-$38.00**

Cake turner, also called a keyhole spatula, blade of whitesmithed iron is shaped like a fat large keyhole, there's a cutout cross in the "ball" of blade, American (?), 8¾"L, very early 19th C. • Cake turners are often called spatulas, although this is technically incorrect, or at least debatable. On the one hand, when you talk about the shape of some fingertips, or certain petals or leaves, they

are spatulate if they broaden at the tip in a spade-like way. That is the cake turner blade shape. A (pan)cake turner has a blade which is almost always longer than it is wide, about 5"L x 4" or 4½"W, and the blade is also almost always slotted or perforated with a number of holes. A cake turner is used to flip food like flapjacks, fried eggs, grilled cheese sandwiches, crab cakes or banana fritters. Many people specialize in the numerous cake turners of the A & J Co, later Edward Katzinger Co. (now EKCO), or of Androck. • For the most part, a spatula is like a wide, flexible or limber dinner knife blade, about 1¼"W, with long slender blade rounded on end, and the most common kitchen uses are icing cakes or scraping work surfaces or grills or cleaning the curved insides of bowls. Some spatulas are also perforated, but longness and flexibility are the basic attributes. • What we might take as our final arbiters, the manufacturers' catalogs of the 19th & 20th C, are divided in terminology. **$65.00-$80.00**

Cake turner, also called a kitchen trowel by manufacturer, ovoid unperforated blade, nickel plated steel, tiller handle "Elevated about 2" from the blade", in trowel fashion, rubberoid handle grip, "Kitchen Kumfort Trowel", mfd by Lasher Mfg. Co., Davenport, IA, about 10"L, patent applied for by 1911. **$10.00-$13.00**

Cake turner, brass with forged iron handle, "F. B. S.", Canton, OH, 14½"L, pat'd 1886. • The style of these looks much older, and there are LOTS of them around, accounting for wide value range, because they look much older, & some people may not be aware of supply. **$50.00-$150.00**

Cake turner, cast aluminum, angled slots in blade, 4 holes at front edge, marked with word "Aluminum" inside a hammer outline, also "D. R. G. M." (for *Deutsches Reichs-Gebrauchsmuster*), German, 10¼"L, early 20th C, prior to 1918, when the mark "D. R. G. M." was superceded. **$10.00-$13.00**

Cake turner, enameled sheet iron, white with pale blue pattern of "Chicken wire", tubular handle, hanging ring, blade spatulate in shape with rounded "shoulder", pattern of perforations is two double rows of stylized wheat berries along outside blade edges, American (?) or European, 13"L, TOC. • This came in various color combinations. The "Chicken wire" effect adds a lot to value here; one with black or dark red handle and plain white blade would be a third as much. **$95.00-$125.00**

Cake turner, forged iron, smallish flat blade with marvelous wing-like shoulders, long shaft that is straight for first few inches, then twisted with big-fat & little-tight twists, rattail loop at end, American, 17''L, 18th C. • **Shrove Tuesday Flapjacks.** — William Hone's 1845 edition of *The Year Book*, for Feb. 3, Shrovetide, has a quote from ''Taylor, the water-poet, in his works, 1630: Shrove Tuesday, at whose entrance in the morning all the whole kingdom is inquiet; but by that time the clocke strikes eleven, which…is commonly before nine, then there is a bell rung, cal'd the pancake bell, the sound whereof makes thousands of people distracted, and forgetful either of manners or humanitie; then there is a thing called wheaten floure, which the cookes do mingle with water, egges, spice, and other tragical, magicall inchantments; and then they put it, by little and little, into a frying-pan of boiling suet, where it makes a confused dismall hissing, untill at last, by the skill of the cooke, it is transformed into the forme of a flip-jack call'd a pancake, which ominous incantation the ignorant people doe devoure very greedily''. **$500.00-$750.00**

Cake turner, forged iron, whitesmithed, polished & filed yet dark in color, shapely strong handle, end has teardrop hanging hole, shovel-shaped rectangular blade with rounded shoulders, slightly flared sides, bold cutouts of rather large diamond near center with 4 round holes near each corner, signed ''E. P. Sebastian'' on handle. Edward Sebastian was noted for openwork ''Spatulas''. Host, Berks County, PA, blade 6¼'' x 5½'' with 14½''L handle, c. 1850s-80s. • Called a ''Spatula'' in the catalog. Most people's inclination, & I'm not excepted, is to call these spatulas, but since that is a very particular kitchen tool, with a long flexible blade about 1¼''W, I want to reserve the term for that. Whether or not you make <u>hotcakes</u> (flapjacks, flatjacks, pancakes, etc.), or just fried eggs, ''Cake turner'' is correct. • Robacker May 1989 price: **$1400.00**

Cake turner, forged iron with wide flat blade, relatively short handle, American (?), 13½''L, 19th C. **$35.00-$45.00**

Cake turner, forged & polished iron, long handle with small heart cutout in end near rattail loop, American; PA (?), 18½''L, early 19th C. **$150.00-$175.00**

Cake turner, forged & polished iron, unusual sideways rectangular blade almost size of playing card, with rounded corners, thin graceful forged iron handle, with small hanging loop, fine inlaid brass floral designs. PA. Blade 4'' x 5¼''W, with 16''L handle, dated ''1854''. • Price achieved at May 1989 Horst auction: **$325.00**

• **Fake Brass Inlays.** — Jeannette Lasansky, (Oral Traditions Project, Court House, Lewisburg, PA 17837) is author of several meticulously researched books on old Pennsylvania crafts. In ''Collectors' notes'', Nov. 1980 *The Magazine ANTIQUES*, she shared her discovery of a number of fake brass inlays found in a disparate group of 18th or early 19th C forged iron implements from different collections. The faking was done at some point after 1860 (determined from fluorescence analysis of the brass involved), and probably in the 20th C . Pieces included cake turners, flesh forks, tasters, ladles and a skimmer, all common forms, with stylistic differences in the design of the forged iron. The significant thing, what brought Lasansky's attention to the fraud, is that ''On all the pieces the brass-inlay technique is identical and the motifs, repetitive.'' The three types of decoration done by the faker are narrow bands with minimal engraved design; wide bands with engraved initials and/or dates (Lasansky says they are all from 1823 through 1829); and wide bands or inset ''lozenges'' with images (hearts, eagles or tulips) engraved on them. From the pictures shown in that article, of pieces in the Titus Geesey Collection at the Philadelphia Museum, and the Abby Aldrich Rockefeller Folk Art Center, Williamsburg, VA, it seems that without Lasansky's eagle eye, and the sharing of artifacts made possible by exhibits, photographs and books, we would never have known. The engraving is of the bright cut variety from the early 19th C, and the style of letters, numbers and pictures mimics the eagerness and slight primitiveness of examples of authentic period engraving. It's scary. I've not seen an update, though Lasansky asked collectors and curators to closely examine their collections. One thing apparent from the pictures is that the pitting, scarring and surface distressing of the polished iron of the handles of the various implements is in sharp contrast to the virtually untouched surfaces of the brass inlays. • I must stress that no item from the Earl F. & Ada F. Robacker Collection was said to have a fake 20th C inlay, and the sharing of Lasansky's observations is not meant to impinge on the value or authenticity of any inlaid piece auctioned by T. Glenn Horst.

Cake turner, handsomely formed tin, with tiny pie-wedge cutouts, stylized heart & bird decorations, ribbed cylindrical handle with little strap hanger, possibly made as a 10th Wedding Anniversary gift, found in Bradford or Sullivan County, NY, 13⅜''L x 2½''W at widest point, c.1860s to 1880s. **$135.00-$150.00**

• **1875 ''Tin Weddings.''** — Passing an extensive house furnishing store twice daily, we most always give a glance at the show-window. Some months ago we saw a most beautifully fashioned shoe on exhibition, which appeared to be made of the finest planished tin. We wondered what it could be for; it was too large for a smoker's ash-receiver, and could hardly be an article for kitchen or table use; several days after, and before we had time to step in and solve the matter, there appeared by the side of the shoe an elegant fan of the same material, at least so far as fine workmanship could make a tin fan elegant; this added to the mystery, but in a day or two all was made plain by the displaying of a card reading 'Articles for Tin Weddings.' All that we know of 'tin weddings' is that the fifth [No, it's the 10th, not the 5th] anniversary of marriage is by some people celebrated, as a sort of burlesque upon silver weddings, by a party, at which the guests made presents of tinware. The presents were formerly of useful articles, but now it seems that the burlesque itself is travestied, and much ingenuity is expended in making articles for tin weddings which can be of no possible use to those who receive them. Quite a large number of these articles are now imported from France; two of these have already been named above; besides these we found on inquiry there were ridiculous bouquets of tin flowers; preposterous necklaces, and other jewelry of skillful workmanship, but all of the same cheap material; a tin saw and other tools for a mechanic; instruments supposed to be emblematic of the medical profession, and other curious, expensive, and equally useless articles are offered. Now we believe in innocent amusement, and if any fun can be had out of a tin wedding — if the parties most concerned are so disposed — so be it, but there should be some sense even to our nonsense, and we must say that we regard this matter of tin shoes, tin bouquets, and the like, as carrying the matter just a little too far.'' — Anonymous editor, *American Agriculturist*, July 1875, offices in NYC, where this tinwares store must have been. This humorless writer would be astounded to see with what high regard collectors today hold these ''nonsensical'' tin objects.

Cake turner, homemade, a flattened tin can side, carefully cutout in a truncated wedge shape, front edge bent, nailed to a peeled & partly whittled stick, extremely well-worn, great patina on handle, wire wrapped around handle as a sort of ferrule, Oregon, 16''L, found around 1965, dates poss. to c.1940s. • Found by collector James R. Holroyd of Oregon, discarded at a camp on the Skyline Trail in the Oregon Cascades. **$10.00-$18.00**

Cake turner, keyhole spatula, twisted forged iron handle, all filed & polished whitesmith's work, pretty silvery appearance, American, 11''L, very early 19th C. • This keyhole shape, sometimes called a thistle shape (with bulbous part down), was used in much later cake turners too — especially in enamelware. **$75.00-$100.00**

Cake turner, metal, adv'g ''Rettberg's Scrapple'', dated 1914. **$12.00-$15.00**

Cake turner, metal, adv'g ''Barnes Coal Co.'', early 20th C. **$7.00-$12.00**

Cake turner, nickel plated steel with wire shank, blue & ivory painted wood handle, Perforation pattern is center straight line of holes flanked by an outward curving line of holes on each side, ''Blutip'', A & J, Binghamton, NY, 14¼''L, c. 1940s. • Price reflects poor condition of paint. The two-tone ones, especially with ivory, seemed to flake off in big chips more readily than the red or green finishes. **$7.00-$8.00**

Cake turner, oblong tin blade, sharp front corners, rounded corners at heel of blade, 2 elongated corrugations lengthwise on blade — according to the ads, ''So the cake cannot slide sidewise'' (hee hee). Paint-enameled turned wood handle, mfd by Handy Things Co., Ludington, MI, blade is 3½''L x 2⅞''W, overall length 11¼'', c.1904. • Remember, ''Cake'' refers to pancake, not layer cake. **$7.00-$10.00**

Cake turner, or peel (?), nicely shaped wrought iron blade with heart-top (or shoulder-padded) shoulders, turned wooden handle, shortish shaft, American, about 12''L, 19th C. **$110.00-$135.00**

Cake turner, or peel (?), very small round disc blade, interesting long handle with short chevron and bull's eye hole, marked ''Levi Lewis'', prob. PA, 14¾''L, 19th C. **$120.00-$150.00**

Cake turner, or peel, whitesmithed iron, well-formed shoulder, initials ''A. W.'' inlaid in brass on handle. From near Stroudsburgh, PA, 13¹³/₁₆''L, early 19th C. **$500.00-$600.00**

Cake turner, or perhaps peel, forged iron, whitesmithed & polished, long handle with broad end & rattail loop, decorated with cut lines & bull's eyes. Round blade has cutout 6 point star or petaled flower, ¾'' wide border decorated with 6 bull's eyes, American, 20½''L overall, blade is 4'' diameter, 18th C. **$300.00-$400.00**

Cake turner, or small peel, perhaps even a dough scraper, though without the latter's customary angled handle. This is whitesmithed iron, nifty large hanging ring, American,

prob. PA, 12¼''L, late 18th C. • The silvery surface comes from being worked, filed, polished, planished and hammered. The hammering & polishing, which gave the surface a very fine texture, is called <u>planishing</u>. Sometimes the smith who did this work was known as a <u>whitesmith</u> or <u>brightsmith</u>. **$95.00-$115.00**

Cake turner, perforated tinned steel & wire, the heavy wire handle wiggles & snakes off at the tip, an elegant solution to heat dispersal problem. ''A good cook will quickly see the merits of this cake turner. The grease passes through it instantly and leaves the food light and tempting. The handle gives a firm, cool grip and is easily cleaned'', say the ads of the time. mfd by Arcade Mfg. Co. (famed toy mfrs), Freeport, IL, 14¾''L, c. 1905. **$15.00-$18.00**

Cake turner, polished, filed, shaped & decorated forged iron, handle has round hanging loop, copper inlaid along handle, small blade with very rounded shoulders & tips, no cutouts, marked ''B. H'' with date, PA. Blade is 4'' x ⅞'', with 12''L handle, dated 1821. • Robacker May 1989 price: **$850.00**

Cake turner, probably a <u>10th Anniversary piece</u>, not for use. Described by the Robackers as a ''Pie peel'', but the blade isn't large enough. The blade is bent to create angled-up shoulder, & is crudely soldered to long dented cylindrical handle, the only redeeming feature being the punctured tin decoration (& that done with no finesse) comprised of a squat, typically Pennsylvania German heart, with the initials ''L'' and ''S'' inside, the heart surmounted by a wavy line indicating a leaf scroll with a small flower in the center, PA, 21⅝''L, with blade about 6¼''L x 4½''W, late 19th C. • Robacker May 1989 price is way over the money in my opinion. **$450.00**

Cake turner, stamped sheet metal, handle riveted to simple blade round shoulder, no finesse to design, but it wouldn't look bad in that Bouquet-of-turner-tulips stuck handle down in a crock, no mark, American, 13''L, c.1890 to 1900. **$6.00-$8.00**

Cake turner, steel blade, turned wood handle, brass ferrule, American, 16''L, 19th C. **$40.00-$50.00**

Cake turner, tin, adv'g ''Quick Meal Ranges'', for Ringen Stove Co., but prob. not made by them, early 20th C. **$12.00-$15.00**

Cake turner, tin & green finished wood, blade is stamped with ridges to add rigidity and is perforated with highly decorative pattern of holes that form a heart reminiscent of Pennsylvania German designs, American, 11¾''L, 20th C. **$8.00-$12.00**

Cake turner, tin with knobby turned wooden handle, baked on white enamel finish with 1/6th of handle at end dipped in rich medium blue, wire shank, shapely shouldered blade with 3 graduated rows of perforations, ''Blutip'', A & J Mfg. Co. (Div. of Edward Katzinger), Binghamton, NY, 13¼''L, c.1930. **$12.00-$15.00**

Cake turner, tin with wire, has 3 long oblong blades with large holes, they are stacked 1 2 3, but when fanned out when you pull the thumb release they almost triple the width of the useable blade. This way you can adjust the width to suit the griddle or frying pan you are using as well as the pancake or omelet, marked ''Coradon'', (the one in Jane Celehar's book was made by Gadget Mfg. Co.), NYC, 12½''L, blade: 6½''L x 2⅝''W, spreads to 8½''W, pat'd Dec. 8, 1936, by Minnie Greene & Lois Udey. • Flap the Jack, Mac, **Lookalike alarm.** — Lehman's

Hardware & Appliances, 4779 Kidron Rd., Kidron, OH 44636 offer a very similar one with stainless steel blades in their 1989 "Non-Electric Good Neighbor Amish Country" catalog, which costs about $2.00. • Another mechanical type has a trigger that you pull which flips the blade; talk about a "lazy elbow" (as the nickname goes for kettle tilters from hearth cooking days)! **$12.00-$18.00**

Cake turner, tinned blade, embossed handle, "Aurora Ice Cream", early 20th C. **$12.00-$15.00**

Cake turner, tinned iron, adv'g "Ira Egger General Merchandise", American, early 20th C. **$7.00-$12.00**

Cake turner, tinned iron with bottle opener handle, adv'g "Clyde Milling Co.", Clyde, KS, early 20th C. **$7.00-$9.00**

Cake turner, tinned iron with bottle opener handle, adv'g "Farmers Mercantile Co.", pat'd Nov. 24, 1914.
$7.00-$12.00

Cake turner, tinned metal, heart-shaped blade with very small heart cutout, bottle opener at other end of handle, looks rather like a Rumford turner, adv'g "Metropolitan Furniture Co. — A Good Place to Trade", American, pat'd Nov. 24, 1914. **$22.00-$28.00**

Cake turner, tinned sheet metal, wire handle stamped flat with embossed design and "Rumford", blade simple with small heart-shaped hole near the riveted joint of handle & blade, "Rumford Baking Powder" adv'g piece, but poss. mfd by Pilgrim Novelty Co., American, 10¾"L x 2¾"W, c. 1914 (?). • You find this same turner without an adv'g message too, but worth less that way. **$18.00-$25.00**

Cake turner, tinned steel blade in pear shape with straight front edge, slightly elevated tiller handle with turned wood grip, Cronk & Carrier Mfg. Co., Geneva, OH, 12½"L x 4"W, c.1920s. **$15.00-$20.00**

Cake turner, tinned steel blade, wire shank, turned wooden handle. The blade is unperforated & if the turner is held upright, blade up, it looks like an abstract tulip. In fact, if someone could come up with an unobtrusive base, which would hold unaltered cake turners much as a flower frog holds roses and carnations, you could have a very wonderful bouquet of cake turners. I'm afraid the base would either obscure the handles, however, or the handles would have to be drilled. Hmmm ... Aarne Anton, wanna try? marked "WB/W", I believe this is probably Waterbury Button & Mfg. Co., Waterbury, CT, 14¼"L, c.1910-30. **$9.00-$13.00**

Cake turner, tinned steel blade with as many perforations as a sieve, nicely turned wooden handle left natural, American, 15"L, c.1910. **$8.00-$12.00**

Cake turner, tinned steel blade with rounded "Fins" at the back end, 3 rows of perforated holes, center one straight, side ones curved out, stamped "Stainless" (which it wasn't), so they crossed that out & stamped it "Rustless" (which it wasn't either), A & J Mfg. Co., Binghamton, NY, 13¼"L x 3½"W, c.1935. • Some of value here is in the social history aspect of the stamped marks.
$12.00-$18.00

Cake turner, tinned steel long oblong blade with 2 sizes of perforations forming diamond pattern, nice shoulder to blade, turned wooden handle, American, 12"L x 3"W, c.1920s. • The reality of collecting is that people still pay more for "Brand names" than unmarked pieces, but I firmly believe that in the long run this is a less successful way to collect. Remember that unknown art always has to be discovered. **$8.00-$12.00**

Cake turner, tinned steel with wood handle, odd extremely rigid near-round blade with truncated end & no perforations, American, 14¼"L x 4"W, c.1910s. **$7.00-$12.00**

Cake turner, cast aluminum with sort of rayed design or perforations, hanging hole in handle, "Royal Brand", German, 12½"L x 3¾"W, I used to think these were c.1930s; now I think c.1910s. **$15.00-$20.00**

• **Country of Origin Marks.** — Part of the widely-debated McKinley Tariff Act, passed by the 51st Congress on October 1, 1890, is of interest to all collectors. From Chapter 1244, Section 6: "That on and after the first day of March, 1891, all articles of foreign manufacture, such as are usually or ordinarily marked, stamped, branded, or labeled, and all packages containing such or other imported articles, shall, respectively, be plainly marked, stamped, branded, or labeled in legible English words, so as to indicate the country of their origin; and unless so marked, stamped, branded, or labeled they shall not be admitted to entry". The name "England" often appeared stamped on export china after 1875, and many English potteries marked "England" after 1880, but all did after 1891.

Cake turner, shapely tinned steel blade with 3 parallel rows of large to small graduated perforations, wooden handle, A & J, Binghamton, NY, 13¼"L, 1930s. • These A & J cake turners came in a variety of sizes and patterns of perforations. Condition of the paint on the wooden handle & size are important to value. **$7.00-$15.00**

Cake turner, tinned steel, wire, wood, blade has pretty design of radiating petal-like lines and small holes, shapely shoulder to blade, marked "WB/W", probably Waterbury Button & Mfg. Co., 12½"L x 3⅛"W, c.1915-20. **$12.00-$15.00**

Cake turner, wrought iron handle with brass blade, perforations in blade form the initials "L.H.", which were probably those of the owner (or recipient of this hand-made gift). American (?), 9⅞"L, 1850s to 1870s.
$200.00-$225.00

Cake turner, wrought steel, rattail handle, 20"L, 19th C.
$40.00-$50.00

Cooking implements, set of 4 in original box, sheet metal with green wooden handles, "Samson Cutlery", Rochester, NY, 20th C. See also Implement racks in Chapter VII, Storage & Containers. **$20.00-$35.00**

Cooking set, handcrafted, a cleaver, large spoon, carving knife & sharpening steel, flesh fork, handles are assembled bands of ivory, pipestone & onyx. American, mid 20th C. **$100.00-$135.00**

Cooking spoon, metal, adv'g "Monarch Stoves", TOC.
$20.00-$25.00

Corn cob handles, cast sterling silver, in shape of husked cobs, set of 12. The American Agriculturist, Sept. 1846, published a tip on "How to Boil Green Corn", with advice on eating it too. "The proper state in which to eat green corn, is, at the time that the milk flows upon pressing the kernels with the thumb nail. It is best when boiled in the ear with the husks on, the latter of which should be stripped off when brought to the table. The ears should then be covered with butter, with a little salt added, and the grains eaten off the cob. Over-refined people think this vulgar, and shave them off, but in so doing they lose much of their sweetness." 2¾"L, late 19th or early 20th C. • Part of the value of any sterling piece is its intrinsic silver bullion value, so it's hard to judge. People have been making these for a long time, but I'm not sure many people ever use them. You have to handle that hot cob to push the handles in, and you might as well go on and lift the cob to your mouth by then. **$120.00-$180.00**

Cream dipper or ladle—See Dipper or ladle for cream.

Dipper, agateware, mottled gray, "Windsor" type, large straight-sided & flat-bottomed bowl with slightly angled, turned wooden handle painted black, American, came in 4 sizes, from 4¼" diameter x 3" deep, up to 6¾" diameter x 3¾" deep, handles approx. 5"L, 1880s-90s.
$45.00-$75.00

Dipper, brass bowl with forged iron handle hooked on end, American (?), 15¼"L, late 18th or early 19th C.
$200.00-$235.00

Dipper, brown enameled ware, "Windsor" style, flat bottom bowl, flat handle, 18"L handle, late 19th C.
$55.00-$80.00

Dipper, carved out ash burl, beautiful patina, turned handle, American, bowl is 3" deep x 6" x 5½", slightly warped oval, unusual 13"L handle, early 19th or late 18th C. **$180.00-$250.00**

Dipper, coconut, small, highly polished after stripped of husk, with turned wooden long handle set at about 30° angle, pointed tip, pewter ferrule, marked "Cleveland Brothers, Providence, RI", mid 19th C. **$250.00-$300.00**

Dipper, copper, for maple sugar, late 19th C. **$80.00-$110.00**

Dipper, dried gourd of ornamental variety, long skinny neck, large hole cut out of main body, it's scraped clean & then dried, old cord through hole at tip of natural handle, American, 10"L, 19th C. • The price for this one is in the gorgeous patina: **$80.00-$100.00**

• Such **dried gourd dippers** were made by many so-called "Native" cultures as well as by country North Americans. An old gourd dipper from Mexico or Central America might be expected to have some decoration carved into its surface, or a more colorful dyed wool cord, or perhaps the gourd itself might be painted on the outside. Now that I need the information, I can't find it, but I believe I read somewhere years ago that the growing of such gourds for making dippers & scoops (as well as birdhouses) once was a cottage industry in certain parts of the country. • If you're interested in growing gourds to make dippers, birdhouses, bowls, rattles, whatever, the organization for you is the American Gourd Society, Box 274, Mount Gilead, OH 43338.

Dipper, dried gourd, polished, ornamental variety, big bowl, curved neck with enough hook to end to hang over edge of bucket, American, 8"L x 3" deep, 19th C.
$65.00-$90.00

Dipper, dried gourd, straight necked ornamental variety, American, 4⅞" deep x 9½"L, 19th C. • **Out Of Your Gourd.** — W. Scott Boyce's *Economic and Social History of Chowan County, North Carolina , 1880-1915*, published in NYC by Columbia University, 1917, says about the 1880s country person: "They improvised by far the greater number of their own dippers, occasionally from conch shells, more frequently from cocoanut hulls, but largely from the common gourd, which was cut, scraped, boiled, scrubbed, and sunned to remove the 'gourdy' taste and smell — said taste and smell, however, in spite of all these efforts, remaining to a more or less degree just as long as there was a piece of the gourd." (p.109). **$40.00-$65.00**

Dipper, forged iron, stamped on handle is maker's name, "H. W. Weaver", 23½"L, early 19th C. • $65.00 at Garth's Auctions, Delaware, OH, April 11-12, 1986.
$50.00-$80.00

Dipper, forged iron, huge round-bottom bowl with 2 quart capacity, long handle with hooked end, American, 24"L handle, early to mid 19th C. **$70.00-$110.00**

Dipper, forged iron with rattail handle, American, 15"L, early 19th C. **$45.00-$60.00**

Dipper, gray graniteware, bent-tip flat handle, deep but small bowl, a few dings & chips, 12"L overall, TOC.
$10.00-$20.00

Dipper, gray graniteware, "Windsor" style, rolled rim, long tubular handle riveted on at almost 45° angle. A "Windsor" has a flat bottom, somewhat flared sides, so that the dipper almost looks like a very small saucepan. American (?), 13"L overall, TOC. **$35.00-$48.00**

Dipper, mottled brown & white enamelware, a few slight dings, possibly "Onyx", Columbian Enameling & Stamping Co., or European, 5¼" diameter bowl, handle 14½"L, late 19th C. **$12.00-$15.00**

Dipper, of flat-bottomed type called a cup dipper, smaller than a "Windsor", stamped tin, slightly bulging sides, rolled rim, long forged iron handle with hanging hole, set about 45° angle to edge of cup. This kind of dipper could be filled, then set down without spilling, with the handle propped against something. Matthai-Ingram Co., 5⅛" diameter cup, 14"L handle, late 19th C. **$15.00-$20.00**

Dipper, often called a cocoa dipper because of round cup/bowl and size of bowl relative to overall size and the rim which is very slightly smaller than the widest part of the bowl, gray & black mottled outside of round-bottom bowl, black rim, black inside bowl, turned wood handle painted black, set into socket set at about 40° to bowl, prob. American, cup 3⅝" diameter, 11"L overall, late 19th C to TOC. **$125.00-$175.00**

Dipper, pieced tin with tubular handle set at angle, American, 9½"L, 2 cup capacity, 19th C. **$30.00-$38.00**

Dipper, robin's-egg blue enamelware with black trim, black enameled tubular handle, probably Lisk Mfg. Co., Canandaigua, NY, 14"L, 20th C. **$20.00-$25.00**

Dipper, speckled burgundy enamelware, 18"L, early 20th C. **$95.00-$125.00**

Dipper, tin, unusual for the stamped message: "Stolen from State Bank", Springfield, MN, 19th or early 20th C.
$18.00-$25.00

Dipper, tin, flat tinned iron handle with hook at end, American, 14"L with 5" diameter bowl, 19th C.
$22.00-$25.00

Dipper, tin, long handled, tubular handle, with half-moon mount, blue paper label with black printing states "Made of Best Quality Charcoal-Plate, Warranted not to rust", "Reed One-Pint", mfd solely by the Reed Mfg. Co., Newark, New York (not NJ), 14"L, dipper is 5⅛"W x 3¼"H, pat'd Nov. 17, 1896. **$20.00-$35.00**

Dipper or ladle for cream, for using with milk bottles, tin, small conical bowl, vertical wire handle with slight curved hook on end, looks rather like a candle snuffer in form and size, mfd by C. A. Chapman, Geneva, NY, c.1908.
$7.00-$10.00

Dipper or ladle for cream, stamped tin, American, dated 1924. **$7.00-$12.00**

Dipper or ladle for cream, stamped tin, "Sweet Clover Condensed Milk", 20th C. **$10.00-$15.00**

Dipper or ladle for cream, stamped tin, for milk bottles to dip off cream that rose to top before pasteurization, small like a gravy ladle for table use as it had to fit down in mouth of milk bottle, "Cream Top," dated 1925. **$7.00-$12.00**

Dipper & skimmer, a pair, forged iron, polished, filed and decorated, stamped on both handles is maker's name, "W. Werntz", 19"L, early 19th C. • Garth's Auctions, Delaware, OH, April 11-12, 1986, for $150.00. **$135.00-$170.00**

Dipper & skimmer, a pair, wrought iron, arrow handle with hooked end, large shallow bowls, the skimmer pierced with concentric rings of small holes, the handles inlaid with brass bands, engraved with initials "T.L." and the date, American, 19¼"L, dated "1823", but see note below. • This pair sold at Garth's Auctions; Delaware, OH, April 11-12, 1986, for $1200.00. Probable value range now is extremely difficult to assess. If they are recently-decorated iron pair, they're good only for a study collection, and valued between $20.00-$30.00. If they are legitimate (and I'm not doing anything here but speculating that they might not be) the range for a pair with brass inlay would be: **$1000.00-$1500.00**

•**Uh-oh, the Dreaded "1823".**— While the two implements may be genuinely old (and they do have authentic-looking distressing, pitting, tiny scratches, etc.), the inlaid brass date & maker bands are possibly modern en-forgings, to coin a phrase. Jeanette Lasansky did some work on the modern addition of faked brass inlays to old implements. She found that the faked dates fall within the limited range of dates: 1823 through 1827.

Dipper & skimmer, matched pair, wrought iron with brass inlay, "T. L.," American, 19¼"L, dated 1823, but the inlay may be fake and the date too. 1986 auction price: **$1200.00**

Doughnut lifter, bowed or curved slender wand of wood, with turned handle, for poking into kettles of boiling fat to remove doughnuts when they are just so, Mennonite, 30"L, 19th C. **$120.00-$150.00**

Doughnut lifter, scissor action with 4 long hooked prongs, cast iron & wire. The new identification of this (which I called a pie lifter in the 2nd edition) comes from Phyllis & Jim Moffet, who say it was used to "Turn, lift & remove doughnuts & such from the hot cooking oil." The Moffets are thorough, diligent collectors & researchers, & while I have not had a chance to check the patent record, I'm sure they have. American, somewhere between 8" to 11"H (?), pat'd April 14, 1908. • **Measurements in this book.** — Occasionally throughout this book, I use the word "About" in three ways when it refers to the measurement. (l) It is hard to measure because it flops around or you have to include the wingnut or the finial, or (2) I have never seen a real one, only something in a very old trade catalog that didn't mention the size. These guesses are supposed to be what they call "well-educated." (3) I either lost the measurement, forgot to get it, had to estimate it on the run, and can't check it out now. For this piece, which I identified as a pie lifter in the 2nd edition, I apparently forgot to measure it, and am recalling it viscerally. **$40.00-$55.00**

Dried fruit or sugar auger, or dried fruit loosener, forged iron, with wooden crossbar handle (like on an old push lawnmower), 2 twirly prongs with straight pointed prong

extension of handle, looks like a dancing post hole auger, pat'd by H. J. White, sometimes called the "Hiddleson's Dried Fruit Auger", agented by S. W. Sheldon, NYC (but we don't know where made), 16¼" to 17"L (measured examples), pat'd July 27, 1875. • Also called a sugar devil, obviously because of its whirling dervish appearance. (Or ballet dancer, for the gentler soul). Also called & used as a "Fruit lifter", to tear into a keg of hard sugar, or stuck-together dried fruit to break it up. I've seen one other version of these. • In the last edition, I said 1873 or 1875, because the mark wasn't clear. Now I've seen 2 more that also appear to say 1873, so it is possible that a fault in the casting was made. July 27 was on Tuesday in 1875, and Tuesday is patent-awarding day in America. **$125.00-$175.00**

Dried fruit or sugar auger, wrought iron, 2 curved out-and-in prongs, wooden T handle like old lawnmower handle, pat'd by William McCormick, Blair, NE, about 16"L, pat'd May 23, 1876. • Another type was made by Enterprise Mfg. Co. in Philadelphia, PA. It has a T handle, long shaft with crosspiece at bottom with short prong in center, and 4 curved short wider blades along the bar. Theirs is probably 1890s. **$125.00-$165.00**

Egg lifter, spring steel wire, squeeze action, the 2 clasping ends are concave coils of wire, looks like an insect of some extreme kind, American, 12½"L, c.1890s to 1920s. **$12.00-$15.00**

Fish slice, enameled steel, cobalt blue tubular handle which is relatively short compared to white blade, diamond pattern of 9 perforations in center, blade and handle stamped out of one piece, some dimension given to blade, handle curled to make tube, American or European, 11½"L, TOC. **$65.00-$85.00**

Fish slice, perforated tin with wooden handle, wire hanging ring, design is a fabulous outline of fish with 2 fins, gill, eye in the small holes on blade, American, 12½"L, 19th C. **$135.00-$175.00**

Flesh fork, for hearth, forged iron, twisted & stepped handle with elongated chevron, rattail loop, 3 tines, the 2 outer ones straight & simple, the center one partly split or reticulated, finished by whitesmith, American, 18½"L, late 18th or early 19th C. **$225.00-$350.00**

Flesh fork, forged iron, 2 prongs, long handle is arrow shaped, from arrowhead point (where it joins tines) to fletch. Very end of handle is heart with small hanging hole, and a smaller heart is punched into flat surface near end of handle, American, 16¼"L, early 19th C. • Garth's Auctions, Delaware, OH, April 11-12, 1986, for $750.00. **$650.00-$1200.00**

Flesh fork, forged iron, 2 tined, shaped handle, end shaped like fletching on an arrow (the trimmed feather part), prob. PA, 16¾"L, early 19th C. • **Lookalike alarm.** — You see a lot of iron flesh forks for sale, for about $15.00, which have little or no detailing, & the handles of which are an expeditiously-hammered rod. Often they seem to be painted black. They are new, decorator items, not necessarily made to fool you. Old ones: **$45.00-$50.00**

Flesh fork, forged iron, 2 tines, elongated chevron and bull's eye handle, American (?), late 18th C. **$85.00-$120.00**

Flesh fork, forged iron, 2 tines, elongated diamond & bull's eye end to handle, plus heart, very decorative, signed "Nathan Putnam", prob. PA, dated 1749. **$2000.00-$2500.00**

Flesh fork, forged iron, very long handle with figural finial of man's head with pop eyes & pork pie hat, large hanging ring cutout a few inches below head, 2 tines, not signed, prob. PA, 29⅛"L, prob. 1840s-1870s. • Offered for sale in 1981 by David A. Schorsch, Greenwich, CT. Price range mine. **$3500.00-$4500.00**

Flesh fork, iron or wire with wooden or wire handles, more of the type you'd expect to use with a hotdog over a campfire than a really hard-working one, American (?), about 18"L, c.1920s to 1950s. **$7.00-$12.00**

Flesh fork, wrought iron, 2 prong, with arrow shape handle or shaft, terminating in marvelous generous heart with a small hanging hole. Almost too good to be true. American (?), PA (?), 16½"L, 19th C or poss. late 18th. • Price from 1986 Garth's auction: **$750.00**

Flesh fork, wrought iron, unusual with 4 tines of type found on much later dinner forks, rattail hanging loop, decoratively marked handle, 21"L, 18th C or early 19th. **$175.00-$200.00**

Flesh forks, for hearth, forged iron, 2 or 3 tines, long handles, American or European, about 15" to 18"L, 18th or 19th C. • **Flesh Fork Variations:** • Very simple with no nifty touches • Simple but with some nice detail like a rattail handle • Some punch design to shaft • Very elegantly finished by a whitesmith (planisher) with some decorations, nice handle & maybe something special about the shoulder to the fork. **$55.00-$125.00**

Foam scraper, for beer suds, molded celluloid, adv'g "Grain Belt Beer", 20th C. **$12.00-$15.00**

Fork, cast iron handle with simple scroll design, meant for table, American, 7½"L, mid 19th C. **$7.00-$10.00**

Fork, twisted wire with ingenious push-off action when you squeeze both handles, 2 tines, American, 9 1/4"L, pat'd June 11, 1895. **$16.00-$22.00**

Implements—See Implement racks in Storage & Container chapter.

Ladle, brass bowl, iron shaft with turned wood handle, American, 16"L, 19th C. **$75.00-$90.00**

• **Ladle or Dipper?** — Euphony? Quantity? First of all, 20th century dictionaries don't seem to make much of a thing about defining the differences. In fact, the terrific Webster's Second even gives as one of the definitions of dipper — "A ladle", and for ladle, they say it is used to ladle out or dip out liquids — from soup to molten iron! In fact, popular usage over a long period seems to decide the question, Is it a ladle or a dipper? "Soup" and "Punch", for example, seem to be coupled with "ladle", while "Chocolate" and "water" go with "dipper". Did someone long ago decide that "Soup dipper" sounded strange? There is, to some extent, a hint of quantification about the two words, so that "dipper" implies a smaller amount (dip, sip, nip), while "ladle" implies a greater amount. Richard H. Thornton, in *An American Glossary, Being An Attempt to Illustrate Certain Americanisms Upon Historical Principles*, London: Francis & Co., 1912, lists "Dipper" with the meaning "A ladle", first citation of usage 1801. He doesn't give "Ladle" its own listing. John Bartlett's *Dictionary of Americanisms. A Glossary of Words and Phrases Usually Regarded As Peculiar to the United States*, Boston: Little Brown, 1887, defines a dipper as "A vessel, generally with a handle, used to dip water or other liquor." "Ladle" is not accorded a definition. In the 1859 edition of Bartlett's book, "dipper" is not listed. Checking out the *Oxford English Dictionary*, I found that as in Bartlett, the first printed reference to "dipper" is cited as belonging to George Mason's *A Supplement to Samuel Johnson's Dictionary*. In 1801, Mason said it was "A spoon made in a certain form. Being a modern invention, it is not often mentioned in books." So he gave no printed earlier source, but by inference we can assume it to be earlier. It's not that a word "dipper" hadn't existed before; it's just that the meaning was different. The *OED* cites a 1611 use — for a person who dips, or moistens. • Nowadays it seems that the primary difference lies in the angle of the handle. Both dippers and ladles have handles long in relation to bowl size, but the ladle's handle is set either at right angles (90°) to the bowl, or on the same horizontal plane as the rim of the bowl. A dipper seems to be set at between 15° and about 40°. Size of bowl probably has something to do with the definition, ladles being generally larger than dippers.

Ladle, cast aluminum, marked "G. M. T. & Bro." (G. M. Thurnauer, in *Thomas' Register* as a "Manufacturer", made in Germany (for Thurnauer?) & imported, as most GMT wares were. TOC. **$9.00-$12.00**

Ladle, cast aluminum, ovoid bowl, long upright handle with short prong off side about 4 inches from end, to hook on side of kettle, German, 10¾"L, c.1910-1915. **$10.00-$22.00**

Ladle, cast aluminum, ovoid bowl, with one side distinctly more rounded that other side, long handle with cast-in ridge in center, upright from bowl, sometimes only marked with country of origin, "Made in Germany", 10¾"L, c. 1910-1915. **$9.00-$18.00**

Ladle, dark blue spattered enamelware, 13"L, 19th C. **$28.00-$40.00**

Ladle, enamelware, long black hooked handle, bowl is white inside outside with blue blobs with brown & white veining called "Turtle, Tortoise or Chickenwire" by collectors, but "Duchess" by manufacturer, Vollrath Co., Sheboygan, WI, TOC. • "Now architects and decorators decree that beauty belongs in the kitchen too! … that even pots and pans can be interesting and attractive." Ad for Vollrath, 1928. **$50.00-$80.00**

Ladle, pewter bowl with socket-fitted turned wooden handle, American (?), 15"L, mid 19th C. **$90.00-$125.00**

Ladle, possibly a tallow spoon, wrought iron, wonderful upcurving long handle with arched foot toward end, rather deep bowl with pouring spout rests perfectly horizontally on hearth or table, American, 4½"D bowl, 19½"L overall, 18th or very early 19th C. • This is another rarity found by Clara Jean Davis. The description is adapted from her sale list, in which she also says "Rather crudely made, doubtless a country blacksmith, however, interesting work. … Done all in one piece of iron pounded out to make the bowl. … Most likely used as tallow spoon. Very early iron, impure, likely 18th C." • Price range below is not Davis'. **$150.00-$200.00**

Ladle, tan enamelware with green trim, 1930s. **$10.00-$18.00**

Ladle, white enamelware with black handle & rim, 10"L, 20th C. • **German vocabulary** — Schopfloffel: literally, cup spoon. **$10.00-$18.00**

Love spoon, carved wood, painted & decorated, 5 glass windows set in over 4 printed blue & brown calico scraps plus a damask pink & white scrap, hex signs, little XXX borders & a tree of life, plus the initials, are picked out in red paint or lac (possibly mixed with gum or wax), Welsh, 11"L, 18th or very early 19th C. • I think this is the most extraordinary Welsh love spoon I've ever seen, I guess it's the charm of the little pieces of material set under glass that does it for me. The price at a show in 1983 was $950.00. Value has increased. **$1500.00-$1800.00**

Maple syrup taster, brass, American or Canadian, 19th C. **$35.00-$45.00**

Marrow spoon, carved & decorated wood (possibly cherry), American (?), 10"L, late 18th C. **$85.00-$120.00**

Marrow spoon, very fine-grained wood with good patina, lathe turning on end of handle, American or English, 11¼"L, late 18th or early 19th C. **$85.00-$110.00**

Meat fork, forged iron, 2 tine, long handle with wooden grip, American (?), 35"L, early 19th C. **$65.00-$100.00**

Meat fork, forged iron, ring handle, 2 long tines, American (?), 21"L, early 19th C. • Impossible, I believe, to determine origin of these pieces. There have now been so many brought in by dealers from other countries in the last few years. **$45.00-$55.00**

Meat fork, planished forged iron, light-color, whitesmith or brightsmith work, 2 tines, ring handle, American (?), 15"L, early 19th C. • **Whitesmith or Brightsmith Work.** — According to Carl W. Drepperd, in *Primer of American Antiques*, originally a whitesmith was the same as a whitster, who was a "Planisher, one who hammered iron white", and only later did a whitesmith come to mean a worker in tin, tin plate, or any other white metal. **$45.00-$60.00**

Meat fork, tinned sheet metal, "Rumford", American, 20th C. **$18.00-$22.00**

Olive fork, for pickles, cherries, olives, nickeled iron, long rod looped at one end to make a grip, end split to make 2 short sharp tines, mounted on original card, "No. 185-M", "Just the Tool for Small Mouth Bottles", American, 8"L, c.1915. **$2.00-$4.00**

Olive or pickle fork, tinned steel, 2 prong, American (?), 8"L, prob. 20th C. **$2.00-$3.00**

Olive or pickle fork, twisted wire, American, 10"L, prob. 19th C. **$4.00-$8.00**

Pancake server, Black Americana, metal Aunt Jemima, 20th C. • The best Halloween costume I ever saw was a duet in the famed parade through the West Village in NYC. One very tall man was dressed as Aunt Jemima, in perfect detail, and the other man was the pancake, and with a stuffed cloth cake turner, Aunt Jemima walked the whole length of the parade route whopping that pancake upside the head and down the other, making it twirl and flip. **$35.00-$45.00**

Peel, carved pine, somewhat charred on blade end, nice used patina on handle, for removing bread from oven, American, 51"L, 19th C. **$110.00-$145.00**

Peel, carved wood, probably pine, European (?), blade only 13"L, with 5"L handle, late 19th C. **$25.00-$35.00**

Peel, for bread or pies, wrought iron, long handle with a fat ball end, American (?), 48"L, late 1700s. **$125.00-$175.00**

Peel, made in one piece instead of joined handle, wooden, with very long bakery handle, front edge of blade straight & thinned, 54"L, c. 1800. **$75.00-$150.00**

Peel, short handled, one piece wooden, rather like a round paddle with hole for hanging, good patina & slight scorching. 15¼"L, of which only about 5¼" is handle. 19th C. **$75.00-$85.00**

Peel, wrought iron, fat knob on end of long handle, American (?), 51"L, late 18th or early 19th C. • This peel, being 51"L, is obviously not going to be confused with a cake turner, but that is a possibility for short-handled & small-bladed peels. In fact, I don't know how to tell you it couldn't be a cake turner. And who knows? Maybe those skilled cooks back in the 1780s or the 1810s used small peels for all kinds of purposes. **$100.00-$125.00**

Peel, wrought iron, long ram's horn handle, the commonest type found, ranging in size widely. American (?), 22"L; 25"L; 29½"L; 35"L, early 19th C. • The 1st price range is for about 2 feet long & under; 2nd range for 2 feet & over, especially over 4 feet. **$40.00-$65.00** • **$75.00-$250.00**

Peel, wrought iron, ram's horn handle, wide blade, "Londonderry" (NH?), 35"L, late 18th C. **$120.00-$150.00**

Picnic fork, shaped thin wood with 3 stubby tines, pencil writing on back from souvenir-saving child reads, charmingly, "September, 8, 1942, Sun Set Large" (sic), mark burned into handle "Bentwood Forks", with a daisy, American, 4⅞"L, c.1941. • Believe it or not, this is a nice little subfield for collectors — wooden picnic spoons and forks. I have quite a number of them, but this is the first marked one. **$1.00-$3.00**

Pie lifter, blackened sheet steel, like a big oblong pan or cookie sheet, & possibly used as such, rounded front end like some oven peels have, very low raised sides, the end, or handle, raised at about 45 degree angle with curled under end, embossed on handle "I. W. MCNESS", American, 15"L x 10"W, looks early 20th C, but may be later. **$10.00-$15.00**

Pie lifter, forged iron, 2 widely-spaced tines to support the pie (though not so's I'd want to depend on it when taking a hot one from the oven), twisted handle, broken ring loop at end, American, 14"L, c.1840s. **$125.00-$150.00**

Pie lifter, heavy spring steel wire with cast iron fingers, & sliding hook that slides along handle & grips pie pan, American, 16"L, pat'd 1883. **$25.00-$35.00**

Pie lifter, tinned metal combination tool, with long handle with crown cap opener at one end, & narrow rounded cake-serving knife flat blade, with small heart cutout, at other end. stamped into the two narrow parts of handle's shank is "Use Omar Wonder Flour. Puts Magic In Your Baking", early 20th C. **$12.00-$18.00**

Pie lifter, hexagonal tin platform to support pie, green wooden handle, adjustable side grips, "Sure-Grip," American, 20"L, TOC. • This pie lifter is the lifter of choice, with all kinds of built-in crash-proof features. (Wish my computer had the same thing. I could use a double-sided 30 MB hexagonal tin platform to support my data. Can't tell you how many crashes we've had while assembling this book, and the hardest part is it's all taking place invisibly, so you can't reach out and make a save, or grab it with your knees, like Tom Sawyer.) **$22.00-$30.00**

Pie lifter, wire with wooden handle, a sort of fork, with 2 long prongs that fit under the pie plate, American (?), 17½"L, 19th C. **$15.00-$22.00**

Pie lifter, wooden handle, heavy gauge wire, TOC. **$22.50-$30.00**

Pie lifter & lid lifter combined, hinged cast iron, with hook ends, openwork casting in handles, 8"L, c.1880s. **$50.00-$65.00**

Pie lifter or hot pan lifter, heavy wire flapping wings or arms, black-painted turned wood handle, spring action thumb piece to work the arms, which we hope won't flap while you carry your blue ribbon pie from oven to table, American, 12½"L x 6"W (each wing), late 19th or early 20th C. **$18.00-$22.00**

Pie or cake slicer, wire, sets down over a pie or single layer of cake and creates a guide for a separate (not included) knife to cut 8 equal wedges, TOC. **$12.00-$18.00**

Pie or hot plate lifter, heavy spring steel wire arms and long double-shaft wooden handle, looks like it ought to have something to do with clothes hangers, but it actually grips around opposite sides of the pie plate (or other hot plate), "Triumph", sold through Montgomery Ward, or with adv'g for a store, American, 13½"L, c.1890s.
$22.00-$30.00

Pie server, metal, baked right in pan under the pie, wedge-shaped & bent to conform to sides of pie pan, Shera Corp., Hohokus, NJ, for a 9" pie pan, but the peculiar thing is that it is so wide it only allows for 5 wedges, "Patent applied for", c.1940s (?). **$5.00-$7.00**

> "An apple-pie without some cheese
> Is like a kiss without a squeeze."
> *Old English rhyme*

Pie server, tinned metal, green wood tiller handle, cutouts in blade, "Rumford" adv'g piece, manufacturer not known, early 20th C. **$7.00-$10.00**

Punch bowl hook, twisted steel wire with large curve at one end to fit over edge of punch bowl, smaller end is hooked for punch cup, plated in nickel, made by mfr, C. T. Williamson Wire Novelty Co., Newark, NJ, early 20th C. • Daniel Morrell wrote "Report on the Iron and Steel Exhibits at Paris", for the 1878 Universal Exposition held in Paris of manufacturing and industrial products of the whole world. It appeared in a set of books containing all the "Reports" in different categories, including ceramics, glass, textiles, etc., published by the Government Printing Office in Washington DC, 1880. Unfortunately, the company mentioned in the following paragraph, quoted from the London Times of Aug. 22, 1878, wasn't further identified. "Close by [the flexible shaft display] stands Clough & Williamson's 'wire cork-screw machine,' which catches a straight piece of steel wire and throws it out as a corkscrew of such temper that it may be driven through an inch deal plank and not yield a hair's breath. The deftest waiter will take as long to pull a cork as this machine to make half a dozen cork-screws of an exceptionally good quality". I ran the names through the computer Metal Maker records, and found the names already connected somehow, but unclearly. I believe the company was a short-lived partnership, and was in Newark, NJ, and after splitting up Clough went to NH, Williamson stayed in Newark. **$2.00-$3.00**

Roasting fork, for hearth, brass & steel, 3 tines, telescoping handle with some turning & detail, hanging ring, English (?), 12" extends to 20"L, 19th C. • For a while in the late 1970s you saw a good number of these at antique shows; they don't appear much anymore, maybe the sources have dried up. **$55.00-$100.00**

Sauerkraut auger, very like a sugar auger, probably interchangeable, iron & wood, with twirled tongs that were stuck into kraut barrel, twisted, & used to bring up big batch of dripping sauerkraut to transfer to pot or serving dish, American, 3rd quarter 19th C. **$150.00-$175.00**

Serving fork, aluminum, graceful bold handle of twisted aluminum rod, with tendril and bud terminal, "Buenilum", Made in U. S. A., 8"L, c.1940s. **$8.00-$12.00**

Skimmer, shallow brass bowl with holes pierced in concentric rings, simple iron handle with punched stipple decoration, Adams County, PA, 17"L, 2nd to 3rd quarter19th C. **$120.00-$135.00**

Skimmer, slightly ovoid shallow brass bowl, pierced decoration of 6 point star against background of tight concentric rings of holes, simple iron handle, prob. PA, 23"L, 2nd to 3rd quarter19th C. **$225.00-$250.00**

Skimmer & fork combined, metal, long handle, for stew or soup, you flipped up the skimmer to reveal the meat fork, good for poking out potatoes & meaty chunks from the pot, American, 19th C. **$45.00-$60.00**

Spatula, embossed metal, message is "Merry Christmas, Happy New Year", 10"L, 20th C. **$18.00-$28.00**

Spatula, embossed metal, (seen spelled two ways), "Swans Down Makes Better Cakes", "Swansdown", Igleheart Brothers, Evansville, IN, 12"L x 1¼"W, 20th C.
$18.00-$28.00

Spoon, carved from horn, very old repair with riveted iron bands, American, 7"L, late 18th or early 19th C.
$25.00-$35.00

Spoon, for stirring powdered seltzer into water, long handle, marked "Bromo Seltzer Cures Headache!", c.1920s.
$20.00-$25.00

Spoon, pressed wood fiber, end of handle has 4 crosses marked on it, shaft stamped "Sanispoon", mfd by American Container Co., NYC, NY, 5"L (they also made a 3½"L one), 1918. **$3.00-$5.00**

Spoon, wrought iron, round bowl, rattail back attachment where handle is forged to bowl, American (?), 7"L, late 18th C. **$45.00-$60.00**

Spoon, wrought iron spoon, very crude, possibly not finished, some white stuff in crevices, American, 9⅛"L, early 19th C. • **White Sediment.** — Every once in a while I come upon an old iron piece with this white substance, which really isn't powdery. I wonder if it's some sort of flux used when working the iron, and if its presence indicates a piece was never finished, and therefore never used? Anyone know? Here's a possibility, just found in a Southern recipe book: • **To Prevent Rust in Iron Utensils.** — "To prevent their rusting when not in use: Mix half a pound of lime with a quart of warm water; add sweet oil until it looks like cream. Rub the article with this; when dry, wrap in paper, or put over another coat." Mrs. A. P. Hill, *Mrs. Hill's New Family Receipt Book*, NY: 1870.
$18.00-$22.00

Spoon & fork combined, scissor action, carved of baleen with ivory pin, English or American whaling vessel product, 8¼"L, second half 19th C. **$125.00-$150.00**

Spoon & ladle set, blue & white speckled enamelware, hanging holes in both handles, 20th C. • For the pair:
$55.00-$90.00

Spoon rest, stamped aluminum, instructions: "Place on kitchen table or range. Easy to clean. Unbreakable. Burn proof." American, 20th C. **$2.00-$3.00**

Spoon rest, stamped tin, with loop hook for side of pot or pan, egg shaped bowl with 7 drain holes, adv'g "Rumford the Wholesome Baking Powder", 3"L, early 20th C. • Summer 1988 show price $75.00. I think even for a highly desirable Rumford piece this is way too high. But at least it's now on record. More reasonable value range:
$20.00-$30.00

Suckit spoon, a spoon & fork combination, one at either end, light-colored whitesmithed iron, shallow bowl, Pennsylvania version of an English form, 16⅜"L with 2⅝" diameter spoon, early 19th C. **$500.00-$700.00**

Table cutlery, knives & forks only, steel with fancy inlaid bone handles, 21 pieces, American (?) or English, late 19th C. **$50.00-$65.00**

Taster, also called a tasting spoon, for hearth use originally, but a type of spoon still in use, forged iron, smallish bowl, long straight shank with widening at end, rattail hook, incised with zigzags & highly polished or planished by whitesmith, also called a brightsmith, American, 18"L, late 18th C. **$125.00-$160.00**

Taster, forged iron, long straight handle ending in rattail loop, shallow bowl is turnip shaped, American, 21"L, early 19th C. **$75.00-$100.00**

Taster, ovoid bowl, very long handle with ridge up center, set in almost horizontal position to bowl, for right-handed cooks to pour from small end of bowl into mouth, Made in Germany, 13½"L, c.1910-1915. **$9.00-$12.00**

Taster, small brass bowl, riveted to forged iron long handle, American (?), about 18"L, early 19th C. **$100.00-$125.00**

Taster, tinned brass, or latten bowl, forged iron handle riveted to bowl in 3 places, very attractive shape to tapered flat handle with hooked end, crudely engraved, and dated, American, 7¾"L, "1862." • **Pennsylvania ?—** Everyone likes to know where a piece comes from, and some places are "Sexier" than others hype-wise. Pennsylvania as provenance has been very popular for a long time; Ohio, South Carolina, Alabama, Georgia, Texas, West Virginia and Tennessee are upcomers. And there are probably many more out West, though we in the East are last to hear about it. But you have to think. People everywhere used utensils and implements, and there was a constant emigration generally westward all through the 19th C, when most of our antiques were made. The combination of brass and iron often proves to be Pennsylvanian; but this piece could be a "Country" piece from practically anywhere. • Sold for $375.00 at Garth's Auctions, Delaware, OH, April 11-12, 1986. **$350.00-$450.00**

Taster, tinned brass spoon bowl, wrought iron handle, American, 7¾"L, dated 1862. • **Added value. —** Pricier with tinning & date. Other tasters, with brass or copper bowls, might bring slightly less. A taster has a somewhat shallow and perfectly round spoon bowl, riveted to the perfectly straight handle that lies along the same horizontal plane as the bowl. The shallow bowl means the food to be tasted didn't have to be cooled a long time. **$185.00-$225.00**

Taster & scraper (?), forged iron, with spoon at one end, a sort of cake turner, scraper at other end, marked "C. Monk", American (?), 7"L, 19th C. **$35.00-$45.00**

Toasting fork, 3 ply heavy twisted wire, decorative handle, of type made in England, but dealer found in Ohio & said that 3 strands & the heaviness of the wire were "Typical of Ohio work", so prob. Ohio, 17⅜"L, c.1860s to 1880s. • I happen to have bought this one, & like it a lot better than the ones I've seen that were admittedly English imports. The wire is more substantial. **$75.00-$100.00**

Toasting fork, 3 tines, decorative long handle, forged iron, 23⅜"L, c.1820s to 1830s. **$250.00-$350.00**

Toasting fork, for hearth cooking, wrought iron, 2 tines, American (?), 19"L, early 19th C. **$60.00-$75.00**

Toasting fork, for hearth cooking, wrought iron with wooden handle, 3 tines, American (?), 55"L, early 19th C, poss. late 18th C. **$85.00-$120.00**

Toasting fork, forged iron tines & shaft, wooden handle, American (?), 20"L, early 19th C. **$75.00-$100.00**

Toasting fork, forged iron, turned wooden handle, brass hanging hook, 4 prongs form a cube's outline, American (?) or English (?), 26"L, 19th C. **$150.00-$175.00**

Toasting fork, tinned metal, "Rumford", adv'g piece, American, 20th C. **$18.00-$25.00**

Toasting fork, twisted 2 ply wire handle forms hanging ring at end, little metal sleeve or collar pulls down to release or open its prongs, English, 20⅛"L, c.1880s (?). **$35.00-$45.00**

Toasting forks, set of 4, all forged iron with 2 tines. (1) The tines on the "Marshmallow fork" are long, very slender, slightly curved, with suggestion of hooks at ends, the rod of the shaft is twisted ⅓ of way up from tines, and looped handle is twisted around shaft. (2) The "Little Colonial Fork" is very lightweight, has short tines, loop ring with tip twisted around shaft, which has another twist above tines. (3) The "Twist rod fork" is made of a length of iron rod, the ends forming the tines, a loop for hanging, the shaft's 2 wires twisted in 2 places to hold together. (4) The "Twist handle fork" has beaten tines to flatten and broaden them somewhat, loop handle, 2 twists to shaft. A "Colonial" set for "Bungalow & camping parties". The Arden Forge, Arden, DE, respectively: 30"L, 15"L, 24"L and 30"L, advertised in Sept. 1923 *House Beautiful*. • **Lookalike alarm. —** You'd not know which were made by Arden Forge (I'm sure other Colonial Revival forges made similar forks for fireplace or campfire), unless you found in original packaging with name. But this listing will alert you to the fact that even the least of old kitchen implements were replicated or approximated by 20th C commercial companies. • Price range for set. **$7.00-$15.00**

Tongs, for cooking, metal, adv'g "Ney's Restaurant", Bad Axe, MI, early 20th C. **$7.00-$12.00**

Tongs, iron, adv'g "Only Gas Costs Less", early 20th C. **$7.00-$12.00**

Whatzit spoon & fork, wooden spoon at one end, 3 tined fork at other, spoon is like a scoop & when dealer accidentally set implement in sunny place, tallow came out. The chip carving forms zigzags, hole in broad part of fork for hanging up, English (?), 20⅞"L, with 6"L tines, mid 19th C (?). **$55.00-$70.00**

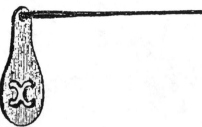

XIII-1
Apple butter stirrer.

Sketch that appeared in the "Ladies' Department" of American Agriculturist, 9/1847. "Any handy lad of fourteen years can easily make one for his mother. The handle should be about six feet long, in order that the cook may keep from the heat and danger of fire. The other part should be of heavy oak-board, six inches broad, with two transverse slits in the lower part, and long enough to reach the bottom of the kettle, so that while it moves, the handle has need only of a steady horizontal motion." The "kettle" referred to, by the way, was outside and suspended or supported above a fire; it held from a half barrel to nearly a barrel of cider. I once made apple butter from a gallon of cider; it took 15 hours! **$45.00-$90.00**

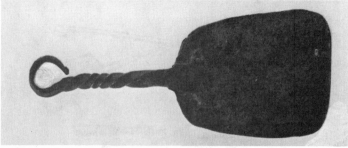

XIII-4.
Tasting spoon & cake turner,

often also called a spatula. Wrought iron, rat-tail handles, both with twisted shanks for strength, both 8"L. American, late 18th C. Picture courtesy of Robert W. Skinner Inc., Auctioneers, Bolton, MA. Range for either: **$90.00-$140.00**

XIII-2.
Asparagus holder.

"Champion" wire tongs, mfd. by A. H. Brinkmann & Co., Baltimore, MD. House Furnishing Reveiw, 1903. See also Chapter V on Measuring tools. **$15.00-$20.00**

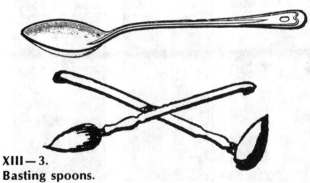

XIII—3.
Basting spoons.

Distinguishing feature is rather shallow bowl with horizontal long handle on most. From top: (1) Graniteware stamped steel, 16"L, hanging hole. Mfr. unidentified; from Sethness Co., Chicago, catalog, 1925. (2) Tinned stamped sheet iron, 12"L, 13 3/4" or 15 1/4"L, from Savory, Inc., Newark, c.1925-28. (3) Very similar to #1 in handle design. 10", 12", 14", or 16"L, mfd. by Central Stamping Co., 1920. Both (2) and (3) were described in catalogs as being "threaded," supposed to have a ridge stamped in lengthwise— for strength. (4) Crossed "French Basting spoons—Deep and with side handles," from American Home Cook Book, 1854. Probably iron. Note shaped handles, and what appears to be hooked tip of handle. **$8.00-$20.00**

XIII-5.
Cake turners or short peels.

All are forged iron. (L) Heart-shaped shoulders, turned wood handle possibly newer than others. 16"L. Mid 19th C. Collection of Meryle Evans. (M) and (R) have hooked handles. One with spatulate blade, 17 1/2"L, other with cut & filed decorated handle, including abstract heart or arrowpoint at center. Oblong blade unusual. 22"L. Both late 18th, early 19th C. Photo courtesy Litchfield Auction Gallery, Litchfield, CT. Ex-Harold Corbin Collection, auctioned 1/1/1989. Second price was realized for Corbin pieces. **$120.00-$150.00 and $425.00**

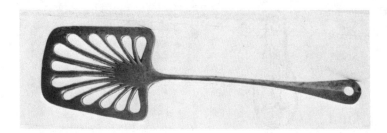

XIII-6.
Cake turners & egg slices.
(T) All metal one (17"L), and the one at bottom (blade 4 3/4" x 4 1/8") are both egg slices. Both have perforated blades. c.1904-10. Wood handle one at (T) is 21"L, a "hotel" cake turner. c.1901-10. One with pear-shaped nickel-plated blade is the "Kitchen Kumfort Trowel," with rubberoid tiller handle. "The old fashioned turner was originally invented to lift and turn cakes on an old fashioned flat griddle. Now as the number of articles which are either fried or cooked in hot fat, such as croquettes, meat balls, omelets, etc., have increased, the cake turner has been used to handle such articles simply because there was no other utensil at hand. Experiments with a turner having the handle elevated about two inches from the blade resulted in this lifter." Lasher Mfg. Co., Davenport, IA, 1911 ad. Other is the "Jewel", with "flat serpentine handle that gives a good grip." Steel, Arcade Mfg. Co., 1905.
$10.00-$22.00

XIII-8.
Cake turners.
Both cast aluminum. (T) marked "Royal Bra–", probably Royal Brand, and "Made in Germany." 12 1/2"L, c.1910. (B) Angled straight-front blade. Word "Aluminum" appears in hammer-shaped mark on back, also "D.R.G.M. Germany." 10 1/4"L, c.1910s.
$12.00-$20.00

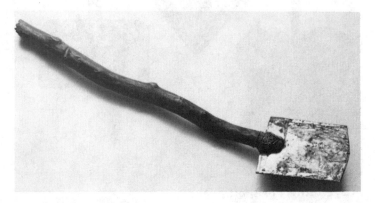

XIII-7.
Homemade cake turner.
My personal favorite. Made from flattened and trimmed tin can, whittled stick, wire and a nail. Found by Oregon collector, Jim Holroyd, at "a camp on the Skyline Trail in the Oregon Cascades, around 1965." 16"L. **$10.00-$18.00**

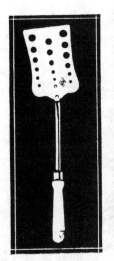

XIII-9.
Cake turners.
*All nickel-plated steel, with turned wood handles with "three coats of highest grade enamel" in 2-tone Blutip colors. All made with or without holes. Long perforated "kitchen tool" with tiller handle, 11"L overall. Plain small one is 11 1/4"L. Third one is 13"L. All "Ekco," Edward Katzinger Co., Chicago, in "A & J Blutip Kitchen Tools" catalog, 1930. A & J was division of Ekco.***$6.00-$15.00**

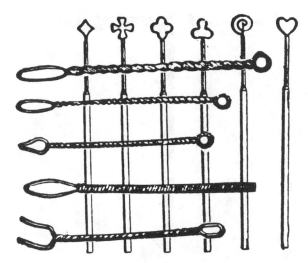

XIII-10.
Bon Bon dips or dipping forks,
tinned wire or brass, for lifting coated candies out of coating. Plain ones are from candymakers' supplier S. Joseph Co. catalog, c.1927. Fancy ones from T. Mills, Philadelphia, 1930. Almost identical ones date well back into 19th C. **$4.00-$20.00**

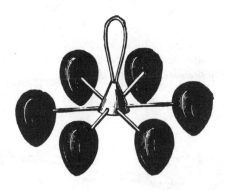

XIII-11.
Candy egg dipper,
or **egg hook,** *for coating cream eggs with chocolate. Heavy tinned wire, with hanging loop (to hang on rack). "Small" to accommodate 6 eggs, for 1¢ 2¢, 3¢ or 5¢ eggs; and "large" for 4 eggs of 10¢ size. Mills, 1930.* **$8.00-$12.00**

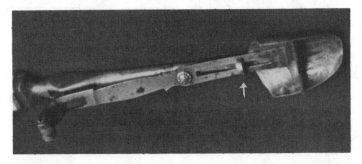

XIII-12.
Cheese scoop.
Steel mechanical scoop, bone or ivory handle (shaped like table knife handle). Tiny rivet has cut decorations & facets. Thumbscrew (small piece where arrow points) holds follower on track inside spade-like scoop and can be turned to lift follower for thorough cleaning. 10 1/16"L overall; scoop 1 5/8"L x 1 1/4"W. English, 19th C. Courtesy Louise Bibb, of Virginia. **$40.00-$55.00**

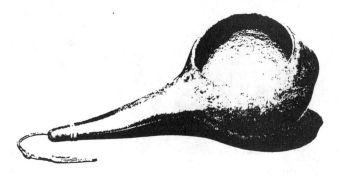

XIII-13.
Dipper.
Dried goard. Late 19th C. Picture courtesy of the National Museum of American History, Smithsonian Institution. Value for similar pieces: **$50.00-$90.00**

XIII-14.
Dippers.
(L) Pieced tin, both with flat bottoms and braced tubular handles. Top has long handle with shovel-like half-loop handle. 1 3/8 quart capacity; bowl 3 5/8"H x 6 1/2" diameter. Central Stamping Co., 1920. (R) Bent maple with turned maple handle and pine bottom. Copper tacks hold lap joint together. Shaker, mid to third quarter 19th C. **$15.00-$30.00; $250.00-$500.00**

XIII-15.
Dippers,
most with round-bottomed bowls. From top: (1) Tin, tubular handle, 2 qt. size. From Butler Brothers catalog, 1899. (2) Large water dipper in "Pearl Agate," which came in different pale colors, all with black-enameled wood handle, nickel or silver plated fittings. Manning, Bowman & Co., c.1892. (3) Smaller gray enamelware handle, very like the previous one, but not so well made — at least, original wholesale price was 5¢ each, as opposed to $1.10 each. Butler, 1899. (4) "Copper dipper," with tubular socket handle. Sizes from 4" to 10" diameter. Duparquet, Huot & Moneuse, c.1904-1910. Flat one (R) is Agateware, turned wood handle; 4 sizes from 3"H x 4 1/4" diameter to 3 3/4"H x 6 3/4". Lalance & Grosjean, c.1890. **$30.00-$120.00**

XIII-16.
Suds dipper.
Pieced tin, for laundry work. Tin, two sizes, 3 5/8" x 6 1/2" and 4"H x 6 7/8". Savory, Inc., Newark, c.1925-28. **$15.00-$30.00**

XIII-19.
Dried fruit lifter or sugar auger.
Looks like a whirling dervish. Malleable cast iron, wood handles, 16 3/4"L. Pat'd 7/27/1875. Used to extricate stuck-together dried apricots or apples from a keg or barrel, or similarly, for damp-stuck sugar. Stab it in & twist. Collection of Meryle Evans. **$120.00-$175.00**

XIII-17.
Doughnut lifter.
Misidentified as "pie lifter" in last edition; ID corrected by collectors Phyllis & Jim Moffet. It was used to "turn, lift and remove doughnuts and such from the hot cooking oil." 8"H, pat'd 4/14/1908. Should have been in Disney movie Dark Crystal — as a moonwater strider. Collection of Meryle Evans. **$45.00-$75.00**

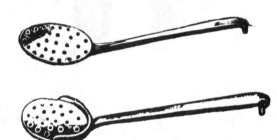

XIII-20.
Egg slices,
or slicers. Completely tinned perforated copper blades & iron handles. (T) Nine sizes, from 3" to 7" diameter. (B) only two sizes: 4" and 4 1/2" diameter. Henry Rogers, Sons & Co., Wolverhampton, England, 1914 catalog. **$20.00-$45.00**

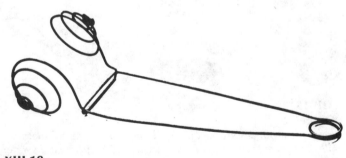

XIII-18.
Egg lifter.
*or **egg tongs.** Spring wire, for retrieving hardboiled eggs — or dumplings! 12 1/2"L, c.1890-1920. Collection of Meryle Evans.* **$12.00-$18.00**

XIII-21.
Fish slice,
also called a fish carver. Shape of blade fairly typical of fish slices. Tin with turned wood handle, perforated design of fish. 12 1/2"L, late 19th C. Very unusual. Collection of Meryle Evans. **$135.00-$175.00**

XIII-22.
Flesh fork & tasting spoon.
Forged iron fork, late 18th C. Brass bowl & iron handle spoon, c.1800. Picture courtesy of Georgia G. Levett, Levett's Antiques, Camden, ME. **$100.00-$150.00**

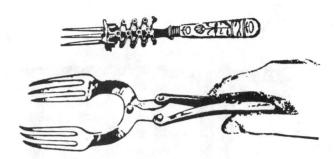

XIII-24.
Forks
with mechanical actions. (T) Sandwich fork, with lazy-elbow push-off. Blue & white Meissen handle, came in small and large size. Ritzinger & Grasgreen, importers, c.1906-07. (B) "Duplex Serving Fork," wire spring, steel tines, nickeled handle. "For lifting vegetables from boiling water; for lifting fruit jars in canning; for serving." 10 1/2"L. Washburn Co., 1927. **$8.00-$35.00**

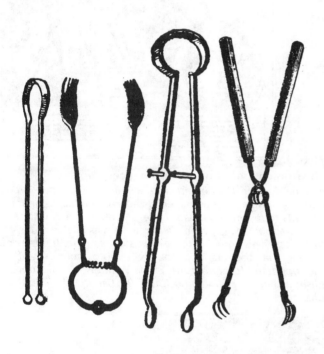

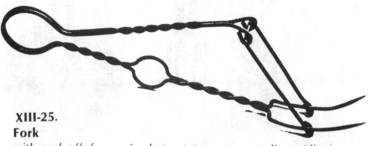

XIII-25.
Fork
with push-off, for serving hot potatoes, or meat slices. All wire, 9 1/4"L, pat'd 6/11/1895. Collection of Meryle Evans. **$20.00-$30.00**

XIII-23.
Beefsteak tongs.
Simplest pair from American Home Cook Book, 1854. "To turn a steak, to avoid puncturing holes with a fork, which lets the juice escape." Middle are "spring tongs," 18"L, from Duparquet, Huot & Moneuse, c.1904-1910. Next to last are from Warne's Model Cookery, ed. by Mary Jewry. London: 1868. (R) are for "taking various articles out of boiling water, roasting oysters, taking fish out of brine, ...as a dish-washer, and particularly to wash out the inside of fruit jars, pitchers." Spring activated, long wooden handles. "Ladies' Favorite," mfd. and invented by Mr. G.J. Capewell, Cheshire, CT. American Agriculturist, 12/1876. **$40.00-$70.00**

XIII-26.
Cake turner & flesh fork.
Forged iron. Cake turner with wonderful winged shoulders to blade, 17"L. American, late 18th or early 19th C. Fork, 3-tinned, twisted and stepped handle with chevron that echoes cutout of reticulated center tine. Beautiful rat-tail loop. 18 1/2"L. Late 18th C. Picture courtesy of Robert W. Skinner Inc., Auctioneers, Bolton, MA. **$300.00-$600.00**

XIII-27.
Implements & rack.
Forged iron. Rack with decorative hearts riveted on, has sharp ends to be driven into wall. Narrow-bladed cake turner & flesh fork have decorative detailing, done with chisel or file, on handles. Not a set, but that would have been rare even in late 18th or early 19th C when these were made. Probably Pennsylvania. Photo courtesy of Pat Guthman Antiques, Southport, CT.

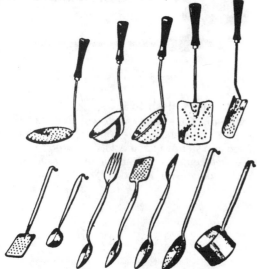

XIII-28.
Implements.
(T) skimmer, ladle, strainer ladle & cake turner two views show crooked handle) are stamped aluminum. "Mirro," Aluminum Goods Mfg. Co., 1927. (B) described in its catalog as "1. Copper Slice. 2. Sauce Ladle. 3. Spoon with Fork. 4. Spoon with Slice. 5. Double Spoon. 6. Pierced Spoon. 7. Stock Ladle." Probably all tinned iron, with copper blade of first "slice" (or cake/egg turner), also tinned. William S. Adams & Son, London, England. c.1860-61.
$15.00-$20.00; $40.00-$60.00

HVMANI VICTVS INSTRVMENTA.

XIII-29.
"Instruments of Human Sustenance: Cooking."
Etching done in 1569 by artist in "circle of" Guiseppe Archimboldo — Italian artist who specialized in assemblages of objects or fruits to resemble human figures. Painting which inspired etching was done by Giovanni da Monte Cramasco. Part of the verse translates "This is not an image, this is not a figure. It is the noble makings in the art of cooking." Photo courtesy of The Metropolitan Museum of Art, Elisha Whittelsey Collection, The Elisha Whittelsey Fund, and Harris Brisbane Dick Fund, by exchange, 1977.

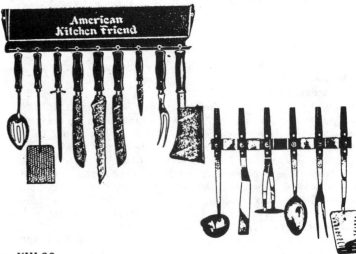

XIII-30.
Implement sets.
(T) "American Kitchen Friend," "our new flat handled kitchen outfit," with japanned tin rack, tinned steel blades, wood handles, brass rivets. Imported, probably German. Thurnauer wholesaler ad from House Furnishing Review, 12/1909. (B) almost 50 years later: "Flint Stainless Steel Kitchen Tools — tall, tapered, and terrific. So good they're guaranteed for fifteen years." From "Flint" line of Ekco, mfd. by Ekco Products Co. 1958.

XIII-31.
Strainer ladle, ladle & cake turner or peel.
Wonderful long-beaked tin strainer has wood handle set into tubular socket. 13 1/4"L overall. Brass ladle has steel or white–smithed iron handle, marked "8" only. 13"L. Cake turner or short peel is steel, marked "Levi Lewis", 14 3/4"L. Early 19th C. Strainer ladle is best piece. Collection of Meryle Evans.$175.00-$225.00;
$100.00-$150.00

XIII-33.
Ladles.
(L) From "Androck Balanced" line. Oval with pouring lip at each end, nickel plated, upright handle with tapered enameled wood grip. 10 1/2"L, with handle in choice of green, yellow, red, green with ivory band, or yellow with blue band. Washburn Co., 1936. (R) from top: tinned iron "French Gravy Ladle," 3 sizes with bowls 1 3/8" deep, from 2 3/8" to 3 1/8" diameter. Sexton, Stove & Mfg. Co., Baltimore, c.1930s. but this is much older cut. Next a tin soup ladle, threaded handle. Bowl 3 3/4" diameter. Central Stamping Co., 1920. Bottom: Welded iron handle with hook, tinned all over, 4 sizes from 3 1/4" to 4 1/16" diameter. Savory, c.1925-28.
$5.00-$20.00

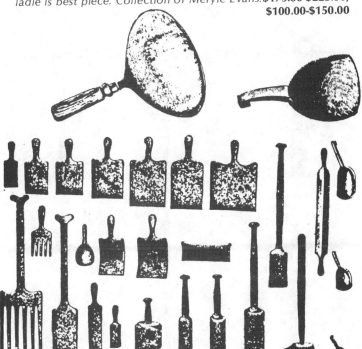

XIII-34.
Syrup ladles.
Tinned, with riveted iron socket handles to take long wooden handles. (L) advertised for "sugar planters." Matthai-Ingram, c.1890. (R) more common spouted form for syrup ladles. From Urbain Debois' La Patisserie D'Aujourd'hui, Paris, c.1860s-90.
$30.00-$60.00

XIII-32.
Ladles & packers for dairies.
Wood, in familiar forms we see today often described as mid or early 19th C. All from 1921 Cherry-Bassett Co. catalog of dairy supplies except top right, a hooked-handle butter ladle "in the New York Style. 1905 catalog. Top (L) is "transfer ladle" for icecream or butter. Other pieces include butter hands, dairy & factory size ladles, from 12" to 16"L, a butter fork 11 1/4"L. A striker for tubs or printer looks like a rolling pin in picture; 27 1/2"L. Also assorted square & round dairy packers, etc. Value range shown is what it should be for such recent items.$10.00-$50.00

XIII-35.
Syrup ladle.
Copper with socket handle & 2 spouts. Iron bail. 7"H x 9" diameter. Ex-Wiggins Tavern Collection, Northampton, MA. Courtesy Glenna Fitzgerald. Photograph Luella McCloud Antiques, Shelburn Falls, MA.

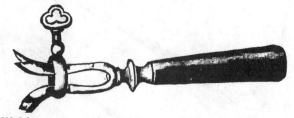

XIII-36.
Leg of mutton holder.
Nickeled steel or iron, wood handle. Fitted over end of bone, tightened, and thus allowed you to hold it securely for carving. Ritzinger Grasgreen importers' catalog, c.1906-07. **$8.00-$15.00**

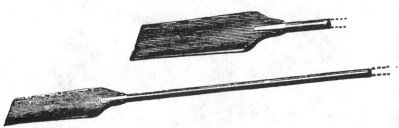

XIII-39.
Peel blade & peel.
Replaceable tapered blades, which wore down & chipped along front edge, came in five sizes: 6", 8", 10", 12" and 14" wide. Handles were — get this! — 12 feet long. c.1904-1910. Very similar wooden pieces, albeit narrower in blade, were candy stirring paddles & scrapers. Many were from 36" to 46"L. **$20.00-$40.00**

XIII-37.
Lifter.
Twisted wire. 15 1/4"L, c.1900. From stock of Carol Bohn, Mifflinburg, PA. **$25.00-$35.00**

XIII-40.
Pie plate lifter.
"Eureka." Wooden handle with 2 wire prongs wiht stamped tin support (?) for pie plate. Heinz & Munschauer's, Buffalo, 1882, who were famous for their birdcages. **$15.00-$30.00**

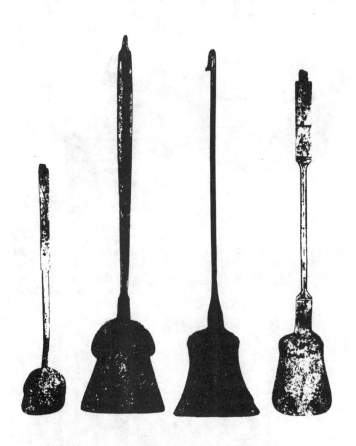

XIII-38.
Short peels or cake turners,
and one **baker's shovel.** *Forged iron, late 18th or early 19th C. From 10 1/2" to 14 1/2"L. Ex-Linden collection. Photo courtesy Christie, Manson & Woods, International Inc. Each:***$40.00-$150.00**

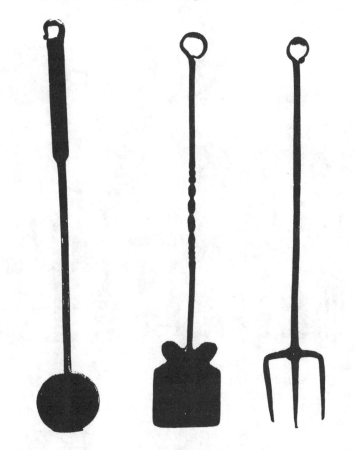

XIII-41.
Tasting spoon, cake turner, flesh fork.
Forged iron. Tasting spoon with zigzag incised, whitesmith-finished handle, 18"L. Cake turner with wonderful winged shoulders to blade, 17"L. Fork with 3 tongs, 16 3/4"L. Sold at auction in early 1980s for $125.00; $600.00; and $75.00. American, late 18th or early 19th C. The most remarkable piece, the cake turner, would probably still command that much, but probably not more. Picture courtesy of Robert W. Skinner Inc., Auctioneers, Bolton, MA.

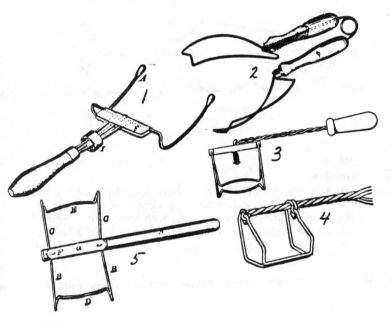

XIII-42.
Pie plate lifters.
All wire & spring action. Top (L) has finger & thumb holes, and works okay as long as pie isn't heavy. (And what pie, sigh, isn't?) 14 3/4"L. (R) Slightly springier; no stronger. 14 3/4"L. Bottom is least trustworthy. I wouldn't carry a mud pie with it. 16 1/2"L. Collection of Meryle Evans. **$25.00-$45.00**

XIII-43.
Plate lifter patents.
(1) "Improvement in Forks for Handling Heated Plates." Pat'd 11/11/1856. G.W. Hyatt. (2) A "plate or dish lifter" pat'd 11/6/1877, William Beattie, Portage, WI. Looks like a grip strengthener. (3) "Pie turner," pat'd 9/27/1887, George H. Thomas, Chicopee Falls, MA. Has "spirally-grooved rod." (dark part between the "plate engaging arms"). (4) "Pie plate holder." pat'd 9/22/1874, Joseph L. Daughtery, Newry, PA. To fit in narrow column of Official Gazette, his handles were cut off in drawing. Even so, it still looks unworkable. (5) Plate lifter, pat'd 3/5/1867, Daniel Welch, Lowell, MA, assignor to H.A. Hildreth, Lowell, & W. J. Johnson, Newton, MA. One jaw fixed, other adjustable "to accomodate itself to varying plates."

XIII-44.
Pie turner & lifter.
"Locke's Automatic," W.E. Thomas & Co., Boston, MA. "The wire jaws are put around the pie plate, and the weight of the pie when lifted causes it to turn, on account of the ingenious spiral attached to the handle. I'd call this "Tenterhooks Hopeful Pie Lifter." The Metal Worker, 11/15/1890. **$20.00-$35.00**

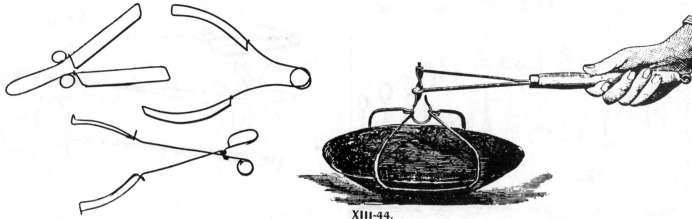

XIII-45.
Woodenware street seller print.
Note woman's woodenwares, from (L) to (R): Mixing spoons; knobbed chocolate mullers; —?—; perforated spoons; rolling pins. The man holds a grass rake. Unidentified engraving, "Published as the Act directs June 1773. Published by John Heywood & Son. Excelsior Works, Manchester. (England.)"

XIII-46.
Roaster & toaster.
Forged iron. (T) Serpentine tine makes it useful as roaster. Damaged ram's-horn handle. 26"L, late 18th C. Ex-Keillor Collection. (B) Toasting fork, 3 prongs, 22"L. Early 19th C. See Hearth chapter. **$250.00-$400.00**

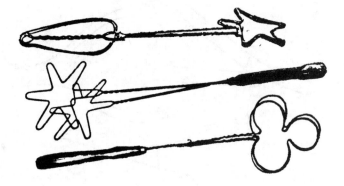

XIII-49.
Toasting fork patent & toasters.
(T) "Toaster & broiler," pat'd 9/18/1877, by Samuel Poole, Brooklyn, NY. (M) Star toaster, wire wood, 19"L x 5 1/8", c.1910. Courtesy Carmille S. Zaino. (B) Wire, wood, 16 1/2"L x 4 3/4"W, late 19th C. Ex-Keillor Collection. **$25.00-$50.00**

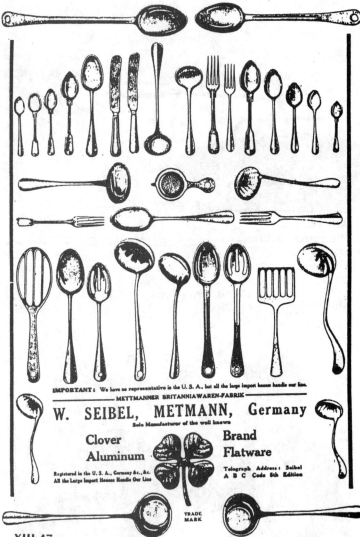

XIII-47.
Spoons, ladles, tableware.
All cast aluminum, "Clover Brand." Mfd. by W. Seibel, Metmann, Germany, who also made Britannia wares. House Furnishing Review, *3/1914.*

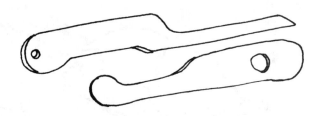

XIII-50.
Spurtles.
Typical shapes for carved flat wooden spatula or stirring tool, originally Scottish. Used for turning griddle cakes, or stirring porridge. Verb spurtle means "to cover with spatterings," which is what usually happens when I make pancakes. Still being made. **$5.00-$25.00**

XIII-48.
"Home-made Toasting Fork."
"A fork that will hold bread, cakes, muffins, or even chops, steaks and slices of bacon, that are to be toasted, before, a fire, be made of any refuse piece of tin, as the bottom of a sardine box, or the side of a fruit can. A piece of tin of convenient size, 6 to 8 inches long, and 3 to 4 inches wide, for instance, is flattened out; the corners are cut off, and the edges are turned up as shown in the engraving. This is done to make it stiffer, so that it will hold its shape. Three angular (triangular) pieces are then cut and bent up, and three wires are fastened into the holes, and then twisted to form a handle. This is a little useful thing for the boys to exercise their ingenuity on." American Agricultuirst, *7/1877.* **$10.00-$20.00**

D. COOKING

XIV. COFFEE, TEA & CHOCOLATE

Well, it's about time to take a break. This chapter has two of the most popular collecting fields in it: coffee mills (or grinders), and enamelware tea kettles and coffee pots. Many people who collect food-related items are attracted to coffee, tea and chocolate. They use books on coffee-growing, or the tea ceremony or the history of the chocolate trade, to broaden the historical and social interest of their collections. Trade cards are an important part of chocolate-collecting.

The growing market in exotic blends of imported coffees, and the proliferation of specialized coffee bean shops around the country, is accompanied by increased interest in coffee utensils and gadgets. Apparently there are many new theme collectors of coffee-related stuff...including caterers, and owners of the bean shops. They like to assemble old roasters and mills, sometimes for their window-decorating potential, which is not to say they aren't truly interested in the objects themselves. There has been a shift to collecting from primarily late 19th or early 20th century mills to much earlier pieces. Consequently, prices have gone up across the board.

The enamelware, or — more popularly — "graniteware" market has shot up amazingly since the second edition of this book was published. There is still some shaking out to do, which means that ready buyers have to be found for the very most expensive pieces and the commonest and least sought-after forms have to have a price drop. Still, among the most desirable and expensive pieces are coffee pots, teapots or kettles. Chocolate pots are very high on collectors' lists.

There's still room for entry level collectors of things in this chapter, such as smaller pieces like tea steepers.

Advertising teapot, miniature size, saltglazed stoneware with 2 color decoration, "Van Dyke Coffee & Tea Co.", early 20th C. **$75.00-$90.00**

Bracket for tea kettle, backplate is cutout heavy guage copper in form of simple 2 handled ewer, 4 holes to screw to wall. Coming from center is a swinging bracket that pivots full 180°, sliding hook for tea kettle or teapot handle, English (?), 6 3/16"H x 6 1/8"W, with 7 7/8"L swinging bracket, 2nd to 3rd quarter 19th C. **$110.00-$135.00**

Chocolate grater—See Cut & pare chapter.

Chocolate molds—See Mold & shape chapter.

Chocolate pot, copper with steel handle, with what could be the original wooden muller (or muddler), English, 7"H, mid 18th C. **$180.00-$210.00**

Chocolate pot, in its own nickel plated castor, brown & white agateware with nickeled collar, lid & spout, "Manning Patent", Manning & Bowman, American, 11"H, TOC. **$200.00-$300.00**

Chocolate pot, pear-shaped body, cast & machined brass, 3 brazed-on short legs with fat ball feet, side handle of heavy ebonized turned wood, hinged spout lid, lid with finial & thumb hinge, French or Swiss, 8 7/8"H, c.1730s. **$325.00-$475.00**

Chocolate pot, tin, side handle with turned wood grip, small "trapdoor" in lid to allow muddler, American, c.1870. **$150.00-$165.00**

Chocolate pot, brown sponged enamelware, nickeled copper, nickel plated lid, spout & handle, Manning, Bowman & Co., late 19th C. **$250.00-$350.00**

Chocolate sauce pan, gray graniteware, pouring lip, American, 9 1/4" diameter, late 19th C. **$35.00-$50.00**

Coffee biggin, French style, tall cylindrical body, enameled a soft sage green with black chicken wire design overlaid, with rows of white dogwood blossoms, partially fluted nickeled white metal mountings — spout & handle, tall white metal insert & domed lid, enameled white inside, Manning, Bowman & Co., Meriden, CT, capacity 2 pts., c. 1880s. • Price on these highly decorative pieces is hard to determine. Partly this is because many advanced collectors prefer the subtleties of plainer wares, but to the "outsider" it seems as if the fancy ones ought to bring the most. . **$250.00-$400.00**

Coffee biggin, gray graniteware pot with gooseneck spout, tin cylindrical vessel (the biggin part) with domed top, drip style coffee maker, invented by a Mr. Biggin around 1800, this one from Matthai-Ingram catalog and American,

others imported, came in different sizes for capacities from 1/2 to 5 qts., this one about 8"H plus another 5" for tin part, c.1870s or 1880s. **$125.00-$200.00**

• **Biggins.** — "Two cylindrical tin vessels, one fitting into the other; the bottom of the upper one is a fine strainer, another coarser strainer is placed on this with a rod running upwards from its center; the finely ground coffee is put in, and then another strainer is slipped on the rod, over the coffee, the boiling water is poured on the upper sieve and falls in a shower upon the coffee, filtering through it to the coarse strainer at the bottom, which prevents the coffee from filling up the holes of the finer strainer below it." *Practical Housekeeping,* Minneapolis: 1884. • "If you use a coffee-biggin, let the coffee be ground very fine and packed tight in the strainer; pour on boiling water, stop the spout of the pot, shut the lid close, and place it upon a heater kept for the purpose. This is made at table." Mrs. Cornelius, *The Young Housekeepers Friend, or, A Guide to Domestic Economy & Comfort,* Boston & NY: 1846.

Coffee boiler, blue agateware, wire bail handle & fixed side handle, tapered body, American, 10"H x 8 3/4" diameter at base, late 19th C. **$70.00-$130.00**

Coffee boiler, blue & white swirl enamelware, with small "V-neck" lip or spout, American or European, late 19th C. **$75.00-$135.00**

Coffee boiler, gray graniteware, bail handle with wooden grip, American, 1 1/2 gal. capacity, late 19th or early 20th C. • A one gallon size almost same price range. **$50.00-$80.00**

Coffee boiler, gray graniteware, with typical V-neck lip or spout, "Granite Iron Ware", mfd by St. Louis Stamping Co., St. Louis, MO, 8 1/2"H, pat'd May 30, 1876, May 8, 1877. **$55.00-$80.00**

Coffee boiler, mottled blue enamelware, enamelware lid with wooden finial, enameled handle, American or European, late 19th or early 20th C. **$75.00-$115.00**

Coffee boiler, powder blue & white speckled enamelware, tin lid, wire bail handle with wooden grip, large size, early 20th C. **$80.00-$130.00**

Coffee boiler, tin, side V-neck lip or spout, American, c.1870s. **$22.00-$35.00**

Coffee boiler, tin with wide strap handle, plus small strap "tipper" opposite lip to ease pouring, from F. A. Walker catalog, imported or American, different sizes, including 6, 8, 10 & 12 qt. capacity, c.1870s.

• **"The Tin Pan Nuisance.** — 'If I were Duke of this country,' began a friend, as we rode through an elegant section of the country, 'I would punish with banishment every man or woman who threw tin trumpery into the street.' — 'Amen,' said I, 'and send them out of the country with a string of oyster cans for a necklace.' This was no new spectacle — we had seen the like a hundred times before — but in this instance it was especially aggravating. There was a large country-house, with a beautiful lawn extending to the fashionable avenue, and at one side to a public road, not fashionable, but greatly traveled, and in a small ravine that made a gap under the fence and opened into the roadside gutter, was tumbled a melange of old tin-ware — coffee and tea-pots, pans, cups, watering pots, innumerable fruit and vegetable cans, and broken crockery. It was an ugly blotch on the otherwise fair beauty of the place. ...What to do with such old trumpery, that cannot be burnt, seems to be an unsolved riddle with the majority of country people. In cities, the housemaid stuffs it in a barrel, which the ash and garbage-men carry away. In the country, it is commonly pitched into some out of the way place, under porch floors, into vacant cellars, under currant bushes, etc., but always where in some moment it will be discovered....

"So far as I know, there is no better way to dispose of broken and worn out wares, than to put them into a well dug for the purpose — one which has a cover, and which, when full, can be earthed and grassed over. Such a receptacle has its advantages — one always knows where to look for old basins and pans, if they are needed, for broken pottery when pieces are required for drainage, while bits of glass are thus put forever out of the way of children's feet.

"The sight of old tin 'lying around loose' [must] have a charm for some people, judging from the way they distribute it in their backyards and front ditches. A man's back-yard is his private property; if he chooses to make it a hideous looking place, it is his own affair; but the man who makes a public highway the receptacle of his trumpery, should be prosecuted by the Commissioner of Roads, and punished as a polluter of public morals. It is as manifest [an] indelicacy to allow such broken & worn out domestic utensils to public view, as to throw old shoes in the street." — MWF, *American Agriculturist*, Apr. 1878.   **$25.00-$35.00**

Coffee boiler, white & blue enameled sheet metal, V-neck spout, wire bail handle as well as large strap tipping handle opposite lip, American, early 20th C.   **$65.00-$100.00**

Coffee boiler, white & brown speckled enamelware, nickeled base & lid, wood finial & fancy handle, Manning, Bowman & Co., 9"H, pat'd 1889.   **$175.00-$225.00**

Coffee boiler, white & sky blue marbleized enamelware, bail handle with turned wooden grip, American, 13"H, late 19th or early 20th C.   **$155.00-$225.00**

Coffee cup, china, large size, with caricature of NYC's Boss Tweed and a spoofing quote, on other side, from the time of the Tammany Hall political boss's downfall. Quote in tradition of 200 years of politically-related engravings & plates & cups: "I am not greedy, but I like a lot" American, early 1870s (?). • Price probably less in area of the country with no interest in Boss Tweed, although his name became nationally synonymous with political graft.
                                              $100.00-$125.00

Coffee cup or mug, graniteware, white background with dark green (or black?) transfer picture of pine tree, etc., adv'g "Dickenson's Ace Clover, Extra-Recleaned, A Trade Winner" & "Dickenson's Pine Tree" Timothy Seed, Average Purity Test, 99½%, It Stands Alone" (the lone pine tree symbolizes this). Dickenson's, American, 19th C. • They must have made a lot of these, because you see them fairly regularly.   **$45.00-$75.00**

Coffee dispenser, wall built-in, aluminum, "Club Aluminum Utensil Co.", Chicago, IL, 2nd quarter 20th C.
                                              $10.00-$15.00

Coffee drip maker, individual size, aluminum, little non-folding legs, one of which serves as handle, snug-fitting lid, put coffee grounds in cup, which is marked with measuring line on side, pour water in, put lid on, no maker name, 3"H x 3⁷⁄₁₆" diameter, 1940s. • My mother's note inside reads "In the early days of WWII, a teacher at Hutchinson School (Memphis) gave me this to send to my mother to make her one-cuppa."   **$4.00-$6.00**

Coffee & hot beverage urn, for restaurants & hotels, copper & brass, "Mason's", American, 18"H, including little feet, TOC. • These were used for hot water, coffee, even clam broth. Some of these were nickel plated.
                                              $150.00-$250.00

Coffee maker, electric drip style, chrome 4 legged urn, the sides flaring up & out, drop ring handles on each side, 2 side by side spigots — one for coffee, one for hot water to "dilute to taste" or for making tea, "Edicraft Menlo Siphonator", mfd in the Laboratories of Thomas A. Edison, Inc., Orange, NJ, 9 cup capacity, c.1930. • The original cost was $45.00 — a very high price in Depression years. For $42.50 more you could also get a sugar, creamer & a sort of truncated oval tray to match. • For other electric wares not related to coffee, see separate Electrical Gadget & Appliance chapter.   **$45.00-$65.00**

Coffee maker, for dining room, on stand with 4 cabriole legs, over alcohol lamp, all copper except for "fishbowl" glass globe top through which passes the vertical tube which circulated the boiling water through the grounds, "Empress Ware, No. 2", New York Stamping Co., Brooklyn, NY, pat'd March 2, 1893 and Sept. 17, 1895. • **Very similar pieces** with alcohol lamps were made by other companies. Manning-Bowman made the "Meteor Circulating Coffee Percolator", with a sort of sugar bowl-shaped glass top; another was the "American Coffee & Tea Extractor", by Buffalo Mfg. Co., Buffalo, NY, advertised in January 1903; a third was the "Auto Vac Glass Coffee Filter", maker unknown, advertised in 1917; then the "Paramount Percolator", NYC, with a glass top and bottom, advertised in 1915; a fifth was advertised by F. A. Walker, "housefurnishers" in Boston who imported many of their goods This was the "French Steam Coffee Pot", of copper or silver-plated copper, with a glass sugar-bowl like top part. It came in sizes from 2 cups to 20. Sternau, a NYC company known to us for "Sterno", made a handsome coffee maker outfit on a stand with columns at each corner of the stand & a sugar bowl-shaped top part. Sterno got a Feb. 17, 1865 patent for the fuel part, and a Nov. 10, 1908 patent for the rest. • All such decorative wares were aimed at the new market that liked to cook at the table — newly servantless hostesses, who could also set up chafing dishes, waffle makers, and other pieces, heated by alcohol lamps or electricity.   **$45.00-$65.00**

Coffee maker, tin with turned wood handle, strainer inside, American, c.1910 to 1915. **$15.00-$20.00**

Coffee maker, vacuum type, 2 globular glass sections, glass rod filter, black plastic handle, measuring cup & lid, Cory Glass Coffee Brewer Co., Chicago, IL, early 1940s. **$5.00-$12.00**

Coffee measure, aluminum, adv'g "Schillings Best", for A. & C. Schilling, San Francisco, CA, c. 1930s. **$12.00-$15.00**

Coffee mill, box or lap type, mahogany, pewter hopper, cast iron crank handle, "Celsor Cook & Co.", American (?), 19th C. • **Box mills** are also called <u>table mills, lap mills</u> or <u>French mills</u>, but many early catalogs called them "box mills" to differentiate them from wall-mounted side mills, or those which clamped to a table top. **$120.00-$145.00**

Coffee mill, box type, brass with wooden handle, European (?), c.1920s. **$30.00-$40.00**

Coffee mill, box type, cast iron, pat'd by J. R. Adams, NYC, NY, pat'd Dec. 1, 1867. • Joseph F. Glidden, who invented barbed wire, may have had an Adams' mill. Stephen L. Goodale, *Chronology of Iron and Steel*, (Pittsburgh: Pittsburgh Iron & Steel Foundries, 1920), wrote about Glidden's two 1874 patents for barbed wire: "The first barbs were made on an old coffee mill, and the wire was twisted with the crank of an old grindstone. The barbs were put on one at a time, and set in place with a hammer. It was first manufactured under the name Barb Fence Co., at De Kalb, Illinois." (p. 185). **$120.00-$165.00**

Coffee mill, box type, cast iron & wood, hopper & crank on top, very plain, probably a cheap proprietary model made for a mail order house, American, TOC or early 20th C. • **Reproduction alert I.** — This extremely simple box style with bowl-like hopper, is being made today, & one that's being sold by Cumberland General Store of Crossville, TN has "satin black finish" cast iron, is 6"H x 4" square, & sells for about $35.00. • **Alert II.** — Lehman's Hardware & Appliances, 4779 Kidron Rd., Kidron, OH 44636 offer a $24.00 + 7"H x 4¾" square box mill with "dovetailed corners" (which are actually box jointed) in their 1989 "Non-Electric Good Neighbor" catalog. • **Alert III.** — A 1968 ad in *McCall's Needlework & Crafts*, shows a box-joint wooden coffee mill, drawer with wood knob, ornate cast iron top, top crank with white porcelain knob, handle grip, hopper inside box, described by "The Country Cousin" dealer as "Decorative coffee mill really works, has a hand-rubbed antique walnut finish. 7" high. $9.95. ppd." **$25.00-$35.00**

Coffee mill, box type, cast iron & wood, side crank out of side of wooden box instead of more usually seen out of top of hopper, side handle, "Parkers Columbia Rapid Grinder, No. 260", sold through Montgomery Ward catalog, Meriden, CT, 1 lb. size, c.1890s. **$55.00-$65.00**

Coffee mill, box type, chromolithographed tin depicts coffee plant on front & convivial scene of man & woman drinking the brew on the sides, sunken hopper with crank, small drawer, "None-Such", mfd by Bronson-Walton Co., Cleveland, OH, c.1904. **$65.00-$75.00**

Coffee mill, box type, dovetailed cherry wood, cast iron, American, 8¼"H x 7" x 7", 19th C. **$75.00-$85.00**

Coffee mill, box type, dovetailed hardwood, entire top is cast iron finished in bronze lacquer, sunken hopper has pivoting cover, handle on top, "Imperial Mill No. 705", mfd by Arcade Mfg. Co., Freeport, IL, box 5"H x 6" square, c.1903-04. **$60.00-$80.00**

Coffee mill, box type, dovetailed wood, japanned cast iron, "Parker's Union Coffee Mill No. 25", 6¼"H, c.1908. **$25.00-$35.00**

Coffee mill, box type, dovetailed wood, with drawer, iron handle, brass, American, 15"H x 8½" square, 19th C. **$250.00-$300.00**

Coffee mill, box type, forged iron box on base plate supporting 4 corner columns with brass fleur-de-lis finials, large capacity high mortar-shaped hopper also houses mill, with serpentine scroll supports & side handle of flat iron also shaped like fleur-de-lis, central crank has turned wooden knob, French, 16"H. If for home use, certainly not for small family (although Emile Zola drank 40 + cups a day), late 1600s or early 1700s. **$650.00-$900.00**

Coffee mill, box type, "French style" with raised hopper, wood with ornate cast iron top, bad condition, with warped wood, poor finish, drawer knob missing, Amerian, 19th C. • Even with everything wrong, still can bring real money as decorative shelf piece. **$25.00-$40.00**

Coffee mill, box type, grain painted tin in bold red & black, hopper filled at top, but bottom has a snap-on hinged lid which you open to release the ground coffee from the box, sort of like you empty crumbs from the toaster, marked only "P B" on front, in block letters, poss. for Parker, looks European, 4½" square, late 19th C. • The dealer had another like it, somewhat smaller, rather dully finished in brown paint, for much less. **$125.00-$145.00**

Coffee mill, box type, hand wrought iron bowl &crank, American, mid 19th C. • **"A French coffee-mill,** which is simple and durable, is a necessity where filtered coffee is made. This will grind coarse or exceedingly fine. Easily adjusted and so simple that a child can use it." Maria Parloa, *Kitchen Companion*, Boston: Estes & Lauriat, 1887. **$80.00-$95.00**

Coffee mill, box type, heavy cast iron, square with slightly slanted sides, 2 cast-in flanges for bolting to board or table, cast iron drawer, brass hopper, brass oval medallion with regal looking rampant lion, "A Kenrick & Sons Patented Coffee Mill", England, 6½"H, prob. c.1860s to 1870s (?). **$55.00-$75.00**

Coffee mill, box type, iron, wood, "Arcade IXL", 11"H with 7½" square base, 19th C. **$150.00-$165.00**

Coffee mill, box type, low wooden box with box joints, cast iron mill, hopper inside, cranked on top with "self adjusting spiral spring", drawer for grounds, "Chicago Double Grinder, No. 60", Chicago Coffee Mill Co., IL, pat'd Oct. 19, 1886, but began making in 1890. **$75.00-$90.00**

Coffee mill, box type modern style, dark maroon Bakelite® (or other molded phenolic resin plastic), nickel plated handle, metal works inside, wooden knob, "The PE-DE Coffee Grinder, Dienes-Reform D. R. G. M. R. P.", German, 8"H, 1930s. • **German vocabulary** — <u>Kaffeemuhle:</u> coffee mill. • I have not been able to track down the meaning of the last two letters, R. P., unless it's *Reichspatent*. The D. R. G. M. stands for *Deutsches Reichs-Gebrauchsmuster* (or Registered Trademark of Germany). *Dienes-Reform* means Reformed Office. The whole thing (probably meaning Reformed Office of German Registered Trademarks and Patents) might have been used between WWI, when D. R. G. M. was used by itself, and WWII, after which Germany was divided. **$65.00-$80.00**

Coffee mill, box type, ornate cast iron top & dovetailed wood, tin drawer with wooden front & knob, top handle, "Challenge Fast Grinder", Sun Mfg. Co., Greenfield, OH, 1 pound size, late 19th C. • In 1891 Jno. M. Waddel Mfg. Co., also of Greenfield, OH, sent out letters informing dealers that the Sun Novelty Works of Greenfield was infringing their patents on their "Greenfield" mill. **$45.00-$55.00**

Coffee mill, box type, painted wood, turned wooden hopper, iron works & crank, not marked, American (?), TOC. **$100.00-$120.00**

Coffee mill, box type, plain, pale beech wood, drawer below, chromed-plated stamped sheet metal top, chromed top crank, Made in Germany, c.1961. • This box mill was offered in *House Beautiful* magazine; also in cherry or walnut. The 3 woods cost $4.95, $7.95 and $8.95 originally. **$12.00-$18.00**

Coffee mill, box type, stamped steel with black enamel finish, sunken hopper, crank on top, wood knob, "Universal #109", Landers, Frary & Clark, New Britain, CT, 5¼"H x 5¼" square box, pat'd Feb. 15, 1905. **$55.00-$65.00**

Coffee mill, box type, very ornate beautifully carved wood, probably mahogany, decorated with angel's heads at each corner of the lower box part, then carved into tower part housing mill works, with acanthus leaves coming down from top, 4 tiny feet, iron screw-on top with graceful iron crank with turned wood knob, ring handle on little drawer. This mill — with the almost furniture-like look, and the tall tower broadening out with undulations into the little box — is what is called a "Louis XIV" type mill because that is when this style appeared, marked "Tivelier Jeune" (Tivelier Jr.), St. Etienne, France, 10 ⅜"H, c.1830s-1850s. **$350.00-$400.00**

Coffee mill, box type, with wide shelf base & lid, cast iron sunken hopper, lid, crank & top grip, door below swings out to reveal tin pan on little shelf that pivots out when you open the door, "Greenfield Coffee Mill, No. 91", mfd by Jno. M. Waddel Mfg. Co., Greenfield, OH, 9½"H, prior to 1890. • See the similar mill by Sun Mfg. Co. **$110.00-$140.00**

Coffee mill, box type, wood & cast iron, original red paint, pin-striping & other decoration on iron, Landers, Frary & Clark, New Britain, CT, 12"H, late 19th C. **$200.00-$250.00**

Coffee mill, box type, wood drawer with brass pull, lid, sunken hopper, cast iron crank & mill works, nice surface decoration, American, 19th C. • **Reproduction alert.** — A very close reproduction of this type is being made and sold now through Cumberland General Store (and probably other outlets). Like this one there's a ¾" wide border around varnished wood box base, side grip handle cast as one piece with cast iron top. There's a double locknut regulator between the crank and the top. This repro box is 5" x 5" square, 5"H exclusive of handle. The new one goes for about $40.00. **$75.00-$90.00**

Coffee mill, box type, wood & iron, original paper label on box, "Home Coffee Mill #767", mfd by Arcade Mfg. Co., pat'd June 5, 1884. **$65.00-$80.00**

Coffee mill, box type, wood with chamfered top, turned cast brass tower, called a "collar", forged iron crank with turned wood knob, iron decoration on 4 sides of box, & brass ring handle on little drawer, Spanish (?), about 8"H, early 18th C. **$350.00-$400.00**

Coffee mill, box type, wooden, cast iron finished with thin copper plating, sunken hopper, crank in top, "Parker's National Coffee Mill No. 430", only 4½"H, TOC. **$35.00-$45.00**

Coffee mill, cabinet side mount, cast iron, folding handle, marked "Geo. W. M. Vandecrift", American, c.1870s-80s, though it looks older. **$85.00-$115.00**

Coffee mill, cast iron, 4 legged, frame screwed to long board with 3 fingerholes at each end, huge crank, tin drawer slides underneath between the legs, key at side to take works apart for cleaning, cup-shaped hopper, an extraordinarily handsome mill, not marked, Pennsylvania, mill is 6¾"H (exclusive of crank) x 5½" x 5⅞", mid 19th C. **$150.00-$200.00**

Coffee mill, cast iron, brass, looks like a cannon, "Persepolis Coffee Grinder", late 19th C. **$275.00-$350.00**

Coffee mill, cast iron cup or hopper & bracket to screw to board, this example mounted to thick wooden paddle, porcelain knob on crank, sawtoothed opening in bottom of hopper, marked "ADAMS" on handle, opposite the word "PATENT", 12½"L with 4½" diameter hopper, date 1840 on underside. • Puzzle. Dealer Bob "Primitive Man" Cahn found it. He discovered that ADAMS also made paint mills of a portable kind (perhaps also larger sizes). In the Index to the Official Gazette, up to 1873, there is but one Adams, a J. R., who is credited with a coffee mill, and that not until 1867 [see a few entries back]. There is no extension, reissue or improvement listed for any coffee mill, mill, paint mill or grinding mill for an Adams or anything patented in 1840. This makes me think this is probably English. • Price range mine not Cahn's. **$225.00-$275.00**

Coffee mill, cast iron, single wheel, huge for store use, American, 6 feet high, 19th C. **$400.00-$600.00**

Coffee mill, cast iron with original paint & stenciled designs, double wheel, drawer below, body "breaks" in center, hopper lid surmounted by eagle, "Enterprise #7", 21½"H, 17" diameter wheel, dated 1873, still selling, with replacement parts, at least in c.1905. • **Replacement parts for coffee mills.** — Every part was replaceable. Perhaps of most interest to the general collector is the fact that 20 eagles were offered, from 25¢ each for the small mills up to 60¢ for larger ones. Looking closely at catalog pages, you can see **differences in eagles:** (1) Flying with wings spread wide & up curved; (2) flying, wings out in downstroke position; (3) standing with wings way out; or (4) tucked in partway, heads left, heads right. What a warehouse find these spare part eagles would be! **$450.00-$550.00**

Coffee mill, cast iron & wood, double wheel, painted blue, "S. H. Co.", St. Louis, MO, 13"H, late 19th C. **$300.00-$450.00**

Coffee mill, clamps to table, wood & iron, "S. H. Co.", St. Louis, MO, TOC. **$120.00-$140.00**

Coffee mill, counter type with double flywheels, painted & decorated cast iron, hinged lid for hopper, drawer below, "Coles No. 2", mfd by Coles Mfg. Co., Philadelphia, PA, c.1906. • Coles also made smaller & larger mills, for coffee & spices. **$225.00-$300.00**

Coffee mill, countertop, cast iron, double wheel with open-work 5 petal flower gear design, shapely body painted red and black, with gold pinstripes, wheels, with name cast around outside rim, rich dark blue with letters picked out in gold, the vase-shaped hopper above is painted light & dark blue with design of sun's rays in red on top, instead of being polished brass. Eagle & flag decals on body. Elgin National Coffee Mill, 26"H, 1880s to TOC. **$600.00-$900.00**

Coffee mill, countertop double wheel type, openwork wheels with 6 petal flower, red painted cast iron, brass knobs on pull-out drawer, & hopper lid, wood crank handle, marked on wheel "John Wright, Wrightsville, PA", 11"H x 7"W, advertised in 1973. **$50.00-$70.00**

Coffee mill, countertop for commercial use, red painted cast iron, spectacular double wheels, stately plinth base, cylindrical bean hopper with domed lid, with blue & yellow paint trim, & applied landscape & portrait bust decals on hopper & grounds box, "Lane Brothers & Co. #15", Poughkeepsie, NY, 29½"H, wheels 16½", pat'd Feb. 9, 1875. **$900.00-$1300.00**

Coffee mill, countertop for home, painted & decorated cast iron, double wheel, drawer in base, breaks apart in middle, no eagle on hopper top, "Family Mill No. 2", Enterprise Mfg. Co., 4 oz. hopper, 12½"H, 8¾" wheels, late 19th C. **$125.00-$145.00**

• **Lookalike alarm.** — Hammacher Schlemmer advertises a single wheel grinder thus: "Exact replica of the coffee grinder used during the turn-of-the-century. Fire engine red body and black wheel, topped with chrome hopper. Hardwood base drawer and handle. 12"H, 7" square base." It sells for about $40.00. Well! Even it it weren't for the chrome hopper, you'd never mistake this for an old one, and I cannot, after diligent search, find what this one is an "exact replica" of. Anyway, it works and it's fine as long as you aren't misled. **Reproduction alert.** — Cumberland General Store has a 2 wheeler, cast iron with wooden drawer, daisy petal spoked wheels, that comes in red with ivory trim or black with gold. It's 11"H x 7" square, and sells for over $100.00.

Coffee mill, countertop store model, 2 wheels, cast iron, original red & black paint, Landers, Frary & Clark, New Britain, CT, 10½"D wheels, TOC. **$400.00-$600.00**

Coffee mill, double wheel store model, countertop but with funnel opening to lower compartment instead of drawer, painted & stenciled cast iron, eagle on top same as others, "Enterprise No. 12", Enterprise Mfg. Co., 32"H with 25" diameter wheel, late 19th C but sold into 20th C. **$600.00-$1000.00**

Coffee mill, electric, cast iron painted white, with glass jar, looks almost like some modern flashlight & birdfeeder combined, "KitchenAid", division of Hobart Mfg. Co., Troy, Ohio, 1938. **$28.00-$35.00**

Coffee mill, electric, enameled cast iron base, screw-on clear glass bean holder above, a glass tumbler marked off in measures sits under chute in left side, "KitchenAid", early 1940s. **$28.00-$35.00**

• **Wartime dates.** — It is problematic to date any American, Canadian, English, French, Italian product to the years of the World Wars. • WWI had been going on for three long years before the U.S. declared against Germany. I suspect that all metals, as well as glass & cloth, were in short supply for making housewares in any involved country between 1914 & 1918. Ads in trade magazines such as *House Furnishing Review* reflect the trade restrictions imposed on products of the Central Powers. • WWII really started long before Germany in-

vaded Poland in 1939. I'd like to read a study of trade practices between what became the Allied Nations and the main Axis powers, Germany & Italy, starting, say in 1935. At any rate, the war was almost two years old when the U.S. landed troops in Iceland, and over two years old when we declared war in December 1941. Probably a great percentage of manufacturers of household appliances and wares suspended domestic production to turn to suitable war materiel manufacturing. Strategic raw materials were severely restricted. Many ads of the early 1940s talk about what goodies would come after the war was over. Any products made of vital materials (iron, steel, copper, rubber, etc.) sold in the U.S. between c.1940 and 1946 may have been made before that period. I don't know what the government did during the metal & rubber drives when objects made of metal or rubber were solicited from the general populace ... whether or not they asked the same thing of manufacturers & their warehoused finished products. In a September 1944 ad in *Better Homes & Gardens,* The headline is "War or no war — Mrs. Jones keeps 'selling' KitchenAids! KitchenAid has gone to war — but enthusiastic KitchenAid users haven't stopped 'selling' their friends. What do they say? They say that a KitchenAid is more than a kitchen 'gadget.' It's a kitchen machine, strong enough and powerful enough to take the elbow-grease out of the really hard ... jobs — mixing, mashing, juicing, whipping, and such. ... They say — but why go on? The fact remains there still isn't a single KitchenAid to sell. But someday there will be — and then remember to talk to a KitchenAid user before you buy any mixer."

Coffee mill, electric, enameled cast iron, with glass top, "KitchenAid", No. A-9, Hobart Mfg. Co., Troy, OH, 1938. **$50.00-$65.00**

Coffee mill, electric, for supermarket use, in shape of big fancy coffee pot with high domed lid & curved short "duckneck" spout, has 4 grinds — coarse, boil, perk & drip. Panel lights up in back to tell what grind to use: "Extra fine for glass maker, fine for drip, medium for perk, coarse for pot", but the terms don't match up. "American Duplex Electric Coffee Cutter", mfd by American Duplex Co., Louisville, KY, 30"H, c.1940-1942. • The dealer said it was one of only about 200 to 250 made. I don't know; I've actually seen two , plus two more advertised. Maybe a store chain suddenly closed up a few years ago, releasing these into the atmosphere? • **Duckneck spout.** — What better name for a short, almost vestigial gooseneck spout than duckneck? **$500.00-$750.00**

Coffee mill, floor model on 4 legs, ornate cast iron base in original paint, huge double flywheels, flared vase-shaped hopper is right, I believe, but looks rather small for the wheels, stepped dome lid with wings-up eagle, "Enterprise #18", 5 feet 8" H, 31" wheels, TOC. • I've seen one advertised as size 18½; could this be later model? If you think you'll buy one through the mail, it weights 233 lbs, and was originally "packed in two crates and one box." **$1200.00-$1600.00**

Coffee mill, floor standing model on intricate cast iron base, 2 wheels. Cast iron with brass hopper & tall finial, "John C. Dell & Son", American, 33"D wheels, pat'd 1884. **$1000.00-$1250.00**

Coffee mill, floor standing store model, 2 wheels, cast iron with all original black & red paint, "Elgin National", mfd by Woodruff & Edwards Co., Elgin, IL, 65"H x 27½"W, TOC. • Very unusual in this size & style.

$1300.00-$1600.00

Coffee mill, floor standing store model, ornate lyre base, double flywheels (the petal spokes of which are much fatter than on the Enterprise), large brass hopper with eagle finial, all original red paint, "Elgin National Coffee Mills", 60"H, TOC. **$1000.00-$1300.00**

Coffee mill, for home use, cast iron, painted black with some fancy gold trim & stencils, no wheels on this smallest model, urn body & hopper breaks (comes apart) at fattest part, where crank is, for cleaning, etc. Capacity of hopper is only 4 oz. of coffee, "Enterprise #1", American,12½"H, crank 6"L, TOC. • $2.25 was the original cost. **$225.00-$275.00**

Coffee mill, japanned & stenciled cast iron, like the #00 but with screw clamp, hopper built in, but a bowl must be put below chute during use, "Enterprise #0", Enterprise Mfg. Co., 11½"H, c.1898. **$35.00-$45.00**

Coffee mill, japanned & stenciled cast iron, wall mount side mill with hopper above balanced by receiving cup below, crank in middle, one of their many "rapid grinding and pulverizing mills", possibly usable as spice mill, "Enterprise Mfg. Co. #00", 9"H, hopper holds 4 oz., "pat. applied for", shown in their 1898 catalog cookbook.

$30.00-$40.00

Coffee mill, screw clamps to table, cast iron, with decorative decal, "Universal #30", Landers, Frary & Clark, TOC.

$35.00-$45.00

Coffee mill, store model for countertop, cast iron painted red & stenciled, with 2 large daisy petal spoked wheels, convex round hopper has domed top, with cast eagle on top, white porcelain knob on drawer below, regulated to grind coarse or fine, "seventy-five turns by hand will granulate a pound of Coffee as fine as required" ... "and by power (larger Grinders being supplied) fifty turns." "Enterprise Mfg. Co., #9", wheels are 19½"D, overall 24"H, TOC. • This is the 4th from biggest overall size of this type with lower drawer; the larger are the #10, 28"H, 19½" wheel, concave flared urn hopper; #209 & #210, which both have 25"D wheels. #209, 33"H, has an iron wheel, fat, urn-shaped hopper surmounted with an eagle with wings spread. #210, 37"H, is even more spectacular, as it has a nickel-plated hopper, in a concave-sided urn-shape, surmounted by eagle with wings partly folded down. There are also smaller ones. The full range of capacity is 1¾ lbs. to 7½ lbs. coffee. Then there are floor-standing models with their own fancy cast iron bases. For those, the added value would be considerable, probably double, even triple, the countertop styles. **$350.00-$500.00**

"Coffee" mill, stump- or box-top, cast iron, with one wheel, simple angular open cast body, shallow wide hopper, for cracking bones, shells, corn, etc., for poultry feed, "Enterprise #750", 17¼"H, with 19"D wheel, TOC. • **Confusable.** — "Coffee" is in quotes, because this **Bone, Shell, Root, Bark, Salt & Corn Grinder** is sometimes confused with a coffee grinder. Enterprise made 3 of these grinders — one wall-mounted, the #650, which was 11"H; and the #750, as above, & the #550 with a crank, instead of a flywheel, which was also 17¼"H. The identifying number is on the hopper. **$75.00-$120.00**

Coffee mill, tabletop, lithographed tin, cast iron, "Grand Union Tea Company", Brooklyn, NY, early 20th C.

$175.00-220.00

Coffee mill, tabletop, small 2 wheeler, painted cast iron, mfd by Swift, Poughkeepsie, NY, TOC. **$275.00-$350.00**

Coffee mill, "telephone" novelty type, wall mounted, side crank, all wood with side crank, of course it looks like an old oak wall crank telephone dating only a few years before the mill itself. brass plate gives name and dates, "The Telephone Coffee Mill", pat'd by F. J. Hollis, Kansas City, MO, 16"H x 6¼"W, pat'd April 18, 1892 (2 years after Arcade's desirable telephone mill). **$175.00-$225.00**

Coffee mill, "telephone" novelty type, wall or shelf mounted, ornate cast iron front to wooden box, "Telephone Mill", mfd. by Arcade Mfg. Co., Freeport, IL, 13"H, pat'd Sept. 25, 1888, April 15, 1890, & April 11, 1898. • Thanks to collector Dorothy Bloom for measurements & other information. **$450.00-$600.00**

Coffee mill, very primitive wooden body with punched iron decorative sides, wide flaring hopper with crank, the whole thing mounted to seat-sized paddle. It is, in fact, a seat, to be straddled while working. Turkish, 18th C. • **Turkish Imports.** — I include a Turkish mill because in the last three or four years of the 1980s, lots of kitchen antiques began showing up in flea markets, imported from Turkey. At the time of this writing (Fall 1988), most of these antique imports are copper frying pans with interestingly braced iron handles, or similar saucepans, or the more familiar exotic coffee pots. Some wholesalers are pricing these by the pound. In addition, around the turn of the century, many wares, mostly copper and brass, were imported to the U.S., and sold chiefly by dealers in NYC's brass district, down on Allen Street. This was true well into the 1960s, and people shopped there for samovars for 60 years or more. Turkey shared a border with Russia, so it is likely that some Turkish wares showed up in the emigre shops.

Other Turkish coffee mills are much fancier, reflecting ancient Byzantine and Persian crafts of inlay and mosaic; some are made of several kinds of wood, even with bone decoration and brass fittings. A star and crescent moon decoration easily identify a piece as Turkish, but this symbol was not adopted for their flag until 1936. I don't know how long ago the symbols were popularly used. To confuse things, a popular American fraternal order, the Shriners, use as their emblem a Turkish scimitar (curve upwards) with a downpointing crescent moon with 5-point star pendent from the scimitar's blade. The Shriners wear a fez, which is also Turkish. Some decorative arts of American origin have the scimitar insignia or emblem. **$350.00-$550.00**

Coffee mill, wall mounted side mill (hereafter "wall/side"), sheet & cast iron, painted black & mounted to natural-finish wood block, partly carved & painted so that it "mirrors" shape of the sheet iron hopper front, brass ID plate: "Wilson's Improved Patent Coffee-Mill", mfd by Increase Wilson, or Wilson's Foundry, New London, CT, mill and hopper are 6"H, hopper is 4"W, crank is 4½"L. 1840s to 1860s (?). • The only dated Wilson coffee mill patent I found was March 6, 1818, but this isn't anywhere near that old. **$60.00-$85.00**

Coffee mill, wall/side, cast iron bean box above iron mill housing, spring & screw clamp holder below for cut crystal container for the grounds. Ornate casting depicts a hand bell surrounded with Art Nouveau scrolls, etc., & the word "BELL", one of 70 styles mfd by Arcade Mfg. Co., in their "Crystal" line, Freeport, IL, c.1908. **$125.00-$175.00**

Coffee mill, wall/side, cast iron, "Brighton", TOC. **$40.00-$55.00**

Coffee mill, wall/side, cast iron mill housing & crank & bracket, finished in black, white or blue enamel, clear glass upper bean container has screw-on lid on top & its bottom screws into iron center part, with clear glass grounds holder below, "Enterprise Mfg. Co. #100", 14½"H, early 20th C. **$30.00-$50.00**

Coffee mill, wall/side, cast iron with glass canister, marked "Crystal No. 3" on glass, mfd by Arcade, American, TOC. • Arcades are the most commonly found coffee mills, in various models and sizes. Having "Crystal" on the glass canister means added value, as they are easily broken, and could be replaced with other glass jars. **$60.00-$75.00**

Coffee mill, wall/side, cast iron works, tin hopper & housing, mounted — as many are — on a wooden board with 3 holes. Lots of side mills are found mounted to a board, sometimes with three holes in a sort of zigzag on one side. This way, the mill could easily be put up on the side of a cupboard, or the wall of a pantry or kitchen, & moved more easily. • An 1841 article on side mills, the design of which hardly changed for 60 or 70 years, says "It is sold without a frame, & is so constructed as to be fastened to a post or board in any part of the house, or it can be attached to a simple frame." "S. J.", TOC.• **$22.00-$28.00**

Coffee mill, wall/side, Delft blue & white pottery, with iron works & crank, Dutch, English or German — prob. the latter, 1930s.• **Reproduction alert.** — A box mill is being made today with large porcelain bowl hopper, white with blue flowers, painted sheet iron base with drawer, top handle. It is 8"H x 5½" square. **$35.00-$55.00**

Coffee mill, wall/side, glass & cast iron, "Arcade #3", Arcade Mfg. Co., late 19th C. **$100.00-$135.00**

Coffee mill, wall/side, looks rather like the Wilson mill but backplate is cast iron as is the hopper, & there is a thumb-screwed "collet" or washer to regulate coarseness of grind, marked "James Carrington, Wallingford, CT", pat'd April 3, 1829. **$165.00-$200.00**

Coffee mill, wall/side, metal, "Regal #44", TOC or early 20th C. **$45.00-$55.00**

Coffee mill, wall/side, mounted on board, iron, large glass canister with red lettering "Koffie", Dutch (?), TOC. **$65.00-$85.00**

Coffee mill, wall/side, mounted to board, blue, red, green & white lithographed tin oblong canister above, depicts fat Dutch girl & sea scenery, cast iron mill & catch-can below in bracket, marked "Holland Beauty" under woman's image, mfd by Bronson-Walton Co., Cleveland, OH, pat'd July 9, 1901. • Value is mostly in the fine condition of the lithographed tin canister. **$40.00-$50.00**

Coffee mill, wall/side, on board, sheet iron hopper, cast iron mill & S crank, no lid on hopper, but doesn't appear there ever was one, embossed "L. Holts Improved Coffee Mill", eagle & banner saying "Patent". (Holt-Lyon? No

Holt in *Patent Index*), looks 1850s; no patent record 1790-1873. (If Holt-Lyon, c.1890s.) **$40.00-$55.00**

Coffee mill, wall/side, painted or bronzed japanned cast iron, oblong upper box holds beans above grinder, cast iron front has shield cutout with glass window to show beans, below mill is spring-tension screw with plate that holds cup or can tightly against bottom of mill to catch grounds, "Golden Rule Blend Coffee. The Finest Blend in the World", Citizen's Wholesale Supply Co., Columbus, OH, 17½"H, early 20th C. **$175.00-$225.00**

Coffee mill, wall/side, red & black tin & iron, "Aroma #9", Cleveland, OH, late 19th C. **$55.00-$75.00**

Coffee mill, wall/side, screwed to board, oblong lithograph-ed sheet metal canister top, in exaggerated grainy wood, oval glass viewing window, below is plain cast iron mill housing & crank, with grounds cup that matches top, mfd by Bronson-Walton Co., Cleveland, OH, pat'd July 9, 1901, with other patents pending. • A slightly fancier version of this has a little cast iron support for the grounds catcher cup. **$40.00-$55.00**

Coffee mill, wall/side, screwed to board, oblong lithograph-ed tin canister above, cast iron mill housing, canister marked "Silver Lake" with four leaf clover, mfd by Bronson-Walton Co., c.1901-1905. • The works & the shape were, I think patented July 9, 1901. I'm sure that different styles or decorations for the lithographed canister were introduced at least yearly. **$20.00-$30.00**

Coffee mill, wall/side, screwed to board, sheet & cast iron, cast iron crank, marked "P. S. & W. Co. No. 6", Peck, Stow & Wilcox, CT, 5½"H, 3rd to 4th quarter 19th C. **$45.00-$60.00**

Coffee mill, wall/side, screwed to piece of wood which is then screwed to the wall, japanned cast iron, "Sun No. 94", Sun Mfg. Co., Greenfield, OH, c.1900. **$15.00-$18.00**

Coffee mill, wall/side, sheet metal & cast iron, screwed to board, oblong box with a small drawer below the mill to catch the grounds, & a larger storage drawer for the coffee beans on the side, cast iron X crank handle, brass plate on mill's hopper embossed "John Luther's Coffee Mill, Warren, RI", 12"H x 16"L overall, "pat'd Aug. 11, 1848". **$125.00-$165.00**

Coffee mill, wall/side, sheet steel canister, painted black, cast iron grinder & crank, with wooden knob, green & white label on canister, "Universal, #0012", Landers, Frary & Clark, 13¼"H, pat'd Feb. 14, 1905. **$65.00-$90.00**

Coffee mill, wall/side, tin & iron, "Parker #60", Meriden, CT, c.1860s to 1900. • This looks like the Eagle side mill pat'd by J. & E. Parker, Meriden, on Feb. 7, 1860, and so marked on round stamped brass ID disc on hopper. The "Eagle" came in four sizes: #50, #60, #70 & #80, and sold in the Dover Stamping Co. catalog of 1869. **$50.00-$65.00**

Coffee mill, wall/side, unusual fold down type, adjustable mill parts, deep hopper & crank of cast iron, these 3 basic elements fitted to a wooden platform which is hinged to fold up against the wall. It would have to be mounted somewhere where a receptacle could be placed, & may have seemed more ingenious that it was in practice, "Lone Star", J. M. Waddel Mfg. Co., c.1890. **$50.00-$65.00**

Coffee mill, wall/side, with crank handle coming out of wooden box. This is a new one, being made today, & has an iron hopper and a "walnut stained hardwood body" mounted to a board & decorated with molding, described as being "Colonial styled with antique finish." American-made (?), 1980s. • **Lookalike** advertised in Cumberland General Store catalog. New price about: **$30.00**

Coffee mill, wall/side, wood, drawer & crank have white china knobs, signed "I. D. Post, Lahaska, PA", last quarter 19th C. **$165.00-$220.00**

Coffee mill, wall/side, wooden box with iron lid & with one glass side for viewing the beans above the cast iron mill housing and crank, simple iron receptacle for grounds below. Advertised as "A reliable grinder at a very low price ... for customers of limited means." "X-Ray Mill" mfd by Arcade Mfg. Co., Freeport, IL, c.1908. **$60.00-$75.00**

Coffee mill, wall/side, wrought iron, American, about 6"H, early 19th C. **$160.00-$175.00**

Coffee mill, wood base, vertical post that supports sheet iron hopper with snap-on hinged lid. Below the hopper are the horizontal works in a cylinder, with side crank; very delicate looking, George Washington had one almost the same that is now in the Smithsonian, possibly made from an illustration, & description in the famed 1750s Diderot's Encyclopedia, French or even poss. American, about 23"H, late 18th C. **$600.00-$800.00**

Coffee or teapot, pieced tin lighthouse shape body, made of 8 soldered vertical strips, thin strap handle, straight spout originating almost halfway up body, American, mid 19th C. **$100.00-$125.00**

Coffee or teapot, straight sides, Britannia trim and curved fluted spout, fancy handle, celadon green enamelware body with blue & pink morning glories with green leaves, Manning-Bowman, Meriden, CT, 9"H, 1890s. **$250.00-$350.00**

Coffee percolator, aluminum, green Depression glass percolator lid, turned wooden handle, 4 little feet, no maker's name, 14"H, 1930s. **$18.00-$22.00**

Coffee percolator, copper and brass, urn shaped with wooden handles, finial & spigot handle, nice footed base, on stand, Manning & Bowman, 13"H, pat'd 1906. **$85.00-$110.00**

Coffee percolator, dark blue spattered graniteware, early 20th C. **$65.00-$100.00**

Coffee percolator, electric, 2 glass globes with red phenolic plastic handles & swing or swivel lid for lower globe, black plastic base, percolating tube goes up through center, very handsome, "Silex" glass, "Automatic Coffee Percolator" mfd by General Electric, c.1940s (?). **$85.00-$100.00**

Coffee percolator, electric, chrome plated brass & copper ball on high flared foot, with funny tapered perky spout, balanced on opposite side by arched white plastic handle, knurled knob on lid, "Table Electric" by Chase Brass & Copper Co., Inc., division of Kennecott Copper Corp., 7 cup capacity, c.1937. • A non-electric companion to this was a tea kettle, a large chromium ball, same kind of tapered spout, much smaller ring foot, white plastic handle forms arches a few inches from spout to backside, describing an arch approximately ⅛ of the diameter of the kettle. **$65.00-$85.00**

Coffee percolator, electric, round, Labelle Silver Co., Brooklyn, NY, 1950s. **$20.00-$30.00**

Coffee percolator, light blue speckled enamelware, "Universal", L. F. & C., Landers, Frary & Clark, pat'd first in 1894. **$125.00-$165.00**

Coffee percolator, pale green enameled iron, nickeled copper lid & trim, paneled body, tubular handle painted black, aluminum basket, glass top, called in catalog the "High Pattern-Cold Water Type", glass insert in lid is "Fire King", function of the odd little tippy pedestal base was to draw heat up, separating the pedestal from the top is some kind of insulating material, Reed Mfg. Co., Newark, New York (not NJ), 9⅞"H, 6 cup capacity, c. 1927. • (It also came in white.) This particular color, sometimes called closet green by stove manufacturers, was called "blue" in the Reed catalog. **$45.00-$75.00**

Coffee percolator, red & white swirled enamelware, glass insert in lid, 20th C.• Red & white enamelware is high among the most sought-after colors. **$90.00-$150.00**

Coffee percolator, stamped aluminum, paneled sides, domed percolator lid set with green glass, turned wood handle, V-neck spout or lip, "A. A. W. Peerless Co., The Better Ware", American Aluminum Ware Co., Newark, NJ, 9"H x 4⅞" diameter, c.1915-1930. **$10.00-$15.00**

Coffee percolator, stamped aluminum, slanting sides rounded at bottom, percolator lid, clear glass, somewhat straightened out gooseneck spout, "C" shaped black-finished wood handle, No. 69, Landers, Frary & Clark, 7½"H x 5¾" diameter, c.1915-1930. **$10.00-$15.00**

Coffee percolator, straight sides, green & tan enamelware, green glass in lid, all interior parts present, American, 1930s. **$20.00-$35.00**

Coffee percolator, with rather fat slant-sided metal body, long tapered straight spout originating near bottom, simple strap handle above which is an attached tin funnel — the aperture through which water is poured into a sort of pocket within the pot. Above is a rather short cylinder with hinged lid, which is where the grounds are & where the tube with perforated top terminates. Pour water in, it is forced up tube & percolates out strainer through the coffee grounds. As a 1911 article stated, the difference between this early percolator & later ones is that in the 1875 one the water only dripped through one time, instead of over & over. Manning-Bowman & Co., Meriden, CT, available in 1875, pat'd in 1876. • **Archaeological Find.** — In a large ad featuring a brand new percolator for 1911, come three tantalizing paragraphs in small print, entitled "A Chance Discovery and Its Meaning. (1) While making changes in our factory at Meriden a short time ago, workmen opened up a long forgotten vault in the wall. (2) In the vault were a number of Manning-Bowman Coffee Percolators made from 1865 to 1876. Weird productions compared with modern designs, they show the wonderful progress we have made in Coffee Percolator building since 40 years ago. (3) The next time you are in Meriden, or New York, do not fail to drop in and inspect them." Oh boy, wouldn't you love to have that time machine now? **$80.00-$100.00**

Coffee percolator, yellow enamelware with green trim, glass top, 20th C. **$30.00-$45.00**

Coffee percolator or maker, 2 "fishbowl" shaped glass globes, one above the other, scalloped red plastic "skirt" for the lower globe, part of the handle assembly, cover of top globe is also red, has odd little tabletop "gas" stove, with 2 handles, called the "Bride's Special", with "Pyrex" glass, "Moldex" plastic, mfd by The Silex Co., Hartford, CT, about 18"H, late 1930s. • **Silex made several models** — gas & electric — at the time. A fancy

"De Luxe Lido" model had chrome instead of the "Moldex" & a sort of saucered chrome base. Another model, the "Buffet Service", for parties, had 2 bottom pouring pots, with one top globe. This model came on a 2 burner electric stove with black plastic base & small black handles at each end. **$18.00-$25.00**

Coffee pot, 2 tone gray spotted graniteware, pewter spout, base, trim, handle, crown collar & lid, American (?), 8 3/4"H, 19th C. **$130.00-$175.00**

Coffee pot, a sort of combined French biggin & drip percolator, conical metal body with long straight spout originating near bottom of pot, fancy openwork scrolled cast iron handle, long "stove pipe" drip cylinder, with wooden rod or pressure block used to force hot water through the grounds placed in the perforated interior strainer, Manning-Bowman & Co., Meriden, CT, pat'd 1873. • "Burnett's Coffee Clearer. A Woman's Invention. A patented combination of Cod Fish Skins and White of Eggs. The Best article for Settling Coffee. Eggs saved and no patent coffee pots needed. At a daily expense of less than ½¢ per family." Feb. 1889 ad of Joseph Burnett & Co., Boston. The pot: **$100.00-$135.00**

Coffee pot, a sort of percolating drip type, nickeled copper, straight sided cylinder with beading around top edge, straight tapered spout set midway up, vertical bracket handle of ebonized turned wood, ball valve in spout is a real marble, very fine wire mesh (called wire gauze) filter compartment gets filled with grounds & put down in pot, then strainer with vertical pipe — the "air tube" — put in on top of filter. Domed cover with knob. Medallion on side: "Marion Harland Tea & Coffee Pot", mfd by Silver & Co., Brooklyn, NY, 4 cup capacity, c.1890, but made over a 30 year period or more. • This also came in polished copper (tinned inside), or in what they called "Old English" finish, which was not defined in catalogs or ads. Possibly a sort of dull pewtery finish? This pot was also advertised with the curved "question mark" handle. **$18.00-$35.00**

Coffee pot, actually a coffee maker, tin, perfectly cylindrical shape, with a perforated grounds cup insert, percolating funnel tube, slightly tapered straight spout originating near bottom, slightly domed lid with pretty little cast metal finial, graceful question-mark shaped handle. Manufacturer's brochure states that "In using a new pot a slight taste of tin impairs the flavor of the coffee. After a few times using, (or after boiling coffee in the pot a few hours) this entirely disappears." Also stated is that the 2 extra pieces, filtering cup & tubed funnel, "are of a form easily kept clean, durable, and, if necessary, easily repaired or renewed by an ordinary tinsmith." "The Windsor", mfd by Hubbard & McClary, Windsor, CT, 9 sizes — from one to 16 qts., c.1870s. **$30.00-$45.00**

• "Tinkering Made Easy. —

Holes in sauce pans or other tinwares, is a small thing. Those who will take the trouble to learn, can easily do small jobs at soldering, but many have not the needed gumption, and spoil the job. These will find the 'Magical Patching Plate' a great convenience. It is a thin sheet of solder prepared for the purpose, from which a bit is to be cut out large enough to well cover the hole; the surface of the ware is scraped bright, the patch put on, a poker or other hot iron held upon it, and when the solder melts, the job is done." *American Agriculturist,* 1877.

Coffee pot, agateware with colorful depiction of Statue of Liberty, ornate pewter spout, domed lid & handle, American, Statue of Liberty Commemorative, 1886. • Would Have Been Great Investment — Offered in 1982 for sale by Al & Nancy Schlegel, Willow Hollow, Penacook, NH. The price then was only $225.00. It would most likely have jumped to double in 1986, for the centennial of the statue. Probable value now: **$400.00-$650.00**

Coffee pot, aluminum with Bakelite® or other molded phenolic resin handle, 2 part, top is "biggin" drip container, lower has V-neck pouring spout. (Another version, reportedly only 11"H, has green wooden finial and handle.) "Drip-O-Lator, The Better Coffee Maker", Enterprise Aluminum Co., Massillon, OH, 12"H, pat'd by R. F. Krause, Jan. 14, 1930. **$20.00-$22.00**

Coffee pot, biggin drip maker type, tin, cast white metal handle originally painted black. There's a cork stopper which is kept in a little dead end funnel on the straight spout's bridge or brace strut, except when it's transferred to spout when coffee has to be kept hot inside, "Chesterman's Coffee Pot", W. Chesterman, Centralia, IA, 9⅜"H, pat'd July 19, 1859, & Jan. 24, 1860. **$85.00-$100.00**

Coffee pot, biggin type, silvery plated (tin? Britannia?) copper, straight-sided cylindrical lower body, slightly smaller diameter drip top, curved handle, straight spout, large round knob on lid, American, prob. CT, 11"H, mid to 3rd quarter 19th C. **$200.00-$235.00**

Coffee pot, black & white enamelware, American, large size, c.1910 to 1930s. **$40.00-$65.00**

Coffee pot, blue & white enamelware in slant-sided shape, with moss roses on both sides, doesn't look like Manning-Bowman wares, prob. European, late 19th C. **$165.00-$250.00**

Coffee pot, blue & white enamelware with flower design, tin lid, gooseneck spout, European or American, late 19th C. **$155.00-$220.00**

Coffee pot, bluish-gray graniteware, tin top with wooden finial, unusual one-cup size, late 19th C. **$65.00-$120.00**

Coffee pot, brown graniteware with a few chips. 12"H, 19th C.• Nice color, but a shelf piece. **$25.00-$30.00**

Coffee pot, brown speckled enamelware, with Britannia mountings, including lid, handle & spout. Protective band around base is brass — undoubtedly once nickel-plated, probably Manning, Bowman & Co., c.1890-1900. **$155.00-$225.00**

Coffee pot, brown & white agateware, white metal lid, copper base, shell & column motif on throat of spout & handle, probably Manning & Bowman, 10"H, late 19th C. **$275.00-$350.00**

Coffee pot, brown & white spattered agateware, domed "golden" pewter lid, spout & handle, golden-colored tin "skirt", possibly colored by some kind of japanning. American, 11⅜"H, late 19th C. • This is another piece offered for sale by the Schlegels in 1982. Price range mine: **$300.00-$375.00**

Coffee pot, brown & white speckled enamelware, gooseneck spout, nickeled white metal mountings, probably Manning, Bowman, late 19th C. **$140.00-$190.00**

Coffee pot, brown & white swirled enamelware, with gooseneck spout, probably "Onyx", Columbian Enameling & Stamping Co., TOC. **$150.00-$190.00**

Coffee pot, ceramic, decorated with modernistic, almost Art Deco, flamingos, "Ohio Potteries", Zanesville, OH, late 1920s or early 1930s. **$55.00-$65.00**

Coffee pot, cobalt enamelware, with gold trim, gooseneck spout, prob. European, late 19th C. **$115.00-$165.00**

Coffee pot, copper, hinged lid, green Depression glass insert in lid, mark is indistinct, looks like "MERID--", could be name Meriden or possibly the place, Meriden, Ct., 1925. **$15.00-$18.00**

Coffee pot, copper, roundish body, wood finial & handle, Manning & Bowman, makes only one cup, late 19th C. **$30.00-$45.00**

Coffee pot, copper with brass hinge, wood finial on lid & wood handle, brass ferrule on handle, crooked neck spout, "James S. Shaw Co.", 5½"H, 19th C. **$70.00-$85.00**

Coffee pot, copper, with brass trim, & nifty turned wooden handles painted black, American, 11½"H, TOC. **$45.00-$55.00**

Coffee pot, copper, with Britannia (pewter-like) lid, gooseneck spout & handle, very fancy, American, late 19th or early 20th. **$75.00-$85.00**

Coffee pot, dark brown enamelware flecked with white, hinged lid, possibly "Onyx" by Columbian Stamping, or possibly Manning, Bowman & Co., or even European, early 20th C. **$90.00-$150.00**

Coffee pot, dark turquoise enamelware, with gooseneck spout, European or American, TOC. **$95.00-$155.00**

Coffee pot, electric, chrome, with sugar & creamer to match, "Edison General Electric Hotpoint", 20th C. **$22.00-$30.00**

Coffee pot, electric, chrome with tan handles & spigot, shaped like a football, "Forman Brothers Inc.", Brooklyn, NY, 2nd quarter, 20th C. **$20.00-$25.00**

Coffee pot, electric, floral patterned china, chrome base & spigot, matching creamer and covered sugar bowl, (china by Fraunfelter) "Royal Rochester", mfd by Robeson Rochester Corp., (Zanesville, OH), Rochester, NY, pat'd Aug. 12, 1924. **$135.00-$150.00**

Coffee pot, enamelware in mulberry color, lighthouse shape, black painted turned wood handle & wood finial, 9"H, TOC or a bit earlier. **$150.00-$250.00**

Coffee pot, enamelware with white background & floral design, white metal mountings at collar, gooseneck spout, base, handle, (these were also offered with nickel plated mountings at a slight extra cost), Manning-Bowman, pat'd June 5, 1883, registered Jan. 13, 1885. **$175.00-$225.00**

• **"New Art Enameled Ware.** Beautiful Creations That Prophesy Great Developments in Ornamental Novelties of Steel. — It is refreshing to turn away for a brief while from ... ordinary enameled ware ... & contemplate the possibilities that lie in enameled ware as an article for decorating & beautifying homes. Not much of the latter is yet shown in this country, & probably none of it will ever be made by the American manufacturer whose mind runs more toward the question of profit than the production of truly artistic wares. (!) But the Austrians have devoted considerable time of late to the making of beautifully decorated vases, pitchers, urns, mugs, etc., that at first glance can scarcely be distinguished from pottery or fine china, although made of drawn steel.

"It is decorative in every sense of the word and possesses all the charm of ... ceramic ... (plus) indestructability, for this new art enameled ware can be dropped to the floor or knocked about with impunity. ... (On display at a NY firm, Stransky & Co., is a collection of) various kinds of enameled ware that are sold in foreign countries.

In America the housewife is satisfied with her white and white, blue and white, gray mottled, etc., but abroad ... tastes are more exacting, and each country demands its own particular designs.

"In Japan, for example, the vogue is for flowery patterns in all the pleasing colors of the Sunrise Kingdom, and the Stransky collection contains a series of basins bearing characteristic pictures. Some are purely floral but others portray boating scenes and sketches of Japanese life, every detail being worked out even more minutely than is possible on pottery.

"If the limits of this article permitted, it would be highly interesting to describe separately the enameled ware fashions of each country: China, Little Asia, Turkey, Singapore, Siam, the Balkan States, Hungary, etc., all have their individuality, running the gamut from the fantastic dragon patterns of China to the thick, heavy designs of Russia. It is amazing how well the colors are produced, and the effect of real china is so cleverly simulated that even a trained eye could be readily deceived. The Stransky collection will be appreciated by those of the trade who are interested in something more than enameled ware which sells at nineteen cents, marked down from a quarter." *House Furnishing Review*, Feb. 1906.

Coffee pot, engraved tin, with designs including tulips, eagle, flag, peacock, vines & leaves, PA German, prob. mid 19th C. **$3000.00-$4500.00**

Coffee pot, filter percolator, plated metal tripod base, double-globe glass coffee maker in 2 parts — the filter part & the serving part, both decorated with leaves, scrolls & chrysanthemums in "silver deposit" on clear glass. The glass parts sit over alcohol heater in base, or can be used on a gas, coal or electric stove, "Auto Vac Glass Coffee Filter", mfd by Auto Vacuum Freezer Co., NYC, NY, c.1917. **$35.00-$45.00**

Coffee pot, for students, tin with brass trim, wooden handle sticks straight out halfway down cylindrical body, straight side spout attached at bottom of pot, looks sort of like an espresso coffee pot, from F. A. Walker catalog, four sizes: 2, 4, 6 and 8 cup capacity, c.1870s or 1880s. • I have always thought that F. A. Walker was only an importer & wholesaler. But here's an enlightening news item from *The Metal Worker*, Oct. 21, 1882. "Messrs. F. A. Walker & Co., 83 Cornhill, Boston, manufacturers and refinishers of brass goods, have a very fine display of brass fenders, fire screens, fire sets, coal vases, tea urns, placques, brass-trimmed bellows, &c. Several specimens of Benerez brasswork shown by this firm are very fine indeed, and attract marked attention." **$30.00-$45.00**

Coffee pot, gray graniteware, tin cover, graceful shape, American, 9"H, early 20th C. **$85.00-$135.00**

Coffee pot, gray graniteware, tin lid with white porcelain knob, hollow cast iron handle was originally painted black, American (?), 8½"H, late 19th or early 20th C. **$85.00-$135.00**

Coffee pot, gray graniteware with tin lid, brass ring around base, a few dings, late 19th C. **$45.00-$65.00**

Coffee pot, gray spattered graniteware, tin lid, large size, late 19th C. **$125.00-$160.00**

Coffee pot, green & white striped enamelware, small size, European, prob. Czechoslovakian, early 20th C to 1930s. **$135.00-$145.00**

Coffee pot, hammered copper, pewter lined (looks like tin), foreign looking pot with round globular lower body, small ring foot, topped by slightly flared high neck with big beak spout, domed lid, thin handle curves out from near rim and "falls" inward to middle of globe, a reproduction based on a Russian pot from sometime in 19th C, which in turn reflects Middle Eastern & Turkish influence, B. Paleschuck, NYC, NY, 10"H, one qt. capacity, early 1930s, based on 19th C form. **$25.00-$35.00**

Coffee pot, large tin one with unusual copper bottom coming 2 inches up sides. The copper protected the tin solder & conducted heat better besides, American, 19th C. **$35.00-$45.00**

Coffee pot, lavender or mauve (hey! what would you call mauve? Oscar Wilde said it was pink trying to be lavender; and Thomas Beer, who in 1926 wrote *The Mauve Decade*, about the 1890s in America, said it was "pink turning to purple". Some dictionaries say mauve is lilac.). Anyway, pale browny lavender speckled enamelware, tin spout & tin lid with turned wooden finial, wooden handle, probably Manning & Bowman, American, 9"H, late 19th C. **$170.00-$250.00**

Coffee pot, lighthouse shape, decorated tin, or tole. Dark brown japanned background (least desirable color) with polychromatic flowers, & swagged border, strap handle with grip, nice crooked spout, stepped low dome lid with brass knob finial, amazingly unworn finish, American, 10⅝"H, 19th C pot with period decoration, though faked finishes are known. • Brought $3700.00 at Garth's Auctions, Delaware, OH, April 11-12, 1986. **$3000.00-$4000.00**

Coffee pot, lighthouse shape with crooked neck spout, domed lid, braced strap handle, painted tin with flowers, fruits, leaves in color on black asphaltum background, American, 11½"H, mid 19th C. **$800.00-$1400.00**

Coffee pot, lighthouse (slant-sided) style, copper, with wire bail & turned wooden handle, ring finial on lid,10 cup capacity, mid 19th C. **$65.00-$75.00**

Coffee pot, lighthouse style, enamelware, dark chocolate brown spattered with white, TOC. **$145.00-$175.00**

Coffee pot, lighthouse style, tin with black japanning, crooked neck spout, slightly domed hinged lid with brass knob, American, poss. CT, 10"H, 19th C. • Not as desirable to collectors as would be one with either a red background, or painted decorations over the japanned background. **$165.00-$195.00**

Coffee pot, lighthouse style with perky — even impertinent — pieced, crooked neck spout & extra large curved handle, brown japanning & polychrome flowers, brass mushroom finial to lid, American, 10⅝"H, 19th C. • Not anywhere near as desirable as one with red or blue japanned background color. But surface is very good, & original. • I use the term crooked neck or crooked only with an angled spout having a seam at the elbow (to mix similes), occasionally at "wrist" also. Sometimes these are called cock's head spouts. Many crooked spouts on copper tea kettles look just as angular, but do not have a circumferential elbow seam. These are called gooseneck spouts, and there is a wide latitude in the use of the term. Some goosenecks are more stuck-out, more curious, more aggressive than others — more ganderish (?); some are more graceful and plump at the bend; still others are small and timid, perhaps gosling necks? The crooked neck or crooked spout is, I'm sure, the tinsmiths' adaptation of

the coppersmiths' gooseneck spout, which could not be copied exactly, because it was much more difficult, perhaps impossible, to hammer out the extreme angle, in tin plate, and keep the integrity of the plating. **$2500.00-$3000.00**

Coffee pot, nickel plated copper, covered spout, turned wooden handle & knob on lid, "Rome 4" on bottom, Rome, NY, early 20th C. **$18.00-$28.00**

Coffee pot, painted tin with scrolls & flowers on dark green ground, somewhat worn, tapering sides, nice scrolled strap handle, deep conical lid, very handsome, American, 11"H, mid 19th C. **$800.00-$1500.00**

Coffee pot, peacock blue & white enamelware, gooseneck spout, American, early 20th C. **$140.00-$175.00**

Coffee pot, pieced tin, extreme conical body with funnel top, strap handle, hinged lid with strap handle, curved spout support from neck where cone meets funnel, for drip coffee, extraordinary piece. American, 11"H, 19th C. **$300.00-$500.00**

Coffee pot, pieced tin, very tall & thin, Shaker style, American, 12"H, early 19th C. **$55.00-$70.00**

• Shortly after the McKinley Tariff went into effect, a budding industry of rolling out iron & steel plates, then tin plating them, needed to grow quickly to satisfy the enormous demands of the consumers — tinsmiths & factory makers of pots, pans & cans. This article appeared in Jan. 1892 *The Metal Worker*: **"Tin Plate Sizes.** — Tin-plate manufacturers are still feeling their way with reference to sizes and gauges and nomenclature in general. A few concerns are turning out 14 x 20 and 20 x 28 plates of IC and IX gauge (a common grade and a better but not best grade), but greater thought is being given to the wants of the consumers in this matter than any one outside of a very small circle would suppose. No one seems inclined to erect (tin plate) works which shall be restricted to the sizes of plates heretofore current, (which would make) it impossible to produce larger sizes on occasion. All are disposed to so manage that they can turn out whatever a consumer may desire. The year that is just opening (1892) will, no doubt, decide many of the questions which are still open. Gauge designations have already been partially established upon a basis differing from that of British manufacturers." Next the journal listed all the "tin-plate works in operation and projected" — a scant 32 of them, mostly in Ohio & Pennsylvania. • To give the other side, they quoted from a circular sent out by a group of tin plate consumers: "If the tin-plate industry can be transferred to this country within a reasonable time and without damage to our business and the hundreds of thousands of American workmen employed at our factories, giving us a cheap raw material as that obtained before the increased tax was levied on it, we realize we will be the greatest beneficiaries. ... It is a matter of business that we have had to pay (since the McKinley bill passed) over $10,000,000 more for the tin plates we use in our factories and workshops, and that the present duty will add every year over 15 million to the cost of our material.

"At the present moment (Dec. 10), not one sheet of coke tins, which constitute over half of our entire requirements, has yet been put on the market by the American manufacturers and the present output of all kinds by American manufacturers) does not constitute 1%

of the entire consumption of tin plate in America."

Coffee pot, pieced tin with diagonal seams, straight spout with thin brace at top, slanted sides, braced handle. If this is not early 19th C, at least it was made from small pieces of tin. (Tin was only available in small sheets during 18th & early 19th Cs, imported , mostly?, from England. But nothing would stop a frugal tinsmith from using pieced scrap tin from larger, later sheets.) Style sometimes called "Shaker", American, 9½"H, early 19th C.   **$75.00-$95.00**

• **Tin Plate Sizes.** — All the main writers on tin disagree on sizes of imported sheet tin available at different times to American smiths, except that in earliest days of American tinsmithing (the latter part of the 18th C), and for 90 + years in the 19th C, sheets tended toward the small. It is supposed that most if not all tinwares in use in America prior to the 1st quarter of the 18th C were finished wares imported from England (although sometimes made with German tinplate). Shirley Spaulding DeVoe (see Bibliography), who has written the most about it, reproduced a size chart from c.1817, in *The Tinsmiths of Connecticut*, pp.188-189. She writes that American tinsmiths imported tin plate, from Britain (Wales) & Germany, until America had its own rolling mills after 1890s. • DeVoe gives the commonest size of early 19th C tin plate as 10" x 13¾". Heavier plate was 15" x 11". "When or if the early tinsmith ever used a tin sheet larger … than 15 x 11", she writes, "cannot be determined but it was probably first imported when tin was admitted duty-free by the Tariff Act of 1833." (p. 126, DeVoe's *The Art of the Tinsmith, English and American*). The 1890 McKinley Tariff act(s) raised tariffs on tin needed by tin plate-consumers (utensil & can makers, etc.), forcing an American tin plate industry into being. • Jeannette Lasansky, in *To Cut, Piece, & Solder* (see Bibliography) "Tinsmith(s) always worked with small sheets of metal, initially a 16" square. By 1915 the tinplate sheet had increased in size to a standard 14" x 20". Terneplate (roofing tin plated with a lead & tin alloy, not meant for cookware) came … as large as 28" x 40". These larger sizes meant that some shapes could be cut out in one piece, but generally the tinsmith was always restricted in this regard, having to make many of his forms out of seamed pieces." (p.76). • P. W. Flower (p. 156, *History of the Trade In Tin*, 1880) gives two 1870s sizes to show the range: 10" x 14" for a tin can to 40" x 28" for roofing "in the Western states of America."

Coffee pot, pink agateware with handpainted petunias, nickeled brass & copper trim including breast-band, spout, lid & base, probably Manning & Bowman, late 19th C.   **$225.00-$350.00**

Coffee pot, polished cast aluminum, sort of egg shaped body, flat on bottom, in what manufacturer called a "graceful Dutch shape", hinged stepped lid made with perforated strainer appendage that fits exactly over small lip or spout, turned wooden handle, "which can readily be replaced if accidentally charred" (and I've seen quite a few with the handles charred on the lower end). "Monar-cast", mfd by Monarch Aluminum Ware Co., Cleveland, OH, c.1915.   **$20.00-$25.00**

Coffee pot, punched tin, simply decorated with strong tulip and leaves on upper part of body, flowers with 6 petals below, spiraled ring border around flared foot, crooked spout, braced strap handle, nearly flat lid with button finial, out & in body pieced from 2 truncated cones (also called an inverted cone body by some cataloguers), the shorter below, joined at the "waist", ⅓ way from bottom, marked with two initials "A" and "R", probably those of owners, Pennsylvania, about 10"H, dated 1867. • This piece from the Lamb collection was sold at Pennypacker's in 1976. Price then was $2,300.00. A similar pot, 11"H, with punched design of flower pots with tulips, very attractive curve to spout, was in the Richard Withington March 4, 1989 auction at Andover, MA, and sold for a low $1100.00. Very surprising because it is right as right can be.   **$3000.00-$5000.00**

Coffee pot, punched tin, slightly battered but still graceful crooked neck spout, design of small pot with large tulip & leaves punched on one side (perhaps on both?), braced strap handle, traces of "old black paint & light rust". **Punched tin is not punctured tin.** It refers to a very rare form of decoration, done by tapping a small punch along the outlines of flowers, urns, birds, eagles, on what will be the inside of the vessel, in order to make a raised beaded line. Pennsylvania, 11"H, mid 19th C. • Sold at Garth's, July 28, 1989 for: **$2600.00**

Coffee pot, purplish brown enamelware, domed enameled top, turned wooden handle, possibly Manning, Bowman & Co., 9"H, late 19th C.   **$180.00-$255.00**

Coffee pot, red enamelware, gooseneck, nickeled lid, 20th C.   **$75.00-$120.00**

Coffee pot, robin's egg blue & white agateware, gooseneck spout, American, 19th C.   **$125.00-$165.00**

Coffee pot, sky blue & white speckled enamelware, gooseneck spout, bail handle with wood grip, late 19th C, early 20th.   **$130.00-$185.00**

Coffee pot, slant-sided, copper with tin lid with unusual copper ring finial, wire bail with wooden handle, American, mid 19th C.   **$75.00-$100.00**

Coffee pot, so-called French style, cast aluminum in 4 parts, viz. lid (which looks like a fat biscuit cutter), perforated drip insert, urn shaped pot with black handle & funny fat little spout or lip up at top rim, separate sort of flared ruffled base, "makes coffee without boiling" by putting ground coffee in the cylindrical insert and pouring in water. Wagner Ware, 3 pt. capacity, 1930. • A nearly identical pot, except for a more traditional gooseneck spout & rounder handle, was reported by collector Mozelle Bamber, of MA. Hers, which is marked on the bottom "Super Maid Cook-Ware", is 10½"H or 11¼"H on base, which is about 4" diameter. Another collector from New Hampshire wrote to report one that is unmarked except for "Made in Canada".   **$30.00-$40.00**

Coffee pot, straight spout, japanned & polychrome decorated tin, American, prob. CT or PA, 8⅝"H, 19th C.   **$1750.00-$2000.00**

Coffee pot, straight-sided, tin, with copper bottom, turned wooden handle painted black, American, late 19th C.   **$45.00-$55.00**

Coffee pot, teal & white swirled agateware, 11½"H, TOC.   **$200.00-$300.00**

Coffee pot, thresher's boiler type — that is, a very big one for the harvest crew, green & white swirl enamelware, American (?), TOC.   **$165.00-$200.00**

Coffee pot, tin, 3 loop tin finial on the lid, prob. CT, 6"H, c.1830s to 1850. **$95.00-$125.00**

Coffee pot, tin & Britannia, E. B. Manning, Meriden, CT, mid 19th C. **$65.00-$85.00**

Coffee pot, tin, conical shape with straight side spout, strap handle, simple but very unusual, the design as spare & elegant as the sleek Italian designs of 100 years later, American, 8¾"H, prob. 2nd quarter 19th C. **$95.00-$125.00**

• **The Thirteenth Annual Report of the Commissioner of Labor.** *1898. Hand and Machine Labor*, Volume 1 (Washington: GPO, 1899) compares two methods of making a 2-quart coffee pot from tin. The conical pot above is about the same age as the "primitive" one described below. "Under the modern method the bodies of the pots were cut with a steam cutting machine in 15 minutes. Under the primitive method the tin was cut with stock shears by hand and required 4 hours, but before the tin could be cut ... it was necessary to mark it out, and this required an additional ... 2 hours and 40 minutes, so that ... the hand work required nearly 27 times as long as the machine work." The "primitive" method dates to 1840; the machine method to 1895. *The Report* lists a tinsmith's 30 production steps — using tools from an awl & hatchet stake to swage & peening hammer — as: Marking out bodies of pots; — cutting out bodies; — turning top edges for wire; — putting in wire; — peening down top edges; — swaging bead around tops; — forming bodies; — cutting out handles, spouts, and rim; — forming spouts; — turning edges of handled for wire; — putting in wire and forming hinges; — peening down edges of handles; — cutting out hinges; forming tin lips on hinges; — forming handles; — marking out covers; — cutting out covers; — raising covers; — turning edges of covers; — peening down edges of covers; — putting knobs on covers; — soldering spouts and seams in bodies; — turning edges for bottoms; marking out bottoms; — edging bottoms; — snapping on bottoms; — peening down edges of bottoms; — double-seaming bottoms; — soldering all seams. • The 22 steps for machine-making, taken by 27 different workers with 18 job descriptions, are: Cutting out bodies; perforating for spouts; edging bodies for wire; forming bodies; grooving bodies together; wiring tops; notching bodies for hinge; boring bodies for bottom; cutting out bottoms; double-seaming bodies, cutting out spouts; forming spouts; cutting out handles; beading handles; forming handles; cutting out covers; drawing covers; crimping covers; notching covers; punching covers & putting in knobs; soldering all seams; testing pots; *plus overseeing establishment; furnishing power; and firing boiler (for steam power)."* Note that the soldering was also done by hand in the factory setting of 1895.

Coffee pot, tin, finial is a grape cluster, brass ID plate with an eagle, and reads "The National Tea and Coffee Pot Company", J. B. Smith's, Milwaukee, WI, 1859 patent #22737 (or 22787?), & Nov. 19, 1867's #71236 & #71237. Smith patented this & at least two more coffee pots later. **$85.00-$100.00**

Coffee pot, tin, lighthouse (or slanted sides) shape, with domed lid & ring finial, wire bail handle, great braced handle, American. 3 qt. capacity.early to mid 19th C. Even plain, this is quite a looker, especially the braced handle. A lot of modern designers — even (or especially?) architects — could learn something by studying such a coffee pot as this. **$45.00-$65.00**

Coffee pot, tin, "out-and-in" body of 2 different height truncated cones, the bottom one upside down, joined at the large ends around the "waist", with crooked spout originating in lower part, braced strap handle with grip, hinged high conical lid with scrolled double ring finial, rather high foot. Elaborately decorated with an eagle(?) & foliage in wrigglework or wriggle work, accomplished by tapping a small chisel-like tool with a mallet or hammer so that it makes tiny bounces or skips & cuts a sort of chased zigzaggy line in the metal somewhat similar to brightwork in silver. This is probably the most highly desired type of tinware, more than painted tin, and is sometimes called wrigglesware - unmarked, but if Lansansky is correct, "M.B." is the maker, therefore prob. PA, 10¾"H, 19th C. • According to Jeanette Lasansky, in her *To Cut, Piece, and Solder*, "Only one maker of tinware used this (wriggle work) technique ... unfortunately ... (his) identity ...remains a mystery — only two of his pieces have initials (M.B.), and none are dated." (p. 72) Her book shows four pieces. **$5000.00-$7000.00**

Coffee pot, tin, slanted sides, straight spout, scroll-y handle with spur lid rest, American, mid 19th C. **$70.00-$85.00**

Coffee pot, tin, brass ID plate reads "The Young America", American, dated 1859. • There's a town in Minnesota, known to devotees of sweepstakes, called "Young America", but I couldn't find, among the several coffee pots patented in 1859, any from that state. **$65.00-$80.00**

Coffee pot, tin with copper bottom to aid heat conduction, American, late 19th or early 20th C. • **German vocabulary** — Kaffeekanne: coffee pot. **$35.00-$45.00**

Coffee pot, tin with fluted spout, delicate mushroom finial on lid, cast iron handle with spur lid rest, beautifully made, elegant detail, American, late 19th C. **$75.00-$90.00**

Coffee pot, tole, decorated tin, decorations in perfect condition, red, yellow & green on black asphaltum ground, braced strap handle, attractive finial, American, early 19th C. • **Color & Added Value.**—These vary in price considerably. Generally speaking, blue background — most $$, red is 2nd, yellow 3rd, black 4th, & brown last. Price range below for most tole-decorated, well-formed, good condition pots. • For this black one: **$1000.00-$2000.00**

Coffee pot, turquoise & white spattered enamel deep blue trim, American, late 19th or early 20th C. **$200.00-$255.00**

Coffee pot, white & black enamelware, tall & thin, American, 19th C. **$150.00-$170.00**

Coffee pot trivet, cast iron, 5 legs, Griswold, late 19th, early 20th C. **$55.00-$75.00**

Coffee roaster, cast iron, 3 part, pot with 3 legs, wire bail handle, pivoting agitator with tall vertical handle, slotted lid, pat'd by F. Humphrey of Philadelphia, mfd by I. A. Sheppard & Co., marked Philadelphia, PA (Baltimore was another Sheppard location). Size #1: 5¼"H x 8½" diameter, pat'd Mar. 13, 1866. **$175.00-$225.00**

Coffee roaster, cast iron frame with 3 legs & thin wire bail, side handles that are held clamped together by the slip-on long dogleg crank, cast iron 2 piece globe shaped container rests in frame, looks like something from a planetarium, "Woods Patent", mfd by Roys & Wilcox & Co., Thomas R. Wood (Cincinnati, OH) R&W in Berlin, CT, ball: 6½" diameter with 5¼"L handles; frame: 2¾"H x 9" diameter, pat'd April 17, 1849. • Another very similar one seen is marked Roys & Wilcox, plus a patent date of May 17, 1859. This roaster was featured in the 1869 Dover Stamping Co. catalog. A handsome example was for sale by a dealer with a verv discerning eye and fabulous iron stock. **$350.00-$600.00**

Coffee roaster, for hearth, sheet iron cylinder with sliding "trap" door, long crooked crank handle out of one end, short iron rod out of other, fit into spit holder or other iron frame, Canadian or American, 20"L tip to tip, cylinder itself is 8¾"L x 6¼" diameter, sliding hatch opens to 2½", c.1840 to 1860. • **German vocabulary** — Kaffee-rostmaschine: coffee roaster. **$275.00-$350.00**

Coffee roaster, for hearth, sheet iron, cylindrical, long shaft & wooden handle knob, American (?), 50"L, early 19th C. **$200.00-$275.00**

Coffee roaster, heavy cast iron, straight sides, top crank that moves the 4 stirring "fingers" inside, 2 large upright fixed ring handles, looks like a cross between an ironclad Civil War submarine & a pirate's chest, not marked, American, 11"H x 8¾" diameter, mid-19th C. **$150.00-$175.00**

Coffee roaster, heavy sheet iron, looks like a sauce pan with a crank handle up from the lid, American, mid 19th C. • The Sept. 1846 *American Agriculturist* has a recipe for **Dandelion Coffee,** sent in by a reader of an British periodical, Cottage Gardening. "Dr. Harrison, of Edinburgh, prefers dandelion coffee to that of Mecca; and many persons all over the Continent prefer a mixture of succory* and coffee to coffee alone. Dig up the roots of dandelion, wash them well, but do not scrape them, dry them, cut them into the size of peas, and then roast them in an earthen pot, or coffee roaster of any kind. The great secret of good coffee, is, to have it fresh burnt and fresh ground." (*I don't know if "succory" is the same as "chicory".) **$140.00-$175.00**

Coffee roaster, heavy sheet iron, sauce pan or frying pan style with long handle, fitted lid with small oval trap door, crank in top, American, 8" diameter, (another of these is 7½" diameter x 2½" deep, with overall length 16" including handle), c.1870s or 1880s. • **Reproduction alert.**— This sauce pan roaster has been reproduced in heavy steel, with same long handle. **$45.00-$55.00**

Coffee roaster, key wound clockwork mechanism, sets over 2 range eyes, cast iron frame, tall housing of works at one end, long horizontal wire mesh cylinder holds beans, hemi-cylindrical pieced tin cover with strap handle fits down over the wire canister, diagonal revolving plates inside to move the beans around, "American Coffee Roaster", pat'd by C. A. Mills, Hazel Green, WI, 9"H x 18½"L, pat'd Nov. 7, 1863 & April 28, 1868. • In his specifications, Mr. Mills wrote "The frame and upright plates may be cast iron, the vessel of sheet metal, and the wheels of the clock mechanism may be of cast or wrought metal, the teeth being cut. I do not, however, confine myself to any particular material or mode of manufacture." **$350.00-$425.00**

Coffee roaster, sheet iron & brass, aluminum, alcohol heating lamp in base, clockwork action, corrugated drum inside bounces beans around, snap lid, looks like a percolator inside, detachable crank looks like a Victrola handle, has 2 speeds, "Rapide" & "Lente" plus "Arrette" (stop), French, TOC. **$175.00-$225.00**

Coffee roaster, sheet iron can & cast iron frame, fits over range eye, sliding door in the canister body, side crank,

Griswold Mfg. Co., 9" diameter, c.1880s. • **German vocabulary** — Kaffee-Brenner, also Kaffee-Roster: coffee scorcher/burner, or coffee roaster. **$85.00-$100.00**

Coffee roaster, sheet iron, lid with hinged trapdoor for beans, brass gear in center operates iron stirrers inside, American, about 2" deep x 10" diameter, mid 19th C. **$150.00-$170.00**

Coffee roaster, sheet iron, pan shape, fitted lid, lower handle is a pointed shaft, as if it once had wooden handle, no mark, American (?), pan is 7¼" diameter, 20¼"L overall. mid 19th C. **$75.00-$95.00**

Coffee roaster, sheet iron pan style, hinged trapdoor opening in fixed lid through which blades inside are visible, cast iron crank has old repair, marked "#22", American, 19th C. **$75.00-$100.00**

• **Old Repair.**— When it doesn't qualify as a make-do or a repaired piece with some quirkiness or idiosyncracy or charm in the repair, an "old" repair takes away less value than a recent repair. As to whether or not it is an old or new repair, you must examine all the elements — method, metal, condition — to decide. Because cast iron is so friable, and pieces tend to crack or break off, legs, stanchions, rods, wingnuts, finials & handles all tend to "go missing" as they say in British mysteries. Old repairs are likely to be frankly repairs; modern repairs, by collectors or dealers, are likely to be much less obvious, and cast in iron from a matching part, or from another piece, or even from a carved pattern mold. It is not bad form to ask if anything is a replaced part, or at least to examine things for which you are paying a lot with a magnifying glass. **$75.00-$100.00**

Coffee roaster, stove top, sheet iron oblong box, shallow, with longish handle with ring at end. Hinged lid has pierced holes in it, American, about 20"L including handle, 19th C. • The pierced lid gave Mary Earle Gould pause, in *Antique Tin and Tole Ware*, and she thought this might have been a "fire carrier" or "coal carrier" but certain stains inside led her to believe it might have served a double duty. She also had heard it might be a corn popper. Although she didn't mention any names, she wrote that some of these had been found with manufacturers' names stamped in the metal. **$75.00-$100.00**

Coffee urn, chrome plated, orange Bakelite® (or other molded phenolic resin) handles & spigot handle, "Champion", looks c.1930s but can't find in directories between 1932 & 1944. **$25.00-$30.00**

Coffee urn, copper body, tinned inside, with slender vertical open top cylinder into which fits a heated cast iron slug (looks like a sash weight) that would keep the coffee hot. Cast brass handles & spigot, side handles have opalescent knobby white glass grips, spigot has more opaque white knob, square base with 4 small feet, high decorative rather churchy dome lid with high copper finial, King Manufactory, Hull, England, 16"H, c. mid 19th C (?). **$275.00-$350.00**

Coffee urn, copper & brass, domed lid, cabriole legs (that is, a crookt leg with a pronouncedly curved or bent "knee"), nice detail, American, late 19th C. **$150.00-$200.00**

Coffee urn, copper, brass spigot, wooden handles, on stand with solid fuel burner underneath, mfd by Sternau, NYC, TOC. **$185.00-$225.00**

Coffee urn, electric, chrome plated brass & copper ball, on fluted base, white plastic handles, knob on top, spigot handle, and ring base with 4 small ball feet, looks like a little robot baby, but would "put poise in your parties"! "Table Electric" by Chase Brass & Copper Co., Inc., division of Kennecott Copper Corp., 25 cup capacity, c.1937. • Crossover interest from Art Deco, Art Moderne, & Chase name brand collectors. **$65.00-$85.00**

Coffee urn, electric, nickel plated, very ornate, with matching creamer & sugar, "Universal", mfd by Landers, Frary & Clark, only 11"H, patents from 1910 to 1920s. **$35.00-$45.00**

Coffee urn, for restaurant or hotel use, copper with brass trim & handles & spout, very lovely graceful form, American, 21"H. TOC. **$200.00-$225.00**

Coffee urn, heavy polished aluminum, electric heating unit concealed in slightly flared perforated base, tall with 2 body sections, each with black plastic side handles, domed lid with black plastic knob, glass viewing tube above spigot, West Bend Aluminum Co., West Bend, WI, made 48 cups, late 1940s. **$15.00-$20.00**

Conjurer kettle, or Camp Kettle, heavy tin tea kettle in odd shape — a very very short cylinder with flat bottom, flat top with small "biscuit cutter" lid, curved spout comes out of top, with normally sized & placed forged iron handle. This was supposed to set down into a tall cylindrical portable sheet iron stove, with very short strap iron feet, in the base of which was built a small fire over a draft hole. Conjurers, or conjurors, were meant for cooking in non-kitchen settings, and were said to require but 3 sheets of paper to cook a steak. English (?), 8" diameter, mid 19th C. **$30.00-$40.00**

• **"The Conjuror, or Camp Kettle.**— Some years ago, an apparatus of this name was very generally sold in London, where some may yet be found at the ironmongers, and is remarkable for the expedition with which a small piece of meat may be dressed in it; sufficient for one person may be done in less than five minutes; and a pint of water can be boiled in the same time, the only fuel being half a sheet of thick brown paper. In the interior of a cylinder of sheet iron, an iron cone ..., perforated, is placed over a hole in the bottom. A shallow dish of tin, with its [flat] cover, holds the meat, suppose a beefsteak, and fits exactly into the top of the cylinder. There is a little door on the side, through which the paper wrapped round the cone is set fire to; the door is then shut. The heat of the flame being confined altogether within the cylinder, very soon cooks the meat, an effect which is assisted by the steam being confined by the cover of the dish. The smoke passes off by a pipe. ... This little machine has been found extremely useful, not only in fishing or shooting parties, and other occasions where a dinner might be required at a distance from home, but likewise in numberless instances in the house where cooked meat or hot water may be wanted quickly, and when it is inconvenient to light a fire, particularly in summer. It is, perhaps, impossible to carry economy, convenience, and expedition farther than by this apparatus; but it must be admitted that by this process the meat is neither roasted, fried, baked, nor stewed; but it is completely done, and, with proper management, very palatable for those who have a good appetite." *Webster & Parkes, An Encyclopedia of Domestic Economy.* 1848 NY edition of English book of 1845. Sounds for all the world like a microwave oven! • Price range for kettle, which in a pure sense, is incomplete — not being with its conjurer. **$30.00-$40.00**

Funnel for percolators, enamelware, looks like long cone divided so the top half is like a coffee cup with handle, then a wide flange or lip almost like a saucer, then long conical neck with very small opening at bottom. The flange allowed the percolator funnel to rest on the edge of various size coffee pots, to turn them into percolators. Matthai - Ingram, but not marked, about 6½" or 7"L x 4½" diameter, c.1890s. **$35.00-$50.00**

Hot beverage urn, for restaurant or hotel, copper with brass fittings, brass spigots, domed covers with knobs, American, 20"H x 18"W, TOC. **$400.00-$500.00**

Hot water kettle, cast iron, pit bottom, magnificent & beautiful round body, short gooseneck spout, falling forged iron bail, hinged lid lifts up, hinge opposite spout, the flattish lid has name, plus a beaded design in a circle, "Abbott & Noble", Philadelphia, 10¾"H x about 9½" diameter, late 19th C. **$115.00-$145.00**

Percolator urn, alcohol burner below, plated metal, antique style body with rounded belly, cabriole legs, side handles, glass percolator top, "Universal Percolator Co.", Landers, Frary & Clark, 12"H, pat'd 1907-1910. **$135.00-60.00**

Percolator urn, electric, chromium plated paneled Georgian style urn, ebonized wood handles & spigot handle, on 3 legged base, Royal Rochester Co., No. E639, mfd by Robeson Rochester Corp., Rochester, NY, 15"H, c.1930s. **$30.00-$45.00**

Percolator urn, electric, copper, tinned inside, with straight-sided "milk can" style urn, glass dome, black Bakelite® (?) side handles & spigot handle, on rather heavy brass tripod stand, "Universal", mfd by Landers, Frary & Clark, New Britain, CT, pat'd May 22, 1899. • This almost looks Arts & Crafts, and the period is right, so possibly it has some extra value now to the avid A&C collector. **$75.00-$110.00**

Percolator urn, electric, nickel plated, on 3 long cabriole (so-called "Queen Anne") legs, glass percolating top with high domed metal lid & finial, plug screws into bulb socket, Simplex Electric Heating Co., Cambridge, MA, 1906. **$45.00-$55.00**

Percolator urn, electric, silver plated, octagonal base, octagonal paneled urn, Georgian style (of late 18th or early 19th C), "Automatic Percolator", Hotpoint, Edison Electric Appliance Co., 12"H, c.1930s. **$50.00-$65.00**

Percolator urn, electric, nickeled brass and iron, glass, turned wood, very handsome metal urn with spigot, surmounted by sugar-bowl shaped glass percolating bowl, lion's paw feet, side handles, "Type ECP", mfd by General Electric, c.1918-1919. **$60.00-$80.00**

Tea ball, perforated spun aluminum acorn with chain, 1920s or 1930s. **$5.00-$7.00**

Tea ball, sterling silver, in shape of fancy teapot, hexagonal body with canted sides, classical handle, high domed lid lifts off for tea leaves, the whole body perforated with fine holes, The Watson Co., Attleboro, MA, about 1½"H, c.1930. **$25.00-$30.00**

Tea bowl, mocha decoration in blue on white band, yellowware, small foot, English, 7⅞" diameter, mid 19th C. **$275.00-$300.00**

Tea caddy, chromolith decorated tin with image of a flag and a man, American, 1880s-90s. **$35.00-$45.00**

Tea caddy, enameled copper, very Oriental-looking, with birds, butterflies & flowers on white & turquoise background, 4½"H x 5"D, late 19th C. **$85.00-$100.00**

Tea & coffee pot, shiny tin plate, black wooden handle and knob, marked only "Extra Tin Plate", American, 2 qt. capacity, TOC. **$25.00-$35.00**

Tea kettle, blue & white enameled heavy cast iron, late 19th C. • A lot of these big kettles are actually <u>water kettles,</u> meant to heat water for tea (or anything else). **$75.00-$125.00**

Tea kettle, blue & white swirl agateware, white lining, swivel lid, "Wrought Iron Range Co.", St. Louis, MO, 4 qt. capacity, late 19th C. **$125.00-$175.00**

Tea kettle, brass & copper, possibly stripped of nickel plating, forged iron bail with turned wood grip, white porcelain knob on lid, 5½"H including knob, late 19th C. **$40.00-$55.00**

Tea kettle, brown & white enameled cast iron, European or American, 2 qt. size, TOC. **$125.00-$155.00**

Tea kettle, cast aluminum, high bail handle with wooden grip, "Colonial", Wagner Ware, Sidney, OH, 5 qts., c.1902 to 1920. **$20.00-$25.00**

Tea kettle, cast aluminum, lid swivels sideways, neat little filling hole & lid at top of spout, falling wire bail handle with turned wooden grip, flat bottom, "Colonial Design, Safety Fill #8", Griswold Mfg. Co., Erie, PA, 9¾" diameter, 6 qt. capacity, pat'd Sept. 9, 1913. **$45.00-$55.00**

Tea kettle, cast aluminum, rounded body with small flat part under spout, hinged lid, short fat gooseneck spout, coiled wire bail, "No. 330", Wear-Ever, T. A. C. U. Co. (Aluminum Cooking Utensil Co., sales division of Pittsburg Reduction Co.), 8¼" diameter, 1903-1915. **$35.00-$45.00**

Tea kettle, cast aluminum, side-swiveling lid, wire bail handle with wooden grip, "Colonial Tea Kettle", Wagner Ware, 6 qt. size, pat'd 1902. **$28.00-$35.00**

Tea kettle, cast aluminum, sliding lid, turned wood handle with wooden knob, oblong shaped kettle, very dramatic, "Wagner Ware Grand Prize Tea Kettle", 12⅝"L x 8⅞"W, pat'd Sept. 28, 1916. **$70.00-$80.00**

Tea kettle, cast aluminum, smooth sides, slightly domed swingaway lid, flat bottom, wire bail with turned wood grip, "Griswold #6", 8⅞" diameter at bottom, c.1920. **$40.00-$55.00**

• **Contenders for First Aluminum Casting.**— A 1917 article on Griswold in *House Furnishing Review* states "During the period 1890 to 1894, the Griswold Manufacturing Company in conjunction with the original Pittsburgh Aluminum Company — now the Aluminum Company of America — first made, in an experimental way, aluminum ware. This aluminum ware was cast in sand molds, and was the first cast aluminum ware known to have been made in the world. A few of these first pieces of cast aluminum ware were offered to the trade during those years, and after long years of service, they have still been found to be in perfect condition.

"A process of hardening the surface of aluminum ware was later discovered. After casting, by a secret electrical treatment, the surface is tempered, hardening and closing all the pores of the metal. This 'tempered surface,' as it is called, is positive proof against discoloration or absorption, and the ware remains for all time a silvery gray." The article adds "the first big trade on Griswold cast aluminum tempered ware came through their London office" and only later became known all through the world!

• Auburn Hollow Wax Co., of Auburn, NY, made at least one exhibition piece of cast aluminum — a tea kettle, and it may have actually been the first cast aluminum kitchen piece made. This was reported in *The Metal Worker*, April 30, 1892; they may have made a typo with Wax instead of Ware, but I can't find the name elsewhere to check.

Tea kettle, cast aluminum, very modern style, low arched handle, large hole in molded spout, for filling & pouring, "Magnalite #4135", mfd by Wagner Ware, 10" diameter, c.1930s. **$45.00-$55.00**

Tea kettle, cast aluminum, with domed lid, Wagner Ware, small size. 20th C. **$25.00-$35.00**

Tea kettle, cast aluminum with highly polished finish on rounded body, lovely iron wire falling bail handle in "chef's hat" profile characteristic of kettles from the early 19th C, coiled grip, long inquisitive gooseneck spout, "Wear-Ever", T. A. C. U. Co. (The Aluminum Cooking Utensil Co.), 9" diameter, c.1920. **$35.00-$45.00**

Tea kettle, cast iron, "Rhine Mfg. Co.", 19th C. **$35.00-$45.00**

Tea kettle, cast iron, "Foxell, Jones & Millard", York, NY (?), (Troy, NY?), 1870s, **$40.00-$55.00**

Tea kettle, cast iron, 3 very short peg feet, long casting gate on bottom, very pronounced angular gooseneck, forged bail, vertical casting seams on both sides, circumferential casting seam around middle, and including lower part of spout, domed lid with riveted cast brass knob, no mark, American, 7"H, 2nd quarter 19th C. • The value here is in the age, the nice form, & especially the spout. **$200.00-$250.00**

Tea kettle, cast iron, 'bowler hat' profile wire bail handle, domed lid with spoked ridges out from squared finial, pit bottom, "Higgins, Foxell & Martin", Troy, NY, c.1860. **$65.00-$85.00**

Tea kettle, cast iron, brass cover, fixed handle, 19th C. • **German vocabulary** — <u>Tee kessel</u>: tea kettle; <u>Eisener kessel</u>: iron kettle; and <u>Messinger kessel</u>: brass kettle. **$95.00-$120.00**

Tea kettle, cast iron, bulbous with gooseneck spout, small feet, iron handle, prob. American, mid-19th C. **$195.00-$220.00**

Tea kettle, cast iron, enameled, swirled cobalt blue & white, bail handle, short 'duckneck' spout, marked "St. Louis Stove Works", MO, early 20th C, poss. late 19th. **$65.00-$80.00**

Tea kettle, cast iron, flat bottom, duckneck (short fat gooseneck) spout, casting line curves down & around close to bottom at back, falling bail of nickeled wire with heat-dissipating coil for hand grip, swivel lid covers entire top, and pivots at back where handle is attached, with knob at opposite edge. The center part of the lid, like a mesa, rises up & has sizeable flat top — touted as being a place where you could set something else to keep it hot, "Favorite", Favorite Stove & Range Co., Piqua, OH, advertised July 1890. • This line was available in pit bottom style, & in various finishes: plain cast iron, "milled" iron (?), galvanized, nickel plated, & nickel plated with white porcelain enamel inside. • **Wagner Too?**— In Jan.

1892, an editorial notice in *The Metal Worker*, told about a new company's new line of "high grade hollow ware, high polish or nickeled finish, including a tea kettle available flat bottom or pit bottom, in seven sizes from 8 to 30 gallons. The linecut used to illustrate the kettle is as close to identical as possible to the linecut showing the Favorite Piqua kettle 18 months before, considering that two differerent firms of cut engravers made the pictures. In addition, a low kettle with bail, round tipping handle and 3 peg feet is shown; it is also the same as an earlier Favorite, though engraved by a different firm. The use of the same linecuts was widespread in retail catalogs, but one wonders what's the case here? Did Wagner copy Favorite's kettles themselves, detail for detail? Did they only make a similar one and require of their engravers to furnish them with "an engraving like this one here" … tossing the Favorite one on the artist's desk? No mention is made in *Metal Worker* about the similarity; but this is no surprise as many trade magazines then, as now, were a mix of advertising, editorial puffery, editorial posturing, and serious facts. **$55.00-$65.00**

Tea kettle, cast iron, flat bottom, hexagonal dome on flat flanged lid, forged bail, marked "B " on bottom & a large "4" on side, American, 5½"H exclusive of lid, mid 19th C **$140.00-$160.00**

Tea kettle, cast iron, forged bail handle, hinged lid, nice little one, marked "I. Brandt & M'Dowell", 4 qt. capacity, 19th C. **$75.00-$85.00**

Tea kettle, cast iron, forged bail with turned wood grip, side-swing or pivoting hinged lid, pit bottom, heavily incrusted on outside, marked on lid "John A. Goewey, #8", Albany, NY, 19th C. **$75.00-$90.00**

Tea kettle, cast iron, forged iron handle, sideswing lid with no knob, 3 short peg legs, long straight casting gate on bottom is filed down, on side is a sort of palm leaf decoration cast in, marked only "S.C.", which may be Spencer Cole, poss. CT, poss. late 18th C or early 19th. **$350.00-$400.00**

Tea kettle, cast iron, gooseneck, 3 short feet, forged bail, American, 8"H x 10" diameter, 19th C. **$100.00-$120.00**

Tea kettle, cast iron, gooseneck spout, marked only "B romwich", must be Bromwich, England, where at least 2 iron foundries were. 2 qt. capacity, 19th C. **$45.00-$60.00**

Tea kettle, cast iron, gooseneck spout, bail handle, 3 small feet, American, late 18th or early 19th C. **$300.00-$350.00**

Tea kettle, cast iron, gooseneck spout, forged bail, "J. J. Siddons", "West Bromwich" , England, 2 qt. capacity, 19th C. • **Using a Gazetteer.** — Because there was some possibility that this was American, I checked a very useful reference book I bought not too long ago, called *The Centennial Gazetteer of the United States*, by A. von Steinwehr, published by J. C. McCurdy & Co. in 1875. It contains "a geographical and statistical encyclopedia of the states, territories, counties, townships, villages, post-offices, mountains, rivers, lakes, etc., in the American Union" and can be checked for place names from the 18th C through 1875. I checked because Bromwich is such a Connecticut-type name, but there was no Bromwich or West Bromwich anywhere in the "Union". **$75.00-$100.00**

Tea kettle, cast iron, gooseneck spout, forged iron bail handle unusual in that it's fixed in place, American, 7½"H overall, very small 1½ pt. capacity, early 19th C. **$190.00-$220.00**

Tea kettle, cast iron, pit bottom, chubby body with short duckneck spout, flat falling bail handle, levered lid with small thumb piece, "S. W. Ransom & Co. #8", pat'd by A. Ransom & R. D. Granger, Albany, NY, pat'd Mar. 19, 1861. **$60.00-$80.00**

Tea kettle, cast iron, pit bottom, decorative swivel lid with scrolls rather finely cast on it, "A. Bradley & Co., Pittsburg, PA", 1866. **$55.00-$80.00**

Tea kettle, cast iron, pit bottom, hinged lid, flat forged bail, "I. A. Sheppard & Co., Baltimore, MD" (they also had a foundry in Philadelphia), mid 19th C. • According to Leander Bishop's book on early manufacturing, Baltimore had, in 1860, 10 iron foundries (including stove makers), five brass founders, and 37 tin, copper, and sheet iron wares manufacturers. **$55.00-$75.00**

Tea kettle, cast iron, pit bottom, ornate scrolled casting on top of sides, 3 tiny peg feet, forged bail, slightly domed lid with tab handle, no mark, American, 7"H exclusive of lid, mid to late 19th C. **$80.00-$110.00**

Tea kettle, cast iron, slide away or swing lid, flat bail handle, interesting shape with a sort of decoy-like swooping line, pit bottom, no number or mfr's mark, American, 11" diameter including spout, 19th C. **$35.00-$45.00**

Tea kettle, cast iron, straight sides, high gooseneck spout, almost serpentine in its curves, with fabulous very wide flat "tu-tu" rim or flange making the kettle a pit bottom for range top, falling bail strap handle, American, very early 19th C, transition from hearth to range. **$300.00-$400.00**

Tea kettle, cast iron, swingaway pivoting lid, short stubby spout, pit bottom, small separate washer-like disc fits in depression at back end of lid where forged bail hooks on to lug, "Joseph Bell & Co. #9, Wheeling, WV", pat'd June 23, 1863. **$55.00-$75.00**

Tea kettle, cast iron, swinging lid, shallow pit bottom, fat spout, falling forged iron bail, "Bussey & McLeod", stove makers, Troy, NY, 8"H , pat'd Jan. 1, 1861. • **"To remove rust from Iron Ware and Stoves.**— New stove or range furniture is sometimes so much rusted as to make the use of it very inconvenient. Put into a rusty kettle as much hay as it will hold, fill it with water and boil many hours. At night set it aside, and the next day boil it again. Rub the rusty spots on a stove with sandpaper and then with sweet oil." Mary Hooker Cornelius, *The Young Housekeepers Friend*, Boston & NY: 1871, a later edition of the 1846 book. • **Seasoning New Ironwares.**— By 1884, the hay tip had become a recipe for seasoning a new cast iron utensil: "Boil Ashes or a bunch of hay or grass in a new iron pot before cooking in it; scour well with soap and sand, then fill with clean water, and boil one or two hours." *Practical Housekeeping*, 1884. • **Another recipe for seasoning:** "The best way to prepare a new iron kettle for use is to fill it with clean potato-peelings, boil them an hour or more, then wash the kettle with hot water, wipe it dry and rub it with a little lard; repeat the rubbing for six times after using. In this way you will prevent rust, and all the little annoyances liable to occur in the use of a new kettle." Emma Whitcomb Babcock, *Household Hints*, NY: Appleton, 1881. **$85.00-$120.00**

Tea kettle, cast iron, swivel lid, forged handle, casting gate on bottom, "Wisher & Co.", Philadelphia, PA, 1 gal. size, 6⅝"H, number "50" on bottom, pat'd 1861. • "Among the … colonists of New England many domestic utensils of Iron, with which the humblest dwellings are now (1868) supplied, were quite unknown. Others were comparatively rare, and were prized accordingly. The inventories of property, and the wills of many persons of good estate, particularly enumerate such articles as Iron pots, of which one or two appear frequently to have comprised the whole stock. These were often bequeathed to some member of the household as a mark of esteem. The exclusive use of wrought-iron tea-kettles, and the extreme rarity of iron vessels a century ago (1768), are evidences of the limited product of cast-iron ware, even in the parent country, whence the colonists were supplied with such things as were then in common use. The profusion of such wares in every department of culinary service at this time is the result of comparatively recent improvements in this branch of metallurgy, and is due to the substitution of coke, and still more of anthracite, for charcoal in the reduction of ores.'' pp. 488-89, Vol. I, Leander J. Bishop, *A History of American Manufactures from 1608-1860.* (Philadelphia, 1868). **$65.00-$80.00**

Tea kettle, cast iron, swivel lid, short spout, pit bottom, falling wire bail handle, ''Hardwick Stove Co.'', Cleveland, TN, TOC. **$55.00-$65.00**

Tea kettle, cast iron, swivel top, forged falling bail handle, pit bottom with long casting gate, ''Ohio Stove Co.'', Portsmouth, OH, 19th C. **$30.00-$40.00**

Tea kettle, cast iron, tapered sides, half circle hinged lid on top, forged bail, short duckneck spout with flat beveled underside, ''Leibrandt - M'Dowell'' on lid, Philadelphia, PA, late 19th C. **$45.00-$60.00**

Tea kettle, cheap, thin aluminum with nifty molded black plastic chef's head whistle-stopper, copper bottom, cane-wrapped handle, ''Raineland'' with 3 stars, 7¾''H, 20th C. **$15.00-$18.00**

Tea kettle, chrome body, copper bottom, strap handle painted red, plastic bird's head whistle, ''Revere'', 20th C. **$28.00-$35.00**

Tea kettle, chromium plated solid copper, red strap handle, copper bottom, very Art Deco design, cast white metal bird whistle, ''Made in U. S. A.'', 20th C. **$28.00-$35.00**

Tea kettle, cobalt blue enamelware, marked only ''Iron Range Company'', probably same as ''Wrought Iron Range Co.'', (St. Louis, MO), late 19th C. **$115.00-$145.00**

Tea kettle, cobalt enamelware, small size — sometimes called a ''Five-O'clock'', American, late 19th, early 20th C. **$50.00-$60.00**

Tea kettle, cobalt & white swirl agateware, 19th C. **$100.00-$150.00**

Tea kettle, copper, beautiful slender gooseneck spout, fixed handle, domed & ridged lid with high acorn finial, mid 19th C. **$140.00-$160.00**

Tea kettle, copper, dovetail seam, gooseneck spout, signed ''J M W E'', English (?), 19th C. **$100.00-$135.00**

Tea kettle, copper, dovetail seam, high dome lid, pit bottom, little hinged cover for spout, no marks, but hinged lid on spout prob. means English, 8 1/4''H, 2nd quarter 19th C. **$75.00-$100.00**

Tea kettle, copper, dovetail seams, forward thrust gooseneck spout, extremely well-formed falling strap handle of copper, more in profile of a bowler hat than a chef's hat, a few dings, marked ''G. Ebert'', PA, 6 1/2''H exclusive of handle, 19th C. • Went for $450.00 at Garth's Auctions, Delaware, OH, April 11-12, 1986. **$400.00-$550.00**

Tea kettle, copper, gooseneck spout, ''Finnemore, Granbrook'', 5 qt. capacity, early 19th C. **$225.00-$265.00**

Tea kettle, copper, gooseneck, with brass finial, unsigned (look on handle usually for stamped maker's name), prob. PA, marked #5, 1830s-40s. • Marked wares bring highest prices. **$295.00-$400.00**

Tea kettle, copper, highly polished, turned wooden grip on wire bail handle, porcelain knob on lid, ''Majestic'', TOC. **$85.00-$100.00**

Tea kettle, copper, on stand, with alcohol burner, meant for sideboard or tea table, Swedish, TOC. **$95.00-$110.00**

Tea kettle, copper, pieced, with horizontal seam in middle of widest part, cast brass handle frame & handle, no marks, 2 qt. size, 9'' diameter, mid 19th C or earlier. **$70.00-$90.00**

Tea kettle, copper, ringed around & shaped like a woven strawgrass bee skip, with birdwhistle in spout, early 20th C. **$28.00-$40.00**

Tea kettle, copper, tin inside, shaped like a squatty bell, with a very wide (impossible to tip over) base & a narrow opening, strap handle with grip, very large coffee boiler type spout, close fitting flat lid. I've never seen a real one or even seen a picture of an old one. An ad featuring this reproduction has explanatory notes. ''A replica of those (the copper captain's kettles) used aboard Nantucket Whalers during the 1800's. Use in the Captain's private pantry for warming his tea or grog.'' Landfall Collection, S. Norwalk, CT, Feb. 1975, *Early American Life* magazine. American (?), 10''H including handle, 10'' diameter at base, 1975. • A ship's decanter has a squatty, wide-bottomed body so that the center of gravity is as low as possible. I believe this ad is legitimate & that old kettles like this, dating to the early to mid 19th C exist. Price range is for repro, which sold for $47.75 ppd in 1975. **$30.00-$50.00**

Tea kettle, copper with brass finial, gooseneck spout, pit bottom, American (?), 6 qt. size, 19th C. **$200.00-$250.00**

Tea kettle, copper with brass trim, bail handle with black finished turned wood grip, wooden knob on lid, marked ''Rome'' where handle is attached, Rome, NY, 1898. • Possibly originally nickeled, as many are found that way. It is also possible they were offered both ways. **$45.00-$60.00**

Tea kettle, copper with gooseneck spout, falling handle, ''J. Gable, Lancaster, PA'', 14⅜''H with handle upright, 1843. • Marked, dated & good form = high price. **$450.00-$600.00**

Tea kettle, copper, with hollow copper handle, acorn finial on lid, gooseneck spout, English, late 19th C. **$95.00-$125.00**

Tea kettle, copper with iron bail handle, wood grip, lid with strap handle, short ''duckneck'' spout, marked ''Old Colony'', sounds like a Colonial Revival reproduction, (possibly Old Colony Foundry), (Bridgewater, MA), 7½''H x 89 ¼'' diameter, c.1920s. **$35.00-$45.00**

Tea kettle, copper with iron whistling bird in spout, late 19th C. • ''As arsenic frequently enters metallic compositions, especially those of copper and tin, it were much to be wished, that such compound metals could for ever be banished, at least from our Kitchens.'' Anthony Florian Madinzer Willich, *The Domestic Encyclopedia; or A Dictionary of Facts & Useful Knowledge... ,* 1st American edition, Philadelphia: W. Y. Birch & A. Small, 1803-04. **$65.00-$80.00**

Tea kettle, copper with simple scrolly handle, gooseneck spout, acorn finial, PA, prob. Philadelphia, 2 cup size, late 18th or early 19th C. • **Finial Shapes.**— In the "Silver" chapter of *The Complete Encyclopedia of Antiques*, compiled by *The Connoisseur*, edited by L. G. G. Ramsey, Hawthorn Books 1962, there is a short entry on finials, applicable to silver wares, but — factoring in the time lag for decorative elements being adopted for other metals, and an even longer lag involved in reaching America — we can use the facts when we study other metals. The timetable for finial shapes, as given in the *Encyclopedia*, is: Early 18th C = acorn; Rococo Period, Mid to Late 18th C = flame and pineapple; Classic Period, Late 18th to Early 19th C = urn, pine cone. For application to American copper tea kettles, you would probably be safe adding 50 to 100 or so years to the widespread use of acorns; then a much shorter time, say 30 to 50 years for the flame and pineapple; by the time you get to urns and pine cones, the period is only about 15 to 25 years behind in America compared to the Continent. As with all such "rules" of thumb, it's not true in every case. **$125.00-$150.00**

Tea kettle, copper, with unusual (probably replacement) green & white enameled lid, gooseneck spout, "Majestic", American, 5 qt. capacity, TOC. **$95.00-$125.00**

Tea kettle, deep blue & white enamelware over cast iron, low & squat, "Wrought Iron Range Co.", St. Louis, MO, 7" diameter, 4th quarter 19th C. **$85.00-$140.00**

Tea kettle, deep green agateware, white enameled interior, gooseneck spout, high domed hinged lid, "Made in Yugoslavia", early 20th C. **$50.00-$75.00**

Tea kettle, deep midnight blue enameled cast iron, low & squat of the type sometimes called a bachelor kettle, fixed handle with wooden grip, very short pouring lip or spout, American, 8" diameter base, late 19th C. **$50.00-$75.00**

Tea kettle, electric, chrome-plated metal, very modern in appearance. Electrical element is in back end of handle, & the kettle could also be used stovetop like any other tea kettle. "Speedmaster", (Waters - Genter?), (Minneapolis?), 1930s. **$35.00-$45.00**

Tea kettle, electric, silver plated copper in hammered finish, 8 sided & footed, with plain fat gooseneck spout, high rattan wrapped handle, acorn finial made of oak, designed by Peter Behrens, German, 1909. **$450.00-$600.00**

Tea kettle, galvanized cast iron, pit bottom, swoopy curved pouring spout with outthrust lower lip, falling bail handle with heat-dissipating "Alaska" coil grip, Matthai - Ingram, came in No's 6, 7, 8 and 9, c.1890s. • *Seeger & Guernsey's Cyclopaedia of the Manufactures and Products of the United States*, published in 1890, gives a very long list of stove & range founders; then a long list of **makers of cast iron hollowware,** some of whom also made stoves. It is probably by no means complete, but might be interesting to see here, and to check against your own collections. • Abendroth Brothers; Albany Stove; Belleville Stove; Samuel Booth; Bouton Foundry; Bramhall Deane; Broadway Machine Co.; Budke Mfg. Co.; Chamberlain Stove Co.; Cleveland Co-op Stove Co.; Clipper Mfg. Co.; Columbus Iron Works; Cribben, Sexton; Culter & Proctor Stove Co.; Defiance Machine Works; Great Western Stove Co.; Griswold Mfg. Co.; Highland Foundry; Hill, Whitney & Co.; Hoy & Co.; F. & L. Kahn & Bros.; Keokuk Stove Works; Lithgow Mfg. Co.; Magee Furnace; Manning, Bowman & Co.; Marietta Casting Co.; Marietta

Hollow Ware & Enamelling Co.; Mount Penn Stove Works; Ohio Stove Co.; Patton Mfg. Co.; J. S. & M. Peckham; Rathbone, Sard & Co.; John Savery's Son; I. A. Sheppard & Co.; Standard Mfg. Co. • A few years later, in *The Buyers' Guide (of) Thomas' Register of American Manufacturers*, NYC: 1905, the only listings are Atlanta Stove Works, Georgia; Blacklock Foundry Co., South Pittsburg, TN; Marietta Casting Co., and Marietta Holloware & Enamelling Co., Marietta, PA; Mobile Stove & Pulley Mfg. Co., Alabama; possibly Phillips & Buttorff Mfg. Co., Nashville; and Wagner Mfg. Co., Sidney, OH. **$35.00-$50.00**

Tea kettle, gray granite, bell-bottomed, gooseneck, bail handle, 19th C. • This particular one is a "shelf", or should I say "hob" piece, as the bottom has holes all over it. **$12.00-$15.00**

Tea kettle, green & tan enamelware, gooseneck spout, 1930s. **$25.00-$45.00**

Tea kettle, heavy pieced tin, gooseneck, same "chef's hat" or popover-shape outline to the fixed handle as is found on American copper teapots of the period, American, 5½"D at bottom, sides cant slightly outward as they go upward. 9⅜"H including handle, prob. 1st quarter of 19th C. • **Cleaning Copper With Love Apples.**— While waiting for dishes to be served in a restaurant in NYC's Chinatown, we used to amuse ourselves cleaning pennies with the Louisiana Hot Sauce that was a standard condiment on the table. The darkest penny will turn bright and pink (and unshiny) in seconds. Earl Proulx, in his *Yankee* column, "Plain Talk", Dec. 1987, gives a tip on cleaning a very darkened copper bath tub: "For the inside of the tub, scour it with ketchup." **$150.00-$165.00**

Tea kettle, mottled green agateware, tiny flakes chipped off, early 20th C. Condition lowers value. **$35.00-$55.00**

Tea kettle, odd square shape with 1" wide flange angled from back to front down sides and top, meant to fit into a specific base burner, forged iron bail handle hooks to end of spout and to hinge of lid, "Spoor's Patent #5114", mfd by Spoor, and by license by A. Ingraham & Co., Troy, NY, 7"H x 6"W x 10"L including spout, c.1850. • **Classic.** — This is a spectacular must-have for tea kettle collectors. Spoor also designed and patented a sort of flanged inserted niche that went into the stove, and could be used as a shelf with a tea steeper or a flat iron or a square frying pan. Oooo wheee! See page 547. **$250.00-$325.00**

Tea kettle, or hot water kettle, cast aluminum, side-swiveling lid, short coffee-boiler style "V" neck lip or spout, wire handle with wooden grip, very simple slanted straight sides, looks thick & it is, Wagner Mfg. Co., 10" diameter at base, c.1910. **$35.00-$40.00**

Tea kettle, pieced tin, long straight high angle spout, hinged lid, strapwork falling bail handle, strapwork ring finial on lid, American, 6¼"H x 3¾" diameter, mid 19th C. • **Early Tin.**— "The Dutch or Irish emigrant far away in his tent on the boundless prairies of the West, the boatman barging down his cotton over the bosom of the Mississippi, the Father of Waters, the rough miners of Nevada fighting with nature to extract the virgin silver from the heart of the Rocky Mountains, all require tinware in its rudest form, a tea-pot, a kettle, a pannikin, a wash-bowl, and requiring them are well aware that they will find them ready when desired at the nearest country store. ... There is no doubt that the immense modern increase in the manufacturing and consumption of tin plates has resulted from the rapid increase of population in the U.S.A." P. W. Flower, *A History of the Trade in Tin*, 1880. (The "plates" are pieces of tin plated iron, not dinner plates.) **$65.00-$80.00**

Tea kettle, red enameled thin metal, little aluminum snap-on whistle with turned wood knob, you have to take whistle off to pour, no mark, 6⅞" diameter across bottom, c.1930s or 1940s. **$12.00-$15.00**

Tea kettle, sheet iron, unusual inner & outer bodies, pipe vent connects hole in bottom center of outer body & passes through inner body at angle, with exit & entry holes brazed to seal; pipe vent ends up at one of holes around rim near the lid. It draws heat up through the water in the inner kettle, working like a percolator. Kettle has straight spout in 2 sections, with holes around lower section (part of outer pot) evidently to increase air draft & efficiency in heating the water, nicely-shaped fixed bail handle, like handles from American 1820's teapots, turned wooden grip & hanging ring of wire, lift out lid in center of top of pot, like an ironclad battleship with its airholes & heavy sheet iron. "R. Wall, #568", Grove City, PA, about 6½"H including lid x 10" diameter, c.1880s (?) or poss. a little earlier? • *The Journal of the Franklin Institute of Philadelphia*, Aug. 1828, reported on an "**Improvement in the Tea Kettle,** and other vessels for culinary purposes" as follows: "A Mr. Gordon, of London (England), is manufacturing tea-kettles, and other culinary vessels, which are said to be very economical; the improvement consists simply in enclosing vessels of the ordinary kind, such as tea-kettles, stew-pans, &c., with an outer casing surrounding their sides, but open at the bottom, for the flame of a lamp (alcohol or spirit) to act upon it. When heat is applied to vessels so constructed, the plate of air between the cases becomes highly rarified, and the heat, having no tendency to descend, accumulates in the upper part to such an intense degree, as to be capable of melting a rod of glass if passed up the cavity. In vessels of the usual construction, the greater part of the heated air escapes without producing any useful effect; in these, however, it is detained, and the water may in consequence be boiled in a very short space of time. The chief advantages of the new construction are, therefore, economy of heat, or of the inflammable matter employed in producing it, economy of time, and convenience; the value of these may be variously estimated by different individuals, but all will acknowledge that they are important." **$150.00-$175.00**

Tea kettle, stainless steel body & spout in round-topped wide-bottomed cone shape, with ring of embossed dots just up from bottom, high straight spout terminated by red plastic bird whistle, high ¾ round handle, part of which has Wedgwood blue plastic handgrip with finger holds on underside, & red balls at each end, designed by American architect Michael Graves for Alessi, 2 qt. capacity, ©1985. • An editorial note in 1986 said that 25,000 + of these $100.00 to $125.00 kettles had been sold in the first three or so months since its introduction late August 1985. **$100.00-$150.00**

Tea kettle, tin, painted black, "Kreamer", American, 2 cup capacity, 20th C. **$25.00-$32.00**

Tea kettle, tin, with range eye pit bottom made of copper, strap handle, domed lid, American, late 19th C. **$65.00-$75.00**

Tea kettle, urn-like, in that there is a spigot instead of a spout, copper, American, mid 19th C. **$85.00-$100.00**

Tea kettle, very architectural looking, beige enamelware with black trim & black interior, chrome handle with Art Deco Bakelite® (or other molded phenolic resin) knob, canted back handle with plastic grip, strainer holes in spout, no mark, 8½"H exclusive of handle, c.1930s (?). **$45.00-$60.00**

Tea kettle, very low & broad, gooseneck spout, wide falling strap handle, stamped & pieced tin, "for oil stoves", Matthai - Ingram, 8½" diameter, 3 qt. capacity, c.1890s. **$35.00-$45.00**

Tea kettle, bulbous cast iron body, 3 short feet, gooseneck, forged iron handle, no maker's mark, American, late 18th, early 19th C. **$150.00-$200.00**

Tea kettle, cast iron, swiveled or pivoted copper cover, gooseneck spout, American, 9"H, 19th C. **$80.00-$90.00**

Tea kettle, cast iron with tin cover, heavy bail handle, long gooseneck spout, American, 5½"H, late 19th C. **$55.00-$70.00**

Tea kettle, whistling type, steel body decoratively enameled as worried setting hen, handle arches over lid, spout has cast phenolic resin chicken head, the comb attached with a rachet device thumb activated to pull back for pouring, wings in black lines on white body, "TeaBird® ", M. Kamenstein, made in Taiwan, 2½ qts. capacity, 1986. • **Futurewatch.**— Anything with figural details, whether it's useful or useless will probably have collector value sometime in the future. Original price of this is $30.00. Discounted to $23.00 in 1989. Secondhand market in perfect condition, possibly close to that. But wait 50 years, and never use it, and it may gain 200% on your investment. But maybe not. **$20.00-$30.00**

Tea kettle, white enameled iron, cobalt handle & knob, on bottom in black is a transfer print of a dreaming woman in a corset, with title "Dream of Comfort", adv'g "The 'Specialite Corset' ", and on bottom in cobalt is mark "20 C III", 7⅞" diameter, early 20th C. • For a similar motif, see the "Mademoiselle Worth" pitcher in the Container chapter. I think if corset collectors (they do exist, don't they?) discovered these pieces the prices would go up. **$75.00-$150.00**

Tea kettle & kettle tilter combined, cast & forged iron, swivel ring on top of tilter, American (?), late 18th C. **$450.00-$600.00**

Tea kettle or hot water kettle, cast iron, nearly straight sides, simple slightly domed lid with ring finial, curved lever on top, right above spout, which is the attached kettle tilter, forged iron bail handle with ring top, at right angles to the spout, to be hung from trammel or pot hook, American, prob. New England, about 15"H x 12" diameter, late 18th or early 19th C. **$350.00-$450.00**

Tea kettle & teapot, matched pair, shaded blue ombre enamelware, American, 6"H and 6½"H, early 20th or late 19th C. **$175.00-$265.00**

Tea kettle, teapot & coffee pot set, sky blue enamelware with cobalt knobs, coffee pot has glass lid made by H. C. Fry Co., Rochester, PA, 20th C. **$165.00-$250.00**

Tea kettles, cast aluminum, various styles, mfd by Griswold, Wagner or Wear-Ever T.A.C.U. Co. (The Aluminum Cooking Utensil Co.), about 8¼" to 10" diameter, 1903 (when trade name came in) to about 1915. • When I wrote my first book, I only knew one person who collected them, Paul Persoff, my photographer. He used to buy them at Englishtown (NJ) flea market for under $5.00. • General ball-park value range for this type of kettle: **$35.00-$45.00**

Tea or water kettle, cast iron, bail handle marked with place and date, Vermont, 3 qt. size, 1875. **$45.00-$60.00**

Tea or water kettle, copper, tinned inside, dovetail seams, lid with brass acorn finial, gooseneck spout, marked "J. C. & W. Lord", Birmingham, England, 7"H x 5¾" diameter, late 19th C. • **Reproduction alert.**— A London company, John Hancock Reproductions Ltd., advertises that they are the "leading specialist wholesaler of reproduction antiques", with "more than 6,000 separate lines", of repros of "brass & copperware, pots, jardiniers, novelties" among many other lines. A brass schoolmarm's bell and brass twisted-shaft candlesticks are the only things in the picture which might apply to our subjects here, but I suspect that much of what is coming from England in containers now is reproduction. Unfortunately this is a signal that the end of a collecting cycle is coming, because it's too dangerous to enter the field. So far, not enough of our "territory" has been encroached upon to make it hard to collect kitchen & housewares, but if you step outside, just a few figurative inches, *caveat emptor.* Study Study Study. And if you buy mail order, insist on return privileges for any reason. **$100.00-$145.00**

Tea or water kettle, copper with brass handle, gooseneck, "Majestic", American, 20th C. **$65.00-$85.00**

Tea or water kettle, nickeled brass & copper, gooseneck style, "Gilchrist", large size, 1903. **$25.00-$40.00**

Tea set, with teapot with brave straight spout & long gently-arched ribbed plastic handle, sugar bowl with round lid, creamer, designed by Russell Wright for Chase Copper & Brass, Waterbury, CT, c.1930s. • Designer's name is the $$-maker here. **$225.00-$300.00**

Tea steeper, cobalt blue enamelware, early 20th C (?). **$35.00-$65.00**

Tea steeper, dark green enamelware with white loopy streaks or swirls, white inside, "Chrysolite", American, TOC. **$85.00-$135.00**

Tea steeper, white enamelware with blue trim, TOC. **$12.00-$22.00**

Tea strainer, gray graniteware, TOC. **$20.00-$30.00**

Tea strainer, tin with red wooden handle, depicts teapot & cups on the strainer cup, 1930s-40s. **$15.00-$18.00**

Tea strainer spoon, silverplate, advertises "Tetley Tea", 20th C. **$20.00-$25.00**

Tea strainer & stand, nickeled metal, Main Tool & Mfg. Co., (Brooklyn, NY?), 20th C. **$4.00-$6.00**

Tea urn, a sort of English samovar, brass urn is round tinned inside, set up on 4 pillars, square base, alcohol burner below bolted to base, English, 14"H x 7½" diameter, c.1840s. • In silver this form might be as much as 40 years older. **$170.00-$225.00**

Tea urn, brass plated globe on straight legs, sort of Art Deco or Arts & Crafts space station, strips of bamboo wrapped around spigot, heating alcohol lamp below, Austrian, early 20th C. **$175.00-$200.00**

Tea urn, copper with brass handles, spigot & trim, on 4 legs, English, 21"H, late 19th C. **$165.00-$185.00**

Tea urn, tin, grape cluster molding, cast iron handles, brass spigot, American (?), 15"H, c.1870s (?). **$100.00-$125.00**

Teapot, 3 metals — tin, brass and copper, brass finial on lid, footed & very graceful, 19th C. **$85.00-$100.00**

Teapot, black & white speckly enamelware, with Britannia collar & lid, strainer inside gooseneck spout, 8½"H, 19th C. **$150.00-$180.00**

Teapot, blue enamelware, with Britannia mountings, Manning - Bowman, late 19th C. **$125.00-$175.00**

Teapot, blue glazed earthenware, lid chipped & repaired, double wire bail handle with black painted turned wood grip, no marks, 5½"H to finial top, 19th C. • **"LUTE — A Matter to Mend Broken Vessel.**— Take any quantity of white of eggs, and beat them well to a froth. Add to this soft curd cheese, and quicklime, and begin beating a-new all together. This may be used in mending whatever you will, even glasses, and will stand both fire and water ... **Another,** for the same purpose, which resists water. — Take quicklime, turpentine, and soft curd cheese. Mix these well together; and, with the point of a knife, put of this on the edges of the broken pieces of your ware, then join them together." James Cutbush, *The American Artists Manual, or Dictionary of Practical Knowledge ....* (Philadelphia, 1814). • **Mending With Brads.**— The most common (or at least visible) repair found on any ceramic wares utilizes the brad — a metal staple-like object made of a fairly soft metal. At a recent auction I saw a lovely Willow Ware soup tureen on stand, with a high domed lid which had a very old brad repair that held the two halves together. The brads, about 10 of them, were set fairly close together, just under an inch apart, and were about ⅝" wide straddling the break line. The technique is probably very ancient, and probably found in every country where ceramics existed. In the October 1946 *National Geographic Magazine,* on p. 540, there's an interesting picture of an Afghanistan workman sitting on a pad on the floor, holding a broken cup with the toes of one foot while he uses a beautiful bow drill to "bore small cavities into either side of the crack. Brads of soft copper are hammered in, binding the pieces. From Iran to Tientsin (85 miles S.E. of Beijing, China), this is a common repair." The article, "Back to Afghanistan", is by Maynard Owen Williams. **$350.00-$385.00**

Teapot, blue & white enamelware swirl, gooseneck, 19th C. **$115.00-$160.00**

Teapot, blue & white swirl agateware, hinged lid, 7"H, late 19th or early 20th C. **$165.00-$225.00**

Teapot, Britannia, wonderful melon-ribbed shape, small curved feet, "James Dixon", early to mid 19th C. • In 1836, the *Journal of the Franklin Institute* published a short report of interest to people trying to date Britannia (and other metal) teapots. **"Tea-pots made by steam.** Britannia metal tea-pots are now made by steam; the round bodies are spun, and the wooden handles and knobs are cut up by powerful steam engines. A good workman can spin twenty dozen of pot-bodies in a day." A complex melon shape like this might possibly have been made with a spun blank. **$85.00-$110.00**

Teapot, canal boat or barge china, with dark brown glaze and thickly decorated blue flowers and birds, and pink and white flowers, very small teapot finial on lid, medallion or scroll on front reads "A Present From A Friend 1790", English, 12⅜"H, 1790. • **Barge china.**— This colorful pot is an example of many decorative, exuberant pottery wares used by the thousands of people who lived on the barges and flat-bottomed boats that plied up and down the vast inner canal system in England. The pieces date well into the 19th C. **$375.00-$425.00**

Teapot, cast iron, black, very pebbly surface like a warty toad, lift off lid, forged bail handle, round with faintly squashed shape, short gooseneck spout, Japanese, small, maybe 2 pt. capacity, 19th or 20th C. • These are beginning to show up regularly at shows. They sometimes have a very dark brown finish to the iron. They are finely made, and there is little that would alert the first time viewer that they are Japanese. They sometimes have a faintly different ringing sound when you put the lid back on. I don't know if the Japanese iron workers added something to the metal. I have never seen one without the pebbly surface — this is perhaps the most conclusive evidence to share with you. I am suspicious that there may be Japanese-made reproductions or lookalikes are being made. For export to the U. S., they would have to have country of origin marked somewhere. • A very charming miniature of this already small teapot is actually a water vessel, perhaps an inch or so in height, used by sumi painters and calligraphers to moisten the ink blocks. They have a tiny regulating hole, which the user covers with forefinger, while holding lid on too. By removing the finger briefly, the pressure inside is relieved and the water comes out the tiny spout. These miniatures (a teapot is only one form the little water vessel may take — some are figural animals or birds or mythological beings) are sold for upwards of $400.00. I saw one for $800.00. In Japanese metal work, as in so much else of their artisanry, the master, whose name is signed in a teensy mark, makes up most of the value. This is a very sophisticated market. • Most of the 1, 2 or 3 pt. sizes are priced in the upper range: **$65.00-$120.00**

Teapot, cinnamon colored enamelware on outside, white inside, turned wood handle with black finish, tin plated or nickeled brass lid & base, Manning - Bowman, 6½"H to top of finial, pat'd May 21, 1889. **$220.00-$260.00**

Teapot, cinnamon colored enamelware on outside, white inside, turned wood knob on lid is possibly replacement, Manning - Bowman, 10"H, pat'd May 21, 1889. **$250.00-$350.00**

Teapot, cobalt enamelware, white flower decorations, gold trim, hinged lid, European, 7"H, TOC. •

Czechoslovakian Enamelware.— It took a while, but American collectors of enamelware seem to finally have wholeheartedly welcomed European wares made from the mid 19th C up through the early 1930s to their collections. These are wares imported in the waning years of the 19th C and up to WWI, wares imported during a short resumption of trade, and finally wares only recently imported by containerload, specifically for the collector market. This latest wave of importing will probably include old marked pieces once made for possible export (hence, after 1891 bearing name of country of origin), as well as more truly antique pieces dating back as far as the mid 19th C. While there were probably hundreds of European enamelware manufacturers in the late 19th C, there were only a handful in all of the United States, and none that I know of in Canada. • For today's collectors (perhaps enamored of other "gaudy" wares), Czechoslovakian pieces are especially interesting, having been made in really spectacular patterns & bold colors, with skilled, confident painting, peasant or "country look" designs. Sometimes sets are found, recently imported to the U.S. Plaids in cobalt blue & white, or red & white, colorful polkadots, flowers, leaves, stripes, geometric border patterns, often with contrasting colors for spout, handle and finial, are very desirable. Trade journal ads, c.1900, showed imported German, Austrian & Swedish imported wares. • A provision of the 1890 McKinley Tariff Act raised an already stiff tariff on imported enamelware. Although American enamelware brought in $4 million yearly, the Times added "It is not very durable, the base being of iron, and the profit is very heavy." Of "Bohemian" enamelware they wrote, "nearly all ... foreign ware is ... blue & white...more attractive than the mottled (American) graniteware." Steel-based imports were considered three times as durable. McKinley's tariff raised the 45% rate already in effect. In 1890, stores stockpiled foreign enamelware to sell at prices lower than would be seen for a long time. • In 1890, St. Louis Stamping Co.'s Imperial Decorated Iron Ware was touted as "closely approximating French china in weight and grace of form...The...original color decorations in flowers, &c., are in pleasing contrast with the pure white enamel surface." • Container chapter has more on Tariff Act. **$175.00-$250.00**

Teapot, copper, square base, square spout, angular handle with Bakelite® grip, truncated pyramidal shape, the sides not simple triangles, but faceted, very hard to describe, impossible to forget, & my camera jammed as I was photographing it at a show, English, from near Brighton, 7¾"H, base is 8¾" measured diagonally up to 5" diagonal at top, c.1920s. **$500.00-$600.00**

Teapot, decorated china, hinged metal lid with large finial knob with hole in it, odd spout turns down like a faucet, "Royle's Patent Self Pouring Teapot", mfd by Doulton Potteries, Manchester, England, 7½"H, pat'd 1886 in England by A.J. Royle. • Classic. — This fabulous piece was advertised as "a boon for mothers of large families" (as most families of the time were. You didn't have to pick up the teapot to pour the tea; instead, you merely lifted the lid, put your finger over the hole in the finial knob, then closed the lid and the tea came out the downturned spout. Woe to the M.o.l.f. if she'd forgotten the cup. • An article in Spinning Wheel in October 1969, showed examples made of Britannia, by Meriden Britannia and told about one marked "Asbury - Paine Mfg Co., Phila. PA" with a patent date of April 3, 1888. This patent date is the American one, and was used on self-pouring teapots made of various materials. **$250.00-$400.00**

Teapot, electric, "American Electrical Heater Co.", Detroit, MI, 1904. **$25.00-$35.00**

Teapot, enamelware, white background with gorgeous raspberries, blackberries & leaves in brilliant colors, pewter lid, copper bottom rim to protect from chipping, Manning - Bowman, 9¼"H to finial top, pat'd May 21, 1889, in late 1890s catalog as are others. **$325.00-$400.00**

Teapot, "end of day" enamelware with swirls of several bright colors, predominately cobalt & red, with orange & yellow, American (?), small, 19th C. • **End of Day.—** The popular, but not necessarily accurate, term for swirled multicolored enamelwares (as well as blown glass wares) is "End of Day" pieces. I have not seen documentary contemporary evidence that would back up a somewhat romantic notion that the dog-tired artisan, at the end of a 10 or 12 hour workday, would be lively enough, and adequately enough supplied with "leftovers", or even allowed, to work past quitting time to make a whimsical end of day piece for a loved one. I am speculating here, just as everyone else does, but it is possible that the first few of this type of thing became so much the rage that artisans everywhere wanted to make or were asked to make such things during regular working hours. Diaries, documents, worksheets, inventories — all would help answer our questions. Do you keep a diary? • More subtle color mixtures don't seem to bring the high prices that brighter ones do. **$150.00-$200.00**

Teapot, globe-shaped, blown-molded glass, with engraved floral spray on sides, press-molded lid with knob, "Pyrex", English, 5½"D; 1½ pt. capacity, c. 1930. • This earliest Pyrex teapot is the only one with engraved flowers. **$60.00-$75.00**

Teapot, gray graniteware with pewter cover, spout, breast band & handle, copper bottom, footed, handle is scrolled, domed lid with nice finial, body is a beautiful, nearly round form, American, late 19th C. **$150.00-$200.00**

Teapot, gray graniteware with tin spout, handle, lid, breastband & base rim, American, 19th C. **$155.00-$225.00**

Teapot, japanned tin, big foot, stamped inside lid with mark — probably maker not owner (?), carpenter's dividers straddling a rising sun, also initials "W & S", American (?), 14"H, c.1840s. **$400.00-$500.00**

Teapot, nickeled copper, double walled, wood handle, decorative nickeled cast pot-metal finial on lid, "Sweeney Mfg. Co.", Brooklyn, NY, 3 pt. size, early 20th or late 19th C. **$20.00-$28.00**

Teapot, olive drab green enamelware, white inside, pewter handle, nickled brass base, wooden "heat sink" where handle joins lid, "Quality #5", mfd by Manning - Bowman, Meriden, CT, 8¾"H, late 19th C. **$175.00-$265.00**

Teapot, pale green & white marbleized enamelware, gooseneck spout, "Elite", marked Austria, TOC. **$170.00-$250.00**

Teapot, spun aluminum with wooden handle, chain that feeds through finial of lid is attached to small domed tea ball perforated with circles of holes, looks like The Little King of comic strip fame, "Merit", American, 7¼"H x 8½"W including spout and handle, c.1920s. **$16.00-$22.00**

Teapot, very bulbous shape, bright blue agateware, with Britannia trim — lid, spout, part of handle, Manning - Bowman, 1889. **$125.00-$150.00**

Teapot, white & blue speckled enamelware, also called speckleware, possibly United States Stamping Co., Moundsville, WV, 1st quarter 20th C. **$155.00-$185.00**

Teapot, with clawfoot stand & alcohol warming lamp, copper, late 19th C. **$145.00-$165.00**

Teapot, yellow enamelware with red poppies & green trim, gooseneck spout, prob. European, 20th C. **$50.00-$70.00**

Trivet, for teapot at table, ornate cast iron, with name around edge, "Midget", American, 3¾"D, TOC. **$35.00-$45.00**

Water kettle, cast iron, hinged top, coiled wire handle, squared gooseneck spout, pit bottom, "M'Dowell", Philadelphia, 8"H to slightly domed lid x 12" diameter, pit bottom is 1½"H x 9" diameter, 19th C. • **German vocabulary** — Wasserkessel: water kettle. **$135.00-$155.00**

Water kettle, cast iron with brass handle & lid, marked "Cannon Deepfields", English, "No. 2, 5 pints" on bottom, mid 19th C. **$150.00-$175.00**

Whistle for tea kettle, stamped & pieced brass, bird has a "stem" to fit into spout, American, 3½"H, pat'd 1923. **$20.00-$30.00**

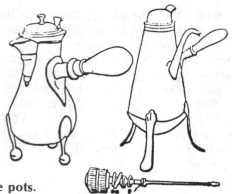

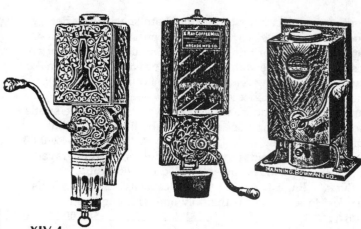

XIV-1.
Chocolate pots.

both have typical rounded bottom, which accommodated the muddler (stirrer). (L) Cast & turned brass, pyriform body with 3 ball feet, side spout, hinged lid with thumb-piece, ebonized wooden handle, 8 7/8"H. Probably French or Swiss, c.1730. Drawn from ad of reknowned brass antique dealer, Rupert Gentle, Wiltshire, England. (R) Pieced tin with hinged lid, slender gooseneck side spout, wooden handle. Probably American, early 19th C. Drawn from ad of Pat Guthman Antiques, Southport, CT. At bottom is drawing of Mexican all-in-one piece carved wood muller or muddler, about 8 1/2"L. Three rings marked with dots are loose, and twirl when the stick, held vertically, is rubbed between the palms. The rings do not slip off end. Note corrugated wide bands at bottom. Chocolate, of course, originated in South America. **$175.00-$500.00**

XIV-4.
Coffee mills.

(L) "Bell", ornate cast iron front to oak box. Glass receptacle inside. (M) "X-Ray," with glass box above ornate cast iron mill. Both Arcade Mfg. Co., Freeport, IL. They made 70 "different varieties of coffee mills and 400 house furnishing specialties." Ads in House Furnishing Review, *1908.* **$200.00-$400.00**

"The Telephone Mill," for coffee or spices. "Made of hard wood, highly finished and nickel trimmed, and is the only boxed mill which can be fastened equally well on Table, Shelf or Wall...It is easily regulated to pulverize if desired." Name plate says "The Telephone Mill. Ring Up For Coffee. Freeport, IL." Arcade Mfg. Co., appeared in Manning-Bowman 1892 catalog. Original price in 1890 was only $2.50. More desirable one has fancy cast iron front. **$200.00-$300.00**

XIV-2.
"Mr. Garnet Terry's Mill."

A hand mill, for coffee beans, spices etc., of wood and sheet iron. Invented by Londoner Garnet Terry, c.1800-01. Illustration published in Anthony Willich's The Domestic Encyclopedia, *1803-04, which was a practical work meant for men who were used to making most of their own tools and household items.*

Coffee or spice mill,

"but will grind grain of any kind. It is sold without a frame, and is so constructed as to be fastened to a post or board in any part of the house, or it can be attached to a simple frame. "Sheet iron with revolving cast iron corrugated "plates" which could be ordered separately. From article in Journal of the American Institute, *9/1841.* **$25.00-$50.00**

XIV-5.
Coffee mill.

"Lone Star Side Mill," which "may readily be attached to the face of a door, window casing, or the wall" and may be "folded up when not in use." Projects 4" from wall when folded. John M. Waddel Mfg. Co., Greenfield, OH, article in The Metal Worker, *6/14/1890.* **$30.00-$60.00**

XIV-6.
Coffee mill,

Shelf or table-mounted. Cast iron with bell-shaped hopper. Maker not known; picture form Harrod's Stores 1895 catalog. London. **$50.0-$75.00**

XIV-3.
Wall-mounted coffee mill.

"The Crystal," so-named because of glass hopper/canister and receiving cup. Ornate cast iron mill. Arcade Mfg. Co., Freeport, IL. Ad in Thomas' Register of American Manufacturers...Buyers' Guide, *1905-06.* **$60.00-$80.00**

"ENTERPRISE"
Rapid Grinding and
Pulverizing Mills

Capacity of Hoppers—1 lb. of Coffee

Mills illustrated on this page
will "Pulverize"

Will Granulate ¾ lb. of Coffee
per minute.

Adapted for Steamboats, Butchers, Lumber Camps or wherever it
is desirable to save space.

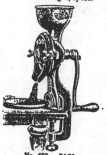

No. 350, $3.50
Height, - - 16½ inches
Weight, 17 lbs.

No. 235, $6.00
Height, 18 in., Diam. of Wheel, 17 in.
Weight, 29 lbs.
The No. 235 was designed especially for Butchers' use in grinding
spices.

No. 450, $4.50
Height, - - 21 inches
Weight, 19½ lbs.

XIV-7.
Coffee mills.
*Various grinding & pulverizing styles of cast iron mills mfd. by
Enterprise Mfg. Co., Philadelphia. Early 20th C. catalog.*
$70.00-$150.00

XIV-8.
Coffee mills.
*(L) "Double Grinding" mill for tabletop use. Decorated cast iron.
Silver & Co., Brooklyn, c.1910. It gets its name by being "a new
departure in 'Grinding Mills.' Has two inlets for the Coffee Bean
and two outlets for the Ground Coffee." Adjustable for coarse
to powdered grinds. (R) "Crown No. 11", mfd. by Landers, Frary
& Clark, New Britain, CT. Painted & decorated cast iron, 12 1/2"H,
drawer in base. From Pick catalog, 1909.* **$60.00-$100.00 and
$40.00-$70.00**

XIV-9.
Coffee mills.
*(L) Enterprise Mfg. Co. No.8, with double iron flywheels, brass
canister/hopper (which may be nickel-plated), bulbous cast iron
mill housing hinged in center. Style came in 3 numbers — 8, 10,
and 210, which would grind 1 lb., 1 1/2 lbs., and 1 3/4 lbs. per
minute. Offered in Duparquet, Huot and Moneuse catalog,
c.1904-1910.
(R) "Swift Mills," Lane Brothers. Large, double-wheeled mill,
painted cast iron with drawer in box base. About 22"H. Early 20th
C ad, but mill probably dates to 3rd quarter 19th C.*
$400.00-$600.00

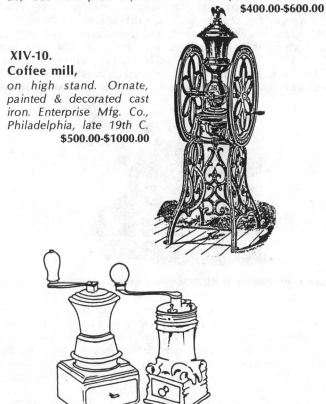

XIV-10.
Coffee mill,
*on high stand. Ornate,
painted & decorated cast
iron. Enterprise Mfg. Co.,
Philadelphia, late 19th C.*
$500.00-$1000.00

XIV-11.
Coffee mills.
*Small cylindrical mills of wood, about 7" to 9"H. (L) A simple
turned wood mill made in Provence district of France, in very early
18th C. It was supposedly based on earlier Italian models. (R)
Carved wood mill from the 18th C. It looks as if it could have
been made by a furniture or frame-carver. Both are drawn from
a wonderful article, "Les moulins a cafe," by Edith Mannoni, that
appeared in the French magazine Art & Decoration,
August/September 1982. It is filled with unusual mills, mostly un-
familiar to American collectors.* **$125.00-$200.00**

XIV-12.
Coffee mill.

Box type, cast iron with closed-top hopper, tin drawer slides underneath. Key at side for taking apart for cleaning. Screwed to oblong board with shaped ends and 3 holes at each end, perhaps for fingerholds for carrying? Mill 6 3/4"H exclusive of crank; base 5 1/2" x 5 7/8", Pennsylvania, mid 19th C. Courtesy of dealer Darryl G. Dudash, Alaquippa, PA, who specializes in Pennsylvania cast iron. Value range mine.   **$200.00-$300.00**

XIV-13.
Box type coffee mill.

"No. 1050 Improved," mfd. by John M. Waddel Mfg. Co., Greenfield, OH. "This is designed for a good, low priced mill, with burr and shell so constructed as to grind coffee very fine. The point is made of a new feature in this mill, consisting of a device for firmly locking the grinding shell and large retinned hopper to the box, holding the shell firmly to its place and making a bearing for the burr shaft." Open door and round tin cup automatically slides out. This feature was typical of Waddel mills. From writeup in The Metal Worker, 8/16/1890.   **$30.00-$40.00**

X-14.
Box mill.

Raised hopper, wooden box with ornate cast iron top and slanted sides, shallow drawer. Marked on medallion above door, but I can't read. English made, from Harrod's Stores 1895 catalog. Probably A. Kenrick.   **$45.00-$60.00**

XIV-15.
Box mills.

(L) "Favorite No. 700," raised hopper with cover, and with handle for firm grip, wood box-jointed body with drawer, box 4 1/4"H x 6 1/4" square. Pat'd 1880 & 1888. Top (R) "Imperial No. 147," sunken hopper with hinged cover, white walnut box, cast iron top finished with "French gold bronze." 4 3/4"H x 7" square, pat'd 1888. Lower (R) Simplest type, "No. 257," japanned iron open hopper, hardwood box, 3 1/4"H x 6" square. All Manning, Bowman & Co., from 1892 catalog.   **$30.00-$65.00**

XIV-16.
Coffee mills.

Lap or box types. (L) "None-Such," mfd. by Bronson-Walton Co., Cleveland, OH. Chromolithographed decorative box with scene of coffee-drinkers. Domed hopper with top crank. (R) "Universal No. 110," mfd. by Landers, Frary & Clark, New Britain, CT. Black enameled sheet steel with iron handle & crank. 8 1/2"H. Both in ads from 1905. The colorful one is worth much more than the plain one, particularly in near mint condition.   **$25.00-$100.00**

XIV-17.
"Turkish" coffee mill.

"Patterned after Oriental models, heavily japanned, has black enamel finish, and is handsomely decorated." Maker unknown, but it appeared in the Albert Pick catalog, 1909. **$20.00-$40.00**

XIV-18. Souvenirs.

of huge coffee pot in Winston-Salem, NC. Black-painted cast pot metal and cast brass version, both 5 1/4"H. I suspect brass one is older. **$5.00-$15.00**

**XIV-19.
Coffee pot.**

Pieced tin, squared short curved spout, unusual fanciful curve to handle. Brass mushroom finial to convex lid, 10"H. Pennsylvania, mid 19th C. Courtesy Carol Bohn, Mifflinburg, PA. Value range mine, not Bohn's. While this one is not decorated on the surface, the extra wiggle in the handle adds great sculptural charm, which many people pay extra for. **$150.00-$300.00**

**XIV-20.
Post card of "The Big Coffee Pot"**

in Winston-Salem, NC. Color lithograph, reprinted over fairly long period. This one was mailed in 1940. The conical coffee pot itself, with the braced crooked neck spout and handle with reinforced grip, is made of painted tin and was erected in 1858 and still stands today, off Main Street. Merchant Julius Mickey, who wanted to attract custom to his roofing, tin and stove business, had it built (or perhaps built it himself). Fortunately, it lasted through two metal drives and various vicissitudes. The pot, probably based on a Moravian style, is 7' 3"H x 27" diameter at top & 64" diameter at bottom. It is calculated that it would hold 740½ gallons of coffee.

**XIV-21.
Coffee pots.**

Both Pennsylvanian pieced tin with inverted cone bodies and crooked-neck spouts. (L) Pot with flared footed base. Its funnel-like hinged lid, which gives it a slightly comical appearance, is uncommon. Note extra brace to handle. The style of decoration is called wriggled. Signed with serpentine maker's mark, early to mid 19th C. 10 3/4"H. (R) Jauntier pot, 11 3/4"H, has maker's smoothly domed lid. Its decoration called "punchwork." Signed in beautiful capital serif letters by "W(illoughly) Shade for Mary Shade," and dated March 18, 1848. We do not know who Mary was, but such coffee pots were usually, if not always, presentation pieces given to brides. In wriggleswork, the graving tool was skidded across surface, making a jiggedy mark to outline & fill shapes of flowers, leaves, etc. Punchwork is done with a punch, but although it is hit hard enough to make a dimple on the tin's surface, it is not allowed to puncture or pierce it. Photograph courtesy Sotheby Parke-Bernet, NYC. Prices realized at 10/26/1984 auction. **$2200.00 and $2400.00**

XIV-22.
Pieced tinwares,
including coffee pots, and unusual conical vessel. Photograph courtesy of Oveda Maurer Antiques, San Anselmo, CA.

XIV-24.
Tinwares.
Note low-originating straight spout on coffee pot at right. But for me, of special interest is the funny spout and its serpentine brace on the vessel at left. It appears to be an oiler or lamp filler of some kind. This dealer always has unusual metalwares. Photographed courtesy Oveda Maurer Antiques, San Anselmo, CA.

XIV-23.
Coffee pot.
Paint-decorated tin, short straight spout, hinged lid with curled-tin knob. Note diagonal piecing seam under handle, indicative of small sheets of tin. Note also the faint light circle behind the flowers: this is thought by some to be near-proof of Pennsylvania origins, and yet coffee pots having this circle and with exactly this kind of border near the top, are said by others to be typical of Connecticut provenance. Generally speaking, it seems that the straight spout tends to be Connecticut, while the crooked spout is Pennsylvania. Remember: wares were made in CT for "Western" trades, and peddled in NY & PA. 8 7/8"H, 19th C. Picture courtesy of the National Museum of American History, Smithsonian Institution.

XIV-25.
Coffee pot,
or at least so identified by the Smithsonian. I believe it may be a large lamp filler. At any rate, a tinsmith's work of art. Funnel top (for making drip coffee? or for safer filling with the lamp oil?. Hinged lid, strap handle, braced spout. I think it's a lamp filler because of the smallness of the spout's tip, and the angle of the spout. 11"H, 19th C. Picture courtesy of the National Museum of American History, Smithsonian Institution.

XIV-26.
Coffee boiler & tea pot.
Enameled graniteware, with paint-enameled turned wooden handles, gadrooned domed hinged lids. St. Louis Stamping Co., St. Louis, MO. Ad in The Metal Worker, 8/20/1892. **$50.00-$100.00**
(R) Biggin,
for drip-style coffee making. Graniteware and tin, from Matthai-Ingram catalog, c.1890. **$125.00-$200.00**

XIV-28.
Biggin coffee maker,
and possibly a lamp filler, both in pieced tin. Note the delightful zigzag brace to the long spout at right. 19th C. Photograph couresy Oveda Maurer Antiques, San Anselmo, CA.

XIV-27.
Coffee pot,
in 'gaudy' decorated Rockingham ceramic called "barge" or "canal craft," used on British canal barges. Besides the flowers and the mini-pot finial is the legend "A Present from a Friend" on the side. 10 1/2"H x 6 1/2"W, English, 19th C. Ex-Keillor Collection.

XIV-29.
Coffee makers.
When the factories of Manning-Bowman & Co., at Meriden, CT., were remodeled in the early 20th C, a "vault was discovered that had become bricked up at some time in the past and forgotten. In this vault were found a large number of coffee percolators and other household apparatus, which was made by Manning-Bowman & Co. as far back as the Civil War." (The company was started back in 1849.) Shown here, and in the article in House Furnishing Review, 8/1911, are (L) a combined French biggin & drip percolator, pat'd in 1873. The coffee was "extracted by pressure of a wooden block forced down by wet coffee grounds." (R) "A nearer approach to the modern coffee percolator, made by Manning-Bowman in 1875 and patented in 1876. It proves quite conclusively that contrary to general belief (in 1911), the percolator is not a recent contraption. This model has a center tube with spray top, and a water spreader on the cover to distribute the water that is forced up through the tube. It differs radically from the present day percolators in the fact that the water, after it is poured in the funnel shaped aperture on the side" is percolated only once through the grounds, instead of "making a continuous percolation as the modern ones do." **$75.00-$125.00**

XIV-30.
"Infuser for tea or coffee,"

two views. "By the insertion of the stopper into the spout of the pot, the water poured into the (upper chamber) infuser is retained there until it has dissolved all the desirable properties of the tea or coffee. By withdrawing the stopper the prepared beverage is allowed to run into the pot, from which it may be served in the usual way. This infuser is made in three styles — tin, enameled ware and stoneware, and it comes in various sizes." Imported from Europe by G.M. Thurnauer & Bro. NYC wholesalers of housewares. Article in *House Furnishing Review*, 7/1905.

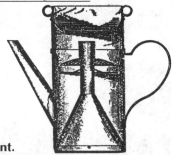

XIV-31.
Coffee pot patent.

Pat'd 12/29/1885, by Philip A. Covington, Fort Worth, TX, assignor of one-half to Albert H. Iverson. "A coffee-pot having a cone-shaped chamber perforated and provided with an upright tube, a perforated cup surrounding the same, a flaring cap connected to the tube and bottom of cup, a perforated retaining-plate, and a condensing-vessel formed with a convex bottom." For making a type of percolated coffee. *Official Gazette*.

XIV-32.
"French coffee pot."

Graniteware with planished tin. White metal or nickel-plated mountings Made in 5 sizes — from 2 to 6 pints. Manning, Bowman & Co., 1892. **$100.00-$150.00**

XIV-33.
Coffee pot patent.

Pat'd 8/9/1887, by Jeremiah Boudinot, Springfield, IL. "A coffee-pot having a steam-pipe, opening into the upper and lower ends thereof, and a removable diaphragm suspended in the lower portion of the pot at a point above the lower end of the steam-tube." Note the double spout, one which I believe is the steam tube.

XIV-34.
Biggin coffee pot.

"Chesterman's, "pat'd 7/19/1859 and 1/24/1860 by W. Chesterman, Centralia, IA. 9 3/8"H. **$85.00-$100.00**

XIV-35.
"French coffee pot."

Nickel-plated copper, "extra well made and the up-to-date thing." Hinged cover, ebony (perhaps ebonized) handle. 1 pt. or 2pts. From Albert Pick catalog, 1909. You know if you see one in an antique shop now, the nickel (oooh,icky proletarian) plating will have been surgically removed to reveal the copper and improve the price. **$40.00-$65.00.**

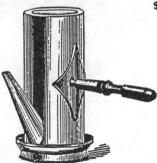

XIV-36.
"Student's coffee pot."

Brass and tin, with wood side handle. 2, 4, 6 and 8 cups. From F.A. Walker catalog, c.1870s. **$35.00-$50.00.**

The Kin-Hee Coffee Pot

is a triumph of genius. It is unlike other Coffee Pots. If you can boil water you can in one minute make Coffee in it fit for a king. By actual test it costs only seven-tenths of a cent per cup. It is, therefore, the best to drink and the least expensive.

Demonstrated at Pan-American Exposition

This shows the coffee pot upside down, the top filled with boiling water and coffee submerged. It stands for one minute, straining cloth is put on, then the bottom. Then the entire pot is turned right side up and the coffee is ready to serve. A child can do it. *Patented May 22, 1900.*

XIV-37.
Coffee pot.
"Kin-Hee" pot, mfd. by James Heekin & Co, Cincinnati, OH, and in Canada, The Eby, Blain Co., Ltd., Toronto. They also sold a mocha-java coffee blend in 1 lb. cans.

XIV-38.
Coffee pot.
Easily confused with a butter melter or some other saucepan. Copper, in the "Turkish pattern," made in six sizes, holding from 1 to 6 cups. Henry Rogers Sons & Co., Wolverhampton, England, 1914 catalog. **$20.00-$40.00**

XIV-39.
Coffee pot.
"French style," cast aluminum, 3 parts with inner basket, 3-pt. capacity. Mfd. by Wagner, Sidney, OH. "It makes coffee without boiling by the French (drip) method. It keeps coffee hot for a long time. The pot also is a beautiful pitcher. It will keep lemonaide, etc., cold for a long period. It may be used also for ice water by putting the cracked ice in the basket."; 1930 ad. Similar pots with the scalloped bottom edge were made by other companies. **$20.00-$40.00**

XIV-40.
Tea & coffee pot.
"Marion Harland" pot, mfd. by Silver & Co., Brooklyn, NC. In their c. 1910 catalog. Made of copper with ebonized wood handlesl. Could be had in plain, nickelplated or "Old English" finish. Tinned inside. It was sort of a percolating infuser. **$20.00-$40.00.**

XIV-41.
"Self-pouring" tea of coffee pot.
"Royle's Patent," this "Boston No. 1" model sold by Paine, Diehl & Co., Philadelphia, out of their 1888 catalog. It was probably made for them by William Vogel & Brothers, Brooklyn. The patent was granted 4/3/1888 in America, but was two years earlier in England. There the self-pourers were made by James Dixon & Sons, Sheffield, for the patentee, J.J.Royle, Manchester. Wherever made, most seem to be made of Britannia metal, which could be left plain, or plated with nickel or silver. Meriden Britannia Co. and the Boston Co. were other makers in the U.S. It was sometimes called a "mother's helper" because "mother"(the person designated to pour tea at teatime) needed only pull up the pump in the top of the finial, place the cup under the spout, and push the piston down. I imagine it took a bit of practice. **$85.00-$135.00**

XIV-42.
Coffee & tea filtering system.
"Boston," all glass, mfg. by The Silex Co., Boston, MA. Came in 4 and 6 cup sizes. *House Furnishing Review, 5/19/1917.*
$40.00-$100.00

XIV-43.
"Tricolator" coffee makers.
Filtering percolation pot. "Norfolk" 9-cup electric. Mfd. by Tricolor Co., Inc., NYC. They had at least a couple dozen styles, with glazed & decorated china pots, Pyrex® pots, and metal upper parts. 1933 brochure. **$20.00-$30.00**

XIV-44.
Coffee roaster.

"Woods Patent," Roys & Wilcox Co., Harrington's Import, Berlin, Ct. Pat'd. 5/12/1859. Cast iron, hinged "cannon ball" in frame, with bail handle & 3 legs. Ball has long handles which clamp together by the crank. Frame 2 3/4"x 9" diameter; ball 6 1/2" diameter with 5 1/4"L handles. Courtesy Darryl G. Dudash, Alaquippa, PA. Prices vary widely; range given here is general average.**$400.00-$600.00**

XIV-45.
Coffee roaster.

This depicted in F.A. Walker & Co.'s catalog, 1880s. The Thomas R. Wood 4/17/1849 patent? Or J.D. Harrington's of 5/17/1859.?

XIV-46.
Coffee roaster,

saucepan type. Sheet iron with cast iron crank and probably wrought iron long handle. Depicted in American Home Cook Book, By an "American lady", 1854. Directions said to add "to each pound of coffee one table-spoonful of water. The coffee will throughly roast without being burned."

XIV-47.
Coffee roaster.

"Patent Flue" roaster to use on cookstoves or ranges. Cast & sheet iron, high carrying handle on top, crank at one end. Mfd. by Stuart, Peterson, & Co., of Philadelphia, PA, and Burlington, NJ, who made stoves and stove hollowware. They made this roaster in 4 sizes: a round one to fit a 8" or 9" hole; and ovals to fit two 6" holes, two 7" holes, and two 9" holes. Catalog picture of 1875. There is a great similarity in this style of roaster to confectioners' roasters for "burnt" almonds, and other nuts. **$200.00-$350.00**

XIV-48.
Coffee roaster,

"American Coffee Roaster," pat'd. 4/28/1863 and 11/7/1865, by C.A.Mills, of Hazel Green, Wi and then Bristol, CT. Clockwork mechanism wound by key seen at right. Sets over 2 eyes of range. You load the heavy wire canister with coffee beans, set it into the cast iron frame, slip tin cylindrical cover over it, wind it, and let'er roll. 9"H x 18 1/2"L. Collection of Meryle Evans.
$350.00-$550.00

X-49.
Partial coffee roaster.

Misidentified in last edition as a "kettle with scraper," this is really a coffee roaster missing its lid. Cast iron, 3 short legs. 5 1/4"H x 8 1/2" diameter. Pat'd. 3/13/1866 by K. Humphrey, and mfd. by I.A.Sheppard & Co., Philadelphia. Picture courtesy of the Museum of History and Technology, The Smithsonian Institution.
$175.00-$250.00

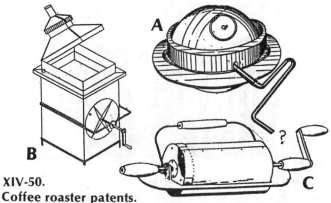

XIV-50.
Coffee roaster patents.

(A) Pat'd 11/8/1881, by George A. Bridler, Middletown, PA. This patent application had a model—perhaps you'll be lucky enough to find it. Note the resemblance to the Woods Patent in XIV-44. This is a "two-part roasting-vessel provided with a (round) door and a cranked stirring rod with double circular flanged base support, which is reversible. I put a question mark at the end of the crank, not knowing how it was supposed to end. Offical Gazette.

(B) Pat'd 10/27/1885, by Samuel S. Kingery, Cincinnati, OH. Inventor patented it a a "coffee-roaster," but refers to it throughout the application as nut-roaster," and a "peanut-roaster." There was no patent model, alas.

(C) Pat'd 1?.../1885, by Matthew J. Clark, Clermontville, OH. A metallic cylinder in 2 separate longitudinal sections, riveted together, each section "provided with an inwardly-projecting flange formed integral with the section." In addition, one end of the cylinder has a detachable head or cover.

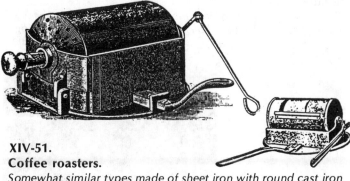

XIV-51.
Coffee roasters.

Somewhat similar types made of sheet iron with round cast iron frames to fit over range eye, and cranked cylinders. (L) "Imperial Family" roaster, by T.B.C. Burpee, Philadelphia. Ad in Century, *10/1892. (R) Maker not known, but sold through the Albert Pick catalog, 1909. It was made in 3 sizes, with cylinders 6"L x 5 1/2" diameter; 8" x 5 1/2"; and 9 1/2" x 7". All under $2.00 originally.*
$65.00-$150.00

XIV-52.
Portable coffee roaster,

all-in-one stove with revolving cylinder "suspended on a crane over fire, and can be swung outward for filling or discharging." Made for hand-cranking or power-hookup. Came in four sizes, for roasting 20-30 lbs., 30-60 lbs., 75-135 lbs., and 150-270 lbs. Wow! From Duparquet Huot & Moneuse hotel supply wholesale catalog, c.1904-1910.
$150.00-$350.00

XIV-53.
Coffee roaster.

Pit bottom style, meant to sit down into eye of range. Heavy cast iron, with crank in lid that stirred beans with four fingers. Hinged lid, upright lifting rings. 11"H x 8 3/4" diameter, possibly English if not American, mid 19th C. Collection of Meryle Evans.
$200.00-$350.00

XIV-54
Coffee roaster.

Sheet iron with holding handle and crank handle. The crank turned the bevel gears in the center of the top, turning the stirrer fingers inside. Note trapdoor. 9" diameter, 20"L overall. Picture contributed by The Primitive Man, Bob Cahn. **$150.00-$250.00**

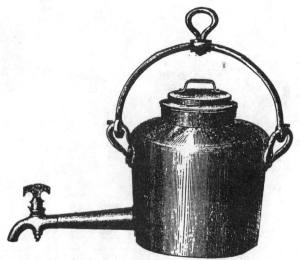

XIV-55.
Tea or hot water boiler,
of early type that was originally made to hang inside fireplace, although it would work on a range top too. The bail with eye on this 20th C. one meant it could be hung on a hook somewhere convenient. Copper, with tinned iron heavyweight bail, long spigot. Henry Rogers Sons & Co., Wolverhampton, England, 1914 catalog. **$150.00-$250.00**

XIV-57.
"Tea & Coffee Urns in Batteries,"
meaning in a connected group. Copper & brass with nickel plating overall. Made in 4 set sizes: 3-gallon urns, 5-, 8- and 10-gallons. S.B. Sexton Stove & Mfg. Co., Baltimore, c.1930s. It's not much of a leap of imagination to think of them as The Ladies Come to Tea. Value is hard to give; they would probably be worth most as second-hand restaurant supplies, bought to put into use. Required house-room (the "real-estate-factor") has to be calculated when pricing large items of no particular use. **$100.00-$400.00**

XIV-58.
"Canteen" urn.
Nickeled copper, shaped like barrel on stand. Two-gallon capacity, so just the right size for a house. From Albert Pick 1909 catalog. **$150.00-$350.00**

XIV-56.
Tea or hot water boiler,
also sometimes called a hot water urn. Copper, slightly tapered body with long tapered spigot. Flat lid with bracket handle, forged iron bail handle with swivel ring in center. Smithsonian dates between 1854 and 1894, but we see from XIV-55 that it could be much later. 11 1/8"H exclusive of bail x 21 1/4" overall with faucet. Picture courtesy of the National Museum of American History, John Paul Remensnyder estate.

XIV-59.
Coffee percolator,
and server. Chrome, electric, mfd. by Labelle Silver Co., Brooklyn, NY, c.1950s. It's possible that this company is related to Silver & Co. **$40.00-$80.00**

XIV-60.
Tea kettle.

Copper, tinned inside, brass finial on domed lid, falling handle of flat copper forming chef's hat shape. This one rakish by being bent — whether that was the intention of the maker or early user or an accident we don't know, but it might make it easier to pour from. Marked in relief on top of handle "John W. Schlosser." 11 3/4"H when handle up, early 19th C. Photograph by Jennifer Oka. Picture courtesy of the National Museum of American History, Smithsonian Institution, John Paul Remensnyder estate.

XIV-61.
Tea kettles.

Both copper with barrel handles. (L) "New Shape Round" kettle, made in capacities from 2 to 10 pints. (R) "Range" kettle "with well." Made to hold from 6 to 12 pints (skipping 11). Henry Rogers Sons, Wolverhampton, England, 1914 catalog. **$85.00-$200.00**

XIV-62.
Tea kettles.

All square ones. Top two are seamless, and meant for gas stoves, made of copper, with gooseneck spouts. (L) To be had with barrel or ebonized wood handle. (R) To be had with amber or "opal" (probably opalescent glass) handle. Bottom (L) is "all copper except tinned iron handle and tinned iron swan neck spout. (R) "Square block tin kettle with copper bottom." All were made in several sizes, generally from 4 to 12 pints. Also Henry Rogers, 1914. **$85.00-$200.00**

XIV-63.
Tea kettle.

Pit bottom body to fit down into range eye or "pit." Copper, rounded body, flattop finial to stepped domed lid, tentative, graceless gooseneck spout. Flat falling bail with rolled edge, marked on handle on a fixed medallion "Bramhall, Deane & Co. New York," who were manufacturing suppliers to hotels and restaurants. 12 13/16"H overall x 12 5/8"W. Probably late 19th C. Photograph by Jennifer Oka. Picture courtesy of the Naional Museum of American History, Smithsonian Institution, John Paul Remensnyder estate.

XIV-64.
Tea kettle.

Copper, oval cylinder with flat bottom & top, gooseneck spout, fixed handle with barrel grip flanked by small spurs. Small lid with turned wooden knob plus an opening on opposite side which is the top of an inverted funnel. It's a sort of double-boiler vessel within the outer pot. 10 1/4"H overall x 10"L. Embossed medallion fixed on top says "The Cyprus No. 341. 1879. Patented Jan. 28." Probably English. Photographed by Jennifer Oka. Picture courtesy of the National Museum of American History, Smithsonian Institution, John Paul Remensnyder estate.

XIV-65.
Tea kettle.
Cast iron, globular body with wonderful spout. Fitted tin lid, wire bail, 3 short legs. Photograph courtesy Pat Guthman Antiques, Southport, CT.

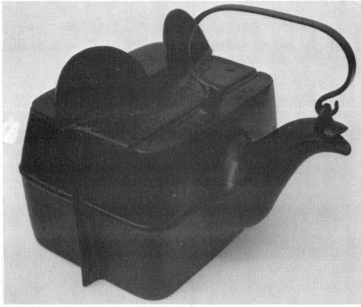

XIV-66.
Tea kettle.
*Cast iron, oblong, with Mickey Mouse ears. These fins actually form, along with the rib down the sides, a partial heat seal. The kettle was made for a specific type of stove, and was stuck partway into its heat box. The collector was told, when he bought it, that it "came off a barge on the Erie Canal." Such stoves may have been used on canal boats. This was patented as a **boiling kettle,** 2/23/1869, by S. Spoor, Phelps, NY. Photograph courtesy of David Smith.*

XIV-68.
Tea kettles.
"Ripley's New" kettles, from 1860 announcement that patent was being extended to March 14, 1867. "The objection for many years existing to the use of the old fashion Cast Iron Tea Kettle, owing to the difficulty in moulding the spout, its liability to clog or fill, especially when use of lime water is made, were fully removed by the production of the Kettle in the above, which was the invention of Mr. Ezra Ripley, to whom letters patent were granted on the 14th of March, 1846. The breast of the Kettle may be so shaped as to prevent any possibility of filling with sediment, and ensuring the greatest rapidity of pouring. The cost of moulding is reduced at least six cents per Kettle, a very material difference from former prices. The pattern may be made in any shape desired, but will be composed of two parts, the spout being connected with the body of the Kettle. Each part of the pattern can be removed from the green sand core separately, leaving the cores of the spout and body of the Kettle together in one entire core, which prevents the old necessity of setting a dry sand core for the spout. The pattern may be made to part vertically or longitudinally at the option of the manufacturer. The spouts being spacious admit of being enameled with the inner surface of the body if desired...We are prepared to dispose of foundry rights; patterns and Flasks can be furnished on reasonable terms." Signed Ezra Ripley, Fuller, Warren & Co., Troy, NY, March 15, 1860. A circular sent to "stove and hollow ware manufacturers."

XIV-67.
Kettle tilter.
Wrought iron, swivel ring at top, "S" curved handle with ball tip, approx. 14"L. Late 18th or early 19th C. Ex-Keillor Collection.
$125.00-$225.00

XIV-69.
Tea or water kettle.
Cast iron, pit bottom, hinged lid, coiled heat-dissipating bail handle. Nice squat bulbous body. Squared gooseneck (or "swan" as in England?) spout. Marked "M'Dowell, Phila. PA." 8"H overall to slightly domed lid x 12" diameter. Part that fits down into range eye is 9" diameter x 1 1/2"H. Courtesy of dealer Jean Hatt, Hatt's Hutt, Denver, PA. **$85.00-$100.00**

XIV-70.
Closeup of spout (previous picture).
Note marks of filing to smooth out casting lines; also the small knurled knob to lid.

XIV-71.
Tea kettle.
Enameled cast iron, deep midnight blue, barrel handle. American, late 19th C. Courtesy Darwin Urffer. **$45.00-$65.00**

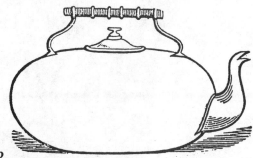

XIV-72.
Tea kettle.
Depicted without caption in <u>American Home Cook Book</u>, 1854.

XIV-73.
Tea kettle.
Cast iron with forged iron handle, bronze lid. 5 1/4"H x 6" diameter. Early 19th C. Japanese. **$80.00-$150.00**

XIV-74.
Tipping kettle. *Cast iron, bail is flat forged iron. American, early 19th C. Photograph courtesy Pat Guthman Antiques, Southport, CT.*

XIV-75.
Tea kettle.
Cast iron, small globular body with 3 short feet. Cast in 3 sections, see vertical & horizontal seams. Crookneck spout, flat forged falling bail, stepped dome lid — intriguingly chained to handle. "A.T." cast on side. 6 1/8" x 12 1/4"L. Photograph by Jennifer Oka. Picture courtesy of the National Museum of American History, Smithsonian Institution, John Paul Remensnyder estate.

XIV-76.
Teapot.
Gray graniteware with white metal (probably Britannia) spout, handle, lid, breast-band and base rim. Late 19th C. From the collection of Susan Kistler, Lenhartsville, PA. **$75.00-$125.00**

XIV-77.
Teapot.
"Patent decorated pearl agateware," mfd. by Manning, Bowman & Co., in their 1892 catalog. Pat'd in 1883. This style was one of several occasion-related pieces. People could pay extra and really personalize them. **$125.00-$200.00**

XIV-78.
"Toddy kettle" & gas lamp heater.
The "Union Attachment" bracket fits to the gas fixture and provides a place for a smallish (and definitely light weight) tea kettle. Mfd. by Standard co., NYC. *The Metal Worker, 7/8/1882.*

XIV-79.
Tea kettle.
"Puritan," cast aluminum, wooden grip on wire bail. "Automatic lid permits opening and closing of lid by means of the bail." Wagner Mfg. Co., Sidney, OH. 1923 ad. **$35.00-$50.00**

XIV-80. Tea kettle.
Cast aluminum, wood, bail handle. 10" diameter, c.1910. Wagner Mfg. Co., Sidney, OH. Collection of Paul Persoff, who photographed my first book so long ago. **$35.00-$50.00**

XIV-81. Tea kettle.
Cast aluminum, wood. Note small filling hole with its own lid, and larger swiveling lid, good for cleaning lime deposits out of interior. 8 1/2" diameter, 4 quart size. "Colonial Design, Safety Fill," mfd. by Griswold, Erie, PA. Pat'd 9/9/1913. Collection of Paul Persoff. **$35.00-$50.00.**

XIV-82.
Electric tea kettle,
on Art Nouveau-styled stand, mfd. by "Simplex." From Maud Lanacaster's Electric Cooking, 1914.   **$45.00-$75.00.**

XIV-83.
Electric tea kettle.
"Speedmaster," with "independent electric heating element, but is so constructed that it may also be used on any stove the same as the ordinary type of kettle." From The Electric Home, E.S. Lincoln, 1936.   **$25.00-$45.00.**

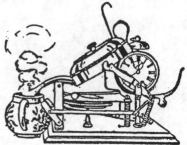

XIV-84.
"The Clock That Makes Tea."
"Most people seem to think that America has cornered the world market on Yankee inventive genius, but it remains for our British cousins to cap the climax of inventions intended to permit the weary sojourner on this terrestial ball to roll over and take another nap again" by means of the clock teapot. "Johnny Bull likes his cup of tea upon rising, (and with this) the clock wakes him up, lights a lamp, boils a pint of water, pours the water into handy teapot, puts out the lamp, and rings a gong announcing that tea is ready." This was in House Furnishing Review, 2/1908, and whether it's true or a ruse, I don't know. But they've got 'em now!

XIV-85.
"Bird tea kettle."
An old idea in a new design—the whistling plastic (or metal in older ones) bird in the spout who whistles when the water is boiling. This stainless steel one with colored plastic handle & bird designed by architect Michael Graves, copyrighted 1985.
          $100.00-$150.00

XIV-86.
Tea or coffee pot stands.
Twisted wire in various shapes, available in different sizes. Mfd. by Sherwood, Worcester, MA, mid 19th C and made for long period.   **$20.00-$45.00.**

XIV-87.
Tea or coffee pot stand.
Nickeled cast brass horeshoe design, with expected "Good Luck." Heinz & Munschauer, Buffalo, NY, 1882 catalog. **$20.00-$45.00**

D. COOKING
COUNT RUMFORD'S COFFEE DRIPOLATORS

The following article is part of a much larger one by the late Sanborn C. Brown, Associate Professor of Physics at M.I.T. that appeared in the Harvard Library Bulletin, *Vol. IX, No. 3, Autumn 1955, Cambridge, MA. In the original Bulletin printing, the Council of the American Academy of Art & Sciences, the Rumford Fund, was credited for awarding a grant that made it possible to publish the drawings. The article is reprinted here, with illustrations, and Conclusions, explaining the significance of the cache of drawings. The Rumford Chemical Works, of Providence, RI, which made Rumford Baking Powder, took its name from renowned chemist Count Rumford, but there is otherwise no known connection.*

The phrase "the present writer" refers to Sanborn Brown. However, italicized remarks or notes in parentheses are by author of this book, L.C. Franklin, or are adapted from the 11th edition of the Encyclopedia Britannica's *article on Rumford. That article would be worth reading, for it details some of Rumford's untiring work to better the condition of the poor in Bavaria (Germany), whereas Professor Brown's short biography below makes him seem more of a priveleged elitist and "soldier of fortune".*

***

COUNT RUMFORD'S DESIGNS FOR COFFEE MAKERS

The Harvard College Library has recently acquired, through the generosity of David P. Wheatland, '22, a remarkable collection fo working drawings made by Benjamin Thompson, Count Rumford. This is the only collection of Rumford material of this sort that has come to light and provides real insight into the working habits and methodology of invention of a man whose greatest achievement was to show how the scientific method could be put to practical uses. ...

Count Rumford was born Benjamin Thompson in Woburn, Massachusettes, on 26 March 1753. His boyhood experience as a dry-goods clerk in Salem and Boston showed that his talents lay in other fields. [*Apparently he "occupied himself in chemical and mechanical experiments" throughout his boyhood. EB]* Although Thompson was never officially enrolled at Harvard we know that he attended at least a few of Professor Winthrop's lectures on natural philosophy...Thompson's marriage *(1772)* to a rich widow in Concord [at that time, Rumford], New Hampshire, brought him to prominence in the colonies. He embraced the Tory cause the first week of the Revolution, and left for England in 1776 to spend his life as scientist and soldier of fortune.

At the close of the Revolution...he was retired on half pay from the British Army. He was knighted by George III, but spent his most productive years in the service of [*Prince Maximilian*] the Elector of Bavaria [mainly in Munich]. A prolific investigator, he wrote over fifty papers, many of which appeared at different times in English, German, French, and Italian. Of these papers, thirty were on the subject of heat, six on light, and seven on the formation and operation of scientific and charitable institutions.

In 1799 Thompson,...by then made a Count of the Holy Roman Empire [*who had chosen his own name from his wife's American township*] by the grateful [Maximilian], was sent to England as Bavarian minister. George III refused to accept one of his own subjects as foreign representative, and Rumford, after declining an offer to become director of the United States Military Academy, occupied his enforced leisure in organizing the Royal Institution of Great Britain — a forerunner of our present museums of science.

Count Rumford spent the last years of his life near Paris. His American wife had died years before, and he married Mme. Lavoiser, widow of the famous French chemist. This proved a violently unhappy match, and lasted only a few years. Count Rumford died at Auteuil, outside Paris, on 21 August 1814. When he made his will in France in 1812, he bequeathed the whole residue of his property to the President and Fellows of Harvard College, whom he appointed his residuary legatee for the purpose of setting up the Rumford Professorship of the Physical and Mathematical Sciences as applied to the Useful Arts.

The drawings which are the subject of this article were obtained from an undisclosed original source, but there seems little doubt that Rumford worked on these ideas during the fairly brief period of his French marriage (1805-09). Some of the sheets bear dates within these years and most of the undated drawings have notations in French. It was only at this time that Rumford wrote his private notes and correspondence in French.

...We know that for several months in the winter of 1808-09 Rumford was gravely ill, and it seems reasonable to assume that during his convalescence he turned his attention to the design of coffee makers and stoves which make up the bulk of the documents we are discussing here.

The material was received by the Harvard Library as a completely undocumented and random collection. It has been the attempt of the present writer to bring together the drawings of similar subjects and to put them into a logical sequence so that their significance both in this collection and in terms of Rumford's published works becomes evident. There remains undiscussed a number of sketches of parts of apparatus unrecognizable to the author...

In physical state, the drawings present a very heterogeneous appearance, on paper of various shapes, sizes, and colors, sometimes crowded several to a page, and even occasionally overlapping. In the reproductions printed herewith relative arrangement of drawings has not necessarily been preserved, nor all tentative pencilings, guide lines, and so forth. In certain reproductions numbered arrows have been added by the present writer [Brown], for clarity of discussion.

COFFEE MAKERS

Most of the design sketches of the coffeepots are dated and signed by Rumford and provide a delightful sequence of the evolution of his ideas in producing an efficient and simple coffee maker. In his essay *Of the Excellent Qualities of Coffee, and the Art of Making It in the Highest Perfection,* pubished separately in 1812 (and reprinted in Volume IV of *The Complete Works of Count Rumford,* Boston: American Academy of Arts and Sciences, 1870-75), Rumford tells us that he had spent fifteen years studying the science of coffee making. He had found by experiment that the flavor of coffee was concentrated in the volatile oils which were lost from the coffee on contact with the air. Some years earlier, Rumford had been the discoverer of convection currents in unevenly heated liquids, whereby hot liquid rose and cool liquid fell, setting up a thermal motion of the fluid. He reasoned that the dripolater type of coffee maker was ideal because boiling water sealed up the coffee in such a way that the volatile oils could not escape. He realized further that when the unit was uncovered convection currents in the hot liquid coffee would impair flavor by bringing too much coffee in contact with air at the top. This detail was too important for Rumford's precise mind to ignore, and he designed a hot-water jacket to equalize temperature, thus reducing this destructive thermal activity. It is clear from these newly found manuscript sketches that Rumford's scientific ideas for the design of coffee makers were thoroughly worked out by early 1809. The attempts illustrated here are concerned with questions of convenience and compactness and show no further development of his already completed basic theories of coffeepot construction.

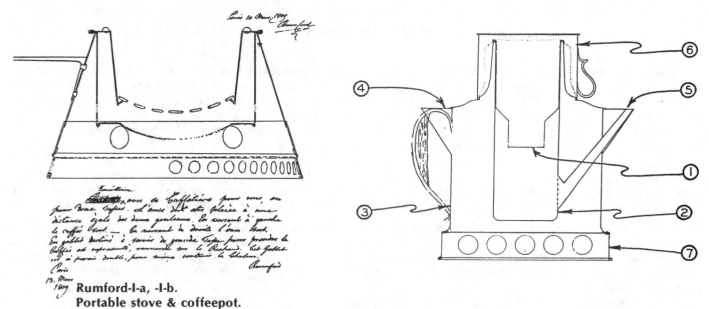

Rumford-I-a, -I-b.
Portable stove & coffeepot.
Sketches dated March 10, and March 13, 1809. The slanted sides of the stove (left) give it stability. Note evidence of a handle sticking off from left side. (Right) is a coffee pot Count Rumford drew March 13. Circled numbers & arrows are Sanborn Brown's, and refer to parts described below in the text. All pictures are reprinted with permission from the Harvard Library Bulletin, Vol. IX, No. 3, 1955. French text by Rumford describes layout and proportions of a "boiler and coffee-maker for one, or for two, cups."

The sketches of 10 and 13 March 1809, **Rumford-I-a** and **Rumford-I-b,** show a complete portable coffee maker, **I-a** illustrating the stove and **I-b** the coffeepot itself. In the essay…*Of the Excellent Qualities of Coffee,* Rumford described this coffee maker in detail:

"Now, when coffee is made in the most advantageous manner, the ground coffee is pressed down in a cylindrical vessel which has its bottom pierced with many small holes so as to form a strainer (shown faintly in the original drawings, and labeled "1" by the present writer), and a proper quantity of boiling hot water being poured cautiously on this layer of coffee in powder the water penetrates it by degrees, and after a certain time begins to filter through it…

These strainers must be suspended in their reservoirs which are destined for receiving the coffee, and at such a height that after all the coffee has passed through the strainer the bottom of the strainer may still be above the surface of the coffee in the reservoir… (reservoir is indicated by 2) and just large enough above to receive the strainer in such a manner that it may be suspended in the reservoir by means of a narrow projecting brim.

The boiler (3) in which the reservoir is suspended may likewise be made…of such diameter above as to receive the reservoir in such a manner as to be firmly united to it…

The small quanitiy of water which it will be necessary to put into the boiler, in order that the reservoir for the coffee may be surrounded by steam, may be introduced be means of a small opening on one side of the boiler (4)…

The spout through which the coffee is poured out passes through the side of the boiler, and is fixed to it by soldering (5). The cover of the boiler (6) serves at the same time as a cover for the reservoir and for the cylindrical strainer; and it is made double, in order more effectually to confine the heat."

The explanation quoted here is a much more accurate description of this manuscript illustration than of any figure published in the essay. The manuscript sketch differs somewhat, however, from the description, since the cover of the coffeepot becomes a double-walled cup (6) into which the coffee could be poured for drinking. To return to Rumford's own words:

The boiler is fixed below to a hoop, made of sheet brass, which is pierced with many holes. This hoop (7), which is one inch in width, and which is firmly fixed to the boiler, serves as a foot to it when it is set down on a table…

When the boiler is heated…over a small portable furnace (**Rumford-I-a**) In which charcoal is burned, as the vapour from the fire will pass off through the holes made in the sides of the hoop, the bottom of the hoop will always remain quite clean, and the table-cloth will not be in danger of being soiled when this coffee-pot is set down on the table."

The effort of March 13 (**Rumford-I-b**), which Rumford described with such care in his essay, was unquestionably cumbersome, with its reservoir and boiler soldered together to form a single unwidely unit. Rumford must have seen the disadvantages at once, for the sketches of the next few days show him working on a device which could be taken apart. Even before

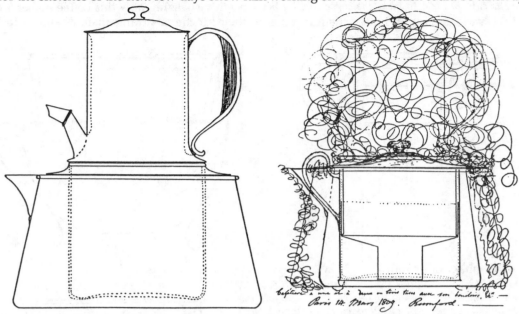

Rumford-II-a, -II-b.
Coffeepot set down into boiler.
Sketch dated March 14, 1809. (L) -II-a Sanborn Brown's "tracing of one of the complete coffeepots shown in II-b" (R). Figure II-a clearly shows features we are familiar with — the strap handle with grip, and the mushroom finial on the domed lid, which was probably meant to be cast brass. Brown's tracing is probably the earlier complete setup in the sketch, later scribbled out, and -II-b on the (R) is the first version of Rumford's compact self-contained design with interior funnel dripper and the cup handle (at left). It is shown by itself in the next illustration.

he had finished another sketch (**Rumford-II-a,** traced by the present writer to clarify the confusion in **Rumford-II-b**), it apparently occurred to him that even this was too clumsy, and that he could easily develop a design in which the pot would become a cup with the boiler and strainer fitted inside. In **Rumford-II-b** we see him scratching out his first idea as this portable design took shape in his mind. By blanking out all but his final unscribbled design of March 14, we get **Rumford-III-a.**

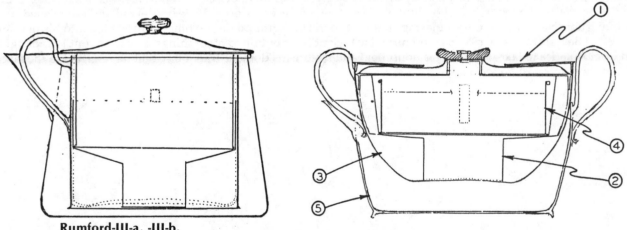

Rumford-III-a, -III-b.
Portable coffeepot.
(L) is design "obtained by suppressing the unwanted lines of "previous picture. Done by Sanborn Brown from Rumford's March 14, 1809 scribbled sketch. (R) March 15, 1809. Preliminary design of portable coffeepot, showing new shape of lid, and the hole in it, as well as two handles.

New ideas were coming fast by this time. He toyed with the thought that an alcohol lamp could be designed to be stored inside the strainer, and he sketched it in lightly, as may be seen dimly in **Rumford-II-b**. The next day he continued the engineering of his portable coffee maker. First he modified his ideas of the previous day by adding a cover (**1** of **Rumford-III-b**) with a large hole in it. When the parts were reassembled in the process of making coffee, the strainer (2) would fit into this hole, which would hold it over the cup (3) as the water dripped through from the top. Then it occured to him that if he was going to keep the coffee hot with an alcohol lamp (4), he could eliminate the boiler (5) completely. **Rumford-IV-a** shows his completed design of a compact coffee maker, whose parts could be placed inside each other for portability and storage. He was satisfied with this device, and he titled, signed, and dated the sketch: 'Une Grande Tasse a Caffe, de fer-blanc renfermant une Machine a faire le Caffe et une Lampe a l'esprit de vin pour chauffer l'eau dans la tasse, pour faire le Caffe. Paris 15 Mars 1809 Rumford —' [*'A large cup for coffee, a self-contained tin device for making coffee and a spirit lamp for heating water in the cup, in order to make the coffee'. LCF.*] For ease in visualizing how this coffee maker went together in use, I have traced the various parts and fitted them together in their functional arrangement as shown in **Rumford-IV-b.**

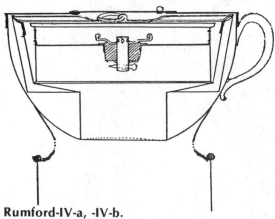

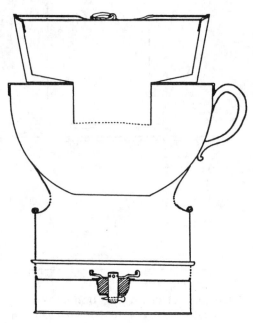

Rumford-IV-a, -IV-b.
Portable or compact coffeepot.
March 15, 1809. (L) This sketch is the one Rumford lableled "A large cup for coffee, a self-heating tin device..." It shows all the parts of the compact coffee maker as fit together for storage. Note the ring handle to the lid of the funnel that would hold the coffee "powder". (R) Sanborn Brown's "tracing of the various parts" of the illustration at left, assembled in their functional position.

One might well suspect that Rumford had this particular coffee maker in mind when he wrote: 'It is a curious fact, but it is nevertheless most certain, that in some cases, spirits of wine is cheaper, when employed as fuel, even than wood. With a spirit lamp constructed on [Ami] Argand's principle [in which the air was drawn up to the intensity of the light many fold], but with a chinmey made of thin sheet iron, which I caused to be made about seven years ago. [c.1807]...I heated a sufficient quantity of cold water to make coffee for the breakfast of two persons, and kept the coffee boiling hot one hour after it was made with as much spirits of wine as cost *two sous*, or one penny English money.' These Harvard drawings are the only Rumford illustrations which combine a coffee maker with a spirit lamp.

It is not too surprising that Count Rumford found neither the time nor the inclination in March 1809 to continue designing coffeepots to the point of writing an essay on the subject. As was mentioned before, his life was in a turmoil at the time. As soon as he was well enough to move, Rumford left Mme. Lavoiser's stormy Paris household and established himself in the Parisian suburb of Auteuil. Coffee making slipped into the background for the time, as he settled into his new surroundings, visited Bavaria for a few months, and turned his scientific attention to other things. It was not until his daughter had arrived from America to take charge of his household and restore his dometic tranquility that he returned to the fascinating question of how to make good coffee.

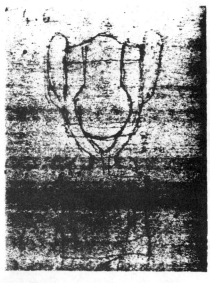

Rumford-V.
Sketches of various coffeepots and urns.

The six Rumford sketches, done on various colors of paper (c. 1809-1812), show an interesting range of designs. Three are like classical funerary urns, and are directly related to neo-Greco-Roman designs in favor in the early 19th century by designers of ornament for furniture, textiles, and ceramics. Top right appears to have two spouts, which is not unheard of. About others of this type of coffee pot, it was said that a "choice of spouts, (allowed) the mistress of the house (to) pour in the English or the French way at pleasure." (Esther Singleton, Russell Sturgis, Furniture of Our Fathers. 1900). Bottom left looks like a little tugboat pot; bottom right closely resembles coffee pots from the 1930s.

The remainder of the drawings of coffeepots and urns are preliminary sketches for those published in Rumford's essay. **Rumford-V** shows most of these. The similarities are evident in **Rumford-VI,** in which Rumford's final manuscript drawing (a) and a published plate (b), both of 1812, are placed side by side.

Colléctive pour 1. 2. 3. 4. 5. ou 6 Tasses from Mons: Bordas
Lumlond 10 Avril
1812.

Rumford-VI-a, -VI-b.
Drip coffee maker.

(L) April 10, 1812. This careful drawing, of a coffee maker for 1, 2, 3, 4, 5, or 6 cups, is the final drawing Rumford did for the manuscript of his published essay. (R) The published engraving. Note the elongation of the pot, the change in shape of the spout and the finial, and the change in the vent holes for the self-contained spirit lamp. Rumford not only studied chemistry and mechanical arts as a young man, he also took up engraving. It is not known if this particular engraving might have been done by him.

In 1802, six years before the date of the working drawings in the present collection, Count Rumford published Part III of his *Essay X* 'On the Construction of Kitchen Fire-Places and Kitchen Utensils.' A good many pages are spent in discussing small portable kitchen furnaces and pots and pans designed for maximum efficiency and convenience. The basic pan shapes which Rumford had achieved at this time are shown in **Rumford-VII.** The pan of **VII-a** was

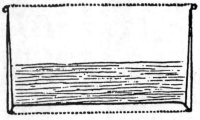
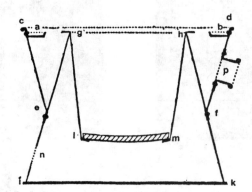

Rumford-VII-a, -VII-b.
Cooking pot & portable stove.
1802 published illustrations. Top is the nearly straight-walled cooking pan meant to fit on top of the portable stove shown at bottom. The pan was "Figure 73" in the published Rumford Essay X, On the Construction of Kitchen Fire-places and Kitchen Utensils. *The stove was "Figure 63."*

constructed to fit into a sand rim (a-b) at the top of the stove of **-VII-b**, thus forming a heat-tight joint between the stove and the pan. The fire was built on the grate (**1-m**). The flame rose to the bottom of the pan, giving up maximum heat by being forced to reverse its direction around the bottom of the pan and the rim (**g,h,**) before being drawn to the chimney through the flue pipe (**p**).

Until these present manuscripts came to light, there was no evidence to show that Rumford ever again turned his attention to stove design, but we can see now that he explored the subject much further in 1809 than he had in 1802. The dates on many of the sketches suggest strongly that Rumford's study of portable stoves for coffeepots was the factor which set him thinking again about types of portable stoves. This sequence of drawings (**Rumford-VIII to -X**) shows vividly how his ideas developed, until he could write of **Rumford-X-b**: 'Je regarde ce Rechaud comme le plus parfait que j'ai fait construire, jusqu'à present.' [*'I consider this stove to be the most perfect that I have made, up to the present.' LCF. By the way, the modern meaning of rechaud is "hot plate."*]

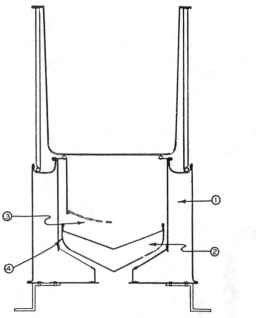
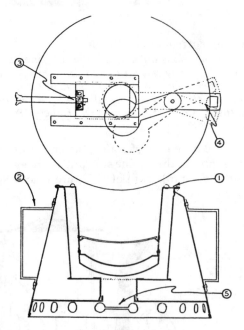
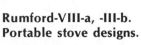

Rumford-VIII-a, -III-b.
Portable stove designs.

(L) Design from 1809, reworking some problematic parts of the stove design in previous illustration. Sanborn Brown's numbered areas are described fully in the text below. (R) More modifications, including damper.

The design of **Rumford-VIII-a** shows a stove not unlike that of **-VII-b** supporting a pot of the same general form as **-VII-a.** As we bear in mind that the two preceding illustrations were published some years before, we can see from the additional lines of **Rumford-VIII-a** that Rumford was worried about the loss of heat outward through the sides of his stove. To overcome this, he began to work in methods of insulation, using jackets full of ashes to prevent the heat loss. In this first drawing he planned to insulate not only the walls (1) of the furnace but the bottom (2) below the grate (3) as well.

This posed a serious problem in controlling the flow of air, which was supposed to rise to the grate from between the bottom and side insulated jackets through the narrow empty passage (4). Construction became very difficult, particularly that of the bottom jacket. He therefore tried supporting the bottom jacket on the same member as the grate (**Rumford VIII-b**). The cooking pot was to rest on the top rim (1), instead of setting within the high walls of **Rumford-VIII-a.** He also added carrying handles (2) and attacked the problem of controlling the air flow to the fire. He tried several shcemes for this, two of which (3) and (4) are shown in the horizontal plan of the stove bottom appearing in the upper half of **Rumford-VIII-b**. In (3) the air intake is opened and closed with a slide, in (4) with a pivoted damper. It can be surmised that the slot in the bottom of the stove (5) was to allow the motion of the handle of the damper (4). He worked on one other more elaborate damper (not reproduced here) before making a major change in design by eliminating the bottom insulator completely.

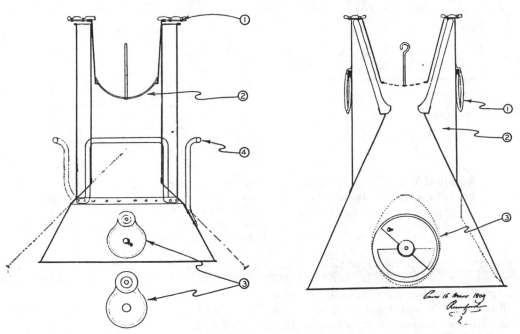

**Rumford-IX-a, -IX-b.
Portable stove designs.**

1809. (L) Rumford worked with the idea of raising the "grate" up high (on what look like two ionic columns), and works on a design for the adjustable vent or damper at bottom. (R) March 16, 1809. Much more stable design, but still not perfect.

Rumford-IX-a shows this next step. The cooking kettle was to be placed on the top rim. (1), and the grate (2) was raised very high to provide plenty of space for air insulation below it. Complicated sliding and pivoting damper arrangements gave way to the simple type (3) Rumford had recommended for his furnaces in 1802. Although the simpler operation of this stove was an improvement over his previous ideas, Rumford must have seen how dangerously unstable this device would prove in use, with a heavy cooking kettle full of food on the top of a tall, thin, pipe-shaped heater, whose lower part was filled with nothing heavier than several cubic feet of air. The carrying handles (4) were mounted very low on the stove to keep them well away from the hot grate. The next drawing, **Rumford-IX-b**, was signed and dated from Paris on 16 March 1809. The handles (1) of this stove are high on the sides, well insulated (2) from the heat, and the damper (3) is of the register design he had described in *Essay X*. When we visualize how tall and thin this stove would be with a pan on top, we can see that although its bottom is wider than in **Rumford-IX-a** the stability question was far from solved.

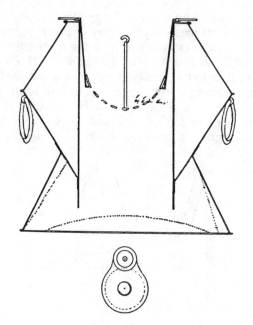

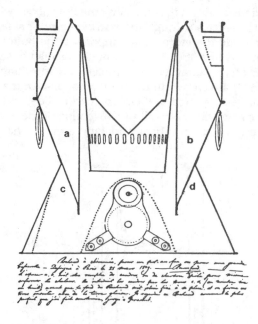

Rumford-X-a, -X-b.
Portable stove designs.

(L) March 1809. Almost completed design, still adjusting placement of handles and broadness of base. Design of damper or vent back to an earlier design. (R) March 25, 1809. This was the final model. I have enhanced the letters "a, b, c, and d" so that the references in the text will be clearer.

Within the next few days, Rumford managed to solve the rest of his problems. In **Rumford-X-a** he broadened the base of his stove still more, giving it a shape which would be less likely to tip over in use. The greater width gave the handles more insulation, and the damper was again his simplest type.

The final model **(Rumford-X-b)** was dated 'Paris le 25 Mars 1809.' The sand rim at the top hold the cooking vessel and the reversing smoke flow to the vent pipe at the side were characteristic of his earlier designs. The dotted parabola denotes a flattened section to provide for the motion of the damper. Constructional details were added at the bottom: 'L'espace a, b, doit etre remplie de cendres, ou de charbon pile pour mieux la chaleur. On introduit les cendres par les trous c, d, (en nombre six ou huit), avant que le fond du Rechaud soit fixe a sa place, et on ferme ces trous ensuite avec de la terre glaise.' [*The hollow spaces a, b, are to be filled with cinders, or with crushed charcoal, to better preserve the heat. One puts the cinders into the openings c, d, (in number, six or eight), before the base of the stove is fixed in its place, and one closes the openings afterward with the earthen clay.' LCF.*] We have no evidence that this stove was ever actually built and put into use, but it satisfied Rumford.

FIREPLACES

Count Rumford's name has been quite rightly associated with the modern fireplace. It was he who analyzed carefully the air currents and the flow of warm and cold gases in a fireplace and consequently introduced the throat, smoke shelf, and damper which characterize a well designed chimney. In his own day he was famous for this, and during one brief period in 1795 and 1796 he claimed to have rebuilt over two hundred smoky chimneys in the houses of Great Britain alone.

The sketches included in **Rumford-XI and -XII** are important because they show us for the first time how Rumford thought a new fireplace should be built, rather than how an old one should be changed. These detailed drawings provide a valuable graphic summary of the conclusions to which his extensive earlier thinking and writing on the rebuilding of unsatisfactory fireplaces had led.

Rumford supervised personally most of his early fireplace modifications, but no record exists of the details of the individuals changes. On 9 February 1796, Sir John Sinclair, then President of the Board of Agriculture in England, wrote to Rumford, asking him to prepare detailed instructions to bricklayers on how best to modify existing fireplaces so that 'the knowledge of so useful an art may be as rapidly and as extensively diffused as possible.' Rumford, vacationing in England from his military duties in Munich, undertook this at once with great enthusiasm, producing the essay 'Of Chimney Fire-Places' in little over a week.

When the Count came back to England in 1798 he wrote a short paper, 'Supplementary Observations concerning Chimney Fire-places,' to point out the errors that were being made by builders who were not following his instructions carefully enough. Although one would suspect that his interest in fireplace construction might have continued, we had no evidence of any further interest until Harvard acquired these drawings. The sketches illustrated in **Rumford-XI** are working drawings (c. 1806) which Rumford must have made for the benefit of workmen engaged in 'Rumfordizing' the estate on Rue d'Anjou in Paris where Mme Lavoisier and Rumford made their home...

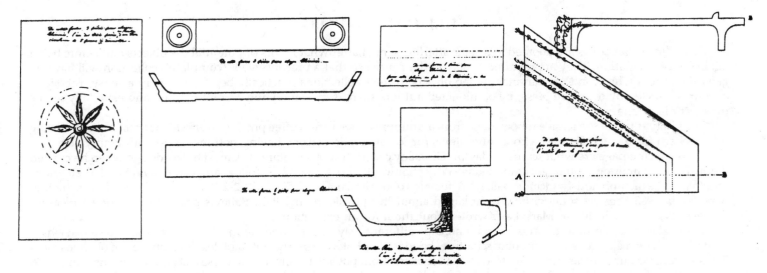

Rumford-XI.
Fireplace designs & decorations.

Most important, from functional viewpoint, is the sketch at upper right, which shows the angle of the chimney coving. Most of the other drawings represent decoration.

The assemblage of drawings, including designs and decorations, brought together in **Rumford-XI** from several different sheets of originals, shows how carefully Rumford worked out even the minutiae which he required his workmen to follow. It is obvious from his handwritten instructions that a considerable number of chimneys were being modified.

Rumford had good reason to be precise in his instructions. His second fireplace essay...shows us how exasperated he had been in 1798 with the mistakes of workmen...[who] were not taking the trouble to read his instructions carefully enough:

It is likewise very important to *"round off the breast of the chimney,"* though this I find is very often intirely (sic) neglected, even by workmen who have had much practice in the construction of (my) fire-places...

Another very common fault that I have observed in chimney fire-places, that have been altered on what have been called my principles, and which has a direct tendency to bring dust, and even smoke, into the room, is the sloping of the covings too much...I have said, in my Essay on Chimney Fire-places, that where chimnies are well constructed, and well situated, and have never been apt to smoke, the covings should be placed *less obliquely*, in respect to the back...But most of the workmen who have altered chimnies seem to have paid little attention to these distinctions...

...if the passage of the air down a chimney in which there is no fire, is occasioned by strong eddies of wind, there is no remedy for that evil but...closing up the throat of the chimney occasionally, by a door made for that purpose of sheet-iron.

If the door-way...be closed with a flat piece of cast iron, or of plate iron, fixed at its lower end, to the lower end of the door-way, by a hinge, or moveable on two gudgeons; this plate may easily be so contrived as to serve occasionally as a register, or door, for diminishing, or closing, the throat of the chimney.

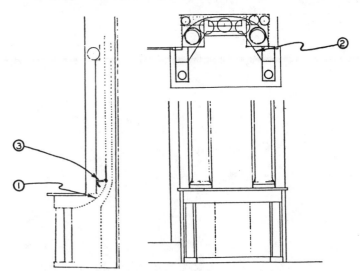

Rumford-XII.
Elevations & section of a Rumford fireplace.
At left and top right are sections of the fireplace showing, as Brown says, "a very round breast" (1) and a 125° angled coving (2) and the built-in damper or "door-way" as Rumford termed it. What would we do without a damper?

Rumford's second fireplace essay was published without any drawings, but we find among these sketches (in the Harvard collection) the front and side elevations and cross-section of a fireplace **(Rumford-XII)**which could well serve as an illustration emphasizing the points quoted above. It shows a fireplace with a very round breast (1), the covings at 125° with the back (2) — well below his 135° maximum, and a built-in damper (3), the invention of which Rumford first described *(as a "door-way" of plate or cast iron)* in the passage quoted above. These Harvard drawings are the only known Rumford illustrations of a new fireplace.

URNING A LIVING

Slot-filling collectipiles are doomed to a static afterlife — no matter what merits or potential the objects had before being taken out of circulation. They are required to stay in their place so that a preconceived "complete" collection will have no gaps. Collectors who won't give an inch, when objects in their collections practically beg for it, are in a sense, robotic — creatures directed by the trade press, by opinionated authors such as myself, by the current market, and especially by the prospect of fortune.

The photograph of the female robots made from aluminum coffee urns, coffee pots, vacuum cleaner nozzles and serving trays is here for those collectors who acquire items for idiosyncratic reasons having nothing to do with empty slots.

On the facing page are what sculptor Clayton G. Bailey called "robot secretaries" almost a decade ago when he created them. Too, too limiting, you might think today. Why shouldn't "T-T" and "2-2" follow any career suitable to their wants and talents (which obviously include ballet)? A female robot similar to "T-T" and "2-2" was kicked out of an exhibit at Berkeley in 1983 because some visitors complained about her physiognomy. Bah. Bailey's sculptures "exude a pleasant domesticity," as art historian Mark Levy wrote about them for an exhibition.

These gleaming aluminum forms are an amusing, different way to see things found in more prosaic guise elsewhere in this book. The major gene pool for robot sculpture, besides old photocopiers and automobiles, is comprised of old household items — from vacuum cleaner attachments to cocktail shakers, from pot lids to percolators. Presumably, the artist uses (mostly?) broken or incomplete objects, the scavenging of which we as collectors should have no quarrel with. And if not, there are, as Bailey says, many more parts than there are robot-makers (or kitchen collectors, for that matter).

The components of " 'as-is' minor appliances," as Bailey describes them, are reassembled into portraits we may already have glimpsed rough sketches of in the objects crowded under a flea market table. The anthromorphic sentiment evoked by a starving-orphan home appliance *who* can be adopted and loved as never loved before, is not entirely unknown to avid collectors.

Bailey's *The Robot Builder's Manual* contains an artist's statement which echoes the paranormal experience many collectors have had with certain pieces in their collections. Saying that old stoves, toasters, etc., are the "mechanical molecules" that go into his robots (some of which are not humanoid, but zoomorphic), Bailey claims that "these 'molecules' from which a robot is constructed have a past life or history. Regardless of how carefully or cleverly these objects are…transformed…, a memory of their history and their past lives remains and provides the Robot with its 'soul.' "

Do you want to get started building kinetic (or stationary) robots? Order a copy of Bailey's *The Robot Builder's Manual* for $10.00 postpaid from Wonders of the World, P.O. Box 69, Port Costa, CA 94569.

Robots "T-T" (L) and "2-2", by Clayton G. Bailey, a sculptor who lives near San Franscisco, in Port Costa, CA. Each is approx. 62"H x 20"W. Made primarily of polished aluminum parts from coffee urns, coffee pots, trays, etc., and various tubes and cones. Other materials include plastic, glass, rubber and electric lights. Bailey's work may be seen at the Joseph Chowning Gallery in San Francisco. Photograph by Greg MacGregor.

E. PRESERVING:

XV. CHILL & FREEZE

A very early way to preserve food was by lowering its temperature (in ice or cold water) to stop decomposition; some anthropologists even believe that those early humans who followed the Ice Age "harvested" mastodon and other animals preserved (perhaps even for thousands of years) in glacial ice.

Just two or three hundred years ago, people built ice houses — below ground ice 'wells', where huge chunks of sawn or chopped lake or pond ice could be stored (insulated to some extent with straw or marsh grasses or whatever relatively clean vegetable matter could be used to protect the ice from the air), and where it might be expected to last well into the summer. Thick domed stone tops to these wells or pits, insulated further with thick layers of earth and sod, helped protect the ice. This ice was probably used more to cool drinks and make desserts than to preserve food, at least for more than a few hours. Smoking and drying were more common methods of preserving food for the long term. (See next chapter.)

The most popular collectibles within this chapter are small <u>ice chippers</u>, shredders and shavers, <u>ice tongs</u>, and ice cream freezers. Prices haven't moved very much in these categories since the last edition of the mid 1980s, except for 18th or early 19th century forged iron ice tools, which have become much more expensive (as have their cousins, the hearth tools). I have placed a **Futurewatch** on ice cube trays — aluminum, rubber, and any other material I'm not aware of.

The least popular category is still ice boxes and refrigerators — which implies nothing about their artistic or historic merit, merely (and it ain't so mere) their size. For most people, one or two ice boxes is the limit; and most people seek decorative oak ones that go with Arts & Crafts or Mission furniture. They use them as bars or storage cabinets in their living or dining rooms. There are sufficient known collectors of large 20th century appliances, however, to encourage Charles Diehl, Jr., of Baltimore, MD, to attempt to organize a club. And if he knows of, say, 50 people collecting major appliances, we all know that means that — like an iceberg — there are many who aren't known. If you care to write Mr. Diehl about your interest, his address is 13 S. Potomac St., Baltimore, MD 21224.

Please: always use an SASE when writing to enquire for information from a fellow collector. I hesitate sometimes to tell people the addresses I know; if I give an address and 100 people write wanting information (let's say about something I have incorrectly described, or that never got off the ground), that's $30.00 out-of-pocket for the person who has to answer ... just for postage. It's not that we (the people whose addresses you have) don't like getting your letters; and, yes, we mean well about answering mail. But to get a stack of 30 or 50 or 100 letters, all wanting help, means that a suitable stack of envelopes has to be bought, 30, 50 or 100 stamps have to be bought, addresses have to be deciphered and written on the envelopes, and replies must be researched and written. This is a tremendous amount of work for a single individual, month after month.

If you are reading this book from back to front, you may have expected to find <u>ice cream molds</u>, and <u>dishers or scoops</u>, in this chapter. They are in Chapter IV — Form, Mold, Shape & Decorate.

Freezer, fabulous streamlined design with 2 round deep cylinders flanking a finned motor, all in white enameled steel, colored top lids on both compartments, "no food more than 9 inches away from all-surrounding source of cold", 1945 ad states. "You store two units with food. You use the food out of one unit. When this is consumed, you turn it off and start using the food in the second unit." "Deepfreeze", mfd by Deepfreeze Division of Motor Products Corp., North Chicago, IL, interior of compartments 30"H x 18" diameter, overall 41¼"H x 65⅝"L x 26¹¹⁄₁₆" diameter, began making c.1938. **$65.00-$85.00**

Ice box, ash, enameled metal interior, 2 door, 57"H, TOC. • I believe that some **old refrigerator hardware,** including some name plates of cast brass, can still be bought through the mail from: Constantine's, 2050 Eastchester Rd, Bronx, NY 10461; The Antique Hardware Store, 43 Beridge St, Frenchtown, NJ 08825; and The 19th Century Hardware & Supply Co., POB 599, Rough and Ready, CA 95975. Ask also about their catalogs, for which you must pay a fee. **$175.00-$220.00**

Ice box, oak, 4 doors, "Northey Duplex", 6 feet 2½" H x 4 feet 1½"W x 2½ feet deep, TOC. **$350.00-$400.00**

Ice box, oak, porcelainized interior, lift top lid with zinc-lined box, one door, wire shelves, 47"H x 27½" wide, TOC. • Once I did something very bad (or could you call it "urban archaeology", as they do now?). I was living in Memphis in the early 1960s, and a few of us were out late one night with nothing to do, even though there was an all-night supermarket and a 24-hour launderette. A row of

old turn-of-the-century houses were slated for demolition in a neighborhood not far from ours. We drove up in one of the driveways, and, with our flashlights, went inside one of the houses, which was completely open. The house was filled with boards, doors, piles of lath strips, wires ripped out, presumably all junk, but there was an old oak icebox like the one described here, which we carried out, loaded onto sun roof of my long-suffering VW and drove home. It was rusted inside, and covered with mildew, but cleaned up nicely. This was 1963, and I don't still have it; I left it behind when I moved to NYC. **$175.00-$220.00**

Ice box, pine with zinc lining, lift top, 1 door, wire shelves, 42"H, TOC. **$135.00-$150.00**

Ice box, unusual tall cupboard type, door over door, oak with paneled sides, bracket feet, M. M. Whitman & Co., Worcester, MA, 60"H x 28½"W x 23½" deep, TOC. **$400.00-$500.00**

Ice box, which could be converted to electricity with a compressor, motor & gas coils, large boxy enameled (ivory, grey, blue or green) steel cabinet on casters, 4 hinged doors, lined with white "quarried" stone, "White Mountain", Maine Mfg. Co., Nashua, NH, c.1927. **$75.00-$100.00**

Ice box, white enamel painted steel inside and out, insulated with cork, 4 stumpy bath tub-like legs with casters, lid lifts off top part where ice goes, hinged door in side reveals 2 (1916 one seems to have 3) round revolving nickel plated shelves inside, later ones had a spigot on

side of top part to draw off ice cold water for drinking (you'd have to trust your ice man!), in 1920 ad, glass water cooler with removable top shown adjacent to the ice compartment, "White Frost", mfd by Metal Stamping Co., Jackson, MI, 43"H x 23" diameter, pat'd Sept. 11, 1906, Nov. 6, 1906 and June 23, 1908. • Advertisements claimed that the White Frost was used by the government during work on the Panama Canal. By 1916 the company was called White Frost Refrigerator Co., and by 1920 it was the Home Products Corporation. Still selling in 1920 in nearly the same form. Condition of original baked-on enamel paint, and condition of inside affects value.
$55.00-$100.00

Ice box, zinc alloy, nickeled brass hardware, 2 doors with wire shelves, 4 legs, TOC. **$150.00-$170.00**

Ice bucket, metal, shaped like a medieval knight's helmet, top opens to reveal ice, 20th C. **$40.00-$55.00**

Ice chipper, cast iron, "Gilchrist #50", Newark, NJ, 20th C. **$20.00-$25.00**

Ice chipper, cast iron, brass ferrule, wooden handle, "Briddell #60", Charles D. Briddell, Inc., Crisfield, MD, late 19th or early 20th C. **$6.00-$8.00**

Ice chipper, steel with wood handle, wicked looking, "Crown", mfd by North Brothers, Philadelphia, PA, c.1900. **$10.00-$15.00**

Ice chipper & bottle opener combined, iron, wooden handle, "Coolerator", Duluth Refrigerator Corp., Duluth, MN, early 20th C. **$5.00-$8.00**

Ice chisel, steel, turned wood handle, downturned chisel head fitted on back with a much shorter head with 4 very broad sharp teeth, "Crown Ice Chipper", mfd by American Machine Co., Philadelphia, PA, pat'd April 8, 1884. **$12.00-$15.00**

Ice chisel, polished steel blade, turned wooden handle with iron band to keep it from splitting when hit with mallet, 4 wicked sharp beveled teeth, Matthai-Ingram Co., c.1890s. **$14.00-$18.00**

Ice chopper, heavy clear glass tumbler with 3 red bands & 2 black bands indicating ounce measurements, chromed lid, fitted with heavily weighted nickeled metal cross bladed chopper with knob handle, blades have teeth, American, 20 oz. capacity, 9"H, c.1930s to 1940s. **$10.00-$14.00**

Ice cracker, long springy chromed steel handle with plastic grip and with heavy round head, used with ice in palm of hand or on towel, "Tap-Icer", Williamsport, PA, c.1960. **$3.00-$5.00**

Ice cream can, gray graniteware, container for ingredients which could be put into some kinds of ice cream freezers. 1 qt. size, late 19th C. **$70.00-$90.00**

Ice cream carrier, for picnics, oak box, zinc lining, side door swings open to put in block of ice cream, then you lift off top & pack in ice, "The Bradley Ice Cream Cabinet, Patented", mfd by the Bradley Mfg. Co., New Haven, CT, 8 ½"H x 11" x 9", late 19th C. • Ice cream is a high ticket area of specialization in kitchen collections. For collector club, see Ice cream molds in Mold chapter.
$225.00-$275.00

Ice cream freezer, "North Pole", Alaska Freezer Co., Winchendon, MA, 20th C. **$45.00-$55.00**

Ice cream freezer, "Champion", Arlington, NJ, early 20th C. **$60.00-$70.00**

• **Makers of Ice Cream Freezers.** — In the *Thomas' Register of American Manufacturers*, for 1905-06, there are but 14 makers of ice cream freezers listed: White Mountain, Nashua, NH; Treman, King & Co., Ithaca, NY; Cordley & Hayes, NYC, who made them of Indurated Fibre ware; Crandall & Godley, and Slotkin & Praglin, both also of NYC; E. C. Stearns & Co., Syracuse, NY; Dana Mfg., H. Day & Co., Kingery Mfg. Co., and The Samuel C. Tatum Co., all of Cincinnati, OH; and J. P. Anderson & Co., Thomas Mills & Brother, North Brothers Mfg. Co., and Charles W. Packer, all 4 of Philadelphia.

Ice cream freezer, all metal, galvanized iron outer box, "reinforced cover", heavy tin round "paint can" cylinder inside with a "friction cover which is absolutely water tight", tinned iron dasher and crank with wooden knob, the crank being outside the box's side, "The Snow Flake Freezer" stenciled on side, mfd by Snow Flake Mfg Co., came in 1, 2, 3 and 4 qt. sizes, c.1907-1908. **$40.00-$50.00**

Ice cream freezer, clamps to table, "Liberty Can Co.", Lancaster, PA, 2 qt. size, pat'd 1920 and 1921. • **Doughboys Love Ice Cream.** — "Ice cream has played a great part in this war (WWII) and is recognized as a morale builder, unsurpassed. The importance of ice cream has been testified to by the enormous amounts of prepared mix and portable equipment for freezing provided by the army and used so close to combat lines that battle weary men just back of the front have been able to have a dish of ice cream in the protection of the nearest foxhole." Dr. H. A. Ruehe, American Butter Institute, *The Sealtest Food Adviser*. Fall 1945. **$55.00-$65.00**

Ice cream freezer, galvanized metal canister, snug fitting lid, vertical crank with wooden knob, wire bail handle, "Glacier Freezer Triple Action", mfd by Sunburst Alcohol Stove Co., T. W. Houchin, NYC, NY, c.1912.
$25.00-$35.00

Ice cream freezer, galvanized tin, blue painted lid, outer body, crank, paper label says "Kwik Freeze", 20th C.
$45.00-$55.00

Ice cream freezer, horizontal heavy tin "duplex" cylinder with stationary dasher blade inside each half, cylinder (which fits into malleable cast iron screw clamp frame) turns freely when cranked, while the dashers remain stationary, oblong hinged hatch in middle for putting in salt & ice, close-fitting caps at each end for adding ingredients for 2 flavors of ice cream, "Acme", mfd by Palmer Hardware Mfg. Co., Troy, NY, c.1892. **$100.00-$125.00**

Ice cream freezer, japanned & stenciled tin canister, with imitation graining & bronze decorations and label. Heavy porcelain knob with gilding on close-fitting lid, galvanized interior, long cone-shaped insert to hold ingredients with salt packed around, cast iron side handles, "Automatic Ice Cream Freezer", mfd by Treman King & Co, "System Dr. Meidinger" (refers to a patent?), Ithaca, NY, 13½"H x 6" diameter, c.1880s. They were s.i.b. in 1905. **$165.00-$225.00**

Ice cream freezer, looks like horizontal barrel churn with straight cylindrical sides, on A frame, all wood but for iron bands on freezer, iron crank in end. A small size one is tabletop & mounted to board. "Tingley's Patent Horizontal", mfd by the churn maker Charles G. Blatchley as "Blatchley's Horizontal", Philadelphia, PA, sizes from 3 to 40 qts., pat'd by J. Tingley of Philadelphia Feb. 11, 1868 and June 6, 1871. Advertised by Blatchley in 1874, and as late as 1911. **$125.00-$140.00**

• "**Directions for Freezing Ice-Creams and Custards.** — Ice-creams, custards and water are so delightful and refreshing for summer desserts and tea, it is to me a matter of astonishment that every family is not supplied with a patent ice-cream freezer, of which there are many in the market. By the use of one of these, the process of freezing is rendered so much more expeditious and satisfactory as to more than compensate for the trifling expense involved in its purpose. If not provided with this convenience, a small quantity of ice-cream can be frozen in a tin bucket, taking care that there are no holes in it to let in the water, and spoil the cream. Set this bucket in a wooden tub or bucket several inches larger. On the bottom of this place a layer of pounded ice and salt; set in the bucket containing the cream, or custard, and pack closely around its sides a mixture of pounded ice and salt (mixed in the proportion of six pounds of ice to one of salt), extending to within two inches of the top of the freezer. Cover the freezer, and keep it in constant motion, removing the cover frequently to scrape the congealed cream from the sides with a silver spoon or wooden paddle, taking care to keep the sides clear, and stirring it well to the bottom. Keep the tub well filled with salt and ice outside the freezer, and take great care that none of the salt water gets in to spoil the cream. The outside tub or bucket should have a hole in or near the bottom, from which the bung can be removed to allow the water to pass out as the ice melts. After the cream is well frozen, it may be packed in moulds, and set in salt and pounded ice. When you wish to serve it, wrap the mould with a hot cloth, turn out the cream and serve immediately.

"For making ice-cream, genuine cream is, of course, preferable. But in the absence of this, equal parts of milk and cream may be used; or, the milk may be heated, and, while hot, perfectly fresh sweet butter added to it in sufficient quantity to give it the richness of cream. Boiled milk or custards must be allowed to become perfectly cold before putting them in the freezer. Sour cream or buttermilk may be used by stirring into them enough soda to correct their acid before sweetening and flavoring. Custards and creams for freezing should be sweetened and flavored more highly than when not frozen." Mrs. A. P. Hill, *Mrs. Hill's New Family Receipt Book*. NY: 1870.

Ice cream freezer, pail shaped, crank on top, frame of malleable cast iron, pail is tinned wrought sheet iron, Isaac S. Williams & Co., Philadelphia, pat'd June 21, 1881.

Ice cream freezer, staved wooden bucket with wire bail handle, tinned cast iron works, crank turns numerous horizontally-fixed beater blades, "Rapid", Clement & Dunbar, Philadelphia, 4 gal. capacity, c.1880s.
$35.00-$45.00

Ice cream freezer, tin, "Kress", poss. Philadelphia, pat'd July 23, 1912. **$30.00-$35.00**

Ice cream freezer, tin cylinder, wooden crank top, "Acme", mfd by Ritter, Philadelphia, 2 gal. capacity, pat'd Feb. 15, 1910. Later patent shown on others is July 3, 1912.
$35.00-$45.00

Ice cream freezer, wood bucket with cast iron works, "Arctic", mfd by White Mountain Freezer Co., Nashua, NH, pat'd 1889. They were still in business 1905. • **German vocabulary** — Eismaschinen: Ice machine. **$35.00-$45.00**

Ice cream freezer, wood & galvanized metal, "Frost King", Richmond Cedar Works, Richmond, VA, 20th C. (Still making them in 1930s.) • "A Freezing Tub must be made oblong or oval, the sides to be as upright as possible; may be made to hold two or three sabbatiers, or freezing pots, in length, leaving a sufficient space for the ice; it must have a false bottom with some holes in it; in the side of the tub, near the bottom, make a hole for a peg, by which means you may constantly draw off the water, a precaution highly necessary when freezing, to prevent the water from ever getting into the sabbatier. Sabbatiers, ice moulds, and ice spoons, may be supplied by any experienced pewterer." Joseph Bell, *A Treatise on Confectionary* Newcastle, England, 1817. • "**To freeze Ices.** — If only one sort of ice, set the freezing pot in a small upright pail, made as above, with two bottoms, &c.,is two or three sorts, set your pots at a proper distance in the long pail; fill up the space with ice well beat, mix in three or four handfuls of salt, and press both well down; then take a clean cloth and make the tops of the pots clear of ice and salt; take off the tops; and put into each the creams or waters previously mixed for them; please to observe, that pots must not be more than half full; then replace the top to each; draw the tub a little to one side, and turn each pot as quickly, as possible; if you have two pots in, turn one with each hand; if three, let one stand alternately; when you have turned the pots ten minutes, take off the tops, and scrape the frozen cream down from each with an ice spoon; if the cream appears hard and flinty, you may conclude it is not rich enough mixed; if, on the other hand, it does not freeze, it is over rich, and in either case must be rectified; if right, proceed as before directed, and every ten minutes, scrape it down; when the cream in the pots appears nearly frozen, keep off the covers, and work well with the ice spoon, making the pots turn round in the ice, this will make the cream both smooth and light; as soon as it appears pretty stiff, put on the tops, and cover the pots well up with more ice and salt, until you prepare your moulds to receive it. N.B. It may be necessary here to note, that you must have an ice spoon for each pot; or must be careful to wash it every time, to prevent a mixture of tastes." Joseph Bell, *A Treatise on Confectionary*. Newcastle, England, 1817. • For Bell's tips on molding ice cream, see an Ice cream mold entry in the Mold chapter. **$45.00-$55.00**

Ice cream freezer, wood, metal, "Auto Vacuum", pat'd Jan. 2, 1912. **$30.00-$40.00**

Ice cream freezer, wood with cast iron crank & frame, 2 gal. size, dated 1858 — probably one pat'd by H. B. Masser of Sunbury, PA, on Jan. 19, 1858. The three earliest patents for freezers were granted in 1848: E. M. Manigle of Philadelphia got one May 30; A. H. Austin of Baltimore got one Sept. 19; and H. B. Masser got his first one Dec. 12, 1848, then this one 10 years later, then one in 1861 and another in 1867. **$125.00-$150.00**

Ice cream freezer, wooden tub or bucket, bail handle, iron crank and frame, "American", mfd by American Machine Co., Philadelphia, PA, c.1880s. **$35.00-$45.00**

Ice cream holder, tin, bail handle, insulated inside, "Thermopak", Joe Lowe Co., Inc., Brooklyn, NY, 1st third 20th C. **$15.00-$20.00**

Ice cream jar, glass, "Ice Cream in Glass", American, 1 pt. capacity. **$15.00-$18.00**

Ice cream maker, glass canister with feet, wire frame, with original recipe & instruction folder inside, "Sanitary Crystal Glass Ice Cream Freezer", mfd by "Consolidated Mfg. Co.", American (poss. Dayton, OH; poss. Quincy, IL), early 20th C. **$50.00-$65.00**

Ice Cream mixer, cast aluminum, used with CO_2 cartridges, that came in boxes of 5, then put in freezer tray after mixing, "One Smoothie Whip is required for making. ... When the Whip has been discharged and removed from the holder it can be thrown out, as it cannot be used again." Marked with decal of name "Smoothie" superimposed over a green sundae dish with ice cream in it, "The Smoothie. The Instant Home Mixer of " 'Satin Smooth' Ice Cream", mfd by Ralmac Corp., Grand Rapids, MI, no date, c. 1950s. **$45.00-$55.00**

Ice cream molds & ice cream dishers See Form & Mold chapter.

Ice cream packing tins, set of 4, tin, American, 4 qt., 1 pt., ½ pt. & ¼ pt. capacity, early 20th C. **$35.00-$50.00**

Ice crusher, cream-colored painted cast metal, wood handle crank, on a stand with place for a tumbler, "National Ice-Crusher", 9"H, pat'd 1936. **$28.00-$32.00**

Ice crusher, iron, "Alaska #1", Alaska Freezer Co., Winchendon, MA, 19th C into 1st third 20th C. **$35.00-$40.00**

Ice cube breaker, cast iron base, with green glass ice hopper, "Lightning", North Brothers Mfg. Co., Philadelphia, PA, 1932 design patent #86599. **$40.00-$50.00**

Ice cube breaker, enameled steel frame and platform, fitted with square green Depression glass container, hopper above with crank, "Lightning", North Brothers (?), 1933 patent #1980952. **$35.00-$40.00**

Ice cube breaker, nickel plated brass, "Coolerator", Duluth Refrigerators, Duluth, MN, 20th C. **$28.00-$35.00**

Ice cube crusher, all cast iron, oblong jaws with "waffled" treads inside, "Stover Ice Cube Kracker", Freeport, IL, 7 ¾"L, early 20th C. **$18.00-$25.00**

Ice cube tray, aluminum, dividers so niftily jointed it looks like a millipede, no maker mark, 12⅛"L, 1938 patents #214795, #2265705, #2212424, and #2212425. • **German vocabulary** — Eiswurfel-schale or Eiswurfel-lade: ice tray. **$3.00-$5.00**

Ice cube tray, green rubber with metal wire puller or grip, "FlexoTray", mfd by Inland Mfg. Co., Dayton, OH, 10½"L, 1929 reissue patent #17273. • According to a 1931 ad, the "FlexoTray" was made for Westinghouse, Kelvinator, Leonard, Electrolux, Servel, Copeland, Universal & other refrigerators. Inland also made the "Quickube Tray" for Frigidaire, and the "DuFlex" for General Electric. These various flexible rubber trays were "supplied by all leading automatic refrigerator makers". **$4.00-$8.00**

Ice cube tray, natural colored brownish rubber, very flexible, makes 21 cubes, each cup has interconnecting hole in inner walls, "Flexo Tray", mfd by The Inland Mfg. Co., Dayton, OH, 1¾" deep x 12¼"L x 3¾"W, 1929 reissue patent # s 17278 and 17279. **$8.00-$10.00**

Ice grinder, cast metal alloy, Dazey, the churn people, St. Louis, MO, 1940s. **$20.00-$30.00**

Ice pick, all metal, steel pick, cast heavy metal handle, adv'g "Coca-Cola", 20th C. **$4.00-$6.00**

Ice pick, iron with turned wooden knob handle, spring action, punch it down & shaft telescopes to increase pounds-per-square-inch force, in F. A. Walker catalog, c.1870s. **$15.00-$18.00**

Ice pick or hammer, brass, long rod handle with ruffled cuff ferrule and small cast fist holding large tack-shaped thing with point and flat top, English or Continental, about 10"L overall, with fist about 3"L, prob. mid 19th C. **$100.00-$135.00**

Ice pick & scraper, nickeled iron with wooden handle, looks like a sort of fork with a frame over top of tines, has a small maw to catch shavings, mfd by & advertising "Coolerator. The Air Conditioned Refrigerator", Coolerator Co., Duluth, MN, 12"L, 20th C. **$15.00-$18.00**

Ice picks, nickeled steel, all steel or steel with wooden handles, with advertising, early 20th C or late 19th. • Advertising picks are valued the highest. **$8.00-$12.00**

Ice scoop, corrugated galvanized tin with wooden handle, long bowl with high slightly rounded sides, flat heel, American, 9"L, c.1890s. **$8.00-$12.00**

Ice scraper & chipper, cast iron with wooden handle, "White Mountain", Nashua, NH, late 19th or early 20th C. **$10.00-$15.00**

Ice shaver, cast iron, "Arctic Ice Shave #3", Grey Iron Casting Co., Mount Joy, PA, late 19th C. **$15.00-$20.00**

Ice shaver, cast iron base with steel shaving table, stands high on 4 beautiful scrolled cabriole legs, mid 19th C. **$100.00-$135.00**

Ice shaver, cast iron, steel, Griswold, Erie, PA, late 19th or early 20th C. **$35.00-$40.00**

Ice shaver, cast iron & steel, hand-cranked rotary type, Clawson Machine Co., Flagtown, NJ, early 20th C. **$75.00-$100.00**

Ice shaver, heavy cast iron, tinned, lid has a monogram, "ACW" for A. C. Williams Co., Ravenna, OH, 7⅝"L, TOC. **$15.00-$20.00**

Ice shaver, nickeled cast iron, hinged hopper, removeable blade, "Gem", mfd by North Brothers Mfg. Co., Philadelphia, patent applied for. **$15.00-$20.00**

Ice shaver, cast metal, big cup with adjustable and sharpenable steel blade, "Morgan-Strowbridge Iron Co. #2", New Brighton, PA, TOC. **$7.00-$10.00**

Ice shaver or plane, galvanized cast iron (they also made one of cast aluminum) with double edged tool steel blade, hinged angled top that encloses compartment that catches the shavings, looks almost identical to one made by Stover, "No. 77", Gilchrist Co., Newark, NJ, c.1906. **$7.00-$10.00**

Ice shaver, tongs & hammer combined, cast iron, American, 13¼"L, pat'd June 1878. **$75.00-$90.00**

Ice shredder, tinned cast iron, cone-shaped with lid, shaving blade is in lid so held cone tip up to work, slightly curved double handles hinged at end, one attached to cone, one to lid, held together while scraping, "after the Shredder is scraped full of ice, tap the small end of cone so as to make contents solid", after which you release handle to reveal snow cone, which fits then into paper holder, "especially adapted for the use of vendors selling 'Snow Balls,' as by hole in the small end of cone the ball can be readily flavored and easily ejected." "Enterprise Hardware Co. #43", Philadelphia, c.1890s, sold into 20th C. **$22.00-$30.00**

Ice shredder or shaver, tinned cast iron cup with curved handle, looks like little saucepan with hinged lid, steel shaver teeth inside, makes snow balls for snow cones, or ice for icing oysters on the half shell, or celery, fruits, drinks, marked "Enterprise Mfg. Co. #33" on lid, 7¾"L overall, cup is 3½" diameter x 2½" deep, sold at least by July 1892; pat'd July 4, 1893, lucky patent date for ice cold treat! • The same size #34 was nickeled, & cost 3 times as much when new, but not now. **$30.00-$45.00**

Ice tongs, cast & forged iron, American, 21"L, TOC. **$20.00-$25.00**

Ice tongs, iron, "Butler Ice Co.", 14"L, TOC. **$15.00-$20.00**

Ice tongs, iron with wooden handle, adv'g "Dixie Gem Coal, Ice & Fuel Co.", 14"L, early 20th C. **$20.00-$25.00**

Ice tongs, scissor type with 2 handle grips, flat forged iron, 12"L, 20th C. **$15.00-$22.00**

Ice tongs, simple forged bar iron, early 20th C. **$25.00-$45.00**

Ice tongs, wrought iron with decorative twisting, American, 14"L, 19th C. **$35.00-$50.00**

Ice water bottle, green glass, oblong with big rounded top, embossed pebbly surface except for depiction of Monitor Top refrigerator, & words "WATER ... for use with the GENERAL ELECTRIC REFRIGERATOR" on the front, measures from 1 cup (½ pt.) to 3 cups (½ pts.) on back, GE, 8½"H x 5"W, 1927. **$75.00-$85.00**

Nursery refrigerator, japanned sheet steel chest with lifting handles at each end, looks like oak graining with pin striping, hasped lid lifts to reveal one compartment of porcelainized steel for ice water or other cold liquid, another compartment for food, insulated with mineral wool (asbestos), mfd by James R. Wotherspoon, Philadelphia, PA, very early 20th C. • Fries & McAleer made these too, almost identical in appearance. **$15.00-$22.00**

Refrigerator, box on short cabriole legs, motor housing on top is shaped like the Capitol dome in Washington, DC, white enameled steel, "Ice-O-Matic" in Capitol Model, mfd by Williams Oil-O-Matic Heating Corp., Bloomington, IL, small, c.1930. • **It's What's On Top That Counts.** — The most famed refrigerator with motor housing on top is the GE Monitor Top, but it is also the most commonly found. According to a 1930 ad, you can have the motor "unit on top of its good-looking cabinet; in the lower compressor compartment or in the basement." **$75.00-$100.00**

Refrigerator, electric, but looks just like large icebox, white enameled steel, tall box with nickeled-steel binding around each of 6 doors, plated hinges & handles, louvered motor compartment underneath, upper right door reveals ice cube tray, glass in all doors makes this look like professional restaurant refrigerators sold today to upscale housewives, Servel Corp. (soon to be Electrolux Servel), factories in Evansville, IN, Carteret, NJ, Newburgh, NY, c.1925. • **German vocabulary** — Kuhlschrank: cold cupboard (refrigerator). **$55.00-$75.00**

Refrigerator, white enameled steel, stepped streamline shape, black base, bin compartment with pull-down door at bottom, main door reveals small central freezer compartment, several shelves, many nickeled wire shelves built into drawer, amazing part is the radio built into the top front of the refrigerator, WOW!!! "Crosley Shelvador", Crosley Radio Corp., Cincinnati, OH , c.1938. Because of the radio this has great crossover collector value, even if the radio needs tubes. **$350.00-$425.00**

Refrigerator bottle, green glass, pat'd Sept. 15, 1931. **$15.00-$20.00**

Refrigerator bowl, gray graniteware, with cover, TOC. **$45.00-$65.00**

Refrigerator container, pale blue "crystal" glass, with lid, "Fire-King", Anchor Hocking Glass Corp., 4½" x 5", 1940s-50s. **$10.00-$15.00**

Refrigerator container, glass, "Westinghouse", 1930s. **$10.00-$15.00**

Refrigerator ice water dispenser, glass with fired-on opaque pastel green finish, chrome spigot with red rubber gasket, clear glass (called "crystal") lid molded with concentric rings, sort of a glass shoebox that lies on its side with spigot at one end, for getting cold water. In old refrigerators this might fit under the tiny freezer compartment, mfd by Hall, 12"L, c.1930s. • **"Jadite"** generally refers to a color, most usually, a pale green that can be opaque "milk" glass or painted on the inside (as is this refrigerator container), but it is also a trade name for an opaque green that Jeannette Glass Co. (Jeannette, PA) made, and the name "Jade-ite" was used by Anchor Hocking. Other pieces in opaque green were made by Fenton Glass Co., who used simply "Jade"; and McKee Glass Co. used "Jade Green". Collectors tend to use it for a wide range of very pale to rather richly green opaque but translucent glass. When used in ads it often doesn't mean the Jeannette brand name. **$65.00-$80.00**

Refrigerator ice water dispenser, pebbly-textured clear, or "crystal", glass body, plain "crystal" lid, white rubber gasket, c.1930s. **$30.00-$45.00**

Refrigerator jar, saltglazed stoneware, small size, Red Wing, MN, 20th C. **$100.00-$110.00**

Refrigerator jar, saltglazed stoneware with 2 blue bands, bail handle, "Red Wing Refrigerator Jar, Compliments of Semon's Fair Store, Athens, Wisc.", mfd in MN, 5¾"H, early 20th C. **$100.00-$300.00**

Refrigerator pan, galvanized steel, looks like dog feeding dish for a St. Bernard, round with bowl bottom set in side, 2 side ear handles, catches drips from melting ice, New England Enameling Co., Middletown, CT, TOC. • "A strictly modern newspaper item tells of a bride who declined an invitation to a picnic because she could never be away from the apartment for more than five hours and twenty minutes at a stretch. Her inquisitive friends asked why. 'Well', she explained reluctantly, 'you see, every five hours and twenty-one minutes, the refrigerator-pan overflows.' " Frances Lester Warner, "When Equipment Overflows", *House Beautiful*, Feb. 1927. **$7.00-$10.00**

Refrigerator water bottle, rich green Depression glass, embossed design of old-fashioned well, American, 1930s. **$25.00-$30.00**

Refrigerator water jug, swirled cobalt blue Depression glass, with spigot, 20th C. **$145.00-$175.00**

Water cooler, blue & gray stoneware, depiction of woman & well (Rebecca?), Robinson Clay Products, OH, early 20th C. **$275.00-$350.00**

Water cooler, blue & white pottery, with metal spigot, Western Pottery Mfg. Co., Denver, CO, 3 gal. capacity. **$100.00-$150.00**

Water cooler, blue & white saltglazed stoneware, 3 gal. size, late 19th C. **$120.00-$240.00**

Water cooler, blue & white earthenware, of the relatively softer type, relief molded with depiction of man at a wall and flowers. I don't think I've ever seen one without a few chips, especially on the raised parts of the design, American, 12"H, last quarter 19th C. **$75.00-$95.00**

Water cooler, japanned tin urn, stenciled "Ice Water", with cast iron finial to ridged, domed tin lid & cast iron spigot, in F.A. Walker catalog, 8 sizes: 2, 3, 4, 6, 8, 10, 15 & 20 gal., c.1870s. • This also came with a porcelain liner, in 2, 3, 4, 6, 8 and 10 gallon sizes. **$45.00-$65.00**

Water cooler, saltglazed stoneware, Red Wing, MN, 6 gal. size, 20th C. **$250.00-$300.00**

Water cooler, saltglazed stoneware, blue striped, American, 14½"H x 10" diameter, late 19th C.   **$65.00-$90.00**

Water cooler, saltglazed stoneware jug with ear handles, on wonderful turned stoneware pedestal base, metal spigot, gray with cobalt blue birds on branches, incised & colored, marked with capacity number ''4'', PA, 21½"H, mid 19th C. • $500.00 at auction in early 1980s.
$750.00-$1200.00

Water cooler, saltglazed stoneware with cobalt blue flower design, pewter spigot, no lid, 4 gal. size, 19th C.
$200.00-$300.00

Water cooler, saltglazed stoneware, name stenciled in cobalt, ''Fort Dodge Stoneware Co.'', American, 4 gallon size, 2nd half 19th C. • Two other companies' coolers to look for, also made of stoneware with various shaped exteriors, are Gate City Stone Filters, NYC, and John C. Jewett Mfg. Co. coolers, Buffalo, NY. The latter, advertised in 1888 as the ''New Era'', was supposedly the ''only cooler for milk, lemonade & all summer drinks.''
$225.00-$275.00

Water cooler, spongeware with metal spigot, Monmouth Pottery, 10 gal. capacity.   **$375.00-$425.00**

Water cooler, white pottery with blue rings, metal spigot, matching lid, American, 3 gal. capacity, TOC.
$95.00-$120.00

Water cooler, white & blue spongeware, ''Avery & Winter Pottery Co. #6'', NYC, NY, 19th C.   **$300.00-$400.00**

Water filter & cooler, blue & white glazed pottery, shapely breasted container with spigot hole near bottom, ''The Allen Germ-Proof Filter'', Toledo, OH, 13½"H x 10¼" diameter, late 19th C. • When I lived in Toledo I only saw one of these, the lidless one I bought. Since then, at flea markets all over, I have seen a number of them, all without lids.   **$175.00-$300.00**

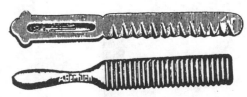

XV-2.
Eis-Dressiermess, or ice-breaking knife.
Two types from A. Bertuch catalog of specialties mainly for ice cream makers & confectioners. Berlin, Germany, c.1904. Cast metal.   **$15.00-$30.00**

XV-3.
Ice box.
"White Frost Sanitary", mfd. by C.A. Carey, Home Products Corp., Jackson, MI. Ladies' Home Journal ad, 5/1920: " 'Our iceman says, 'This is the only refrigerator in town. People could afford to throw their ice boxes away and save the price of a White Frost in ice.' A doctor says, 'From a sanitary standpoint, it cannot be beaten.' " Steel, granulated cork insulation, nickel trim, white glass water cooler, removable top, shelves revolve.   **$250.00-$450.00**

XV-1.
"Closet or Upright Refrigerator," and Ice box.
(L) "The door on the side insures ventilation, and the closet form is most convenient to arrange dishes." American Home Cook Book, 1854. (R) "Glacier Refrigerator." Northern Refrigerator Co., Grand Rapids, MI. Their motto: "As far ahead of all others as the electric light excels the candle." I wonder if work was already in progress trying to make an electric refrigerator. Century, 5/1892.
$200.00-$400.00

XV-4.
Ice cutter or breaker.
No. 1 of 4 sizes. This one "for hotel keepers, confectioners, wine merchants, refreshment rooms, ships' cabins, butlers' pantries, & etc.," Cast iron, cast iron legs with lion's head knees. Circular ring underneath is for pan to catch the ice. Largest styles had drawers underneath. No.3 "will take a piece of ice about 5" x 6" x 8", breaking it into pieces about the size of a chestnut." Ad in Mrs. A.B. Marshall's Cookery Book, London, c.1900.   **$150.00-$300.00**

XV-5.
Ice chippers.

"Lightning" (L & R), & "Crown" (M)). North Brothers Mfg. Co., Philadelphia. "They take the place of the old-time bag and hatchet, and quickly reduce the ice to uniformly small pieces, about the size of a peanut." Lightning made in No.1, for families; No.2, with 48"L handle for confectioners, hotels, restaurants. North's promo-cookbook *Dainty Dishes For All the Year Round,* by Mrs. S.T. Rorer. **$10.00-$18.00**

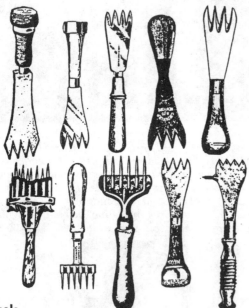

XV-6.
Ice chisels.

Most are versions of 4-toothed style. Those with flat-ended handles were used by hitting with mallet. (L) to (R) top first. (1) Polished steel blade, iron band around handle kept it from splitting when hit. Matthai-Ingram, c.1890. (2) Steel blade, tinned "cap" to wood handle, 10 1/2"L. (3) Steel blade, wood handle, choice of 6", 8", or 10" blades, with 8", 10" or 12" handles, 12" handle. Landers, Frary & Clark. (2) & (3) Sexton catalog, 1930s. (4) Steel, iron ferrule, C.W. Dunlap & Co., NYC. c.1904-1910. (5) Steel & wood. Heinz & Munschauer, 1882. (6) Galvanized iron, hardwood handle, steel points "securely fastened & interchangeable." 9", 11 1/2" or 48"L. Sold by Albert Pick, 1909. (7) "Gilchrist's Needle Point Ice Chipper No.50," also for "caked salt, sugar, etc." Sexton catalog, 1930s. (8) "Ice Pick Chipper," tinned steel, 9 1/2"L x 3"W. Pick, 1909. (9) "Four-Point Ice Shaver," tempered steel, nickeled iron band & ferrule to wood handle. On cap: "N. White City & Co." (?) Pick, 1909. (10) Combo shave & pick, nickeled malleable iron. 6 1/2"L blade; 12"L overall. Pick, 1909. **$5.00-$25.00**

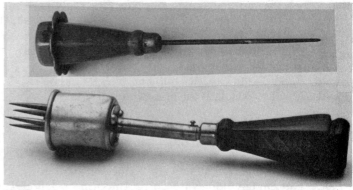

XV-7.
Ice picks.

(T) Needle point, wood handle with scalloped cap of metal which is a crusher head. 7 5/8"L. Probably Androck, c.1930s. (B) Mechanical one, with protective housing when not in use. Wood handle with flat top for mallet, steel prickers & shank, aluminum housing. To reveal pick points, you push aluminum cup up shaft, and twist it. Bayonet locking device. 8"L. Located by Primitive Man, Bob Cahn, Carmel, NY. **$7.00-$15.00; $20.00-$40.00**

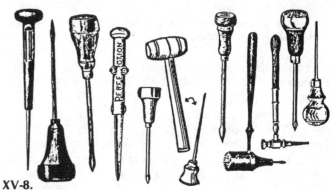

XV-8.
Ice picks.

(L) to (R): (1) "Unique", steel needle point, malleable cast iron handle slides up & down, serves as a hammer. 8 1/2"L. Albert Pick, 1909. (2) Patented, iron bound wood handle, pick with slight "arrowhead" or spear point — the other type of pick point. John Van Range Co., 1914. (3) 5"L pick. Sexton, c.1930. (4) "Perfection", all iron handle. Mfd. by W.G. Browne Mfg. Co. 1910. (5) "Ice Pick — Steel Awl," 8 3/4"L, tinned cap. Sexton, c.1930. (6 & 7) connected by arrows, "Ice mallet with pick that slides into the handle" of the mallet. Most valuable one here. *American Home Cook Book,* 1854. (8) Steel point, wood handle. Without iron band. Matthai-Ingram, c.1890. (9) "Steak pounder & ice mallet No.4." Steel pick in head of hammer. Heinz & Munschauer, 1882. (10) Ice hammer & pick, rosewood handle, tempered steel point, silver-plated hammer & shank. 2nd most valuable. 8 1/2"L x 2 7/8"W. (11) "Spear point" steel pick, nickeled iron band & ferrule. 8 1/2"L. Has "N. White City & Co." cap mark. (12) Needle pick, steel, hardwood knob handle, 9 1/4"L. Last 3 all Pick, 1909. **$5.00-$65.00**

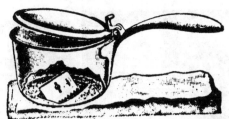

XV-9.
Ice shaver or shredder.
Tinned or nickeled cast iron 'cup' like saucepan, hinged lid. A cutaway view shows adjustable (& removable) blade inside. Enterprise Mfg. Co., Philadelphia. It is "only necessary to draw the blade upon the ice, the pressure applied producing fine or coarse pieces, as desired. To remove the finely cut ice from the cup the shredder is grasped firmly in the right hand, striking it inverted upon the left, being careful to keep the lid closed. The ice is then scraped into some convenient receptacle. It is not necessary to take the ice out of the refrigerator, as the cup may be filled from the side or top of the cake." **$25.00-$45.00**

XV-10.
Ice planes.
(R) Nickeled iron legs, steel top & blade, wood base. 7 1/2"H x 14 1/2" x 6 1/4"W. Albert Pick, 1909 catalog. (L) "Keith's Registered Plane," English. "The ice plane is as simple in its construction as its application, being merely rubbing the ice to and fro rapidly upon the surface, when the snowlike flakes will descend into the vessel below. **Sherry Cobblers, Mint Juleps, & etc.** *— It will be found of great utility wherever ice is used (more especially the Wenham Lake ice), as it is rendered into a more elegant, agreeable, and useful form at table than the irregular masses which are less sightly. It will be found indispensable for the preparation of the American beverages, sherry cobblers, mint juleps, &c. Mr. Keith is decidely at the head of the ice department in this country, and has been so spirited in his enterprises as to keep completely at bay his numerous imitators." The Lady's Newspaper, 6/15/1850. Ice from "Wenham Lake" (I could find no information) presumably was very fine, as it was contrasted with "common rough ice."* **$20.00-$50.00 and $75.00-$150.00**

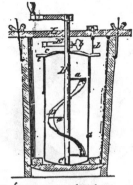

XV-11.
Ice cream or sorbetiere freezer, freezer patent.
(L) Cedar tub, large cranked wheel with bevel gears. It is called a turbine in the book it's in — Dubois, Patisserie d'Aujourd'hui, c.1860s-70s. (R) Pat'd 6/10/1856, by Joseph Parisette, Indianapolis, IN. Features spiral scraper which revolves & scrapes sides of can, as well as forcing to the bottom the frozen cream so that the unfrozen will "rise to the top to be mixed and equally frozen."

XV-12.
Ice cream freezer.
"Jack Frost", 2 quart size. Wood & cast iron. Note depiction of winter play scene inside lid. "It takes very little ice and salt, being constructed on an entirely new principle. Instead of having the ice and salt on the outside of the can, the can is on the outside, and the ice and salt inside." The Housewife, 7/1891. **$125.00-$200.00**

XV-13.
Ice scoop.
Galvanized crimped tin, wood handle, 9"L, c.1890-1920. Other prettier ones of the period, with turned wood handles, were made of nickeled copper and cast aluminum. **$7.00-$15.00**

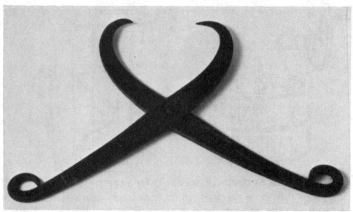

XV-14. Ice tongs.

Forged iron, handles have what cataloguer called "pigtail ends." 19"L. Photo courtesy Litchfield Auction Gallery, Litchfield, CT. Ex-Harold Corbin Collection, auctioned 1/1/1989. Price realized is approximate, as it was sold in a lot. **$30.00-$50.00**

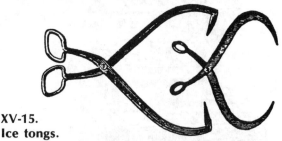

XV-15.
Ice tongs.

Wrought iron, but not blacksmith made like previous pair. Medium & large size. c.1900-1910. **$10.00-$30.00**

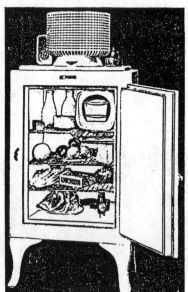

XV-16.
Refrigerator classic.

A General Electric "Monitor Top." 1927 Ladies' Home Journal reads: "Here is a new development in electric regrigerators for the home. ...It marks an entirely new conception. ...an entirely new type of icing unit — unlike any other you have ever seen. The entire mechanism of the GE Icing Unit is housed on top of the cabinet in one hermetically sealed casing. That is all the mechanism — none below the box. None in the basement. There are no pipes, no drains, no attachments. All bulky machinery is eliminated — virtually no servicing. The result of fifteen years of intensive research." Electric Refrigeration Dept., GE Co., Cleveland, OH. By 1929, There were 6 sizes to choose from; at least one opened to the left instead of right.

XV-17.
Refrigerators.

(L) From 1935 ad comes this "New G-E Model X-4" designed for small homes and apartments. (R) "Ice-O-Matic Capitol Model," mfd. by Williams Oil-O-Matic Heating Corp., Bloomington, IL. Much as I like the GE for looks, this is even better. You could have the motor "on top" as illustrated; "in the lower compressor compartment or in the basement." Country Life, 1930. I would think the value would be greater than the GE Monitor Top.

XV-18.
Refrigerator with radio.

"Shelvado ... just open the door. There, at your finger-tips, are your most-often-needed foods. No reaching. No searching." This model with "built-in radio." Crosley Electric Refrigerators, mfd. by Crosley Radio Corp., Cincinnati, OH. McCalls, 6/1938 (Shelvadors introduced c.1936).

XV-19.
Home freezer.
The trade name for it became a generic term for home freezers: "Deepfreeze." Two cylinders, each 18" diameter x 30" deep. You used all food in one unit & turned it off, then switched over to food in 2nd unit. Deepfreeze Division, Motor Products Corp., North Chicago, IL Country Gentleman ad, 1945.

XV-21.
Water filter & water coolers.
Top (L) Stoneware filter, for "purifying cistern water for cooking or table use." (R) "Water cooler, filled in with charcoal, preserves the ice and keeps water icy cold. — The water is kept cooler than the atmosphere without ice." The cooler looks like japanned sheet metal, but may be stoneware. Both pictures from American Home Cook Book, 1854. Often coolers and filters were combined. Lower (L) "Improved Sanitary," gray stoneware, blue bands, mfd. by Fulper Pottery Co., Flemington, NJ. House Furnishing Review, 4/1908. (Fulper was established in 1805). (R) Stoneware with leaf decoration, nickeled faucet. 12 sizes, from 2 gallons to 50 gallons. Also Pick catalog, 1909.

XV-20.
Water cooler.
Stoneware with cobalt flower decoration, rare exaggerated ovoid shape, 2 handles. Made by I. Seymour, Troy, NY, 18"H, 19th C. A perfectly beautiful form, sensual & almost figural. Photo courtesy Litchfield Auction Gallery, Litchfield, CT. Ex-Harold Corbin Collection. Auctioned 1/1/1990. Price realized: **$6000.00**

XV-22.
"Lady Franklin Family Ice Urns."
"Perfection" granite ironware & "Pearl Agateware" with quadruple silverplate fittings, mfd. by Manning, Bowman & Co., 1892 catalog. (L) & (M) show detached parts — including "shell" which fit down over handled reservoir, and footed stand. Two sizes, for 6 pints or 8, and had matching footed goblets. (R) "Assorted decorations in winter scenes," 9-pint size with goblets to match, you could order "plain silver band just above the faucet" engraved however you liked. **$400.00-$1000.00**

E. PRESERVING:

XVI. CAN & DRY

It seems a bit funny, etymologically, that practically everything in this category has to do with 'jarring', not 'canning', food! But that is only because the so-called fruit jars (also called canning jars) are the most widely-collected food preserving items, and old food cans don't have any potential to become that. Occasionally you see a very old food can, contents intact if not edible, and there are collectors (mainly identifying themselves with country store and/or advertising collectors). But they are rare. The not inconsiderable number of cans of tomato sauce, beets, blackeyed peas, and other things I tend to keep around, that have sprung leaks or bulges after no more than three or four years (!), make me afraid of having a collection of canned foods from the 1920s, say. I'm even afraid to open such cans for disposal, thinking they might explode and knock my block off, and I don't want to pour them into the toilet because I might become the Noxious Valdez of Botulism Spills and cause great damage to the environment. What do you *do* with old cans of gone-bad food?

Glass fruit jars are widely collected partly because for decades, bottle and glass collectors have been digging them up and cataloguing them. The fastest upcoming collectible that you might have expected to find here is can openers — about which we hope for a book in the next few years. It's possible that if a census of gadgets for the household was taken for the years between, say, 1860 and 1920, that can openers would outnumber everything else; especially if you added corkscrews. So big is this category that I've put them in their own chapter. The mechanical go-withs for fruit jars *are* included in this chapter; see fruit jar wrenches and lifters.

Can openers—See Open & Close chapter, page 372.

Canner, tin & cold-rolled copper, 2 canisters (they came in other sizes & numbers of canisters) of tin set down into rectangular water reservoir, glass canning jars were set, lidless, into the metal cans for heating. Expensive models had copper bottoms, came with wood, iron & leather strap jar wrench, also booklet of recipes & instructions, "Mudge Patent Processor", mfd by John L. Gaumer Co., Philadelphia, PA, 14¾"H x 13¼"L x 8"W, box is 4"H, pat'd July 27, 1886. • Self-proclaimed as a "household necessity. ... The cheapest, most efficacious, most economical system of putting up high standard goods." It came in several models, which ranged in price from $3.00 to $12.00, and which differed in size, number of canners, quality and quantity of the "tin plate, cold-rolled copper bottoms, copper tops and steam whistles." You put the processor box on the range, added water, then the carefully-filled cans into the water with the covers place over them. "Have water boiling to generate steam before using. Keep well boiling vigorously while using the canner as you must have sufficient steam to do good work. Put fruit or vegetables in the jar raw. Place jar on a dry folded towel while pouring in the hot syrup or water to prevent breakage. Pour in slowly. In cooking or canning dry, be careful to temper glass jars before subjecting to the action of the steam. Place wooden blocks on the canner under the jars to prevent breaking. Do not put the lids on the jars while processing. ... Be careful to sterilize lids and rubbers before sealing. Never allow water to boil away. If steam escapes through the whistle, it is time to refill (the well) to keep the bottom from burning. ... Be sure to wipe the canner dry after using before putting away. Read Mrs. Rorer's directions carefully." Finally, to catch every possible purchaser, the booklet claimed "While this apparatus is called a cannery, it is an admirable contrivance for cooking vegetables, meats and making tea and coffee. It saves time and fuel and preserves flavor and color." The jar holder that came with the canner claimed "Our adjustable jar holder will be appreciated by those who have burnt their fingers in lifting hot jars. They are leather lined, strongly bound by tin with wooden handles. The adjustment is made so they will fit any size jar. Handy for sealing and removing jar lids too." The jar holder originally cost 25 cents. **$225.00-$300.00**

Canning jar—See Fruit jar; also Preserve jar.

Canning rack, wire, rectangular & meant for use in a 2 hole boiler, late 19th or early 20th C. **$10.00-$15.00**

Corn dryer, all twisted wire, the sharp points were made by clipping the wire at an angle. Hanging ring at top, American, c.1910. **$8.00-$15.00**

Corn dryer, or seed corn tree, wooden rod with short iron pins stuck crosswise through it to hold 28 ears of corn, iron T-handle, American, about 20"L, pat'd Feb. 4, 1908 by James C. Blackford. **$18.00-$25.00**

Corn dryer, forged iron with 10 long sharp chiseled hooks, eye hole at top, hangs from ceiling hook, looks like a fish backbone, American, 20"L with 4"L hooks at a 40° angle from vertical, very early 19th C. • **Reproduction alert.** — Hard to tell age on these. Late 19th and 20th C examples may also be wrought iron, but they look machine-made perfect. There are modern reproductions being made and sold today. I won't spend my money to write off for one, so can't describe it minutely. Value of late 19th or early 20th C examples of forged iron, with some aesthetic merit, would be up to $35.00. Wire ones shouldn't be more than $15.00. **$100.00-$125.00**

Cup, for jellies & jams, pressed wood fiber with impressed design of Classical Greco-Roman woman next to tall stand, lid, & "although the Kleen Kup is made of wood fibre, it may be filled with heated jam, marmalade, jelly, or the like as any glass tumbler may be filled, and under the same conditions. The jelly may be heated to almost any degree Fahrenheit, and during the filling process it is unnecessary to immerse the kup in cold water, or wrap it in cold, wet cloths. ... The use of paraffine wax on top of the cooled jelly is optional." Called the "Wedgewood (sic) Kleen Kup", mfd by Mono-Service Co., Newark, NJ, 1918. • Came originally in a cardboard box of one dozen. See also Jelly glasses. Price range for one: **$3.00-$7.00**

Fruit dryer, galvanized tin base to set over stove top, wooden frame with 8 wood drawers with wire screening for bottoms. Used to dry sliced fruit or pitted, halved apricots, pears, etc. paper label mostly gone, American, 25¼"H x 18½"L x 14"W, TOC. **$65.00-$85.00**

Fruit dryer, tin frame with wire screen, 3 shelves, removeable trays, for drying sliced apples & other fruits, "Arlington Oven Dryer" on brass ID plate, Arlington, MA, 9"H x 14" x 10½", 19th C. **$120.00-$150.00**

Fruit jar, also called a canning jar, yellow amber glass, wax sealer, no lid, "Putnam Glass Works", Zanesville, OH, 1 qt. size. • According to Alice Creswick, there are two different ambers for this jar: a "deep olive amber" and a "deep yellow amber". This one is a rich yellow, but not what I'd call "deep". **$300.00-$400.00**

Fruit jar, amber glass, square base & sides with arched shoulders & screw-on metal lid has milky, almost opalescent, insert, jar marked with large monogram of intertwined A, G & S and "Full Measure", mfd by A. G. Smalley & Co., Boston, MA, 2 qt. size, also has 2 patent dates: Dec. 13, 1892, and April 7, 1896. **$40.00-$50.00**

Fruit jar, aqua glass, cylindrical body goes in at abruptly rounded shoulder, then goes out again at mouth, wax sealer type with rather deep moat for melted wax, glass stopper lid, missing the iron yoke clamp with hooked-under arms, that was tightened by wingnut to hold lid in place, marked "Millville Atmospheric", also "Whitall's Patent", with date. Inventor J. M. Whitall was from Philadelphia. 1 qt. size, "Preserve-jar" patent granted June 18, 1861. Whitall got a patent for a "Fruit-jar Stopper" on April 11, 1865. • According to Creswick, a cobalt blue example of this sold for $10,000 in 1982. Wow! **$35.00-$50.00**

Fruit jar, aqua glass, cylindrical with abruptly rounded shoulder, glass & metal stopper, best thing about this is it's stopper. A much more valuable "Lafayette" has an embossed portrait profile bust of the French hero of the American War of Independence. "Lafayette" in signature script, 1 qt. size. 1880s. **$100.00-$130.00**

Fruit jar, aqua glass, iron yoke clamp & glass lid. The yoke clamp, with 2 curved arms that hook under flange just below rim of jar, acts as a press to hold lid against rim, and is tightened by a thumbscrew rather than a wingnut like on the Millville Atmospheric. marked "Eagle" in nice serif cap letters, along with dates, "patd Dec. 28th, 1858. Reisd [reissued] June 16, 1868". • I guess this is the J. K. Jenkins patent for "preserving fruit". I can't find anything else that fits the date & the classification. **$90.00-$120.00**

Fruit jar, aqua glass, shaped like a Mason, embossed "Swayzee's Improved Mason", Swayzee Glass Co. , Swayzee, IN, TOC. • Lots of fruit jar makers thought they could "improve" on the several patents of J. L. Mason, which were granted beginning in January 1869. So, after counting variations of jars with "Mason's Patent" embossed on the front, next most numerous might be those with "Improved Mason's" within their names. **$10.00-$15.00**

Fruit jar, aqua glass, slowly sloping shoulder, screw-on cap, the top rim is slightly beveled out, there is no wider flange or ring below the screw threads on the glass, marked "Mason's Patent", 1 qt. size, pat'd Nov. 30, 1858 but made for a long time. • This is only one of scores of various "Mason" jars. The very name is sometimes used as a generic term for fruit jar, so well is it known. The best of these, although they are all so well-formed and simply functional, are the biggest, the smallest, those in unusual colors (various blues, citron, even black), and those with rare embossed marks. You will have to study, study and go to every show and talk to dealers and other collectors if you want to get into this field. I never knew but one fruit jar collector; his name was Chuck Pogue,

and I haven't seen him in 30 years, but I clearly remember the excitement with which he talked about digging for bottles. I don't know how many collectors still depend on bottle digs for great finds, but they are about the closest to old-fashioned archaeology as we find in the collecting world. **$5.00-$10.00**

Fruit jar, aqua glass, wire bail clip handle, "Trademark Lightning Putnam #31". The "Putnam' is Henry W. Putnam, inventor. Pat'd April 25, 1882. (Earlier patents 1875 & 1877.) • I can't find a #31 in Creswick, but I'm sure that's what I saw. **$8.00-$14.00**

Fruit jar, aqua glass, wire clip, that without the lid looks like a 2-strand bail handle, embossed "Trade Mark Lightning", Bennington, VT, 1 qt. size, last quarter 19th C. **$5.00-$10.00**

Fruit jar, aqua glass, zinc screw-on lid, embossed "Mason's Patent", so-called "midget" 1 pint, dated Nov. 30, 1858. • One of the earliest uses for **rolled zinc,** a sheet form of this rustproof metal, was as lids for canning jars. After long exposure to corrosives, a white powdery film develops which is peculiarly unpleasant to the touch. • See also the Toy chapter for Miniature fruit jars. **$25.00-$35.00**

Fruit jar, bluish-aqua glass (color called "Ball Blue" by Creswick), uses the "Lightning" wire bail lid clip, glass lid, "McDonald New Perfect Seal", pat'd July 14, 1908. **$8.00-$12.00**

Fruit jar, clear or "crystal" glass with wax seal groove in lip, "Rau's Improved Groove", American, TOC. • **German vocabulary** — <u>Weckglas</u>: (glass) preserve jar. **$35.00-$45.00**

Fruit jar, glass, rubber, dried clay, American, c.1880. • **Hypothetical entry.** — I assume this was made; has anyone seen one? It was described in the pages of the Oct. 1880 *Scribner's Monthly* magazine as "A new device for preserving fruit in its natural condition [that] consists of a glass jar or tumbler, having a cover with a rubber packing-ring, secured to the jar by a screw clamp. At the bottom of the jar is a hole, designed to be closed air-tight by a suitable stopper, and inside the jar is placed a layer of dried clay, to absorb the moisture that may escape from the fruit. The grapes or other fruits are hung up inside the jar, the cover is put on, and air is withdrawn by means of an air-pump, when the opening in the bottom is closed and sealed." If it exists: **$65.00-$85.00**

Fruit jar, medium cobalt blue glass, glass lid with little notch in high thick "fin", wire bail clip, "The Canton Electric Fruit Jar", 1880s. • You probably won't see one of these, they're so extremely rare, but it's nice to dream that you might find one at a yard sale! Of course, cobalt blue is a choice color for wretched fakes. So far as I know, the "Canton Electric" hasn't been replicated. **$2500.00 on up!**

Fruit jars, or canning jars, glass — clear (or "crystal"), aqua, amber, cobalt blue, citron & brown. A few 19th C patents are behind most jars & lids that were made well into the 20th C (some still being made). Lids are glass, zinc, plated steel, aluminum, vitreous pottery, etc. • This is a very specialized field with established market prices & price guides (See Alice Creswick's *Red Book of Fruit Jars* in Bibliography). Knowledge is widely shared about the jars themselves, closures, seals, marks & colors. It seems arcane to anyone (like me) who has not studied glass at all,

let alone glass fruit or canning jars. Unless you are prepared to study them, buy only for decorative or useful value. Obviously, very very large ones, or very early ones, or those in unusually colored glass, or with figural embossing, will usually be worth the most, but you have to get into the "loop" of other collectors and dealers so that information on repros will get to you in time to save an expensive mistake. • **Turn of Century Makers.** — According to *Thomas' Register of American Manufacturers,* 1905-06, quite a number of companies made glass fruit jars. As listed, they are: Hermetical Closure Co., J. A. Landsberger Co., and Vacuum Jar & Fruit Package Co., all of San Francisco, CA; Illinois Glass Co., Alton, IL; Port Glass Works, Bellville, IL; Safe Glass Co., Chicago, IL; Penna Glass Co., Anderson, IN; Western Flint Glass Co., Eaton, IN; Greenfield Fruit Jar & Bottle Co., Greenfield, IN; Sneath Glass Co., Hartford City, IN; Louis Hollweg, Indianapolis, IN; Marion Fruit Jar & Bottle Co., Marion, IN; Ball Brothers Glass Mfg. Co., Muncie, IN; Red Key Glass Co., Red Key, IN; Swayzee Glass Co., Swayzee, IN; Terre Haute Glass Mfg. Co., Terre Haute, IN; Safe Glass Co., Upland, IN; Upland Co-Operative Glass Co. [which may have included Safe], Upland; Skillin-Goodin Glass Co., Yorktown, IN; Hemingway Glass Co., Covington, KY; A. G. Smalley & Co., Boston; Victor Jar Co., Detroit, MI; Cumberland Glass Mfg. Co., Bridgeton, NJ; Moore Brothers Glass Co., Clayton, NJ; Gilchrist Improved Jar Co., Elmer, NJ; Consolidated Fruit Jar Co., New Brunswick, NJ; Woodbury Bottle Works, Woodbury, NJ; F. H. Palmer, Brooklyn, NY; R. G. Wright & Co., Buffalo, NY; Poughkeepsie Glass Works, Poughkeepsie, NY; Crystal Glass Co., Bridgeport, OH; W. Glenny Glass Co., Cincinnati, OH; Kearns-Gorsuch Bottle Co., Zanesville, OH; Co-operative Flint Glass Co., Ltd., Beaver Falls, PA; Gilchrist Improved Jar Co. & Hero Fruit Jar Co., both of Philadelphia, PA; D. Cunningham Glass Co., National Glass Co., Weightman Glass Co., & Wormser Glass Co., all of Pittsburg, PA; Hazel-Atlas Glass Co., Wheeling, WV & Washington, PA; S. George Co., Wellsburg, WV; and Weston Glass Co., Weston, WV. • Many of the same companies were making jars in the early 1930s.
$1.00-$10,000.00

Fruit jar holder, wire, looks like a doll stand, only the arms come around neck of jar, not waist of doll, 6"H, TOC.
$10.00-$12.00

Fruit jar lifter, iron, "E-Z Lift". **$3.00-$5.00**

Fruit jar lifter, little one-jar basket, with loop-de-loop sides that form feet for carrier, twisted side pieces with wire bail handle, wooden grip, American, about 5"H, 19th C. • **Reproduction alert.** — An exact copy is made by Mathews Wire, of Frankfort, IN. Only the turned wooden handle looks too new, and there are no dings, sags, shrugs or banged-up bends in the wire. **$12.00-$18.00**

Fruit jar lifter, metal, "Simplex", mfd by Gorman Mfg. Co., Boston, MA, late 19th C. **$10.00-$15.00**

Fruit jar opener, works like pliers, metal with rubber grips, "The Cunnard Co.", (saw in one record as "Gunnard"), pat'd 1936. **$7.00-$10.00**

Fruit jar sealer & wrench, nickeled malleable cast iron, plier handle, looks like a short-handled snake catcher with wire hoop that adjusts to fit, one side marked "Up for wrench", mfd by Stockland (?), Minneapolis, MN, 6⅝"L, no date, but early 20th C (?). **$15.00-$18.00**

Fruit jar wrench, cast iron, "Wilson's", Wilson Mfg. Co., Niles, OH, early 20th C (?). **$12.00-$15.00**

Fruit jar wrench, cast iron (malleable?), leather strap, 8½"L, TOC. **$10.00-$13.00**

Fruit jar wrench, galvanized metal strips, adjustable band, plier handles, 9¾"L, 20th C. **$10.00-$15.00**

Fruit jar wrench, geared mechanical, cast metal, "Speedo", TOC. • This information is taken from ad; See also the "Speedo" jar opener in the Open chapter. I don't know if it could be the same piece. **$8.00-$12.00**

Fruit jar wrench, green painted iron, 2 sets of arms, the lower pair has white rubber sleeves to hold jar safely, upper metal arms swivel or pivot and turn the lid without the lower arms moving. Very ingenious, 8¼"L, 20th C. **$14.00-$18.00**

Fruit jar wrench, iron, in original box, "Presto", mfd by Cupples, (possibly Cupples Co.), (St. Louis, MO), 20th C. **$5.00-$8.00**

Fruit jar wrench, iron, mechanical, C. A. Powell. 19th C. **$5.00-$7.00**

Fruit jar wrench, iron & wire, cast iron and wire, marked with "on" and "off" position, "Best S. Co.", Lancaster, PA, 7¾"L, pat'd May 8, 1917. **$10.00-$15.00**

Fruit jar wrench, iron with wooden handle, teeth hold the jar lid, 8½"L, late 19th or early 20th C. **$8.00-$13.00**

Fruit jar wrench, metal, "Triumph Fruit Can Wrench", mfd by Benjamin P. Forbes (Chocolate) Co., Cleveland, OH, 6½"L, patent pending, early 20th C. In 1932-33 *Thomas' Register.* • NOTE: This was pat'd Nov. 3, 1903 as the "Triumph Fruit Jar Wrench", with the manufacturer given on it as "Benj. P. Forbes, Cleveland, O." I don't know where, if or when "Chocolate" came into the name. • Forbes also made, c.1903, the "Perfection Fruit Jar Wrench" and the "Perfection Fruit Jar Holder", meant to fit "any Mason jar made." The wrench is flat metal, with handle used to adjust size of flat ring that goes on lid; the holder has a band of metal that holds the jar, and plier handles of cast iron.
$10.00-$15.00

Fruit jar wrench, nickeled steel, adjustable, "Winchester's of Carthage", Carthage, MO. **$10.00-$15.00**

Fruit jar wrench, plated iron, adjustable, using screw driver, small wheel set at angle runs around edge of glass jar, American, 7 3/8"L, pat'd Mar. 5, 1907. **$10.00-$15.00**

Fruit jar wrench, red rubber over heavy wire, "Daisy Jar Opener", 20th C. **$5.00-$7.00**

Fruit jar wrench, simple hoop of cast iron, with handles, looks like something to pinch on a hog's nose. American, 5½"L, "patent applied for", c.1900. **$10.00-$15.00**

Fruit jar wrench, tin & wire, 2 rubber arms inside grip jar, 8"L, 20th C. **$7.00-$10.00**

Fruit jar wrench, tinned iron, flat metal, adjustable diameter loop, mfd by A. C. Williams, Ravenna, OH, 8"L, c.1910. **$7.00-$10.00**

Fruit jar wrench & can opener combined, cast iron frame, steel blade, adjustable leather strap, "Mason Jar Sealer and Opener", c.1912. **$15.00-$18.00**

Funnel or fruit jar filler—See in Measure & Weigh chapter.

Herb drying rack, wood with original old blue paint, 28"L, 19th C. Auction notices are always noting "Shaker herb drying rack", but probably very few (if any) are Shaker. • The price on this is determined more than anything else by the blue paint. **$350.00-$500.00**

Jelly glasses, also called jellies, jelly jars or jelly tumblers, blown or press-molded glass, mostly in clear ("crystal"), but also medium blue, light & dark green, and "Ball Blue", to borrow from fruit jar-collecting. They are the size and shape, usually, of small tumblers, with slightly slanted sides. Others are bell-shaped, some like cups, some are footed and have stems like goblets. Some are half-size, like low-walled custard cups. The most collectible have a design of some sort — from flutes or thumbprints to very detailed fruit, berries, flowers or patriotic patterns. Although some old jelly glasses were used as molds, and the jelly turned out onto a serving dish in all its quivery beauty, often as not the design is not on the inside (where it would impress the gelatin), but on the outside. There are also jelly glasses known as table jellies, which are among the oldest types (late 18th C in this country), and were individual dessert glasses. Lids are often not present, and for some jellies (as the collectors call them), it is not known what kind of lid was original — metal or glass — or even if there were a lid at one time. For such an ubiquitous household object, it amazes me how few I see at even the largest of flea markets. I feel even less qualified to write anything about jellies than I do about fruit jars, although they both are related to kitchen collectibles. For the most information, a charming and reliable self-published looseleaf book by Barbara Bowditch is highly recommended. *American Jelly Glasses: A Collector's Notebook* may be obtained from Mrs. Bowditch at 1173 Peck Road, Hilton, NY 14468. Please send SASE when enquiring about cost & availability. Very clear line drawings by George Bowditch, as well as color photos, show us side views as well as patterns on the bottom or lid. For me, the most delightful and desirable of all the jellies are the Kerr "Angel & Crown", a name referring to a figural trademark embossed on the outside bottom of what would otherwise be rather plain glasses. There are many variations, as each mold-carver made his own version; I have at least 12, and mark-rubbings by Dennis Smith, for Barbara Bowditch, show many more. • A collectors' group is the **Jelly Jammers,** with a newsletter. Please use SASE when enquiring of Betty Landis, Rte 1, Box 8A, Hinton VA 22831 or Sonia Force, 105A Highway 31, Flemington, NJ 08822. • Prices for most jellies are toward the low end of this range: **$3.00-$50.00**

Meat curing pump, metal, in original cardboard tube with instructions, "Morton Salt", American, 20th C.
$20.00-$25.00

Preserve jar, brown saltglazed stoneware, wax seal type with ridged flat rim into which wax or paraffin was melted; then the lid was pushed down before wax solidified, "Minnesota Stoneware", MN, 1½ quart size, late 19th C. • **Brown saltglaze** was made like gray or buff stoneware, but with one extra step. Instead of firing the plain clay vessel, and throwing salt in to vaporize as a glaze, a brown slip was brushed on or the object was dipped in it, allowed to dry, then put in the kiln just like other pieces, and at the right time the salt was thrown in.
$30.00-$45.00

Preserve jar, redware, "Galena", Illinois (?), 9"H, late 19th C.   **$120.00-$135.00**

Preserve jar, saltglazed stoneware, with double rim with recess for wax, called a "wax sealer", with original lid, some nicking where sharp tool has been used over years of use to dig out hardened wax, American (?), 1 qt. size,

late 19th C. • **Several companies made earthenware** or stoneware canning jars at the turn of the century. The only two listed in *Thomas' Register of American Manufacturers*, 1905-06, are Chicago Pottery Co., Chicago, IL; and Weir Pottery Co., Monmouth, IL. • The 1932-33 *Thomas'* had a few more: Robinson Clay Product Co., of NY, NJ, CT, OH; Western Stoneware Co., Monmouth, IL; White Hall Pottery Works, White Hall, IL; Louisville Pottery Co., Louisville, KY; Dorchester Pottery Works, Boston, MA; Red Wing Union Stoneware Co., Red Wing, MN; United States Stoneware Co., Akron, OH; Logan Pottery Co., Logan, OH; Hyssong Pottery Co., Bloomsburg, PA; and Sherwood Brothers Co., New Brighton, CT. **$40.00-$50.00**

Preserve jar, saltglazed stoneware, with lid and wire fastener, "Weir", Monmouth, IL, 1 qt. size, pat'd Mar. 21, 1892.   **$30.00-$40.00**

Preserve jar, saltglazed stoneware with stenciled blue capacity number "1", blue flowers, "Hamilton & Jones", Greensboro, PA, one gal. capacity, c.1870s (?).
$135.00-$160.00

Preserve jar, saltglazed stoneware, with stoneware lid, wire clamp-on lever to hold lid on, top of jar (which is like a jug) slants up, and lid is only about ⅓ diameter of jar itself, "The Weir Stone Fruit Jar", mfd by Weir Pottery Co., Monmouth, IL, 1 qt. size, (came also in 2, 4 & 8 qts., & the full range was from 1 pt. to 10 gal.), 1892 into early 20th C. • I saw one advertised with a "amber glass lid" which is not original.   **$25.00-$30.00**

Preserve jar, stoneware, saltglazed in shades of brown, 12 paneled sides, Peoria Pottery Co., Peoria, IL, 7"H x 4½" diameter, last quarter 19th C.   **$45.00-$55.00**

Tipping copper, or soldering iron, copper bullet-like or wedge-shaped pointed head, sometimes with hexagonal sides like a large copper crystal, has heavy iron wire shaft or handle, sometimes with wooden grip at end, used to solder closed the hole left in the top of the early cans. The tin cans were boiled, filled with hot food, and the top soldered on. Then a steam hole was punched in the lid and the can boiled again, and steam escaped from the hole. The hole was then immediately soldered closed, using a heated tipping copper and solder. If a can was found with 2 holes, both soldered up, it indicated that someone had taken a spoiled batch of food, re-heated and re-sealed the can. About 8" to 10"L, 19th and 20th C. Such tools are still made.   **$5.00-$10.00**

XVI-1.
Canner.
"Mudge Patent Processor, for Canning and Cooking Fruit & Vegetables," John L. Gaumer Co., Philadelphia, PA. A two-vessel style with iron wire bail handles. Cold-rolled copper bodies and tin lids, 14 3/4"H overall x 13 1/4"L x 8"W. Included here is the all wood jar wrench, 9"L, and Mrs. Sara T. Rorer's instruction & recipe booklet. Note steam whistle lower left corner of box's top. Original prices ranged from $3.00 to $12.00, depending on number of cans, size, and the amount of copper. Collection of Meryle Evans. Collector Dolores Thomas sent me pictures of her 4-can completely tinned set, including recipe booklet. Her cans have no bails, but the lids have bracket strap handles. Value for either about evens out: **$200.00-$300.00**

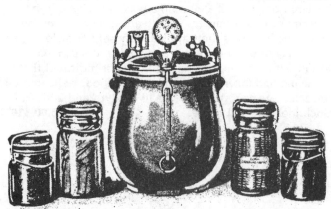

XVI-2.
Fruit preserving apparatus.
"Payne's 'Common Sense' Fruit Preserver," sold through Williams & Chase, NYC. The "approved apparatus for preserving by steam, an arrangement regarded by scientific judges as the most complete ever offered to the public. Its construction is perfectly simple and easy to manage. Six or more jars can in as many minutes be preserved, with one-fourth the labor and fuel. The fruits retain all their Solidity, Flavor & Beauty, requiring no sugar, unless preferred. When perfect jars are used (those represented in the cut, also Mason's Union and Standard, are regarded by the inventor as among the best." Came in 1-pipe, 2-pipe, 4-pipe and 6-pipe sizes. Pat'd 9/3/1867; 10/26/1860. 1870 ad in Peterson's Ladies' Magazine.   **$40.00-$70.00**

XVI-3.
Canner.
"Iron Horse Cold Pack" canner, mfd. by Rochester Can Co., Rochester, NY, c.1930. "With this the uncooked fruit can be placed directly in the jars, the syrup added and the cooking done directly in the jars, practically eliminating the labor formerly required." Made of charcoal (blackened) tin, bottom double-seamed, wood handle grips at side. Rack for seven quart jars, and a wire jar lifter. 9"H x 13 3/4" diameter. They also made them of copper or galvanized steel. I believe the picture is probably a printed paper label — most desirable to have.   **$40.00-$80.00**

XVI-4.
Cup for jellies or jams.
"The Wedgewood Kleen Kup," mfd. by Mono Service Co., Newark, NJ. "Decorated wood fibre with classical Greco-Roman lady. "The jelly may be heated to almost any degree Fahrenheit, and during the filling process it is unnecessary to immerse the kup in cold water, or wrap it in cold, wet cloths. It is suggested, however, that the filled kups be allowed to stand over night, or until thoroughly cold, before the lids are inserted. The use of paraffine wax on top of the cooled jelly is optional." House Furnishing Review ads, 1918. Per cup: **$3.00-$7.00**

XVI-5.
Fruit Evaporator & Preserver.
Coleman Evaporating & Fruit Preserving Co. of Western Maryland, Hagerstown, MD. A substantial oak cabinet with shelves, fitted to stove or hot-air heater pipe. For private homes. (Another is for restaurants) In 1870s-80s flyer. This appears to have drawers for drying, and a bucket and pipe for liquids. Oddly, it has a fluted bake pan on top shelf, muffins on another, and a tea kettle at bottom, on what may have been used as a warmer, since the hot air goes in at the bottom.

XVI-6.
Fruit dryer.
Wood with galvanized tin base and wire mesh screening in each of eight drawers. Used on top of range to dry sliced fruit or pitted, halved apricots, etc. 26"H, early 20th C. **$80.00-$120.00**

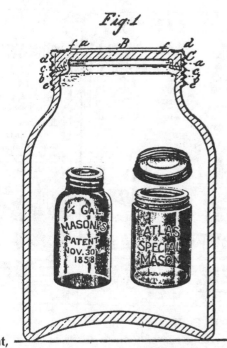

XVI-7.
Fruit jar patent,
and examples of other Mason jars. In this collage of pictures, the outer drawing is John L. Mason's patent drawing for #102,913, issued to Mason on May 10, 1870 for an improvement in his earlier fruit jar. He sold the patent to Consolidated Fruit-Jar Co., who sued another maker, Wright, for using the patent. The case went to the U.S. Supreme Court, who decided the merits of the suit on the basis of the patentee (Mason) forfeiting his "right to the invention if he constructs it and vends it to others to use, or if he uses it publicly himself in the ordinary way" up to two years before applying for a patent. Poor Mr. Mason had "completed his invention in June 1859, at which time he had at least two dozen jars made. Some of the jars he gave away; others he sold to get the money they yielded and to test salability in the market. Mason failed to file a patent application until January 15, 1868," almost 10 years later! The case was decided against Consolidated, and Mason in favor of Wright. From a 1947 book by C. D. Tuska, Patents for Engineers, from Official Gazette *records.*

XVI-8.
Fruit jar.
"Squire's Patent," mfd. by John B. Bartless, NYC. Undated flyer from c.1860.

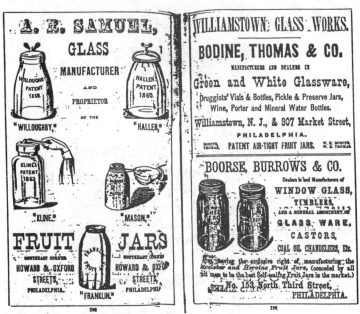

XVI-9. Fruit jars.

Two facing pages from an 1860s book *Philadelphia and Its Manufacturers*. See the "Willoughby", the Kline," the "Franklin", the "Mason" and the "Haller" in A.E. Samuel's ad; and the "Heroine," and "Excelsior," jars of Boorse, Burrows & Co.

XVI-10.
Fruit jars.

"Mason's Improved Butter Jar," and "Millville Atmospheric Fruit Jar." The Mason's has a metal screw-band seal and glass lid, and probably dates to the turn of the century. The Millville, with a glass lid held by yoke and thumbscrew, dates to about 1862. Picture courtesy of the National Museum of American History, Smithsonian Institution.

XVI-11.
Hermetically sealed glass jar.

for cheese. "American Club House Cheese," Chandler & Rudd Co., Cleveland, OH. "A full size jar will be sent to any point in the United States, charges prepaid, on receipt of 50¢." Picture and words probably printed on outside of glass. Ad from *Century* magazine, c.1891.

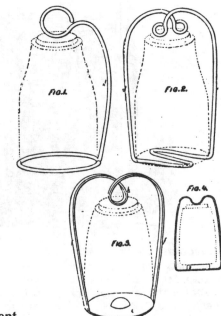

XVI-12.
Jar holder patent,

actually called by inventor a "dish holder," but obviously with fruit jars sketched in. Pat'd 4/26/1870, by W.P. Walter. Spring wire bails of different types to fit different shapes of fruit jars.

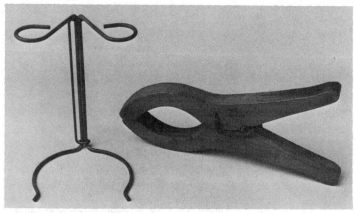

XVI-13.
Jar holders.

All wire, like a doll stand, 9"H. Other one like blanket pin is mostly wood — see Mudge canner XVI-1. It grips really tight. These were used for handling hot jars — the one at left for lifting from canner, could be left in while canning.

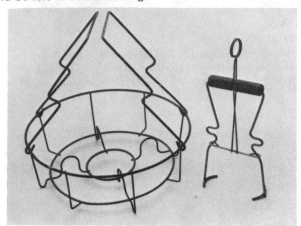

XVI-14.
Jar rack & lifter.

Wire, rack holds 4 jars for sterilizing. Basket part is 3 1/4"H x 10 1/4" diameter. The lifter works with one hand; your thumb goes through hole at top while fingers pull up on wooden grip. 10"H, early 20th C. **$18.00-$28.00**

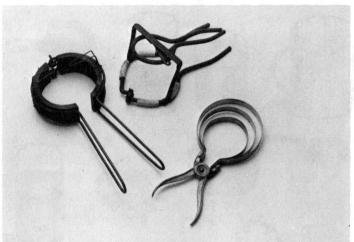

XVI-15.
Jar wrenches.
(L) Wood with heavy wire handles. Top (R) Wire with leather. A double gripper that grips the jar with the bigger wrench and the lid with the pivoting upper wrench. 9 1/2"L. Bottom (R) with 3 bands is copper. The band can be selected to fit the circumference of the jar to be opened. 9 1/2"L. All located by The Primitive Man, Bob Cahn, Carmel, NY. **$28.00-$75.00**

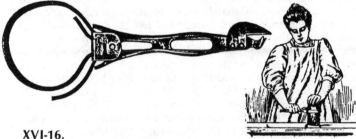

XVI-16.
Mason Jar Sealer & Can Opener combined.
Made of "New Process White Metal," which is "strong, will not break, takes a high polish, and will last a lifetime." Leather strap and malleable cast iron frame. From F.W. Seastrand drummers' catalog, c.1912. **$10.00-$20.00**

XVI-17.
Fruit jar wrenches.
Top: Unmarked one of nickeled metal. Note bottle crown cap opener at top. (M) Looks like a lariat — wire & malleable cast iron. Best & Co., pat'd 1917. (B) Nickeled steel, mfd. by A.C. Williams, New Jersey, c.1900. They specialize in corkscrews and bottle openers. **$8.00-$20.00**

XVI-18.
"Angel & crown" Kerr jelly glass bottoms.
Pure folk art. These are only five of an estimated 58 different patterns. molded in bottom (inside of glasses, outside of tumblers) of the jellies. Tumblers are 3 3/4"H x 2 7/8" diameter at top. The smaller glasses, with fluted sides, range from about 2 1/4"H x 3 1/4" diameter to 2 3/8"H x 3 1/2" diameter.

The mold-makers at A.H. Kerr & Co., Sand Springs, OK, interpreted the crown and angel, seemingly a different way each time. I am deeply indepted to the Jelly Jammers club, and to Betty Landis for giving me my first one, and setting me off. Especial thanks go to Barbara Bowditch, author of a remarkable book on American Jelly Glasses, which includes rubbings done by Dennis Smith, of 58 of the angel and crown, as well as much more. (See bibliography.) I was unable to do rubbings. Bottoms illustrated here were done on photocopy machine with a disk of black paper inside bottom of tumbler, and a white piece of paper with circle cut out, laid on top of copier's glass.

I have collected folk art for about 15 years, and this is the first time I've ever seen anything like these angels on a mass-produced object. The variety of treatment of hair, wings, face-shape, gown, star and crown are remarkable. See XVI-19 for some parallel angels. **$2.00-$5.00**

XVI-19.
Other folk art angels & crowns.
These greatly reduced drawings are done from a fraktur-like draw-
ing (top) of the Pennsylvania Germans, and from four gravestone
carvings from the mid-to-late 18th C, in Connecticut. There are
many other New England gravestone carvings of similar subjects.
The A.H. Kerr glass company, of Oklahoma, supposedly used the
motif taking it from the family coat of arms, but I have no con-
firmation of that. Interesting how almost Mayan or Aztec the
angels look here! For further reading, see Allan I. Ledwig's Graven
Images. New England Stonecarving and its Symbols, 1650-1815.
Middletown, CT: Wesleyan University Press. And Scott T. Swank,
et. al., Arts of the Pennsylvania Germans. *Winterthur: 1983.*

XVI-20.
Soldering tool patent.
Pat'd 1/13/1880, by William Painter, Baltimore, MD, assignor of
one half of right to Louis B. Keizer. A "hand soldering device for
capping cans, the combination of a soldering tool whose edge
is curved to conform to the groove in the can-top, and is the sole
guide of the tool, with a handle."

XVI-21.
Tipping copper,
for soldering can lids in home canning, or for mending tinwares.
The sharp long tip was copper, which conducted heat very well;
held in iron cleft, wood handle. The "pointed portion is to be
'tinned', as the workmen say, which means that it is to be coated
with solder. To tin the point, file it smooth, heat the tool hot
enough to melt solder, then quickly file the surface bright, and
rub it on a small lump of solder that has been placed on board
for the purpose, using rosin, or a few drops of a zinc solution."
American Agriculturist, *2/1870.*

XVI-22.
"Uses for Old Fruit Cans."
Make-dos, from article in American Agriculturist, *1/1875. Cup at*
top left was from AA, 1880. "Take round fruit, or vegetable, cans
and melt off the top; bend a hickory withe for a handle, as shown
in the engraving, and fasten it with wire or rivets. This makes a
useful dipper, pitcher, measure, or vessel for many purposes about
the barn or house; one may be made for the flour barrel; another
for sugar; others for feed, grain, etc." Others: (1) Emptied can,
showing old-type hole in top which was soldered on after cann-
ing. You would melt other solder and flatten the tin, which is
useful for "covering mouse and rat-holes," etc. If you lived in an
old apartment in NYC, you'd find tin can lids nailed down over
holes in the floor and wall. (2) "Little bucket or paint pot." (3)
Scoop. (4) Saucepan "for small messes." (5) A fruit-picker. (6)
Coarse grater "for crackers, dry bread, horseradish, and the like."
The tin is tacked to board. (7) "Muffin and cake-rings." Strips cut
and held by rivets. (8) Lantern, with a piece of "stove mica" set
into side."

XVI-23.
Fruit can soldering machine,
sometimes described as a cylinder-scraper for automobiles, which
indeed it may have been used for. "Allens'". mfd. by Hull
Brothers, Webster & Co., Cleveland, OH. "The only machine ever
made which will finish the can completely with one handling.
By the use of it the can only requires one handling to finish solder-
ing. Adjusts to size of both top and bottom; they will not spring
off while being soldered." I've seen one — its about 9" or 10"L,
nice wooden handle, and it rattles when turned quickly back and
forth, so it may be mistaken for some kind of noisemaker. The
Metal Worker, *7/8/1882.* **$40.00-$65.00**

F. FURNISHING
XVII. CHAIRS, TABLES, CUPBOARDS & CABINETS

You may doubt that there are "collectors" of furniture. But, like a surprising number of people, I happen to collect chairs (mostly not kitchen chairs, however), and I have good friends in Massachusetts who collect wall-hung wooden cupboards that are mainly a couple of centuries old. Most people are constrained by money and room, and find it hard to visualize a collection of tables, for example, arranged anywhere in the house. (Some of my chairs are hung on the wall; some are in storage against the time when one of my dreams — a Chair Room — can be made real.)

A good percentage of collectors of kitchen implements of the 20th century own, or would like to own, at least one period piece of furniture which helps set the smaller pieces in a natural context. The most popular item is a "Hoosier"-type cabinet, made by Hoosier or one of many other companies.

For collectors of 19th century implements and hollowware, a scrubbed-top table, a pie safe, or some Windsor-style kitchen chairs are goals. Hutch tables and wall cupboards with wrought hardware are favored by collectors of 18th and early 19th century wares. These pieces help set the scene.

What makes up a collection of furniture? Some people say you have to have at least two pieces; others say three or more are needed. I tend to agree with the latter. A pair of something, even an unmatched pair, isn't really a collection. Various assembled pieces of furniture, all in original green paint, or all made of bird's-eye maple, or all with turned legs, or all made in North Carolina — that's a collection.

Baker's cupboard, very like a pie safe, pine with one large door, slatted shelves & screened sides, for cooling fresh-baked bread loaves, TOC. **$450.00-$550.00**

Baker's rack, iron, sides look like intertwined grapevines, 5 shelves, European or poss. American, 6 1/2 feet H x 5 feet W, early 20th C. **$375.00-$425.00**

Butcher block, deep, solid maple on strong thick turned legs, worn & scarred, 20" square, 19th C. **$300.00-$400.00**

Cabinet, all original finish, double doors above, flanking flour bin with oval glass window, slightly arched top, bins below, 4 drawers, sifter, spice rack, etc., "Hoosier", early 20th C. **$800.00-$1000.00**

Cabinet, also called a kitchen piano, varnished wood, porcelainized iron counter top, original sifter and bin, revolving spice rack for 7 containers with shaker tops, flour & sugar containers, perfect condition, "Hoosier", either Albany, IN, or shortly thereafter, New Castle, IN, very early 20th C. • An ad in a 1902 *Ladies Home Journal* said that "Household Economy is as much a matter of saving your steps as of thrifty living. There is more time and strength left for these things if you have a Hoosier Kitchen Cabinet." Another ad, in *House Furnishing Review,* Jan. 1908, said that the "Hoosier kitchen cabinet saves as many steps as a bicycle. It is as necessary a convenience as a sewing machine." **$475.00-$600.00**

Cabinet, maple, bottom has 2 bins, 2 drawers & 2 molding boards for rolling out dough, top section has 8 drawers flanking small cupboard with door, American, 48"W, late 19th C. **$250.00-$350.00**

Cabinet, oak in original finish, flour bin & sifter, roll front that works very well, "Hoosier", early 20th C. **$350.00-$45.00**

Cabinet, painted wood, doors above, bins, pull out pastry board, "Sellers", early 20th C. • Win & Gin Dahlquist, 618 49th Avenue, N.W., Puyallup, WA 98371 have (as of 1989) replacement sifters & sugars & sifter bowls made from the old dies. Use SASE when writing for information about these parts. **$300.00-$375.00**

Cabinet, stepback hutch top, 2 doors above, 2 utility drawers over bin, nice legs, Larkin, early 20th C. **$375.00-$450.00**

Cabinets, Hoosier-type, wood, either varnished natural finish or painted white, some with enameled or porcelainized iron work surface, varying numbers of built-in accessories, from spice containers & flour sifters to shopping aids, many companies besides Hoosier, in various places, mostly Indiana, from TOC, but most date after 1910s but before built-in cabinets in 1940s. • **Makers of kitchen cabinets and/or safes in early 1900s** are listed below. Only a few advertised nationally. The generic name often to applied to all kitchen cabinets comes from Hoosier Mfg. Co., New Castle, IN. Others include: G. P. McDougall, Indianapolis & Frankfort, IN; G. I. Sellers, Elwood, IN; Cardinal's Mother Hubbard's, Wabash, IN; Coppes, Zook & Mutschler's "Nappanee", Nappanee, IN; Kompass & Stoll, Niles, MI ; Ariel, Peru, IN; Acme, Wilkinson, IN; Campbell, Smith & Ritchie, Lebanon Mfg. Co., and A. H. Meyer, all 3 from Lebanon, IN; McCure Mfg. Co., as well as Union Cabinet Co., both of Marion, IN; C. A. Hubbard, Martinsville, IN; Andrews, in Andrews, IN; L. A. Jennings, New Castle, IN; Jonathan Koontz Sons, Union City, IN; Dubuque Cabinet Makers' Assoc., Dubuque, IA; Helmers Mfg. Co., Leavenworth, KS; Alles Bros. (made kitchen safes), Henderson, KY; Ft. Smith Folding Bed & Table Co., and McLoud & Sparks (who made safes), both of Ft. Smith, AR; Bisk Corp., Brockton, MA; Ware Mfg. Co. (safes), Atlanta, GA; Mound City Furniture Co. (safes), Mound, IL; McNown Mfg. Co., Columbia, IN; Evansville Furn. Co. (safes), Globe Furn. Co., as well as Indiana Furn. Co., all 3 of Evansville; Paul Mfg. Co., Ft. Wayne, IN; I-X-L, and Goshen Pump Co. (latter also made safes), both Goshen, IN; Bagby Furn. Co. (safes), Baltimore; Minneapolis Furn. Co., MN; Aude Furn. Co., R. E. Lasher & Co. (safes), Koenig Furn. Co., and Charles Sueme (safes), all 4 from St. Louis; Bryant Furn. Co., Truxton, NY; High Point Mantel & Table Co. (safes), High Point, NC; Fitts-Crabtree Mfg. Co. (safes), Sanford, NC; Kesslers & Sons (safes), Logan, OH; Marysville Cabinet Co., Marysville, OH; Tipp Bldg. & Mfg. Co., Tippecanoe City, OH; A. D. Deemer Furn. Co., Brookville, PA; Acme Kitchen Furn. Co., Chattanooga, TN; Parker-Battle-Talbot Mfg. Co. (safes), Tullohoma, TN; House & Herrmann, Wheeling, WV; Tillman Bros. (safes), La Crosse, WI; Winter Lumber Co., Sheboygan, WI. • Value ranges widely; those at the low end are plain or in poor condition. Rather expensive manufactured ones are "possum bellies" — large, with rounded bins, built-in sifters, racks & extra details. The most expensive of all are handmade, maybe pieced of different colors of wood in a mosaic, or with carved decoration. Avoid the irreversibly refinished. **$250.00-$500.00**

Cabinets or chests for spice—See Container & Storage chapter.

Cupboard, also called a pantry cupboard, wall hung, primitive pine, stripped, alas, of original paint, hence much lower in value. It is possibly English — countless (except by U.S. Customs) container loads of stripped pine "country" pieces are being brought over each year. American, Scandinavian or English, 19th C. • **German vocabulary** — Kuchen Schrank: kitchen cupboard. **$150.00-$175.00**

Cupboard, brown painted wood, top has crested back & side board and a pair of drawers with turned wood knobs; overhangs lower part by a little over an inch, scalloped apron, very short feet, 2 doors with 2 tins each in punctured star-in-circle design, West VA, 19th C. **$1400.00-$1700.00**

Cupboard, cherry in original finish, stepback consisting of a blanket chest or bin with hinged board lid on bottom, 2 shelf cupboard above with molded cornice, 2 doors with 3 punctured tins each door, footed basket with droopy flowers design, PA (?), 19th C. **$3500.00-$4200.00**

Cupboard, red painted walnut (?) with molded cornice, 2 top doors glazed with 6 panes each, 2 drawers in middle with wooden knobs, scalloped apron & bracket feet, 2 lower doors with punctured tins painted green, American, 94"H x 60"W, 19th C. • **Walnut plus.** — Walnut is one of the cachet woods, like boxwood or apple wood. A cupboard or old country chair or knife box of walnut has added value over one of pine, in most cases. Even when it's been painted. **$2700.00-$3500.00**

Cupboard, red painted wood, tall, scalloped apron in front and sides almost to floor, 2 tall doors with 4 punctured tins each door, plus 4 tins on each side, flat board top, punctured design is X with 2 hearts & 2 diamonds filling in spaces between the crossed lines, Ohio (?), 60"H x 42"W x 17"D, 19th C. • Dealers Robb and Alice Guss, Youngsville, NY, sold this in 1984. Price range mine. **$2800.00-$3500.00**

Cupboard, stepback of curly cherry, highly figured wood, bottom has scalloped apron, 2 doors, long drawer below counter top, above has molded cornice, 2 doors with 3 punctured tins each, simple concentric curved lines of quarter circles, made by John Richey, Hammersville, OH, 19th C. • Sold at Garth's, Nov. 1983, at the Ron Klapmeir Sale, for $2300.00. Now? **$4000.00-$5500.00**

Cupboard, walnut, 2 pieces, 12 small glass windows & 3 spice drawers of tiger maple in top, 3 tiger maple drawers for cutlery in 2 door base, Pennsylvania Dutch, 19th C. **$3500.00-$4000.00**

Cupboard or meat safe, hung from beam, tan painted wood frame has short feet, but at top the sides extend like upside down legs, each having a hole for bolting to a beam, 2 shelves, 4 tins with slits in 10 concentric circles, corners with odd X marks, Ohio, mid 19th C to 3rd quarter. • Dealer Cornelia Mott offered this in 1984. Price range mine. **$650.00-$900.00**

Dry sink, child size, wood with cupboard underneath with 2 doors with knobs, sea green paint inside sink, counter & splash board, brown & ochre grain-painted outside, American, 20"H x 22"W, c.1860s. **$375.00-$450.00**

Dry sink, dovetail construction, 2 doors, painted in old red over original imitation graining, 19th C. **$500.00-$700.00**

Dry sink, painted pine, zinc lining, one drawer, cupboard below with 2 doors, prob. American, 19th C. • Value ranges widely due to paint color & appearance, style, details such as drainboard and drawer, origin, and size. **$250.00-$1200.00**

Dry sink, pine with cast iron liner to well, traces of old gray paint, very plain & handsome, 19th C. • The iron liner is unusual; most are zinc or tin or painted wood. **$275.00-$400.00**

Dry sink, wood painted olive drab underneath, sink painted white inside, original tacked-on sink lining, probably metal, probably zinc, now missing, small drawer to right for scouring materials, square drawer knob replaced, American, prob. PA, 43¾"W, c.1860s or 1870s. **$1000.00-$1200.00**

Dry sink & cupboard, beautiful glowing old red paint, zinc sink, compartment with lid at left of sink for cleaning materials, cupboard was built-in & upper shelves have no back, taken out of an old Easton, PA home, 9 feet high, 19th or very early 20th C. • Dealers Jack and Vicky Pilarski in 1986 was asking only $800.00 for this, which was way way under the money then, and still is. It is a superb piece with beautiful color. **$2200.00-$3000.00**

Flour bins — See Storage & Container chapter.

Hanging cupboard, old green paint over pine, 3 shelves with one door, simple iron latch, Maine, 19th C. **$275.00-$350.00**

Hanging cupboard, pine with grayish blue old paint, one simple paneled door, no molding, brass keyhole possibly adapted from another piece of furniture, simple door latch, American (?), c.1830s to 1850s. **$550.00-$700.00**

Hanging cupboard, simple pine butt joints, blue milk paint, 2 door, 2 shelves, prob. PA, European heritage, 1870s or 1880s. **$350.00-$450.00**

Hutch table, 2-plank top, red over old blue paint, rosehead nails and turned pegs, butterfly cleats on underside hold planks together. Tabletop made to be lifted into upright position to provide a seat when not serving as a table. Really convertible furniture! American, 37½" diameter, this one c.1830s, but the form is much older. • **Hutch.** — The "hutch" in hutch cupboard is probably from words in Middle English and Latin that mean "care, keeping, guard", and would therefore be related to a hutch in the sense of a storage chest or coffer, or a "box or box-like pen or 'house' in which an animal is confined." *Oxford English Dictionary*. Or a hutch as a kneading trough for dough. *op cit.* "Hutch" in hutch table is probably from other words, and is related to what the OED calls an "obsolete phonetic variant of hulch ... meaning hunched or humped, as in "hutch back." When the tabletop of a hutch table is in its vertical position, the already anthromorphic shape of the bench or chair underneath takes on a somewhat round-shouldered, even "hunch-backed" appearance. • **Huck.** — Mountain or Piedmont Virginians, to this day say "huck", as in "huck table" or "huck chair". **$4000.00-$5500.00**

Hutch table, pine in original finish, American, c.1730s. **$2000.00-$3500.00**

Hutch table, pine & maple in original red stain, circular top above bench base, New England, 27"H x 45¼" diameter top, late 18th C. **$5000.00-$7000.00**

Ice cream parlor interior, carved oak backbar, marble columns, bevel glass mirrors outined in neon, candy cases, leaded stained glass window panels, etc., with all equipment, European-made, with American equipment, 36 feet long, 1911, with 1940s booths & soda fountain. • This parlor interior was advertised in *Antique Trader Weekly* in 1983, by a private seller — possibly owner or a going-out-of-business parlor, or demolition company representative. Asking price: **$35,000.00**

Ice cream table, & 2 chairs, child's size, oak seats & tabletop, metal rims to seats, with heavy gauge twisted iron wire, painted white, for legs & backs, TOC into 3rd decade 20th C. • Companies making "ice cream" sets, for adults, and possibly for children too, in the early 1930s were: Royal Metal Mfg. Co., Chicago; Frank Rieder & Sons, Philadelphia; A. H. Andrews & Co., Chicago. **$175.00-$250.00**

Jam cupboard, bootjack ends, 5 shelves with 2 doors, stripped exterior, alas, but possibly original light blue inside, American, 50"H, TOC. **$235.00-$400.00**

Kitchen cabinet, wood, painted green with green & black marbleized enameled iron work surface, casters on legs, arched doors, clock set in frame at top, wonderful looking, "Keystone Cabinet Co." with truncated arrowhead-like keystone logo, Littlestown, PA, 39¾"W, pat'd Feb. 2, 1922. • A spectacular greenie piece for a Depression glass kitchen. Or for any other room; this is a beauty. Price in 1986 was $1400.00. **$1400.00-$1600.00**

Kitchen cabinet table, elm with maple top, cast iron handles, zinc bin drawer at bottom, 3 drawers at left, door on right half reveals 2 shelves, paneled sides, from Montgomery Ward catalog, 2 feet 8"H x 4 feet 4"L x 2 feet 4" deep, c.1895. • When the bins' curved fronts show, a popular name for these tables is possum belly tables; the name also applies to bin tables with cabinets above. **$90.00-$120.00**

Kitchen table, wide plank pine drop-leaf top, turned sturdy legs, pull-out bread boards each end, with utility drawers for implements at each end. At each end of this tea-cake-for-two working table is a big possum belly flour or meal bin. All drawers, including bins, have single cast iron dog's head pull, American, c.1880 to 1900. • The dog's head pulls are what give this table that extra punch. A single such pull sold in a mixed lot of iron at the June 1989 Robacker auction, with a shutter dog and a stirrup for only $65.00. The table at antique show late summer 1989 for: **$450.00**

Lamp, tin & glass, wall mounted reflector oil lamp, American, 1860s-70s. • We tend to overlook lamps for the kitchen; ones like this were mounted above work tables, sink, and cook stove. **$35.00-$150.00**

Lamps, nickeled brass, double light, reflectors painted white inside, outside enameled dark green, reflector angled light down onto stove, and could be set on the hob shelves, Boston, MA (?), 18"H, c.1840s. • Some have mirrored reflectors. **$200.00-$300.00**

Meat safe, "a back porch piece" according to dealer, green painted wood, tall legs, 18 punctured tins in geometric design with rough side out, bottom of legs dipped in tar for setting in pans of water to keep ants out, brass catch on door, once had keyhole, iron catch inside, from New Berne, Craven County, NC, 71½"H x 36½"W x 26½" deep, c.1830s to 1860. **$1200.00-$1500.00**

Meat safe hook, cast iron, long screw for beam or ceiling with curvy hook at bottom & cup in middle for bug-deterring water (ever see a roach that couldn't swim an inch?), patented by Joseph C. Moulton as a "suspension hook & insect insulator", Fitchburg, MA, pat'd Oct. 28, 1859. **$7.00-$12.00**

Milk cupboard, also called a milk or **cheese safe,** tall wooden case, square top, louvred sides and door, lined with thin muslin, central shaft or axle, around which revolve the 8 round shelves, for holding milk pans, meat or other food needing a safe, pat'd by E. H. Nash, Westport, CT, about 50"H x 22" square, pat'd July 27, 1858. **$200.00-$35.00**

Milk cupboard, wood with original mustard color paint, 6 shelves, open back & front for air circulation, prob. PA-European heritage, 70"H, 19th C. **$1700.00-$2000.00**

Milking stool, cast iron, 3 sproingy insect-like legs, doughnut seat with big hole in center, "E. A. Kaestner Co.", Baltimore, MD, 12"H, 19th or early 20th C. **$30.00-$40.00**

Nursing lamp, tin lamp with inserted double boiler like heating pan of copper, brass burner inside, "Badger", American (?), 9"H, 19th C. **$150.00-$200.00**

Pie safe, almost Biedermeier or Empire in form, with paneled pilasters flanking the 2 doors, 2 drawers above, with keyholes, very short round feet, poss. cut down, 4 tins with punctured pattern of sort of fattened & straightened-out fylfot (pinwheels) & triangular corner spandrels, Southwest VA or East TN, mid 19th C. **$1000.00-$1500.00**

Pie safe, black painted wood, 2 drawers, 2 three tin doors with punctured 8 point stars & quarter-round spandrels in corners, latches on both doors, stenciled inside one drawer "J. Zitzer & Son, Furniture Dealer & Undertaker", West Alexandria, OH, 19th C. • $900.00 at auction at Garth's in 1984. **$1500.00-$2000.00**

Pie safe, folding, oak with wire screening, sides fold in half, patented but no legible mark, American, late 19th C (?). • Aaron Osborne, of Georgetown, CT, patented this July 5, 1881, "as a new article of manufacture, a provision-safe having its sides hinged, and adapted to fold together without being detached one from the other ... in combination with a collapsible body ... a board or stretcher adapted to fit within the body and to hold the same in an expanded condition. ..." • An 1891 *Ladies' Home Journal* ad reads: "Mother wants it. Wright's Kitchen Safe, Refrigerator and dumb Waiter combined or separate. Can be instantly lowered into cellar from any part of room floor. — Cochran Safe Co., Cochran, IN." **$450.00-$600.00**

Pie safe, green painted wood, 12 tins, 3 on each side, 3 on both doors, punctured holes & slits, depicting footed bowls with tulips, from MD (?), 42¾"W, c.1860s. **$2800.00-$4000.00**

Pie safe, low counter height cupboard, short bracket feet, one shelf, 2 doors with single oblong punctured tin in each door, double repeat pattern of 6-point flower in circle with 6 bull's eyes in each door, PA, 40"H x 54"W, 19th C. **$1500.00-$2000.00**

Pie safe, painted wood, 8 tins, 2 on each side, 2 in each door, long drawer at bottom, long straight legs, simple punctured geometric design, marked "John M. Smythe Co.", Chicago, IL, TOC. **$400.00-$650.00**

Pie safe, painted wood case in dark greenish black, scalloped apron, interesting long legs with 2 turned bands slightly thicker than legs, flat top, one central door with odd old hardware, screen & mesh panel openings framed with molding — 6 in door, 3 flanking each side of door, almost looks like some kind of hutch or bird cage, but no place for feeding the animals, American, 52"H x 39½"W x 17½"D, 19th C. • NYC's Ricco-Johnson Gallery, which often comes up with interesting folk art pieces, had this for sale in early 1984. Price range mine. **$3800.00-$4500.00**

Pie safe, painted wood frame, hangs from beams, sides & front with slit pierced tin panels, single door, 5-point stars or 6-point petals within circles, very free & graphic, perhaps Lancaster, PA, 19th C. **$1400.00-$1700.00**

Pie safe, pine, 12 panels of punctured tin in front & sides, unexceptional concentric circles, etc., geometric pattern, 2 doors, American, 58"H x 37"W, 19th C. • You shouldn't say only "American" now because of scholarship that's been done on regional pie safes. (For example: Roddy Moore's well-illustrated "Wythe County, Virginia, punched tin: its influence and imitators", *The Magazine ANTIQUES*, Sept. 1984). I can't make a more complete study myself, and urge you to read everything you can before plunking down big money. • **Reproduction alert.** — Beware the faked country-look tins. An old pine safe can be stripped of its old tins, then be gussied up with distressed tin pierced with valuable eagle, animal, flag, human forms. I saw such a one the summer of 1987 in Charlottesville. The body was old, nice long legs and small 2 shelf box, with 4 front panels and 2 on each side. The tins had coffee cups, forks, spoons, dogs, birds, flowers ... just too too TOO. Over it all was a layer of what looked like old blue milk paint, scratched and distressed. The price was just high enough to almost seem OK, but too low if this were for real. (It was $1800.00.) You must develop a sixth sense about the look of the tins. • **Punched & Punctured.** — The adjective "punched" is slightly misleading. Pie safes have punctured holes in their "punched tins"; that is, the holes were punched [verb] all the way through. There is a need to differentiate between punched and punctured because the word punched is used specifically to describe a certain kind of tinsmith's decorative work, usually on coffee pots, where a punch [the tool] has been used to make a raised or pimply mark that could be used to make a textured design. A grater (of tin or brass, for example) can have both punctured holes and pierced holes or perforations. The latter two do not have the rough, ragged edge of a punctured hole. The tools used to punch and to puncture are different in that the former is used to make a mark and has a flattened or rounded tip, perhaps even one cast with a letter or symbol or other mark, and the latter must have a point sharp enough to go through the metal. Dealers, & authors of auction catalogs & articles describe the tins in pie safes as "punched". They also use "punched" when describing a kind of tin ware decoration where a punch is used to make a dimple or tiny bump. I will fly in the face of common and widely-accepted usage and use the slightly clumsy "punctured" in this book. I'm not really being stubborn about this, though I expect to get some pooh-pooh reaction. Part of my reason is based on the ease of retrieving exact information when searching the computer; part of it is to make clear what I mean, with no further explanation needed. I do not expect to change common usage, nor do I want you to think that only an ignoramus would say "punched tins". **$375.00-$450.00**

Pie safe, pine, 12 panels of punctured tins, front & sides, stars & crescent moons, 2 door, American, 55"H, 19th C. **$2200.00-$3000.00**

Pie safe, pine, 3 punctured tin panels on each side & 3 panels on both front doors, whirligig design with quarter-circle spandrels (designs filling each corner of tins), 3 shelves, clean & not refinished, 4 legs all in good condition at bottom, not rat chewed or water rotted, American, 47"H, 19th C. **$700.00-$1200.00**

"To Get Rid of Ants. — Wash the shelves with salt and water; sprinkle salt in their paths. To keep them out of safes: Set the legs of the safe in tin cups; keep the cups filled with water." Mrs. A. P. Hill, *Mrs. Hill's New Family Receipt Book*, NY: 1867, 1870. • "If ants are troublesome, set legs in cups of water." Catherine Beecher & Harriet Beecher Stowe, *American Woman's Home*, 1869.

Pie safe, pine, 6 punctured tins, star designs on doors only, wood on sides, 4 very long legs, 2 shelves, American, 50"H, 19th C. **$450.00-$550.00**

Pie safe, pine with 3 fancy geometric punctured tin panels on each side & in both doors, 3 shelves, original finish, legs in good condition, American, 19th C. **$600.00-$700.00**

Pie safe, red painted wood, 12 tins, 3 on each side, 3 on both doors, punctured petaled-flower design adapted to fit rectangular shape (sometimes called a butterfly pattern), white porcelain knobs (could be original or not), southern IL, 19th C. **$900.00-$1200.00**

Pie safe, red stained sycamore & maple, straight case with medium-length legs, long single drawer at bottom, overhanging board top, 2 interesting doors, each with 3 punctured tins in design of clock face with Arabic numerals & curved horn, the time reading 12 minutes to 12 on each one, crescent moons in corners, dealers have called such designs "New Year" tins, maybe OH (?), late 19th or early 20th C. • Dealers Tim & Barb Martien, Western Reserve Antiques, Burton, OH, had this for sale in 1984. Price range mine. **$3000.00-$4500.00**

Pie safe, red stained wood, turned feet but straight case and board top, 2 large doors with single tin panel each, punctured with characteristic urn with ear handles & tall multi-stemmed tulip design, star spandrels in corners, side panels punctured too, southwestern VA, prob. Wythe County, 19th C. • This is the classic **Wythe County** design, and a very desirable piece. Fine Wythe County safes deserve praise, and Roddy Moore's 1984 article gave them added cachet, translating to much increased prices. • An urn of this type (with a nice rounded bowl body, flared stem, pedestal base, & two vertical handles) is sometimes called a chalice, although to my mind an urn would be a bigger piece by far, though perhaps it is context that determines the name. I recently saw a graphite drawing of what I would have thought was a cast iron or stone urn, with several doves drinking from it or flying about it, and the dealer described it as "doves and chalice", which somehow seems to have a much more religious context than a simple garden scene would have. **$3500.00-$5000.00**

Pie safe, refinished wood, alas, straight-sided case with turned feet, flat board top, 2 large doors with single large tin on each, punctured as if with 4 panels each, centered pinwheels (fylfot), with round spandrels in corners, keyhole in door, Wythe County, VA, 54″W, 19th C. • Refinished wood always reduces value. **$700.00-$900.00**

Pie safe, simple wooden case with straight medium-length legs, molded top, fancy scalloped apron or skirt, 2 doors, each with 2 punctured tins, design an 8 petaled flower within circle, 2 shelves, 2 drawers at top with wooden knobs, PA (?), early 19th C. • **Reproduction alert.** — Newly-made punctured tins have been used to make an old cupboard into a more desirable pie safe; they have also been used to replace very simple designs with designs that seem folk arty and unique. Beware especially of any pie safe with figural or zoomorphic, or pictorial tins, such as men in stovepipe hats, forks and spoons, cows, pigs, dogs and eagles. Know your dealer, ask about provenance, inspect tins carefully on both sides with magnifying glass. For people who want to make their modern kitchen cupboards into mini pie safes, new punctured tin panels may save some trouble. Watch for ads in the "Miscellaneous Specialty Items" section of *Antique Trader Weekly*. **$850.00-$1000.00**

Pie safe, small, wood case & legs with 2 shelves, 8 tins punctured with design of star in a star in a circle, stars in each corner as spandrels, American, 19th C.
$550.00-$675.00

Pie safe, tall elegant piece, dark varnish, suitable for parlor, with molded cornice, 2 doors, each with one square tin in center with punctured rectangular tins above & below, bull's eye (one in square, 2 in rectangles) framed with quarter- & half-round spandrels, plus 6 narrow oblong punctured tins in panels flanking doors, in ad of Georgia dealer, perhaps GA provenance, about 80″ to 90″H, late 19th C. Appleberry Hill Antiques, Atlanta, GA, advertised this in 1984. Price range is not that of Lebby Harrison, dealer, but mine. **$3500.00-$5000.00**

Pie safe, tall simple wood case, flat board top, straight legs, long drawer across top, 2 doors, each with 3 tins, punctured design of a footed sugar bowl with ear handles & domed lid with large round finial & footed cream jug, both with concentric rings forming body, the decoration making you think this might be a cupboard for dairy products, a cheese or butter safe, found in Arkansas, late 19th or early 20th C. • According to Carl W. Drepperd's *A Dictionary of American Antiques*, the "butter cupboard" dating to 15th C England or the Continent, was for storing butter or cheese. Made entirely of oak (or other woods), they had pierced doors for air circulation. In *Primer of American Antiques*, Drepperd said that pie safes or butter cupboards were known in 17th C America, and probably were first offered as a "commercial product" as late as 1880s. Related are the meat safe or meat keep, and the *gard-manger*. • Dealer Joan Gould, Summer Kitchen Antiques of Little Rock, said another in this pattern was found in Arkansas. At $595.00 in 1984, it seems way under the money. **$1200.00-$1600.00**

Pie safe, varnished pine, straight board top, straight simple case & medium length legs, single drawer below cupboard, 2 doors with 3 punctured tins, design of each is a 5 point star within circle, plus 4 smaller stars around circle, smallest star within big star, with 3 straight rows of holes

for border, Colorado, 55⅛″H, c.1875. • Described from picture of one in collection of the State Historical Society of Colorado. The value range is mine, not the Society's.
$1700.00-$2000.00

Pie safe, walnut, 12 tins with tulip & vase (or basket) design, 2 shelves, 2 drawers, short turned wooden legs, not refinished but cleaned up, simple iron latch, American, poss. PA (?), 54″H, mid 19th C.
$1200.00-$1500.00

Pie safe, walnut & poplar, straight case with flat board top, shortish straight legs, long dovetailed drawer across top, 2 three tin doors, punctured design of many petaled flower or butterfly, in horizontal rectangles, poss. from the South, or IL, 19th C. **$900.00-$1200.00**

Pie safe, wood with traces of green paint, 2 shelves above double drawers, 2 doors with 3 punctured tin panels, base constructed of cutout boards instead of legs, American, 53″H x 40″W, mid 19th C. • "A closet, called a safe, for keeping food in the cellar, is an important convenience for keeping meat, milk, bread and various articles in daily use." Mrs. Cornelius, *The Young Housekeepers Friend, or, A Guide to Domestic Economy & Comfort*, Boston & NY: 1846.
$500.00-$700.00

Portable pantries—See Storage & Container chapter.

Shelf paper, various patterns & colors, also shelf edge papers — printed, scalloped, pleated, or lace. All these are collectible, if unnoticed to this time, and nothing adds a more authentic touch to a shelf with a collection of 1920s or 30s or 40s gadgets and implements than authentic shelf paper, or at least edge papers, thumbtacked neatly in place with colored tacks. 1910s to 1950s. • **Yo, Bounty!** — "The uses of paper in the home are not so many. Shelving in the pantry or kitchen can be kept in renewed health with paper laces. The bungalow, motor trip or picnic can well be supplied with paper or fibre plates. Rather would we warn you against paper uses; such as wrapping up your ice to preserve it, for it doesn't; wrapping up your food stuff in paper in refrigerator; greasing muffin pan with paper, for which you should use a brush. Sometimes, however, a piece of paper will clean off the top of the stove very efficiently, yet even here a brush would be far better. Clean brown paper to absorb French fried potatoes is quite indispensible. The paper napkin has made its place even in the homes of wealth. Wax paper is a delight to wrap up sandwiches and keep breadstuffs and cakes fresh for touring or picnics. Paper lining for drawers is necessary. The pretty paper lace doily for under finger bowls, cake and bread is delightfully pretty and saves the linen, the laundress and the laundry list." Ethel R. Peyser, "Tinware, Rubber and Paper for the Kitchen", *House & Garden*, June 1922. **$2.00-$8.00**

Shopping list aid, also called a <u>daily reminder or household reminder</u>, tin, lithographed in blue & white with flowers, flat oblong device, with tabs along left & right sides that are pulled out to mark those things on the printed lists to be bought, such as Rice & Sago, Lemons, Blacking, Oatmeal or Wash Blue, named "The Housekeeper's Friend", this one prob. European, c.1908. **$12.00-$15.00**

Shopping list aid, lithographed cardboard, adv'g "Doe-Wah-Jack" stoves, TOC. **$25.00-$30.00**

Shopping list aid, paper, meant for a Hoosier cabinet & marked "Hoosier", early 20th C. **$22.00-$30.00**

Shopping list aid, plastic disc with tiny blue plastic knobs to indicate which of the many things printed around the circumference are needed, adv'g ''Watkins Awning & Sign Co., Farmville, VA'', maker name not shown, 3⅜'' diameter not counting little knobs, c.1948. **$5.00-$8.00**

Step stool or folding stool, painted wood, 3 steps, slightly cutout step shape, very attractive, American, about 1910-1920. • In the middle 1980s, a For Sale ad appeared in a collector newspaper for a ''Folding kitchen stool used by James Dean before his movie fame; from Fairmount, IN. personal friend. Offers considered, collectors only.'' I don't know what eventually happened, but this is an example of the <u>Absurd Rub-Off Theory of Collectible Objects</u> which is behind the very high prices of things once belonging to a famous person. Andy Warhol's cookie jars went for 10 times market price, and it's quite possible he never even touched them, merely pointed to them before buying. When James Beard's cookbooks were auctioned, the auction house glued in cheapo copies of his bookplate, despite the fact that Beard himself had chosen to put bookplates in very few books. (At that sale, a box of tatty old dirty bowties sold for hundreds of smackeroos.) While fabulous prices are being paid for Van Gogh's and Picasso's and Frank Stella's paintings, works that were actually created by and intimately ''touched'' by the masters, objects supposed to have been touched by, or known to have been owned by, famous people who had nothing to do with the objects' creation, are selling for outrageous prices. Auras don't rub off. **$12.00-$15.00**

Table and 4 chairs, enamelware top, drop leaf & extension, nice geometric or abstract floral design on top in red or black, American, c.1910-1940s. • These have gone up greatly in popularity. Sets, with four kitchen chairs and a table (often without extension leaves), varnished or painted in snowy white, show up at every big antique show and sell for many hundreds of dollars. They are in with the modern and Deco stuff at the big shows in NYC. **$400.00-$1000.00**

Table, birch with single wide birch plank top, 2 side drawers, turned legs, late 19th C, Memphis, TN, 28⅞''H x 59½''L x 30''W, TOC. • My Franklin grandfather worked for a lumber mill in Memphis, and had this table made with an extraordinarily wide single plank top just shy of 1'' thick. Unfortunately refinished. **$300.00-$400.00**

Table, child's, wood with blue & white graniteware top, American, early 20th C. **$100.00-$125.00**

Table, drop leaf, green paint, very deep overhang at ends, American, 36''L, mid 19th C. **$400.00-$500.00**

XVII-1

"A Method of Arranging a Kitchen,"

from the American Agriculturist, *4/1876. A farmhouse kitchen designed by L.D.Snook to suit the farmer's wife—as a complement to city kitchens "arranged with great care to facilitate the work of servants." "E" is wood or iron sink, and if wood, treated with linseed oil inside. "An iron pump is placed in at the end near the window." Below the sink is a "closet" with two doors, and to the right of that is a china closet ("H") and a lower "closet" for kettles, tinware, and the various cooking utensils. The oiled wooden rack "B" below the window is slatted, and for draining dishes. "F" is a pass-through to the pantry seen through the door. On the lowest shelf in there appears to be a bread dough raiser. What about the stove? "For convenience the stove should be placed upon the side of the room occupied by the closets (cupboards), or near where the table stands in the illustration."*

XVII-3.

Butcher blocks.

Clockwise from top (L): (1) "Made from 1 1/2" strips of best grade white maple, glued & bolted together," turned legs. Seven sizes: from 15" square to 30" x 40". S.B. Sexton catalog, Baltimore c.1930s. (2) Not so described, but looks like section of tree trunk. Five diameters, from 18" to 30"; and (3) "Square sectional" block in 3 sizes, from 20" x 25" to 25" x 30", bolted through, on turned legs. (4) "Butcher Bench," thick plank 24"W x any length. Braced with iron rods, on heavy turned trestle legs. Last three all from Duparquet, Huot & Moneuse suppliers' catalog, c.1904-1910. (5) A high sectionnal maple block, called a **chef block** *18" x 10"deep; 34"H overall. Also Sexton, c.1930s. Distress from use & age don't devalue.* **$40.00-$400.00**

XVII-2.

Plate dresser & work table,

as depicted in a wood engraving from an 1833 edition of a chapbook, Mother Goose's Melodies, *published in England. The caption reads "Sing, Sing!—What shall I sing? The Cat's run away with the Pudding-Bag String."*

XVII-4.

This multipurpose cupboard shows how an awkward corner between doors leading to a dining room and to a pantry, was made to "be comprehensive, compact, capacious, and convenient.' (A) covers a flour barrel and is a swing-out curved door. (B) is the hinged cover. (C) is the top of a "case of drawers" (G), but just under it, in (E), is a "space for the bread pan and the moldingboard, which slides in on cleats; these are reached by the door (D), which lifts, and is provided with a spring-catch.

XVII-5.
"Possum-belly" cabinet tables.

Clockwise from top (L), with original price: (1) "Princess," made mostly of ash, with sanded top — what became known as a scrub-top. Base finished "antique oak." 27" x 47"L. Two "sliding extension boards; two partitioned sliding bins which may be used for potatoes, etc." $5.65. (2) "Domestic new-style Combination Kitchen Cabinet," made of ash, 18" x 45" with drop leaf shown up; sliding bins and extension carving boards. $6.90. (3) "Kitchen Queen," seasoned white wood. One large drawer above sliding flour bin. Top unfinished; rest "golden oak." $2.95. (4) "Convenient," ash, plain top, "antique color" base, 27" x 42" top, two 50-lb bin drawers," $5.90. All from Albert Pick mail order catalog, 1909. **$150.00-$350.00**

XVII-6
Combination table & cabinet.

Upper part an open dresser meant mainly for china, but here there is a lift-up door for the big middle shelf. Lower table part is what was called a cabinet table, with bin drawers. Unidentified English illustration, c.1890s. **$200.00-$500.00**

XVII-7.
Combination cabinet tables.

(L) to (R) from top: (1) "Ever Ready Table and Shelf." Overall it's 66"H; table 28 1/2"H x 42" x 26" deep. Bass or cottonwood, light or dark finish. (2) "Locker," of oak, with base consisting of one tin-lined tilting bin, 2 drawers, 2 pull-out molding boards, 2 compartments. 83"H overall, "golden oak" finish. (3) "Triumph," with more drawers that the others, glass-fronted cupboard, 81"H overall. Bass or cottonwood, light or dark finish. (4) "Winner," of oak, sanded table top, tilting 100-lb flour bin with tin lining, glass & wood-panelled cupboard doors, 83"H x 48"W. (5) "Handy," for china, glass, cutlery, linens, but with no work surface. 79"H. (6) "Utility," with all sizes of drawers, many features not in any others, including drawers on side, and removable extension boards "for many purposes." Oak, in "golden oak" finish. 75 1/2"H x 42"W. Originally the most expensive at $17.25; others ranged from $6.95 to $16.80. Albert Pick catalog, 1909. **$200.00-$500.00**

XVII-8.
Cabinet.

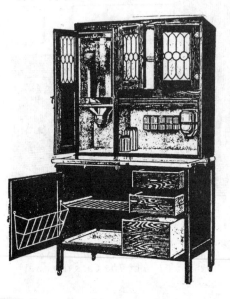

"I-XL" Co., Goshen, IN. Golden oak finish, nickeled hardware, "drop roll curtain" in middle right section. Glass jar equipment includes "swinging sugar bin with metal cap and cut-off, one coffee, one tea, and five spice jars." Tilting metal sifter flour bin with glass front. Sliding top of "polished metal or white porcelain." "Special bracket and block for food grinder." Sliding bread board, metal-lined drawers. 70"H x 40"W. Also available in golden oak finish." From c.1916 catalog, Note leaded glass panels, resembling house fenestration of the time. **$250.00-$350.00**

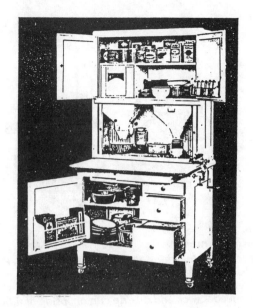

XVII-9.
"Hoosier cabinet,"
this one really mfd. by Hoosier. Called by them their "Thirty-Six-Inch Hoosier." 71 1/2"H x 37"W, finished in white enamel, but available in "light golden oak." "Equipment includes (fixed?) white Porcelain top; mouse-proof construction; ant-proof casters; shaker flour sifter; 9-piece glassware set; package rack on lower door; shallow utensil tray suspended from work-table." Has meat grinder clamped to work surface, and you can see the spice rack on upper right door. Hoosier Mfg. Co., Newcastle, IN, 1922 catalog. Value range is for unrefinished white original finish, which is not as highly prized as the wood. **$250.00-$400.00**

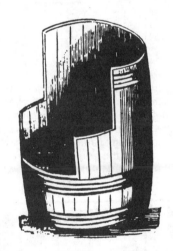

XVII-10.
Barrel chair.
"Homemade easy chair," reads heading in American Agriculturist, 3/1865. Quite possibly not for the kitchen, but it's made from "a good flour barrel," with a few staves cut away. "A small opening or door can be made under the seat, which will furnish a convenient work box." The article advises nailing the hoops to each stave before commencing the making of such a chair! Value would depend on age of original barrel, its patina or finish, skill of making, and possibly the upholstered cushion. **$90.00-$250.00**

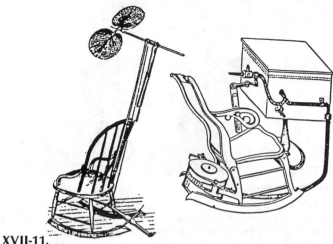

XVII-11.
Chair patents.
(L) "Fly Fan and Rocking Chair" pat'd in 1899, by James T. Cowan, Boston, MA. Patent #622,123. (R) "Ventilating Rocking Chair," pat'd 11/24/1857, by D. Kahnweiler, Wilmington, DE. #18,696. Official Gazette. A new combination rocking chair & fan was patented about every seven years. Other combos included rocking chairs with churns, cradles and even one that was also a trunk, and one that played music.

XVII-12.
Ice cream parlor tete-a-tete chair.
"A new creation...a novelty that will please." Two bow-back chairs connected by tiny table. Seat and tabletop in oak or birch with mahogany finish, and available with three metal finishes: "Japanese copper," brass or nickel. Manufacturer unknown, but picture from confectioners' supply catalog, Jaburg Brothers, 1908. **$150.00-$200.00**

XVII-13.
Hutch table.
Trestle foot (with variation shown at right), with 3-board round top. Pin goes all the way across (shown in black here). Other hutch tables are found with other types of legs or feet, including, most rarely, four turned legs. They also have square, oblong or oval tops, though most are round. Some have storage in the seat, accessible through drawer or lifting lid. Many have two much shorter pivoting pins that don't go all the way across. The rarest, and oldest, were made from such huge trees that a single board, or at most two, was wide enough to make even a 50" top. Late 18th or very early 19th C. **$2000.00-$10,000.00**

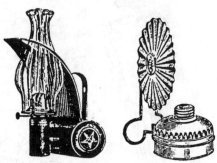

XVII-14.
Kitchen lamps.

(L) The designation "kitchen lamp" is not commonly found in old ads, but the lamp at left, of an old type was so names. The ad read "Tin kitchen lamps. Strong, neat, well made, durable. Made by Geuder & Paeschke Mfg. Co. Tin Wares, Milwaukee, WI." The Metal Worker, 1/9/1892. Note horizontal cylindrical reservoir for fuel, with star on end, and the reflector that would put more light where it was needed. It could be set down on a work surface, even a shelf or windowsill, or hung on wall where needed. (R) "Jaxon" reflector lamp, "made from one piece of 7-guage steel wire very strong and springy, complete with 7" bright tin reflector and 4 1/2" front, made for No. 2 burner. New and a ready seller." In mail order catalog of Butler Brothers, 1899.
$50.00-$135.00

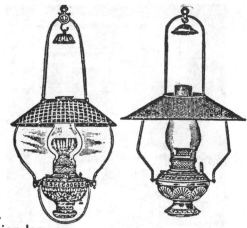

XVII-16.
Suspension lamps,

suitable for many locations, including a kitchen. (L) " 'Pittsburgh' store or hall lamp, absolutely non-explosive. Burns over 10 hours without refilling." 20" diameter tin shade. (R) " 'Banner' store lamp, with extra feeder wick and oil drip cup on inside of tube to carry any overflow back to the wick. 20" tin shade, No. 3 burner, font wick and chimney." The second would have been nice for a kitchen, but probably only very rarely used for one, at least in a private home. Both also in Butler Brothers catalog, 1899.

XVII-15.
"A Useful Piece of Furniture."

"In many rural households, the space allotted to the kitchen is often cramped and narrowed too much. A piece of kitchen furniture that will answer three distinct purposes is a great convenience. Here is one that is at once a settee, trunk, and an ironing table or bake board. There is a box or trunk, in which one may stow away many things that usually lie about, having no special place otherwise. The lid of this trunk forms the seat of the settee. The ends are raised up, forming the arms. The back of it is pivoted upon one side of the ends, and when it is turned down it forms a table. When it is turned down, it is held in place by two small hooks." American Agriculturist, 11/1874. **$200.00-$800.00**

XVII-17.
Meat safe.

Wood and wire, "to protect food from mice, insects, &c." Wood with wire gauze screens. No. 79 in list of kitchen requisites given in American Home Cook Book, by an American Lady. NYC: Dick & Fitzgerald, 1854. This would probably have almost no value unless something interesting had been done to the surface (carving or painting), or unless the iron wire gauze had rusted out and been replaced by homemade punctured tins, which may or may not have predated metal screening.

XVII-18.
"Wooden Meat Screen,

lined with tin." Trestle feet with what appear to be casters. Note iron handle on right side for pulling it. The measurement is given as 3'9", but whether that is height or length I don't know. London dealers William S. Adams & Son, "Outfitters for Kitchens," advertised this in small booklet called Francatelli's Cook's Guide Advertiser, c.1860-61.

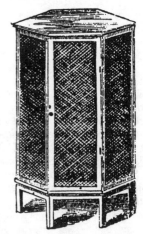

XVII-19.
"Milk Shelves for the Kitchen."
"In many farm-houses the kitchen is obliged to...serve as the dairy, in which the milk is set, and the cream is kept, especially in the winter, when it is the warmest spot in the house. There is nothing objectionable in this, if the kitchen is kept scrupulously clean, and well ventilated. But a well-contrived cupboard, kept specially for the milk and cream where they may be safe from dust and drafts, and yet have proper ventilation, will be a great advantage." This one is six-sided, and *"wide enough to hold two ten-quart pans across it, or four upon each shelf. This will be nearly or quite 3 feet outside measure. This will be ample for winter use, where ten cows are kept."* There's a center post that turns, having a pointed bottom that fits into a small socket in which is put some *"fine chips of soap, or a little powdered black lead. "Five round shelves are fixed to it. Under the shelves, which are rather close together, is space for two "cream crocks," of stoneware.* American Agriculturist, *12/1875.*

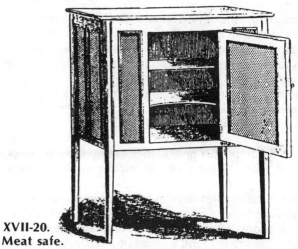

XVII-20.
Meat safe.
Wood with wire screening. L.H. Mace catalog, 1880s.
$100.00-$300.00

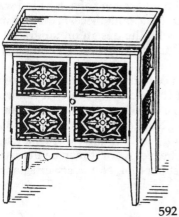

XVII-21.
Sideboard & provision safe.
Wood (probably poplar) with punctured tin panels for decoration & ventilation. Sideboard is 4'6"H x 3'1"W x 1'2" deep. "Tin provision safe" is 4'9"H x 2'6"W x 1'2" deep. Bagby & Rivers, Baltimore, 1882 catalog. Baltimore, by the way, is still famous for painted window & door house screens, usually a form of rural landscape. These paintings do not obstruct the vision from the inside looking out, but serve both to decorate the outside, and to a small extent, make less visible the interior. I have never seen a pie safe with painted screening in its doors or sides.
$400.00-$1000.00

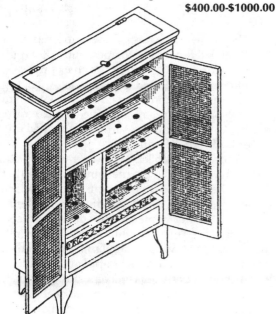

XVII-22.
"Insect-proof Closet & Safe" patent.
Pat'd 8/30/1881, by Charles H. Larrabee, Napa City, CA, assignor to Hamilton W. Crabb, same place. Bottom drawer serves as a "water-containing tank." Holes served to circulate air from shelf to shelf. Official Gazette.
$100.00-$200.00

XVII-23.
"Perforated plate for kitchen-safes" patent.
Pat'd 11/11/1884, by George W. Knapp, Baltimore, MD. No.307,959. Knapp's claim was for "The method of ornamenting perforated plates for safes, consisting in first applying a colored design to a surface of the plate, and then making the ventilating-perforations with respect to the features of the said colored design, and producing on the same surface a burr projecting about each perforation, so located as to avoid marring the said colored design." Official Gazette. *I've never seen a pie safe with the punctured tins painted in other than the same or contrasting color to the case...not that the idea is odd. NOTE recessed top. Value — dependent greatly on patina and original ploychromed tins — not necessarily this low.*
$500.00-$1000.00

XVII-24.
Pie safe.
It is not upside down; it's meant to be bolted to rafters and hang from them. Painted wood case with punctured tins on all four sides, larger than most. Three shelves inside. Front door has flower-stars in the corners to match the center; the sides have fan-shaped, rayed spandrels in the corners. 34"H x 36"W x 22" deep. Ex-collection of Earl F. & Ada F. Robacker, auctioned by T. Glenn, Horst Auctions, Farmersville, Lancaster County, PA, on 6/23-24/1989. Measurements from catalog, prepared by Clarence E. Spohn. Price realized was very low. **$475.00**

Pie Safe Tin Designs
Filling Empty Rectangles With Patterns

The following pictures show four common design categories used for punctured pie safe tins, including simple geometrics, stars, petaled flower-like shapes, and fylfot (pinwheels). These four form a large proportion of tin designs, but this short over view describes but a couple dozen examples.

I have also included a single category of figural — urn-and-flower designs (XVII-29) — although many more figurals are to be found, including horsemen, chickens, and cups & saucers. The urn-and-flowers are included because of Wytheville-area safes, which are at the time of this writing the only ones to have been written about in a scholarly way (J. Roderick Moore, "Wythe County, Virginia, punched tin: its influence and imitators," *The Magazine ANTIQUES*, 9/1984), and they are advertised rather frequently.

Before I began collecting and arranging pictures by pattern type, I theorized that the obvious similarities to other repeating geometric patterns were meaningful rather that coincidental, even to the extent that comparison would prove that pie safe tin punchers copied their designs from something previously existing. I assumed that such post hoc likenesses would become especially evident when pie safe designs were compared with quilts and jacquard coverlets. I thought that I would be able therefore to offer names for the designs, based on established quilt design names.

This turned out to be impossible, except in the most simplistic way, matching a star to a star, for example. I was surprised and pleased to find close similarities between stitch-like slits and holes and quilting stitches (which subtly overlay more easily visible pieces, patches or appliques and hold batting or lining in place) — especially in fan and petal motifs.

Although both quilt-makers and tin-punchers were concerned with filling up squares or rectangles with pattern, the methodology behind ventilating a sheet of tin and making a quilt are very different. Tin punchers break up the surface of a square or oblong blank with rounded or angular shapes defined by holes or slits. Quilt-makers assemble a whole by fitting cut shapes, most of which are straight-edged and angular, together.

The elements of geometric designs include circles, diamonds, triangles, squares, and lines, which may be connected or not, parallel or divergent/convergent (as for 'rays'). Petals and pie wedges are formed by combining triangles and circles. All geometric designs, and parts of figural ones, can be laid out with tools no more complex than a pair of dividers, probably found in nearly every 19th century homeowner's toolbox, a straight-edge of some kind, and a scribe or pencil. Fan-shaped spandrels filling the corners of so many tins are easy to do with a compass or dividers. One point is placed at the corner, the other leg is adjusted, and a curve is lightly scratched onto the tin, to be traced with holes.

The several tins of one pie safe may be so alike that you know a tracing of some kind was done. One way would be with a set of cutout tin templates like those for making identical multiple quilt pieces. Another way would be to use heavy paper, rubbed with powdered graphite on the side against the tin, with the design on top traced again and again. With some pie safes, although each tin has the same overall design, all were drawn individually, and have obvious differences in measurement or placement.

Probably a majority of geometric designs are a consequence of the tools used and the given shape of the tins, as well as the need to make the tin function as a ventilated screen. For corroborating evidence, look at wood-frame footwarmers with tin sides punctured for ventilation. A motif vocabulary of 5-, 6-, or 8-point stars, hearts, and stylized, geometric flowers was available to most people, no matter whether they were making blanket chests, fraktur, candlewick spreads, pie safes or quilts, but each motif may or may not have any especial meaning for its user. In other words, it may be subjective and hence figural, or it may be a pleasing gap-filler. A star may be patriotic or heavenly, or it may be there because it could be made to fit an empty space, or simply because it was easy to do by means of a tool. Not every artisan is an "artist" also.

Generally speaking, most pie safe tin designs, like patterns filling any empty rectangles or squares, are not culture-specific, but are found on ancient tiles, pattern glass, Amerindian as well as Persian rugs, and architectural friezes from Abyssinia to China. It is arguable that some pie safe tin designs are expanded doodles! Flipping through my old high school notebooks, I see page corners and blank spaces filled with pattern-making dots, lines, triangles, circles, fans, tendrils and even fylfot-like squiggles.

The more figural designs *are*, in a way, culture-specific, although more than one culture may claim such figures as hearts, tulips, lilies, grapes, urns, horses etc., and probably would assign different symbolic meaning to them (just as they do to the simpler geometrics).

By conducting this small survey, and studying quilt books throughout, I've learned that when comparing different classes of objects, similarity of final appearance does not prove similitude of intent or technique. Patterns of some pie safe tins and some quilts may be strikingly similar when the two are viewed together, but it's sophistry to therefore assume that one was a model and the other a copy. Instead, it seems more nearly true to say that all decorative arts draw on a large but nevertheless finite 'dictionary' of design elements.

All drawings here are of pie safe tins, and were done by me, as photo-tracings, or from actual safes. The former are generally more accurate, although often the perspective is very slightly skewed off from a perfect rectangle, and occasionally the photo may have misled me with small shadows or scratches. I've used dashes (- = = =) for slits or slots, and dots, big or little (• ...) for nail holes or other basically round holes. An X represents crossed slits in the original. All dealer or collector sources are noted in individual captions.

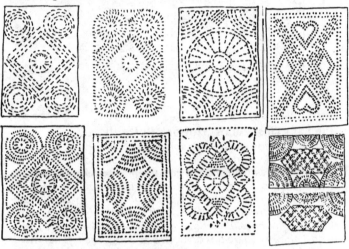

XVII-25. Pie Safe Tins: Simple Geometrics.

Four of these are square diamonds with circle or fan spandrels in the corner. Two have a petaled or rayed round center medallion, one with fan spandrels, one inside a diamond with half-rounds forming a sort of lovers' knot. One has a large X with hearts & diamonds. The last shows two tins, the one above is completely drawn, the lower tin is only half-drawn, to show how 2 adjacent tins may make corner quarter-rounds into half-rounds. I credit each tin to its dealer or owner and tell how many tins the particular safe has in front, a note about construction feature, and where the ad appeared, beginning (L) to (R), top row then bottom. (A) Calico Cat Antiques, Ann & Dick Wardrop, Wexford, PA, (8), shaped apron, (Ohio) Antique Review, 5/1990. (B) Loy's Auction Sales, Kernersville, NC, Jean Craddock photo, (4), 2 drawers above doors, Antique Week, 3/27/1989. (C) Vicki & Bruce Waasdorp, Clarence, NY, (6), long drawer below doors, long legs, New York-Pennsylvania Collector, 11/1989. (D) Robb & Alice Guss, Youngsville, NY, (8), cupboard has shaped apron, very short legs, Antiques and Arts Weekly, 7/20/1984. (E) In "Antiques in Dutchland," by Earl & Ada Robacker, Pennsylvania Folklife, Fall 1961. (6), shallow drawer beneath doors, long legs. (F) Made by John Richey of Hammersville, OH, Garth's Auctions, Inc., Delaware, OH, Ron Klapmeir Sale Plus Additions, 11/25-26/1988, (6), step back cupboard with tins for upper doors, Ohio Antique Review, 1/1984. (G) Sheppheards, Schellsburg, PA, (6), drawer below doors, (Ohio) Antique Review, 10/1990. (H) Collection of John Little, Jr., Fig. 23 in article by J. Roderick Moore, from Sullivan County, TN, (8), Empire style 1840-60 cupboard with four tins on both of two doors in lower part of cupboard. The Magazine ANTIQUES, 9/1984. A full circle is formed in the center of each door by the conjunction of four spandrels. The tins are not divided by wood molding or framework. Elongated hexagonal design in center of the 8 tins are marked in a diamond pattern familiar from cut and pressed glass.

XVII-26.
Pie Safe Tins: Stars.

Three of these feature 5-point stars; two are 6-point stars; one has 8 points. In all but one, the star is encircled, and in the other the spandrels are quartered circles and the interior pattern of small slits was apparently done in a circular fashion. The strangest design is the one with a rayed sunburst in the center of big star, which is surrounded by kite-like shapes with crosses. (L) to (R) from top: (A) Tim Martien, Burton, OH, (4), Odd cupboard/safe with top half having 2 doors with the tins, divided from lower half by drawer. Lower half has wood paneled doors. Each side has 4 stacked tins over single wood panel. Thought to be from Tennessee. (Ohio) Antique Review clipping not dated. (B) Antique Associates, at West Townsend & Joslin Tavern (group shop), (8), 70"H cupboard, 4 over 4, with long drawer in middle, between 2 sets of doors. New York-Pennsylvania Collector, 5/1990. (C) Muleskinner, Clarence, NY, (6), long drawer under 2 doors. Maine Antique Digest, 8/1989. (D) Collection State Historical Society of Colorado, (6), very shallow drawer below 2 doors. Sides not tinned. Unidentified clipping, probably from The Magazine ANTIQUES. (E) Labeled inside. "J. Zitzer & Son, Furniture Dealer and Undertaker, West Alexandria, Ohio." Ohio collector's consignment to Garth's Auctions, Inc., Delaware, OH, 1/6/1984 sale. (6) long drawer under 2 doors. Ohio Antique Review, 2/2984. (F) The Blue Door, Mudge Saver, Sunbury, OH, (6) drawer above 2 doors. (Ohio) Antique Review, 10/1990. Note: Charles A. Muller, the editor of the (Ohio) Antique Review (the name of which was changed in the mid-1980s), is knowledgable about pie safes himself, and his collector paper has the most pie safe ads of any. Perhaps this is because the majority of pie safes seem to come from the midwest.

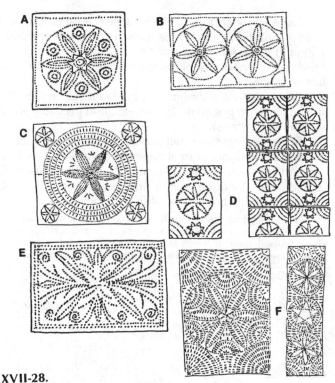

XVII-27.
Pie Safe Tins: Pinwheels or Fylfots.
All five designs include the goodluck fylfot design, known in another variation as a swastika (not the Nazi kind). It is an ancient design, found in Egypt and Amerindian arts, and was very popular in late Victorian times. Because of the method of making these drawings, the direction of the pinwheels in A, B, C and E are all reversed. two (A, C) that now go clockwise go counterclockwise on the originals, and two (B,E) that now go counterclockwise, go clockwise on original tins. (A) Thomas C. Queen, (3), this is actually a sideboard with 3 doors side by side. From Lee County, VA, c.1850. Maine Antique Digest updated clip. (B)Wiltshire Antiques, Milford, OH, (8), two drawers above 2 doors, shallow shaped apron, tapered legs. (Ohio) Antique Review, 4/1986. (C) Kenneth W. Farmer auc tion, Radford, VA, 2/2-3/1985. (8), low sideboard style with 2 doors, each with 4 tins not divided by molding or framework. (Ohio) Antique Review, 4/1985. (D) Mary Mac & Robert Franklin, VA, (6), short turned legs, found in central Virginia. (E) Muleskinner, Ronald Korman, prop., Clarence, NY, (4), long drawer under 2 doors, tall turned legs, believed to be of Southern origin. Maine Antique Digest, 4/1987.

XVII-28.
Pie Safe Tins: Petals, Flowers, Butterfly.
The 6-petal flower design is sometimes referred to as a star, but because of the rounded edges, I identified them as flowers. All are encircled. Lower left is a design sometimes referred to as a "butterfly", which is a sort of stretched flower & tendril design. It reminds me of folded-paper blot pictures done by psychologists with ink and by kindergartners with paint. (L) to (R) from top: (A) Belmont Antiques, Belmont, VT, (4), low, bracket-foot cupboard with 2 almost square tins on both of 2 doors, the tins not divided by molding or framework. Pennsylvania origin. Unidentified clipping, probably from New York-Pennsylvania Collector. (B) Private collector, Long Beach, CA, (6), short legged cupboard with exceptionally oblong tins, 3 on each door. Wonderful use of doubled design to fill otherwise awkward space. Safe found in Michigan. (C) Ex-Collection Earl F. Ada F. Robacker. (1), single large panel on front of wall or rafter-hung safe, which has tins on other 3 sides also. Two oblong sheets of tin are joined along the horizontal axis to form one outside tin about 3 1/2" wide. From Pennsylvania Folklife. Spring 1961. A design very similar to (A) and (C) is in the Bybee Collection, in the von Rosenberg kitchen, at Round Top, TX. (D) Charles Gerhardt Antiques, Lebanon, OH, (10), but arranged in what may be a unique fashion — with 4 1/2 panels on each of 2 doors. See the larger drawing at the right that shows how the parts are assembled. (Ohio) Antique Review, 1/1990. (E) Dogwood Antiques, Sparta, TN, (6), shallow drawer above 2 doors. Unidentified clipping, possibly Mid-Atlantic Antiques, or Antiques Gazette. (F) Gus Knapp, Hudson, OH, (3), large hanging safe with large tin on door and a narrower panel (with a star in the center) on either side. Undated (Ohio) Antique Review clipping.

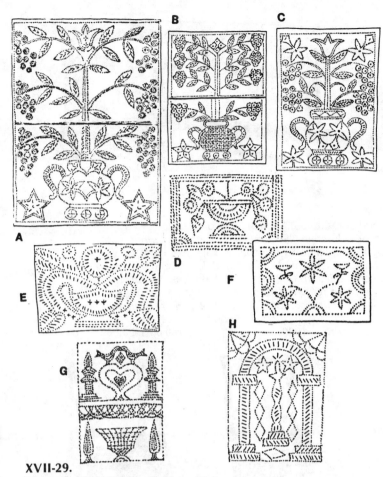

ANTIQUES, 9/1984. (H) K & K Antiques, Springfield, OH. (8), 4 tins joined without molding or framework to create effect of one large tin for each door. Short turned legs, sideboard type of safe with low gallery backplate on sides & back of the top. Siever County, TN origin. *Maine Antique Digest*, 4/1989.

XVII-30.
Pie Safe Case Types.

(L) to (R) from top: (A) Four tins in 2 doors, tins separated by framework (or molding), with 2 drawers above doors, short legs. (B) Six tins in 2 doors, bracket feet, shaped apron. (C) Hanging safe with large tin (or joined tins) on single door. Other tins usually on other vertical sides. Hung from rafters. (D) Six tins in 2 doors, above long drawer, long tapered legs. (E) Twelve tins joined without framework or molding to form 2 large tins in 2 doors, turned feet. (F) Wythe County (and neighboring counties), Virginia-type case with 2 drawers above 2 doors, and distinctive urn & grapes (urn & flowers, urn & stars) pattern. Turned feet not always found on type. Single drawer sometimes found. All drawings of composite type not taken from any single model.

XVII-29.
Pie Safe Tins: Urns, Flowers, Columns.

Virginia, Pennsylvania, and possibly, Ohio safes. The first three drawings are beautiful examples of classic Wythe County area urn & flower or urn & grape designs, with stars (or starflowers). Here the stars are separate from the stems; in some similar examples, pinwheels or stars may take the place of some of the grapes or flowers. Sometimes hearts take the place of or are used along with, stars, grapes or flowers. In the lower, and sometimes upper corners, one finds stars, pinwheels, flowers or columns resembling candles, and which may relate to the Fraternal Order of Masons. One constant, in all the examples I saw but one, is that the vertical stalk/stem is made with three lines, possibly signifying the Trinity. (A) From article about Roddy Moore's research into Southwest VA and East TN safes, prior to the *ANTIQUES* article. *Antique Gazette* 3/1984. (B) Just Us, J. & S. Schneider, Tucson, AZ, (4), 2 doors with 2 short drawers above, short turned legs. Wythe County area. The 2 tins on each door are joined (and obviously not lined up) horizontally across center, with no molding or framework. Note diapered checker design inside urn. *Maine Antique Digest*, 10/1984. (C) Kenneth Farmer auctioneer, Radford, VA, 2/2/1985 sale. (4 tins joined to make 2), with side panels. Wythe County area. This is a drawing of the side tin, showing the star flowers. The front tins have stars instead of flowers; interior decoration of the urn is the same. Note how the 'kite'-like shapes attached to the lower part of the flowers resemble those in the upper part of the urn/vase in (A). *Maine Antique Digest*, 4/1985. (D) Don & Janie Noyes, Glenford, OH. (6), a stepback cupboard, extremely severe case design, lower part being a lift-top chest. Tins set into 2 upper doorst. Probably Pennsylvania. *Maine Antique Digest*, 3/1986. (E) Leland Schmidt, Rockford, IL, number of tins not shown, possibly (6) unidentified clipping, possibly New York-Pennsylvania Collector, or (Ohio) *Antique Review*, 6/1988. (G) Collection of Carl & DeEtta Pace, fig. 16 in Moore's *ANTIQUES* article. (2), long drawer above 2 doors. Depiction of footed compote, possibly meant to represent one in pressed glass. Garlands, lovebirds, hearts, a diamond, 2 candles and 2 trees resembling Cedars of Lebanon complete the striking design. *The Magazine*

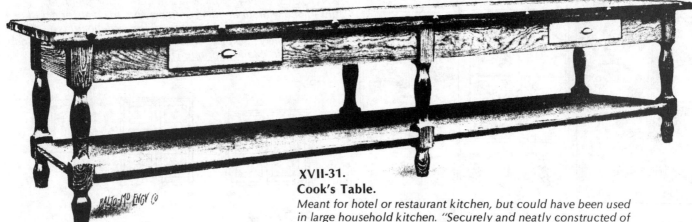

XVII-31.
Cook's Table.

Meant for hotel or restaurant kitchen, but could have been used in large household kitchen. "Securely and neatly constructed of natural wood, resting on heavy turned legs, with dish shelf below. Tops are of three strips, tongued and grooved, leaded and securely bolted together. Tables up to 8' in length have one drawer and four legs; those 10' to 16' have two drawers and three sets of legs. Came in choice of 3 widths — 30", 36", and 42", and in 8 lengths — 5', 6', 7', 8', 10', 12', 14', and 16'L. Catalog of S. B. Sexton Stove & Mfg. Co., Baltimore, c.1930s. **$100.00-$500.00**

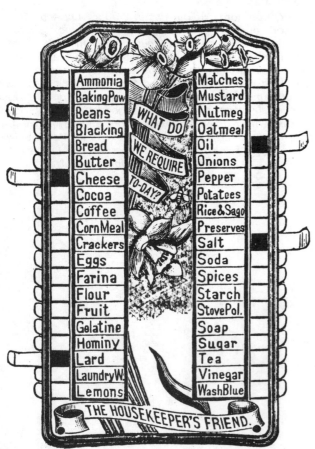

Ammonia	Matches
BakingPow	Mustard
Beans	Nutmeg
Blacking	Oatmeal
Bread	Oil
Butter	Onions
Cheese	Pepper
Cocoa	Potatoes
Coffee	Rice&Sago
CornMeal	Preserves
Crackers	Salt
Eggs	Soda
Farina	Spices
Flour	Starch
Fruit	StovePol.
Gelatine	Soap
Hominy	Sugar
Lard	Tea
LaundryW.	Vinegar
Lemons	WashBlue

WHAT DO WE REQUIRE TO-DAY?

THE HOUSEKEEPER'S FRIEND.

XVII-32.
Shopping list aid or reminder.

"The Housekeeper's Friend." Probably printed celluloid. Advertised by wholesale importer G.M. Thurnauer & Brother who supplied kitchenwares to the trade. The NYC firm imported from Germany and France. Ad in House Furnishing Review, 11/1909. **$15.00-$30.00**

XVII-33.
Convertible step ladders.

*(T) Folding step ladder chair, shown in both positions, were manufactured by Tucker & Dorsey Mfg. Co., Indianapolis, who made all kinds of woodenwares including ironing boards and pastry boards. Advertised in The Metal Worker, 6/21/1890. Same linecuts used in 1909 Albert Pick wholesale catalog, advertised as "solid and substantial; it is a good hall chair. As a step ladder it is heavy enough to be used without danger of upsetting. Finished in oak." (B) Called **"utility steps"** in F.A. Walker wholesale catalog, Boston, 1870s. Instead of folding, the steps slid under the stool Finish and condition account for value.* **$40.00-$150.00**

I have had this February 17, 1973 cartoon on my bulletin board for 16 years, for even though I don't collect old electrical appliances, it is a glorious image of a man with a secret obsession. He may be a collector or not; he may have been given these for a wedding that never took place; he may just be a compulsive shopper.

What is most interesting to me about this category of collecting is the social history behind it. First, there were the marketing efforts of power companies who could see the Future and knew it had to be Electric for their own survival. So power companies in the first quarter of a century drummed up business by actively selling that Electric Future. It's amusing to read articles written for their own trade journals (a couple of which are excerpted in this chapter). Such articles offer background to our understanding of public ad campaigns in the first third of the 20th century.

For example, an article in the *Edison Electric Institute Bulletin* of September 1934, tells about the development of a "distinctive and appealing character" — "Reddy Kilowatt, the Electrical Servant". Reddy, also spelled "Ready" by some companies, formed the basis for a "program... to humanize the utility approach to the public by translating... the complicated business of serving electricity to all types of customers." Reddy's appeal holds strong today, although it is the rare customer who has a choice about whether or not to use electricity.

Nowadays, power companies issue occasional brochures on "saving energy", and then spend the rest of their time lobbying before state assemblies asking for rate increases because of decreased usage, or fighting people who want to sell them excess power generated by privately-owned windmills. They are otherwise mired in a bureaucracy of meter-reading and kilowatt hours . Obviously they neither have the time nor do they need to fund their own test kitchens as in the old days, or pay well-known cookbook authors to prepare promotional cookbooks. And thankfully they have not used old Reddy to try to humanize nuclear power plants and high tension electric lines. Talk about zap.

The second aspect of the social history of household electricity is the utopian view that it would replace what was a dwindling supply of cheap servants and that it would make the housewife's life easier. For the majority of plugged-in households in the teens and early 1920s, life in general was pretty trig, and electricity only made it more so. It is to laugh to see the retouched, vignette photographs in old power-company booklets, showing cute young things, in pre-Flapper outfits, sitting at their dressing tables curling their hair, or standing at a tea table, ogled by admiring friends while making waffles, or posing beside tabletop washing machines in which you can be sure there are some dainty silk stockings.

Once electricity was available in a community, probably the biggest problem in selling electrical appliances in the earliest days was that there was virtually no-one to do repairs. And undoubtedly many people were afraid of shocks and electrocution. Find a copy of James Thurber's story "The Car We Had to Push", which appears in a collection of stories published in 1933 called *My Life and Hard Times*. In the story, Thurber tells about one of "the victims and martyrs of the wild-eyed Edison's dangerous experiments" — his mother's mother, who "lived the latter years of her life in the horrible suspicion that electricity was dripping invisibly all over the house. It leaked, she contended, out of empty sockets if the wall switch had been left on." In fact, if you want to be charmed completely, get copies of all of Thurber's wonderful stories and read them again.

Toasters are the big thing here, as you are well aware from booths at shows and ads in trade papers. I use an old (c.1941) toaster myself, with perfect satisfaction. It's not very outre to look at, but it's easy to use, easy to fix, and easy to clean. In selecting the couple dozen toasters listed here, I just made notes on the ones I saw at flea markets or antique shows — trying to pick out aesthetic or techno-historical winners; there are also a number that aren't rare but which add breadth (and perhaps a bit of cheapth) to a collection.

In the next few years, other small electrical appliances, many dating well into the 1940s, will become increasingly collectible. There's still time to scout them out at fleas and thrift shops.

Baby food warmer, small pitcher-like vessel set on electric base, gray & white agateware that looks like moss agate, 4 wooden button feet screwed on to base, odd plug with flat prongs, many marks, "AGL, #2510", "Triangle Lektrik Baby Food Warmer", mfd by American Electrical Heater Co., Detroit, MI, 4½"H, early 20th C. **$50.00-$60.00**

Baker, round-cornered oblong chromium box like a big shoe box, with slide out baking tray drawer, black plastic handle on drawer, 4 little feet, temperature dial on top, "Redi-Baker", mfd by Knapp Monarch NESCO, St. Louis, MO, c.1963. **$12.00-$15.00**

Barber mug, white enamelware with cobalt trim, pat'd 1905. • Patent prob. refers to heating element, not mug's design. **$65.00-$75.00**

Beater, heavy metal motor housing with black wooden knob on top, sets down in Akro Agate glass bowl with green & rusty pumpkin swirls, original wiring, no mark, bowl is 4½"H, overall height including knob is 7⅝"H, 20th C. See also Eggbeater, this chapter. **$35.00-$45.00**

Beater, paneled custard slag container, with ivory-painted metal motor housing with shaped knob, simple beater blades, "Vidrio", Vidrio Products Corp. (the glass parts), Cicero, IL, 1920s-30s. • The only time I've seen the name Vidrio it's been on small electric appliances with glass. According to *Thomas' Directory*, 1932-33, glass products were Vidrio's beat. So I don't know who made the electrical parts. **$45.00-$55.00**

Beater or mixer, cobalt blue panelled glass container fitted with single squiggly beater blade attached to housed motor, strap handle, lid has hole for pouring ingredients in with funnel, "Vidrio Products Corp.", Catalog #E30, Chicago, IL, 2 cup capacity, 1933 patent #1935857. • This also came with a Depression green glass jar with green-painted metal lid and motor housing. That one is valued at about a ⅓ or ½ of value of one with blue jar. **$75.00-$85.00**

Bottle warmer, chromed metal, plastic knobs, temperature gauge on top, "Sunbeam", Chicago Flexible Shaft, 12 ¹⁵⁄₁₆"H, developed 1951; this one early 1950s. **$200.00-$250.00**

Casserole, tan, brown & black enameled body with chrome & red Art Deco design of woman serving steaming casserole dish on front, 2 Bakelite® Deco black handles & lid knob, inner bowl, electric cord, high & low settings for heat, "NESCO Thrifty Cook Casserole #B40", National Enamel & Stamping Co., Milwaukee, WI, c.1940s. **$60.00-$70.00**

Corn popper, heavy tinned short cylindrical steel body, crank in top with a bent blade of heavy wire, like a dough mixer, green wood handles, mark stamped on bottom but illegible, American, 8" diameter, c.1928 to 1935. **$30.00-$35.00**

Corn popper, metal straight-sided body on short legs, 2 handles, lid, heating element inside at bottom, perforated with band of holes," Dominion Electric Co.", Minneapolis, MN, 1930s. **$35.00-$45.00**

Corn popper, nickeled steel with perforations, straight-sided basket pan on heating stand with 3 legs, wooden side handle, lid through which top crank comes, green wood & green cord, "Betsy Ross", mfd by Central Flatiron Mfg. Co., Johnson City, NY, 6 1/2"H x 8 1/2" diameter, introduced June 1930. **$35.00-$45.00**

Doughnut maker, electric, oval black sheet metal base, 2 round lids, sort of works like waffle maker, only it makes 7 "donuts", the base & upper molds having the 7 rings with convex centers which touch when closed to create the hole, Wallace Ray Co., Waseca, MN, 1968 ad in *McCall's Needlework & Crafts* magazine. Just 20 + years ago, but the ad copy seems so dated & funny today. The screaming headlines, above the smiling bob-haired woman gazing upon the maker, is **"MAKE MONEY MAKING DONUTS.** - New! - Greaseless! - Different! No experience needed ! New electric machine bakes 14 dozen per hour, all kinds: Plain, Iced, Raisin, etc. Costs you only 16¢ per doz. YOU earn up to $125.00 a month SPARE TIME ... MUCH MORE FULL TIME! Start in own kitchen. Sell to restaurants, grocers, drugstores, cafeterias, plants, etc. No bookkeeping! Collect cash profits daily! Machine guaranteed. Add more as needed. Write today for Free Recipes, details. No obligation." **$18.00-$28.00**

Drink mixer, electric, various metals, some enameled, "Drinkmaster", Hamilton Beach, Racine, WI, 1926. **$50.00-$60.00**

Egg boiler, electric, metal, "El Eggo", mfd by Pacific Electric Heating Co., Ontario (?), CA, late 1890s. **$35.00-$45.00**

Egg cooker, red ceramic, chrome lid, metal poaching rack inside and ceramic insert, includes instruction booklet, Fiesta Ware ceramic; cooker itself "#599", Hankscraft Co., Good Housekeeping Institute Seal of Approval, Madison, WI, c.1930s. • The same cooker, in orange or light blue, about the same price; in yellow, slightly less; in pale seafoam green, about $10.00 less. **$30.00-$40.00**

Eggbeater, single stainless steel blade, white glass beater jar, cast with rocket-like 4 strut bottom for stability, red wood knob handle, "K-M", Knapp-Monarch Co., St. Louis, MO, 9 1/2"H, 20th C. **$15.00-$20.00**

Fan, kerosene burner in base to power fan with hot air, floor model, 4 large brass blades, wiggly cage wires, almost as large as its 'plant stand' wrought iron base that has 4 twisted legs. "Lake Breeze #16", Chicago, IL, c.1914 #20 (?). (There was also a Lake Breeze alcohol-powered table fan.) Although the kerosene fan isn't electric, I included it here for comparison with much commoner electric fans, which might be from the same period. One kerosene fan sold at a benefit auction for the Owls Head Museum, in July 1989, for $2900.00, plus 10% premium for the buyer. **$3000.00-$4000.00**

Fan, kerosene lamp powered, floor model, iron stand, 3 brass blades, does not work continuously, but in cycles, decal reads "Radio Fan", "Made in Germany", 53"H x 34" diameter, 20th C. **$275.00-$350.00**

Fan, marbleized glass base, metal blades, maker unknown, (could it be Vidrio?), American (?), 20th C. **$85.00-$100.00**

Fan, nickel-plated table fan to be used as a centerpiece, with the brass blades set horizontally, & a removable cut or pressed glass bowl fitted on the top. The bowl did not revolve, but I'd hate to reach carelessly for a summer peach & miss the bowl. "White Cross No. 289", mfd by Lindstrom-Smith Co., Chicago, IL, 10½"H x 9½" diameter, 1915. **$150.00-$200.00**

Fan, originally meant for bank tellers, horizontal blades so money wouldn't be blown away, brown finished metal pedestal base with globe top with openwork slots, "Savory Airator", Buffalo, NY, pat'd 1926. **$250.00-$400.00**

Fan, oscillating, cast iron base, with cage, hinged so as to be used on desktop or mounted to wall, mfd by Diehl Mfg. Co., Division of Singer Mfg. Co., Elizabethport, NJ, 1930s. **$35.00-$45.00**

Fan, tabletop, all brass, "Emerson-Trojan", St. Louis, MO. • The Fan Man Inc., Mr. Kurt House, 4606 Travis, Dallas, TX 75205, has a catalog of antique fan parts for sale, also a book on mechanical fans, & information on an association. Please use SASE when writing. **$100.00-$125.00**

Fan, tabletop, cast iron base with brass blades & guard wires, Westinghouse, early 20th C. **$45.00-$65.00**

Fan, tabletop personal fan, brown Bakelite® with 3 loops of heavy ribbon attached to revolving head, which would serve as blades without being at all dangerous, no cage needed, "Ribbonaire", sold through Sears, mfd by Diehl Mfg. Co., Division of Singer Mfg. Co., Elizabethport, NJ, 1930s to 1950s. • Diehl sold them under their own name too, "Airflow Safan", during same period. **$175.00-$225.00**

Flour sifter, electric—See in Strain & sift chapter.

Food warmer, copper with black molded phenolic resin (one famous tradename is Bakelite) handles, 3 compartments, Chase Brass & Copper, with centaur logo, 1940s. **$40.00-$55.00**

Fudge sauce warmer, "Johnston's", (could this be Robert A. Johnston Co.?), (Milwaukee, WI?), 1920s? **$35.00-$40.00**

Griddle, chromed metal, small rectangle on short legs, "Electrahot" Style 512, Electrahot Mfg. Co., Minneapolis, MN, c.1930s. **$15.00-$20.00**

Hot dog cooker, black metal base, green pottery insert with side cup handle & 4 brass feet that fit into holes in metal base, probably something to do with the electrical connection, black plastic handle, "The Lightning Wiener Cooker", mfd by Lightning Cooker Co., Cleveland, OH, holds 3 hot dogs, c.1920s or 1930s. No patent numbers. **$20.00-$30.00**

Hot dog steamer, white enameled metal house with heavy-duty molded plastic red plastic peaked roof with steam vent chimneys, marked 'Dog House"on front, "Sunbeam", Chicago Flexible Shaft Co., 7"H x 7¾"L, 1980s. • This is a perfect example of an almost instant collectible. It is not a "Snoopy" item, but plays only on word "Dog". Faddish and figural and extremely well-made. Wish now I'd bought the one I saw in 1983; it was the last one they had, and was cheap ... under $15.00. Now?... **$20.00-$30.00**

Juicer, A. F. Dormeyer Co., Chicago, IL, 1930s. **$20.00-$25.00**

Juicer, green Jadite glass, dark green enameled motor housing with chrome trim, cream ceramic reamer, alternating current only, "Sunkist Juicit", mfd by Chicago Electric Mfg. Co., a "Handy Hot" Product, Chicago, IL, 8¾"H, 1934 patents #1943270 and #1962856. **$28.00-$40.00**

Liquid mixer, enameled iron base for motor, glass top, base looks like a streamlined locomotive front, Hollywood Liquefier Co., South Pasadena, CA, 1930s. **$20.00-$30.00**

Malt mixer, "Hamilton Beach #51", 20th C. **$50.00-$60.00**

Malt mixer, metal & glass, "Arnold #15", Arnold Electric Co., subsidiary of Hamilton Beach, 1930s. **$45.00-$60.00**

Malted milk machine, green porcelainized cast iron, has 2 containers, Hamilton Beach Mfg. Co., Racine, WI, early 1930s-40s. **$70.00-$100.00**

Marshmallow toaster, sheet metal "campstove" like thing on 4 wire legs, red rubber feet on legs, 2 little wire forks to hold marshmallows, 150 volts, 345 watts, "Angelus-Campfire Bar-B-Q Marshmallow Toaster", early 20th C. **$65.00-$80.00**

Milk shake mixer, triple head & 3 speed, green or cream enameled steel, glass, this triple head type was for a soda fountain not the home, Hamilton Beach, 1930s. **$150.00-$250.00**

Milk shake mixer, white porcelain base, glass, metal, Arnold Mfg. Co., adv'g "Horlicks, The Original Malted Milk", 20th C. **$100.00-$125.00**

Milk shaker mixer, various metals, glass, Gilchrist, Newark, NJ, 1922. **$100.00-$125.00**

Mixer, cast metal base with detachable mixer, juicer attachment, set of ceramic, heat-proof mixing bowls & lids that could be put directly in oven, Sears' "Powermaster DeLuxe", late (?) 1930s. **$45.00-$65.00**

Mixer, cast & sheet metal, nickel plated, with turned wood spade handle; a portable food mixer in its own heavy wire stand (rather like a doll stand), that allowed it to be used in vertical position with a tumbler or other fairly low container. They advertised "Used on stand or in the hand." To be plugged into lamp socket. "Whip-All", mfd by Air-O-Mix, Wilmington, DE, 1923 to about 1926-27. Very short-lived, hence very rare. **$75.00-$90.00**

Mixer, countertop, cast metal base with mixer that, when first introduced, came with 2 stainless steel mixing bowls, and one attachment: a juicer. That was soon to be joined by other attachments: a food chopper, grater, potato peeler, knife sharpener, polisher, can opener, drink mixer & coffee grinder. "Mixmaster", mfd by the Chicago Flexible Shaft Co. (later Sunbeam), Chicago, IL, 1930-31. (By 1936, all the other attachments were available.) • According to Earl Lifshey, author of *The Housewares Story* (see Bibliography), "By 1936 'Mixmaster' sales reached to more than 300,000 units." So there are plenty of old ones out there for collectors; the trick is finding the attachments. **$125.00-$150.00**

Mixer, enameled cast metal, with opaque green custard glass reamer & mixing bowl, Manning Bowman & Co., Meriden, CT, 1930s-40s. •**German vocabulary** — Ruhr-apparat or Mixer: mixing appliance. **$45.00-$55.00**

Mixer, green cast iron frame, green Jadite bowl, green wooden handle, like a small KitchenAid, "Mixette", mfd by F. A. Smith Mfg. Co., Rochester, NY, c.1930s. **$50.00-$65.00**

Mixer, plated metal stand has tall post to which multi-speed beater motor clamped at any height, revolving metal mixing bowl, "Star-Rite Magic Maid", Fitzgerald Mfg. Co., Torrington, CT, c.1931. **$30.00-$40.00**

Mixer, with instruction booklet and many attachments, including ricer, meat grinder, mixing bowls of creamy green glass, "Sunbeam Model FC4", Chicago Flexible Shaft Co., 1934 patent #1926910 is latest patent number given. Their first "Mixmaster" was 1930. **$80.00-$90.00**

Mixer, with original glass bowl, "Lindstrom', Chicago, IL, 1920s. • In a 1919 speech, Raymond Marsh, Secretary of the American Washing Machine Manufacturers' Association, said "A wonderful story could be told about how women went into factories and recovered entirely from their awe and fear of machinery. Experience has shown that women are and can be efficient at running machinery. ... During the war, women rendered efficient service working hydraulic presses, heating and charging furnaces, welding brass, forging chains, molding bricks, constructing compasses ... and a thousand and one other important and necessary tasks." Marsh's point was that WWI encouraged the use of labor saving devices in the kitchen because women had lost their fear of machines and they had no household servants when every able-bodied woman in the U.S., England and France (and probably Germany too) went to work in war-industry factories. **$10.00-$15.00**

Mixer & food processor, enameled cast iron base and motor housing, holder for mixing bowls, 3 speeds & attachments to beat eggs or mix batters, whip cream, mix dough, strain fruits, sieve & puree vegetables, slice potatoes, chop meats or nuts, make ice cream, grind coffee, shred or grate, extract citrus fruit juice, make applesauce ... yep, sounds like a you-know-what. KitchenAid division of Hobart Mfg. Co., Troy, OH, early model introduced c.1920; this large one c.1930. **$75.00-$100.00**

Mixer or beater, iron housing lid with strap handle, looks like part of an old hair dryer, activates 2 wing blade, glass jar, works perfectly, hums quietly, "Challenge", mfd by CEM Co., "Tyre Avub" (? whur's this, hey! Sounds like a Biblical land of gluttony & sloth). "CEM" is Chicago Electrical Manufacturing Co., Chicago, IL, 8 1/2"H, with 3 cup capacity, 1930s? (CEM est. c.1903.). • "Use Electric Mixer to WAX, POLISH, SAND" — so advertised Towle Mfg. Co., Walnut Creek, CA, in Sept. 1960. Their device, a "slip-on TOOLZON", was fitted on the shaft of "any mixer" so that you could "let your kitchen mixer wax furniture, floors, auto; polish silver, glass, brass; sand wood, metal, ceramics.' (I can just see the warranties now.) In theory it's a great Idea. **$15.00-$20.00**

Outlet, cast iron, figural with 3 outlets & 2 lions' heads, American or English, 3"L, late 19th C (?). **$65.00-$80.00**

Outlet, twin outlet porcelain plug for appliances, in original box depicting woman demonstrating the plug hanging from a ceiling fixture (shades of George Booth cartoons). "Permits the Use of Two Electrical Conveniences at the Same Time." "GE", Schenectady, NY, 4"L, 1916. • The best information on the **development of electrical plugs** is found in the July 1986 issue of *Technology and Culture* quarterly of the Society for the History of Technology, in an article by Dr. Fred E. H. Schroeder of the U. of Minnesota, entitled "More 'Small Things Forgotten': Domestic Electrical Plugs and Receptacles, 1881-1931". Reprints may be ordered for $5.00 or less (the price has probably gone up since 1986 when it was a dollar), from The University of Chicago Press, 5801 South Ellis Avenue, Chicago, IL 60637. For anyone interested in electrical appliances, I would highly recommend this. **$35.00-$45.00**

Ovenette, stand with 3 cabriole legs, rack inside over holes to let heat rise, high cover, wooden knob, plated metal, temperature gauge on side, between 2 legs, "Stanley Ovenette", mfd by Stanley Savage Mfg Co., Chicago, IL, about 8" diameter, 1930s. **$25.00-$30.00**

Potato baker, insulated oven in casserole or chafing dish shape, on 3 sheet metal legs, molded phenolic resin side handles & lid knob, heating element in bottom part, "Knapp-Monarch", St. Louis, MO, 1930s. **$35.00-$45.00**

Sandwich grill, oblong streamlined body, thick, heavy lid is removable (for washing) grill surface, inside is smooth, of course, 4 legs, "tassel-like" molded phenolic resin "Bakelite®" lid handle, also has accessory broiling and frying grids, "Edicraft", Edison Electric, NJ, 1930s. • With all grids & grills: **$45.00-$55.00**

Teapots, coffee pots, electric—See Coffee & tea chapter.

Toaster, boxy body, almost as long as high, (came with choice of nickel or chrome finish), on wide base with 4 small button feet, embossed on sides with decorative border & medallion that looks for all the world like a Georgian wall mirror, toast holder for one slice pulls out of end, holds bread vertically, clockwork timer, adjustable for brownness; a gussied up & automatic version of the simpler E942. "Universal E9422", Landers, Frary & Clark, New Britain, CT, late 1920s to 1930. • This style looks so neo-Georgian/Victorian, it is hard to believe that it was being made at the same time as much more streamlined electric toasters. **$25.00-$35.00**

Toaster, brightly chromed, Art Deco, side loading, "Son-Chief", Winsted, CT, 1920s-30s. • In 1983, Charles P. Fisher, an engineer with a special understanding of and fondness for toasters, wrote me that he was beginning work on a book devoted to electric toasters. The book is *Hazlecorn's Price Guide to Old Electric Toasters* (See Bibliography), on which Mr. Fisher's name appears only in tiny type & abbreviated, on the title page. But Fisher is the expert. I have referred to him a few times in the following toaster entries. **$35.00-$45.00**

Toaster, chrome, black Bakelite® handles, leaping deer Art Deco decoration on door, does only one piece of toast at a time, toast holder controlled by lever handle, tilt down to insert bread, push up to insert holder in toaster, dial on side for degree of toastedness, using letters of alphabet from A to K instead of numbers, GE Appliances Co., 6¾"H, late 1920s. **$40.00-$50.00**

Toaster, chrome & black Bakelite®, high round top body with flat sides and flat bottom, shapely black base, one slice, handles on both ends, Merit-Made Co., Buffalo, NY, early 1940s. **$30.00-$40.00**

Toaster, chrome & black-painted sheet metal, tray base, flip down doors, does 4 slices, "Victorian, Model A65", Bersted Mfg. Co., Chicago, IL, 12"L x 6¾"W, looks c.1940s, may be a bit earlier. **$20.00-$25.00**

Toaster, chrome body, black plastic base, does only one piece at a time, bread is inserted in one end & comes out other end of narrow body (which is an elongated oval seen from above), after a rather jerky trip through the length of the toaster ... a trip you can observe through a very small porthole in the side. Adjustable light & dark lever. Has a fan inside that cools the works (but not the toast). "Toast-O-Lator, Model J", pat'd by Alfredo DeMatteis, and mfd by Toast-O-Lator Corp., Long Island City, NY, about 11"H, c.1940. **$200.00-$235.00**

Toaster, chrome body, brown Bakelite® handles, "Faultless Appliances, Model #1249", St. Louis, MO, 1930s-40s. **$30.00-$35.00**

Toaster, chrome half-round body, flat sides, black Bakelite base and handles, red signal light on one side, near base, hinged crumb tray, could be set for "pops toast up" or "keeps toast warm", 2 slices, styling by George Scharfenberg, "Sunbeam", Chicago Flexible Shaft Co., Chicago, IL, 1940. **$30.00-$40.00**

Toaster, chrome, makes 2 pieces of toast, has 6 toasting darkness degrees, "Edicraft Automatic", mfd by Thomas A. Edison Inc., Orange, NJ, 7⅛"H x 10¼"L, early 20th C. **$120.00-$140.00**

Toaster, chrome oblong boxy body with control end slightly truncated at top corner, one slice capacity (they also made a 2 slice model), 5 fluted vertical panels on both sides, "Toastmaster Model 185", mfd by Waters-Genter Co., division of McGraw Electric Co., Minneapolis, MN, 1931. **$35.00-$45.00**

Toaster, chromed brass pedestal base with ball feet not at corners, embossed fancy decoration on sides, pendant handles at each end, toasting frame is like an abstract slice of toast turned diamond-wise, with point facing down, arched top, basket-flipping operated with pushbutton, "Universal E-9419", mfd by Landers, Frary & Clark, New Britain, CT, c.1928-29. • It is probably safe to say that collectibles utilizing metal made just before a war, or fancy items made just before a financial crash, have rarity added by events which almost certainly halt production. **$225.00-$300.00**

Toaster, chromed sheet metal, peaked tent shape with pull down doors decorated with 2 vertical bands with sort of wheat berry design, the dished tray on top — for buttering prepared toast or keeping it warm — lifts off for cleaning, dial control for light, brown or medium sticks out under one side, "Serv-Hot Toast Tray" & "Queen Mary" pattern, "Royal-Rochester" toaster, mfd by Robeson-Rochester Corp, Rochester, NY, c.1937. **$20.00-$28.00**

Toaster, cylindrical shape, revolves on its base and was probably used in center of breakfast table, black plastic knob on top and 3 oblong feet, chrome plated, 4 swingout 'car' doors with slot for toast (where car window would be), heating element in central core, "Elem", German, 1958. **$40.00-$55.00**

Toaster, enameled black metal base and top, very boxy, chromium body with 2 sets of 4 vertical stamped lines or stripes on both sides (design called the "Beaumonde Pattern"), Bakelite® (or other molded phenolic resin) knob on end door, end-loading for 2 slices, "Double-Quick", Universal Electric, mfd by Landers, Frary & Clark, c.1935. **$20.00-$30.00**

Toaster, fabulous 3 slicer, black baked enameled steel 3-sided box frame and base, 3 decorated chrome doors, triangular top of chrome with knob, mica heating element, "Delta", mfd by Kamco Inc., Unionville, CT, c.1935. •
Mica is a silicate crystal, built up by nature in thin, somewhat flexible leaves or sheets. It was early used for translucent panels in oven doors, heating stoves & lanterns as well as later for heating elements in electric toasters. **$55.00-$70.00**

Toaster, gorgeously simple open-sided metal box on base with curled strap metal legs, black baked enamel finish, toasting elements visible like a modern art sculpture, "Cookenette", no mfr's name, 1920s or 30s, but not in 1930 *House Furnishing Review Buyer's Directory*. **$60.00-$70.00**

Toaster, green painted sheet metal, "The Handy Hot", Chicago Mfg. Co., (or Chicago Electric Mfg. Co.), Chicago, IL, c.1930s. **$20.00-$25.00**

Toaster, high & skinny, porcelain base, chromed openwork metal with 6 small cutout stars on top, 2 toast doors are loaded, then you turn to other side, turning knobs on top are molded plastic, "Star-Rite, the Star Electric Toaster", mfd by Fitzgerald Mfg Co., Torrington, CT, 9"H, c.1929 (?). • In early 1986, a dealer in Pennsylvania placed an ad offering to pay $20.00 each (this would be her wholesale price) for the first 200 chrome electric toasters with openwork sides that were offered to her. The seller had to pay shipping. **$40.00-$50.00**

Toaster, moderately interesting Art Deco design, in original box, "Speed Master", mfd by Son Chief Electric Co., Winsted, CT, 1930s. **$22.00-$30.00**

Toaster, nearly square chromed box with slightly sloped sides, 4 corner columns rising from little black rolling feet, what the manufacturer called "artistic" pendent handles on 2 sides, lever to cause toast to pop up, 2 slices, automatic switch-off with bell, adjustable for doneness, "Auto-Toastmaker", Bersted Mfg. Co., Chicago, IL, new in 1930. **$25.00-$35.00**

Toaster, hot plate & warming oven combined, cast iron base, white enameled metal with black trim, black Bakelite handles, "darker" and "lighter" switch, push down lever for toast, nickeled plate on oven door says "LASKO Toaster Combination", mfd by Lasko Toaster Co., 7½"H x 9⅜" x 13"W, c.1930s. **$85.00-$100.00**

Toaster, nickel plated, blue wooden knobs, swing-out baskets with pivoting hinges so that toast could be "turned over" by pushing the baskets back in the opposite way. This pivoting action is interesting relative to pivoting toe toasters of hearth cooking times. "Electrex", United Drug Co.; or "Torrid Pushomatic", by Frank E. Wolcott Mfg. Co.; or Beardsley-Wolcott, so Boston, MA or Waterbury, CT, 7"H x 8"L x 4¼"W, 1920 & 1927 patents, Fisher says "Pushomatic" used 1928 to c.1930. • Classic. — Pleasing to know that one of only two old toasters I ever bought, is considered by the undisputed expert, Charles Fisher, whose list provided the various markings above, as "an interesting and important toaster." I love it. **$55.00-$65.00**

Toaster, nickel plated, single slice, boxy end-loading oven type, with pull out rack, "Universal E942", Landers, Frary & Clark, pat'd in 1925. • German vocabulary — Toaster or Brotroster: toaster. **$28.00-$35.00**

Toaster, nickeled metal, flip-down doors perforated with 7 long popsicle stick vertical slots, warming platform on top, "patented attachment turns the toast automatically" is activated by touching door handles , "Electric Flipflop Model 65" (by 1922 called the "Marion Flipflop"), mfd by Rutenber Electric Co., Marion, IN, 1917. **$25.00-$35.00**

Toaster, plain white porcelain base, high sided wire basket rack with 11 upright wires on both sides, with heating elements in center, "General Electric D-12", Oct. 20, 1908 patent is for heating element. **$250.00-$300.00**

Toaster, plump but sleek, black bottom, chrome upper, 2 slicer pop-up, with brown plastic handles each end, one is also the pushdown, tiny dial at bottom, this is the toaster I use every day, since buying it at a thrift shop in the 1970s. And I can fix it myself if something goes wrong. "Toaster with the Tester", Manning-Bowman, about 7½"H, prior to WWII, suspended, then in production again. • **After the War.**— A 1944 ad in *House & Garden*, is interesting because of insight into effect of war on domestic appliance production. "Watch for the return of the famous 'Toaster with the Tester' and other top-quality Manning-Bowman appliances. They'll be back (soon we hope) when our production facilities are no longer needed by the armed forces....Manning-Bowman — Means Best. Keep on buying war bonds!" **$10.00-$15.00**

Toaster, pop-up, nickeled or chromed, interesting one slice top-loader with 6 horizontal louvers on each side, one end squared neatly, the other end rounded off at top, 2 lever control — to set timer and to lower basket inside, "Toastmaster Automatic, Model 1A1", mfd. by Waters-Genter, Minneapolis, MN, pat'd 1926 by Charles Strite. • "A 2" slice model was also made. **$45.00-$55.00**

Toaster, pyramid, aluminum, does 2 pieces of toast, black painted base, black handles, "Riverside Mfg. Co.", Ypsilanti, MI, 20th C. **$15.00-$20.00**

Toaster, shapely ceramic body, with resemblance to Oriental temple, 4 feet, mica elements, outstanding underglaze decoration in version of "Blue Willow" pattern, with the typical arched footbridge, 2 figures on bridge, temples & trees, Pan Electrical Mfg. Co., Cleveland, OH, c.1920s. **$200.00-$300.00**

Toaster, sheet metal base — black baked enamel over copper, fancy floral embossed doors, openwork top, wooden knobs, "Universal", mfd by Landers, Frary & Clark, 1930s. • **A children's book** that you toaster & electric appliance collectors should try to add to your collection is the delightful *The Brave Little Toaster*, by Thomas M. Disch, illustrated by Karen Lee Schmidt, (Doubleday 1986). Ad says the story "recounts the adventures of an indomitable two-slice toaster and its four friends, obsolete household appliances all." **$30.00-$35.00**

Toaster, simple heavy wire frame with finer wires crisscrossing inside, "General Electric X-2", pat'd Nov. 9, 1915. • Mr. Charles P. Fisher corrects GE's own misinformation that this one was patented in 1905 (as I stated in the last edition, based on their statements); the patent date is actually 1915. This is the value of specialization in research. Fisher asks, in the caption to this toaster in his book, "Rare? nonexistent?" Perhaps the photo GE sent me was of a prototype or office model. **$200.00-$300.00**

Toaster, toast warmer rack above for 6 slices, put toast in wire frame of door, it comes down on a spring, you flip it and push it back up to the heating elements, "The Reversible Toaster", Manning -Bowman Co., Meriden, CT, pat'd Dec. 28, 1920, & Dec. 4, 1923. **$25.00-$32.00**

Toaster, very Art Deco, black metal base and top, chrome sides with leaping deer decoration, loads one slice on end, adjusts for brownness, "Hotpoint", mfd by GE, Edison General Electric Appliance Co., Inc., Chicago, 1931. **$20.00-$30.00**

Toaster, very Art Deco, chrome and black painted tin, very odd, angled truncated pyramid shape, red Bakelite (or other molded phenolic resin) double knobs on the 2 doors, engraved with wheat design, 4 little button feet, Nelson Machine & Mfg. Co., Cleveland, OH, c.1930s. **$40.00-$50.00**

Toaster, white porcelain base, high frame wire basket with 6 vertical wires on both sides, heating elements in center, does 2 slices of toast, "General Electric D-12", c.1910 according to C. Fisher. This was, he says, 2nd version of D-12. • Add $75.00 or so for detachable wire warming rack; add $100.00 or so for floral decorated porcelain base. **$175.00-$225.00**

Toaster, white porcelain base, wire basket with low sides and 6 vertical wires, with detachable wire warming rack above, "General Electric D-12" (3rd version, according to Fisher), 2 patent dates, for heating elements, 1908 & 1909. Toaster c.1912 until -?- • Take off $75.00 or so for missing toast rack; add $100.00 or more for floral-decorated porcelain. • Price range for "D-12": **$175.00-$250.00**

Toaster, with possible other functions, handsome chrome body in shape of 2 near-halves of ball spread apart with vertical "valley", zig zag wire toast warming shelf above, long black handle on one side, short handle for other hand on other side, at least 3 insert trays, one with wire arches to hold a piece of toast, one a shallow oblong tray or cradle with arched sides, one a perforated metal box that would fit sideways into the "valley", all with long black handles, the 2 halves "look like 2 reflectors opposite each other with a shelf in between with holes." label reads "A. Mecky Co.", Philadelphia, PA, pat'd Aug. 1921. • Collector and paper dealer Tom Secondo, of Enfield, CT, wrote me about this piece in the mid 1980s, but I have not investigated the patent, and have never seen one. Quite an interesting appliance. **$75.00-$125.00**

Toaster, egg cooker & bacon cooker combined, metal, 3 tiered appliance, cooks 4 eggs on the bottom, toast in the middle, bacon on the top, stamped "Hotpoint", mfd by Edison Electric Appliance Co., Catalog #116G10W 660V110, pat'd Nov. 4, 1913. • Collector Pat Castagnola brought this to my attention, and sought information about it. **$45.00-$55.00**

Toaster stove, little rectangular cooker on cabriole legs, tray and comfit mesh screen, Westinghouse Electric & Mfg. Co., East Pittsburg, PA, early 20th C. **$45.00-$55.00**

Toaster, nickel plated, 2 openwork flip-down doors, openwork warming shelf above, mica & wire elements, 4 knurled Bakelite knobs at bottom corners of doors, "Westinghouse Turnover Toaster, Model S372788B", mfd by Westinghouse Electric Mfg. Co., Mansfield, OH, This model dates to c.1925. • Westinghouse made several "Turnover" toasters, earlier ones with wire doors, the very earliest with ceramic heating elements, the slightly later ones have doors with less openwork. • **Limp versus Crisp.** — An interesting sidenote: Mr. C. Fisher, who wrote what is now called *Hazelcorn's Price Guide to Old Electric Toasters, 1908-1940*, says that because of the greater air intake through toaster doors with a lot of openwork, toast was crisper when made in them, although it took longer. Toaster doors without openwork, or with very little, was in aid of faster, less crispy toasting. In England,

people are accustomed to, and prefer, crisp toast. Perhaps early in the 20th C, Americans preferred it the English way, whereas later in the century maybe they were looking for ways to save electricity, and persuaded themselves to prefer limper toast! **$35.00-$45.00**

Toasters, non-electric—See Pots & Pans chapter for stovetop types; also Hearths & Fireplaces.

Waffle irons, electric—See Mold & Form chapter.

Illustration by Eric Nitsche, for article in House Beautiful, *5/1937.*

XVIII-1.
Reddy Kilowatt,

with added avoirdupois. This version is a painted cutout plywood sign, probably unique, and meant to be propped in window. About 28"H. 1930s-40s. **$100.00-$200.00**

XVIII-3.
Chafing dishes.

Styled exactly like traditional ones using alcohol lamps, these were touted for making "dainty dishes" right on the table. (L) General Electric Co., Schenectady; (R) Landers, Frary & Clark "Universal". Both have ebonized wooden handles and finials, and are somewhat in the Georgian mode of the 1830s. Pictures from Electric Cooking, 1914. **$100.00-$175.00**

XVIII-4.
Egg cooker.

Ceramic bottom by Fiesta Ware, chromed metal parts including lid and poaching rack. Mfd. by Hankscraft Co., Madison, WI. Ceramic came in variety of colors,; cream or pastel green is most common, bright Fiesta red most desirable. A small "casserole dish" came with this unit, for making coddled eggs or custards, but I've never seen one for sale with that. They do work, but they're a nuisance to clean and maintain. Electric Home, 1936. Hankscraft also made a bottle warmer along the same lines. **$20.00-$40.00**

A FEW THINGS A CENT'S WORTH OF ELECTRICITY WILL DO

It will bring to a boil two quarts of water.

It will run the electric boiler for six minutes.

It will operate a twelve-inch fan for ninety minutes.

It will operate an electric griddle for eight minutes.

It will operate a luminous radiator for eight minutes.

It will make a Welsh rarebit in an electric chafing dish.

It will operate a sewing machine motor for three hours.

It will keep an eight-inch disc stove hot for **seven minutes, or** long enough to cook a steak.

It will operate a seven-inch frying pan for twelve minutes.

It will make four cups of coffee in an electric coffee percolator.

It will keep a foot-warmer hot for a quarter of an hour.

It will keep a six-pound electric flatiron hot for **fifteen minutes.**

It will heat an electric curling iron once a day for **two weeks.**

It will clean seven pairs of boots on a boot polisher.

It will clean five hundred knives on a knife cleaner.

It will carry a passenger up and down about three times in an eighty-foot house elevator.

It will run an electric clock one year.

It will run a small office ventilating fan about two hours.

It will warm sufficient water for shaving three mornings.

It will light three hundred cigars.

It will iron three silk hats.

It will fill and cork twenty-five dozen pint bottles.

It will pump ten gallons of water to a height of twenty-five feet.

It will run or operate an electric piano for one hour.

XVIII-2.
One cent of electricity—

what it would do in 1914. You can see from the list that much was done by electricity, at what may seem a very early date. I love the juxtoposition of old & new fangles—top hats to ventilating fans! From Electric cooking, Heating & Cleaning. A Manual of Electricity in the Service of the Home, by Maud Lancaster, 1914. This book will be referred to in succeeding captions as Electric Cooking, 1914.

XVIII-5. Dining room set, *consisting of chafing dish (ECD), a type of hot plate called a "stove" (ES), and a coffee percolator urn (ECP). General Electric, 1918-1919. ES under $20.00; ECD & ECP* **$60.00-$80.00**

XVIII-6.
Table fans.

(L)White Cross Breezer Fan No. 60, "especially adapted for use in small rooms, offices, state rooms, telephone booths, by the bedside, on the desk and enclosed motor boats and automobiles. It is equipped with starting and speed-regulating device and is particularly adapted as a portable electric fan, from the fact of it being lighter in weight than the average eight inch fan. Angle adjustable. Nickeled or oxidized copper, cast iron & tool steel. (R)White Cross Table Fan No. 289, "for use on table as a center piece." AC or DC, any cycle, and was furnished for any voltage from 100 to 220. Three speeds. Nickeled cast iron, brass blades, removable pressed glass bowl on top. 10 1/2"H x 9 1/2" diameter. Both mfd. by Lindstrom-Smith Co., Chicago. Editorial note in House Furnishing Review, *5/1915.* **$25.00-$35.00 and $125.00-$200.00**

XVIII-7.
Hot air, kerosene lamp fan.

The famous "Lake Breeze" floor-standing fan with wrought iron base. This looks like many items of the same period for use on the porch—plant stands and furniture, and its independence of electricity or water meant that it could be used outdoors. The kerosene lamp below caused rising hot air, which eventually caused the blades to turn. It is considered a very desirable collectors' fan, and brings thousands of dollars at auction. Lake Breeze Motor, Chicago, IL. Mfd. between about 1914 and 1920. **$2000.00-$3500.00**

XVIII-8.
Frypan & frittering pan.

"Eclipse" deep frying pan, made by the Electric & Ordnance Accessories Co., Birmingham, England, & unidentified frittering (deep frying) pan, heating elements in their bases. Pictures from a book which combines American and English appliances, cooking techniques and vocabulary—Maud Lancaster's Electric Cooking, Heating & Cleaning, 1914. The indistinct picture of the frittering pan appears to show glass marbles forming the feet. Lancaster gives a list of electrical appliance makers: English—Amorduct Mfg. Co.; Benham & Sons; A.F.Berry, "Tricity"; British Prometheus Co. (founded in 1892); The Carron Co.; Dowsing Radiant Heat Co. & Mssrs. Crompton & Co. (pioneer mfr. exhibited at Crystal Palace in 1891); Eastman & Warne; The Electric & Ordance Accessories Co.; The Electrical Co.; The Falkirk Iron Co., Ferranti; Jackson Electric Stove Co.; Phoenix Electirc Heating Co. (founded 1894); Purcell & Nobbs; Simplex Conduits; Spagnoletti; The British Thomason-Houston Co. American— The Automatic Electric Cook Co.; The Berkeley Electric Cooker Co.; The Cook Stove Co.; The General Electric Co. (there was also GE of Great Britain); The Hot-point Electric Heating Co.; The Hughes Electric Heating Co.; The Prometheus Electric Co.; The Simplex Electric Heating Co.; The Vulcan Electric Heating Co.; The Western Electric Co.; The Westinghouse Electric Co. She does not mention Edison Electric, probably because most of her list was of companies entering the business "within the last five years" (i.e. about 1907).   **$30.00-$50.00**

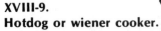

XVIII-9.
Hotdog or wiener cooker.

"Here we have the use of electricity in its simplest form where the 'hot dogs' are cooked by running the electricity through them. Alternating current should be used. The electricity boils the water contained in the food and causes it to do its own cooking. Such a cooker has another automatic feature inasmuch as the carrying handle also controls the switch. When the handle is in its vertical position the current is on, and when the wieners are cooked the handle is put to one side or the other of the device, automatically shutting off the current and leaving free space for handling the wieners. These devices are furnished in different sizes and colors to suit one's fancy." Electric Home, 1936. **$30.00-0.00**

XVIII-10.
Juicer.

"Sunkist Juicit" deluxe model No. BM-21, in the Handyhot line, by Chicago Electric Mfg. Co. "Included in its construction is a Magic Automatic Strainer that oscillates rapidly back and forth, whipping the juice cells of the pulp against sharpened edges of strainer holes, first releasing every drop of juice, and, secondly, cutting the health-giving pulp into tiny particles." Chrome with "French Ivory" glass juice collector bowl and reamer. "Powerful induction type motor does not interfere with radio reception and operates only on 110-120 volts, 50-60 cycle alternating current. Toggle switch. Cord and plug cap attached." Handyhot catalog AA, 1940.   **$30.00-$55.00**

XVIII-11.
Electric kitchen,

of Mr. H.J. Dowsing, England. 1894. "In 1891 Mr. H.J. Dowsing, one of the pioneers of heating and cooking and founder of the Dowsing Radiant Heat Co., had a stand at the Crystal Palace Electrical Exhibition at which were shown Electric cookers and heaters. He certainly had far-seeing ideas. ...Certainly Messrs. Crompton, who were responsible for the manufacture of these articles, fully grasped the possibilities of Electricity being applied for perfect cooking in the future..."Lancaster, Electric Cooking, 1914. In fact, the appliances shown here, including the stove at left, the wall oven, and the saucepan or frying pan at near right, are the commercially-produced electrical wares placed on the market in 1894 by Dowsing.

XVIII-12.
Combination tabletop appliance.

For grilling, making pancakes, poaching eggs, heating liquids. Nickeled steel with black painted wooden handles. 3 feet pads of nonducting "fibre." Three heat levels with "snap switch," removable rack with 4 separate pans for egg poaching. Shape and size (8" diameter) of stove plate permits use of round aluminum vessels. Depths of the 3 pans are 1/4", 1 1/4" and 2"D. D.J. Barry jobber catalog, 1924. Manufacturer not given, but probably Universal (Landers, Frary & Clark).   **$30.00-$50.00**

XVIII-13.
Electric kitchen,

sketched from one in operation in a private home in 1896. I found the picture and the caption, but do not know from whence it came. I think it was probably Harper's Century or Scribner's Monthly from the style of the drawing and appearance of the type.

XVIII-15.
Mixer.

General Electric's "DeLuxe Hotpoint Mixer" — a "complete Kitchen Power Unit, designed for thorough mixing, beating, juice-extracting, and numerous other duties." Baked-on enamel in 3 color combinations: green with black trim, cream with green trim, green with cream trim. Three speed motor in base, AC or DC, rubber cord, Pyrex® bowls. G-E catalog, 1935-36. **$95.00-$165.00**

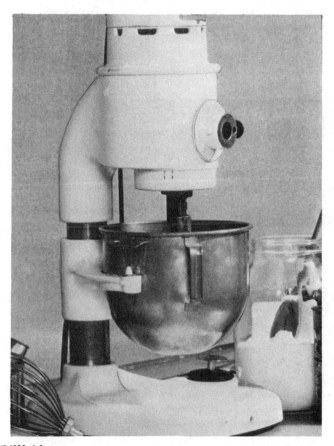

XVIII-14.
Mixer & Juicer attachment, on stand.

Enameled metal. Note hinged stanchion. General Electric, 1919. Picture courtesy G.E. **$75.00-$120.00**

XVIII-16.
Mixer beater.

"Quick-Mix" with one speed and one beater. The eye at left of motor housing is for hanging it on a hook when not in use. Manufacturer not known, name not in Thomas' Register of American Manufacturers of the same period. Pictured in book Electric Home, 1936. **$35.00-$50.00**

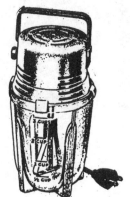

XVIII-17.
Mixer beater whipper.

"Handyhot" deluxe combination mixer, clear glass beater jar with graduated markings for 3 cups. White motor housing with nickeled handle. 110-120 volts, 50-60 cycle AC current. Chicago Electric Manufacturing Co., 1938 catalog. **$35.00-$50.00**

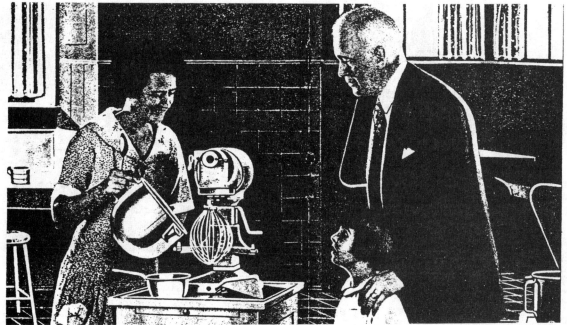

XVIII-18.
Mixer & food preparer.
Also the KitchenAid — showing the whipping blades. Notice the detachable
funnel lying on the right of the work stand. "The kitchen is too often a drab kind of place. Yet surely, considering the hours spent there,...It ought to be the cheerfullest room in the house. In KitchenAid homes, the kitchen has come into its own. It is Mother's workshop — a place where drudgery has given way to self expression — where cooking and baking has become a joy — new recipes a real sport. It is no longer a lonely place. Dad, who admires mechanical ingenuity, likes to watch KitchenAid's deft, steel hands at work — or to 'run' it himself, especially in freezing ice cream. You will find 'Junior' and 'sister' there, too, and very often a guest." KitchenAid catalog, 1928. **$100.00-$175.00**

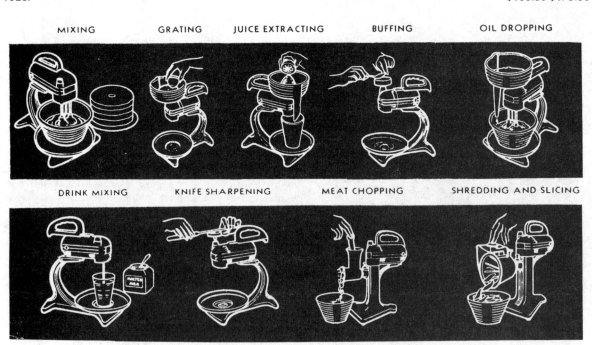

XVIII-19.
Mixer in many roles.
Page decorations for the G—E "Hotpoint Portable Mixer." 1935-36 catalog.

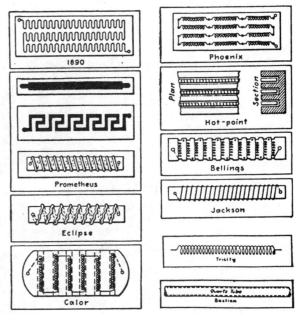

XVIII-20.
Mixer.

Single stainless steel blade, red wooden knob, white glass beater jar, cast with rocket-like design base — for stability and style. 9 1/2"H. "K-M", Knapp-Monarch Co., St. Louis, MO, c.1940s.
$35.00-$45.00

XVIII-21.
"Preparing dinner with Electric Cooker."

These are called "electric cookers" in the book from which the English picture comes, but they function like stoves. For other stoves, see Chapter XI. General Electric Co. of Great Britain photo, in Electric Cooking 1914.

XVIII-22.
Electric heating elements.

From Electric Cooking and Heating, 1914. 1890. "Early electric heating elements...for self-contained utensils (were made of) fine German silver wire embedded in enamel in the form in sketch." Prometheus: Three forms introduced by the Prometheus Co. (American). (1) Strip "consisting of a deposit of gold and platinum on strips of mica"; (2) ribbon in the "key pattern form used for flat irons, hot-plates, etc."; (3) finally, "oven elements took the form of special high resistance wire or tape wound over mica, varnished and encased with thin steel." Eclipse: "High resistance ribbon crimped to give greater length and free-air space, wound over mica strips with the ends connected to heavy eyelet terminals as in sketch."Calor: "A base of fireclay with grooves into which spirals of fine high resistance wire are placed." Phoenix: "Spiral wire coiled held lightly at short intervals by porcelain insulators mounted on a suitable base." Hot-point. "Nichrome wire or ribbon, wound lightly around thin strips of mica; further covered with a thin mica covering and inserted very tightly into grooves or slots made in the hot-plate or iron base to receive the finished strips." Belling: "Fireclay strip with spirals of nichrome wire stretched across width of base, notches being provided in the base for receiving ends of the spiral and holding them tightly in position." Jackson: "Has a different class of fireclay base with quite a smooth surface, the section of the strips, being a flat oval, wire or ribbon of nichrome, is wound tightly over strip in one continuous length and clamped between heavy terminals at each end." Tricity: "Nichrome ribbon wound over thin mica and clamped between thin sheets of mica and metal." Bastian or Quartzalite: "Spiral of nichrome wire or ribbon coated with film of oxide insulation & held in or on a quartz tube...to give it a 'hot-rod' appearance."

XVIII-23.
Toaster & other appliances.

From bottom (L): Early toaster with high sided basket (like the "Eclipse"), flower-decorated white porcelain base. General Electric. According to engineer Charles P. Fisher (who wrote, with his wife, Hazelcorn's Price Guide to Old Electric Toasters, 1908-1940), this is the second version of the G-E D-12, dating to "about 1910", not 1908 as reported in my last edition. Note the high "railing" of the toast-holding basket. The third version, says Fisher, looks almost the same but has considerably lower sides. It probably dates to about 1912. By the way, an even rarer decorated porcelain toaster would be the one in Blue Williow pattern made by Pan Electrical Mfg. Co., Cleveland, OH, c.1925. Above, seemingly floating in air (but on Plexiglass) is a "Universal E947" made by Landers, Frary & Clark. Fisher describes this toaster as "the loveliest and most durable of swingers," and I agree. The base alone is beautiful; it's worth buying the toaster for those angled nonconductive disks forming the feet. This dates to between 1922-29. Center is an "Angelus Campfire Bar-B-Q Marshmallow Toaster," with red fubber feet on wire legs. "Pat. Appl. For", c.1920s-1930s. Angelus Campfire Co., Inc., Chicago. The pedestal base waffle iron is heavily chromed and has a decorative porcelain insert in the lid. It is undated, but is probably about 1930. Collector Susan Lewis wrote me about hers, similar but with lovebird design, made by "SuperLectric." Hers is also undated. The electric iron is not described by G-E, who provided the photograph. Three value ranges are for the 2 toasters and the waffle iron. **$275.00-$400.00; $45.00-$75.00; $85.00-$150.00**

VXIII-24.
Toaster.

General Electric, Model X-2, pat'd 11/9/1915 (not 1905 as stated in 2nd edition). I thank Charles P. Fisher, again, for correcting this error, which resulted because G-E itself gave me a 1905 date. According to Fisher, it may never have been marketed, although obviously the toaster itself exists or G-E couldn't have sent me a picture! If it exists, the value would be very high. **$200.00-$400.00**

XVIII-25.
First electric toaster—

at least according to the Cologne, Germany auction house Auction Team Breker, which sold this "Eclipse" toaster from 1893 at auction, April 28, 1990. **The estimated price was $900.00 to $1200.00.** *"Eclipse" was trade name used by the Electric & Ordnance Accessories Co., Birmingham, England, but according to the Lancaster book of 1914, E & O didn't get into the business of electrical appliances until after about 1905. See drawings of various heating elements used in toasters & some other small appliances. The "Eclipse" element, fifth down, has crimped "high resistance ribbon...wound over mica strips," which (at least in the picture) matches up. Drawing done from photograph; there should be only 11 turned rings in all on the handle. "Value" is price achieved at the 1990 auction.* **$2165.00**

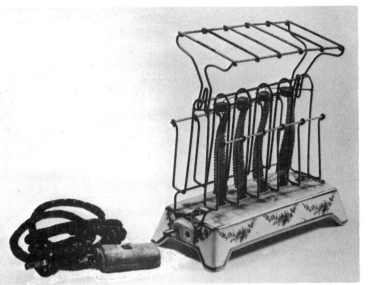

XVIII-26.
Toaster.

General Electric, 2nd version of D-12, c 1910. Detachable wire warming rack in place. Painted poreclain base. Picture courtesy of G-E shows plug and cord which I am not sure are original because I don't think they had the black cloth-wrapped cords with white dots, as shown here, at the time. **$275.00-$400.00**

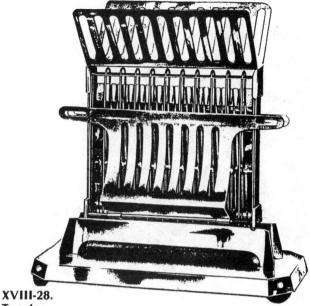

XVIII-28.
Toaster.

"Thermax" No. 1942, by Landers, Frary & Clark. In the "Universal" catalog of 1914, but this toaster was in their not-so-well-known "Thermax" line. Available like the previous one in nickel or silver plate, but with 6′L "flexible cord." Triple contact terminal plug. Note slotted rack above and the nifty sleek slotted doors. **$45.00-$60.00**

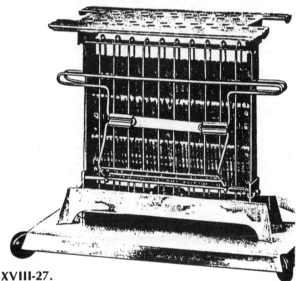

XVIII-27.
Toaster.

"Universal" E941, by Landers, Frary & Clark with perforated top plate for keeping toast warm. This is a primitive "flipdown" door type for two slices. Note the angled feet disks—terrific styling. This 340 watt toaster could be nickel plated or "silver plated", but I don't know if the many toasters offered in silverplate were "German silver" or sterling silver. Came with 6′L "mercerized silk finish flexible cord, triple contact terminal plug." 1914 catalog. LF&C also offered a "twin" style, with two identical E941 toasters mounted to a single oblong flat base. **$45.00-$60.00**

XVIII-29.
Toaster.

Nickel plated, blue wooden knobs, 7"H x 8"L x 4 1/4"W, 1920 & 1927 patents. "Electrix" by United Drug Co. (See price listing for more on other names.) **$50.00-$65.00**

XVIII-30.
Toaster,

with flat bed. Bread held in horizontal basket, rather than vertical. Not a very efficient toaster for the time, but rather stylish in appearance. Picture from Louise J. Peet & Lenore E. Sater's _Household Equipment,_ 1934, 1940. **$15.00-$25.00**

XVIII-31.
Toaster.

"Marion Giant Flipflop #66," mfd. by Rutenber Electric Co., Marion, IN. According to Charles Fisher, many versions of this were made, with vertical cutouts in the door, cutouts in the bases, different flat tops. Nickel plated, c.1925-31. From unidentified catalog page. **$18.00-$25.00**

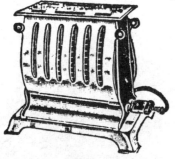

XVIII-32.
Toaster.

The maker of this "economical, thoroughly dependable" toaster was not given in the general merchandise catalog in which I found the picture, but it is to my eye very attractive. It resembles, in some respects, the products of a wide range of manufacturers, but I couldn't find it in Fisher's book, nor in any of my other catalogs. "Sparkling nickel plate," 7 1/2" x 7 1/2" x 4 1/4", 6'L cord, 2-piece plug. "All complicated and fragile moving parts are eliminated. Being standard size, it takes a full slice of bread without trimming. Women appreciate its artistic design and quiet elegance." Possibly Linderman & Hoverson, of Milwaukee, or possibly Russell Electric, Chicago. From Slack Mfg. Co., c.1925 catalog. I don't think they actually made electric appliances. **$18.00-$25.00**

XVIII-33.
Toaster.

The "new and improved" pop-up Toastmaster, from 1930. "It comes in 1 and 2-slice sizes and is a revelation in simplicity and smartness. Of the hundreds of thousands who saw the remarkable first model which revolutionized toastmaking in America, not one would have believed it could ever have been improved on. Yet— that has been done! With the new model, all you do is drop in the bread and press but a single lever. And forget about it!" Waters-Genter Co., Division of McGraw Electric Co., Minneapolis, MN. 10/1930 ad in Good Housekeeping. **$55.00-$75.00**

XVIII-34.
Toy toaster.

Note the feet like the "Universal. This was described in the 6/1930 House Furnishing Review, shortly after they began covering the toy market. "The Excel Electric Co., Muncie, IN, makes the Excel Toastoy, a toy electric toaster, for toasting half slices of bread. Nickeled throughout, with nichrome heating element, 150-watt capacity complete with plug and silk cord. Retails at $1.00." Nickel finish; 5"H x 6"L x 3"W. The "Toastoy" had apparently been for sale in 1929 also, and they continued making them for several years, at least until 1933. **$120.00-$175.00**

XVIII-35.
Toaster,

for one slice; automatic. Toastmaster 1A1, 1926. This was McGraw-Edison's first domestic toaster, and was the result of mechanic Charles Strite's inventiveness. In 1918, Mr. Strite built an automatic pop-up toaster, and the principle of its operation, using a spring motor and switch, was patented in 1919. Commercial toasters were made soon after, for restaurants and lunch counters, and sold under the Strite name. Not until 1926 did this first automatic pop-up appear in housewares departments. It sold in 1926 for the then-whopping $12.50 **$45.00-$65.00**

**XVIII-36.
Toaster.**

"Delta," mfd. by Kamco Inc., Unionville, CT, c.1935. Chrome doors in black-enameled frame. Originally only $2.39. House Furnishing Review, 7/1935. **$55.00-$75.00**

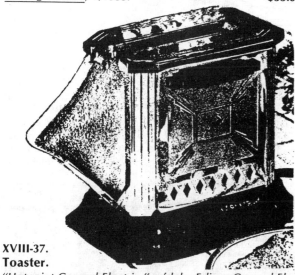

**XVIII-37.
Toaster.**

"Hotpoint General Electric," mfd. by Edison General Electric Appliance Co., Chicago, IL, 1931. Chromed steel. Note Art Deco leaping stag design in center of side. Ad from Ladies' Home Journal, 3/1931. **$45.00-$75.00**

**XVIII-38.
Toasters.**

(L) Unidentified maker. Styling similar to many other non-automatic toasters requiring the doors to be lowered. (R) Toastmaster automatic. Both pictures from Electric Home, by E. S. Lincoln, 1936. **$20.00-$65.00**

**XVIII-39.
Toaster.**

"The Hotpointer" No. 129T41, automatic, 2 slices, General Electric. "The thermostat, placed right against one slice of the bread, regulates the color of the toast as determined by the setting of the Control Knob...Hotpointer signal light, on top, glows a ruddy red when the current is on, and fades out when the current turns off. Tiny bell concealed in base of toaster chimes gently when toast is done. The Hotpointer is absolutely silent in operation, except for this soft musical chime note." Chromed finish, black Calmold® plastic knob and handle, nichrome wire with mica, 6'L detachable cord set with G-E moulded rubber attachment plug and miniature Calmold appliance plug. 850 watts, 115, 125 volts. 1935-36. **$35.00-$55.00**

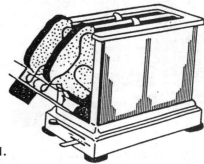

**XVIII-40.
Toaster.**

"Hotpointer" semi-automatic, similar exterior styling to preceding one. Permanently attached cord set. Came with recipe booklet. It does one side of toast at a time, and when the thermostat shuts off the current, you "lower the doors, which turns the toast, and the current immediately comes on again, to toast the other side." Here they call the thermostat a "Taste Control." General Electric, 1935-36 catalog. **$25.00-$55.00**

**XVIII-41.
Toaster.**

Neat tipping action. Safe retrieval of non-pop-up toast was a concern of consumers and manufacturers. Probably a "Universal" model by Landers, Frary & Clark, c.1935. Picture from Peet's book Household Equipment, 1940. **$30.00-$45.00**

XVIII-44.
Toaster.

"Toastwell", manufactured by Utility Electric Co., St. Louis. It's completely automatic and "super silent — no 'ticking' annoyance found in the ordinary toasters." Pop-up, chrome plated with Bakelite® handles & base. 7"H x 11 1/2"L. 725 watts; 110-125 volts AC or DC, detachable cord & plug. It also came in a 4 slice style, which was simply elongated to 13 3/8"L, and 7 1/4"H. Pictures from Dearborn catalog, 1942. The 4-slice style would bring more.
$30.00-$50.00

XVIII-42.
Toaster.

Two views. Note spider web design. General Electric, 1940.
$30.00-$45.00

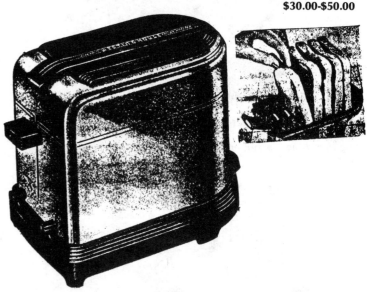

XVIII-45.
Toaster & toast server-top.

Westinghouse "Pop-Up", with automatic "crisper for regular or Melba toast." Streamline design, chrome finish, Bakelite® base & handles, curved end for easy parking. Bakelite cover-server is seen protecting innards (L), and being used upside down as toast server at (R) — a really excellent idea. In Dearborn catalog, 1940.
$55.00-$85.00

XVIII-43.
Toaster.

"Universal Turn-Easy" model E1321 in the Coronet pattern. "Second to none in styling. Its design follows the modern trend with artistic chasing." Came with matching percolator, waffle iron, etc. Chrome plated, "smart black handles & feet" (they don't mention Bakelite®, used in describing others on same page), 6'L cord and plug. Lowering doors turns toast over. From Ft. Dearborn Mercantile catalog, 1942.
$25.00-$45.00

Either "POPS UP" THE TOAST or KEEPS IT WARM IN THE TOASTER-OVEN as you choose!

THE CRISPIEST, CRUNCHIEST TOAST YOU EVER TASTED! EVEN TOASTING ALL OVER— NOT EVEN THOSE USUAL WHITE GUIDE-WIRE TRACINGS

EFFORTLESS OPERATION A LIGHT TOUCH ON THE LEVER IS ALL IT TAKES

LOOK! YOU CAN SET IT TO "POP UP" THE TOAST OR TO KEEP IT WARM INSIDE THE TOASTER 'TIL WANTED

AND THERE'S A BUTTON HERE THAT SETS IT FOR ANY SHADE OF TOAST YOU WANT

AND THERE'S A HINGED CRUMB-TRAY ON THE BOTTOM FOR EASY CLEANING

THIS RED SIGNAL LIGHT TELLS YOU WHEN THE TOAST IS DONE IF YOU DON'T WANT IT TO "POP UP"!

AND ISN'T THIS DESIGN THE LOVELIEST YOU EVER SAW!

EVERY SLICE THE SAME UNIFORM GOLDEN BROWN NO MATTER HOW MANY YOU DO

XVIII-46.
Toaster.

"Sunbeam," by Chicago Flexible Shaft Co. "The lovely oval design (is) the last word in modern styling by George Scharfenberg." (Imagine a 1990s toaster ad giving the designer's name, unless it was a famous architect and the toaster was $250.00) Ad claimed "every slice of toast the identical shade of every other slice, whether it's first or last." That was useful when making party canapes, I guess. Could be had also as part of a "stunning buffet set including four new intaglio crystal lap trays, 3-compartment appetizer dish and large, roomy walnut tray." The really nifty feature was you could set this one to pop-up or to keep the toast inside until wanted. Saturday Evening Post, 1940. $30.00-$50.00

XVIII-47.
Portable hot water heater.

Unit for heating a pail of water. The "Premier" by the National Ideal Co., Toledo, OH. Ad from Farm Journal, 11/1947. $10.00-$20.00

H. HOUSECLEANING
XIX. SWEEP, DUST, VACUUM & THROW OUT

These pages will be expanded, along with material on LAUNDERING, CLOSETING & BATHROOMS, into a book, to be published as soon as possible. The remaining pictures and captions, with no separate price listings, are just the barest hint of what will follow in the full book, *300 Years of Housekeeping Collectibles*. Important subjects for collectors are dustpans, carpet beaters, and vacuum cleaners. The first two deserve a **Futurewatch** flag.

I want to hear from any man, woman or child who has opinions about neatness and housecleaning — particularly how these may have affected your hospitality, sociability, private guilt feelings, leisure time, creativity.

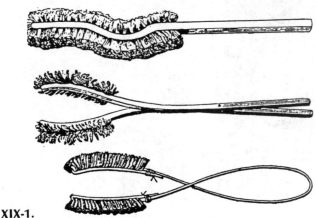

XIX-1.

Kerosene lamp brushes.

"A good kerosene lamp gives a light so fine and steady that those who live in the country need not regret the absence of gas. It is true that the care of lamps takes a little time. By a ...few simple contrivances the labor...is reduced to a trifle. In trimming the wick, do not use scissors, but simply scrape off the charred crust with a knife. The metallic tube which enclosed the wick, whether flat or circular, should be kept free of all incrustation...(And) the chimneys must be kept clean." Brushes of (M) fit inside the chimney globe by compressing the handles. (T) is curved wood with lamp wick or *"coarse worsted threads"*. Homemade, from *American Agriculturist*, 9/1867.   **$5.00-$15.00**

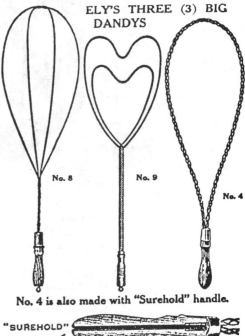

ELY'S THREE (3) BIG DANDYS

No. 8   No. 9   No. 4

No. 4 is also made with "Surehold" handle.

"SUREHOLD"

THEO. J. ELY MFG. CO.,   Girard, Pa.

XIX-3.

Carpet beaters.

Three "big Dandy" styles, wire or braided wire. Mfd. by Theo. J. Ely Mfg. Co., Girard, PA. The middle one shows that a heart shape was indeed used early on, but note its difference from modern fakes. Braided one sold at least as early as 1903 and is about 30"L. This ad from HFR, 4/1909.   **$25.00-$45.00**

XIX-2.

Dust bunny drawing.

I not only collect dustpans and dust, I also like drawings related to dusting, et al. This is by Terry Ackerman, showing her cat Rufus making critters compounded of NYC dust and his own long hair. 1990.

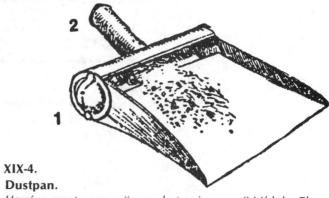

XIX-4.

Dustpan.

Here's a great one—a "germ-destroying gem." Mfd. by Thomas Clover, Philadelphia. Clover believes that after sweeping up the germs, the user should "be provided with some means of destroying them." There is, therefore, a "concealed chamber beneath the flat surface, which receives the dust, and (the) entrance to this chamber is gained through the cyclindrical head at the rear. Inside this head is a slotted tube, which closes the end, while the handle (2) serves as a reservoir for a liquid disinfectant." After sweeping in the dust, you tilted the pan so it fell into the slot, whereupon it was disinfected. HFR, 4/1903.   **$65.00-$100.00**

XIX-5.
Fly traps.
(L) "Balloon" trap of wire screen and japanned tin. Mfd. by National Mfg. Co., Worcester, MA, and advertised by them as being theirs in HFR, 4/1904. Eleven years later, Wire Goods Co. of Worcester, which may have been the later incarnaton of National, advertised them. (M) "American" trap, with large tin base with wooden bottom and tin trucated cone, and wire gauze dome, the whole japanned in blue with bronze striping. Mfd. by Geuder & Paeshcke Mfg. Co., Milwaukee. Picture from _The Metal Worker_, 6/4/1890. (R) "Harper," with tin bottom, also made by Wire Goods Co., c.1915. **$50.00-$100.00**

XIX-7.
Wastebaskets.
All are "retinned" wire, mfd. by the Andrews Division of the Washburn Co., Rockford, IL. (L) Large wastebasket, solid tin bottom, 1" mesh, 24"H x 18" diameter at top, or 18"H x 16 1/2" diameter at top. (M) Curved top basket, tin bottom, 1" mesh, in four sizes: 30"H x 22" square; 27"H x 20" square; 24"H x 18" square; 18"H x 14" square. Per dozen, thes cost from $6.30 up to $55.00 (for the Janitor's biggest). Starting price for collectors now would surprise Pick-Barth! **$45.00-$75.00**

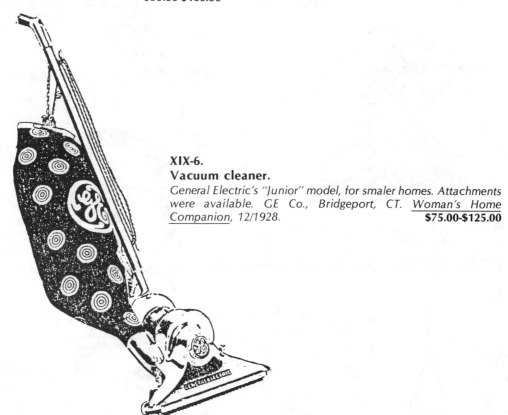

XIX-6.
Vacuum cleaner.
General Electric's "Junior" model, for smaler homes. Attachments were available. GE Co., Bridgeport, CT. Woman's Home Companion, 12/1928. **$75.00-$125.00**

These two pages introduce a subject which will soon be featured in a large Housekeeping book. For further information, read the introductory note to the preceding mini-chapter on Housecleaning tools.

One writer on collectibles, Harry Rinker, says that we collect in order to recapture our childhoods. I believe this as regards my long interest in kitchen and housekeeping tools. In retrospect, some of my happiest times of childhood were spent in the breakfast room, near the open back door, learning to iron under the capable and kindly tutleage of Mrs. T.B. Burton. In 40 years I have *never* set up the ironing board and ironed (which I find very relaxing) without thinking of her.

Sadirons, sadiron stands, clothespins and washboards are probably the most popular subject areas here.

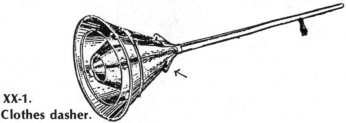

XX-1.
Clothes dasher.
"Rapid Vacuum Washer," heavy tin, beechwood handle with cross handle bolted on. Handle 40"L. Note hooded covers near top of cone, which cover air holes meant to "introduce air into the water, forcing steam, water and air through the clothes thoroughly cleaning them." From catalog of Excelsior Stove & Mfg. Co,. Quincy, IL, c.1916. **$35.00-$60.00**

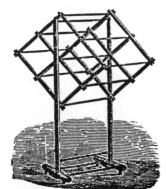

XX-2.
Clothes dryer.
(Creak, creeeeaaak, crRASH.) "To the many devices for holding clothes while drying, we add this one that gives a large amount of hanging room for the floor space it occupies." Hardwood foot pieces and upright standards, light pine kite-box frame. Folding. Published as a do-it-yourself project in American Agriculturist, 4/1881.

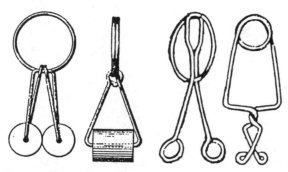

XX-3.
Clothespin patents.
(L-1 & 2) Pat'd 2/6/1877, by S.B. Hunt, NYC, assignor to A.W. Billings, Brooklyn, NY. Bent wire with wooden rollers that form the clamp. Great idea! (M) Pat'd 10/28/1890, by George W. McCord, Baker City, OR. (R) Pat'd 8/1/1876, by George A. Lambert, Worcester, MA. Another item patented the same day by Lambert was a sort of jailor's keyring with a ring to fit around arm at the crook of the elbow, suspended from which was a partially-closed ring over which one slipped the small loop of his wire clothespins. **$5.00-$15.00**

XX-4.
Fluting machine.
"Empire Fluter," mfd. & sold by Heinz & Munschauer, Buffalo, NY. Nickeled cast iron plate & roller, wooden T. handle. Hinged base plate, two heating plates. Base 6 3/4"L x 3 1/4"W; roll 2 1/2" diameter x 3 1/4"W. **$90.00-$125.00**

MRS. POTTS IRON   COMMON IRON

POLISHER   FLOUNCE IRON

XX-5.
Various kinds of irons.
This illustration is from Approved Methods for Home Laundering, by Mary Beals Vail. Cincinnati: Procter & Gamble, 1906. Relative prices were given to help the consumer decide on an iron: 2" sad irons, 8 lbs., 40¢ each; 2 sad irons, 6 lbs., 30¢ each; 1 sad iron, 4 lbs., 20¢; 1 flounce iron, narrow and long, 25¢; 1 or 2 polishers, 45¢ each; set of 3 irons, with detachable handle.

XX-6.
Stands for sadirons.
Twisted wire, German, and although they look 1870s, the auction cataloguer says they date to c.1920-30. About 9 3/4"L. Photograph courtesy Waltraud Boltz Auction House, Bayreuth, Germany. From the Loercherbach Collection, auctioned May 1987.
$40.00-$60.00

XX-8.
Washing machine.
"Doty's Clothes Washer." Won first prize for washing machines at the American Institute Fair of 1865. All wood. American Agriculturist 3/1866.

XX-7.
Washboard patents.
(L) Pat'd 1/30/1877, by Samuel A. Gould, Osgood, IN. Zinc with "serpentine ridges." (R) Pat'd 1/30/1877, by Thomas M. Webb, Norwalk, OH, assignor to L.T. Farrand, Norwalk. There are "acorn-shaped projections formed on the upper face of the board"; and "triangular figures embossed on the lower face." stamped sheet metal, the claim for which was based on the new patterns. Official Gazette.

XX-9.
Wringer.
Galvanized iron, with cog wheels. "Sherman's Improved," available through, and possibly mfd. by Haley, Morse & Co., NYC. Came in four sizes — two "Family" ones, with rollers either 10"L x 1 7/8" or 11"L x 1 7/8"; and two "Hotel" ones, with rollers 12"L x 2 1/4", and 14"L x 2 1/4". Flyer c.1863.
$40.00-$90.00

I. LAUNDERING & MENDING:
XXI. SEWING TOOLS & COLLECTIBLES MADE OF CLOTH

Once a 20 page chapter with 50 pictures, this too has been reduced to a mini chapter. (See introduction to Housecleaning for fuller explanation).

Sewing birds, figural measuring tapes, darning eggs, aprons and potholders are probably the most popular items from this category.

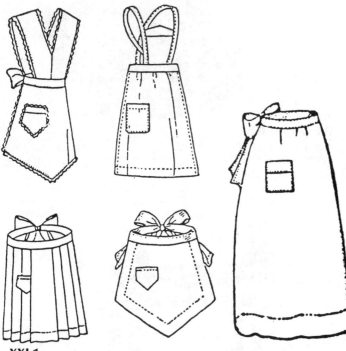

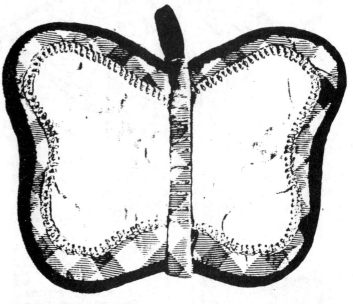

XXI-2.
Pot holder.
Pieced cotton butterfly, handsewn with brown & white check, dark brown border, tan inside, black & gold floss embroidery. 5 3/4" x 7 1/8", c.1930s. **$3.00-$5.00**

XXI-1.
Aprons.
Clockwise from top (L): (1) Heavy linen tea room apron, with long streamer ties, edges trimmed with white rickrack. Small pocket on both sides of skirt, making the apron reversible. (2) Heavy linen reversible apron with pin-back waistband. 27"L from waist. (3) Linen full-length apron, pockets inside & out making it reversible. 38"L x 44"W. (4) and (5) White cotton soda & tea room aprons, with streamer ties. Pointed bottom one 17"L; pleated one, 18"L. Not reversible. All from Albert Pick-Barth Co. hoteliers supply catalog, 1929. **$4.00-$6.00**

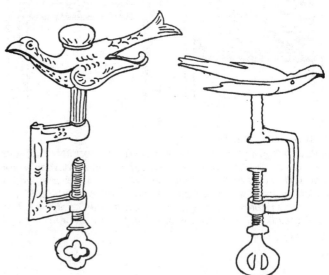

XXI-3.
Sewing birds.
(L) Gilded cast metal, possibly firegilt brass, with green plush pincushion. Bird may represent a gold finch. About 5 1/2"H. 1840s. (R) Steel, no cushion, very sleek bird, 6"H, 1830-50s. **$160.00-$225.00**

J. CLOSETING:
XXII. TAKE IT OFF & HANG IT UP

The material contained in this mini chapter opens a whole new field for many collectors. I have a growing collection myself of coat hangers, shoe trees and shoeshine boxes — and a **Futurewatch** is put on all of them. What is shown is but a tiny sampling. See Housecleaning mini chapter for fuller explanation of new book coming soon!

XXII-1.
Bootjack.
Cast iron bug bootjack. That appeared in the 1874 Henry Arthur catalog of cobblers' tools, etc.; it was made by an unidentified foundry. Note the wrinkled neck and forehead and the pigmy-hippo-type feet with wrinkles. A reproduction design very like this was (perhaps still is) made by John Wright foundry in Wrightsville, PA, in the late 1970s. **$35.00-$125.00**

XXII-2.
Shoe shine box.
Homemade, black-painted wood with 4 compartments. Angled footrest. Words "Shoe Shine" spelled out in upper & lower case letters on one side, with faceted brass upholstery tacks. 7 1/2"H x 13 1/2" x 9 1/2"W. 20th C. Found in Georgia. **$75.00-$125.00**

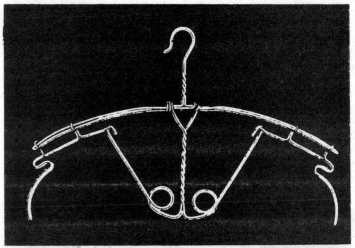

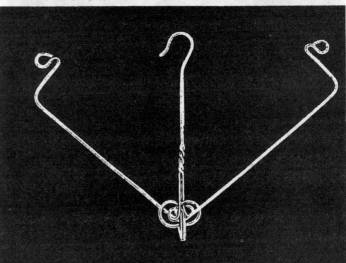

XXII-3.
Clothes hangers.
(T) "Vassar" ladies' suit hanger, for skirts and jackets — "entirely adjustable, and will allow the garments to hang in their natural form, retaining pleats and folds as when worn. Adjusting by the skirt's own weight to any size (waist) band, it leaves no mark nor causes any strain on the skirt." Meant to be good for travelers too because the hook folds down. Steel wire. Originally sold for $.10. (B) "Princess" ladies' skirt hanger, steel wire, adjusts automatically to skirt size. A very stylized bird form. Both mfd. by Pittsburg Wire Mfg. Co., Pittsburg, PA. Ad in House Furnishing Review, 8/1906. **$25.00-$50.00**

K. PLAYING AT KEEPING HOUSE:
XXIII. TOYS, MINIATURES & SALESMAN'S SAMPLES

This fittingly miniaturized chapter will be a separate book with hundreds of illustrations and a great deal of collecting information that will help kitchen collectors to get into the dollsize market. If you have started reading this book from the back, you will be struck by how much material the publisher and I were forced to remove from the central subject — cooking tools. In a way, this is a blessing, because it means that I can truly concentrate on these separate (no matter how interrelated) subjects in greater detail.

You will find a few references throughout the "kitchen book" to salesman's samples and models; most examples will go into the new book on small versions of big kitchen things, which will also include toy and miniature gardening and laundry equipment.

The selection of entrancing items shown here represent only 40 years or so of toy implements and toy stoves — if they tickle your fancy, you will love having an entire book on the subject.

XXIII-1.
Kitchen utensil set.
Blue enameled metal, sewn to cardboard and in cardboard box. Box 16"L x 11"W, with 21 pieces. They also offered sets with 5 pieces, 7 pieces, and 11 pieces. McClurg, 1908-09 wholesale jobber's catalog. **$200.00-$300.00**

XXIII-3.
Baking or pastry sets.
All rock maple. "Clean made goods — not the trashy, made-to-sell kind." Rolling pin & masher with black handles, board is 10" x 7", masher 5 1/2"L, rolling pin 8"L, bowl 3 1/4" diameter, "extra deep." "Ours are better goods as well as lower prices." They weren't kidding: 38¢ and 72¢ a dozen sets. Wholesale catalog of Butler Brothers, Chicago, 1899. **$30.00-$50.00**

XXIII-2.
Baking & kitchen sets.
Ann Drock's No. 4 set, with perforated cake turner, perforated kitchen spoon, egg beater & tea strainer.(Very similar to A & J products, marketed as "Mother's Little Helper" sets, c.1923 until the 1930s.) These sets are from the Washburn Co. "Sno-Cap" catalog of the "new Androck Line" of kitchen equipment. Worcester, MA & Rockford, IL, 1927. "Sno-Cap" referred to the snowy white "cap" tipping off a beautiful blue handle. These sets are no longer in the Washburn catalog of 1936. **$30.00-$50.00**

XXIII-4.
Cooking ranges.
Stamped, painted tin, with cabriole feet, high backs hung with utensils, and other utensils on the range. These came packed by the dozen, for about wholesale, with 2/3 of them in red, and 1/3 in assorted colors (blue, green, gold). Range is 6 1/2" x 4 1/2" with back 7 1/2"H. Two ovens, 4 covered stew pans, tea kettle with lid, grater, tart pans, oblong cake pan, dustpan, and long-handled stew pan. Same color distribution. An even larger one, not pictured in catalog, almost became a toy kitchen, and had 10 miscellaneous things hanging on back, and a "fire pan," presumably for lighting a real fire. Butler Brothers, 1899. **$75.00-$150.00**

L. GARDENING

XXIV. WATER, SPRINKLE, MOW, CLIP, WEED & DECORATE

The publisher and I have decided that because of the importance of the subject, and the vast amount of material available that we should do an entire book on the subject, to come out shortly after the books on housekeeping and cooking antiques.

The eleven pictures selected to stand in for the coming book, and to titillate beginning collectors of gardening collectibles, pretty fairly represent the range of things which will be covered. Just about everything, except boot scrapers, deserves a **Futurewatch** flag. One subject which I have not included in this miniscule sampling is lawn sprinklers. They have come up quickly as a collecting specialty in the last half of the 1980s, and the prices for many desirable figural ones are astronomical. It's a situation ripe for rip-off and fakery, so keep your eyes open.

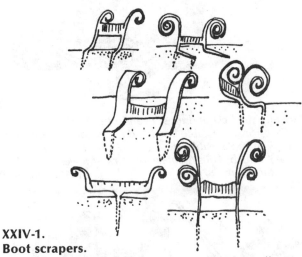

XXIV-1.
Boot scrapers.
A variety of simple wrought scrapers, all with scrolls. Most have spikes to drive into concrete or mortar. All late 18th or early 19th C, all American. Most unusual is the single spiker. Drawings done from articles on real colonial "footscrapers" from early magazines. These have been reproduced since the 1920s, so beware. Value depends on provenance and age; if old: **$80.00-$180.00**

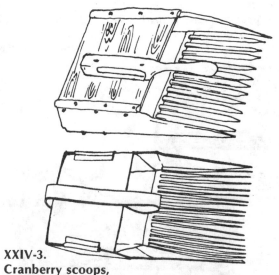

XXIV-3.
Cranberry scoops,
*also called **berry rakes.** (T) Made of turned and carved wood, metal nails. Handle is type associated with Shaker woodenwares. Probably mid 19th C. (B) Tinned sheet iron with sliding back. 19 tines or teeth. 17"L x 6 3/4"W. American. Collection Evelyn King.* **$150.00-$350 and $100.00-$200.00**

XXIV-2.
Chicken waterer or poultry fountain.
"The Flowing Spring," pat'd 10/1/1867 and 12/27/1870 by B. Van Gaasbeek, NYC. Fully galvanized iron. Came in 1 or 2-gallons for chicks & ducklings; in 2, 4, & 5-gallons for chickens. Ad in American Agriculturist, 5/1871. **$35.00-$55.00**

XXIV-4.
Garden faucet.
One of many figurals from late 1920s & early 30s. They're enjoying a revival now, and expensive new cast bronze ones are found everywhere, although the casting is relatively poorly finished. This burnished bronze one, 8"H, was designed by sculptor Sylvia Shaw Judson, design pat. #75428. Advertised in 1929. **$35.00-$100.00**

XXIV-5.
Garden vases or urns.
Just two of many hundreds of original styles. Cast iron. (L) Chase Bros. & Co., Boston. 1855-57 ad. (R) E.T. Barnum Iron Works, Detroit. 1923 catalog. Casting marks usually obscured by many layers of paint, or are in inaccessible place. Full range for almost all types: **$500.00-$4000.00**

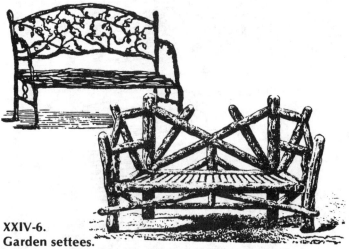

XXIV-6.
Garden settees.
(T) Cast iron rustic, copying so-called "twig" construction. Chase Bros. & Co., Boston Ornamental Iron Works, 1855-57 ad. (B) Rustic red cedar, bark on, 5' long. B.K. Bliss & Sons catalog, 1876. Iron valued higher than wood; size, design & condition determines value. **$300.00-$1000.00**

XXIV-7.
Weeders.
One collectible category of hand tool. (R) Forged iron, 3-prong claw fork. (L) A "Brown's Easy Weeder" with thin-blade — "too dull to damage plant stems," although OK to cut weeds. Size not given in catalog, so I don't know if it might be confused with pillow beater. Both 1905 Breck catalog. **$3.00-$10.00**

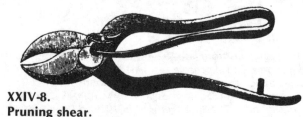

XXIV-8.
Pruning shear.
"Perfection," imported from France. One of scores, if not hundreds, of different designs. This one is particularly unusual, and was written up in American Agriculturist, *3/1882.* **$30.00-$50.00**

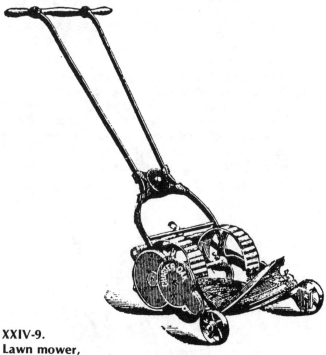

XXIV-9.
Lawn mower,
"emphatically the best and most beautiful Lawn Mower in the World." Cast iron, adjustable iron handle, 3-bladed solid revolving cutter with replaceable steel edges, gear train. "The New Charter Oak," mfd. by Hills Archimedean Lawn-Mower Co., c.1875. Catalog picture from 1876. **$150.00-$500.00**

XXIV-10.
Watering pots or cans.
Painted or japanned pieced tin, both with 2 strap handles with reinforced grips. Both made in 10 sizes, from 1 pint to 16 quarts. (L) Long angled spout with copper rose (sprinkling head); (R) Short braced spout, allover red color. Both English, from 1895 Harrod's catalog. At shows and in ads you will often see water cans (meant for supplying toilette water into washbowls in bedroom or bathroom) called "watering cans." **$55.00-$125.00**

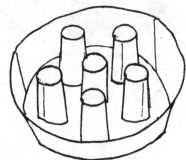

XXIV-11.
Whatzit flower-arranging contrivance.
Pieced, galvanized (zinc-coated) sheet iron. 6 slightly conical tubes soldered to bottom. 2 1/2"H x 8 1/4" diameter; cones 2 7/8"H. Very worn & used but not rusted. Thought by some to be a kind of mold, but there are no openings in bottom. **$60.00-$125.00**

This is a brief preview of the subject which will soon be featured in its own collector's guide and will detail many subjects not covered in recent books on collecting cookbooks. One special section, which I am thrilled to be able to complete for you now that I have the luxury of a complete book, will be what I call a "Concordance to Old Cookbooks."

This Concordance will feature twenty 18th and 19th century cookbooks, analyzed and dissected, in a way, to reveal all the wonderful descriptions of and usages for hundreds of kitchen utensils, implements and gadgets. When Eliza Leslie calls for the use of a "patty pan" in a recipe, you will get a chance to connect the pan itself to the recipe made in it. Many hidden secrets are to be found by leisurely reading old cookbooks; this is a great deal of the pleasure in them, and it means that you can successfully collect old cookbooks for content, not just for their antiquarian value.

The pictures shown here are views of kitchens, as found in cookbooks, dating from about 1700, 1854, and 1869. As you will have noticed, I have used many illustrations from the paperback *American Home Cook Book*. It was one of the best and most exciting purchases I have ever made.

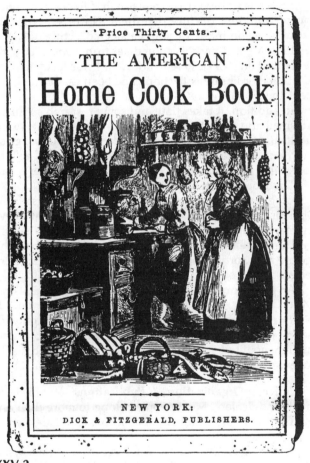

XXV. 1.
Chapbook illustration
from the early 18th C, perhaps as early as 1690. This is the title page of a small, 'cheap' book entitled A Choice Collection of Cookery Receipts, printed at New Castle, in England. I found it, but with no more information, in John Ashton's Chap Book of the Eighteenth Century, London: Chatto & Windus, 1882. Upper left appears to be someone in the pantry, with a pie (with vent cut in the crust), a leg of mutton or a ham, and a loaf of bread. Right is the cook at the hearth, with a cauldron suspended from a hook and a haunch of meat on one of the spits before the fire. Bottom left is the maid in the distillery, and at right is the noble family at table, waiting for their meal (?). **$100.00-$250.00**

XXV-2.
The American Home Cook Book.
By an American Lady. NYC: Dick & Fitzgerald, 1854. Printed paper wraps shown, depicting interior of old-style kitchen of the time. The artistic arrangement — truly a 'still-life' of dead fish, hung fowl, and uprooted vegetables — is shown on the floor and hanging above the cookstove exactly as were similar displays shown in 18th C kitchen pictures. Note original price! **$40.00-$60.00**

XXV-3.
Beecher, Catherine E., & Harriet Beecher Stowe.
American Woman's Home, or Principles of Domestic Science. NYC: J.B. Ford & Co., 1869. Showing an "enlarged plan of the sink and cooking-form. Two windows make a better circulation of air in warm weather, by having one open at top and the other at the bottom." Also seen are what are believed to be the first built-ins. I question the idea of draining dishes above the flour bin, or rolling pastry over the corn and rye, but it sure looks more sanitary than the kitchen in XXVII-2. **$55.00-$85.00**

N. DOCUMENTING:

XXVI. TRADE CATALOGS

What are widely known as "trade catalogs" are, for me, the real goal of the treasurehunt known as collecting. This is partly because they take up a lot less room than the real things they depict. More importantly, they document objects, and help collectors, curators and dealers identify, qualify, quantify and date particular items. Additionally, they depict things which may not have been seen in a century, or only by a very few people. So they have become a new kind of "wish book" (as mail order catalogs in the late 19th C were called by customers) — books with all the things we'd love to find.

There are **several types** of trade catalogs:

(1). Retail mail order catalogs for consumers, bypassing a store.

(2). Manufacturers' specialty catalog booklets or brochures aimed at the ultimate retail consumer to encourage his trade at a retail establishment. This kind was often stamped with the name of a retailer and given away free by them to shoppers.

(3). Manufacturers' wholesale catalogs featuring only their own goods, aimed at wholesalers and/or retailers,

(4). Wholesalers' or jobbers' catalogs, with goods made by more than one company, aimed at the retailer or store owner.

Each has its own place in research. I happen to prefer type (3) manufacturers' catalogs because they get you right to the source, and then *you* interpret them. However, type (1) and type (4) offer much more variety between two covers, and in a way give you more for your catalog-collecting dollars. I have a few hundred catalogs, of which most are manufacturers' catalogs. Most of my collection dates from about 1880 to the 1940s. Catalogs older than that are so exceedingly rare that I may never find one, or be able to afford it. I was lucky to have begun collecting them about 1972 — long after some fabulous institutional or library collections had been established, but before many private collectors had turned to documents to augment their "hardware".

In addition, it takes time and some research sophistication to come to appreciate unillustrated catalogs, many of which are small and tantalizingly matter-of-fact price lists (none of which are given in the lists below). Early price lists (say from the 1840s to 1860s) for ceramics, metalwares, lamps, glasswares, clothing, textiles, tools and hardware are not exactly abundant, but they can be found because they are still relatively unpopular with collectors. Prices usually range under $50.00, depending on the subject, date, and manufacturer's name, but they can be priced much higher.

The words "supercedes all previous catalogs", or "please discard all earlier listings", often found on the title page of a catalog, make us cringe nowadays. All those wastebaskets (collectible themselves) ... all those lost sources of information! Obviously many retailers from the last 120 years saved everything, regardless of what the directions said. Interestingly, there are many more dealers in old trade catalogs now than there were when I first began. I think this is because more attention has been given to the field, and book dealers who might not have paid any special attention to old trade catalogs 20 years ago are now sorting them out and even issuing detailed catalogs with scores of listings. See "Sources" of trade catalog dealers at the end of this introduction.

An as-yet-unparalleled book on these monuments of business ephemera is Lawrence B. Romaine's *A Guide to American Trade Catalogs, 1744-1900.* (NYC: R. R. Bowker Co., 1960). This has recently been reprinted; old copies are for sale — for upwards of $50.00. If you are interested, I highly recommend getting a copy, no matter what it costs. It contains information on thousands of catalogs, many in specific, named library collections, broken down by subjects from "Agricultural Implements" to "Windmills". A lot can be learned just by browsing the book itself, although there are no illustrations, and no excerpts from the catalogs themselves. Romaine made many informative observations in his annotated entries.

Collector Organizations & Publications. — Some large organizations serve generalist paper collectors (private & institutional) and dealers. Most people belong to more than one. They are The Ephemera Society of America, Inc., (EPHSOC of America), POB 37, Schoharie, NY 12157, and its related society, The Ephemera Society of Canada, Inc., c/o Barbara Rusch,

XXVI-1.

Sharing a trade catalog with a friend.

This genteel picture actually appeared in a slim mail order catalog — from S.W. Seastrand, c.1910s — a sort of Walter Drake for kitchen gadgetry. Their caption read: "To the Housekeeper: We have used great care and caution in the preparation of this catalogue — to make it complete and to supply you with good practical contrivances that you can use, thereby saving time and money. Consider the comfort and convenience of making your selection and ordering by mail. In your leisure moments, during the day or in the evening when your family is gathered around the evening table you can bring out the catalogue and discuss and decide the merits of the different articles listed in the catalogue. You make up your order in a quiet manner and in due time your goods come to you clean and new, all ready to use. You can make up club orders from the catalogue and earn handsome premiums. Show it to your friends and make your selection. Hang the catalogue in a convenient place always and you will find that it is a welcome addition to your household."

36 Macauley Drive, Thornhill, Ontario, CAN., L3T 5S5; The <u>Ephemera Society</u> [England's parent organization], c/o Maurice Rickards, 12 Fitzroy Square, London, England, W1P 5HQ; The <u>Ephemera Society of Australia</u>, c/o Honor Godfrey, 345 Highett Street, Richmond, Victoria, Australia, 3121; and <u>P.A.C.</u> (National Association of Paper & Advertising Collectors), POB 500, Columbia, PA 17552. In addition to the publications of those organizations, there is another useful monthly called <u>Paper Collectors' Marketplace</u>, POB 127, Scandinavia, WI 54977. Another periodical is the Paper Pile Quarterly, Box 337, San Anselmo, CA 94960.

Dating the Undated. — Often trade catalogs are not dated. And although sometimes the catalog number (for example #27, for the Reed one under "Utensils" below) actually corresponds to the year of publication (in that case 1927), this is by no means usual.

• The next simplest way to date an undated catalog is to compute with two clues often found on the first couple of pages: an "established" date for the company, and a phrase in a preface or introduction which says something like, "Thirty-two years ago ..."; it's simple arithmetic.

• Sometimes you will find testament letters in the front or back of a catalog, but these are rarely dated so that the best of then could be used over and over in all kinds of advertising.

• Sometimes you will see a page of premiums or medallic awards won by the company for its products; these are often long in the past, and are only occasionally useful. For example, a catalog from the 1920s may still brag about a Gold Medal awarded at an international fair in the 1890s.

• Another way is to put a magnifying glass to the engravings or linecuts to look for patent dates that may show up on the body or handle of an illustrated items; at least you know that the catalog cannot have been made before the patent.

• According to many experts on old printing, there are often dating clues to be found on the back cover (inside or out) or the last page — code numbers and letters used by the printer of the catalog. I have never found enough of such codes to depend on them. In fact, I put a random pile of 25 catalogs on my desk to test this, and not one of them has a code number. It is possible that it is mainly 20th C catalogs with the codes; most of mine are earlier.

• Yet another way to estimate a date is to look at depictions of women that may appear, and judge from their clothing what decade the catalog belongs to. This can often be misleading because old illustrations may be used for longer than a decade.

• Finally, a date can be estimated by experienced people based on the graphic style of the typeface and the cover design. This will sometimes get you to a decade, at least. However, to confuse things, often what's inside looks 20 or 30 or even 50 years older than the cover. This is because of the variety of illustrations culled from the company's files and used over and over — some of those illustrations being generics that could be purchased from engraving houses specializing in catalog art, and used by different companies to represent their own product. (Can you imagine that today?). In addition, some companies made the same product for decades.

Kinds of Illustrations. — Catalogs may be illustrated in as many as six ways — all under one cover. Old generic linecut engravings from the previous century, or at least several decades old; old specific linecuts from the past; new linecuts or drawings; halftone photographs (sometimes retouched); black & white lithographs; and chromolithographs (also call chromoliths, or color lithographs). Because so many catalog illustrations are attractive, you will occasionally find orphaned catalog pages mixed in with art print bins. Because of their decorative value they have been removed from catalogs. I buy and ask questions later, if the price is reasonable (say under $10.00). But I really don't like the common practice of breaking old books or catalogs down to pictures unaccompanied by text.

Cataloging the Catalogs. — Although it is a good idea to do it for everything you buy for your collection, it is almost imperative to catalog your catalogs, as if you were a librarian. You can do this on 3 x 5 cards or on your computer. I find it best to list the manufacturer first and alphabetize the listing under the manufacturer, with perhaps cross-references to such extremly well-known trade or model names as "Universal" (a brand name used by Landers, Frary & Clark). You might also want to arrange it by subject category, as the small list of catalogs was done for this chapter.

Document Files. — It is very useful to go through a catalog carefully and Xerox pages of slightly unexpected goods to file in subject folders. Often a catalog will be devoted, say, 95% to pots and pans, but have a few pages of gadgets in the back. I would Xerox the gadgets and note on the sheets what catalog they are from, then file them individually under the gadgets. I have my "document" collection arranged alphabetically in about 350 file folders, from "Advertising" and "Artwork" through "Enamelware" and "Hearth Cooking" to "Toasters" and "Yellowware", plus "A Miscellaneous", "B Miscellaneous", etc. Every time I come across something that I can either clip or Xerox, I do it for the files. I couldn't have done this third edition without my files of ads, articles, pictures, trade cards, advertising brochures, and photocopied catalog pages, instruction sheets, and labels.

Caring for Catalogs. — Unless you really want to get involved in making a perfect climate for your catalogs, you will have to expect some deterioration with time. All the catalogs from the mid 19th C on, especially those printed on uncoated paper, will darken with time and become brittle. (Coated paper will too, it just takes longer.) I use vertical file boxes, and try not to crowd too many catalogs into a space. Some elbow room, or air, is good. Catalogs, like any printed matter, should be kept in a dry but not heated place, and definitely not where sun or mildew can get to them. Only the most fragile of my catalogs get any special treatment. For them I try to use a supportive piece of acid-free cardboard inside an archival plastic bag, so that they will not be stressed or bent.

Pricing Catalogs. — When pricing catalogs, condition affects price, but is nowhere near as important as completeness, subject and age. These are truly primary research resources, treasured for their content. This is a world of rampant substance abuse, by everyone from glitz queens (who abuse the privilege their wads of money bring them, and 'feel good' because they have labels, shoes, jewelry, furs, houses, cars, makeup, hair and other externals to prove their worth), to poor souls on drugs (who, believing they have no worthy substance or content, turn to drugs to temporarily give them a substitute for both). Style can be like rust, and we must constantly reaffirm our faith in substance, content and meaning.

BUYING OLD CATALOGS

Lawrence B. Romaine, a bookseller in Middleboro, Massachusetts, shared the fruits of a quarter century of pleasure in selling and tracking down American catalogs prior to 1900, in a book published by R. R. Bowker in 1960. *A Guide to American Trade Catalogs, 1744-1900,* has over 10,000 catalogs listed, divided by category and cross-referenced in the index. Romaine was not the first to be interested in the catalogs; maybe the first was Bella C. Landauer, a New York state woman who in the early 20th century collected hundreds of thousands of ephemeral paper items, and whose collections are now in the New York Historical Society. Many libraries across the country also have sizeable collections — in Business Divisions and/or in Local History Divisions. Many are not cataloged, but are bound as miscellaneous pamphlets, or filed in boxes.

Romaine's book was ground-breaking because it publicized the presence of, and need to preserve, manufacturers', wholesalers', and retailers' catalogs for study of American business history. He wrote that he hoped a movement to locate trade catalogs "may eventually sweep the country. This means that at long last these lowly give-aways will be acknowledged as historical records from coast to coast." Apparently something of the sort did sweep the country, because it is terribly difficult now to find old catalogs in popular subject areas.

A growing number of dealers are specializing in old catalogs, if not all the time, at least once a year with saved-up offerings assembled over months of buying old books and paper ephemera of other types.

One dealer, Robert C. Bailey of Hillcrest Books, has been sending out catalogs from which I've been buying for over 20 years. Like many catalog dealers, it's mail order only. Bailey has been in business since October 1, 1959. apparently he and Romaine were on the same wavelength, because it was just a few months later that Romaine's already compiled & written book was published.

The greater demand has meant increased prices. Catalog dealers are being asked to pay sizeable amounts for what once were thrown into cheap box lots, and they must ask ever higher prices from us. Added to this is the fact that since 1980 there has been a formalized recognition of the importance of paper stuff, and collector organizations for general and narrow-field paper documents. A discouraging reality is that attics, barns, leased storage units, filing cabinets, desks, and basements can disgorge only so many more 19th and early 20th century paper collectibles before being emptied. If you think it's hard to find tinwares, or old iron, or treen, the situation for ephemeral paper goods is even worse, because they are fragile and subject to water, fire and sun ... as well as neatophilia (the love of throwing out!).

To receive dealers' periodic lists, expect to buy regularly, or pay from $2.00 to $5.00 for the privelege of being on their mailing lists. The often detailed bibliographic listings are expensive to compile and mail, and become a fine record worth a good deal of money in their own right. When you write a dealer for information, or to tell them your wants, be as specific as you can about what you want, and enclose a SASE (a self-addressed stamped envelope).

Over the years I've tried to find dealers who specialize in trade catalogs, or who put out special lists from time to time. I have tripled the list from the first edition of this book, but undoubtedly there are even more out there. I would like to state at this time, because of the suspicious minds of some people, that I have never benefited from providing this list to you — either by a reduced special price to me, or by early or private notice of any catalog. I have, in a way, cut off my nose to spite my face by sharing my sources with you. But in the long run, the finding of good foster homes for these treasures of American business history, is the most important thing. I hope that you will consider gifting or willing your collection to a library or other suitable institution, such as the Smithsonian Museum of American History. This will help ensure that the future won't be bereft of this history.

SOURCES: In Alphabetical Order

Jonathan Alk
1515 S. Webster
Green Bay, WI 54301

Peter G. Boody
The Paper Tiger
POB 99
Wakefield, MA 01880

Bookworm & Silverfish
Jim Presgraves, Prop.
POB 639
Wytheville, VA 24382

Fred P. Elwert
POB 254
Rutland, VT 05701

Steve Finer
Box 758
Greenfield, MA 01302

Fortunate Finds Bookstore
Mildred E. Santille
16 W. Natick Road
Warwick, RI 02886

High Ridge Books
POB 286
Rye, NY 10580

Hillcrest Books*
R. C. Bailey
Route 2, Box 162
Spring City, TNB 37381

Dennis Holzman
240 Washington Avenue
2nd Floor
Albany, NY 12210

Kenneth Leach
Rare Book Scout
POB 78
Brattleborough, VT 05301

Peter L. Masi — Books
POB B
Montague, MA 01351

Harold R. Nestler, Inc.
13 Pennington Avenue
Waldwick NJ 07463

The Paper Chase
Norm Martinus
628 Down Patrick Lane
Raleigh, NC 27615

Francis Patrick Antiques
POB 833
Gaithersburg, MD 20760
or
Box 197
Hinsdale, MA 01235

Kenneth E. Schneringer
271 Sabrina Court
Woodstock, GA 30188

John Whiting
POB 25058
Richmond VA 23260

Ximenes
19 E. 69th Street
NYC, NY 10021

Please don't forget SASE.
* Trade catalogs exclusively

Abbreviations: **Cat.** *catalog;* **pp** *pages;* **prof.** *profuse;* **illus.** *illustrations;* **(M)** *Manufacturer's catalog;* **(R)** *Retailer's;* **(RMO)** *Retailer's Mail Order;* **(W)** *Wholesaler's.*

Bakers', Candy-makers & Confectioners' Supplies

H. Heug & Co.'s "Book of Designs for Bakers & Confectioners", (M). fantastical decorations for cakes & candies, NYC, NY, 48 pp, many illus., 1896. **$38.00-$50.00**

Herman Heug & Co., "Ornamental Confectionery and The Art of Baking", (M), 41 pp, prof. illus., remainder is cookbook in English & German, NYC, 1905. **$30.00-$50.00**

Jaburg Brothers, "The Best of Everything for Bakers (Cat. #2)", (M, W), machinery, fixtures, pans (which Jaburg made), ovens, plus interesting little decorations, bride & groom figures, paper doilies, etc., 160 pp, prof. illus., NYC, n.d. [1908]. **$75.00-$100.00**

Joseph Middleby Jr., Inc., "Cat. #42B Bakers' Supplies, Tools, Fixtures, Machinery", (W), 176 pp, prof. illus. with every kind of supply — many found in home kitchens too. Boston, 1927. **$35.00-$50.00**

Sethness Co., "The Sethness Candy Maker", (M), large assortment of candy equipment, mostly commercial, 64 pp, prof. illus., Chicago, 1925. **$25.00-$40.00**

Wood & Selick, "Confectioners Machinery & Utensils", (M), 183 pp, including photographs, NYC, 1915. **$35.00-$50.00**

Campers' Supplies

David T. Abercrombie, "Complete Outfit for Campers, Hunters, Surveyors, Prospectors", (W, R), stoves, etc., large format, illus., NYC, 1908. **$40.00-$55.00**

Sterno (Sternau) Corp., (M), camp & solid fuel cooking devices, NYC, small size, 1930. **$12.00-$18.00**

Dairy Equipment & Churns

T. Crafts & Co., (M), churns, pitchers, other earthenware, broadside price listing, no pictures, Nashua, NH, 1845. • After years of buying catalogs with pictures, and passing up price lists, I wish I could go back again. Not as fun to look at, maybe, but extremely valuable for the information, including range of products, terminology, style names, choice of finishes, and prices. • Added value. — Certain subjects much higher in price than others; especially crockery or stoneware. **$45.00-$60.00**

A. H. Reid, "Creamery Supplies", (M), dairy equipment & vessels, 38 pp, Philadelphia, 1889. **$22.00-$30.00**

A. H. Reid, (M), dairy fixtures, etc., 12 pp, 1883. **$28.00-$35.00**

Vermont Farm Machine Co., (M), churns & dairy fixtures, Bellows Falls, VT, 12 pp, 1877. **$30.00-$40.00**

Electrical Appliances & Gadgets

Bibber-White Co., (W), electric stuff, from lamps to novelties, Boston, 132 pp, 1898. **$135.00-$150.00**

Chicago Electric Mfg. Co., (M), "The Handyhot Line, Cat. M", electric household appliances of all types, 18 pp, large format, Chicago, 1938. **$12.00-$18.00**

Chicago Flexible Shaft Co., "Sunbeam", "Electrical Products Cat. #96", (M), irons to heating pads, grill & toaster, 16 pp, large format, Chicago, 1928. **$12.00-$18.00**

General Electric "Electrical Heating & Cooking", (M), toasters, stoves, irons, etc., 62 pp, 1912. **$55.00-$75.00**

General Electric, "The Matchless Kitchen", (M), electric kitchens, 35 pp with photographs, 1917. **$45.00-$60.00**

Hotpoint (Edison General Electric), (M), electrical conveniences & appliances, from toasters to ranges, 64 pp, large format, lots of illus., Chicago, 1927-28. **$40.00-$65.00**

Landers, Frary & Clark, "Universal Household Helps", (M), electric appliances & hand-operated gadgets, 32 pp, New Britain, CT, 1920s. **$22.00-$40.00**

Marietta Manufacturing Co., "The New Crescent Electric Fans", (M), 32 pp, many illus., OH, 1899. **$150.00-$175.00**

Furniture

Acme Kitchen Furniture Co., (M), oak cupboards, safes, tables, etc., 20 pp, 1910. **$25.00-$45.00**

The Hoosier Mfg. Co., "Hoosier Kitchen Cabinets", (M), many cabinets, tables, and closeups of housewife demonstrating features, bl/wh photos, 32 pp, Newcastle, IN, c.1920. **$20.00-$35.00**

Lammert Furniture Company, (M), including kitchen & bathroom furniture, St. Louis, 204 pp, 1894. **$100.00-$135.00**

Marietta Chair Co., (M), furniture, including kitchen pie safes with tin panels, Marietta, OH, 98 pp, 1884. **$135.00-$165.00**

Ice Boxes, Refrigerators & Ice-Related Supplies
(For Ice Cream See Soda Fountain Category)

Bostwick Refrigerating Co., (M), ice boxes of all styles, Mishawaka, IN, 1877. **$55.00-$75.00**

Bowen Mfg., (M), hardwood refrigerators, ice chests, for home & commercial use, 70 pp, Fond du Lac, WI, 1900. **$50.00-$65.00**

Gifford & Wood Co., (M), picks, tongs, scales, plus commercial machinery for handling ice, 48 pp, Hudson, NY, 1911. **$40.00-$55.00**

Frigidaire Corporation, (M), booklet, Dayton, OH, 1927. **$12.00-$18.00**

Kelvinator Corp., "Kelvinator Refrigerates Without Ice", (M), 14 pp, illus., Detroit, MI, c.1920. **$15.00-$25.00**

Lockwood & Hall, "Refrigerators, Blacking Cases & Commodes", (M), 40 pp, illus., 1885. **$40.00-$55.00**

G. M. Shirk Mfg. Co., "North Star Refrigerators", (M), oak ice boxes, 48 pp, Chattanooga, TN, 1893. **$28.00-$45.00**

Implements

A. & J.—See next section.

Lewis Dean Co., (M), wire goods, 8 pp, Worcester, MA, 1875. **$35.00-$50.00**

Gilbert & Bennett Mfg. Co., (M), wire goods, sieves, etc., small size, Georgetown, CT, 1887. **$40.00-$50.00**

Sargent Co., "Gem Chopper", (M), 92 pp, New Haven, CT, 1902. **$22.00-$35.00**

The Washburn Company, "Androck Balanced Kitchenware", (M), 56 pp, prof. illus., Worcester, MA, or Rockford, IL, 1936. **$50.00-$70.00**

The Washburn Co., (M), kitchen utensils, 102 pp, illus., 1926 **$40.00-$50.00**

Labor Savers, Gadgets & Implements

The A & J Mfg. Co., "Blutip Kitchen Tools. Colorful Kitchen Tools of Quality. Cat. #1", (M), implements of all types, plus eggbeaters & glass beater jars, also "complete" line of children's baking sets & implements. 88 pp, prof. illus. in color & bl/wh, (company by then part of Edward Katzinger Co. of Chicago), Binghamton, NY, n.d. (1930). **$100.00-$150.00**

American Machine Co., (M), "Perfection" meat chopper, "Gem" cake pans, "American" cake mixer, etc., 100 pp, plus many recipes, Chicago, c.1890. **$40.00-$55.00**

D. J. Barry & Co., "Supplies for Engineers, Janitors, Laundries, Garages, Housekeepers, Institutions, Factories, Office buildings & Contractors", (W, M), everything from ash cans & brooms to spittoons, wooden bowls, enamelware, wheelbarrows & wastebaskets. I was unable to tell what they actually manufactured though they claimed to be manufacturers as well as jobbers. 173 pp, prof. illus., NYC, n.d. (1924). **$40.00-$60.00**

Butler Brothers, (R-MO), general merchandise along with lots of kitchen things, NYC & Chicago, December 1918. • Always fun to find Christmas catalogs, for all the variety of novelties, most of which have nothing to do with kitchens.

$115.00-$140.00

Butler Brothers, (R-MO), general merchandise, with lots of kitchen things, 422 pp, 1922. • Look for other general merchandise catalogs which have sections on kitchen wares. Sears Roebuck, Montgomery Ward (both of which have been reproduced), Larkin Company, Wanamaker Stores, Siegel-Cooper Company, Baltimore Bargain House, and Stern Brothers catalogs are all good bets. Some catalog dealers offer these humongous catalogs broken up into sections so that collectors can choose their specialty at an affordable price. **$100.00-$125.00**

Dover Stamping Co., "Dover Stamping Co's Cook Book", (M), 48 pp combined catalog & cookbooklet with illus. of egg beaters, dish drainers, etc., Boston, MA, 1899.

$20.00-$30.00

Fairbanks Scales, (M), all sorts of scales, from family & grocer to large platform, 914 pp, Chicago, 1914.

$95.00-$150.00

Enterprise Mfg. Co. of Pennsylvania & Iron Founders, (M), all kinds of gadgets & tools, 32 pp, prof. illus., Philadelphia, 1881. **$85.00-$120.00**

Enterprise Mfg. Co., (M), coffee mills, food choppers, ice tools, many other implements, 78 pp, 10"H x 7"W, 1927.

$45.00-$65.00

William Frankfurth Hardware Co., various goods, 1752 pp in all (144 pp on kitchenwares), 1917. **$175.00-$250.00**

Haslet, Flanagen & Co., (W), tinware, enameled tin, apple corers, etc., 100 pp, Philadelphia, c.1886. **$95.00-$125.00**

Hibbard, Spencer, Bartlett & Company, (M), apple parers, slicers, choppers, etc., Chicago, 1884. **$95.00-$125.00**

Hodges Co., (W), various tin wares, gadgets, egg openers, cream whips, egg separators, etc., 107 pp, 10"H x 7"W, illus., Philadelphia, 1929. **$50.00-$65.00**

John Jewett Mfg Co., (M), novelties, umbrella stands, japanned tinwares, etc., 64 pp, Buffalo, 1883.

$120.00-$150.00

S. Joseph Co., Inc., "Hotel, Baker & Restaurant Supplies. House Furnishing Goods & Specialties", (W), wide variety in wire, wood & tin, 91 pp, prof. illus., NYC, c.1927.

$40.00-$55.00

Edward Katzinger Co., "Geneva Forge" cutlery, "Ovenex", "Ekco", "A & J", "Katzinger", (M), variety of implements, 50 pp, Chicago, 1940. **$85.00-$100.00**

Ketcham Co., (W), tinware, lamps & lanterns, coffee mills, ice cream freezers, much more, 250 pp, 1888.

$125.00-$150.00

"Kitchen Specialties", (W), equipment of all types for hotel, restaurant & home use, 107 pp, large format 10" x 7", early 20th C. **$50.00-$75.00**

Landers, Frary & Clark, "Universal Household Helps" — See Electrical section.

L. L. Lewis & Co., (R), dealer in ice cream freezers, sewing machines, ice boxes, etc., 96 pp, illus., Sacramento, CA, 1896. • Always great to find a California catalog as they are few and far between (or at least East of the Mississippi). Pre-Quake is especially desirable. **$95.00-$150.00**

Paine, Diehl & Co., "What It Is, What Is Said About It." (M), Self-pouring coffee & teapots, various wire wares — trivets, sadiron stands, toast racks, egg stands, etc., recipes for using eggs, etc. 36 pp, prof. illus., Philadelphia, PA, (1888). **$45.00-$60.00**

Albert Pick & Co., "E-6 General Catalog", goods of great variety from a "specialty catalog house, catering principally to the wants of Hotels, Restaurants, Dining Cars, Clubs and Saloons", all kinds of glassware, cooking utensils & implements, urns, cupboards, furniture, floor coverings, lighting, etc.. Much of the stuff is the same as what was available retail to the retail customer buying for her own kitchen. One fun aspect is seeing the photographs of many major hotels & institutions "supplied" by Pick, viz. The Gayoso in Memphis, The Sherman hotel & The Union Club in Chicago, etc., etc. My copy incomplete, goes only to p.586; original had at least 672 pp. Prof. illus., Chicago, 1909. Remember, we're buying information here, so as-is condition value range: **$45.00-$65.00**

F. W. Seastrand, (W) for traveling salesmen, with all sorts of kitchen related gadgets, small size, South Manchester, CT (also Buffalo, NY) c.1913. I have several of these, all slightly different. **$30.00-$45.00**

S. B. Sexton Stove & Mfg. Co.—See Stove section.

Shapleigh Hardware Co., "Fall Catalog No. 161", (M - W, R), mixed "Diamond" brand items of their manufacture, ie. edge tools, cookwares, gadgets, etc., and other goods found in a hardware establishment, the catalog seemingly printed with retail prices (even though by the dozen) because accompanying it is price booklet that is printed "Keep out of the hands of the public". It has prices slightly less than half what is shown in the catalog. 316 pp, prof. illus. on extremely thin paper, St. Louis, MO, 1914. **$65.00-$80.00**

Silver & Co., "Silver's Housefurnishings, Homeware Cat. #18", (M), 128 pp, tall skinny format, prof. illus. with cuts, Brooklyn, NY, c.1910s-20s. **$50.00-$75.00**

Simmons "Keen Kutter", (M), whole line of hardware specialties, including edge tools, St. Louis, 1939.

$125.00-$150.00

Gordon Vantine Co. "Home Conveniences", 80 pp, 1918.

$25.00-$38.00

F. A. Walker & Co., (W), imported & domestic tinwares, brass and copper wares, wooden wares, etc., prof. illus., the 1871 one has 130 pp full. Boston, c.1870s & 1880s, first (?) is 1871.

wonderful huge catalogs is an important find. For any of 100 pages or more: **$200.00-$400.00**

Wheaton & Hickox, "The Housekeeper's Own Book", (R), every kind of tin bath, kitchen & serving wares, 36 pp, really fabulous, Worcester, MA, c.1845. **$175.00-$200.00**

Wickwire Brothers, (M), wire screening, plus various things made of wire — from sieves to bird cages, 24 pp, illus., Cortland, NY, 1890. **$30.00-$40.00**

Soda Fountain & Bar Supplies

"Benedict Silver", Benedict Mfg. Co., (M), silverplated wares, many soda fountain supplies, (East Syracuse, NY), 1931. **$75.00-$100.00**

Cleveland Faucet Co., (M), bar fixtures, 40 pp, illus., Cleveland, OH, late 1880s. **$75.00-$95.00**

E. Compiegne (successor to Cadot), "Moules en Etain, Turbines la Glacer et Sorbetieres", (M), tin ice cream molds, etc., 28 pp, prof. illus., Paris, 1900. **$70.00-$100.00**

Gilchrist, (M), soda fountain equipment, ice cream dippers, etc., Newark, NJ, 1916. **$95.00-$130.00**

Kingery Mfg Co., (M), milk shake & soda fountain equipment, corn poppers, etc., 32 pp, illus., Cincinnati, OH, 1899. **$85.00-$120.00**

Charles Lippincott & Co., (W), fancy soda fountains & plated wares, etc., 218 pp, prof. illus., Philadelphia, c.1890. **$200.00-$300.00**

Liquid Carbonic Co., "Soda Fountain Specialties & Supplies", (W), ice cream tables & chairs, pumps, etc., 96 pp, illus., Chicago, IL, 1915. **$140.00-$185.00**

Joe Lowe Corp., "Presenting a Complete Listing of Metal Molds for Ice Cream With Composition Display Models", "Jo-lo Molds", (M), 32 pp, with laid-in sheet of "new designs" (including 'Whistler's Mother'), photo illus., Brooklyn, NY, n.d. (late 1920s or early '30s). **$40.00-$60.00**

Meyer Brothers Drug Co., (W), soda fountain glasswares, etc., 816 pp, St. Louis, 1889. • Part of high value in some catalogs comes from age & size, of course, but also because in them some collectors see a worthwhile opportunity for reprint — especially in a very popular, well-organized field with high ticket items. **$250.00-$350.00**

Thos. Mills & Bro., Inc., "Ice Cream Manufacturers' Equipment, Cat. 31", (M), pumps, tubs, molds, spoons, etc., prof. illus. on thin paper, 60 pp, Philadelphia, c.1930s. **$15.00-$25.00**

James W. Tufts Co., "Arctic Soda Water Apparatus", (M), fabulous soda fountains, 176 pp, illus., Boston, 1876. **$250.00-$350.00**

Stoves, Ranges & Some Related Hollowware

American Range Co., "Sanico Ranges", (M), Shakopee, MN, 1922. **$12.00-$18.00**

Assorted stove foundries, (M), including Gold Coin, Abrams & Cox, Union, Welcome, Buckwalter, Liberty. American, from the early 1890s to c. 1915. • Price range is somewhat narrow, unless a really "hot" stove foundry is involved, and prices vary mainly because of date, number of pages and especially variety & quality of illustrations. **$65.00-$250.00**

H. A. Bartlett & Co., (M), stove related stuff: stove polish, blacking, etc., 12 pp, Philadelphia, NYC, Boston, 1876. **$12.00-$18.00**

Broomell, Schmidt & Co., "The Heatencook Range", (M), 32 pp, NYC, York, PA, 1899. **$65.00-$80.00**

Buffalo Stove Co., "Potbellied Parlor Stoves, & Kitchen Ranges", (M), 54 pp, 8" x 5 1/4", well illus., Buffalo, NY, 1894. **$45.00-$65.00**

William Campbell Co., "The Rapid Fireless Cooker", (M), 64 pp, with recipes, 1915. **$28.00-$40.00**

Cole's Hot Blast stoves, (M), 40 pp, Chicago, 1924. **$30.00-$40.00**

"Doe-Wah-Jack" stoves, (M), 60 pp, illus., plus price list, Dowagiac, MI, 1922. **$45.00-$65.00**

Engman Range Eternal Co., (M), Goshen, IN, c.1915. **$30.00-$45.00**

Excelsior Mfg. Co., G. F. Filley, "Charter Oak Ranges & Stoves, Cat. #9", (M), 194 pp., St. Louis, MO, (poss. 1870s?). **$85.00-$120.00**

Excelsior Stove & Mfg. Co., "Cat. #6", (M, W), featuring "Monarch", "National", etc. stoves & stove accessories, kitchen cabinets, poultry supplies, cobblers' tools, etc., etc., a wholesale catalog with many things besides those mfd by Excelsior. 136 pp, illus., Quincy, IL, c.1936 (?) **$40.00-$55.00**

Garland Stoves, (M), 168 pp, Detroit, MI, 1892. **$120.00-$140.00**

Great Western Stove Co., (M), 215 pp, plus price listing, Leavenworth, KS, 1912. **$65.00-$95.00**

"Howard Overdraft" stoves, (M), 48 pp, Syracuse, NY, 1921. **$45.00-$55.00**

"Howard Ranges, Heaters, & Furnaces", (M), 81pp, n.d. (c. 1920s). **$55.00-$65.00**

"Majestic Range Repair", (M), 24 pp, St. Louis, MO, 1926. **$40.00-$50.00**

Monarch Ranges, (M), Mansfield, OH, 1931. **$15.00-$25.00**

J. L. Mott Iron Works, (M), cast iron of all kinds, andirons, fenders, grates, etc., 167 pp, NYC, 1882. **$200.00-$300.00**

Omaha Stove Repair Works, "Cat. #0", (M), 547 pp, Omaha, NE, n.d. **$75.00-$95.00**

"Perfection Stoves, Ovens, Heaters", (M), 58 p, color illus., Cleveland, OH, 1927. **$35.00-$65.00**

The S. B. Sexton Stove & Mfg. Co., "Hotel Ranges & Kitchen Appliances for Hotels, Restaurants, Institutions, Clubs and Steamships", (M, W), their own stoves, ranges, sinks, hot & steam tables, etc., plus wares by Landers, Frary & Clark, Fearless Dishwasher Co., Elgin, Creasey, etc., etc., 136 pp, prof. illus. with linecuts & bl/wh halftone photos. Baltimore, MD, n.d. (c.1920). **$40.00-$60.00**

Shakopee Stove Co., (M), Shakopee, MN, 1928. **$15.00-$25.00**

Shear, Packard & Co., (M), stoves, illus., Albany, NY, 1856. **$70.00-$85.00**

Sheeler, Buckwalter & Co., (M), stoves & hardware, 8 pp, Royer's Ford, PA, 1875. **$40.00-$55.00**

Sterling-Stewart Corp., "Stewart Stoves & Ranges", (M), 74 pp, Rochester, NY, 1924. **$35.00-$55.00**

The John Van Range Co., "Wrought Steel Portable Ranges", also "implements for culinary purposes", (M), 143 pp of all kinds of things, Cincinnati, OH, 1914. **$55.00-$70.00**

Wrought Range Stove Company, (M), "Home Comfort" ranges, & many cooking utensils, 126 pp, illus., St. Louis, MO, 1896. **$140.00-$180.00**

Aluminum Cooking Utensil Company, "Wear-Ever", (M, R), various utensils & their advantages, booklet, New Kensington, PA, 1903. **$18.00-$22.00**

Aluminum Cooking Utensil Company, "Wear-Ever Specialties Cat. #30", (M, R), various goods, 45 pp, prof. illus., 1916. **$30.00-$45.00**

Atlantic Stamping Co., (M), galvanized pails, drip pans, garbage cans, tea pots & kettles, copper wash boilers, 48 pp, color illus., Rochester, NY, 1919. **$85.00-$100.00**

Bramhall Deane Co., (M, W), lots of copper utensils for home & restaurants, 40 pp, Brooklyn, NY, 1906. In this catalog you would see many sauce pans & cook pots which people try to sell as 100 years older than they are. **$45.00-$55.00**

Bramhall Deane Co., "Galley Equipment for Yachts", etc., 24 pp, 1919. **$25.00-$40.00**

Bronson-Walton Company, (M), "Never-Burn", pans, also coffee mills & roasters, large illus., Cleveland, OH, 1905. **$50.00-$65.00**

Brown Oil Can Co., "Tinware Specialties", (M), household decorated tin, including dustpans, toilette sets, etc., 82 pp, Toledo, OH, 1903. **$50.00-$75.00**

Buehler, Bonbright & Co., tinware, enameled iron wares, waffle irons, etc., 12 pp, Philadelphia, 1872. Old, interesting, & with sought-after subjects, so size isn't as important in pricing. **$100.00-$130.00**

Central Stamping Co., "Cat. #43", (M), tinware of all kinds & other kitchenwares, 236 pp, prof. illus., NYC, 1920. **$75.00-$95.00**

Cleveland Metal Products, (M), numerous aluminum products, small size, Cleveland, OH, 1920. **$18.00-$25.00**

Cordley & Hayes, "Indurated Fibre Ware", (M), buckets, slop jars, measures, etc., 48 pp, illus., NYC, NY, c.1886. **$30.00-$50.00**

Crandell & Godley Mfg. Co., (M), wares for commercial & home kitchens, 260 pp, NYC, c.1886. **$125.00-$150.00**

J. B. Foote Foundry Co., (M), various wares for traveling salesmen, 32 pp, Frederickstown, OH, 1906. **$75.00-$90.00**

Gage & Co., (M), bowls, woodenwares, 16 pp, Henniker, NH, 1888. **$20.00-$35.00**

Geuder, Paeschke & Frey Company, "Cream City Ware", (M), enameled wares, copper & tin wares, 256 pp, including some color illus., Milwaukee, WI, 1926. **$170.00-$225.00**

Griswold Mfg. Co., "Heart-Star Waffles", (M, R), recipes for the heart-star waffle iron, patty iron, & heart-star gem pans, 8 pp — covers, color & bl/wh illus., Philadelphia, c.1920s. **$18.00-$25.00**

Janney, Semple & Co., (W), enamelwares, iron wares, gadgets, Minneapolis, MN, 1887. **$65.00-$90.00**

Keystone Works, (M), coffee roasters, coal scuttles, wash boilers, etc., 18 pp, Philadelphia, 1873. **$50.00-$75.00**

Lalance & Grosjean Mfg. Co., (M), many assorted utensils in various finishes, 360 pp, 6 1/8" x 5", flexible cloth cover, NYC, "February 15, 1890". **$135.00-$195.00**

List Mfg. Co., (M), all types of tin kettles, pots & pans for kitchen, 127 pp, 9" x 6", Canandaigua, NY, 1901. **$50.00-$70.00**

Matthai-Ingram & Co., (M), all types of sheet metal wares, 277 pp, great illus., Baltimore, MD, c.1890. **$140.00-$170.00**

National Enameling & Stamping Co. (NESCO), (M), complete line of kitchen utensils, card stock printed in mottled "enamelware" for cover, Milwaukee, 1903. **$95.00-$150.00**

National Enameling & Stamping Co., (M), complete line of kitchen utensils, coffee pots, condiment sets, pails, 414 pp, some color illus., 1924. **$100.00-$175.00**

C. S. Osborne & Co., (M), cast iron wares for cooking & other purposes, Newark, NJ, c.1890. **$40.00-$60.00**

C. B. Porter Co., (M), tinwares, enameled tin, water coolers, bread bins, etc., 82 pp, Philadelphia, 1920s. **$100.00-$125.00**

Reed Mfg. Co., "Matchless Metalware Cat. #27", (M), 160 pp of cookwares in stamped steel wares & some enamelwares (some in color), prof. illus., Newark, NY, 1927. **$35.00-$55.00**

Henry Rogers, Sons & Co. Ltd., "Book No. E5528", (M), all kinds of copper, brass & tin cooking & serving wares, many kettles, 87 pp, prof. illus., Wolverhampton, England, 1914. **$100.00-$135.00**

St. Louis Stamping Co., (M), enameled wares, tinwares, wire goods, etc., 316 pp, St. Louis, MO, 1890. **$150.00-$175.00**

Seavey & Co., (M), all kinds of tinwares, 104 pp, many illus., Boston, 1885. **$165.00-$190.00**

"Wear-Ever Specialties"—See Aluminum Cooking Utensil Company.

BIBLIOGRAPHY
OF BOOKS RECOMMENDED AND/OR CONSULTED

I can't recommend all the following, except as picture sources. Some books contain information which is incorrect or romanced from thin air. Many valuable secondary research sources are articles published in periodicals. They have been credited throughout the text. Trade catalogs are invaluable and irrefutable. The few hundred I have collected since 1970 are my treasure trove.

A & J Mfg. Co. *Colorful Kitchen Tools* Catalog. Binghampton, NY & Chicago: Edward Katzinger Co., A & J Division, 1930.

Adams & Son, William S. *Francatelli's Cook's Guide Advertiser*. London, England: c.1860-61.

American Agriculturist. Monthly. NYC: Orange Judd & Co., 1840s-80s.

American Home Cook Book, by an American lady. NYC: Dick & Fitzgerald, 1854.

Ames, Alex. *Collecting Cast Iron*. England: Moorland Pub., 1980.

Anthoine, A. *Moules a Glaces en Etain*. Catalog. Paris: c.1900. May have been jobbers, not manufacturers.

Antique Metalware Brass, Bronze, Copper, Tin Wrought & Cast Iron. Edited by James R. Mitchell. NYC: Universe Books, c.1976. Anthology of metal-related articles from *The Magazine ANTIQUES*, 1922-1976.

Arthur, Eric & Thomas Ritchie. *Iron, Cast & Wrought Iron in Canada from the Seventeenth Century to the Present*. Toronto: University of Toronto Press, 1982.

Baker, Frank T. *Hooks, Rings & Other Things. ...N.E. Iron, 1660-1860.* Hanover, MA: Christopher Pub., 1988. Some descriptions to be taken with a grain of salt.

Barry, D.J. & Co. *Hotel Supplies* Catalog. NYC: 1924. Manufacturers, jobbers, importers of housefurnishings.

Beard, James, Milton Glaser, et. al, ed. *The Cook's Catalogue*. NYC: Harper & Row, 1975.

Beard, James, intro. *The International Cooks' Catalogue*. NYC: Random House, 1977. Perhaps even more useful than the other, as it shows today's exotic utensils we might think are much older.

Bertuch, A. *Katalog A*. Berlin, Germany: c.1904.

Bishop, John Leander. *A History of American Manufacturers from 1608-1860*. Philadelphia: E. Young & Co., 1861.

Bosker, Gideon. *Great Shakes: Salt & Pepper for All Tastes*. NYC: Abbeville, 1986.

Bowditch, Barbara. *American Jelly Glasses: A Collector's Notebook*. 1173 Peck Rd., Hilton, NY, 14468. Author, 1986.

Breck, Joseph & Sons. *Agricultural Hardware, Implements, Woodenware*. Catalog. Boston: 1903; 1905.

Bull, Donald. *A Price Guide to Beer Advertising Openers & Cork-screws*. Trumbull, CT: Author, 1981.

Bunn, Eleanor. *Metal Molds, Ice Cream, Chocolate, Barley Sugar, Cake*. Paducah, KY: Collector Books, 1981.

Burgess, Fred W. *Chats on Household Curios*. NYC: F.A. Stokes Co., 1914.

Butler Brothers. *Christmas Catalog*. Chicago: 1899. Thousands of mail order household items.

Campbell, Susan. *Cooks' Tools. Complete Manual of Kitchen Implements & How to Use Them*. NYC: William Morrow, 1980. Modern tools; old uses.

Carson, Jane. *Colonial Virginia Cookery*. Williamsburg, VA: Williamsburg Research Studies, 1968.

Celehar, Jane. *Kitchens & Gadgets. 1920 to 1950*. Des Moines, IA: Wallace-Homestead, 1982. Handle shapes, dates, company histories good.

Celehar, J. *Kitchens & Kitchenware*. Lombard, IL: Wallace-Homestead, 1985.

Central Stamping Co., *Catalog No. 43*. NYC: 1920.

Cherry-Bassett Co., *Complete Catalog of Equipment for Milk Plants, Ice Cream Plants ...No. 53*. Baltimore, Philadelphia: 1921.

Chiurazzi, J & Fils/S. De Angelis & Fils. *Artistic Founding*. Catalog. Naples, Italy: 1910-11. Reproductions of ancient metalwares found at Pompeii & Herculaneum.

Christensen, E.O. *The Index of American Design*. NYC: Macmillan, 1950.

Clad, V. & Sons, Inc. *Clad's Advertising Pamphlet*. Philadelphia: c.1890-1900.

Clark, Hyla. *The Tin Can Book*. NYC: New American Library, 1977.

Coffin, Margaret. *The History & Folklore of American Country Tinware, 1700-1900*. Camden, NJ: Thomas Nelson & Sons, 1968.

Consentino, Geraldine, & Regina Stewart. *Kitchenware: A Guide for the Beginning Collector*. NYC: Golden Press, 1977.

Creswick, Alice. *The Collector's Guide to Old Fruit Jars*. (Also called the Red Book of Fruit Jars.) 0-8525 Kenowa S.W., Grand Rapids, MI 49504. Author, 1986. Any edition desirable. Drawings by Howard Creswick are exquisitely done.

Curtis, Will & Jane Curtis. *Antique Woodstoves*. Ashville, ME: Cobblesmith, 1975.

DePasquale, Dan & Gail, & Larry Peterson. *Red Wing Collectibles*. Paducah, KY: Collector Books, 1985.

DeVoe, Shirley Spaulding. *Tinsmiths of Connecticut*. Middletown, CT: Wesleyan, 1968.

Divone, Judene. *Chocolate Moulds. A History & Encyclopedia*. Oakton, VA: Oakton Hills Pubns., 1987. Divone also compiled & reprinted an Anton Reiche catalog of schokoladenformen.

Dover Stamping Co. *Cook Book*. Boston: 1899.

Dow, George Francis. *The Arts & Crafts in New England, 1704-1775. Gleanings from Boston Newspapers*. Topsfield, MA: Wayside Pr., 1927.

Dubois, Urbain. *La Patisserie D'Aujourd'hui*. 7th ed. Paris: c.1890-93. Most illustrations date to c.1860s-70s.

Duparquet, Huot & Moneuse. *Catalog* of house furnishings mainly for hotels & restaurants. NYC: c.1904-1910.

Early Unnumbered Patent Index. Woodbridge, CT: Research Publications, 1980.

Enterprise Mfg. Co. *Catalog*. Philadelphia: c.1900-1910. Another, 1881.

Fearn, Jacqueline. *Domestic Bygones*. Aylesbury, England. Shire, 1977.

Field, Rachel. *Irons In the Fire. A History of Cooking Equipment.* London: Crowood Press, 1984.

Festliches Backwerk. Holzmodel, Formen aus Zinn, Kupfer und Keramik, Waffel-und Oblateneisen. Nurnberg, Germany: Germanisches National Museum, 1981. Baking molds in tin, copper, ceramic, cast iron.

Fisher, Charles. *Early American Electric Toasters. 1906-1940.* Teaneck, NJ: HJH Publications, c.1980s. Now known as "Hazelcorn's Price Guide to Old Electric Toasters."

Florence, Gene. *Kitchen Glassware of the Depression Years.* 2nd & 3rd editions. Paducah, KY: Collector Books, 1983; 1987.

Forty, Anne. *Treen & Earthenware.* Midas Books, 1979.

Franklin, Linda Campbell. *From the Hearth to Cookstove: An American Domestic History of Gadgets & Utensils...1700-1930.* Florence, AL: House of Collectibles, 1976, 1978. You may find a copy of this book with my name removed & the publisher's son's name as author. Don't believe it.

Franklin, L.C., ed. *Kitchen Collectibles News.* NYC: 1984-86. 18 issues.

Fredgant, Don. *Electrical Collectibles.* San Luis Obispo, CA: Padre Productions, 1981.

Fuller, John. *Art of Coppersmithing.* 4th ed. NYC: David Williams Co., 1911. First published 1889-90.

Gallo, John. *Nineteenth & Twentieth Century Yellow Ware.* Oneonta, NY 13820. Author, 1985.

Gaston, Mary Frank. *Antique Brass.* Paducah, KY: Collector Books, 1985.

Gentle, Rupert, & Rachel Feild. *English Domestic Brass, 1680-1810.* NYC: E. P. Dutton, 1975.

Geuder, Paeschke & Frey Co. *Cream City Ware.* Catalog. Milwaukee, WI: 1925.

Giedion, Siegfried. *Mechanization Takes Command.* NYC: Oxford University, 1948.

Gordon, Bob. *Early Electrical Appliances.* Aylesbury, England: Shire, 1984.

Gottesman, Rita Susswein. *The Arts & Crafts in New York, 1726-1776.* NYC: New-York Historical Society, 1938. Also, *1777-1799.* 1954.

Gould, Mary Earle. *Antique Tin & Tole Ware.* Rutland, VT: Charles E. Tuttle, 1962.

Gould, M.E. *Early American Wooden Ware & Other Kitchen Utensils.* Rutland, VT: Tuttle, 1962.

Graham, J.T. *Scales & Balances. A Guide to Collecting.* Aylesbury, England: Shire, 1981.

Greaser, Arlene & Paul H. *Cookie Cutters & Molds.* Allentown, PA: 1969.

Green, Harvey. *The Light of the Home: An Intimate View of the Lives of Victorian Women in America.* NYC: Pantheon, 1983.

Griswold Mfg. Co. *1928 Catalog Reprint.* Chuck Wafford, 1936 "H" St., Springfield, OR 97477. 1985.

Groft, Tammis Kane. *Cast with Style. Nineteenth Century Cast-Iron Stoves from the Albany Area.* Rev. ed. Albany, NY: Albany Institute of History, 1984.

Greguire, Helen. *The Collector's Encyclopedia of Granite Ware.* Paducah, KY: Collector Books, 1990. Full color.

Handwrought Object, 1776-1976, The. Exhibit catalog, curated by Nancy Neumann Press. Ithaca, NY: Herbert F. Johnson Museum, Cornell, 1976.

Harned, Bill & Denise. *Griswold Cast Collectibles.* POB 340, Edinboro, PA 18412. 1985.

Harrison, Molly. *The Kitchen in History.* NYC: Charles Scribner's, 1972.

Heuring, Jerry & Elaine. *Keen Kutter. Illustrated Price Guide.* Paducah, KY: Collector Books, 1984.

House Furnishing Review. NYC: c.1890-1930. Trade journal for buyers in hardware stores & housefurnishings departments.

Hueg, Henry & Co. *Book of Designs for Bakers & Confectioners.* Catalog. NYC: 1896.

Hueg, Henry & Co., *The Little Confectioner.* NYC: 1921.

Hughes, Therle. *Sweetmeat & Jelly Glasses,* Guildford, England: Lutterworth Press, 1981.

Jaburg Brothers. *Best of Everything for Bakers.* Catalog. NYC: 1908.

Jones, Joseph C., Jr. *American Ice Boxes.* Humble, TX: Jobeco Books, 1981.

Joseph, S. Co. *Hotel, Bakery & Restaurant Supplies .... Catalog.* NYC: c.1927.

Kate-von Eicken, Brigitte ten. *Kuchengerate um 1900.* Stuttgart: Walter Hadecke Verlag, (1979?)

Katzinger Co., Edward. *Katzinger Co. Price List 53.* Chicago: 1940.

Kauffman, Henry J. *American Copper & Brass.* Reprint of 1968 edition. NYC: Crown, 1979.

Kauffman, H.J. *Early American Ironware, Cast & Wrought.* Rutland, VT: Charles E. Tuttle, 1966.

Kauffman, H.J. *The American Fireplace: Chimneys, Mantelpieces, Fireplaces & Accessories,* NYC: Galahad Books, 1972.

Kauffman, Henry J. & Quentin H. Bowers. *Early American Andirons and Other Fireplace. Accessories.* NYC: Thomas Nelson, 1974.

Kevill-Davies, Sally. *Jelly Moulds.* Guildford, England: Lutterworth Press, 1983.

Kindig, Paul E. *Butter Prints & Molds.* West Chester, PA: Schiffer, 1986. A near perfect book.

Klever, Ulrich. *Alte Kuchengerate, Backen und Kochen.* Munich: Wilhelm Heyne Verlag, 1979. Cooking & baking utensils & molds.

Knight, Edward H. *American Mechanical Dictionary.* 2 vol. NYC: J.B. Ford & Co., 1874, etc.

Kruger, Laura. *Vom Zauber Alten Hausgerats.* Freiburg im Breisgau: Rombach & Co., 1981.

Ladies' Home Journal. Monthly. Philadelphia: Curtis Pub. Co., 1887-1920 consulted.

Lalance & Grosjean Mfg. Co. Catalog. NYC: 1890.

Lancaster, Maud. *Electric Cooking, Heating & Cleaning.* NYC: D. Van Nostrand, 1914.

Lantz, Louise K. *Old American Kitchenware, 1725-1925.* NYC: Thomas Nelson, 1970. This is accompanied by a price guide booklet which has been updated periodically & published by the author.

Lasansky, Jeannette. *Made of Mud. Stoneware Potteries in Central Pennsylvania, 1831-1929.* Lewisburg, PA: Oral Traditions, 1979. All Lasansky's books are extremely informative & attractive.

Lasansky, J.. *To Cut, Piece, & Solder. Work of the Rural Pennsylvania Tinsmith 1778-1908.* Lewisburg, PA: Oral Traditions, 1982.

Lasansky, J.. *To Draw, Upset, & Weld. Work of the Pennsylvania Rural Blacksmith 1742-1935.* Lewisburg, PA: Oral Traditions, 1980.

Lasansky, J.. *Willow, Oak & Rye. Basket Traditions in Pennsylvania.* Lewisburg, PA: Oral Traditions, 1979.

Leibowitz, Joan. *Yellow Ware. The Transitional Ceramic.* Exton, PA: Schiffer, 1985.

Lifshey, Earl. *The Housewares Story: A History of the American Housewares* Industry. Chicago, IL: Nat'l Housewares Mfrs. Assoc., 1973. An incredibly useful trade-sponsored history.

Lincoln, E.S. & Paul Smith. *The Electrical Home. A Standard Ready Reference Book.* NYC: Electric Home Pub'g, 1936.

Lindsay, J. Seymour. *Iron & Brass Implements of the English & American House.* Bass River, MA: C. Jacobs, 1964.

Lord, Priscilla Sawyer, & Daniel J. Foley. *The Folk Arts and Crafts of New England.* NYC: Chilton, 1965.

Manning, Bowman & Co. *Perfection Granite Ironware. Decorated Pearl Agateware.* Catalog. Meriden, CT: c.1892.

Marque C.C. *Fabrique Speciale de Moules en Etain.* Catalog. Paris: 1900.

Marshall, Jo. *Kitchenware. Collecting for Tomorrow.* London: BPC Publishers, 1976.

Marshall, Mrs. A.B. *Cookery Book.* 45th-thousandth. London: c.1900. Most of it dates to c.1887.

Marshall, Mrs. A.B. *Larger Cookery Book of Extra Recipes.* 10th-thousandth printing. London: c.1902.

Marshall, Mrs. A.B. *The Book of Ices. Including Cream & Water Ices, Sorbets, Mousses, Iced Souffles.* 14th Ed. London: c.1900-1902.

Matthai-Ingram Co. *Illustrated Catalogue of Sheet Metal Goods.* Catalog 41. Baltimore: c.1890.

Matthews, Mary Lou. *American Kitchen Collectibles.* Gas City, IN: L-W Promotions, 1973.

McNerney, Kathryn. *Antique Iron. Identification & Values.* Paducah, KY: Collector Books, 1984.

Mercer, Henry C. *The Bible in Iron.* Doylestown, PA: Bucks County Historical soc., 1914. Third edition with additions by Joseph E. Sanford, 1961. Cast iron 5, 6 and 10 plate stoves, also firebacks.

Metal Worker, Plumber & Steam Fitter, The, NYC: 1882. Trade journal. Assorted dates consulted.

Mills, Thomas & Bro. *Ice Cream Manufacturers' Equipment.* Catalog 31. Philadelphia: c.1915. A larger one dates to 1930.

Moore, Jan. *Antique Enameled Ware,* Paducah, KY: Collector Books, 1975.

Moore, N. Hudson. *Old Pewter, Brass, Copper & Sheffield Plate.* Garden City, NY: Garden City Pub. Co., 1933.

Mussey, Barrows, ed. *Yankee Life By Those Who Lived It.* NYC: Alfred Knopf, 1947. Excerpts from journals, autobiographies, letters, etc.

North Bros. Mfg. Co. *Dainty Dishes For All the Year Round,* by Mrs. S.T. Rorer. Philadelphia: 1912. Cookbooklet with catalog pages.

Objects for Preparing Food. Exhibit catalog, with intros by Curator Sandra Zimmerman & Mimi Shorr (Sheraton). Washington, D.C.: Renwick Gallery, 1972. Done in conjunction with the Museum of Contemporary Crafts of the American Crafts Council, NYC.

Official Gazette. Washington, D.C.: U.S. Patent Office, 1850s-on.

Pearson-Page Co., Ltd. *New Catalog.* Birmingham & London, England: 1925. Cast brass reproductions of 1000s of household items & decorations.

Peet, Louise Jenison, & Lenore E. Sater. *Household Equipment.* NYC: John Wiley & Sons, 1934; 1940.

Peirce, Josephine H. *Fire On the Hearth. Evolution ... of the Heating-Stove.* Springfield, MA: Pond-Ekberg, 1951.

Perry, Evan. *Collecting Antique Metalware.* NYC: Doubleday, 1974.

Perry, Evan. *Corkscrews & Bottle Openers.* Aylesbury, England: Shire, 1980.

Phipps, Frances. *Colonial Kitchens, Their Furnishings, and Their Gardens.* NYC: Hawthorn, 1972.

Pick, Albert & Co., *E-6 General Catalog. Hotel, Restaurant, Bar, Fountain Furnishings & Kitchen Utensils.* Chicago: 1905; 1909. Jobber & wholesaler with 1000s of items.

Pick-Barth Co. *General Catalog E-32.* Chicago: 1929.

Pinto, Edward H. *Treen & Other Wooden Bygones.* London: Bell & Hyman, 1969. Reprinted in 1979. Huge & informative.

Porter Co., C.B. *Catalogue Illustrating & Describing Plain Enameled Tinware, ...Water Coolers. ..* Philadelphia: 1920.

Prime, Alfred Coxe. *The Arts & Crafts in Philadelphia, Maryland, and South Carolina, 1720-1785.* Topsfield, MA: Walpole Society, 1929. Also — *1786-1800.* 1932.

Putnam, J. Pickering. *The Open Fireplace in All Ages.* Ticknor & Co., 1886.

Reed Mfg. Co. *Matchless Metalware Catalog 27.* Newark, NY & Canadaigua, NY: 1927.

Revi, Albert Christian, ed. *Spinning Wheel's Collectible Iron, Tin, Copper & Brass.* Castle Books, 1974. Anthologized articles from lamented defunct magazine.

Ritzinger & Grasgreen. *Catalog of Household Goods & Novelties.* NYC: c.1906-07. Importers & jobbers for door-to-door salesmen.

Robacker, Earl R. *Pennsylvania Dutch Stuff, A Guide to Country Antiques.* NYC: A.S. Barnes, 1944.

Rogers, Henry, Sons & Co. *Book No. E5528.* Wolverhampton, England: 1914.

Romaine, Lawrence B. *Guide to American Trade Catalogs 1744-1900.* NYC: R.R. Bowker, 1960. Recently reprinted.

Russell & Erwin Mfg. Co. *Illustrated Catalog of American Hardware.* New Britain, CT: 1865. A facsimile reprint was published by Assoc. for Preservation Technology, 1980.

Russell, Loris S. *Handy Things to Have Around the House. Oldtime Domestic Appliances of Canada and the U.S.* NY: McGraw-Hill Ryerson Ltd., 1979.

Schiffer, Peter, Nancy & Herbert. *Antique Iron. Survey of American & English forms, fifteenth through nineteenth centuries.* Exton, PA: Schiffer, 1979. Excellent pictures as usual but scant information.

Schiffer, Peter, Nancy & Herbert. *The Brass Book, American, English & European, 15th Century to 1850.* Exton, PA: Schiffer, 1978.

Scientific American. Weekly. NYC: Munn & Co., c.1850s-on. 19th C. issues almost always contain something on a household improvement.

Seymour, John. *The National Trust Book of Forgotten Household Crafts.* London: Dorling Kindersley, 1987.

Silver & Co. *Silver's House Furnishings. Catalog No. 18.* Brooklyn, NY: c.1910.

Smith, Elmer Lewis, ed. *Early American Butter Prints.* Witmer, PA: Applied Arts, 1971.

Smith, Elmer & Mel Horst. *Early Iron Ware.* Lebanon, PA: Applied Arts, 1971. Others: *Household Tools & Tasks,* and *Tinware, Yesterday & Today.*

Smith, Wayne. *Ice Cream Dippers. An illustrated History & Collector's Guide.* Box 418, Walkersville, MD 21793. Author. 1986. Beautifully photographed & well-researched.

Sonn, Albert H. *Early American Wrought Iron.* 3 vol. NYC: Charles Scribner's, 1928. Reprinted in 1979.

Sparke, Penny. *Electrical Appliances. Twentieth Century Design.* London: Unwin Hyman, 1987.

Stoudt, John Joseph. *Early Pennsylvania Arts & Crafts.* NYC: A.S. Barnes, 1964.

Stuart, Peterson & Co. *Celebrated Tinned, Enameled, Turned & Plain Hollow Ware*. NYC: 1975. Also 1866; 1876 & 1888.

Subject-Matter Index of Patents for Inventions. Issued by the U.S. Patent Office, 1790 to 1873, Inclusive. 3 volumes. NYC: Arno Press, 1976.

Tefft, Gary & Bonnie. *Red Wing Potters & Their Wares*. Locust Enterprises, 1981.

Thompson, Frances. *Antiques from the Country Kitchen*. Des Moines: Wallace-Homestead, 1985.

Thornton, Don. *The Eggbeater Book. The First and Last Word About Man's Greatest Invention*. NYC: Arbor House, 1983. Terrific book which publisher cut too short.

Toller, Jane. *Turned Woodware for Collectors. Treen & Other Objects*. Cranberry, NJ: A.S. Barnes, 1975.

Toulouse, Julian Harrison. *A Collector's Manual: Fruit Jars*. Hanover, PA: Everybody's Press, 1969.

Trice, James E. *Butter Molds; An Identification & Value Guide*. 2nd edition. Paducah, KY: Collector Books, 1980. Great variety pictured; little information.

Ure, Andrew. *A Dictionary of Arts, Manufactures & Mines*. 2 vol. England: 1839. NYC: D. Appleton, 1854.

Viel, Lyndon C. *The Clay Giants. The Stoneware of Red Wing, Goodhue County, Minnesota. Book 2*. Des Moines, IA: Wallace-Homestead, 1980.

Vogelzang, Vernagene, & Evelyn Welch. *Graniteware. Collector's Guide with Prices*. Wallace-Homestead, 1981. *Book II*, 1986. Great pictures and storehouse of in-depth information.

Walker, F.A. Various catalogs & flyers. Boston: c.1870s-90s. Large undated catalog of housewares, many imported from France & England; some mfd. by Walker.

Wallance, Don. *Shaping America's Products*. NYC: Reinhold, 1956.

Warne's Model Cookery & Housekeeping Book, compiled & edited by Mary Jewry. People's Edition. London: Frederick Warne & Co., 1868.

Warren, Geoffery. *Kitchen Bygones*. London: Souvenir Press, 1984.

Washburn Co. *Sno-Cap. The New Androck Line of Kitchen Equipment*. Worcester, MA & Rockford, IL: 1927.

Washburn Co. *The Androck Line. Balanced Kitchenware. No. 225*. 1936.

Weaver, William Woys. *America Eats. Forms of Edible Folk Art*. NYC: Harper & Row, 1989. Cookbook profusely & beautifully illustrated with utensils & decorated, molded food.

Weaver, W.W...*The Christmas Cook. Three Centuries of American Yuletide Sweets*, NYC: Harper & Row, 1990. Molded & painted cookies.

Weiner, Piroska. *Carved Honeycake Moulds*. Budapest, Hungary: 1964.

Westfall, Ermagene. *Cookie Jars*. Paducah, KY: Collector Books, 1983.

Wetherill, Phyllis Steiss. *Cookie Cutters & Cookie Molds*. Exton, PA: Schiffer, 1985. Encyclopedia for more modern cutters; much detail.

Wetherill, Phyllis Steiss. *Encyclopedia of Cookie Shaping*. 5426 27th St., N.W., Washington, D.C. 20015. Author. 1981.

Willich, Antony Florian M. *The Domestic Encyclopedia. ... 5 vol*. Philadelphia: W.Y. Birch & A. Small, 1803-04.

Wills, Geoffrey. *Collecting Copper & Brass*. NYC: Bell, 1962.

Wire Goods Co. *''Sherwood'' Wire Hardware. Wire Kitchen Ware. Catalog 7*, Worcester, MA: 1915. Also a supplement, 1915.

Wright, Lawrence. *Home Fires Burning. History of Domestic Heating & Cooking*. London: Routledge & Kegan Paul, 1964.

Yarwood, Doreen. *500 Years of Technology in the Home*. London: Batsford, 1983.

Yarwood, Doreen. *The British Kitchen. Housewifery Since Roman Times*. London: Batsford, 1981.

SUPPLEMENTARY NOTES
Use this space to list books or periodicals references you have found useful.

UNITED STATES PATENT NUMBERS

Table showing the First Patent,
Design Patent, Reissue and Trademark Numbers
Issued in Each Year from 1836 to 1945, inclusive.

DATE	PATENT	DESIGN	REISSUE	TRADEMARK
1836	1			
1837	110			
1838	546		1	
1839	1,061		7	
1840	1,465		20	
1841	1,923		30	
1842	2,413		36	
1843	2,901	1	49	
1844	3,395	15	60	
1845	3,873	27	67	
1846	4,348	44	78	
1847	4,914	103	91	
1848	5,409	163	105	
1849	5,993	209	128	
1850	6,981	258	158	
1851	7,865	341	184	
1852	8,622	431	209	
1853	9,512	540	229	
1854	10,358	626	258	
1855	12,117	683	286	
1856	14,009	753	337	
1857	16,324	860	420	
1858	19,010	973	517	
1859	22,477	1,075	643	
1860	26,642	1,183	674	
1861	31,005	1,366	1,106	
1862	34,045	1,508	1,253	
1863	37,266	1,703	1,369	
1864	41,047	1,879	1,596	
1865	45,685	2,018	1,844	
1866	51,784	2,239	2,140	
1867	60,658	2,533	2,430	
1868	72,959	2,858	2,830	
1869	85,503	3,304	3,250	
1870	98,460	3,810	3,784	1
1871	110,617	4,547	4,223	122
1872	122,304	5,452	4,687	608
1873	134,504	6,336	5,216	1,099
1874	146,120	7,083	5,717	1,591
1875	158,350	7,969	6,200	2,150
1876	171,641	8,884	6,831	3,288
1877	185,813	9,686	7,452	4,247
1878	198,733	10,385	8,020	5,463
1879	211,078	10,975	8,529	6,918
1880	223,211	11,567	9,017	7,790
1881	236,137	12,082	9,523	8,139
1882	251,685	12,647	9,994	8,973
1883	269,820	13,508	10,265	9,920
1884	291,016	14,528	10,432	10,822
1885	310,163	15,678	10,548	11,843
1886	333,494	16,451	10,677	12,910
1887	355,291	17,046	10,793	13,939
1888	375,720	17,995	10,892	15,072
1889	395,305	18,830	10,978	16,131
1890	418,665	19,553	11,053	17,360

DATE	PATENT	DESIGN	REISSUE	TRADEMARK
1891	443,987	20,439	11,137	18,775
1892	466,315	21,275	11,217	20,537
1893	486,976	22,092	11,298	22,274
1894	511,744	22,994	11,397	23,951
1895	531,619	23,922	11,461	25,757
1896	552,502	25,037	11,520	27,586
1897	574,369	26,482	11,581	29,399
1898	596,467	28,113	11,646	31,070
1899	616,871	29,916	11,706	32,308
1900	640,167	32,055	11,798	33,957
1901	664,827	33,813	11,879	35,678
1902	690,385	35,547	11,960	37,606
1903	717,521	36,187	12,070	39,612
1904	748,567	36,723	12,189	41,798
1905	778,834	37,280	12,299	43,956
1906	808,618	37,766	12,428	48,446
1907	839,799	38,391	12,587	59,014
1908	875,679	38,980	12,738	66,892
1909	908,436	39,737	12,906	72,083
1910	945,010	40,424	13,066	76,267
1911	980,178	41,063	13,189	80,506
1912	1,013,095	42,073	13,346	84,711
1913	1,049,326	43,425	13,504	89,731
1914	1,083,267	45,098	13,668	94,796
1915	1,123,212	46,813	13,858	101,613
1916	1,166,419	48,358	14,040	107,875
1917	1,210,389	50,177	14,238	114,666
1918	1,251,458	51,629	14,417	120,005
1919	1,290,027	52,836	14,582	124,066
1920	1,326,899	54,359	14,785	128,274
1921	1,364,063	56,844	15,018	138,556
1922	1,401,948	60,121	15,257	150,210
1923	1,440,362	61,478	15,513	163,003
1924	1,478,996	63,675	15,739	177,848
1925	1,521,590	66,346	15,974	193,596
1926	1,568,040	69,170	16,240	207,437
1927	1,612,790	71,772	16,515	222,401
1928	1,654,521	74,159	16,841	236,987
1929	1,696,897	77,347	17,176	251,129
1930	1,742,181	80,254	17,550	265,655
1931	1,787,424	82,966	17,917	278,906
1932	1,839,190	85,903	18,312	290,313
1933	1,892,663	88,847	18,705	299,926
1934	1,941,449	91,258	19,038	309,066
1935	1,985,878	94,179	19,409	320,441
1936	2,026,516	98,045	19,804	331,338
1937	2,066,309	102,601	20,226	342,070
1938	2,104,004	107,738	20,610	353,324
1939	2,142,080	112,765	20,959	363,536
1940	2,185,170	118,358	21,311	374,062
1941	2,227,418	124,503	21,683	384,047
1942	2,268,510	130,989	21,992	392,581
1943	2,307,007	134,717	22,242	399,378
1944	2,338,081	136,916	22,415	404,974
1945	2,366,154	139,862	22,585	411,001
	(to 2,391,855)	(to 143,385)	(to 22,795)	(to 418,493)